| | GROSS DOMESTIC PRODUCT | | PRICES AND INFLATION | | | |
| | | | GDP DEFLATOR | | CONSUMER PRICE INDEX | |
YEAR	1992 PRICES (BILLIONS OF DOLLARS)	ANNUAL REAL RATE OF GROWTH	INDEX (1992 = 100)	ANNUAL PERCENTAGE CHANGE	INDEX (1982–84 = 100)	PERCENTAGE CHANGE (DEC. TO DEC.)
1959	2,212.3	5.5	23.0	2.8	29.1	1.7
1960	2,261.7	2.2	23.3	1.4	29.6	1.4
1961	2,309.8	2.1	23.6	1.2	29.9	0.7
1962	2,449.1	6.0	23.9	1.3	30.2	1.3
1963	2,554.0	4.3	24.2	1.2	30.6	1.6
1964	2,702.9	5.8	24.6	1.5	31.0	1.0
1965	2,874.8	6.4	25.0	1.9	31.5	1.9
1966	3,060.2	6.4	25.7	2.8	32.4	3.5
1967	3,140.2	2.6	26.6	3.2	33.4	3.0
1968	3,288.6	4.7	27.7	4.4	34.8	4.7
1969	3,388.0	3.0	29.0	4.7	36.7	6.2
1970	3,388.2	0.0	30.6	5.3	38.8	5.6
1971	3,500.1	3.3	32.1	5.2	40.5	3.3
1972	3,690.3	5.4	33.5	4.2	41.8	3.4
1973	3,902.3	5.7	35.4	5.6	44.4	8.7
1974	3,888.2	−0.4	38.5	8.9	49.3	12.3
1975	3,865.1	−0.6	42.2	9.4	53.8	6.9
1976	4,081.1	5.6	44.6	5.8	56.9	4.9
1977	4,279.3	4.9	47.5	6.4	60.6	6.7
1978	4,493.7	5.0	50.9	7.3	65.2	9.0
1979	4,624.0	2.9	55.3	8.5	72.6	13.3
1980	4,611.9	−0.3	60.4	9.3	82.4	12.5
1981	4,724.9	2.5	66.1	9.4	90.9	8.9
1982	4,623.6	−2.1	70.2	6.3	96.5	3.8
1983	4,810.0	4.0	73.2	4.2	99.6	3.8
1984	5,138.2	6.8	75.9	3.8	103.9	3.9
1985	5,329.5	3.7	78.6	3.4	107.6	3.8
1986	5,489.9	3.0	80.6	2.6	109.6	1.1
1987	5,648.4	2.9	83.1	3.1	113.6	4.4
1988	5,862.9	3.8	86.1	3.7	118.3	4.4
1989	6,060.4	3.4	89.7	4.2	124.0	4.6
1990	6,138.7	1.3	93.6	4.4	130.7	6.1
1991	6,079.0	−1.0	97.3	3.9	136.2	3.1
1992	6,244.4	2.7	100.0	2.8	140.3	2.9
1993	6,383.8	2.2	102.6	2.6	144.5	2.7
1994	6,604.2	3.5	105.0	2.3	148.2	2.7
1995	6,739.0	2.1	107.5	2.4	152.4	2.5

Source: *Economic Report of the President, 1996.*

JAMES D. GWARTNEY
Florida State University

RICHARD L. STROUP
Montana State University

with the assistance of
A. H. STUDENMUND
Occidental College

RUSSELL S. SOBEL
West Virginia University

economics

PRIVATE AND PUBLIC CHOICE

EIGHTH EDITION

THE DRYDEN PRESS
Harcourt Brace College Publishers

Fort Worth Philadelphia San Diego New York Orlando Austin San Antonio
Toronto Montreal London Sydney Tokyo

Executive Editor: Emily Barrosse
Acquisitions Editor: Daryl Fox
Developmental Editor: Stacey Sims
Project Editor: Jim Patterson
Art Director: Brian Salisbury
Production Manager: Carlyn Hauser
Art & Literary Rights Editor: Adele Krause
Product Manager: R. Paul Stewart
Editorial Assistant: Cristin Westhoff
Marketing Coordinator: Virginia Warren

Copyeditor: Carolyn Crabtree
Proofreader: Jennifer Moorhouse
Indexer: Linda Webster
Compositor: GTS Graphics
Text Type: 10/12 Palatino

Address for orders:
The Dryden Press
6277 Sea Harbor Drive
Orlando, FL 32887-6777
1-800-782-4479, or 1-800-433-0001 (in Florida)

Address for editorial correspondence:
The Dryden Press
301 Commerce Street, Suite 3700
Fort Worth, TX 76102

ISBN: 0-03-019269-2

Library of Congress Catalog Card Number: 96-84460

Credits appear on page 1025, which constitutes a continuation of the copyright page.

Printed in the United States of America

8 9 0 1 2 3 4 5   048   9 8 7 6 5 4

The Dryden Press
Harcourt Brace College Publishers

This is an exciting time to study economics. Lower transport and communication costs are shrinking the size of our world. There is now more interaction and trade between people in different nations than at any time in history. How will these developments affect you? How will increased trade with less developed countries like Mexico influence your future job opportunities? People in Latin America, Eastern Europe, and the former Soviet Union have moved toward democracy. Will the adoption of democratic political institutions improve economic conditions in these areas? In recent decades, the per capita income of several Asian countries has grown substantially while that of most African and Latin American nations has stagnated. Why have some countries prospered while others have regressed? What is the recipe for economic growth? As we proceed, we will use the tools of economics to address these and many other important issues that affect our lives.

EIGHTH EDITION

Two objectives dominated our thought process during this revision. First, we wanted to make the core material shorter and clearer. We have always sought to communicate ideas in an understandable manner; reviewers tell us this is a major strength of the text. Nonetheless, precision and clarity were priorities in this revision. We literally went over every sentence and paragraph asking ourselves if it was really necessary and how we might make the central points easier for readers to grasp. As a result, the core theory chapters are about 10 percent shorter than in the last edition.

Second, this edition is more visual. We want to make it easier for readers to "see" important relationships. Our teaching experience has shown us that we instructors often take too much for granted. Students often miss major points embodied in even simple tables—points that seem obvious to us. Thus, more than in previous editions, we have used graphs and other visual aids to highlight key relationships. We also carefully prepared and designed Illustrated Exhibits that introduce each section. We believe that these exhibits will provide background and set the stage for the forthcoming material.

As in prior editions, our central objective is to help the reader develop the economic way of thinking. While this method of thinking is in many ways simply common sense, it is a powerful tool of analysis when woven together logically. We have sought to present the material in a manner that will stimulate students, challenge their reasoning ability, and teach them to think like economists. Examples are used freely to illustrate the power and relevance of economic analysis. Real-world data are employed to analyze and test the implications of economic theory. We think this approach will enliven the study of economics for both the student and the teacher.

Many instructors have informed us that they like to structure their course around issues and applications. Of course, we stress the application of economics throughout the text. In addition, this edition includes a new chapter, "Current Issues and Policy Debates," that focuses on several of the central issues of our day. Features on the approaching social security crisis, income inequality, provision of health care, the flat tax, and welfare reform are included in this chapter.

This edition has a more international flavor. Cross-country comparisons are often used to highlight general applications of economic theory. Increasingly, students are interested in the economies of other countries—their performance and how their economic organization and policies differ from those of the United States. We believe that the additional material on these topics will make the study of economics both more informative and stimulating.

CHANGES IN THE CORE MACROECONOMICS

While the organization of the core macroeconomics has changed little from the previous edition, several new features have been incorporated into this edition. The following list highlights a number of the specific changes.

■ Chapter 12 outlines some of the problems and ambiguities involved in defining and measuring the money supply. The significance of currency held abroad, highly liquid stock and bond mutual funds, and the increasing use of debit cards (and electronic money) is highlighted in this edition.

■ The material on monetary policy (Chapter 13) has been revised to reflect the potential importance of changes in exchange rates and credit rationing as well as interest rates in the transmission of monetary policy.

■ Several nations have adopted various structural monetary reforms (for example, the introduction of index bonds, exchange rate targeting, and legalization of alternative currencies). Chapter 15 discusses these reforms and analyzes their effect on the conduct of monetary policy.

■ Given the global nature of modern financial markets, credit markets are a source of fiscal discipline, particularly when a nation's debt to GDP ratio is high. This point is highlighted in this edition.

■ Chapters 8 and 9 present the basic aggregate demand/aggregate supply model used throughout the core macro. We worked hard to make this material briefer and more easily understandable.

CHANGES IN THE CORE MICROECONOMICS

The following changes were made in the core microeconomics:

■ The industrial organization material of this edition is presented in the price taker/price searcher framework. This approach highlights the importance of entry barriers, while reducing the significance of a downward sloping demand curve *facing the firm*. It also avoids the use of "monopolistic competition," which is a confusing term to describe markets characterized by low barriers to entry and intense competition among rival suppliers.

■ The role of the entrepreneur as both one who discovers opportunities overlooked by others and introduces innovative products and production methods is highlighted more fully in this edition. In addition, Chapter 20 contains a feature on the achievements and strategies of several highly successful entrepreneurs. Surveys indicate that many students taking introductory economics would like to own and operate a business. Our emphasis on entrepreneurship should be of particular interest to these students.

■ The importance of competition as a process is stressed in this edition. Sometimes while emphasizing the mechanics and beauty of the purely competitive equilibrium conditions, we overlook the discipline that competition imposes on firms that do not (a) produce at a low cost, (b) supply goods that consumers value highly (relative to cost), and (c) innovate and adopt better ways of doing things. These are important functions that we must communicate to students.

■ We condensed the discussion and analysis of antitrust and expanded the material on regulation in Chapter 22. New features on the regulation of taxicabs and the use of the chemical alar will enhance student understanding of the regulatory process.

■ Chapter 27 presents data on both the static income comparisons at a point in time and the dynamic movement of people up and down the income ladder. The discussion accompanying this material highlights both the significance and limitations of these data.

DISTINGUISHING FEATURES OF OUR APPROACH

As we mentioned previously, clarity and brevity are a priority with us. We seek to write in a manner that is easily understandable, using examples and illustrations to reinforce basic concepts. Simplicity, however, has not been substituted for depth. Rather, our aim is to highlight the power, accessibility, and relevance of economic concepts. Where complex ideas are essential to our analysis, they are developed fully. We believe that economics can be comprehensible to the student as well as challenging and applicable to the real world.

Economic reasoning is central to our approach. Although models, theories, and exercises are important, they are only tools with which to develop the economic way of thinking. We have avoided abstractions and mechanical exercises that obscure basic concepts. On the other hand, we have integrated applications and real world data in an effort to make the basic concepts come alive to the reader.

The tools of economics are relevant to both the market and political processes. Most textbooks tell students how an ideal market economy would operate, how real-world markets differ from the hypothetical ideal, and how ideal public policy can correct the shortcomings of the market. In addition to discussing these three basic issues, we analyze what real-world public policy is likely to do. We think this approach enlivens the study of economics.

ORGANIZATIONAL FEATURES

We have employed several organizational features designed to make the presentation both more interesting and more understandable.

1. **Myths of Economics**   In a series of boxed articles, commonly held fallacies of economic reasoning are dispelled. Each myth is followed by a concise explanation of why it is incorrect and each one is presented within a chapter containing closely related material.

2. **Applications in Economics** These boxed features apply economic theory to real-world issues and controversies. They add breadth to topics of special interest and illustrate the relevance of basic principles to the world in which we live.

3. **Measures of Economic Activity** Measurement is an important element of economics. These features explain how important economic indicators such as the consumer price index, the unemployment rate, and the index of leading indicators are assembled.

4. **Chapter Focus Questions and Closing Summaries** Each chapter begins with several questions that summarize the focus of the chapter. A summary, which provides the student with a concise statement of the material (chapter learning objectives), appears at the end of each chapter. Reviewing the focus questions and chapter summaries will help the student better understand the material and integrate it into the broader economic picture.

5. **Key Terms** The terminology of economics is often confusing to introductory students. Key terms are introduced in the text in bold type; simultaneously, each term is defined in the margin opposite the first reference to the term. A glossary containing the key terms also appears at the end of the book.

6. **Critical Analysis Questions** Each chapter concludes with a set of discussion questions and problems designed to test the student's ability to analyze economic issues and to apply economic theory to real-world events. Appendix B at the end of the text contains suggested answers for approximately half of the critical analysis questions. We think these answers, illustrating the power of economics, will interest students and will help them develop the economic way of thinking.

SUPPLEMENTARY MATERIALS

COURSEBOOKS. Prepared by Professor A. H. Studenmund of Occidental College, the Coursebooks—available as splits covering microeconomics and macroeconomics—are more than study guides. Each Coursebook includes numerous multiple choice, true/false, and discussion questions permitting students to self-test their knowledge of each chapter. Answers and short explanations for most questions are provided in the back of the Coursebooks. Each chapter also contains problem and project exercises designed to improve the student's knowledge of the mechanics. A set of short readings chosen to supplement the classroom teaching of important topics is also included. Several of the readings are arranged in a debate format and cover areas of controversy in economics. Like the textbook, the Coursebooks are designed to help students develop the economic way of thinking.

TEST BANK. The Test Banks for the Eighth Edition were prepared by Russell Sobel, J. J. Bethune, Edward Bierhanzl, and James Gwartney. The two Test Banks contain approximately 7,000 questions—multiple-choice and short answer—most of which have been class tested. Within each chapter, the questions correspond to the major subheadings of the text. A comprehensive quiz covering the material of each chapter is included. Of course, both Test Banks are available on computer diskette for both IBM and Macintosh users. The ExaMaster system makes it easy to create tests, print scrambled versions of the same test, modify questions, and reproduce graphic questions.

INSTRUCTOR'S MANUAL. The Instructor's Manual was prepared by Gary Galles of Pepperdine University and Russell Sobel of West Virginia University. It is divided into three parts. The first part, which is also available on computer diskette, is a detailed outline of each chapter in lecture-note form. It is designed to help instructors organize and structure their current lecture notes according to the format of the Eighth Edition of *Economics: Private and Public Choice.* Instructors can easily prepare a detailed, personalized set of notes by revising the computerized form of the notes. The second part of the Instructor's Manual contains teaching tips, sources of supplementary materials, and other helpful information. Part 3 provides instructors with several games designed to illustrate and enliven important economic concepts. Suggested answers to most of the critical analysis questions that were not answered in Appendix B of the text are also provided in the Instructor's Manual.

COLOR TRANSPARENCIES. Color transparencies of the major exhibits of the Eighth Edition have been especially prepared for overhead projectors. They are available to adopters upon request in sets for microeconomics and macroeconomics.

TUTORIAL ANALYTICAL AND GRAPHICAL (TAG) SOFTWARE. This award-winning software by Tod Porter and Teresa Riley of Youngstown State University has been significantly enhanced in this edition. An Economics in the News feature applies the tools of a given chapter to a recent news event. Hotspots are sprinkled throughout the selection that ask students to identify the concepts involved and whether the author has used them correctly. In the Econoquest section, students are given a problem and a file cabinet of tools and data they may need to solve it. Students must correctly identify the tools and data required before attempting to solve the problem. The software also includes annotated multiple-choice questions in addition to the extensive chapter-by-chapter tutorials, hands-on graphing sections in which students are actually required to draw curves (with key strokes or a mouse), calculation and analysis practice problems, and practice exams for each section that make up the standard features of the program. TAG automatically tracks and evaluates student responses for each of the various components. It can be used with Windows 3.1® and Windows '95®.

PRESENTATION SOFTWARE IN POWERPOINT®. Prepared by Tony Zambelli of Cuyamaca College, this software provides bulleted lecture notes and figures selected from the text, ready for classroom presentation using the PowerPoint® Viewer, which we provide. While all instructors can select the information they wish to cover, those with the full version of PowerPoint® can actually customize the lecture notes to reflect their personal course goals.

LASER DISC. This package contains a macroeconomics disc. It focuses on the core principles and presents the information interactively. A brief 5–7 minute video from CBS begins each learning section. Related animated graphics follow.

Once students understand the concepts, they are then challenged with critical-thinking questions.

The Dryden Press will provide complimentary supplements or supplement packages to those adopters qualified under our adoption policy. Please contact your sales representative to learn how you may qualify. If as an adopter or potential user you receive supplements you do not need, please return them to your sales representative or send them to:

Attn: Returns Department
Troy Warehouse
465 South Lincoln Drive
Troy, MO 63379

For more information about this and other economics titles from The Dryden Press visit our web site at: www.dryden.com/econ

ACKNOWLEDGMENTS

A project of this type is a team effort. Several people contributed substantially to the development of this edition. Russell Sobel of West Virginia University assisted us with all phases of the project, including updating of exhibits, drafts for several text features, and preparation of questions for the Test Bank. Once again, Woody Studenmund of Occidental College prepared the Coursebook and provided valuable direction and insightful comments. As in the prior edition, Gary Galles of Pepperdine University co-authored the Instructor's Manual. The teaching tips and special games (and projects) contained in the manual reflect his creativity, communication skills, and talent for the teaching of economics. J. J. Bethune of University of Tennessee—Martin and Ed Bierhanzl of Florida A&M University also played a major role in the development of the Test Bank.

We would also like to express our appreciation to David Macpherson, who supplied us with computerized tabulations from the *Survey of Current Population* for the updating of several exhibits. Barry Hirsch provided us with valuable comments and data used to update exhibits in the factor market section. Barbara Morgan assisted us with the preparation of several exhibits. Tim Sass supplied us with a number of high-quality questions for the Test Bank. Jennifer Troyer and Brian Nottage also assisted us with the Test Bank.

We have often revised material in light of suggestions made by reviewers, users, friends, and even a few competitors. In this regard, we would like to express our appreciation to the following people for their contributions to the Eighth Edition: Robert N. Baird, Case Western Reserve University; John W. Dodge, Jr., University of Sioux Falls; Charles J. Ellard, the University of Texas—Pan American; T. Windsor Fields, James Madison University; Joseph Fuhrig, Golden Gate University; Ralph C. Gamble, Jr., Fort Hays State University; Joseph D. Greene, Augusta College; Anthony L. Ostrosky, Illinois State University; Robert C. Rencher, Jr., Liberty University; Torsten Schmidt, University of New Hampshire; Paul M. Taube, the University of Texas—Pan American; Donna Thompson, Brookdale Community College; Roger Trenary, Kansas State University.

We are also indebted to the excellent team of professionals at The Dryden Press. Emily Barrosse, executive editor; Daryl Fox, acquisitions editor; Stacey Sims, developmental editor; Jim Patterson, project editor; and Cristin Westhoff, editorial assistant provided us with editorial assistance and encouragement. We would also like to thank Carlyn Hauser, production manager; Adele Krause, art and literary rights editor; Brian Salisbury, art director; and R. Paul Stewart, product manager, who have worked together to create the finest edition of this textbook yet.

Finally, we would like to acknowledge the assistance of Valerie N. Colvin, Amy Gwartney, and Jane Shaw Stroup, all of whom contributed in numerous ways to the success of this project. Without their assistance and encouragement, we would have been unable to meet the demands and deadlines of this project.

A NOTE TO STUDENTS

This text contains several features that we think will help you maximize (a good economic term) the returns derived from your study effort. Our past experience indicates that awareness of the following points will help you to use the book more effectively.

- Each chapter begins with a series of focus questions that communicate the central issues of the chapter. Before you read the chapter, briefly think about the focus questions, why they are important, and how they relate to the material of prior chapters.
- The textbook is organized in the form of an outline. The headings within the text (highlighted with a color background) are the major points of the outline. Minor headings are subpoints under the major headings. In addition, important subpoints within sections are often set off and numbered. *Bold italics* is used to highlight material that is particularly important. Sometimes thumbnail sketches are included to help the reader better organize important points. Careful use of the headings, highlighted material, and the thumbnail sketches will help you master the material.
- A summary appears at the end of each chapter. Use the summary as a checklist to determine whether you understand the major points of the chapter.
- A review of the exhibits will also provide you with a summary of each chapter. The accompanying legend briefly describes the content and analysis of each exhibit. After studying the chapter, briefly review the exhibits to ensure that you have mastered the central points.
- The key terms introduced in each chapter are defined in the margins. As you study the chapter, go over the marginal definition of each key term as it is introduced. Later, you may also find it useful to review the marginal definitions. If you have forgotten the meaning of a term introduced earlier, consult the glossary at the end of the book.
- The boxed features provide additional depth on various topics without disrupting the flow of the text. In general, the topics of the boxed features have been chosen because of their relevance as an application of the theory or because of past student interest in the topic. Reading the boxed features will supplement the text and enhance your understanding of important economic concepts.
- The critical analysis questions at the end of each chapter are intended to test your understanding of the economic way of thinking. Solving these questions and problems will greatly enhance your knowledge of the material. Answers to approximately half of these questions are provided in Appendix B.

If you need more practice, be sure to obtain a Coursebook and solve the questions and problems for each chapter. The Coursebook also contains the answers to the multiple-choice questions and a brief explanation of why an answer is correct (and other choices incorrect). In most cases, if you master the concepts of the test items in the Coursebook, you will do well on the quizzes and examinations of your instructor.

APPLICATIONS IN ECONOMICS

MEASURES OF ECONOMIC ACTIVITY

MYTHS OF ECONOMICS

RELATIONSHIP BETWEEN MAIN EDITION AND MACRO/MICRO VERSIONS.

Note that the chapter numbers of the course book and test bank correspond to those of the macro and micro versions.

economics

PRIVATE AND
PUBLIC CHOICE

EIGHTH EDITION

The United States is a rich country. In 1994, the per person income of the United States was approximately 25% greater than that of Japan and Germany, three times that of Mexico, and ten times that of China.

SOURCE: Robert Summers and Alan Hesten, *Penn World Tables* (Cambridge, National Bureau of Economic Research, 1994). The figures were updated by the authors.

EXHIBIT I–A

THE INCOMES OF AMERICANS ARE THE HIGHEST IN THE WORLD

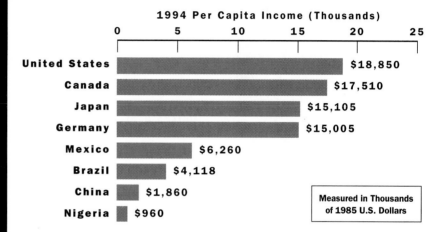

1994 Per Capita Income (Thousands)

United States	$18,850
Canada	$17,510
Japan	$15,105
Germany	$15,005
Mexico	$6,260
Brazil	$4,118
China	$1,860
Nigeria	$960

Measured in Thousands of 1985 U.S. Dollars

Measured in 1987 dollars, the income per person in the United States in 1995 was a little more than three times the figure for 1929. The 1995 per capita income level was 47% greater than the comparable figure for 1969.

SOURCE: *Economic Report of the President.*

EXHIBIT I–B

THE INCOME PER CAPITA OF THE UNITED STATES HAS INCREASED SUBSTANTIALLY DURING THE LAST 65 YEARS

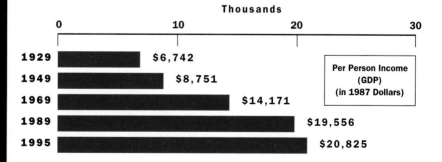

Thousands

1929	$6,742
1949	$8,751
1969	$14,171
1989	$19,556
1995	$20,825

Per Person Income (GDP) (in 1987 Dollars)

During the last 15 years, South Korea, Thailand, Singapore, Hong Kong, Indonesia, and Malaysia have achieved the highest growth rates in the world. As the accompanying graph illustrates, the per capita income of these countries has grown much more rapidly than that of the United States and other high-income industrial nations, including that of Japan.

SOURCE: World Bank, *World Tables: 1995*.

EXHIBIT I-C

THE PER CAPITA INCOME OF SEVERAL ASIAN COUNTRIES IS GROWING MUCH MORE RAPIDLY THAN THAT OF THE UNITED STATES

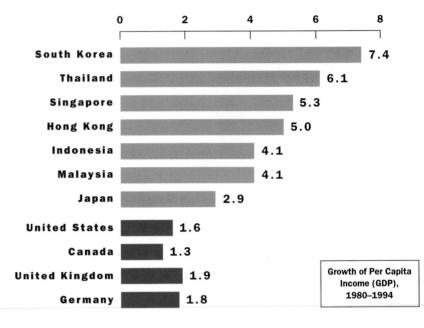

Growth of Per Capita Income (GDP), 1980–1994

As we will discuss in Chapter 2, investment can provide future workers with more and better tools, machines, and physical structures, and thereby increase their productivity. Other things constant, countries that invest more will tend to grow more rapidly. As the graph illustrates, the high growth countries of Asia invest a much larger share of their output than the United States and most other high-income industrial countries.

SOURCE: International Monetary Fund, *International Financial Statistics Yearbook, 1995*.

EXHIBIT I-D

HIGH INVESTMENT RATES ARE PROPELLING THE GROWTH IN THE ASIAN ECONOMIES

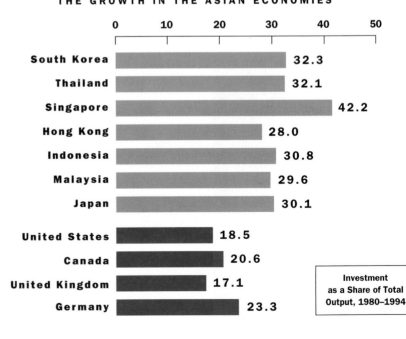

Investment as a Share of Total Output, 1980–1994

EXHIBIT I-E

During the 15 years following the Second World War, there was a sharp increase in the number of births. As a result, almost one-third (32.5%) of Americans were age 15 years and younger in 1960. Since that time, the proportion of young Americans has steadily declined. The baby boom generation contributed to the sharp increase between 1960 and 1990 in the proportion of the population aged 25 to 44 years. Between 1990 and 2010, there will be a substantial increase in the size of the 45 to 64 age group and in the years following 2010 there will be a dramatic increase in the proportion of Americans aged 65 years and older, more than twice the figure for 1960.

What impact will these demographic changes have on the American economy?

SOURCE: *Statistical Abstract of the United States.*

THE BABY BOOMERS AND THE CHANGING COMPOSITION OF THE U.S. POPULATION

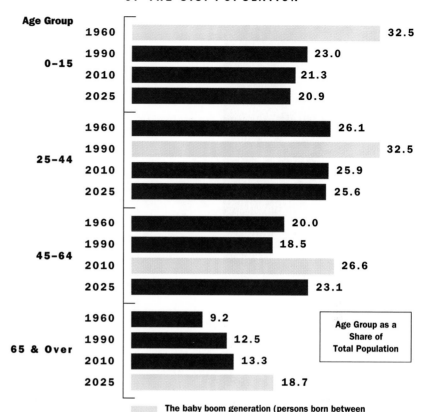

The baby boom generation (persons born between 1946 and 1960) are included in this group.

EXHIBIT I-F

In 1950 less than one in four (23.8%) married women worked outside of the home. The figure has steadily increased during the last four decades. In 1994, more than 60% of married women worked in the labor force.

What impact does this increase in the workforce participation of married women have on the economy?

THE DRAMATIC INCREASE IN THE LABOR FORCE PARTICIPATION OF MARRIED WOMEN

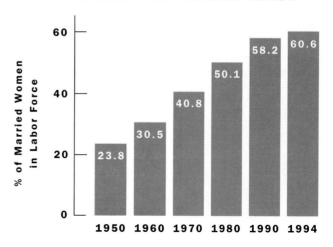

3

The composition of the activities and expenditures of the federal government have changed dramatically since 1960. In 1960, federal expenditures on income transfers (social security is the largest program in this area), medical and health care programs, and net interest summed to 29% of the total. By 1995, the expenditures in these three areas accounted for 68% of the federal expenditures. During the same time period, expenditures on national defense fell from 55.4% to 18.5% of the total.

How does this shift in federal activities from national defense to the provision of transfer payments and health care affect the U.S. economy?

SOURCE: *Economic Report of the President.* Expenditures on International Affairs are included in the national defense figure. The Medicare and Medicaid programs comprise the bulk of the expenditures on medical and health.

EXHIBIT I-G

THE FEDERAL GOVERNMENT AS A PROVIDER OF INCOME TRANSFERS AND HEALTH CARE

Percentage of Federal Expenditures

1960 | 1975 | 1995

1960:
- All Other (15.6)
- National Defense (55.4)
- Medical & Health (<1.0)
- Net interest (7.5)
- Income Transfers (20.6)

1975:
- All Other (22.4)
- National Defense (28.2)
- Net Interest (7.0)
- Medical & Health (7.8)
- Income Transfers (34.6)

1995:
- All Other (13.3)
- National Defense (18.5)
- Net Interest (14.9)
- Medical & Health (17.6)
- Income Transfers (35.7)

EXHIBIT I-H

The world is shrinking. Long-distance transportation and communication costs have fallen dramatically in recent decades. As a result, Americans are increasingly buying from and selling to foreigners. The size of the international trade sector (exports plus imports) more than doubled between 1960 and 1990.

SOURCE: *Economic Report of the President.*

THE INCREASING IMPORTANCE OF INTERNATIONAL TRADE

Exports + Imports as a Percentage of U.S. Economy

1960	1970	1980	1990	1995
9.4	12.4	16.2	22.0	22.2

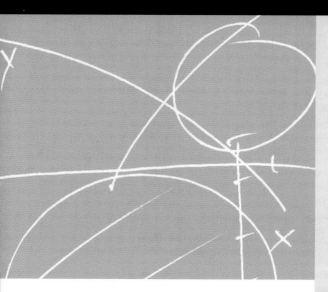

CHAPTER FOCUS

■ Why is scarcity a key economic concept, even in an affluent economy?

■ How does scarcity differ from poverty? Why does scarcity necessitate rationing and, therefore, competition?

■ What are the basics underlying the economic way of thinking? What is different about the way economists look at choices and human decision making?

■ What is the difference between positive and normative economics?

[Economics] is not a body of concrete truth, but an engine for the discovery of concrete truth.

ALFRED MARSHALL[1]

---

[1] Alfred Marshall, *The Present Position of Economics* (1885), p. 25.

This is an exciting time to study economics. Recent political campaigns in the United States have centered on such economic issues as budget deficits, the structure and level of taxes, and policies toward international trade. Economic issues also occupy center stage in other countries. The market economies of Western Europe are struggling to develop a single, integrated economy with a common currency and legal structure. Several countries of Eastern Europe and the former Soviet Union are attempting to move from socialist central planning to a market-directed economy. Latin American and African leaders are searching for economic prescriptions that will generate prosperity and upgrade living standards.

Simultaneously, economies around the world are becoming more and more interrelated. Many of the goods at your favorite shopping mall are produced, at least in part, by people who speak a different language and live in a country far from your own. Similarly, many Americans work for companies that market their products in Europe, Japan, Latin America, or Africa. Ownership shares of American companies are traded not only in New York but also on stock exchanges in London, Tokyo, and throughout the world.

How will our current economic policies and rapidly changing world affect the economic status of Americans? What impact will the globalization of our economy have on our living standards, lifestyles, and future opportunities? This book will help you better understand the world in which you live. This is not to imply that economics provides easy answers for problems. As Alfred Marshall stated more than a century ago, economics is a discovery process—a way of thinking—rather than a "body of concrete truth" (see chapter opening quote). Our goals are to present the tools of economics and illustrate how the economic way of thinking can enhance your understanding of our rapidly changing world.

WHAT IS ECONOMICS ABOUT?

[Economics is] the science which studies human behavior as a relationship between ends and scarce means which have alternative uses.

LIONEL ROBBINS[2]

Economics is about people and the choices they make. The unit of analysis in economics is the individual. Of course, individuals group together to form collective organizations, such as corporations, labor unions, and governments. Individual choices, however, still underlie and direct these organizations. Thus, even when we study collective organizations, we will focus on the ways in which their operation is affected by the choices of individuals.

SCARCITY AND CHOICE

Would you like some new clothes, a nicer car, and a larger apartment? How about better grades and more time to watch television, go skiing, and travel abroad? Most of us would like more of all these goods. The human desire for

---

[2]Lionel Robbins, *An Essay on the Nature and Significance of Economic Science* (1932).

goods is virtually unlimited. We cannot, however, have more of everything. Both individually and collectively we face a constraint called **scarcity.** Goods are scarce because people's desire for things is far greater than what is freely available from nature. Since scarcity prevents us from having as much as we would like of **economic goods,** we are forced to choose among a restricted set of potential alternatives. **Choice,** the act of selecting among alternatives, is the logical consequence of scarcity. These two—*scarcity* and *choice*—are the basic ingredients of an economic topic.

Resources are inputs used to produce goods and services. In essence, they are tools that we can use to battle scarcity. There are three general categories of resources. First, there are human resources—the productive knowledge, skill, and strength of human beings. Second, there are physical resources—things like tools, machines, and buildings that enhance our ability to produce goods. Economists often use the term *capital* when referring to these human-made resources. Third, there are natural resources—things like land, mineral deposits, oceans, and rivers. The ingenuity of humans is often required in order to make these natural resources useful in production. Recognizing the best ways to produce goods, and which goods to produce under changing circumstances, are as important to production as the existence of the resources themselves.

With the passage of time, investment activities can increase the availability of resources; but more investment requires the sacrifice of additional current consumption. If we use more of today's resources to produce education and skill enhancement, or tools, machines, and factories, then fewer resources will be available to produce goods for consumption now. Economics is about trade-offs. **Exhibit 1–1** lists some desired goods and limited resources.

During the past 250 years, we have loosened the grip of scarcity a little. Think for a moment what life was like in 1750. People all over the world struggled 50, 60, and 70 hours a week to obtain the basic necessities of life—food, clothing, and shelter. Manual labor was the major source of energy. Animals provided the means of transportation. Tools and machines were primitive by today's standards. As the English philosopher Thomas Hobbes had stated earlier, life was "solitary, poor, nasty, brutish, and short."[3]

Throughout much of South America, Africa, and Asia, economic conditions continue to make life difficult. In North America, Western Europe, Oceania, and some parts of Asia, however, substantial economic progress has been made. Of course, scarcity is still a fact of life in these areas, too; the desire for goods and services still far outstrips the ability of people to produce them. But from a material standpoint, life is now safer and more comfortable. Modern energy sources and means of transportation are available there. Subsistence levels of food, shelter, and clothing are taken for granted, and the typical family there can worry instead about financing summer vacations, obtaining a large-screen television with a videocassette recorder, and providing for the children's college education.

It is important to note that scarcity and poverty are not the same thing. Poverty implies some basic level of need, either in absolute or relative terms. Absence of poverty means that the basic level has been attained. In contrast, the absence of scarcity would imply that we have as much of all goods as we would like. Both individuals and countries may win the battle against poverty—people may achieve income levels that allow them to satisfy a basic level of need.

Scarcity
Fundamental concept of economics that indicates that a good is less freely available than consumers would like.

Economic good
A good that is scarce. The desire for economic goods exceeds the amount that is freely available from nature.

Choice
The act of selecting among alternatives.

Resource
An input used to produce economic goods. Land, labor, skills, natural resources, and capital are examples. Our history is a record of our struggle to transform available, but limited, resources into things that we would like to have—economic goods.

---

[3]Thomas Hobbes, *Leviathan* (1651), Part I, ch. 13.

History is a record of our struggle to transform available, but limited, resources into things that we would like to have—economic goods.

EXHIBIT 1-1

A GENERAL LISTING OF DESIRED ECONOMIC GOODS AND LIMITED RESOURCES

ECONOMIC GOODS	LIMITED RESOURCES
Food (bread, milk, meat, eggs, vegetables, coffee, etc.)	Land (various degrees of fertility)
Clothing (shirts, pants, blouses, shoes, socks, coats, sweaters, etc.)	Natural resources (rivers, trees, minerals, oceans, etc.)
Household goods (tables, chairs, rugs, beds, dressers, television sets, etc.)	Machines and other human-made physical resources
Space exploration	Nonhuman animal resources
Education	Technology (physical and scientific "recipes" of history)
National defense	Human resources (the knowledge, skill, and talent of individual human beings)
Recreation	
Leisure time	
Entertainment	
Clean air	
Pleasant environment (trees, lakes, rivers, open spaces, etc.)	
Pleasant working conditions	
More productive resources	

But it is painfully obvious that we will not triumph over scarcity. Even in the wealthiest of countries, productive capabilities cannot keep pace with material desires. People always want more goods, for themselves and others they care about, than can be produced with available resources.

SCARCITY NECESSITATES RATIONING

Rationing
An allocation of a limited supply of a good or resource to users who would like to have more of it. Various criteria, including charging a price, can be utilized to allocate the limited supply. When price performs the rationing function, the good or resource is allocated to those willing to give up the most "other things" in order to obtain ownership rights.

When a good (or resource) is scarce, some criterion must be set up for deciding who will receive the good (or resource) and who will do without it. Scarcity makes **rationing** a necessity.

There are several possible criteria that could be used in rationing a limited amount of a good among citizens who would like to have more of it. The rationing criterion chosen will influence human behavior. If the criterion were first-come, first-served, goods would be allocated to those who were fastest at getting in line or to those who were most willing to wait in line. If beauty were used, goods would be allocated to those who were thought to be most beautiful. The political process might be used, and goods would be allocated on the basis of political status and ability to manipulate the political process to personal advantage. In a market setting, price is used to ration things; goods and resources are allocated to those willing to pay the highest prices. One thing is certain: Scarcity means that methods must be established to decide who gets the limited amount of available goods and resources.

COMPETITION RESULTS FROM SCARCITY

Competition is a natural outgrowth of scarcity and the desire of human beings to improve their conditions. Competition exists in every economy and every society. It exists both when goods are allocated by price in markets and when they are allocated by other means—political decision making, for example.

Moreover, the rationing criterion will influence which competitive techniques will be used. When the rationing criterion is price, individuals will engage in income-generating activities that enhance their ability to pay the price. The market system encourages individuals to provide goods and services to others in exchange for income. In turn, the income will permit them to procure more scarce goods.

A different rationing criterion will encourage other types of behavior. When the appearance of sincerity, broad knowledge, fairness, good judgment, and a positive television image are important, as they are in the rationing of elected political positions, people will use resources to project these qualities. They will hire makeup artists, public relations experts, and advertising agencies to help them compete. We can change the form of competition, but no society has been able to eliminate it, because no society has been able to eliminate scarcity and the resulting need for rationing. When people who want more scarce goods seek to meet the criteria established to ration those goods, competition occurs.

Economists recognize that how people compete in the rationing process has an important impact on production. They may not agree on which form of competition is best in a particular situation. However, recognition that the rationing criterion will affect the actions of people will influence how economists think about scarcity and related issues.

THE ECONOMIC WAY OF THINKING

It [economics] is a method rather than a doctrine, an apparatus of the mind, a technique of thinking which helps its possessor to draw correct conclusions.

JOHN MAYNARD KEYNES[4]

One does not have to spend much time around economists to recognize that there is an "economic way of thinking." Admittedly, economists, like others, differ widely in their ideological views. A news commentator once remarked that "any half-dozen economists will normally come up with about six different

---

[4]John Maynard Keynes (1883–1946) was an English economist whose writings during the 1920s and 1930s exerted an enormous impact on both economic theory and policy. Keynes established the terminology and the economic framework that are still widely used when economists study problems of unemployment and inflation.

Economic theory
A set of definitions, postulates, and principles assembled in a manner that makes clear the "cause-and-effect" relationships of economic data.

policy prescriptions." Yet, in spite of their philosophical differences, there is a common ground in the approach of economists.

That common ground is **economic theory,** developed from basic postulates of human behavior. Economic theory, like a road map or a guidebook, establishes reference points indicating what to look for, and how economic issues are interrelated. To a large degree, the basic economic principles are merely commonsense. When applied consistently, however, these commonsense concepts can provide interesting and powerful insights.

EIGHT GUIDEPOSTS TO ECONOMIC THINKING

The economic way of thinking requires the incorporation of certain guidelines—some would say the building blocks of basic economic theory—into one's thought process. Once these guidelines are incorporated, we believe that economics can be a relatively easy subject to master. Students who have difficulty with economics have almost always failed to assimilate these principles. We will outline and discuss eight principles that characterize the economic way of thinking and that are essential to understanding the economic approach.

1. THE USE OF SCARCE RESOURCES TO PRODUCE A GOOD IS ALWAYS COSTLY.
Economists sometimes refer to this as "There Ain't No Such Thing As A Free Lunch," or the "TANSTAAFL" principle. The use of resources to produce one good diverts the resources from the production of other goods that are also desired. No option is free of cost. The highest valued alternative that must be sacrificed is the **opportunity cost** of the option. For example, if you use one hour of your scarce time to study economics, you will have one hour less time to watch television, read magazines, sleep, work at a job, or study other subjects. Time spent working at a job, or even time spent sleeping, might be viewed as your highest valued option forgone. The cost of an action is always the highest valued option lost if you choose the action.

Opportunity cost
The highest valued alternative that must be sacrificed as a result of choosing among alternatives.

It is important to recognize that the "scarce resources have a cost" concept is true regardless of who pays for the good or service produced. In many countries, various kinds of schooling are provided free of charge *to students*. However, provision of the schooling is not free *to the community*. The scarce resources (for example, buildings, equipment, and skills of teachers) used to produce the schooling could have been used instead to produce more recreation, entertainment, housing, or other goods. The cost of the schooling is the highest valued option that must now be given up because the resources required for its production were instead used to produce the schooling.

By now the central point should be obvious. Economic thinking recognizes that the use of a scarce resource always involves a cost. The use of more resources to do one thing implies fewer resources with which to achieve other objectives. In the next chapter we will look more closely at this key concept and some of its implications.

2. DECISION MAKERS CHOOSE PURPOSEFULLY; THEREFORE THEY WILL ECONOMIZE. Since resources are scarce, decision makers seek to choose wisely and avoid wasting their valuable resources. Recognizing the restrictions imposed by the limited resources available to them (income, time, talent, and so on), they try

Reprinted by permission: Tribune Media Services.

to select the options that best advance their own personal objectives. In turn, the objectives or preferences of individuals are revealed by the choices they make. **Economizing behavior** results directly from purposeful (rational) decision making. Economizing individuals will seek to accomplish an objective at the least possible cost to themselves. When choosing among things that yield equal benefit, an economizer will select the cheapest option. For example, if a pizza, lobster dinner, and a sirloin steak are expected to yield identical benefits (including the enjoyment of eating them!), economizing behavior implies that the cheapest of the three alternatives, probably the pizza, will be chosen. In the same way, when choosing among alternatives of equal cost, economizing decision makers will select the option that yields the greatest benefit. Purposeful decision makers will not deliberately pay more for something than is necessary.

Purposeful choosing implies that decision makers have some basis for their evaluation of alternatives. Economists refer to this evaluation as utility, the benefit or satisfaction that an individual expects from the choice of a specific alternative. The **utility** of an alternative is highly subjective, often differing widely from person to person.

3. INCENTIVES MATTER—CHOICE IS INFLUENCED IN A PREDICTABLE WAY BY CHANGES IN ECONOMIC INCENTIVES.   This guidepost to clear economic thinking might be called the basic postulate of all economics. *As the personal benefits from choosing an option increase, other things constant, a person will be more likely to choose that option. In contrast, as the personal costs associated with the choice of an item increase, the individual will be less likely to choose that option.* For a group, this basic economic postulate suggests that making an option more attractive will cause more people to choose it. In contrast, as the cost of a selection to the members of a group increases, fewer of them will make this selection.

This basic postulate of economics is a powerful tool because its application is so widespread. Incentives affect behavior in virtually all aspects of our lives, ranging from market decisions about what to buy to political choices concerning for whom to vote.

According to this basic postulate, how will consumers react if the price of beef increases (relative to other goods)? Since the higher beef prices make beef consumption more expensive, the basic postulate indicates that consumers will be less likely to choose it. The predicted result is a decline in the amount of beef consumed as the result of the increase in its price.

Economizing behavior
Choosing with the objective of gaining a specific benefit at the least possible cost. A corollary of economizing behavior implies that, when choosing among items of equal cost, individuals will choose the option that yields the greatest benefit.

Utility
The benefit or satisfaction expected from a choice or course of action.

To show its broad application, we can apply this basic postulate of economics to the examination process. If a classroom instructor makes it more costly to cheat, students will be less likely to do so. There will be little cheating on a closely monitored, individualized, essay examination. Why? Because it is difficult (that is, costly) to cheat on such an exam. Suppose, however, that an instructor gives an objective "take-home" exam, basing students' course grades entirely on the results. Among the same group of students, more will be likely to cheat because the benefits of doing so will be great and the risk (cost) minimal.

The "incentives matter" postulate is just as applicable to human behavior under socialism as under capitalism. For example, at one time in the former Soviet Union, the managers of glass plants were rewarded according to the tons of sheet glass produced. Not surprisingly, most plants met their tonnage goals more cheaply, by making sheet glass so thick that one could hardly see through it. The rules were then changed so that the managers were rewarded according to the square meters of glass produced. Under the new rules, Soviet firms stretched their resources, producing very thin glass that was cheaper per square meter, but was easily broken. Incentives matter in both capitalist and socialist countries. (The boxed feature "Do Incentives Matter?" gives yet another application of this principle.)

Marginal
Term used to describe the effects of a change in the current situation. For example, the marginal cost is the cost of producing an additional unit of a product, given the producer's current facility and production rate.

4. ECONOMIC THINKING IS MARGINAL THINKING. Fundamental to economic reasoning and economizing behavior are the effects of decisions made to change the status quo. Economists describe such decisions as **marginal.** Marginal choices always involve the effects of net additions to or subtractions from the current conditions. In fact, the word *additional* is often used as a substitute for marginal.

THE FAMILY CIRCUS®   **By Bil Keane**

"Everybody wants to be sick.
I'm using M&M's for pills."

Reprinted with special permission of King Features Syndicate.

DO INCENTIVES MATTER?

How generally can we apply the "incentives matter" principle? Does it apply, for example, to drinking and driving? Will changing the incentives with regard to drinking and driving change behavior? Consider the case of Norway, the country that has the toughest drunk-driving laws in the Western world.[1] Drinking a single can of beer before driving can put a first offender in jail for a minimum sentence of three weeks. These drivers generally lose their licenses for up to two years and often get stiff fines as well. Repeat offenders are treated even more harshly. These laws are far more draconian than those of the United States. And the results?

1.   One out of three Norwegians arrives at parties in a taxi, while nearly all Americans drive their own cars.

2.   One out of ten Norwegian partygoers spends the night at the host's home; Americans seldom do.

3.   In Norway, 78 percent of drivers totally avoid drinking at parties, compared to only 17 percent of American drivers.

Norwegians do like to drink, though they consume only half as much alcohol as Americans. The strong incentives built into Norwegian law, however, clearly make a difference in the incidence of drunken driving in that country. Once again, incentives do matter, and matter in a big way.

---

[1]The information in this feature is from L. Erik Calonius, "Just a Bottle of Beer Can Land a Motorist in Prison in Norway," *The Wall Street Journal*, August 16, 1985, p. 1.

For example, we might ask, "What is the marginal (or additional) cost of producing one more automobile?"

Marginal decisions may involve large or small changes. The "one more unit" could be a new plant or a new stapler. It is marginal because it involves additional costs and additional benefits. Given the current situation, what marginal benefits (additional sales revenues, for example) can be expected from the plant, and what will be the marginal cost of constructing it? The answers to these questions will determine whether building the new plant is a good decision.

It is important to distinguish between *average* and *marginal*. A manufacturer's current average cost of producing automobiles (total cost divided by total number of cars produced to date) may be $20,000, but the marginal cost of producing an additional automobile (or an additional 1,000 automobiles) might be much lower, say $5,000 per car. Costs associated with research, testing, design, molds, heavy equipment, and similar factors of production must be incurred whether the manufacturer is going to produce 1,000 units, 10,000 units, or 100,000 units. Such costs will clearly contribute to the average cost of an automobile. However, since these activities have already been undertaken to produce the manufacturer's current output level, the cost of producing additional units will change them very little. Thus, the manufacturer's marginal cost may be substantially less than the average cost. When determining whether to expand or reduce the production of a good, the choice should be based on marginal costs, which indicate the change in total cost due to the decision rather than the current average cost.

We often confront decisions involving a possible change from the current situation. The *marginal benefits* and *marginal costs* associated with the choice will determine the wisdom of our decisions. What happens at the margin is there-fore an important element of the economic way of thinking.

5. ALTHOUGH INFORMATION CAN HELP US MAKE BETTER CHOICES, ITS ACQUI-SITION IS COSTLY.   Thus we will almost always make choices based on limited knowledge. Information that will help us make better choices is valuable. Like other resources, however, it is also scarce and therefore costly to acquire. As a result, individuals will economize on their search for information just as they economize on the use of other scarce resources. For example, when purchasing a pair of jeans, you may check price and evaluate quality at several different stores. At some point, though, you will decide that additional shopping—that is, acquisition of additional information—is simply not worth the trouble. You will make a choice based on the limited knowledge that you already possess.

The process is similar when individuals search for a place to eat, a new car, or a roommate. They will seek to acquire some information, but at some point, they will decide that the expected benefit derived from still more information is simply not worth the cost. When individual choice is likely to make an impor-tant difference to the decision maker, more time and effort will be spent to make a better individual decision. Even then, limited knowledge and resulting uncer-tainty about the outcome characterize the decision-making process.

6. ECONOMIC ACTIONS OFTEN GENERATE SECONDARY EFFECTS IN ADDITION TO THEIR IMMEDIATE EFFECTS.   Failure to consider these secondary effects is the most common source of economic error. Frederic Bastiat, a nineteenth-century French economist, stated that the difference between a good and a bad economist is that the bad economist considers only the immediate, visible effects, whereas the good economist is also aware of the **secondary effects,** effects that result from the initial policy, but may be seen or felt only with the passage of time.

Perhaps a simple example involving both immediate and secondary effects will help us grasp this point. The immediate effect of an aspirin is a bitter taste in one's mouth. The secondary effect, which is not immediately observable, is relief from a headache. The immediate effect of drinking six quarts of beer might be a warm, jolly feeling. The secondary effect, for many, would be a pounding headache the next morning.

In economics, the immediate, short-term effects that are highly visible are often quite different from the long-term effects. Changes in economic policy

Secondary effects
Economic consequences of an economic change that are not immediately identifiable but are felt only with the passage of time.

Reprinted with special permission of King Features Syndicate.

often alter the structure of incentives, which indirectly affect things like how much people work, earn, invest, and conserve things for the future. But the impact of the secondary effects is often observable only after the passage of time—and even then only to those who know what to look for.

Consider tariffs, quotas, and other restrictions that limit imports. Proponents of such restrictions argue that they will increase employment; and, indeed, at first they do. If, for example, the supply of foreign-produced automobiles to the U.S. market were restricted, Americans would buy more American-made automobiles, increasing output and employment in the domestic auto industry. These would be the immediate, easily identified effects. But consider the secondary effects. The restrictions would also reduce supply to the domestic market and increase the price of both foreign- and American-made automobiles. As a result of the higher prices, many auto consumers would pay more for automobiles and thus be forced to curtail their purchases of food, clothing, recreation, and literally thousands of other items. These reductions in spending would mean less output and employment in those areas. There would also be a secondary effect on sales to foreigners. Since foreigners would be selling fewer automobiles to Americans, they would acquire fewer dollars with which to buy American-made goods. U.S. exports, therefore, would fall as a result of the restrictions on automobile imports.

Once the secondary effects are considered, the net impact on employment of the import restrictions is no longer obvious. The restrictions will increase employment in the auto industry, but they will also reduce employment in other industries, particularly export industries. Primarily, they will reshuffle employment rather than increase it. As this example illustrates, consideration of secondary effects is an important ingredient of the economic way of thinking.

7. THE VALUE OF A GOOD OR SERVICE IS SUBJECTIVE. Preferences differ, sometimes dramatically, between individuals. How much is a ticket to see tonight's performance of the Bolshoi Ballet worth? Some would be willing to pay a very high price, while others might prefer to stay home and avoid the ballet performance, even if tickets were free! Circumstances can change from day to day, even for a given individual. Alice, a ballet fan who usually would value the ticket at more than its price of $20, is invited to a party, and suddenly becomes uninterested in the ballet tonight. Now what is the ticket worth? If she knows a friend who would give her $5 for the ticket, it is worth at least that much. If she advertises on a bulletin board and gets $10 for it, a higher value is created by seeing that the ticket is used by the higher-valued user. But if someone who doesn't know of the ticket would have paid even more, then a potential trade that would have created even more value is missed. One thing is certain: The value of the ticket depends on several things, including who uses it and under what circumstances.

Seldom will one individual know how others would value an item. Consider how difficult it often is to know what would make a good gift, even for a close friend or family member! So, arranging trades, or otherwise moving items to higher-valued users and uses, is not a simple task. The entrepreneurial individual who can correctly anticipate what people would pay if offered the choice, and who arranges for resources to flow to higher-valued uses, can create huge increases in value from existing resources. In fact, how society promotes such coordination in the behavior of individuals who can buy and sell or produce and consume is a key subject in many of the chapters that follow.

8. THE TEST OF A THEORY IS ITS ABILITY TO PREDICT. Economic thinking is **scientific thinking.** The proof of the pudding is in the eating. The usefulness of an economic theory is proved by its ability to predict the future consequences of economic action. Economists develop economic theory from scientific thinking, using basic postulates to analyze how incentives will affect decision makers, and comparing the analysis against events in the real world. If the events in the real world are consistent with a theory, we say that the theory has *predictive value* and is therefore valid.

If it is impossible to test the theoretical relationships of a discipline, the discipline does not qualify as a science. So, since economics deals with human beings, who can think and respond in a variety of ways, can economic theories really be tested? The answer to this question is yes, if, on average, human beings respond in predictable and consistent ways to certain changes in economic conditions. The economist believes that this is the case even though not all individuals will respond in a specified manner. Economics usually does not try to predict the behavior of a specific individual; instead, it focuses on the general behavior of a large number of individuals.

How can we test economic theory when controlled experiments with all the interactions of real life are not feasible? This is a problem, but economics is no different from astronomy in this respect. Astronomers must also deal with the world as it is. They cannot change the course of the stars or planets to see what impact the change would have on the gravitational pull of the earth. And so it is with economists, who cannot arbitrarily change the price of cars or unskilled labor services just to observe the effect on quantity purchased or level of employment. However, economic conditions (for example, prices, production costs, technology, transportation costs, and so on), like the location of the planets, do change from time to time. As actual conditions change, economic theory can be tested by comparing its predictions with real-world outcomes. Just as the universe is the laboratory of the astronomer, the real economic world is the laboratory of the economist.

Scientific thinking
Development of theory from basic postulates and the testing of the implications of that theory as to their consistency with events in the real world. Good theories are consistent with and help explain real-world events. Theories that are inconsistent with the real world are invalid and must be rejected.

POSITIVE AND NORMATIVE ECONOMICS

A positive science may be defined as a body of systematized knowledge concerning what is; a normative or regulative science is a body of systematized knowledge relating to criteria of what ought to be, and concerned therefore with the ideal as distinguished from the actual.

JOHN NEVILLE KEYNES[5]

---

[5]John Neville Keynes, *The Scope and Method of Political Economy*, 4th ed. (1917), pp. 34–35.

Economics as a social science is concerned with predicting or determining the impact of changes in economic variables on the actions of human beings. Scientific economics, commonly referred to as **positive economics,** attempts to determine "what is." Positive economic statements postulate a relationship that is potentially verifiable or refutable. For example: "If the price of butter were higher, people would buy less." Or, "As the money supply increases, the price level will go up." We can statistically investigate (and estimate) the relationship between butter prices and sales, or between the supply of money and the general price level. We can analyze the facts to determine the correctness of a statement about positive economics.

Positive economics
The scientific study of "what is" among economic relationships.

Normative economics involves the advocacy of specific policy alternatives, because it uses ethical or value judgments as well as knowledge of positive economics. Normative economic statements concern "what ought to be," given the preferences and philosophical views of the advocate. Value judgments may be the source of disagreement about normative economic matters. Two persons may differ on a policy matter because one is a socialist and the other a libertarian, because one wants cheaper food while the other favors organic farming, or even because one values wilderness highly while the other wants more improved campsites that can be easily reached by roads. They may agree as to the expected outcome of altering an economic variable (that is, the positive economics of an issue), but disagree as to whether that outcome is "good" or "bad."

Normative economics
Judgments about "what ought to be" in economic matters. Normative economic views cannot be proved false, because they are based on value judgments.

In contrast with positive economic statements, normative economic statements cannot be tested and proved false (or confirmed to be correct). "Business firms should not maximize profits." "The use of pesticides on food to be sold in stores should not be allowed." "More of our national forests should be set aside for wilderness." These normative statements cannot be scientifically tested, since their validity rests on value judgments.

Positive economics does not tell us which policy is best, although by increasing our knowledge of policy options, it can eliminate one source of disagreement about policy matters. This knowledge can also reduce policy mistakes based on false expectations.

Our normative economic views can sometimes influence our attitude toward positive economic analysis. When we agree with the objectives of a policy, it is easy to overlook warnings of potential problems implied by positive economics. Desired objectives, though, are not the same as workable solutions. The actual effects of policy alternatives often differ dramatically from the objectives of their proponents. A new law forcing employers to pay all employees at least $15 per hour might be intended to help workers, but the resulting decline in the number of workers employed (and increase in the number unemployed) would be disastrous despite the good intentions. Proponents of such a law, of course, would not want to believe the economic analysis that predicted the unfortunate outcome.

The task of the professional economist is to expand our knowledge of how the real world operates, both in the private and the public sectors. If we do not fully understand the implications, including the secondary effects, of alternative actions, we will not be able to choose intelligently. Yet, it is not always easy to use economic thinking to isolate the impact of a change in an economic variable or policy. Let us consider some of the potential pitfalls to avoid in economic thinking.

PITFALLS TO AVOID IN ECONOMIC THINKING

VIOLATION OF THE CETERIS PARIBUS CONDITION

Ceteris paribus
A Latin term meaning "other things constant," used when the effect of one change is being described, recognizing that if other things changed, they also could affect the result. Economists often describe the effects of one change, knowing that in the real world, other things might change and have their effects, too.

Economists often preface their statements with the words **ceteris paribus,** a term from Latin meaning "other things constant." "Other things constant, an increase in the price of housing will cause buyers to reduce their purchases." Unfortunately for the economic researcher, we live in a dynamic world. Other things seldom remain constant. For example, as the price of housing rises, the income of consumers may also be increasing. Each of these factors—higher housing prices and an expansion in consumer income—will have an impact on housing purchases. In fact, we would generally expect them to have opposite effects: higher prices reducing housing purchases but the rise in consumer income increasing the demand for housing. The task of sorting out the specific effects of two or more variables when all are changing at the same time is difficult, though with a strong grip on economic theory, some ingenuity, and enough data, it can often be done. In fact, the major portion of the day-to-day work of many professional economists consists of statistical research.

ASSOCIATION IS NOT CAUSATION

In economics, causation is very important, and statistical association alone cannot establish causation. Perhaps an extreme example will illustrate the point. Suppose that each November a witch doctor performs a voodoo dance designed to arouse the cold-weather gods of winter, and that soon after the dance is performed the weather in fact begins to turn cold. The witch doctor's dance is associated with the arrival of winter, but does it cause the arrival of winter? Most of us would answer in the negative, even though the two are linked statistically.

Unfortunately, cause-and-effect relationships in economics are not always self-evident. For example, it is sometimes difficult to know whether a rise in income has caused people to buy more or, conversely, whether an increase in people's willingness to buy more has created more business and caused incomes to rise. Similarly, economists sometimes argue whether rising money wages are a cause or an effect of inflation. Economic theory, if rooted to the basic postulates, can often help to determine the source of causation, even though competing theories may sometimes suggest differing directions of causation.

FALLACY OF COMPOSITION

What is true for the individual (or subcomponent) may not be true for the group (or the whole). If you stand up for an exciting play during a football game, you will be better able to see. But what happens if everyone stands up at the same time? What benefits the individual does not necessarily benefit the group as a whole. When everyone stands up, the view for individual spectators fails to improve; in fact, it probably becomes even worse.

People who argue that what is true for the part is also true for the whole may be mistaken because of the **fallacy of composition.** Consider an example from economics. If you have an extra $10,000 in your bank account, you will be better off. But, what if everyone suddenly has an additional $10,000? This increase in the money supply will result in higher prices, as people with more money bid against one another for the existing supply of goods. Without an increase in the availability (or production) of scarce economic goods, the additional money will not make anyone better off. What is true for the individual can be misleading and is often fallacious when applied to the entire economy.

Potential error associated with the fallacy of composition highlights the importance of considering both a microview and a macroview in the study of economics. Because individual decision makers are the moving force behind all economic action, the foundations of economics are clearly rooted in a microview. Analysis that focuses on a single consumer, producer, product, or productive resource is referred to as **microeconomics.** As Professor Abba Lerner put it, "Microeconomics consists of looking at the economy through a microscope, as it were, to see how the millions of cells in the body economic—the individuals or households as consumers, and the individuals or firms as producers—play their part in the working of the whole organism."[6]

As we have seen, however, what is true for a small unit may not be true in the aggregate. **Macroeconomics** focuses on how the aggregation of individual micro-units affects our analysis. Like microeconomics, it is concerned with incentives, prices, and output. Macroeconomics, however, aggregates markets, lumping all 100 million households in this country together to study such topics as consumption spending, saving, and employment. Similarly, the nation's 20 million firms together are considered "the business sector."

What factors determine the level of aggregate output, the rate of inflation, the amount of unemployment, and interest rates? These are macroeconomic questions. In short, macroeconomics examines the forest rather than the individual trees. As we move from the microcomponents to a macroview of the whole, it is important that we beware of the fallacy of composition.

Fallacy of composition
Erroneous view that what is true for the individual (or the part) will also be true for the group (or the whole).

Microeconomics
The branch of economics that focuses on how human behavior affects the conduct of affairs within narrowly defined units, such as individual households or business firms.

Macroeconomics
The branch of economics that focuses on how human behavior affects outcomes in highly aggregated markets, such as the markets for labor or consumer products.

ECONOMICS AS A CAREER

If you find yourself doing well in this course, and find economics an interesting field of study, you may want to think about majoring in economics. Graduating with a major in economics provides a variety of choices. Many students go on to graduate school in economics, business, public administration, or law. Graduate M.B.A. and law programs find economics majors particularly attractive candidates because of their strong analytical skills.

A graduate degree (a master's or doctorate) in economics is typically required to pursue a career as a professional economist. About one-half of all

---

[6]Abba P. Lerner, "Microeconomy Theory," in *Perspectives in Economics*, ed. A. A. Brown, E. Neuberger, and M. Palmatier (New York: McGraw-Hill, 1968), p. 29.

professional economists are employed by colleges and universities as teachers and researchers. Professional economists also work for the government or private businesses. Most major corporations have a staff of economists to advise them in business decisions, while governments employ economists to analyze the impact of policy alternatives. The federal government has a Council of Economic Advisers whose purpose is to provide the president with analyses of how the activities of the government influence the economy. The chairmanship of the Council of Economic Advisers is a cabinet-level position.

Students who major in economics, but who do not pursue graduate school, have many job opportunities. Because economics is a way of thinking, knowledge of economics is a valuable decision-making tool on almost any job. Undergraduate majors in economics typically work in business, government service, banking, or insurance. There are even increasing opportunities for persons with only undergraduate economics majors to teach economics at the high school level.

The average salary offer for a beginning economics graduate is comparable to those with finance and accounting majors, and is generally higher than for management or marketing. The average undergraduate economics major employed as a business economist eventually earns approximately $40,000 annually. Professional economists with graduate degrees in economics who work for private business average approximately $60,000 per year, and those who choose to work as teachers and researchers at colleges and universities earn approximately $50,000 annually. While salaries vary substantially, the point is that a career in economics can be rewarding both personally and financially. If you are

MYTHS OF ECONOMICS

"ECONOMIC ANALYSIS ASSUMES PEOPLE ACT ONLY OUT OF SELFISH MOTIVES. IT REJECTS THE HUMANITARIAN SIDE OF HUMANKIND."

Probably because economics focuses on the efforts of individuals to satisfy material desires, many casual observers of the subject argue that its relevance hinges on the selfish nature of humankind. But economists recognize that people act for a variety of reasons, some selfish and some humanitarian. The point is that actions of whichever type will be influenced by costs and benefits, as viewed by the decision maker. As an activity becomes more costly, it is less likely to be chosen. As it becomes more attractive, it is more likely to be chosen.

The choices of both the humanitarian and the egocentric individual will be influenced by changes in personal costs and benefits. For example, both will be more likely to try to save the life of a small child in a three-foot swimming pool than in the rapid currents approaching Niagara Falls. Both will be more likely to give a needy person their hand-me-downs rather than their best clothes. Similarly, both will be more likely to

support a policy that generates benefits for others (farmers, the poor, the elderly) when the personal cost of doing so is low. Incentives matter for both the humanitarian and the egocentric person.

Observation would suggest that the right to control one's destiny is an "economic good" for most persons. Most of us would prefer to make our own choices rather than have someone else decide for us. But is this attitude necessarily greedy and selfish? If so, why do people often make choices in a way that is charitable toward others? After all, many people freely choose to give a portion of their wealth to the sick, the needy, the less fortunate, and to religious and charitable institutions. Economics does not imply that these choices are irrational. It does imply that if you make it more (less) costly to act charitably, fewer (more) persons will do so.

Economics deals with people as they are—not as we would like to remake them. Should people act more charitably? Perhaps so. But this is not the subject matter of economics.

interested in learning more about a major in economics, and the job opportunities available for economics majors, you might visit your school's career center or speak with your school's undergraduate adviser in economics.

Even if you choose not to major in economics, you will find that your economics courses will broaden your horizons and increase your ability to understand and analyze what is going on around you in the world of politics, business, and human relations. Economics is a social science, often overlapping with the fields of political science, sociology, and psychology. Because the economic way of thinking is so useful in making sense of the abundance of available economic data, and because there is ample opportunity for productive research using economic science in the real world, economics has sometimes been called the "queen of the social sciences." Reflecting the scientific nature of economics, the Swedish Academy of Science in 1969 instituted the Nobel prize in economic science. The men and women of genius in economics now take their place alongside those in physics, chemistry, physiology and medicine, peace, and literature.

OUTSTANDING ECONOMIST

THE IMPORTANCE OF ADAM SMITH, THE FATHER OF ECONOMICS

Economics is a relatively young science. The foundation of economics was laid in 1776, when Adam Smith (1723–1790) published *An Inquiry Into the Nature and Causes of the Wealth of Nations*. Smith presented what at that time was a revolutionary view. He argued that the wealth of a nation did not lie in gold and silver, but rather in the goods and services produced and consumed by people. According to Smith, coordination, order, and efficiency would result without the planning and direction of a central authority.

Adam Smith was a lecturer at the University of Glasgow, in his native Scotland. Morals and ethics actually were his concern before economics. His first book was *The Theory of Moral Sentiments*. For Smith, self-interest and sympathy for others were complementary. However, he did not believe that charity alone could provide the essentials for a good life. He stressed that free exchange and competitive markets would harness self-interest as a creative force. Directed by the "invisible hand" of market prices, individuals, *pursuing their own interests*, would be encouraged to produce the goods and supply the resources that others value most highly (relative to costs).

Ideas have consequences. Smith's ideas greatly influenced not only Europeans but also those who mapped out the structure of the U.S. government. Since then, the effectiveness of the "invisible hand" of the market has become accepted as critical to the prosperity of nations.[1]

---

[1]For an excellent biographical sketch of Adam Smith, used to prepare this feature, see David Henderson, ed., *The Fortune Encyclopedia of Economics* (New York: Warner Books, 1993), pp. 836–838.

LOOKING AHEAD

The primary purpose of this book is to encourage you to develop the economic way of thinking so that you can separate sound reasoning from economic nonsense. Once you have developed the economic way of thinking, economics will be relatively easy. Using the economic way of thinking can also be fun. Moreover, it will help you become a better citizen. It will give you a different and fascinating perspective on what motivates people, why they act the way they do, and why their actions sometimes go against the best interest of the community or nation. It will also give you some valuable insight into how people's actions can be rechanneled for the benefit of the community at large.

CHAPTER SUMMARY

1. Scarcity and choice are the two essential ingredients of an economic topic. Goods are scarce because desire for them far outstrips their availability from nature. Because scarcity prevents us from having as much of everything as we would like, we must choose among the alternatives available to us. Any choice involving the use of scarce resources requires an economic decision.

2. Because people want more of scarce goods than are freely available, a rationing mechanism is necessary. Competition is the natural outgrowth of the necessity for rationing scarce goods. A change in the rationing mechanism used will alter the form of competition, but it will not eliminate competitive tactics.

3. Scarcity and poverty are not the same thing. Absence of poverty implies that some basic level of need has been met. Absence of scarcity would mean that all our desires for goods have been met. We may someday be able to eliminate poverty, but scarcity will always be with us.

4. Economics is a method of approach, a way of thinking. The economic way of thinking emphasizes the following:

   a. Among economic goods, there are no free lunches. Someone must give up something if we are to have more scarce goods.

   b. Individuals make decisions purposefully, always seeking to choose the option they expect to be most consistent with their personal goals.

   c. Incentives matter. People will be more likely to choose an option as the benefits expected from that option increase. In contrast, higher costs will make an alternative less attractive, reducing the likelihood that it will be chosen.

   d. Marginal costs and marginal benefits (utility) are fundamental to economizing behavior. Economic reasoning focuses on the impact of marginal changes.

   e. Since information is scarce, uncertainty will be present when decisions are made.

   f. In addition to their initial impact, economic events often alter personal incentives in a manner that leads to important secondary effects that may be felt only with the passage of time.

   g. The value of a good or service is subjective and will differ among individuals.

   h. The test of an economic theory is its ability to predict and to explain events in the real world.

5. Economic science is positive. It attempts to explain the actual consequences of economic actions and alternative policies. Positive economics alone does not state that one policy is superior to another. Normative economics is advocative; using value judgments, it makes suggestions about "what ought to be."

6. Testing economic theory is not an easy task. When several economic variables change simultaneously, it is often difficult to determine the relative importance of each. The direction of economic causation is sometimes difficult to ascertain. Economists consult economic theory as a guide and use statistical techniques as tools to improve our knowledge of positive economics.

7. Microeconomics focuses on narrowly defined units, such as individual consumers or business firms. Macroeconomics is concerned with highly aggregated units, such as the markets for labor or goods and services. When shifting focus from micro- to macro-units, one must beware of the fallacy of composition. Both micro- and macroeconomics use the same postulates and tools. The level of aggregation is the distinction between the two.

8. The origin of economics as a systematic method of analysis dates to the publication of *The Wealth of Nations* by Adam Smith in 1776. Smith argued that production and wealth would increase if individuals were left free to work, produce, and exchange goods and services. He believed that individuals pursuing their own interests would be led by the "invisible hand" of market incentives (prices) to employ their productive talents in a manner "most advantageous to the society." Smith believed a market economy would bring individual self-interest and the public interest into harmony.

CRITICAL ANALYSIS QUESTIONS

1. Indicate how each of the following changes would influence the incentive of a decision maker to undertake the action described.

a. A reduction in the temperature from 80 degrees to 50 degrees on one's decision to go swimming.

b. A change in the meeting time of the introductory economics course from 11:00 A.M. to 7:30 A.M. on one's decision to attend the lectures.

c. A reduction in the number of exam questions that relate to the text on the student's decision to read the text.

d. An increase in the price of beef on one's decision to have steak.

e. An increase in the rental price of apartments on one's decision to build additional housing units.

*2. "The government should provide goods such as health care, education, and highways because it can provide them free." Is this statement true or false? Explain your answer.

3. Is the following disagreement between Senator Dogooder and Senator Donothing positive or normative? Explain.

Senator Dogooder: I favor an increase in the minimum wage because it would help the unskilled worker.

Senator Donothing: I oppose an increase in the minimum wage because it would cause the unemployment rate among the young and unskilled to rise.

*4. Some groups in the United States have asked for an increase in the personal income tax exemption provided to parents for each dependent child. According to the basic postulate of economics, how would this change affect the birth rate?

*5. "The economic way of thinking stresses that good intentions lead to sound policy." Is this statement true or false? Explain your answer.

6. Economic theory postulates that self-interest is a powerful motivation for action. Does this imply that people are selfish and greedy? Do self-interest and selfishness mean the same thing?

*7. Congress and government agencies often make laws to help protect the safety of product consumers. New cars, for example, are required to have many safety features before they can be sold in the United States. These rules do indeed provide added safety for buyers, although they also add to the cost and price of the new vehicles. But can you think of secondary effects of the laws that tend to undercut or reduce the intended effect of increasing auto safety?

*8. "Individuals who economize are missing the point of life. Money is not so important that it should rule the way we live." Evaluate this statement.

*9. "Positive economics cannot tell us which agricultural policy is better, so it is useless to policymakers." Evaluate this statement.

10. "I examined the statistics for our basketball team's wins last year and found that, when the third team played more, the winning margin increased. If the coach played the third team more, we would win by a bigger margin." Evaluate this statement.

---

*Asterisk denotes questions for which answers are given in Appendix B.

ADDENDUM
UNDERSTANDING GRAPHS

Economists often use graphs to illustrate economic relations. Graphs are like pictures. They are visual aids that can communicate valuable information in a small amount of space. A picture may be worth a thousand words, but only to a person who understands the picture (and the graph).

This addendum illustrates the use of simple graphs as a way to communicate. Many students, particularly those with some mathematics background, are already familiar with this material, and can safely ignore it. This addendum is for those who need to be assured that they can understand graphic economic illustrations.

THE SIMPLE BAR GRAPH

A simple bar graph helps us to visualize comparative relationships and to understand them better. It is particularly useful for illustrating how an economic indicator varies among countries, among time periods, or under alternative economic conditions.

Exhibit 1A–1 is a bar graph illustrating economic data. Part a presents a table of data on the income per person in 1994 for several countries. Part b uses a bar graph to illustrate the same data. The horizontal scale of the graph indicates the total income per person in 1994. A bar is made indicating the income level of each country. The length of each bar is in proportion to the per person income of the country. Thus, the length of the bars provides a visual illustration of how per capita income varies across the countries. For example, the extremely short bar for Tanzania shows immediately that income per person there is only a small fraction of the comparable income figure for the United States, Canada, Switzerland, and several other countries.

LINEAR GRAPHIC PRESENTATION

Economists often want to illustrate variations in economic variables with the passage of time. A linear graph with time on the horizontal axis and an economic variable on the vertical axis is a useful tool to indicate variations over time. **Exhibit 1A–2** illustrates a simple linear graph of changes in consumer prices (the inflation rate) in the United States between 1960 and 1995. The table of the exhibit presents data on the percentage change in consumer prices for each year. Beginning with 1960, the horizontal axis indicates the time period (year). The inflation rate is plotted vertically above each year. Of course, the height of the plot (line) indicates the inflation rate during that year. For example, in 1975 the inflation rate was 6.9 percent. This point is plotted at the 6.9 percent vertical distance directly above the year 1975. In 1976 the inflation rate fell to 4.9 percent. Thus, the vertical plot of the 1976 inflation rate is lower than for 1975. The inflation rate for each year (part a) is plotted at the corresponding height directly above the year. The linear graph is simply a line connecting the points plotted for each of the years 1960 through 1995.

Source: Robert Summers and Alan Heston, *The Penn World Tables* (Cambridge: National Bureau of Economic Research, 1995). The original data were for 1992. They were updated to 1994 by the authors.

EXHIBIT 1A–1

INTERNATIONAL COMPARISON OF INCOME PER PERSON

COUNTRY	TOTAL INCOME PER PERSON, 1994 (IN 1985 DOLLARS)
United States	$18,850
Canada	17,510
Switzerland	15,980
Japan	15,105
Germany	15,005
Sweden	13,930
United Kingdom	13,430
Mexico	6,260
China	1,860
India	1,335
Tanzania	470

(a)

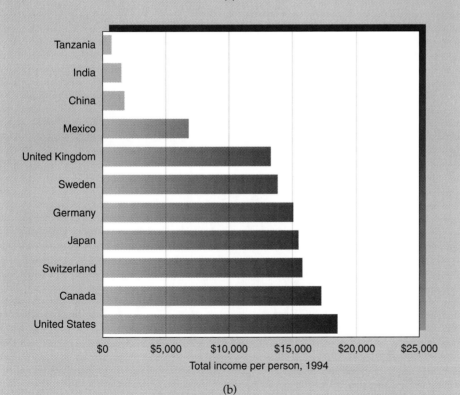

(b)

The tabular data (a) of the inflation rate is presented in graphic form in (b).

Source: *Economic Report of the President, 1991*, Table B-61; and *Economic Report of the President, 1996*, Table B-62.

EXHIBIT 1A–2

CHANGES IN LEVEL OF PRICES IN UNITED STATES, 1960–1995

YEAR	PERCENT CHANGE IN CONSUMER PRICES	YEAR	PERCENT CHANGE IN CONSUMER PRICES
1960	1.4	1978	9.0
1961	0.7	1979	13.3
1962	1.3	1980	12.5
1963	1.6	1981	8.9
1964	1.0	1982	3.8
1965	1.9	1983	3.8
1966	3.5	1984	3.9
1967	3.0	1985	3.8
1968	4.7	1986	1.1
1969	6.2	1987	4.4
1970	5.6	1988	4.4
1971	3.3	1989	4.6
1972	3.4	1990	6.1
1973	8.7	1991	3.1
1974	12.3	1992	2.9
1975	6.9	1993	2.7
1976	4.9	1994	2.7
1977	6.7	1995	3.0

(a)

(b)

The linear graph is a visual aid to understanding what happens to the inflation rate during the period. As the graph shows, the inflation rate rose sharply between 1967 and 1969, in 1973–1974, and again in 1977–1979. It was substantially higher during the 1970s than it was in the early 1960s or the mid-1980s. Although the linear graph does not communicate any information not in the table, it does make it easier to see the pattern of the data. Thus, economists often use simple graphics rather than tables to communicate information.

DIRECT AND INVERSE RELATIONSHIPS

Economic logic often suggests that two variables are linked in a specific way. Suppose an investigation reveals that, other things constant, farmers supply more wheat as the price of wheat increases. **Exhibit 1A–3** presents hypothetical data on the relationship between the price of wheat and the quantity supplied by farmers, first in tabular form (part a) and then as a simple two-dimensional graph (part b). Suppose we measure the quantity of wheat supplied by farmers on the x-axis (the horizontal axis) and the price of wheat on the y-axis (the vertical axis). Points indicating the value of x (quantity supplied) at alternative values of y (price of wheat) can then be plotted. The line (or curve) linking the points illustrates the relationship between the price of wheat and the amount supplied by farmers.

In the case of price and quantity supplied of wheat, the two variables are directly related. When the y-variable increases, so does the x-variable. When two variables are directly related, the graph illustrating the linkage between the two will slope upward to the right (as in the case of SS in part b).

Sometimes the x-variable and the y-variable are inversely related. A decline in the y-variable is associated with an increase in the x-variable. Therefore, a curve picturing the inverse relationship between x and y slopes downward to the right.

Exhibit 1A–4 illustrates this case. As the data of the table indicate, consumers purchase less as the price of wheat increases. Measuring the price of wheat on the y-axis (by convention, economists always place price on the y-axis) and the quantity of wheat purchased on the x-axis, the relationship between these two variables can also be illustrated graphically. If the price of wheat was $5 per bushel, only 60 million bushels would be purchased by consumers. As the price declines to $4 per bushel, annual consumption increases to 75 million bushels. At still lower prices, the quantity purchased by consumers will expand to larger and larger amounts. As part b illustrates, the inverse relationship between price and quantity of wheat purchased generates a curve that slopes downward to the right.

COMPLEX RELATIONSHIPS

Sometimes the initial relationship between the x- and y-variables will change. **Exhibit 1A–5** illustrates more complex relations of this type. Part a shows the typical relationship between annual earnings and age. As a young person gets work experience and develops skills, earnings usually expand. Thus, initially, age and annual earnings are directly related; annual earnings increase with age.

As the table (a) indicates, farmers are willing to supply more wheat at a higher price. Thus, there is a direct relation between the price of wheat and the quantity supplied. When the x- and y-variables are directly related, a curve mapping the relationship between the two will slope upward to the right like SS.

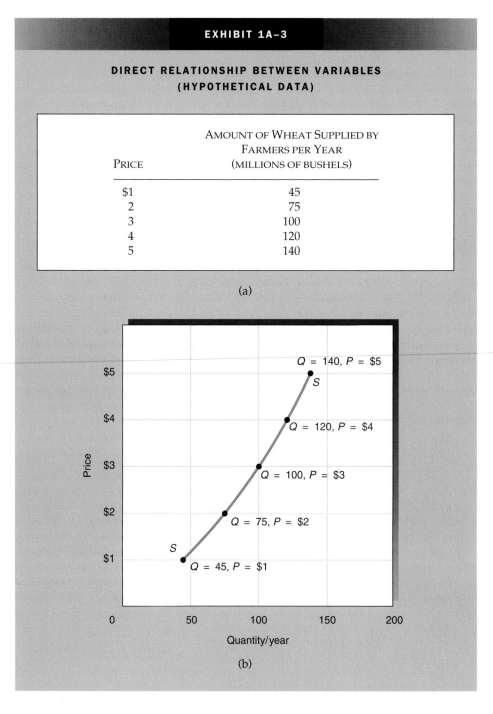

EXHIBIT 1A–3

**DIRECT RELATIONSHIP BETWEEN VARIABLES
(HYPOTHETICAL DATA)**

PRICE	AMOUNT OF WHEAT SUPPLIED BY FARMERS PER YEAR (MILLIONS OF BUSHELS)
$1	45
2	75
3	100
4	120
5	140

(a)

(b)

However, beyond a certain age (approximately age 55), annual earnings generally decline as workers approach retirement. As a result, the initial direct relationship between age and earnings changes to an inverse relation. When this is the case, annual income expands to a maximum (at age 55) and then begins to decline with years of age.

Part b illustrates an initial inverse relation that later changes to a direct rela-

EXHIBIT 1A–4

INVERSE RELATIONSHIP BETWEEN VARIABLES
(HYPOTHETICAL DATA)

PRICE	AMOUNT OF WHEAT DEMANDED BY CONSUMERS PER YEAR (MILLIONS OF BUSHELS)
$1	170
2	130
3	100
4	75
5	60

(a)

As the table (a) shows, consumers will demand (purchase) more wheat as the price declines. Thus, there is an inverse relationship between the price of wheat and the quantity demanded. When the x- and y-variables are inversely related, a curve showing the relationship between the two will slope downward to the right like DD.

(b)

tionship. Consider the impact of travel speed on gasoline consumption per mile. At low speeds, the automobile engine will not be used efficiently. As speed increases from 5 mph to 10 mph and on to a speed of 40 mph, gasoline consumption per mile declines. In this range, there is an inverse relationship between speed of travel (*x*) and gasoline consumption per mile (*y*). However, as speed increases beyond 40 mph, air resistance increases and more gasoline

At first, an increase in age (and work experience) leads to a higher income, but later earnings decline as the worker approaches retirement (a). Thus, age and annual income are initially directly related but at approximately age 55 an inverse relation emerges. Part (b) illustrates the relationship between travel speed and gasoline consumption per mile. Initially, gasoline consumption per mile declines as speed increases (an inverse relation), but as speed increases above 40 mph, gasoline consumption per mile increases with the speed of travel (direct relation).

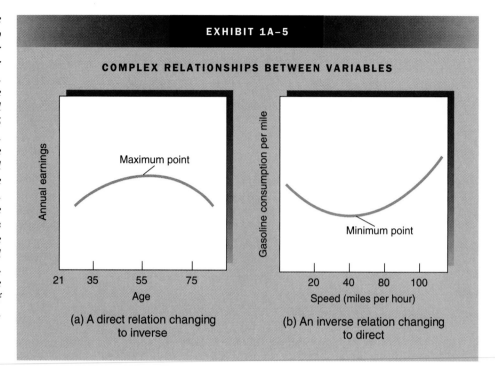

EXHIBIT 1A–5

COMPLEX RELATIONSHIPS BETWEEN VARIABLES

(a) A direct relation changing to inverse

(b) An inverse relation changing to direct

per mile is required to maintain the additional speed. At very high speeds, gasoline consumption per mile increases substantially with speed of travel. Thus, gasoline consumption per mile reaches a minimum, and a direct relationship between the *x*- and *y*-variables describes the relationship beyond that point (40 mph).

SLOPE OF A STRAIGHT LINE

In economics, we are often interested in how much the *y*-variable changes in response to a change in the *x*-variable. The slope of the line or curve reveals this information. Mathematically, the slope of a line or curve is equal to the change in the *y*-variable divided by the change in the *x*-variable.

Exhibit 1A–6 illustrates the calculation of the slope for a straight line. The exhibit shows how the daily earnings (*y*-variable) of a worker change with hours worked (the *x*-variable). The wage rate of the worker is $5 per hour, so when 1 hour is worked, earnings are equal to $5. For 2 hours of work, earnings jump to $10, and so on. A 1-hour change in hours worked leads to a $5 change in earnings. Thus, the slope of the line ($\Delta y / \Delta x$) is equal to 5. (The symbol Δ means "change in.") In the case of a straight line, the change in *y*, per unit change in *x*, is equal for all points on the line. Thus, the slope of a straight line is constant for all points along the line.

Exhibit 1A–6 illustrates a case in which there is a direct relation between the *x*- and *y*-variables. For an inverse relation, the *y*-variable decreases as the *x*-variable increases. So, when *x* and *y* are inversely related, the slope of the line will be negative.

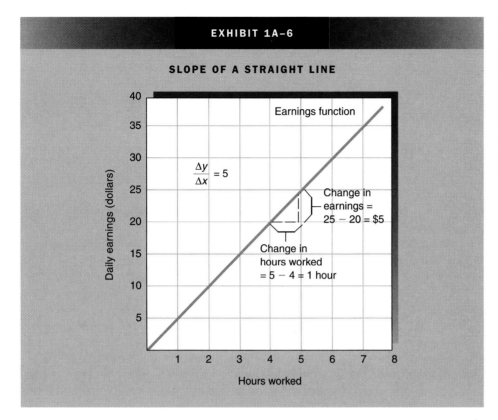

EXHIBIT 1A–6

SLOPE OF A STRAIGHT LINE

Earnings function

$\dfrac{\Delta y}{\Delta x} = 5$

Change in earnings = 25 – 20 = $5

Change in hours worked = 5 – 4 = 1 hour

Daily earnings (dollars)

Hours worked

The slope of a line is equal to the change in y divided by the change in x. The line opposite illustrates the case in which daily earnings increase by $5 per hour worked. Thus, the slope of the earnings function is 5 ($5 ÷ by 1 hr). For a straight line, the slope is constant at each point on the line.

SLOPE OF A CURVE

In contrast with a straight line, the slope of a curve is different at each point along the curve. The slope of a curve at a specific point is equal to the slope of a line tangent to the curve at the point, meaning a line that just touches the curve.

Exhibit 1A–7 illustrates how the slope of a curve at a specific point is determined. First, consider the slope of the curve at point A. A line tangent to the curve at point A indicates that y changes by one unit when x changes by two units at point A. Thus, the slope ($\Delta y/\Delta x$) of the curve at A is equal to one-half unit.

Now consider the slope of the curve at point B. The line tangent to the curve at B indicates that y changes by two units for each one unit change in x at point B. Thus, at B the slope ($\Delta y/\Delta x$) is equal to 2. At point B, a change in the x-variable leads to a much larger change in y than was true at point A. The greater slope of the curve at B reflects this greater change in y per unit change in x at B relative to A.

GRAPHS ARE NOT A SUBSTITUTE FOR ECONOMIC THINKING

By now you should have a fairly good understanding of how to read a graph. If you still feel uncomfortable with graphs, try drawing (graphing) the relationship

The slope of a curve at any point is equal to the slope of the straight line tangent to the curve at the point. As the lines tangent to the curve at points A and B illustrate, the slope of a curve will change from point to point along the curve.

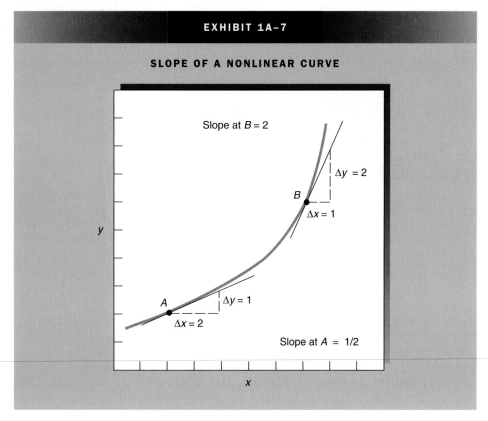

EXHIBIT 1A–7

SLOPE OF A NONLINEAR CURVE

Slope at *B* = 2

B

Δ*y* = 2

Δ*x* = 1

y

A

Δ*y* = 1

Δ*x* = 2

Slope at *A* = 1/2

x

between several things with which you are familiar. If you work, try graphing the relationship between your hours worked (*x*-axis) and your weekly earnings (*y*-axis). Exhibit 1A–6 could guide you with this exercise. Can you graph the relationship between the price of gasoline and your expenditures on gasoline? Graphing these simple relationships will give you greater confidence in your ability to grasp more complex economic relationships presented in graphs.

This text uses only simple graphs. Thus, there is no reason for you to be intimidated. Graphs look much more complex than they really are. In fact, they are nothing more than a simple device to communicate information quickly and concisely. One cannot communicate anything with a graph that cannot be communicated verbally.

Most important, graphs are not a substitute for economic thinking. Although a graph may illustrate that two variables are related, it tells us nothing about the cause-and-effect relationship between the variables. To determine probable cause and effect, we must rely on economic theory. Thus, the economic way of thinking, not graphs, is the power station of economic analysis.

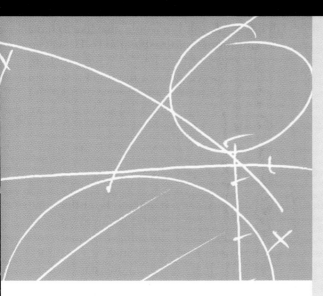

CHAPTER FOCUS

■ What is opportunity cost? Why do economists place so much emphasis on it?

■ Why do people engage in exchange?

■ How does private ownership affect the use of resources?

■ What does a production-possibilities frontier demonstrate?

■ How does exchange create value and promote economic progress?

■ What three economic decisions are faced by every nation?

■ What are the two major methods of economic organization? How do they differ?

The goods people sell usually are made by processes using a high proportion of the skills they are gifted in, whereas the goods people buy usually are made by processes they are comparatively ungifted in.

ROBERT A. MUNDELL[1]

---

[1]Robert A. Mundell, *Man and Economics: The Science of Choice* (New York: McGraw-Hill, 1968), p. 19.

I n the preceding chapter, you were introduced to the economic approach. In this chapter, we discuss some important tools that will help you develop the economic way of thinking.

WHAT SHALL WE GIVE UP?

Scarcity calls the tune in economics. We cannot have as much of everything as we would like. Most of us would like to have more time for leisure, recreation, vacations, hobbies, education, and skill development. We would also like to have more wealth, a larger savings account, and more consumable goods. However, all of these things are scarce, in the sense that they are limited. Our efforts to get more of one will conflict with our efforts to get more of the others. We can have more leisure time if we sacrifice some wealth. We can increase our current consumption if we reduce our rate of saving. Choosing more of one alternative requires us to give up something of the other.

OPPORTUNITY COST

An unpleasant fact of economics is that the choice to do one thing is, at the same time, a choice not to do something else. Your choice to spend time reading this book is a choice not to spend the time playing tennis, listening to a math lecture, or attending a party. These things must be given up because of your decision to read. As we indicated in Chapter 1, the highest valued alternative sacrificed in order to choose an option is the opportunity cost of that choice.[2]

Costs are subjective. (So are benefits. After all, a cost is a sacrificed benefit!) A cost exists in the mind of the decision maker. It is based on expectation—the expected value of the forgone alternative. Cost can never be directly measured by someone other than the decision maker because only the decision maker can place a value on what is given up.[3] Others, including experts and elected officials, who try to choose for the individual (or group of individuals), face an exceedingly difficult information problem. Individuals differ in the trade-offs they prefer to make, and those preferences change with time and circumstances. Only individuals are in a position to properly evaluate options for themselves, and to decide whether a specific trade-off is a good thing for them, in their specific circumstances of time and place.

Cost, however, often has a monetary component that enables us to approximate its value. For example, the cost of attending a ballet (or a football game) is the highest valued opportunity lost as a result of (1) the time necessary to attend and (2) the purchasing power—the money—necessary to obtain a ticket. The monetary component is, of course, objective and can be measured. So long

---

[2]See also David Henderson, "Opportunity Cost," in *The Fortune Encyclopedia of Economics*, ed. David Henderson (New York: Warner Books, Inc., 1993), pp. 44–45.

[3]See James M. Buchanan, *Cost and Choice* (Chicago: Markham, 1969), for an analysis of the relationship between cost and choice.

as individuals are paying the money price in voluntary exchange, and the good is available to others at that price, it represents for them a true opportunity cost. When nonmonetary considerations are relatively unimportant, the monetary component will approximate the total cost of an option. We should notice, though, that, to a buyer (or to one who refuses to sell), the item is probably worth more than the market price. To a seller (or one who does not buy), though, at the same time the item is worth less than the market price.

OPPORTUNITY COST AND THE REAL WORLD

Is real-world decision making influenced by opportunity cost? Remember, the basic economic postulate states that an option is more likely to be chosen when its cost to the decision maker is less. So economic theory does tell us that differences (or changes) in opportunity cost will influence decisions. So recognizing opportunity costs can help us to understand decisions—those made by college students, for example.

Consider your own decision to attend college. Your opportunity cost of going to college is the value of the next best alternative, which could be measured as the salary you would earn if you had chosen to work rather than go to college. Every year you stay in college, you give up what you could have earned by working that year. Changes in the opportunity cost of going to college will affect students' decisions to go to college. Suppose, for example, that you received a job offer today for $250,000 per year as an athlete or an entertainer, but the job would require so much travel that school would be impossible. Would this change in the opportunity cost of going to college affect your continuation in school? For many students it would; such a large increase in the cost of remaining in school would cause many students to leave. It is clear that one of the most important costs of attending college is the value of the next best alternative: the opportunity cost.

Even when their parents pay all the monetary expenses of their college education, some students are surprised to learn that they are actually incurring more of the total cost of going to college than their parents. For example, the average monetary cost (tuition, room and board, books, and so forth) for a resident student attending a public four-year college is about $10,000 per year. Even if the student's next best alternative was working at a job that only paid $15,000 per year, then over a four-year college career, he or she will incur $60,000 of the cost of college in the form of forgone earnings, while the parents will incur only about $40,000 of the cost.[4]

Now consider another decision made by college students—whether to attend a particular meeting of class. The monetary cost of attending a class (bus fare or parking and gasoline, and so on) remains fairly constant from day to day. Why then do students choose to attend class on some days and not on others? Although the monetary cost remains fairly constant, the opportunity cost

---

[4]From the standpoint of the family's total economic cost of sending a child to college, some of the monetary costs, such as room and board, should actually not be included in the calculation. At least some of these costs are not truly marginal costs; that is, they would be incurred by the family whether or not the student went to college. Which member of the family pays may, however, change.

changes each day. Because the opportunity cost of attending class on a given day is the value of the next best alternative (such as the value of sleeping later, working at a part-time job, or watching TV), on some days attending class may carry a small opportunity cost, while on other days the opportunity cost will be substantially larger. Using this concept, it is easy to understand why the last day of class before a holiday break, or the day following a big party or concert, usually has a lower attendance rate.

Failure to consider opportunity cost often leads to unwise decision making. Suppose that your community builds a beautiful new civic center. The mayor, speaking at the dedication ceremony, tells the world that the center will improve the quality of life in your community. Persons who understand the concept of opportunity cost may question this view. If the center had not been built, the resources could have been used to build a new hospital, improve the educational system, or perhaps provide better housing for low-income families. Will the civic center contribute more to the well-being of the people in your community than these other facilities? If so, it was a wise investment. If not, however, your community will be worse off than it might have been had a higher valued project (that must now be forgone) been built instead.

These examples highlight the fact that good decisions, as well as accurate predictions about human choices, often require consideration of opportunity costs. Frequently, monetary costs of a choice are only a portion of what must be sacrificed in order to make that choice. And even when money is a good measure, what really matters is the alternatives sacrificed when the money is spent.

TRADE CREATES VALUE

We learned in the preceding chapter that preferences are subjective, they are known only to the individual, and they differ among individuals. That is why the value of an item can vary greatly from one person to another. In turn, this means that simply trading—rearranging goods and services among people to get them to higher valued uses and users—can create value. In our Chapter 1 example, the value to Alice of a ticket to attend the Bolshoi Ballet performance was zero once she received the party invitation, but the value to other individuals had not declined. Suppose the value of the ticket to Jim, who bought it at the advertised price of $10, was $14. An unforeseen change in Alice's schedule had destroyed the value of the performance that evening for her, but trading (selling) the ticket to Jim created $10 in value for her, and it netted $4 in value for Jim—the $14 value he placed on the performance minus the $10 he gave to Alice. The performance remained the same, and the seats available remained the same, but trade had created value just as surely as if an additional seat had been made available. It is wrong to assume that a particular good or service has a fixed value just because it exists.[5] As the example of the ballet ticket illustrates, the value of goods and services generally depends on who uses them, and on

[5]An illuminating discussion of this subject, termed the "physical fallacy," is found in Thomas Sowell, *Knowledge and Decisions* (New York: Basic Books, 1980), pp. 67–72.

circumstances such as when and where they are used, as well as on the physical characteristics of the item.

TRANSACTION COSTS—A BARRIER TO TRADE

Unfortunately, Alice did not know about Andrew, another ballet fan, who would have been willing to pay $17 for the ticket. Andrew lives off campus and failed to see the bulletin board ad, so the potential for another $3 increase in value failed to materialize. But if Jim and Andrew happen to meet and talk about the ballet before the show, the additional $3 in value for the ticket might be created by another transaction: Jim trading the ticket to Andrew. Such a transaction is unlikely, because getting together requires either good luck or costly measures such as searching bulletin boards. Of course, new and cheaper marketing methods, such as electronic bulletin boards, can reduce the cost and increase the frequency of value-creating trades. Still, not every trade that could potentially create value will be discovered and made.

Although exchange creates value, it is also costly. The costs of the time, effort, and other resources necessary to search out, negotiate, and conclude an exchange are called **transaction costs.** *Transaction costs reduce our ability to produce gains from potential trades.*

Transaction costs
The time, effort, and other resources needed to search out, negotiate, and consummate an exchange.

Because of transaction costs, we should not expect all potentially valuable trades to take place, any more than we expect all useful knowledge to be learned, all safety measures to be taken, or all potential "A" grades to be earned. Frequent fliers know that if they never miss a flight, they are probably spending too much time waiting in airports. Similarly, the seller of a car, a house, or a ballet ticket knows that to find that one person in the world who would be willing to pay the most money is not worth the enormous effort required to locate that buyer. The cost of perfection in exchange, as in most things we do, is just too high.

MIDDLEMAN AS COST REDUCER

Because there are gains from exchange, some people, called **middlemen,** specialize in providing information and arranging trades. People sometimes think that middlemen just add to the buyer's expense without helping the buyer. Now that we recognize transaction costs, however, we can see the fallacy of this view. The auto dealer, for example, can help both the makers and the buyers of cars. By keeping an inventory of autos, and by hiring knowledgeable salespeople, the dealer lowers the cost for the car shopper to learn about the many cars offered, and how each car looks, performs, and "feels." (Don't forget that, because preferences are subjective, they are not objectively known to others.) Car buyers also like to know that the local dealer will honor the warranty and provide parts and service for the car when they are needed. The car maker, by using the dealer as a middleman, is able to concentrate on designing and making cars, leaving to middlemen—that is, dealers—the task of marketing and servicing them in each community.

Middleman
A person who buys and sells, or who arranges trades. A middleman reduces transaction costs, usually for a fee or a markup in price.

Grocers also provide middleman services. Each of us could avoid the grocer by dealing with food producers directly and buying in large quantities, perhaps shopping through catalogs to choose what we want. If we did, though, we wouldn't be able to squeeze the tomatoes! Besides, we would all need giant refrigerators, freezers, and storerooms at home to hold huge quantities of food. Or, perhaps we could form consumer cooperatives, banding together to eliminate the middleman, using our own warehouses and our own volunteer labor to order, receive, display, redistribute, and collect payment for the food. In fact, some cooperatives like this do exist, but most people prefer instead to pay the grocer to provide all of these middleman services.

Stockbrokers, publishers of the Yellow Pages, and merchants of all sorts are middlemen—specialists in selling, guaranteeing, and servicing the items traded. For a fee, they reduce transaction costs both for the shopper and for the seller. By making exchange cheaper and more convenient, middlemen cause more efficient trades to happen. In so doing, they themselves create value.

PROPERTY RIGHTS

Property rights
The right to use, control, and obtain the benefits from a good or service.

The buyer of an automobile or an apple may take the item home. The buyer of a steamship or an office building, though, might never touch it. When exchange occurs, it is really the rights—the **property rights**—to the item that change hands. In a market system of property rights, whoever wants to use a resource or a good must own it, or obtain permission from the owner. Trade occurs as one person seeks the use of one item, offering another item (or more often, money) in trade. In a market setting, it is property rights and the signals from market prices that cause individuals to take into account how others are affected by the owner's use of property. In a community that does not recognize private property rights, whoever has the power or the political authority can simply take command of an item, regardless of the wishes of the producer, or the person in possession, or of other potential users. In a community with private property rights, conditions are very different.

Private property rights
Property rights that are exclusively held by an owner, or group of owners, and that can be transferred to others at the owner's discretion.

Private property rights involve three things: (1) the right to exclusive use, (2) legal protection against invaders—those who would seek to use or abuse property without the owner's permission, and (3) the right to transfer (exchange) to another. *Private ownership links responsibility with the right of control.* Private owners cannot do anything they want with their property. Most significantly, they cannot use their property in a manner that invades or infringes on the property of another. For example, I cannot throw the hammer that I own through the television set that you own because, if I did, I would be violating your property right to your television. Since an owner has the right to control the use of a good, the owner also must accept responsibility for the outcomes of that control.

Powerful incentive effects follow from private ownership of goods. The following four factors are particularly important.

1. Private owners can gain by employing their resources in ways that are beneficial to others. On the other hand, owners bear the opportunity cost of ignoring the wishes of others.   If someone values an asset more than its current owner, the current owner can gain by paying heed to the wishes of others. For example, suppose Ed owns a car that others would also like to have. What incentive is there for Ed to pay attention to the desires of the others? If someone else values the car at $2,000, while Ed values it at only $1,500, then Ed can gain by selling the car at any price higher than $1,500. Turning down the offer of $2,000 costs Ed $500. In fact, if transaction costs are low (if search is cheap and easy), Ed might gain by searching for people (potential buyers) who want the car more than he does. If he fails to yield to the desires of others, Ed "pays" the opportunity cost for continued ownership of the car by not receiving the $2,000. Failing to consider the wishes of others may penalize the potential buyer, but it would also hurt Ed. When potential buyers and sellers know that cars are privately owned and thus easily transferable, each has every incentive to search out mutually advantageous trades. After all, if they find such a trade, only the buyer and seller have to approve the deal, and both will gain.

As a second example, suppose Ed owns a house and will be out of town all summer. Will the house stay vacant, or will Ed let someone else use it during those months? We don't know, but we do know that Ed can rent the house to someone else if he chooses, and that if he does not, he will incur the opportunity cost—the rental payments he could get, minus any damages, added upkeep, and transaction costs. Even if he is unwilling to rent the house, ownership of the private property rights again faces Ed with the opportunity costs of not renting it out, and provides him with a strong incentive to consider the wishes of others regarding the use of his property.

2. The private owner has a strong incentive to care properly for the item he or she owns.   Will Ed change the oil in his car? Will he take care to see that the seats do not get torn? Probably so, since being careless about these things would reduce the car's value, both to him and to any future owner. The car and its value—the sale price if he sells it—belong just to Ed, so he would bear the burden of a decline in the car's value if the oil ran low and ruined the engine, or if the seats were torn. Similarly, he would capture the value of an investment that improves the car, such as providing a new paint job to make the car more attractive. As the owner, Ed has both the authority and the incentive to protect the car against harm or neglect, and even to enhance its value. Private property rights give the owner a strong incentive for good stewardship.

3. The private owner has an incentive to conserve for the future if the item is expected to be worth more then.   Suppose our man Ed owns a case of very good red wine, which is only two years old. Age will improve it substantially if he

"Their house looks so nice. They must be getting ready to sell it."

From *The Wall Street Journal*— permission, Cartoon Features Syndicate.

puts it in his cellar for another five years. Will he do so? Well, if he does not, he will personally bear the consequences. He (and presumably his friends) will drink wine sooner, but they will sacrifice quality. Also, Ed will forgo the chance to sell the wine later for much more than its current worth. The opportunity cost of drinking the wine now is its unavailability later, for drinking or for sale. Ed bears that cost. Private property rights assure that Ed has the authority to preserve the wine, and that he gains the benefits if he does so. If the greater quality is expected to be worth the wait, then Ed can capture the benefits of not having the wine "before its time."

In a similar way, if Ed owns land, or a house, or a factory, he has a strong incentive to bear costs now, if necessary, to preserve the asset's value. His wealth is tied up in its value, which reflects nothing more than the net benefits that will be available to the owner in the future. So Ed's wealth depends on his willingness and ability to look ahead, maintain, and conserve those things that will be highly valued in the future.

4. With private property rights, the property owner is accountable for damage to others through misuse of the property.   Ed, the car owner, has a right to drive his car, but he has no right to drive in a drunken or reckless way that injures Alice. A chemical company has control over its products, but exactly for that reason, it is legally liable for damages if it mishandles the chemicals. Courts of law recognize and enforce the authority granted by ownership, but they also enforce the responsibility that goes with that authority. Once again, property rights hold accountable the person (owner) with authority over property.

These incentives provided by private ownership of property rights are very useful, and in fact are critical for market coordination of an economy. Private property rights and the resulting market for exchanges make possible what F. A. Hayek, the 1988 Nobel laureate in economics, called the "extended order." The ability of individuals to cooperate in mutually beneficial ways is extended worldwide in a market setting, without the need to meet each other, and without any detailed knowledge of trading partners. Private property rights eliminate the need to like one's trading partners, to respect the way they live, or to pass judgment about them. All that is required for peaceful and productive cooperation is that each person respect the legal rights of the others.

When private property rights are not present or are not enforced, other methods must be found to provide the incentives for good stewardship of property, and for proper concern for others by the users of property. For example, when the owner of an automobile or a factory pollutes the air and is not made to pay for damage to the property of others, then property rights are not being enforced. Without effective property rights, other measures may be needed to control polluting behavior. We will return to this problem in Chapter 4.

PRODUCTION POSSIBILITIES CURVE

The resources of every individual are limited. Purposeful decision making and economizing behavior imply that individuals seek to get the most from their limited resources. They do not deliberately waste resources.

The nature of the economizing problem can be made more clear by the use of a conceptual tool, the production-possibilities diagram. A **production possibilities curve** from this diagram reveals the maximum amount of any two products that can be produced from a fixed set of resources, and the possible trade-offs in production between them.

Exhibit 2–1 illustrates the production possibilities curve for Susan, an intelligent economics major. This curve indicates the combinations of English and economics grades that she thinks she can earn if she spends a total of 10 hours per week studying for the two subjects. Currently she is choosing the material to study in each course that she expects will help her grade the most, for the time spent, and she is allocating 5 hours of study time to each course. She expects that this amount of time, carefully spent on each course, will allow her to earn a B grade in both, indicated at point *T*. But if she took some time away from studying one of the two subjects and spent it studying the other, she could raise her grade in the course receiving more time. If she spent more hours on economics and fewer on English, for example, her expected economics grade would rise as a result, while her English grade would fall.

Susan's production possibility curve indicates that the additional study time required to raise her economics grade by one letter, to an A (point *S*), would require giving up two grades in her English class, not just one grade, reducing her English grade to a D. As she shifts more time away from English, she gives up some time that would have been spent studying the most important (grade-increasing) material. In contrast, as she reallocates more and more study time to economics, much of that time is spent studying additional material that is likely to be a little less helpful in producing grade points than the material chosen at point *T*. The curve is flatter to the left of point *T*, and steeper to the right,

Production possibilities curve
A curve that outlines all possible combinations of total output that could be produced, assuming (1) the utilization of a fixed amount of productive resources, (2) full and efficient use of those resources, and (3) a specific state of technical knowledge. The slope of the curve indicates the rate at which one product can be traded off to produce more of the other.

The production possibilities for Susan, in terms of grades, are illustrated for 10 hours of total study time. If Susan studied 10 hours per week in these two classes, she could attain (1) a D in English and an A in economics (point S), (2) a B in English and a B in economics (point T), or (3) a D in economics and an A in English. [Note: Spending even more of her 10 hours on economics than at point S, moving along the curve to the left, would decrease her English grade toward an F, but could not improve her A in economics. Similarly, spending more time on English than at point U, moving her downward on the curve from there, would decrease her economics grade toward an F, but could not increase her A in English, so we assume that Susan will not choose to spend time on these parts of her production-possibilities curve.]

   Could Susan move the entire curve outward, making higher grades in both? Yes, if she were willing to apply more resources, perhaps by giving up some leisure or her job.

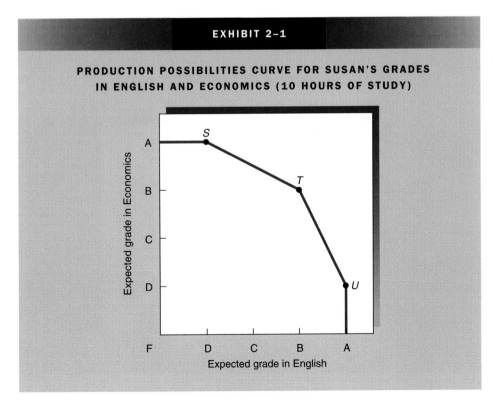

EXHIBIT 2–1

PRODUCTION POSSIBILITIES CURVE FOR SUSAN'S GRADES IN ENGLISH AND ECONOMICS (10 HOURS OF STUDY)

showing that, as she takes more and more of her resources (time in this case) from one course and puts it into the other, she must give up greater and greater amounts of productivity in the course getting fewer resources.

Of course, Susan could study more economics *without* giving up her English study time, if she gave up some leisure, or study time for other courses, or her part-time job in the campus bookstore. If she gave up leisure or her job to add to the 10 hours of study time for economics and English, the entire *STU* portion of the curve in Exhibit 2–1 would shift outward. She could get better grades in both classes by devoting more of her scarce time to studying for both of them.

Can the production-possibilities concept be applied to the entire economy? The answer is yes. We can grow more soybeans if we grow less corn, since both can be grown on the same land. Beefing up the military requires the use of resources that otherwise could be used to produce nonmilitary goods. When scarce resources are being used efficiently, more of one thing requires the sacrifice of others.

Exhibit 2–2 shows a production possibilities curve for an economy producing only two goods: food and clothing. The curve is convex, or bowed out from the origin, just as Susan's was in the previous exhibit. Why? Changing production in an efficient manner implies taking advantage of the least cost way to produce another unit. When the least cost production shifts have been undertaken, the next few in the same direction will probably be more costly in terms of the sacrifice required, just as they were for Susan in Exhibit 2–1.

Resources are not equally well suited to produce food and clothing. Consider an economy that is using all of its resources to produce clothing. At that point *(S)*, food production can be expanded by transferring those resources that are best suited for production of food (and least suitable for clothing produc-

When an economy is using its limited resources efficiently, production of more clothing requires the economy to give up some other goods—food in this simple example. With time, a technological discovery, expansion of the economy's resource base, or improvement in its economic organization could make it possible to produce more of both, shifting the production possibilities curve outward.

Or the citizens of the economy might decide to give up some leisure for more of both goods. These factors aside, limited resources will constrain the production possibilities of an economy.

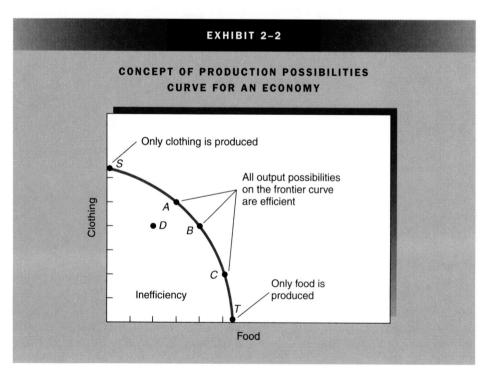

EXHIBIT 2-2

CONCEPT OF PRODUCTION POSSIBILITIES CURVE FOR AN ECONOMY

tion) from clothing to food production. Since the resources transferred are highly productive in food and not very productive in clothing, in this range the opportunity cost (clothing forgone) of producing additional food is low. However, as more and more resources are devoted to food production, and successively larger amounts of food are produced (moving from *S* to *A* to *B* and so on), the opportunity cost of food will rise. This results because as more and more food is produced, additional food output can be achieved only by using resources that are less and less suitable for the production of food relative to clothing. Thus, as food output is expanded, successively larger amounts of clothing must be forgone per unit of additional food.

What restricts the ability of an economy, once resources are fully utilized, from producing more of everything? The same thing that kept Susan from making a higher grade in both English and economics—lack of resources. There will be various maximum combinations of goods that an economy will be able to produce when:

1. It uses some fixed quantity of resources.
2. The resources are not unemployed or used inefficiently.
3. The level of technology (discussed later in this chapter) is constant.

When these three conditions are met, the economy will be at the edge of its production possibilities frontier (points such as *A, B,* and *C* in Exhibit 2–2). Producing more of one good, such as clothing, will necessitate less production of other goods (for example, food).

When the resources of an economy are unemployed or used inefficiently, the economy is operating at a point inside the production possibilities curve—point *D*, for example. Why might this happen? It happens if the economy is not properly solving the economizing problem. A major function of economic decision making is to help us get the most out of available resources, to move us out to the production possibilities frontier. We will return to this problem again and again.

SHIFTING THE PRODUCTION POSSIBILITIES CURVE OUTWARD

Could an economy ever have more of all goods? In other words, could the production-possibilities curve be shifted outward? The answer is yes, under certain circumstances. There are four major possibilities.

1. An increase in the economy's resource base would expand our ability to produce goods and services. If we had more and better resources, we could produce a greater amount of all goods. Many resources are human-made. If we were willing to give up some current consumption, we could invest more of today's resources into the production of long-lasting physical structures, machines, education, and the development of human skills. This **capital formation** would provide us with better tools and skills in the future and thereby increase our ability to produce goods and services. **Exhibit 2–3** illustrates the link between capital formation and the future production possibilities of an economy. The two economies illustrated start with the same production possibilities curve (*RS*). However, since Economy A (part a) allocates more of its resources to investment

Capital formation
The production of buildings, machinery, tools, and other equipment that will enhance the ability of future economic participants to produce. The term can also be applied to efforts to upgrade the knowledge and skill of workers and thereby increase their ability to produce in the future.

Here we illustrate two economies that initially confront identical production-possibilities curves (RS). The economy illustrated on the left allocates a larger share of its output to investment (I_a, compared to I_b for the economy on the right). As a result, the production possibilities of the high-investment economy will tend to shift outward by a larger amount than will be true for the low-investment economy.

EXHIBIT 2–3

INVESTMENT AND PRODUCTION POSSIBILITIES IN FUTURE

(a) Economy A, high investment

(b) Economy B, low investment

Technology

The technological knowledge available at any given time. The level of technology establishes the relationship between inputs and the maximum output they can generate.

Invention

The creation of a new product or process, often facilitated by the knowledge of engineering and scientific relationships.

Innovation

The successful introduction and adoption of a new product or process; the economic application of inventions and marketing techniques.

than does Economy B, A's production-possibilities curve shifts outward with the passage of time by a greater amount. The growth rate of A—the expansion rate of the economy's ability to produce goods—is enhanced because the economy allocates a larger share of its output to investment. Of course, more investment in machines and human skills requires a reduction in current consumption. (See Illustrated Exhibits I-C and I-D for evidence that high rates of investment tend to increase economic growth.)

2. Advancements in technology can expand the economy's production possibilities. **Technology** determines the maximum physical output obtainable from any particular set of resource inputs. New technology can make it possible to get more from our given base of resources.[6] An important form of technological change is **invention,** the use of science and engineering to create new products or processes. Sending information instantly and cheaply by satellite, getting more oil from a well, and growing more corn from newly developed hybrid seed are all examples of technological advances resulting from inventions. Each one has pushed our production possibilities curve outward.

An economy can also benefit from technology change through **innovation,**

---

[6]Without modern technical knowledge, it would be impossible to produce the vast array of goods and services responsible for our standard of living. Thomas Sowell makes this point clear when he notes:

> *The cavemen had the same natural resources at their disposal as we have today, and the difference between their standard of living and ours is a difference between the knowledge they could bring to bear on those resources and the knowledge used today.*

See Thomas Sowell, *Knowledge and Decisions* (New York: Basic Books, 1980), p. 47.

the practical and effective adoption of new techniques. Such innovation is commonly carried out by an **entrepreneur**—one who seeks profit by introducing new products or improved techniques to satisfy consumers at a lower cost.[7] To prosper, an entrepreneur must undertake projects that convert and rearrange resources in a manner that will increase their value, thus expanding our production possibilities. Some examples will help us explain.

One entrepreneur, Henry Ford, changed car-making technology by pioneering the assembly line. With the same amount of labor and materials, Ford made more cars, more cheaply. Another entrepreneur, the late Ray Kroc, founded the McDonald's hamburger chain. In addition to a popular restaurant menu, he provided information to potential customers. By carefully designing a limited menu that could be prepared according to strict formulas, setting up a training school (Hamburger University, outside Chicago) for managers, and providing a program for regular inspection of restaurants, he could guarantee uniformity (known products and quality level) to each customer. Once the McDonald's reputation spread, hungry people knew what to expect at the "golden arches" without even having to enter the restaurant. Trying McDonald's in one location provides information on thousands of others. Nationwide franchises and quality control make it easy for McDonald's fans to find these quick, cheap meals. The same information makes it easy for those who dislike the formula to avoid it. There is no need to sample each restaurant's offerings. In both cases, we benefit from Mr. Kroc's entrepreneurship—an innovative way to guarantee quality and to transmit instant information cheaply.

Another type of entrepreneur takes inventions produced by others and applies them more effectively. Steven Jobs, cofounder of the Apple Computer Corporation, is an example. He and his firm used the new computer technology to create personal and small-business computers, and pioneered the "user-friendly" software needed by most of us to use such machines. Selling the combination helped make computers useful to millions of people, both at home and on the job, and brought the new technology within their financial reach. Once again, entrepreneurship expanded our production possibilities.

3. An improvement in the rules under which the economy functions can increase output. The legal system of a country influences the ability of people to cooperate with one another and produce desired goods. Changes in legal institutions that promote social cooperation and enhance the incentive of people to produce will shift the production possibilities curve outward.

Historically, legal innovations have been an important source of economic progress. During the eighteenth century, a system of patents provided inventors with a private property right to their ideas. At about the same time, the recognition of the corporation as a legal entity reduced the cost of forming large firms that were often required for the mass production of manufactured goods. Both of these legal changes improved economic organization and thereby accelerated the growth of output (that is, shifted the production possibilities curve outward more rapidly) in Europe and North America.

Entrepreneur
A profit-seeking decision maker who decides which projects to undertake and how they should be undertaken. A successful entrepreneur's actions will increase the value of resources.

---

[7]This French-origin word literally means "one who undertakes." The entrepreneur is the person who is ultimately responsible. Of course, this responsibility may be shared with others (partners or stockholders, for example) or it may be partially delegated to technical experts. Nevertheless, the success or failure of the entrepreneur is dependent on the outcome of the choices he or she makes.

Sometimes governments, perhaps as the result of ignorance or prejudice, adopt legal institutions that reduce production possibilities. Laws that restrict or prohibit trade among various groups provide an illustration. For example, the laws of several southern states prohibited the employment of African Americans in certain occupations, and restricted other economic exchanges between blacks and whites for almost 100 years following the Civil War. This legislation was not only harmful to African Americans, it retarded progress and reduced the production possibilities of these states. Research across nations shows that economies in which governments allow more economic freedom produce more output per person, and have faster rates of economic growth.[8]

4. By working harder and giving up current leisure, we could increase our production of goods and services. Strictly speaking, this is not an expansion in the production frontier because leisure is also a good. We are giving up some of that good to have more of other things.

The work effort of individuals depends not only on their personal preferences but also on public policy. For example, high tax rates may induce individuals to increase their leisure by reducing their work time. The basic economic postulate implies that, as high tax rates reduce the personal payoff from working (and earning taxable income), individuals will shift more of their time to other, untaxed activities, including the consumption of leisure, moving the production possibilities curve for market goods inward. (Recall, from Exhibit 2–1, how Susan's production possibilities for grades would shift *outward* if she changed from 10 hours of study per week to more than 10 hours.) Any reduction in market work time not only reduces output directly, but is likely also to reduce the gains from the division of labor, as more people do more work for themselves because doing so is untaxed. We turn now to look at why such a reduction is important.

DIVISION OF LABOR, SPECIALIZATION, AND PRODUCTION POSSIBILITIES

In a modern economy, individuals do not produce most of the items we consume. Instead, we sell our labor services (usually agreeing to do specified productive work) and use the income we get in exchange to buy what we want.

GAINS FROM THE DIVISION OF LABOR AND ADOPTION OF MASS PRODUCTION PROCESSES

Division of labor
A method that breaks down the production of a commodity into a series of specific tasks, each performed by a different worker.

Specialization, exchange, and the **division of labor** often allow us to produce far more goods and services through cooperative effort than we could if each house-

---

[8]See, for example, James Gwartney, Robert Lawson, and Walter Block, *Economic Freedom of the World: 1975–1995* (Washington, D.C.: Cato Institute, 1996).

hold produced its own food, clothing, shelter, transportation, and other desired goods. Observing the operation of a pin manufacturer more than 200 years ago, Adam Smith noted that specialization and division of labor permitted far more output. When each worker specialized in a productive function, ten workers were able to produce 48,000 pins per day, or 4,800 pins per worker. Without specialization and division of labor, Smith doubted an individual worker could produce even 20 pins per day.[9]

The division of labor separates production tasks into a series of related operations. Each worker performs one or a few out of perhaps hundreds of tasks necessary to produce a commodity. There are several reasons why the division of labor often leads to enormous gains in output per worker. First, specialization permits individuals to take advantage of their existing abilities and skills. (Put another way, specialization permits an economy to take advantage of the fact that individuals have different skills.) Different types of work can be assigned to those individuals who are able to accomplish them most efficiently. Second, a worker who specializes in just one narrow area becomes more experienced and more skilled in that task with the passage of time. Third, and perhaps most important, the division of labor lets us adopt complex, large-scale production techniques unthinkable for an individual household. As our knowledge of technology and the potential of machinery expands, capital-intensive production procedures and the division of labor permit us to attain living standards undreamed of just a few decades ago.

GAINS FROM SPECIALIZATION AND COMPARATIVE ADVANTAGE

Economizing means getting the most out of our available resources. How can this be accomplished? How can we reach our production possibilities frontier and get more value from our productive activities? To answer these questions, we must understand a basic truth known as the **law of comparative advantage,** which lies at the heart of economizing behavior for any economy. Initially developed in the early 1800s by the great English economist David Ricardo, this law states that the total output of a group of individuals, an entire economy, or a group of nations will be greatest when the output of each good is produced by the person (or firm) with the lowest opportunity cost.

If a product, any product made in the economy, can be produced by someone else with a lower opportunity cost, the economy is giving up more than necessary. It is not economizing. Economizing, or economic efficiency, requires that output always be generated by the producer who has the lowest opportunity cost.

Once we have thought about it, the law of comparative advantage is almost common sense. It simply means that if we want to get a job done (something produced) with the smallest sacrifice, each of us should specialize in that part of the job that we do best, comparatively speaking.

The principle of comparative advantage is universal. It is just as valid in socialist countries as it is in capitalist countries. It is just as applicable to trade

Law of comparative advantage
A principle that states that individuals, firms, regions, or nations can gain by specializing in the production of goods that they produce cheaply (that is, at a low opportunity cost) and exchanging those goods for other desired goods for which they are a high-opportunity-cost producer.

---

[9]See Adam Smith, *An Inquiry into the Nature and Causes of the Wealth of Nations* (1776; Cannan's ed., Chicago: University of Chicago Press, 1976), pp. 7–16, for additional detail on the importance of the division of labor.

among individuals as trade among nations. Consider the situation of an attorney who can type 120 words per minute. The attorney is trying to decide whether to hire a secretary, who types only 60 words per minute, to complete some legal documents. If the lawyer does the typing job, it will take four hours; if a secretary is hired, the typing job will take eight hours. At first glance, we might think that the cost of the typing is less if the lawyer does it (4 hours) than if the secretary does it (8 hours). Certainly, the lawyer can do the job more quickly than the prospective employee. The *cost* of her time, though, is the $50 per hour she can earn when working as a lawyer, while the typist's time is worth just $7 per hour as a typist.

Although she is a fast typist, the attorney is still a high-opportunity-cost producer of typing service. If she types the documents, the job will cost $200, the opportunity cost of four hours of lost time as a lawyer. Alternatively, the cost of having the documents typed by the typist is only $56 (eight hours of typing service at $7 per hour). The lawyer's comparative advantage thus lies in practicing law. She will increase her own productivity, and gain income accordingly, by hiring the typist and spending her own time specializing in the practice of law.

DIVISION OF LABOR, SPECIALIZATION, AND EXCHANGE

It is difficult to exaggerate the gains derived from division of labor, specialization, and exchange in accordance with the law of comparative advantage. These factors are the primary source of our modern standard of living. Can you imagine the difficulty involved in producing one's own housing, clothing, and food, to say nothing of radios, television sets, dishwashers, automobiles, and telephone services? Yet, most families in North America, Western Europe, Japan, and Australia enjoy these conveniences. They are able to do so largely because their economies are organized in such a way that individuals can cooperate, specialize, and trade, thereby reaping the benefits of the enormous increases in output—both in quantity and diversity—thus produced.

Gains from trade are a key to economic progress. Human-made obstacles that retard exchange also retard the realization of gains from specialization, comparative advantage, and division of labor. Countries that impose such trade barriers fail to realize their full potential. (See the "Myths of Economics" box concerning gains from trade.)

PERSONAL MOTIVATION, SPECIALIZATION, AND EXCHANGE

Economic thinking implies that people will choose an option only if they expect the benefits (utility) of the choice to exceed its opportunity cost. Purposeful decision makers will be motivated by the pursuit of personal gain. They will never knowingly choose an alternative when they expect the opportunity cost to exceed the benefits. To do so would be to make a choice with the full awareness that it meant the sacrifice of another, preferred course of action. That simply would not make sense.

"IN EXCHANGE, WHEN SOMEONE GAINS, SOMEONE ELSE MUST LOSE."

People tend to think of making, building, and creating things as productive activities. Agriculture and manufacturing are like this. They create something genuinely new, something that was not there before. On the other hand, trade—the mere exchanging of one thing for another—does not create anything new. Therefore, some conclude that it is a zero-sum game in which one person's gain is necessarily a loss to another. A closer look at the motivation for trade helps one see through this popular myth. Exchange is based on agreement and the expectation of gain. If the parties did not expect the trade to improve their well-being, they would not agree to it. Because trade is mutually advantageous, it must be a positive-sum productive activity.

There are three major reasons why trade is a positive-sum activity.

First, trade channels goods and services to those who value them most. It is easy to think of material things as wealth, but material things are not wealth until they are in the hands of someone who values them. The preferences, knowledge, and goals of people vary widely. A good that is virtually worthless to one may be a precious gem to another. For example, a highly technical book on electronics that is of no value to an art collector may be worth several hundred dollars to an engineer. Similarly, a painting that is unappreciated by an engineer may be of great value to an art collector. Therefore, a voluntary exchange that moves the electronics book to the engineer and the painting to the art collector will increase the value of both goods. Simultaneously, the transaction creates wealth for both the trading partners and the nation because it channels goods to persons who value them more highly.

Second, exchange permits trading partners to gain from a larger total output as the result of specialization in those areas where they have a comparative advantage. A group of individuals, regions, or nations will be able to produce a larger joint output when each specializes in those productive activities that it does best. In turn, the larger total output allows both trading parties to gain when they produce those goods they can provide at a low cost and use the revenue generated from their sale to purchase desired products that they could produce only at a high cost. For example, exchange permits a skilled carpenter to concentrate on building house frames, while contracting for electrical and plumbing services from others who have comparative advantages in those areas. Similarly, trade permits a country such as Canada to specialize in the production of wheat, while Brazil specializes in coffee. Since the joint output of the two countries is enlarged as the result of this specialization, both can gain from the exchange of Canadian wheat for Brazilian coffee.

Third, voluntary exchange makes it possible for individuals to produce more goods through division of labor and adoption of mass production methods. In the absence of exchange, productive activity would be limited to the individual household. Self-provision and small-scale production would be the rule. Exchange permits business firms to sell their output over a broad market area; therefore, they are able to plan for large outputs and adopt complex large-scale production processes. Adoption of such mass production procedures often leads to a more efficient application of both labor and machinery and enormous increases in output per worker. Without exchanges, these gains could not be achieved.

When an individual's interest, aptitudes, abilities, and skills make it possible to gain by exchanging low-opportunity-cost goods for those things that he or she could produce only at a high opportunity cost, pursuit of the potential gain will motivate the individual to trade precisely in this manner. If free exchange is allowed, it will not be necessary for people to be ordered to perform the "right" job. In a market setting, individuals will find it in their interest—their income will be higher—if they produce and sell items for which they have a comparative advantage (items they can produce cheaply). Similarly, they will find it in their interest to buy those things that others can produce more cheaply.

Trade makes it possible for individuals, regions, and nations to gain from specialization, division of labor, and adoption of mass production techniques.

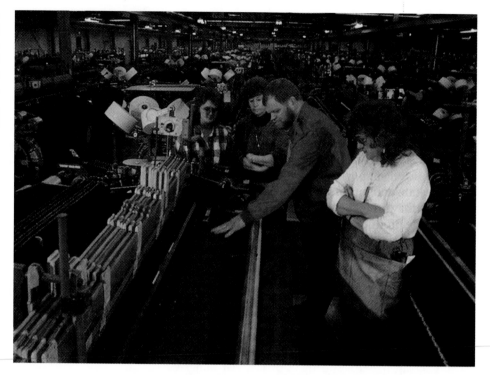

THREE ECONOMIC QUESTIONS

We have outlined several basic concepts that are important if one is to understand the economizing problem. In this section, we outline three general economic questions that every nation, regardless of its institutions, must answer.

1. What will be produced? We cannot produce as many goods as we desire. So what goods should we produce and in what quantities? Should we produce more food and less clothing, more consumer durables and less clean air, more national defense and less leisure? Or, should we use up some of our productive resources, producing more consumer goods today even though it will mean fewer goods in the future? If our economy is operating efficiently (that is, on its production-possibilities curve), the choice to produce more of one commodity will reduce our ability to produce others. Sometimes the impact may be more indirect. Production of some goods will not only require productive resources but may, as a by-product, reduce the actual availability of other goods. For example, production of warmer houses and more automobile travel may, as a by-product, increase air pollution and thus reduce the availability of clean air (another desired good). Use of natural resources (water, minerals, trees, and so on) to produce some goods may simultaneously reduce the availability of wildlife habitat. In every economy, these and similar questions concerning what should be produced must be answered.

2. How will goods be produced? Usually, different combinations of productive resources can be used to produce a good. Education could be produced with less labor by the use of more television lectures, recording devices, and books. Wheat could be raised with less land and more fertilizer. Chairs could be constructed with more labor and fewer machines. Thus, decisions must be made as to which combinations of alternative productive resources will be used to produce the goods of an economy.

After the decision to produce, resources must be organized and people must be motivated. How will the resources of an economy be transformed into the final output of goods and services? Economies may differ as to the combination of economic incentives, threats of force, and types of competitive behavior that are permissible, but all still face the problem of how their limited resources can be used to produce desired goods.

3. For whom will goods be produced? Who will actually consume the available products? This economic question is often referred to as the *distribution* problem. Property rights for resources, including labor skills, might be established and resource owners permitted to sell their services to the bidder making the best offer. Income from the sale of resource services then would be used to bid for goods. In this case, prices and resource ownership would be the determining factors of distribution. Alternatively, goods might be split on a strict per capita basis, with each person getting an equal share of the pie. Or they might be divided according to the relative political influence of citizens, with larger shares going to those who are more persuasive and skillful than others at organizing and obtaining political power. They could also be distributed according to need, with a dictator or even an all-powerful, democratically elected legislature deciding which citizens have which needs.

INTERRELATEDNESS OF THE ECONOMIC QUESTIONS

One thing is clear—these three questions are highly interrelated. How goods are distributed will exert considerable influence on the "voluntary" availability of productive resources, including human resources. The choice of what to produce will influence how resources are used. In reality, these three basic economic questions must be resolved simultaneously, and all economies, whatever their other differences, must somehow answer them. There are many ways to set up the institutions—the "rules of the game"—by which an economy makes these decisions. Each will result in a different set of answers to the universal questions.

TWO METHODS OF MAKING DECISIONS—THE MARKET OR GOVERNMENT PLANNING

Two prominent ways to organize economic activity are through the market mechanism and collective decision making. Let us briefly consider each of these methods.

Market mechanism
A method of organization that allows unregulated prices and the decentralized decisions of private property owners to resolve the basic economic problems of consumption, production, and distribution.

Capitalism
An economic system based on private ownership of productive resources and allocation of goods according to the signals provided by market prices.

Collective decision making
The method of organization that relies on public-sector decision making (voting, political bargaining, lobbying, and so on). It can be used to resolve the basic economic problems of an economy.

Socialism
A system of economic organization in which (1) the ownership and control of the basic means of production rest with the state, and (2) resource allocation is determined by centralized planning rather than by market forces.

Private ownership, voluntary contracts (often these contracts are verbal), and reliance upon market prices are the main features of the **market mechanism,** or of *capitalist economies,* as they are often called. Under market **capitalism,** people have private ownership rights to consumption goods, to their own labor, and to productive assets.[10] Private parties are permitted to buy and sell ownership rights at mutually agreeable prices in unregulated markets. The role of government is limited to that of a referee—a neutral party enforcing the rules of the game. The government recognizes, defines, and protects private ownership rights, enforces contracts, and protects people from fraud. But the government is not an active player; the political process will not be used to modify market outcomes or favor some at the expense of others. For example, the government will not prevent a seller from using price reductions and quality improvements to compete with other sellers. Nor will the government prevent a buyer from using a higher price to bid a product or productive resource away from another potential buyer. Legal restraints (for example, government licensing) will not be used to limit potential buyers or sellers from producing, selling, or buying in the marketplace. Under market organization, planning by a central authority is absent. The three basic economic questions are answered through the market coordination of the decentralized choices of buyers and sellers.

The major alternative to market organization is **collective decision making,** the use of political organization and government planning to allocate resources. The economic system in which the government owns the income-producing assets (machines, buildings, and land) and directly determines what goods they will produce is called **socialism.** Alternatively, the government may maintain private ownership in name, but use taxes, subsidies, and regulations to impose its own answers for the basic economic questions. In both instances, political rather than market forces are used to direct the economy. In both cases, the decision to expand or contract the output of education, medical services, automobiles, electricity, steel, consumer durables, and thousands of other commodities will be made by government officials and planning boards. This is not to say that the preferences of individuals have no importance. If the government officials and central planners are influenced by the democratic process, they have to consider how their actions will influence their election prospects. Otherwise, like the firm in a market economy that produces a product that consumers do not want, their tenure of service is likely to be a short one.

In most economies, including that of the United States, many decisions are made through both the decentralized pricing system and the public sector. Both exert considerable influence on how we solve fundamental economic problems. Although the two arrangements are different, in each case the choices of individuals acting as decision makers are important. Economics is about how people make decisions, and how the tools of economics can be applied to both market- and public-sector action. Constraints on the individual and incentives to pursue various types of activities will differ according to whether decisions are made politically in the public sector or in the marketplace. Still, people are people; changes in personal costs and benefits will influence their choices. In turn, the acts of political participants—voters, lobbyists, and politicians—will influence public policy and its economic consequences.

---

[10]*Capitalism* is a term coined by Karl Marx.

LOOKING AHEAD

The next chapter presents an overview of the market sector. Chapter 4 focuses on how the public sector—the democratic collective decision-making process—functions. It is not enough merely to study how the pricing system works. To understand the forces influencing the allocation of economic resources in a country such as the United States, we must apply the tools of economics to both market- and public-sector choices.

We think this approach is important, fruitful, and exciting. How does the market sector really work? What does economics say about which activities should be handled by government? What types of economic policies are politically attractive to democratically elected officials? Is sound economic policy sometimes in conflict with good politics? We will tackle all these questions.

CHAPTER SUMMARY

1. Because of scarcity, when an individual chooses to do, to make, or to buy something, that individual must simultaneously give up something else that might otherwise have been chosen. The highest valued activity sacrificed is the opportunity cost of the choice. Differences in opportunity costs (and changes in those costs) help explain human behavior observed in the real world.

2. Mutual gain is the foundation of trade. Parties to an exchange agree to the trade because they anticipate that it will improve their economic well-being.

3. Transaction costs—the time, effort, and other resources necessary to search out, negotiate, and conclude an exchange—are an obstacle to the realization of gains from trade. People who specialize in making exchange cheaper and more convenient—often called middlemen—reduce transaction costs and thereby create value by expanding the realization of gains from trade.

4. Private property rights allow owners to use or exchange their property as they see fit, as long as they do not invade or infringe upon the ownership rights of others. However, private ownership also provides owners with a strong incentive to use their resources in ways that are beneficial to others, to maintain and take good care of things, and to conserve resources for the future.

5. The production possibilities curve reveals the maximum combination of any two products that can be produced with a fixed quantity of resources, assuming that the level of technology is constant. When an individual or an economy is operating at maximum efficiency, the com-

bination of outputs chosen will be on the production possibilities curve. In such cases, greater production of one good will necessitate a reduction in the output of other goods.

6. The production possibilities curve of an economy can be shifted outward by (1) current investment that expands the future resource base of the economy, (2) technological advancement, (3) improved institutions, and (4) the forgoing of leisure and an increase in work effort. The last factor indicates that the production possibilities constraint is not strictly fixed, even during the current time period. It is partly a matter of preference.

7. Production can often be expanded through division of labor and cooperative effort among individuals. With division of labor, production of a commodity can be broken down into a series of specific tasks. Specialization and division of labor often lead to an expansion in output per worker because they (1) permit productive tasks to be undertaken by the individuals who can accomplish those tasks most efficiently, (2) lead to improvement in worker efficiency as specific tasks are performed numerous times, and (3) facilitate the efficient applications of machinery and advanced technology to the production process.

8. Joint output of individuals, regions, or nations will be maximized when goods are exchanged between parties in accordance with the law of comparative advantage. This law states that total output is maximized when parties specialize in the production of goods for which they are low-opportunity-cost producers and exchange these for goods for which they are high-opportunity-cost producers.

9. Voluntary exchange is an important source of economic progress. It creates value and wealth by (1) channeling goods to the individuals who value them most, (2) enabling the trading partners to produce more as the result of specialization in areas where they have a comparative advantage, and (3) expanding production as the result of division of labor and the adoption of mass production processes. Pursuit of personal gain will encourage people to specialize and trade in a manner that will lead to the realization of gains from these sources.

10. Every economy must answer three basic questions: (1) What will be produced? (2) How will goods be produced? (3) How will the goods be distributed? These three questions are highly interrelated.

11. There are two basic methods of making economic decisions: the market mechanism and public-sector decision making. The decisions of individuals will influence the result in both cases. The tools of economics are general. They are applicable to choices that influence both market- and public-sector decisions.

CRITICAL ANALYSIS QUESTIONS

1. "If Jones trades $2,000 to Smith for a used car, the items exchanged must be of equal value." Is this statement true, false, or uncertain?

*2. Economists often argue that wage rates reflect productivity. Yet, the wages of housepainters have increased nearly as rapidly as the national average, even though these workers use approximately the same methods that were applied 50 years ago. Can you explain why the wages of painters have risen substantially even though their productivity has changed so little?

3. It takes one hour to travel from New York City to Washington, D.C., by air, but it takes five hours by bus. If the air fare is $55 and the bus fare is $35, which would be cheaper for someone whose opportunity cost of travel time is $3 per hour? For someone whose opportunity cost is $5 per hour? $7 per hour?

4. Explain why the percentage of college-educated women employed outside the home exceeds the percentage of women with 8 years of schooling who are engaged in outside employment.

*5. "People in business get ahead by exploiting the needs of their consumers. The gains of business are at the expense of suffering imposed on their customers." Evaluate this statement from the producer of a prime-time television program.

6. With regard to the use of resources, what is the objective of the entrepreneur? What is the major function of the middleman? Is the middleman an entrepreneur?

7. If you have a private ownership right to something, what does this mean? Does private ownership give you the right to do anything that you want with the things that you own? Explain. How does private ownership influence the incentive of individuals to (a) take care of things, (b) conserve resources for the future, and (c) develop and modify things in ways that are objectionable to others? Explain.

*8. Does a 60-year-old tree farmer have an incentive to plant and care for Douglas fir trees that will not reach optimal cutting size for another 50 years?

*9. What forms of competition does a private-property, market-directed economy authorize? What forms does it prohibit?

10. What is the law of comparative advantage? According to the law of comparative advantage, what should be the distinguishing characteristics of the goods that a nation produces? What should be the distinguishing characteristics of the goods that the nation imports? How will international trade of this type influence the level of production and living standard of the populace? Explain.

11. What are the three major sources of gains from trade? Why is exchange important to the prosperity of a nation? How do physical obstacles (such as rivers, mountains, and bad roads) that increase transaction costs influence gains from trade and the prosperity of a nation? How do human-made obstacles (for example, tariffs, quotas, and legal restrictions limiting trade) that increase transaction costs influence gains from trade and prosperity?

12. "The rancher, who owns his grazing land, may overgraze it [let the cattle eat so much of the grass that erosion ruins the land] if he is desperate to make money now. Private ownership of land is dangerous." Evaluate this statement.

*13. "Really good agricultural land should not be developed for housing. Food is far more important." Evaluate this statement.

14. The United States imposes tariffs (taxes) on textiles, automobiles, computer chips, and many other imported products. Other trade restraints prohibit the importation of sugar and cheese products. How do these trade restraints affect the economic well-being of Americans?

*15. "When you're dealing with questions related to human life, economic costs are irrelevant." Evaluate this statement made by a congressman.

16. In many states, the resale of tickets to sporting events at prices above the orginal purchase price ("ticket scalping") is prohibited. Who is helped and who is hurt by such prohibitions? Can you think of ways ticket owners who want to sell might get around the prohibition? Do you think it would be a good idea to extend the resale prohibition to other things—automobiles, books, works of art, or stock shares, for example? Why or why not?

17. Consider the questions below:
   a. Do you think that your work effort is influenced by whether there is a close link between personal output and personal compensation (reward)? Explain.
   b. Suppose the grades in your class were going to be determined by a random draw at the end of the course. How would this influence your study habits?
   c. How would your study habits be influenced if everyone in the class were going to be given an A grade? How about if grades were based entirely on examinations composed of the multiple-choice questions in the coursebook for this textbook?
   d. Do you think the total output of goods in the United States is affected by the close link between productive contribution and individual reward? Why or why not?

---

*Asterisk denotes questions for which answers are given in Appendix B.

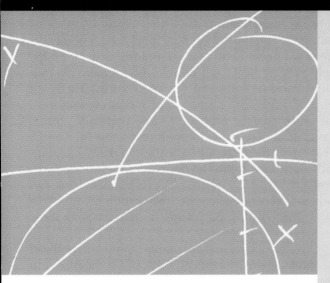

CHAPTER FOCUS

■ What do economists mean when they talk about the laws of supply and demand? How is the market price of a good determined?

■ How do market prices respond to changes in supply and demand?

■ Why is there a tendency for the market price of a good to move toward the per unit cost of producing the good?

■ As buyers and sellers respond to changes in supply and demand, what role does time play in the adjustment process?

■ What happens when prices are fixed above or below the market level?

■ What is the "invisible hand" principle?

I am convinced that if it [the market system] were the result of deliberate human design, and if the people guided by the price changes understood that their decisions have significance far beyond their immediate aim, this mechanism would have been acclaimed as one of the greatest triumphs of the human mind.

NOBEL LAUREATE FRIEDRICH HAYEK[1]

From the point of view of physics, it is a miracle that [seven million New Yorkers are fed each day] without any control mechanism other than sheer capitalism.

SCIENTIST JOHN H. HOLLAND AT THE SANTA FE INSTITUTE

---

[1]Friedrich Hayek, "The Use of Knowledge in Society," *American Economic Review* 35 (September 1945), pp. 519–530.

Computer scientist John H. Holland and other scientists use *chaos theory* and other computerized mathematical techniques to study how complex systems develop and operate without central direction. Along with biological questions, such as "How do the many kinds of specialized cells in a tree organize themselves into leaves?", they also consider economic questions, such as "How are the millions of people of New York City fed day after day with very few shortages or surpluses despite a lack of central planning of food supply and distribution?" The signals and incentives of a working market perform so well that the scientists who study complex systems are generally amazed. Their reaction adds emphasis to Professor Hayek's view, expressed in 1945, that if the market system had been designed by people, it would be "acclaimed as one of the greatest triumphs of the human mind."

The difficulty of coordinating the components of a national economy is enormous. Consider the awesome task of coordinating the economic activity of 260 million Americans with widely varying goals and desires. About half (135 million) are workers, each having various skills and job preferences. There are roughly 7 million businesses producing a vast array of products ranging from toothpicks to supercomputers. How can the actions of these economic participants be coordinated in a sensible manner? How do producers know how much of each good to produce? What keeps them from producing too many ballpoint pens and too few bicycles with reflector lights? Who directs each labor-force participant to the job that best fits his or her skills and preferences? How can we be sure that business firms will choose the correct production methods? In this chapter, we analyze how a market-directed pricing system answers these questions.

In the ideal market economy, no individual, planning board, or political authority tells the participants what to do. Markets are free and competitive, in the sense that there are no legal restrictions limiting the entry of either buyers or sellers. The economic role of government is limited to defining property rights, enforcing contracts, protecting people from fraud, and similar activities that establish the rules of the game.

Even economies that are strongly market-oriented, such as the U.S. economy, use a combination of market- and public-sector answers to the basic economic questions. Nonetheless, it is important to understand how a free-market pricing system functions, how it motivates people, and how it allocates goods and resources. Market prices drive the system, but how are these prices determined? We look first at buyers, and the demand side of price determination.

HOW MARKET PRICES ARE DETERMINED: I. CONSUMER CHOICE AND LAW OF DEMAND

Our desire for goods is far greater than the purchasing power of our income. Even rich consumers cannot purchase everything that they would like. We are all forced to make choices.

To get as much satisfaction (value) as possible from our limited income, we make such choices purposefully, choosing the alternatives that we expect to enhance our welfare the most, relative to their cost. Clearly, prices influence our decisions. A higher price of a desired good, relative to the price of other goods, means that purchasing it will require a greater sacrifice of other goods.

The basic postulate of economics says that an increase in the cost of an alternative reduces the likelihood that it will be chosen, so higher prices will reduce consumption. In contrast, lower prices reduce the opportunity cost of purchasing a good, stimulating the consumption of it. The inverse relationship between the price of a good and the amount of it that consumers are willing to buy is called the **law of demand.**

Law of demand
A principle that states there is an inverse relationship between the price of a good and the amount of it buyers are willing to purchase.

The availability of *substitutes*—goods that perform similar functions—is the main reason that consumers buy less of a product as its price increases. No single good is absolutely essential (see Myths of Economics box below). To some extent, each good can be replaced by other goods. Margarine can be substituted for butter.

MYTHS OF ECONOMICS

"THE DEMAND CURVE FOR SOME GOODS IS VERTICAL, BECAUSE FIXED AMOUNTS OF THEM ARE NEEDED FOR CONSUMPTION."

Noneconomists often ignore the impact of price and make statements implying that, for some goods, there is a fixed amount that must be available for consumption. "During the next five years the United States will need 30 million barrels of oil." "Next year the United States will need 20,000 more physicians." Have you ever heard popular commentators make statements like these, implying that the demand for some commodity is vertical—that some fixed quantity is absolutely required, regardless of the price or cost of the good?

Two points should be recognized when evaluating such statements. *First, we live in a world of substitutes.* There are alternative ways of satisfying needs. The amount of each good that it makes sense for an individual to consume is influenced by the price and availability of other goods. Often the substitutes are seemingly unrelated. For example, reading, staying home and watching television, and backyard picnics are substitutes for gasoline used for a Sunday drive to the park ten miles away. In varying degrees, there are substitutes for everything.

Second, since scarcity and limited income restrict our options, each of us will have to forgo many things that we "need"—or at least think we need. Given our limited income, purchasing them would mean that we would have to give up other things that we value more highly and therefore apparently need more urgently.

The concept of need changes with differences in income, preferences, and cultural factors. In affluent countries, families are thought to need at least one bathroom with hot and cold running water, sink, toilet, and bath or shower. Yet the typical family in many poorer countries would perceive that to be a luxury.

What about a good like water? Don't people need water to live? They do, but there are substitutes for water and people buy varying amounts depending on its price. When water is cheap and abundantly available, people will use it for not only drinking, cleaning, and cooking, but also washing cars, watering lawns, and irrigating crops. On the other hand, when it is expensive, consumers will use water constrictors for their showers, substitute cactus gardens for lush green lawns, wash their cars less often, and use sophisticated irrigation methods to conserve its usage. The quantity of water demanded, like the quantity demanded of other goods, is inversely related to its price.

Demand is important precisely because it provides information about the preferences of people—how much they value alternative scarce goods and how much they are willing to give up of some in order to have additional units of others. We all want many goods, but our incomes are limited and there are substitutes for each good. So the amount of each good that each of us will choose to purchase will depend upon its price. The vertical demand curve, like the unicorn, is a myth.

Wood, aluminum, bricks, and glass can take the place of steel. Car pools, slower driving, bicycling, and smaller cars are substitutes for gasoline, allowing households to reduce their gas consumption. When the price (and therefore the consumer's opportunity cost) of a good increases, people turn to substitute products that serve almost as well and economize on their use of the more expensive good. A larger price increase leads to more substitutions. Prices really do matter.

MARKET DEMAND SCHEDULE

Exhibit 3–1 shows a hypothetical demand schedule for videocassette recorders (VCRs) with three differing prices and the quantities that consumers would demand at each price. In the table, when the price of a VCR is $1,400, consumers would purchase 480,000 of them. But if the price were lower, $650 for example, then sales would increase to 4,020,000 units. If the price of VCRs reached $390, people would watch a lot of movies at home! VCR sales would reach 12,300,000 at that price, according to the table.[2]

Using the hypothetical data of Exhibit 3–1, **Exhibit 3–2** provides a graphic presentation of the law of demand. When representing the demand schedule graphically, economists measure price on the vertical, or *y*-axis, and the amount demanded on the horizontal, or *x*-axis. Because of the inverse relation between price and amount purchased, the demand schedule will slope downward to the right. The demand curve indicates how many additional units of the good—VCRs in our example—consumers are willing to purchase as the price declines.

The entire market demand schedule is not something that can be observed directly by government planners or decision makers of a business firm. At any

At a lower price for VCRs, consumers will purchase more of them. The consumption level of VCRs (and other products) is inversely related to their price, as consumers substitute more costly alternative ways to satisfy their wants with the good whose price is falling. At the lower price, we would expect people to watch more movies on VCRs and fewer movies at the theater, to watch fewer network TV shows, and to attend fewer sports events, for example.

EXHIBIT 3–1

CONSUMER DEMAND SCHEDULE FOR VCRs

VCR PRICE	VCR SALES
$1,400	480,000
650	4,020,000
390	12,300,000

---

[2]In the previous edition, we noted that in constant 1987 dollars, these three prices and quantity combinations were approximately correct in the United States for 1979, 1983, and 1987, and that *if we assumed that demand conditions (income, other prices, etc.) had remained constant during that time period,* then this hypothetical demand schedule would have been accurate for that time period. A number of our teaching colleagues pointed out that, although we might be technically correct, given our stated assumptions, the result could easily be misinterpreted by a student if our strong assumptions about changes in demand factors were not remembered. Recognizing this problem, we now treat the numbers as hypothetical, depicting alternative prices and quantities *at a given time.*

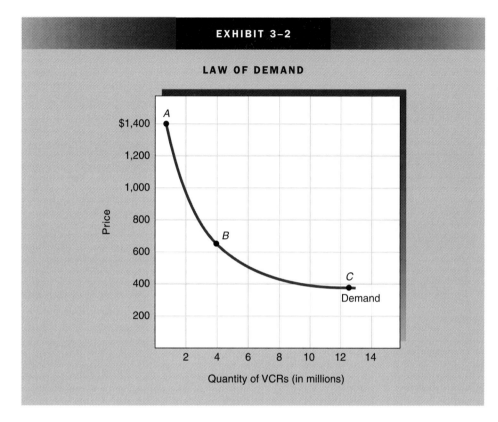

EXHIBIT 3–2

LAW OF DEMAND

Quantity of VCRs (in millions)

This demand curve shows graphically the demand schedule data from Exhibit 3–1 (points A, B, and C), fitted with a curve to indicate that other possible combinations of price and quantity along that curve could also be chosen.

point in time, only the amount purchased at the current price is observed. Nonetheless, the choices of consumers reveal important information about their preferences—their valuation of goods. *The height of the demand curve indicates the maximum price that consumers are willing to pay for an additional unit of a product.* If consumers value an additional unit of a product highly, they will be willing to pay a large amount (a high price) for it. Conversely, if their valuation of an additional unit of the good is low, they will be willing to pay only a small amount for it.

HOW MARKET PRICES ARE DETERMINED: II. PRODUCER CHOICE AND LAW OF SUPPLY

How does the market process determine the amount of each good that will be produced and offered on the market? We cannot answer this question properly unless we understand the factors that influence the choices of those who supply goods. Producers of goods and services, often using the business firm,

1. organize productive inputs, such as labor, land, natural resources, and intermediate goods,

2. transform and combine these factors of production into goods desired by households, and

3. sell the final products to consumers for a price.

Production involves the conversion of resources into commodities and services. Producers have to pay the owners of scarce resources a price that is at least equal to what the resources could earn elsewhere. Stated another way, each resource employed has to be bid away from all other uses; its owner will have to be paid its opportunity cost. The sum of the amounts paid by the producer for each productive resource, including the cost of production coordination and management, will equal the product's opportunity cost. That cost represents the value of those things given up by society to produce the product.

Profit

An excess of sales revenue relative to the cost of production. The cost component includes the opportunity cost of all resources, including those owned by the firm. Therefore, profit accrues only when the value of the good produced is greater than the sum of the values of the individual resources utilized.

All economic participants have a strong incentive to undertake activities that generate **profit,** which can be viewed as a residual "income reward" earned by decision makers who produce a good or service that is valued more highly than the resources that were required for its production. Profit is what is left over after all costs have been paid. If an activity is to be profitable, the revenue derived from the sale of the product must exceed the cost of employing the resources that have been bid away from other uses to make the product. Sometimes decision makers use resources unwisely. They use resources to produce an output that consumers value less than the opportunity cost of the resources used. **Losses** result, because the sales revenue derived from the project is not enough to pay the opportunity cost of the resources.

Loss

Deficit of sales revenue relative to the cost of production, once all the resources used have received their opportunity cost. Losses are a penalty imposed on those who use resources in lower, rather than higher, valued uses as judged by buyers in the market.

Losses discipline even the largest of firms. For example, in 1985, the Coca-Cola Company announced its carefully planned multimillion-dollar strategy to replace its main product, Coca-Cola, with "New Coke," which had a slightly different taste. There was a lukewarm reception to the new product, consumers complained that they missed the old Coke, and investors were sufficiently worried about the decision that the firm's stock quickly fell in value by $500 million. Most of that loss was regained when the company wisely went back to its earlier product, but the company had spent and lost millions of dollars by then.

In 1987, General Motors launched the Cadillac Allanté as a $54,700 coupe that would appeal to car buyers shifting their demands to European cars in that price range. But the car did not have the qualities consumers wanted at that price. It never sold even half of the 7,000 cars per year that General Motors planned. In 1993 the Allanté went out of production. Once again, a giant corporation had been taken to the woodshed and forced to learn a costly lesson.

The Allanté was on the market for only six years, but that is longer than many new products last. Innovative products can be extremely profitable, but many are not. Marketing studies have found that only about 55 to 65 percent of new products introduced are still on the market five years later.[3] Losses from the unsuccessful introduction of a new product and other unwise business decisions can lead to business failure. In 1994, for example, more than 71,500 busi-

---

[3]See "Flops," the *Business Week* cover story, August 16, 1993, pp. 76–82, for a history and explanation of new-product failures in the United States.

nesses failed in the United States. That was only 74 out of every 10,000 firms, but many more had losses and were taken over by new owners.

SUPPLY AND THE ENTREPRENEUR

As we learned in the previous chapter, entrepreneurs undertake production organization, deciding what to produce and how to produce it. The business of the entrepreneur is to figure out which projects will be profitable, and then to convince a corporation, or bankers, or individual investors to invest the resources needed to give the new idea a chance. Since the profitability of a project is affected by the price consumers are willing to pay for a product, the price of resources required to produce it, and the cost of alternative production processes, successful entrepreneurs must either be knowledgeable in each of these areas or be able to obtain the advice of others who have such knowledge.

To prosper, business entrepreneurs must convert and rearrange resources in a manner that will increase their value. An individual who purchases 100 acres of raw land, puts in a street and a sewage-disposal system, divides the plot into one-acre lots, and sells them for 50 percent more than the opportunity cost of all resources used is clearly an entrepreneur. This entrepreneur "profits" because the value of the resources has been increased. Sometimes entrepreneurial activity is less complex. For example, a 15-year-old who purchases a power mower and sells lawn service to the neighbors is also an entrepreneur seeking to profit by increasing the value of resources—his time and equipment. In a market economy, profit is the reward to the entrepreneur who discovers and acts upon an opportunity to produce a good or service that is valued more highly than the resources required for its production. Profit also provides an incentive for rival entrepreneurs to enter the market.

MARKET SUPPLY SCHEDULE

How will producer-entrepreneurs respond to a change in product price? *Other things constant, a higher price will increase the producer's incentive to supply the good.* New entrepreneurs, seeking personal gain, will enter the market and begin supplying the product. Established producers will expand the scale of their operations, leading to an additional expansion in output. Higher prices will induce producers to supply a greater amount. The direct relationship between the price of a product and the amount of it that will be supplied is termed the **law of supply.**

Exhibit 3–3 presents a graphic picture of this law. The *supply curve* summarizes information about production conditions. Unless the profit-seeking producer receives a price that is at least equal to the opportunity cost of the resources employed, the producer will not continue to supply the good. *The height of the supply curve indicates both (1) the minimum price necessary to induce producers to supply a specific quantity and (2) the opportunity cost of producing the marginal unit of the good.* The minimum supply price will be high (low) if the opportunity cost of supplying the marginal unit is high (low). Of

Law of supply
A principle that states there is a direct relationship between the price of a good and the amount of it offered for sale. As the price of a product increases, other things constant, producers will increase the amount of the product supplied to the market.

As the price of a product increases, other things constant, producers will increase the amount of the product supplied to the market.

EXHIBIT 3–3

SUPPLY CURVE

course, the opportunity cost of each unit represents valuation of the resources required for its production.

HOW MARKET PRICES ARE DETERMINED: III. SUPPLY AND DEMAND INTERACT

Market

An abstract concept that encompasses the trading arrangements of buyers and sellers that underlie the forces of supply and demand.

Consumer-buyers and producer-sellers make decisions independent of each other, but markets coordinate their choices and influence their actions. To the economist, a **market** is not a physical location, but an abstract concept that encompasses the forces generated by the buying and selling decisions of economic participants. A market may be quite narrow (for example, the market for razor blades), or it may be quite large when it is useful to aggregate diverse goods into a single market, such as the market for "consumer goods." There is also a broad range of sophistication among markets. The New York Stock Exchange is a highly computerized market in which each weekday buyers and sellers, who seldom formally meet, exchange shares of corporate ownership worth billions of dollars. In contrast, the neighborhood market for lawn-mowing services may be highly informal, since it brings together buyers and sellers primarily by word of mouth.

Equilibrium

A state of balance between conflicting forces, such as supply and demand.

Equilibrium is a state in which conflicting forces are in balance. When a market is in equilibrium, the decisions of consumers and producers are brought into harmony with one another. In equilibrium, it will be possible for both buyers and sellers to realize their choices simultaneously.

SHORT-RUN MARKET EQUILIBRIUM

The great English economist Alfred Marshall pioneered the development of supply and demand analysis. Stressing the importance of time in the production process, Marshall introduced the concepts of *short run* and *long run*. The **short run** is a time period of such short duration that business decision makers do not have enough time to build a new plant or to obtain new "made-to-order" heavy equipment for their existing facility. *In the short run, producers are stuck with their existing facility.* They are able to alter the amount of a good supplied *only* by using more (or less) labor and raw materials with their existing plant and heavy equipment.

As Exhibit 3–2 illustrates, the amount of a good demanded by consumers will be inversely related to its price. On the other hand, a higher price will induce producers to use their existing facilities more intensively in the short run. As Exhibit 3–3 shows, the amount of a good supplied will be directly related to its market price.

The market price of a commodity will tend to change in a direction that will bring the rate of consumer purchases into balance with the rate producers are willing to supply. That is, price will tend to move toward equilibrium. If the price is too high, the quantity supplied will exceed the quantity demanded. Producers will be unable to sell as much as they would like unless they reduce their price. Alternatively, if the price is too low, the quantity demanded will exceed the quantity supplied. Some consumers will be unable to get as much as they would like, unless they are willing to pay a higher price. Thus, there will be a tendency for the price in a market to move toward the price that brings the quantity demanded by consumers into balance with the quantity supplied by producers.

Exhibit 3–4 illustrates short-run supply and demand curves in the market for oversize playing cards. At a high price—$12, for example—card producers will plan to supply 600 decks of the cards per month, whereas consumers will choose to purchase only 450. An excess supply of 150 decks will result. Production exceeds sales, so inventories of producers will rise. To reduce undesired inventories, some of the oversize card producers will cut their price in order to increase their sales. Other firms will have to lower their price also, or sell even fewer decks. The lower price will make production of the cards less attractive to producers. Some of the marginal producers may go out of business, while others will reduce their current output. How low will the price go? When it has declined to $10, the quantity supplied by producers and the quantity demanded by consumers will be in balance at 550 decks per month. At this price ($10), the choices of buyers and sellers are brought into harmony. The amount that producers are willing to supply is just equal the amount that consumers want to purchase.

What will happen if the price per deck is lower—$8, for example? The amount demanded by consumers (650 units) will exceed the amount supplied by producers (500 units). An excess demand of 150 units will be present. Some consumers who are unable to purchase the cards at $8 per unit because of the inadequate supply would be willing to pay a higher price. Recognizing this fact, producers will raise their price. As the price increases to $10, producers will expand their output and consumers will cut down on their consumption. At the $10 price, short-run equilibrium will be restored.

Short run
A time period of insufficient length to permit decision makers to adjust fully to a change in market conditions. For example, in the short run, producers will have time to increase output by using more labor and raw materials, but they will not have time to expand the size of their plants or to install additional heavy equipment.

The table indicates the supply and demand conditions for oversize playing cards. These conditions are also illustrated by the graph. When the price exceeds $10, an excess supply is present, which places downward pressure on price. In contrast, when the price is less than $10, an excess demand results, which causes the price to rise. Thus, the market price will tend toward $10, at which point supply and demand will be in balance.

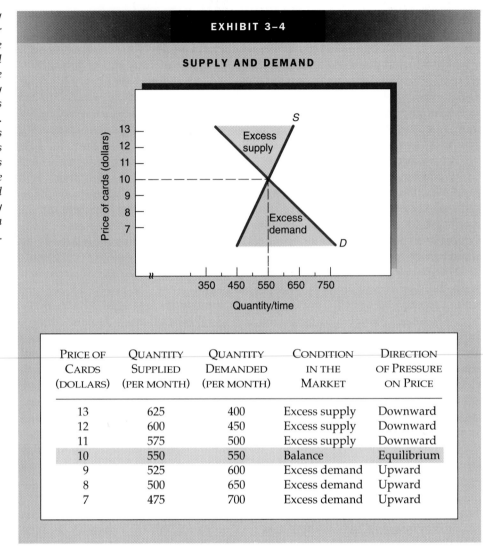

EXHIBIT 3–4

SUPPLY AND DEMAND

PRICE OF CARDS (DOLLARS)	QUANTITY SUPPLIED (PER MONTH)	QUANTITY DEMANDED (PER MONTH)	CONDITION IN THE MARKET	DIRECTION OF PRESSURE ON PRICE
13	625	400	Excess supply	Downward
12	600	450	Excess supply	Downward
11	575	500	Excess supply	Downward
10	550	550	Balance	Equilibrium
9	525	600	Excess demand	Upward
8	500	650	Excess demand	Upward
7	475	700	Excess demand	Upward

LOCAL, NATIONAL, AND WORLD MARKETS

Price equalization principle

The tendency for markets, when trade restrictions are absent, to establish a uniform price for each good throughout the world (except for price differences due to transport costs and differential tax treatment of the good).

Will prices differ from one neighborhood to another, or from one city to another, or one nation to another? If prices do differ, there may be a profit opportunity for the entrepreneur who moves goods from where they cost less to where they sell for more. When there are no trade barriers (legal restrictions limiting exchange), transportable goods will tend to trade for the same price in all markets, except for price differences caused by transportation costs and taxes. This **price equalization principle** reflects the fact that profits can be made (and value created) by transporting goods to where they are worth more. Any inequality across markets in the price of a good, for reasons other than taxes and transport costs, creates such a profit opportunity. Entrepreneurs can profit if they buy the good where the price is low and sell it in the market where the price is high. The additional buying will push the good's price upward in the low-price market, and the additional supply will drive its price down in the high-price market. Thus, profit-seeking behavior will tend to equalize the price of a transportable good across all markets—local, national, and international—except for price differences reflecting transport costs and taxation (or trade restrictions) among markets.

The price equalization principle explains why, if it costs 5 cents to transport oranges from Florida to Wisconsin, oranges will not sell for 25 cents in Florida and 50 cents in Wisconsin. If those prices were present, entrepreneurs would buy the oranges at the cheap Florida price and ship them to Wisconsin, driving the price up in Florida while decreasing the Wisconsin price. This continues to be profitable until the price differential between the two locations is reduced to only the cost of transportation (assuming similar tax treatment between the two states).

LONG-RUN MARKET EQUILIBRIUM

In the **long run,** decision makers have time to adjust fully to a change in market conditions. Thus, they can alter their output not only by using their current plant more intensively, but also by changing its size and/or its equipment. *In other words, the long run is a time period long enough to permit producers to expand the size of their capital stock (the physical structure and heavy equipment of their plant).*

A balance between amount supplied and amount demanded will bring about market equilibrium in the short run. However, for the current market price to persist in the future—that is, in the long run—an additional condition must be present: The opportunity cost of producing the product must equal the market price.

If the market price of a good is greater than the opportunity cost of producing it, suppliers will gain from an expansion in production. Attracted by the opportunity for profit, entrepreneurs will invest heavily in such an industry. The flow of capital into the industry will lead to new plant capacity and additional output. The expansion in output will continue until the additional supply lowers the market price sufficiently to eliminate the economic profit. At this point, capital invested in this market will once again earn only a normal return.

In contrast, if the market price is too low to cover the good's full opportunity cost of production, including durable capital such as specialized machinery, then suppliers will lose money if they continue to produce the good.[4] The losses will keep some producers from replacing their capital as it wears out or becomes obsolete. Over time, capital will flow away from the industry. Eventually the shrinkage in the capital base (durable productive assets) of the industry and the resulting decline in supply will push prices upward and eliminate the losses.

Long run
A time period of sufficient length to enable decision makers to adjust fully to a market change.

---

[4]Bear in mind that economists use the opportunity-cost concept for *all* factors of production, including those owned by the producers. Therefore, the owners are receiving a return equal to the opportunity cost of their investment capital even when profits are zero. Zero profits therefore mean that the capital owners are being paid precisely their opportunity cost, precisely what they could earn if their resources were employed in the highest-valued alternative that must be forgone as the result of current use. Far from indicating that a firm is about to go out of business, zero economic profits imply that each factor of production, including the capital owned by the firm and the managerial skills of the owner-entrepreneur, is earning the market rate of return.

In a market economy, characterized by freedom of entrepreneurs to enter
and exit each market, there will be a tendency for the price of products to converge toward the opportunity cost of producing the marginal units. Furthermore,
the movement of capital from low-return to higher-return markets causes the
after-tax rate of return on investment to move toward a uniform rate, the competitive rate of return. *Neither abnormally high nor abnormally low after-tax
returns will persist for long periods of time.* This tendency for returns on investment capital to move toward a uniform, normal rate is sometimes referred to as
the **rate-of-return equalization principle.**

It is easy to see why there is a tendency for abnormal investment returns—
that is, both profits and losses—to be eliminated with the passage of time in a
competitive environment. Suppose the after-tax investment return on capital was
abnormally high in the retail clothing industry and abnormally low in the publishing industry. The high return in retail clothing would cause existing suppliers to expand and would attract additional investors (rival suppliers). Supply in
the clothing industry would expand, causing both prices and returns on investment to decline. Eventually, prices would be driven down to the level of opportunity costs and normal returns would be restored in the clothing industry. Conversely, the abnormally low return in the publishing industry would cause
investment flight and a reduction in supply. This shrinkage of the capital base
and decline in supply in the publishing industry would continue, leading to
higher prices, until the remaining firms in the industry would once again be able
to cover their opportunity costs and earn returns equal to those elsewhere.

**Rate-of-return
equalization principle**
*The tendency for capital
investment in each market to
move toward a uniform, or
normal, rate of return. An
abnormally high return in a
market will attract additional
investment, which will drive
returns down. Conversely, an
abnormally low return will
result in investment flight
from the market, which will
eventually lead to the
restoration of normal returns.*

SHIFTS IN DEMAND VS. CHANGES IN QUANTITY DEMANDED

A *demand curve* isolates the impact of *price* on the amount of a product purchased.
Of course, factors other than price—for example, number of consumers, consumer income, tastes, taxes on the purchase of the product, availability and
prices of related goods, and expectations as to the future price of a product—
also influence the decisions of consumers. Until now, we have assumed that
these factors stay the same. If one of them changes, though, the entire demand
curve will shift. Economists refer to such shifts in the demand curve as a change
in *demand*.

Let us take a closer look at some of the factors that would cause the demand for a product to change. More consumers moving into a market will increase the demand in that market. Expansion in consumer income makes it possible for consumers to purchase more goods at current prices. They usually respond by increasing their spending on a wide cross section of products. A tax on the purchase of a product, such as a luxury tax on certain autos, will make buyers less willing to pay the market price for the product, decreasing the demand—the willingness to pay the seller—by the amount of the tax (shifting the demand curve to the left). Changes in prices of closely related products also influence the choices of consumers. If the price of butter were to fall, more consumers would use it in place of margarine. The demand for margarine would decline (shift to the left) as a result. Since VCRs and videocassette movies are used together, a rise in the price of cassettes (or their rental) may decrease the demand for VCRs, since watching movies on VCRs will become more costly.

Our expectations about the future price of a product also influence our current decisions. For example, if you learn that the price of an automobile you have considered buying is going to rise by 10 percent next month, this will increase your incentive to buy now, before the price rises. In contrast, if you think that the price of a product is going to decline, you will demand less now, as you attempt to move your purchase into the future, when prices are expected to be lower.

Failure to distinguish between a change in *demand* and a change in *quantity demanded* is one of the most common mistakes made by beginning economics students.[5] A change in *demand* is a shift in the entire demand curve. A change in *quantity demanded* is a movement along the same demand curve.

Exhibit 3–5 clearly demonstrates the difference between the two. The demand curve D_1 indicates the initial demand (the entire curve) for doorknobs. At a price of $3, consumers would purchase Q_1. If the price declined to $1, there would be an increase in *quantity demanded* from Q_1 to Q_3. Arrow A indicates the change in *quantity demanded*—a movement along demand curve D_1. Now, suppose that there is a 20 percent increase in income that causes a housing boom. The *demand* for doorknobs would increase from D_1 to D_2. As indicated by the B arrows, the entire demand curve would shift. At the higher income level, consumers would be willing to purchase more doorknobs at $3, at $2, at $1, and at every other price than was previously true. The increase in income leads to an increase in *demand*—a shift in the entire curve.

How will a market adjust to a change in demand conditions? Using bicycles as an example, **Exhibit 3–6** illustrates how the market for a product will react to an increase in demand. Initially, the market for bicycles reflected the demand D_1 and supply S. Given the initial market conditions, the equilibrium price of bicycles was P_1. Now suppose that consumer incomes increase or that people suddenly decide that they want to exercise more or engage in more recreational activities. As a result, the demand for bicycles increases from D_1 to D_2. This increase in demand will disrupt the initial equilibrium. After the increase in demand, consumers will want to purchase a larger quantity of bicycles than producers are willing to supply at the initial price (P_1). The excess demand will push the price of bicycles up to P_2. At the higher price, producers are willing to supply

---

[5]Questions designed to test the ability of students to make this distinction are favorites of many economics instructors. A word to the wise should be sufficient.

Arrow A indicates a change in quantity demanded, a movement along the demand curve D₁, in response to a change in the price of doorknobs. The B arrows illustrate a change in demand, a shift of the entire curve, in this case due to a housing boom.

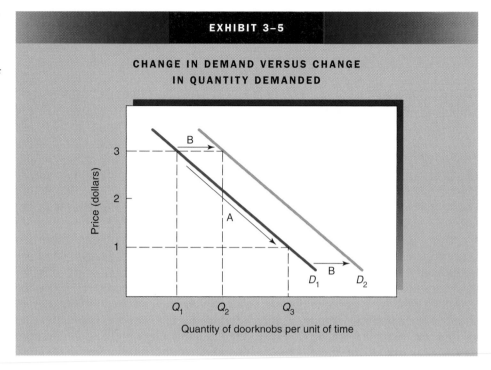

EXHIBIT 3–5

CHANGE IN DEMAND VERSUS CHANGE IN QUANTITY DEMANDED

a larger quantity (Q_2 rather than Q_1). The higher price will also moderate the increase in purchases by consumers. At the price of P_2, the quantity demanded by consumers will again be brought into balance with the quantity supplied by producers. The pricing system responds to the increase in demand by providing (1) producers with a stronger incentive to supply more bicycles and (2) con-

Initially the market for bicycles reflected demand D₁ and supply S. Suppose that there is an increase in demand for bicycles (shift from D₁ to D₂), perhaps as the result of an increase in income or an exercise craze. The higher level of demand would increase both the equilibrium price (from P₁ to P₂) and the quantity supplied (from Q₁ to Q₂) in the market for bicycles.

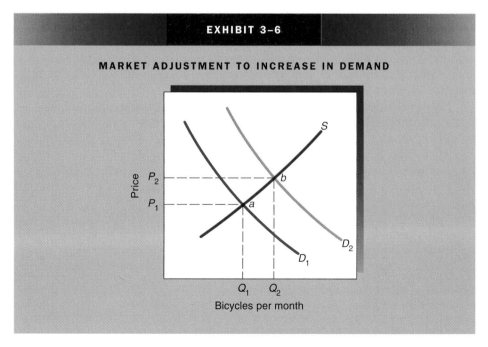

EXHIBIT 3–6

MARKET ADJUSTMENT TO INCREASE IN DEMAND

sumers with more incentive to search for substitutes and to moderate their additional purchases.

When the demand for a product declines, the adjustment process will provide buyers and sellers with just the opposite signals. A decline in demand (a shift to the left) will lead to lower prices. In turn, the lower prices will reduce the incentive of producers to supply the goods and moderate the decline in purchases by consumers.

SHIFTS IN SUPPLY

Other things constant, the supply curve summarizes the willingness of producers to offer a product at alternative prices. As with demand, it is important to note the difference between (1) a change in *quantity supplied* and (2) a change in *supply*. A change in *quantity supplied* is a movement along the same curve in response to a change in price. A change in *supply* indicates a shift in the entire supply curve.

What factors would cause a shift in the entire supply curve? How does the market for consumer goods adjust to a shift in supply? We now turn to an analysis of these two questions.

We previously indicated that a profit-seeking entrepreneur will produce a good only if the sales price of the good is expected to exceed its opportunity cost. Factors that increase the opportunity cost of producers will discourage production and decrease supply (shift the entire curve to the left). Similarly, changes that decrease the opportunity cost of producers will increase supply (shift the entire curve to the right).[6]

Let us consider a number of important factors that will shift the supply curve.

CHANGES IN RESOURCE PRICES

Resource and product markets are closely linked. Firms demand labor, machines, and other resources because they contribute to the production of goods and services. In turn, individuals supply resources in order to earn income.

---

[6]Expected future prices affect both demand and supply, but they affect supply in several rather complex ways. Thus, we will not introduce *changes in the expected future price* as a factor that shifts the supply schedule at this time. A suddenly appearing expectation that the price will rise in the future will exert conflicting influences on current producers and sellers. On the one hand, holding inventory off today's market to sell in the future becomes more attractive, reducing current supply. On the other hand, *production* (but not sales) should rise as sellers increase current output in order to build inventory for sale at the higher future price. For goods not easily stored in inventory, building more production capability for future production may increase availability now, even at prices that do not fully cover today's costs. For example, in preparation for the Olympic Games of 1996, when hotel and motel prices were expected to rise dramatically for several months, new hotels and motels were constructed in and near Atlanta in 1995. Thus the *expected* price increase for hotel rooms in 1996 (and probably for labor as the Olympics approached) increased the supply in 1995 beyond the level that the 1995 prices themselves would have warranted. As we proceed, we will consider this factor and related issues in the micro section.

In resource markets, the demand curve is typically downward-sloping and the supply curve upward-sloping, just as it is in product markets. An inverse relationship will exist between the amount of a resource demanded and its price because businesses will substitute away from a resource as its price rises. Less of the resource will be used at higher prices. In contrast, there will be a direct relationship between the amount of a specific resource supplied and its price. An increase in the price of a resource—for example, the labor services of an automotive mechanic—will make the prospect of supplying the resource more attractive. Some people who would choose other work when the wage (price) of automotive mechanics is low will be willing to supply the resource (or more of the resource) when the payoff from doing so improves.

Just as in markets for consumer goods, prices will coordinate the choices of business firms and households in resource markets. There will be a tendency for the price of each resource to move toward an equilibrium, where the amount of the resource supplied by households is in balance with the amount demanded by businesses.

How will an increase in the price of a resource affect product markets? Higher resource prices will increase the opportunity cost of producing consumer goods that use the resource. The higher costs will reduce supply and increase price in the product market. **Exhibit 3–7** illustrates this point. The wages of low-skill workers are increasing in some markets, primarily because there are fewer youthful workers (teenagers and persons in their early twenties). As part a illustrates, a reduction in the supply of low-skill workers pushes their wage rates upward (from $4.85 to $5.75). The higher price of this resource increases the opportunity cost of hamburgers at fast-food restaurants, such as McDonald's and Wendy's. In turn, the higher opportunity cost reduces supply (from S_1 to S_2) and increases hamburger prices at fast-food establishments (part b).

Suppose a reduction in the supply of low-skill labor pushes the wage rates of workers hired by fast-food restaurants upward (a). In the product market (b), the higher wage rates will increase the restaurant's opportunity cost, causing a reduction in supply (shift from S_1 to S_2), leading to higher hamburger prices.

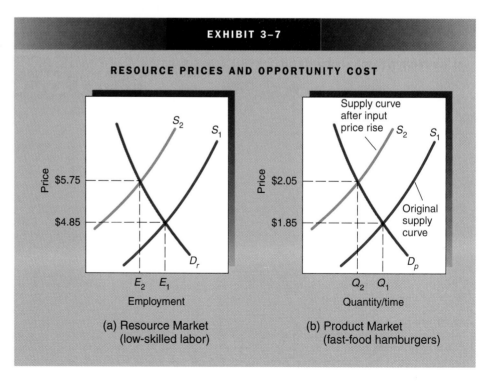

EXHIBIT 3–7

RESOURCE PRICES AND OPPORTUNITY COST

(a) Resource Market (low-skilled labor)

(b) Product Market (fast-food hamburgers)

Of course, lower resource prices would exert the opposite effect in the product market. A reduction in resource prices will reduce costs and expand the supply (a shift to the right) of consumer goods using the lower-priced resources. The increase in supply will lead to a lower price in the product market.

CHANGES IN TECHNOLOGY

Technological improvements—the discovery of new, lower-cost production techniques—will reduce the opportunity cost of production and increase supply (shift the supply curve to the right) in the product market. Previously we showed how consumers would increase their purchases of VCRs if prices for them declined (see Exhibit 3–1). **Exhibit 3–8** illustrates why VCR prices might fall. Technological improvements that substantially reduce the opportunity cost of producing VCRs will make the prospect of producing VCRs more attractive for entrepreneurs. Established firms will expand output. New firms will begin production, further contributing to the expansion of supply. The supply curve will shift to the right (from S_1 to S_2). At the old $1,400 price, consumers would not buy the larger supply of VCRs. A reduction in price to $390 is needed to bring the desires of producers to expand production into line with consumers' willingness to purchase the output. At that price, coordination of buyer and seller decisions will be achieved.

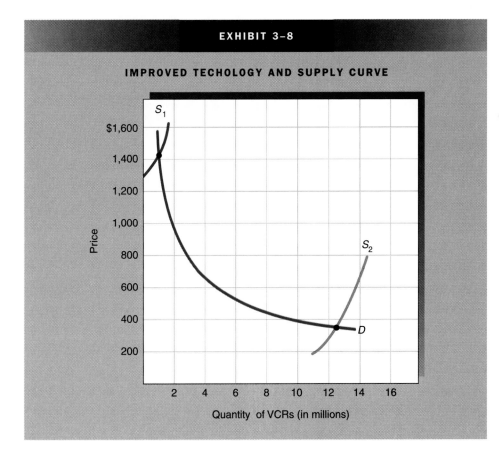

EXHIBIT 3–8

IMPROVED TECHOLOGY AND SUPPLY CURVE

As technological improvements substantially reduced the production costs of VCRs, the supply curve shifted to the right (from S_1 to S_2). Prices declined, inducing consumers to purchase a larger quantity.

ELEMENTS OF NATURE AND POLITICAL DISRUPTIONS

Natural disasters and changing political conditions may also alter supply, sometimes dramatically. For example, in 1986 a drought hit Brazil, destroying a substantial portion of that year's coffee crop. War and political unrest in Iran exerted a major impact on the supply of oil in the late 1970s, as did the invasion of Kuwait by Iraq in 1990.

In the early 1980s there was substantial overfishing in the Atlantic haddock fishery off Georges Bank, off the coasts of New England and Canada. No one owned the fishery; no one controlled access. As a result, too many fishing boats took too many fish. The breeding stock fell, and by 1986 the catch was much smaller than it had been earlier. At the 1981 price, there would have been an excess demand for haddock. As **Exhibit 3–9** shows, price rose sharply in response to the reduction in supply (shift from S_1 to S_2). Consumers cut back on their consumption of the more expensive good. Some switched to substitutes— in this case probably other varieties of fish. By 1986 the price of haddock had risen to more than twice its 1981 level, rationing the smaller supply of haddock to those most willing to pay the higher price. Balance was maintained in the market, despite the sharp drop in the supply of haddock.

CHANGES IN TAXES ON SELLERS

If the government increases the taxes on the sellers of a product, the result will be the same as any other increase in the cost of doing business. The added tax to be paid by sellers will reduce their willingness to sell at any given price. At

Overfishing of the Atlantic haddock fishery off Georges Bank in the early 1980s caused the number of haddock to decline dramatically. Supply was reduced (the supply curve shifted upwards) so that 1986 prices were more than double those of 1981. The smaller supply was rationed to buyers willing to pay the higher prices. Other buyers shifted to cheaper substitutes.

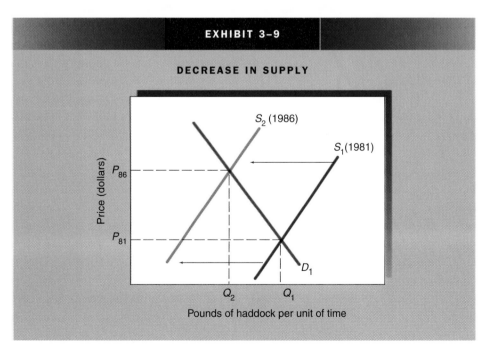

EXHIBIT 3–9

DECREASE IN SUPPLY

S_2 (1986)

S_1(1981)

Price (dollars)

P_{86}

P_{81}

D_1

Q_2 Q_1

Pounds of haddock per unit of time

THUMBNAIL SKETCH

These factors increase (decrease) the demand for a good:

1. A rise (fall) in the number of consumers in the market
2. A rise (fall) in consumer income
3. A rise (fall) in the price or decline in availability of a good used as a substitute
4. A fall (rise) in the price of a complementary good often used with the original good
5. A rise (fall) in the expected future price of the good

These factors increase (decrease) the supply of the good:

1. A fall (rise) in the price of a resource used in producing the good
2. A technological change allowing cheaper production of the good
3. Favorable weather (bad weather or a disruption in supply due to political factors, or war)
4. A reduction (increase) in the taxes imposed on the producers of the good

---

each price, only those units for which the price covers all opportunity costs, including the tax, will be offered for sale. For example, the Superfund law placed a special tax on petroleum producers based on petroleum output (not on the producer's past or present pollution level). That raised the cost of producing petroleum products, and decreased the supply (shifted the supply curve to the left), raising the price of those products.

The accompanying "Thumbnail Sketch" summarizes the major factors causing shifts in demand and supply.

TIME AND THE ADJUSTMENT PROCESS

The signals that the pricing system sends to consumers and producers will change with market conditions. The market-adjustment process will not be completed instantaneously, though. Sometimes various signals are sent out and acted upon only gradually, with the passage of time.

Using gasoline as an example, **Exhibit 3–10** illustrates the role of time as market participants adjust to a decline in supply. During the late 1970s, political turmoil in Iran—an important oil producer—caused a reduction in supply, represented by the shift from S_1 to S_2. This led to sharply higher prices for gasoline. Adjusted for inflation, gasoline prices rose from $.70 in 1978 to $1.20 in 1980. *Initially,* consumers responded to rising prices by cutting out some unnecessary trips and leisure driving, and by driving more slowly in order to get better gasoline mileage. Adjustments like these allowed consumers to reduce their consumption of gasoline, but only by a small amount (from 7.4 million to 7.0 million barrels per day), moving them up D_{sr} from point a to point b. The quantity

Here we illustrate the adjustment of a market to an unanticipated reduction in supply, such as occurred in the market for gasoline during 1978–1982. Initially, the price of gasoline was 70 cents (equilibrium a). Supply declined (shifted from S_1 to S_2) as the result of military conflict and political unrest in the Middle East. In the short run, prices rose sharply to $1.20, and consumption declined by only a small amount (equilibrium moved from a to b). In the long run, however, the demand for gasoline was more responsive to the price change. As a result, in the long run the price increase was more moderate (equilibrium moved from b to c).

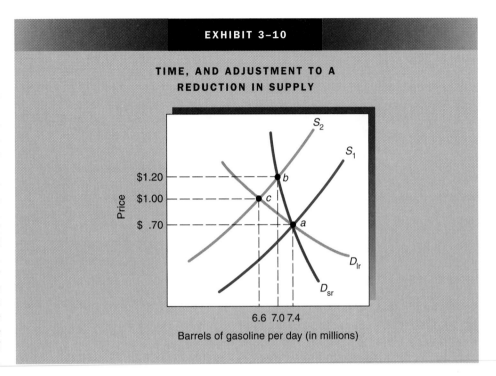

EXHIBIT 3–10

TIME, AND ADJUSTMENT TO A REDUCTION IN SUPPLY

demanded of gasoline in the short run was not very responsive to the change in price.

Given additional time, however, consumers were able to make other adjustments that influenced their consumption of gasoline. For example, as larger cars that used a lot of gasoline became old and worn out, new car purchases shifted toward smaller cars with better gas mileage. Adjustments like this caused a more price-responsive long-run demand for gasoline. By late 1981, consumption of gasoline had declined to 6.6 million barrels per day, and there was downward pressure on prices.

This adjustment process for gasoline was a typical one. The consumption response to a price change will usually be smaller in the short run than over a longer period of time. As a result, an unexpected reduction in the supply of a product will generally push the price up more in the short run than in the long run.

Similarly, the adjustments of producers to changing market conditions take time. Suppose that specialized new computer software is developed that causes an increase in demand for notebook computers. How will this change be reflected in the market? **Exhibit 3–11** provides an overview. The increase in demand is shown by the shift from D_1 to D_2. Initially, suppliers of notebooks see a decline in their inventories as the computers move off their shelves more rapidly. Discounts will be more difficult to find, deliveries to buyers will be slower, and prices will begin to rise as sellers ration their limited supplies among the increased number of buyers. The market price rises from P_1 to P_2.

A few aggressive entrepreneurs in the computer producing business may quickly expand their production of notebooks. They increase the quantity supplied quickly, by rush orders of new materials, having employees work over-

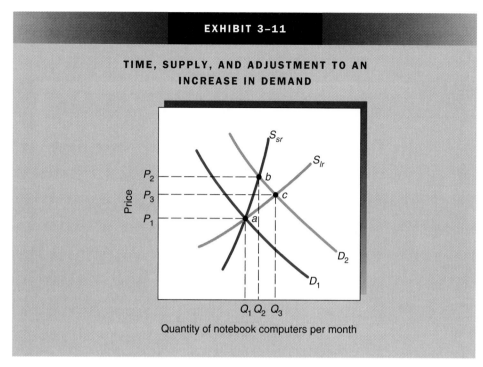

EXHIBIT 3–11

TIME, SUPPLY, AND ADJUSTMENT TO AN INCREASE IN DEMAND

Quantity of notebook computers per month

It takes time for producers to respond to an increase in price. Therefore, supply is generally more responsive to a price change in the long run than in the short run. If the market for notebook computers was initially in equilibrium at P_1 and Q_1, an unexpected increase in demand would push the price of the notebooks up sharply to price P_2 (moved from a to b). Given more time, however, producers will expand output by a larger amount in response to higher prices. The long-run supply curve will be more responsive to a price change than the short-run curve (S_{lr} rather than S_{sr}). The more responsive supply will place downward pressure on price (moved from b to c) with the passage of time.

time, and so on. But since it is costly to expand output quickly, the higher market price (P_2) will lead to only a modest increase in output from Q_1 to Q_2 in the short run. The higher prices and improved profitability, however, will encourage other, more deliberate efforts to supply more notebooks. *With the passage of time,* more resources will be brought into notebook computer production. Some resource prices will have to be bid higher in order to obtain larger quantities. This raises costs, but over time relatively efficient expansion will take place. In the long run the quantity supplied will be more responsive (S_{lr} rather than S_{sr}) and the price increase will be more moderate (P_3 rather than P_2). All these responses will take time, however, even though economists sometimes talk as if the process were instantaneous.

REPEALING THE LAWS OF SUPPLY AND DEMAND

Buyers often believe that prices are too high, while sellers complain that they are too low. Unhappy with prices established by market forces, individuals may seek to have prices set by legislative action. Fixing prices seems like a simple, straightforward solution. However, do not forget the phenomenon of secondary effects.

A **price ceiling** is a legal restriction that prohibits exchanges at prices greater than a designated price—the ceiling price. When imposed below the market equilibrium, the price ceiling will alter the operation of the market. **Exhibit 3–12,** part a, illustrates the impact of fixing a price of a product below its equilibrium

Price ceiling
A legally established maximum price that sellers may charge.

When price is fixed below the equilibrium level by a price ceiling, shortages will develop (a). In panel a, the price is not allowed to go above P₁, and the quantity demanded at that ceiling price is greater than the quantity supplied. On the other hand, if price is fixed above its equilibrium level by a price floor, then a surplus will result (b). In panel b, the price is not allowed to go below P₁, and the quantity supplied at this floor price exceeds the quantity demanded. When ceilings and floors prevent prices from bringing about a market equilibrium, nonprice factors will play a more important role in the rationing process.

EXHIBIT 3–12

IMPACT OF PRICE CEILINGS AND PRICE FLOORS

(a) Price ceiling

(b) Price floor

level. Of course, the price ceiling does result in a lower price than market forces would produce, at least in the short run. However, that is not the end of the story. At the below-equilibrium price, producers will be unwilling to supply as much as consumers would like to purchase. A **shortage** ($Q_D - Q_S$ in part a) of the good will result, a situation in which the quantity demanded by consumers exceeds the quantity supplied by producers *at the existing price*. Normally, competing buyers would bid up the price. Fixing the price will prevent that, but it will not eliminate the rationing problem. Nonprice factors will now become more important in the rationing process. Producers must discriminate on some basis other than willingness to pay as they ration their sales to eager buyers. Sellers will be partial to friends, to buyers who do them favors, and even to buyers who are willing to make illegal black-market payments.

In addition, the below-equilibrium price reduces the incentive of sellers to expand the future supply of the good. Fewer resources will flow into the production of this good, because higher profits will be available elsewhere. With the passage of time, the shortage conditions will worsen as suppliers direct resources away from production of this commodity and into other areas.

What other secondary effects can we expect? *In the real world, there are two ways that sellers can raise prices. First, they can raise their money price, holding quality constant. Or, second, they can hold the money price constant while reducing the quality of the good.* (The latter could include a reduction in the size of the product, such as a decline in the size of a candy bar or loaf of bread.) Confronting a price ceiling, sellers will rely on the latter method of raising prices. Rather than do without the good, some buyers will accept the lower-quality

Shortage

A condition in which the amount of a good offered by sellers is less than the amount demanded by buyers at the existing price. An increase in price would eliminate the shortage.

MYTHS OF ECONOMICS

"RENT CONTROLS ARE AN EFFECTIVE METHOD OF ENSURING ADEQUATE HOUSING AT A PRICE THE POOR CAN AFFORD."

Over 200 American cities maintain rent controls, intended to protect residents from high housing prices. However, economic theory suggests that when rents (a price for a good) are set below the equilibrium level, the amount of rental housing demanded by consumers will exceed the amount landlords will make available. Initially, if the mandated price is not very much below equilibrium, the impact of rent controls may be barely noticeable. With the passage of time, however, their effects will grow. Inevitably, controls will lead to the following results.

1. The future supply of rental houses will decline. The below-equilibrium price will discourage entrepreneurs from constructing new rental housing units. Private investment will flow elsewhere, since the controls have depressed the rate of return in the rental housing market. In the city of Berkeley, rental units available to students of the University of California reportedly dropped 31 percent in the first five years after the city adopted rent controls in 1978.[1]

2. Shortages and black markets will develop. Since the quantity of housing supplied will fail to keep pace with the quantity demanded, some persons who value rental housing highly will be unable to find it. Frustrated by the shortage, they will seek methods by which they may induce landlords to rent to them. Some will agree to prepay their rent, including a substantial damage deposit. Others might agree to rent or buy the landlords' furniture at an exorbitant price in order to obtain an apartment. Still others will make under-the-table (black market) payments to secure the cheap housing.

3. The quality of rental housing will deteriorate. Economic thinking suggests that there are two ways to raise prices. The nominal price can be increased, quality being held constant. Alternatively, quality can be reduced, while the nominal price is maintained. When landlords are prohibited from adopting the former, they will use the latter. Normal maintenance and repair service will deteriorate. Tenant parking lots will be eliminated (or rented). Eventually, the quality of the rental housing will reflect the controlled price. Cheap housing will be of cheap quality.

4. Nonprice methods of rationing will increase in importance. Since price no longer plays its normal role, other forms of competition will develop. Prohibited from price rationing, landlords will have to rely more heavily on nonmonetary discriminating devices. They will favor friends, persons of influence, and those with lifestyles similar to their own. In contrast, applicants with many children, unconventional lifestyles, or perhaps dark skin will find fewer landlords who cater to their personal requirements. Since the cost to landlords of discriminating against those with characteristics they do not like has been reduced, such discrimination will become more prevalent in the rationing process.

5. Inefficient use of housing space will result. The tenant in a rent-controlled apartment will think twice before moving. Why? Even though the tenant might want a larger or smaller space, or might want to move closer to work, he or she will be less likely to move because it is much more difficult to find a vacancy if rent control ordinances are in effect. So turnover will be lower, and even those who gain financially from living in rent-controlled units may find themselves in locations and in apartments not well suited to their needs.

6. Long-term renters will benefit at the expense of newcomers. People who stay for lengthy time periods in the same apartment often pay rents substantially below market value (because the controls restrict rent increases), while newcomers are forced to pay exorbitant prices for units sublet from tenants, or for the limited supply of unrestricted units—typically newly constructed and thus temporarily exempted. Distortions and inequities result. A book on housing and the homeless by William Tucker reports several examples, such as "actress Ann Turkel, who paid $2,350 per month for a seven-room, four-and-a-half bathroom duplex on the East Side (of New York City). . . . Identical apartments in the building were subletting for $6,500."[2] Turkel had been spending only two months each year in New York. "Former mayor Edward Koch . . . pays $441.49 a month for a large, one-bedroom apartment . . . that would probably be worth $1,200 in an unregulated market. Koch kept the apartment the entire twelve years he lived in Gracie Mansion (the official mayor's residence)." Tucker uses these and many other such cases to illustrate the distortions brought on by the control of rental prices.

(continued)

Rent controls may appear to be a simple solution, but many problems result, including a decline in the supply of rental housing, poor maintenance, and shortages. In the words of Swedish economist Assar Lindbeck: "In many cases rent control appears to be the most efficient technique presently known to destroy a city—except for bombing."[3] Though this may overstate the case somewhat, economic analysis suggests that the point is well taken.

[1]William Tucker, *The Excluded Americans* (Washington, D.C.: Regnery Gateway, 1990), p. 162. For a more detailed exposition on rent controls, see Walter Block, "Rent Controls," in *Fortune Encyclopedia of Economics*, ed. David Henderson (New York: Warner Books, 1993).
[2]Tucker, *The Excluded Americans*, p. 248.
[3]Assar Lindbeck, *The Political Economy of the New Left* (New York: Harper and Row, 1972), p. 39.

product. It is not easy to repeal the laws of supply and demand. (See the accompanying Myths of Economics box.)

It is important to note that a shortage is not the same as scarcity. **Scarcity is inescapable.** Scarcity exists whenever people want more of a good than nature has provided. This means, of course, that almost everything of value is scarce. **Shortages, on the other hand, are avoidable if prices are permitted to rise.** A higher, unfixed price (P_0 rather than P_1 in part a of Exhibit 3–12) would (1) stimulate additional production, (2) discourage consumption, and (3) ration the available supply to those willing to pay the higher price. These forces, an expansion in output and a reduction in consumption, would eliminate the shortage. But when the price ceiling (P_1) does not allow the price to rise (and when no "cheating" on quality, quantity, or illegal payment occurs), the shortage is inevitable.

Price floor
A legally established minimum price that buyers must pay for a good or resource.

While price ceilings set a maximum price, **price floors** establish a minimum price that can legally be charged. Part b of Exhibit 3–12 illustrates the case of a price floor, which fixes the price of a good or resource above the market equilibrium level. At the higher price, sellers will want to bring a larger amount to the market, while buyers will choose to buy less of the good. A **surplus** ($Q_S - Q_D$) will result. Agricultural price supports and minimum wage legislation are examples of price floors. Predictably, nonprice factors will again play a larger role in the rationing process than would be true without a price floor. Buyers can now be more selective, since sellers want to sell more than buyers, in aggregate, desire to purchase. Buyers can be expected to seek out sellers willing to offer them favors (discounts on other products, easier credit, or better service, for example). Some sellers may be unable to market their product or service.[7] Unsold merchandise and underutilized resources will result.

Surplus
A condition in which the amount of a good that sellers are willing to offer is greater than the amount that buyers will purchase at the existing price. A decline in price would eliminate the surplus.

Note that a surplus does not mean the good is no longer scarce. People still want more of the good than is freely available from nature, even though they desire less, *at the current price,* than sellers desire to bring to the market. A decline in price would eliminate the surplus but not the scarcity of the item.

---

[7]Our theory indicates that minimum wage legislation (a price floor for unskilled labor) will generate an excess supply of inexperienced, low-skilled workers. The extremely high unemployment rate of teenagers—a group with little work experience—supports this view.

HOW THE MARKET ANSWERS THE THREE BASIC ECONOMIC QUESTIONS

How does the market's pricing mechanism resolve the three basic economic questions introduced in Chapter 2—*what* goods will be produced, *how* will they be produced, and *for whom* will they be produced?

In a market economy, what will be produced is determined by the consumer's evaluation of a good (demand) relative to its opportunity cost (supply). If consumers value a good (in terms of money) more than its price, they will choose to purchase it. Simultaneously, profit-seeking producers will supply a good as long as consumers are willing to pay a price that is sufficient to cover the opportunity cost of producing it. The result: There is an incentive to produce those goods, and only those goods, to which consumers attach a value at least as high as the production costs of the goods.

How goods will be produced is determined by the economizing behavior of suppliers. Suppliers have a strong incentive to use production methods that minimize costs, because lower costs will mean larger profits. Thus, producers can be expected to organize production efficiently—to use division of labor, to invent and adapt new technologies, and to choose labor–capital combinations that will result in lower production costs.

What assurances are there that producers will not waste resources or exploit consumers by charging high prices? Competition provides the answer. Inefficient producers will have higher costs. They will find it difficult to meet the price competition of sellers who use resources wisely. Similarly, in a market with rival sellers, competition among firms will tend to keep prices in line with per unit production costs. When prices are above the opportunity costs of a good, profits for the producers will result. As we have discussed, the profits will attract additional suppliers into the market, driving the price down.

To whom will the goods be distributed? Goods will be allocated to consumers willing and able to pay the market price. (The accompanying Applications in Economics box titled, "Repealing the Laws of Supply and Demand," highlights this point.) Of course, some consumers will be better able to pay the market price—they have larger incomes (more "dollar votes") than others. The unequal distribution of income among consumers is directly related to what is produced and how. The income of individuals reflects the extent of their provision of resources to others. Those who supply large amounts of highly valued resources—resources for which market participants are willing to pay a high price—will have high incomes. In contrast, those who supply few resources or resources that are not valued by others will have low incomes.

As long as the preferences and productive abilities of individuals differ, a market solution will lead to unequal incomes. Many people are critical of the pricing system because of the income inequality that results. But unequal incomes are not unique to a market economy. In virtually all systems, unequal income shares exist and provide at least some of the incentive for individuals to undertake productive activities. Because efforts to alter the allocation of income will also affect supply conditions, this issue is highly complex. As we proceed, we will investigate it in more detail.

APPLICATIONS IN ECONOMICS

REPEALING THE LAWS OF SUPPLY AND DEMAND: PRICE CONTROLS DURING HURRICANE HUGO

In the fall of 1989 Hurricane Hugo struck the coast of South Carolina, causing massive property damage and widespread power outages lasting for weeks. The lack of electric power meant that gasoline pumps, refrigerators, cash registers, ATM machines, and many other types of electrical equipment did not work. In the hardest hit coastal areas such as Charleston, the demand for such items as lumber, gasoline, ice, batteries, chain saws, and electric generators increased dramatically. Stores that remained open using backup gasoline-powered generators sold out of most items immediately. Goods that began to flow in from other cities were being sold by some sellers at much higher prices. A bag of ice that sold for $1 before the hurricane went up in price to as much as $10, plywood went up in price to about $200 per sheet, and gasoline sold for as much as $10.95 per gallon. Individual citizens from other states were renting trucks, buying supplies in their home state, driving them to Charleston, and making enough money to pay for the rental truck and the purchase of the goods, and to compensate them for taking time off from their regular jobs.

In response to consumer complaints of "price gouging," the mayor of Charleston signed emergency legislation making it a crime, punishable by up to 30 days in jail and a $200 fine, to sell goods at prices higher than their pre-hurricane levels in the city. The price ceilings kept prices down, but also stopped the flow of goods into the area almost immediately. Shippers of items such as ice would stop outside the harder hit Charleston area, to avoid the price controls, and sell their goods. Shipments that did make it into the Charleston area were often greeted by long lines of consumers, many of whom would end up without the good after waiting in line for up to five hours. Shortages became so bad that military guards were required to protect the goods and maintain order when a shipment did arrive.

The price controls resulted in serious misallocations of resources such as electricity, which, during the emergency, could be gotten mainly from emergency generators. Grocery stores could not fully open because of the lack of electric power, and inside the stores, food items were spoiling—thousands of dollars' worth, in some stores. Gasoline pumps require electricity to operate, so, although there was fuel in the underground tanks, there was a shortage of gasoline because of the inability to pump it. Consumers were faced with problems of obtaining money, as ATM machines and banks could not operate without electric power. Hardware stores that sold electric generators before the hurricane typically had only a few in stock, but suddenly hundreds of businesses and residents wanted to buy them. The price ceilings would not allow the store owners to ration the few generators they had by raising the price, so the owners had to allocate the sale of their generators in other ways. It was not uncommon for the owner of the store to take one generator home, and to sell the others to his or her friends. While these families used the generators for household uses, gasoline stations, grocery stores, and banks were closed because of their inability to buy a generator. Thousands of consumers could not get goods they urgently wanted because these businesses were closed. Without price controls, we would expect the price of generators to be bid up to the point that they would (a) be purchased by those who had the most urgent uses for them, and (b) be imported into the city rapidly enough to keep the price from rising still further.

The secondary impacts of the price controls used during Hurricane Hugo in Charleston, South Carolina, highlight the importance of understanding economics and the role of prices in our economy. Despite pleas from economists in local newspapers and in *The Wall Street Journal*, the price controls remained in effect, increasing the suffering and retarding the recovery of the areas most severely damaged by the hurricane.[1]

---

[1]See, for example, David N. Leband, "In Hugo's Path, a Man-Made Disaster," *The Wall Street Journal*, September 27, 1989, p. A22; and Tim Smith, "Economists Spurn Price Restrictions," *The Greenville News*, September 28, 1989, p. C1.

INVISIBLE HAND PRINCIPLE

More than 200 years ago, Adam Smith, the father of economics (see page 21), stressed that personal self-interest *when directed by the market prices* is a powerful force promoting economic progress. In a famous passage in his *Wealth of Nations,* Smith put it this way:

> *Every individual is continually exerting himself to find out the most advantageous employment for whatever capital he can command. It is his own advantage, indeed, and not that of the society which he has in view. But the study of his own advantage naturally, or rather necessarily, leads him to prefer that employment which is most advantageous to society. . . . He intends only his own gain, and he is in this, as in many other cases, led by an invisible hand to promote an end which was not part of his intention. By pursuing his own interest he frequently promotes that of the society more effectually than when he really intends to promote it.[8]*

Using the terminology employed by Smith, economists refer to the tendency of competitive markets to direct the actions of self-interested individuals and bring them into harmony with the general welfare (economic progress) as the **invisible hand principle.** Let us take a closer look at how markets perform this function.

Invisible hand principle
The tendency of market prices to direct individuals pursuing their own interests into productive activities that also promote the economic well-being of the society.

COMMUNICATING INFORMATION TO DECISION MAKERS

Communication of information is one of the most important functions of markets. Markets register information reflecting the choices of consumers, producers, and resource suppliers and tabulate it into a summary statistic called the *market price.* This statistic provides decision makers with valuable information that would be difficult to obtain by any other means. Even though the preferences of consumers cannot be directly observed, market prices communicate up-to-date information about consumers' valuation of additional units of each commodity. Similarly, we cannot turn to an engineering equation in order to calculate the opportunity cost of alternative commodities. But resource prices tell the business decision maker the relative importance others place on production factors (skill categories of labor, natural resources, and machinery, for example). With this information, and knowledge of the relationship between potential input combinations and the output of a product, producers can make reliable estimates of their opportunity costs. Without the information provided by market prices, it would be impossible for decision makers to determine how intensively a good was desired relative to its opportunity costs—that is, relative to other things that might be produced with the resources required to produce the good.

---

[8]Adam Smith, *An Inquiry into the Nature and Causes of the Wealth of Nations* (New York: Modern Library, 1937), p. 423.

COORDINATING ACTIONS OF MARKET PARTICIPANTS

Market prices also coordinate the choices of buyers and sellers, bringing their decisions into line with each other. Excess supply will lead to falling prices, discouraging production and encouraging consumption until the excess supply is eliminated. Alternatively, excess demand will lead to price increases, encouraging consumers to economize on their uses of the good and encouraging suppliers to produce more of it, eliminating the excess demand and bringing the choices of market participants into harmony.

The combination of product and resource prices will determine profit (and loss) rates for alternative projects and thereby direct entrepreneurs to undertake the production projects that consumers value most intensely (relative to their cost). If consumers really want more of a good—for example, luxury apartments—the intensity of their demand will lead to a market price that exceeds the opportunity cost of constructing the apartments. The profitable opportunity thus created will soon be discovered by entrepreneurs who will undertake the construction, expanding the availability of the apartments. In contrast, if consumers want less of a good—large cars, for example—the opportunity cost of supplying such cars will exceed the sales revenue from their production, penalizing entrepreneurs who undertake such unprofitable production.

An understanding of the importance of the entrepreneur also sheds light on the market-adjustment process. Since the future is not fully predictable, and information is imperfect, the move toward equilibrium will typically be a groping process. With time, however, successful entrepreneurial activity will be more clearly identified. Successful methods will be copied by other producers. Learning-by-doing and trial-and-error will help producers sort out attractive projects from "losers." The process, though, will never quite be complete. By the time entrepreneurs discover one intensely desired product (or a new, more efficient production technique), change will have occurred elsewhere, creating other unrealized profitable opportunities. The wheels of dynamic change never stop.

MOTIVATING ECONOMIC PLAYERS

As many leaders of centrally planned economies discovered, people must be motivated to act before production plans can be realized. Market prices establish a reward-penalty (profit-loss) structure that induces participants to work, cooperate with others, use efficient production methods, supply goods that are intensely desired by others, and invest for the future.

No government agency needs to tell business decision makers to use resources wisely and thereby minimize the cost of producing their product. The pursuit of profit will encourage them to produce what buyers want, and to economize while doing so. Those who fail to do so, as even giant firms have learned, will be unable to compete successfully with more cost-effective rivals.

Similarly, no one has to tell resource suppliers to invest and develop productive resources. Why are many young people willing to undertake the necessary work, stress, late hours of study, and financial cost to acquire a medical or law degree, or an advanced degree in economics, physics, or business administration? Why do others seek to master a skill requiring an apprentice program?

Why do individuals save to buy businesses, machines, and other capital assets? The expectation of financial reward is not the only factor, but it is an important stimulus, providing motivation to work, create, develop skills, and supply capital assets to those productive activities most desired by others.

PRICES AND MARKET ORDER

How is it that grocery stores in thousands of different locations have approximately the right amount of milk, bread, vegetables, and other goods—an amount sufficiently large that the goods are nearly always available but not so large that spoilage and waste are a problem? How is it that refrigerators, automobiles, and VCRs, produced at diverse places around the world, are supplied in the U.S. market in approximately the same amount that they are demanded by consumers? The answer is that the invisible hand of market prices directs self-interested individuals into cooperative action and brings their choices into harmony.

The invisible hand principle is difficult for many people to grasp because there is a natural tendency to associate order with central direction. Surely some central authority must be in charge. But this is not the case. *The pricing system, reflecting the choices of literally millions of consumers, producers, and resource owners, is providing the direction.* The market process works so automatically that most give little thought to it. They simply take it for granted that the goods most people value will be produced in approximately the quantities that consumers want to buy them.

Perhaps an illustration will enhance your understanding of both the operation and importance of the invisible hand principle. Visualize a busy limited-access highway with four lanes of traffic moving in each direction. No central planning agency assigns lanes and directs traffic. No one tells drivers when to shift to the right, middle, or left lane. Drivers are left to choose for themselves. Nonetheless, they do not all try to drive in the same lane. Why? Drivers are alert for adjustment opportunities that offer personal gain. When traffic in a lane slows due to congestion, some drivers will shift to other lanes and thereby smooth out the flow of traffic among the lanes. Even though central planning is absent, this process of mutual adjustments by the individual drivers results in order and social cooperation. In fact, the degree of social cooperation is generally well beyond what could be achieved if central coordination were attempted—if, for example, each vehicle were assigned a lane.

Market participation is a lot like driving on the freeway. It is often necessary to alter one's actions in light of the choices made by others. Success is dependent upon one's ability to act upon opportunities. Like the amount of traffic in a lane, profits and losses provide market participants with information concerning the advantages and disadvantages of alternative economic activities. Losses indicate that an economic activity is congested, and as a result, producers are unable to cover their costs. Successful market participants will shift their resources away from such activities toward other, more valuable uses. Conversely, profits are indicative of an open lane, the opportunity to experience gain if one shifts into an activity where price is currently high relative to per-unit cost. As producers and resource suppliers shift away from activities characterized by congestion and into those characterized by the opportunity for gain (profit), they smooth out economic activity and enhance its flow. Order is the result, even though central planning is absent. This coordination brought about by market prices is precisely what Adam Smith was referring to when he spoke of the "invisible hand" more than 200 years ago.

QUALIFICATIONS

In this chapter, we have focused on the operation of a market economy. *The efficiency of market organization is dependent on (1) competitive markets and (2) well-defined private property rights.* Competition, the great regulator, can protect both buyer and seller. The presence (or possible entry) of independent alternative suppliers protects the consumer against a seller who seeks to charge prices substantially above the cost of production. The existence of alternative resource suppliers protects the producer against a supplier who might otherwise be tempted to withhold a vital resource unless granted exorbitant compensation. The existence of alternative employment opportunities protects the employee from the power of any single employer. Competition can equalize the bargaining power between buyers and sellers.

Understanding the information, coordination, and motivation results of the market mechanism helps us see all the more clearly the importance of property rights, the things actually traded in markets. Property rights force resource users—including those who own them—to bear fully the opportunity cost of their actions and prohibit persons from engaging in destructive forms of competition. When property rights are well defined, secure, and tradeable, suppliers of goods and services will be required to pay resource owners the opportunity cost of each resource employed. They will not be permitted to seize and use scarce resources without compensating the owners—that is, without bidding the resources away from alternative users. Neither will they be permitted to use violence (for example, to attack or invade the property of another) as a means to achieve an economic objective.

LOOKING AHEAD

Lack of competition and poorly defined property rights will reduce the ability of a market economy to function well, making it less efficient. Government plays an important part in securing property rights, and can reduce the problems that result when markets do not function properly. In the following chapter, we will consider cases where the invisible hand does not work so well and analyze how the political process works as a potential alternative to the market.

CHAPTER SUMMARY

1. The law of demand holds that there is an inverse relationship between price and the amount of a good pur-

chased. A rise in price will cause consumers to purchase less because they now have a greater incentive to use substitutes. On the other hand, a reduction in price will induce consumers to buy more, since they will substitute the cheaper good for other commodities.

2. The law of supply states that there is a direct relationship between the price of a product and the amount supplied. Other things constant, an increase in the price of a product will induce established firms to expand their output and new firms to enter the market. The quantity supplied will then expand.

3. Market prices will bring the conflicting forces of supply and demand into balance. If the quantity supplied to the market by producers exceeds the quantity demanded by consumers, price will decline until the excess supply is eliminated. On the other hand, if the

quantity demanded by consumers exceeds the quantity supplied by producers, price will rise until the excess demand is eliminated.

4. If there are no restrictions on the movement of a good, the good will tend to sell for the same price in all markets, except for variations resulting from differences in transport costs and taxes.

5. Two conditions are required for long-run equilibrium in a market: (a) the quantity demanded must equal the quantity supplied, and (b) the producer's opportunity cost must equal the market price. If the opportunity cost of supplying the good is less than the market price, profits will accrue. The profits will attract additional suppliers, which will expand supply and reduce price until profit is eroded. On the other hand, if the opportunity cost of producing a good exceeds the market price, suppliers will experience losses. The losses will induce producers to leave the market, causing price to rise until long-run equilibrium is restored.

6. Changes in consumer income, prices of closely related goods, preferences, and expectations as to future prices will cause the entire demand curve to shift. An increase (decrease) in demand will cause prices to rise (fall) and quantity supplied to increase (decline).

7. Changes in input prices, technology, and other factors that influence the producer's cost of production will cause the entire supply curve to shift. An increase (decrease) in supply will cause prices to fall (rise) and quantity demanded to expand (decline).

8. The constraint of time temporarily limits the ability of consumers to adjust to changes in prices. With the passage of time, a price increase will usually elicit a larger reduction in quantity demanded. Similarly, the market supply curve shows more responsiveness to a change in price in the long run than during the short-term time period.

9. When a price is fixed below the market equilibrium, buyers will want to purchase more than sellers are willing to supply. A shortage will result. Nonprice factors such as waiting lines, quality deterioration, and illegal transactions will play a more important role in the rationing process. When a price is fixed above the market equilibrium level, sellers will want to supply a larger amount than buyers are willing to purchase at the current price. A surplus will result.

10. The pricing system answers the three basic allocation questions in the following manner.

   a. What goods will be produced? Additional units of goods will be produced only if consumers value them more highly than the opportunity cost of the resources necessary to produce them.

   b. How will goods be produced? The methods that result in the lowest opportunity cost will be chosen. Since lower costs mean larger profits, markets reward producers who discover and utilize efficient (low-cost) production methods.

   c. To whom will the goods be distributed? Goods will be allocated to individuals according to the quantity and price of the productive resources they supply in the marketplace.

11. Market prices communicate information, coordinate the actions of buyers and sellers, and provide the incentive structure that motivates decision makers to act. Market prices establish a reward-penalty system, which induces individuals to cooperate with each other and motivates them to work efficiently, invest for the future, supply intensely desired goods, economize on the use of scarce resources, and use efficient production methods. As Adam Smith noted long ago, market prices, reflecting the decentralized choices of consumers, producers, and resource suppliers, are generally able to bring the personal self-interest of individuals into harmony with the general welfare. The efficiency of the system is dependent on (1) competitive market conditions and (2) securely defined private-property rights.

CRITICAL ANALYSIS QUESTIONS

*1. Which of the following do you think would lead to an increase in the current demand for beef: (a) higher pork prices, (b) higher incomes, (c) higher feed grain prices, (d) a banner-year corn crop, (e) an increase in the price of beef?

2. What is being held constant when a demand curve for a specific product (like shoes or apples, for example) is constructed? Explain why the demand curve for a product slopes downward to the right.

3. What is the law of supply? How many of the following "goods" do you think conform to the general law of supply: (a) gasoline, (b) cheating on exams, (c) political favors from legislators, (d) the services of heart specialists, (e) children, (f) legal divorces, (g) the services of a minister? Explain your answer in each case.

*4. A drought during the summer of 1988 sharply reduced the 1988 output of wheat, corn, soybeans, and hay. Indicate the expected impact of the drought on the following:

   a. Prices of feed grains and hay during the summer of 1988.

   b. Price of cattle during the summer and fall of 1988.

   c. Price of cattle during the summer and fall of 1989.

5. What is being held constant when the supply curve is constructed? Explain why the supply curve slopes upward to the right.

*6. To be meaningful, a price ceiling must be below the market price. Conversely, a meaningful price floor must be above the market price. What impact will a meaningful price ceiling have on the quantity exchanged? What impact will a meaningful price floor have on the quantity exchanged? Explain.

7. Carefully define profit. How does the economist's concept of profit differ from that of the accountant? If the accounting statement of a large corporation indicates that the net income of the firm is positive, does this mean that the firm is making a profit? Explain.

*8. "The future of our industrial strength cannot be left to chance. Somebody has to develop notions about which industries are winners and which are losers." Is this statement by a newspaper columnist true? Who is the "somebody"?

9. What is the necessary condition for short-run equilibrium to exist in the market for a specific good like shoes or bread? What additional condition is necessary for long-run equilibrium in the market? Explain why this additional condition is necessary for long-run equilibrium.

*10. "Production should be for people and not for profit." Answer the following questions concerning this statement:
a. If production is profitable, are people helped or hurt? Explain.
b. Are people helped more if production results in a loss than if it leads to profit?
c. Is there a conflict between production for people and production for profit?

11. If a market for dress shirts was initially in equilibrium, how would an unexpected increase in the demand for dress shirts influence: (a) the price of the shirts, (b) the quantity of shirts produced in the short run, (c) the profits of the shirt manufacturers, (d) the amount of capital investment of shirt manufacturers, and (e) the output of the shirt manufacturers in the long run? Construct diagrams to illustrate your answers.

*12. Suppose a drought destroyed half of the wheat crop in France. What is the expected impact on the market price of wheat in France?

13. **What** goods will be produced in a market economy? What determines whether or not a good will be produced? **How** will resources be combined and what production methods and forms of business organization will be used to produce goods and services in a competitive market economy? **To whom** does a market economy allocate goods?

*14. When the price of a commodity (for example, rental housing or campus parking) is below equilibrium, then waiting in line rather than monetary payments will play a greater role in the allocation of the good. What is a major disadvantage of rationing by having consumers wait in line rather than by raising prices? (Hint: How do the alternative methods affect future supply?)

15. What is the *invisible hand principle?* Does it indicate that "good intentions" are necessary if one's actions are going to be beneficial to others? What are the necessary conditions for the invisible hand to work well? Why are these conditions important?

*16. A popular California winery, and the restaurant on its grounds, can be reached only by a tram with gondola cars, similar to those used at ski resorts. Suppose the owners are charging $3 to winery visitors and restaurant diners alike, but are thinking about providing "free rides" to diners. Explain how this change would affect the following conditions:
a. The demand for dining at the restaurant
b. The price and quantity of meals served at the restaurant

17. The county commission recently voted $15 million for the construction of a new civic center. The chairperson of the commission stated, "We are undertaking this project because the community needs a civic center and the 500 new jobs the project will create." Answer the following questions about this news item:
a. Does a "need" for a project mean it should be undertaken?
b. What is the opportunity cost of the project?
c. Will the project actually expand employment by 500 workers?

18. **What's Wrong with This Way of Thinking?** "Economists claim that when the price of something goes up, producers bring more of it to the market. But the last year in which the price was really high for oranges, there were not nearly as many oranges as usual. The economists are wrong!"

19. **What's Wrong with This Way of Thinking?** "Economists argue that lower prices will necessarily result in less supply. However, there are exceptions to this rule. For example, in 1970, ten-digit electronic calculators sold for $100. By 1995 the price of the same type of calculator had declined to less than $15. Yet business firms produced and sold five times as many calculators in 1985 as in 1970. Lower prices did not result in less production or in a decline in the number of calculators supplied."

---

*Asterisk denotes questions for which answers are given in Appendix B.

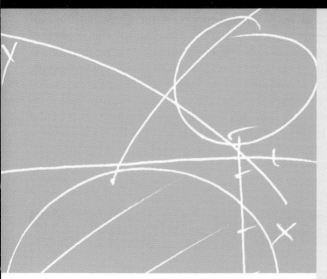

■ What does the economic way of thinking have to say about economic efficiency?

■ When do markets fall short of the ideal of economic efficiency?

■ Can government action improve on the efficiency of the market? When is it most likely to do so?

■ What is public-choice analysis? What does it reveal about how the political process works and how it compares with the market process?

■ Is there sometimes a conflict between good economics and good politics? Why?

A century ago there was little federal regulation of private economic activity: today, federal nonmarket control of the private sector is very nearly ubiquitous.

JONATHAN HUGHES[1]

[Public choice] analyzes the motives and activities of politicians, civil servants and government officials as people with personal interests that may or may not coincide with the interest of the general public they are supposed to serve. It is an analysis of how people behave in the world as it is.

ARTHUR SELDON[2]

---

[1]Jonathan Hughes, "Do Americans Want Big Government?" in *Second Thoughts,* ed. Donald N. McCloskey (New York: Oxford University Press, 1993), p. 115.

[2]Preface to Gordon Tullock, *The Vote Motive* (London: Institute of Economic Affairs, 1976), p. x.

T he economic role of government is pivotal. The government sets the rules of the game. It recognizes and protects property rights, which are necessary for the smooth operation of markets. It can also be an important determinant of economic stability. The government sometimes uses subsidies to encourage the production of some goods while it applies special taxes that reduce the availability of others. In a few cases—education, the mail service, and local electric power, for example—the government becomes directly involved in the production process. As the quote from economic historian Jonathan Hughes suggests, the economic involvement of government has been growing for many decades in the United States. The rest of the world has had a similar experience.

Government's broad economic role and increasing size make it vital for us to understand how it works and when it might increase (or decrease) the efficiency of the allocation of resources. In this chapter, we examine the shortcomings of the market and the potential of government policy as an alternate means for resolving economic problems. Issues involving market- and public-sector organization will be discussed repeatedly throughout this book. Public-choice analysis, as suggested in the quotation from British economist Arthur Seldon, is an important way of using economics to better understand the workings of the political sector. Political economy—the study of how the public sector works, and how its workings compare with those of the market—is an integral and exciting aspect of economic analysis.

IDEAL ECONOMIC EFFICIENCY

Economic efficiency
Economizing behavior. When applied to a community, it implies that (1) an activity should be undertaken if the sum of the benefits to the individuals exceeds the sum of their costs and (2) no activity should be undertaken if the costs borne by the individuals exceed the benefits.

We need a criterion by which to judge alternative institutional arrangements—that is, market- and public-sector policies. Economists often use the standard of **economic efficiency.** The central idea is straightforward. It simply means that, for any given level of effort (cost), we want to obtain the largest possible benefit. A corollary to this is that we want to obtain any specific level of benefits with the least possible effort. Economic efficiency simply means getting the most value from the available resources—making the largest pie from the available set of ingredients, so to speak.

Why efficiency? Economists acknowledge that people generally do not have the efficiency of the economy as a primary goal. Rather, each person wants the largest possible "piece of the pie." All might agree that a bigger pie is preferred, however, particularly if they are allowed a larger slice as a result. Thus, efficiency can be in everyone's interest because it makes a larger pie possible.

What does efficiency mean when applied to the entire economy? Individuals are the final decision makers of an economy, and individuals will bear the costs and reap the benefits of economic activity. When applied to the entire economy, two conditions are necessary for ideal economic efficiency to exist:

RULE 1. *Undertaking an economic action will be efficient if it produces more benefits than costs for the individuals of the economy.* Such actions make it possible to improve the well-being of at least some individuals without creating reductions in the welfare of others. Failure to undertake such activities means that potential gain has been forgone.

RULE 2. *Undertaking an economic action will be inefficient if it produces more costs than benefits to the individuals.* When an action results in greater total costs than benefits, somebody must be harmed. The benefits that accrue to those who gain are insufficient to compensate for the losses imposed on others. Therefore, when all persons are considered, the net impact of such an action is counterproductive.

When either Rule 1 or Rule 2 is violated, economic inefficiency results. The concept of economic efficiency applies to each and every possible income distribution, although a change in income distribution may alter the precise combination of goods and services that is most efficient.[3] Positive economics does not tell us how income should be distributed. Of course, we all have ideas on the subject. Most of us would like to see more income distributed our way. Agreement on what is the best distribution of income is unlikely, but for any particular income distribution, there will be an ideal resource allocation that will be most efficient.

MARKETS, INCENTIVES, AND EFFICIENCY

A closer look at the way in which markets work can help us to understand the concept of efficiency and the role markets play in providing incentives for individuals to make efficient production and consumption decisions. When property rights are privately owned, competitive market forces represented by supply and demand provide the signals needed for decision makers to use resources efficiently, and the incentive to let those signals guide their actions.

The supply curve reflects producers' opportunity costs. Each point along the supply curve indicates the minimum price for which the units of a good could be produced without a loss to the seller. The cost, which must be paid by producers, pushes them to economize on the use of valuable inputs. On the other side of the market, each point along the demand curve indicates the consumer's valuation of an extra unit of the good—the maximum amount the consumer is willing to pay for the extra unit. Consumer willingness to pay urges producers to add to output. The necessity for payment restrains consumer demands. Any time the consumer's valuation exceeds the producer's opportunity cost—the producer's minimum supply price—producing and selling more units of the good can generate mutual gain.

When only buyers and sellers are affected by production and exchange, and the options are known to each, they are directed by the market forces of supply

---

[3]Note to students who may pursue advanced study in economics: Using the concept of efficiency to compare alternative policies typically requires that the analyst estimate costs and benefits that are difficult or impossible to measure. Costs and benefits are the values of opportunities forgone or accepted by individuals, *as evaluated by those individuals.* Then, these costs and benefits must be added up across all individuals, and compared. But does a dollar's gain for one individual really compensate for a dollar's sacrifice by another? Some economists simply reject the validity of making such comparisons. They say that neither the estimates by the economic analyst of subjectively determined costs and benefits nor the adding up of these costs and benefits across individuals is meaningful. Their case may be valid, but most economists today nevertheless use the concept of efficiency as we present it. No other way to use economic analysis to compare policy alternatives has been found.

and demand to produce the efficient output level. All potential gains from production and exchange are realized. **Exhibit 4–1** illustrates why this is true. Suppliers of a good, bicycles in this example, will produce additional units as long as the market price exceeds the production cost. Similarly, consumers will gain from the purchase of additional units as long as their benefits, revealed by the height of the demand curve, exceed the market price. Market forces will result in an equilibrium output level of Q: All units providing benefits to consumers that exceed the costs to suppliers will be produced. Rule 1 is met, since all potential gains from exchange (the shaded area) between consumers and producers are fully realized. If more than Q bicycles were produced, however, Rule 2 would be violated and inefficiency would result. Consumers would value the additional units (beyond Q) less than their cost. With competitive markets, suppliers will find it unprofitable to produce units beyond Q because the cost of the additional units will exceed revenues from those units.

Consumers and producers alike will thus be guided by the pricing system to output level Q, just the right amount. The market works beautifully. Individuals, pursuing their own interests, also promote the general welfare. This was Adam Smith's "invisible hand" message of more than 200 years ago.

WHY MIGHT THE INVISIBLE HAND FAIL?

Is the invisible hand still working today? Why might it fail? There are four important factors that can limit the ability of the invisible hand to perform its magic.

When competitive forces are present, price will tend toward the supply-demand intersection P. At that price, the seller's opportunity cost of producing the last unit will just equal the buyer's evaluation of that unit. All potential mutual gains from production and exchange are realized. If producers and users are paying the full cost of their actions and receiving the benefit of the value they produce, then such trading is efficient.

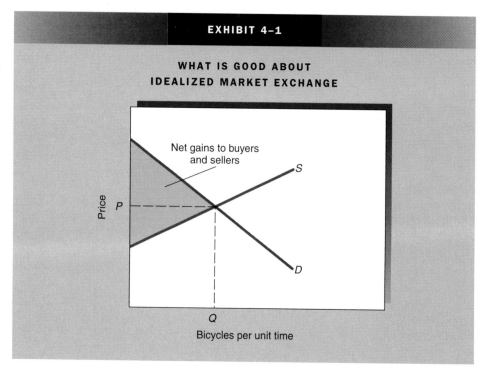

EXHIBIT 4–1

WHAT IS GOOD ABOUT IDEALIZED MARKET EXCHANGE

Net gains to buyers and sellers

Price

P

S

D

Q

Bicycles per unit time

LACK OF COMPETITION

Competition is vital to the proper operation of the pricing mechanism. It is competition among sellers that drives the prices for consumer goods down to the level of their cost. Similarly, competition in markets for productive resources prevents (1) sellers from charging exorbitant prices to producers and (2) buyers from taking advantage of the owners of productive resources. The existence of competing buyers and sellers reduces the power of both to rig the market in their own favor.

Since competition is the enemy of prices higher than costs, sellers have a strong incentive to escape from its pressures. When there are only a few firms in a market, rather than competing, sellers may be able to collude effectively. Efforts in this direction should be expected. Competition is something that is good when the other guy faces it. Individually, each of us would prefer to be loosened from its grip. Students do not like stiff competitors at exam time, when seeking entry to graduate school, or in their social or romantic lives. Similarly, sellers prefer few real competitors.

Exhibit 4–2 illustrates how sellers can gain from collusive action. If a group of sellers could eliminate the competition from new entrants to the market, they would be able to raise their prices. The total revenue of sellers is simply the market price multiplied by the quantity sold. The sellers' revenues may well be greater, and their total costs would surely be lower, if the smaller, restricted output Q_2 were sold rather than the competitive output Q_1. The artificially high price P_2 reflects not only resource scarcity, but also the reduction in output brought on by collusion among sellers.

It is in the interest of consumers and the community that output be expanded to Q_1, the output consistent with economic efficiency. It is in the interest of

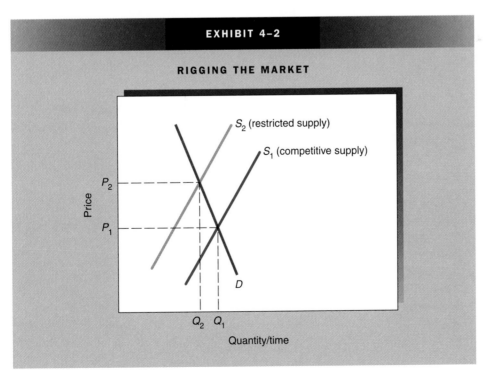

EXHIBIT 4–2

RIGGING THE MARKET

S_2 (restricted supply)

S_1 (competitive supply)

Price

P_2

P_1

D

Q_2 Q_1

Quantity/time

If a group of sellers can restrict the entry of competitors and connive to reduce their own output, they can sometimes obtain more total revenue by selling fewer units. Note that the total sales revenue P_2Q_2 for the restricted supply exceeds the sales revenue P_1Q_1 for the competitive supply, in this case. Such behavior reduces the gains from trade, making the market less efficient as a result.

sellers, though, to make the good artificially scarce and raise its price. If sellers can use collusion, government action, or other means of restricting supply, they can gain. However, the restricted output level would violate Rule 2. Inefficiency would result. There is a conflict between the interests of sellers and what is best for the entire community.

When there are only a few firms in the industry, and competition from new entrants can be restrained, sellers may be able to, at least partially, escape competitive pressures. What can the government do to preserve competition? Congress has enacted a series of antitrust laws, most notably the Sherman Antitrust Act and the Clayton Act, making it illegal for firms to collude or attempt to monopolize a product market. For the most part, economists favor the principle of government action to ensure and promote competitive markets. There is considerable debate, however, about the effectiveness of past public policy in this area. Many economists believe that, by and large, antitrust policy has been ineffective. Others stress that government regulatory policies have often restricted entry, protected existing producers, and limited price competition. These critics charge that by doing so, the government has actually reduced the competitiveness of markets.

EXTERNALITIES—FAILURE TO SOLVE THE INCENTIVE PROBLEM

Externalities

The side effects, or spillover effects, of an action that influence the well-being of nonconsenting parties. The nonconsenting parties may be either helped (by external benefits) or harmed (by external costs).

When property rights are not fully enforced, the actions of a producer or consumer might harm the property (or the person) of another. In this situation, production and consumption of some goods will result in spillover effects that the market prices fail to register. These spillover effects, called **externalities,** are present when the actions of one individual or group harm the property of others without their consent. The presence of externalities means that the incentive problem has not been solved, so that decision makers will not confront the proper cost and price incentive structure.

Examples of externalities abound. If you live in an apartment house and the noisy stereo of your next-door neighbors keeps you from studying economics, your neighbors are creating an externality. Their actions are imposing an unwanted cost on you. Similarly, driving your car during rush hour increases the level of congestion, thereby imposing a cost on other motorists.

The existence of externalities implies the lack of property rights, or of enforcement of those rights. The apartment dweller who is bothered by a neighbor's noise either does not have a right to quiet, or is unable to enforce the right. In either case, the maker of the noise is not forced to take into account the resulting discomfort of neighbors. Similarly, each motorist adding his or her car to heavy traffic will not be forced to consider the effects on others, unless there is a highway access fee reflecting the costs of congestion. When enforceable property rights are not present, externalities are a normal result.

Not all externalities result in the imposition of a cost. Sometimes human actions generate benefits for nonparticipating parties. The homeowner who keeps a house in good condition and maintains a neat lawn improves the beauty of the entire community, and thereby provides benefits for other community members. A flood-control dam project built by upstream residents for their benefit may also generate gains for those who live downstream. Scientific theories benefit their authors, but the knowledge gained also contributes to the welfare of others who do not help to pay for their development costs. Again, a lack of enforceable property rights keeps the producers of the goods or services that provide the positively valued externalities from reaping fully the benefits of them.

Why do externalities create problems for the market mechanism? **Exhibit 4–3** can help answer this question. With competitive markets in equilibrium, the cost of a good (including the opportunity cost borne by the producer) will be paid by consumers. Unless consumer benefits exceed the opportunity cost of production, the goods will not be produced. What happens, though, when externalities are present?

Suppose that a business firm discharges unwanted smoke into the air or sewage into a river. Valuable resources—clean air and pure water—are used essentially for garbage disposal. When those downwind or downstream who are harmed cannot successfully sue for damages, neither the firm nor the consumers of its products will pay for these costs. As part a of Exhibit 4–3 shows, the supply curve will understate the opportunity cost of production when these external costs are present. Since the producer has to consider only the cost to the firm, and can ignore the cost imposed on secondary parties, supply curve S_1 will result. If the producer had to pay all costs, supply would be S_2. The actual supply curve S_1 will not reflect the full opportunity cost of producing the good. For the producer, the opportunity cost paid is low enough to merit an increase in supply. Output will be expanded beyond Q_2 (to Q_1), *even though the buyer's valuation of the additional units is less than their full opportunity cost.* The second efficiency condition, Rule 2, is violated. Inefficiency in the form of excessive air and

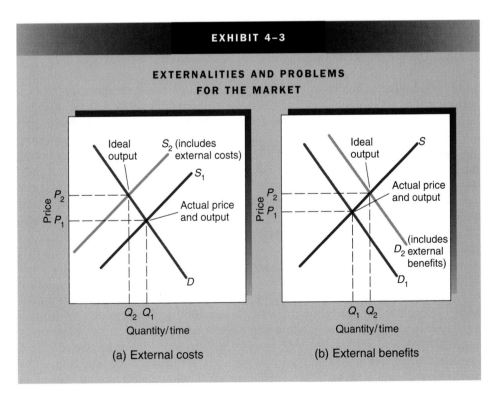

EXHIBIT 4–3

EXTERNALITIES AND PROBLEMS FOR THE MARKET

(a) External costs

(b) External benefits

When external costs are present (a), the output level of a product will exceed the desired amount. Some units (beyond Q_2) will be produced even though their costs exceed the benefits they generate, causing reduced efficiency. In contrast, market output of goods that generate external benefits (b) will be less than the ideal level. Production that could generate more benefits than costs is not undertaken, and a lack of efficiency results.

water pollution results. In the total picture, the harm caused by the added pollution outweighs the net benefits derived by buyers and sellers from the production of units beyond Q_2. To repeat, this problem is caused by the failure of the courts to protect the property rights of those downstream who are harmed.

As part b of Exhibit 4–3 shows, external benefits often result in opportunities forgone. A good such as a flower garden in the front yard of a home may be intended for private consumption. But when others also benefit without paying, some of the benefits are external. Then, as in the case of part b, the market demand curve D_1 will not fully reflect the total benefits, which include those who receive the benefits without helping to pay for their cost. Output Q_1 will result. Could the community gain from a greater output of the product? Yes. The demand curve D_2 reflects both the direct benefits to paying consumers and the benefits bestowed on secondary, nonpaying parties. Expansion of output beyond Q_1 to Q_2 would result in a net gain to the community. But since neither producers nor paying consumers can capture the secondary benefits, consumption level Q_1 will result. The potential net gain from the greater output level Q_2 will be lost. Rule 1 of our ideal efficiency criterion is violated. Once again, the failure of property rights enforcement causes the problem. In this case, producers are unable to collect payment from some of those who enjoy the goods or the service they produce.

Summarizing, competitive markets will fail to give consumers and producers the correct signals and incentives when property rights are not fully defined and enforced, creating externalities. The market will tend to overallocate resources to the production of goods that impose external costs on nonconsenting parties and underallocate resources to the production of goods with external benefits.

PUBLIC GOODS—MORE PROBLEMS FOR THE MARKET

Public goods
Jointly consumed goods that are not diminished when one person enjoys their consumption. When consumed by one person, they are also made available to others. National defense, flood control dams, and scientific theories are all public goods.

Some goods are difficult to provide commercially through the marketplace because there is no way to exclude nonpaying customers. Goods that (a) must be provided jointly to all, if anyone is to get them, and (b) are not diminished by any person's consumption, are called **public goods.** National defense, the judicial and legal systems, and the monetary system are examples of public goods. The national defense that protects you also protects others. Unlike candy bars, national defense cannot be provided only to the citizens who pay and not to others, and enjoyment of defense protection by one does not diminish its availability to others. Similarly, the actions of a central monetary authority are a public good. The monetary system that provides price stability (or instability) for you also provides it for others.

Why are public goods troublesome for the market? Typically, in the marketplace, there is a direct link between consumption and payment. If you do not pay, you do not consume. It is the payments of consumers that provide signals and the incentive to supply products. Public goods, however, are consumed jointly. If a public good is made available to one person, it is simultaneously made available to others. Since those who do not pay cannot be excluded, no one has much incentive to help pay for such goods. This will be true even if the good were quite valuable. Think for a moment—why would you or any other citizen voluntarily pay a "fair share" for national defense, the courts, or police protection if these goods were provided only through the market? From your viewpoint, if others contribute a large amount, these public goods will be provided pretty much regardless of what you do. If others do not pay, your actions will not make much difference anyway. Each person thus has an incentive to pay little or nothing for a public good.

When everybody pays little or nothing, what happens? Not very much of the public good is produced. This is precisely why the market cannot handle public goods very well. Resources will be underallocated to their production because self-interested consumers, recognizing that their specific contribution will have little effect on the quantity supplied, will fail to contribute to their costs. But when many people follow this course, too little of the public good is produced. Thus, the nature of public goods causes a conflict between self-interest and the public interest of economic efficiency.

ECONOMIC INSTABILITY

If markets are to function well, individuals need to know the value to others of what they are buying or selling. For market prices to convey this information, a stable monetary exchange system must be provided. This is especially true for the many market exchanges that involve a time dimension. Houses, cars, consumer durables, land, buildings, equipment, and many other items are often paid for over a period of months or even years. If the purchasing power of the monetary unit, the dollar in the United States, gyrated wildly, previously determined prices would not represent their intended values. Few would want to make transactions involving long-term commitments because of the uncertainty. The smooth functioning of the market would be retarded.

The government's spending and monetary policies exert a powerful influence on economic stability. If properly conducted, these policies contribute to economic stability, full and efficient utilization of resources, and stable prices. Improper stabilization policies, though, can cause massive unemployment, rapidly rising prices, or both.

Economists are not in complete agreement on the extent to which public policy can stabilize the economy and promote full employment. They often debate the impact of various policy tools. All agree, however, that a stable economic environment is vital to a market economy. Those pursuing a course in macroeconomics will find both the potential and the limitations of government action as a stabilizing force in the economy discussed further in Part Two.

THE ECONOMICS OF COLLECTIVE ACTION

The pricing system will fail to meet our ideal efficiency standards if (1) markets are not competitive, (2) externalities are present, (3) public goods necessitate joint consumption, or (4) the aggregate economy is characterized by instability and the resultant uncertainty. If public-sector action can correct these deficiencies, net gains for the community are possible.

Just because it is *possible to visualize* that public-sector action will promote economic welfare, it does *not* follow that real-world governments, including those organized democratically, *will necessarily institute* sound policies. Government is not a "supra-individual" that will always make decisions in the "public interest," however that nebulous term might be defined. Neither will it necessarily operate as a corrective device available for use when market organization fails to achieve a desired outcome. It is instead an alternative method of social organization—an institutional process through which individuals collectively make choices and carry out activities.

The information and incentive structure facing decision makers in the public sector are typically imperfect, just as they are in the private sector. For a hint at why, consider the fact that controlling government programs to serve the general public (rather than serving just the specific providers or recipients of each program at the expense of the public) requires individual voters to study issues, monitor the programs, and be willing to vote unselfishly. Yet that control is a service that benefits everyone. Control is determined by the total vote, not the vote of the individual who is asked to sacrifice time, effort, and self-interest. Such "good citizenship" control is a service that resembles a public good, and, like other public goods, it may be underprovided. We will now turn the spotlight of economic analysis on how government works, and how it differs from the workings of markets.

If we are going to make meaningful comparisons between market allocation and collective action, we need to develop a sound theory that will help us understand both forms of economic organization. **Public-choice analysis** has significantly advanced our understanding of the collective decision-making process in recent years. Something of a cross between economics and political science, public-choice theory applies the principles and methodology of economics to collective choices.

In a democratic setting, individual beliefs and preferences will influence the outcome of collective decisions, just as they influence outcomes in the market. Public-choice theory postulates that individual behavior in the political arena will be motivated by considerations similar to those that influence market behavior. If self-interest is a powerful motivator in the marketplace, there is every reason to believe it will also be a motivating factor when choices are made collectively. If market choices are influenced by differences in projected personal costs relative to benefits, we can expect that such differences will also influence choices made by voters, politicians, and civil servants in government. Public-choice theory, in other words, suggests that the number of saints and sinners in the two sectors will be comparable.

In analyzing the behavior of people in the marketplace, economists develop a logically consistent theory of behavior that can be tested against reality. Through theory and empirical testing, we seek to explain various economic actions of decision makers and, in general, how the market operates.

In the public sphere, our purpose should be the same: to explain how the collective decision-making process really operates. This means developing a logically consistent theory linking individual behavior to collective action, analyzing the implications of that theory, and testing these implications against events in the real world.

Since the theory of collective decision making is not as well developed as our theory of market behavior, our conclusions will not be as well defined. But

Public-choice analysis

The study of decision making as it affects the formation and operation of collective organizations, such as governments. The discipline bridges the gap between economics and political science. In general, the principles and methodology of economics are applied to political science topics.

JAMES BUCHANAN (1919–)

James Buchanan is a key figure in the "public choice revolution." His most famous work, *The Calculus of Consent* (1962), coauthored with Gordon Tullock,[1] argues that, unless rules bring the self-interest of the political players into harmony with the wise use of resources, government will go awry. This and related contributions won him the 1986 Nobel Prize in economics.

[1]J. M. Buchanan and G. Tullock, *The Calculus of Consent* (Ann Arbor: University of Michigan Press, 1962).

in the past 40 years, social scientists have made great strides in helping us to understand resource allocation by the public sector.[4] Currently, this subject is often dealt with at a more advanced academic level. Even on an introductory level, though, economic tools can be used to shed light on how the public sector handles economic activities.

DIFFERENCES AND SIMILARITIES BETWEEN MARKET AND COLLECTIVE ACTION

There is at least one important similarity between the market and the public sectors: The motivations of individuals will influence outcomes in both. But there are basic structural differences.[5] Voluntary exchange, coordinated by prices, is the key in a market economy. In contrast, when collective action occurs in a democratic setting, majority rule is the key, either directly or through legislative procedures. Let us take a look at both the differences and similarities between the two sectors.

1. **Competitive behavior is present in both the market and public sectors.** The market sector is sometimes called the "competitive sector," but competitive behavior is present in both sectors. Politicians compete for elective office. Bureau chiefs and agency heads compete for additional taxpayer dollars. Public-sector employees compete for promotions, higher incomes, and additional power, just as they do

---

[4]The contributions of Kenneth Arrow, James Buchanan, Duncan Black, Anthony Downs, Mancur Olson, Robert Tollison, and Gordon Tullock have been particularly important.

[5]The Public Choice section, later in this book, analyzes the topics of alternative forms of economic organization—market versus collective action—in more detail.

in the private sector. Lobbyists compete for program funding, for favorable bureaucratic rulings, and for favorable legislation for the interest groups they represent—including both private and government clients. (See the "Applications in Economics" box.) The nature of the competition and the criteria for success do differ between the two sectors. Nonetheless, competitive behavior is present in both sectors.

2. **Public-sector organization can break the individual consumption-payment link.** In the market, a consumer who wants to obtain a commodity must pay the price. In this respect, there is a fundamental difference between market and collective action. The government usually does not establish a one-to-one relationship between the individual's payment and receipt of a good. For example, your tax bill will be the same whether you like or dislike the national defense, agriculture, or antipoverty policies of the government. Some individuals will receive very large benefits (either monetary or subjective) from a government action without any signifi-

---

APPLICATIONS IN ECONOMICS

PERSPECTIVES ON THE COST OF POLITICAL COMPETITION

We all have our own ideas about how government should be run. Because government is such an extremely important force in our economy and in our lives, individuals and groups try to influence election outcomes by voting, by contributing to political campaigns, and by ringing doorbells, among other activities. In addition, legislative and executive branch decisions can be influenced directly, by lobbying.

Competition for elective office is fierce, and campaigns are expensive. In preparation for the 1992 elections, for example, candidates for House and Senate positions spent $678 million. Unlike bidders in a market auction, winners and losers alike pay the full costs of the election bid. It is common for lobbying groups to donate to opposing candidates in a close race.

During and after the election, lobbying groups compete for the attention—the ear—of elected officials. In fact, the greatest portion of campaign funds raised by incumbents is not raised at election time; rather, it accrues over their entire term in office. A large campaign contribution may not be able to "buy" a vote, but it certainly enhances the lobbyist's chance to sit down with the elected official to explain the power and the beauty of the contributor's position. In the competitive world of politics, the politician who does not at least listen to helpful "friends of the campaign" is less likely to survive.

Campaign contributions are only the tip of the lobbying iceberg. In Washington, D.C., alone, tens of thousands of individuals, many of them extremely talented, hard-working, and well paid, are dedicated to lobbying Congress and the executive branch of the federal government. Trade associations, for example, have more than 3,000 offices and 80,000 employees in Washington. Of these associations, at least 30 pay their highest officials between $400,000 and $900,000 per year.[1] Another indicator of the enormous amount of time and effort allocated to influencing government is that 65 percent of *Fortune* 200 chief executive officers travel to Washington at least every two weeks, on average. Billions of dollars in budgets, in taxes, and in expenditures required by regulation are at stake. When Congress and the agencies wield such power, competition to obtain the prizes and avoid the penalties naturally results in huge expenditures designed to influence government policy.

---

[1]The salary range is from Peter H. Stone, "Payday!" *National Journal* (December 17, 1994): pp. 2948–2961. More details on campaign finance can be found in Michael Barone and Grant Ujifusa, *The Almanac of American Politics: 1996* (Washington, D.C.: National Journal, 1995). See also David Boaz, "Spend Money to Make Money," *The Wall Street Journal*, November 13, 1983.

cant impact on their personal tax bill. Others will pay substantial taxes while receiving much smaller benefits. In contrast with the market, the amount one pays does not determine the amount received in the public sector.

3. **Scarcity imposes the aggregate consumption-payment link in both sectors.** Although the government can break the link between an individual's payment for a good and the right to consume the good, the reality of the *aggregate consumption–aggregate payment* link will remain. There are no free lunches. Someone must pay the cost of providing scarce goods, regardless of the sector used to produce (or distribute) them. Free goods provided in the public sector are "free" only to certain individuals. They are certainly not free from the viewpoint of society.

4. **The element of compulsion is present in the public sector.** Governments possess an exclusive right to the use of coercion. Large corporations like Exxon and General Motors are economically powerful, but, unlike government, they cannot require citizens to pay for their products. In contrast, in the political arena, if a legislative majority decides on a particular policy, the minority must accept the policy and help pay for its cost, even if that minority strongly disagrees. If $10 billion is allocated by the legislative branch for the development of a superweapon system (or for welfare programs, farm subsidies, or foreign aid), the dissenting minority is required to pay taxes that will help finance the project. When issues are decided in the public sector, those who disagree must, at least temporarily, yield to the current dominant view.

5. **When collective decisions are made legislatively, voters must choose among candidates who represent a bundle of positions on issues.** On election day, the voter cannot choose the views of Representative Frank Free Lunch on poverty and business welfare and simultaneously choose the views of challenger Amanda Austerity on national defense and tariffs. *Inability to support a candidate's views on one issue while rejecting his or her views on another greatly reduces the voter's power to make preferences count on specific issues.* Since the average representative is asked to vote on roughly 2,000 different issues during a two-year term, the enormity of the problem is obvious. The situation in a market is quite different. A buyer can purchase some groceries or items of clothing from one store, while choosing related items at different stores. There is seldom a bundle purchase problem in markets.

6. **Income and power are distributed differently in the two sectors.** Individuals who supply more highly valued resources in the marketplace have larger incomes. The number of dollar votes available to an individual will reflect his or her abilities, ambitions, skills, perceptiveness, past savings, inheritance, good fortune, and willingness to produce for others, among other things. An unequal distribution of consumer power is the result. In a democratic public sector, ballots call the tune. One citizen, one vote is the rule. This does not mean, however, that political power or the benefits derived from the political process are allocated equally to all citizens. Some individu-

als are much better than others at using the political process to personal advantage. The political process gives the greatest rewards to those who best use persuasive skills, organizational abilities, and financial contributions to help politicians get votes. Persons who have more money and skills of this sort—and are willing to spend them in the political arena—can expect to benefit more handsomely from the political process than individuals who lack these personal resources. In the public sector as in the market, there is an unequal distribution of influence and "income," although the sources of success and influence differ between the two sectors.

SUPPLY OF AND DEMAND FOR PUBLIC-SECTOR ACTION

Political good
Any good (or policy), whether a public good or a private good, supplied through the political process.

In markets, consumers use their dollar votes to demand goods. Producers supply goods in exchange for revenue. In a democratic political system, voters and legislators are counterparts to consumers and producers. Voters demand **political goods** using their political resources—votes, lobbying, contributions, and organizational abilities. Vote-conscious legislators are suppliers of political goods.

How does a voter decide which political supplier to support? Because there is no evidence that entrance into a voting booth or participation in the political process causes a personality transformation, there is sound reason to believe that the motivation of participants in the market and political processes is similar. The voter who selects among political alternatives is the same person who selects among market alternatives. If John Jones is influenced by expected personal benefits and costs when he makes choices in the department store, it makes sense that he will be similarly influenced by personal benefits and costs when he makes choices in the voting booth.

Other things constant, voters will support those candidates whom they expect to provide them with the most benefits, net of cost. The greater the expected gains from a candidate's election, the more voters will do to ensure the candidate's success. A voter, like the consumer in the marketplace, will ask the supplier, "What can you do for me and how much will I pay?"

SUPPLY OF PUBLIC SECTOR ACTION

The goal of the political supplier is to put together a majority coalition—to win the election. Vote-seeking politicians, like profit-seeking business decision makers, will have a strong incentive to cater to the views of politically active constituents. The easiest way to win votes, both politically and financially, is to give the constituents—or at least appear to give them—what they want. A politician who pays no heed to the views of his or her constituents is as rare as a businessperson selling swimsuits in the Arctic.

Once the legislature has made the political decision to provide a good or service, or simply to write checks to specified recipients, it uses the services of an agency in the executive branch of government to carry out its orders. The agency is essentially a seller of services to the political sector. The legislators budget tax dollars for the agency to spend, and grant some agencies the authority to regulate citizens. Legislators also monitor the agency, providing oversight on behalf of their constituents. Decisions about the day-to-day operation of the agency, however, must be left to the nonelected civil servants (bureaucrats) who lead the agency. Agency leaders have much narrower interests, and face much more focused political pressures, than elected legislators.[6]

DEMAND FOR PUBLIC SECTOR ACTION

Voters are likely to turn to public-sector economic organization for two major reasons: (1) to reduce waste and inefficiency stemming from noncompetitive markets, externalities, public goods, and economic instability and (2) to redistribute income.

Public-sector action that corrects, or appears to correct, the shortcomings of the market will be attractive. If properly conducted, it will generate more benefits than costs to the community. Much real-world public policy is motivated by a desire to correct the shortcomings of the market. Antitrust action is designed to promote competition. Government provision of national defense, crime prevention, a legal system, and flood-control projects is related to the public-good nature of these activities. Similarly, externalities help justify public-sector action in such areas as pollution control, pure research, and disease control. Furthermore, the tax, spending, and monetary policies of the government are generally used to influence the level and stability of economic activity in most Western nations.

Demand for public-sector action may also stem from a desire to change the income distribution. There is no reason to presume that the unhampered market will lead to the most desirable distribution of income. In fact, the ideal distribution of income is largely a matter of personal preference. There is nothing in positive economics that tells us that one distribution of income is better than another. Some people may desire to see more income allocated to low-income citizens. Others may desire public-sector redistribution for less altruistic reasons—they may seek to enhance their own personal incomes. Whatever the motivation for politically controlled income redistribution, there is reason to believe that economic waste will result. There are three major reasons why large-scale redistribution is likely to reduce the size of the economic pie.

First, income redistribution weakens the link between productive activity and reward. When taxes take a larger share of one's income, the tax revenues are spread among all beneficiaries, so the benefits to the individual from hard work and productive service are reduced. The basic economic postulate suggests that when benefits allocated to producers are reduced (and benefits to nonproducers are raised), less productive effort will be supplied.

Second, as public policy redistributes a larger share of income, individuals will allocate more resources to **rent seeking**.[7] *Rent seeking* is a term used by

Rent seeking
Actions by individuals and interest groups designed to restructure public policy in a manner that will either directly or indirectly redistribute more income to themselves.

---

[6]Later in this book, in the Public Choice section, we will further analyze the operation and interests of agencies.

[7]See Charles K. Rowley, Robert D. Tollison, and Gordon Tullock, *The Political Economy of Rent-Seeking* (Boston: Kluwer Academic Publishers, 1988), for additional details on rent seeking.

economists to denote those actions designed to change public policy—tax structure, composition of spending, or regulation—in a manner that will redistribute income toward favored individuals. Resources used for lobbying and other means of rent seeking (perhaps "favor seeking" would be more descriptive) will not be available to increase the size of the economic pie.

Third, higher taxes to finance income redistribution and an expansion in rent-seeking activities will induce taxpayers to focus less on income-producing activities, and more on actions to protect their income. More accountants, lawyers, and tax-shelter experts will be retained as people seek to limit the amount of their income that is redistributed to others. Like the resources allocated to rent seeking, resources allocated to protecting one's wealth from public policy will also be wasted. They will not be available for productive activity. Therefore, the incentives generated by large-scale redistribution policies can be expected to reduce the size of the economic pie.

CONFLICTS BETWEEN GOOD ECONOMICS AND GOOD POLITICS

While collective decision making has the potential to improve economic efficiency, current economic and political research reveals factors that limit our ability to use government to correct shortcomings of the market. We deal with these factors in more detail in a later chapter, but three important characteristics of the political process are introduced here.

THE RATIONAL IGNORANCE EFFECT

Less than one-half of the American electorate can correctly identify their representatives to Congress. Even fewer can state where those representatives stand on various issues. Why are so many people ignorant of the simplest facts regarding the political process? The reason is not a lack of intelligence on the part of the average American. The problem stems from the incentives confronting the voter. Most citizens recognize that their vote is unlikely to determine the outcome of an election. So they have little incentive to spend much effort seeking the information needed to cast an informed ballot. Economists refer to this lack of incentive as the **rational ignorance effect.**

Rational ignorance effect
Voter ignorance resulting from the fact that people perceive their individual votes as unlikely to be decisive. Therefore, they rationally have little incentive to seek the information needed to cast an informed vote.

The rationally ignorant voter is exercising good judgment as to how his or her time and effort will yield the most personal benefits. The voter's failure to acquire political knowledge is like the farmer's inattention to the factors that determine the weather. Weather is often the most important factor determining the income of an individual farmer, yet it makes no sense for the farmer to spend time studying atmospheric science. Even the farmer who understands the weather cannot control it, so learning how weather systems work will not help the farmer avoid the problems they bring. So it is with the average voter. The voter stands to gain little from learning more about a wide range of issues that are decided in the political arena.

Just as farmers rely on brief weather reports, most voters simply rely on information that is supplied to them freely by candidates (via political advertising) and the mass media, as well as conversations with friends and coworkers. It is not surprising, then, that few voters can accurately describe the consequences of raising tariffs on automobiles or of abolishing the farm price support program. In using their time and efforts in ways other than studying these policy issues, voters are merely responding to economic incentives.

THE PROBLEM OF SPECIAL INTERESTS

A **special interest issue** is one that generates substantial personal benefits for a small number of constituents while imposing a small individual cost on a large number of other voters. A few gain a great deal individually, while a large number lose a little individually.

Special interest issue
An issue that generates substantial individual benefits to a small minority while imposing a small individual cost on many other voters. In total, the net cost to the majority might either exceed or fall short of the net benefits to the special interest group.

Special interest issues are very attractive to politicians who are eager to win elections. Voters who have a small cost imposed on them by a policy favoring a special interest will not care enough about the issue to examine it, particularly if the policy is complex, making its cost difficult to identify. Because information is costly, most of those harmed will not even be aware of their legislators' views on such an issue. On the other hand, those most strongly affected by such an issue will let the candidate (or legislator) know that it is important to them. Because they are a small group, they may be able to organize to give financial and other help to politicians receptive to their ideas, while opposing those who are not.

What would you do if you wanted to win an election? You would have a strong incentive to support the special interest groups, milk them for financial resources, and use those resources to promote your candidacy among the uninformed majority of voters. This would often be true even if the total community benefit from the special interest program were less than its cost. Even if the policy is counterproductive, it might still be a political winner.

What about the interests of the large majority, many of whom are harmed a little by the program benefiting the special interest? Most of these voters are uninformed (remember the rational ignorance effect) on the issue and unlikely to care much about it. Because the cost imposed on them is small, even the few who are informed are unlikely to place much importance on this issue or do much to help politicians who supported their best interests get elected. Recognizing this, astute politicians will generally support various special interest groups.

Thus, the political process tends to work in favor of special interest groups, even when their programs are inefficient. This means that sometimes there is a conflict between good politics (winning elections) and ideal public policy. Throughout, as we consider public-policy alternatives, we will remind you to consider how public policy is likely to operate when special interest influence is strong.

POLITICAL GAINS FROM SHORTSIGHTED POLICIES

The complexity of many issues makes it difficult for voters to identify the future benefits and costs. Can a change in tax rates lead to a greater rate of economic growth? Will a change in environmental policy now lead to a healthier environment for our grandchildren, or just to slower economic growth? What impact will an increase in the national debt have on future prosperity? These questions are hard to answer. The difficulty of predicting the future results of current policies acts to reinforce the rational ignorance effect. Few voters will seriously research and analyze the long-run implications of complex policy alternatives having impacts mainly in the future.

There is a strong contrast here with market investments. The choice to buy or sell a share of stock in a corporation belongs to the individual, and will affect that individual's personal wealth and income. The corporation's decisions are judged by buyers and sellers every day in the stock market. The value of the stock reflects the expectations of all investors, each with personal wealth riding on a correct judgment. The corporation that makes a decision that investors believe is a bad one will see its stock price fall. The firm gets immediate feedback. By contrast, there is no market to judge, day by day, the quality of government's decisions about future directions. Government decisions of this kind seldom generate serious analysis by voters. An individual's mistaken vote, unlike a mistaken investment decision, seldom makes a difference in the outcome for that individual. Instead of studying issues to project the impact of a candidate's views on their future, voters generally rely on current conditions when judging the performance of incumbents.[8] To the voter, the most easily seen indicator of performance is, "How are things now?"

Accordingly, politicians seeking reelection have a strong incentive to support policies that generate current benefits in exchange for future costs, particularly if the future costs will be difficult to identify on election day. Public-sector action will therefore be biased in favor of legislation that offers immediate (and easily identifiable) current benefits in exchange for future costs that are complicated and difficult to identify. Simultaneously, there is a bias against legislation that involves immediate and easily identifiable costs (for example, higher taxes) while yielding future benefits that are complex and difficult to identify. Economists refer to this bias inherent in the collective decision-making process as the **shortsightedness effect.**

What if shortsighted policies lead to serious problems after an election? This can be sticky for politicians, but is it not better to be an officeholder explaining why things are in a mess than a defeated candidate trying to convince people who will not listen why you were right all the time? The political entrepreneur has a strong incentive to win the next election and worry about the problems later, as they arise.

Shortsightedness effect

Misallocation of resources that results because public-sector action is biased (1) in favor of proposals yielding clearly defined current benefits in exchange for difficult-to-identify future costs and (2) against proposals with clearly identifiable current costs but yielding less concrete and less obvious future benefits.

---

[8]As we will see in more detail in the later chapter on public choice, the public sector lacks a market in stock ownership. It is the ability to buy or sell stock that gives stockholders the incentive to monitor current corporate decisions that affect future corporate costs and benefits, so that they can individually sell their corporate stock if they think bad decisions are currently being made, or buy more stock if they think current decisions will produce net future benefits for the corporation. Their buying and selling activities cause the stock price to rise or fall, sending an instant signal and incentive to corporate management to avoid decisions that are shortsighted, in order to avoid falling prices for their corporate stock. Such market signals cannot be generated in the public sector.

IMPLICATIONS OF PUBLIC CHOICE

It is important to distinguish between ordinary politics and constitutional rules. Constitutions establish the procedures that will be utilized to make decisions. They also may reduce the negative results from the problems just discussed, by limiting the reach of the majority. They do so by placing certain matters (for example, the taking of private property without compensation, restrictions on freedom of speech or worship, and various restrictions on voting) beyond the reach of majority rule or normal legislative procedures.

Both bad news and good news flow from public-choice analysis. The bad news is that, for certain classes of economic activity, unconstrained democratic government will predictably be a source of economic waste and inefficiency. Not only does the invisible hand of the market sometimes fail to meet our ideal efficiency criteria, so, too, does political decision making. That makes the growth of government (noted by Jonathan Hughes in the chapter-opening quote) worrisome. But there is also some good news arising from public-choice theory: Properly structured constitutional rules can improve the expected result from government. So the study of how people behave when they make collective choices "in the world as it really is" suggests constructive alternatives for improving the government process.

Whether political organization leads to desirable or undesirable economic outcomes is critically dependent upon the structure of the political (constitutional) rules. In government as elsewhere, proper incentives are critical to good decision making. When the structure of the political rules harmonizes the self-interest of individual voters, politicians, and bureaucrats with the general welfare, government will promote economic prosperity. On the other hand, if the rules fail to bring about this harmony, political allocation will lead to both waste of resources and conflict among citizens. The challenge before us is to develop political economy institutions that are more consistent with economic prosperity. Public choice theory provides us with insight concerning how this objective might be achieved. Needless to say, this general topic is one of the most exciting and potentially fruitful areas of study in economics.

LOOKING AHEAD

In the next chapter, we will examine the government's actual spending and tax policies. In subsequent chapters, the significance of economic organization and issues of political economy will be highlighted. The tools of economics are applied to government with a dual objective. We will point out what government ideally might do, but we will also focus on what government can be expected to do. Not surprisingly, the two are not always identical. *Political economy*—the use of economic tools to explain how both the market and the public sectors actually work—is a fascinating subject. It helps us to understand the "why" behind many of today's current events. Who said economics is the dismal science?

CHAPTER SUMMARY

1. Economic efficiency—creating as much value as possible from a given set of resources—is a goal by which alternative institutions and policies can be judged. Two

conditions must be met to achieve economic efficiency: (1) all activities that produce more benefits than costs for the individuals within an economy must be undertaken and (2) activities that generate more costs than benefits to the individuals must not be undertaken. If only the buyer and the seller are affected and competition is present, the incentives built into market production and exchange are consistent with the ideal efficiency criteria.

2. Lack of competition may make it possible for a group of sellers to gain by restricting output and raising prices. When competition is absent, the self-interest of sellers often conflicts with economic efficiency.

3. When property rights are imperfectly defined or enforced, market exchange will tend to underallocate resources to the production of goods with external benefits and overallocate resources to those products that generate external costs.

4. Public goods are troublesome for the market to handle because nonpaying customers cannot easily be excluded. Since the amount of a public good that each individual receives is largely unaffected by whether he or she helps pay for it, many individuals will contribute little. The market will thus tend to undersupply public goods.

5. The public sector will improve the operation of markets if it provides a stable economic environment.

6. The public sector is an alternative means of organizing economic activity. Public-sector decision making will reflect the choices of individuals acting as voters, politicians, financial contributors, lobbyists, and bureaucrats. Public-choice analysis applies the principles and methodology of economics to group decision making to help us understand collective organizations.

7. Successful political candidates will seek to offer programs that appeal to voters. Voters, in turn, will be attracted to candidates who reflect the voters' own views and interests. In a democratic setting, there are two major reasons voters will turn to collective organization: (1) to reduce waste and inefficiency stemming from noncompetitive markets, externalities, public goods, and economic instability and (2) to alter the income distribution.

8. Public-sector action may sometimes improve the market's efficiency and lead to an increase in the community's welfare, all individuals considered. However, the political process is likely to conflict with ideal economic efficiency criteria when (1) voters have little knowledge of an issue, (2) special interests are strong, and/or (3) political figures can gain from following shortsighted policies.

9. The democratic political process is not perfect, but the problems that result from its imperfect incentives can be limited by constitutional restraints on its procedures and on the reach of majority rule.

CRITICAL ANALYSIS QUESTIONS

1. What is allocative efficiency and when is it present? Why might a market economy fail to achieve the ideal conditions of economic efficiency?

*2. If producers are to be provided with an incentive to produce a good, why is it important for them to be able to prevent nonpaying customers from receiving the good?

3. Explain in your own words what is meant by external costs and external benefits. Why may market allocations be less than ideal when externalities are present?

4. Do you think special interest groups exert much influence on local government? Why or why not? As a test, check the composition of the local zoning board in your community. How many real-estate agents, contractors, developers, and landlords are on the board? Are there any citizens without real-estate interests on the board?

*5. "Economics is a positive science. Government by its very nature is influenced by philosophical considerations. Therefore, the tools of economics cannot tell us much about how the public sector works." Do you agree or disagree with this statement? Why?

*6. Which of the following are public goods: (a) an antimissile system surrounding Washington, D.C.; (b) a fire department; (c) tennis courts; (d) Yellowstone National Park; (e) elementary schools? Explain, using the definition of a public good.

7. "A democratic government is a corrective device used to remedy inefficiencies that arise when market allocation is not working well." Is this statement true or false? Explain.

8. Incentives are important in both the market and political sectors. Discuss the similarities and differences in the incentives of the following pairs of people to use resources efficiently and provide value to others.

    a. The president of General Motors and the president of a large state university.

    b. A member of the board of directors of IBM and a congressional representative.

    c. The general manager of Walt Disney World and the superintendent of Yellowstone National Park.

    d. The president of a textbook-publishing company and the superintendent of public schools in your state.

*9. How can you determine if a market action is efficient? How can you determine if a government action is efficient? If the majority of the citizens favor a project, does this indicate it is productive?

10. English philosopher John Locke argued that the protection of each individual's person and property was the primary function of government. Why is the secure pro-

tection of each individual's person and property (that is, property acquired without the use of violence, theft, or fraud) important to the efficient operation of an economy?

*11. Does the democratic political process incorporate the invisible hand principle? Is the presence or absence of the invisible hand principle important? Why or why not?

*12. "The average person is more likely to make an informed choice when he or she purchases a personal computer than when he or she votes for a congressional candidate." Evaluate this statement.

13. Are well-organized special interest groups likely to exert a disproportional influence on the democratic political process? Why or why not? Explain.

14. Suppose that Abel builds a factory next to Baker's farm, and air pollution from the factory harms Baker's crops. Is Baker's property right to the land being violated? Is an externality present? What if the pollution invades Baker's home and harms her health? Are her property rights violated? Is an externality present? Explain.

---

*Asterisk denotes questions for which answers are given in Appendix B.

Our Constitution is in actual operation; everything appears to promise that it will last; but in this world nothing is certain but death and taxes.

BENJAMIN FRANKLIN, 1789

CHAPTER FOCUS

▪ How big is government? What goods and services do we provide through government? How are they financed?

▪ Why has the size of government grown more rapidly than our economy during the past several decades? Does government now provide more goods and services than it did in the past? Does it redistribute more income?

▪ How do taxes influence the behavior of people? If a tax rate is increased by 10 percent, will revenue from the tax increase by 10 percent?

▪ How did tax legislation passed during the 1980s affect the taxes paid by the rich?

▪ How does the size of government in the United States compare with the size of government in other countries?

T he activities of government have an enormous impact on our lives. Governments levy taxes and organize the production of many goods and services. Governments often tax income away from some people and transfer it to others. Governments also provide the legal infrastructure for economic activity. Laws against theft, fraud, and violence greatly influence how markets work and the degree of cooperation and conflict among economic participants. Similarly, the monetary framework and regulatory activities of government are vitally important. In fact, in its role as rule maker and referee, government probably exerts more influence on the economic prosperity of a nation than it does as a producer of goods and services.

Nevertheless, taxation and government expenditures are the most direct means by which the government influences the economy. Analysis of the government's spending policies and methods of finance will reveal a great deal about the size and nature of government.

THE GROWTH OF GOVERNMENT

Prior to the 1930s, government expenditures generally amounted to less than 10 percent of our gross domestic product (GDP).[1] Except during times of war, federal government expenditures were quite small in the early part of this century. As **Exhibit 5–1** illustrates, the total government expenditures were only 10.1 percent of GDP in 1929, and federal expenditures accounted for less than one-third of the total.

During the 1930–1970 period, both the size and composition of government changed dramatically. By 1970 total government expenditures comprised 30.8 percent of our economy, more than triple the level of 1929. Most of this growth of government took place at the federal level. *As a share of our economy,* federal expenditures tripled during the 1930s, while state and local expenditures increased by only a small amount. Between 1940 and 1970, federal expenditures more than doubled in size (from 9.5 percent to 20.6 percent) as a share of our economy. State and local spending grew more slowly, advancing from 9.0 percent of GDP in 1940 to 10.2 percent in 1970. In contrast with 1929, when government expenditures were small and mostly at the local level, by 1970 government spending summed to nearly one-third of our total output, and most of this spending was undertaken by the federal government.

Since 1970 the growth of government as a proportion of our economy has continued, albeit at a slower rate. *In 1995 total government expenditures comprised 32.2 percent of GDP, up from 30.8 percent in 1970. More than two-thirds of the government spending in 1995 was undertaken at the federal level.*

---

[1]GDP is discussed in Chapter 6. For now, it can be thought of as a measure of total output produced during a period.

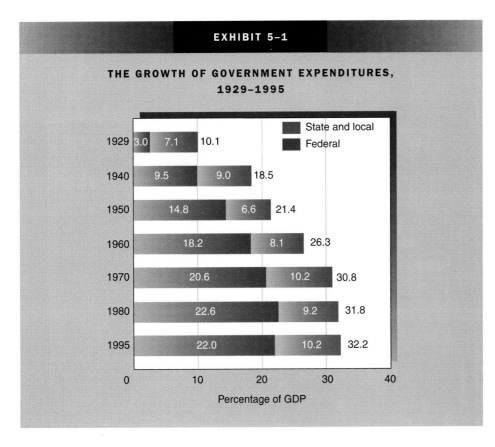

EXHIBIT 5-1

THE GROWTH OF GOVERNMENT EXPENDITURES, 1929-1995

Year	State and local	Federal	Total
1929	3.0	7.1	10.1
1940	9.5	9.0	18.5
1950	14.8	6.6	21.4
1960	18.2	8.1	26.3
1970	20.6	10.2	30.8
1980	22.6	9.2	31.8
1995	22.0	10.2	32.2

Percentage of GDP

In 1929 total government spending summed to 10.1 percent of total output. During the 1930–1970 period, the size of government as a share of the U.S. economy rose substantially, reaching 30.8 percent of GDP in 1970. In 1995 total government spending was 32.2 percent of GDP.

Source: *Economic Report of the President,* various issues. Grants to state and local governments are included in federal expenditures.

FEDERALISM AND GOVERNMENT EXPENDITURES

The economic functions of government in the United States vary among the different levels. The United States has a federalist system of government. Although many economic activities are conducted at the federal level, the primary responsibility for other functions remains with state and local governments. The expenditure data of **Exhibit 5–2** and **Exhibit 5–3** highlight the functional differences among the levels of government.

Exhibit 5–2 shows the broad categories of federal expenditures for fiscal year 1995. The federal government is solely responsible for national defense. A little more than one-fifth (22.1 percent) of federal expenditures went for defense and related areas (space, veterans' benefits, and foreign affairs) in 1995. The largest item in the federal budget was cash-income maintenance—social security, unemployment payments, and public assistance to the poor and the disabled. These income transfers accounted for 35.7 percent of the total federal budget. Expenditures on health-care programs (primarily Medicare and Medicaid) made up 17.6 percent of all federal spending in 1995. Thus, spending in these two categories—cash-income transfers and health-care spending—accounted for more than half (53.3 percent) of the federal expenditures. Net interest payments on the national debt accounted for another 14.9 percent of the total federal outlays.

The breakdown of the 1995 fiscal year federal budget is presented here. Defense accounted for 22.1 percent of federal spending. More than half of the federal tax dollar was spent on cash-income maintenance and health care.

Source: *Economic Report of the President, 1996*, Table B-77.

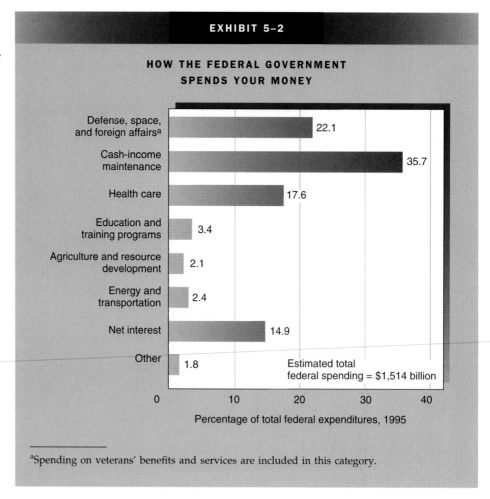

EXHIBIT 5–2

HOW THE FEDERAL GOVERNMENT SPENDS YOUR MONEY

Category	Percentage
Defense, space, and foreign affairs[a]	22.1
Cash-income maintenance	35.7
Health care	17.6
Education and training programs	3.4
Agriculture and resource development	2.1
Energy and transportation	2.4
Net interest	14.9
Other	1.8

Estimated total federal spending = $1,514 billion

Percentage of total federal expenditures, 1995

[a]Spending on veterans' benefits and services are included in this category.

The figures reveal a great deal about the nature of the federal government in the mid-1990s. Nearly 70 percent of federal expenditures go for just three things: (1) income transfers, (2) health care, and (3) net interest on the national debt. When defense is added to these three items, the four categories account for 90 percent of the federal expenditures. This means that expenditures on everything else—the federal courts, national parks, highways, education, job training, agriculture, energy, natural resources, federal law enforcement, and numerous other programs—account for only 10 percent of the federal budget.

Exhibit 5–3 highlights the functional responsibilities of state and local governments. In the United States, public education has traditionally been the responsibility of state and local governments. Twenty-nine percent of state and local government expenditures were allocated to education during fiscal year 1992. State governments supplement federal allocations in the areas of social welfare, public welfare, and health. These social welfare expenditures composed 21 percent of the total spending of state governments during 1992. Highways, utilities, insurance trust funds, law enforcement, and fire protection are other major areas of expenditure for state and local government.

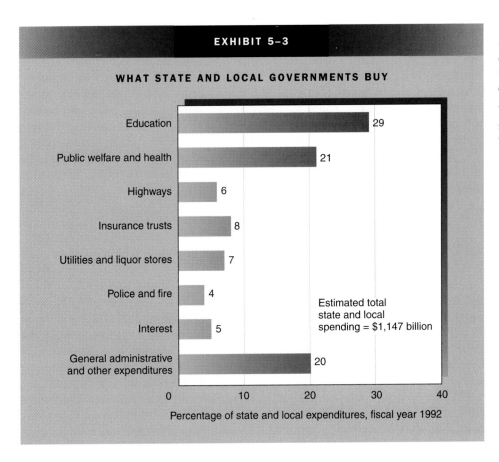

EXHIBIT 5–3

WHAT STATE AND LOCAL GOVERNMENTS BUY

Education — 29
Public welfare and health — 21
Highways — 6
Insurance trusts — 8
Utilities and liquor stores — 7
Police and fire — 4
Interest — 5
General administrative and other expenditures — 20

Estimated total state and local spending = $1,147 billion

Percentage of state and local expenditures, fiscal year 1992

Education and public welfare (including health) expenditures compose the major budget items of state and local governments.

Source: U.S. Department of Commerce.

GOVERNMENT PURCHASES AND TRANSFER PAYMENTS

It is important to distinguish between (1) government purchases of goods and services and (2) transfer payments. **Government purchases** occur when either consumption or investment goods are supplied through the public sector. Government supplied consumption goods would include government expenditures on items such as police and fire protection, medical services, and administration. Government investments would include the provision of long-lasting goods such as highways, jet planes, and buildings. The resources used to supply consumption and investment goods through the public sector have alternative uses. Thus, these government purchases directly reduce the supply of resources available to produce private goods and services.

Transfer payments are transfers of income from taxpayers to recipients who do not provide current goods and services in exchange for these payments. Simply put, transfer payments take income from some to provide additional income to others. Social security benefits, pensions of retired government employees,

Government purchases
Current expenditures on consumption and investment goods provided by federal, state, and local governments; they exclude transfer payments.

Transfer payments
Payments to individuals or institutions that are not linked to the current supply of a good or service by the recipient.

and Aid to Families with Dependent Children (AFDC) are examples of transfer payments.

Unlike government purchases, transfer payments do not directly reduce the resources available to the private sector. They do, however, alter the incentive structure of the economy and almost certainly exert an indirect impact on the size of the economic pie. The taxes necessary to finance transfer payments reduce the personal payoff from saving, investing, and working. In addition, when receipt of a transfer payment is inversely related to one's income, transfers will also reduce the recipient's incentive to earn taxable income. As we proceed, we will investigate the link between aggregate output and the incentive structure in more detail.

ALTERNATIVE MEASURES OF GOVERNMENT'S SIZE

Exhibit 5–4 presents four alternative measures of government size. In 1994 the purchases of federal, state, and local governments amounted to $1,315 billion, or 19 percent of total U.S. output. Government purchases thus consumed a little less than one-fifth of our resources. Government employment offers a second gauge by which we can measure the size of government. In 1994 a little more than one out of every six workers (16.8 percent) was employed by a government unit.

As we have already pointed out, government purchases fail to tell the whole story. Governments not only employ people and provide goods and services, they also tax the income of some and transfer it to others. Once transfer payments are included, total government expenditures (the third measure of size)

Source: *Economic Report of the President, 1996* (Washington, DC: U.S. Government Printing Office, 1996), and *Monthly Labor Review* (U.S. Department of Labor, October 1995). Intergovernmental transfer payments (i.e., federal grants to state and local governments) are not counted twice.

EXHIBIT 5–4

FOUR MEASURES OF SIZE OF GOVERNMENT: FEDERAL, STATE, AND LOCAL, 1994

1. Government purchases of consumption and investment goods	(a) Billions of dollars	$1,315
	(b) Percentage of GDP	19.0
2. Government employment	(a) Millions of employees	19.1
	(b) Percentage of total employment	16.8
3. Total government expenditures, including transfer payments	(a) Billions of dollars	$2,218
	(b) Percentage of GDP	32.0
4. Total taxes and other revenues	(a) Billions of dollars	$2,128
	(b) Percentage of GDP	30.7

in 1994 summed to $2,218 billion, or 32 percent of GDP.[2] The total tax bill (the fourth measure of size) was slightly less, accounting for 30.7 percent of GDP. Therefore, during 1994 approximately one-third of the national output was channeled through the public sector.

On a per capita basis, government expenditures were equal to $8,530 in 1994. If government expenditures in 1994 had been divided equally among the 95 million households in the United States, each household would have received $23,350.

THE CHANGING COMPOSITION OF GOVERNMENT

For many years, government has been involved in providing national defense, police and fire protection, roads, education, and other jointly consumed goods and services. Because defense is a classic example of a public good, it is not surprising that this good is supplied through the public rather than through the private sector. Police and fire protection, road maintenance, and education have traditionally been financed and distributed by state and local governments. Many would argue that these goods either generate external spillover effects or exhibit public-good characteristics.

Interestingly, these traditional public-sector functions are not responsible for the growth of government in recent years. As **Exhibit 5–5** shows, the growth of government during the past several decades stems from its increased involvement in income-transfer activities. Perhaps surprisingly to some, government purchases of consumption and investment goods have declined from approximately 28 percent of GDP in the late 1950s to less than 20 percent of GDP in the early 1990s. Most of this decline in government purchases is the result of reductions in defense expenditures, which fell from approximately 14 percent of GDP in the late 1950s to less than 5 percent in 1995. As Exhibit 5–5 illustrates, nondefense government purchases of goods and services fluctuated within a narrow band around 14 percent of GDP. In contrast with the reductions in defense expenditures, income transfers grew from less than 6 percent of GDP in the late 1950s to almost 14 percent in the early 1990s. Put another way, the government taxes approximately 14 percent of total output away from producers and channels it to the elderly, the unemployed, farmers, children in single-parent families, persons with disabilities, and other transfer recipients.

Taken together, Exhibits 5–2 and 5–5 shed light on both (1) the changing nature of government and (2) future problems that will have to be confronted. For several decades, the government has increased its expenditures on income transfers (the social security retirement program accounts for the bulk of spending in this category) and health care (primarily Medicare and Medicaid). (See

---

[2]The public administration costs associated with income-transfer programs do involve the direct use of resources, and they therefore are counted as government purchases. Only the redistribution portion is counted as a transfer payment.

During the past several decades, defense expenditures have declined as a share of the economy. In 1995, defense spending consumed approximately 5 percent of output, less than half the comparable figure of the 1960s. In contrast, income transfers have grown from approximately 6 percent of GDP in the early 1960s to nearly 14 percent in the early 1990s.

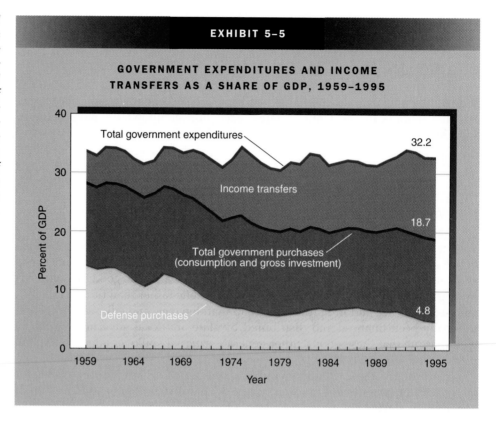

EXHIBIT 5-5

GOVERNMENT EXPENDITURES AND INCOME TRANSFERS AS A SHARE OF GDP, 1959–1995

Illustrated Exhibit I–G on page 4 for additional evidence on this point.) In the past, growth of expenditures in these two areas has been financed with reductions in defense expenditures and increases in national debt. This will not be possible in the future. Additional cuts in defense will be very difficult, and the growth of the debt is now pushing the government's interest cost upward.

As Exhibit 5–2 illustrates, nearly 70 percent of federal expenditures are now consumed by income transfers, health-care expenditures, and net interest on the debt. In the mid-1990s, the federal government basically transfers income and helps pay health-care bills. The typical working taxpayer who pays most of the cost of these programs receives few benefits in return. This factor helps to explain why so many people are dissatisfied with government, particularly the federal government, in the mid-1990s.

Unfortunately, the situation is almost certain to worsen unless the current programs are modified. Beginning around 2010 the baby boom generation—those born between 1946 and 1960—will move into the retirement phase of their lives. As this happens, there will be a sharp increase in the proportion of the population age 65 years and over. (See Illustrated Exhibit I–F on page 3 for evidence on this point.) Unless the current programs are modified, expenditures on social security and Medicare, the two largest programs driving the growth of income transfers and health-care expenditures, will soar. Given that the bulk of federal expenditures are already consumed by these two categories, additional spending will surely encounter taxpayer resistance.

FINANCING GOVERNMENT EXPENDITURES

There are no free lunches. Government provision of goods, services, or income transfers must be financed. Governments use three major sources of funds to pay for their expenditures: (1) taxes, (2) user charges, and (3) borrowing.[3] In the United States, taxes are by far the largest source of government revenue. The power to tax sets governments apart from private businesses. Of course, a private business can put whatever price tag it wishes on its products; but no private business can force you to buy. With its power to tax, a government can force citizens to pay, regardless of whether they receive a "good" of equal or greater value in return.

Let's take a closer look at the taxes levied by governments and at the other sources of revenues available for the finance of government activities.

PERSONAL INCOME TAXES

The largest single source of revenue for governments is the personal income tax. This tax is particularly important at the federal level, where it accounts for 44 percent of federal budget receipts (see **Exhibit 5–6**). Since the Second World War, the income tax has also become an important source of revenue at the state level, where it now accounts for 10 percent of the tax receipts collected by the states. Only six states (Florida, Nevada, South Dakota, Texas, Washington, and Wyoming) now fail to levy a state income tax.

The rate structure of the federal income tax is progressive. A **progressive tax** takes a larger percentage of income from high-income recipients. For example, using the rate structure applicable to income in 1995, the tax liability of a single person with $20,000 of taxable income is $3,004. The **average tax rate (ATR)** can be expressed as follows:

$$ATR = \frac{\text{tax liability}}{\text{taxable income}}$$

The single person's ATR on $20,000 of income is 15.02 percent ($3,004 ÷ $20,000). Because the federal income tax structure is progressive, the ATR will increase with taxable income. For example, the tax liability (1995) of a single person with a taxable income of $40,000 is $8,172, resulting in an ATR of 20.4 percent, higher than the ATR for $20,000 of taxable income.

The economic way of thinking stresses that what happens at the margin is of crucial importance in personal decision making. The **marginal tax rate (MTR)** can be expressed as follows:

$$MTR = \frac{\text{change in tax liability}}{\text{change in income}}$$

Progressive tax
A tax that requires those with higher taxable incomes to pay a larger percentage of their incomes to the government than those with lower taxable incomes.

Average tax rate (ATR)
One's tax liability divided by one's taxable income.

Marginal tax rate (MTR)
Additional tax liability divided by additional income. Thus, if $100 of additional earnings increases one's tax liability by $30, the marginal tax rate is 30 percent.

---

[3]In addition to borrowing from private sources, the federal government also may borrow from its central bank. As we will see later, borrowing from a central bank is equivalent to the finance of government via the creation of money.

EXHIBIT 5-6

SOURCES OF GOVERNMENT REVENUE

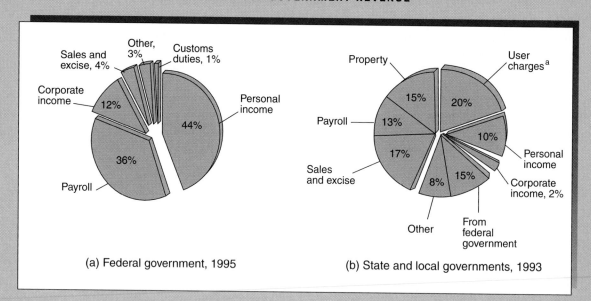

(a) Federal government, 1995

(b) State and local governments, 1993

Personal income and payroll taxes are the major sources of revenue for the federal government. User charges, sales taxes, property taxes, and grants from the federal government provide the major revenue sources for state and local governments.

ᵃRevenues from government-operated utilities and liquor stores are included in this category.

Source: *Statistical Abstract of the United States, 1995,* and *Economic Report of the President, 1996.*

The MTR reveals both how much of one's *additional* income must be turned over to the tax collector and how much is retained by the individual. For example, when the MTR is 25 percent, $25 of every $100 of additional earnings must be paid to the taxing authority. The individual is permitted to keep $75 of his or her additional income.

With progressive taxation of income, inflation will persistently push taxpayers into higher tax brackets. **Indexing** is a procedure designed to prevent this from happening. (See accompanying feature on indexing of taxation.)

Indexing
The automatic increasing of money values as the general level of prices increases. Economic variables that are often indexed include wage rates and tax brackets.

PAYROLL TAXES

Although income from all sources is covered by the income tax, only earnings derived from labor are subject to the payroll tax. Interest, dividends, rents, and other income derived from capital are not subject to payroll taxes. Payroll taxes on the earnings of employees and self-employed workers finance social security (including Medicare) and unemployment-compensation benefits. Payroll taxes constitute the second largest, and most rapidly expanding, source of tax revenue. In 1995 payroll taxes constituted 36 percent of all federal revenues, compared to only 16 percent in 1960.

INDEXING, INFLATION, AND THE TAXES PEOPLE PAY

After the inflation of the 1970s pushed taxpayers into higher and higher tax brackets, Congress finally moved to index the personal income tax structure beginning in 1985. Indexing increases the nominal income tax brackets (and the personal-exemption allowance) in proportion to the general increase in prices. This widening of the tax brackets each year in order to compensate for the impact of inflation on nominal incomes reduces the increase in taxes resulting from inflation. (*Note:* The current indexing does not eliminate higher taxes as the result of inflation. See the Applications in Economics box on capital gain taxation.)

Perhaps an example will help clarify how this indexing works. Suppose a marginal tax rate of 10 percent is applied to the initial income bracket of $0 to $10,000, and also suppose that a 20 percent marginal tax rate is applicable for incomes between $10,000 and $25,000. Still higher rates may be applicable at still higher levels of income. Consider what would happen if prices and wages double (perhaps over a period of several years) and, as a result of this inflation, the taxable income of a worker expands from $10,000 to $20,000. If the tax structure is not indexed, this worker's tax liability will increase from $1,000 (10 percent of the $10,000 income) to $3,000 (10 percent of $10,000 plus 20 percent of the next $10,000 of taxable income). Even though this worker's nominal income, like the general level of prices, merely doubled, the tax liability tripled because the inflation pushed the worker into a higher tax bracket. As the result of the inflation, both the average and marginal tax rates are increased.

Indexing widens the tax brackets to offset the effects of inflation and thereby keeps inflation from pushing taxpayers with incomes of constant purchasing power into higher tax brackets. With indexing, the $0–$10,000 income bracket would be expanded to $0–$20,000 when prices increase by 100 percent. So when inflation increases the income of a taxpayer by 100 percent, the taxpayer's average and marginal tax rates remain constant. The objective of indexing is to protect taxpayers from unlegislated tax increases that, under a progressive tax system, would otherwise be automatically imposed by inflation.

The payroll tax encompasses both proportional and regressive features. A **proportional tax** is one that takes the same percentage of income from all taxpayers, regardless of income level. Until the maximum taxable income ceiling is reached, the payroll tax is proportional. For example, in 1995, both employees and their employers paid a tax rate of 7.65 percent on all employee earnings up to $61,200. (Self-employed workers paid a 15.3 percent rate.) Beyond that taxable income ceiling, no additional payroll tax is levied.[4] So a worker earning $10,000 incurs a payroll tax of $765, whereas one earning $20,000 is taxed twice that amount, or $1,530. Until the taxable income ceiling is met, all workers (and their employers) pay exactly the same tax rate.

A **regressive tax** takes a smaller percentage of income from those in high-earnings brackets than it does from low-income recipients. Because the social security payroll tax does not apply beyond the maximum income ceiling, it is regressive for incomes beyond that point. For example, a person with an income twice the taxable ceiling will pay exactly the same amount of social security payroll taxes (and only one-half the average tax rate) as another individual whose earnings are equal to the taxable ceiling. All people with earnings above the taxable ceiling will pay a lower average tax rate than people with earnings below the ceiling. Thus, for incomes beyond the earnings ceiling, the payroll tax is regressive.

Proportional tax
A tax for which individuals pay the same percentage of their income (or other tax base) in taxes, regardless of income level.

Regressive tax
A tax that takes a smaller percentage of income as income level increases. Thus, the proportion of income allocated to the tax would be greater for the poor than for the rich.

---

[4]Actually, the payroll tax has two components: a 6.2 percent social security tax that applies only to earnings up to the $61,220 ceiling and a 1.45 percent Medicare tax that applies to all earnings, including those beyond the ceiling. Since both the employee and the employer are subject to these rates, essentially the effective payroll tax rates are twice the rates visibly imposed on the employee.

SALES AND EXCISE TAXES

Taxes levied on consumption expenditures for a wide range of goods and services are called sales taxes. A tax levied on specific commodities, such as gasoline, cigarettes, or alcoholic beverages, is called an excise tax. There is little difference between the two, except that one is a general tax and the other is quite specific.

Sales and excise taxes provided 17 percent of the revenue for state and local governments in 1992. They are particularly important at the state level, where they account for almost one-third of the revenue raised by state governments.

PROPERTY TAXES

Despite their unpopularity, property taxes still constitute the bulk of local tax revenues. In 1992, 75 percent of the tax revenue raised by local governments was generated from this source. Property taxes are often criticized because they are cumbersome. The assessor must set a value on taxable property. This generally involves a certain amount of arbitrary judgment. During a period of rising prices, property that has been recently exchanged is likely to receive a higher valuation than similar property without an easily identifiable indicator of current value. High administration costs and problems in providing equal treatment for similarly situated taxpayers are associated with property taxes.

CORPORATE INCOME TAX

The corporate income tax is levied on the net income—that is, the income after deductions for the business expenses accompanying the provision of goods or services. It might also be properly thought of as a tax on the accounting profit of corporate firms.

Corporate incomes in the United States have been taxed since 1909. The tax currently generates approximately 12 percent of all federal tax receipts and 2 percent of the revenue of state and local governments (see Exhibit 5–6).

The structure of the corporate income tax is relatively simple. In 1995 the first $50,000 of corporate profit was taxed at a rate of 15 percent. Corporate earnings in the range from $50,000 to $75,000 were taxed at a rate of 25 percent, and earnings above $75,000 but less than $100,000 were taxed at a 34 percent rate. For earnings above $100,000, the rate was approximately 35 percent.[5]

Many public finance economists are critical of the corporate income tax because it discriminates against the corporate business structure. The owners of business firms organized as proprietorships or partnerships pay only personal income taxes on their business earnings. In contrast, the income generated through the corporate business structure is taxed twice—once as net income of the business firm and again when it accrues to shareholders as dividends or appreciation in the value of the stock.

---

[5]For a short, readable summary of the history and impact of the corporate income tax, see Rob Norton, "Corporate Taxation," in *The Fortune Encyclopedia of Economics,* ed. David R. Henderson (New York: Warner Books, 1993).

The double-taxation feature of the corporate tax can result in very high marginal rates of taxation. For example, if a corporation earns $1,000 for a shareholder, only $660 will remain after a 34 percent corporate tax is paid. If the individual is in the 36 percent personal income tax bracket, payment of the $660 in dividends would generate only $422.40 in after-tax earnings for the shareholder. Thus, taxes take almost 58 percent of the original business earnings.

Because federal tax procedures do not allow businesses to take the opportunity cost of equity as an expense, the corporate income tax encourages corporate firms to use debt financing rather than equity ownership. A corporation that uses debt to finance a capital expenditure will incur an interest cost, which will reduce its accounting profits and tax liability. In contrast, if the same firm uses equity financing (that is, raises financial capital by issuing additional stock), the interest cost will not appear on the firm's accounting statement. Therefore, even though there is an opportunity cost of capital, regardless of whether it is raised by equity financing or by debt, only the latter will reduce the tax liability of the firm.

USER CHARGES

Not all government revenue comes from taxes. For some services, governments charge consumers a price, just as private businesses do. **User charges** differ from taxes in that one's payment is directly linked to the consumption of a good or service. Citizens who do not consume the government-provided good or service do not have to pay for it. User charges are particularly important at the state and local level, where they account for 20 percent of government revenue. Local governments often provide utility services, garbage pickup, hospital care, and bus transportation. These government-operated businesses—many of which are in competition with private firms—are often partially or entirely financed by prices charged to the users of these services. In general, when the nature of the good permits, economists favor user charges rather than taxes, since the former provide better information on whether consumers value the good or service produced more than its cost of production.

Sometimes taxes can be used to approximate the effects of a user charge. For example, an excise tax on gasoline used to finance roads imposes the cost of the roads on individuals roughly in proportion to their consumption (use). Similarly, if a civic auditorium is operated by the government, a ticket tax used to finance the arena's cost approximates a user charge.

User charge
A payment that users (consumers) are required to make if they want to receive certain services provided by the government.

BORROWING

In addition to taxes and user charges, government has one other method of financing expenditures: borrowing. When the total spending exceeds revenue from taxes and user charges, the government will have to borrow to cover its budget deficit. Governments generally borrow by issuing interest-bearing bonds. With borrowing, governments can affect the timing of taxation, but the burden cannot be escaped. In essence, borrowing commits the government to higher future taxes in order to meet the interest obligations on the outstanding debt.

In recent years, the federal government has borrowed funds to cover a major proportion—approximately 20 percent during the past decade—of its expenditures. Constitutional provisions often limit the borrowing powers of state governments. Thus, state and local governments borrow much less than the federal government. In fact, state and local governments in aggregate have generally run a budget surplus in recent years.

ISSUES OF EFFICIENCY AND EQUITY

There are two major factors to consider when choosing among taxation alternatives. First, taxes should be consistent with economic efficiency. Taxes should not encourage people to use scarce resources wastefully. A tax system is inconsistent with economic efficiency if it encourages individuals (1) to buy goods costing more than their value to consumers and/or (2) to channel time into tax-avoidance activities. We will examine these issues in detail later in this section.

Second, a tax system should be equitable; that is, it should be consistent with widely accepted principles of fairness. Economists often speak of "horizontal" and "vertical" equity. Horizontal equity means equal treatment of equals. If two parties earn equal incomes, for example, horizontal equity implies that the two should be taxed equally. The corollary concept of vertical equity requires that persons who are situated differently should be taxed differently. It encompasses what economists refer to as the **ability-to-pay principle,** the seemingly straightforward idea that taxes should be levied according to the ability of the taxpayer to pay. Deciding exactly what this means, however, is at least partially subjective. Most people find it reasonable that the rich should pay more taxes than the poor. This would be the case under a proportional (or flat) tax system. Under a flat tax system, those with higher incomes would pay proportionally more taxes. For example, a taxpayer with twice the income of another would pay twice as much in taxes.[6] Many would also find it reasonable that the rich should pay a higher proportion in taxes as their income increases. Of course, progressive taxation incorporates this concept. But how much higher should the rate be for those with higher incomes? At this point, the consensus breaks down. There is little agreement among either the general public or economists about the proper degree of tax progressivity.

Moreover, the ability-to-pay principle—particularly the view that some should be forced to pay a larger proportion of their income for government—often conflicts with another broad notion of fairness, the **benefit principle.** According to the benefit principle, those benefiting from government services should be the ones to pay for them. In this case, taxes are thought of as a pay-

Ability-to-pay principle
The equity concept that people with larger incomes (or more consumption or more wealth) should be taxed at a higher rate because their ability to pay is presumably greater. How much higher the rate of taxation should be as income increases is subjective.

Benefit principle
The concept that those who receive government services should pay taxes or user charges for their provision according to the amount of the service or benefit derived from the government activity.

[6]A flat or single-rate tax system could be progressive if there were allowances for personal exemptions. For example, suppose that each taxpayer was permitted to exclude from taxation $5,000 of income for each family member. This would mean that a family of four could earn $20,000 before they were liable for any income tax. Since the single tax rate would only apply to the income above that level, the average tax rate would continuously rise (and eventually approach the single rate) as income increased. Most single-rate tax proposals are of this type.

ment for government services. People who use more government-supplied services—like garbage collection, highways, schools, retirement benefits, and agricultural programs—should pay more because, after all, they are the beneficiaries. Why should such users expect others to pay for things that they do not consume? Of course, the benefit principle suggests that, whenever possible, the government should finance services that it provides with the aforementioned user charges.

Although the concept of equity, or fairness, is ambiguous and subject to different interpretations, it cannot be ignored. People will have a more positive view toward government and be more likely to comply voluntarily with tax and regulatory policies if they believe that the policies are reasonable and equitable. In contrast, the enforcement costs of a tax system that is widely perceived as unreasonable or unfair are certain to be extremely high.

Equity, though, must be balanced with efficiency. A tax system that ignores economic efficiency—one that encourages wasteful use of resources—will also be extremely costly to an economy. There are various ways that tax systems may promote the wasteful use of resources. For example, they might encourage individuals to purchase tax-deductible (or business expense) items, such as housing, business travel, medical service, and luxury cars, even though they are not valued highly relative to their cost. Similarly, a system is inefficient if it encourages individuals to allocate more time and money to investments that reduce the tax burden (depreciable assets, municipal bonds, tax-free retirement plans, and so on), and less time and money to savings and work activities that generate taxable income.

Unfortunately, it is exceedingly difficult to devise a tax system that would not, to some degree, distort the incentive of individuals to use resources wisely. Probably the only tax that would not distort the incentive of individuals to work, earn, and spend wisely is a **head tax**—an equal lump-sum tax on all individuals, poor or rich (or the same liability on those who consume few goods as on those who consume many goods). Because a head tax conflicts with the concept of vertical equity—the view that persons who are situated differently should be taxed differently—it fails to pass our test of fairness.

Thus, we generally tax such things as income, consumption, and property. However, taxes on these items distort pricing signals and thereby cause individuals to forgo productive activities. Economists refer to this inefficiency and the accompanying reduction in private-sector output over and above the tax revenue collected as the **excess burden of taxation.** It is easy to think of cases that illustrate the excess burden of taxation. For example, if two individuals decide to forgo a mutually advantageous exchange because a tax makes the transaction unprofitable, they incur a burden from the taxation even though they do not pay a tax, because the transaction did not take place. Similarly, if a taxpayer decides to allocate more time to leisure or to household production and less time to market work—because the tax system limits the individual's ability to retain income generated by market work—a burden over and above tax revenues collected from the individual is imposed. Income from market work is lost to the individual, and whatever benefits for others that might have resulted from the work are sacrificed. Excess burdens reflect economic inefficiency, relative to our hypothetical ideal. They impose a **deadweight loss** on an economy, because they reflect a cost imposed on some individuals without any offsetting benefit to others.

Head tax
A lump-sum tax levied on all individuals, regardless of their income, consumption, wealth, or other indicators of economic well-being.

Excess burden of taxation
A burden of taxation over and above the burden associated with the transfer of revenues to the government. An excess burden usually reflects losses that occur when beneficial activities are forgone because they are taxed.

Deadweight loss
A net loss associated with the forgoing of an economic action. The loss does not lead to an offsetting gain for other participants. It thus reflects economic inefficiency.

Here we illustrate the impact of a 50-cent tax (per pack) on cigarettes. Since the tax increases the cost of supplying cigarettes for consumption, the supply curve is shifted vertically by the amount of the tax. At the higher price, however, consumers reduce their consumption. The equilibrium price increases from $1.00 to $1.25 per pack. Consumers pay 25 cents more per pack and sellers receive 25 cents less as the result of the 50-cent tax. In addition, consumers and producers lose the mutual gains from exchange (triangle ABC) because the tax reduced the volume of trade between cigarette producers and consumers.

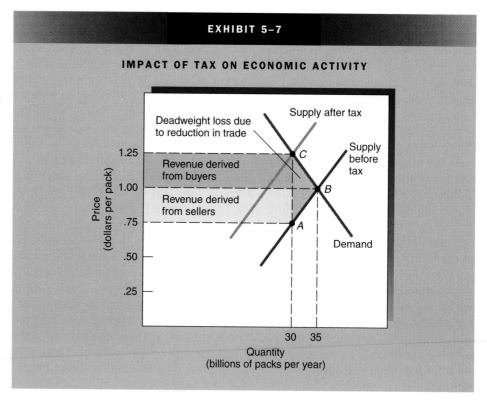

EXHIBIT 5–7

IMPACT OF TAX ON ECONOMIC ACTIVITY

Exhibit 5–7 illustrates the distinction between the tax burden associated with the transfer of purchasing power and the excess burden of taxation. Here we show the impact of a 50-cent tax imposed on each pack of cigarettes. Prior to the imposition of the tax, 35 billion packs of cigarettes were produced and sold to consumers at a market price of $1.00 per pack. The cigarette tax increases the cost of supplying and marketing cigarettes by 50 cents per pack. Thus, the supply curve of cigarettes shifts vertically by the amount of the tax. Consumers, however, would not continue to purchase as many cigarettes at the higher price. So when the supply curve shifts vertically, the market price of cigarettes rises by less than the amount of the tax. Since the number of cigarettes demanded is thus responsive to the higher price, some of the tax burden will fall on cigarette producers. In our hypothetical example, the new equilibrium price for cigarettes will become $1.25 per pack, with an annual output rate of 30 billion packs of cigarettes. The tax will raise $15 billion (50 cents times 30 billion packs) of revenue. Buyers will pay 25 cents more per pack for the 30 billion packs of cigarettes purchased after the tax is imposed. Simultaneously, sellers will receive 25 cents less per pack. The tax thus transfers $15 billion of revenue from cigarette buyers and sellers to the government.

Note, though, that the quantity of cigarettes produced and consumed has fallen by 5 billion packs. The mutually advantageous gains that would have accrued to producers and consumers from these unrealized trades (the triangle *ABC*) are lost. (Remember that trade is a positive-sum game, so a reduction in the volume of trade will result in economic loss.) This loss of welfare (triangle

IS THE CURRENT TAXATION OF CAPITAL GAINS FAIR AND EFFICIENT?

A capital gain (or loss) is experienced when individuals sell an asset such as real estate or stocks for more (or less) than they paid for it. In the United States, nominal capital gains are fully taxable (up to 28 percent) as personal income, while capital losses are deductible against one's income subject to a maximum deduction of $3,000 during any one year (excess losses can be carried forward to future years). Prior to 1987, capital gains were taxed at a lower rate than other forms of income.

Since capital gains take place over a time period—and sometimes the period is lengthy—the real gains of taxpayers can be substantially distorted by inflation. This will be true even if the rate structure is indexed (see Applications in Economics on page 119). For example, suppose that Susan Brown bought a plot of land for $10,000 in 1980 and sold the land for $20,000 in 1997. Since prices doubled during this period, the investor's real capital gain is zero. The $20,000 sale price of the land will not buy any more goods and services in 1997 than the $10,000 purchase price would have in 1980. Nonetheless, Susan will be subject to a capital gains tax on the nominal gain. If she is in the 28 percent tax bracket, she will owe an additional tax bill of $2,800, even though she reaped no real gain from the transaction.

Alternatively, suppose the land was sold for $25,000. In this case, measured in 1997 dollars, the investor's in-

flation-adjusted capital gain would be $5,000 ($25,000 minus a $20,000 purchase price in terms of 1997 dollars) and her additional tax liability $4,200 (28 percent of the $15,000 nominal gain). She is liable for $4,200 in additional taxes even though her real capital gain in current dollars is only $5,000. In fact, her marginal tax rate is 84 percent, not 28 percent.

The current taxation of nominal capital gains often leads to exceedingly high marginal taxation of capital gains, rates that substantially reduce the incentive of investors to fund new projects. These rates also encourage people to continue holding assets (until death or retirement) that they otherwise would like to sell. This problem would be eliminated if the initial purchase price were indexed—if it were adjusted for the rate of inflation.

The United States taxes capital gains much more heavily than do other countries. Among the high-income developed countries, Belgium, Italy, and the Netherlands totally exempt capital gains from taxation, and Germany exempts capital gains on assets held for six months or more. Hong Kong, Singapore, South Korea, and Malaysia—four of the most rapidly growing economies in the world—also exclude capital gains from taxation. Canada, Japan, and France impose much lower rates of taxation on capital gains than the United States. Most economists think the United States should reconsider the current policy and either index the initial asset purchase price or tax the gains at a lower rate.

ABC) associated with the unrealized exchanges imposes an excess burden on buyers and sellers over and above the burden accompanying the transfer of revenue to the government. The triangle *ABC* is a deadweight loss, since it is not accompanied by an offsetting gain in the form of additional tax revenue for the government.

In our example, the burden of the tax was divided equally between sellers and buyers. This will not always be the case. If the demand curve were steeper (and the supply curve flatter), the price of the taxed good would rise by a larger amount, imposing more of the burden on buyers. In contrast, if the demand curve were flatter (and the supply curve steeper), the market price would rise by a smaller amount, and a larger share of the tax burden would fall on sellers.

Thus, the burden of taxes is not always borne by the person who writes a check to the Internal Revenue Service. Economists use the term **tax incidence** to describe how the burden of a tax is distributed among parties. Since the distribution of the tax burden is dependent on the slope of the supply and demand curves for the activity being taxed, it is not easy to determine how it is distributed among parties.

Tax incidence
The manner in which the burden of the tax is distributed among economic units (consumers, employees, employers, and so on). The tax burden does not always fall on those who pay the tax.

TAX RATES, TAX REVENUES, AND THE LAFFER CURVE

Governments generally levy taxes in order to raise revenues. The basic postulate of economics indicates that when an activity is taxed more heavily, people will choose less of it because the tax will make it more expensive. Thus, it is important to distinguish between a change in tax rates and a change in tax revenues. A higher **tax rate** will lead to a shrinkage in the size of the **tax base**—the quantity or level of the activity that is being taxed. If there are attractive substitutes for the activity that is taxed, the decline in the tax base due to the higher tax may be substantial.

Tax rate
The per unit or percentage rate at which an economic activity is taxed.

Tax base
The level of the activity that is taxed. For example, if an excise tax is levied on each gallon of gasoline, the tax base is the number of gallons of gasoline sold. Because higher tax rates generally make the taxed activity less attractive, the size of the tax base is inversely related to the rate at which the activity is taxed.

Perhaps a real-world example will help clarify the importance of this point. In 1981 the District of Columbia increased the tax rate on gasoline from 10 cents to 13 cents per gallon, a 30 percent increase. Tax revenues, however, increased not by 30 percent, but by only 12 percent. Why? The higher tax rate discouraged motorists from purchasing gasoline in the District of Columbia. There was a pretty good alternative to the purchase of the more highly taxed (and therefore higher-priced) gasoline—the purchase of gasoline in Virginia and Maryland, where the tax rates (and therefore prices) were slightly lower.

The revenue the government derives from a tax is equal to the tax base multiplied by the tax rate. When taxpayers can easily shift to substitutes or escape the tax by altering their behavior, the tax base will shrink significantly as rates are increased. As the result of this erosion of the tax base, an increase in tax rates will generally lead to a less than proportional increase in tax revenues.

Economist Arthur Laffer has popularized the idea that, beyond some point, higher tax rates will shrink the tax base so much that tax revenues will decline when tax rates are increased. The curve illustrating the relationship between tax rates and tax revenues is called the **Laffer curve. Exhibit 5–8** illustrates the concept of the Laffer curve as it applies to income-generating activities. Obviously, tax revenues would be zero if the income tax rate were zero. What is not so obvious is that tax revenues would also be zero (or at least very close to zero) if the tax rate were 100 percent. Confronting a 100 percent tax rate, most individuals would go fishing—or find something else to do rather than engage in taxable productive activity, since the 100 percent tax rate would completely remove the material reward derived from earning taxable income.

Laffer curve
A curve illustrating the relationship between tax rates and tax revenues. The curve reflects the fact that tax revenues are low for both very high and very low tax rates.

As tax rates are reduced from 100 percent, the incentive to work and earn taxable income increases, income expands, and tax revenues rise. Similarly, as tax rates increase from zero, tax revenues expand. Clearly, at some rate greater than zero but less than 100 percent, tax revenues will be maximized (point *B* in Exhibit 5–8). This is not to imply that the tax rate that maximizes revenue is ideal. In fact, as rates are increased and the maximum revenue point (*B*) is approached, relatively large tax rate increases will be necessary to expand tax revenue by even a small amount. In this range, the excess burden of taxation in the form of reductions in gains from trade will be substantial.

The Laffer curve suggests that under a progressive income tax system, the impact of a change in tax rates on tax revenues will vary across tax brackets (and income groupings). When people confront a low tax rate (for example, the 25 percent rate associated with point *A* in Exhibit 5–8), a rate reduction will reduce

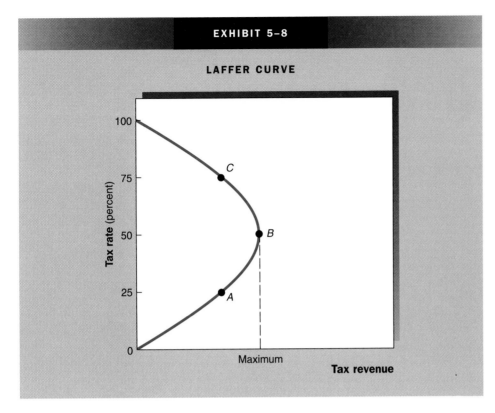

EXHIBIT 5-8

LAFFER CURVE

Tax rate (percent)

100

75 — ●C

50 — ●B

25 — ●A

0

Maximum

Tax revenue

Since taxation affects the amount of the activity being taxed, a change in tax rates will not lead to a proportional change in tax revenues. As the Laffer curve indicates, beyond some point (B), an increase in tax rates may actually cause tax revenues to fall. Since large tax rate increases will lead to only a small expansion in tax revenue as B is approached, there is no presumption that point B is an ideal rate of taxation.

revenues. Similarly, a rate increase from, say, 25 percent to 30 percent will increase tax revenues. On the other hand, for high-income taxpayers confronting extremely high rates (for example, the 75 percent rate associated with point C in the exhibit), a rate reduction would actually increase the revenues collected from this group. Similarly, an increase in the high tax rate would reduce the revenues the government would collect from high-income groups.[7]

When the rates of some taxpayers are above and others are below the revenue maximum point (B in the exhibit), the implications of the Laffer curve are significant. Under these circumstances, a general reduction in tax rates would reduce the revenues collected from low-income taxpayers, while increasing the

---

[7]Similar percentage reductions in income tax rates will generally increase the incentive to earn taxable income in the upper tax brackets more than it will in the lower brackets. Consider how a reduction in a marginal tax rate from 70 percent to 50 percent would influence the incentive of a high-income professional or business executive to earn taxable income. When confronting a 70 percent marginal tax rate, the taxpayer gets to keep only 30 cents of each additional dollar earned by cutting costs, producing more, or investing more wisely. However, after the tax cut, take-home pay from each dollar of taxable income jumps to 50 cents—a whopping 67 percent increase in the incentive to earn. In contrast, consider the incentive effects of an identical percentage rate reduction in lower tax brackets. Suppose the 14 percent marginal rate were cut to 10 percent. Take-home pay, per dollar of additional earnings, would expand from 86 cents to 90 cents, only a 5 percent increase. Since the incentive effects are greater in the upper brackets, changes in the tax base (taxable income) will tend to, at least partially if not entirely, offset changes in revenues resulting from increases (and decreases) in high marginal tax rates.

revenues derived from high-income taxpayers. A general tax increase would have just the opposite effect—more revenue would be collected from those in lower income brackets, while less would be collected from the rich.

THE LAFFER CURVE AND TAX CHANGES IN THE 1980S

It is interesting to view the tax changes instituted in the United States during the past 15 years within the framework of the Laffer curve. During the 1980s the top marginal tax rates—the rates confronted by high-income taxpayers—were reduced sharply by major legislation passed in 1981 and 1986. At the beginning of the 1980s, the United States had 14 different marginal tax brackets ranging from a beginning rate of 14 percent to a top rate of 70 percent. By 1988 the number of brackets had been reduced to only three, with marginal rates of 15, 28, and 33 percent. The personal-exemption allowance for each taxpayer, spouse, and dependent and the standard deduction (the amount of tax-free income granted each taxpayer) were also increased. In effect, these latter changes reduced the tax rates of low-income taxpayers. In many cases, the tax liabilities of low-income recipients were completely eliminated.

Focusing on the sharp reduction in the top rates (from 70 percent to 33 percent during the decade), critics charged that the 1980s' tax policies were a bonanza for the rich. In analyzing the position of the critics, once again it is important to distinguish between changes in tax rates and changes in tax revenues. As the Laffer curve indicates, reduction in high marginal tax rates can sometimes increase the tax revenue collected from high-income taxpayers. This is true because the incentive to earn additional income as the rates are reduced will be particularly strong in the upper tax brackets. Both additional work effort and a decline in tax-avoidance activities contribute to the expansion in the tax base when marginal rates are reduced. Some taxpayers will work more hours or accept a higher paying position involving more responsibility and fewer nonpecuniary benefits. In other instances, spouses may choose to enter the labor force because they are now permitted to keep more of what they earn.[8] At the lower marginal rates, less money is spent on tax-deductible items like plush offices, Hawaiian business conferences, and various fringe benefits (for example, a company luxury automobile, business entertainment, and a company retirement plan). As taxpayers make adjustments like these, their "true" income becomes more visible and their taxable income base expands. In turn, the expansion in the tax base, at least partially, replaces revenues lost as a result of the rate cuts.[9]

Exhibit 5–9 presents data on the real tax revenue collected from various income categories for 1980, 1985, and 1990. *Measured in 1982–1984 dollars,* the income tax revenue collected from high-income taxpayers rose throughout the decade. Even though their marginal rates were cut sharply, the real tax revenue

---

[8]According to a Brookings Institution study by Barry Bosworth and Gary Burtless, in 1988 men between the ages of 25 and 64 worked 5.2 percent more hours than they would have under the tax rate structure of 1980; women aged 25 to 64 worked 5.8 percent more; and married women worked 8.8 percent more. See Barry Bosworth and Gary Burtless, *Effects of Tax Reform on Labor Supply, Investment, and Savings* (Washington, D.C.: Brookings Institution, 1990).

[9]See Joel B. Slemrod, ed., *Do Taxes Matter?: The Impact of the Tax Reform Act of 1986* (Cambridge, Mass.: MIT Press, 1990) for an excellent set of readings on the impact of the tax changes adopted during the 1980s.

EXHIBIT 5-9

CHANGE IN FEDERAL INCOME TAX REVENUE DERIVED
FROM VARIOUS INCOME GROUPS, 1980–1990

INCOME GROUP	TAX REVENUE COLLECTED FROM GROUP (IN BILLIONS OF 1982–1984 DOLLARS)			PERCENT CHANGE 1980–1990	
	1980	1985	1990	GROUP	PER RETURN[a]
TOP 10 PERCENT OF EARNERS	149.0	154.0	191.9	+28.8	+5.6
Top 1 Percent	57.6	65.3	87.2	+51.4	+24.1
Top 5 Percent	111.4	116.0	151.4	+35.9	+11.4
NEXT 40 PERCENT	132.0	123.8	133.5	+1.1	−17.1
BOTTOM 50 PERCENT	21.3	21.4	19.5	−8.5	−25.0
TOTAL	302.3	299.2	344.9	+14.1	−6.5

[a]The number of returns in each category increased by 22 percent between 1980 and 1990.   Source: U.S. Department of Treasury, Internal Revenue Service.

collected from the top 1 percent of earners rose a whopping 51.4 percent between 1980 and 1990. Per tax return, the real taxes paid by this top group increased 24.1 percent. During the decade, the real revenues collected from the top 5 percent and top 10 percent of returns rose by 35.9 percent and 28.8 percent, respectively. The real revenues per return in these categories also increased.

The picture was quite different for other taxpayers. While the real revenues for those between the 50th and 90th percentiles changed little, the bottom 50 percent of taxpayers paid less in 1990 than in 1980. Per return, the average real tax liability of the bottom 90 percent of taxpayers declined between 1980 and 1990.

The pattern of the response to the lower rates—the increase in real (inflation-adjusted) tax revenue collected from high-income Americans and reduction in revenues collected from those with lower incomes—is highly consistent with the implications of the Laffer curve. This pattern indicates that a reduction in low marginal rates—say, rates of 30 percent or less—led to less revenue. (Note the 17 percent and 25 percent reduction in tax liability per return for the bottom 90 percent of taxpayers.) In contrast, however, the cuts in high marginal rates—say, rates of 45 percent or more—increased the revenues derived from those facing the high rates.[10]

[10]Harvard economist Lawrence Lindsey, now a governor of the Federal Reserve System, estimates that, in the United States, marginal personal income rates above 43 percent reduce tax revenues. See Lawrence Lindsey, *The Growth Experiment: How the New Tax Policy Is Transforming the U.S. Economy* (New York: Basic Books, 1989).

Beginning in 1990, the United States began to reverse the tax policy adopted during the 1980s. The 1990 legislation—which reflected a budget agreement between Congress and the Bush administration—increased the top marginal rate in 1991 from 28 percent to 31 percent and subjected additional income of top earners to taxation. In 1993 legislation was adopted providing for two additional tax brackets—a 36 percent rate that would take effect at $140,000 for a married couple filing jointly and a 39.6 percent rate that would apply at a still higher level of income ($250,000 for married couples). Counting a recently adopted 2.9 percent Medicare payroll tax, the top marginal tax rate imposed by the federal government has now been pushed back up to 42.5 percent (the 39.6 percent rate plus the 2.9 percent Medicare rate).

Both the 1990 and 1993 rate increases generated far less revenue than was projected. In fact, the real tax revenue collected from high-income taxpayers fell following the rate increases mandated by the 1990 legislation. Thus far, the 1993 rate increases, which applied only to high-income taxpayers, have generated less than one-third of the revenue forecast by the Clinton administration. Furthermore, a recent study by Harvard's Martin Feldstein indicates that the economy suffered a deadweight loss of $2 for every $1 of revenue generated by the rate increases.[11]

WHO PAYS THE TAX BILL?

How is the overall burden of taxation distributed among income groupings? This is not an easy question to answer. As we have discussed, several different types of taxes are levied, and it is difficult to identify who actually bears the burden of many taxes. In some cases, taxes are designed to act as a proxy for a user charge for public services. Motor fuel taxes to finance roads provide an example. Taxes of this type allocate costs to users, independent of income.

The late Joseph Pechman of the Brookings Institution conducted a detailed study of the U.S. tax structure that found it to be within the proportional-to-mildly-progressive range.[12] Even Pechman's assumptions that yielded his most progressive estimates indicated that high-income recipients paid only slightly higher average tax rates—27.3 percent compared with 20.6 percent—than households with much lower incomes.

Edgar Browning of Texas A&M and William Johnson of the University of Virginia dispute the findings of the Pechman study.[13] They claim that the U.S. tax structure is highly progressive, with high-income groups paying approximately three times the average rate of low-income groups.

---

[11]See Martin Feldstein and Daniel Feenberg, *The Effect of Increased Tax Rates on Taxable Income and Efficiency: Preliminary Analysis of the 1993 Tax Rate Increases* (Cambridge, Mass.: National Bureau of Economic Research, 1995); and Martin Feldstein, *Tax Avoidance and the Deadweight Loss of the Income Tax*, (Cambridge, Mass.: National Bureau of Economic Research, 1996).

[12]Joseph Pechman, *Who Paid the Taxes, 1966–85?* (Washington, D.C.: The Brookings Institution, 1985).

[13]Edgar Browning and William R. Johnson, *The Distribution of the Tax Burden* (Washington, D.C.: American Enterprise Institute, 1979).

"THIS NEW TAX PLAN SOUNDS PRETTY GOOD... WE GET A 9% CUT AND BUSINESS PICKS UP THE BURDEN...."

All taxes are paid by people in their roles as consumers, earners, or owners of assets.

By John Trever, *Albuquerque Journal.* Reprinted by permission.

A study by the Congressional Budget Office (CBO) also indicates that federal taxes are quite progressive, though somewhat less so than during the 1970s.[14] The CBO study estimated that personal income, corporate income, payroll, and excise taxes account for 93 percent of federal tax revenue. According to CBO projections, these four federal taxes consumed between 25 percent and 26.6 percent of the income of the top decile (top 10 percent) of wage earners in 1988, compared with slightly less than 10 percent for the bottom decile of earners. Taxpayers in middle-income groupings paid average rates ranging from 13 percent (the third decile) to 24 percent (the ninth decile).

With regard to the burden of taxation, two additional points should be noted. *First, middle-income and upper-middle-income taxpayers earn the bulk of income and pay the bulk of the tax bill.* In 1992, 55 percent of households in the United States had incomes between $25,000 and $80,000. These households earned approximately 70 percent of the total income, and they shouldered slightly more than 70 percent of the tax burden. The findings of both Pechman and Browning and Johnson are consistent with this view.

Second, although politicians sometimes speak of imposing taxes on businesses, as if part of the tax burden could be transferred from individuals to nonpersons (business firms), people pay all taxes. Like all other taxes, business taxes are paid by individuals. A corporation or business firm may write the tax check to the government, but it does not pay the taxes; it merely collects the money from people—customers, employees, or stockholders—and transfers it to the government. It makes good political rhetoric to talk about "businesses" paying taxes, but the hard fact is that individuals provide all tax revenues.

---

[14]Congressional Budget Office, *The Changing Distribution of Federal Taxes: 1975–1990* (Washington, D.C.: U.S. Government Printing Office, October 1987).

THE COST OF GOVERNMENT

Do taxes measure the cost of government? One might think so, but the answer to this question is, in fact, "not entirely." Our old friend—the opportunity-cost concept—will help us understand why. There are three types of costs incurred when governments provide goods and services.

First, there is the opportunity cost of the resources used to produce goods supplied through the public sector. When governments purchase missiles, education, highways, health care, and other goods, resources to provide these goods must be bid away from private-sector activities. If these resources were not tied up producing goods supplied through the public sector, they would be available to produce private-sector goods. Note that this cost is incurred regardless of whether the provision of the public-sector goods is financed by current taxes, by an increase in government debt, or by money creation. This cost can be diminished only by reducing the size of government purchases.

Second, there is the cost of resources expended in the collection of the tax. Tax laws must be enforced. Tax returns must be prepared and monitored. Resources used to prepare, monitor, and enforce tax legislation are unavailable for the production of either private- or public-sector goods. In the United States, studies indicate that these compliance costs amount to between 5 percent and 7 percent of the tax revenue raised.

Finally, there is the excess burden cost due to price distortions emanating from the levying of taxes (and the provision of transfers). Less output will result because the tax-transfer structure will cause individuals to forgo productive activities and engage in counterproductive action (for example, tax-avoidance activities).

In essence, the cost of government activities is the sum of (1) the opportunity cost of resources used to produce government-supplied goods and services, (2) the cost of tax compliance, and (3) the excess-burden cost of taxation. Thus, government purchases of goods and services generally cost the economy a good bit more than either the size of the tax bill or the level of budget expenditures implies.

THE SIZE OF GOVERNMENT IN THE UNITED STATES VERSUS OTHER COUNTRIES

There is substantial variation in the size of government across countries. In a few countries, government does little more than provide a legal structure and a few goods like roads and national defense, items that are difficult to provide through the private sector. In other countries, the government is involved in all sorts of activities, including the operation of businesses like hotels, theaters, mining, airlines, radio and television broadcasting, and steel manufacturing.

As **Exhibit 5–10** illustrates, government spending sums to more than three-fifths of the total output in Sweden and Denmark. More than one-half of the total

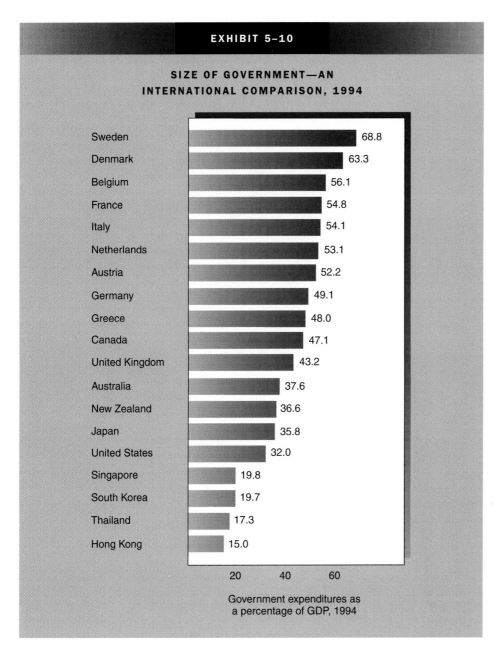

EXHIBIT 5–10

SIZE OF GOVERNMENT—AN INTERNATIONAL COMPARISON, 1994

Country	
Sweden	68.8
Denmark	63.3
Belgium	56.1
France	54.8
Italy	54.1
Netherlands	53.1
Austria	52.2
Germany	49.1
Greece	48.0
Canada	47.1
United Kingdom	43.2
Australia	37.6
New Zealand	36.6
Japan	35.8
United States	32.0
Singapore	19.8
South Korea	19.7
Thailand	17.3
Hong Kong	15.0

20   40   60

Government expenditures as
a percentage of GDP, 1994

The size of government varies substantially across countries. Government expenditures constitute more than 60 percent of GDP in Sweden and Denmark, and approximately 55 percent in Belgium and France. In contrast, government spending amounts to only about one-third of GDP in the United States, Japan, and New Zealand. In Singapore, Thailand, South Korea, and Hong Kong, four rapidly growing Asian countries, the size of government is still smaller.

Source: Organization for Economic Cooperation and Development (OECD) *Economic Outlook*, (December 1995); Government Information Services. Hong Kong, *Hong Kong 1995*; and International Monetary Fund, *Government Finance Statistics, Yearbook*, 1995.

income of Belgium, France, Italy, the Netherlands, and Austria is channeled through the public sector. Government spending as a share of GDP is also quite large in Germany, Greece, Canada, and the United Kingdom. The high level of government spending in these countries primarily reflects greater public-sector involvement in the provision of housing, health care, retirement benefits, and aid to the poor and unemployed. The size of the public sector in Australia, Japan, and New Zealand is only slightly larger than in the United States. Interestingly, the size of government in South Korea, Singapore, Thailand, and Hong Kong, four Asian nations where income has grown very rapidly in recent decades, is substantially smaller than in the United States.

LOOKING AHEAD

Government expenditures and tax rates are important determinants of an economy's output and employment. They also influence the price and output of consumer goods and income of resource suppliers. As we proceed, we will investigate these topics in greater detail.

CHAPTER SUMMARY

1. Government expenditures have grown more rapidly than the U.S. economy during this century. In 1929 government spending accounted for only 10 percent of GDP; since then, it has expanded every decade. In the early 1990s approximately one-third of the total output of the United States was channeled through the public sector.

2. Government purchases of goods and services constitute approximately 20 percent of the national output. Approximately one out of every six Americans works for the local, state, or federal government. Taking into account transfer payments, total 1995 government expenditures amounted to 32 percent of the GDP.

3. During the past three decades, government spending in traditional areas, such as national defense, highways, police and fire protection, and the provision of other goods and services, has declined relative to the size of the economy. The growth of government in recent decades is the result of increased government involvement in the redistribution of income and financing of health care.

4. Personal income taxes, payroll taxes, and corporate income taxes are the major sources of federal tax revenues. Sales taxes provide the major tax base for state governments, whereas local governments still rely primarily on property taxes for their revenue.

5. Payroll taxes constitute the most rapidly expanding source of tax revenues. In 1994 payroll taxes constituted 36 percent of the total tax revenue at the federal level. The social security payroll tax is a proportional tax up to the $60,200 earnings cutoff and then it is regressive beyond that income level.

6. As the marginal tax rates increase, the proportion of income individuals are permitted to keep for private use declines. Because it determines the share of earnings available for private expenditures, the marginal tax rate exerts a major impact on the incentive of individuals to earn.

7. Both efficiency and equity should be considered when choosing among taxation alternatives. A tax system that induces inefficient behavior will be costly to a society. Similarly, it will be costly to induce compliance with a tax system that is perceived as unreasonable or unfair.

8. Ideally, a tax system that does not distort prices or induce individuals to channel scarce resources into tax-avoidance activities is preferable. However, a tax on productive activity will always alter some prices. Our goal should be to adopt an equitable system that will minimize the inefficiency effects.

9. It is important to distinguish between a change in tax rates and a change in tax revenues. The size of the tax base will generally be inversely related to the rate of taxation. Therefore, an increase in tax rates will lead to a less than proportional increase in tax revenues, particularly if there are viable substitutes for those things that are taxed.

10. At very high rates of taxation, it is possible that an increase in tax rates will cause a reduction in tax revenues, because people will make substantial shifts away from the activity that is being taxed. The Laffer curve illustrates this possibility.

11. The cost of government activities encompasses the following components: (a) the opportunity cost of resources used to produce public-sector goods and services, (b) the compliance costs of taxation, and (c) the excess burden costs associated with price distortions and inefficiencies emanating from taxation. Generally, these costs will exceed both the size of the government budget and the dollar amount of the tax revenue collected.

12. Government expenditures as a share of the economy in the United States are smaller than for other high-income industrial nations and substantially smaller than for most Western European countries. As a share of GDP, government expenditures are smallest in the high-growth countries of Asia (Hong Kong, Thailand, Singapore, and South Korea).

CRITICAL ANALYSIS QUESTIONS

1. Major categories of government spending include (a) national defense, (b) education, and (c) income transfers and antipoverty expenditures. Why do you think the public sector has become involved in these activities? Why not leave them to the market?

*2. People can avoid local taxes and, to a lesser degree, state taxes by moving. In comparison with the federal government, how does this characteristic influence people's abilities to achieve value for their tax dollar at these levels of government?

*3. "User charges are simply another name for taxes. It makes no difference whether a government activity is financed by taxes or user charges." Evaluate this statement.

4. "Transfer payments exert no influence on our economy because they merely transfer income from one group of individuals to another." Evaluate this statement.

5. Do you think your college should cover the cost of

providing campus parking through user charges, higher tuition for all students, or taxation? Should waiting in line (that is, time spent hunting for a parking space) play a substantial role in the allocation of parking spaces? Discuss this issue.

*6. "A government project financed by taxation should be undertaken only if the expected value of the project is somewhat greater than the outlay necessary for its finance." Evaluate this statement.

*7. How would a reduction in marginal tax rates influence the incentive of a taxpayer to incur a tax deduction expenditure?

8. Currently nominal capital gains (income from assets sold for a higher nominal price than they were purchased) are taxed at the same rate as other income. Do you think the current taxation of capital gains is fair? Is it consistent with economic efficiency? Why or why not?

9. How would each of the following affect the ability of the "invisible hand" to bring self-interest and helping others into harmony?
   a. A tax transfer system that equalized incomes
   b. High tax rates and a large public sector that allocated most goods and services

*10. A popular sticker on trucks reads, "This truck pays $6,775 (or some other figure) in annual road-use taxes." Is this statement true?

11. Under current tax law, the interest income on municipal bonds (bonds issued by cities and other local governments) is not taxable. How does this tax exemption influence the attractiveness of these bonds to potential investors? How does it affect the interest yield of the bonds? Who is the major beneficiary of this tax exemption? Explain.

12. Both the initial tax structure and the tax structure after a 20 percent rate reduction are indicated in the following table.

	INITIAL TAX STRUCTURE		TAX STRUCTURE AFTER A 20 PERCENT RATE CUT	
ANNUAL TAXABLE INCOME (IN DOLLARS)	MARGINAL TAX RATE	PERCENTAGE OF ADDITIONAL EARNINGS TAXPAYERS KEEP	MARGINAL TAX RATE	PERCENTAGE OF ADDITIONAL EARNINGS TAXPAYERS KEEP
Less than 10,000	10	____	8	____
10,000 to 20,000	20	____	16	____
20,000 to 30,000	30	____	____	____
30,000 to 50,000	50	____	____	____
50,000 to 70,000	70	____	____	____
More than 70,000	90	____	____	____

   a. Fill in the missing blanks.
   b. By what percentage did the tax cut increase the amount of additional earnings that people making less than $10,000 were allowed to keep?
   c. By what percentage did the tax cut increase the amount of additional earnings that people making more than $70,000 were allowed to keep?
   d. How will the tax cut affect the revenues derived from people making less than $10,000 per year? Be specific. How will the rate cut affect the revenues derived from those making more than $70,000 per year? Explain.

13. Smith purchased 500 shares of stock in 1982 and sold them in 1994. The nominal purchase and sales prices are indicated in the following table.

	PRICE OF 500 SHARES OF STOCK	PRICE INDEX (1982 = 100)	REAL PRICE OF STOCK (1994 DOLLARS)
Bought in 1982	$2,500	100	_____
Sold in 1994	$4,950	180	_____

   a. If Smith is liable for a 28 percent tax on the nominal capital gain derived from the stock, calculate her capital gain tax liability as the result of the stock sale.
   b. Fill in the blanks in the last column of the table. What was Smith's real capital gain measured in 1994 dollars?
   c. What was Smith's marginal tax rate on the real capital gain?
   d. If the inflation rate and the increase in the nominal price of the stock had both been 20 percent greater during the 1982–1994 period, what would have happened to Smith's marginal tax rate on her real capital gain?

*Asterisk denotes questions for which answers are given in Appendix B.

Real GDP is the broadest and most widely used measure of output. Since 1950 the annual growth rate of real GDP has averaged approximately 3 percent. But the growth has been uneven. As the shaded areas indicate, since 1950, the United States has experienced 8 recessions, periods of falling real GDP.

SOURCE: *Economic Report of the President.*

Here we illustrate the length (in months) of both the expansions and recessions since 1950. As the graph indicates, the length of both varies substantially, although the expansions have generally been longer.

What causes these fluctuations? How might their intensity be reduced? We will analyze the questions in Part II.

EXHIBIT II-A

GROWTH IN REAL GDP

EXHIBIT II-B

FLUCTUATIONS IN THE OUPUT OF THE UNITED STATES

Period of Expansion or Recession	Length of Recession (in Months)	Length of Expansion (in Months)
Oct '49 to July '53		44
July '53 to May '54	10	
May '54 to August '57		39
August '57 to April '58	9	
April '58 to April '60		24
April '60 to February '61	10	
February '61 to Dec '69		105
Dec '69 to November '70	10	
Nov '70 to Nov '73		36
Nov '73 to March '75	16	
March '75 to January '80		58
January '80 to July '80	6	
July '80 to July '81		12
July '81 to November '82	16	
Nov '82 to July '90		92
July '90 to March '91	9	

Here we illustrate the average annual rate of inflation (as measured by the consumer price index) during various time periods. The inflation rate was high during 1941–1947 and it soared to an average annual rate of 9.2 percent during 1973–1981.

What causes inflation and why is the rate high during some periods and low during others? We will address this issue in Part II.

Until recent decades, the federal government balanced its budget or ran only small deficits *except during periods of war.* This has not been the case during the last couple of decades. The average size of the federal deficit as a percent of GDP increased sharply during the 1970s and 1980s.

What impact do these deficits have on the economy?

Measured as a share of the economy, the federal government debt owed to the general public rose sharply during World War II. Following the war, it declined steadily during the 1950s and 1960s. Since the mid-1970s the large deficits (see prior exhibit) have pushed the net federal debt upward.

Is this rising debt dangerous? How will it affect your future?

EXHIBIT II–C

ANNUAL RATE OF INFLATION (AVERAGE ANNUAL RATE OF CHANGE IN CONSUMER PRICE INDEX)

EXHIBIT II–D

THE GROWTH OF FEDERAL BUDGET DEFICITS

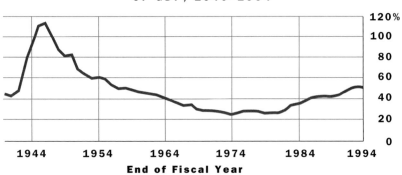

EXHIBIT II–E

FEDERAL DEBT HELD BY PUBLIC AS PERCENTAGE OF GDP, 1940–1994

End of Fiscal Year

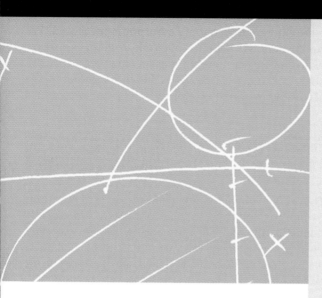

It has been said that figures rule the world; maybe. I am quite sure that it is figures which show us whether it is being ruled well or badly.

JOHANN WOLFGANG GOETHE, 1830

Measurement is the making of distinction; precise measurement is making sharp distinctions.

ENRICO FERMI[1]

---

[1]As quoted by Milton Friedman in Walter Block, ed., *Economic Freedom: Toward a Theory of Measurement* (Vancouver, B.C.: The Fraser Institute, 1991), p. 11.

O ur society likes to keep score. The sports pages supply us with the win-loss records that reveal how well the various teams are doing. We also keep score on the performance of our economy. The scoreboard for economic performance is the *national income accounting system*. Just as a firm's accounting statement provides information to assess the firm's performance, national income accounts supply similar information for the entire economy.

Simon Kuznets, the winner of the 1971 Nobel Prize in economics, developed the basic concepts and outlined the measurement procedures of national income accounting during the 1920s and 1930s (see Outstanding Economist feature). Through the years, these procedures have been modified and improved. The national income accounts provide a measuring rod for national output. In this chapter, we will explain how the flow of an economy's output is measured. We will also explain how changes in national income that reflect changes in production are separated from those that reflect merely inflation (changes in prices). Finally, we will analyze the strengths and weaknesses of the measurement tools used to assess the performance of our national economy.

GDP—A MEASURE OF OUTPUT

Gross domestic product (GDP)

The total market value of all final goods and services produced domestically during a specific period, usually one year.

The **gross domestic product (GDP)** is the most widely used measure of economic performance. It is the market value of goods and services produced domestically during a specific time period, usually a year. GDP estimates in the United States are prepared quarterly and released a few weeks following the end of each quarter. The numbers are widely reported and closely watched, particularly in the business and financial communities.

GDP is a "flow" concept. By analogy, a water gauge measures the amount of water that flows through a pipe each hour. Similarly, GDP measures the market value of production that "flows" through the economy's factories and shops each year (or quarter).

WHAT COUNTS TOWARD GDP?

Because GDP measures only current production, it cannot be arrived at merely by summing the totals on all the nation's cash registers. Many transactions have

OUTSTANDING ECONOMIST

SIMON KUZNETS (1901–1985)

Simon Kuznets provided the methodology for modern national income accounting and developed the first reliable national income measures for the United States. He is often referred to as the "father of national-income accounting." A native Russian, he immigrated to the United States at the age of 21 and spent his academic career teaching at the University of Pennsylvania, Johns Hopkins University, and Harvard University.

to be excluded. GDP (1) counts only the goods and services purchased by their ultimate, or final, users; (2) counts only the goods and services produced during the specified period; and (3) excludes all financial transactions and income transfers.

FINAL MARKET GOODS AND SERVICES. If output is to be measured accurately, all goods and services produced during the year must be counted once and only once. Most goods go through several stages of production before they end up in the hands of their ultimate users. To avoid double-counting, care must be taken to differentiate between **intermediate goods**—goods in intermediate stages of production—and **final market goods and services,** which are those purchased for final use rather than for resale or further processing.

Sales at intermediate stages of production are not counted by GDP because the value of the intermediate goods is embodied within the final-user good. Adding the sales price of both the intermediate good and the final-user good would exaggerate GDP. For example, when a wholesale distributor sells steak to a restaurant, the final purchase price paid by the patron of the restaurant for the steak dinner will reflect the cost of the meat. Double-counting would result if we included both the sale price of the intermediate good (the steak sold by the wholesaler to the restaurant) and the final purchase price of the steak dinner.

Exhibit 6–1 will help clarify the accounting method for GDP. Before the final good, bread, is in the hands of the consumer, it will go through several intermediate stages of production. The farmer produces a pound of wheat and sells it to the miller for 30 cents. The miller grinds the wheat into flour and sells it to the baker for 65 cents. The miller's actions have *added* 35 cents to the value of the wheat. The baker combines the flour with other ingredients, makes a loaf of bread, and sells it to the grocer for 90 cents. The baker has *added* 25 cents to the value of the bread. The grocer stocks the bread on the grocery shelves and provides a convenient location for consumers to shop. The grocer sells the loaf of bread for $1, *adding* 10 cents to the value of the final product. Only the final market value of the product—the $1 for the loaf of bread—is counted by GDP. This price reflects the value added at each stage of production. The 30 cents *added* by the farmer, the 35 cents by the miller, the 25 cents by the baker, and the 10 cents by the grocer sum to the $1 purchase price.

ONLY GOODS PRODUCED DURING THE CURRENT PERIOD ARE INCLUDED IN GDP. Keep in mind that GDP is a measure of current production. Therefore, transactions that merely involve the exchange of goods or assets produced during an earlier period or the transfer of ownership rights are excluded because they do not contribute to current production. Thus, secondhand sales are excluded. The purchase of a used car produced last year will not enhance current GDP, nor will the sale of a "used" home, constructed five years ago. Production of these goods was counted at the time they were produced and initially purchased. Resale of such items produced during earlier years merely changes the ownership of the goods or assets. It does not add to current production. (*Note:* If a sales commission is involved in the exchange of a used car or home, the commission would add to current GDP because it involves a service during the current period.)

Because GDP counts long-lasting goods, such as automobiles and houses, when they are produced, it is not always an accurate gauge of what is currently being consumed. During an economic slowdown, few new durable assets will

Intermediate goods
Goods purchased for resale or for use in producing another good or service.

Final market goods and services
Goods and services purchased by their ultimate user.

Most goods go through several stages of production. This chart illustrates both the market value of a loaf of bread as it passes through the various stages of production (column 1) and the amount added to the value by each intermediate producer (column 2). GDP counts only the market value of the final product. Of course, the amount added by each intermediate producer (column 2) sums to the market value of the final product.

EXHIBIT 6-1

GDP AND STAGES OF PRODUCTION

Stage of Production	Sales receipts at each stage of production (1)	Amount added to the value of the product (equals income created) (2)
Stage 1: Farmer's wheat	$.30	$.30 — Value added by farmer
Stage 2: Miller's flour	$.65	$.35 — Value added by miller
Stage 3: Baker's bread (wholesale)	$.90	$.25 — Value added by baker
Stage 4: Grocer's bread (retail)	$1	$.10 — Value added by grocer
	Total consumer expenditure = $1	Total value added = $1

be produced. However, the consumption of durable goods that were produced and counted during an earlier period will continue. During good times, there will be a rapid expansion in the production of durable assets, which will generally provide consumption benefits for several years in the future. Because of this cycle, GDP tends to understate consumption during an economic decline and overstate it during a rapid expansion in economic activity.

FINANCIAL TRANSACTIONS AND INCOME TRANSFERS ARE EXCLUDED BECAUSE THEY ARE NOT ADDITIONS TO CURRENT OUTPUT. GDP does not count purely financial transactions, since they do not involve current production. For example, the purchases and sales of stocks, bonds, and U.S. securities are not counted as part of GDP because such transactions merely transfer ownership rights; they do not add to current production. Similarly, both private- and public-sector income transfers are excluded because they do not enhance current production. If your aunt sends you $100 to help pay for your college expenses, your aunt has less wealth and you have more, but the transaction adds nothing to current production. Thus, it is not included in GDP. Neither are government income transfer payments like social security, welfare, and veterans' payments. The recipients of these transfers are not producing goods in return for the transfers. Therefore, it would be inappropriate to add them to GDP.

DOLLARS—THE COMMON DENOMINATOR FOR GDP

In elementary school, each of us was instructed about the difficulties of adding apples and oranges. Yet, this is precisely the nature of aggregate output. Literally millions of different commodities and services are produced each year. How can the production of apples, oranges, shoes, movies, roast beef sandwiches, automobiles, dresses, legal services, education, heart transplants, astrological services, and many other items be added together?

The vastly different goods and services produced in our modern world have only one thing in common: Someone pays a price for them. Therefore, when measuring output, units of each good are weighted according to their purchase price. If a consumer pays $20,000 for a new automobile and $20 for a nice meal, production of the automobile adds 1,000 times as much to output as production of the meal. Similarly, production of a television set that is purchased for $1,000 will add 1/20 as much to output as the new automobile and 50 times the amount of the meal. *Each good produced increases output by the amount the purchaser pays for the good. The total spending on all goods and services produced during the year is then summed, in dollar terms, to obtain the annual GDP.*

GNP—A CLOSELY RELATED MEASURE TO GDP

Prior to 1991 the United States used **gross national product (GNP)** as its primary measure of output. *GDP and GNP are very closely related. GDP is a measure of the output that is produced domestically, while GNP measures the output that is produced by the "nationals" of a country.* Put another way, GDP is a measure of the output that is produced by labor and capital *within the geographic borders of a country,* regardless of whether the laborer or the owner of the capital is a citizen of the country or a foreigner. On the other hand, GNP measures the output generated by the labor and capital *owned by the citizens of the country,* regardless of whether that output is produced domestically or abroad.

Written in equation form:

$$\text{GNP} = \text{GDP} + \begin{array}{l}\text{Income received by citizens} \\ \text{for factors of production} \\ \text{supplied abroad}\end{array} - \begin{array}{l}\text{Income paid to foreigners} \\ \text{for their contribution} \\ \text{to domestic output}\end{array}$$

Thus GNP includes (a) income earned by citizens from their work and investments abroad, but omits (b) income earned by foreigners from their work and investments domestically. GDP does just the opposite.

Gross national product (GNP)
The total market value of all final goods and services produced by the citizens of a country. It is equal to GDP plus the income the nationals earned abroad minus the income foreigners earned domestically.

TWO WAYS OF MEASURING GDP

There are two ways of looking at and measuring GDP. First, the GDP of an economy can be reached by totaling the expenditures on goods and services produced during the year. National-income accountants refer to this method as the *expenditure approach. Alternatively, GDP can be calculated by summing the income payments to the resource suppliers and the other costs of producing those goods and services.* Production of goods and services is costly because the resources required for their production must be bid away from their alternative uses. These costs generate incomes for resource suppliers. Thus, this method of calculating GDP is referred to as the *resource cost-income approach.*

GDP derived by the resource cost-income approach will equal GDP derived by the expenditure approach. It is easy to see why this will be the case. From an accounting viewpoint, when a good is produced and sold, the total payments to the factors of production (including the producer's profit or loss) must be equal to the sales price generated by the good.[2] This is true for each good or service produced, and it is also true for the aggregate economy. This is a fundamental accounting identity.

$$
\begin{array}{ccc}
\text{Dollar flow of} & & \text{Dollar flow of} \\
\text{expenditures} & = \text{GDP} = & \text{producer's cost} \\
\text{on final goods} & & \text{on final goods}
\end{array}
$$

This relationship highlights two important characteristics of GDP. *First, GDP is a measure of the value of the goods and services that were purchased*

---

[2]In the national-income accounts, the terms *profit* and *corporate profit* are used in the accounting sense. Thus, they reflect *both* the rate of return on assets owned by a business firm (which is sometimes referred to as normal profit) *and* the firm's economic profit and loss, which was discussed in Chapter 3.

GDP is a measure of current production. It counts only goods and services produced during the year. Exchanges involving ownership rights to previously produced goods and assets are not included in GDP.

by households, investors, governments, and foreigners. These purchasers valued the goods and services more than the purchase price; otherwise they would not have purchased them. *Second, GDP is also a measure of aggregate income.* Production of the goods involves human toil, wear and tear on machines, use of natural resources, risk, managerial responsibilities, and other of life's unpleasantries. Resource owners have to be compensated with income payments in order to induce them to supply these resources.

Exhibit 6–2 summarizes the components of GDP for both the expenditure and resource cost-income approaches. Except for a few complicating elements that we will discuss in a moment, the revenues business firms derive from the sale of goods and services are paid directly to resource suppliers in the form of wages, self-employment income, rents, profits, and interest. We now turn to an examination of these components.

EXPENDITURE APPROACH

When derived by the expenditure approach, there are four components of GDP: (1) personal consumption expenditures, (2) gross private domestic investment, (3) government consumption and gross investment, and (4) net exports to foreigners. The left side of **Exhibit 6–3** presents the values in 1995 for these four components. Later we will discuss the right side, which deals with the resource cost-income approach.

EXHIBIT 6–2

TWO WAYS OF MEASURING GDP

EXPENDITURE APPROACH	RESOURCE COST-INCOME APPROACH
PERSONAL CONSUMPTION EXPENDITURES	INCOME PAYMENTS TO RESOURCE OWNERS (AT FACTOR COST)
+	Compensation of employees (wages and salaries)
GROSS PRIVATE DOMESTIC INVESTMENT	Income of self-employed proprietors
+	Rents
GOVERNMENT CONSUMPTION AND GROSS INVESTMENT	Profits
+	Interest
NET EXPORTS OF GOODS AND SERVICES	+
=	NONINCOME COST ITEMS
GDP	Indirect business taxes
	Depreciation
	+
	GNP-GDP ADJUSTMENT
	=
	GDP

There are two methods of calculating GDP. It can be calculated either by summing the expenditures on the "final-user" goods and services purchased by consumers, investors, governments, and foreigners (net exports) or by summing the income payments and direct cost items (plus the GNP-GDP adjustment) that accompany the production of goods and services.

EXHIBIT 6-3

TWO WAYS OF MEASURING GDP—
1995 DATA (BILLIONS OF DOLLARS)[a]

EXPENDITURE APPROACH			RESOURCE COST-INCOME APPROACH	
PERSONAL CONSUMPTION		$4,924	EMPLOYEE COMPENSATION	$4,209
Durable goods	$ 606		PROPRIETORS' INCOME	478
Nondurable goods	1,486		RENTS	122
Services	2,832		CORPORATE PROFITS	589
GROSS PRIVATE INVESTMENT		1,065	INTEREST INCOME	401
Fixed investment	1,028		INDIRECT BUSINESS TAXES	613
Inventories	37			
GOV. CONS. & GROSS INV.		1,359	DEPRECIATION	
Federal	517		(CAPITAL CONSUMPTION)[b]	826
State and local	842		GNP-GDP ADJUSTMENT	
NET EXPORTS		−102	(MINUS NET INCOME EARNED ABROAD)	8
GROSS DOMESTIC PRODUCT		$7,246	GROSS DOMESTIC PRODUCT	$7,246

[a]The left side shows the flow of expenditure and the right side the flow of income payments and indirect costs (plus the GNP-GDP adjustment). Both procedures yield GDP.
[b]Includes $679 billion for the depreciation of privately owned capital and $147 billion for depreciation of government-owned assets.

Source: U.S. Department of Commerce. These data are also available in the *Federal Reserve Bulletin,* which is published monthly.

Personal consumption
Household spending on consumer goods and services during the current period. Consumption is a flow concept.

CONSUMPTION PURCHASES. **Personal consumption** purchases are the largest component of GDP; in 1995 they amounted to $4,924 billion. Most consumption expenditures are for nondurable goods or services. Food, clothing, recreation, medical and legal services, and fuel are included in this category. These items are used up or consumed in a relatively short time. Durable goods, such as appliances and automobiles, comprise approximately one-eighth of all consumer purchases. These products are enjoyed over a longer period of time even though they are fully counted at the time they are purchased.

Private investment
The flow of private sector expenditures on durable assets (fixed investment) plus the addition to inventories (inventory investment) during a period. These expenditures enhance our ability to provide consumer benefits in the future.

GROSS PRIVATE INVESTMENT. The next item in the expenditure approach, **private investment,** is the construction or manufacture of capital goods that provide a "flow" of future consumption or production service. Unlike food or medical services, they are not immediately "used." Business plants and equipment are investment goods because they will provide productive services in the future. Similarly, a house is an investment good because it will also provide a stream of services long into the future. Increases in business inventories are also classified as investment since they measure goods that will provide future consumer benefits.

Gross investment includes expenditures for both (1) the replacement of machinery, equipment, and buildings worn out during the year and (2) net additions to the stock of capital assets. Net investment is simply gross investment minus an allowance for **depreciation** and obsolescence of machinery and other physical assets during the year.

Net investment is an important indicator of the economy's future productive capability. Substantial net investment indicates that the capital stock of the economy is growing, thereby enhancing the economy's future productive potential (shifting the economy's production-possibilities frontier outward). In contrast, a low rate of net investment, or, even worse, negative net investment, implies a stagnating or even contracting economy. Of course, the impact of investment on future income will also be affected by the productivity of investment—whether the funds invested are channeled into wealth-creating projects. Other things the same, however, countries with a large net investment rate will tend to grow more rapidly. (See Illustrated Exhibits I–C and I–D, page 2 for evidence that high rates of investment generally promote more rapid growth of GDP.) Income levels in countries with a low or negative net investment rate will tend to stagnate or even regress. In 1995 gross private investment expenditures in the United States were $1,065 billion, 14.7 percent of GDP. Of course, a large portion ($679 billion) of this figure was for replacement of private assets worn out during the year. Thus, net private investment was $386 billion, only 5 percent of GDP.

Because GDP is designed to measure current production, allowance must be made for goods produced but not sold during the year—that is, for **inventory investment,** changes during the year in the market value of unsold goods on shelves and in warehouses. If business firms have more goods on hand at the end of the year than they had at the beginning of the year, inventory investment will be positive. This inventory investment must be added to GDP. On the other hand, a decline in inventories would indicate that the purchases of goods and services exceeded current production. In this case, inventory *disinvestment* would be a subtraction from GDP. In 1995 the United States invested $37 billion in additions to inventories.

The inventory component of investment varies substantially. At the beginning of an unexpected recession, inventories often rise as the result of weak demand. Later in the recession, businesses reduce their inventories in response to weak sales. In contrast, businesses generally rebuild their inventories during prosperous times when strong future sales are anticipated.

Many goods possess both consumer- and investment-good characteristics. There is not always a clear distinction between the two. National accounting procedures have rather arbitrarily classified business purchases of final goods as private investment and considered household purchases, except housing, as personal consumption.

GOVERNMENT CONSUMPTION AND GROSS INVESTMENT. In 1995 federal, state, and local government consumption and investment summed to $1,359 billion, approximately 19 percent of total GDP. The purchases of state and local governments exceeded those of the federal government by a wide margin. The government component includes both investment and consumption services. Thus, current public-sector expenditures on missiles, highways, and dams for flood control, as well as the operation of veterans' hospitals, public schools, and law enforcement agencies, are all included in the government component. Because transfer payments are excluded, the total expenditures of the public sector are substantially greater than government purchases of goods and services.

Depreciation
The estimated amount of physical capital (for example, machines and buildings) that is worn out or used up producing goods during the period.

Inventory investment
Changes in the stock of unsold goods and raw materials held during a period.

Net exports
Exports minus imports.

Exports
Goods and services produced domestically but sold to foreigners.

Imports
Goods and services produced by foreigners but purchased by domestic consumers, investors, and governments.

NET EXPORTS. The final item in the expenditure approach is **net exports,** or total exports minus imports. **Exports** are domestically produced goods and services sold to foreigners. **Imports** are foreign-produced goods and services purchased domestically. We want GDP to measure only the domestic production of a nation. Therefore, when measuring GDP by the expenditure approach, we must (1) add exports (goods produced domestically that were sold to foreigners) and (2) subtract imports (goods produced abroad that were purchased by Americans). For national-income accounting purposes, we can combine these two factors into a single entry:

$$\text{Net exports} = \text{Total exports} - \text{Total imports}$$

Net exports may be either positive or negative. When we sell more to foreigners than they buy from us, net exports are positive. In recent years, net exports have been negative, indicating we were buying more goods and services from foreigners than we were selling to them. In 1995 net exports were −$102 billion.

RESOURCE COST-INCOME APPROACH

Exhibit 6–3 illustrates how, rather than summing the flow of expenditures on final goods and services, we could reach GDP by summing the flow of costs incurred and income generated. Labor services play a very important role in the production process. It is therefore not surprising that employee compensation, $4,209 billion in 1995, provides the largest source of income generated by the production of goods and services.

Self-employed proprietors undertake the risks of owning their own businesses and simultaneously provide their own labor services to the firm. Their earnings in 1995 contributed $478 billion to GDP, 6.6 percent of the total. Together, employees and self-employed proprietors accounted for approximately two-thirds of GDP.

Machines, buildings, land, and other physical assets also contribute to the production process. Rents, corporate profits, and interest are payments to persons who provide either physical resources or the financial resources with which to purchase physical assets. Rents are returns to resource owners who permit others to use their assets during a time period. Corporate profits are compensation earned by stockholders, who bear the risk of the business undertaking and who provide financial capital with which the firm purchases resources. Interest is a payment to parties who extend loans to producers.

Not all cost components of GDP result in an income payment to a resource supplier. There are two major indirect costs: indirect business taxes and the cost of depreciation.

Indirect business taxes
Taxes that increase the business firm's costs of production and therefore the prices charged to consumers. Examples would be sales, excise, and property taxes.

INDIRECT BUSINESS TAXES. Taxes imposed on the sale of a good that increase the cost of the good to consumers are called **indirect business taxes.** The sales tax is a clear example. When you make a $1.00 purchase in a state with a 5 percent sales tax, the purchase actually costs you $1.05. The $1.00 goes to the seller to pay wages, rent, interest, and managerial costs. The 5 cents goes to the government. Indirect business taxes boost the market price of goods when GDP is calculated by the expenditure approach. Similarly, when looked at from the factor-cost view-point, taxes are an indirect cost of supplying the goods to the purchasers.

DEPRECIATION. Using machines to produce goods causes the machines to wear out. Depreciation of capital goods is a cost of producing current goods, but it is not a direct cost because it reflects what is lost to the producer when machines and facilities become less valuable. Depreciation does not involve a direct payment to a resource owner. It is an estimate, based on the expected life of the asset, of the decline in the asset's value during the year. In 1995 depreciation (sometimes called *capital consumption allowance*) of private and public sector capital amounted to $826 billion, approximately 11 percent of GDP.

GNP-GDP ADJUSTMENT. Last, adjustment has to be made for the difference between GNP and GDP. The sum of employee compensation, proprietors' income, rents, corporate profits, and interest yields the income of Americans, regardless of whether that income was earned domestically or abroad. If depreciation and indirect business taxes—the two indirect cost components—are added to national income, the result will be gross national product (GNP) rather than GDP. As we previously discussed, GDP and GNP are slightly different. GDP includes the domestic income of foreigners and omits the income that Americans earn abroad, while GNP does just the opposite. GNP counts the income that Americans earn abroad, but it omits the income foreigners earn in the United States. Therefore, when deriving GDP by the resource cost-income approach, we must subtract the net income Americans earned abroad. This net income figure is equal to the income Americans earned abroad minus the income that foreigners earned in the United States. Since it is net income, it may be either positive or negative.

If Americans earned more income abroad than foreigners earned in the United States, the net income of Americans would be positive. Since this net income adds to GNP but not GDP, it must be subtracted when GDP is derived by the resource cost-income method. When the citizens of a country earn net income abroad, GDP will be less than GNP.

Of course, the domestic earnings of foreigners may exceed the earnings of the domestic nationals abroad. If this is true, the figure for net earnings abroad will be negative. When net income earned abroad is negative, it should be added (subtraction of a negative number yields a plus) when GDP is derived by the resource cost-income approach. This was the case in 1995. The earnings of foreigners in the United States exceeded the earnings of Americans abroad by $8 billion. Thus, $8 billion is added when deriving GDP (see Exhibit 6–3, right column). In 1995, GNP was $7,238 billion, $8 billion less than GDP.

RELATIVE SIZE OF GDP COMPONENTS

Exhibit 6–4 shows the average proportion of GDP accounted for by each of the components during 1992–1995. When the expenditure approach is used, personal consumption is by far the largest and most stable component of GDP. Consumption accounted for 68 percent of GDP during 1992–1995, compared to only 14 percent for private investment and 19 percent for government purchases. When GDP is measured by the resource cost-income approach, compensation to

EXHIBIT 6-4

**MAJOR COMPONENTS OF GDP IN THE
UNITED STATES, 1992–1995**

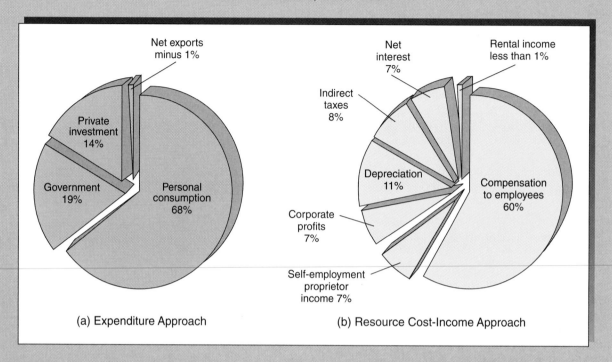

(a) Expenditure Approach

(b) Resource Cost-Income Approach

The relative sizes of the major components of GDP usually fluctuate within a fairly narrow range. The average proportion of each component during 1992–1995 is demonstrated here for both (a) the expenditure approach and (b) the resource cost-income approach.

Source: *Economic Report of the President, 1996.*

employees is the dominant component (60 percent of GDP). During 1992–1995, rents, corporate profits, and interest combined to account for 14 percent of GDP.

DEPRECIATION AND NET DOMESTIC PRODUCT

Net domestic product (NDP)
Gross domestic product minus a depreciation allowance for the wearing out of machines and buildings during the period.

The inclusion of depreciation costs in GDP points out that it is indeed a "gross" rather than a "net" measure of economic production. Because GDP fails to allow for the wearing out of capital goods, it overstates the net output of an economy. The **net domestic product (NDP)** is a concept designed to correct this deficiency. It is the total market value of the goods and services produced domestically and purchased by consumers, governments, and foreigners, plus any net additions to the nation's capital stock. In accounting terms, net domestic product is simply GDP minus depreciation.

Because NDP counts only net additions to the nation's capital stock, it is less than GDP. Net investment—the additions to capital stock—is always equal to gross investment minus depreciation. NDP counts only net investment.

WHEN WILL GDP AND GNP DIFFER?

In most cases, the overwhelming bulk of output is produced domestically, and it is produced with resources owned by the nationals of the country. Thus, the difference between the GDP and the GNP of a country is usually quite small. As **Exhibit 6–5** illustrates, the difference is 1.5 percent or less for the United States, Germany, Japan, United Kingdom, France, Netherlands, and Spain.

The two output measures, however, will differ significantly when there is a substantial difference between the income citizens earn abroad and the domestic income generated by foreigners. This will generally be true if the country has attracted either a relatively large number of foreign workers or a large amount of foreign investment. Under these circumstances, the incomes of foreigners

Source: Derived from the International Monetary Fund, *International Financial Statistics Yearbook 1995.*

EXHIBIT 6–5

THE RELATIONSHIP BETWEEN GDP AND GNP FOR SELECTED COUNTRIES

COUNTRY	GDP AS A PERCENT OF GNP (1994 DATA)	PERCENT DIFFERENCE (GDP − GNP)
United States	100.1	+ 0.1
Germany	101.1	+ 1.1
Japan	99.2	− 0.8
United Kingdom	98.5	− 1.5
France	100.7	+ 0.7
Netherlands	99.6	− 0.4
Spain	101.0	+ 1.0
Indonesia	104.0	+ 4.0
Malaysia	105.2	+ 5.2
Australia	103.4	+ 3.4
Canada	103.6	+ 3.6
Kuwait	84.4	− 15.6
Switzerland	96.0	− 4.0

within a country will tend to be large relative to the earnings of domestic citizens abroad. As a result, the country's GDP will exceed its GNP. In recent years, foreign investment in Indonesia, Malaysia, Australia, and Canada has been quite large. Therefore, foreigners earn more in these countries than domestic nationals earn abroad. This investment income of foreigners contributes to GDP, but not GNP. Therefore, as Exhibit 6–5 illustrates, the GDP of these countries is somewhat larger than their GNP.

In contrast, when the citizens of a country have made substantial investments abroad, or if a relatively large number of them work abroad, the earnings from these activities will add to GNP, but not GDP. Under these circumstances, a country's GDP will tend to be less than its GNP. Kuwait and Switzerland are examples of countries where substantial income from investments abroad results in GNP that is significantly greater than GDP.

REAL AND NOMINAL GDP

Nominal values
Values expressed in current dollars.

Real values
Values that have been adjusted for the effects of inflation.

Nominal GDP
GDP expressed at current prices. It is often called money GDP.

Real GDP
Gross domestic product adjusted for changes in the price level.

GDP deflator
A price index that reveals the cost of purchasing the items included in GDP during the period relative to the cost of purchasing these same items during a base year (currently, 1992). Since the base year is assigned a value of 100, as the GDP deflator takes on values greater than 100, it indicates that prices have risen.

It is important to distinguish between real and nominal economic values. **Nominal values** (or *money values*, as they are often called) are expressed in current dollars. Over time, nominal values reflect both (1) changes in the real size of an economic variable and (2) inflation—a change in the general level of prices. In contrast, **real values** eliminate the impact of changes in the price level, leaving only the real changes in the size of an economic variable. *Whenever economists use the term* real *(for example,* **real GDP** *and* **real income**), *this means that the data have been adjusted for the effects of inflation. When comparing data at different points in time, it is nearly always the real changes that are of most interest.*

Perhaps an example will help clarify the difference between real and nominal values. In 1995 per capita **nominal GDP**—that is, GDP expressed at current prices—in the United States was $27,541, compared to only $2,913 in 1960. Does this mean we produced more than nine times as much output per person in 1995 as we did in 1960? No. In 1995 the general level of prices was 4.64 times the level of 1960. *Measured in terms of the price level in 1960,* **real GDP**—that is, GDP adjusted for the effects of inflation—per person in 1995 was $5,936, only about twice the GDP per person of 1960.

Nominal GDP will increase if either (1) more goods and services are produced or (2) prices rise. Typically, both factors will contribute to an increase in GDP. Because we are usually interested in comparing only the output or actual production during two different time intervals, GDP must be adjusted for the change in prices.

How can we determine how much the prices of items included in GDP have risen during a specific period? We answer this question by constructing a price index called the **GDP deflator.** The Department of Commerce estimates how much of each item included in GDP has been produced during a year. This bundle of goods will include automobiles, houses, office buildings, medical services, bread, milk, entertainment, and all other goods included in the GDP, in the quantities actually produced during the current year. The Department of Commerce then calculates the ratio of (1) the cost of purchasing this representative bundle of goods at current prices divided by (2) the cost of purchasing the same bundle at the prices that were present during a designated earlier base year. The base year chosen (currently 1992 for the GDP deflator) is assigned the value 100. The GDP deflator is equal to the calculated ratio multiplied by 100. If prices are, on average, higher during the current period than they were during the base year, the GDP deflator will exceed 100. The relative size of the GDP deflator is thus a measure of the current price level compared to the price level during the base year. (See Measures of Economic Activity box on the following page for additional detail on how the GDP deflator and another important price index, the **consumer price index (CPI),** are constructed.)

We can use the GDP deflator together with nominal GDP to measure real GDP: GDP in dollars of constant purchasing power. If prices are rising, we simply deflate the nominal GDP during the latter period to account for the effects of inflation.

Exhibit 6–6 illustrates how real GDP is measured and why it is important to adjust for price changes. Between 1992 and 1995, the nominal GDP of the United States increased from $6,244 billion to $7,246 billion, an increase of 16.0 percent. However, a large portion of this increase in nominal GDP reflected inflation rather than an increase in real output. The GDP deflator, the price index that measures changes in the cost of all goods included in GDP, increased from 100 in the 1992 base year to 107.5 in 1995. This indicates that prices rose by 7.5 percent between 1992 and 1995. To determine the real GDP for 1995 in terms of 1992 dollars, we deflate the 1995 nominal GDP for the rise in prices:

$$\text{Real GDP}_{95} = \text{Nominal GDP}_{95} \times \frac{\text{GDP deflator}_{92}}{\text{GDP deflator}_{95}}$$

Because prices were rising, the latter ratio is less than 1. Measured in terms of 1992 dollars, the real GDP in 1995 was $6,739 billion, only 7.9 percent more than in 1992. So although money GDP (nominal GDP) expanded by 16.0 percent, real GDP increased by only 7.9 percent.

Consumer price index (CPI)
An indicator of the general level of prices. It attempts to compare the cost of purchasing the market basket bought by a typical consumer during a specific period with the cost of purchasing the same market basket during an earlier period.

EXHIBIT 6–6

**CHANGES IN PRICES AND REAL GDP OF
UNITED STATES, 1992–1995**

	NOMINAL GDP (BILLIONS OF DOLLARS)	PRICE INDEX (GDP DEFLATOR, 1992 = 100)	REAL GDP (BILLIONS OF 1992 DOLLARS)
1992	$6,244	100.0	$6,244
1995	7,246	107.5	6,739
Percent Increase	16.0	7.5	7.9

Between 1992 and 1995, nominal GDP increased by 16.0 percent. But when the 1995 GDP is deflated to account for price increases, we see that real GDP increased by only 7.9 percent.

Source: U.S. Department of Commerce.

MEASURES OF ECONOMIC ACTIVITY

TWO KEY PRICE INDEXES—THE GDP DEFLATOR AND THE CONSUMER PRICE INDEX

When making comparisons of output and expenditures between periods, it is important to adjust for price changes. Economists measure changes in prices by constructing a price index, which measures the cost (or value) of a given "bundle of goods" at a point in time relative to the cost of the same bundle of goods during a prior base year. The base year is assigned a value of 100. If prices are higher during the current period (that is, if the cost of purchasing the given bundle of goods has risen), the value of the price index during the current period will exceed 100.

Consider the following simple example. Imagine that students at your college purchase only four items: hamburgers, T-shirts, blue jeans, and compact discs (CDs). In recent years, the prices of some of these goods have risen. Suppose we wanted to measure how much prices have risen between 1985 (the base year) and 1996. A careful sampling of prices was used to determine the average price of the four items in both 1985 and 1996. These data are presented in Chart 1. Note that price changes varied among the goods. The price of hamburgers doubled between 1985 and 1996, while the price of jeans remained unchanged. T-shirt prices rose by 80 percent (from $10 to $18), but the price of CDs declined between 1985 and 1996.

A price index reveals the cost of purchasing a market basket (or "bundle") of goods at a point in time compared to the cost of purchasing the identical market basket during an earlier base period. What market basket should be used? One obvious possibility would be the market basket consumed by students during the base period. Suppose that a 1985 survey of the student population indicated that, on average, students purchased 60 hamburgers, 4 T-shirts, 2 pairs of blue jeans, and 1 compact disc monthly during the 1985 base year. This information allows us to calculate the cost of the market basket purchased by the typical student in 1985 *at both 1985 and 1996 prices.* Chart 1 presents these calculations. The market basket consumed by the typical student in 1985 cost $200 at 1985 prices. At 1996 prices, the identical market basket costs $324. The current-year price index is equal to:

CHART 1

THE 1996 PRICE INDEX (1985 = 100) BASED ON TYPICAL MARKET BASKET CONSUMED BY COLLEGE STUDENTS IN 1985 (HYPOTHETICAL DATA)

MONTHLY PURHASES, 1985	AVERAGE PRICE		COST OF 1985 MARKET BASKET	
	1985	1996	1985 PRICES	1996 PRICES
60 hamburgers	$ 1.60	$ 3.20	$ 96.00	$192.00
4 T-shirts	10.00	18.00	40.00	72.00
2 jeans	24.00	24.00	48.00	48.00
1 compact disc	16.00	12.00	16.00	12.00
		Total	$200.00	$324.00

$$\text{PRICE INDEX IN 1996} = \frac{324}{200} \times 100 = 162$$

(1985 = 100)

$$\frac{\text{current cost of purchasing the typical bundle}}{\text{base year cost of purchasing the same bundle}} \times 100$$

Because the cost of the base-year market basket in 1996 was $324, compared to a cost of $200 in 1985, the 1996 College Student Price Index (CSPI) is equal to 162 (the ratio of 324 divided by 200 multiplied by 100). This indicates that, on average, prices were 62 percent higher in 1996 than in 1985.

ALTERNATIVE TYPICAL MARKET BASKETS Rather than using the base-year market basket, we might have used the market basket purchased during the current year (1996) to weight the 1985 and 1996 prices. Consumers will systematically reduce their purchases of those items (like hamburgers in our example) that increase the most in price. Similarly, they will tend to expand their consumption of commodities (like CDs) that become relatively cheaper. As a result, use of the current-year quantities rather than those of the base year to calculate the cost of purchasing the typical bundle will generally provide a lower estimate for the current-year price index.

There is still another procedure that might be used to calculate a price index. One might always use *last year's* prices to determine how much the cost of purchasing *this year's* typical bundle has changed. For example, the prices in 1993 and 1994 might be used to calculate the change in the cost of purchasing the 1994 market basket. Similarly, 1994 and 1995 prices would be used to calculate the change in the cost of the 1995 market basket. Economists refer to this as the *chain-weight index method* because, as you move through time, the data for each year are chained to that of the prior year.

THE CONSUMER PRICE INDEX AND GDP DEFLATOR
The consumer price index (CPI) is the most widely used index of price changes over time. It is prepared monthly by the Bureau of Labor Statistics of the Department of Labor. The methodology underlying the CPI is much like that illustrated by Chart 1 except that the market basket for the CPI is much broader. The composition (quantities) of that market basket is based on the Consumer Expenditure Survey of urban consumers conducted during 1982–1984. This survey identified 364 items that composed the typical bundle purchased by urban consumers during 1982–1984.[1]

Each month, some 250 survey workers call or visit approximately 21,000 stores in urban areas selected to represent all urban places in the United States. Alto-gether, the CPI each month uses approximately 125,000 prices in order to derive the average price for each of the 364 food items, consumer goods and services, housing, and property taxes included in the CPI. Just as we illustrated for the four-item market basket of Chart 1, the cost of purchasing the 364-item market basket at current prices is then compared with the cost of purchasing the same market basket at base-year prices. The result is a measure of current prices compared to base-year prices.

In 1995 the value of the CPI was 152.4, compared to the 100 during the 1982–1984 base period. This indicates the price level in 1995 was 52.4 percent higher than the price level of 1982–1984.

The GDP deflator is a broader price index than the CPI. It is designed to measure the change in the average price of the market basket of goods included in GDP. In addition to consumer goods, the GDP deflator includes prices for goods and services purchased by businesses and governments. Thus, such items as large computers, airplanes, welding equipment, and office space are included in the GDP deflator. Since 1995 the Department of Commerce has used the chain-weight method to calculate the GDP deflator. The cost of purchasing the typical bundle of goods included in this year's GDP is always compared with the cost of purchasing that same bundle at last year's prices. Thus, substitution away from more expensive goods is incorporated each year. It is believed that this procedure will yield a more accurate measure of price changes.

COMPARISON OF THE CPI AND GDP DEFLATOR
Chart 2 presents data for both the CPI and GDP deflator during the last 15 years. Even though they are based on different market baskets and procedures, the two measures of the annual rate of inflation are quite similar. Inspection of the annual rate of inflation as measured by each index indicates that they tend to move together and that, during the past 15 years, the difference between the two measures has usually been only a few tenths of a percent.

The CPI and GDP deflator were designed for different purposes. Choosing between the two depends on what we are trying to measure. If we want to determine

---

[1] Actually, the Bureau of Labor Statistics now publishes two indexes of consumer prices—one for "all urban households" and the other for "urban wage earners and clerical workers." The two differ slightly because the typical bundles of goods purchased by the two groups are not identical.

MEASURES OF ECONOMIC ACTIVITY (continued)

CHART 2

CONSUMER PRICE INDEX AND GDP DEFLATOR:
1981–1995

YEAR	CPI (1982–84 = 100)	INFLATION RATE (PERCENT)	GDP DEFLATOR (1992 = 100)	INFLATION RATE (PERCENT)
1981	90.9	10.3	66.1	10.0
1982	96.5	6.2	70.2	6.2
1983	99.6	3.2	73.2	4.1
1984	103.9	4.3	75.9	3.7
1985	107.6	3.6	78.6	3.6
1986	109.6	1.9	80.6	2.5
1987	113.6	3.6	83.1	3.1
1988	118.3	4.1	86.1	3.6
1989	124.0	4.8	89.7	4.2
1990	130.7	5.4	93.6	4.3
1991	136.2	4.2	97.3	4.0
1992	140.3	3.0	100.0	2.8
1993	144.5	3.0	102.6	2.6
1994	148.2	2.6	105.0	2.3
1995	152.4	2.8	107.5	2.4

Source: Economic Report of the President, 1996.

A change in money GDP tells us nothing about what is happening to the rate of real production unless we also know what is happening to prices. Money income could double while production actually declines if prices more than double. On the other hand, money income could remain constant while real GDP increases if prices fall. *Data on both money GDP and price changes are essential for a meaningful comparison of real income between two time periods.*

PROBLEMS WITH GDP AS A MEASURING ROD

GDP is not a perfect device for measuring current production and income. Some items that involve current production are excluded because their value is difficult to determine. The introduction of new products complicates the use of GDP *how rising prices affect the money income of consumers, the CPI would be most appropriate because it includes only consumer goods. However, if we want an economy-wide measure of inflation with which to adjust GDP or national-income data, clearly the GDP deflator is the appropriate index because it includes a broader set of goods and services.*

SOME PROBLEMS WITH PRICE INDEXES   Because they are so widely used to adjust wage rates, pension benefits, and government programs, it is especially important that price indexes are as accurate as possible. There are two general problems that complicate this task. First, price indexes like the CPI that are based on a fixed base-year market basket do not make an allowance for the tendency of consumers to substitute away from goods that become more expensive and toward those that become relatively cheaper. Economists refer to this deficiency as the *substitution bias*. As the result of the substitution bias, price indexes tend to overstate the rate of inflation and the impact of the price increases on our living standards. (*Note:* This is less of a problem for the GDP deflator than for the CPI because the former is derived by the chain-weight method.)

Second, price indexes generally fail to make an adequate allowance for improvements in the quality of goods and introduction of new products. As new and improved products replace others, consumer welfare is enhanced. In fact, these changes are an important source of the improvement in our modern living standards. Although some adjustments are made for this factor, most economists believe that they are inadequate.

A recent blue ribbon committee headed by Michael Boskin, a former chairman of the president's Council of Economic Advisers, analyzed these issues. *The committee estimated that the CPI has overstated the annual rate of inflation in recent years by approximately 1.5 percent.*[2] As a result, pressure is building to adopt revised procedures that will yield more accurate estimates in the future.

---

[2]Advisory Committee to Study the Consumer Price Index, Michael Boskin, Chairman, *Toward a More Accurate Measure of the Cost of Living*, Interim Report to the Senate Finance Committee, September 1995.

---

as a measuring rod. Also, when production involves harmful "side effects" that are not fully registered in the market price of inputs, GDP will fail to accurately measure the level of output. These limitations are particularly important when GDP is used as an indicator of economic well-being, rather than as simply a measure of the rate of *market* output over time or across countries. Let us consider some of the major limitations of GDP.

NONMARKET PRODUCTION

The GDP fails to count household production because such production does not involve a market transaction. Because of this, the household services of millions of people are excluded. If you mow the yard, repair your car, paint your house, pick up relatives from school, or perform similar productive household activities, your labor services add nothing to GDP, because no market transaction is involved. To the extent that women work more than men in the home, this omission leads to an understatement of their productive contribution. Such nonmarket productive activities are sizable—10 percent or 15 percent of total GDP, perhaps more.

Furthermore, their exclusion results in some oddities in national-income accounting. For example, if a woman marries her gardener, and if, after the marriage, the spouse-gardener works for love rather than for money, GDP will decline because the services of the spouse-gardener will now be excluded: There is no longer a market transaction. If a family member decides to enter the labor force and hire someone to perform services previously provided by household members, there will be a double-barreled impact on GDP. It will rise as a result of (1) the market earnings of the new labor-force entrant plus (2) the amount paid to the person hired to perform the services that were previously supplied within the household.

The omission of many nonmarket productive activities makes comparisons over time and across countries at various stages of market development less meaningful. For example, compared to the situation 30 or 40 years ago, people are now more likely to eat out at a restaurant rather than prepare their own food; hire a lawn service rather than mow their own lawn; and purchase an automatic dishwasher rather than do the dishes by hand. These and many other similar changes involve the substitution of a market transaction, which adds to GDP, for self-provision, which is excluded. Because the share of total production provided within the household has declined relative to production that involves market transactions, current GDP, even in real dollars, is overstated relative to the earlier period.

Similarly, GDP comparisons overstate the output of developed countries when compared to that of underdeveloped countries. A larger share of the total production of underdeveloped countries originates in the household sector. For example, Mexican families are more likely than their U.S. counterparts to make their own clothing, raise and prepare their own food, provide their own child-rearing services, and even build their own homes. These productive labor services, originating in the household sector, are excluded from GDP. Therefore, GDP understates total output in Mexico even more than it does in the United States.

THE UNDERGROUND ECONOMY

Underground economy
Unreported barter and cash transactions that take place outside recorded market channels. Some are otherwise legal activities undertaken to evade taxes. Others involve illegal activities, such as trafficking in drugs and prostitution.

Some people attempt to conceal various economic activities in order to evade taxes or because the activities themselves are illegal. Economists refer to these unreported and therefore difficult to measure activities as the **underground economy.**

Because cash transactions are difficult for government authorities to trace, they provide the lifeblood of the underground economy. This is why drug trafficking, smuggling, prostitution, and other illegal activities are generally conducted in cash. Not all underground economic activity is illegal. A large portion of the underground economy involves legal goods and services that go unreported to avoid taxes. The participants in this legal-if-reported portion of the underground are quite diverse. Taxicab drivers and waitresses may pocket fees and tips. Small-business proprietors may fail to ring up and report various cash sales. Craft and professional workers may fail to report cash income. Employees ranging from laborers to bartenders may work "off books" and accept payment in cash in order to qualify for income-transfer benefits or evade taxes (or allow their employers to evade taxes).

Even though they are often productive, these unreported underground activities are not included in GDP. Estimates of the size of the underground economy in the United States range from 10 percent to 15 percent of total output. The available evidence indicates that the size of the underground economy is even larger in Western Europe (where tax rates are higher) and South America (where regulations often make it more costly to operate a business).

LEISURE AND HUMAN COSTS

GDP excludes leisure, a good that is valuable to each of us, and the human cost associated with the production of goods and services. Simon Kuznets, the "inventor" of GDP, believed that this omission substantially reduced the accuracy of GDP as a measure of economic well-being. One country might attain a $20,000 per capita GDP with an average workweek of 30 hours. Another might attain the same per capita GDP with a 50-hour workweek. The market output per person of the two countries would be identical. In terms of economic well-being, however, the first country would be better off because it "produces" more leisure, or sacrifices less human cost. GDP, though, does not reflect this fact.

The average number of hours worked per week in the United States has declined steadily over the years. The average nonagricultural production worker spent only 34.5 hours per week on the job in 1995, compared to more than 40 hours in 1947—a 14 percent reduction in weekly hours worked. Clearly, this reduction in the length of the workweek raised the American standard of living, even though it did not enhance GDP.

GDP also fails to take into account human costs. On average, jobs today are less physically strenuous and are generally performed in a safer, more comfortable environment than was true a generation ago. To the extent that working conditions have improved through the years, GDP figures understate the growth of real income.

QUALITY VARIATION AND INTRODUCTION OF NEW GOODS

In a dynamic world, changes in quality and the introduction of new goods make income comparisons over time more difficult. During the past 10 or 20 years, there have been substantial changes in the quality and availability of products. Today, new automobiles are more fuel-efficient and generally safer than were new automobiles 20 years ago. Dental services are generally much less unpleasant than was true 20 years ago. Some commodities—compact disc players, video recorders, personal computers, and fax machines, to name a few—simply were unavailable. Statisticians devising price indexes attempt to make some allowance for quality improvements. Many economists believe, however, that failure to fully adjust for quality improvements and the introduction of new products results in an overestimation of the inflation rate by as much as 1 percent or 2 percent annually.

When the bundle of goods available differs substantially between years, the significance of income comparisons is reduced. As **Exhibit 6–7** shows, per capita

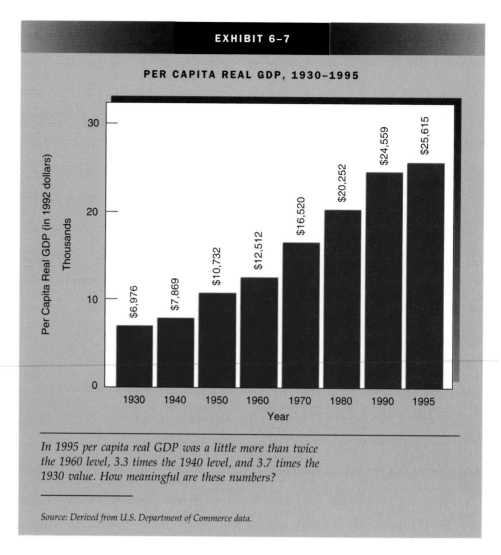

EXHIBIT 6–7

PER CAPITA REAL GDP, 1930–1995

In 1995 per capita real GDP was a little more than twice the 1960 level, 3.3 times the 1940 level, and 3.7 times the 1930 value. How meaningful are these numbers?

Source: Derived from U.S. Department of Commerce data.

real GDP in 1930 was only about one-fourth the figure for 1995. Does this mean that, on average, Americans produced and consumed almost four times as much in 1995 than in 1930? Caution should be exercised before arriving at this conclusion. In the 1930s there were no jet planes, television programs, automatic dishwashers, personal computers, videocassette players, or fax machines. In 1930 even a millionaire could not have purchased the typical bundle consumed by Americans in 1995.[3] On the other hand, in 1930 there were plenty of open spaces, trees, uncongested (but rough) roads, pure-water rivers, hiking trails, and areas

---

[3]The following quotation from Mancur Olson, professor of economics at the University of Maryland, illustrates this point:

The price level has risen about eight times since 1932, so a $25,000 income then would be the "equivalent" of an income of $200,000 today—one could readily afford a Rolls-Royce, the best seats in the theater, and the care of the best physicians in the country. But the 1932 Rolls-Royce, for all its many virtues, does not embody some desirable technologies available today in the humblest Ford. Nor would the imposing dollar of 1932 buy a TV set or a home videocassette recorder. And if one got an infection, the best physicians on 1932 would not be able to prescribe an antibiotic.

with low crime rates. Thus, many goods were available in 1995 that were not available in 1930, and vice versa. Under such circumstances, comparative GDP statistics lose some of their relevance.

HARMFUL SIDE EFFECTS AND ECONOMIC "BADS"

GDP makes no adjustment for harmful side effects that sometimes arise from production, consumption, and the events of nature. If they do not involve market transactions, economic "bads" are ignored in the calculation of GDP. Yet, in a modern industrial economy, production and consumption sometimes generate side effects that either detract from current consumption or reduce our future production possibilities. When property rights are defined imperfectly, air and water pollution are sometimes side effects of economic activity. For example, an industrial plant may pollute the air or water while producing goods. Automobiles may put harmful chemicals into the atmosphere while providing us with transportation. GDP makes no allowance for these negative side effects. In fact, expenditures on the cleanup of air and water pollution, should they be undertaken, will add to GDP.

Similarly, GDP makes no allowance for destructive acts of nature. Consider the impact of Hurricane Andrew, which left a path of destruction as it roared through South Florida during the fall of 1992. Numerous buildings, bridges, and homes were destroyed or damaged. Yet nothing was subtracted from GDP, because it makes no allowance for losses that operate outside of market channels. In fact, Andrew probably increased GDP in late 1992 and throughout 1993. Several hundred million dollars were poured into the reconstruction efforts that went on for more than a year. The cleanup and replacement of items lost undoubtedly caused people to work longer and purchase more goods and services than otherwise would have been the case. Because GDP ignored the destruction, but counted the rebuilding activities, it tended to overstate the change in living standards during the period.

THE GREAT CONTRIBUTION OF GDP

When considering the function of the GDP data, it is important to keep in mind what the data are intended to measure. GDP is not a measure of economic welfare or happiness of the citizenry. It is not even primarily a measure of economic well-being. Indeed, a number of things like leisure and household production that obviously influence the well-being of people are omitted.

GDP was designed to measure the value of the goods and services produced in the market (or business) sector. In spite of its shortcomings and limitations, real GDP is a reasonably precise measure of the rate of output in the market sector and how that output rate is changing.

Adjusted for changes in prices, annual and quarterly GDP data provide the information required to track the performance level of the economy. These data allow us to compare the current output of goods and services relative to the rate of output in the recent past. This is a vitally important contribution. Without this information, policymakers would be less likely to adopt productive policies and many business decision makers would be less able to determine the future direction of demand for their product. In the words of Kenneth Boulding, this contribution is significant enough to rank GDP as "one of the great inventions of the twentieth century, probably almost as significant as the automobile and not quite as significant as TV."[4]

RELATED INCOME MEASURES

National income
The total income payments to owners of human (labor) and physical capital during a period. It includes both the domestic and foreign income earned by the nationals (citizens).

Personal income
The total income received by individuals that is available for consumption, saving, and payment of personal taxes.

Disposable income
The income available to individuals after personal taxes. It can either be spent on consumption or saved.

Exhibit 6–8 illustrates the relationship among five alternative measures of aggregate income. GDP, of course, is the broadest and most frequently quoted index of economic performance. As we previously discussed, the net domestic product (NDP) is simply GDP minus depreciation. NDP measures the total purchases of consumers, governments, and foreigners, plus the net additions to the capital stock. It values the production of goods and services of the economy at market prices. These prices, however, include indirect business taxes, which boost market prices but do not represent the cost of using a factor of production. When these indirect taxes are subtracted from NDP and the net income earned abroad added (or subtracted if the net earnings abroad are negative), the resulting figure is the **national income**. National income thus represents net output valued at factor cost. It includes the income that domestic citizens (nationals) earn domestically as well as abroad. As Exhibit 6–8 shows, the sum of employee compensation, interest, self-employment income, rents, and corporate profits also yields national income.

Although national income represents the earnings of all resource owners, it is not the same as **personal income**, which is the total of all income received by individuals. This is the income with which individuals consume goods, add to savings, and pay taxes. It differs from national income in two respects. First, some income is earned but not directly received. Stockholders, for example, do not receive all the income generated by corporations. Corporate taxes take a share. Additional profits are channeled back into the business, remaining undistributed to the stockholder. Social security taxes, as another example, are deducted from the employee's paycheck, forming a component of income earned but not directly received. These factors must be subtracted when calculating personal income.

Second, some income is received even though it was not earned during the current period. Government transfer payments, including social security and interest payments, are included in this category. By the same token, dividends received add to personal income, regardless of when they were earned. These components must be added to yield personal income.

As most workers know, the amount shown on your paycheck does not equal your salary. Personal taxes must be deducted. **Disposable income** is the income

---
[4]Kenneth Boulding, "Fun and Games with the Gross National Product—The Role of Misleading Indicators in Social Policy," in *The Environment Crisis*, ed. Harold W. Helfrich Jr. (New Haven, Conn.: Yale University Press, 1970), p. 157.

EXHIBIT 6–8

FIVE ALTERNATIVE MEASURES OF INCOME

	Net exports	Depreciation	Indirect business taxes minus net income earned abroad			Personal taxes
	Personal consumer expenditures		Employee compensation	Minus Corporate profits and social insurance taxes → Plus Transfer payments, net interest, and dividends		
	Gross private domestic investment		Proprietors' income			
			Interest			
	Government consumption & investment		Rents			
			Corporate profits			
	Gross Domestic Product	Net Domestic Product	National Income		Personal Income	Disposable Income
1995 (billions)	$7,246	$6,420	$5,799		$6,102	$5,307

The bars illustrate the relationship among five alternative measures of national income. The alternatives range from the gross domestic product, which is the broadest measure of output, to disposable income, which indicates the funds available to households for either personal consumption or saving.

that is yours to do with as you please. It is simply personal income minus personal taxes.

There are thus five alternative measures of domestic output and income:

1. Gross domestic product
2. Net domestic product
3. National income
4. Personal income
5. Disposable income

Each of the five alternatives measures something different, but they are all closely related. Movement of one nearly always parallels movement of the other indicators. Because the five measures move together, economists often use only GDP or the terms *income, output,* or *aggregate production* when referring to the general movement of all five indicators of productive activity.

LOOKING AHEAD

GDP and the related income concepts provide us with a measure of economic performance. In the next chapter, we will take a closer look at the movements of prices and real output in the United States and in other countries. As we proceed, we will investigate the factors that underlie these movements. Models that rely heavily on the interrelationships among household consumption, business investment, and government expenditures will be central to our analysis. As we compare the implications of our analysis with the real world, measurement of GDP and related indicators of income will help us sort out sound theories from economic nonsense.

CHAPTER SUMMARY

1. Gross domestic product (GDP) is a measure of the market value of final goods and services produced domestically during a specific time period, usually a year.

2. Because GDP is designed to measure output, only the production of final-user goods and services produced during the period are counted. Dollars act as a common denominator for GDP. Production of each final product is weighted according to its selling price. GDP excludes income transfers, exchanges involving purely financial transactions, and goods produced during earlier periods because they do not represent current production.

3. GDP can be calculated either by adding up the market value of the final-user goods and services purchased during the period, or by summing the income payments—broadly defined to include both the accounting profits of producers, allowance for depreciation, and indirect business costs—to those who contributed to the production. The two methods sum to an identical result. They also highlight the fact that GDP is a measure of both aggregate output and aggregate income.

4. Gross national product (GNP) is closely related to gross domestic product. While GDP measures the output produced domestically (including that produced with resources supplied by foreigners), GNP measures the output produced by the nationals (domestic citizens) of a country. Because the overwhelming bulk of output is usually pro-

duced domestically by the nationals of a country, in most cases, GDP and GNP are similar.

5. When GDP is measured by the expenditure approach, it has four major components: personal consumption, gross private investment, government consumption and gross investment, and net exports.

6. When GDP is calculated by the resource cost-income approach, it is equal to (a) the direct income components (wages and salaries, self-employment income, rents, interest, and corporate profits), plus (b) the indirect business costs (depreciation and indirect business taxes), minus (c) the net income earned abroad by the nationals of the country.

7. When comparing income and output data over time, it is important to distinguish between real and nominal values. Changes in nominal values reflect changes in the general level of prices as well as changes in the economic variable. In contrast, data measured in real terms have been adjusted to eliminate the impact of changes in the price level. Because economics focuses primarily on real changes, economists generally use real data to measure income, output, and other variables influenced by the level of prices.

8. In effect, price indexes compare the cost of purchasing a typical bundle of goods during a time period relative to the cost of the same bundle during an earlier base year. The base-year price level is assigned a value of 100. Thus, if prices have risen relative to the base year, the price index will exceed 100. The two most widely used price indexes in the United States are the GDP deflator and the consumer price index (CPI).

9. GDP may increase because of an increase in either output or prices. The GDP deflator can be used to convert nominal GDP to real GDP. Measured in period 1 dollars:

$$\text{Real GDP}_2 = \text{nominal GDP}_2 \times \text{GDP deflator}_1 \, / \, \text{GDP deflator}_2$$

10. GDP is an imperfect measure of current production. It excludes household production and the underground (unreported) economy. It fails to take leisure and human costs into account. It adjusts imperfectly for quality changes and it fails to account for the negative side effects of current production, such as air and water pollution, depletion of natural resources, and other factors that do not flow through markets. GDP comparisons are less meaning-

ful when the typical bundle of available goods and services differs widely between two time periods (or between two nations).

11. Despite all its limitations, GDP is vitally important because it is an accurate tool in enabling us to identify short-term fluctuations in the output of goods and services supplied in the market sector. Without such an indicator, our understanding of business fluctuations and their underlying causes would be substantially limited.

12. Economists frequently refer to four other income measures that are related to GDP: net domestic product (NDP), national income, personal income, and disposable income. All these measures of income tend to move together.

CRITICAL ANALYSIS QUESTIONS

*1. Indicate how each of the following activities will affect this year's GDP:
   a. The sale of a used economics textbook to the college bookstore
   b. Smith's $500 doctor bill for setting her son's broken arm
   c. Family lawn services provided by Smith's 16-year-old child
   d. Lawn services purchased by Smith from the neighbor's 16-year-old child who has a lawn-mowing business
   e. A $5,250 purchase of 100 shares of stock at $50 per share plus the sales commission of $250
   f. A multibillion-dollar discovery of natural gas in Oklahoma
   g. A hurricane that causes $10 billion of damage in Florida
   h. $50,000 of income earned by an American college professor teaching in England

2. What does GNP measure? How does it differ from GDP? Under what circumstances would the GDP of a country be substantially greater than GNP? When would GDP be less than GNP? In the case of the United States, is there much difference between GDP and GNP? Why or why not?

*3. A large furniture retailer sells $100,000 of household furnishings from inventories built up last year. How does this sale influence GDP? How are the components of GDP affected?

4. If a nation's gross investment exceeds its depreciation (capital consumption allowance) during the year, what has happened to the nation's stock of capital during the year? How will this affect future output? Is it possible for the net investment of a nation to be negative? Explain. What would negative net investment during a year imply about the nation's capital stock and future production potential?

*5. Why might even real GDP be a misleading index of changes in output between 1900 and 1994 in the United States? Of differences in output between the United States and Mexico?

6. Suppose a group of British investors finances the construction of a plant to manufacture skateboards in St. Louis, Missouri. How will the construction of the plant affect GDP? If the construction project is carried out with American workers, how will it affect GNP? Suppose the plant generates $100,000 in corporate profits this year. Will these profits contribute to GDP? Will they contribute to GNP? Explain.

*7. In 1982 the average earnings of private nonagricultural workers was $267.26 per week. By 1995 the average earnings of private nonagricultural workers had risen to $395.37. In 1995 the CPI was 152.4, compared to 96.5 in 1982. What were the real earnings of private nonagricultural workers in 1995 measured in 1982 dollars?

8. Consider an economy with the following data:

	NOMINAL GDP (IN TRILLIONS)	GDP DEFLATOR
1995	$7.00	120
1996	$7.25	125

   a. What was the 1996 GDP in constant 1995 dollars?
   b. What was the growth rate of real GDP between 1995 and 1996?
   c. What was the inflation rate between 1995 and 1996?

*9. How much do each of the following contribute to GDP?
   a. Jones pays a repair shop $1,000 to have the engine of her automobile rebuilt.
   b. Jones spends $200 on parts and pays a mechanic $400 to rebuild the engine of her automobile.
   c. Jones spends $200 on parts and rebuilds the engine of her automobile herself.
   d. Jones sells her four-year-old automobile for $5,000 and buys Smith's two-year-old model for $10,000.
   e. Jones sells her four-year-old automobile for $5,000 and buys a new car for $10,000.

10. What is the distinction between all market transactions and final-good transactions? Which is a better measure of the economy's rate of production? Why? What is the relationship between final-good transactions and the sum of the value added of producers?

*11. Indicate whether the following statements are true or false:
   a. "For the economy as a whole, inventory investment can never be negative."
   b. "The net investment of an economy must always be positive."
   c. "An increase in GDP indicates that the standard of living of people has risen."

*12. How do the receipts and expenditures of a state-operated lottery affect GDP?

13. Distinguish between the consumer price index (CPI) and the GDP deflator. Which is the better measure of price increases?

*14. Indicate how each of the following will affect this year's GDP:

    a. You suffer $10,000 of damage when you wreck your automobile.

    b. You win $10,000 in a state lottery.

    c. You spend $5,200 in January for 100 shares of stock ($5,000 for the stock and $200 for the sales commission) and sell the stock in August for $8,300 ($8,000 for the stock and $300 for the sales commission).

    d. You pay $300 for this month's rental of your apartment.

    e. You are paid $300 for computer services provided to a client.

    f. You receive $300 from your parents.

    g. You get a raise from $4 to $5 per hour and simultaneously decide to reduce your hours worked from 20 to 16 per week.

    h. You earn $2,000 working in Spain as an English instructor.

15. GDP does not count productive services such as child care, food preparation, cleaning, and laundry provided within the household. Why are these things excluded? Is GDP a sexist measure? Does it understate the productive contributions of women relative to men? Discuss.

16. "GDP counts the product of steel but not the disproduct of air pollution. It counts the product of automobiles but not the disproduct of 'blight' due to junkyards. It counts the product of cigarettes but not the disproduct of a shorter life expectancy due to cancer. Until we can come up with a more reliable index, we cannot tell whether economic welfare is progressing or regressing." Explain why you either agree or disagree with this view.

*17. Would you rather have a $40,000 income in 1929 or in 1994, assuming you could buy only the goods that were available during each of those years? Explain your answer.

18. Explain why the rate of growth in GDP in *current* dollars can sometimes be a misleading statistic.

19. The accompanying chart presents 1994 data from the national-income accounts of the United States.

COMPONENT	(BILLIONS OF DOLLARS)
Personal consumption	$4,699
Employee compensation	4,008
Rents	159
Gov. consumption & investment	1,315
Imports	818
Depreciation	819
Corporate profits	527
Interest income	393
Exports	722
Gross private investment	1,014
Indirect business taxes	602
Self-employment income	415
Net income of Americans abroad	−9

    a. Indicate the various components of GDP when it is derived by the expenditure approach. Calculate GDP using the expenditure approach.

    b. Indicate the various components of GDP when it is derived by the resource cost-income approach. Calculate GDP using the resource cost-income approach.

*20. Fill in the blanks in the following table:

YEAR	NOMINAL GDP (IN BILLIONS)	GDP DEFLATOR (1992 = 100)	REAL GDP (BILLIONS OF 1992 DOLLARS)
1960	$ 526.6	23.3	a. _____
1970	$1,035.6	30.6	b. _____
1980	$2,784.2	c. _____	$4,611.9
1990	d. _____	93.6	$6,138.7
1992	$6,244.4	e. _____	$6,244.4
1994	$6,931.4	105.0	f. _____

_____

*Asterisk denotes questions for which answers are given in Appendix B.

ECONOMIC FLUCTUATIONS, UNEMPLOYMENT, AND INFLATION

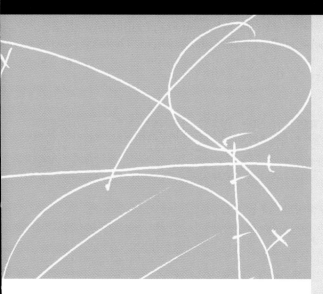

■ What is a business cycle? How much economic instability has the United States experienced?

■ Why do we experience unemployment? Are some types of unemployment worse than others?

■ What do economists mean by full employment? How is full employment related to the natural rate of unemployment?

■ How is the rate of inflation measured? What is the difference between anticipated and unanticipated inflation?

■ What are some of the dangers that accompany inflation?

Prosperity is when the prices of the things that you sell are rising; inflation is when the prices of the things that you buy are rising. Recession is when other people are unemployed; depression is when you are unemployed.

ANONYMOUS

Measures of output, employment, and the level of prices are widely used to assess the performance of an economy. Key indicators, such as growth of real GDP, the rate of unemployment, and the inflation rate, are closely watched by investors, politicians, and the media. In this chapter, we will explain how several key economic indicators are derived and analyze their significance.

What happens to output, employment, and prices is closely related to the economic stability of a nation. Our goal in this chapter is to provide the reader with basic knowledge of economic instability—how it is measured and what impact it has on our lives. As we proceed, we will develop a model of our economy that will help us better understand the causes of economic instability and the potential of government policy as a stabilizing force.

Most governments are committed to the achievement of rapid growth in output, a high level of employment, and relatively stable prices. There is, however, substantial disagreement about what governments can do to accomplish these objectives. In subsequent chapters, this issue will be analyzed in detail.

SWINGS IN THE ECONOMIC PENDULUM

During this century, the growth rate of real GDP in the United States has averaged approximately 3 percent. The rate of growth, however, has not been steady. During the first 50 years of this century, the annual growth rate of real GDP exceeded 6 percent on several occasions. In other instances, output as measured

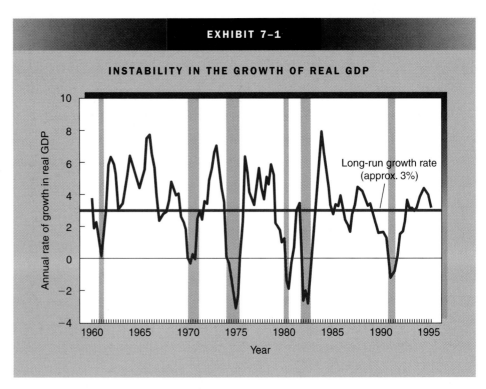

EXHIBIT 7-1

INSTABILITY IN THE GROWTH OF REAL GDP

While real GDP fluctuates substantially, periods of positive growth outweigh the periods of declining real income. Since 1960, the U.S. growth rate of real GDP has averaged approximately 3.0 percent annually. Economists refer to periods of declining real GDP as recessions. The recessionary periods are shaded.

Source: *Economic Report of the President,* various issues.

by real GDP actually declined. During the Great Depression, economic growth plunged. Real GDP declined by 7.5 percent or more each year between 1930 and 1932. In 1933 it was almost 30 percent less than it was in 1929. The 1929 level of real GDP was not reached again until 1939. The Second World War was characterized by a rapid expansion of GDP, which was followed by a decline after the war. Real GDP did not reach its 1944 level again until 1953, although the output of consumer goods did increase significantly in the years immediately following the war.

As **Exhibit 7–1** illustrates, real GDP has continued to grow at an annual rate of approximately 3 percent during 1960–1995. Economic ups and downs also continued during this period. Real GDP grew rapidly throughout most of the 1960s, 1972–1973, 1976–1977, 1983–1988 and 1992–1995. There have been six periods (1960, 1970, 1974–1975, 1980, 1982, and 1991) of falling real GDP since 1960. Compared to the first half of this century, the growth of real GDP has been more stable during the last four decades. During this period, the annual fluctuations in real GDP have fallen within the range of *minus* 2 percent to *plus* 6 percent. This is a definite improvement.

A HYPOTHETICAL BUSINESS CYCLE

Although the real GDP of the United States and other modern economies has grown, the pattern of the growth has been uneven. Periods of economic expansion and growth of real GDP do not last forever. Inevitably, they have been followed by economic slowdown and contraction. Economists refer to these swings in the rate of output as the **business cycle.** Periods of growth in real output and other aggregate measures of economic activity followed by periods of decline are the distinguishing characteristics of business cycles.

Exhibit 7–2 illustrates a hypothetical business cycle. When most businesses

Business cycle
Fluctuations in the general level of economic activity as measured by such variables as the rate of unemployment and changes in real GDP.

In the past, ups and downs have often characterized aggregate business activity. Despite these fluctuations there has been an upward trend in real GDP in the United States and other industrial nations.

EXHIBIT 7–2

BUSINESS CYCLE

are operating at capacity level and real GDP is growing rapidly, a *business peak,* or boom, is present. As aggregate business conditions slow, the economy begins the *contraction,* or recessionary, phase of a business cycle. During the contraction, the sales of most businesses fall, real GDP grows at a slow rate or perhaps declines, and unemployment in the aggregate labor market increases.

The bottom of the contraction phase is referred to as the *recessionary trough.* After the downturn reaches bottom, and economic conditions begin to improve, the economy enters the *expansion* phase of the cycle. Here business sales rise, GDP grows rapidly, and the rate of unemployment declines. The expansion eventually blossoms into another business peak. The peak, however, peters out and turns into a contraction, beginning the cycle anew.

Recession

A downturn in economic activity characterized by declining real GDP and rising unemployment. In an effort to be more precise, many economists define a recession as two consecutive quarters in which there is a decline in real GDP.

Depression

A prolonged and very severe recession.

The term **recession** is widely used to describe conditions during the contraction and recessionary trough phases of the business cycle—that is, a period during which real GDP declines. Many economists specify that a recession means a decline in real GDP for two or more successive quarters.[1] When a recession is prolonged and characterized by a sharp decline in economic activity, it is called a **depression.**

In one important respect, the term *business cycle* is misleading. *Cycle* generally implies that there is some regularity—like that indicated by the hypothetical business cycle of Exhibit 7–2—in the timing and duration of the activity. In the real world, as Exhibit 7–1 illustrates, this is not the case. The observed fluctuations in real output are irregular and unpredictable. The expansions and contractions last varying lengths of time, and the swings differ in terms of their magnitudes. For example, the recessions of 1961 and 1982 were followed by approximately eight years of uninterrupted growth of output. In contrast, the recession of 1980 was followed by an expansion that lasted only 12 months. The expansionary phase following the recessions of 1970 and 1974–1975 fell between these two extremes.[2] See Illustrated Exhibits II-A and II-B (page 137) for additional details on the timing and duration of both recessions and expansions since 1950.

ECONOMIC FLUCTUATIONS AND THE LABOR MARKET

Civilian labor force

The number of persons 16 years of age and over who are either employed or unemployed. In order to be classified as unemployed one must be looking for a job.

Fluctuations in real GDP influence the demand for labor and employment. In our modern world, people are busy with jobs, household work, school, and other activities. **Exhibit 7–3** illustrates how economists classify these activities in relation to the **civilian labor force,** defined as the number of persons age 16 years and over who are either employed or seeking employment. The noninstitutional civilian adult population is grouped into two broad categories: (1) persons not in the labor force and (2) persons in the labor force. There are a variety of reasons why individuals may not currently be in the labor force. Some are retired.

---

[1]See Geoffrey H. Moore, "Recessions," in *The Fortune Encyclopedia of Economics,* ed. David R. Henderson (New York: Time Warner Inc., 1993), for additional information on recessions in the United States.

[2]See Robert J. Gordon, ed., *The American Business Cycle: Continuity and Change* (Chicago: University of Chicago Press, 1986), for an excellent set of readings on the topic of business cycles.

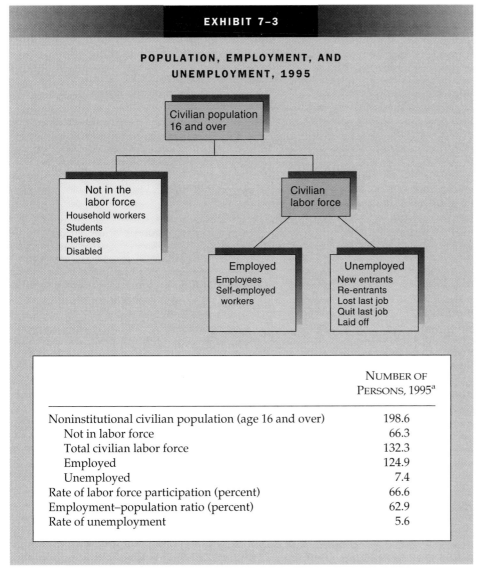

EXHIBIT 7–3

POPULATION, EMPLOYMENT, AND UNEMPLOYMENT, 1995

Civilian population 16 and over

Not in the labor force
Household workers
Students
Retirees
Disabled

Civilian labor force

Employed
Employees
Self-employed workers

Unemployed
New entrants
Re-entrants
Lost last job
Quit last job
Laid off

	NUMBER OF PERSONS, 1995[a]
Noninstitutional civilian population (age 16 and over)	198.6
Not in labor force	66.3
Total civilian labor force	132.3
Employed	124.9
Unemployed	7.4
Rate of labor force participation (percent)	66.6
Employment–population ratio (percent)	62.9
Rate of unemployment	5.6

The accompanying diagram illustrates the alternative participation-status categories for the adult population.

*Data are measured in millions, except those expressed as percentages. U.S. Department of Labor, Monthly Labor Review, April 1996.

Others may be working in their own household or attending school. Still others may not be working as a result of illness or disability. Although many of these people are quite busy, their activities are outside the market labor force.

As Exhibit 7–3 illustrates, **unemployed** workers who are seeking work are included in the labor force along with employed workers. The **labor force participation rate** is the number of persons in the civilian labor force (including both the employed and the unemployed) as a percentage of the civilian population 16 years of age and over. In 1995, the population (16 years of age and over) of the United States was 198.6 million, 132.3 million of whom were in the labor force. Thus, the U.S. labor force participation rate was 66.6 percent (132.3 million divided by 198.6 million).

The labor-force participation rate varies substantially across countries. For example, in 1993 the labor force participation rate was 66 percent in both Canada and the United States, but only 55 percent in Germany and 49 percent

Unemployed
The term used to describe a person not currently employed who is either (1) actively seeking employment or (2) waiting to begin or return to a job.

Labor force participation rate
The number of persons in the civilian labor force 16 years of age or over who are either employed or actively seeking employment as a percentage of the total civilian population 16 years of age and over.

in Italy. The percent of married women in the labor force is generally smaller in countries like Italy and Germany that have a low labor-force participation rate.

In the United States, one of the most interesting labor-force developments of the post–Second World War era is the dramatic increase in the labor force participation rate of women. **Exhibit 7–4** illustrates this point. In 1995, 59.2 percent of adult women worked outside the home, up from 32.7 percent in 1948. Married women accounted for most of this increase. More than half of all married women now are in the labor force, compared to only 20 percent immediately following the Second World War. While the labor force participation of women rose, the rate for men has fallen. In 1995, the labor force participation rate of men was 75.4 percent, down from 83 percent in 1960 and 87 percent in 1948. Clearly, the composition of work-force participation within the family has changed substantially during the last five decades.

Rate of unemployment

The percent of persons in the labor force who are unemployed. Mathematically, it is equal to

$$\frac{\text{Number of persons unemployed}}{\text{Number in the labor force}} \times 100$$

The **rate of unemployment** is a key barometer of conditions in the aggregate labor market. This notwithstanding, the term is often misunderstood. At the most basic level, it is important to note that unemployment is different from not working. As we have already indicated, there are several reasons—including household work, school attendance, retirement, and illness or disability—why a person may be neither employed nor looking for a job. These people, though not employed, are not counted in the unemployment tally.

Moreover, persons must either be employed or unemployed before they are counted as part of the labor force. The rate of unemployment is the number of persons unemployed expressed as a percentage of the labor force. In 1995 the rate of unemployment in the United States was 5.6 percent (7.4 million out of a labor force of 132.3 million). (See the Measures of Economic Activity box for information on how the Bureau of Labor Statistics derives the unemployment rate.)

As the chart illustrates, the labor-force participation rate for women has been steadily increasing for several decades, while the rate for men has been declining.

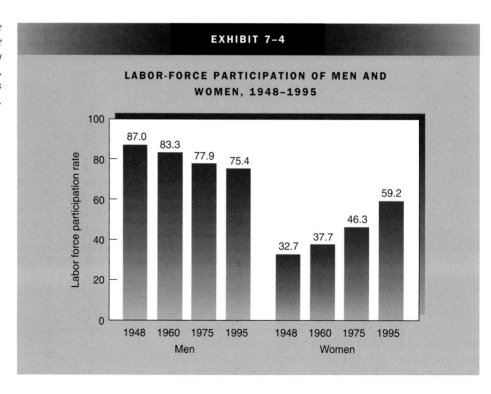

EXHIBIT 7–4

LABOR-FORCE PARTICIPATION OF MEN AND WOMEN, 1948–1995

MEASURES OF ECONOMIC ACTIVITY

DERIVING THE UNEMPLOYMENT RATE

Each month, the Bureau of Labor Statistics (BLS) of the U.S. Department of Labor calculates the number of people employed, unemployed, and not in the labor force. Because it would be too burdensome, the BLS does not contact each person in the United States to determine his or her employment status. Instead, it randomly samples 59,500 households drawn from 729 different locations in the United States. The survey is designed to reflect geographic and demographic groups in proportion to their representation in the nation as a whole.

Specially trained interviewers pose identical questions in the same order to each of the 59,500 households (which include approximately 100,000 adults). Questions designed to determine if a person is employed, unemployed, or not in the labor force are asked of each participant. People are considered employed if they (1) worked at all (even as little as one hour) for pay or profit during the survey week, (2) worked 15 hours or more without pay in a family-operated enterprise during the week, or (3) have a job at which they did not work during the survey week because of illness, vacation, industrial disputes, bad weather, time off, or personal reasons.

People are considered unemployed if they (1) do not have a job, (2) are available for work, and (3) have actively looked for work during the past four weeks. Looking for work may involve any of the following activities: (1) registration at a public or private employment office, (2) meeting with prospective employers, (3) checking with friends or relatives, (4) placing or answering advertisements, (5) writing letters of application, or (6) being on a union or professional register. In addition, those not working are classified as unemployed if they are either waiting to start a new job within 30 days or waiting to be recalled from a layoff.

Only people in the labor force—that is, only those classified as either employed or unemployed—enter into the calculation of the unemployment rate, which is the number of people unemployed divided by the number of people in the civilian labor force. Based on its survey, the BLS calculates the unemployment rate and other employment-related statistics monthly. States use the BLS survey data and employment figures from industries covered by unemployment insurance to construct state and area employment statistics based on BLS guidelines. The *Monthly Labor Review* and *Employment and Earnings,* publications of the U.S. Department of Labor, are the primary sources of data on employment and labor market conditions.

REASONS FOR UNEMPLOYMENT

Not all people who are unemployed lost their last job. A dynamic economy will be characterized by considerable labor mobility as workers move (1) from contracting to expanding industries and (2) into and out of the labor force. Spells of unemployment often accompany such changes.

The Department of Labor indicates five reasons why workers may experience unemployment. **Exhibit 7–5** indicates the share of unemployed workers in each of these five categories in 1995. Interestingly, 7.8 percent of the unemployed workers were first-time entrants into the work force and 34.1 percent were reentering after exiting for additional schooling, household work, or other reasons. Thus, 42 percent of the unemployed workers were experiencing unemployment as the result of entry or reentry into the labor force. Approximately 11 percent of the unemployed quit their last job. People laid off and waiting to return to their previous positions contributed 13.9 percent to the total. Workers terminated from their last job accounted for only one-third (33 percent) of the unemployed workers.

In a dynamic world where information, like most other things, is scarce and people are free to choose among jobs, some unemployment is inevitable. As new products are introduced and new technologies developed, some firms are

This chart indicates the various reasons why persons were unemployed in 1995. Only one-third (33 percent) of the persons unemployed were terminated from their last job. More than two-fifths (42 percent) of the unemployed workers were either new entrants or reentrants into the labor force.

Source: *Monthly Labor Review,* April 1996.

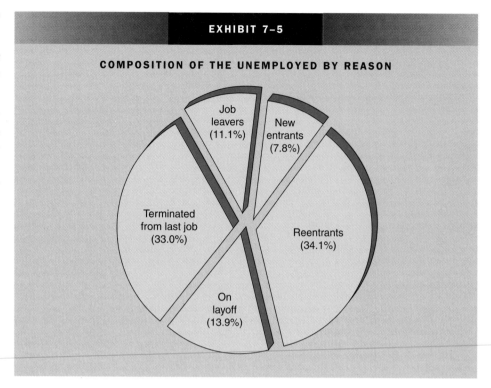

EXHIBIT 7–5

COMPOSITION OF THE UNEMPLOYED BY REASON

Job leavers (11.1%)

New entrants (7.8%)

Terminated from last job (33.0%)

Reentrants (34.1%)

On layoff (13.9%)

expanding while others are contracting. Still other firms may be going out of business. This process results in the creation of new jobs and the disappearance of old ones. Similarly, at any point in time potential workers are switching from school (or nonwork) into the labor force, while others are retiring or taking a leave from the labor force. As long as workers are mobile—as long as they can voluntarily quit and search for better opportunities in a changing world, switching from one job to another and reallocating work responsibilities within the family—some unemployment will be present.

There is a positive side to job search and unemployment: It generally permits individuals to better match their skills and preferences with the requirements of a job. Such job moves enhance both employee productivity and earnings.

Young workers often switch jobs and move between schooling and the labor force as they search for a career path that best fits their abilities and preferences. As the result of this job switching, the unemployment rate of younger workers is substantially higher than for more established workers. As **Exhibit 7–6** shows, in 1995 the unemployment rate of workers 20–24 years of age was more than twice the rate for their counterparts age 25 years and over. The unemployment rate for teenagers was approximately four times the rate of older workers.

THREE TYPES OF UNEMPLOYMENT

Although some unemployment is perfectly consistent with economic efficiency, this is not always the case. Abnormally high rates of unemployment generally reflect weak demand conditions for labor, counterproductive policies, and/or the

Source: *Monthly Labor Review*, April 1996.

EXHIBIT 7–6

UNEMPLOYMENT RATE BY AGE AND SEX, 1995

GROUP	CIVILIAN RATE OF UNEMPLOYMENT, 1995 (PERCENT)
Total, all workers	5.6
Men, Total	5.6
Ages 16–19	18.4
Ages 20–24	9.2
Ages 25 and over	4.3
Women, Total	5.6
Ages 16–19	16.1
Ages 20–24	9.0
Ages 25 and over	4.4

inability or lack of incentive on the part of potential workers and potential employers to arrive at mutually advantageous agreements. To clarify matters, economists divide unemployment into three categories: frictional, structural, and cyclical. Let us take a closer look at each of these three classifications.

FRICTIONAL UNEMPLOYMENT. Unemployment that is caused by constant changes in the labor market is called **frictional unemployment.** It occurs because (1) employers are not fully aware of all available workers and their job qualifications and (2) available workers are not fully aware of the jobs being offered by employers. In other words, the basic cause of frictional unemployment is imperfect information. The number of job vacancies may match the number of persons seeking employment. The qualifications of the job seekers may even meet those required by firms seeking employees. Nonetheless, frictional unemployment will still occur because persons seeking jobs and firms hiring employees with the qualifications of the job seekers do not know about each other. Seeking to improve their options, both employers and employees will search for better alternatives.

Employers looking for a new worker seldom hire the first applicant who walks into their employment office. They want to find the "best available" worker to fill the opening. It is costly to hire workers who perform poorly. It is sometimes even costly to terminate their employment. So, employers search— they expend time and resources screening applicants in an effort to find the best qualified workers willing to accept their wage and employment conditions.

Similarly, job seekers search for their best option among the potential alternatives. They make telephone calls, respond to newspaper ads, submit to job interviews, use employment services, and so on. Pursuit of personal gain—the landing of a job that is more attractive than the current options of which they are aware—motivates job seekers to engage in job search activities.

Frictional unemployment
Unemployment due to constant changes in the economy that prevent qualified unemployed workers from being immediately matched up with existing job openings. It results from the scarcity of information and the search activities of both employers and employees for information that will help them make better employment choices.

As a job searcher finds out about more and more potential job opportunities, it becomes less likely that *additional search* will uncover a more attractive option. Therefore, the *marginal benefit* derived from job search declines with time spent searching for a job, because it becomes less likely that additional search will lead to a better position. The primary cost of job search is generally the opportunity cost of wages forgone as the result of failure to accept one's best current alternative. This cost will increase as additional search leads to the discovery of better alternatives. Thus, the *marginal cost* of job search will rise with the length of one's job search time, primarily because still more search means forgoing wages on more attractive jobs discovered by prior search.

As the marginal benefit from additional search declines and marginal costs rise, eventually the rational job seeker will conclude that potential gain from additional search is not worth the cost. The best alternative resulting from the search process will be accepted. However, this process takes time, and during this time the job seeker is contributing to the frictional unemployment of the economy. It is important to note that, even though frictional unemployment is a side effect, the job search process typically leads to improved economic efficiency and a higher real income for employees (see Myths of Economics later in this chapter).

Changes that affect the costs and benefits of job search influence the level of unemployment. If, for example, the development of a computerized job listing system made it easier to acquire information about job openings quickly, frictional unemployment would tend to decline. On the other hand, a change that reduced the job seeker's cost of continued search would lead to more lengthy periods of search. For example, an increase in unemployment benefits would make it less costly to continue looking for a preferred job. Other things constant, this reduction in the cost of job search would induce job seekers to expand their search time. As as result, the level of unemployment would be pushed upward.

Structural unemployment
Unemployment due to the structural characteristics of the economy that make it difficult for job seekers to find employment and employers to hire workers. Although job openings are available, they generally require skills that differ from those of the unemployed workers.

STRUCTURAL UNEMPLOYMENT. In the case of **structural unemployment,** changes in the basic characteristics of the economy prevent the "matching up" of available jobs with available workers. It is not always easy to distinguish between frictional and structural unemployment. In each case, job openings and potential workers searching for jobs are present. The crucial difference between the two is that, with frictional unemployment, workers possess the requisite skills to fill the job openings; with structural unemployment, they do not. Essentially, the skills of a structurally unemployed worker have been rendered obsolete by changing market conditions and technology. Realistically, the structurally unemployed worker faces the prospect of either a career change or prolonged unemployment. For older workers in particular, these are bleak alternatives.

There are many causes of structural unemployment. Dynamic change is of course at the top of the list. The introduction of new products, productive methods, and technologies can substantially alter the relative demand for workers with various skills. Changes of this type can affect the job opportunities of even highly skilled workers, particularly if their skills are not easily transferable to other industries and occupations. The "computer revolution" has dramatically changed the job opportunities of many workers. The alternatives available to workers with the skills required to operate and maintain high-tech equipment have improved substantially, while the prospects of those without such skills have, in some cases, deteriorated drastically.

Shifts in public sector priorities can also cause structural unemployment. As changing international conditions permitted the United States to significantly reduce national defense expenditures in the early 1990s, these expenditure cuts resulted in reduced incomes and job prospects of workers in defense and related industries. Regions such as southern California that were heavily dependent on the defense industry were particularly hard hit. Since the skills of many workers who lost their jobs in defense-related industries were not well suited for employment in expanding sectors of the economy, structural unemployment was a result.

Institutional factors that reduce the ability of employees to obtain skills necessary to fill existing job openings also increase structural unemployment. For example, minimum wage legislation may reduce the incentive of business firms to offer on-the-job training to low-skill workers, thereby contributing to structural unemployment.

CYCLICAL UNEMPLOYMENT.   When there is a general downturn in business activity, **cyclical unemployment** arises. Because fewer goods are being produced, fewer workers are required to produce them. Employers lay off workers and cut back employment.

Unexpected reductions in the general level of demand for goods and services are the major cause of cyclical unemployment. In a world of imperfect information, adjustments to unexpected declines in demand will be painful. When the demand for labor declines generally, workers will at first not know whether they are being laid off because of a specific shift in demand away from their previous employer or because of a general decline in demand. Similarly, they will not be sure whether their current bleak employment prospects are temporary or long-term. Workers will search for employment, hoping to find a job at or near their old wage rate. If their situation was merely the result of shifts among employers in demand, or if the downturn is brief, terminated workers will soon find new employment similar to their old jobs. When there is a general decline in demand, however, most workers' search efforts will be fruitless and the duration of their unemployment will be abnormally long.

With time, unemployed workers will lower their expectations and be willing to accept some reduction in wages. However, when the decline in aggregate demand is substantial, the adjustment process may be lengthy and a substantial increase in the unemployment rate is the expected result. As we proceed, we will investigate potential sources of cyclical unemployment and consider policy alternatives to reduce it.

Cyclical unemployment
Unemployment due to recessionary business conditions and inadequate aggregate demand for labor.

EMPLOYMENT FLUCTUATIONS—THE HISTORICAL RECORD

Employment and output are closely linked over the business cycle. If we are going to produce more goods and services, we must either increase the number of workers or increase the output per worker. Although productivity, or output per worker, is an important source of long-term economic growth, it changes slowly from year to year. Thus, rapid increases in output, such as those that

"UNEMPLOYED RESOURCES WOULD NOT EXIST IF THE ECONOMY WERE OPERATING EFFICIENTLY."

Nobody likes unemployment. Certainly, extended unemployment can be a very painful experience. Not all unemployment, however, reflects waste and inefficiency. If the resources of an economy are going to be used effectively, the skills of workers must be matched with the jobs of employers. People must end up working on jobs that fit their knowledge, skills, and preferences. Similarly, firms must employ workers that are well suited for their jobs. Waste will result if, for example, a person with high-level computer skills ends up working as a janitor while someone else with minimal computer skills is employed as a computer programmer.

Prospective employees searching for the right job need information on job requirements and availability, wage rates, work environment, and so on. This information is scarce and is generally acquired by "shopping"—by searching for employment. In essence, job seekers are using their time to acquire valuable information that will help them find employment that fits their skills, earning capabilities, and preferences.

Similarly, employers shop when they are seeking labor services. They, too, acquire information about available workers that will help them select employees whose skills and preferences match the demands of the job. The shopping of job seekers and employers results in some unemployment, but it also communicates information that leads to a better match between the characteristics of job seekers and job requirements. Improvement in the match between employees and jobs will lead to an expansion in real output and higher wage rates. Thus, job search can yield a return (in excess of its cost) to both the individual and the society. Such job search, even though it often involves unemployment, is a natural part of an efficiently operating labor market.

Perhaps thinking about the housing market will help the reader better understand why search time can be both beneficial and productive. As with the employment market, the housing market is characterized by dynamic change. New housing structures are brought into the market; older structures depreciate and wear out. Families move from one community to another. In this dynamic world, it makes sense for renters from time to time to shop among the available accommodations, seeking the housing quality, price, and location that best fit their preferences and budgets. Similarly, landlords search among renters, seeking to rent their accommodations to those who value them most highly. "Frictional unemployment" of houses is inevitable, but does it indicate inefficiency? No. It results from people's attempts to acquire information that will eventually promote an efficient match between housing units and renters.

Of course, some types of unemployment, particularly cyclical unemployment, are indicative of inefficiency. However, this is not the case with frictional unemployment. The job searching (and frictional unemployment that accompanies it) helps both job seekers and employers make better choices and it leads to a more efficient match of applicants with job openings than would otherwise be possible. It is perfectly consistent with economic efficiency.

---

occur during a strong business expansion, generally require an increase in employment. As a result, output and employment tend to be positively related. Therefore, the unemployment rate generally increases when the economy dips into a recession.

The empirical evidence of **Exhibit 7–7** illustrates the inverse relationship between output and rate of unemployment. When output declines during a recession, the unemployment rate generally rises. During the recession of 1960–1961, the rate of unemployment rose to approximately 7 percent. In contrast, it declined throughout the economic boom of the 1960s, only to rise again during the recession of 1970. During the recession of 1974–1975, the unemployment rate jumped to more than 9 percent. Similarly, it soared to nearly 11 percent during the severe recession of 1982 and to 7.6 percent during the aftermath of the 1991 recession. Conversely, it declined substantially during the expansions of the 1960s, 1976–1978, 1983–1989, and 1993–1995.

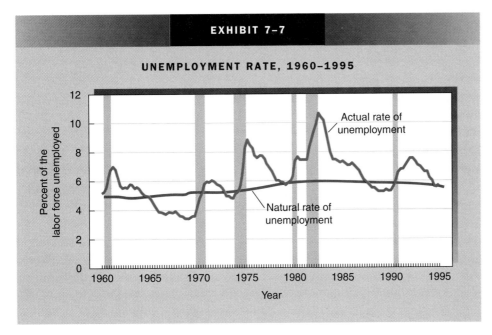

EXHIBIT 7-7

UNEMPLOYMENT RATE, 1960–1995

Actual rate of unemployment

Natural rate of unemployment

Percent of the labor force unemployed (y-axis: 0, 2, 4, 6, 8, 10, 12)

Year (x-axis: 1960, 1965, 1970, 1975, 1980, 1985, 1990, 1995)

Here we illustrate the rate of unemployment during the 1960–1995 period. As expected, the unemployment rate rose rapidly during each of the six recessions (the shaded years indicate periods of recession). In contrast, soon after each recession ended, the unemployment rate began to decline as the economy moved to an expansionary phase of the business cycle. Also note that the actual rate of unemployment was substantially greater than the natural rate during and immediately following the recessions.

Source: *Economic Report of the President, 1996*; and Robert J. Gordon, *Macroeconomics* (Boston: Little Brown, 1990).

THE CONCEPT OF FULL EMPLOYMENT

Full employment, a term widely used by economists and public officials alike, does not mean zero unemployment. As we have noted, in a world of imperfect information, both employees and employers will "shop" before they agree to accept a job or hire a new worker. Much of this shopping is efficient, since it leads to a better match between the skills of employees and the skills necessary to carry out productive tasks. Some unemployment is thus entirely consistent with the efficient operation of a dynamic labor market. *Consequently, economists define full employment as the level of employment that results when the rate of unemployment is normal, considering both frictional and structural factors. In the United States, most economists put this figure at 94 to 95 percent of the labor force.*

The concept of full employment implies that some unemployment is perfectly normal in a world of dynamic change and imperfect information. Even if the labor market is working quite efficiently, the "shopping" of employees and employers will lead to some unemployment. Economists refer to the amount of unemployment that reflects this job shopping in a world of imperfect information and dynamic change as the **natural rate of unemployment.** The natural or normal rate of unemployment is closely related to the concept of full employment. In fact, it is the unemployment rate that is associated with the full employment of resources. It reflects both frictional and structural unemployment, *but not cyclical unemployment. The natural rate of unemployment is not a temporary high or low; it is a rate that is sustainable into the future. Economists sometimes refer to it as the unemployment rate accompanying the economy's "maximum sustainable rate of output."*

Full employment
The level of employment that results from the efficient use of the labor force after allowance is made for the normal (natural) rate of unemployment due to information cost, dynamic changes, and the structural conditions of the economy. For the United States, full employment is thought to exist when between 94 and 95 percent of the labor force is employed.

Natural rate of unemployment
The long-run average unemployment rate due to frictional and structural conditions of labor markets. This rate is affected both by dynamic change and by public policy. It is sustainable into the future. The current natural rate of unemployment in the United States is thought to be between 5 percent and 6 percent.

The natural rate of unemployment, though, is not immutably fixed. It is influenced both by the structure of the labor force and by changes in public policy. For example, youthful workers experience more unemployment because they change jobs and move in and out of the labor force often (refer to Exhibit 7–6), so the natural rate of unemployment increases when youthful workers compose a larger proportion of the work force. This is precisely what happened during the 1960s and 1970s. In 1958 youthful workers (ages 16 to 24) constituted only 15.6 percent of the labor force. As the postwar "baby boom" generation entered the labor market, youthful workers as a share of the labor force rose dramatically. By 1980 one out of every four workers was in the youthful-worker grouping. In contrast, prime-age workers (over age 25) declined from 84.4 percent of the U.S. work force in 1958 to only 75.3 percent in 1980. Studies indicate that this increased representation of youthful workers pushed the natural rate of unemployment up by approximately 1.5 percent during the 1958–1980 period. (See the estimated natural rate of unemployment in Exhibit 7–7.)

Public policies also affect the natural rate of unemployment. Policies that (1) encourage workers to reject job offers and continue to search for employment, (2) prohibit employers from offering wage rates that would induce them to employ (and train) low-skill workers, and (3) reduce the employer's opportunity cost of using layoffs to adjust rates of production will increase the natural rate of unemployment. With regard to these points, most economists believe that increases in the legislated minimum wage and higher unemployment benefits push the natural rate of unemployment upward.

Exhibit 7–7 illustrates the relationship between the *actual* unemployment rate and the *natural* unemployment rate during the past five decades. The actual unemployment rate fluctuates around the natural rate, in response to cyclical economic conditions. The actual rate generally rises above the natural rate during a recession and falls below the natural rate when the economy is in the midst of an economic boom. For example, the actual rate of unemployment was substantially above the natural rate during the recessions of 1974–1975 and 1982, while the reverse was the case during the economic boom of the 1960s. As we proceed, we will often compare the actual and natural rates of unemployment. In a very real sense, macroeconomics studies why the actual and natural rates differ and attempts to discern the factors that cause the natural rate to change with the passage of time.

Without detracting from the importance of full employment—in the sense of maximum sustainable employment—we must not overlook another vital point. Employment is a means to an end. We use employment to produce desired goods and services. Full employment is an empty concept if it means employment at unproductive jobs. It is a meaningful concept only if it refers to productive employment that will generate goods and services desired by consumers at the lowest possible cost.

UNEMPLOYMENT AND MEASUREMENT PROBLEMS

The definition of unemployment is not without ambiguity. Remember that persons are counted as unemployed only if they are (1) available for and seeking work or (2) awaiting recall from a layoff. These criteria can lead to some para-doxical outcomes. For example, a person who quits looking for work because his or her job-seeking efforts have been discouraging is not counted as unemployed. On the other hand, a well-paid northern construction worker drawing unem-ployment compensation while vacationing in Florida during an annual winter-weather layoff is numbered among the unemployed.

One can argue that the statistical definition of unemployment results both in (1) people being excluded even though they would prefer to be working (or working more) and (2) people being included who are not seriously seeking employment. **Discouraged workers** are those whose employment prospects are so bleak that they no longer consider it worthwhile to search for employment. Though not counted as unemployed, many of them would be willing to accept employment were it available. When the economy turns down, the number of workers in the discouraged category rises substantially. For example, during the 1991 recession, the Department of Labor estimated that there were one million discouraged workers (approximately 0.8 percent of the labor force) in the United States, up from 715,000 prior to the recession.

The method of classifying part-time workers may also result in an under-statement of the number of unemployed workers. Part-time workers who desire full-time employment are classified as employed rather than unemployed if they work as much as a single hour per week. Yet these people are certainly under-employed, if not unemployed.

On the other hand, some people who claim to be searching for work and are thus classified as unemployed are not seriously seeking employment. For exam-ple, an individual who rejects available employment because it is less attractive than the current combination of household work, continued job search, unem-ployment benefits, food stamps, and other government welfare programs is numbered among the unemployed. Since recipients of several government income-assistance programs, including food stamps and Aid to Families with Dependent Children (AFDC), are required to register for employment, many of them are classified as "unemployed" even though they have no plans to search for and accept employment. According to a study by Lawrence Summers and Kim Clark of Harvard University, these work-registration requirements push the official unemployment rate up by approximately 0.5 to 0.8 percent (600,000 to 1 million potential employees).[3]

The measurement of unemployment is also complicated by other factors. Unemployment insurance benefits tend to increase the measured unemployment rate by reducing the incentive of recipients to accept available jobs as long as they qualify for the benefits. If they are not otherwise gainfully employed, peo-ple engaged in criminal activities (for example, drug pushers, gamblers, and prostitutes) or working "off the books" in the underground economy may also be classified as unemployed. Although estimates are difficult to project, some researchers believe that as many as one million people fall into this category.

As a result of these ambiguities, some economists argue that the **employ-ment/population ratio**—the number of persons age 16 and over who are

Discouraged workers
Persons who have given up searching for employment because they believe additional job search would be fruitless. Because they are not currently searching for work, they are not counted among the unemployed.

Employment/population ratio
The number of persons 16 years of age and over employed as civilians divided by the total civilian population 16 years of age and over. The ratio is expressed as a percentage.

---

[3]Lawrence H. Summers and Kim B. Clark, "Labor Market Dynamics and Unemployment: A Recon-sideration," *Brookings Papers on Economic Activity* 1 (1979): 13–60. Also see Lawrence H. Summers, *Understanding Unemployment* (Cambridge, Mass.: MIT Press, 1990).

employed expressed as a percentage of the civilian population 16 years and over—is a more objective and meaningful indicator of job availability than is the rate of unemployment. Both the number employed and the population age 16 and over are well defined and readily measurable. Their measurement does not require a subjective judgment as to whether a person is actually "available for work" or "actively seeking employment."

The rate of employment is relatively free of several defects that may distort the unemployment figures. For example, when a large number of discouraged job seekers stop looking for work, the rate of unemployment drops. The employment/population ratio, however, does not follow such a misleading course.

Which of the two figures should the wise observer follow? The answer is both. Our economy has been undergoing several structural changes that contribute to the diversity of the unemployed population and affect both the rate of unemployment and the employment/population ratio. Monitoring both of these variables will help one avoid invalid conclusions and more fully understand labor market conditions.

ACTUAL AND POTENTIAL GDP

If an economy is going to realize its potential, full employment is essential. When the actual rate of unemployment exceeds the natural rate, the actual output of the economy will fall below its potential. Some resources that could be productively employed will be underutilized.

Potential output
The level of output that can be achieved and sustained into the future, given the size of the labor force, expected productivity of labor, and natural rate of unemployment consistent with the efficient operation of the labor market. For periods of time, the actual output may differ from the economy's potential.

The Council of Economic Advisers defines the **potential output** as: "The amount of output that could be expected at full employment. . . . It does not represent the absolute maximum level of production that could be generated by wartime or other abnormal levels of aggregate demand, but rather that which would be expected from high utilization rates obtainable under more normal circumstances."

The concept of potential output encompasses two important ideas: (1) full utilization of resources, including labor, and (2) an output constraint. Potential output might properly be thought of as the maximum *sustainable* output level consistent with the economy's resource base, given its institutional arrangements.

Estimates of the potential output level involve three major elements: the size of the labor force, the quality (productivity) of labor, and the natural rate of unemployment. Since these factors cannot be estimated with certainty, there is some variation in the estimated values of the potential rate of output for the U.S. economy. Relying on the projections of potential output developed by the Council of Economic Advisers, **Exhibit 7–8** illustrates the record of the U.S. economy since 1965. During the latter half of the 1960s, output expanded and even temporarily exceeded the sustainable potential output rate of the economy. However, during the recessions of 1969–1970, 1974–1975, 1982, and 1991, output fell well below the economy's potential.

Note the similarity in the pattern of the actual real GDP data of Exhibit 7–8 and the hypothetical data of an idealized business cycle of Exhibit 7–2. Although the actual data of Exhibit 7–8 are irregular compared to the hypothetical data,

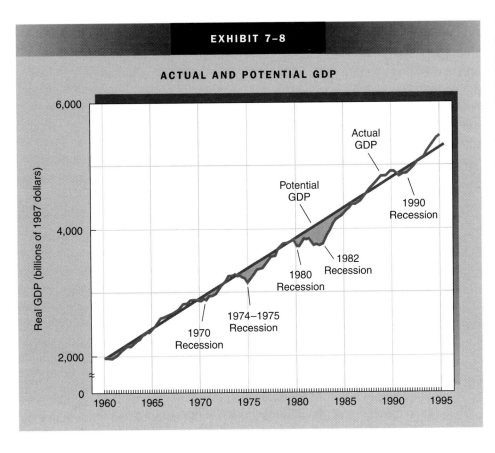

EXHIBIT 7–8

ACTUAL AND POTENTIAL GDP

Real GDP (billions of 1987 dollars)

6,000

Actual
GDP

Potential
GDP

1990
Recession

4,000

1982
Recession

1980
Recession

1974–1975
Recession

1970
Recession

2,000

0

1960   1965   1970   1975   1980   1985   1990   1995

Here we illustrate both the actual and potential GDP. Note the gap (shaded area) between the actual and potential GDP during periods of recession.

Source: U.S. Department of Commerce, Bureau of Economic Analysis.

nonetheless periods of expansion and economic boom followed by contraction and recession are clearly observable. During the boom phase, actual output expands rapidly and may temporarily exceed the economy's long-run potential. In contrast, recessions are characterized by an actual real GDP that is less than potential. As we proceed, we will focus on how we can achieve the maximum potential output while minimizing economic instability.

EFFECTS OF INFLATION: AN OVERVIEW

Inflation is a continuing rise in the general level of prices, such that it costs more to purchase the typical bundle of goods and services that is produced and/or consumed. Of course, even when the general level of prices is stable, some prices will be rising and others will be falling. During a period of inflation, however, the impact of the rising prices will outweigh that of falling prices. Because of the higher prices (on average), a dollar will purchase less than it did previously. Inflation, therefore, might also be defined as a decline in the value (the purchasing power) of the monetary unit.

Inflation
A continuing rise in the general level of prices of goods and services. The purchasing power of the monetary unit, such as the dollar, declines when inflation is present.

How do we determine whether prices, in general, are rising or falling? Essentially, we answered that question in the last chapter when we indicated how a price index is constructed. When prices are rising, on average, the price index will also rise. The annual inflation rate is simply the percent change in the price index (PI) from one year to the next. Mathematically, the inflation rate (i) can be written as:

$$i = \frac{\text{this year's PI} - \text{last year's PI}}{\text{last year's PI}} \times 100$$

So if the price index this year was 220, compared to 200 last year, the inflation rate would equal 10 percent:

$$\frac{220 - 200}{200} \times 100 = 10$$

The consumer price index (CPI) and the GDP deflator are the price indexes most widely used to measure the inflation rate in the United States. Since the CPI and the GDP deflator are calculated monthly and quarterly, respectively, we often compare their value during a specific month (or quarter) with their value during the same month (or quarter) one year earlier to calculate the inflation rate during the most recent 12 months.

How rapidly have prices risen in the United States? **Exhibit 7–9** illustrates the record since the early 1950s. During the 1950s and into the mid-1960s, the annual inflation rate was generally low. The average inflation rate during the

Here we present the annual rate of inflation for the last four decades. Between 1953 and 1965, prices increased at an annual rate of only 1.3 percent. In contrast, the inflation rate averaged 9.2 percent during the 1973–1981 era, reaching double-digit rates during several years. Since 1982, the rate of inflation has been lowered (the average annual rate was 3.6 percent during 1982–1995) and more stable.

Source: Derived from computerized data supplied by FAME ECONOMICS. Also see *Economic Report of the President* (published annually).

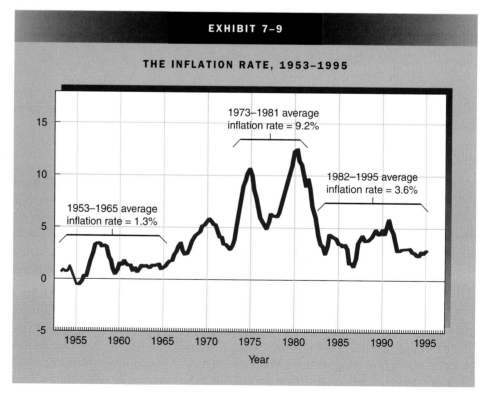

EXHIBIT 7–9

THE INFLATION RATE, 1953–1995

1953–1965 period was 1.3 percent. Beginning in the latter half of the 1960s, inflation began to accelerate upward, jumping to 12 percent or more during 1974, 1979, and 1980. During the 1973–1981 period, the inflation rate averaged 9.2 percent. Price increases moderated again in the mid-1980s, as the inflation rate averaged 3.6 percent during 1982–1995.

The rate of inflation varies widely among countries. **Exhibit 7–10** provides data on the annual inflation rates during 1987–1994 for Japan, Singapore, the United States, Germany, Canada, and Thailand—six countries with low rates of inflation. The annual inflation rate of these countries was generally less than 5 percent during this period, and, moreover, the year-to-year variation was relatively small. The inflation rate of these countries seldom changed by more than 1 or 2 percent from one year to the next.

Exhibit 7–10 also presents parallel inflation rate data for six high-inflation countries: Venezuela, Turkey, Mexico, Brazil, Argentina, and Zaire. In contrast with the low-inflation countries, the inflation rate of the high-inflation countries was not only higher, it varied substantially more from one year to another. For example, consider the data for Venezuela. The inflation rate of Venezuela

---

EXHIBIT 7–10

VARIATION IN ANNUAL INFLATION RATE OF SELECTED COUNTRIES, 1987–1994

COUNTRY	RATE OF INFLATION							
	1987	1988	1989	1990	1991	1992	1993	1994
LOW INFLATION								
Japan	0.1	0.7	2.3	3.1	3.3	1.7	1.3	0.6
Singapore	0.5	1.5	2.4	3.5	3.4	2.3	2.4	3.6
United States	3.6	4.1	4.8	5.4	4.2	3.0	3.0	2.6
Germany	3.3	2.7	3.5	3.4	3.2	2.4	2.1	2.3
Canada	4.4	4.0	5.0	4.8	5.6	1.5	1.8	0.6
Thailand	2.6	3.8	5.4	5.9	5.7	4.1	3.6	5.3
HIGH INFLATION								
Venezuela	28.4	29.5	84.3	40.8	34.2	31.4	38.1	60.8
Turkey	38.8	75.4	63.3	60.3	66.0	70.1	66.1	106.3
Mexico	131.8	114.2	20.0	26.7	22.7	15.5	9.8	7.0
Brazil	229.8	682.8	1,286.9	2,928.4	440.7	1,008.7	2,148.4	2,668.5
Argentina	131.6	342.7	3,079.2	2,311.3	171.7	24.9	10.6	4.2
Zaire	90.4	82.7	104.1	81.3	2,154.7	4,129.7	1,986.9	23,773.0

Source: International Monetary Fund, *International Financial Statistics,* August 1995. The consumer price index was used to measure the inflation rate of each country.

jumped from 29.5 percent in 1988 to 84.3 percent in 1989, before receding to 40.8 percent in 1990 and 34.2 percent in 1991. By 1994, the rate had again soared to 60.8 percent. In Brazil the inflation rate rose from 229.8 percent in 1987 to 682.8 percent in 1988 and 2,928.4 percent in 1990. This latter figure indicates that the general level of prices in Brazil in 1990 was more than 29 times the level of just one year earlier! Brazil's inflation rate continued to fluctuate wildly during the early 1990s. The data of Exhibit 7–10 reflect a general pattern. *High rates of inflation are almost always associated with wide year-to-year swings in the inflation rate.*

ANTICIPATED AND UNANTICIPATED INFLATION

Unanticipated inflation
Increase in the general level of prices that was not expected by most decision makers.

Before examining the effects of inflation, it is important that we distinguish between unanticipated and anticipated inflation. **Unanticipated inflation** is an increase in the price level that comes as a surprise, at least to most individuals. For example, suppose that, based on the recent past, most people anticipate an inflation rate of 4 percent. If the actual inflation rate turns out to be 10 percent, it will catch people off-guard. When the rate of inflation is high and variable, like the rates for the high-inflation countries of Exhibit 7–10, it will be virtually impossible for decision makers to anticipate future rates accurately, and long-range planning will be extremely difficult.

Anticipated inflation
An increase in the general level of prices that was expected by most decision makers.

Anticipated inflation is a change in the price level that is widely expected. Decision makers are generally able to anticipate slow steady rates of inflation—such as those present in Japan, Singapore, the United States, Germany, Canada, and Thailand during 1986–1992—with a high degree of accuracy.

Contrary to the satirical statement at the beginning of the chapter, inflation will affect the prices of things we sell as well as the prices of goods we buy. Both resource and product prices are influenced by inflation. Before we become too upset about inflation "robbing us of the purchasing power of our paychecks," we should recognize that inflation influences the size of those paychecks. The weekly earnings of employees would not have risen at an annual rate of 7 percent during the 1970s if the rate of inflation had not increased rapidly during that period. Wages are a price, also. Inflation raises both wages and prices.

HARMFUL EFFECTS OF INFLATION

Simply because money income initially tends to rise with prices, it does not follow that there is no need to be concerned about inflation, particularly high rates of inflation. Inflation causes problems! Our modern living standard is the result of gains from specialization, division of labor, and mass production processes. Realization of gains from these sources is dependent upon trade and a smooth functioning system of exchange. High and variable rates of inflation will generate uncertainty and weaken the link between income and productive activity. There are three major reasons why inflation will have a harmful impact on the economy.

1. Because unanticipated inflation alters the outcomes of long-term projects like the purchase of a machine or investing in a business, it will increase the risks and retard the level of such productive activities.   When the price level rises 15 percent one year, 40 percent the next year, and then increases again by 20 or 25 percent the following year, no one knows what to expect. Unanticipated changes of even 5 percent or 10 percent in the rate of inflation can often turn an otherwise profitable project into a personal economic disaster. Given the uncertainty that it creates, many decision makers will simply forgo capital investments and other transactions involving long-term commitments when the rate of inflation is highly variable and therefore unpredictable. As a result, mutually advantageous gains from trade will be lost and the efficiency of markets reduced.[4]

2. Inflation distorts the information delivered by prices.   Prices communicate important information concerning the relative scarcity of goods and resources. Some prices can be easily and regularly changed. But this will not be true for others—particularly those set by long-term contracts. For example, there will be time delays before the prices accompanying rental lease agreements, items sold in catalogs, mortgage interest rates, and collective bargaining contracts can be changed. Since some prices will respond quickly to inflationary policies while others will change more slowly, an unanticipated change in the rate of inflation will change *relative prices* as well as the *general price level*. The distorted relative prices will be a less reliable indicator of relative scarcity. As a result of these unreliable price signals, producers and resource suppliers will often make choices that they will later regret and the allocation of resources will be less efficient than would be the case if the general level of prices was more stable.

3. People will respond to high and variable rates of inflation by spending less time producing and more time trying to protect themselves from inflation. Since the failure to accurately anticipate the rate of inflation can have a substantial effect on one's wealth, individuals will divert scarce resources from the production of desired goods and services to the acquisition of information on the future rate of inflation. The ability of business decision makers to forecast changes in prices becomes more valuable relative to their ability as managers and organizers of production. Speculative practices are encouraged as people try to outguess each other with regard to the future direction of prices. Funds flow into speculative investments such as gold, silver, and art objects rather than into productive investments (buildings, machines, and technological research) that expand the investor's ability to produce goods and services. Such practices are socially counterproductive. They reduce our production possibilities.

Although the initial effects of inflation can sometimes be positive, high and variable rates of inflation will inevitably exert a negative impact on real output and the level of prosperity. Economists have coined the term **stagflation** to describe the phenomenon of rapid inflation and sluggish economic growth. The 1970s were a period of stagflation in the United States. Two recessions (1974–1975 and 1979–1980) and sluggish growth accompanied the double-digit inflation rates of the 1970s.

Stagflation
A period during which an economy is experiencing both substantial inflation and either declining or slow growth in output.

---

[4]See Robert Higgs, "Inflation and the Destruction of the Free Market Economy," *The Intercollegiate Review* (spring 1979), for an excellent discussion of this point.

WHAT CAUSES INFLATION?

We must acquire some additional tools before we can answer the question of what causes inflation in detail, but at this point we can outline a couple of theories. First, economists emphasize the link between aggregate demand and supply. If aggregate demand rises more rapidly than supply, prices will rise. Second, nearly all economists believe that a rapid expansion in a nation's stock of money causes inflation. The old saying is that prices will rise because "there is too much money chasing too few goods." The hyperinflation experienced by South American countries and, more recently, the countries of the former Soviet Union has mainly been the result of monetary expansion. Once we develop additional knowledge about the operation of our economy, we will consider this issue in more detail.

LOOKING AHEAD

In this chapter, we have examined the historical record for real income, employment, and prices. Measurement problems and the side effects of economic instability were discussed. In the next chapter, we will begin to develop a macroeconomic model that will help us better understand both the sources of and potential remedies for economic instability.

CHAPTER SUMMARY

1. Historically, real GDP in the United States has grown unevenly. Periods of rapid real growth have been followed by economic slowdowns. Nevertheless, the long-term trend has been upward. During the past century, real GDP in the United States has grown at an average annual rate of approximately 3 percent.

2. *Business peak, contraction, recessionary trough,* and *expansion* are terms used by economists to describe the four phases of the business cycle. During an expansion, output increases rapidly and unemployment declines. The highest output rate of an expansion is referred to as a business peak or economic boom. Contraction is characterized by declining real output and increasing unemployment. The bottom of the contraction is referred to as the recessionary trough.

3. Officially, the Commerce Department defines a recession as two successive quarters of declining real GDP. If a recession is quite severe, it is called a depression.

4. Even an efficient exchange economy will experience some unemployment. Frictional unemployment results because of imperfect information about available job openings and qualified applicants. Structural unemployment stems from the presence of factors that prevent the "matching up" of available applicants with available jobs. Currently, frictional and structural unemployment in the United States are thought to involve between 5 and 6 percent of the labor force.

5. Cyclical unemployment results when aggregate demand for labor is insufficient to maintain full employment. A primary concern of macroeconomics is how cyclical unemployment can be minimized.

6. Full employment is the employment level consistent with the economy's natural rate of unemployment, which reflects both frictional and structural factors. The natural rate is neither a temporary high nor low, but rather the rate of unemployment associated with the economy's maximum sustainable rate of output. It is not immutable, but, rather, can be affected by public policies and changes in the composition of the labor force.

7. Employment is a means to an end. The meaningful goal of full employment is productive employment that creates desired goods and services.

8. The definition of *unemployed* is imperfect and involves some subjectivity. Some persons are not counted as unemployed because they are currently too discouraged to actively seek employment. Others are counted even though they may be employed in the underground economy or only casually seeking employment, perhaps because of an incentive structure that makes unemployment more attractive. Because of these ambiguities, some observers believe that the employment/population ratio is a more objective and accurate indicator of current employment opportunities. A prudent observer will consider both measures.

9. The concept of potential output encompasses two important ideas: (a) full utilization of resources and (b) a supply constraint that limits our ability to produce desired goods and services. When the resources of the economy are not fully and efficiently used, output will fall below its potential rate.

10. Inflation is a general rise in the level of prices. Alternatively, we might say that it is a decline in the purchasing power of the monetary unit—the dollar, in the case of the United States. The inflation rate accelerated upward in the United States during the 1970s. Since 1982 it has been more moderate.

CRITICAL ANALYSIS QUESTIONS

11. It is important to distinguish between anticipated and unanticipated inflation. Anticipated inflation involves increases in the general level of prices that are expected by most people. Unanticipated inflation catches decision makers by surprise. When a rate of inflation is anticipated, people will plan for it and adjust their behavior accordingly, prior to the occurrence of the inflation. When it is unanticipated, it will often alter the intended terms of long-term agreements and cause people to make choices that they will later regret.

12. When the inflation rate is high, the year-to-year variability in the rate will generally be large. Since high and variable rates of inflation are unpredictable, they result in unanticipated inflation.

13. Inflation, particularly unanticipated inflation, has harmful effects on an economy. It reduces the gains from trade and productive activity because it (a) increases the uncertainty accompanying investment and other exchanges involving time, (b) distorts relative prices, and (c) consumes valuable resources as individuals use their skills and talents attempting to prevent the erosion of their income and wealth as the result of the inflation.

CRITICAL ANALYSIS QUESTIONS

1. List the major phases of the business cycle and indicate how real GDP, employment, and unemployment change during these phases. Are the time periods of business cycles and the duration of the various phases relatively similar and therefore highly predictable?

*2. Explain why even an efficiently functioning economic system will have some unemployed resources.

3. Classify each of the following as employed, unemployed, or not in the labor force:
   a. Brown is not working; she applied for a job at Wal-Mart last week and is awaiting the result of her application.
   b. Smith is vacationing in Florida during a layoff at a General Motors plant due to a model changeover, but he expects to be recalled in a couple of weeks.
   c. Green was laid off as a carpenter when a construction project was completed. He is looking for work but has been unable to find anything except an $8-per-hour job, which he turned down.
   d. West works 50 to 60 hours per week as a homemaker for her family of nine.
   e. Carson, a 17-year-old, works six hours per week as a route person for the local newspaper.
   f. Johnson works three hours in the mornings at a clinic and for the last two weeks has spent the afternoons looking for a full-time job.

4. What is full employment? How are full employment and the natural rate of unemployment related? Indicate several factors that would cause the natural rate of unemployment to change. Is the actual rate of unemployment currently greater or less than the natural rate of unemployment? Why?

5. Carefully explain how both the rate of unemployment and the employment/population ratio are derived. If the rate of unemployment decreases, does the employment/population ratio necessarily increase? Why or why not? Which is the better indicator of employment opportunity? Why?

*6. "As the inflation proceeds and the real value of the currency fluctuates widely from month to month, all permanent relations between debtors and lenders, which form the ultimate foundation of capitalism, become so utterly disordered as to be almost meaningless; and the process of wealth-getting degenerates into a gamble and a lottery." Do you agree with this well-known economist's view? Why or why not? How high do you think the inflation rate would have to climb before these effects would become pronounced? How does the inflation rate, particularly high rates of inflation, influence the operation of a market economy? Discuss.

*7. How are the following related to each other?
   a. Actual rate of unemployment
   b. Natural rate of unemployment
   c. Cyclical unemployment
   d. Potential GDP

*8. Use the following data to calculate (a) the labor-force participation rate, (b) the rate of unemployment, and (c) the employment/population ratio:

Population	10,000
Labor force	6,000
Not currently working	4,500
Employed full-time	4,000
Employed part-time	1,500
Unemployed	500

*9. Persons are classified as unemployed if they are not currently working at a job and if they made an effort to find a job during the past four weeks. Does this mean that there were no jobs available? Does it mean that there were no jobs available that unemployed workers were qualified to perform? What does it mean?

*10. Indicate how an unanticipated 5 percent jump in the inflation rate will influence the wealth of the following:
   a. A person whose major asset is a house with a 30-year mortgage at a fixed interest rate.
   b. A family holding most of its wealth in long-term fixed yield bonds.
   c. A retiree drawing a monthly pension.
   d. A heavily indebted small-business owner.
   e. The owner of an apartment complex with substantial outstanding debt at a fixed interest rate.
   f. A worker whose wages are determined by a three-year union contract ratified three months ago.

11. Is the natural rate of unemployment fixed? Why or why not?

12. If a group of employees has a relatively low oppor-

tunity cost of job search, how will this affect their unemployment rate? How do you think the opportunity cost of job search of teenagers living with their parents compares with that of a prime earner with several dependents? How will this affect the unemployment rate of teenagers?

*13. How will each of the following affect a job seeker's decision to reject an available job offer and continue searching for a superior alternative?

    a. The rumor that a major firm in the area is going to expand employment next month

    b. The availability of food stamps

    c. Optimism about the future of the economy

*14. "My money wage rose by 6 percent last year, but inflation completely erased these gains. How can I get ahead when inflation continues to wipe out my increases in earnings?" What's wrong with this way of thinking?

15. Suppose that the consumer price index at year-end 1996 was 140 and by year-end 1997 had risen to 150. What was the inflation rate during 1997?

16. Data for the nominal GDP and the GDP deflator (1990 = 100) in 1993 and 1994 for six major industrial countries are presented in the accompanying Table A.

    a. Use the data provided to calculate the 1993 and 1994 real GDP of each country measured in 1990 prices. Place in the blanks provided.

    b. Use the data for the GDP deflator to calculate the 1994 inflation rate of each country. Place in the blanks provided.

    c. Which country had the highest growth rate of real GDP during 1994? Which had the lowest growth rate?

    d. Indicate the countries that had the highest and the lowest inflation rates in 1994.

    e. Which one of the countries had the most inflation during the 1990–1994 period?

17. The accompanying Table B presents the 1994 population and labor-force data for several countries.

    a. Calculate the number of people in the labor force for the United States, Canada, and Japan in 1994.

    b. Calculate the 1994 rate of labor-force participation for each country and place in the blanks provided. Which country had the highest rate of labor force participation? Which country had the lowest?

    c. Calculate the rate of unemployment in 1994 for each country, and place in the blanks provided. Which country had the highest rate of unemployment? Which had the lowest?

_____

*Asterisk denotes questions for which answers are given in Appendix B.

TABLE A

	NOMINAL GDP (BILLIONS OF LOCAL CURRENCY UNITS)[a]		GDP DEFLATOR (1990 = 100)		REAL GDP (IN 1990 CURRENCY UNITS)		INFLATION RATE
COUNTRY	1993	1994	1993	1994	1993	1994	1994
United States	6,343.3	6,738.4	109.1	111.4	_____	_____	_____
Canada	712.9	750.1	105.3	105.9	_____	_____	_____
Japan	466.0	469.2	104.0	104.0	_____	_____	_____
Germany	2,853.7	2,977.7	111.9	114.2	_____	_____	_____
France	7,082.8	7,380.3	108.1	109.7	_____	_____	_____
United Kingdom	630.7	668.9	114.8	117.2	_____	_____	_____

[a]The data for Japan are in trillions of yen.

TABLE B

COUNTRY	POPULATION 16 YEARS AND OVER (IN MILLIONS)	NUMBER EMPLOYED (IN MILLIONS)	NUMBER UNEMPLOYED (IN MILLIONS)	RATE OF LABOR-FORCE PARTICIPATION (PERCENT)	RATE OF UNEMPLOYMENT (PERCENT)
United States	194.0	123.1	8.44	_____	_____
Canada	21.2	13.3	1.49	_____	_____
Japan	102.8	63.3	1.38	_____	_____
Germany	55.6	34.9	2.60	_____	_____
France	44.8	22.4	2.36	_____	_____
United Kingdom	45.1	25.4	2.35	_____	_____
Italy	49.6	20.0	2.65	_____	_____

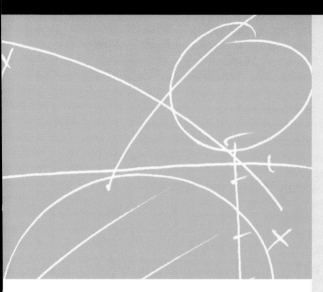

CHAPTER FOCUS

■ What are the major markets that coordinate macroeconomic activities?

■ Why is the aggregate demand for goods and services inversely related to the price level?

■ Why is an increase in the price level likely to expand output in the short run, but not in the long run?

■ What determines the equilibrium level of GDP of an economy?

■ How is the natural rate of unemployment related to the concept of long-term aggregate supply?

■ What is the difference between the real interest rate and the money interest rate? Does inflation help borrowers relative to lenders?

Macroeconomics is interesting . . . because it is challenging to reduce the complicated details of the economy to manageable essentials. Those essentials lie in the interactions among the goods, labor, and assets [loanable funds] markets of the economy.

RUDIGER DORNBUSCH AND STANLEY FISCHER[1]

---

[1]Rudiger Dornbusch and Stanley Fischer, *Macroeconomics* (New York: McGraw-Hill, 1978).

I n Chapter 6 we explained how output is measured and how price indexes are developed and utilized to transform nominal output figures into real measures of output—that is, output adjusted for changes in the general level of prices. In Chapter 7 we presented historical data on fluctuations in real output, employment, and the price level and considered several important implications of these fluctuations. We are now ready to shift from the description of economic performance to an analysis of that performance and the factors that influence it.

UNDERSTANDING MACROECONOMICS: OUR GAME PLAN

Let us develop a simple macroeconomic model—a road map, if you like—that will help us better understand macroeconomic relationships. This model will enhance our understanding of both how our macroeconomy works and the impact of policy changes on important economic variables like output, employment, and the general level of prices.

Fiscal policy
The use of government taxation and expenditure policies for the purpose of achieving macroeconomic goals.

Macroeconomic policy is usually divided into two components: fiscal policy and monetary policy. **Fiscal policy** entails the use of the government's taxation and spending policies in order to achieve macroeconomic goals. In the United States, fiscal policy is conducted by Congress and the president. It is thus a reflection of the collective decision-making process. **Monetary policy** encompasses actions that alter the money supply. The direction of monetary policy is determined by a nation's central bank, the Federal Reserve System in the United States. Ideally, both monetary and fiscal policy are used to promote business stability, high employment, the growth of output, and a stable price level.

Monetary policy
The deliberate control of the money supply, and, in some cases, credit conditions, for the purposes of achieving macroeconomic goals.

Initially, as we develop our basic macroeconomic model, we will assume that monetary and fiscal policies are unchanged. Stated another way, we will proceed as if the government continues to maintain the current tax and spending policies in the future. Similarly, we will assume that policymakers maintain a constant **money supply**—that they follow policies that keep the amount of cash in our billfolds and deposits in our checking accounts constant. Of course, changes in government expenditures, taxes, and the money supply are potentially important. We will investigate their impact in detail in subsequent chapters. For now, though, things will go more smoothly if we simply assume that policymakers are holding government expenditures, taxes, and the supply of money constant.

Money supply
The supply of currency, checking account funds, and traveler's checks. These items are counted as money because they are used as the means of payment for purchases.

THREE KEY MARKETS: RESOURCES, GOODS AND SERVICES, AND LOANABLE FUNDS

Businesses generally purchase resources from households and use them to produce goods and services. In turn, households generally use a substantial portion of the income they earn from the sale of their productive services to purchase goods and services supplied by businesses. Thus, there is a circular flow of output and income between these two key sectors, businesses and households. This circular flow of income is coordinated by three key macroeconomic markets: (1) goods and services, (2) resources, and (3) loanable funds. **Exhibit 8–1** illustrates both the circular flow of income between the household and business sectors and the interrelationships among those key macroeconomic markets.

The bottom loop of this circular-flow diagram depicts the **resource market,** a highly aggregated market that includes the markets for labor services, natural resources, and physical capital. In the resource market, business firms demand resources because of their contribution to the production of goods and services. As we indicated in Chapter 3, the demand for resources is a derived demand— it is derived from the demand for goods and services. While business firms demand resources, households supply them in exchange for income. The forces of demand and supply determine prices in the resource market. The payments to the suppliers of resources—that is, the wages paid for labor services, rents,

Resource market
A highly aggregated market encompassing all resources (labor, physical capital, land, and entrepreneurship) that contribute to the production of current output. The labor market forms the largest component of this market.

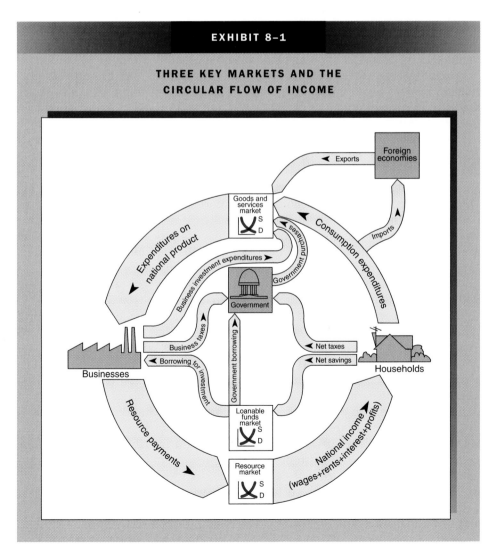

EXHIBIT 8–1

THREE KEY MARKETS AND THE CIRCULAR FLOW OF INCOME

A circular flow of income is coordinated by three key markets. First, the resource market (bottom loop) coordinates the actions of businesses demanding resources and households supplying them in exchange for income. Second, the loanable funds market (lower center) coordinates the saving choices of households and the borrowing decisions of businesses and governments. Finally, households, investors, governments, and foreigners (net exports) purchase products supplied by the business sector. These exchanges are coordinated in the goods and services market (top loop).

Goods and services market
A highly aggregated market encompassing the flow of all final-user goods and services. The market counts all items that enter into GDP. Thus, real output in this market is equal to real GDP.

Loanable funds market
A general term used to describe the market arrangements that coordinate the borrowing and lending decisions of business firms and households. Commercial banks, savings and loan associations, the stock and bond markets, and insurance companies are important financial institutions in this market.

Saving
Disposable income that is not spent on consumption. Saving is a "flow" concept. Thus, it is generally measured in terms of an annual rate.

and interest paid to those who supply physical and financial resources, and the profits earned by corporations and other businesses—sum to national income.

The **goods and services market** comprises the top loop of the circular-flow diagram. In this market, businesses supply goods and services in exchange for sales revenue. Households spend much of their income on consumer goods and housing. These expenditures contribute substantially to the demand for goods and services.

As Exhibit 8–1 illustrates, however, there are also two indirect routes by which funds can flow from the household to the business sector. First, the net savings of households can flow through the **loanable funds market** to (1) business firms purchasing investment goods and (2) governments purchasing public services. **Saving** is that portion of one's disposable income that is not spent on consumption. It is income not consumed. Net saving by the household sector supplies funds to the loanable funds market. In turn, businesses borrow loanable funds to finance investment expenditures. In addition, governments often finance their expenditures by borrowing. When the borrowed funds are spent on investment goods and government purchases, they return to the circular flow. The price of loanable funds is the interest rate. The actions of borrowers and lenders are coordinated by the interest rate in the loanable funds market. The interest rate will tend to rise or fall until it brings the quantity of loanable funds demanded by borrowers into equality with the quantity supplied by lenders.

Second, some of the income of households is taxed in order to transfer purchasing power to governments. In turn, as these revenues are used to finance the purchase (or production) of goods and services provided by governments, they contribute to the demand in the goods and services market.

We live in a world where instant communications and shrinking transportation costs facilitate exchange between trading partners thousands of miles apart. As a result, the exchange partners of modern economies often live in different countries. The import-export loop of Exhibit 8–1 depicts this interaction with foreign economies. Households will import some of the goods and services that they purchase. Similarly, in addition to their domestic sales, business firms will export some of the goods and services that are produced domestically. Net exports are the amount sold to foreigners minus the amount bought from them. If net exports are positive, they will increase the demand for domestically produced goods and services. On the other hand, if net exports are negative, they will decrease the demand for domestically produced goods and services.

As the arrows flowing into the goods and services market (top loop) indicate, there are four major sources of expenditures in this market: (1) household expenditures on consumption (and new housing), (2) business investment, (3) government purchases, and (4) net exports. These expenditures of households, business investors, governments, and foreigners (net exports) compose the aggregate (total) demand for domestic output. As the major components of demand indicate, the goods and services market is a highly aggregated and diverse market. It includes such items as ice cream, pizza, hairstyling, movie tickets, clothing, and television sets—goods purchased primarily by consumers. The goods and services market also includes investment goods that are bought primarily by businesses—such items as machines, tools, heavy equipment, and factory buildings. Finally, items such as highways, fire protection, and national defense, which are usually purchased by governments, are also part of the goods and services market.

As we noted in Chapter 6, there are two ways of measuring gross domestic product (GDP), the aggregate domestic output of an economy. First, GDP can be measured by adding up the expenditures of consumers, investors, governments, and foreigners (net exports) on goods and services produced during the year. This method is equivalent to measuring the flow of output as it moves through the top loop—the goods and services market—of the circular-flow diagram. Alternatively, GDP can be measured by summing the income payments, both direct and indirect, received by the resource suppliers who produced the goods and services. This method uses the bottom loop—the resource market—to measure the flow of output.

AGGREGATE DEMAND FOR GOODS AND SERVICES

What goes on in the aggregate goods and services market is vital to the health of an economy. Indeed, if we could keep our eye on just one market in an economy, we would choose the goods and services market because it exerts a vital impact on our economic opportunity and standard of living.

It is important to note that the "quantity" and "price" variables in this highly aggregated market differ from their counterparts in the market for a specific good. In the goods and services market, the "quantity" variable is real GDP; it is the flow of domestically produced goods and services during a period. The "price" variable in the goods and services market represents the average price of goods and services purchased during the period. In essence, it is the economy's price level, as measured by a general price index (for example, the GDP deflator).

Just as the concepts of demand and supply enhance our understanding of markets for specific goods, they also contribute to our understanding of a highly aggregated market such as the goods and services market. The demand in the goods and services market is composed of the purchases of *domestically produced* goods and services by consumers, investors, governments, and foreigners. The **aggregate demand curve** indicates the various quantities of domestically produced goods and services that purchasers are willing to buy at different price levels. As **Exhibit 8–2** illustrates, the aggregate demand curve slopes downward to the right, indicating an inverse relationship between the amount of goods and services demanded and the price level.

WHY DOES THE AGGREGATE DEMAND CURVE SLOPE DOWNWARD?

The explanation of the downward slope of the aggregate demand (AD) schedule differs from that for a specific commodity, which we discussed previously in Chapter 3. The inverse relationship between price and the amount demanded of a specific commodity—television sets, for example—reflects the fact that consumers will substitute the good for other commodities when a price reduction makes the good less expensive relative to other goods. A price reduction in the

Aggregate demand curve
A downward-sloping curve indicating an inverse relationship between the price level and the quantity of domestically produced goods and services that households, business firms, governments, and foreigners (net exports) are willing to purchase during a period.

As illustrated here, the quantity of goods and services purchased will increase (to Y_2) as the price level declines (to P_2). Other things constant, the lower price level will increase the wealth of people holding the fixed quantity of money, lead to lower interest rates, and make domestically produced goods cheaper relative to foreign goods. All these factors will tend to increase the quantity of goods and services purchased at the lower price level.

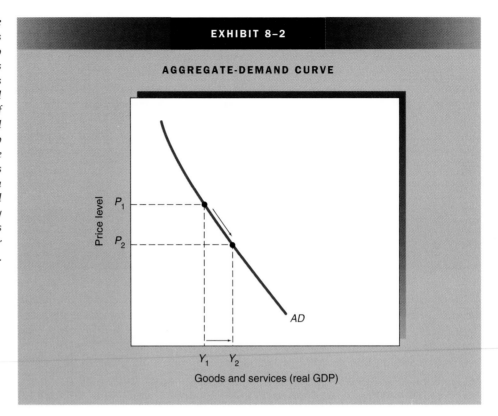

EXHIBIT 8-2

AGGREGATE-DEMAND CURVE

aggregate goods and services market indicates that the level of prices has declined. On average, the prices of all goods are lower. When the prices of all goods produced domestically fall by the same proportion, there will be no incentive for *domestic* purchasers to substitute one good for another.

Be careful! Both the nature of the aggregate demand curve and the explanation for its downward slope differ substantially from that of the demand for a specific commodity. There are three major reasons why a reduction in the price level will lead to an increase in the aggregate quantity of goods and services demanded by purchasers.

1. A lower price level will increase the purchasing power of the fixed quantity of money. As the level of prices declines, the purchasing power of the fixed quantity of money increases. For example, suppose that you have $2,000 in your bank account. Consider how a 20 percent reduction in the level of prices will influence your wealth and spending. At the lower price level, your $2,000 will buy more goods and services. In fact, your $2,000 will buy as much as $2,500 would have purchased at the previous higher level of prices. Other people are in an identical position. As the price level declines, the purchasing power of their money balances also increases.

Real balance effect
The increase in wealth generated by an increase in the purchasing power of a constant money supply as the price level decreases. This wealth effect leads to an inverse relationship between price (level) and quantity demanded in the goods and services market.

Economists refer to this inverse relationship between the price level and the wealth of households and businesses holding a fixed supply of money as the **real balance effect.** It helps to explain the downward slope of the aggregate demand curve. When the price level declines, the purchasing power of money and the real wealth of people holding fixed money balances increases. (Note: Remember we are assuming that the *nominal* supply of money is fixed.) As their wealth increases because their fixed quantity of money will purchase more goods, people will increase their purchases. Therefore, a negative relationship between the price level and the quantity of goods and services purchased emerges from the real balance effect.

2. The Interest Rate Effect: A lower price level will reduce the demand for money and lower the real interest rate, which will stimulate additional purchases during the current period. A reduction in the price level will increase the *real* money supply—the nominal supply of money relative to the level of prices. When the average price of goods and services declines, consumers and businesses will be able to conduct their normal activities with smaller average money balances. Households will be able to get by just fine with a smaller amount of cash and checking account funds since, at the lower price level, they will be spending a smaller nominal amount on food, clothing, and other items regularly purchased. Similarly, businesses will want to reduce their money balances since less funds will now be required to pay employee wages, taxes, and other business expenses at the lower price level. As both consumers and businesses attempt to reduce their money balances, they will channel some of these funds into savings—the loanable funds market. Thus, this decline in the demand for money relative to the fixed supply of money will place downward pressure on interest rates.[2]

What impact will a lower interest rate have on the demand for goods and services? A reduction in the interest rate will make it cheaper to purchase goods and services during the current period, particularly those that are financed. Thus, households can be expected to increase their purchases of interest-sensitive consumption goods such as automobiles and consumer durables. Similarly, firms will expand their current investment expenditures on business expansion and new construction. Thus, a reduction in the price level leads to a lower interest rate that encourages both consumption and investment spending. This interest rate effect also contributes to the downward slope of the aggregate demand curve.

3. Other things constant, a lower price level will make domestically produced goods less expensive relative to foreign goods. At a lower price level, imports will decline as Americans find that many domestically produced goods are now cheaper than products produced abroad. At the lower price level, Americans will tend to purchase fewer Japanese automobiles, Korean textiles, Italian shoes, and other imports since these products are now more expensive relative to domestically produced goods. At the same time, foreigners will increase their purchases of American-made goods that are now relatively cheaper. Therefore, net exports will tend to rise (or net imports decline).[3] This increase in net exports at the lower U.S. price level will directly increase the quantity demanded of domestically produced goods. Thus, the international-substitution effect provides a third reason for the downward slope of the aggregate demand curve.

---

[2]We will provide additional detail on this topic when we analyze the demand for money in Chapter 13.

[3]An increase in exports and decline in imports may cause a nation's currency to appreciate, which will partially offset the international-substitution effect.

THUMBNAIL SKETCH

WHY IS THE AGGREGATE QUANTITY DEMANDED INVERSELY RELATED TO THE PRICE LEVEL?

A decrease in the price level will raise aggregate quantity demanded because

1. The real wealth of persons holding money balances will increase when prices fall; this will encourage additional consumption.

2. A reduction in the demand for money balances at the lower price level will reduce interest rates, which will encourage current investment and consumption.

3. Net exports will expand (since the prices of domestic goods have fallen relative to foreign goods).

THE DOWNWARD-SLOPING AGGREGATE DEMAND CURVE: A SUMMARY

The accompanying Thumbnail Sketch indicates why the price level is inversely related to the amount demanded in the aggregate goods and services market. A lower price level will (1) increase the purchasing power of the fixed money supply, (2) lower interest rates, and (3) reduce the price of domestically produced goods relative to goods produced abroad. Each of these factors will tend to increase the quantity demanded of domestically produced goods and services.

While we have considered the impact of a lower price level on the quantity purchased, the effects would be just the opposite for a higher price level. At a higher price level, (1) the wealth of people holding the fixed supply of money would be less, (2) the demand for money would be greater, which would lead to higher interest rates, and (3) domestic goods would be more expensive relative to those produced abroad. Each of these factors would tend to reduce the quantity demanded of domestically produced goods. Therefore, even though the explanation differs, the quantity demanded in the aggregate goods and services market, like the quantity demanded for a specific product, will be inversely related to price.

AGGREGATE SUPPLY OF GOODS AND SERVICES

Aggregate supply curve
A curve indicating the relationship between the nation's price level and quantity of goods supplied by its producers. In the short run, it is probably an upward-sloping curve, but in the long run most economists believe the aggregate supply curve is vertical (or nearly so).

In light of our discussion of aggregate demand, it should come as no great surprise that the explanation of the general shape of the **aggregate supply curve** differs from that of the supply curve for a specific good. As we have already noted, an increase in price in the goods and services market indicates that the general level of prices has risen, rather than the price of one good relative to all other goods. Thus, the general shape of the aggregate supply (AS) curve is not a reflection of changes in the relative prices of goods.

When considering aggregate supply, it is particularly important to distinguish between the short run and the long run. In this context, the short run is the time period during which some prices, particularly those in labor markets, are set by prior contracts and agreements. Therefore, in the short run, households and businesses are unable to adjust these prices when unexpected changes occur, including unexpected changes in the price level. In contrast, the long run is a time period of sufficient duration that people have the opportunity to modify their behavior in response to price changes. We now consider both the short-run and long-run aggregate supply curves.

AGGREGATE SUPPLY IN THE SHORT RUN

The short-run aggregate supply (SRAS) curve indicates the various quantities of goods and services that domestic firms will supply in response to changing demand conditions that alter the level of prices in the goods and services market. As **Exhibit 8–3** illustrates, the *SRAS* curve in the goods and services market slopes upward to the right. The upward slope reflects the fact that, in the short run, an unanticipated increase in the price level will, on average, improve the profitability of firms. They will respond with an expansion in output.

The *SRAS* curve is based on a specific expected price level, P_{100}, in the case of Exhibit 8–3, and rate of inflation that generates that price level. When the expected price level is actually achieved, firms will earn normal profits and

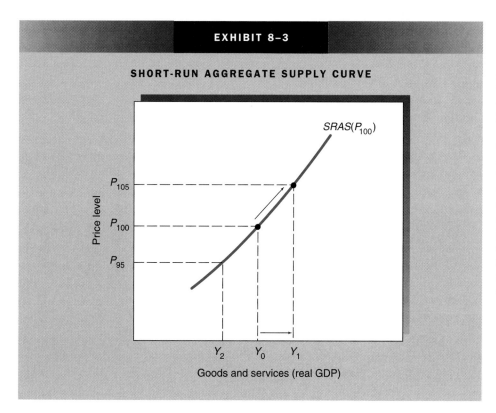

EXHIBIT 8–3

SHORT-RUN AGGREGATE SUPPLY CURVE

The short-run aggregate supply (SRAS) curve shows the relationship between the price level and the production of goods and services by domestic suppliers during the period immediately following the change in aggregate demand leading to the change in the price level. In the short run, firms will generally expand output as the price level increases because the higher prices will improve profit margins since many components of costs will be temporarily fixed as the result of prior long-term commitments.

supply output Y_0. Why will an increase in the price level (to P_{105}, for example) enhance profitability, at least in the short run? Profit per unit equals price minus the producer's per-unit costs. *Important components of producers' costs will be determined by long-term contracts.* Interest rates on loans, collective bargaining agreements with employees, lease agreements on buildings and machines, and other contracts with resource suppliers will influence production costs during the current period. The prices incorporated into these long-term contracts at the time of the agreement are based on the expectation of price level (P_{100}) for the current period. These resource costs tend to be temporarily fixed. *If an increase in demand causes the price level to rise unexpectedly during the current period, prices of goods and services will increase relative to the temporarily fixed components of costs. Profit margins will improve, and business firms will happily respond with an expansion in output (to Y_1).*[4]

An unexpected reduction in the price level to P_{95} would exert just the opposite effect. It would decrease product prices relative to costs and thereby reduce profitability. In response, firms would reduce output to Y_2. Therefore, in the short run, there will be a direct relationship between amount supplied and the price level in the goods and services market.

AGGREGATE SUPPLY IN THE LONG RUN

The long-run aggregate supply (LRAS) *curve indicates the relationship between the price level and quantity of output after decision makers have had sufficient time to adjust their prior commitments where possible, or take steps to counterbalance them, in the light of any unexpected changes in market prices.* A higher price level in the goods and services market will fail to alter the relationship between product and resource prices in the long run. Once people have time to fully adjust their prior commitments, competitive forces will restore the

---

[4]The short-run aggregate supply schedule concerns the output that business firms will supply in response to a change in aggregate demand. Viewed from this perspective, there are other reasons why an increase in aggregate demand will cause firms to produce a larger output in the short run. For the representative firm, an increase in aggregate demand will lead to strong sales for a few weeks or months. Consider how a typical business firm will respond to the strong demand for their product. Initially, the manager of the firm will not know whether the increased sales are temporary or permanent. If the strong sales are only temporary, the firm will be fearful that a large price increase might drive their regular customers to rival suppliers. Therefore, until it is convinced that the temporary increase in sales reflects a genuine long-term increase in demand for its product, the typical business firm will increase its price only moderately, if at all. In the short run, firms will generally supply the larger output that their customers are demanding without much increase in price.

In addition, some firms may be confused by the general increase in demand for products. Mistakenly, they may believe that the demand for their product has increased relative to other products. If this were the case, the firm would be able to purchase the resources required to expand long-term output without much increase in costs. Fooled by the general increase in demand, many firms will hire resources, make investments, and expand output in the short run. Because many other firms are also expanding output, with the passage of time the outcome is going to be higher resource prices and increases in costs. Initially, however, the firms undertaking the expansions in output will be unaware that this will be the case. This factor may also contribute to the positive relationship between the price level and output as firms respond to an increase in aggregate demand in the short run.

usual relationship between product prices and costs. Profit rates will return to normal, removing the incentive for firms to supply a larger rate of output. Therefore, as **Exhibit 8–4** illustrates, the *LRAS* curve is vertical.

The forces that provide for an upward-sloping **SRAS** *curve are absent in the long run.* Costs that are temporarily fixed as the result of contractual agreements will eventually rise. With time, the long-term contracts will expire and be renegotiated. Once the contracts are renegotiated, resource prices will increase in the same proportion as product prices. A proportional increase in costs and product prices will leave the incentive to produce unchanged. Consider how a firm with a selling price of $20 and per-unit costs of $20 will be affected by the doubling of both product and resource prices. After the price increase, the firm's sales price will be $40, but so, too, will its per-unit costs. Thus, neither the firm's profit rate nor the incentive to produce is changed. Therefore, in the long run an increase in the nominal value of the price level will fail to exert a lasting impact on aggregate output.

Reflecting on the production possibilities of an economy also sheds light on why the **LRAS** *curve is vertical. As we discussed in Chapter 2, at a point in time, the production possibilities of a nation are constrained by the supply of resources, level of technology, and institutional arrangements that influence the efficiency of resource use. A higher price level does not loosen these constraints.* For example, a doubling of prices will not improve technology. Neither will it expand the availability of productive resources, nor improve the efficiency of our economic institutions. Thus, there is no reason for a higher price level to increase our ability to produce goods and services. This is precisely what the vertical *LRAS* curve implies. The accompanying Thumbnail Sketch summarizes the factors that underlie both the short-run and long-run aggregate supply curves.

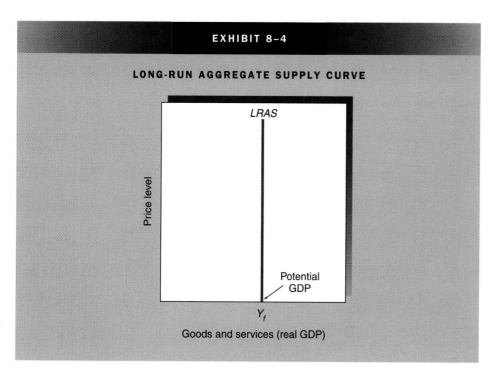

EXHIBIT 8–4

LONG-RUN AGGREGATE SUPPLY CURVE

LRAS

Price level

Potential
GDP

Y_f

Goods and services (real GDP)

In the long run, a higher price level will not expand an economy's rate of output. Once people have time to adjust their prior long-term commitments, resource markets (and costs) will adjust to the higher level of prices and thereby remove the incentive of firms to supply a larger output at the higher price level. An economy's sustainable potential output rate is determined by the supply of resources, level of technology, and structure of institutions, factors that are insensitive to changes in the price level. The vertical LRAS curve illustrates this point.

THUMBNAIL SKETCH

WHY IS THE SHORT-RUN AGGREGATE QUANTITY SUPPLIED DIRECTLY RELATED TO THE PRICE LEVEL?

• As the price level increases, profit margins will improve because *initially* the product prices of firms will rise relative to cost (important components of which are temporarily fixed by long-term contracts).

WHY IS THE LONG-RUN AGGREGATE SUPPLY CURVE VERTICAL?

• Once people have the time to adjust fully to a new price level, the normal relationship between product prices and resource costs is restored.
• The sustainable potential output of a national economy is determined by its quantity of resources, technology, and the efficiency of its institutional structures, not by the price level.

EQUILIBRIUM IN THE GOODS AND SERVICES MARKET

Equilibrium

A balance of forces permitting the simultaneous fulfillment of plans by buyers and sellers.

We are now ready to combine our analysis of aggregate demand and aggregate supply and consider how they act to determine the price level and rate of output. When a market is in **equilibrium,** there is a balance of forces such that the actions of buyers and sellers are consistent with one another. In equilibrium, buyers are willing to purchase all the units that sellers are willing to supply *at the current price.* Because the equilibrium price clears the market—all units produced are sold—some refer to it as the "market clearing price."

EQUILIBRIUM IN THE SHORT RUN

As **Exhibit 8–5** illustrates, short-run equilibrium is present in the goods and services market at the price level *(P)* where the aggregate quantity demanded is equal to the aggregate quantity supplied. This occurs at the output rate *(Y)* where the *AD* and *SRAS* curves intersect. At this market clearing price *(P),* the amount that buyers want to purchase is just equal to the quantity that sellers are willing to supply during the current period.

If a price level of less than *P* were present, the aggregate quantity demanded would exceed the aggregate quantity supplied. Purchasers would be seeking to buy more goods and services than producers were willing to produce. This excess demand would place upward pressure on prices, causing the price level to rise toward *P.* On the other hand, at a price level greater than *P,* the aggregate quantity supplied would exceed the aggregate quantity demanded. Producers would be unable to sell all the goods produced. This would result in downward pressure (toward *P*) on prices. Only at the price level *P* would there be a balance of forces between the amount of goods demanded by consumers, investors, governments, and foreigners, and the amount supplied by domestic firms.

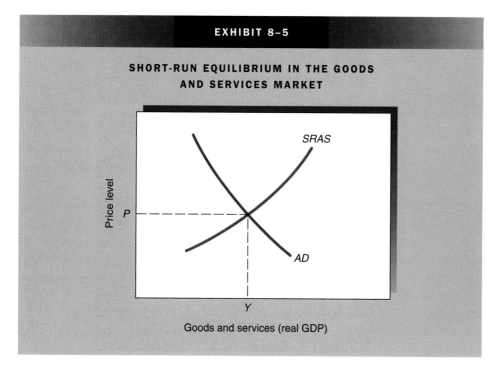

EXHIBIT 8–5

**SHORT-RUN EQUILIBRIUM IN THE GOODS
AND SERVICES MARKET**

Short-run equilibrium in the goods and services market occurs at the price level (P) where AD and SRAS intersect. If the price level were lower than P, general excess demand in goods and services markets would push prices upward. Conversely, if the price level were higher than P, excess supply would result in falling prices.

EQUILIBRIUM IN THE LONG RUN

In the short run, the goods and services market will gravitate toward a market clearing price—one that brings quantity demanded and quantity supplied into balance. *However, a second condition is required for long-run equilibrium: The buyers and sellers must have correctly anticipated the consequences of their prior choices.* If they are unsatisfied as the result of surprise occurrences, they will want to change their actions in the future. Thus, long-run equilibrium requires that decision makers who agreed to long-term contracts influencing current prices and costs must have correctly anticipated the current price level *at the time they arrived at the agreements.* If this is not the case, buyers and sellers will want to modify the agreements when the long-term contracts expire. In turn, their modifications will affect costs, profit margins, and output.

Exhibit 8–6 illustrates a long-run equilibrium in the goods and services market. As in Exhibit 8–3, the subscripts attached to the SRAS and AD curves indicate the price level (an index of prices) that was anticipated by decision makers at the time they made decisions affecting the schedules. In this case, when buyers and sellers made their purchasing and production choices, they anticipated that the price level during the current period would be P_{100}, where the subscript 100 refers to an index of prices during an earlier base year. As the intersection of the AD and SRAS curves reveals, the P_{100} was actually attained.

When the price level expectations embedded in the long-term contracts turn out to be correct, there is no reason for buyers and sellers in resource markets to modify resource prices when their contracts come up for renegotiation. Therefore, the resource prices, costs, and profits will continue into the future. Since the price-cost relationship is unchanged, firms have no incentive to alter either

When the goods and services market is in long-run equilibrium, two conditions must be present. First, the quantity demanded must equal the quantity supplied at the current price level. Second, the price level anticipated by decision makers must equal the actual price level. The subscripts on the SRAS and AD curves indicate that buyers and sellers alike anticipated the price level P_{100}, where the 100 represents an index of prices during an earlier base year. When the anticipated price level is actually attained, current output (Y_f) will equal the economy's potential GDP and full employment will be present.

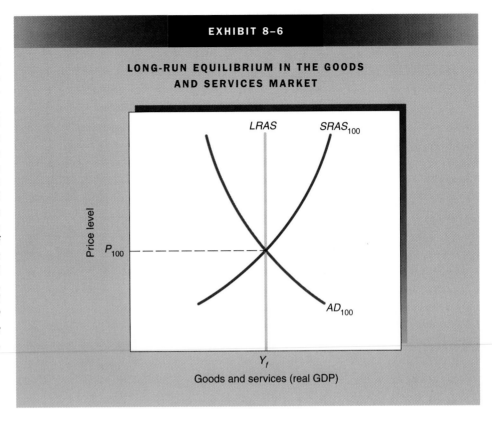

EXHIBIT 8–6

LONG-RUN EQUILIBRIUM IN THE GOODS AND SERVICES MARKET

their product prices or rate of output. Thus, the price level (P_{100}) and output (Y_f) are in long-run equilibrium. They will persist into the future until changes in other factors alter *AD* or *SRAS*.

LONG-RUN EQUILIBRIUM, POTENTIAL OUTPUT, AND FULL EMPLOYMENT

When long-run equilibrium is present, the actual output achieved is equal to the economy's potential GDP. In other words, when a short-run equilibrium (*AD* intersects with *SRAS*) occurs along the economy's vertical aggregate supply curve (*LRAS*), long-run equilibrium will also be present. Exhibit 8–6 illustrates this case.

As we discussed in Chapter 7, potential GDP is equal to the economy's *maximum sustainable output* consistent with its resource base, current technology, and institutional structure. Potential GDP is neither a temporary high nor an abnormal low. Rather, it reflects the normal operation of markets, the situation when decision makers (including those involved in long-term agreements) neither systematically underestimate nor overestimate the current price level.

The long-run equilibrium output rate (Y_f in Exhibit 8–6) also corresponds with the full employment of resources. When full-employment output is present, the job-search time of unemployed workers will be normal, given the characteristics of the labor force and the institutional structure of the economy. Only frictional and structural unemployment will be present; cyclical unemployment will be absent.

When an economy is in long-run equilibrium, the *actual* rate of unemployment will be equal to the *natural* rate. Remember, the natural rate of unemployment reflects the normal job-search process of employees and employers, given the structure of the economy and the laws and regulations that affect the operation of markets. It is a rate that is neither abnormally high nor abnormally low; it can be sustained into the future. When an economy is in long-run equilibrium, this will be the case. Decision makers will have correctly anticipated the inflation rate and the current price level that it generates. Thus, they will have no reason to undertake changes that will affect costs relative to prices. On average, the profitability of firms will be normal. This situation is sustainable into the future.

Therefore, in long-run equilibrium, (a) output will be equal to its potential, (b) full employment will be achieved, and (c) the actual rate of unemployment will be equivalent to the natural rate of unemployment. (See Measures of Economic Activity box.)

ADJUSTMENT WHEN OUTPUT DIFFERS FROM LONG-RUN POTENTIAL

What happens when changes in the price level catch buyers and sellers by surprise? When the actual price level differs from the level forecast by buyers and sellers, some decision makers will enter into agreements that they will later regret—agreements that they will want to change as soon as they have an opportunity to do so.

Consider the situation when the price level *increases* more than was anticipated. Failing to foresee the price increase, lenders in the loanable funds market agree to interest rates that are lower than they are willing to accept once the general increase in prices (inflation) is taken into account. Similarly, anticipating a lower current price level, union officials and employees accept money-wage increases that end up creating lower real wages than were initially perceived. In the short run, the atypically low interest rates and real wages reduce costs relative to product prices. Profit margins are abnormally high, and firms respond with a larger output. Employment expands. Unemployment falls below its natural rate.

But this abnormally large output and high level of employment is not sustainable. The "mistakes," based on a failure to predict the strength of current demand, will be recognized and corrected when contracts expire. Real wages and interest rates will increase and eventually reflect the higher price level and rate of inflation. Profit margins will return to normal. When these adjustments are completed, the temporarily large output rate and high employment level will decline and return to normal.

What will happen if product prices *decline or increase less* rapidly than decision makers anticipate? Anticipating a higher price level (a higher inflation rate

MEASURES OF ECONOMIC ACTIVITY

NATURAL RATE OF UNEMPLOYMENT

The natural rate of unemployment is a theoretical concept and cannot be directly observed. The theory, however, indicates how it can be estimated. The natural rate of unemployment will be present when decision makers correctly anticipate the inflation rate. When the inflation rate of an economy is relatively constant—when it is neither increasing nor decreasing—buyers and sellers will be able to accurately anticipate it and adjust nominal prices, wages, and interest rates accordingly. *Thus, the actual unemployment rate will tend to gravitate toward the economy's natural rate of unemployment when the inflation rate is constant for an extended period of time.*

A statistical equation that links the unemployment rate to the rate of inflation can be used to estimate the natural rate of unemployment. When the *change* in the inflation rate is set equal to zero within this equation, the results will provide an estimate for the natural rate of unemployment. *Statistical estimates of this type indicate that the natural rate of unemployment in the United States is currently between 5 percent and 6 percent.*

Over time, the natural rate is influenced by changes in the demographic composition of the labor force. Since younger workers are more likely than their older counterparts both to switch jobs and enter (and reenter) the labor force, the natural unemployment rate increases when youthful workers grow as a proportion of the labor force. This happened during the 1960s and 1970s, when the baby-boom generation—those born during the 15 years following the Second World War—entered the labor force. Researchers in this area estimate that the large influx of youthful workers during this period pushed the natural rate of unemployment up from approximately 5 percent in the late 1950s to nearly 7 percent in 1980. This situation reversed during the 1980s and 1990s. The natural rate of unemployment declined during this period as the baby-boomers moved into their prime working years and the proportion of youthful workers as a share of the labor force fell. Thus, the current natural rate of unemployment is estimated to be approximately 5.5 percent, similar to the rate during the late 1950s.

than actually occurs), borrowers agree to interest rates that later *in real terms* prove to be unacceptably high. Similarly, employers agree to wage increases that result in higher real wages than expected, since the price level rises more slowly than people thought it would. The abnormally high interest and wage rates increase costs relative to product prices. As profit margins are squeezed, producers reduce output and lay off employees. The *actual rate* of unemployment rises above the *natural rate* of unemployment. Current output falls short of the economy's potential GDP.

Many economists think this is precisely what happened during 1982. After inflation rates of 13 percent in 1979 and 12 percent in 1980, price increases plummeted to 4 percent in 1982. This sharp reduction in the inflation rate caught many decision makers by surprise. Unable to pass along to consumers the large increases in money wages agreed to in 1980 and 1981, employers cut back production and laid off workers. The unemployment rate soared to 10.8 percent in late 1982, up from 7.6 percent in 1981. Eventually, new agreements provided for smaller money wage increases, or even wage reductions, in 1983 and 1984. Unemployment fell. Nevertheless, in 1982 unemployment was well above its natural rate. The necessary adjustments could not be made instantaneously.

In summary, a current output rate will be sustained into the future only when the price agreements of buyers and sellers were based on an accurate forecast of the current price level. If the decision makers were able to accurately forecast the current price level when they arrived at their agreements, then the current resource prices and real interest rates will tend to persist into the future.

Profit rates will be normal. The choices of buyers and sellers will harmonize, and neither will have reason to alter their choices. When this is the case, long-run equilibrium will be present and the economy's sustainable potential rate of output (Y_f in Exhibit 8–6) will be achieved. It is this long-run *maximum sustainable output* that economists are referring to when they speak of "full employment output" or "potential GDP."

RESOURCE MARKET

In addition to the aggregate goods and services market, there are two other basic macroeconomic markets that coordinate the circular flow of income between the household and business sectors. These two markets are the resource market and the loanable funds market. After we discuss the resource market in this section and the loanable funds market in the section that follows, we will be ready to link all three markets together and analyze general macroeconomic equilibrium.

It is not hard to guess that the resource market is a market for resources, but what does that mean? Resources are factors of production, such as labor, natural resources, and machines, so the resource market is nothing more than a place where such items are bought and sold. The resource market thus coordinates the choices of business firms that demand resources and resource owners who supply them. The market for labor services is the dominant component of the resource market. In the United States, the costs of labor make up approximately 70 percent of production costs. Since the labor market is both large and very important, we will often concentrate on it rather than the general resource market.

Why do business firms demand labor and other resources? In a market economy, business firms employ resources because they contribute to the production of goods the firm believes it can sell at a profit. For example, a builder purchases resources, such as lumber, cement, and windows, and hires the labor services of carpenters, bricklayers, and roofers, because they are required in order to produce the houses that the contractor hopes to sell for a profit. The demand for a resource such as labor reflects the law of demand, which says that the higher the price of something, the less the quantity demanded. If the wages that firms must pay for workers increase, the firms will choose to hire fewer workers. In contrast, a lower wage rate will increase the quantity of labor demanded by firms. Therefore, the demand for resources, like the demand for goods and services, slopes downward to the right.

Why are labor and other resources supplied? Most people work and supply resources to earn income. Working, though, requires us to give up something else that is valuable: leisure—time to do nonmarket work and other things. So a trade-off must be made between working for income and spending leisure time on nonmarket activities. Higher real wages increase the opportunity cost of leisure. Because of this, as real wages increase, individuals generally make substitutions that permit them to supply more market work time. Therefore, the quantity of labor and other resources supplied expands as resource prices increase.

Exhibit 8–7 illustrates equilibrium in the aggregate resource market. Price coordinates the actions of buyers and sellers. The equilibrium or market clearing

In general, as resource prices increase, the amount demanded by producers declines and the amount supplied by resource owners expands. In equilibrium, resource price brings the amount demanded into equality with the amount supplied in the aggregate-resource market. The labor market is a major component of the resource market.

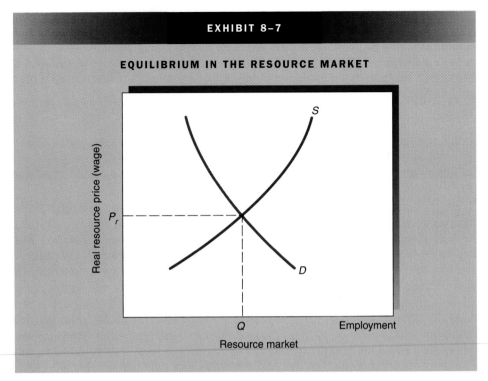

EXHIBIT 8–7

EQUILIBRIUM IN THE RESOURCE MARKET

price brings the amount demanded by business firms into balance with the amount supplied by resource owners. At this price (P_r), the choices of both buyers and sellers in the aggregate resource market harmonize—they are consistent with each other. If the market price were greater than P_r, an excess supply of resources would occur. In turn, this excess supply would push resource prices downward toward equilibrium. In contrast, if resource prices were below equilibrium (less than P_r), excess demand would place upward pressure on the price of resources. Market forces thus tend to move resource prices toward the price that clears the market—the price that brings the amount buyers are willing to purchase into equality with the amount that sellers are willing to supply.

As we discussed in Chapter 3, the markets for resources and products are highly interrelated. The cost of producing goods and services is influenced directly by the price of resources. Other things remaining constant, an increase in resource prices will increase costs and squeeze profit margins in the goods and services market. Aggregate supply will decline (*SRAS* will shift to the left). Conversely, a reduction in resource prices will lower costs and improve profit margins in the goods and services market. An increase in aggregate supply (a shift to the right in *SRAS*) will result.

The demand for resources is directly linked to the demand for goods and services. In fact, the demand for resources is a *derived demand*—it stems from the demand for goods and services. An increase in demand in the goods and services market will generate additional demand for resources. Similarly, a reduction in aggregate demand in the goods and services market will reduce the demand for resources. Since the resource and goods and services markets are highly interrelated, obviously changes in either one of these markets will have repercussions in the other. Much of macroeconomics concerns the interrelations between these two markets and the analysis of how change in one affects the other.

LOANABLE FUNDS MARKET

The loanable funds market coordinates the actions of borrowers and lenders. This market permits households, businesses, and governments to borrow against their assets or against future expected income. As the circular flow of income implies, households are generally net suppliers of loanable funds (see Exhibit 8–1). Businesses and governments often demand loanable funds to finance capital investment projects and other expenditures. Financial institutions (such as savings and loan associations, commercial banks, and insurance companies), pension funds, and the stock and bond markets form the core of this market.

In essence, borrowers are exchanging future income for purchasing power now. Most of us are impatient; we want things now rather than in the future. *From the borrower's viewpoint, interest is the cost paid for earlier availability. From the lender's viewpoint, interest is a premium received for waiting, for delaying possible expenditures into the future.*

The interest rate can also be thought of as the price of credit. Lenders are supplying credit and borrowers are demanding credit. The interest rate brings the choices of borrowers and lenders into harmony.

It is helpful to think of the interest rate in two ways. First, there is the **money interest rate,** the percentage of the amount borrowed that must be paid to the lender in the future, in addition to the principal amount borrowed. Money interest rates are those typically quoted in newspapers and business publications. When there is inflation, the money rate of interest may be a misleading indicator of *real* borrowing costs (remember, *real* means "adjusted for inflation"). Since rising prices shrink the purchasing power of the dollar, inflation reduces the value of the principal and interest paid in the future. Recognizing this fact, borrowers and lenders implicitly agree on an interest premium when they expect inflation. So the inflation leads to a higher money interest rate, which is necessary to compensate the lender for the decline in the purchasing power of money during the lifetime of the loan.

Second, there is the **real interest rate,** which reflects the real burden to borrowers and the payoff to lenders in terms of command over goods and services. The real interest rate is simply the money rate of interest adjusted for the expected rate of inflation.

Perhaps an example will clarify the distinction between the two. Suppose a person borrows $1,000 for one year at a 6 percent interest rate. After a year, the borrower must pay the lender $1,060—the $1,000 principal plus the 6 percent interest. Now, suppose during the year prices rose 6 percent as the result of inflation. Because of this, the $1,060 repayment after a year commands exactly the same purchasing power as the original $1,000 did when it was loaned. In effect, the borrower pays back exactly the same amount of purchasing power as was borrowed. The lender receives nothing for making the purchasing power available to the borrower. In this case, the effective real interest rate was zero.

Money interest rate
The interest rate measured in monetary units. It overstates the real cost of borrowing during an inflationary period. When inflation is anticipated, an inflationary premium will be incorporated into the nominal value of this rate. The money interest rate is often referred to as the nominal interest rate.

Real interest rate
The interest rate adjusted for expected inflation; it indicates the real cost to the borrower (and yield to the lender) in terms of goods and services.

Inflation premium
A component of the money interest rate that reflects compensation to the lender for the expected decrease, due to inflation, in the purchasing power of the principal and interest during the course of the loan. It is determined by the expected rate of future inflation.

Lenders are unlikely to continue making funds available at such bargain rates. When the 6 percent inflation rate is anticipated, lenders will demand (and borrowers will agree to pay) a higher money interest rate to compensate for the decline in the purchasing power of the dollar. This premium for the expected decline in purchasing power of the dollar is called the **inflation premium.** Once borrowers and lenders anticipate 6 percent inflation, for example, they might agree to a 12 percent money interest rate, 6 percent of which reflects an inflationary premium and 6 percent a real interest return. (See Myths of Economics box for further explanation.) We can illustrate the relationship between the real interest rate and the money interest rate as follows:

$$\text{Real interest rate} = \text{Money interest rate} - \text{Inflation premium}$$

The size of the inflation premium, of course, varies directly with the expected rate of future inflation. When inflation is correctly anticipated, it is the real interest rate, not the money rate, that indicates the true burden of borrowers and the true yield to lenders derived from a loan.

MYTHS OF ECONOMICS

"BECAUSE INFLATION ERODES THE BURDEN OF OUTSTANDING DEBT, IT SYSTEMATICALLY HELPS BORROWERS AT THE EXPENSE OF LENDERS."

Like most myths, this one has a grain of truth in it.

Inflation does reduce the purchasing power of the proceeds paid by borrowers and received by lenders during the period while a loan is outstanding. But this is only part of the story. *Inflation also influences money interest rates* and therefore the amount paid by borrowers and received by lenders when funds are borrowed.

When higher rates of inflation are anticipated by decision makers, lenders will demand and borrowers will grant higher interest rates on loans because both parties will expect the value of the dollar to depreciate during the period that the loan is outstanding. If borrowers and lenders accurately anticipate a rate of inflation, they will agree to a money interest rate that will be just high enough to compensate for the effects of inflation on the purchasing power of the loan proceeds during the period the loan is outstanding. For example, suppose a borrower and a lender would agree to a 5 percent interest rate if they anticipated a stable price level in the future. Instead, if both expected prices to rise 10 percent annually, they would agree to a 15 percent interest rate. If their expectations are realized, the real interest rate will be 5 percent in both cases.

Of course, decision makers will not always be able to forecast the future rate of inflation accurately. Sometimes the rate of inflation will be higher than was expected, while in other instances it will be lower. There is no rea-

son, however, to expect that these errors in forecasting future inflation rates will be systematic.

If the actual rate of inflation is higher than was expected, borrowers will tend to gain relative to lenders. For example, suppose borrowers and lenders expect a 3 percent future rate of inflation and therefore agree to an 8 percent interest rate on a loan—5 percent representing the real interest rate and 3 percent the inflation premium. If the actual rate of inflation turns out to be higher than 3 percent—6 percent, for example—the real amount paid by the borrower and received by the lender will decline. *When the actual rate of inflation is greater than was anticipated, borrowers gain relative to lenders.*

But the converse is true when the actual rate of inflation is less than expected. Suppose that after the borrower and lender agree to the 8 percent loan, the price level is stable while the loan is outstanding. In this case, the borrower ends up paying an 8 percent real interest rate, rather than the 5 percent that was anticipated. *When the actual rate of inflation is less than anticipated, lenders gain at the expense of borrowers.*

Thus, it is not inflation per se that produces redistributional effects, but rather the actual rate of inflation relative to the expected rate. *Because there is no reason to believe that borrowers and lenders will systematically either underestimate or overestimate the future rate of inflation, there is no reason to believe that it will systematically help one relative to the other.*

An increase in the real interest rate makes borrowing more costly. Households, investors, and governments will reduce the amount of funds demanded as the real interest rate rises. On the other hand, a higher real interest rate increases the payoff derived from waiting. Lenders will therefore supply more funds as the real interest rate increases. So, as **Exhibit 8–8** illustrates, the supply curve for loanable funds slopes upward to the right, while the demand curve has the usual downward slope. Equilibrium is present in the loanable funds market at the real interest rate that brings the amount of funds demanded by borrowers into equality with the amount supplied by lenders.

Businesses and governments often borrow funds by issuing bonds that yield an interest rate. Issuing bonds is simply a method of demanding loanable funds. In turn, the purchasers of bonds are supplying loanable funds. It is important to note that there is an inverse relationship between bond prices and interest rates. *Higher bond prices are the same thing as lower interest rates.* (See Applications in Economics box for further explanation.)

As was true for the resource market, the loanable funds and the goods and services markets are closely interrelated. We previously indicated that the reduction in the interest rate that generally accompanies a lower price level when the supply of money is constant helps explain why the *AD* curve slopes downward to the right. In addition, the real interest rate may change for other reasons. When it does, it will affect the aggregate demand schedule. The real interest rate influences aggregate demand because people who borrow money generally do so in order to buy things. Since a higher real interest rate would discourage borrowing, it would also discourage spending. As we proceed, we will analyze in more detail the interrelationship between the loanable funds market and the goods and services market.

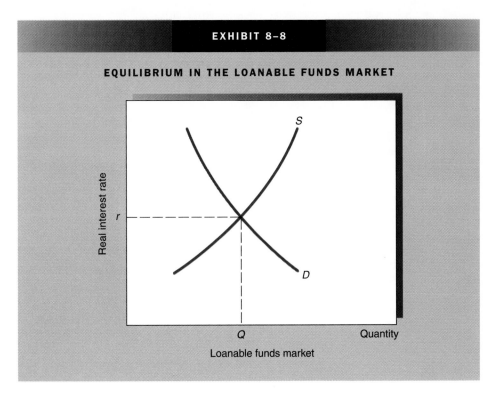

EXHIBIT 8–8

EQUILIBRIUM IN THE LOANABLE FUNDS MARKET

Real interest rate

S

r

D

Q Quantity

Loanable funds market

As illustrated, the quantity of loanable funds demanded is inversely related to the real interest rate. The quantity of funds lenders are willing to supply is directly related to the real interest rate. In equilibrium, the real interest rate (r) will bring the quantity demanded and quantity supplied into balance.

BONDS, INTEREST RATES, AND BOND PRICES

Bonds are simply IOUs issued by firms and governments. Issuing bonds is a method of borrowing money to finance economic activity. The entity issuing the bond promises to pay the bondholder the amount borrowed (called principal) at a designated future date plus a *fixed* amount of interest. Even though interest rates may change with the passage of time, *the bondholder will receive the fixed interest rate as a percent of the original principal throughout the life of the bond.* Some bonds pay the interest at designated intervals (that is, on a specific date each year). Others pay both principal and interest when the bond matures at a specified date in the future.

Even though most bonds are issued for long periods of time, they can be sold to another party prior to their maturity. Each day, sales of previously issued bonds comprise the majority of bonds bought and sold on the bond market.

How does a change in the market interest rate affect the market prices of previously issued bonds? Suppose you bought a newly issued $1,000 bond that pays 8 percent per year in perpetuity (forever) on the $1,000 principal.[1] As long as you own the bond, you are entitled to a fixed return of $80 per year. Let us also assume that after you have held the bond for one year and have collected your $80 interest for that year, the market interest rate in-

creases to 10 percent.[2] How will the increase in the interest rate affect the market price on your bond? Since bond purchasers can now earn 10 percent interest if they buy newly issued bonds, they will be unwilling to pay more than $800 for your bond, which pays only $80 interest per year. After all, why would anyone pay $1,000 for a bond that yields only $80 interest per year when the same $1,000 will now purchase a bond that yields $100 (10 percent) per year? The increase in the interest rate to 10 percent will cause the *market price* of your $1,000 (which earns only 8 percent annually) to fall to $800. At that price, the new owners would earn the 10 percent market rate of interest. In this manner, rising market interest rates cause bond prices to decline.

On the other hand, falling interest rates will cause bond prices to rise. If the market interest rate had fallen to 6 percent, what would have happened to the market value of your bond? (Hint: $80 is 6 percent of $1,333.) Bond prices and interest rates are inversely linked to each other.

---

[1]Undated securities of this sort are available in the United Kingdom. They are called consols.
[2]The astute reader will recognize an oversimplification in this discussion. In reality, the economy supports a variety of interest rates, which usually tend to move together.

EQUILIBRIUM IN OUR THREE-MARKET MACROECONOMY

We have now discussed all three basic macroeconomic markets: the goods and services market, the resource market, and the loanable funds market. From these discussions it would be easy to get the impression that each market exists more or less independently. Nothing could be further from the truth. Instead, the three basic macroeconomic markets are as dependent on one another in the way that they work as the legs of a three-legged stool.

Exhibit 8–9 illustrates equilibrium conditions in the three basic macroeconomic markets of our circular-flow model of Exhibit 8–1. Aggregate demand and aggregate supply are in equilibrium at the price level P_1 and output rate Y_f (part a). Because the P_1 price level was anticipated both by buyers and by sellers, the economy is operating at its long-run (full-employment) capacity. In the resource market, price (P_r) also equates amount demanded and amount supplied (part b). Because the economy is at long-run capacity, only normal unemployment is pre-

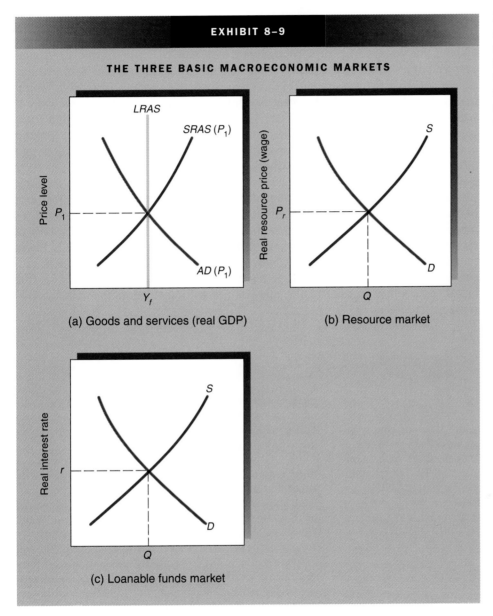

EXHIBIT 8-9

THE THREE BASIC MACROECONOMIC MARKETS

(a) Goods and services (real GDP)

(b) Resource market

(c) Loanable funds market

Here we indicate equilibrium conditions in the three basic markets that coordinate macroeconomic activity. These markets are highly interrelated. Changes in one influence equilibrium conditions in the other two.

sent in the labor market, an important subcomponent of the resource market. Finally, the real interest rate *(r)* has brought the amount demanded and amount supplied into balance in the loanable funds market (part c).

Changes in any one of these three macroeconomic markets will influence the equilibrium price and quantity in the other two. In fact, macroeconomics largely concerns tracing the impact of a change in one market through to other markets, particularly the goods and services market.

When an economy is in long-run macroeconomic equilibrium, interrelationships among the three basic markets—goods and services, resources, and loanable funds—will be in harmony. The price of resources relative to the price of goods and services will be such that business firms, on average, will be just able to cover their cost of production, including a competitive return on their investment. If this were not the case, producers would seek to either contract or expand output. For example, if the prices of resources were so high (relative to producers' prices) that firms were unable to cover their costs, many producers would cut back output or perhaps even discontinue production. Aggregate output would thereby be altered. Conversely, if resource prices were so low that firms were able to earn an above-market return, profit-seeking firms would expand output. New firms would begin production. Again, these forces would alter conditions in the goods and services market.

Similarly, the equilibrium relationship between interest rates in the loanable funds market and product prices must be such that the typical firm is just able to earn normal returns on its investments. In other words, the typical producer's return to capital must equal the interest rate—that is, the opportunity cost of capital. Higher returns would induce producers to expand output, while lower returns would cause them to cut back on production. Therefore, when macroeconomic equilibrium is present, prices in these three markets will be such that buyers and sellers in each of the markets are willing to continue with the current arrangements.

LOOKING AHEAD

In the next chapter, we will consider how our simple aggregate demand/aggregate supply model adjusts to changing conditions. Factors that shift demand and supply in one or more of the markets will be analyzed. The interrelationships among the basic macroeconomic markets will be discussed in more detail. As we proceed, we will use this basic model to analyze such topics as abnormally high unemployment and economic instability.

CHAPTER SUMMARY

1. The circular flow of income illustrates the significance of three highly aggregated markets: (a) goods and services, (b) resources, and (c) loanable funds. In the goods and services market, the demand of households, business investors, governments, and foreigners for products is coordinated with the current supply of commodities produced domestically. The resource market coordinates the exchange of labor and other productive inputs between the household and business sectors. The loanable funds market coordinates the actions of borrowers and lenders, and thereby channels the net savings of households back into the flow of income as investment or government expenditures.

2. The willingness of consumers, investors, governments, and foreigners (net exports) to purchase goods and services determines aggregate demand. The aggregate demand curve indicates the various quantities of domestically produced goods and services that purchasers are willing to buy at different price levels.

3. Assuming the money supply is constant, there are three reasons why the aggregate quantity demanded of goods and services will increase as the price level declines. First, a lower price level will increase the wealth of persons holding the fixed money balances. This increase in wealth will stimulate additional spending on goods and services. Second, at the lower price level, the demand for money will decline relative to the fixed supply, pushing interest rates downward, which will stimulate expenditures on interest-sensitive goods, such as automobiles, homes, and investment projects. Third, a lower price level makes domestic goods less expensive relative to foreign goods, which will lead to an increase in net exports (or a decline in net imports). Each of these factors will increase the quantity of domestically produced goods and services purchased at the lower price level.

4. The aggregate supply (AS) curve indicates the various quantities of goods and services domestic suppliers will produce at different price levels. In the short run, the aggregate supply curve will generally slope upward to the right. This is because a higher price level improves profit margins, since the prices of important cost components are temporarily fixed in the short run.

5. Once decision makers adjust fully to a higher price level, the factors that justified the upward-sloping SRAS

(short-run aggregate supply) curve are no longer present. Output is constrained by such factors as technology and re-source supply. A higher price level does not loosen these constraints. Thus, the *LRAS* (long-run aggregate supply) curve is vertical.

6. Two conditions are necessary for long-run equilibrium in the goods and services market: (a) quantity demanded must equal quantity supplied, and (b) the *actual* price level must equal the price level decision makers *anticipated* when they made buying and selling decisions for the current period.

7. When the economy is in long-run equilibrium, output will be at its maximum sustainable level. Similarly, the *actual rate* of unemployment will equal the *natural rate* (the lowest rate of unemployment that can be sustained over a long period of time). Economists would say that the economy is operating at full employment in this case.

8. The aggregate demand/aggregate supply model reveals the determinants of the price level and real output. In the short run, price and output will move toward an intersection of the aggregate demand *(AD)* and short-run aggregate supply *(SRAS)* curves. In the long run, price and output will gravitate to the levels represented by the intersection of *AD, SRAS,* and *LRAS.*

9. When the current price level differs from what was expected, output will differ from the economy's long-run capacity. When the current price level is *higher* than anticipated, product prices will be unusually high relative to wages and other components of cost. As a result, profits will exceed their normal rate, firms will expand output beyond the economy's long-run capacity, and unemployment will temporarily fall below its natural rate. In contrast, when the current price level is *lower* than was anticipated, product prices will be unusually low relative to costs, causing many firms to experience losses. They will respond by cutting back on both output and employment. Under these circumstances, current output will be lower than the economy's long-run capacity and unemployment will exceed its natural rate.

10. Business firms demand labor and other resources because they contribute to the production of goods and services that the firms hope to sell at a profit. Individuals supply resources in order to earn income. Price in the resource market coordinates the actions of buyers and sellers. The labor market is the largest component of the general resource market.

11. The interest rate in the loanable funds market is the price borrowers pay to obtain purchasing power now rather than in the future. From the lender's viewpoint, interest is a premium one receives for delaying expenditures into the future.

12. It is important to distinguish between real and money interest rates. The real interest rate reflects the real burden to borrowers and the payoff to lenders in terms of command over goods and services. In addition to this real burden, the money rate of interest also reflects the expected rate of inflation during the period the loan is outstanding. The real rate of interest is equal to the money rate of interest minus the inflation premium. The latter depends on the expected rate of inflation.

13. Inflation results in higher nominal interest rates. It only helps debtors when it is underestimated. Since there is no reason to expect decision makers to systematically underestimate the inflation rate, there is no reason to expect that it will systematically be advantageous to debtors.

14. The presence of macroeconomic equilibrium requires that equilibrium be achieved in all three key macroeconomic markets: (a) goods and services, (b) resources, and (c) loanable funds. Changes in any one of these markets will influence price and quantity in the other markets. Macroeconomics is primarily about how these key markets adjust to various changes in economic conditions and alternative policies.

CRITICAL ANALYSIS QUESTIONS

1. In your own words, explain why aggregate demand is inversely related to the price level. Why does the explanation for the inverse relationship between price and quantity demanded for the aggregate demand curve differ from that of a demand curve for a specific good?

2. What are the major factors that influence our ability to produce goods and services in the long run? Why is the long-run aggregate supply vertical?

3. Why does the short-run aggregate supply curve slope upward to the right? If the prices of both (a) resources and (b) goods and services increased proportionally (by the same percent), would business firms be willing to expand output? Why or why not?

*4. Suppose prices had been rising at a 3 percent annual rate in recent years. A major union signs a three-year contract calling for increases in money wage rates of 6 percent annually. What will happen to the real wages of the union members if the price level is constant (unchanged) during the next three years? If other unions signed similar contracts, what will probably happen to the unemployment rate? Why? Answer the same questions under conditions in which the price level increases at an annual rate of 8 percent during the next three years.

5. What is the current money interest rate on 30-year government bonds? Is this also the real interest rate? Why or why not?

6. What is the natural rate of unemployment? Why might the actual rate of unemployment differ from the natural rate of unemployment? If the actual rate of unemployment is less than the natural rate, can this situation be sustained over a long period of time? Why or why not?

*7. In Chapter 3, we indicated the other things that are held constant when the supply and demand schedules for a specific good are constructed. What were they? What are the key "other things" held constant when the AS, LRAS, and SRAS schedules are constructed?

8. If the price level in the current period is higher than what buyers and sellers anticipated, what will tend to happen to real wages and the level of employment? How will the actual rate of unemployment compare with the natural rate of unemployment? Will the current rate of output be sustainable in the future? Why or why not?

9. Suppose that you purchased a $5,000 bond that pays 6 percent interest annually and matures in five years. If the inflation rate in recent years has been steady at 3 percent annually, what is the estimated real rate of interest? If the inflation rate during the next five years remains steady at 3 percent, what real rate of return will you earn? If the inflation rate during the next five years is 6 percent, what will happen to your real rate of return?

*10. How are the following related to each other?
   a. The long-run equilibrium rate of output
   b. The potential real GDP of the economy
   c. The output rate resulting in the equality of the actual and natural rates of unemployment

*11. Can the real interest rate ever be negative? Can you cite any examples of a negative real interest rate? If the interest rate is determined by market forces, is a negative real interest rate likely to persist over a long period of time? Why or why not?

*12. If a bond pays $1,000 per year in perpetuity (each year in the future), what will be the market price of the bond when the long-term interest rate is 10 percent? What would it be if the interest rate were 5 percent?

*13. How are bond prices related to interest rates? Why are they related?

14. The following chart indicates the aggregate demand (AD) and short-run aggregate supply (SRAS) schedules of decision makers for the current period. Both buyers and sellers previously anticipated that the price level during the current period would be P_{105}.

AD_{105}	PRICE LEVEL	$SRAS_{105}$
6,300	90	4,500
6,000	95	4,800
5,700	100	5,100
5,400	105	5,400
5,100	110	5,700
4,800	115	6,000

a. Indicate the quantity of GDP that will be produced during this period.
b. Will it be a long-run equilibrium level of GDP? Why or why not?
c. What will be the relationship between the actual and natural rates of unemployment during the period? Explain your answer.

15. Consider an economy with the following aggregate demand (AD) and aggregate supply (AS) schedules. Decision makers have previously made decisions anticipating that the price level during the current period would be P_{105}.

AD_{105}	PRICE LEVEL	$SRAS_{105}$
6,900	90	4,500
6,600	95	4,800
6,300	100	5,100
6,000	105	5,400
5,700	110	5,700
5,400	115	6,000

a. Indicate the quantity of GDP that will be produced during the period.
b. Is it a long-run equilibrium level of GDP? Why or why not?
c. How will the unemployment rate during the current period compare with this economy's natural rate of unemployment?
d. Will the current rate of GDP be sustainable into the future? Why or why not?

16. Does inflation help debtors relative to lenders? Why or why not? Do you think that inflation will help people with low incomes relative to those with higher incomes? Explain. How will an unanticipated increase in the inflation rate influence the government's liability for the national debt? Is the government helped by inflation? Discuss.

---

*Asterisk denotes questions for which answers are given in Appendix B.

CHAPTER FOCUS

■ What factors will cause shifts in aggregate demand? What factors will shift aggregate supply?

■ How will the goods and services market adjust to changes in aggregate demand?

■ How does the economy adjust to changes in aggregate supply?

■ What causes fluctuations in output and employment?

■ Does a market economy have a self-correcting mechanism that will lead it to full employment?

We might as well reasonably dispute whether it is the upper or under blade of a pair of scissors that cuts a piece of paper, as whether value is governed by [demand] or [supply].

ALFRED MARSHALL[1]

---

[1]Alfred Marshall, *Principles of Economics*, 8th ed. (London: Macmillan, 1920), p. 348.

I n Chapter 8, we focused on the equilibrium conditions in the three basic macroeconomic markets. Equilibrium is important, but we live in a dynamic world that continually wars against it. Markets are always being affected by unexpected changes, such as the discovery of a vastly improved computer chip, shifts in consumer confidence, a drought in Midwestern agricultural states, or changes in defense expenditures as the result of national security conditions. Consequently, equilibrium is continually disrupted. Thus, if we want to understand how the real world works, analysis of how macroeconomic markets adjust to dynamic change is of crucial importance.

We are now ready to consider how macroeconomic markets adjust to changes in aggregate demand and aggregate supply. As in the preceding chapter, we will continue to assume that the government's tax, spending, and monetary policies are unchanged. For now, we want to help the reader understand how macroeconomic markets work. Once this objective is achieved, we will be better able to understand both the potential and the limitations of macroeconomic policy.

ANTICIPATED AND UNANTICIPATED CHANGES

Anticipated change
A change that is foreseen by decision makers in time for them to adjust.

Unanticipated change
A change that decision makers could not reasonably foresee. Thus, choices made prior to the event did not take the event into account.

It is important to distinguish between anticipated and unanticipated changes in markets. **Anticipated changes** are foreseen by economic participants. Decision makers have time to adjust to them before they occur. For example, suppose that, under normal weather conditions, a new drought-resistant hybrid seed can be expected to expand the production of feed grain in the Midwest by 10 percent next year. As a result, buyers and sellers will plan for a larger supply and lower prices in the future. They will adjust their decision-making behavior accordingly.

In contrast, **unanticipated changes** catch people by surprise. Our world is characterized by dynamic change—new products are introduced, technological discoveries alter production costs, droughts reduce crop yields, demand expands for some goods and contracts for others. It is impossible for decision makers to foresee many of these changes.

Economics largely concerns how people respond and markets adjust to changing circumstances. As we will explain in a moment, there is good reason to expect that the adjustment process will differ depending on whether a change is anticipated.

FACTORS THAT SHIFT AGGREGATE DEMAND

The aggregate demand curve isolates the impact of the price level on the quantity demanded of goods and services. However, the price level is not the only factor that influences the demand for goods and services. When we constructed the aggregate demand curve, we assumed that several other factors affecting the choices of buyers in the goods and services market were constant. Changes in these "other factors" will shift the entire aggregate demand schedule, altering the amount purchased at each price level. Let us take a closer look at the major factors that will cause shifts in aggregate demand.

1. Changes in Real Wealth.   In Chapter 8 we indicated that changes in the price level will alter the real value of money balances and therefore the real wealth of people. But the wealth of individuals—the value of their assets—may change for reasons other than a change in the price level. For example, stock prices in the United States increased by more than 30 percent during 1995. This stock market boom increased the real wealth of stockholders. In contrast, both stock prices and housing prices declined during 1990, reducing the real wealth of households.

How will changes in the wealth of households affect the demand for goods and services? As the real wealth of households increases—perhaps as the result of higher prices in stock, housing, and/or real estate markets—people will demand more goods and services. As **Exhibit 9–1** illustrates, this increase in wealth will shift the entire aggregate demand (AD) schedule to the right (from AD_0 to AD_1). More goods and services are purchased at each price level. Conversely, a reduction in wealth will reduce the demand for goods and services, shifting the AD curve to the left (to AD_2) as the result of a decline in the wealth of households.

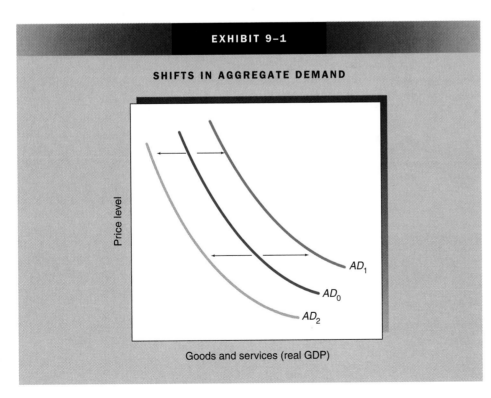

EXHIBIT 9–1

SHIFTS IN AGGREGATE DEMAND

Price level

Goods and services (real GDP)

AD_1

AD_0

AD_2

An increase in real wealth, such as would result from a stock market boom, for example, will increase aggregate demand, shifting the entire curve to the right (from AD_0 to AD_1). In contrast, a reduction in real wealth decreases the demand for goods and services, causing AD to shift to the left (from AD_0 to AD_2).

2. Changes in the Real Interest Rate. As we discussed previously, the major macroeconomic markets are closely related. A change in the real interest rate in the loanable funds market will influence the choices of consumers and investors in the goods and services market. A lower real interest rate makes it cheaper for consumers to buy major appliances, automobiles, and houses now rather than in the future. Simultaneously, a lower interest rate will also stimulate business spending on capital goods (investment). The interest rate influences the opportunity cost of all investment projects. If the firm must borrow, the real interest rate will contribute directly to the cost of an investment project. If the firm uses its own funds, it sacrifices real interest that could have been earned by loaning the funds to someone else had it not undertaken the investment project. Therefore, a lower real interest rate reduces the opportunity cost of a project, regardless of whether it is financed with internal funds or by borrowing.

Because a reduction in the real interest rate makes both consumer and investment goods cheaper, both households and investors will increase their current expenditures in response. In turn, their additional expenditures will increase aggregate demand, shifting the entire schedule to the right. In contrast, a higher real interest rate makes current consumption and investment goods more expensive, which leads to a reduction in aggregate demand, shifting the *AD* curve to the left.

3. Change in the Expectations of Businesses and Households about the Future Direction of the Economy. What people think will happen in the future influences current purchasing decisions. Optimism concerning the future direction of the economy will stimulate current investment. Business decision makers know that an expanding economy will mean strong sales and improved profit margins. Investment today may be necessary if business firms are going to benefit fully from these opportunities. Similarly, consumers are more likely to buy big-ticket items such as automobiles and houses when they expect an expanding economy to provide them with both job security and rising income in the future. So increased optimism encourages additional current expenditures by both investors and consumers, increasing aggregate demand.

Of course, pessimism about the future state of the economy exerts just the opposite impact. When investors and consumers expect an economic downturn (a recession), they will cut back on their current spending for fear of becoming overextended. This pessimism leads to a decline in aggregate demand, shifting the *AD* schedule to the left.

4. Change in the Expected Rate of Inflation. When consumers and investors believe that the inflation rate is going to accelerate in the future, they have an incentive to spend more during the current period. "Buy now before prices go higher" becomes the order of the day. Thus, the expectation of an increase in the inflation rate will stimulate current aggregate demand, shifting the *AD* curve to the right.

In contrast, the expectation of a decline in the inflation rate will tend to discourage current spending. When prices are expected to stabilize (or at least increase less rapidly), the gain obtained by moving expenditures forward in time is reduced. The expectation of a reduction in the inflation rate will thus reduce current aggregate demand, shifting the *AD* curve to the left.

5. Changes in Income Abroad. Changes in the income of a nation's trading partners will influence the demand for the nation's exports. If the income of a nation's trading partners is increasing rapidly, the demand for exports will expand. In turn, the strong demand for exports will stimulate aggregate demand. For example, rapid growth of income in Europe and Japan increases the demand of European and Japanese consumers for U.S.–produced goods. As U.S. exports expand, aggregate demand increases (the *AD* schedule shifts to the right).

Conversely, when a nation's trading partners are experiencing recessionary conditions, they reduce their purchases, including their purchases abroad. Thus, a decline in the income of a nation's trading partners tends to reduce both exports and aggregate demand.

Currently, approximately 10 percent of the goods and services produced in the United States are sold to purchasers abroad. The export sector is still larger for Canada, Mexico, and most Western European countries. The larger the size of the trade sector, the greater the potential importance of fluctuations in income abroad as a source of instability in aggregate demand. If the demand of foreign buyers does not rise and fall at the same time as domestic demand, however, the diversity of markets will reduce the impact of fluctuations in domestic demand.

6. Changes in Exchange Rates. As we previously explained, a change in a nation's price level relative to that of its trading partners will influence both net exports and the quantity of goods and services demanded at home. So will a change in the exchange rate—the value of a nation's currency in terms of the currency of another country. For example, changes in the value of the dollar on the foreign exchange rate market will alter the prices of imports to U.S. consumers and the prices of U.S. exports to foreign consumers.

Consider the impact of an increase in the exchange rate value of the U.S. dollar relative to the British pound. The increase in the exchange rate value of the dollar will make *the dollar price* of British goods cheaper to U.S. consumers because each dollar will now buy more pounds than was previously true. In turn, this reduction in the dollar price of British goods will stimulate U.S. imports. Simultaneously, since it will take more pounds to purchase a dollar than was previously the case, the increase in the exchange rate value of the dollar will make the price tag on U.S. goods (in terms of pounds) more expensive to British consumers. Predictably, British consumers will reduce purchases of American-made goods. Thus, the increase in the exchange rate value of the dollar will stimulate American imports and retard U.S. exports. Net exports will decline, which will retard aggregate demand (that is, shift the *AD* schedule to the left).

A decline in the exchange rate value of the dollar will have just the opposite effect. When there is a decline in the value of the dollar on the foreign exchange market, foreign-produced goods become more expensive for U.S. consumers, while U.S.–produced goods become cheaper for foreigners. As a result, net exports will increase and thereby stimulate aggregate demand (shifting *AD* to the right).[2]

---

[2]Later, when we consider the topic of international finance, we will analyze in more detail the determinants of the exchange rate and consider more fully the impact of changes in the exchange rate value of a nation's currency.

THUMBNAIL SKETCH

WHAT FACTORS WILL INFLUENCE AGGREGATE DEMAND?

These factors will increase (decrease) aggregate demand (*AD*).[a]

1. An increase (decrease) in real wealth.
2. A decrease (increase) in the real rate of interest.
3. An increase in the optimism (pessimism) of businesses and consumers about future economic conditions.
4. An increase (decline) in the expected rate of inflation.
5. Higher (lower) real incomes abroad.
6. A reduction (increase) in the exchange rate value of the nation's currency.

---

[a]The important factors of macroeconomic policy will be considered later.

SUMMARY OF FACTORS THAT SHIFT AGGREGATE DEMAND

The accompanying Thumbnail Sketch summarizes the major factors causing shifts in aggregate demand. Next, we will analyze how the goods and services market adjusts to changes in demand. The government's spending, taxing, and monetary policies also influence aggregate demand. Knowledge of how the goods and services market works will help us better understand how fiscal and monetary policies work.

UNANTICIPATED CHANGES IN AGGREGATE DEMAND

How will unanticipated changes in aggregate demand influence price and output in the goods and services market? It will take time for decision makers to respond fully to unexpected changes. Initially, it may be unclear to decision makers whether a change—an increase in sales, for example—reflects a random occurrence or a real change in demand conditions. It will also take businesses some time to differentiate between temporary fluctuations and more permanent changes. Even after decision makers are convinced that market conditions have changed, time will be required for them to make new decisions and carry them out. In some cases, complete adjustment will also be delayed by the presence of long-term contracts. All these factors will reduce the speed of market adjustments to unexpected changes in demand conditions.

INCREASES IN AGGREGATE DEMAND

Part a of **Exhibit 9–2** illustrates how an economy that is initially in long-run equilibrium will adjust to an unanticipated increase in aggregate demand. Initially the economy is in long-run equilibrium at output Y_f and price level P_{100} (point E_1). Aggregate demand and aggregate supply are in balance. Decision makers have correctly anticipated the current price level, and the economy is operating at its full-employment level of output.

Consider what would happen if this equilibrium were disrupted by a stock market boom or burst of business optimism that caused an unanticipated increase in aggregate demand (shift from AD_1 to AD_2). An excess demand for goods and services would result at the initial price level (P_{100}). Responding to the strong sales and excess demand, businesses would increase their prices. Their profit margins would improve (since product prices increase relative to the cost of resources), and they would expand output along the $SRAS$ curve. As part a of Exhibit 9–2 shows, the economy would move to a short-run equilibrium (e_2), at a larger output (Y_2) and higher price level (P_{105}). (Note: A short-run equilibrium is indicated with a lowercase e, while a capital E is used to designate a long-run equilibrium. This convention will be followed throughout the text.)

For a time, many wage rates, interest payments, rents, and other resource prices would still reflect the initial price level (P_{100}) and the previously weaker demand. Because markets do not adjust instantaneously, these resource prices, and therefore costs, would lag behind prices in the goods and services market. Thus, the higher price level temporarily would improve profit margins, which,

EXHIBIT 9–2

EFFECTS OF UNANTICIPATED INCREASE IN AGGREGATE DEMAND

(a) Short-run effects of increase in *AD*

(b) Long-run effects of increase in *AD*

In response to an unanticipated increase in aggregate demand for goods and services (shift from AD₁ to AD₂), prices will rise (to P₁₀₅) in the short run and output will temporarily exceed full-employment capacity (a). However, with the passage of time, prices in resource markets, including the labor market, will rise as the result of the strong demand. The higher resource prices will mean higher costs, which will reduce aggregate supply to SRAS₂ (b). In the long run, a new equilibrium at a higher price level (P₁₁₀) and an output consistent with the economy's sustainable potential will result. Thus, the increase in demand will expand output only temporarily.

in turn, would provide the incentive for business firms to expand both output and employment in the short run. As a result, the unemployment rate would drop below its natural rate, and output would temporarily exceed the economy's long-run potential output level.[3]

This is not the end of the story, however. The strong demand accompanying this high level of output will place upward pressure on prices in resource and loanable funds markets. With time, the strong demand conditions will push wages, other resource prices, and real interest rates upward. As part b of Exhibit 9–2 illustrates, the rising resource prices and costs will shift the short-run aggregate supply curve to the left (to $SRAS_2$). Eventually, a new long-run equilibrium (E_2) will be established at a higher price level (P_{110}) that is correctly anticipated by decision makers.

Thus, the increase in real GDP above the economy's long-run potential is only temporary. It will last only until there is an opportunity to alter the temporarily fixed resource prices (and interest rates) upward in light of the new stronger demand conditions. As this happens, profit margins return to their normal level, output recedes to the economy's long-run potential, and unemployment returns to its natural rate.

Because an increase in aggregate demand does not alter the economy's productive capacity, it cannot permanently expand output (beyond Y_f). The expansion in demand temporarily expands output, but over the long term its major effect will be higher prices (inflation).

REDUCTIONS IN AGGREGATE DEMAND

How would the goods and services market adjust to an unanticipated reduction in aggregate demand? For example, suppose decision makers become more pessimistic about the future or that an unexpected decline in income abroad reduces the demand for exports. **Exhibit 9–3** will help us analyze this issue.

Once again, we consider an economy that is in long-run equilibrium (E_1) at output Y_1 and price level P_{100} (part a). Long-run equilibrium is disturbed by the reduction in aggregate demand: the shift from AD_1 to AD_2. As the result of the decline in demand, businesses will be unable to sell Y_f units of output at the ini-

---

[3]Thoughtful students may wonder how output (and, by implication, the quantity of resources) can be increased, even temporarily, when real wages and resource prices more generally are declining. There are two reasons why this may be the case. First, in an inflationary environment, workers (and other resource suppliers) may be fooled, at least temporarily, by an increase in money wages (and resource prices) that is less rapid than the inflation rate. Responding to the higher money wages, workers may supply more labor even though their real wages have fallen. Although we have presented the analysis within the framework of a noninflationary environment, the basic linkage between real wages (costs) and SRAS still holds. A reduction in the real wage rate, even when it takes the form of a nominal wage increase that is less than the inflation rate, will reduce real costs, and thereby increase SRAS. Second, the resource base may temporarily expand in response to strong demand conditions because the cost of entering the labor force will decline during this boom phase of the business cycle. Potential new labor-force entrants will be able to find jobs quickly at this time. Thus, the size of the labor force will tend to grow rapidly during an economic expansion. Conversely, the labor force will tend to shrink (or grow less rapidly) during a business contraction, when the cost of entering the labor force will be high.

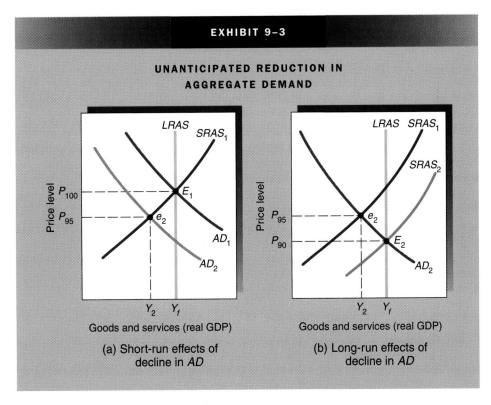

EXHIBIT 9–3

**UNANTICIPATED REDUCTION IN
AGGREGATE DEMAND**

(a) Short-run effects of
decline in *AD*

(b) Long-run effects of
decline in *AD*

*The short-run impact of an
unanticipated reduction in
aggregate demand (shift from
AD_1 to AD_2) will be a
decline in output to Y_2 and a
lower price level, P_{95} (a).
Temporarily, profit margins
will decline, output will fall,
and unemployment will rise
above its natural rate. In the
long run, weak demand and
excess supply in the resource
market will lead to lower
wage rates and resource
prices. This will reduce costs,
leading to an expansion in
short-run aggregate supply
(shift to $SRAS_2$ (b). However,
this method of restoring
equilibrium (E_2) may be both
highly painful and quite
lengthy.*

tial price level of P_{100}. In the short run, business firms will both reduce output
(to Y_2) and cut prices (to P_{95}) in response to the weak demand conditions.
Because many costs of business firms are temporarily fixed, profit margins will
decline. Predictably, firms will cut back on output and lay off workers, causing
the unemployment rate to rise. The actual rate of unemployment will rise above
the economy's natural rate of unemployment. Weak demand and excess supply
will be widespread in resource markets. These forces will place downward pressure on resource prices.

*If resource prices quickly adjust downward in response to weak demand and
rising unemployment, then the decline in output to Y_2 will be brief.* Lower
resource prices will reduce costs and thereby increase aggregate supply (shift to
$SRAS_2$). As part b of Exhibit 9–3 illustrates, the result will be a new long-run
equilibrium (E_2) at the economy's full employment output rate (Y_f) and a lower
price level (P_{90}).

Resource prices, though, may not adjust quickly. Long-term contracts and
uncertainty as to whether the weak demand conditions are merely temporary
will slow the adjustment process. In addition, individual workers and union officials may be highly reluctant to be the first to accept lower nominal wages. *If
resource prices are inflexible in a downward direction, as many economists
believe, the adjustment to a reduction in aggregate demand will be both lengthy
and painful. Prolonged periods of economic recession—below-capacity output
rates and abnormally high unemployment—may occur before the new long-run
equilibrium is restored.*

SHIFTS IN AGGREGATE SUPPLY

What happens if aggregate demand stays the same but aggregate supply changes? The answer to this question depends on whether the aggregate supply change is long run or short run. By a long-run change in aggregate supply, we mean a change in the economy's long-run production possibilities (sustainable potential rate of output). For example, the discovery of a lower-cost source of energy would cause a long-run change in aggregate supply. In such a situation, both long-run (*LRAS*) and short-run (*SRAS*) aggregate supply would change.

In contrast, changes that temporarily alter the productive capability of an economy will shift the *SRAS* curve, but not the *LRAS*. A drought in California would be an example of such a short-run change. The drought will hurt in the short run, but it will eventually end, and output will return to the long-run normal rate. Changes that are temporary in nature will shift only *SRAS*. Let us now consider the major factors capable of shifting the *LRAS* and *SRAS* schedules.

CHANGES IN LONG-RUN AGGREGATE SUPPLY

When constructing the *LRAS* curve, the (1) quantity of resources, (2) level of technology, and (3) institutional arrangements that influence the productivity and efficiency of resource use are held constant. Changes in any of these three determinants of output would cause the *LRAS* curve to shift.

As part a of **Exhibit 9–4** illustrates, changes that increase the economy's productive capacity—its maximum sustainable output at full employment—will

Such factors as an increase in the stock of capital or an improvement in technology will expand the economy's potential output and shift the LRAS to the right (a). Such factors as a reduction in resource prices, favorable weather, or a temporary decrease in the world price of an important imported resource would shift the SRAS to the right (b). Of course, changes that resulted in a decrease in either LRAS or SRAS would shift the respective schedules to the left.

EXHIBIT 9–4

SHIFTS IN AGGREGATE SUPPLY

(a) Increase in *LRAS*

(b) Increase in *SRAS*

shift the *LRAS* curve to the right. With the passage of time, net investment can expand the supply of physical capital, natural resources, and labor (human resources). Investment in physical capital can expand the supply of buildings, machines, and other physical assets. Search, discovery, and technological change can increase the supply of natural resources. With the passage of time, changes in population and labor-force participation may affect the supply of labor. Similarly, education, training, and skill-enhancing experience can improve the quality of the labor force, and thereby expand the supply of human resources.

Such increases in the economy's resource base will make it possible to produce *and sustain* a larger rate of output. Both the *LRAS* and *SRAS* curves will increase (shift to the right). On the other hand, a lasting reduction in the quantity (or quality) of resources will reduce both the current and long-term production capacity of the economy, shifting both *LRAS* and *SRAS* curves to the left.

Improvements in technology—the discovery of economical new products or less costly ways of producing goods and services—also permit us to squeeze a larger output from a specific resource supply. The enormous improvement in our living standards during the last 250 years is, to a large degree, the result of the discovery and adoption of technologically superior ways of transforming resources into goods and services. The development of the steam engine, and later the internal combustion engine, electricity, and nuclear power, has vastly altered our energy sources. The development of the railroad, the automobile, and the airplane dramatically changed both the cost and speed of transportation. More recently, the development of microcomputers, compact disc players, microwave ovens, video cameras and cassette players, and fax machines has vastly expanded our productive capacity and the ways in which we work and play. Improvements in technology enhance our **productivity** and thereby shift the *LRAS* curve to the right.

Finally, institutional changes may also influence the efficiency of resource use and thereby alter the *LRAS* schedule. Public policy increases aggregate supply when it enhances economic efficiency by providing, for example, public goods at a low cost, or police and legal protection against invasions by others, including polluters, who would use resources without the permission of their owners. In contrast, institutional arrangements sometimes promote waste and increase production costs. For example, studies indicate that minimum wage legislation reduces employment and restricts the opportunity for training, particularly in the case of youthful workers. Output restrictions accompanying agricultural price supports generally result in inefficient production methods and reductions in output. Such arrangements reduce aggregate supply.

The long-run growth trend of real GDP in the United States has been approximately 3 percent per year. This indicates that increases in the supply of resources and improvements in productivity have gradually expanded potential real output. Hence, the *LRAS* and *SRAS* curves have gradually drifted to the right at about a 3 percent annual rate, sometimes a little faster and sometimes a little slower.

Productivity
The average output produced per worker during a specific time period. It is usually measured in terms of output per hour worked.

CHANGES IN SHORT-RUN AGGREGATE SUPPLY

Changes can sometimes influence current output without altering the economy's long-run capacity. When this is the case, the *SRAS* curve will shift even though *LRAS* is unchanged. What types of changes would do this?

1. Changes in Resource Prices.   When we derived the *SRAS* schedule in Chapter 8, we noted explicitly that resource prices were being held constant. A change in resource prices will alter *SRAS* but not necessarily *LRAS*. A reduction in resource prices will lower costs and therefore shift the *SRAS* curve to the right, as illustrated in part b of Exhibit 9–4. However, unless the lower prices of resources reflect a long-term increase in the supply of resources, they will not alter *LRAS*. Conversely, an increase in the price of resources will increase costs, shifting the *SRAS* curve to the left. But unless the higher prices are the result of a long-term reduction in the size of the economy's resource base, they will not reduce *LRAS*.[4]

2. Changes in the Expected Rate of Inflation.   As we previously noted, a change in the expected rate of inflation will influence current aggregate demand *(AD)* in the goods and services market. It will also alter *SRAS*. If sellers in the goods and services market expect the future rate of inflation to increase, their incentive to sell at a given price in the *current* period will be reduced. After all, goods that they do not sell today will be available for sale in the future at what they anticipate will be even higher prices (as the result of the increase in the rate of inflation). Therefore, an increase in the expected rate of inflation will reduce the *current* supply of goods, thereby shifting the *SRAS* curve to the left. Of course, a reduction in the expected rate of inflation will have just the opposite impact. When sellers scale back their expectations concerning future price increases, their incentive to sell in the current period is increased. Why wait, if the price is not going to increase very much in the future? Thus, a reduction in the expected rate of inflation will increase short-run aggregate supply (shift *SRAS* to the right).

Supply shock
An unexpected event that temporarily either increases or decreases aggregate supply.

3. Supply Shocks.   Various supply shocks may also alter current output without directly affecting the productive capacity of the economy. **Supply shocks** are surprise occurrences that temporarily increase or decrease current output. For example, adverse weather conditions, a natural disaster, or a temporary increase in the price of imported resources (for example, oil in the case of the United States) will reduce current supply, even though they do not alter the economy's long-term production capacity. They will thus decrease short-run aggregate supply (shift *SRAS* to the left) without directly affecting *LRAS*. On the other hand, favorable weather conditions or temporary reductions in the world price of imported resources will increase current output, even though the economy's long-run capacity remains unchanged.

The accompanying Thumbnail Sketch summarizes the major factors influencing both long-run and short-run aggregate supply. Of course, macroeconomic policy may also influence aggregate supply. As in the case of aggregate demand, we will consider the impact of macroeconomic policy on supply in subsequent chapters.

---

[4]The definition of long-run aggregate supply helps clarify why a change in resource prices will affect short-run aggregate supply, but not long-run aggregate supply. When an economy is operating on its *LRAS* curve, the relationship between resource prices (costs) and product prices will reflect normal competitive market conditions. Because both profit and unemployment rates are at their normal levels, there is no tendency for resource prices to change relative to product prices when current output is equal to the economy's long-run potential. Therefore, when an economy is operating on its *LRAS* schedule, any change in resource prices will be matched by a proportional change in product prices, leaving the incentive to supply resources (and output) unchanged.

IMPACT OF CHANGES IN AGGREGATE SUPPLY

As we have previously stressed, the impact of changes in market conditions will be influenced by whether the changes are anticipated or unanticipated. When a change takes place slowly and predictably, decision makers will make choices based on the anticipation of the event. Such changes do not generally disrupt equilibrium conditions in markets.

ECONOMIC GROWTH AND ANTICIPATED SHIFTS IN LONG-RUN AGGREGATE SUPPLY

With the passage of time, net investment, improvements in technology, and institutional changes that improve the efficiency of resource use induce all of us to achieve and sustain larger rates of output. Such economic growth will shift the economy's *LRAS* curve to the right. When expansions in the productive capacity of an economy take place gradually, they will be anticipated by decision makers. Thus, they need not disrupt macroeconomic equilibrium.

Exhibit 9–5 illustrates the impact of economic growth on the goods and services market. Initially, the economy is in long-run equilibrium at price level P_1 and output Y_{f_1}. The growth expands the economy's potential output, shifting both the *LRAS* and *SRAS* curves to the right (to $LRAS_2$ and $SRAS_2$). Since these changes are gradual, decision makers have time to anticipate the changing market conditions and adjust their behavior accordingly.

When economic growth expands the economy's production possibilities, it will be possible to both produce and sustain a higher rate of real output (Y_{f_2}).

Here we illustrate the impact of economic growth due to capital formation or a technological advancement, for example. The full employment output of the economy expands from Y_{f_1} to Y_{f_2}. Thus, both LRAS and SRAS increase (to LRAS$_2$ and SRAS$_2$). A sustainable, higher level of real output and real income is the result. If the money supply is held constant, a new long-run equilibrium will emerge at a larger output rate (Y_{f_2}) and lower price level (P_2).

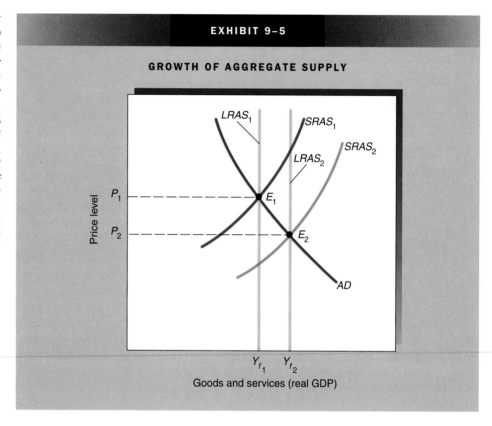

EXHIBIT 9–5

GROWTH OF AGGREGATE SUPPLY

The larger output rate can be achieved even while unemployment remains at its natural rate. If the money supply is held constant, the increase in aggregate supply will lead to a lower price level (P_2).

During the past 50 years, real output has expanded significantly in the United States and other countries. However, contrary to the presentation of Exhibit 9–5, the price level has generally not declined. This is because the monetary authorities have expanded the supply of money. As we will see later, an increase in the money supply stimulates aggregate demand (shifts *AD* to the right) and thereby pushes the price level upward.[5]

UNANTICIPATED CHANGES IN AGGREGATE SUPPLY

In addition to changes that can be anticipated, *un*anticipated disturbances will often influence the level of prices and output in the aggregate goods and services market. Changes in the factors that influence the *SRAS* curve are particularly likely to be unanticipated. By their nature, supply shocks are unpredictable. We now turn to an analysis of unexpected changes in aggregate supply.

---

[5]In subsequent chapters, we will explain how stable prices can be achieved as real output increases.

UNANTICIPATED INCREASES IN SRAS. What would happen if highly favorable weather conditions or a temporary decline in the world market price of oil or some other critical imported resource increased the current output and income of a nation? **Exhibit 9–6** addresses this issue. Because the temporarily favorable supply conditions cannot be counted on in the future, they will not directly alter the economy's long-term production capacity. Given that the favorable supply conditions are temporary, short-run aggregate supply will increase (to $SRAS_2$), while $LRAS$ will remain constant. Output (and income) will temporarily expand beyond the economy's full-employment constraints. This increase in current supply will place downward pressure on the price level.

How will households respond to their *temporarily* higher incomes? Recognizing that they will be unable to maintain their current high level of income, individuals will generally save a substantial portion of it for use at a future time that is not nearly so prosperous. This increased saving will expand the supply of loanable funds (shift to S_2 in part b of Exhibit 9–6), causing the real interest rate to decline. The lower real interest rate will stimulate investment and encourage the purchase of consumer durables, such as automobiles and appliances. In turn, the additional capital formation will expand the future resource base, which will make it possible to spread some of the benefits of the current high level of income into the future.

What would happen if the favorable conditions increasing supply reflected long-term factors? For example, suppose adoption of a new oil production technology resulted in a decline in the price of oil that was expected to be *permanent* rather than temporary. In this case, both the $LRAS$ and the $SRAS$ would increase (shift to the right). This case would parallel the analysis of Exhibit 9–5. A new long-run equilibrium at a higher output would result.

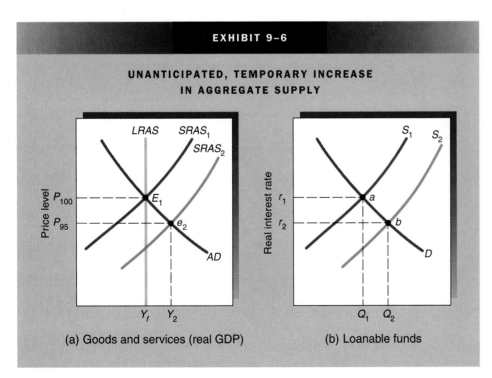

EXHIBIT 9–6

UNANTICIPATED, TEMPORARY INCREASE IN AGGREGATE SUPPLY

(a) Goods and services (real GDP)

(b) Loanable funds

Here we illustrate the impact of an unanticipated, but temporary, increase in aggregate supply such as might result from a bumper crop due to highly favorable weather conditions. The increase in aggregate supply (shift to $SRAS_2$) would lead to a lower price level (P_{95}) and an increase in current GDP to Y_2. Since the favorable supply conditions cannot be counted on in the future, the economy's long-run aggregate supply will not increase. Predictably, decision makers will save a large proportion of their temporarily higher real income, spreading the benefits into the future. Thus, the supply of loanable funds will increase. The real interest rate will fall to r_2, encouraging expenditures on interest-sensitive capital goods and consumer durables.

UNANTICIPATED DECREASES IN SRAS. In recent decades, the U.S. economy has been jolted by several unfavorable supply-side factors. In 1973, and again in 1979, the United States and other oil-importing countries were hit with sharply higher oil prices as the result of unstable conditions in the Middle East. During the summer of 1988, the most severe drought conditions in 50 years resulted in an extremely poor harvest in the U.S. agricultural belt. In August 1990, Iraq suddenly invaded Kuwait and threatened the oil fields of Saudi Arabia. Once again the world price of oil shot up, sharply increasing the cost of energy in the United States and other oil importing countries.

How do such unfavorable supply shocks influence macroeconomic markets? **Exhibit 9–7** illustrates the answer. Both an unfavorable harvest due to adverse weather conditions and a higher world price of oil will reduce the supply of resources (from S_1 to S_2 in part a) in the domestic market. Resource prices will rise to P'_r. In turn, the higher resource prices will reduce short-run aggregate supply (the shift from $SRAS_1$ to $SRAS_2$ in part b) in the goods and services market. Because supply shocks of this type are generally unanticipated, initially they will reduce output and place upward pressure on prices (the rate of inflation) in the goods and services market.

If an unfavorable supply shock is expected to be temporary, as will generally be the case for a bad harvest, long-run aggregate supply will be unaffected. After all, unfavorable growing conditions for a year or two do not represent a permanent change in climate. Therefore, as normal weather patterns return with the passage of time, both supply and price conditions in the resource market will return to normal, permitting the economy to return to long-run equilibrium at output Y_f.

Suppose there is an unanticipated reduction in the supply of resources, perhaps as the result of a crop failure or sharp increase in the world price of a major imported resource such as oil. Resource prices would rise from P_r to P'_r (a). The higher resource prices would shift the SRAS curve to the left. In the short run, the price level would rise to P_{110} (b), and output would decline to Y_2. What happens in the long run depends on whether the reduction in the supply of resources is temporary or permanent. If it is temporary, resource prices will fall in the future, permitting the economy to return to its intitial equilibrium (E_1). Conversely, if the reduced supply of resources is permanent, the productive potential of the economy will shrink (LRAS will shift to the left) and e_2 will become a long-run equilibrium.

EXHIBIT 9–7

EFFECTS OF ADVERSE SUPPLY SHOCK

(a) Resource market

(b) Goods and services (real GDP)

As in the case of the temporary increase in output, people will use the loanable funds market to smooth consumption in response to a temporary reduction in income. Believing that their lower incomes are temporary, households will reduce their current saving level (and dip into past savings) to maintain a current consumption level more consistent with their longer-term perceived opportunities. But when each household reduces its saving level, the supply of loanable funds decreases, causing an increase in the real interest rate. The higher real interest rate will allocate the available loanable funds to those willing to pay the most to maintain their current spending during the economic hard times. Of course, the higher real interest rate will also retard capital investment. A reduction in net investment and an accompanying decline in near-term economic growth are predictable side effects of a temporary reduction in aggregate supply.

When an adverse supply-side factor is more permanent, the long-run supply curve would also shift to the left. For example, an increase in the price of oil imports that is expected to prevail for the next several years would reduce long-run as well as short-run aggregate supply. Under these circumstances, the economy would have to adjust to a lower level of real output.

Regardless of whether the decline in aggregate supply is temporary or permanent, other things constant, the price level will rise. Similarly, output will decline, at least temporarily. Theory thus indicates that the adverse supply shocks of recent years contributed to the sluggish growth and price increases that accompanied the shocks.

DOES A MARKET ECONOMY HAVE A SELF-CORRECTING MECHANISM?

In a dynamic world of changing demand conditions and supply shocks, economic ups and downs are inevitable. Sometimes (during periods of economic boom) output will exceed the economy's long-run capacity, while at other times (during periods of recession) output will fall short of its potential. Are there market forces that will help stabilize an economy and cushion the effects of economic shocks? Does a market economy have a built-in mechanism that will prevent an economic downturn from plunging into a depression? There are three reasons to believe that the answer to both of these questions is yes.

1. Consumption demand is relatively stable over the business cycle. By far, consumption is the largest component of aggregate demand. As incomes fluctuate over the business cycle, there is good reason to expect that consumption spending will be considerably more stable than aggregate income. The **permanent income hypothesis,** developed by Nobel Prize–winning economist Milton Friedman, explains why. According to the permanent income hypothesis, the consumption of households is determined largely by their long-range expected, or permanent, income. Because temporary changes in income, such as those that occur over the business cycle, generally do not exert much impact on long-term

Permanent income hypothesis
The hypothesis that consumption depends on some measure of long-run expected (permanent) income rather than on current income.

expected income, these transitory increases or decreases do not exert a large impact on *current* consumption.[6]

Therefore, when the incomes of many households increase rapidly during an economic expansion, a substantial amount of the above-normal gains in income will be allocated to saving. (Remember "saving"—without an "s" on the end—is income that is not spent on current consumption.) As a result, consumption demand will increase less rapidly than income during the expansion phase of the business cycle. Similarly, when experiencing a temporary decline in income during a recession, many households will reduce their current saving (and draw on their prior savings) in order to maintain a level of current consumption more consistent with their long-term earnings prospects (expected income). Thus, consumer demand will increase less than income during a boom and decline by a smaller amount than income during a recession. This relative stability of the large consumption component will help stabilize aggregate demand over the business cycle.

2. Changes in real interest rates will help to stabilize aggregate demand and redirect economic fluctuations. Previously, we noted that sudden changes in the confidence of consumers and investors were a potential source of instability. However, interest-rate adjustments will, at least partially, offset disturbances arising from this source. Suppose consumers and investors, motivated by a burst of optimism, suddenly decide to spend more of their current income on goods and services. In order to do so, they will either have to reduce their saving or increase their borrowing. But these actions will reduce the supply of loanable funds relative to the demand. Predictably, the real rate of interest will rise. But the higher real interest rate will make current consumption and investment spending more expensive. Thus, the rising real interest rate will tend to offset the additional spending of the more optimistic consumers and investors, and thereby help to stabilize aggregate demand.

Interest-rate changes will also help to offset reductions in aggregate demand stemming from business pessimism. If pessimistic consumers and investors suddenly reduce their spending of current income, other things being constant, an increase in saving and/or a reduction in demand for loanable funds is implied. The supply of loanable funds will increase relative to the demand. Real interest rates will fall, which will stimulate additional current spending and help to offset the reduction in spending as the result of the increased pessimism. Thus, interest rate adjustments will counteract spending changes arising from expectations about the future and help keep the economy on a sustainable growth path.

---

[6]Perhaps a personal application will help explain why it is important to distinguish between temporary and long-term changes in income. Think for a moment how you would adjust your current spending on goods and services if an aunt left you a gift of $10,000 next month. No doubt you would spend some of the money almost immediately. Perhaps you would buy a new stereo or take a nice vacation. However, you would probably also use a significant portion of this temporary (one-time only) increase in income to pay bills or save for future education. Now, consider how you would alter your current spending if your aunt indicated you were to receive $10,000 per year for the next 30 years. Compared to the one-time gift, the annual gift for 30 years increases your long-term expected income by a much larger amount. In this case, you are likely to spend most of this year's $10,000 almost immediately. You might even borrow money to buy an automobile or make some major expenditures, and thereby expand your spending on goods and services this year by more than $10,000.

Perhaps even more important, changes in the real interest rate tend to redirect both recessions and booms. During an economic downturn, business demand for new investment projects and therefore loanable funds is generally quite weak. The weak demand, however, leads to a lower real interest rate. In turn, the lower interest rate both encourages current consumption and reduces the opportunity cost of investment projects, dampening the decline in aggregate demand. On the other hand, the real interest rate increases as many businesses borrow in order to undertake investment projects during an economic expansion. The higher real interest rate discourages both consumption and investment and thereby minimizes the increase in aggregate demand during a business expansion. Thus, the interest rate acts as a shock absorber helping both to stabilize aggregate demand and redirect economic fluctuations.

3. Changes in real resource prices will redirect economic fluctuations. Price adjustments in the resource market will also help keep the economy on an even keel. Exhibits 9–8 and 9–9 illustrate this point. **Exhibit 9–8** depicts the response of resource prices as market conditions change over the business cycle. When the current output of an economy is less than its full employment potential *(Yf)*, weak demand and slack employment in resource markets will place downward pressure on real resource prices. Under these conditions, real wages and other resource prices will decline (or increase at a very slow rate). In contrast, when an economy is operating beyond its full-employment capacity—that is, when unemployment is less than the natural unemployment rate—strong demand will push the real price of labor and other resources up rapidly.

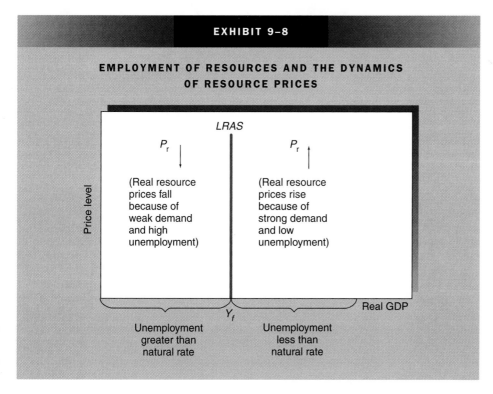

EXHIBIT 9–8

EMPLOYMENT OF RESOURCES AND THE DYNAMICS OF RESOURCE PRICES

When aggregate output is less than the economy's full employment potential (Y$_f$), the weak demand and slack employment in resource markets place downward pressure on wages and other resource prices (P$_r$). Conversely, when output exceeds Y$_f$, strong demand and tight market conditions result in rising real prices in resource markets.

A GRAPHIC PRESENTATION OF THE SELF-CORRECTING MECHANISM

Exhibit 9–9 provides a graphic presentation of the economy's self-corrective mechanism. It illustrates how changes in real interest rates and resource prices direct a market economy toward its full employment sustainable rate of output. Part a illustrates the supply and demand conditions of a goods and services market for an economy initially operating beyond full employment capacity, perhaps as the result of an unanticipated increase in aggregate demand. These are the conditions that one would expect when the expansionary phase of the business cycle results in an unsustainable economic boom. When these conditions are present, the strong demand for goods and services will lead to both a high level of employment and strong demand for investment funds by firms seeking to expand output capacity. As a result, the *actual rate* of unemployment will be

---

EXHIBIT 9–9

THE ECONOMY'S SELF-CORRECTIVE MECHANISM

(a) Output is initially greater than long-run potential

(b) Output is initially less than long-run capacity

In the short run, output may either exceed or fall short of the economy's full employment capacity (Y_f). If output is temporarily greater than the economy's potential (a), higher real interest rates and resource prices will lead to a lower but sustainable rate of output. The higher interest rates will reduce aggregate demand (shift from AD_1 to AD_2). At the same time, the higher resource prices will increase production costs and therefore reduce short-run aggregate supply (shift to $SRAS_2$ [a]). These forces will direct output toward its full employment potential.

When output is less than capacity (b), lower interest rates (reflecting the weak demand for investment funds) will stimulate aggregate demand (causing the shift to AD_2). In addition, lower resource prices (because of weak demand and abnormally high unemployment) will reduce production costs and thereby stimulate short-run aggregate supply (causing the shift to $SRAS_2$). Thus, output will move toward the economy's full employment capacity. However, this self-correction process may require considerable time. As we proceed, we will consider alternative methods of attaining full employment more rapidly.

less than the *natural rate*. However, the strong demand for both loanable funds (to finance investment) and resources will place upward pressure on real interest rates and resource prices, causing both to rise. The higher real interest rates will push up the cost of both investment projects and consumer durables, which will tend to retard the strong demand (shift from AD_1 to AD_2). At the same time, the rising cost of labor and other resources will push production costs upward, causing a reduction in short-run aggregate supply (shift to $SRAS_2$ in part a). As resource prices and costs rise, profit margins will decline to normal competitive rates, and output will recede to its long-run potential. *Eventually, these forces— the higher real interest rates and resource prices—will direct the output of an over-employed economy back to long-run capacity.*

Part b of Exhibit 9–9 illustrates an economy that is initially in a recession. The initial short-run equilibrium (e_1 of part b) takes place at a rate of output (Y_1) well below the economy's full employment capacity. When current output is less than an economy's long-run potential, the demand for investment funds will be extremely weak. This weak demand for loanable funds will result in lower real interest rates, which lead to an increase in aggregate demand (shift to AD_2 in part b). At the same time, the abnormally high unemployment (initially the *actual rate* exceeds the *natural rate*) and weak demand for resources will place downward pressure on real wages and resource prices. Eventually, the excess supply in resource markets will induce suppliers to accept lower wage rates and prices for other resources. This reduction in the real price of resources will reduce costs and lead to an increase in short-run aggregate supply (shift to $SRAS_2$ in part b). *With time, this combination of lower interest rates and resource prices will restore the economy's full employment rate of output (equilibrium E_2 of part b).*

THE BUSINESS CYCLE REVISITED

Our aggregate demand/aggregate supply *(AD/AS)* model enhances our understanding of economic instability. In a dynamic world of changing demand conditions and supply-side shocks, the model indicates that economic ups and downs will be present. Macroeconomic markets do not adjust instantaneously, and decision makers do not always accurately anticipate changes in the price level. Therefore, in the short run, output sometimes exceeds and sometimes falls short of its long-run potential. This is precisely what periods of economic boom and recession imply.

Exhibit 9–10 presents a picture of the economic fluctuations during the past 35 years. It is interesting to reflect on these cycles within the framework of our model. Periods of economic boom, such as were present in the late 1960s, 1973, 1978, and 1986–1989, imply that the *AD* and *SRAS* curves look something like the initial conditions (associated with e_1) of Exhibit 9–9 (part a). The intersection of the *AD* and *SRAS* curves would be at an output rate beyond the economy's full employment potential.

Conversely, when an economy is in a recession, such as was experienced in the United States during 1970, 1974–1975, 1979, 1982, and 1990–1991, conditions similar to the initial situation (associated with e_1) depicted by part b of Exhibit

Here we illustrate the periods of expansion and contraction (recession) since 1960. Note how the reductions in real GDP (shaded periods) in the top graph are associated with increases in the rate of unemployment (bottom graph). During and immediately following these recessionary periods, the actual rate of unemployment is substantially greater than the natural rate. Our analysis indicates that real interest rates and wages will rise during expansions and fall during recessions, and thereby help to stabilize the economy. Exhibit 9–11 presents data on this topic.

Source: Derived from computerized data supplied by FAME ECONOMICS.

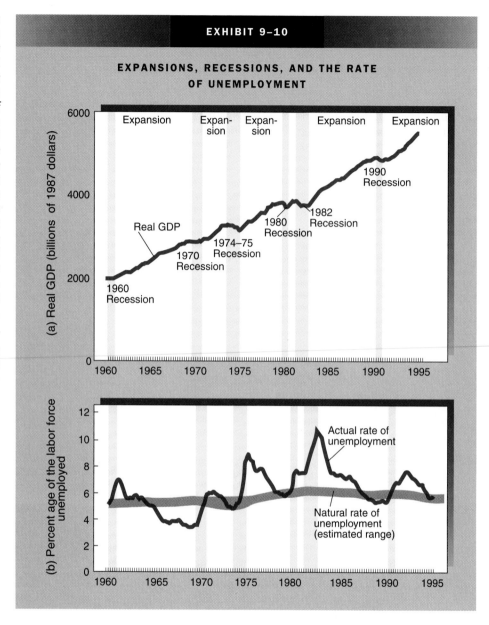

EXHIBIT 9–10

EXPANSIONS, RECESSIONS, AND THE RATE OF UNEMPLOYMENT

9–9 are implied. During a recession, the intersection of the *AD* and *SRAS* curves will be at an output rate that is less than full employment. Therefore, as part b of Exhibit 9–10 illustrates, the unemployment rate will fall below the natural rate during a period of economic boom and rise above the natural rate during recessions. (Note: Since the natural rate of unemployment is not directly observable, a range of estimates is provided in part b of Exhibit 9–10.)

However, our *(AD/AS)* model also indicates that market forces will redirect both an expansionary boom and a recessionary contraction. A boom will not continue to spiral upward. Neither will a contraction continue to plunge downward. During periods of weak resource demand, high unemployment, and output less than the economy's potential GDP, our analysis indicates that real interest rates and real wages will decline (or increase at a sluggish rate). The lower real interest rates will stimulate additional spending on interest-sensitive goods, like investment projects and consumer durables. At the same time, the lower resource prices (relative to the prices of goods and services) will reduce costs. These forces—additional spending due to lower interest rates and additional supply due to lower resource prices and costs—will eventually pull the economy out of the recession.

Conversely, the strong demand accompanying an economic boom will tend to increase both real interest rates and the real prices of resources. In turn, the rising interest rates and resource prices will dampen aggregate demand and increase costs, which will redirect the economy toward its maximum sustainable rate of output—the output associated with the full employment of resources.

Exhibit 9–11 presents data on the estimated *real* interest rate (Aaa corporate bond rate minus the annual rate of inflation during the last three years) for the peaks and troughs of recent business cycles. Data are also presented for the annual rate of change in the *real* hourly compensation of nonfarm employees during the periods of expansion and recession. As our analysis predicts, real interest rates increased during economic expansions and receded during recessionary periods. The estimated real interest rate declined to 1.4 percent

---

EXHIBIT 9–11

CHANGES IN REAL INTEREST RATES AND REAL WAGES OVER THE BUSINESS CYCLE

EXPANSIONS AND RECESSIONS	ESTIMATED REAL INTEREST RATE (AT PEAK FOR EXPANSION AND AT TROUGH FOR RECESSION)	ANNUAL PERCENT RATE OF CHANGE IN REAL COMPENSATION PER HOUR (NONFARM BUSINESS SECTOR)
1966–1969 Expansion (Peak, December 1969)	4.2	2.9
1970 Recession (Trough, November 1970)	1.4	1.0
1971–1973 Expansion (Peak, November 1973)	5.9	2.2
1974–1975 Recession (Trough, March 1975)	0.6	−0.4
1976–1979 Expansion (Peak, December 1979)	3.9	1.8
1979–1982 Recession (Trough, November 1982)	1.7	−1.0
1983–1990 Expansion (Peak, July 1990)	4.4	0.5
1990–1991 Recession (Trough, March 1991)	3.3	−1.1

Source: The real interest rate data were derived from the *Federal Reserve Bulletin*. The estimated real interest rate is the corporate bond Aaa interest rate minus the expected rate of inflation. The average rate of inflation during the last three years was used to estimate the expected rate of inflation. The real compensation data are from the Department of Labor, Bureau of Labor Statistics. The shaded areas indicate the periods of recession.

during the recession of 1970, down from 4.2 percent at the peak of the prior expansion. During the severe 1974–1975 recession, the real interest rate fell to 0.6 percent, compared to 5.9 percent at the peak of the 1971–1973 expansion. The real rate also declined during the 1979–1982 recessionary period and the 1990–1991 downturn.[7]

Real wages also followed the expected pattern. The hourly real compensation of nonfarm employees increased less rapidly during each recession than during the preceding (and subsequent) period of economic expansion. In fact, real hourly compensation actually declined during the 1974–1975, 1979–1982, and 1990–1991 recessions. Clearly, the observed pattern of change for both real interest rates and real wages is consistent with the view that they exert a stabilizing influence on the economy.

THE GREAT DEBATE: HOW RAPIDLY DOES THE SELF-CORRECTIVE MECHANISM WORK?

Following the Great Depression of the 1930s, many economists thought that market economies were inherently unstable. They argued that, unless monetary and fiscal policy were used to stimulate and guide the macroeconomy, prolonged recessions would result. Influenced by both a reevaluation of the 1930s and the experience of the last 50 years, most modern economists reject this stagnation view of market economies.[8] Today, there is a widespread consensus that market economies possess stabilizing forces.

What divides economists is disagreement about how rapidly the self-correcting forces work. This is a key issue. If the self-corrective process works slowly, then market economies will still experience prolonged periods of abnormally high unemployment and below-capacity output. Many economists believe this is the case. As a result, they have a good deal of confidence that discretionary monetary and fiscal policy can help promote stability and prosperity.

Conversely, other economists believe that the self-corrective mechanism of a market economy works reasonably well when monetary and fiscal policy follow a stable course. This latter group argues that macroeconomic policy mistakes are a major source of economic instability. Because of this, they favor policy rules, such as a constant growth rate in the supply of money and balanced budgets, rather than discretionary use of macroeconomic policy. We will return to this debate when we consider the impact of monetary and fiscal policy.

---

[7]Officially, there were two recessions during the 1979–1982 stagnation: one of approximately 6 months' duration in 1980 and a second lasting approximately 18 months during 1981–1982. Because the economy recovered only briefly from the initial recession, the entire period was one economic stagnation.

[8]A detailed analysis of the forces causing and prolonging the Great Depression is presented in Chapter 15.

LOOKING AHEAD

Modern macroeconomics reflects an evolutionary process. The Great Depression and the accompanying prolonged unemployment exerted an enormous impact on macroeconomics. John Maynard Keynes, the brilliant English economist, developed a theory that sheds light on the operation of an economy experiencing high rates of unemployment. The next chapter focuses on the Keynesian theory.

CHAPTER SUMMARY

1. It is important to distinguish between anticipated and unanticipated changes. Anticipated changes are foreseen by decision makers, who can therefore adjust their choices accordingly. In contrast, unanticipated events catch people by surprise, not allowing them to make such adjustments until after the fact.

2. An increase in aggregate demand involves a shift of the entire AD schedule to the right. Other than policy, major factors causing an increase in aggregate demand are (a) an increase in real wealth, (b) a lower real interest rate, (c) increased optimism on the part of businesses and consumers, (d) an increase in the expected rate of inflation, (e) higher real income abroad, and (f) a reduction in a nation's exchange rate. Conversely, if these factors change in the opposite direction, a decrease in aggregate demand will result.

3. When the long-run equilibrium of an economy is disrupted by an unanticipated increase in aggregate demand, output will temporarily increase beyond the economy's long-run capacity and unemployment will fall below its natural rate. However, as decision makers adjust to the increase in demand, resource prices will rise and output will recede to long-run capacity. In the long run, the major impact of the increase in aggregate demand will be a higher price level (inflation).

4. An unanticipated reduction in aggregate demand will temporarily reduce output below capacity and push unemployment above its natural rate. Eventually, unemployment and excess supply in resource markets will reduce wage rates and resource prices. Costs will decline, and output will return to its long-run potential. However, if wages and prices are inflexible downward, less-than-capacity output and abnormally high unemployment may persist for a substantial period of time.

5. Changes that alter the economy's maximum sustainable output will shift the LRAS curve. The following factors will increase LRAS: (a) increases in the supply of labor and capital resources, (b) improvements in technology and productivity, and (c) institutional changes improving the efficiency of resource use.

6. In the short run, output may change as the result of temporary factors that do not directly alter the economy's long-run capacity. The major factors leading to an increase in the short-run aggregate supply (a shift of the SRAS curve to the right) are (a) a reduction in resource prices, (b) a decline in the expected rate of future inflation, and (c) favorable supply shocks resulting from such factors as good weather or a reduction in the world price of a vital imported resource. Conversely, if these factors changed in the opposite direction, SRAS would decline (shift to the left).

7. An increase in output due to economic growth (an increase in the economy's production capacity) will increase both short-run and long-run aggregate supply. The economy will now be able to produce and sustain a larger output level. If the supply of money is constant, a lower price level will result.

8. When an economy in long-run equilibrium experiences an unanticipated favorable supply shock, output (and income) will temporarily rise above capacity and prices will decline. A lower real interest rate is also a predicted result, since a large amount of a temporary increase in income will flow into saving. The lower real interest rate will stimulate capital formation and, other things constant, will lead to more rapid short-run economic growth.

9. An adverse supply shock (decrease in SRAS) will reduce output and increase the price level. If the reduction in income is expected to be temporary, people will increase their borrowing (and reduce their saving) to maintain a consumption level more consistent with their longer-term income. As a result, the real interest rate will rise. Many economists think adverse supply shocks, particularly the sharp increase in the price of imported oil, contributed to the slow rate of growth and rapid increase in the price level during the 1970s.

10. As output fluctuates over the business cycle, the stability of the large consumption component, along with changes in interest rates and resource prices, will help keep a market economy on track. When output and employment exceed the economy's full employment capacity, real interest rates and resource prices (including real wages) will rise. The higher interest rates will restrain demand and the higher resource prices will increase costs. These forces will direct the economy toward its sustainable full employment rate of output. Similarly, when current output is less than the economy's potential GDP, lower real interest rates and falling real resource prices (and wages) will stimulate demand and reduce costs and thereby direct output toward the economy's potential capacity. These forces provide the economy with a self-corrective mechanism, capable of directing it toward the full employment rate of output.

11. Many economists believe the economy's self-corrective mechanism works quite slowly and that discretionary monetary and fiscal policy changes are necessary to

minimize economic instability. Others believe that the self-corrective mechanism works reasonably well and that discretionary policy is likely to do more harm than good.

CRITICAL ANALYSIS QUESTIONS

*1. Explain how and why each of the following factors would influence current aggregate demand in the United States:
   a. Increased fear of recession
   b. Increased fear of inflation
   c. Rapid growth of real income in Japan and Western Europe
   d. A reduction in the real interest rate
   e. A higher price level (be careful)

*2. Indicate how each of the following would influence U.S. aggregate supply in the short run:
   a. An increase in real wage rates
   b. A severe freeze that destroys half the orange trees in Florida
   c. An increase in the expected rate of inflation in the future
   d. An increase in the world price of oil, a major import
   e. Abundant rainfall during the growing season of agricultural states

3. Suppose that the key macroeconomic markets are initially in long-run equilibrium. How will an unanticipated reduction in aggregate demand affect real output, employment, and the price level in the short run? In the long run?

*4. When current output is less than full employment capacity, explain how the self-correcting mechanism will direct output toward the economy's long-run potential. Can you think of any reason why this mechanism might not work? Discuss.

5. What is the difference between an anticipated and an unanticipated increase in aggregate demand? Provide an example of each. Which is most likely to result in a temporary spurt in the growth of real output?

*6. Assume that both union and management representatives agree to wage increases because of their expectation that prices will rise 10 percent during the next year. Explain why the unemployment rate will probably increase if the actual rate of inflation next year is only 3 percent.

7. During 1980–1985, the exchange-rate value of the dollar increased sharply. How did this change influence aggregate demand, output, and the inflation rate during the 1980–1985 period? During 1986–1988, the exchange-rate value of the dollar fell. What impact did this decline have on aggregate demand, output, and inflation?

*8. When the actual output exceeds the long-run potential of the economy, how will the self-correcting mechanism direct the economy to long-run equilibrium? Why can't the above-normal output be maintained?

*9. Are the real wages of workers likely to increase more rapidly when the unemployment rate is high or when it is low? Why?

10. Suppose consumers and investors suddenly become more pessimistic about the future and therefore decide to reduce their consumption and investment spending. How will a market economy adjust to this increase in pessimism? What will happen to the real rate of interest?

11. "Unemployment benefits should replace 100 percent of an employee's earnings from his or her previous job when the employee is terminated or laid off through no fault of his or her own." Evaluate this statement. Do you think the idea expressed is a good one? How would such a practice affect the search time of the unemployed workers? What impact would it have on the unemployment rate?

*12. Suppose that an unexpectedly rapid growth in real income abroad leads to a sharp increase in the demand for U.S. exports. What impact will this change have on the price level, output, and employment in the short run? In the long run?

13. If the real interest rate increases, how will this affect the incentive of consumers and investors to purchase goods and services? How will it affect the *AD* curve?

14. Construct the *AD*, *SRAS*, and *LRAS* curves for an economy experiencing (a) full employment, (b) an economic boom, and (c) a recession.

15. As the result of changing international conditions, there was a decline in real national defense expenditures of approximately 15 percent between 1989 and 1991. What is the expected impact of this decline in defense expenditures on aggregate demand and output in the short run? If the United States is able to spend less on national defense in the future, how will this factor influence the standard of living of Americans? Discuss.

16. Consider an economy with the following aggregate demand (AD) and aggregate supply (AS) schedules. These schedules reflect the fact that, prior to the period in question, decision makers entered into contracts and made choices anticipating that the price level would be P_{105}.

AD_{105} (IN TRILLIONS)	PRICE LEVEL	$SRAS_{105}$ (IN TRILLIONS)
$5.1	95	$3.5
4.9	100	3.8
4.7	105	4.2
4.5	110	4.5
4.3	115	4.8

   a. Indicate the quantity of GDP that will be produced and the price level that will emerge during this period.
   b. Is the economy in long-run equilibrium? Why or why not?
   c. How will the unemployment rate during the cur-

rent period compare with this economy's natural rate of unemployment?

d. What will tend to happen to resource prices in the future? How will this affect the equilibrium rate of output?

e. Will the rate of GDP produced during this period be sustainable into the future? Why or why not?

17. Suppose that the price level that emerges from aggregate demand and aggregate supply conditions during the current period is lower than decision makers had anticipated.

a. Construct *AD*, *SRAS*, and *LRAS* schedules that reflect these conditions.

b. During the current period, how will the actual rate of unemployment compare with the natural rate? How will actual output compare with the economy's potential?

c. As the result of the current conditions, what will tend to happen to resource prices and interest rates? Why?

---

*Asterisk denotes questions for which answers are given in Appendix B.

CHAPTER TEN

KEYNESIAN FOUNDATIONS OF MODERN MACROECONOMICS

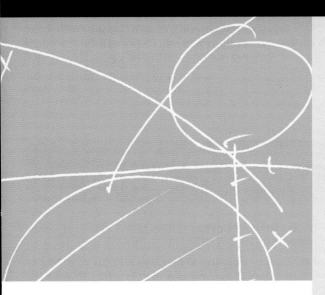

CHAPTER FOCUS

■ What are the major components of the Keynesian model? What is the major factor that causes the level of output and employment to change?

■ What was Keynes's explanation for the high rates of unemployment that persisted during the Great Depression?

■ What determines the equilibrium level of output in the Keynesian model?

■ What is the multiplier principle? Why is it important?

■ Why do Keynesians believe market economies experience business instability?

I believe myself to be writing a book on economic theory which will largely revolutionize—not, I suppose, at once but in the course of the next ten years—the way the world thinks about economic problems.

JOHN MAYNARD KEYNES[1]

---

[1]Letter from John Maynard Keynes to George Bernard Shaw, New Year's Day, 1935.

M odern macroeconomics is the product of an evolutionary process. Prior to the Great Depression of the 1930s, most economists thought market adjustments would automatically guide an economy to full employment within a relatively brief time. The presence of double-digit unemployment rates throughout most of the 1930s undermined the credibility of this view. The experience of the Great Depression also led to the development of a new theory, one capable of explaining the prolonged unemployment of the period.

The new theory, developed by the English economist John Maynard Keynes (pronounced "canes") provided a reasonable explanation for the widespread and prolonged unemployment of the 1930s.[2] It also exerted an enormous influence on the development of macroeconomics. For three decades following the Second World War, Keynesian economics represented the core of macroeconomics. Several basic concepts and much of the terminology we use today can be traced to Keynes. Modern macroeconomics is built on the foundation of Keynesian analysis. This chapter presents the Keynesian view and illuminates its influence on modern macroeconomics theory.

KEYNESIAN EXPLANATION OF THE GREAT DEPRESSION

Classical economists
Economists from Adam Smith to the time of Keynes who focused their analyses on economic efficiency and production. With regard to business instability, they thought market prices and wages would decline during a recession quickly enough to bring the economy back to full employment within a short period of time.

Say's Law
The view that production creates its own demand. Demand will always be sufficient to purchase the goods produced because the income payments to the resource suppliers will equal the value of the goods produced.

Mainstream economists prior to the time of Keynes (often called **classical economists**) emphasized the importance of aggregate supply and paid little heed to aggregate demand. The lack of interest in demand issues by classical economists stemmed from their adherence to **Say's Law,** named for nineteenth-century French economist J. B. Say. According to Say's Law, a general overproduction of goods relative to total demand is impossible, since supply (production) creates its own demand. The reasoning here is that the purchasing power necessary to buy (demand) desired products is generated by production. A farmer's supply of wheat generates income to meet the farmer's demand for shoes, clothes, automobiles, and other desired goods. Similarly, the supply of shoes generates the purchasing power with which shoemakers (and their employees) demand the farmer's wheat and other desired goods.

Of course, producers might produce too much of some goods and not enough of others. But the pricing system would correct such imbalances. The prices of goods in excess supply would fall, and the prices of products in excess demand would rise. According to the classical view, a *general* overproduction of goods was impossible, because the production of the goods would always generate a demand that was sufficient to purchase the goods produced.

Prior to the Great Depression, the classical view seemed reasonable. But the depth and the prolonged duration of the decline during the 1930s challenged its validity and provided the foundation for what we now refer to as Keynesian economics. For those who are familiar only with the relative stability of the past five decades, the depth of the economic decline during the 1930s is difficult to

---

[2]See the classic book, John Maynard Keynes, *The General Theory of Employment, Interest, and Money* (London: Macmillan, 1936), for the presentation of this theory.

JOHN MAYNARD KEYNES (1883–1946)

Keynes might properly be referred to as the "father of macroeconomics." The son of a prominent nineteenth-century economist (John Neville Keynes), he earned a degree in mathematics from King's College, Cambridge, where he would later return and spend most of his career as an economist.

His *General Theory of Employment, Interest, and Money*, published in 1936, revolutionized the way that economists think about macroeconomics. This work, written in the midst of the Great Depression, provided both a plausible explanation for the massive unemployment and a strategy for ending it. Keynes's message married an idea with a moment in time.

Keynes's work was both path-breaking and controversial. His view that governments should run budget deficits during a recession in order to stimulate demand and direct the economy back to full employment challenged the entrenched views of both policymakers and classical economists. Debate concerning the impact of budget deficits continues to this day.

Keynes correctly anticipated that his ideas would, with the passage of time, exert a powerful influence (see the chapter's opening quote). By the 1950s the Keynesian analysis was dominant in academic circles and by the 1960s it formed the foundation for the macroeconomic policy of most Western nations. Keynes died rather suddenly in 1946, so he did not live to observe the enormous impact of his ideas on public policy.

The economic events of the 1970s tempered the confidence of macroeconomists in the basic analysis of Keynes. Nevertheless, his imprint is sure to endure. He revolutionized our way of thinking about macroeconomic issues.

comprehend. *Real* GDP in the United States fell by more than 30 percent between 1930 and 1933. In 1933, 25 percent of the U.S. labor force was unemployed. The depressed conditions continued throughout the decade. In 1939, a decade after the plunge began, per capita income was still nearly 10 percent less than in 1929. Other industrial countries experienced similar conditions.

KEYNESIAN VIEW OF SPENDING AND OUTPUT

Keynes developed a theory that provided an explanation for prolonged depressed conditions like those of the 1930s. Rejecting the classical view, Keynes offered a completely new concept of output determination. *Keynes believed that spending induced business firms to supply goods and services. From this, he argued that, if total spending fell (as it might, for example, if consumers and investors became pessimistic about the future or tried to save more of their current income), then business firms would respond by cutting back production. Less spending would thus lead to less output.*

If unemployment was abnormally high, classical economists believed that wages would fall, reducing costs and lowering prices until the excess supply of labor was eliminated. Keynes and his followers disagreed. They argued that wages and prices were highly inflexible, particularly in a downward direction. Even when demand was weak, Keynesians believed that large business firms and powerful trade unions would resist price and wage reductions. Thus, they rejected the view that flexible wages and prices would automatically direct an economy toward full employment.

Keynes also introduced a different concept of equilibrium and a different mechanism for its achievement. *In the Keynesian view, equilibrium takes place when the level of total spending is equal to current output. When this is the case, producers will have no reason to either expand or contract output.* Keynesians believe that changes in output rather than changes in prices direct the economy to equilibrium. If total spending is less than full-employment output, output will be cut back to the level of spending and, most significantly, it will remain there until the level of spending changes. Therefore, if total spending is deficient, equilibrium output will be less than full-employment output, and high rates of unemployment will continue. This is precisely what Keynes believed was happening during the 1930s.

The message of Keynes can be summarized as follows: Businesses will produce only the quantity of goods and services they believe consumers, investors, governments, and foreigners will plan to buy. If these planned aggregate expenditures are less than the economy's full-employment output, output will fall short of its potential. When aggregate expenditures are deficient, there are no automatic forces capable of assuring full employment. Prolonged unemployment will persist. Against the background of the Great Depression, this was a compelling argument.

BASIC KEYNESIAN MODEL

The key to the basic Keynesian model is the concept of *planned* aggregate expenditures. As with aggregate demand, the four components of planned aggregate expenditures are consumption, investment, government purchases, and net exports. Before we develop the Keynesian model, however, it's useful to make a few assumptions in order to simplify the analysis. First, as with the *AD/AS* model developed in Chapters 8 and 9, we will assume there is a specific full-employment level of output. Only the natural rate of unemployment is present when full-employment capacity is attained. Second, following in the Keynesian tradition, we will assume that wages and prices are completely inflexible until full employment is reached. Once full employment is achieved, though, additional demand will lead only to higher prices. Strictly speaking, these polar assumptions will not hold in the real world. They may, however, approximate conditions in the short run. Finally, we will continue to assume that the government's taxing, spending, and monetary policies are constant.

PLANNED CONSUMPTION EXPENDITURES

The most important component of planned aggregate expenditures is *planned* aggregate consumption. Keynes believed that current income is the primary determinant of consumption expenditures. As he stated:

Men are disposed, as a rule and on the average, to increase their consumption as their income increases, but not by as much as the increase in their income.[3]

According to Keynes, disposable income is by far the major determinant of current consumption. If disposable income increases, consumers will increase their planned expenditures.

This positive relationship between consumption spending and disposable income is called the **consumption function. Exhibit 10–1** illustrates this relationship for an economy. At low levels of aggregate income (less than $4 trillion), the consumption expenditures of households will exceed their disposable income. When income is low, households dissave—they either borrow or draw from their past savings to purchase consumption goods. Because consumption does not increase as rapidly as income, the slope of the consumption function will be less than 1. So the consumption schedule is flatter than the 45-degree line of Exhibit 10–1. As income increases, household aggregate income eventually equals and exceeds current consumption. For aggregate incomes above $4 trillion, saving increases as income rises.

Consumption function
A fundamental relationship between disposable income and consumption, in which, as disposable income increases, current consumption expenditures rise, but by a smaller amount than the increase in income.

PLANNED INVESTMENT EXPENDITURES

Investment encompasses (1) expenditures on fixed assets, such as buildings and machines, and (2) changes in the inventories of raw materials and final products

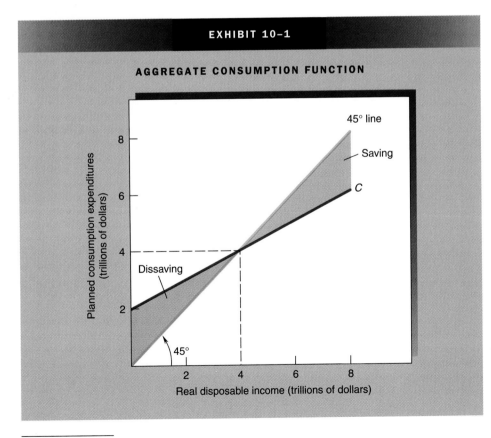

EXHIBIT 10–1

AGGREGATE CONSUMPTION FUNCTION

The Keynesian model assumes that there is a positive relationship between consumption and income. However, as income increases, consumption expands by a smaller amount. Thus, the slope of the consumption function (line C) is less than 1 (less than the slope of the 45-degree line).

---

[3]Keynes, *The General Theory of Employment*, p. 96.

Autonomous expenditures
Expenditures that do not vary with the level of income. They are determined by factors (such as business expectations and economic policy) that are outside the basic income-expenditure model.

not yet sold. Keynes argued that, in the short run, investment was best viewed as an **autonomous expenditure,** one independent of income. In the Keynesian model, planned investment does not change with the level of income. Instead, investment is primarily a function of current sales relative to plant capacity, expected future sales, and the interest rate. Changes in these latter factors would alter investment—they would cause the entire schedule to shift either upward or downward. But when focusing on the forces pushing an economy toward an equilibrium level of output, the basic Keynesian model postulates a constant level of planned investment expenditures.

PLANNED GOVERNMENT EXPENDITURES

As with investment, planned government expenditures in the basic Keynesian model are assumed to be independent of income. These expenditures need not change with the level of income. As we will explain later, Keynesians believe that government expenditures are best viewed as a policy variable determined by the political process. Governments can, and often do, spend more than they receive in taxes. Perceiving government expenditures as autonomous of income allows us to focus more clearly on the stability characteristics of a private economy. Later, we will analyze how changes in government expenditures influence output and employment within the framework of the Keynesian aggregate expenditures model.

PLANNED NET EXPORTS

Exports are dependent on spending choices and income levels abroad. These decisions are, by and large, unaffected by changes in a nation's domestic income level. Therefore, as **Exhibit 10–2** illustrates, exports remain constant when income changes. In contrast, increases in domestic income will induce consumers to purchase more foreign as well as domestic goods. So the level of imports increases as income rises.

Because exports remain constant and imports increase as aggregate income expands, net exports will decline as income expands (see Exhibit 10–2). Accordingly, the Keynesian model postulates a negative relationship between income and net exports.

PLANNED VERSUS ACTUAL EXPENDITURES

It is important to distinguish between planned and actual expenditures. Planned expenditures reflect the choices of consumers, investors, governments, and foreigners, *given their expectations as to the choices of other decision makers.* Planned expenditures, though, need not equal actual expenditures. If purchasers spend a different amount on goods and services than business firms anticipate, the firms will experience unplanned changes in inventories. When this is the case, actual investment will differ from planned investment because inventories are a component of investment in our national-income accounts.

Consider what would happen if the planned expenditures of consumers, investors, governments, and foreigners on goods and services were less than what business firms thought they would be. If this were the case, business firms

EXHIBIT 10-2

INCOME AND NET EXPORTS

TOTAL OUTPUT (REAL GDP IN BILLIONS)	PLANNED EXPORTS (BILLIONS)	PLANNED IMPORTS (BILLIONS)	PLANNED NET EXPORTS (BILLIONS)
$6,600	$350	$150	$200
6,900	350	200	150
7,200	350	250	100
7,500	350	300	50
7,800	350	350	0

Because exports are determined by income abroad, they are constant at $350 billion. Imports increase as domestic income expands. Thus, planned net exports fall as domestic income increases.

would be unable to sell as much of their current output as they had anticipated. Their *actual* inventories would increase as they unintentionally made larger inventory investments than they *planned*. On the other hand, consider what would happen if purchasers bought more goods and services than businesses expected. The unexpected brisk sales would draw down inventories and result in less inventory investment than business firms planned. In this case, *actual* inventory investment would be less than they *planned*.

Actual and *planned* expenditures are equal only when purchasers buy the quantity of goods and services that business decision makers anticipated they would purchase. Only then will the plans of buyers and sellers in the goods and services market harmonize.

KEYNESIAN EQUILIBRIUM

Equilibrium is present in the Keynesian model when planned aggregate expenditures equal the value of current output. When this is the case, businesses are able to sell the total amount of goods and services that they produce. There are no unexpected changes in inventories. Thus, producers have no incentive to either expand or contract their output during the next period. In equation form, Keynesian macroequilibrium is attained when:

$$\underbrace{\frac{\text{Total output}}{\text{Real GDP}}}_{} = \underbrace{\frac{\text{Planned } C + I + G + X}{\text{Planned aggregate expenditures}}}_{}$$

KEYNESIAN EQUILIBRIUM— A NUMERIC EXAMPLE

As an example of Keynesian macroeconomic equilibrium, let's take a look at the hypothetical economy described by **Exhibit 10–3.** To begin, let's focus on columns 1 and 2. At what level of total output is this economy in Keynesian macroeconomic equilibrium? Stop now and attempt to figure out the answer.

Note: All figures are in billions of dollars. Column 2 equals the sum of columns 3 + 4 + 5.

EXHIBIT 10-3

EXAMPLE OF KEYNESIAN MACROECONOMIC EQUILIBRIUM

TOTAL OUTPUT (REAL GDP) (1)	PLANNED AGGREGATE EXPENDITURES (2)	PLANNED CONSUMPTION (3)	PLANNED INVESTMENT + GOVERNMENT EXPENDITURES (4)	PLANNED NET EXPORTS (5)	TENDENCY OF OUTPUT (6)
$6,600	$6,900	$5,000	$1,700	$200	Expand
6,900	7,050	5,200	1,700	150	Expand
7,200	7,200	5,400	1,700	100	Equilibrium
7,500	7,350	5,600	1,700	50	Contract
7,800	7,500	5,800	1,700	0	Contract

The answer is $7,200 billion, because only there is total output exactly equal to planned aggregate expenditures. When real GDP is equal to $7,200 billion, the planned expenditures of consumers, investors, governments, and foreigners (net exports) are precisely equal to the value of the output produced by business firms. To see this, note that only at $7,200 billion do columns 3 + 4 + 5 equal column 1. Because of this equality, the spending plans of purchasers mesh with the production plans of business decision makers. Given this balance, there is no reason for producers to change their plans.

What happens at other output levels? At any output other than equilibrium, the plans of producers and purchasers will conflict. If output is $6,900 billion, for example, planned aggregate expenditures will be $7,050 billion, $150 billion more than the current level of output. When expenditures (purchases) exceed output, inventories will decline. Under these circumstances, firms will expand their output in order to rebuild their inventories to normal levels. Therefore, when aggregate expenditures exceed current output, there will be a tendency for output to expand and move toward equilibrium.

At $7,500 billion, output will be greater than planned aggregate expenditures, and unwanted inventories will accumulate. Of course, business firms will not continue to produce goods they cannot sell, so they will reduce production during the subsequent period, moving the economy toward equilibrium.

EQUILIBRIUM AT LESS THAN FULL EMPLOYMENT

Because Keynesian equilibrium is dependent on equality between planned aggregate expenditures and output, it need not take place at full employment. If an economy is in Keynesian equilibrium, there will be no tendency for output to change even if output is well below full employment capacity.

To see this in our example, assume that full employment is at an output of $7,500 billion, in Exhibit 10–3. Given the current planned spending, the economy will fail to achieve full employment. The rate of unemployment will be high. In the Keynesian model, neither wages nor other resource prices will decline in the face of abnormally high unemployment and excess capacity. Therefore, output will remain at less than the full-employment rate as long as insufficient spending prevents the economy from reaching its full potential.

This is precisely what Keynes thought was happening during the Great Depression. He believed that Western economies were in equilibrium at an employment rate substantially below capacity. Unless aggregate expenditures increased, therefore, the prolonged unemployment had to continue—as it did throughout that period.

KEYNESIAN EQUILIBRIUM— A GRAPHIC PRESENTATION

The Keynesian analysis is presented graphically in **Exhibit 10–4,** where planned aggregate consumption, investment, government, and net export expenditures are measured on the Y-axis and total output is measured on the X-axis. The 45-degree line that extends from the origin maps out all the points where aggregate expenditures (AE) are equal to total output (GDP).

Because aggregate expenditures equal total output for all points along the 45-degree line, the line maps out all possible equilibrium income levels. As long

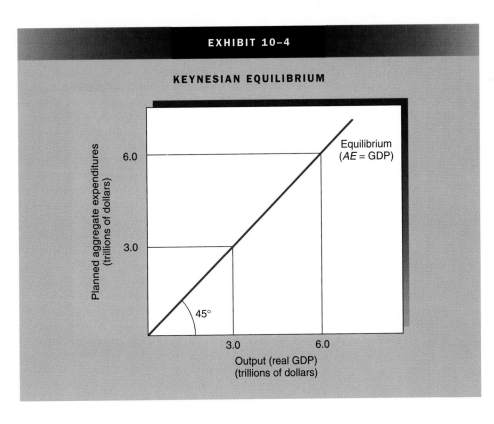

EXHIBIT 10–4

KEYNESIAN EQUILIBRIUM

Planned aggregate expenditures (trillions of dollars)

6.0

3.0

45°

Equilibrium (AE = GDP)

3.0   6.0

Output (real GDP) (trillions of dollars)

Aggregate expenditures will be equal to total output for all points along a 45-degree line from the origin. The 45-degree line thus maps out potential equilibrium levels of output for the Keynesian model.

as the economy is operating at less than its full-employment capacity, producers will produce any output along the 45-degree line they believe purchasers will buy. Producers, though, will supply a level of output only if they believe planned expenditures will be large enough to purchase it. Depending on the level of aggregate expenditures, each point along the 45-degree line is a potential equilibrium.

Using the data of Exhibit 10–3, **Exhibit 10–5** graphically depicts the Keynesian equilibrium. The $C + I + G + X$ line indicates the total planned expenditures of consumers, investors, governments, and foreigners (net exports) at each income level. *Reflecting the consumption function,* the aggregate expenditure (AE) line is flatter than the 45-degree line. Remember, as income rises, consumption also increases, but by less than the increase in income. Therefore, as income expands, total expenditures increase by less than the expansion in income.

The equilibrium level of output will be $7.2 trillion, the point at which the total expenditures (measured vertically) are just equal to total output (measured horizontally). Of course, the aggregate expenditures function $C + I + G + X$ will cross the 45-degree line at the $7.2 trillion equilibrium level of output.

As long as the aggregate expenditures function remains unchanged, no other level of output can be sustained. When total output exceeds $7.2 trillion (for example, $7.5 trillion), the aggregate expenditure line lies below the 45-degree line. Remember that, when the $C + I + G + X$ line is less than the 45-degree line, total spending is less than total output. Unwanted inventories will then

Here the data of Exhibit 10–3 are presented within the Keynesian graphic framework. The equilibrium level of output is $7.2 trillion because planned expenditures (C + I + G + X) are just equal to output at that level of income. At a lower level of income, $6.9 trillion, for example, unplanned inventory reduction would cause business firms to expand output (right-pointing arrow). Conversely, at a higher income level, such as $7.5 trillion, accumulation of inventories would lead to a reduction in future output (left-pointing arrow). Given current aggregate expenditures, only the $7.2 trillion output could be sustained. Note the $7.2 trillion equilibrium income level is less than the economy's potential of $7.5 trillion.

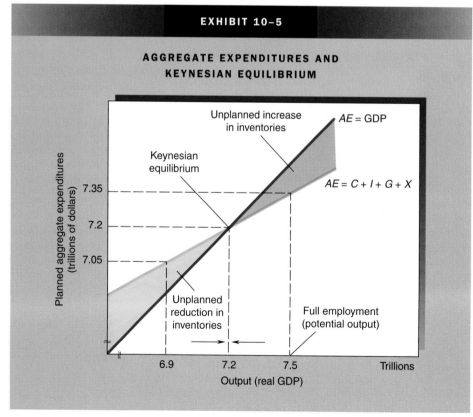

EXHIBIT 10–5

AGGREGATE EXPENDITURES AND KEYNESIAN EQUILIBRIUM

accumulate, leading businesses to reduce their future production. Employment will decline. Output will fall back from $7.5 trillion to the equilibrium level of $7.2 trillion. Note that it is changes in output and employment, not price changes, that restore equilibrium in the Keynesian model.

In contrast, if total output is temporarily below equilibrium, there is a tendency for income to rise. Suppose output is temporarily at $6.9 trillion. At that output level, the $C + I + G + X$ function lies above the 45-degree line. Aggregate expenditures exceed aggregate output. Businesses are selling more than they currently produce. Their inventories are falling. Excess demand is present. They will react to this state of affairs by hiring more workers and expanding production. Income will rise to the $7.2 trillion equilibrium level. Only at the equilibrium level, the point at which the $C + I + G + X$ function crosses the 45-degree line, will the spending plans of consumers, investors, and governments sustain the existing output level into the future.

As Exhibit 10–5 illustrates, the economy's full-employment potential income level is $7.5 trillion. At this income level, though, aggregate expenditures are insufficient to purchase the output produced. Given the aggregate expenditures function, output will remain below its potential. Unemployment will persist. Within the Keynesian model, equilibrium need not coincide with full employment.

AGGREGATE EXPENDITURES, OUTPUT, AND EMPLOYMENT

How could the economy reach its full-employment capacity? According to the Keynesian model, it will not do so unless there is a change in the aggregate expenditures schedule. Because the Keynesian model assumes that prices are fixed until potential capacity is reached, wage and price reductions are ruled out as a feasible mechanism for directing the economy to full employment.

If consumers, investors, governments, and foreigners could be induced to expand their expenditures, output would expand to full-employment capacity. **Exhibit 10–6** illustrates this point. If additional spending shifted the aggregate expenditures schedule (AE) upward to AE_2, equilibrium output would expand to its potential capacity. At the higher level of expenditures, AE_2, total spending would equal output at $7.5 trillion.

What would happen if aggregate expenditures exceeded the economy's production capacity? For example, suppose aggregate expenditures rose to AE_3. Within the basic Keynesian model, aggregate expenditures in excess of output lead to a higher price level once the economy reaches full employment. Nominal output will increase, but it merely reflects higher prices, rather than additional real output. Total spending in excess of full-employment capacity is inflationary within the Keynesian model.

Aggregate expenditures are the catalyst of the Keynesian model. Changes in expenditures make things happen. Until full employment is attained, supply is always accommodative. An increase in aggregate expenditures, caused, for example, by an increase in government expenditures, will thus lead to an increase in real output and employment. Once full employment is reached, however, additional aggregate expenditures lead merely to higher prices.

The Keynesian model implies that regulation of aggregate expenditures is the crux of sound macroeconomic policy. If we could assure aggregate

When equilibrium output is less than the economy's capacity, only an increase in expenditures (a shift in AE) will lead to full employment. If consumers, investors, governments, or foreigners would spend more and thereby shift the aggregate-expenditures schedule to AE_2, output would reach its full-employment potential ($7.5 trillion). Once full employment is reached, further increases in aggregate expenditures, such as indicated by the shift to AE_3, would lead only to higher prices. Nominal output will expand (the dotted segment of the AE = GDP schedule), but real output will not.

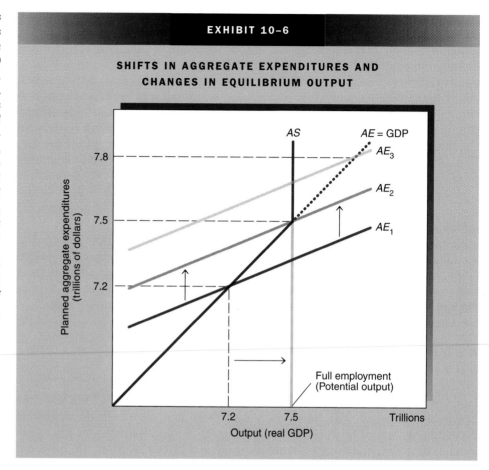

EXHIBIT 10–6

SHIFTS IN AGGREGATE EXPENDITURES AND CHANGES IN EQUILIBRIUM OUTPUT

expenditures large enough to achieve capacity output, but not so large as to result in inflation, the Keynesian view implies that maximum output, full-employment, and price stability could be attained.

THE KEYNESIAN MODEL WITHIN THE *AD/AS* FRAMEWORK

The Keynesian model can also be presented within the now familiar aggregate demand/aggregate supply (*AD/AS*) framework of the previous two chapters. The only difference in the graphic analysis is that the short-run aggregate supply curve (*SRAS*) has a different shape than in previous chapters because of the assumptions of the Keynesian model. Take a look at **Exhibit 10–7.** Note that the *SRAS* is completely flat at the existing price level until full-employment capacity is reached. This is because the Keynesian model assumes that, at less than full-employment output levels, prices (and wages) are fixed since they are inflexible in a downward direction. In essence, firms have a horizontal supply

EXHIBIT 10–7

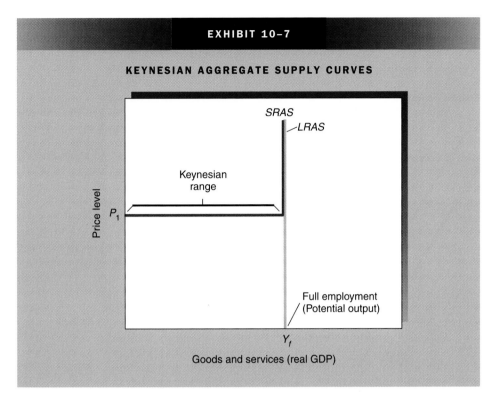

KEYNESIAN AGGREGATE SUPPLY CURVES

The Keynesian model implies a 90-degree angle-shaped aggregate supply curve. Because the model postulates downward wage and price inflexibility, the SRAS curve is flat for outputs less than potential GDP (Y_f). In this range, often referred to as the Keynesian range, output is entirely dependent on the level of aggregate demand. The Keynesian model implies that real output rates beyond full employment are unattainable. Thus, both SRAS and LRAS are vertical at the economy's full employment potential output.

curve when operating below normal capacity, so any change in aggregate demand will lead to a corresponding change in output. Economists sometimes refer to this horizontal segment as the *Keynesian range* of the aggregate supply curve.

What happens to the *SRAS* in Exhibit 10–7 when capacity is reached? In this situation, firms raise their prices to allocate the capacity output to those willing to pay the highest prices. Thus, the economy's *SRAS* is vertical at full employment capacity. So both *SRAS* and *LRAS* are vertical at the full employment rate of output (Y_f in Exhibit 10–7).

Part a of **Exhibit 10–8** illustrates the impact of a change in aggregate demand within the polar assumptions of the Keynesian model. When aggregate demand is less than AD_2 (for example, AD_1), the economy will languish below potential capacity. Because prices and wages are inflexible downward, below-capacity output rates (Y_1, for example) and abnormally high unemployment will persist unless there is an increase in aggregate demand. When output is below its potential, any increase in aggregate demand (for example, the shift from AD_1 to AD_2) brings previously idle resources into the productive process at an unchanged price level. In this range, the Keynesian analysis essentially turns Say's Law (supply creates an equivalent amount of demand) on its head. In the Keynesian range, an increase in demand creates its own supply.

Of course, once the economy's potential output constraint (Y_f) is reached, additional demand would merely lead to higher prices rather than to more output. Because both the *SRAS* and *LRAS* curves are vertical at capacity output, an increase in aggregate demand to AD_3 fails to expand real output.

EXHIBIT 10–8

AD/AS PRESENTATION OF KEYNESIAN MODEL

Goods and services (real GDP)
(a) Polar assumption

Goods and services (real GDP)
(b) Central implication

Part a illustrates the polar implications of the Keynesian model. When output is less than capacity (for example, Y_1), an increase in aggregate demand such as illustrated by the shift from AD_1 to AD_2 will expand output without increasing prices. But, increases in demand beyond AD_2, such as a shift to AD_3, lead only to a higher price level (P_2). Part b relaxes the assumption of complete price inflexibility and short-run output inflexibility beyond Y_f. The SRAS curve therefore turns from horizontal to vertical more gradually. This would imply that unanticipated increases in aggregate demand would lead (1) primarily to increases in output when output is below capacity (for example, Y_1), and (2) primarily to increases in the price level when output is greater than capacity (for example, Y_3).

When constructing models, we often make polar assumptions to illustrate various points. The Keynesian model is no exception. In the real world, prices will not be completely inflexible. Similarly, in the short run, unanticipated increases in demand will not lead solely to higher prices. Nevertheless, the Keynesian model implies an important point that is illustrated more realistically by part b of Exhibit 10–8. The horizontal segment of the *SRAS* curve is an over-simplification intended to reinforce the idea that changes in aggregate demand exert little impact on prices and substantial impact on output when an economy is operating well below capacity. *Therefore, under conditions like those of the 1930s—when idle factories and widespread unemployment are present—an increase in aggregate demand will generally exert its primary impact on output.*

On the other hand, the vertical segment of the aggregate supply curve is a simplifying assumption meant to illustrate the concept that there is an attainable output rate beyond which increases in demand will lead almost exclusively to price increases (and only small increases in real output). *So when aggregate demand is already quite strong (for example, AD_3), increases in aggregate demand will predictably exert their primary impact on prices rather than output.*

THE MULTIPLIER

The multiplier occupies a central position in the Keynesian model. A change in autonomous expenditures—investment, for example—generally leads to an even larger change in aggregate income. The **expenditure multiplier** is defined as the change in total income (equilibrium output) divided by the autonomous expenditure change that brought about the enlarged income.

The multiplier principle builds on the point that one individual's expenditure becomes the income of another. As we previously discussed, consumption expenditures are directly related to income—an increase in income (or wealth) will lead to an increase in consumption. Predictably, income recipients will spend a portion of their additional earnings on consumption. In turn, their consumption expenditures will generate additional income for others who will also spend a portion of it.

Perhaps an example will illuminate the multiplier concept. Suppose that there were idle unemployed resources and that an entrepreneur decided to undertake a $1 million investment project. Because investment is a component of aggregate demand, the project will increase demand directly by $1 million. This is not the entire story, however. The investment project will require plumbers, carpenters, masons, lumber, cement, and many other resources. The incomes of the suppliers of these resources will increase by $1 million. What will they do with this additional income? Given the link between one's income and consumption, the resource suppliers will predictably spend a fraction of the additional income. They will buy more food, clothing, recreation, medical care, and thousands of other items. How will this spending influence the incomes of those who supply these additional consumption products and services? Their incomes will increase, also. After setting aside (saving) a portion of this additional income, these persons will also spend some of their additional income on current consumption. Their consumption spending will result in still more additional income for other product and service suppliers.

The term *multiplier* is also used to indicate the number by which the initial investment would be multiplied to obtain the total summation of the increases in income. If the $1 million investment resulted in $4 million of additional income, the multiplier would be 4. The total increase in income would be four times the amount of the initial increase in spending. Similarly, if total income increased by $3 million, the multiplier would be 3.

Expenditure multiplier
The ratio of the change in equilibrium output to the independent change in investment, consumption, or government spending that brings about the change. Numerically, the multiplier is equal to 1 ÷ (1 − MPC) when the price level is constant.

THE SIZE OF THE MULTIPLIER

The size of the multiplier depends on the proportion of the additional income that households choose to spend on consumption.[4] Keynes referred to this fraction as the **marginal propensity to consume (MPC).** Mathematically:

Marginal propensity to consume (MPC)
Additional current consumption divided by additional current disposable income.

---

[4]For the purposes of simplicity when calculating the size of the multiplier, we will assume that all additions to income are either (1) spent on domestically produced goods or (2) saved. This assumption means that we are ignoring the impact of taxes and spending on imports as income expands via the multiplier process. At the conclusion of our analysis, we will indicate the significance of this assumption.

$$MPC = \frac{\text{Additional consumption}}{\text{Additional income}}$$

For example, if your income increases by $100 and you therefore increase your current consumption expenditures by $75, your marginal propensity to consume is 3/4, or 0.75.

Exhibit 10–9 illustrates why the size of the multiplier is dependent on the MPC. Suppose the MPC is equal to 3/4, indicating that consumers spend 75 cents of each additional dollar earned. Continuing with our previous example, we know that a $1 million investment would initially result in $1 million of additional income in round 1. Because the MPC is 3/4, consumption would increase by $750,000 (the other $250,000 would flow into saving), contributing that amount to income in round 2. The recipients of the round 2 income of $750,000 would spend three-fourths of it on current consumption. Hence, their spending would increase income by $562,500 in round 3. Exhibit 10–9 illustrates the additions to income through other rounds. In total, income would increase by $4 million, given an MPC of 3/4. The multiplier is 4.

If the MPC had been greater, income recipients would have spent a larger share of their additional income on current consumption during each round. Thus, the additional income generated in each round would have been greater, increasing the size of the multiplier. There is a precise relationship between the expenditure multiplier and the MPC. The expenditure multiplier, M, is:

$$M = \frac{1}{1 - MPC}$$

EXHIBIT 10–9

THE MULTIPLIER PRINCIPLE

EXPENDITURE STAGE	ADDITIONAL INCOME (DOLLARS)	ADDITIONAL CONSUMPTION (DOLLARS)	MARGINAL PROPENSITY TO CONSUME
Round 1	1,000,000	750,000	3/4
Round 2	750,000	562,500	3/4
Round 3	562,500	421,875	3/4
Round 4	421,875	316,406	3/4
Round 5	316,406	237,305	3/4
Round 6	237,305	177,979	3/4
Round 7	177,979	133,484	3/4
Round 8	133,484	100,113	3/4
Round 9	100,113	75,085	3/4
Round 10	75,085	56,314	3/4
All Others	225,253	168,939	3/4
Total	4,000,000	3,000,000	3/4

Exhibit 10–10 indicates the size of the multiplier for several different values of MPC.

REAL-WORLD SIGNIFICANCE OF THE MULTIPLIER

Within the framework of the Keynesian model, the multiplier is important because it explains why even small changes in investment, government, or consumption spending can trigger much larger changes in output. The multiplier magnifies the fluctuations in output and employment that emanate from autonomous changes in spending.

There are both positive and negative sides to the amplified effects. On the negative side, the multiplier principle indicates that a small reduction in investment expenditures, perhaps due to a decline in business optimism, can be an important source of economic instability. As a result, many Keynesian economists believe that the stability of a market economy is quite fragile and constantly susceptible to even modest disruptions. On the positive side, the multiplier principle illustrates the potential of macroeconomic policy to stimulate output even if it is able to exert only a small impact on autonomous expenditures.

In evaluating the significance of the multiplier, it is important to keep three points in mind. *First, in addition to saving, leakages in the form of taxes and spending on imports will also reduce the size of the multiplier.* In order to keep things simple, we assumed that all income was either saved or spent on domestically produced goods throughout our analysis. Like saving, taxes and imports will siphon some of the additional income away from spending on domestic goods and services. These leakages from the flow of spending will dampen the effects of the multiplier. Therefore, the actual multiplier will be somewhat smaller than the simple expenditure multiplier of our analysis.

Second, it takes time for the multiplier to work. In the real world, several weeks or perhaps even months will be required for each successive round of

---

EXHIBIT 10–10

A HIGHER MPC MEANS A LARGER MULTIPLIER

MPC	SIZE OF MULTIPLIER
9/10	10
4/5	5
3/4	4
2/3	3
1/2	2
1/3	1.5

spending. Only a fraction of the multiplier effect will be observed quickly. Most researchers believe that only about one-half the total multiplier effect will be felt during the first six months following a change in expenditures.

Third, the multiplier implies that the additional spending brings idle resources into production, leading to additional real output rather than to increased prices. When unemployment is widespread, this is a realistic assumption. However, when there is an absence of abundant idle resources, the multiplier effect will be dampened by an increase in the price level.

MAJOR INSIGHTS OF KEYNESIAN ECONOMICS

Keynesian economics dominated the thinking of macroeconomists for three decades following the Second World War. What are its major insights? Three points stand out.

1. Changes in output, as well as changes in prices, play a role in the macroeconomic adjustment process, particularly in the short run. The classical model emphasized the role of prices in directing an economy to macroeconomic equilibrium. Keynesian analysis highlights the importance of changes in output. Modern analysis incorporates both. Market prices do not adjust instantaneously to economic change. In the short run, changes in output and employment often signal economic change to decision makers and provide the impetus for price adjustments. Hence, modern economists believe that both price and output conditions play a role in the adjustment process.

2. The responsiveness of aggregate supply to changes in demand will be directly related to the availability of unemployed resources. Keynesian analysis emphasizes that, when idle resources are present, output will be highly responsive to changes in aggregate demand. Conversely, when an economy is operating at or near its capacity, output will be much less sensitive to changes in demand. So the *SRAS* curve is relatively flat when an economy is well below capacity and relatively steep when the economy is operating near and beyond capacity (see Exhibit 10–8).

3. Fluctuations in aggregate demand are an important potential source of business instability. Abrupt changes in demand are a potential source of both recession and inflation. Policies that effectively stabilize aggregate demand—that minimize abrupt changes in demand—will substantially reduce economic instability.

THE KEYNESIAN VIEW OF THE BUSINESS CYCLE

Keynesian economists believe that a market economy, if left to its own devices, is unstable and likely to experience prolonged periods of recession. The Keynesian view emphasizes the destabilizing potential of autonomous changes in expenditures powered by the multiplier and changes in optimism. Suppose there is an increase in aggregate demand triggered by what appears to be a relatively minor disruption—for example, higher incomes abroad, an increase in consumer optimism, or a burst of business optimism generated by a new innovation. Keynesians believe that such changes will often lead to an expansion in output that will have a tendency to feed on itself. The initial increase in demand, *magnified by the multiplier,* will lead to an expansion in employment and a rapid growth of income. In turn, the higher incomes will lead to additional consumption and strong business sales. Inventories will decline, and businesses will expand output (to rebuild inventories) and move investment projects forward as they become more optimistic about the future. Unemployment will decline to a low level as the economy experiences a boom.

Can this expansionary phase continue indefinitely? The answer is no. Eventually, full-employment capacity will be reached. Constrained by the availability of both labor and machines, the growth rate of the economy will slow. The slower growth will dampen the optimism of business decision makers and cause them to cut back on fixed investments. Again, the multiplier will magnify the impact of the change in demand. Thus, the reduction in investment and increased pessimism about the future will often lead to a sharp reduction in output. As the economy plunges into a recession, inventories will rise as businesses are unable to sell their goods because of the low level of demand. Workers will be laid off. The ranks of unemployed workers will grow. Bankruptcies will become more common.

This is what Keynes perceived was happening in the 1930s. Consumers were not spending because their incomes had fallen and they were extremely pessimistic about the future. Similarly, businesses were not producing because there was little demand for their products. Investment had come to a complete standstill because underutilized resources and capacity were abundantly available.

Wide fluctuation in private investment is the villain of Keynesian business cycle theory. An economic expansion accelerates into a boom because investment, amplified by the multiplier, stimulates other sectors of the economy. At the first sign of a slowdown, though, investment plans are sharply curtailed. Eventually, machines will wear out and the capital stock will decline to a level consistent with the current level of income. At that point, *additional* investment will be necessary for replacement purposes. The new investment will stimulate additional output and employment, and start the cycle anew. *Keynesian economists believe that the recessionary phase is likely to be quite lengthy and they have little confidence that either lower interest rates or falling resource prices will be able to reverse the tide of the falling incomes.*

EVOLUTION OF MODERN MACROECONOMICS

As we previously discussed, the prolonged unemployment of the Great Depression undermined the classical view that markets will quickly restore full employment. Keynesian analysis provides an explanation for what happened during the 1930s. However, other explanations are also possible. Many economists believe misguided economic policies, particularly monetary policy, contributed to the depth and duration of the Great Depression. According to this view, markets were unable to restore full employment within a reasonable length of time during the 1930s because policies were inadvertently adopted that not only hampered recovery, but actually depressed economic conditions. This monetary view of the business cycle will be presented in Chapters 13, 14, and 15.

The modern view of economic instability is a hybrid, reflecting elements of both classical and Keynesian analysis as well as some unique insights drawn from other areas of economics. As we discussed in the previous chapter, various shocks (unanticipated changes in *AD* or *AS*) can disrupt full-employment equilibrium and lead either to recessionary unemployment or to an inflationary boom in the short run. Furthermore, because macroeconomic markets do not adjust immediately, the short-run disequilibrium conditions may persist for a significant time period, perhaps a year or two. On this point, modern analysis is highly consistent with the Keynesian view.

However, the long-run implications of modern analysis are more consistent with the classical view. In the long run, modern analysis indicates that changes in real wages and interest rates will act as a stabilizing force. When an economy is operating below its potential during a recession, falling real wages and interest rates will help restore full employment. Similarly, rising real wages and interest rates will tend to retard an economic boom.

Economic conditions during the past several decades are consistent with the modern view. We continue to experience economic ups and downs, short-run disequilibrium conditions resulting from various shocks. But economic downturns do not spiral downward and result in prolonged periods of stagnation. The self-corrective characteristics of a market economy are less fragile than was previously thought. Market forces respond and redirect the economy. For example, during the 1991–1992 recession, real wages even in several highly unionized industries declined. Similarly, real interest rates fell. Both of these forces helped to reverse the recessionary forces and direct the economy to a recovery.

In addition, modern macroeconomics indicates that the impact of economic change is more complex than either the earlier classical or Keynesian economists realized. When analyzing the impact of a change, it makes a difference whether the change is anticipated or unanticipated. It is also important whether people expect the change to be temporary or permanent. Today, both Keynesians and non-Keynesians integrate these factors into their analysis.

Several key elements of modern macroeconomics are more easily visualized within the framework of the multimarket *AD/AS* model we developed in Chapters 8 and 9. The *AD/AS* model also makes it easier to understand and distinguish between long-run and short-run conditions. In essence, the Keynesian aggregate expenditure model is a short-run excess-capacity model. It conceals the significance of factors that are important in the long run. In contrast, the *AD/AS* model emphasizes the importance of both "sticky prices" in the short run and price adjustments in the long run. Because the *AD/AS* model is more flexible and will help us address a broader range of economic issues, it will be our primary tool as we seek to develop more depth in our understanding of macroeconomic issues.

LOOKING AHEAD

Although Keynes emphasized that a market economy might fail to automatically reach its potential capacity, he argued that governments could use their tax and expenditure policies to stabilize aggregate demand and assure full employment. Keynes and his followers forced a reluctant economics profession to think seriously about macroeconomic policy. Turning next to this issue, we will begin by considering the potential of fiscal policy as a tool with which to promote full employment, stable prices, and the growth of real output.

CHAPTER SUMMARY

1. Classical economists emphasized the importance of supply because they believed that production created an equivalent amount of current demand (Say's Law) and that flexible wages and prices would assure full employment. The Great Depression undermined the credibility of the classical view.

2. The concept of planned aggregate expenditures is central to the Keynesian analysis. Aggregate expenditures are the sum of spending on consumption, investment, government purchases, and net exports.

3. In the Keynesian model, planned consumption expenditures are positively related to income. As income expands, though, consumption increases by a lesser amount. Both planned investment and government expenditures are independent of income in the Keynesian model. Planned net exports decline as income increases. The Keynesian model postulates that business firms will produce the amount of goods and services they believe consumers, investors, governments, and foreigners (net exports) plan to buy.

4. In the Keynesian model, equilibrium is present when planned total expenditures are equal to output. The equilibrium output level may take place at less than full employment. When it does, the high rate of unemployment will persist into the future. Because the Keynesian model assumes that wages and prices are inflexible downward, reductions in real wages are ruled out as a mechanism to restore full employment. Unless aggregate spending (demand) increases, there is no mechanism for the restoration of full employment.

5. Planned expenditures need not equal actual expenditures. If purchasers spend less than business firms anticipate, unplanned additions to inventories will result. Rather than continuing to accumulate undesired inventories, businesses will cut back output. Income will recede to the equilibrium level.

6. If planned total expenditures temporarily exceed output, businesses will sell more of their products than they anticipate. An unplanned decline in inventories will result. In an effort to restore their abnormally low inventories, businesses will expand future output, and income will rise toward the equilibrium level.

7. Aggregate expenditures are the catalyst of the Keynesian model. Until full employment is attained, supply (real GDP) is always accommodative. Increases in aggregate expenditures thus lead to an expansion in both output and employment as long as the economy is operating below potential capacity. Once capacity is reached, further expansions in expenditures lead only to higher prices, without expanding real output. The Keynesian model implies that maintaining aggregate expenditures at the level consistent with full employment and stable prices is the primary function of sound macroeconomic policy.

8. The expenditure multiplier indicates that independent changes in planned investment, government expenditures, and consumption have a magnified impact on income. Income will increase by some multiple of the initial increase in spending. The multiplier is the number by which the initial change in spending is multiplied to obtain the total amplified increase in income. The size of the multiplier increases with the marginal propensity to consume.

9. In evaluating the importance of the multiplier, it is important to remember that (a) taxes and spending on imports will dampen the size of the multiplier; (b) it takes time for the multiplier to work; and (c) the amplified effect on real output will be valid only when the additional spending brings idle resources into production without price changes.

10. The Keynesian view of the business cycle emphasizes that market forces, once begun, tend to move together, reinforcing either expansion or contraction. Upswings and downswings feed on themselves. During a downturn, business pessimism, declining investment, and the multiplier principle combine to plunge the economy further toward recession. During an economic upswing, business and consumer optimism and expanding investment interact with the multiplier principle to propel the economy further upward. Keynesian theory suggests that a market-directed economy, left to its own devices, will be inherently unstable and fluctuate between economic recession and inflationary boom.

11. Modern macroeconomic analysis incorporates elements of both Keynesian and classical economics. In the short run, market adjustments will not quickly restore full employment. Thus, a less-than-capacity output rate may exist for a period of time, much as the Keynesian model implies. However, in the long run, modern analysis indicates that the changes in real wages and interest rates cushion economic shocks and direct the economy toward full employment, much as the classical model implies.

CRITICAL ANALYSIS QUESTIONS

1. You have just been appointed to the president's Council of Economic Advisers. Write a short essay explaining to the president the Keynesian view concerning why a market economy may be unable to generate the full employment level of income. Be sure to explain why equilibrium may result at less than full employment.

*2. How will each of the following factors influence the consumption schedule?

   a. The expectation that consumer prices will rise more rapidly in the future
   b. Pessimism about future employment conditions
   c. A reduction in income taxes
   d. An increase in the interest rate
   e. A decline in stock prices
   f. A redistribution of income from older workers (age 45 and over) to younger workers (under 35)
   g. A redistribution of income from the wealthy to the poor

3. Why does output change in the Keynesian model? Can the Keynesian model explain prolonged unemployment, such as was present during the 1930s? How?

*4. What is the multiplier principle? What determines the size of the multiplier? Does the multiplier principle make it more or less difficult to stabilize the economy? Explain.

5. "How can the Keynesian model be correct? According to Keynes, falling income, unemployment, and bad times result because people have so much income that they fail to spend enough to buy all of the goods produced. Paradoxically, rising income and good times result because people are reducing their savings, and spending more than they are making. This doesn't make sense." Explain why you either agree or disagree with this view.

6. Widespread acceptance of the Keynesian aggregate expenditures (AE) model took place during and immediately following the Great Depression. Can you explain why? The aggregate expenditures model declined in popularity when many economies experienced both high rates of unemployment and inflation during the 1970s. Was this surprising? Explain.

*7. According to the Keynesian AE model, if people suddenly decide they want to spend more of their current income on consumption, where do they get the funds for the additional spending? What does the model assume with regard to this source of funds?

8. Suppose that individuals suddenly decided to spend less and save more of their current income. Compare and contrast this change within the framework of the Keynesian AE and the AD/AS models.

*9. "Historically, interest rates have generally been higher during periods of economic boom than during recessions. This indicates that higher interest rates stimulate additional investment." Evaluate this view.

10. How would an increase in income abroad influence the equilibrium level of output at home within the framework of the Keynesian AE model? Would the results differ within the framework of the AD/AS model?

11. Economists often state that the Keynesian AE model has its greatest relevance in the short run, while the classical model is most relevant to the long run. In what sense is this true?

*12. In recent years, approximately 25 percent of the income of Canadians has been spent on imports. In the United States, spending on imports constitutes about 10 percent of income. Would you expect the size of the multiplier to be larger or smaller in Canada than in the United States? Explain.

*13. What role do declining real wages and resource prices play in the restoration of full employment in the Keynesian model? If output is currently below the full employment rate, what will direct the economy to full employment in the Keynesian model?

14. In the Keynesian AE model, why does an increase in aggregate spending lead to an equal increase in real GDP as long as output is at less than full-employment capacity? What does this imply about the shape of the aggregate supply curve?

15. The rate of output and planned expenditures for an economy is indicated in the accompanying table.

TOTAL OUTPUT (REAL GDP IN BILLIONS)	PLANNED AGGREGATE EXPENDITURES (IN BILLIONS)
$500	$525
550	550
600	575
650	600
700	625

   a. If the current output rate were $500 billion, what would tend to happen to business inventories, future output, and employment?
   b. If the current output rate were $650 billion, what would tend to happen to inventories, future output, and employment?
   c. What is the equilibrium rate of income of this economy?
   d. If the economy's full-employment rate of output were $600 billion, would the rate of unemployment be high, low, or normal, assuming the current planned demand persisted into the future?
   e. What would happen if there was an autonomous increase in investment of $25 billion?

---

*Asterisk denotes questions for which answers are given in Appendix B.

CHAPTER FOCUS

- How does fiscal policy affect aggregate demand? How does it affect aggregate supply?
- What is the Keynesian view of fiscal policy? How do the crowding-out and new classical models modify the basic Keynesian analysis?
- How difficult is it to time fiscal policy properly? Why is proper timing important?
- Is there a synthesis view of fiscal policy? What are its major elements?
- Are there supply-side effects of fiscal policy?
- How does a large budget deficit affect the use of fiscal policy?

In the early stages of the Keynesian revolution, macroeconomists emphasized fiscal policy as the most powerful and balanced remedy for demand management. Gradually, shortcomings of fiscal policy became apparent. The shortcomings stem from timing, politics, macroeconomic theory, and the deficit itself.[1]

NOBEL LAUREATE PAUL SAMUELSON

---

[1]Paul A. Samuelson and William D. Nordhaus, Economics, 15th ed. (New York: McGraw-Hill, 1995), p. 644.

A s we indicated in Chapter 8, fiscal policy involves the use of the government's spending and taxing authority. We are now ready to use our basic macroeconomic model to investigate the impact of fiscal policy on output, prices, and employment.

Previously, we assumed that the government's taxing and spending policies remained unchanged. We will now relax that assumption. However, we want to isolate the impact of changes in fiscal policy from changes in monetary policy. Because of this, we will continue to assume that the monetary authorities maintain a constant supply of money. We will begin our analysis of monetary policy in the following chapter.

BUDGET DEFICITS AND SURPLUSES

Fiscal policy is reflected through the government's expenditure, tax, and borrowing activities. When the supply of money is constant, government expenditures must be financed with either: (1) taxes and other revenues derived from the sale of services or assets or (2) borrowing. When government revenues from taxes and sales are equal to government expenditures (including both purchases of goods and services and transfer payments), the government has a **balanced budget.** The budget need not be in balance, however. A **budget deficit** is present when total government spending exceeds total government revenue from all sources. When a budget deficit is present, the government must borrow funds to finance the excess of its spending relative to revenue. It borrows by issuing interest-bearing bonds that become part of what we call the national debt. Conversely, a **budget surplus** is present when the government's revenues exceed its total expenditures. The surplus allows the government to reduce its outstanding debt.

The federal budget is much more than a mere revenue and expenditure statement of a large organization. Of course, its sheer size means that it exerts a substantial influence on the economy. Its importance, though, stems from its position as a policy variable. The federal budget is the primary tool of fiscal policy. In contrast with private organizations that are directed by the pursuit of income and profit, the federal government can alter its budget with an eye toward influencing the future direction of the economy.

Changes in the size of the federal deficit or surplus are often used to gauge whether fiscal policy is adding additional demand stimulus or imposing additional demand restraint. When using it as such a gauge, however, it is important to note that changes in the size of the deficit may arise from two different sources. *First, changes in the size of the deficit may merely reflect the state of the economy.* During a recession, tax revenues generally fall substantially as the result of reductions in personal income and business profits. Therefore, even if government expenditures are not increased or tax rates cut, an economic recession will tend to increase the size of the budget deficit. *Second, changes in the deficit may reflect* discretionary fiscal policy. Policymakers may institute deliberate changes in tax laws or spending on government programs in order to alter the size of the budget deficit (or surplus). When we speak of "changes in fiscal policy," we are referring to changes of type—the institution of deliberate changes in government expenditures and/or tax policy that are designed to affect the size of the budget deficit or surplus.

Balanced budget
A situation in which current government revenue from taxes, fees, and other sources is just equal to current government expenditures.

Budget deficit
A situation in which total government spending exceeds total government revenue during a specific time period, usually one year.

Budget surplus
A situation in which total government spending is less than total government revenue during a time period, usually a year.

Discretionary fiscal policy
A change in laws or appropriation levels that alters government revenues and/or expenditures.

KEYNESIAN VIEW OF FISCAL POLICY

Prior to the 1960s, the desirability of a balanced federal budget was widely accepted among business and political leaders. Keynesian economists, though, were highly critical of this view. They argued that the federal budget should be used to promote a level of aggregate demand consistent with the full employment rate of output.

How does the government budget influence the level of aggregate demand? First, the government will directly stimulate aggregate demand if it increases its purchases of goods and services while holding its taxes constant. As the government spends more on highways, flood control projects, education, and national defense, for example, it will increase aggregate demand. Second, changes in tax policy will also influence aggregate demand. For example, a reduction in personal taxes will increase the current disposable income of households. As their after-tax income rises, individuals will spend more on consumption. In turn, this increase in consumption will stimulate aggregate demand. Similarly, a reduction in business taxes increases after-tax profitability, which will stimulate both business investment and aggregate demand.

According to the Keynesian view, fluctuations in aggregate demand are the major source of economic disturbances. Therefore, if demand could be stabilized and maintained at a level consistent with the economy's full employment productive capacity, the major source of economic instability would be eliminated.

Keynesian theory highlights the potential of fiscal policy as a tool capable of reducing fluctuations in demand. When an economy is operating below its potential output, the Keynesian model suggests that government should institute **expansionary fiscal policy.** In other words, the government should either increase its purchases of goods and services and/or cut taxes. Of course this policy will increase the government's budget deficit. In order to finance the enlarged budget deficit, the government will have to borrow from private sources: individuals, business firms, and other sources of loanable funds.[2]

Expansionary fiscal policy
An increase in government expenditures and/or a reduction in tax rates such that the expected size of the budget deficit expands.

Exhibit 11–1 illustrates the case for expansionary fiscal policy when an economy is experiencing abnormally high unemployment due to deficient aggregate demand. Initially, the economy is operating at e_1. Output is below potential capacity, Y_f, and unemployment exceeds its natural rate. As we have previously discussed, if there is no change in policy, abnormally high unemployment and excess supply in the resource market would eventually reduce real wages and other resource prices. The accompanying lower costs would increase aggregate supply (shift to $SRAS_3$) and guide the economy to a full employment equilibrium (E_3) at a lower price level (P_3). In addition, lower real interest rates resulting from weak business demand for investment funds may help stimulate aggregate demand and restore full employment.

---

[2]Alternatively, the government could borrow from its central bank—the Federal Reserve Bank in the United States. However, as we will see in the following chapter, this method of financing a budget deficit would expand the money supply. Since we want to differentiate between fiscal and monetary effects, we must hold the supply of money constant. So for now, we assume that the government deficit must be financed by borrowing from private sources.

Here we illustrate an economy operating in the short run at Y_1, below its potential capacity of Y_f. There are two routes to a long-run full employment equilibrium. First, policymakers could wait for lower wages and resource prices to reduce costs, increase supply to $SRAS_3$, and restore equilibrium at E_3. Keynesians believe this market-adjustment method will be slow and uncertain. Alternatively, expansionary fiscal policy could stimulate aggregate demand (shift to AD_2) and guide the economy to E_2.

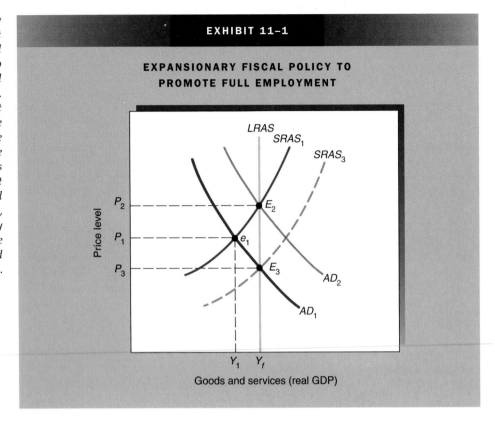

EXHIBIT 11–1

EXPANSIONARY FISCAL POLICY TO PROMOTE FULL EMPLOYMENT

Most Keynesian economists, however, do not believe that this self-corrective mechanism will work very rapidly. Thus, they recommend that policymakers attempt to speed up the process by shifting to a more expansionary fiscal policy. An increase in government purchases would stimulate aggregate demand directly. Alternatively, taxes could be reduced. A reduction in income taxes would expand the after-tax income of households, stimulating consumption. Similarly, business taxes could be reduced, which would help stimulate private investment. Furthermore, both an increase in government purchases and a reduction in taxes would be magnified by the multiplier process. Thus, according to the Keynesian view, the total increase in aggregate demand would be substantially greater than the increase in government purchases and/or the cut in taxes. An appropriate dose of fiscal policy, if timed properly, would stimulate aggregate demand (shift the curve to AD_2) and guide the economy to full employment equilibrium (E_2). *So when an economy is operating below its potential capacity, the Keynesian prescription calls for expansionary fiscal policy— a deliberate change in expenditures and/or taxes that will increase the size of the government's budget deficit.*

The Keynesian view also provides a fiscal policy remedy for inflation. Suppose that an economy is experiencing an inflationary economic boom as the result of excessive aggregate demand. As **Exhibit 11–2** illustrates, in the absence of a change in policy, the strong demand (AD_1) would push up wages and other resource prices. In time, the higher resource prices would increase costs, reduce aggregate supply (from $SRAS_1$ to $SRAS_3$), and lead to a higher price level (P_3).

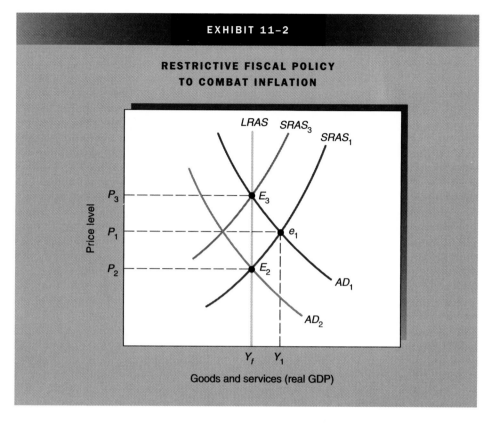

EXHIBIT 11-2

**RESTRICTIVE FISCAL POLICY
TO COMBAT INFLATION**

Strong demand such as AD_1 will temporarily lead to an output rate beyond the economy's long-run potential (Y_f). If maintained, the high level of demand will lead to long-run equilibrium (E_3) at a higher price level. However, restrictive fiscal policy could restrain demand to AD_2 (or better still, prevent demand from expanding to AD_1 in the first place) and thereby guide the economy to a noninflationary equilibrium (E_2).

The basic Keynesian model, however, indicates that **restrictive fiscal policy** could be used to reduce aggregate demand (shift to AD_2) and guide the economy to a noninflationary equilibrium (E_2). A reduced level of government purchases would diminish aggregate demand directly. Alternatively, higher taxes on households and businesses could be used to dampen consumption and private investment. The restrictive fiscal policy—a spending reduction and/or increase in taxes—would tend to shift the government budget toward a surplus (or smaller deficit). *The Keynesian analysis suggests that a shift toward a more restrictive fiscal policy is the proper prescription with which to combat inflation generated by excessive aggregate demand.*

Prior to the Keynesian revolution, it was widely believed that a responsible government would constrain spending within the bounds of its revenues. The Keynesian revolution drastically altered this view, proposing that general economic conditions, rather than the concept of the annually balanced budget, determine the appropriateness of budget policy.

The Keynesian view stresses the importance of **countercyclical policy,** meaning that the government should adopt a more expansionary fiscal policy when the economy is threatened by a recession. On the other hand, fiscal policy should become more restrictive in response to the threat of inflation. When judging whether fiscal policy is expansionary or restrictive, economists generally focus on *changes* in the size of the budget deficit (or surplus). A change in policy is generally described as restrictive if it reduces the size of the budget deficit. For example, a fiscal policy change that reduced the size of the annual budget deficit

Restrictive fiscal policy
A reduction in government expenditures and/or an increase in tax rates such that the expected size of the budget deficit declines (or the budget surplus increases).

Countercyclical policy
A policy that tends to move the economy in an opposite direction from the forces of the business cycle. Such a policy would stimulate demand during the contraction phase of the business cycle and restrain demand during the expansion phase.

from $200 billion to $100 billion would be reflective of restrictive fiscal policy, even though the budget remains in a deficit position. Correspondingly, changes in fiscal policy that increase the size of the budget deficit (or reduce the size of the budget surplus) would be reflective of a more expansionary fiscal policy.

By the early 1960s, the Keynesian view was widely accepted by both economists and policymakers. At that time, it was widely believed that changes in the size of the budget deficit exerted a powerful impact on aggregate demand and output. More recently, however, economists have noted that budget deficits and surpluses often generate important secondary effects in other markets—particularly the loanable funds market—that tend to weaken their impact on aggregate demand. We turn now to an analysis of these secondary effects.

FISCAL POLICY AND THE CROWDING-OUT EFFECT

When the government borrows funds to finance an enlarged deficit, typically it will do so by issuing additional bonds. As we previously discussed, issuing bonds is simply a means of demanding loanable funds. The total demand for loanable funds will increase as government borrowing competes with private borrowing for the available supply of funds. The additional government borrowing to finance a larger deficit will increase the demand for loanable funds and drive up the real rate of interest.

What impact will a higher real interest rate have on private spending? Consumers will reduce their purchases of interest-sensitive goods, such as automobiles and consumer durables, in response to a higher real interest rate. More important, a higher interest rate will increase the opportunity cost of investment projects. Businesses will postpone spending on plant expansions, heavy equipment, and capital improvements. Residential housing construction and sales will also be hurt. Thus, the higher real interest rates caused by the larger deficit will retard private spending. Economists refer to this squeezing out of private spending by a deficit-induced increase in the real interest rate as the **crowding-out effect.**

The crowding-out effect suggests that budget deficits will exert less impact on aggregate demand than the basic Keynesian model implies. Because financing the deficit pushes up interest rates, budget deficits will tend to retard private spending, particularly spending on investment. This reduction in private spending as the result of higher interest rates will at least partially offset additional spending emanating from the deficit. Thus, the crowding-out effect implies that the impact of a budget deficit on demand, output, and employment may *not* be very potent.

Furthermore, the crowding-out effect implies that the budget deficit will change the composition of aggregate demand. As the higher interest rates accompanying the deficits crowd out private investment, the output of capital goods will decline. As a result, the future stock of capital (for example, heavy equipment, other machines, and buildings) will be smaller than would otherwise have been the case. To the extent that budget deficits push up interest rates and crowd out private investment, they will reduce the supply of capital available to future workers and thereby reduce their productivity and income.[3]

Although most modern economists accept the logic of the crowding-out effect, many would argue that it is unlikely to be very important *during a recession.* If expansionary fiscal policy is applied when an economy is operating at less than capacity, then the accompanying demand stimulus will lead to an increase in both real output and income. At the higher income level, households will save more, which will permit the government to finance its enlarged deficit without much upward pressure on interest rates. In addition, when applied during a recession, the demand stimulus may improve business profit expectations and thereby stimulate additional private investment.

The implications of the crowding-out analysis are symmetrical. Restrictive fiscal policy will "crowd in" private spending. If the government increases taxes and/or cuts back on expenditures and thereby reduces its demand for loanable funds, the real interest rate will decline. The lower real interest rate will stimulate additional private investment and consumption. So the fiscal policy restraint will be at least partially offset by an expansion in private spending. *As the result of this crowding in, restrictive fiscal policy may not be very effective as a weapon against inflation.*

Crowding-out effect
A reduction in private spending as a result of higher interest rates generated by budget deficits that are financed by borrowing in the private loanable funds market.

THE CROWDING-OUT EFFECT AND THE INTERNATIONAL LOANABLE FUNDS MARKET

In Chapter 3, we explained that, when legal restraints on trade are absent, there will be a tendency for similar prices to prevail in all markets, except for price differences due to taxes and transportation costs. This price-equalization principle is also applicable to the loanable funds market. People with funds available for loan (or the purchase of bonds) can supply them to markets in London, New York, Toronto, Tokyo, Hong Kong, Sydney, and elsewhere around the world.

---

[3]The impact of budget deficits on capital formation and the well-being of future generations is dealt with in detail in Chapter 16.

Adjusted for taxes and transaction costs (including those of a political nature), the real interest rate in one location will be approximately the same as the real interest rate in other locations (and countries).[4]

Suppose the United States cuts taxes and therefore runs a larger budget deficit. The financing of the deficit increases the demand for loanable funds and pushes up the real interest rate as the crowding-out effect implies. How will foreigners respond to this situation? The higher after-tax real interest yield will attract funds from abroad. In turn, this inflow of loanable funds will moderate the rise in real interest rates in the United States.

But how does the inflow of foreign credit influence the crowding-out effect? Because the inflow of funds moderates the upward pressure on domestic interest rates, it looks, at first glance, as if this factor will tend to minimize the crowding out of private spending. Closer inspection, though, reveals this will not be the case. Foreigners must acquire dollars before they can make financial investments in the United States. Therefore, the higher real interest rates in the United States will not only attract foreign investors, but will also result in an increase in the demand for the U.S. dollar in the **foreign exchange market**—the market that coordinates exchanges of the various national currencies. As foreigners demand more dollars in order to increase their financial investments in the United States, they will bid up the price of the dollar in the foreign exchange rate market. Thus, the dollar will appreciate relative to other currencies.

> **Foreign exchange market**
> *A highly organized market where the currencies of different countries are bought and sold.*

Consider how this increase in the foreign exchange value of the dollar relative to other currencies will influence the net exports of the United States. The appreciation of the dollar will make imports cheaper for Americans. Simultaneously, it will make U.S. exports more expensive for foreigners. Predictably, the United States will import more and export less. Thus, net exports will decline (or net imports increase), causing a reduction in aggregate demand. Therefore, while the inflow of capital from abroad will moderate the increase in the interest rate and the crowding out of private domestic investment, it will reduce net exports and thereby retard aggregate demand.

In summary, the inflow of capital from abroad changes the form of the crowding-out effect, but not necessarily its magnitude. Rather than increased real interest rates crowding out domestic investment and interest-sensitive consumer goods, the appreciation in the foreign exchange value of the dollar crowds out net exports (and stimulates imports). Just as a reduction in private investment tends to offset the demand stimulus emanating from budget deficits, so, too, will the decline in net exports.

Furthermore, our analysis indicates that budget deficits and trade deficits—an excess of imports relative to exports—will tend to be linked. When budget deficits push up interest rates and thereby attract an inflow of foreign capital, they will simultaneously cause a nation's currency to appreciate and its imports to rise relative to its exports.

---

[4]Differences in risk associated with loaning funds in another currency will also contribute to differences in real interest rates across countries. Since the rate of return on a loan extended in foreign currency is also influenced by changes in exchange rates, the risk accompanying such loans is greater. Therefore, foreigners will generally be unwilling to extend such loans unless they receive a somewhat higher interest rate in order to compensate them for the additional risk.

NEW CLASSICAL VIEW OF FISCAL POLICY

Some economists stress still another possible secondary effect of budget deficits—the impact of the deficits on saving. When the government runs a budget deficit and increases its outstanding debt, higher future taxes have to be levied to meet the interest obligations of the larger debt. Until now, we have implicitly assumed that the current saving decisions of taxpayers are unaffected by the higher future taxes implied by budget deficits. Some economists argue that this is an unrealistic view. The 1995 Nobel laureate Robert Lucas (University of Chicago), Thomas Sargent (University of Minnesota), and Robert Barro (Harvard University) have been leaders among a group of economists arguing that taxpayers will reduce their current consumption and increase their saving in anticipation of the higher future taxes implied by the debt financing. Because this position has its foundation in classical economics, these economists and their followers are referred to as **new classical economists.**

In the basic Keynesian model, a reduction in current taxes financed by borrowing increases the current disposable income of households. Given their additional disposable income, households increase their current consumption. New classical economists argue that this analysis is incorrect because it ignores the impact of the higher future tax liability implied by the budget deficit and the interest payments required to service the additional debt. New classical economists stress that debt financing merely substitutes *higher future* taxes for *lower current* taxes. Thus, budget deficits affect the *timing* of taxes, *but not their magnitude.*

A mere change in the timing of taxes will not alter the wealth of households. Therefore, there is no reason to believe that current consumption will change when current taxes are cut and government debt and future taxes are increased by an equivalent amount. According to the new classical view, households will reduce their current consumption in response to additional government debt (and the higher taxes that the debt implies) just as surely as would be the case if an equivalent amount of current taxes were levied. In essence, households will simply save the reduction in their current taxes so they will have the income with which to pay the higher future taxes implied by the additional government debt. Since current consumption declines as the result of the additional debt—just as it would have declined had the equivalent amount of taxes been levied—new classical economists do not believe that the substitution of debt for taxes will stimulate either private consumption or aggregate demand. According to this view, taxes and debt financing are essentially equivalent.

Perhaps an illustration will help explain the underlying logic of the new classical view. Consider the following alternative methods of paying a $1,000 tax liability: (1) a one-time payment of $1,000, or (2) payments of $100 each year in the future. When the interest rate is 10 percent, the opportunity cost of a $100 liability each year is $1,000. Therefore, just as the first option reduces current wealth by $1,000, so, too, does the second.

Now let us consider the impact of the two options on future income. If you dip into your savings to make a one-time $1,000 payment, your future interest

New classical economists
Modern economists who believe there are strong forces pushing a market economy toward full employment equilibrium and that macroeconomic policy is an ineffective tool with which to reduce economic instability.

income will be reduced by $100 each year in the future (assuming a 10 percent interest rate). Just as the second option reduces your future net income by $100 each year, so, too, does the first. In both cases, current wealth is reduced by $1,000. Similarly, in both cases the flow of future net income is reduced by $100 each year. Because of this, the new classical economists believe the two options are essentially the same.

Exhibit 11–3 illustrates the implications of the new classical view as to the potency of fiscal policy. Suppose the fiscal authorities issue $50 billion of additional debt in order to cut taxes by an equal amount. The government borrowing increases the demand for loanable funds (D_1 shifts to D_2 in part b of Exhibit 11–3) by $50 billion. If the taxpayers did not recognize the higher future taxes implied by the debt, they would expand consumption in response to the lower taxes and the increase in their current disposable income. Under such circumstances, aggregate demand in the goods and services market would expand to AD_2. In the new classical model, though, this will not be the case. Recognizing the higher future taxes, taxpayers will maintain their initial level of consumption spending and use the tax cut to increase their savings in order to generate the additional income required to pay the future taxes implied by the $50 billion of additional debt. Because consumption is unchanged, aggregate demand also remains constant (at AD_1). At the same time, the additional saving (to pay the implied increase in future taxes) allows the government to finance its deficit without an increase in the real interest rate. In this polar case, fiscal policy exerts no demand stimulus. In fact, it does not change much of anything. Output, employment, the price level, and even the real interest rate all remain constant.

The new classical view might be summarized as follows: ***The substitution of government debt for current taxes will fail to alter either the wealth or perma-***

New classical economists emphasize that budget deficits merely substitute future taxes for current taxes. If households did not anticipate the higher future taxes, aggregate demand would increase to AD$_2$ (a). However, demand remains unchanged at AD$_1$ when households fully anticipate the future increase in taxes. Simultaneously, the additional saving to meet the higher future taxes will increase the supply of loanable funds to S$_2$ (b) and permit the government to borrow the funds to finance its deficit without pushing up the real interest rate. In this model, fiscal policy exerts no effect. The real interest rate, real GDP, and level of employment all remain unchanged.

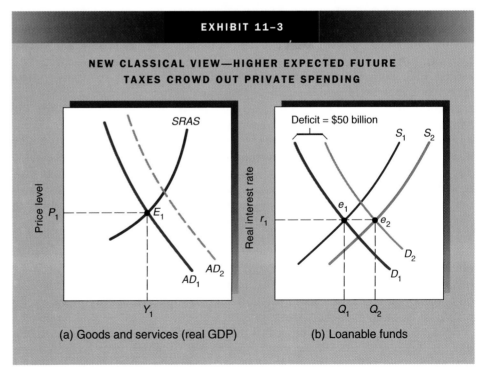

EXHIBIT 11–3

NEW CLASSICAL VIEW—HIGHER EXPECTED FUTURE TAXES CROWD OUT PRIVATE SPENDING

(a) Goods and services (real GDP)

(b) Loanable funds

nent income of the taxpaying households. Households will continue to maintain the same level of consumption even if the government cuts taxes and increases its outstanding debt. Thus, budget deficits will not stimulate aggregate demand. Neither will they affect output and employment. Similarly, the real interest rate is unaffected by deficits since people will save more in order to pay the higher future taxes. According to the new classical view, fiscal policy is completely impotent.

This new classical theory of fiscal policy is controversial.[5] Critics argue that it is unrealistic to expect that taxpayers will anticipate all or even most of the future taxes implied by additional government debt. In addition, even if people did anticipate the higher future taxes, in our world of limited life spans, many would recognize that they will not be around to pay, at least not in full, the future tax liability implied by debt financing. Many economists reject the new classical view of fiscal policy, at least in its pure form. Nonetheless, the significance of the new classical theory and its implications with regard to fiscal policy continue to provide one of the lively topics of debate in modern macroeconomics.

FISCAL POLICY: PROBLEMS OF PROPER TIMING

If fiscal policy is going to reduce economic instability, changes in policy must inject stimulus during a recession and restraint during an inflationary boom. But proper timing of fiscal policy is not an easy task. Because forecasting a forthcoming recession or boom is a highly imperfect science, there is usually a time lag between when a change in policy is needed and when its need is widely recognized by policymakers.

In addition, there is generally a lag between the time when the need for a fiscal policy change is recognized and the time when it is actually instituted. Discretionary fiscal policy requires changes in tax laws and government expenditure programs. The time period required for such changes is likely to be quite lengthy. This will be particularly true for a political structure like that of the United States, with a number of checks and balances built into the system.[6] Congress must act. Experts must study the problem. Congressional committees must meet, hear testimony, and draft legislation. And key legislators may choose to delay action if they can use their positions to obtain special favors for their constituencies. A majority of the lawmakers must be convinced that a proposed

---

[5]See Robert J. Barro, "Are Government Bonds Net Wealth?" *Journal of Political Economy* (November–December 1974): pp. 1095—1117; Robert J. Barro, "The Ricardian Approach to Budget Deficits," *Journal of Economic Perspectives* (spring 1989): pp. 37–44; Alan S. Blinder, "Keynes after Lucas," *American Economic Review* (May 1987): pp. 130–136; James M. Buchanan, "Barro on the Ricardian Equivalence Theorem," *Journal of Political Economy* (April 1976): pp. 337–342; and Gerald P. O'Driscoll, Jr., "The Ricardian Nonequivalence Theorem," *Journal of Political Economy* (February 1977): pp. 207–210.

[6]The time required for the institution of a change in fiscal policy may be shorter under a parliamentary political system, such as that of Canada or the United Kingdom. This is highly likely to be the case if a single party has a parliamentary majority.

action is in the interest of the country, and the details of the policy must be arranged such that they will also believe that their own districts and supporters will not be disadvantaged. All these things take time.

Finally, there is still another factor that adds to the complexity of fiscal policy making: Even after a policy is adopted, it may be six to twelve months before its major impact is felt. If government expenditures are going to be increased, time will be required for competitive bids to be submitted and new contracts granted. Contractors may be unable to begin work right away. Although a tax reduction will generally exert demand stimulus more quickly, it will take time for these effects to work their way through the economy.

Macroeconomic policy making is a little bit like lobbing a ball at a moving target that sometimes changes directions unpredictably. In order to institute fiscal policy in a manner that will help stabilize the economy, policymakers need to know what economic conditions are going to be six, twelve, or eighteen months in the future. Unfortunately, our ability to forecast future economic conditions is limited. Therefore, in a world characterized by dynamic change and unpredictable events, some policy errors are inevitable.

Exhibit 11–4 illustrates the implications of the difficulties involved in the proper timing of fiscal policy. Suppose that policymakers attempt to use expansionary fiscal policy to stimulate aggregate demand during an economic downturn. If inability to forecast a recession and delays accompanying the adoption of a policy change take a substantial period of time, the economy's self-corrective mechanism may already have restored full employment by the time the fiscal stimulus begins to exert its primary impact. If so, the fiscal stimulus will cause excessive demand and inflation. Similarly, restrictive fiscal policy to cool an overheated economy may cause a recession if aggregate demand declines prior to the fiscal restraint.

In the real world, a fiscal policy change is like a two-edged sword; it can both harm and help. If timed correctly, it will reduce economic instability. If timed incorrectly, however, the fiscal change will increase rather than reduce economic instability.

AUTOMATIC STABILIZERS

Automatic stabilizers
Built-in features that tend automatically to promote a budget deficit during a recession and a budget surplus during an inflationary boom, even without a change in policy.

Fortunately, there are a few fiscal programs that tend automatically to apply demand stimulus during a recession and demand restraint during an economic boom. Programs of this type are called **automatic stabilizers.** They are automatic in that, without any new legislative action, they tend to increase the budget deficit (or reduce the surplus) during a recession and increase the surplus (or reduce the deficit) during an economic boom.

The major advantage of automatic stabilizers is that they institute countercyclical fiscal policy without the delays associated with policy changes that require legislative action. Thus, they minimize the problem of proper timing. When unemployment is rising and business conditions are slow, these stabilizers automatically reduce taxes and increase government expenditures, giving the economy a shot in the arm. On the other hand, automatic stabilizers help to apply the brakes to an economic boom, increasing tax revenues and decreasing government spending. Three of these built-in stabilizers deserve specific mention: unemployment compensation, corporate profit tax, and progressive income tax.

EXHIBIT 11-4

WHY PROPER TIMING OF FISCAL POLICY IS DIFFICULT

Goods and services (real GDP)

Here we consider an economy that experiences shifts in AD that are not easy to forecast. Initially, the economy is in long-run equilibrium (E_0) at price level P_0 and output Y_0. At this output, only the natural rate of unemployment is present. However, an investment slump and business pessimism result in an unanticipated decline in aggregate demand (to AD_1). Output falls and unemployment increases. After a time, policy makers institute expansionary fiscal policy seeking to shift aggregate demand back to AD_0. By the time fiscal policy begins to exert its primary effect, though, private investment has recovered and decision makers have become increasingly optimistic about the future. So aggregate demand is already, on its own accord, shifting back to AD_0. Thus, the expansionary fiscal policy over-shifts aggregate demand to AD_2 rather than AD_0. Prices rise as the economy is now overheated. Unless the expansionary fiscal policy is reversed, wages and other resource prices will eventually increase, shifting SRAS to the left, thus pushing the price level still higher (to P_3). Alternatively, suppose an investment boom disrupts the initial equilibrium. The increase in investment shifts aggregate demand to AD_2, placing upward pressure on prices. Policy makers respond by increasing taxes and cutting government expenditures. By the time the restrictive fiscal policy exerts its primary impact, though, investment returns to its normal rate. As a result, the restrictive fiscal policy over-shifts aggregate demand to AD_1 and throws the economy into a recession. Since fiscal policy does not work instantaneously, and since dynamic factors are constantly influencing private demand, proper timing of fiscal policy is not an easy task.

UNEMPLOYMENT COMPENSATION. When an economy begins to dip into a recession, government payments for unemployment benefits will increase as the number of laid off and unemployed workers expands. Simultaneously, the receipts from the employment tax that finances the system will decline because employment falls during a recession. Therefore, this program will automatically run a deficit during a business slowdown. In contrast, during an economic boom, the tax receipts from the program will increase because more people are now working, and the amount paid out in benefits will decline since fewer people are unemployed. Thus, the program will automatically tend to run a surplus during good times. So *without any change in policy*, the unemployment compensation program has the desired countercyclical effect on aggregate demand.[7]

CORPORATE PROFIT TAX. Tax studies show that the corporate profit tax is the most countercyclical of all the automatic stabilizers. This results because corporate profits are highly sensitive to cyclical conditions. Under recessionary conditions, corporate profits will decline sharply, and so will corporate tax payments. This sharp decline in tax revenues will tend to enlarge the size of the budget deficit during the recession. In contrast, when the economy is expanding, corporate profits typically increase much more rapidly than wages, income, or consumption. This increase in corporate profits will result in a rapid increase in the "tax take" from the business sector during the expansion phase of the business cycle. Thus, corporate tax payments will go up during an expansion and fall rapidly during a contraction even though no new legislative action has been instituted.

PROGRESSIVE INCOME TAX. When income grows rapidly, the average personal income tax liability of individuals and families increases. With rising incomes, more people will find their income above the "no tax due" cutoff. Others will be pushed into a higher tax bracket. Therefore, during an economic expansion, revenue from the personal income tax increases more rapidly than income. Other things constant, the budget moves toward a surplus (or smaller deficit), even though the economy's tax rate structure is unchanged. On the other hand, when income declines, many individuals will be taxed at a lower rate or not at all. Income tax revenues will fall more rapidly than income, automatically enlarging the size of the budget deficit during a recession.

FISCAL POLICY AS A STABILIZATION TOOL: A MODERN SYNTHESIS

During the 1960s the basic Keynesian view was widely accepted. Fiscal policy was thought to be highly potent. Furthermore, it was widely believed that political decision makers, with the assistance of their economic advisors, would institute discretionary changes in fiscal policy in a manner that would help stabilize the economy. During the 1970s and 1980s both the operation of fiscal policy and its efficacy as a stabilization tool were analyzed and hotly debated among professional economists. A synthesis view has emerged from that debate. Most macroeconomists—both Keynesian and non-Keynesian—now accept the following three elements of the modern synthesis view.

---

[7]Although unemployment compensation has the desired countercyclical effect on demand, it also reduces the incentive to accept available employment opportunities. As a result, researchers have found that the existing unemployment compensation system actually increases the long-run normal unemployment rate. This issue is discussed in more detail in Chapter 14.

1. Proper timing of discretionary fiscal policy is both difficult to achieve and of crucial importance. Given our limited ability to forecast turns in the business cycle and the political delays that inevitably accompany a change in fiscal policy, the effectiveness of discretionary fiscal policy as a stabilization tool is highly questionable. Therefore, most macroeconomists now place less emphasis on fiscal policy. (Note: The chapter opening quotation from Paul Samuelson, a long-time Keynesian, highlights this point.)

2. Automatic stabilizers reduce the fluctuation of aggregate demand and help to direct the economy toward full employment. Since they are not dependent on legislative action, automatic stabilizers are able consistently to shift the budget toward a deficit during a recession and toward a surplus during an economic boom. Thus, they add needed stimulus during the recession and act as a restraining force during an inflationary boom. Although some question their potency, most all would agree that they exert a stabilizing influence.

3. Fiscal policy is much less potent than the early Keynesian view implied. The current debate among macroeconomists concerning the impact of fiscal policy during normal times is not whether crowding out takes place, but rather how it takes place. The interest-rate crowding-out and new classical models highlight this point. Both models indicate that there are side effects of budget deficits that will substantially, if not entirely, offset their impact on aggregate demand. In the crowding-out model, higher real interest rates and a decline in net exports as the result of currency appreciation reduce private demand and offset the expansionary effects of budget deficits. In the new classical model, higher anticipated future taxes lead to the same result. Both models indicate that fiscal policy will exert little, if any, impact on current aggregate demand, employment, and real output during normal economic times.

SUPPLY-SIDE EFFECTS OF FISCAL POLICY

Thus far, we have focused on the potential demand-side effects of fiscal policy. However, when fiscal changes alter tax rates, they influence the incentive of people to work, invest, and use resources efficiently. Thus, tax changes may also influence aggregate supply. In the past, macroeconomists have often ignored the impact of changes in tax rates, thinking they were of little importance. In recent years, **supply-side economists** have challenged this view.[8] The supply-side argument provided the foundation for the substantial reduction in marginal tax rates in the United States and several other countries during the 1980s.

From a supply-side viewpoint, the marginal tax rate is of crucial importance. As we discussed in Chapter 5, the marginal tax rate determines the breakdown

Supply-side economists
Modern economists who believe that changes in marginal tax rates exert important effects on aggregate supply.

---

[8]See Dwight Lee, ed., *Taxation and the Deficit Economy* (San Francisco: Pacific Institute, 1986); and Lawrence Lindsey, *The Growth Experiment: How the New Tax Policy Is Transforming the U.S. Economy* (New York: Basic Books, 1989) for additional information on supply-side economics.

of one's additional income between tax payments on the one hand and personal income on the other. A reduction in marginal tax rates increases the reward derived from added work, investment, saving, and other activities that become less heavily taxed. People shift into these activities away from leisure (and leisure-intensive activities), tax shelters, consumption of tax-deductible goods, and other forms of tax avoidance. Supply-side economists believe that these substitutions both enlarge the effective resource base and improve the efficiency with which the resources are applied.

The source of the supply-side effects accompanying a change in tax rates is fundamentally different from the source of the demand-side effects. A change in tax policy affects aggregate demand through its impact on disposable income and the flow of expenditures. In contrast, changes in tax rates, particularly marginal tax rates, will affect aggregate supply through their impact on the relative attractiveness of productive activity in comparison to leisure and tax avoidance.

Exhibit 11–5 graphically depicts the impact of a supply-side tax cut, one that reduces marginal tax rates. The lower marginal tax rates increase aggregate supply as the new incentive structure encourages taxpayers to earn additional income and use resources more efficiently. If the tax change is perceived as long-term, both long- and short-run aggregate supply (*LRAS* and *SRAS*) will increase. Real output and income expand.

Of course, the increase in real income will also increase demand (shift to *AD₂*). If the lower marginal rates are financed by a budget deficit, depending on the strength of the crowding-out effect and the anticipation of higher future taxes (new classical theory), aggregate demand may increase by more than aggregate supply. If this is the case, the price level will rise.

Here we illustrate the supply-side effects of a reduction in marginal tax rates. The lower marginal tax rates increase the incentive to earn and use resources efficiently. Since these effects are long-run as well as short-run, both LRAS *and* SRAS *increase (shift to the right). Real output expands. If the lower tax rates are financed by a budget deficit, aggregate demand may expand by a larger amount than aggregate supply, leading to an increase in the price level.*

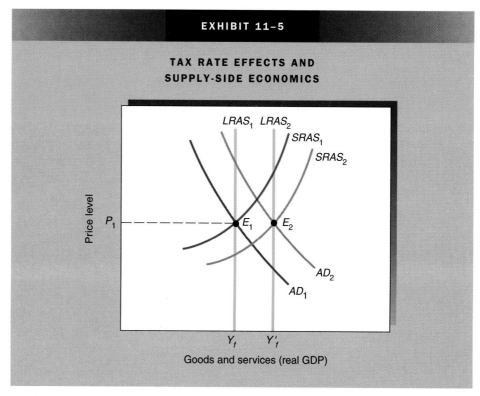

EXHIBIT 11–5

TAX RATE EFFECTS AND SUPPLY-SIDE ECONOMICS

Supply-side economics should not be viewed as a short-run countercyclical tool. It will take time for changing market incentives to move resources out of tax-motivated investments and into higher-yield activities. The full positive effects of lower marginal tax rates will not be observed until labor and capital markets have time to adjust fully to the new incentive structure. *Clearly, supply-side economics is a long-run growth-oriented strategy.*

WHY HIGH TAX RATES TEND TO RETARD OUTPUT

There are three major reasons why high tax rates are likely to retard the growth of output. *First, high marginal tax rates discourage work effort and reduce the productive efficiency of labor.* When marginal tax rates soar to 55 percent or 60 percent, individuals get to keep less than half of what they earn—and when the payoff from working declines, people tend to work less. Some (for example, those with a working spouse) will drop out of the labor force. Others will simply work fewer hours. Still others will decide to take more lengthy vacations, forgo overtime opportunities, retire earlier, or forget about pursuing that promising but risky business venture. In some cases, high tax rates will even drive highly productive citizens to other countries where taxes are lower. High tax rates will also result in inefficient utilization of labor. Some individuals will substitute less-productive activities that are not taxed (for example, do-it-yourself projects) for work opportunities yielding taxable income.

Second, high tax rates will adversely affect the rate of capital formation and the efficiency of its use. When tax rates are high, foreign investment will be repelled and domestic investors will search for investment projects abroad where taxes are lower. In addition, domestic investors will direct more of their time and effort into hobby businesses (for example, collecting antiques, raising horses, or giving golf lessons) that provide both enjoyable activities and tax-shelter benefits. This process will divert investment resources away from projects with a higher rate of return but fewer tax-avoidance benefits. As the result of the tax-shelter benefits, individuals will often be able to gain even though the "investments" reduce the value of resources. Scarce capital is wasted and resources are channeled away from their most productive uses.

Third, high marginal tax rates encourage individuals to substitute less desired tax-deductible goods for more desired nondeductible goods. Here the inefficiency stems from the fact that individuals do not bear the full cost of tax-deductible purchases. High marginal tax rates make tax-deductible expenditures cheap for persons in high tax brackets. Since the personal cost, but not the cost to society, is cheap, taxpayers confronting high marginal tax rates will spend more money on pleasurable, tax-deductible items, such as plush offices, Hawaiian business conferences, and various fringe benefits (for example, a company luxury automobile, business entertainment, and a company retirement plan). Because such tax-deductible purchases reduce their taxes, people will often buy such goods even though they do not value them as much as the cost of producing them.

How important are the supply-side effects accompanying changes in marginal tax rates? Just as economists were divided during the 1970s and 1980s with regard to the demand-side potency of fiscal policy, division currently exists with regard to the importance of the supply-side fiscal incentive effects. Critics of supply-side economics stress that the rate reductions of the 1980s were associated with a modest growth rate of output, a significant reduction in the real tax revenue of the federal government, and large budget deficits. These outcomes do not indicate that the supply-side effects are highly potent. Defenders of the supply-side position respond by noting that the rate reductions of both the 1960s and the 1980s resulted in impressive growth and lengthy economic expansions. Among the major industrial countries, only Japan was able to achieve a growth rate similar to that of the United States during the 1980s. Furthermore, supply-side economists stress that the real tax revenues derived from high-income taxpayers in the top brackets—precisely the area where lower rates have the largest incentive effects—actually increased as the highest rates were reduced during the 1980s. (See Exhibit 5–9 on page 129 for evidence on this point.)

The top marginal tax rates were increased in 1990 by the Bush administration and again in 1993 by the Clinton administration. In both cases, the additional revenue derived from the higher rates was far less than had been projected. (Note: The projections were based on models that failed to include the adjustments of taxpayers to the higher rates.) The 1993 rate increases applied only to taxpayers with high incomes—couples with taxable incomes of more than $140,000 (and singles with more than $115,000). In a study of the high-income taxpayers affected by the rate increases, Martin Feldstein and Daniel Feenberg of the National Bureau of Economic Research found that these taxpayers reported 8.5 percent less income in 1993 than they would have had if their rates had not been increased. As a result, the 1993 tax increase generated less than one-third of the additional revenue that was projected. Furthermore, Feldstein estimated that the economy suffered a deadweight loss (less output and fewer gains from trade) of approximately $2 for every $1 of revenue generated by the rate increases.[9] Like earlier studies of the rate reductions during the 1960s and 1980s, these results indicate that the supply-side response of taxpayers is quite important.

FISCAL POLICY: A CLOSER LOOK AT THE EMPIRICAL EVIDENCE

The accompanying Thumbnail Sketch summarizes the major implications of the alternative theories with regard to the impact of expansionary fiscal policy. In general, the effects of restrictive fiscal policy would be just the opposite. As we previously mentioned, economists use changes in the size of the deficit, rather than the absolute amount of a deficit or surplus, to determine whether fiscal policy is shifting toward expansion or restriction. An increase in the size of the deficit relative to the size of the GDP indicates that fiscal policy is becoming more expansionary. Conversely, a reduction in the size of the deficit relative to GDP would imply a more restrictive fiscal policy.

---

[9]See Martin Feldstein and Daniel Feenberg, *The Effect of Increased Tax Rates on Taxable Income and Efficiency: Preliminary Analysis of the 1993 Tax Rate Increases* (Cambridge, Mass.: National Bureau of Economic Research, 1995); and Martin Feldstein, *Tax Avoidance and the Deadweight Loss of the Income Tax* (Cambridge, Mass.: National Bureau of Economic Research, 1996).

THUMBNAIL SKETCH

IMPACT OF EXPANSIONARY FISCAL POLICY—A SUMMARY

1. *Basic Keynesian model:* An increase in government spending and/or reduction in taxes will be magnified by the multiplier process and lead to a substantial increase in aggregate demand. When an economy is operating below capacity, real output and employment will also increase substantially.

2. *Crowding-out model:* Expansionary fiscal policy will exert little or no impact on aggregate demand and employment because borrowing to finance the budget deficit will push up interest rates and crowd out private spending, particularly investment. In an open economy, the higher interest rates will lead to an inflow of capital, a currency appreciation, and a decline in net exports.

3. *New classical model:* Expansionary fiscal policy will exert little or no impact on aggregate demand and employment because households will anticipate the higher future taxes implied by the debt and reduce their spending (and increase their saving) in order to pay them. Like current taxes, debt (future taxes) will crowd out private spending.

4. *Supply-side model:* A reduction in marginal tax rates will increase the incentive to earn (produce) and improve the efficiency of resource use, leading to an increase in aggregate supply (real output) in the long run.

We are now prepared to take a closer look at the fiscal policy record and consider the actual effects of policy changes more closely. **Exhibit 11–6** provides data on the federal expenditures and revenues for the United States during the past three decades. In general, the data indicate that the budget deficits as a percentage of GDP expanded during recessions (shaded portions of Exhibit 11–6) and contracted during business expansions. For example, revenues declined sharply, leading to a substantial increase in the size of the deficit, during the recession of 1970. In contrast, even though a budget surplus was not achieved, the budget deficit declined as a share of GDP during the 1971–1973 expansion. The deficit also increased sharply during the recessions of 1974–1975, 1980, 1982, and 1990–1991. Correspondingly, it shrank during the periods of prolonged growth following recessions. This pattern of deficits and surpluses indicates that fiscal policy was countercyclical—that it added stimulus during recessions and moved toward restraints during periods of expansion.

However, a review of the record during 1960–1995 indicates that the general countercyclical pattern of fiscal policy was primarily the result of *automatic stabilizers*, rather than active *discretionary* changes in fiscal policy. Judged from the viewpoint of stabilization, the timing of discretionary changes in fiscal policy was often improper.

Perhaps the most effective discretionary fiscal change of recent decades was the 1964 tax cut. Persuaded by his economic advisors, President John F. Kennedy recommended legislation cutting personal income tax rates by almost 20 percent over a two-year period. After President Kennedy's assassination in 1963, the legislation was passed in early 1964. The stimulus provided by the 1964 tax cut worked marvelously. Output increased, and unemployment, which had been hovering near 6 percent, fell below 4 percent in 1966. It was a golden era for economists, particularly Keynesian economists.

Since 1960 the federal budget deficit as a percentage of GDP has generally increased during recessions and declined during periods of economic expansion. (The shaded bars indicate periods of recession.)

Source: *Economic Report of the President,* 1996, tables B–1 and B–77.

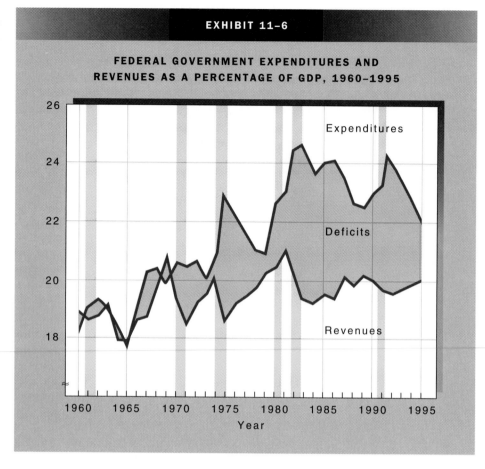

EXHIBIT 11–6

FEDERAL GOVERNMENT EXPENDITURES AND REVENUES AS A PERCENTAGE OF GDP, 1960–1995

Unfortunately, it did not last very long. As Exhibit 11–6 shows, federal expenditures expanded rapidly during 1966–1968, and the budget deficits were quite large during both 1967 and 1968. Even though the economy was operating at a high level of employment, fiscal policy was nonetheless highly expansionary. What is the predicted result of fiscal stimulus when an economy is already operating at capacity? Answer: an increase in the price level. Pushed along by the demand stimulus of both the Vietnam War and Great Society programs, the inflation rate began to accelerate in 1966. In early 1966, many economists—including close advisors of President Lyndon Johnson—called for a tax increase to reduce the fiscal stimulus and retard the rising inflationary pressure. Both President Johnson and Congress failed to heed these early warnings. Finally, after months of delay, President Johnson recommended and Congress passed a temporary (one-year only) 10 percent "surcharge" on personal income tax payments. The tax increase was a case of too little, too late. The temporary tax increase failed to retard consumption spending. In fact, some households borrowed additional funds to pay their higher tax bill while continuing to maintain their current level of consumption. Since the tax increase was not instituted until the deficit was expanding and the inflation rate accelerating, the modest policy shift was unable to turn the tide against the rising prices of the late 1960s.

In 1975 the United States had a similar experience with discretionary fiscal policy—this time in the case of a tax cut. With the economy already in the midst of a serious recession, President Gerald Ford and Congress agreed to a tax-rebate package. The legislation granted taxpayers a partial rebate of their 1974 tax payments and reduced rates for the balance of 1975. The change did little to minimize the effects of the 1974–1975 recession. It came too late—the economy was already beginning to recover when it was instituted. Since the tax cut was temporary, at best, it exerted only a modest impact on current consumption and demand.

Although the discretionary fiscal policy changes of 1964, 1968, and 1975 were motivated by cyclical conditions, the tax changes of the 1980s were overtly tied to the supply-side view that high tax rates retarded long-term economic growth. Nonetheless, the 1982–1984 rate reductions coincided with the sharp deceleration in the inflation rate and a severe recession in 1982. Thus, fiscal policy during and immediately following the 1982 recession was highly expansionary. Government expenditures increased and revenues fell as a share of GDP (see Exhibit 11–6). Later, the Tax Reform Act of 1986 further reduced marginal tax rates, while reducing tax deductions and thus broadening the tax base. Economists who stress the supply-side effects of lower marginal tax rates believe that the rate reductions in the 1980s provided the foundation for the longest peacetime expansion in the history of the United States.

Influenced by the timing difficulties of the 1970s and growth of government debt during the 1980s, the views of both economists and policy makers toward countercyclical fiscal policy have changed dramatically in recent years. In the 1990s, reduction in the size of the budget deficit became the focal point of fiscal policy. In contrast with earlier recessions, Congress and the Bush administration agreed to a *tax increase* and budget accord designed to *reduce* the budget deficit during the 1990–1991 recession. Later, the Clinton Administration *increased* taxes in 1993 and, along with the Republican-controlled Congress, supported policies designed to *reduce* the growth rate of government expenditures in 1995–1996. Even though concern about sluggish growth was widespread, rather than calling for demand stimulus policies, most policy makers sought to reduce the size of the budget deficit in the 1990s.

As Exhibit 11–6 illustrates, the budget deficit declined as a share of GDP during 1992–1995. Of course, a substantial portion of this reduction was the result of the economic recovery, rather than major changes in fiscal policy. Nonetheless, it is clear that fiscal policy is viewed much differently in the 1990s than it was in the 1970s. To a large degree, this change reflects concern about the long run effects of large budget deficits. Reflecting the crowding out theory, many now believe large budget deficits push real interest rates up, slow the rate of capital formation, and lead to economic stagnation. Furthermore, some have expressed concern that continued growth of the national debt *relative to GDP* will eventually reduce the confidence of global investors in the future of the U.S. economy. We will return to this point in the final section of this chapter.

BUDGET DEFICITS AND INTEREST RATES

Do budget deficits cause higher interest rates? The implications of the major fiscal policy models provide different answers to this question. The crowding-out model indicates that deficits will increase the demand for loanable funds and thereby place upward pressure on the real rate of interest. In an open economy, however, the increase in domestic interest rates will be moderated by an inflow of financial capital from abroad. The new classical model implies that the higher expected future taxes will stimulate additional saving and thereby permit the government to expand its borrowing at an unchanged interest rate.

What does the empirical evidence indicate with regard to the relationship between budget deficits and the interest rate? Several studies have addressed this issue. Thus far, the results are mixed. A Congressional Budget Office survey of 24 studies found that only a few indicated that there was a significant positive link between budget deficits and real interest rates. The majority of the studies found no statistically significant relationship.[10] Seemingly, these findings would buttress the new classical view that deficits exert little impact on interest rates. They must, however, be interpreted with caution. When an economy dips into a recession, the budget deficit will tend to rise as the result of the recessionary conditions. When an economy is in a recession, the demand for investment funds is generally weak. In turn, the weak demand for investment will place downward pressure on interest rates. Thus, recessionary business conditions tend to generate both larger budget deficits and lower interest rates. Clearly, this phenomenon makes it more difficult to determine the *independent* impact of budget deficits on interest rates.

Exhibit 11–7 presents data on both the size of the deficit as a share of GDP and the real interest rate during the past three decades. Although the year-to-year linkage between the size of the deficit and the real interest rate is weak, there is some evidence that the generally rising and persistently large deficits of the 1980–1986 period did push the real interest rate upward.[11] Prior to the late 1970s, the real interest rate was generally less than 2 percent. In fact, it hovered in the 2 percent range for three decades following the Second World War. In contrast, during 1981–1986, it fluctuated between 4 percent and 7 percent. In the latter half of the 1980s and in the early 1990s, however, real interest rates were only slightly higher than during the 1960–1980 period, even though the budget deficits were quite large by historical standards. As a sluggish economy contributed to the larger deficits of 1990–1992, the real interest rate continued to decline. As the economy rebounded during 1993–1995, real interest rates rose modestly, but they remained well below the levels of the early 1980s.

Clearly, the evidence indicates that the relationship between budget deficits and real interest rates is weak, at best. Given both the implications of our analysis and the difficulty of isolating the independent impact of the deficit, this is not particularly surprising. After all, even the crowding-out theory indicates that, in an open economy, the upward pressure on interest rates resulting from budget deficits will be moderated by an inflow of capital from abroad.

---

[10]Congressional Budget Office, "Deficits and Interest Rates: Empirical Findings and Selected Bibliography," Appendix A in *The Economic Outlook* (February 1984), pp. 99–102. Also see Charles Plosser, "The Effects of Government Financing Decisions on Asset Returns," *Journal of Monetary Economics* (May 1982); and Paul Evans, "Do Large Deficits Produce High Interest Rates?" *American Economic Review* (March 1985).

[11]Of course, the real interest rate is the money interest rate minus the expected rate of inflation. Since the expected rate of inflation cannot be directly observed, it must be approximated. Exhibit 11–7 uses the actual change in the GDP deflator as a proxy for the expected rate of inflation.

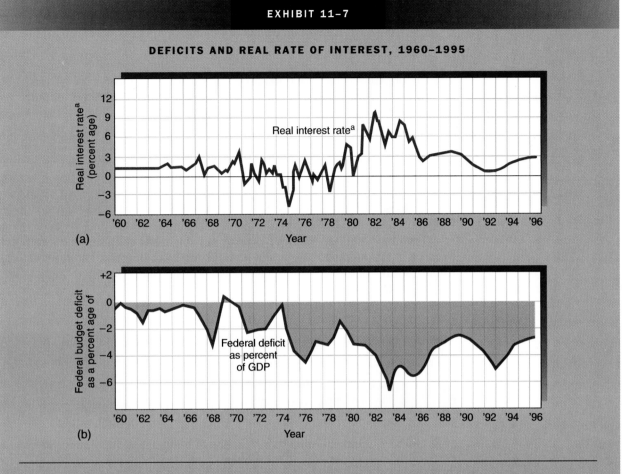

EXHIBIT 11-7

DEFICITS AND REAL RATE OF INTEREST, 1960–1995

(a)

(b)

Although the real interest rate is not closely associated with year-to-year changes in the budget deficit, the persistent large deficits of the 1980–1985 period were associated with high real interest rates.

[a]We use the average quarterly interest rate on 3-month Treasury bills the quarterly change in the GDP implicit price deflator to approximate the minusreal interest rate.

Source: *Board of Governors, Federal Reserve System and the Office of Management and Budget.*

BUDGET DEFICITS, CAPITAL INFLOW, AND NET EXPORTS

What does the evidence say about the inflow of capital during the 1981–1986 period of increasing and persistently large budget deficits? In 1980 the financial investments of Americans abroad exceeded the investments of foreigners in the United States. Thus, there was an outflow of capital. The situation had changed dramatically by the mid-1980s. By 1984 the United States was experiencing an inflow of capital from abroad equal to 2.1 percent of GDP. During the 1985–1987 period, the capital inflow increased to 2.5 percent of GDP. And, just as our theory predicts, this large inflow of capital pushed up the foreign exchange value of the dollar. Between 1980 and 1985, the U.S. dollar appreciated by more than 50 percent (relative to the currencies of our major trading partners) on the foreign exchange market.

As we explained earlier, an appreciation of the dollar will make imports cheaper for Americans, while making American goods more expensive for foreigners. Therefore, appreciation of a currency will depress net exports (or increase net imports). In 1980 the merchandise net imports of the United States were $25 billion—less than 1 percent of GDP. By 1984 the excess of imports relative to exports had jumped to $112 billion, or 3 percent of GDP. During 1985–1987, the net imports of the United States averaged approximately 3.5 percent of GDP.

An inflow of capital, appreciation in currency, and increase in net imports—these are precisely the predicted side effects of large deficits and high real interest rates within the framework of the crowding-out model and an open economy. They indicate that the sharp decline in net exports (increase in net imports) accompanying the inflow of capital and appreciation in the dollar provided the primary source of the crowding out associated with the persistently large deficits of 1980–1986.

DOES A LARGE NATIONAL DEBT LIMIT THE USE OF FISCAL POLICY?

As Exhibits 11-6 and 11-7 illustrate, the size of budget deficits has increased substantially in recent decades. The average federal deficit *as a share of GDP* rose from less than 1 percent in the 1950s and 1960s, to 2.5 percent during the 1970s and approximately 4 percent during the 1980s and 1990s. As the result of these large deficits, the national debt as a share of GDP has been increasing since the mid-1970s (see Illustrated Exhibits II-D and II-E, page 138). *This trend cannot continue. If a nation continues to increase its outstanding debt relative to the size of its economy, at some point its bonds will be downgraded (rated lower because of the weak financial position of the borrower).* If this were to happen, it would be difficult for the nation to borrow funds and it would have to pay an interest rate premium to compensate lenders for the risk associated with the bonds.[12] Although the precise point where these forces will come into play is uncertain, it is clear that credit market pressures place a limit on the ability of a government to continually increase its debt *relative to the size of the economy*.

Some economists think that the United States and several other Western industrial nations, including Belgium, Italy, Greece, Canada, and Sweden, are at or near the point where a substantial increase in their budget deficits (and, there-

---

[12]There is evidence that the large and growing national debts (relative to GDP) of both Italy and Sweden pushed their real interest rates upward in the mid-1990s. See Adrian Orr, Malcolm Edey, and Michael Kennedy, *The Determinants of Real Long-Term Interest Rates* (Paris: Organization for Economic Cooperation and Development, 1996).

fore, outstanding debt) would endanger their credit rating. In essence, credit market pressures could force a government with a large outstanding debt to cut expenditures or raise taxes in order to get its financial house in order. The threat of this factor reduces the ability of a government with a large outstanding debt to follow an expansionary fiscal policy in order to combat a recession. Clearly, under these circumstances, fiscal policy is less viable as a stabilization tool. In Chapter 16, we will take a closer look at the national debt, particularly its impact on the health of an economy and the well-being of future generations.

LOOKING AHEAD

If fiscal policy is now less important, the significance of monetary policy—the other major stabilization weapon—is elevated.[13] We are now ready to integrate the monetary system into our analysis. Chapter 12 will focus on the operation of the banking system and the factors that determine the supply of money. In Chapter 13, we will analyze the impact of monetary policy on real output, interest rates, and the price level.

CHAPTER SUMMARY

1. The federal budget is the primary tool of fiscal policy. Discretionary fiscal policy encompasses deliberate changes in the government's spending and tax policies designed to alter the size of the budget deficit and thereby influence the overall level of economic activity.

2. According to the Keynesian view, fluctuations in aggregate demand are the major source of economic instability. Policies that help to maintain aggregate demand at a level consistent with the economy's full employment capacity will reduce economic instability.

3. Rather than balancing the budget annually, Keynesian analysis indicates that policymakers should use general economic conditions to determine the appropriateness of a budget deficit or surplus. During a recession, Keynesian analysis indicates that expansionary fiscal policy that enlarges the budget deficit would stimulate aggregate demand and help direct the economy to its full employment capacity. Conversely, restrictive fiscal policy—higher taxes and/or a reduction in government expendi-

tures—would be most appropriate during an inflationary boom.

4. Modern macroeconomists stress the potential importance of secondary effects that modify the basic Keynesian analysis. The crowding-out model highlights one of these effects: the increase in demand for loanable funds and upward pressure on real interest rates accompanying larger budget deficits. The higher real interest rates will crowd out private spending, particularly investment, and thereby dampen the stimulus effects of expansionary fiscal policy. Similarly, restrictive fiscal policy will reduce the demand for loanable funds and lower real interest rates, which will stimulate private spending and thereby retard the effectiveness of restrictive policy as an anti-inflation weapon.

5. To the extent that budget deficits lead to higher interest rates, they will encourage an inflow of foreign capital, which will cause the nation's currency to appreciate. Although the inflow of foreign capital will moderate interest-rate increases and the reduction in private investment, the currency appreciation will reduce net exports. Thus, the capital inflow changes the nature of the crowding out, but not necessarily its magnitude.

6. The new classical model introduces another secondary effect—the impact of debt on future taxes. New classical economists argue that substitution of debt for tax financing merely changes the timing, not the level, of taxes. According to this view, taxpayers will anticipate the higher future taxes implied by additional government debt, save more to pay the high future taxes, and, as a result, reduce their current consumption just as if the equivalent taxes had been levied during the current period. The expansion in saving will permit the government to finance its deficit without an increase in the real interest rate. According to the new classical view, substitution of debt for tax financing will leave real interest rates, aggregate demand, output, and employment unchanged.

7. Changes in fiscal policy must be timed properly if they are going to exert a stabilizing influence on an economy. In a world of dynamic change, the effectiveness of discretionary changes in fiscal policy as a stabilization tool

---

[13]With regard to this point, the current view of Paul Samuelson is again revealing. In the 1995 edition of *Economics* (now coauthored with William D. Nordhaus), Samuelson wrote, "Fiscal policy is no longer a major tool of stabilization policy in the United States. Over the foreseeable future, stabilization policy will be performed by Federal Reserve monetary policy" (p. 645).

is reduced because of (a) our limited ability to forecast future macroeconomic conditions, (b) predictable delays that will accompany the institution of a policy change, and (c) a time lag between when a policy change is instituted and when it will exert its primary impact.

8. The problem of proper timing is reduced in the case of automatic stabilizers—programs that apply stimulus during a recession and restraint during a boom even though no legislative action has been taken. Unemployment compensation, corporate profit taxes, and the progressive income tax are examples of automatic stabilizers.

9. With the passage of time, a modern synthesis concerning the impact of fiscal policy as a stabilization tool has emerged. The major points of the synthesis view conclude that (a) during a recession, expansionary fiscal policy is able to stimulate aggregate demand, real output, and employment much as the basic Keynesian model implies; (b) during normal times, higher real interest rates and/or higher expected future taxes substantially dampen the stimulative effects of expansionary fiscal policy; and (c) the difficulties involved in the proper timing of discretionary changes in fiscal policy limit our ability to use it effectively to smooth the economic ups and downs of the business cycle.

10. When fiscal policy changes marginal tax rates, it influences aggregate supply by altering the relative attractiveness of productive activity compared to leisure and tax avoidance. Other things constant, lower marginal tax rates will increase aggregate supply. Most economists believe that the demand-side effects of changes in taxes will dominate the supply-side effects in the short run. Consequently, supply-side economics should be viewed as a long-run strategy, not a countercyclical tool.

11. During the past several decades, the budget deficit has generally expanded as a percentage of GDP during recessions and declined during periods of expansion. This countercyclical pattern of fiscal policy primarily reflects automatic stabilizers rather than discretionary changes in fiscal policy.

12. The year-to-year relationship between budget deficits and the real interest rate is weak. However, the large and increasing deficits of the 1980–1986 period were associated with high real interest rates, an inflow of capital, appreciation in the dollar, and a decline in net exports (increase in net imports). These outcomes are highly consistent with the crowding-out view in an open economy.

13. Discipline applied by credit markets will limit the ability of a government to run large budget deficits that continuously increase outstanding debt relative to the size of the economy. Nations with a large national debt relative to the size of their economy have less flexibility in their use of fiscal policy to combat a recession.

CRITICAL ANALYSIS QUESTIONS

1. Suppose that you are a member of the Council of Economic Advisers. The president has asked you to prepare a statement of "What is the proper fiscal policy for the next 12 months?" Prepare such a statement, indicating (a) the current state of the economy (that is, unemployment rate, growth in real income, and rate of inflation) and (b) your fiscal policy suggestions. Should the budget be in balance? Explain the reasoning behind your suggestions.

*2. What is the crowding-out effect? How does it modify the implications of the basic Keynesian model with regard to fiscal policy? How does the new classical theory of fiscal policy differ from the crowding-out model?

3. Why is it difficult to properly time discretionary changes in fiscal policy? Do you think political factors as well as economic factors limit the use of fiscal policy as a stabilization tool? Why or why not?

*4. What are automatic stabilizers? Explain their major advantage.

5. Outline the supply-side view of fiscal policy. How does this view differ from the various demand-side theories? Explain why a supply-side economist would probably favor a reduction in tax rates financed by the elimination of various tax-deductible items (interest expense, medical expenditures, and state and local taxes, for example).

6. According to the Keynesian view, what fiscal policy actions should be taken if the unemployment rate is abnormally high and real GDP has been flat in recent months?

7. "The economic stimulus of deficit spending is based on money illusion. When the government issues bonds to finance its deficit, it is promising to levy future taxes so that bondholders can be paid back with interest. Bond financing is merely a substitution of future taxation for current taxation. If there are any stimulus effects, they result because taxpayers fail to recognize fully their greater future tax liability and thus they are deceived into thinking that their wealth has increased." Is this view correct? Why or why not?

*8. "If we set aside our reluctance to use fiscal policy as a stabilization force, it is quite easy to achieve full employment and price stability. When output is at less than full employment, we run a budget deficit. If inflation is a problem, we run a budget surplus. Quick implementation of proper fiscal policy will stabilize the economy." Evaluate this view.

9. "Budget deficits may stimulate aggregate demand and output in the short run, but since they divert funds away from capital formation and toward current consumption, they will retard the growth of output in the long run."
   a. Explain why you either agree or disagree with the statement.
   b. Would a proponent of the crowding-out theory agree with this view? Why or why not?

c. Would a new classical economist agree with it? Why or why not?

*10. Some people argue that the growth of output and employment in the 1980s was the result of the large budget deficits. As one politician put it, "Anyone could create prosperity if he wrote $200 billion of hot checks every year." Evaluate this view.

11. In recent years both Republican and Democratic leaders have advocated various proposals to gradually reduce the budget deficit. Suppose the federal deficit was systematically reduced by $25 billion each year until the budget was balanced. What would be the consequences of this policy?

12. If deficits tend to be larger during a recession, how will this affect the relationship between budget deficits and real interest rates?

*13. "If the MPC is .75, a $10 billion increase in government expenditures will stimulate $40 billion of additional expenditures ($10 billion times the multiplier of 4), while a $10 billion tax increase will reduce spending by only $30 billion ($7.5 billion times the multiplier of 4). Thus, a $10 billion increase in both government expenditures and taxes will stimulate aggregate output by $10 billion." Evaluate this statement.

*14. If the impact on tax revenues is the same, does it make any difference whether the government cuts taxes by (a) reducing marginal tax rates or (b) increasing the personal exemption allowance? Explain.

15. Can a nation continually run large budget deficits and increase its outstanding debt (relative to the size of the economy)? Why or why not? Does a large national debt reduce the ability of a government to use expansionary fiscal policy during a recession? Why or why not?

---

*Asterisk denotes questions for which answers are given in Appendix B.

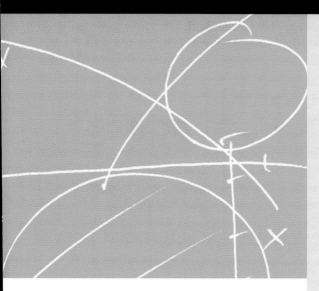

CHAPTER FOCUS

■ What is money? How is the money supply defined?

■ What is a fractional reserve banking system? How does it influence the ability of banks to create money?

■ What are the major functions of the Federal Reserve System?

■ What are the major tools with which the Federal Reserve controls the supply of money?

■ How are financial innovations and other changes affecting the nature of money? What will money be like in the future?

Money is whatever is generally accepted in exchange for goods and services—accepted not as an object to be consumed but as an object that represents a temporary abode of purchasing power to be used for buying still other goods and services.

MILTON FRIEDMAN[1]

[1] Milton Friedman, *Money Mischief: Episodes in Monetary History* (New York: Harcourt Brace Jovanovich, 1992), p. 16.

T he simple model we have developed thus far in this text has three major markets: (1) goods and services, (2) resources, and (3) loanable funds. However, when people make exchanges in any of these markets, they generally use money. Money is used to purchase all types of goods, services, physical assets, and financial assets such as bonds and other savings instruments. Money and monetary policy thus play an important role in the operation of an economy.

This chapter focuses on money and the related issue of how the operation of the banking system and the actions of the central monetary authorities influence the supply of money. In the next chapter, we will analyze how monetary policy affects the level of prices, output, employment, and other important economic variables. But before we are able to deal with this latter topic, we need to know something about the nature of money, how it is measured, and the factors that influence its availability.

WHAT IS MONEY?

Money makes the world go around. Yet, paradoxically, most modern money has no intrinsic worth. Nonetheless, most of us would like to have more of it. Why? Because money is an asset that performs three basic functions: it serves as a medium of exchange, a measuring rod for value, and a means of storing value (purchasing power) for future use.

MEDIUM OF EXCHANGE

Medium of exchange
An asset that is used to buy and sell goods or services.

Money is one of the most important inventions in human history because of its role as a **medium of exchange.** Money simplifies and reduces the costs of transactions. This reduction in transaction cost permits us to realize the enormous gains from specialization, division of labor, and mass-production techniques that underlie our modern standard of living. Without money, exchange would be complicated, time-consuming, and enormously costly. Think what it would be like to live in a barter economy—one without money, where goods were traded for goods. If you wanted to buy a pair of jeans, for example, you would have to first find someone willing to sell you the jeans who is also willing to purchase your labor services or something else you were willing to supply. Such an economy would be highly inefficient.

Money oils the wheels of trade and makes it possible for each of us to specialize in the supply of those things that we do best and to purchase (and consume) a broad cross section of goods and services consistent with our individual preferences. People simply sell their productive services or assets for money and, in turn, use the money to buy the goods and services they want. For example, if a farmer wants to exchange a cow for electricity and medical services, the cow is sold for money, which is then used to buy the electricity and the medical services. Money permits a society to escape the cumbersome procedures of a barter economy.

MEASURING ROD FOR VALUE

Because money is widely used in exchange, it also serves as a unit of measurement—some would say an accounting unit—that can be used to compare the value and cost of things. Just as we use yards or meters to measure distance, units of money are used to measure the exchange value and costs of goods, services, assets, and resources.

Money serves as a common denominator into which the current value of all goods and services can be expressed. If consumers are going to spend their income wisely, they must be able to compare the costs of a vast array of goods and services. Prices measured in units of money help them make such comparisons. Similarly, sound business decisions require cost and productivity comparisons among vastly different productive services. Resource prices and accounting procedures measured in money units facilitate this task.

STORE OF VALUE

Money is a financial asset—a method of storing value and moving purchasing power from one time period to another. There are some disadvantages to using money as a vehicle for storing value (wealth), though. Many methods of holding money do not yield an interest return. During a time of inflation, the purchasing power of money will decline, imposing a cost on those who are holding wealth in the form of money. Money does, however, have the advantage of being a perfectly **liquid asset.** It can be easily and quickly transformed into other goods at a low transaction cost and without an appreciable loss in its nominal value. Because it provides readily available purchasing power for dealing with an uncertain future, most people hold some of their wealth in the form of money.

Liquid asset
An asset that can be easily and quickly converted to purchasing power without loss of value.

WHY IS MONEY VALUABLE?

At various times in the past, societies have used gold, silver, beads, seashells, cigarettes, precious stones, and other commodities as money. When commodities are used as money, people will employ scarce resources—resources that could be used to produce valuable goods and services—trying to produce more of the thing that is used as money. Because of this, the opportunity cost of commodity-based money is high.

If a society uses something as money that costs little or nothing to produce, more scarce resources are available for the production of desired goods and services. Thus, most modern nations use **fiat money,** money that has little or no intrinsic value. A dollar bill is just a piece of paper. Checking account deposits are nothing more than accounting numbers. Coins have some intrinsic value as metal, but in most cases this value is considerably less than their value as money.

How can fiat money be valuable? To a degree, its value is based on the confidence of the people who use it. People are willing to accept fiat money because they know it can be used to purchase real goods and services. Governments issuing fiat money often designate it as "legal tender," meaning it is acceptable for payment of debts.

Fiat money
Money that has neither intrinsic value nor the backing of a commodity with intrinsic value; paper currency is an example.

Money's main source of value, however, is the same as for other commodities; it is determined by demand relative to supply. People demand money because it reduces the cost of exchange. When the supply of money is limited relative to the demand, money will be valuable.

The value of a unit of money—a dollar, for example—is measured in terms of what it will buy. Its value, therefore, is inversely related to the level of prices. An increase in the level of prices and a decline in the purchasing power of a unit of money are the same thing. If the purchasing power of money is to remain stable over time, the supply of money must be controlled. Assuming a constant rate of use, if the supply of money grows more rapidly than the real output of goods and services, prices will rise. In layman's terms, there is "too much money chasing too few goods."

When government authorities rapidly expand the supply of money, it becomes less valuable in exchange and is virtually useless as a store of value. The rapid growth in the supply of money in Germany following the First World War provides a dramatic illustration of this point. During 1922–1923, the supply of German marks increased by 250 percent *per month* for a time. The German government was printing money almost as fast as the printing presses would run. Since money became substantially more plentiful in relation to goods and services, it quickly lost its value. As a result, an egg cost 80 billion marks and a loaf of bread 200 billion. Workers picked up their wages in suitcases. Shops closed at lunch hour to change price tags. The value of money had eroded. More recently, Yugoslavia, Russia, Ukraine (and several other countries of the former Soviet Union), Brazil, Bolivia, Argentina, and Israel among others have experienced this same cycle of rapid growth in the money supply (to pay for government expenditures) and hyperinflation.

M1 (money supply)
The sum of (1) currency in circulation (including coins), (2) checkable deposits maintained in depository institutions, and (3) traveler's checks.

Transaction accounts
Accounts including demand deposits, and interest-earning checkable deposits against which the account holder is permitted to transfer funds for the purpose of making payment to a third party.

Demand deposits
Noninterest-earning checking deposits that can either be withdrawn or made payable on demand to a third party. Like currency, these deposits are widely used as a means of payment.

Other checkable deposits
Interest-earning deposits that are also available for checking.

THE SUPPLY OF MONEY

How is the supply of money defined? There is no straightforward, single answer to this question. Economists and policymakers have developed several alternative measures. We will briefly describe three of the most widely used of these money supply measures.

THE M1 MONEY SUPPLY

Above all else, money is a medium of exchange. The narrowest definition of the money supply, **M1,** focuses on this function. Based on its role as a medium of exchange, it is clear that currency (including both coins and paper bills) and checkable deposits should be included in the supply of money. Deposits that can be drawn from by writing a check are called **transaction accounts.** There are two general categories of transaction accounts. First, there are **demand deposits,** noninterest-earning deposits with banking institutions that are available for withdrawal ("on demand") at any time without restrictions. Demand deposits are usually withdrawn by writing a check. Second, there are **other checkable deposits** that earn interest but carry some restrictions on their transferability.

Interest-earning checkable deposits generally either limit the number of checks written each month or require the depositor to maintain a substantial minimum balance ($1,000, for example). Like currency and demand deposits, interest-earning checkable deposits are available for use as a medium of exchange. Traveler's checks are also a means of payment. They can be freely converted to cash at parity (equal value). ***Thus, the M1 money supply comprises (1) currency in circulation, (2) checkable deposits (both demand deposits and interest-earning checkable deposits), and (3) traveler's checks.***

As **Exhibit 12–1** shows, the total M1 money supply in the United States was $1,125 billion at year-end 1995. Demand and other checkable deposits accounted for approximately two-thirds of the M1 money supply. This large share reflects the fact that most of the nation's business is conducted by check.

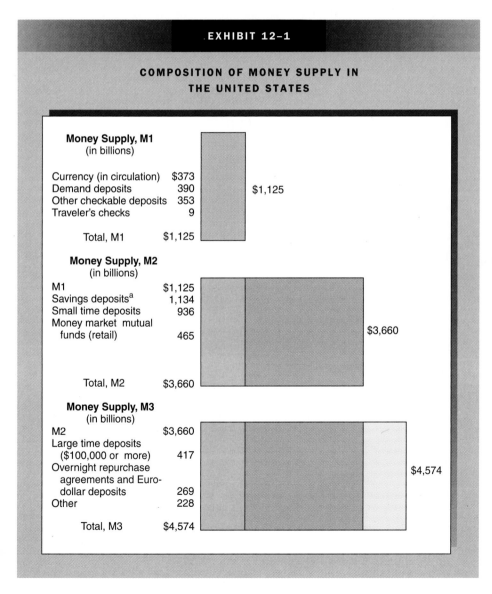

EXHIBIT 12–1

COMPOSITION OF MONEY SUPPLY IN THE UNITED STATES

Money Supply, M1
(in billions)

Currency (in circulation)	$373
Demand deposits	390
Other checkable deposits	353
Traveler's checks	9
Total, M1	$1,125

$1,125

Money Supply, M2
(in billions)

M1	$1,125
Savings deposits[a]	1,134
Small time deposits	936
Money market mutual funds (retail)	465
Total, M2	$3,660

$3,660

Money Supply, M3
(in billions)

M2	$3,660
Large time deposits ($100,000 or more)	417
Overnight repurchase agreements and Euro-dollar deposits	269
Other	228
Total, M3	$4,574

$4,574

The size (as of December 1995) of three alternative measures of the money supply is shown. M1 is the narrowest and most commonly used definition of the money supply. M2, which contains M1 plus the various savings components indicated, is a little more than three times the size of M1. The broadest measure, M3, contains less-liquid forms of savings. M3 is approximately four times the size of M1.

[a]Including money market deposit accounts.

Source: *Federal Reserve Bulletin,* July 1996.

BROADER DEFINITIONS OF MONEY: M2 AND M3

M2 (money supply)
Equal to M1 plus (1) savings deposits, (2) time deposits (accounts of less than $100,000) held in depository institutions, and (3) money market mutual fund shares.

Depository institutions
Businesses that accept checking and saving deposits and use a portion of them to extend loans and make investments. Banks, savings and loan associations, and credit unions are examples.

Money market mutual funds
Interest-earning accounts offered by brokerage firms that pool depositors' funds and invest them in highly liquid short-term securities. Since these securities can be quickly converted to cash, depositors are permitted to write checks (which reduce their share holdings) against their accounts.

M3 (money supply)
Equal to M2, plus (1) time deposits (accounts of more than $100,000) at all depository institutions and (2) large denomination money market mutual funds, (3) overnight loans from customers, and (4) the Eurodollar deposits of U.S. residents.

Eurodollar deposits
Deposits of U.S. dollars by U.S. residents at banks and other financial institutions outside the United States.

In modern economies, several financial assets can easily be converted into checking deposits or currency; therefore, the line between money and "near monies" is often blurred. Broader definitions of the money supply include various assets that can be easily converted to checking account funds and cash. The most common broad definition of the money supply is **M2.** It includes M1 plus (1) savings (including money market deposit accounts), (2) small-denomination time deposits at all **depository institutions,** and (3) money market mutual funds. **Money market mutual funds** are interest-earning accounts offered by brokerage firms that pool depositors' funds and invest them in highly liquid short-term securities. Because these securities can be quickly converted to cash, depositors are permitted to write checks (which reduce their share holdings) against their accounts. In addition to M1, the other components of the M2 money supply provide their owners with funds that can either be used directly as a means of payment or easily and quickly converted for use as a means of exchange. Many economists—particularly those that stress the store-of-value function of money—prefer the broader M2 definition of the money supply to the narrower M1 concept. As Exhibit 12–1 shows, at year-end 1995 the M2 money supply was $3,660 billion, more than three times the M1 money supply.

There is a third method of measuring the money supply, **M3,** which includes M2 plus (1) large-denomination (more than $100,000) time deposits at all depository institutions, (2) large minimum balance ($50,000 or more) money market mutual funds, (3) overnight loans from customers to commercial banks (called *repurchase agreements*), and (4) overnight Eurodollar deposits of U.S. residents. **Eurodollar deposits** are deposits of U.S. dollars by U.S. residents at banks and other institutions outside the United States. The additional assets included in M3 are not quite as liquid as the items that comprise M2. The M3 money supply in December 1995 was $4,574, approximately four times the M1 figure.

CHANGES IN THE NATURE OF M1 AND THE RECENT EMPHASIS ON M2

Developments in financial markets during the past two decades have changed the nature of the M1 money supply. As **Exhibit 12–2** illustrates, during the 1970s M1 was almost entirely composed of currency and demand deposits, neither of which earned interest. The situation changed substantially during the 1980s. Responding to the availability of interest-earning checking accounts, many depositors held some of their savings in these accounts. In recent years these interest-earning checkable deposits have been approximately one-third of the M1 money supply.

Because they earn interest, interest-earning checking accounts are less costly to hold than currency and demand deposits. In essence, interest-earning checking accounts are partly medium-of-exchange money and partly savings. The rapid growth of interest-earning checking accounts during the mid-1980s accelerated the growth rate of the M1 money supply. But they also reduced its comparability with earlier data. Today the M1 money supply has a larger savings

EXHIBIT 12-2

THE CHANGING NATURE OF THE M1 MONEY SUPPLY

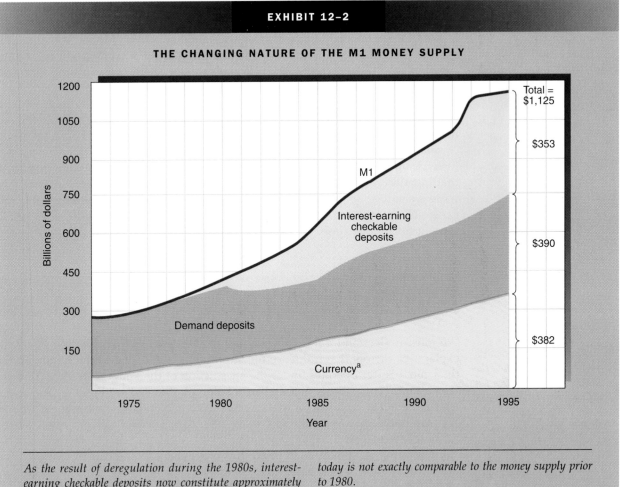

As the result of deregulation during the 1980s, interest-earning checkable deposits now constitute approximately one-third of the M1 money supply. Since the opportunity cost of holding these other checkable deposits is less than for other forms of money, strictly speaking, the money supply today is not exactly comparable to the money supply prior to 1980.

———————————

[a]Traveler's checks are included in this category.

Source: *Federal Reserve Bulletin*, July 1996.

component and a smaller medium-of-exchange component than was true during the 1970s.

The changes in the nature of M1 during the 1980s caused economists and monetary planners to pay more attention to M2. Because both savings and interest-earning checking accounts are components of M2, the financial innovations of the 1980s exerted less impact on M2 than on M1. Most analysts now rely more extensively on M2 (rather than M1) when making comparisons of the money supply (and its growth rate) across time periods that include the 1980s. Reflecting these views, when we use money supply data over the past several decades to assess the impact of monetary policy, we will generally use the M2 definition of money.

CREDIT CARDS VERSUS MONEY

Credit
Funds acquired by borrowing.

It is important to distinguish between money and credit. Money is a financial asset that provides the holder with future purchasing power. **Credit** is liability acquired when one borrows funds. This distinction sheds light on a question students frequently ask: "Because credit cards are often used to make purchases, why aren't credit card expenditures part of the money supply?" In contrast with money, credit cards are not purchasing power. They are merely a convenient means of arranging a loan. When you use your Visa or MasterCard to buy a compact disc player, for example, you are not really paying for the player. Instead, you are taking out a loan from the institution issuing your card, and that institution is paying for the player. Payment is not made by you until you write a check to settle your credit card bill and thereby reduce your money balances. Thus, credit card purchases are not money; they are not an asset representing future purchasing power.

THE BUSINESS OF BANKING

Federal Reserve System
The central bank of the United States; it carries out banking regulatory policies and is responsible for the conduct of monetary policy.

Savings and loan associations
Financial institutions that accept deposits in exchange for shares that pay dividends. Historically, these funds have been channeled into residential mortgage loans. Under banking legislation adopted in 1980, S&Ls are permitted to offer a broad range of services similar to those of commercial banks.

Credit unions
Financial cooperative organizations of individuals with a common affiliation (such as an employer or labor union). They accept deposits, including checkable deposits, pay interest (or dividends) on them out of earnings, and channel funds primarily into loans to members.

We must understand a few things about the business of banking before we can explain the factors that influence the supply of money. The banking industry in the United States operates under the jurisdiction of the **Federal Reserve System,** the nation's central bank. Not all banks belong to the Federal Reserve, but under legislation enacted in 1980 only a nominal difference exists between member and nonmember banks. We will discuss the Fed, as it is often called, in detail later in this chapter.

The banking system is an important component of the capital market. Like other private businesses, banks are profit-seeking operations. Banks provide services (for example, safekeeping of funds and checking-account services) and pay interest in order to attract both checking and savings depositors. They help to bring together people who want to save for the future with those who want to borrow in order to undertake investment projects. Income derived from loans in support of investment projects are the primary sources of revenue for banks.

When deciding whether to fund a project, bankers have a strong incentive to judge both the project's expected profitability and the borrower's creditworthiness. Borrowers may be unable to repay their loans if the funds are channeled into unprofitable investments. In turn, lenders who finance business failures may lose all or part of their funds. Efficient allocation of investment funds is an important source of economic growth. Profitable business projects increase the value of resources and promote economic growth; unprofitable projects have the opposite effect. An efficiently operating capital market, of which the banking system is an integral part, will be good at picking winners—providing funds for profitable rather than unprofitable projects.

In the United States, the banking system consists of savings and loan institutions, credit unions, and commercial banks. **Savings and loan associations** accept deposits in exchange for shares that pay dividends. **Credit unions** are cooperative financial organizations of individuals with a common affiliation (such as an employer) that accept deposits, pay interest (or dividends) on them out of earnings, and channel funds primarily into loans to members. **Commercial banks** offer a wide range of services—including checking and savings accounts and extension of loans—and are owned by stockholders. Under legislation passed in 1980, all of these depository institutions are authorized to offer both checking and savings accounts and to extend a wide variety of loans to customers.

All are now under the jurisdiction of the Federal Reserve System, which applies similar regulations and offers similar services (for example, check clearing and access to borrowing from the Fed) to each type of depository institution. *Therefore, when we speak of the banking industry, we are referring to not only commercial banks, but savings and loan associations and credit unions as well.*

The consolidated balance sheet of commercial banking institutions (**Exhibit 12–3**) illustrates the major banking functions. It shows that the major liabilities of banks are transaction (checking), savings, and time deposits. *From the viewpoint of a bank*, these are liabilities because they represent an obligation of the bank to its depositors. Outstanding interest-earning loans comprise the major class of banking assets. In addition, most banks own sizable amounts of interest-earning securities—bonds issued by either governments or private corporations.

Banking differs from most businesses in that a large portion of its liabilities are payable on demand. However, even though it would be possible for all depositors to demand the money in their checking accounts on the same day, the probability of this occurring is quite remote. Typically, while some individuals are making withdrawals, others are making deposits. These transactions tend to balance out, eliminating sudden changes in demand deposits.

Thus, banks maintain only a fraction of their assets in reserves to meet the requirements of depositors. As Exhibit 12–3 illustrates, **bank reserves**—vault

Commercial banks
Financial institutions that offer a wide range of services (for example, checking accounts, savings accounts, and extension of loans) to their customers. Commercial banks are owned by stockholders and seek to operate at a profit.

Bank reserves
Vault cash plus deposits of the bank with Federal Reserve banks.

Banks provide services and pay interest to attract transaction, savings, and time deposits (liabilities). Most of the deposits are invested and loaned out, providing interest income for the bank. Banks hold a portion of their assets as reserves (either cash or deposits with the Fed) to meet their daily obligations toward their depositors.

Source: *Federal Reserve Bulletin*, July 1996.

EXHIBIT 12–3

FUNCTIONS OF COMMERCIAL BANKING INSTITUTIONS

CONSOLIDATED BALANCE SHEET OF COMMERCIAL BANKING INSTITUTIONS, YEAR-END 1995 (BILLIONS OF DOLLARS)

ASSETS		LIABILITIES	
Vault cash	$ 37	Transaction deposits	$ 809
Reserves at the Fed	20	Savings and time deposits	1,881
Loans outstanding	2,632	Borrowings	695
U.S. government securities	706	Other liabilities	496
Other securities	273	Net worth	360
Other assets	573		
Total	$4,241		$4,241

cash plus reserve deposits with the Federal Reserve—were only $57 billion at year-end 1995, compared to transaction (checking) deposits of $809 billion. Thus, on average, banks were maintaining less than 10 percent of their assets in reserve against the checking deposits of their customers.

FRACTIONAL RESERVE GOLDSMITHING

Economists often like to draw an analogy between our current banking system and the goldsmiths of the past. In the past, gold was used as the means of making payments. It was money. People would store their money with a goldsmith for safekeeping, just as many of us open a checking account for safety reasons. Gold owners received a certificate granting them the right to withdraw their gold anytime they wished. If they wanted to buy something, they would go to the goldsmith, withdraw gold, and use it as a means of making a payment. Thus, the money supply was equal to the amount of gold in circulation plus the gold deposited with goldsmiths.

The day-to-day deposits of and requests for gold were always only a fraction of the total amount of gold deposited. A major portion of the gold simply "lay idle in the goldsmiths' vaults." Taking notice of this fact, goldsmiths soon began loaning gold to local merchants. After a time, the merchants would pay back the gold, plus pay interest for its use. What happened to the money supply when a goldsmith extended loans to local merchants? The deposits of persons who initially brought their gold to the goldsmith were not reduced. Depositors could still withdraw their gold anytime they wished (as long as they did not all try to do so at once). In addition, the merchants were now able to use the gold they borrowed from the goldsmith as a means of payment. *As goldsmiths lent gold, they increased the amount of gold in circulation, thereby increasing the money supply.*

It was inconvenient to make a trip to the goldsmith every time one wanted to buy something. Since people knew that the certificates were redeemable in gold, they began circulating them as a means of payment. The depositors were pleased with this arrangement because it eliminated the need for a trip to the goldsmith every time something was exchanged for gold. As long as they had confidence in the goldsmith, sellers were glad to accept the certificates as payment.

As gold certificates began to circulate as money, the daily withdrawals and deposits with goldsmiths declined even more. Local goldsmiths would keep about 20 percent of the total gold deposited with them so they could meet the current requests to redeem the gold certificates in circulation. The remaining 80 percent of their gold deposits would be loaned out to merchants, traders, and other citizens. Therefore, 100 percent of the gold certificates was circulating as money; that portion of gold that had been loaned out, 80 percent of the total deposits, was also circulating as money. The total money supply, gold certificates plus gold, was now 1.8 times the amount of gold that had been originally deposited with the goldsmith. Since the goldsmiths issued loans and kept only a fraction of the total gold deposited with them, they were able to increase the money supply.

As long as the goldsmiths held enough reserves to meet the current requests of the depositors, everything went along smoothly. Most gold depositors probably did not even realize that the goldsmiths did not have their actual gold and that of other depositors, precisely designated as such, sitting in the "vaults."

Goldsmiths derived income from loaning gold. The more gold they loaned, the greater their total income. Some goldsmiths, trying to increase their income by extending more and more interest-earning loans, depleted the gold in their vaults to imprudently low levels. If an unexpectedly large number of depositors wanted their gold, these imprudent goldsmiths would be unable to meet their requests. As this happened, the system of fractional reserve goldsmithing would tend to break down.

FRACTIONAL RESERVE BANKING

In principle, our modern banking system is very similar to goldsmithing. The United States has a **fractional reserve banking** system. Banks are required to maintain only a fraction of their deposits in the form of cash and other reserves. Just as the early goldsmiths did not have enough gold to pay all their depositors simultaneously, neither do our banks have enough reserves (vault cash and deposits with Federal Reserve banks) to pay all their depositors simultaneously. (Note: As Exhibit 12–3 illustrates, the vault cash plus the reserves held with the Federal Reserve are less than 10 percent of the transaction—that is, checking—deposits of commercial banks.) The early goldsmiths expanded the money supply by issuing loans. So do present-day bankers. The amount of gold held in reserve to meet the requirements of depositors limited the ability of the goldsmiths to expand the money supply. The amount of cash and other **required reserves** limits the ability of present-day banks to expand the money supply.

However, there are also important differences between modern banking and early goldsmithing. Today, the actions of individual banks are regulated by a central bank. The central bank is supposed to follow policies designed to promote a healthy economy. It also acts as a lender of last resort. If all depositors in a specific bank suddenly attempted to withdraw their funds simultaneously, the central bank would intervene and supply the bank with enough funds to meet the demand.

Fractional reserve banking
A system that permits banks to hold reserves of less than 100 percent against their deposits.

Required reserves
The minimum amount of reserves that a bank is required by law to keep on hand to back up its deposits. Thus, if reserve requirements were 15 percent, banks would be required to keep $150,000 in reserves against each $1 million of deposits.

HOW BANKS CREATE MONEY BY EXTENDING LOANS

Under a fractional reserve system, an increase in reserves will permit banks to extend additional loans and thereby create additional transaction (checking) deposits. Since transaction deposits are money, the extension of the additional loans expands the supply of money.

To enhance our understanding of this process, let us consider a banking system without a central bank, one in which only currency acts as a reserve against deposits. Initially, we will assume that all banks are required by law to maintain vault currency equal to at least 20 percent of the checking accounts of their

Required reserve ratio
A percentage of a specified liability category (for example, transaction accounts) that banking institutions are required to hold as reserves against that type of liability.

Excess reserves
Actual reserves that exceed the legal requirement.

depositors. This proportion—the percent of reserves that must be maintained against checkable transaction deposits—is called the **required reserve ratio.** The required reserve ratio in our example is 20 percent. Suppose you found $1,000 that your long-deceased uncle had apparently hidden in the basement of his house. How much would this newly found $1,000 of currency expand the money supply? You take the bills to the First National Bank, open a checking account of $1,000, and deposit the cash with the banker. First National is now required to keep an additional $200 in vault cash, 20 percent of your deposit. However, it received $1,000 of additional cash, so after placing $200 in the bank vault, First National has $800 of **excess reserves,** reserves over and above the amount it is required by law to maintain. Given its current excess reserves, First National can now extend an $800 loan. Suppose it loans $800 to a local citizen to help pay for a car. At the time the loan is extended, the money supply will increase by $800 as the bank adds the funds to the checking account of the borrower. No one else has less money. You still have your $1,000 checking account, and the borrower has $800 for a new car.

When the borrower buys a new car, the seller accepts a check and deposits the $800 in a bank, Citizen's State Bank. What happens when the check clears? The temporary excess reserves of the First National Bank will be eliminated when it pays $800 to the Citizen's State Bank. But when Citizen's State Bank receives $800 in currency, it will now have excess reserves. It must keep 20 percent required reserve ratio, an additional $160, in reserve against the $800 checking account deposit of the automobile seller.

The remaining $640 could be loaned out. Because Citizen's State, like other banks, is in business to make money, it will be quite happy to "extend a helping hand" to a borrower. When the second bank loans out its excess reserves, the deposits of the persons borrowing the money will increase by $640. Another $640 has now been added to the money supply. You still have your $1,000, the automobile seller has an additional $800, and the new borrower has just received an additional $640. Because you found the $1,000 and deposited it in the bank, the money supply has increased by $1,440 ($800 + $640).

Of course, the process can continue. **Exhibit 12–4** follows the potential creation of money resulting from the initial $1,000 through several additional stages. When the reserve requirement is 20 percent, the money supply can expand to a maximum of $5,000, the initial $1,000 plus an additional $4,000 in demand deposits that can be created by extending new loans.

Deposit expansion multiplier
The multiple by which an increase (decrease) in reserves will increase (decrease) the money supply. It is inversely related to the required reserve ratio.

Potential deposit expansion multiplier
The maximum potential increase in the money supply as a ratio of the new reserves injected into the banking system. It is equal to the inverse of the required reserve ratio.

The multiple by which new reserves increase the stock of money is referred to as the **deposit expansion multiplier.** The amount by which additional reserves can increase the supply of money is determined by the ratio of required reserves to deposits. In fact, the **potential deposit expansion multiplier** is merely the reciprocal of the required reserve ratio (r). Mathematically, the potential deposit expansion multiplier is equal to $1/r$. In our example, the required reserves are 20 percent, or one-fifth of the total deposits. So the potential deposit expansion multiplier is 5. If only 10 percent reserves were required, the potential deposit expansion multiplier would be 10, the reciprocal of one-tenth. *The lower the percentage of the reserve requirement, the greater is the potential expansion in the money supply resulting from the creation of new reserves. The fractional reserve requirement places a ceiling on potential money creation from new reserves.*

EXHIBIT 12-4

CREATING MONEY FROM NEW RESERVES

BANK	NEW CASH DEPOSITS: ACTUAL RESERVES	NEW REQUIRED RESERVES	POTENTIAL DEMAND DEPOSITS CREATED BY EXTENDING NEW LOANS
Initial deposit (Bank A)	$1,000.00	$ 200.00	$ 800.00
Second stage (Bank B)	800.00	160.00	640.00
Third stage (Bank C)	640.00	128.00	512.00
Fourth stage (Bank D)	512.00	102.40	409.60
Fifth stage (Bank E)	409.60	81.92	327.68
Sixth stage (Bank F)	327.68	65.54	262.14
Seventh stage (Bank G)	262.14	52.43	209.71
All others (other banks)	1,048.58	209.71	838.87
Total	$5,000.00	$1,000.00	$4,000.00

When banks are required to maintain 20 percent reserves against demand deposits, the creation of $1,000 of new reserves will potentially increase the supply of money by $5,000.

THE ACTUAL DEPOSIT MULTIPLIER

Will the introduction of the new currency reserves necessarily have a full deposit expansion multiplier effect? The answer is no. The actual deposit multiplier will generally be less than the potential for two reasons.

First, the deposit expansion multiplier will be reduced if some persons decide to hold the currency rather than deposit it in a bank. For example, suppose the person who borrowed the $800 in the preceding example spends only $700 and stashes the remaining $100 away for a possible emergency. Only $700 can then end up as a deposit in the second stage and contribute to the excess reserves necessary for expansion. The potential of new loans in the second stage and in all subsequent stages will be reduced proportionally. When currency remains in circulation, outside the banks, it reduces the size of the deposit expansion multiplier.

Second, the actual deposit multiplier will be less than its maximum potential when banks fail to use all the new excess reserves to extend loans. Banks, though, have a strong incentive to loan out most of their new excess reserves. Idle excess reserves do not draw interest. Banks want to use most of these excess reserves so they can generate interest income. **Exhibit 12–5** shows that this is indeed the case. In recent years, excess reserves have accounted for only 1 or 2 percent of the total reserves of banks.

Currency leakages and idle excess bank reserves will result in a deposit expansion multiplier that is less than its potential maximum. However, since

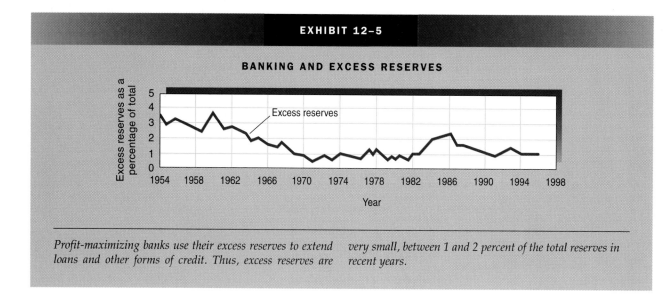

EXHIBIT 12-5

BANKING AND EXCESS RESERVES

Profit-maximizing banks use their excess reserves to extend loans and other forms of credit. Thus, excess reserves are very small, between 1 and 2 percent of the total reserves in recent years.

people generally keep most of their money in bank deposits rather than as currency, and since banks typically eliminate most of their excess reserves by extending loans, strong forces are present that will lead to multiple expansion.

THE FEDERAL RESERVE SYSTEM

Central bank

A bank that accepts deposits and imposes regulations on private commercial banks. The central bank is responsible for the policies that determine the money supply.

Most countries have a central banking authority that controls the money supply and conducts monetary policy. As we previously noted, the **central bank** of the United States is the Federal Reserve System. In the United Kingdom, the central bank is the Bank of England; in Germany, it is the Bundesbank; in Canada, it is the Bank of Canada. Central banks are responsible for the conduct of their nation's monetary policy.

STRUCTURE OF THE FED

The major purpose of the Federal Reserve System (and other central banks) is to regulate the money supply and provide a monetary climate that is in the best interest of the entire economy. Congress has instructed the Federal Reserve, or the Fed, as it is often called, to conduct monetary policy in a manner that promotes both full employment and price stability. Unlike commercial banks, the Federal Reserve is not a profit-making institution. The earnings of the Fed, over and above its expenses, belong to the Treasury.

Exhibit 12-6 illustrates the structure of the Fed. There are three major centers of decision making within the Federal Reserve: (1) the Board of Governors, (2) the district and regional banks, and (3) the Federal Open Market Operations Committee.

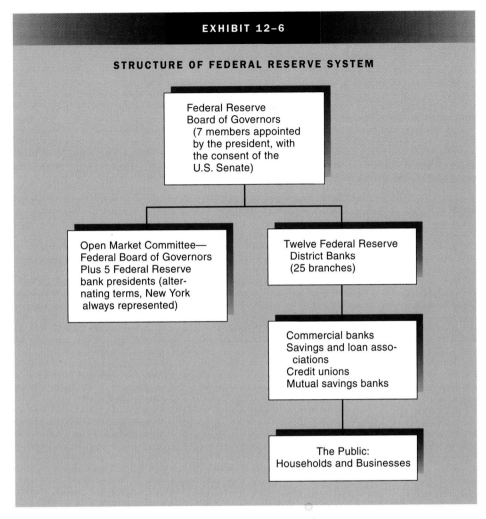

EXHIBIT 12–6

STRUCTURE OF FEDERAL RESERVE SYSTEM

Federal Reserve
Board of Governors
(7 members appointed
by the president, with
the consent of the
U.S. Senate)

Open Market Committee—
Federal Board of Governors
Plus 5 Federal Reserve
bank presidents (alter-
nating terms, New York
always represented)

Twelve Federal Reserve
District Banks
(25 branches)

Commercial banks
Savings and loan asso-
    ciations
Credit unions
Mutual savings banks

The Public:
Households and Businesses

The Board of Governors of the Federal Reserve System is at the center of the banking system in the United States. The board sets the rules and regulations for all depository institutions. The seven members of the Board of Governors also serve on the Federal Open Market Committee, a 12-member board that establishes Fed policy with regard to the buying and selling of government securities, the primary mechanism used to control the money supply in the United States.

1. Board of Governors. The Board of Governors is the decision-making center of the Fed. This powerful board consists of seven members, each appointed to a staggered 14-year term by the president of the United States with the advice and consent of the Senate. The president designates one of the seven members as chair for a four-year term. The Board of Governors establishes the rules and regulations applicable to all depository institutions. It sets the reserve requirements and regulates the composition of the asset holdings of depository institutions. The board is the rule maker, and often the umpire, of the banking industry. Because of the importance of monetary policy and the power of the chair of the Board of Governors, the Fed chair is often said to be the second most influential person—next to the president—in the country. The current chairman of the Board of Governors is Alan Greenspan.

2. Federal Reserve District Banks. There are 12 Federal Reserve District banks with 25 regional branches spread throughout the nation. These district and regional banks operate under the supervision of the Board of Governors.[2] Federal Reserve banks are bankers' banks; they provide banking services for commercial banks. Private citizens and corporations do not bank with Fed. Commercial depository institutions and the federal government are the only banking customers of Federal Reserve banks.

Most depository institutions, regardless of their membership status, usually maintain some deposits with the Fed. Like vault cash, deposits with the Fed count as reserves. The Fed audits the books of depository institutions regularly to assure regulatory compliance and the protection of depositors against fraud. The Federal Reserve banks play an important role in the clearing of checks through the banking system. Since most banks maintain deposits with the Fed, the clearing of checks becomes merely an accounting transaction. The district and regional banks handle approximately 85 percent of all check-clearing services of the banking system.

Federal Open Market Committee (FOMC)

A 12-member board that establishes Fed policy with regard to the buying and selling of government securities, the primary mechanism used to control the money supply in the United States.

3. Federal Open Market Committee (FOMC). The **Federal Open Market Committee** is a powerful committee that determines the Fed's policy with respect to the purchase and sale of government bonds. As we shall soon see, this is the Fed's most frequently used method of controlling the money supply in the United States. This important policy-making arm of the Fed is made up of (1) the seven members of the Board of Governors, (2) the president of the New York District Bank, and (3) four (of the remaining eleven) additional presidents of the Fed's District Banks, who rotate on the committee. Although they do not always have a vote, all 12 Federal Reserve district bank presidents participate in the FOMC meetings, held every five to eight weeks.

THE INDEPENDENCE OF THE FED

Like the Supreme Court, the Federal Reserve operates with considerable independence from both Congress and the executive branch of government. Several factors contribute to this independence. The lengthy terms—14 years—protect the seven members of the Fed's Board of Governors from political pressures. Because their terms are staggered—a new governor is appointed only every two years—even two-term presidents are well into their second term before they are able to appoint a majority of the Fed's governing board. The Fed's earnings on its financial assets, mostly government bonds, provide it with substantially more funding than is needed to cover its operating costs. Thus, it is not dependent on Congress for funding allocations. The Fed does not even have to undergo audits from the General Accounting Office, a government agency that audits the books of most government operations. This independence of the Fed is designed to reduce the likelihood that political pressures will adversely affect its ability to follow a stable, noninflationary monetary policy.

Does the independence of a central bank affect policy? There is considerable variation in the independence of central banks across countries. Like the Fed, the

---

[2]Federal Reserve District Banks are located in Boston, New York City, Philadelphia, Cleveland, Richmond, Atlanta, Chicago, St. Louis, Minneapolis, Kansas City, Dallas, and San Francisco. There are also 25 district "branch banks."

German Bundesbank is largely insulated from the political authorities. In other instances, central banks are directly beholden to political officials. The central banks of many Latin American countries fit into this category. Studies of this topic indicate that when a country's central bank is strongly influenced by political considerations, the bank is more likely to follow inflationary policies.

HOW THE FED CONTROLS THE MONEY SUPPLY

The Fed has three major means of controlling the money stock: (1) establishing reserve requirements for depository institutions, (2) buying and selling U.S. government securities in the open market, and (3) setting the interest rate at which it will loan funds to commercial banks and other depository institutions. We will analyze in detail how each of these tools can be used to regulate the amount of money in circulation.

RESERVE REQUIREMENTS The Federal Reserve System requires banking institutions (including credit unions and savings and loan associations) to maintain reserves against the demand deposits of their customers. The reserves of banking institutions are composed of (1) currency held by the bank (vault cash) and (2) deposits of the bank with the Federal Reserve System. A bank can always obtain additional currency by drawing on its deposits with the Federal Reserve. So both cash-on-hand and the bank's deposits with the Fed can be used to meet the demands of depositors. Both therefore count as reserves.

Exhibit 12–7 indicates the required reserve ratio—the percentage of each deposit category that banks are required to keep in reserve (that is, in the form of either vault cash or deposits with the Fed). As of December 1995 the reserve requirement for transaction accounts was set at 3 percent for amounts under $52 million and 10 percent for amounts in excess of $52 million. Currently, banks are not required to keep reserves against their savings and time deposits.

Why are commercial banks required to maintain assets in the form of reserves? One reason is to prevent imprudent bankers from overextending loans

---

EXHIBIT 12–7

REQUIRED RESERVE RATIO OF BANKING INSTITUTIONS

	TRANSACTION ACCOUNTS	
	$0–$52.0[a] MILLION	OVER $52.0 MILLION
Required reserves as a percent of deposits	3%	10%

Banking institutions are required to maintain 3 percent reserves against transaction-account deposits of less than $52.0 million and 10 percent reserves for transaction deposits over $52.0 million (in effect January 1996).

[a]The $52.0 million dividing point is adjusted each year by 80 percent of the change in total transaction-account deposits in all banking institutions.

Source: *Federal Reserve Bulletin,* July 1996.

and thereby placing themselves in a poor position to deal with any sudden increase in withdrawals by depositors. The quantity of reserves needed to meet such emergencies is not left totally to the judgment of individual bankers. The Fed sets the rules.

The Fed's control over reserve requirements, however, is important for another reason. By altering reserve requirements, the Fed can alter the money supply. The law does not prevent commercial banks from holding reserves over and above those required by the Fed, but, as we have noted, profit-seeking banking institutions prefer to hold interest-bearing assets such as loans rather than excess reserves. Since reserves draw no interest, banks will shave their excess reserves to a low level (see Exhibit 12–5). Because the excess reserves of banks are typically small, an increase in reserve requirements will force them to extend fewer loans. As the volume of loans extended by banks declines, so, too, will the money supply. ***Thus, an increase in the reserve requirements will reduce the supply of money.***

A reduction in reserve requirements will have the opposite impact. When the Fed reduces the reserve requirements, it creates additional excess reserves for banks. Predictably, profit-seeking banks will use a large portion of these newly created excess reserves to extend additional loans. As they do so, their actions will expand the supply of money. ***Thus, lower requirements increase the capacity of banks to lend and, as they extend additional loans, the money supply increases.***

In recent years, the Fed has seldom used its regulatory power over reserve requirements to alter the supply of money. Changes in reserve requirements are a blunt instrument—small changes in reserve requirements can sometimes lead to large changes in the money supply. The magnitude and timing of a change in the money stock resulting from a change in reserve requirements are difficult to predict with precision. For these reasons, the Fed has usually preferred to use other monetary tools.

Open market operations
The buying and selling of U.S. government securities (national debt) by the Federal Reserve.

OPEN MARKET OPERATIONS The most common tool used by the Fed to alter the money supply is **open market operations**—the buying and selling of U.S. securities on the open market. Unlike individuals, businesses, and even other government agencies, the Fed can write a check without funds in its account. When the Fed buys things, it creates money. The primary thing that the Fed buys is the national debt—bonds that were originally issued by the U.S. Treasury and sold to private parties in order to finance budget deficits. As we indicated earlier, Fed policy in this area is conducted by the Federal Open Market Committee (FOMC). The committee, which comprises the 7 members of the Board of Governors and 12 District Bank presidents (only 5 of whom have voting rights), meets every five or six weeks to map out the Fed's policy.

Open market operations affect both the supply of money directly and the reserves available to the banking system. ***When the Fed purchases U.S. securities, it injects "new money" into the economy in the form of an increase in either the currency in circulation or the deposits with commercial banks.*** The sellers of the securities receive checks drawn on a Federal Reserve Bank. If a seller cashes the check, the amount of currency in circulation expands. If, as is more likely to be the case, the seller deposits the check with a commercial bank, the supply of checking-account money increases and new bank reserves are created. When the check is deposited in a bank, the receiving bank acquires a deposit or credit with the Federal Reserve as the check clears. This increases the reserves of the bank, placing it in a position to extend additional loans. As the new loans are extended, the money supply expands by a still larger amount.

Let us consider a hypothetical case. Suppose the Fed purchases $10,000 of U.S. securities from Mary Jones. The Fed receives the securities and Jones receives a check for $10,000, which she deposits in her checking account at City Bank. Her deposit increases the money supply by $10,000, only a fraction of which must be held as required reserves against the new deposits of Jones. Assuming a 10 percent required reserve ratio, City Bank can now extend new loans of up to $9,000 while maintaining its initial reserve position. As the new loans are extended, they too will contribute to a further expansion in the money supply. Part of the new loans will eventually be deposited in other banks, and they also will be able to extend additional loans. As the process continues, the money supply expands by a multiple of the securities purchased by the Fed.

Open market operations can also be used to reduce the money stock. *If the Fed wants to reduce the money stock, it sells some of its current holdings of government securities.* When the Fed sells securities, the buyer pays for them with a check drawn on a commercial bank. As the check clears, both the buyer's checking deposits and the reserves of the bank on which the check was written will decline. Thus, the action will reduce the money supply both directly (by reducing checking deposits) and indirectly (by reducing the quantity of reserves available to the banking system).

The Fed's purchase and sale of U.S. securities determines the size of the **monetary base,** which provides the foundation for the supply of money in the United States. The monetary base is equal to the reserves of commercial banks (vault cash and reserve deposits with the Fed) plus the currency in circulation. Fed purchases of U.S. securities increase the monetary base. Because some of this increase in the monetary base will come in the form of additions to bank reserves, every dollar of securities that the Fed buys will eventually increase the money supply by several dollars. Conversely, every dollar of securities that the Fed sells will reduce the money supply by several dollars.

By how much will the money supply change as the Fed injects and withdraws reserves through open market operations? With time, the money supply will be altered by an amount equal to the change in the size of the monetary base multiplied by the actual deposit expansion multiplier. Given the reserve requirements present in the mid-1990s (see Exhibit 12–7), an increase in the monetary base could potentially expand the money supply (M1) by a multiple of 10 or more. However, as new reserves are injected into the banking system, there is some leakage either because of potential currency reserves circulating as cash or because some banks may be accumulating excess reserves. Thus, the actual size of the deposit expansion multiplier will be substantially less than its potential. As **Exhibit 12–8** shows, since 1970, the money supply (M1) has been between 2.59 and 3.32 times as large as the monetary base, suggesting that the actual deposit expansion multiplier is generally about 3. Therefore, when the Fed's open market operations change the size of the monetary base, the money supply, on average, will tend to change by approximately $3 for each dollar of securities that the Fed either purchases or sells.

Monetary base
The sum of currency in circulation plus bank reserves (vault cash and reserves with the Fed). It reflects the stock of U.S. securities held by the Fed.

DISCOUNT RATE—THE COST OF BORROWING FROM THE FED When banking institutions borrow from the Federal Reserve, they must pay interest on the loan.

EXHIBIT 12–8

HOW BIG IS THE ACTUAL MONEY DEPOSIT MULTIPLIER?

YEAR (DECEMBER)	MONEY SUPPLY (M1) (BILLIONS OF DOLLARS)	MONETARY BASE (BILLIONS OF DOLLARS)	ACTUAL MONEY DEPOSIT EXPANSION MULTIPLIER
1970	214.5	65.0	3.30
1972	249.3	75.2	3.32
1974	274.4	87.5	3.14
1976	306.4	101.5	3.02
1978	358.4	120.4	2.98
1980	408.8	142.0	2.88
1982	474.6	160.1	2.96
1984	552.5	187.2	2.96
1985	620.2	203.6	3.05
1986	724.6	223.7	3.24
1987	750.0	239.9	3.13
1988	786.9	256.9	3.04
1989	794.1	267.7	2.97
1990	826.4	293.1	2.82
1991	897.7	317.4	2.83
1992	1,024.4	351.2	2.92
1993	1,128.6	386.9	2.92
1994	1,148.7	418.7	2.74
1995	1,124.9	435.0	2.59

Between 1970 and 1994, the actual deposit expansion multiplier was between 2.74 and 3.32. Of course, if the reserve requirements were lowered (raised), the deposit expansion multiplier would rise (fall). Note the deposit expansion multiplier has declined during 1994–1995.

Source: Board of Governors of the Federal Reserve System and *Economic Report of the President*, 1996 (Table B-65).

Discount rate
The interest rate the Federal Reserve charges banking institutions for borrowing funds.

The interest rate that banks pay on loans from the Federal Reserve is called the **discount rate.** Borrowing from the Fed is a privilege, not a right. The Fed does not have to loan funds to banking institutions. Banks borrow from the Fed primarily to meet temporary shortages of reserves. They are most likely to borrow from the Fed for a brief period of time while they are making other adjustments in their loan and investment portfolios that will permit them to meet their reserve requirement.

An increase in the discount rate makes it more expensive for banking institutions to borrow from the Fed. Borrowing is discouraged, and banks are more likely to build up their reserves to ensure that they will not have to borrow from the Fed. *An increase in the discount rate is thus restrictive. It tends to discourage banks from shaving their excess reserves to a low level.*

In contrast, a reduction in the discount rate is expansionary. At the lower interest rate, it costs banks less if they have to turn to the Fed to meet a temporary emergency. Therefore, as the cost of borrowing from the Fed declines, banks

FRANK AND ERNEST® by Bob Thaves

Frank and Ernest reprinted by permission of Newspaper Enterprise Association, Inc.

are more likely to reduce their excess reserves to a minimum, extending more loans and increasing the money supply.

The general public has a tendency to overestimate the importance of a change in the discount rate. Many people think an increase in the discount rate means their local banker will (or must) charge them a higher interest rate for a loan.[3] This is not necessarily so. Reserves acquired through transaction and time deposits are the major source of loanable funds for commercial banks. Borrowing from the Fed amounts to less than one-tenth of 1 percent of the available loanable funds of commercial banks. Since borrowing from the Fed is such a negligible source of funds, a 0.5 percent change in the discount rate has something less than a profound impact on the availability of credit and the supply of money. Certainly, it does not necessarily mean that your local bank will alter the rate at which it will lend to you.

If a bank has to borrow to meet its reserve requirements, it need not turn to the Fed. Instead, it can go to the **federal funds market.** In this market, banks with excess reserves extend short-term (sometimes for as little as a day) loans to other banks seeking additional reserves. If the federal funds rate (the interest rate in the federal funds market) is less than the discount rate, banks seeking additional reserves will tap this source rather than borrow from the Fed. In recent years, the Fed has kept its loans to banking institutions at a low level by adjusting the discount rate to match changes in the federal funds rate. As a result, the federal funds rate and the discount rate tend to move together. If the federal funds rate is significantly higher than the discount rate, banks will attempt to borrow heavily from the Fed. Typically, when this happens, the Fed will raise its discount rate, removing the incentive for banks to borrow from it rather than from the federal funds market.

Federal funds market
A loanable funds market in which banks seeking additional reserves borrow short-term (generally for seven days or less) funds from banks with excess reserves. The interest rate in this market is called the federal funds rate.

CONTROLLING THE MONEY SUPPLY—A SUMMARY

As **Exhibit 12–9** illustrates, the foundation of the M1 money supply is the monetary base, primarily composed of the Fed's holdings of U.S. securities. The monetary base can be decomposed into (1) currency in circulation and (2) bank reserves. Of course, the currency in circulation ($382 billion in December 1995)

---

[3]The discount rate is also sometimes confused with the prime interest rate, the rate at which banks loan money to low-risk customers. The two rates are different. A change in the discount rate will not necessarily affect the prime interest rate

The monetary base (currency plus bank reserves) provides the foundation for the money supply. The currency in circulation contributes directly to the money supply, while the bank reserves provide the underpinnings for checking deposits. Fed actions that alter the monetary base will affect the money supply.

[a]Traveler's checks are included in this category.

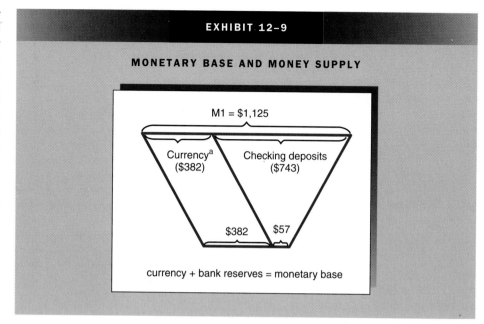

EXHIBIT 12–9

MONETARY BASE AND MONEY SUPPLY

M1 = $1,125

Currency[a] ($382)   Checking deposits ($743)

$382 $57

currency + bank reserves = monetary base

contributes directly to the money supply. In turn, the bank reserves ($57 billion in December 1995) underpin the checking deposits ($743 billion).

The Fed can determine the size of the monetary base through its buying and selling of securities and its discount-rate policy. It can also use adjustments in the reserve requirements to influence the size of checking deposits relative to bank reserves. *If the Fed wants to follow an expansionary policy, it can decrease reserve requirements, purchase additional U.S. securities, and/or lower the discount rate. If it wants to reduce the money stock, it can increase the reserve requirements, sell U.S. securities, and/or raise the discount rate.* Since the Fed typically seeks only small changes in the money stock (or its rate of increase), it typically uses only one or two of these tools at a time to accomplish a desired objective. **Exhibit 12–10** summarizes the monetary tools of the Federal Reserve.

THE FED AND THE TREASURY

Many students have a tendency to confuse the Federal Reserve with the U.S. Treasury, probably because both sound like monetary agencies. The Treasury is a budgetary agency. If there is a budgetary deficit, the Treasury will issue U.S. securities as a method of financing the deficit. Newly issued U.S. securities are almost always sold to private investors (or government trust funds). Bonds issued by the Treasury to finance a budget deficit are seldom purchased directly by the Fed. In any case, the Treasury is primarily interested in obtaining funds so it can pay Uncle Sam's bills. Except for nominal amounts, mostly coins, the Treasury does not issue money. Borrowing—the public sale of new U.S. securities—is the primary method used by the Treasury to cover any excess of expenditures in relation to revenues from taxes and other sources.

EXHIBIT 12–10

SUMMARY OF MONETARY TOOLS OF THE FEDERAL RESERVE

FEDERAL RESERVE POLICY	EXPANSIONARY MONETARY POLICY	RESTRICTIVE MONETARY POLICY
1. Reserve requirements	*Reduce reserve requirements,* because this will create additional excess reserves and induce banks to extend additional loans, which will expand the money supply	*Raise reserve requirements,* because this will reduce the excess reserves of banks, causing them to make fewer loans; as the outstanding loans of banks decline, the money stock will be reduced
2. Open market operations	*Purchase additional U.S. securities,* which will expand the money stock directly, and increase the reserves of banks, inducing bankers in turn to extend more loans; this will expand the money stock indirectly	*Sell previously purchased U.S. securities,* which will reduce both the money stock and excess reserves; the decline in excess reserves will indirectly lead to an additional reduction in the money supply
3. Discount rate	*Lower the discount rate,* which will encourage more borrowing from the Fed; banks will tend to reduce their reserves and extend more loans because of the lower cost of borrowing from the Fed if they temporarily run short on reserves	*Raise the discount rate,* thereby discouraging borrowing from the Fed; banks will tend to extend fewer loans and build up their reserves so they will not have to borrow from the Fed

Whereas the Treasury is concerned with the revenues and expenditures of the government, the Fed is concerned primarily with the availability of money and credit for the entire economy. The Fed does not issue U.S. securities. It merely purchases and sells government securities issued by the Treasury as a means of controlling the economy's money supply. Unlike the Treasury, the Fed can purchase government bonds by writing a check on itself without having deposits, gold, or anything else to back it up. In doing so, the Fed creates money out of thin air. The Treasury does not have this power. The Fed does not have an obligation to meet the financial responsibilities of the U.S. government. That is the domain of the Treasury. The Fed's responsibility is to provide a stable monetary framework for the entire economy. So although the two agencies cooperate with each other, they are distinctly different institutions established for different purposes (see accompanying Thumbnail Sketch).

It is important to recognize that the buying and selling of bonds by the Treasury and by the Fed have different effects on the supply of money. The key point here is that the Treasury and the Fed handle revenues collected from the selling of bonds in a different manner. When the Treasury issues and sells bonds, it does so to pay for federal government expenditures. After all, the Treasury issues the

THUMBNAIL SKETCH

WHAT ARE THE DIFFERENCES BETWEEN THE U.S. TREASURY AND THE FEDERAL RESERVE BANK?

U.S. TREASURY

1. Concerned with the finance of the federal government
2. Issues bonds to the general public to finance the budget deficits of the federal government
3. Does not determine the money supply

FEDERAL RESERVE

1. Concerned with the monetary climate for the economy
2. Does not issue bonds
3. Determines the money supply—primarily through its buying and selling of bonds issued by the U.S. Treasury

bonds in order to generate the required revenue for its spending. The people who buy the bonds from the Treasury have less money, but when the Treasury spends, the recipients of its spending will have more money. Thus, Treasury borrowing and spending does not change the supply of money.

In contrast, when the Fed sells bonds, it, in effect, takes the revenues and holds them, keeping them out of circulation. Because this money is out of circulation and can no longer be used for the purchase of goods and services, the money supply shrinks. On the other hand, if the Fed later wishes to increase the money supply, it can buy bonds, which will increase the availability of bank reserves and the money supply.

AMBIGUITIES IN THE MEANING AND MEASUREMENT OF THE MONEY SUPPLY

In the past, economists have generally used the *growth rate* of the money supply (either M1 or M2) to gauge the direction of monetary policy. A rapid growth rate of the money supply was indicative of expansionary monetary policy—a policy that was adding stimulus to the economy. Conversely, a slow rate of growth, or a decline, in the money stock implied a more restrictive monetary policy. As we discussed earlier, the introduction of interest-earning checking accounts exerted a substantial impact on both the nature and growth rate of the M1 money supply. As interest-earning checking accounts grew in popularity during the mid-1980s, the M1 money supply increased very rapidly. Much of this growth reflected a movement of funds from various forms of savings—most of which were already counted in M2—into the interest-earning checking accounts. These shifts distorted the growth rates of the M1 figures and reduced their reliability as an indicator of monetary policy. Because M2 was less affected by these changes, in recent years economists have generally used M2 to track the direction of monetary policy.

Other structural changes and financial innovations—some of which are already present and others of which are likely to develop in the near future—are altering the nature of money, and therefore the usefulness of the money supply figures (both M1 and M2), as indicators of monetary policy. Let's consider four of these factors.

1. Widespread use of the U.S. dollar outside of the United States. The U.S. dollar is widely used in other countries (see Applications in Economics box, "The Foreign Holdings of U.S. Dollars," on the following page). To a degree, this has been true for a long time. However, a number of countries have recently relaxed legal restraints limiting the domestic use of foreign currencies (and the maintenance of foreign currency bank accounts).[4] As we noted earlier, the currency component of the M1 money supply was approximately $375 billion at year-end 1995. According to a recent study by the Federal Reserve, more than one-half and perhaps as much as two-thirds of this currency is held overseas. The movement of these funds abroad (and our inability to measure it with any degree of precision) substantially reduces the reliability of the M1 money supply figures. (Note: There is also some impact on M2. However, since the currency component is a much smaller proportion of M2 than M1, the distortion of M2 is less severe.)

2. The movement of funds from various interest-earning checking accounts into money market deposit accounts. Recently a substantial number of banks have encouraged customers to move deposits from interest-earning checking accounts into money market deposit accounts. Because the latter are not considered transaction accounts, this reduces the bank's required reserves. Remember, interest-earning checking deposits are included in M1 but money market deposits are not. Therefore, this shift reduces the size of the M1 money supply figures. Many monetary economists believe that this factor is largely responsible for the extremely slow growth of the M1 money supply during 1994 and 1995. (*Note:* Because both the interest-earning checking accounts and money market deposits are included in M2, the M2 figures are not distorted by this shift.)

3. The increasing availability of low-fee stock and bond mutual funds. Until recently, financial investors were generally required to pay a substantial start-up, or load, fee when purchasing stock and bond mutual funds. This reduced their attractiveness relative to the various savings instruments included in the M2 money supply. No-load stock and bond mutual funds—that is, funds without an initial fee—are now increasingly available. Because stock and bond mutual fund investments are not counted in any of the monetary aggregates, movement of funds from various M2 components (money market mutual funds, for example) will distort the M2 money supply figures.[5]

---

[4] The number of countries where it is legal for citizens to maintain a foreign currency bank account rose from 38 in 1985 to 62 in 1995. See James Gwartney, Robert Lawson, and Walter Block, *Economic Freedom of the World: 1975–1995* (Washington, D.C.: Cato Institute, 1996), p. 81

[5] For additional information on this topic, see Sean Collins and Cheryl L. Edwards, "Redefining M2 to Include Bond and Equity Mutual Funds," Federal Reserve Bank of St. Louis *Review*, November/December 1994, pp. 7–30; Kenneth N. Daniels and Neil B. Murphy, "The Impact of Technological Change on the Currency Behavior of Households: An Empirical Cross-Section Study," *Journal of Money, Credit, and Banking* 26 (November 1994): pp. 867–874; and John V. Duca, "Should Bond Funds Be Included in M2?" *Journal of Banking and Finance* 19 (April 1995): pp. 131–152.

THE FOREIGN HOLDINGS OF U.S. DOLLARS

If you have traveled to Mexico, Eastern Europe, or South America lately, you probably noticed that many merchants were willing to accept U. S. dollars as a means of payment. Recent studies indicate that between $200 billion and $250 billion—more than half of the U.S. currency supply—is held abroad.

Why do foreigners want to hold dollars? People in many countries, particularly those with a history of hyperinflation and/or political instability, do not have much faith in their domestic currency. They believe that the U.S. dollar and several other currencies (particularly the German mark and Japanese yen) with a history of relatively stable value are safer ways to store value for the future. Currently, dollars are widely held and, in some cases, used as a means of exchange in Russia (and several other countries of the former Soviet Union), Argentina, Bolivia, Mexico, and other Latin American countries.

How do these holdings of dollars by foreigners affect the U.S. economy? Foreigners acquired the dollars by providing goods and services to Americans. In effect, Americans got valuable goods and services by simply issuing pieces of paper—dollar bills. The dollars held abroad are very much like an interest-free loan to the U.S. government and, indirectly, the taxpayers of the United States. If foreigners were not willing to hold these dollars at a zero interest rate, the U.S. Treasury would have to issue more bonds (perhaps as much as $250 billion more) and pay interest to the bondholders. As a result, the annual interest costs of the federal government would be between $15 billion and $20 billion higher.

---

4. Debit cards and electronic money. Financial innovators are currently developing a more convenient and versatile debit card. A card of this type would transfer funds from the cardholder's bank account to that of the seller. If more and more businesses accept payment via debit cards in the future, Americans will have less reason to hold currency. As less money is held in the form of currency (and more as bank deposits), the money supply will grow rapidly unless the Fed takes offsetting actions. Like the introduction of interest-earning checking accounts, this change in the nature of money may affect the future reliability of the money supply data, particularly the M1 figures, as indicators of monetary policy.

Finally, there is the expected development of electronic money (see Applications in Economics box, "Will Electronic Money Alter Your Future?"). It is difficult to forecast the nature of changes in this area. However, if individuals and businesses can economically and safely use electronic cash, instead of checking deposits and currency, it will clearly change the nature of money and the meaning of the monetary aggregates. If, as is anticipated, these electronic deposits can safely be maintained outside of the banking system, they may also change the major functions of the banking system.

At various times in the past, people have used things ranging from seashells to precious metals as money. Throughout history, major shifts in the nature of money (for example, the shift from precious metals to a fiat currency) have substantially influenced the lives of people. Financial innovations continue to affect the methods of payments that we utilize and the meaning of the various money supply figures. We should keep this in mind as we reflect on the significance and reliability of money supply figures as indicators of monetary policy.

WILL ELECTRONIC MONEY ALTER YOUR FUTURE?

Consider a world where your "paycheck" is deposited in an electronic cash account accessible through your personal computer, but protected with a personal code. With the touch of a few computer keys, you can transfer funds to pay your monthly utility bill, mortgage and auto loan payments, and other regular expenditures. You can also shop on the Internet and use your deposits to pay for magazines, financial advice, and numerous consumer goods. Your funds can also be used to purchase stocks, bonds, mutual funds, and other financial investments. Like your paycheck, earnings from (or future sales of) these investments can be automatically deposited into your electronic cash account. If you want to withdraw some electronic cash, you merely insert a card and load it with transferable purchasing power, which is widely accepted by restaurants, recreation facilities, retail stores, and other business establishments. If you want to give or receive funds from family or friends, you simply merge their "cash cards" with yours and the funds will be added to one card and subtracted from the other. In effect, your electronic money allows you to do anything you can currently do with currency or checking deposits; and you can do it faster, safer, and more conveniently.

Many think that this world, or something very much like it, is only a few years away. If true, it will certainly change the nature of money and reduce the importance of the banking system. It may even limit the ability of central banks to conduct monetary policy.

BANK RUNS, BANK FAILURES, AND DEPOSIT INSURANCE

Between 1922 and 1933, more than 10,000 banks (one-third of the total) failed. Most of these failures were the result of "bank runs," panic withdrawals as people lost confidence in the banking system. Remember, under a fractional reserve system, banks do not have a sufficient amount of reserves to redeem the funds of all (or even most) depositors seeking to withdraw their funds at the same time.

The bank failures of the 1920s and 1930s led to the establishment of the **Federal Deposit Insurance Corporation (FDIC)** in 1934. The FDIC guarantees the deposits of banking customers up to some limit—currently $100,000 per account. Even if the bank should fail, the depositors will be able to get their money (up to the $100,000 limit). Member banks pay an insurance premium to the FDIC for each dollar on deposit, and the FDIC uses these premiums to reimburse depositors with funds in a bank that fails. The FDIC restored confidence in the banking system and brought bank runs to a halt. As a result, bank failures were extremely rare during the 1940–1980 period.

After declining to only a trickle—less than 15 per year during the 1940–1980 period, the number of bank failures increased sharply during the 1980s, soaring to more than 200 per year during 1986–1988. In contrast with the earlier wave of bank failures, the bank failures of the 1980s were generally the result of loan defaults (rather than bank runs). When banks finance investments that turn sour, borrowers are often unable to repay their loans. The bank loses funds when borrowers default. Banks that extend a high percentage of such bad loans will eventually fail.

Federal Deposit Insurance Corporation (FDIC)
A federally chartered corporation that insures the deposits held by commercial banks and thrift institutions.

Why were there so many commercial bank failures and loan defaults during the 1980s? There were several contributing factors. The inflation of the 1970s pushed up both nominal interest rates and the cost of funds. This increase in the cost of funds really put the squeeze on depository institutions that used short-term deposits to finance long-term loans *previously issued at lower interest rates.* While this factor was particularly important in the savings and loan industry, it also exerted an impact on the financial stability of a number of banks.[6] As the result of financial innovations and deregulation, there was a sharp increase in the competitiveness of the banking industry in the 1980s. Many banks were ill-prepared to deal with the more competitive environment. Economic instability in oil markets was also a contributing factor. Bad loans extended to oil interests as the price of oil soared during the 1970s turned sour when oil prices collapsed during the 1980s.

Paradoxically, many economists believe that the structure of the FDIC's premium system also contributed to the bank failures of the 1980s. Unlike the premiums for other forms of insurance, the FDIC charges banks a single premium on deposits, regardless of the risk accompanying the loan portfolio of the bank. During the 1980s, this single-premium element of the deposit insurance system actually encouraged a type of "reverse bank run"—the movement of funds from low-risk to high-risk depository institutions. When banks (and other depository institutions) got into financial trouble during the 1980s, they often attracted funds by offering depositors higher interest rates and sought to restore their financial health by investing these funds in high-yield, risky areas (for example, junk bonds and businesses with low credit ratings). With time, these actions increased both the number of bank failures and the liability of the FDIC. These same forces were even more important in the savings and loan industry.[7]

Economists have been in the forefront of those urging reform in the deposit insurance system so that the premiums charged banking institutions for the insurance will reflect the riskiness of their asset portfolio. Under legislation adopted in 1991, Congress instructed the FDIC to introduce risk-based premiums. To date, it has failed to do so. In essence, the single-rate system provides an implicit subsidy to banks that make risky (or imprudent) investments at the expense of healthy institutions. Removal of this implicit subsidy would encourage banks to evaluate loan applications more carefully, extend fewer risky loans, and follow sounder banking practices.

---

[6]In the 1970s, long-term, fixed-interest-rate mortgages provided the primary source of income for S&Ls. Unsurprisingly, income from these assets failed to keep up with rising interest costs of the period.

[7]For additional analyses of the problems accompanying the current deposit insurance system, see Edward Kane, *The Gathering Crisis in Federal Deposit Insurance* (Cambridge: MIT Press, 1985); R. Dan Brumbaugh, Jr., Andrew S. Carron, and Robert E. Litan, "Cleaning Up the Depository Institutions Mess," *Brookings Papers on Economic Activity,* 1989, no. 1; and David O. Beim, "Beyond the Savings-and-Loan Crisis," *The Public Interest,* spring 1989, pp. 88–99.

LOOKING AHEAD

In this chapter, we focused on the banking industry and the mechanics of monetary policy. We are now ready to analyze the impact of monetary policy on output, growth, and prices. What factors does the Fed consider when deciding whether to expand or contract the money supply? Have Fed policies exerted a stabilizing influence on the economy? These topics will be considered in subsequent chapters.

CHAPTER SUMMARY

1. Money is a financial asset that is widely accepted as a medium of exchange. It also provides a measuring rod for value and a means of storing purchasing power into the future. Without money, exchange would be both costly and tedious.

2. There is considerable debate among economists as to precisely how the money supply should be defined. The narrowest definition of the money supply (M1) includes only (a) currency in the hands of the public, (b) checkable deposits (both demand and interest-earning) held in depository institutions, and (c) traveler's checks. None of these categories of money has significant intrinsic value. Money derives its value from its scarcity relative to its usefulness.

3. The broader M2 money supply includes M1 plus (a) savings and small-denomination time deposits, (b) money market mutual funds shares, (c) money market deposit accounts, (d) overnight loans of customers to commercial banks, and (e) Eurodollar deposits. The introduction of interest-earning checkable deposits has changed the nature of M1 and reduced the comparability of M1 data over time. As a result, most analysts now rely more extensively on M2 data when making comparisons of money supply growth rates across time periods that include the 1980s.

4. Banking is a business. Banks provide their depositors with safekeeping of money, check-clearing services on demand deposits, and interest payments on time deposits. Banks derive most of their income from the extension of loans and investments in interest-earning securities.

5. Under legislation adopted in 1980, savings and loan associations and credit unions are permitted to provide essentially the same services as commercial banks. The Federal Reserve System now regulates all these depository institutions and is legally required to apply uniform reserve requirements to each. In essence, they are all part of an integrated banking system.

6. Under a fractional reserve banking system, banks are required to maintain only a fraction of their deposits in the form of reserves (vault cash or deposits with the Fed). Excess reserves may be invested or loaned to customers. When banks extend additional loans, they create additional deposits and thereby expand the money supply.

7. The Federal Reserve System is a central banking authority designed to provide a stable monetary framework for the entire economy. The Fed is a banker's bank. The structure of the Fed is designed to insulate it from political pressures so that it will have greater freedom to follow policies more consistent with economic stability.

8. The Fed is responsible for monetary policy. It has three major tools with which to control the money supply.

   a. *Establishment of the required reserve ratio.* Under a fractional reserve banking system, reserve requirements limit the ability of banking institutions to expand the money supply by extending more loans. When the Fed lowers the required reserve ratio, it creates excess reserves and allows banks to extend additional loans, expanding the money supply. Raising the reserve requirements has the opposite effect.

   b. *Open market operations.* The open market operations of the Fed can directly influence both the money supply and available reserves. When the Fed buys U.S. securities, the money supply will expand because bond buyers will acquire money and the reserves of banks will increase as checks drawn on Federal Reserve Banks are cleared. When the Fed sells securities, the money supply will contract because bond buyers are giving up money in exchange for securities and the reserves available to banks will decline (causing them to extend fewer loans).

   c. *The discount rate.* An increase in the discount rate is restrictive because it discourages banks from borrowing from the Fed to extend new loans. A reduction in the discount rate is expansionary because it makes borrowing from the Fed less costly.

9. The Federal Reserve and the U.S. Treasury are distinct agencies. The Fed is concerned primarily with the money supply and the establishment of a stable monetary climate. The Treasury focuses on budgetary matters—tax revenues, government expenditures, and the financing of government debt.

10. Historically, the rate of change of the money supply has been used to judge the direction and intensity of monetary policy. However, recent financial innovations and other structural changes (for example, the widespread use of U.S. currency in other countries) have blurred the meaning of money and reduced the reliability of the various money supply measures. In the Computer Age, continued change in this area is likely.

CRITICAL ANALYSIS QUESTIONS

*1. What is meant by the statement, "This asset is illiquid"? List some things that you own, ranking them from most liquid to most illiquid.

2. What determines whether or not a financial asset is included in the M1 money supply? Why are interest-earning checkable deposits included in M1, while interest-earning savings accounts and Treasury bills are not?

*3. What makes money valuable? Does money perform an economic service? Explain. Could money perform its function better if there were twice as much of it? Why or why not?

4. "People are poor because they don't have very much money. Yet, central bankers keep money scarce. If people had more money, poverty could be eliminated." Evaluate this view. Do you think it reflects sound economics?

5. Why can banks continue to hold reserves that are only a fraction of the demand deposits of their customers? Is your money safe in a bank? Why or why not?

*6. Suppose you withdraw $100 from your checking account. How does this transaction affect (a) the supply of money, (b) the reserves of your bank, and (c) the excess reserves of your bank?

7. Explain how the creation of new bank reserves would cause the money supply to increase by some multiple of the newly created reserves.

*8. How will the following actions affect the money supply?
a. A reduction in the discount rate
b. An increase in the reserve requirements
c. Purchase by the Fed of $100 million of U.S. securities from a commercial bank
d. Sale by the U.S. Treasury of $100 million of newly issued bonds to a commercial bank
e. An increase in the discount rate
f. Sale by the Fed of $200 million of U.S. securities to a private investor

9. What's wrong with this way of thinking? "When the government runs a budget deficit, it simply pays its bills by printing more money. As the newly printed money works its way through the economy, it waters down the value of paper money already in circulation. Thus, it takes more money to buy things. Budget deficits are the major cause of inflation."

*10. If the Federal Reserve does not take any offsetting action, what would happen to the supply of money if the general public decided to increase its holdings of currency and decrease its checking deposits by an equal amount?

11. If market interest rates on short-term loans (including the federal funds rate) are declining, does a reduction in the discount rate indicate that the Fed is trying to increase the money supply? What will happen to the amount of reserves borrowed from the Fed if it does not reduce its discount rate? Explain.

*12. If the Fed wants to expand the money supply, why is it more likely to do so by purchasing bonds rather than by lowering reserve requirements?

*13. Are the following statements true or false?
a. "You can never have too much money."
b. "When you deposit currency in a commercial bank, cash goes out of circulation and the money supply declines."
c. "If the Fed would create more money, Americans would achieve a higher standard of living."

14. "The bank failures of the 1980s are a replay of the 1920s and 1930s." Evaluate this statement.

15. How has the nature of the M1 money supply changed in recent years? How have these changes influenced the usefulness of M1 as an indicator of monetary policy? Why do many analysts prefer to use M2 rather than M1 when comparing the monetary policy of the 1980s with that of earlier periods?

16. Why do foreigners often hold U.S. dollars? How does the holding of dollars by foreigners affect the welfare of Americans?

*17. Suppose that the Federal Reserve purchases a bond for $100,000 from Donald Truck, who deposits the proceeds in the Manufacturer's National Bank.
a. What will be the impact of this transaction on the supply of money?
b. If the reserve requirement ratio is 20 percent, what is the maximum amount of additional loans that the Manufacturer's Bank will be able to extend as the result of Truck's deposit?
c. Given the 20 percent reserve requirement, what is the maximum increase in the quantity of checkable deposits that could result throughout the entire banking system as the result of the Fed's action?
d. Would you expect this to happen? Why or why not? Explain.

18. Suppose that the reserve requirement is 10 percent and the balance sheet of the People's National Bank looks like the accompanying example.

Assets		Liabilities	
Vault cash	$ 20,000	Checking deposits	$200,000
Deposits at Fed	30,000	Net worth	15,000
Securities	45,000		
Loans	120,000		

a. What are the required reserves of People's National Bank? Does the bank have any excess reserves?
b. What is the maximum loan that the bank could extend?
c. Indicate how the bank's balance sheet would be altered if it extended this loan.

d. Suppose that the required reserves were 20 percent. If this were the case, would the bank be in a position to extend any additional loans? Explain.

*19. Suppose that the reserve requirements are 10 percent and that the Federal Reserve purchases $2 billion of additional securities on a given day.

a. How will this transaction affect the M1 money supply?

b. If the brokerage firm that sold the bonds to the Fed deposits the proceeds of the sale into its account with City Bank, what is the maximum amount of additional loans that City Bank will be able to extend as the result of this deposit?

c. If, as additional loans are extended throughout the banking system and the proceeds are always redeposited back into a checking account, by how much will the M1 money supply increase if banks use all their additional reserves to extend new loans?

d. Suppose that banks use all their additional reserves to extend new loans but that 10 percent of the loan proceeds (and the additional funds of the brokerage firm) are held as currency rather than being redeposited into a checking account. When this is the case, by how much will the Fed's action increase the money supply?

e. Finally, suppose that banks use 5 percent of their additional reserves to build up their excess reserves and that 10 percent of the proceeds of new loans (and the initial bond sale) end up circulating as currency rather than being redeposited into a checking account. When this is the case, by how much will the Fed's action increase the money supply? Indicate the size of both the potential and actual money deposit multiplier in this case.

f. Why is the actual money deposit multiplier generally less than the potential multiplier?

20. How would the following influence the growth rates of the M1 and M2 money supply figures over time?

a. An increase in the quantity of U.S. currency held overseas

b. A shift of funds from interest-earning checking deposits to money market mutual funds

c. A reduction in the holdings of currency by the general public because debit cards have become more popular and widely accepted

d. The shift of funds from money market mutual funds into stock and bond mutual funds because the fees to invest in the latter have declined

---

*Asterisk denotes questions for which answers are given in Appendix B.

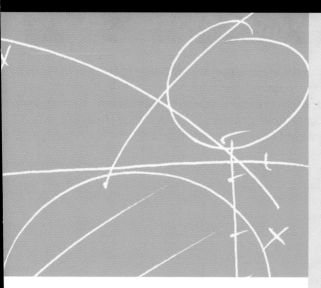

CHAPTER FOCUS

- What are the determinants of the demand for money? How is the supply of money determined?
- How does monetary policy affect interest rates, output, and employment?
- Can monetary policy stimulate real GDP in the short run? Can it do so in the long run?
- Does it make any difference whether people quickly anticipate the effects of a change in monetary policy? Why?
- Does an increase in the stock of money cause inflation?

The conventional wisdom once held that money doesn't matter. *Now there is wide agreement that monetary policy can significantly affect real economic activity in the short run, though only price level in the long run.*

DANIEL L. THORNTON AND DAVID C. WHEELOCK[1]

---

[1]Daniel L. Thornton and David C. Wheelock, "Editor's Introduction," *Federal Reserve Bank of St. Louis: Review*, May/June 1995, p. vii.

Now that we have an understanding of the banking system and the determinants of the money supply, we can relax our prior assumption that the monetary authorities hold the supply of money constant. In this chapter, we will integrate monetary policy into our basic macroeconomic model. After considering factors underlying the demand for and supply of money, we will briefly discuss some of the early views concerning the impact of money on the economy. The primary focus of this chapter is an analysis of how monetary policy works—how shifts in monetary policy affect interest rates, output, and prices.

DEMAND FOR MONEY

Demand for money

The amount of wealth that people desire to hold in the form of money balances—that is, cash and checking-account deposits (or other highly liquid assets in the case of broad measures of the money supply). The quantity demanded is inversely related to the interest rate.

The amount of wealth that households and businesses desire to hold in the form of money balances is called the **demand for money.** Why do individuals and businesses want to hold cash and checking-account money rather than stocks, automobiles, buildings, and consumer durables? When considering this question, it's important not to confuse (1) the demand for money balances with (2) the desire for more wealth (or income). Of course, all of us would like to have more wealth, but we may be perfectly satisfied with our holdings of money in relation to our holdings of other goods, *given our current level of wealth.* When we say people want to hold more (or less) money, we mean that they want to restructure their wealth toward larger (smaller) money balances.

Money provides us with instant purchasing power. Therefore, at the most basic level, we hold money so we can conduct transactions. Households demand money so they can pay for the weekly groceries, the monthly house payment, gasoline for the car, lunch for the kids, and other items purchased regularly. Businesses demand money so they can meet the weekly payroll, pay the utility bill, purchase supplies, and conduct other transactions. Money balances are necessary for transaction purposes because we do not always receive our income at the time we want to buy things. So we keep a little cash or money in the bank to bridge the gap between everyday expenses and payday.

Money balances are like other goods in that price influences the amount demanded. The price, or perhaps more accurately, the opportunity cost of holding money, is directly related to the nominal interest rate. As the nominal interest rate rises, the cost of holding currency and demand deposits (which do not earn interest) increases. Even if you are maintaining money balances in an interest-earning checking account, you could earn a higher rate of interest if you were willing to tie up the funds in a bond or some other less liquid form of savings. *Because higher interest rates make it more costly to hold money, individuals and businesses will try to manage their affairs with smaller money balances when interest rates rise.* Therefore, as part a of **Exhibit 13–1** illustrates, there is an inverse relationship between the quantity of money demanded and the interest rate.

Other things constant, the demand for money balances will increase with the nominal value of transactions. If prices remain constant, while the quantity of goods bought and sold increases, larger money balances will be required to conduct the larger volume of business. Similarly, if wages and prices increase, more money will be required by households to purchase the costlier weekly market

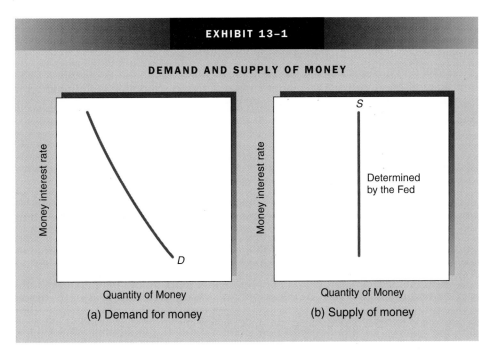

EXHIBIT 13–1

DEMAND AND SUPPLY OF MONEY

(a) Demand for money

(b) Supply of money

The demand for money is inversely related to the money interest rate (a). The supply of money is determined by the monetary authorities (the Fed) through their open market operations, discount-rate policy, and reserve requirements (b).

basket and more money will be required by businesses to pay the larger wage bill. In essence, as nominal GDP increases as the result of either the growth of real output or higher prices, the demand for money balances will also increase— that is, the entire demand for money schedule will shift to the right. Conversely, a decline in nominal GDP will decrease the demand for money, shifting the schedule to the left.

With the passage of time, changes in institutional factors will also influence the demand schedule for money. Both evidence and logic indicate that changes in institutional arrangements have reduced the demand for money in recent years. The widespread use of general-purpose credit cards makes it easier for households to reconcile their bills with their receipt of income. Readily available short-term loans have reduced the need to maintain a substantial cash balance for emergencies. The movement away from agriculture means that more families have a steady income every two weeks or so, rather than an unpredictable income two or three times per year. This steady income makes planning easier. These factors have reduced the need for households to maintain large cash balances (shifting the demand for money schedule to the left).

SUPPLY OF MONEY

Part b of Exhibit 13–1 illustrates the supply schedule for money. Because the money supply is determined by the monetary authorities (the Fed in the United States), and is not affected by changes in the money interest rate, the supply curve is vertical. The money supply is a policy variable; the Fed decides what the supply of money will be. Once the Fed determines the money supply, the nominal interest rate will gravitate toward a level that will bring the quantity of money demanded into balance with the quantity supplied.

How will a change in the money supply affect the economy? Like the modern view of fiscal policy, the modern view of monetary policy is the product of an evolutionary process. Let us consider prior views that have contributed to our modern outlook on the importance of money.

QUANTITY THEORY OF MONEY

For centuries, both laymen and economists recognized that increases in the money supply were a major determinant of changes in price level. Prior to Adam Smith, early social philosophers such as David Hume argued that rapid growth in the supply of money caused inflation. Nearly a hundred years ago, the great classical economists, Englishman Alfred Marshall and American Irving Fisher, formalized a theory in support of this view. According to this early **quantity theory of money,** an increase in the supply of money will lead to a proportional increase in the price level.

Quantity theory of money
A theory that hypothesizes that a change in the money supply will cause a proportional change in the price level because velocity and real output are unaffected by the quantity of money.

The quantity theory of money can be more easily understood once we recognize that there are two ways of viewing GDP. As we previously discussed, nominal GDP is the sum of the price, P, times the output, Y, of each final-product good purchased during the period. In aggregate, P represents the economy's price level, while Y indicates real income or real GDP. There is also a second way of visualizing GDP. When the existing money stock, M, is multiplied by the number of times, V, that money is used to buy final products, this, too, yields the economy's nominal GDP. Therefore,

$$PY = GDP = MV$$

Velocity of money
The average number of times a dollar is used to purchase final goods and services during a year. It is equal to GDP divided by the stock of money.

The **velocity of money** (V) is simply the average number of times a dollar is used to purchase a final product or service during a year. Velocity is equal to nominal GDP divided by the size of the money stock. For example, in 1995 GDP was equal to $7,246 billion, while the M1 money supply was $1,125 billion. On average, each dollar in the M1 money supply was used 6.4 times to purchase final-product goods and services included in GDP. The velocity of the M1 money stock therefore was 6.4. The velocity of the M2 money stock can be derived in a similar manner. In 1995 the M2 money stock was $3,660 billion. Thus, the velocity of M2 was 2.0 ($7,246 billion divided by $3,660 billion).

The concept of velocity is closely related to the demand for money. When decision makers conduct a specific amount of business with a smaller amount of money, their demand for money balances is reduced. Each dollar, though, is now being used more often. Therefore, the velocity of money is increasing. Thus, for a given income level, when the demand for money declines, the velocity of money increases.

Equation of exchange
$MV = PY,$ *where*
M *is the money supply,*
V *is the velocity of money,*
P *is the price level, and*
Y *is the output of goods and services produced.*

When considering the behavior of prices, output, money, and velocity over time, we can write the quantity theory equation in terms of growth rates:

Growth rate of real output + Rate of inflation =
    Growth rate of the money supply + Growth rate of velocity

The $MV = PY$ relationship is simply an identity, or a tautology. Economists refer to it as the **equation of exchange,** because it reflects both the monetary and real sides of each final-product exchange. The quantity theory of money, though, postulates that Y and V are determined by factors other than the amount of money in circulation. Classical economists believed that real output Y was determined by such factors as technology, the size of the economy's resource base, and the skill of the labor force. These factors were thought to be insensitive to changes in the money supply.

Similarly, classical economists thought the velocity of money was determined primarily by institutional factors, such as the organization of banking and credit, the frequency of income payments, the rapidity of transportation, and the communication system. These factors would change quite slowly. Thus, classical economists thought that, for all practical purposes, the velocity, or turnover rate, of money in the short run was constant.

If both Y and V are constant, the $MV = PY$ relationship indicates that an increase in the money supply will lead to a proportional increase in the price level. Classical economists saw the link between the money supply and the price level as being quite mechanical. An increase in the quantity of money led to a proportional increase in the price level. Of course, they recognized that the link might not always be exact. For the purposes of theory, though, it was considered to be a reasonably close approximation to reality.

EARLY KEYNESIAN VIEWS ON MONEY

The Keynesian revolution emphasized the importance of aggregate demand. This notwithstanding, early Keynesians had little confidence in the ability of changes in the money supply to stimulate additional demand, particularly during a recession. During the 1950s, it was popular to draw an analogy between monetary policy and the workings of a string. Like a string, monetary policy could be used to pull (hold back) price increases and thereby control inflation. However, just as one cannot push with a string, according to this popular view, monetary policy could not be used to push (stimulate) aggregate demand.

In his *General Theory*, John Maynard Keynes offered a plausible explanation for why monetary policy might be an ineffective method of stimulating demand. What if the direction of changes in velocity were opposite to the direction of changes in the money stock? If a 5 percent increase in the supply of money led to a 5 percent reduction in velocity, monetary policy would directly influence neither real income nor the price level. Keynes himself recognized this was a highly atypical situation; he rejected the view that changes in the money supply were of no consequence.[2] In the shadow of the Great Depression, though, many of his early followers took the unusual to be typical.

VIEWS OF THE MONETARISTS

Beginning in the late 1950s, economists hotly debated the potency of changes in the supply of money. Led by Milton Friedman, later a Nobel laureate, a group

---

[2]Keynes thought that money did matter, even during a recession. He stated, "So long as there is unemployment, employment will change in the same proportion as the quantity of money, and when there is full employment, prices will change in the same proportion as the quantity of money." *The General Theory of Employment, Interest, and Money* (New York: Harcourt, 1936), p. 296.

Monetarists

A group of economists who believe that (1) monetary instability is the major cause of fluctuations in real GDP and (2) rapid growth of the money supply is the major cause of inflation.

of economists, subsequently called **monetarists,** challenged the existing Keynesian view. In contrast with the early Keynesians, the monetarists argued that changes in the stock of money exerted a powerful influence on both nominal and real GDP, as well as on the level of prices. Indeed, the monetarists charged that erratic monetary policy was the primary source of both business instability and inflation. Milton Friedman proclaimed in his 1967 presidential address to the American Economic Association,

> *Every major contraction in this country has been either produced by monetary disorder or greatly exacerbated by monetary disorder. Every major inflation has been produced by monetary expansion.*[3]

Discretionary monetary policy

Changes in monetary policy instituted at the discretion of policymakers. The policy is not predetermined by rules or formulas.

Although monetarists believe that monetary policy exerts a powerful influence on the economy, they reject active use of **discretionary monetary policy** as an effective stabilization tool. According to the monetarist view, there are *lengthy and unpredictable time lags* between the implementation of a monetary policy change and the observation of its primary effects. When policymakers change the direction of monetary policy, it may be between 6 and 18 months before the change exerts much effect on output. Correspondingly, the effects on the price level may not be felt for 12 to 36 months. During such lengthy time periods, market conditions may change dramatically. Thus, monetarists argue that it is a mistake for decision makers to alter monetary policy in light of current economic conditions.

MODERN VIEW OF MONETARY POLICY

Expansionary monetary policy

A shift in monetary policy designed to stimulate aggregate demand. Bond purchases, creation of additional bank reserves, and an increase in the growth rate of the money supply are generally indicative of a shift to a more expansionary monetary policy.

After nearly four decades of debate between Keynesians and monetarists concerning various aspects of monetary policy, a consensus view has emerged. *Both modern Keynesians and monetarists agree that monetary policy exerts an important impact on our economy.*[4]

TRANSMISSION OF MONETARY POLICY

The modern view indicates that monetary policy exerts an impact on the economy through its influence on interest rates, exchange rates, asset prices, and credit conditions in the loanable funds market. Suppose that the Fed shifts to an **expansionary monetary policy.** When the Fed increases the money supply, it generally does so through open market operations—the purchase of bonds in

---

[3]Milton Friedman, "The Role of Monetary Policy," *American Economic Review,* March 1968, p. 12.

[4]Prior to the 1970s, most Keynesian economists thought that fiscal policy was far more important than monetary policy. This is no longer the case. The evolution of the views of Paul Samuelson, who might properly be regarded as the father of American Keynesian economics, illustrates this point. Commenting on the 12th edition of his classic text in 1985, Samuelson stated:

> *In the early editions of the book* [his best-selling text], *fiscal policy was top banana. In later editions that emphasis changed to equality. In this edition we've taken a stand that monetary policy is most important.*

MILTON FRIEDMAN (1912–   )

Provocative and energetic, Friedman is perhaps the most influential spokesman for a free market economy in the twentieth century. The 1976 recipient of the Nobel Prize, Friedman maintains that business fluctuations are the result of monetary instability. His popular books *Capitalism in Freedom* (1962) and *Free to Choose* (1980), co-authored with his wife Rose, are classical treatises in support of economic freedom. After spending years at the University of Chicago, he is now on the faculty at Stanford University.

the open market. The bond purchases directly increase the money supply and they also increase the reserves available to the banking system. As banks use the additional reserves to extend loans, there will be a further increase in the supply of money.

How will the expansionary monetary policy influence the loanable funds and goods and services markets? **Exhibit 13–2** sheds light on the question. Initially, we consider the situation where the money interest is equal to the real interest rate (r_1), indicating that the expected rate of inflation is zero. When the Fed purchases bonds in order to increase the money supply (shift from S_1 to S_2 in part a), it bids up bond prices and supplies additional reserves to the banking system. The higher bond prices directly reduce the interest rate [Remember: Higher bond prices imply lower interest rates], and the additional reserves place banks in a position to extend additional loans. This combination of factors—higher bond prices and additional reserves that the banks will use to extend loans—will increase the supply of loanable funds (shift to S_2 as shown in part b of Exhibit 13–2). In the short run, the real interest rate will fall to r_2.

How will the Fed's bond purchases, creation of additional bank reserves, and lower real interest rate influence the demand for goods and services? As part c of Exhibit 13–2 illustrates, aggregate demand will increase (shift from AD_1 to AD_2). Economists point to four factors that contribute to this increase in aggregate demand.[5]

1. The lower real interest rate will make current investment and consumption cheaper relative to future spending.   At the lower interest rate, entrepreneurs will undertake some investment projects they otherwise would have forgone. Spending by firms on structures and equipment will increase. Similarly, consumers will decide to expand their purchases of automobiles and consumer durables, which can now be enjoyed with smaller monthly payments.

2. The lower interest rate may also lead to a depreciation in the exchange rate value of the dollar, which will stimulate the net export component of aggregate

---

[5]Although there is general agreement concerning the impact of monetary policy on interest rates, aggregate demand, and output, economists continue to debate precisely how monetary policy is transmitted to the goods and services market. For an excellent set of papers summarizing alternative views and the current state of this debate, see the *Federal Reserve Bank of St. Louis: Review*, May/June 1995, and *Journal of Economic Perspectives* (fall 1995).

When the Fed shifts to a more expansionary monetary policy, it will generally buy additional bonds. This will supply the banking system with additional reserves. Both the Fed's bond purchases and the banks' use of the additional reserves to extend new loans will increase the supply of loanable funds (shift from S_1 to S_2, part b) and place downward pressure on the real rate of interest. As the real interest rate falls (to r_2), aggregate demand increases (to AD_2 in part c). Since the effects of the monetary expansion were unanticipated, the expansion in AD leads to both an increase in current output (to Y_2) and higher prices (inflation) in the short run.

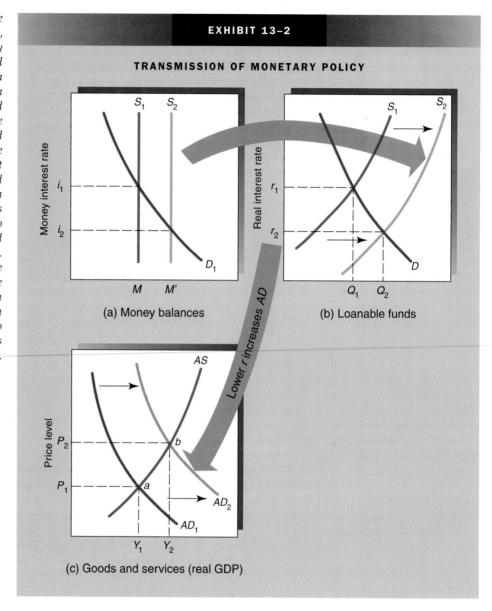

EXHIBIT 13–2

TRANSMISSION OF MONETARY POLICY

(a) Money balances

(b) Loanable funds

(c) Goods and services (real GDP)

demand. As domestic interest rates fall, both domestic and foreign investors will shift some of their financial investments to other countries where rates of return are more attractive. As investors shift funds abroad, they will supply dollars and demand foreign currencies in the exchange-rate market. This will cause the dollar to depreciate. In turn, the depreciation in the exchange-rate value of the dollar will make imports more expensive for Americans and U.S. exports cheaper for foreigners. As a result, U.S. imports will decline and exports will expand. This increase in net exports will also stimulate aggregate demand.

3. The lower interest rates will tend to increase asset prices—for example, the prices of stocks, houses, and other structures—which will also stimulate cur-

rent demand.   As the prices of real and financial assets rise, household wealth increases, which will stimulate additional consumption. Perhaps more important, the higher prices of houses and other physical assets will make new construction of these assets more profitable. As entrepreneurs respond to this increased profitability, the new construction will increase aggregate demand.

4. The increase in bank reserves will make credit more readily available to small and medium-size businesses, enabling them to undertake projects that had previously been delayed.   Banks are the primary source of financing for businesses that are too small to have ready access to the stock and bond markets. When bank reserves are tight, it is therefore difficult for these businesses to obtain bank loans. Many of these firms may simply have to delay investment projects that they believe will be profitable. In contrast, as the Fed supplies additional reserves to the banking system, it will be easier for these small firms to obtain bank financing. This, too, may contribute to the expansion in aggregate demand when the Fed shifts to a more expansionary monetary policy.

UNANTICIPATED EXPANSIONARY MONETARY POLICY

As we have previously discussed, modern macroeconomic analysis stresses the importance of whether a change is anticipated or unanticipated. If people do not anticipate the increase in aggregate demand accompanying an expansionary monetary policy, costs will rise less than prices in the short run. Profit margins will improve. Businesses will respond with an expansion in the output of goods and services (as illustrated by the increase in real output from Y_1 to Y_2 in part c of Exhibit 13–2).

Modern analysis indicates that an unexpected increase in the supply of money will reduce the real rate of interest and increase the availability of credit, thereby triggering an increase in the demand for goods and services. In turn, the increase in aggregate demand will expand real output and employment in the short run.

Part a of **Exhibit 13–3** illustrates the potential of expansionary monetary policy to direct a recessionary economy to full employment. Consider an economy initially at output Y_1, below full employment capacity (Y_f). Expansionary monetary policy will increase aggregate demand (to AD_2). Real output will expand (to Y_f). In essence, the expansionary monetary policy provides an alternative to the economy's self-corrective mechanism. In the absence of demand stimulus, declining resource prices and real interest rates would eventually restore full employment. But many economists believe that this mechanism works quite slowly. If so, expansionary monetary policy may be able to restore long-run, full employment equilibrium more rapidly.

How would a shift to expansionary monetary policy influence output and the price level if the economy were already at full employment? Although this is generally not a desirable strategy, nonetheless, it is interesting to analyze the outcome. As part b of Exhibit 13–3 illustrates, in the short run, an unanticipated increase in aggregate demand resulting from a shift to a more expansionary monetary policy will *temporarily* push real output to Y_2, beyond the economy's long-run capacity of Y_f. Since important components of costs (for example, union

If the impact of an increase in aggregate demand accompanying expansionary monetary policy is felt when the economy is operating below capacity, the policy will help direct the economy to a long-run full-employment equilibrium (a). In this case, the increase in output from Y_1 to Y_f will be long term. In contrast, if the demand-stimulus effects are imposed on an economy already at full employment (b), they will lead to excess demand and higher product prices. Output will temporarily increase (to Y_2). However, in the long run, the strong demand will push up resource prices, shifting short-run aggregate supply to $SRAS_2$. The price level will rise to P_3 and output will recede (to Y_f) from its temporary high.

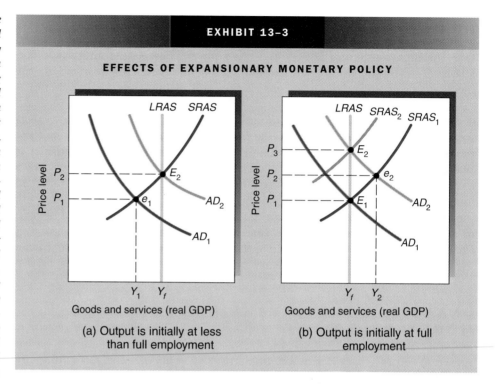

EXHIBIT 13–3

EFFECTS OF EXPANSIONARY MONETARY POLICY

(a) Output is initially at less than full employment

(b) Output is initially at full employment

wage contracts, fixed-interest loans, and lease agreements) are fixed in the short run, the strong demand for goods and services will temporarily increase product prices relative to costs. Profit margins will improve, providing the incentive for business firms to produce the larger output. Unemployment will fall below the natural rate of unemployment.

However, the high rate of output (Y_2) and employment will not be sustainable. Eventually, long-term contracts based on the previously weaker demand (AD_1) will expire. New agreements will reflect the stronger demand. Resource prices will rise, shifting $SRAS$ upward to the left. Eventually, long-run equilibrium (E_2) will result at a higher price level (P_3). Output will recede to Y_f. We can conclude that when an economy is already at full employment, an unexpected shift to a more expansionary monetary policy will temporarily increase output, but in the long run it merely leads to higher prices. Hence, the wisdom of a shift to a more expansionary monetary policy is highly questionable when an economy is already operating at (or beyond) its full-employment capacity.

UNANTICIPATED RESTRICTIVE MONETARY POLICY

Restrictive monetary policy
A shift in monetary policy designed to reduce aggregate demand and place downward pressure on the general level of prices (or the rate of inflation). Bond sales, a decline in bank reserves, and a reduction in the growth rate of the money supply are generally indicative of a restrictive monetary policy.

Suppose the Fed moves toward a more **restrictive monetary policy.** It would generally do so by selling bonds to the general public, which will reduce both the supply of money and the reserves of banks. As the Fed action reduces bond prices and drains reserves from the banking system, real interest rates will rise and availability of credit will tighten. The higher real interest rates will tend to reduce current spending on both investment and consumer durables. They are also likely to cause an inflow of capital and appreciation in the exchange-rate value of the dollar. In turn, this appreciation of the dollar will encourage imports and discourage exports, leading to a reduction in net exports (and aggregate demand). The higher interest rates may also reduce the prices of housing and other assets, thereby discouraging new construction. Finally, the decline in the availability of bank credit may choke off possible investment projects by businesses dependent on bank financing. All these factors will tend to reduce aggregate demand in the goods and services market.

Exhibit 13–4 illustrates the impact of a shift to a more restrictive monetary policy on the loanable funds and goods and services markets. When the Fed sells bonds, its actions will simultaneously decrease the money supply, push bond prices downward, and reduce the quantity of bank reserves. These actions will reduce the supply of loanable funds and increase the real interest rate (from r_1 to r_2) in the loanable funds market (part a of Exhibit 13–4). In turn, the higher interest rates (and tighter credit) will reduce aggregate demand (shift from AD_1 to AD_2 in part b of Exhibit 13–4) in the goods and services market.

The unexpected decline in the demand for goods and services will place downward pressures on prices, squeeze profit margins, and reduce output in the goods and services market. As part b of Exhibit 13–4 illustrates, the price level will decline (to P_2) and output will fall (to Y_2) as the result of the restrictive monetary policy.

The appropriateness of a restrictive policy depends on the initial state of the economy. **Exhibit 13–5** illustrates this point. When an economy is experiencing upward pressure on prices as the result of strong demand, restrictive policy is an effective weapon against inflation. Suppose that, as illustrated by part a of

EXHIBIT 13–4

SHORT-RUN EFFECTS OF A MORE RESTRICTIVE MONETARY POLICY

(a) Loanable funds market

(b) Goods and services (real GDP)

When the Fed shifts to a more restrictive policy, it sells bonds, which reduces the reserves available to banks, decreases the supply of loanable funds, and places upward pressure on interest rates (a). The higher interest rates will decrease aggregate demand (shift to AD_2 in b). When the reduction in aggregate demand is unanticipated, real output will decline (to Y_2) and downward pressure on prices will result.

The stabilization effects of restrictive monetary policy depend on the state of the economy when the policy exerts its primary impact. Restrictive monetary policy will reduce aggregate demand. If the demand restraint comes during a period of strong demand and an overheated economy, then it will limit or even prevent the occurrence of an inflationary boom (a). In contrast, if the reduction in aggregate demand takes place when the economy is at full employment, then it will disrupt long-run equilibrium, reduce output, and result in a recession (b).

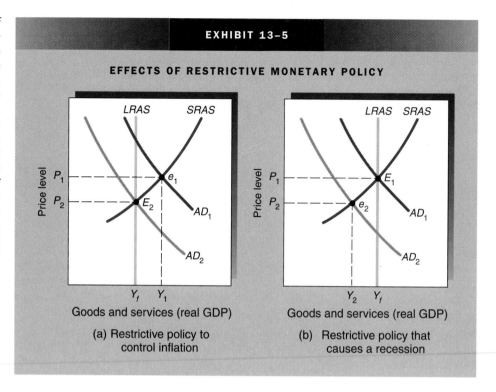

EXHIBIT 13–5

EFFECTS OF RESTRICTIVE MONETARY POLICY

(a) Restrictive policy to control inflation

(b) Restrictive policy that causes a recession

Exhibit 13–5, an economy is temporarily operating at e_1 and Y_1, beyond its full employment real GDP of Y_f. Strong aggregate demand is placing upward pressure on prices. The problem is inflation, not recession. Under these circumstances, restrictive policy makes good sense. It would help control the inflation. If the proper dosage is timed correctly, restrictive policy would retard aggregate demand (to AD_2) and direct the economy to a noninflationary, long-run equilibrium at P_2 and Y_f (that is, E_2).

As part b of Exhibit 13–5 illustrates, however, an unanticipated shift to restrictive policy would be damaging if applied to an economy in full employment equilibrium. If the output of an economy is at full employment (or worse still, at less than full employment), a shift to restrictive policy would reduce aggregate demand (shift to AD_2) and throw the economy into a recession. Real GDP would decline from Y_f to Y_2. Output would fall below the economy's full employment capacity, and unemployment would rise above the natural rate of unemployment.

PROPER TIMING

As with fiscal policy, monetary policy must be properly timed if it is to help stabilize an economy. Exhibits 13–3 and 13–5 emphasize this point. When an economy is operating below its long-run capacity, expansionary monetary policy can stimulate demand and push the output of the economy to its sustainable potential (part a of Exhibit 13–3). Similarly, if properly timed, restrictive monetary policy can help control (or prevent) inflation (part a of Exhibit 13–5).

If it is timed improperly, however, monetary policy can be destabilizing. Expansionary monetary policy is a source of inflation if the effects of the policy are felt when the economy is already at or beyond its capacity (part b of Exhibit 13–3). Similarly, if the effects of a restrictive policy come when an economy is operating at its potential GDP, recession is the likely outcome (part b of Exhibit 13–5). Worse still, the impact of restrictive policy may be disastrous if imposed on an economy already in the midst of a recession.

Proper timing of monetary policy is not an easy task. In contrast with fiscal policy changes requiring time-consuming congressional action, the Federal Reserve can institute a change in monetary policy quite rapidly. However, as an economy drifts toward a recession or an inflationary boom, policymakers may not immediately recognize the need for a change. Therefore, there may be a time lag of several months between the change in economic conditions and the time that policymakers at the Fed recognize that change. More important, there will be an additional time lag between the institution of a policy and when it begins to exert a significant impact on aggregate demand. Economists who have studied this issue estimate that this impact lag will be five or six months at a minimum. Some economists, particularly monetarists, estimate that the primary impact of a change in monetary policy on output and employment is often as much as 12 to 18 months after the change is instituted. In terms of its impact on the price level and rate of inflation, the estimated impact lag is even longer, perhaps as much as 36 months. Given our limited ability to forecast the future, such lengthy time lags clearly reduce the potential effectiveness of discretionary monetary policy as a stabilization tool.

MONETARY POLICY IN THE LONG RUN

Thus far, we have focused on the impact of monetary policy in a static framework. Of course, in a static framework, an increase in the price level implies inflation. However, inflation is a dynamic concept—a rate of increase in prices, not a once-and-for-all movement to a higher price level. It is also important to distinguish between the static and dynamic with regard to the money supply. Static analysis focuses on the change in the supply of money. In a dynamic setting, though, a change in the *growth rate* of the money supply is more indicative of the direction of monetary policy.

In this section, we want to recast our analysis slightly so we can better illustrate both dynamic factors and the long-run adjustment process. We will begin with a simple dynamic case. Suppose that the output of an economy is growing at a 3 percent annual rate and that the monetary authorities are expanding the money supply by 3 percent each year. In addition, let's assume that the velocity of money is constant. This would imply that the 3 percent annual increase in output would lead to a 3 percent annual increase in the demand for money. Under these circumstances, the 3 percent monetary growth would be consistent with stable prices (zero inflation). Initially, we will assume that the economy's real interest rate is 4 percent. Because the inflation rate is zero, the nominal rate of interest is also equal to 4 percent. **Exhibits 13–6** and **13–7** illustrate an economy initially (Period 1) characterized by these conditions.

Here we illustrate the long-term impact of an increase in the annual growth rate of the money supply from 3 to 8 percent. Initially, prices are stable (P_{100}) when the money supply is expanding by 3 percent annually. The acceleration in the growth rate of the money supply increases aggregate demand (shift to AD_2). At first, real output may expand beyond the economy's potential (Y_f). However, abnormally low unemployment and strong demand conditions will create upward pressure on wages and other resource prices, shifting aggregate supply to AS_2. Output will return to its long-run potential, and the price level will increase to P_{105} (e_2). If the more rapid monetary growth continues in subsequent periods, AD and AS will continue to shift upward, leading to still higher prices (e_3 and points beyond). The net result of this process is sustained inflation.

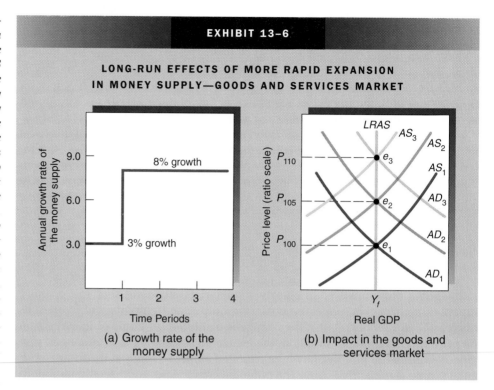

EXHIBIT 13-6

LONG-RUN EFFECTS OF MORE RAPID EXPANSION IN MONEY SUPPLY—GOODS AND SERVICES MARKET

(a) Growth rate of the money supply

(b) Impact in the goods and services market

What will happen if the monetary authorities permanently increase the growth rate of the money supply from 3 percent to 8 percent annually (see part a of Exhibit 13–6, beginning in Period 2)?[6] In the short run, the expansionary monetary policy will reduce the real interest rate and stimulate aggregate demand (shift to AD_2), just as we previously explained (Exhibits 13–2 and 13–3). For a time, real output may exceed the economy's potential. However, as they confront strong demand conditions, many resource suppliers (who previously committed to long-term agreements) will want to modify these agreements in light of the strong demand conditions. With the passage of time, more and more resource suppliers (including labor represented by union officials) will have the opportunity to alter their prior contracts. As this happens, wages and other resource prices will increase. As they do, costs will rise and profit margins will recede to normal levels. The higher costs will reduce aggregate supply (shift to AS_2). As the rapid monetary growth continues in subsequent periods (Periods 3, 4, and so on), both AD and AS will shift upward. The price level will rise to P_{105}, P_{110}, and on to still higher levels as the money supply continues to grow more rapidly than the monetary growth rate consistent with stable prices. The

---

[6]In the preceding chapter, we noted the difficulties involved in the measurement of the money supply (both M1 and M2). Changes in the growth rate of the money supply may not always be indicative of a shift in monetary policy. More generally, the example presented in the text assumes that the Fed has shifted to a more expansionary monetary policy—one that will lead to an acceleration in the rate of inflation—regardless of whether the monetary aggregates as currently measured reflect this shift.

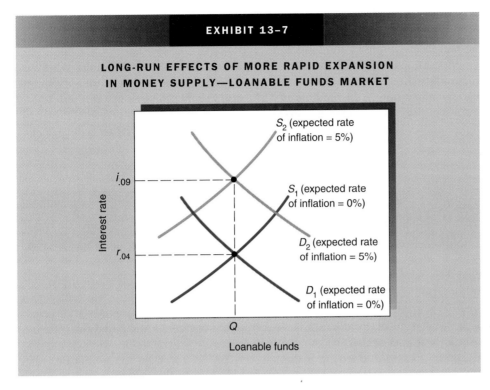

EXHIBIT 13–7

LONG-RUN EFFECTS OF MORE RAPID EXPANSION IN MONEY SUPPLY—LOANABLE FUNDS MARKET

S_2 (expected rate of inflation = 5%)

$i_{.09}$

S_1 (expected rate of inflation = 0%)

D_2 (expected rate of inflation = 5%)

$r_{.04}$

D_1 (expected rate of inflation = 0%)

Interest rate

Q

Loanable funds

When prices are stable, supply and demand in the loanable funds market are in balance at a real and nominal interest rate of 4 percent. If more rapid monetary expansion leads to a long-term 5 percent inflation rate (see Exhibit 13–6), borrowers and lenders will build the higher inflation rate into their decision making. As a result, the nominal interest rate (i) will rise to 9 percent—the 4 percent real rate plus a 5 percent inflationary premium.

continuation of the expansionary monetary policy leads to a higher and higher price level—that is, a sustained inflation.

Suppose an inflation rate of 5 percent eventually emerges from the more rapid growth rate (8 percent rather than 3 percent) of the money supply. With the passage of time, more and more people will adjust their decision making in light of the persistent 5 percent inflation. In the resource market, both buyers and sellers will eventually incorporate the expectation of the 5 percent inflation rate into long-term contracts such as collective bargaining agreements. Once this happens, resource prices and costs will rise as rapidly as prices in the goods and services market. *When the inflation rate is anticipated fully, it will fail to either reduce real wages or improve profit margins. Unemployment will return to its natural rate.*

Exhibit 13–7 illustrates the adjustments in the loanable funds market once borrowers and lenders expect the 5 percent inflation rate. When lenders anticipate a 5 percent annual increase in the price level, a 9 percent interest rate will be necessary to provide them with as much incentive to supply loanable funds as 4 percent interest provided *when stable prices were expected.* Thus, the supply of loanable funds will shift vertically by the 5 percent expected rate of inflation. Simultaneously, borrowers who were willing to pay 4 percent interest on loans when they expected stable prices will be willing to pay 9 percent when they expect prices to increase by 5 percent annually. The demand for loanable funds will therefore also increase (shift vertically) by the expected rate of inflation. Once borrowers and lenders anticipate the higher (5 percent) inflation rate, the equilibrium money interest rate will rise to 9 percent. Of course, the real interest rate is equal to the money interest rate (9 percent) minus the expected rate of inflation (5 percent). In the long run, a 4 percent real interest rate will emerge with inflation, just as it did with stable prices.[7] Inflation, then, will fail to reduce the real interest rate in the long run.

Modern analysis indicates that the long-run effects of rapid monetary growth differ from the short-run effects of an unanticipated move to a more expansionary monetary policy. *In the long run, the major consequences of rapid monetary growth—that is, a more expansionary monetary policy—are inflation and higher nominal interest rates. Rapid monetary growth will neither reduce unemployment nor stimulate real output in the long run.*

MONETARY POLICY WHEN EFFECTS ARE ANTICIPATED

Thus far, we have assumed that decision makers come to anticipate the effects of monetary policy only after they begin to occur. For example, we assumed that borrowers and lenders began to anticipate a higher inflation rate only after prices began to rise more rapidly. Similarly, resource suppliers anticipated the inflation only after it had begun.

What if enough decision makers in the market catch on to the link between expansionary monetary policy and an acceleration in the inflation rate? What if, in effect, they learn the model that you have learned? Suppose borrowers and lenders start paying attention to the money-supply figures and other monetary policy indicators. Observing a shift toward a more expansionary monetary policy, they revise upward their expectation of the future inflation rate. Lenders become more reluctant to supply loanable funds. Simultaneously, borrowers increase their demand for loanable funds at existing rates of interest because they also anticipate a higher rate of future inflation and they want to buy now before prices rise. Under these circumstances, a reduction in supply and an increase in demand for loanable funds will quickly push up the money interest rate. If borrowers and lenders quickly and accurately forecast the future rate of inflation accompanying the monetary expansion, the real interest rate will decline for only a short period of time, if at all.

If buyers and sellers in the goods and services market also anticipate a shift to a more expansionary monetary policy, they too may anticipate its inflationary consequences. As buyers anticipate future price increases, many will buy now rather than later. Current aggregate demand will rise. Similarly, expecting an acceleration in the inflation rate, sellers will be reluctant to sell except at premium prices. Current aggregate supply will fall. This combination of factors will quickly push prices of goods and services upward.

Simultaneously, if buyers and sellers in the resource market believe that more rapid monetary growth will lead to a higher rate of inflation, they too will build this view into long-run contracts. Union officials will demand and employ-

---

[7]Higher rates of inflation are generally associated with an increase in the variability of the inflation rate. Thus, greater risk (the possibility of either a substantial gain or loss associated with a sharp change in the inflation rate) accompanies exchange in the loanable funds market when inflation rates are high. This additional risk may result in higher real interest rates than would prevail at lower rates of inflation. The text discussion does not introduce this consideration.

ers will pay an inflationary premium for future money wages, based on their expectation of inflation. Alternatively, they may write an **escalator clause** (sometimes called cost-of-living adjustments) into their collective bargaining agreements. Such provisions will automatically raise money wages when the inflation transpires. If decision makers in the resource market correctly anticipate the inflation, real resource prices will not decline once prices accelerate upward.

As **Exhibit 13–8** illustrates, when individuals correctly anticipate the effects of expansionary monetary policy *prior to their occurrence*, the short-run impact of monetary policy is much like its impact in the long run. The price level will increase, pushing up money income (P_2Y_1), but real income (Y_1) will be unchanged. Nominal interest rates will rise, but real interest rates will be unchanged. Thus, when the effects of expansionary monetary policy are fully anticipated, they exert little impact on real economic activity.

Are people likely to anticipate the effects of monetary policy? This is a topic of hot debate among economists, and we will consider it in more detail in the next chapter. Because the effects of monetary policy differ substantially depending on whether they are anticipated, the question is clearly a very important one.

Escalator clause
A contractual agreement that periodically and automatically adjusts money wage rates upward as the price level rises. They are sometimes referred to as cost-of-living adjustments or COLAs.

INTEREST RATES AND TIME LAGS OF MONETARY POLICY

Can the Fed control interest rates? How quickly will a shift in monetary policy exert a significant impact on output and prices in the goods and services market? These two questions are linked. Let us begin with the interest rate question.

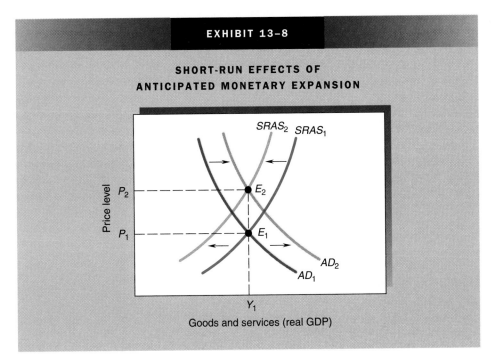

EXHIBIT 13–8

SHORT-RUN EFFECTS OF ANTICIPATED MONETARY EXPANSION

When decision makers fully anticipate the effects of monetary expansion, the expansion does not alter real output even in the short run. Suppliers, including resource suppliers, build the expected price rise into their decisions. The anticipated inflation leads to a rise in nominal costs (including wages), causing aggregate supply to decline (shift to $SRAS_2$). While nominal wages, prices, and interest rates rise, their real counterparts are unchanged. The result: inflation without any change in real output (Y_1).

Thus far, we have proceeded as if there were only a single interest rate. In the real world, of course, there are numerous interest rates reflecting loans of differing risk and time length. For example, there are short-term interest rates, such as those present in the federal funds, Treasury bills, and savings deposit markets. In addition, there are longer-term rates, such as those for home mortgages and long-term bonds.

When the Fed moves toward a more expansionary policy—when it purchases bonds and injects additional reserves into the system—there is an immediate impact on the reserve position of banks. Fewer banks will have reserve deficiencies and more banks will have excess reserves. Rather quickly, these forces will place downward pressure on the interest rate in the federal funds market, a market where banks with excess reserves extend short-term loans to banks with insufficient reserves. As the federal funds rate declines, so too will other short-term interest rates—for example, the rates on savings deposits, three-month Treasury bills, and bank certificates of deposit (CDs).

However, the impact of the expansionary monetary policy on long-term interest rates, such as home mortgages and ten-year bonds, will be more modest and less predictable. There are two reasons for this: First, the long-term rates are influenced more by real factors, such as the demand for investment funds, rather than monetary factors. Second, to the extent that monetary factors influence long-term interest rates, they operate primarily through their impact on the expected rate of inflation. The expected long-term future rate of inflation is an important component of long-term nominal interest rates. If people expect a higher future rate of inflation as the result of the shift to a more expansionary policy, long-term rates may rise rather than fall. Thus, although a shift in Fed policy is able to exert a substantial impact on short-term interest rates rather quickly, its impact on longer-term rates is both less certain and likely to occur with a substantially longer time lag. Because the long-term rates are most relevant for the investment decisions of businesses and households, the ambiguity concerning the impact of monetary policy on these rates is particularly important.

Furthermore, the impact of the change in short-term nominal interest rates on the velocity of money adds an additional complication. A reduction in the short-term rates will reduce the opportunity cost of holding money balances. Predictably, the velocity of money will decline, which will tend to dampen the initial stimulus effects of the monetary expansion. Of course, if the more expansionary monetary policy persists, a combination of lower real interest rates—particularly short-term rates—and more readily available credit will eventually stimulate aggregate demand (see Exhibit 13–2). With time, the additional demand will place upward pressure on prices, which will also serve to increase both the expected rate of inflation and nominal interest rates, including short-term nominal rates. When this happens—and several quarters may pass before it does—the higher short-term nominal interest rates will increase the velocity of money and amplify the demand-stimulus effects of the policy. It is at this point in time that the primary effects of the expansionary monetary policy will be most potent.

The same forces are also present in the case of a shift to a more restrictive monetary policy. When the Fed shifts to a more restrictive policy, it typically drains reserves from the banking system, which will quickly place upward pressure on the federal funds rate and other short-term interest rates. The restrictive policy, however, will generally exert less impact on longer-term interest rates. If people perceive that inflation is less of a threat as the result of the more restrictive monetary policy, this factor will place downward pressure on long-term interest rates, which will at least partially offset the restraining effects emanating from the increase in the short-term rates.

At the same time, the higher short-term rates will increase the opportunity cost of holding money and, as a result, its velocity. This increase in the velocity of money will promote additional spending, which will, *for a time*, tend to dampen the restrictive effects of the policy. Of course, the restrictive policy, if continued, will eventually begin to retard inflation and lower nominal interest rates (including short-term rates), which will reduce the velocity of money. Once this happens, and many months may pass before it does, the restrictive policy will be highly potent—it will substantially reduce aggregate demand, output, and prices.

All these factors suggest that the linkage between a change in monetary policy and a change in output and prices is likely to be both lengthy and variable. When there is a shift in monetary policy, the potency of the short-run effects may differ substantially from the potency of the policy shift over a longer period of time. Obviously, these factors will complicate the job of monetary policymakers and make it more difficult for them to institute changes in a manner that will exert a stabilizing influence on the economy.

EFFECTS OF MONETARY POLICY—A SUMMARY

The accompanying Thumbnail Sketch summarizes the theoretical implications of our analysis. The impact of monetary policy on major economic variables is indicated for three alternatives: (1) the short run when the effects are unanticipated, (2) the short run when the effects are anticipated, and (3) the long run. Note that the impact of monetary policy in the latter two cases is the same. When decision makers quickly anticipate the effects of monetary policy, the adjustment process speeds up, and therefore the short-run effects are identical to the long-run effects. Under these circumstances, only nominal variables (money interest rates and the inflation rate) are affected. Real variables (real GDP, employment, and the real interest rate) are unaffected.

Five major predictions flow from our analysis:

1. An unanticipated shift to a more expansionary (restrictive) monetary policy will temporarily stimulate (retard) output and employment.   As Exhibits 13–2 and 13–3 illustrate, an increase in aggregate demand emanating from an unanticipated increase in the money supply will lead to a short-run expansion in real output and employment. Conversely, as Exhibit 13–4 shows, an unanticipated move toward more restrictive monetary policy reduces aggregate demand and retards real output.

THUMBNAIL SKETCH

WHAT IS THE IMPACT OF MONETARY POLICY?

	SHORT-RUN EFFECTS WHEN POLICY IS UNANTICIPATED (1)	SHORT-RUN EFFECTS WHEN POLICY IS ANTICIPATED[a] (2)	LONG-RUN EFFECTS (3)
IMPACT OF EXPANSIONARY MONETARY POLICY ON			
Inflation rate	Only a small increase, particularly if excess capacity is present	Increase	
Real output and employment	Long-term increase if excess capacity is present; otherwise they increase only temporarily	No change	
Money interest rate	Short-term rates will probably decline.	Increase	
Real interest rate	Decrease	No change	
IMPACT OF RESTRICTIVE MONETARY POLICY ON			
Inflation rate	Only a small decrease	Decrease	
Real output and employment	Decrease, particularly if economy at less than capacity	No change	
Money interest rate	Short-term rates will probably increase.	Decrease	
Real interest rate	Increase	No change	

[a]Beginning from long-run equilibrium

2. The stabilizing effects of a change in monetary policy are dependent upon the state of the economy when the effects of the policy change are observed. If the effects of an expansionary policy come when the economy is operating at less than capacity, then the demand stimulus will push the economy toward full employment. However, if the demand stimulus comes when the economy is operating at or beyond capacity, it will contribute to an acceleration in the inflation rate. Correspondingly, restrictive policy will help to control inflation if the demand-restraining effects are felt when output is beyond the economy's long-run capacity. On the other hand, restrictive policy will result in recession if the reduction in demand comes when the economy is at or below long-run capacity.

3. Persistent growth of the money supply at a rapid rate will cause inflation. Although the short-run effects of expansionary monetary policy may be primarily on output, particularly if excess capacity is present, a persistent expansion in the money supply at a rate greater than the growth of real output will cause inflation. The more rapid the sustained growth rate of the money supply (relative to real output), the higher the accompanying rate of inflation.

4. Money interest rates and the inflation rate will be directly related. As the inflation rate rises, money interest rates will eventually increase because both borrowers and lenders will begin to expect the higher rate of inflation and build it into their decision making. Conversely, as the inflation rate declines, a reduction in the expected rate of inflation will eventually lead to lower money interest rates. Therefore, when monetary expansion leads to an acceleration in the inflation rate, it will also result in an increase in nominal interest rates.

5. There will be only a loose year-to-year relationship between shifts in monetary policy and changes in output and prices. It takes time for markets to adjust to changing demand conditions. Some prices in both product and resource markets are set by long-term contracts. Obviously price responses in these mar-

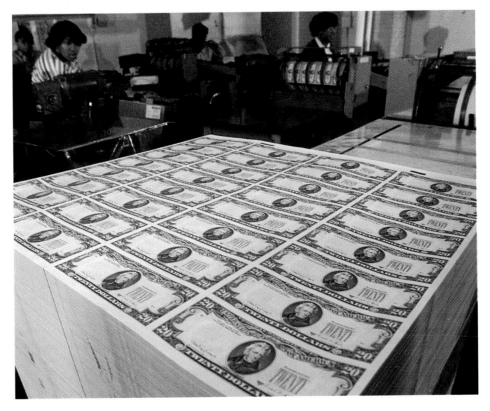

Persistent increases in the quantity of money are the primary cause of inflation.

kets will take time. In some cases, people may anticipate the effects of a policy change and adjust quickly; in others, the reaction to a policy change may take more time. Differences in this area will weaken the year-to-year relationship between monetary indicators and important economic variables.

In addition, a monetary policy shift will initially exert a far greater impact on short-term interest rates than on longer-term rates. Movements in the short-term nominal rates are likely to cause changes in the velocity of money that will tend to dampen the initial effects of a monetary policy shift. This, too, will tend to weaken the year-to-year link between changes in monetary policy and changes in output and prices. Therefore, even though our analysis indicates that monetary policy does influence output and prices, the year-to-year relationships are likely to be weak.

TESTING THE MAJOR IMPLICATIONS OF MONETARY THEORY

Is the real world consistent with our analysis? The next four exhibits provide evidence on this topic.

Our analysis indicates that a shift to a more expansionary monetary policy will initially stimulate output, while a shift to monetary restriction will retard it. **Exhibit 13–9** shows the relationship between changes in the growth rate of the money supply and real output since 1960 for the United States. Because the introduction of interest-earning checking accounts changed the nature of M1 (and affected its growth rate) during the 1980s, the M2 money-supply measure is used here. Of course, factors other than monetary policy (for example, supply shocks, fiscal policy, or changes in incomes abroad) will influence the growth of output. Thus, the relationship between changes in the money supply and the growth of real GDP will be fairly loose. However, close inspection of the data reveals that periods of sharp acceleration in the growth rate of the money supply were generally associated with an acceleration in the growth rate of real GDP. For example, an acceleration in the growth rate of the money supply during 1961–1964, 1971–1972, 1976, and 1983 was associated with an increase in the growth rate of real GDP during each of the periods. The converse was also true: Periods of sharp deceleration in the growth rate of the money supply were generally associated with (or followed by) economic recession. A decline in the growth rate of the money supply preceded the recessions of 1960, 1970, and 1974–1975. Similarly, a sharp decline in the growth rate of the money stock from 12 percent in 1976–1977 to less than 8 percent in 1978–1979 preceded the back-to-back recessions and sluggish growth of 1979–1982. Most recently, the recession and sluggish growth of 1989–1991 was preceded by a substantial deceleration in the growth rate of the money supply. Hence, just as our theory predicts, there does appear to be a relationship between shifts in monetary policy and changes in real GDP.

Exhibit 13–10 presents a graphic picture of the relationship between monetary policy and the inflation rate for the United States. Although our theory indicates that persistent, long-term growth of the money supply will be closely asso-

EXHIBIT 13–9

MONETARY POLICY AND REAL GDP

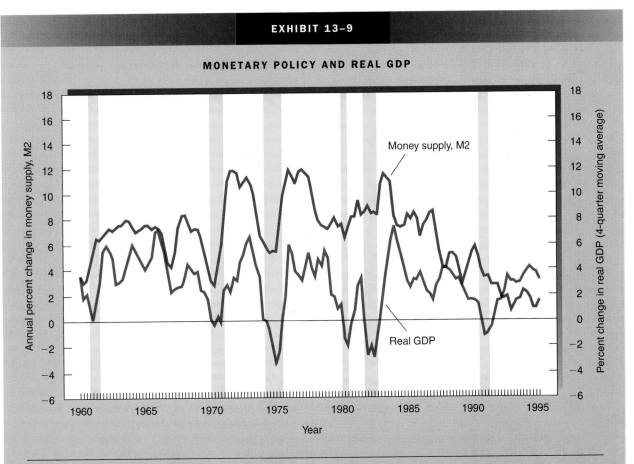

Sharp declines in the growth rate of the money supply such as those of 1968–1969, 1973–1974, 1977–1978, and 1988–1991 have generally preceded reductions in real GDP and periods of recession (indicated by shading). Conversely, periods of sharp acceleration in the growth rate of the money supply, such as 1971–1972 and 1976, have often been followed by a rapid growth of GDP. Note how the monetary authorities have generally increased the growth rate of the money supply during recessions.

Source: Derived from computerized data supplied by FAME ECONOMICS. Also see *Economic Report of the President* (published annually).

ciated with inflation, it also indicates that time is required for a monetary expansion (or contraction) to alter demand relationships and impact prices. Most economists believe that the time lag between shifts in monetary policy and observable changes in the level of prices is often two or three years. Reflecting these views, Exhibit 13–10 compares the current money supply (M2) data with the inflation rate three years in the future. Once again, though the linkage is far from tight, it definitely exists. Most noticeably, the rapid monetary acceleration during 1971–1972 was followed by a similar acceleration in the inflation rate during 1973–1974. Similarly, the sharp monetary contraction of 1974–1975 was accompanied by not only the recession of 1974–1975, but also a sharp deceleration in the inflation rate during 1976–1977. However, as monetary policy again

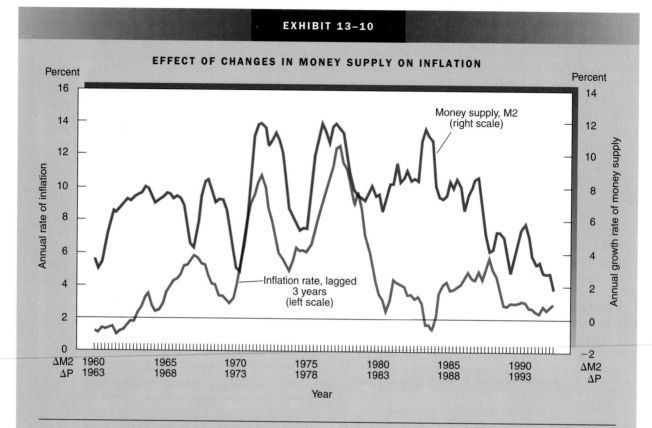

EXHIBIT 13–10

EFFECT OF CHANGES IN MONEY SUPPLY ON INFLATION

Here we illustrate the relationship between the rate of growth in the money supply (M2) and the annual inflation rate three years later. While the two are not perfectly correlated, the data do indicate that periods of monetary acceleration (for example: 1971–1972 and 1975–1976) tend to be associated with an increase in the inflation rate about three years later. Similarly, a reduction in the growth rate of the money sup-

ply, like that of the early 1990s, is often associated with a decline in the rate of inflation.

Source: Derived from computerized data supplied by FAME ECONOMICS. Also see *Economic Report of the President* (published annually). The consumer price index was used to measure the rate of inflation.

shifted toward expansion in 1976–1977, the double-digit inflation rates of 1979–1980 were soon to follow.

During the 1980–1986 period, the linkage between monetary growth and the inflation rate a few years later appeared to weaken. To some degree this may reflect the financial innovations and changing nature of money during this period. There is some evidence that the relationship is once again becoming more predictable now that the transition period to interest-earning checking accounts has been completed. During the 1989–1993 period, the annual growth rate of the money supply (M2) decelerated from approximately 6 percent to less than 2 percent. With a lag, the inflation rate followed a similar path during this period.

Exhibit 13–11 shows the relationship between the inflation rate (change in CPI) and the nominal interest rate. Because our measure of inflation is the annual rate of change in the price level, we will compare it with a short-term nominal interest rate—the three-month Treasury bill rate. Our theory implies that nominal interest rates will tend to rise with the rate of inflation. The empirical evi-

EXHIBIT 13–11

INFLATION RATE AND THE MONEY INTEREST RATE

The expectation of inflation (a) reduces the supply and (b) increases the demand for loanable funds, causing money interest rates to rise (see Exhibit 13–7). Note how the short-term money rate of interest has tended to increase when the inflation rate accelerates (and decline as the inflation rate falls).

Source: Derived from computerized data supplied by FAME ECONOMICS. Also see *Economic Report of the President* (published annually). The consumer price index was used to measure the rate of inflation.

dence indicates that is indeed the case. As the inflation rate rose significantly during the late 1960s, so also did the nominal rate of interest. During the 1970s, sharp increases in the inflation rate, particularly during 1977–1980, were accompanied by substantial increases in the nominal interest rate. Similarly, as the inflation rate decelerated from the double-digit levels of the late 1970s, the money interest rate also plunged during the 1980–1987 period. Later, a modest increase in the inflation rate during 1988–1990 resulted in a similar modest increase in short-term interest rates. Finally, as the inflation rate declined to its lowest level in 30 years in 1993, so did nominal interest rates. These data provide strong evidence that, just as our theory predicts, the choices of borrowers and lenders are strongly influenced by the inflation rate and expectations concerning its path in the future.

A major implication of our analysis is that rapid growth rates in the money supply over long periods of time will be associated with high rates of inflation. **Exhibit 13–12** presents data on the annual growth rate of the money supply (adjusted for the growth rate of the nation's output) and the rate of inflation

EXHIBIT 13–12

MONEY AND INFLATION—AN INTERNATIONAL COMPARISON, 1980–1993

COUNTRY (RANKED ACCORDING TO LOW RATE OF MONEY GROWTH)	AVERAGE ANNUAL GROWTH RATE OF MONEY SUPPLY[a]	AVERAGE ANNUAL INFLATION RATE	COUNTRY (RANKED ACCORDING TO LOW RATE OF MONEY GROWTH)	AVERAGE ANNUAL GROWTH RATE OF MONEY SUPPLY[a]	AVERAGE ANNUAL INFLATION RATE
Senegal	1.9	4.9	Madagascar	15.5	16.1
Côte d'Ivoire	2.4	1.5	Portugal	15.5	16.4
Cameroon	3.1	4.0	Haiti	15.6	12.4
Germany	4.2	2.7	South Africa	15.7	14.7
Japan	4.2	2.0	Iran	15.8	17.1
Switzerland	4.3	3.9	Philippines	16.0	13.6
United States	4.5	3.8	Zimbabwe	16.5	14.4
France	4.7	5.1	Egypt	17.1	13.6
Belgium	5.1	4.0	Guatemala	17.6	16.8
Sweden	5.2	6.9	Syria	18.5	14.0
Canada	5.5	3.9	Indonesia	20.5	8.5
Netherlands	5.7	1.7	Venezuela	20.6	23.9
Malaysia	6.4	2.2	Greece	21.0	17.3
Pakistan	8.2	7.4	Chile	24.0	20.1
Italy	8.3	8.8	Dominican Republic	26.5	25.0
Australia	8.4	6.1	Ecuador	36.4	40.4
Spain	8.5	8.4	Ghana	38.5	37.0
Thailand	11.0	4.3	Zambia	54.0	58.9
India	11.5	8.7	Turkey	56.0	53.5
Tunisia	11.8	7.1	Mexico	56.2	57.9
United Kingdom	12.3	5.6	Poland	63.4	69.3
Kenya	12.6	9.9	Israel	74.5	70.4
Korea	12.8	6.3	Uganda	82.8	83.1
Bangladesh	13.8	8.6	Bolivia	206.0	187.1
Hungary	13.8	12.8	Peru	297.1	316.1
New Zealand	14.7	8.5	Argentina	355.9	374.3
Nigeria[b]	15.3	12.7	Brazil	698.0	423.4
			Zaire	747.0	652.7

[a]The money-supply data are for the actual growth rate of the money supply minus the growth rate of real GDP. Thus, it is the actual supply of money adjusted to reflect the country's growth rate of real output.
[b]Data are for 1980–1991.

Source: World Bank, *World Development Report: 1995* (Washington, D.C.: World Bank, 1995); and International Monetary Fund, *International Financial Statistics Yearbook* (Washington, D.C.: International Monetary Fund, 1995). Only countries with a population of more than 6 million were included.

during the period 1980–1993. The 55 countries (with a population of 6 million or more) for which the data were available are included in the exhibit. The results clearly illustrate the linkage between monetary policy and inflation. Just as our analysis implies, countries with low rates of monetary growth tend to experience low rates of inflation. The average annual growth rate of the money supply during 1980–1993 was between 1 percent and 7 percent for 13 of the countries (Senegal, Côte d'Ivoire, Cameroon, Germany, Japan, Switzerland, United States, France, Belgium, Sweden, Canada, Netherlands, and Malaysia). The accompanying annual inflation rates for each of these countries fell with a similar range (1.5 percent to 6.9 percent).

As the growth rate of the money supply rose, so too did the rate of inflation. Countries with annual money growth rates of between 8 percent and 15 percent experienced annual inflation rates of similar magnitude. As a country's average rate of money growth rose to the 15 percent to 25 percent range, so too did its inflation rate. Countries with monetary growth rates in the 25 percent to 100 percent range tended to experience rates of inflation within this same range. The money supply of five countries (Bolivia, Peru, Argentina, Brazil, and Zaire) expanded at average annual rates of between 200 percent and 750 percent. The inflation rates of these countries ranged from 187 percent to 653 percent.

Just as economic theory indicates, in the long run, rapid expansion in the money supply will lead to high rates of inflation. This is one of the more consistent empirical relations in all of economics.

LOOKING AHEAD

As we discussed in this chapter, theory indicates that the impact of monetary policy will be influenced by whether economic agents anticipate its effects. Thus far, we have said little about how decision makers form expectations about the future. The next chapter will consider this important issue.

CHAPTER SUMMARY

1. The quantity of money demanded is inversely related to the nominal interest rate and directly related to nominal income (GDP). The quantity of money supplied is determined by the central monetary authority (the Fed in the United States).

2. Classical economists developed the quantity theory of money that postulated that the velocity of money was constant (or approximately so) and that real output was independent of monetary factors. According to the quantity theory, therefore, an increase in the stock of money resulted in a proportional increase in prices, while output remained unchanged.

3. The impact of a shift in monetary policy is generally transmitted through interest rates, exchange rates, asset prices, and the availability of credit in the loanable funds market.

4. When instituting a more expansionary monetary policy, the Fed generally buys bonds, which will both increase bond prices and create additional bank reserves, placing downward pressure on real interest rates. The lower real interest rates will (a) encourage investment and the purchase of consumer durables, (b) cause an outflow of capital, which will lead to a depreciation in the exchange-rate value of the dollar and an expansion in net exports, and (c) place upward pressure on asset prices, which will encourage new construction. The additional bank reserves may also increase the availability of bank credit for small businesses. All these factors will tend to stimulate aggregate demand.

5. In the short run, an *unanticipated* shift to a more expansionary policy will stimulate aggregate demand and thereby increase output and employment. In the long run, as markets adjust to the higher level of demand, the primary impact of a more expansionary monetary policy will be a continuous increase in the price level (inflation).

6. When instituting a more restrictive monetary policy, the Fed sells bonds, which will depress bond prices and drain reserves from the banking system. Higher interest rates, an appreciation in the dollar and decline in net exports, falling asset prices (which will discourage new

construction), and a reduction in the availability of bank credit are the expected results. When unanticipated, a shift to a more restrictive monetary policy will reduce aggregate demand, output, and employment in the short run.

*7. Monetary policy is a potential tool of economic stabilization. If the effects of expansionary monetary policy are felt when aggregate output is at less than capacity, then the policy will stimulate demand, and push the economy toward full employment. Correspondingly, if restrictive monetary policy is properly timed, then it can help to control inflation.

8. In the long run, the primary impact of monetary policy will be on prices rather than on real output. When expansionary monetary policy leads to rising prices, decision makers eventually anticipate the higher inflation rate and build it into their choices. As this happens, money interest rates, wages, and incomes will reflect the expectation of inflation, so real interest rates, wages, and output will return to their long-run normal levels.

9. When the effects of expansionary monetary policy are anticipated prior to their occurrence, the short-run impact of an increase in the money supply is similar to its impact in the long run. Nominal prices and interest rates rise, but real output remains unchanged. Thus, theory indicates that the short-run impact of monetary policy is dependent on whether the effects of the policy are anticipated.

10. The empirical evidence indicates that changes in monetary policy influence real GDP in the short run. Shifts toward a more expansionary monetary policy tend to be associated with a temporary increase in the growth rate of real GDP. Conversely, shifts toward monetary contraction have generally been associated with a slowdown in real output.

11. Both the U.S. experience and international comparisons strongly indicate that persistent, rapid growth in the money supply is closely linked with inflation. The U.S. data illustrate that shifts to rapid monetary growth *for an extended period of time* are generally followed by an acceleration in the inflation rate. Similarly, the international data show that countries with low (high) rates of growth in the money supply tend to experience low (high) rates of inflation.

CRITICAL ANALYSIS QUESTIONS

1. Why do people hold money? How will an increase in the interest rate influence the amount of money that people will want to hold?

*2. How would each of the following influence the quantity of money that you would like to hold?
a. An increase in the interest rate on checking deposits
b. An increase in the expected rate of inflation
c. An increase in income

d. An increase in the differential interest rate between money market mutual funds and checking deposits

*3. What is the opportunity cost of the following: (a) obtaining a $100,000 house, (b) holding the house during the next year, (c) obtaining $1,000, and (d) holding the $1,000 in your checking account during the next year?

4. What do economists mean when they say "the demand for money has increased"? How will an increase in the demand for money affect the velocity of money?

5. What impact will an unanticipated increase in the money supply have on the real interest rate, real output, and employment in the short run? How will expansionary monetary policy affect the economy when the effects are widely anticipated? Why does it make a difference whether the effects of monetary policy are anticipated?

6. How rapidly has the money supply (M1) grown during the past 12 months? How rapidly has M2 grown? Do you think the monetary authorities should increase or decrease the growth rate of the money supply during the next year? Why? (The data necessary to answer this question for the United States are available in the Federal Reserve Bulletin.)

*7. If the Fed shifts to a more restrictive monetary policy, it will generally sell bonds in the open market. How will this action influence each of the following? Briefly explain each of your answers.
a. The reserves available to banks
b. Real interest rates
c. Household spending on consumer durables
d. The exchange rate value of the dollar
e. Net exports
f. The prices of stocks and real assets like apartment or office buildings
g. Real GDP

8. Historically, shifts toward more expansionary monetary policy have often been associated with increases in real output. Why? Would a more expansionary policy increase the long-term growth rate of real GDP? Why or why not?

9. Political officials often call on the monetary authorities to expand the money supply more rapidly so that interest rates can be reduced. Nonetheless, the highest interest rates in the world are found in countries that expand the supply of money rapidly. Can you explain these seemingly contradictory facts?

*10. Many economists believe that there is a "long and variable time lag" between when a change in monetary policy is instituted and when the change exerts its primary impact on output, employment, and prices. If true, how does this long and variable time lag affect the ability of policymakers to use monetary policy as a stabilization tool?

*11. "Historically, when interest rates are high, the inflation rate is high. High interest rates are a major cause of inflation." Evaluate this statement.

*12. If the supply of money is constant, how will an increase in the demand for money influence aggregate demand?

*13. Suppose that innovations in financial management during the 1990s permit individuals and business firms to conduct a given volume of transactions with an increasingly smaller average money balance. As a result, the velocity of the M1 money supply increases at a 3 percent annual rate during the decade. If the monetary authorities want to maintain stable prices, what growth rate of the M1 money supply should they choose?

14. Will a budget deficit be more expansionary if it is financed by borrowing from the Federal Reserve or from the general public? Explain.

15. The accompanying chart presents data on the money supply, price level, and real GDP for three countries during the 1987–1990 period.
   a. Fill in the missing data.
   b. Which country followed the most expansionary monetary policy?
   c. Which country experienced the highest annual rate of inflation for the years 1988, 1989, and 1990?
   d. Which country experienced the most rapid increase in real output during the 1987–1990 period?

	MONEY SUPPLY (IN BILLIONS OF LOCAL CURRENCY)	GDP DEFLATOR (1987 = 100)	NOMINAL GDP (IN 1987 CURRENCY UNITS)	REAL GDP (IN 1987 CURRENCY UNITS)	RATE OF CHANGE MONEY SUPPLY	RATE OF CHANGE PRICE LEVEL
UNITED STATES						
1987	2,910.8	100.0	4,539.9	_____	X	X
1988	3,071.1	103.9	4,900.4	_____	_____	_____
1989	3,227.3	108.5	5,250.8	_____	_____	_____
1990	3,339.0	113.2	5,522.2	_____	_____	_____
TURKEY						
1987	17,992.0	100.0	56,763.0	_____	X	X
1988	27,881.0	166.7	97,929.0	_____	_____	_____
1989	47,958.0	273.0	164,067.0	_____	_____	_____
1990	72,618.0	423.4	277,890.0	_____	_____	_____
ARGENTINA						
1987	48.4	100.0	163.5	_____	X	X
1988	259.9	490.0	773.0	_____	_____	_____
1989	5,958.4	15,919.0	22,892.6	_____	_____	_____
1990	70,000.0	322,000.0	480,000.0	_____	_____	_____

Source: World Bank, *World Tables, 1992.*

---

*Asterisk denotes questions for which answers are given in Appendix B.

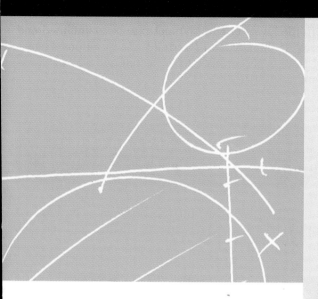

Inflation does give a stimulus . . . when it starts from a condition that is noninflationary. If the inflation continues, people get adjusted to it. But when people get adjusted to it, when they expect rising prices, the mere occurrence of what has been expected is no longer stimulating.

SIR JOHN R. HICKS[1]

_____

[1] J. R. Hicks, "Monetary Theory and Keynesian Economics," in *Monetary Theory*, ed. R. W. Clower (Harmondsworth: Penguin, 1969), p. 260.

CHAPTER FOCUS

■ Why does it make a difference whether a change in macroeconomic policy is anticipated or unanticipated?

■ How do individuals form expectations about what will happen in the future?

■ Can a nation reduce its unemployment rate if it is willing to pay the price of a higher inflation rate?

■ How can one explain the simultaneous occurrence of inflation and a high rate of unemployment? Is this occurrence inconsistent with economic theory?

■ Can economic policy reduce the natural rate of unemployment? If so, how?

■ How has the natural rate of unemployment changed in recent years? How is it likely to change during the 1990s?

People make decisions on the basis of perceptions: the perceived costs and benefits associated with choices. What individuals think is going to happen in the future is important because it affects the choices they make in the present. Sometimes the results of those choices are different than expected. When this occurs, people will often modify their future choices. In this chapter, we will explicitly incorporate the idea that expectations about the future influence the choices of individuals who think and learn from previous experience. We will consider alternative theories about how expectations are formed and investigate their implications.

What impact will a shift to a more expansionary macroeconomic policy have on output and employment? Can expansionary policies reduce the unemployment rate? If so, how long can the lower unemployment rate be maintained and at what cost? Expectations provide the key to answering these questions. Hence, it will help to more fully integrate expectations into our economic way of thinking about output, employment, and prices.

UNANTICIPATED AND ANTICIPATED DEMAND STIMULUS

Throughout this text, we have carefully differentiated between unanticipated and anticipated changes. **Exhibit 14–1** illustrates why this distinction is crucial.

When expansionary policies catch decision makers by surprise, the increase in aggregate demand will lead to an increase in real GDP (from Y_f to Y_2, in the short run (a). In contrast, when resource suppliers correctly anticipate the inflationary impact of demand-stimulus policies, nominal costs will rise, causing a decline in aggregate supply (shift to SRAS$_2$) (b). When the effects are anticipated, demand-stimulus policies merely increase prices without altering the rate of output.

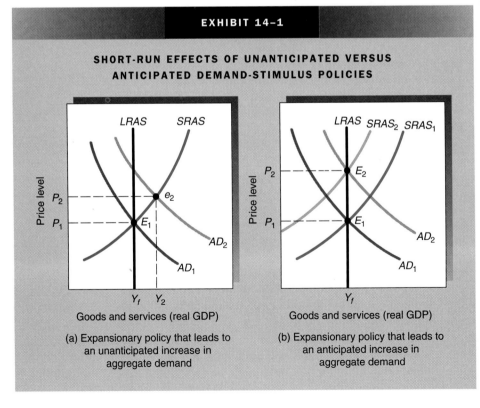

EXHIBIT 14–1

SHORT-RUN EFFECTS OF UNANTICIPATED VERSUS ANTICIPATED DEMAND-STIMULUS POLICIES

(a) Expansionary policy that leads to an unanticipated increase in aggregate demand

(b) Expansionary policy that leads to an anticipated increase in aggregate demand

Beginning from a position of long-run equilibrium, the impact of expansionary macroeconomic policy is indicated under two alternative assumptions. Part a assumes that decision makers fail to anticipate the effects of the expansionary policies and therefore they do not expect the resulting cost and price increases. As we have previously discussed, unanticipated increases in aggregate demand will temporarily increase both output and employment. For a time, output will expand to a rate (Y_2) beyond the economy's long-run potential. Correspondingly, employment will expand and unemployment will recede below the economy's natural rate. When the effects of expansionary policy are unanticipated, both output and employment increase in the short run.

Part b of Exhibit 14–1 illustrates the impact of expansionary macroeconomic policy under the assumption that decision makers anticipate its effects prior to their occurrence. Recognizing that expansionary policies will strengthen demand and lead to inflation, market participants alter their choices accordingly. Agreements specifying future wage rates and resource prices immediately make allowance for an expected increase in the price level. These agreements may even include escalator clauses providing for automatic cost-of-living increases in nominal wages tied to the general price level. When buyers and sellers in the resource market fully anticipate and quickly adjust to the effects of the demand-stimulus policies, wage rates and resource prices will rise as rapidly as product prices. Profit margins will fail to improve. The rising nominal costs will decrease aggregate supply, offsetting the impact of the demand stimulus on output. The result: a higher price level, while real output is unchanged (see the shift from E_1 to E_2 in part b of Exhibit 14–1).

Thus, the impact of expansionary macroeconomic policy depends on whether (and how quickly) decision makers anticipate the eventual effects. *If decision makers fail to anticipate the strong demand and the increase in the price level that will eventually accompany the expansionary policy, the demand stimulus will temporarily increase output and reduce unemployment. In contrast, when the inflationary side effects of expansionary policies are anticipated quickly, the primary impact of the demand stimulus will be an increase in the price level* (see this chapter's opening quote by Nobel laureate Sir John R. Hicks).

HOW EXPECTATIONS ARE FORMED

As Exhibit 14–1 illustrates, expectations concerning the future exert an important impact on the effectiveness of macroeconomic policy. Thus, it is vitally important that we understand how expectations are formed. There are two general theories in this area. Let us outline the essentials of each.

ADAPTIVE EXPECTATIONS

The simplest theory concerning the formation of expectations is that people rely on the past to predict future trends. According to this theory, which economists call the **adaptive-expectations hypothesis,** decision makers believe that the best indicator of the future is what has happened in the recent past. For example, people would expect the price level to be stable next year if stable prices had

Adaptive-expectations hypothesis
The hypothesis that economic decision makers base their future expectations on actual outcomes observed during recent periods. For example, according to this view, the rate of inflation actually experienced during the past two or three years would be the major determinant of the rate of inflation expected for next year.

been present during the past two or three years. Similarly, if prices had risen at an annual rate of 4 or 5 percent during the past several years, people would expect similar increases next year.

Exhibit 14–2 presents a graphic illustration of the adaptive-expectations hypothesis. In period 1, prices were stable (part a). Therefore, on the basis of the experience of period 1, decision makers assume that prices will be stable in period 2 (part b). However, the actual rate of inflation in period 2 jumps to 4 percent. Continuation of the 4 percent inflation rate throughout period 2 (the periods may range from six months to two or three years in length) causes decision makers to change their expectations. Relying on the experience of period 2, they anticipate 4 percent inflation in period 3. When their expectations turn out to be incorrect (the actual rate of inflation during period 3 is 8 percent), they again alter their expectations accordingly. Then, during period 4, the actual rate of inflation declines to 4 percent, less than the expected rate. Again, decision makers adjust their expectations as to the expected rate of inflation in period 5.

Of course, one would not expect the precise mechanical link between past occurrences and future expectations outlined in Exhibit 14–2. Rather than simply using the inflation rate of the immediate past period, people may use a weighted average of recent inflation rates when forming their expectations about the future. It is the structure, however, that is important. If the adaptive-expectations hypothesis is correct, decision makers will always expect the next period to be pretty much like the recent past.

Under adaptive expectations, forecasts of the future rate of inflation will exhibit systematic error—that is, an error that is made over and over again in a regular methodical way. When the inflation rate is accelerating, decision makers will systematically tend to underestimate the future inflation rate. In contrast,

According to the adaptive-expectations hypothesis, the actual occurrence during the most recent period (or set of periods) determines people's future expectations. Thus, the expected future rate of inflation (b) lags behind the actual rate of inflation (a) by one period as expectations are altered over time.

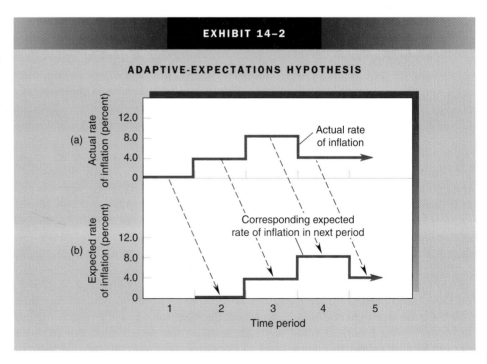

EXHIBIT 14–2

ADAPTIVE-EXPECTATIONS HYPOTHESIS

when the rate of inflation is decelerating, individuals will tend systematically to overestimate its future rate. We will investigate the implication of this occurrence as we proceed.

RATIONAL EXPECTATIONS

The idea that people form their expectations concerning what will happen in the future on the basis of all available information, including information about how policy changes will affect the economy, is called the **rational-expectations hypothesis.** According to this view, rather than merely assuming the future will be pretty much like the immediate past, people also consider the expected effects of changes in policy. Based on their understanding of economic policy, people alter their expectations with regard to the future when the government, for example, runs a larger deficit, expands the supply of money more rapidly, or cuts the size of its expenditures. Just as a football team alters its strategy in response to moves by an opponent, rational decision makers alter their expectations and strategies in response to policy developments.

Perhaps an example will help clarify the rational-expectations hypothesis. Suppose prices had increased at an annual rate of 6 percent during each of the past three years. In addition, assume that decision makers believe there is a relationship between the growth rate of the money supply and rising prices. They note that the money stock has expanded at a 12 percent annual rate during the last nine months, up from the 7 percent rate of the past several years. According to the rational-expectations hypothesis, they will then integrate the recent monetary acceleration into their forecast of the future inflation rate and will thus project an acceleration in the inflation rate, perhaps to the 10 percent to 12 percent range. In other words, they will expect the future inflation rate to respond to the more rapid growth of the money supply. In contrast, the adaptive-expectations hypothesis implies that people would expect the inflation rate for the next period to be the same as that for the last period (or the last several periods).

The rational-expectations hypothesis does not assume that forecasts will always be correct. We live in a world of uncertainty. Even rational decision makers will err. But they will learn from their past mistakes; they will not continue to make the same types of errors. Thus, the rational-expectations hypothesis assumes that the errors of decision makers will tend to be random. For example, sometimes decision makers may overestimate the increase in the inflation rate caused by monetary expansion, and at other times they may underestimate it. But because they learn from prior experience, people will not continue to make systematic errors year after year.

ADAPTIVE VERSUS RATIONAL EXPECTATIONS—A CONTINUING DEBATE

Are expectations determined adaptively or rationally? The question is one of continuing debate among economists. Rational-expectations proponents charge that the adaptive-expectations hypothesis is naive. They find it difficult to accept the notion that individuals look only at past price changes while ignoring information on variables (for example, changes in the money supply, interest rates, and exchange rates) that play an important role in the actual generation of inflation.

Rational-expectations hypothesis
The hypothesis that economic decision makers weigh all available evidence, including information concerning the probable effects of current and future economic policy, when they form their expectations about future economic events (such as the probable future inflation rate).

ROBERT LUCAS (1937–   )

The 1995 Nobel laureate, Robert Lucas is generally given credit for the introduction of the rational-expectations theory into macroeconomics. His technical work integrating rational expectations into macroeconomic models, has substantially altered the way economists think about macroeconomic policy. He is a long-time professor of economics at the University of Chicago.

The advocates of adaptive expectations reply that the rational-expectations theory implies that individuals possess an inordinate amount of information about highly complex issues. They note that the average person neither keeps up with the latest moves of the Fed nor forecasts changes in the federal budget. The proponents of adaptive expectations charge that it is unrealistic to assume that most people will (1) develop reliable theories about the operation of a highly complex economy, (2) monitor the necessary policy variables, and (3) consistently make the implied adjustments to changes in macroeconomic policy. They believe most people will find a simple rule of thumb, such as "inflation next year will be about the same as that of the recent past," to be both sensible and "rational."

The proponents of rational expectations are unmoved by this argument. They believe that it overlooks several facts. After all, business firms and labor unions hire specialists to make forecasts about the future. Predictions made by prominent economists are often widely disseminated via television news and daily newspapers. Because of this, even relatively uninformed citizens, whether they realize it or not, develop a view on the expected rate of inflation.

This debate is likely to continue. As we will soon see, in some cases the implications of the two theories differ substantially. But this is not always the case. As the following section indicates, this is particularly true with regard to the long-run implications of the two theories.

PHILLIPS CURVE—THE DREAM AND THE REALITY

The integration of expectations into our analysis places us in a position to better understand the effects of inflation on unemployment. In an influential article published in 1958, the British economist A. W. Phillips noted that there had been an inverse relationship between the rate of change in wages and the unemployment rate for nearly a century in the United Kingdom.[2] When wages were rising rapidly, unemployment was low. Correspondingly, wage rates rose more slowly when the unemployment rate was high. Others noted that a similar

---

[2]A. W. Phillips, "The Relationship between Unemployment and the Rate of Change of Money Wages in the United Kingdom, 1861–1957," *Economica* 25 (1958): pp. 238–299.

inverse relationship was present between inflation and unemployment during the post–Second World War period in the United States. Because it is based on Phillips's earlier work, a curve indicating the relationship between the rate of inflation and the rate of unemployment is known as the **Phillips curve.**

Phillips curve
A curve that illustrates the relationship between the rate of change in prices (or money wages) and the rate of unemployment.

EARLY VIEWS ABOUT THE PHILLIPS CURVE

Phillips did not draw any policy implications from his analysis, but others did. During the 1960s many economists thought that demand-stimulus policies would permanently reduce the rate of unemployment. As early as 1959, Paul Samuelson and Robert Solow (each of whom would later win a Nobel Prize in economics) argued that we could trade a little more inflation for less unemployment. Samuelson and Solow told the American Economic Association,

> In order to achieve the nonperfectionist's goal of high enough output to give us no more than 3 percent unemployment, the price index might have to rise by as much as 4 to 5 percent per year. That much price rise [inflation] would seem to be the necessary cost of high employment and production in the years immediately ahead.[3]

During the 1960s many leading economists thought that expansionary macroeconomic policy—that is, budget deficits and rapid growth in the money supply—would stimulate output and reduce the rate of unemployment if we were willing to tolerate a little higher rate of inflation. As **Exhibit 14–3** indicates, even the prestigious annual *Economic Report of the President* argued that moderate inflation would reduce the unemployment rate.[4] At the time, most economists thought the inflation-unemployment relationship was stable. In other words, they thought that the short-run equilibrium presented in part a of Exhibit 14–1 was, in fact, a long-lasting relationship (a long-run equilibrium).

For a while, it did seem that demand-stimulus policies could reduce the unemployment rate. Both monetary and fiscal policy were more expansionary during the latter half of the 1960s. As Exhibit 14–3 illustrates, the unemployment rate declined while the inflation rate increased, just as the proponents of the inflation-unemployment trade-off theory had predicted.

ADAPTIVE EXPECTATIONS AND THE PHILLIPS CURVE

Integration of expectations into the Phillips curve analysis enhances our understanding of the relationship between inflation and unemployment. First, let us consider the implications of the adaptive-expectations hypothesis. Suppose the

---

[3]Paul A. Samuelson and Robert Solow, "Our Menu of Policy Changes," *American Economic Review* (May 1960).

[4]Not all economists accepted the view that there was a trade-off between inflation and unemployment. At the height of its popularity, the theoretical underpinning of the alleged trade-off was independently challenged by both Edmund Phelps and Milton Friedman. See Edmund S. Phelps, "Phillips Curves, Expectations of Inflation and Optimal Employment over Time," *Economica* 3 (1967), pp. 254–281; and Milton Friedman, "The Role of Monetary Policy," *American Economic Review* (May 1968): pp. 1–17.

This exhibit is from the 1969 Economic Report of the President, prepared by the President's Council of Economic Advisers. Each dot on the diagram indicates, as a coordinate point on the graph, the inflation rate and unemployment rate for the year. The report stated that the chart "reveals a fairly close association of more rapid price increases with lower rates of unemployment." Economists refer to this link as the Phillips curve. In the 1960s it was widely believed that policymakers could pursue expansionary macroeconomic policies and thereby permanently reduce the unemployment rate. More recent experience has caused most economists to reject this view.

Source: *Economic Report of the President, 1969*, p. 95. The Phillips curve is fitted to the points to illustrate the relationship.

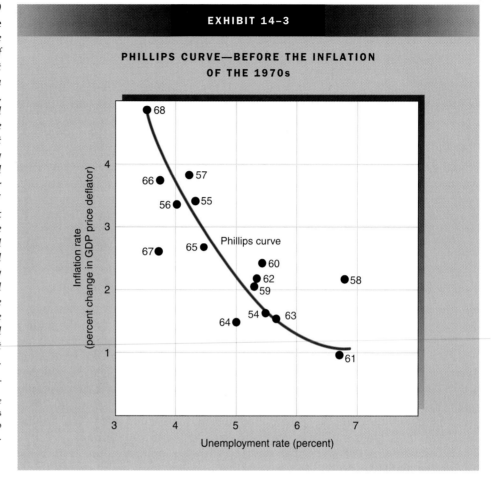

EXHIBIT 14-3

PHILLIPS CURVE—BEFORE THE INFLATION OF THE 1970s

monetary authorities shift to a more expansionary policy that soon leads to an increase in the rate of inflation. Because the adaptive-expectations hypothesis assumes that the next period will be pretty much like the recent past, people will fail to anticipate the increase in the rate of inflation. Therefore, *for a time*, decision makers will systematically *under*estimate the rate of inflation according to the adaptive-expectations hypothesis.

When labor-market participants underestimate the inflation rate, there are two reasons why inflation will stimulate employment. First, unanticipated inflation will reduce the real wages of workers employed under long-term contracts and thereby stimulate employment. Union wage contracts and other wage agreements, both explicit and implicit, often determine money-wage rates over periods ranging from one to three years. Unanticipated inflation means that the impact of wage and price inflation has not been fully factored into long-term money-wage agreements. Once an employer-employee agreement establishes money rates, an unexpected increase in the inflation rate will reduce the employee's real wage rate and the employer's real wage costs.

Suppose that employees and employers anticipate a 4 percent inflation rate during the next year. From this, they concur on a collective bargaining agreement calling for money wages of $10 during the current year and $10.40 for the year beginning 12 months from now. If the actual inflation rate this year equals the 4 percent expected rate, the $10.40 money-wage rate 12 months from now translates to a $10 real-wage rate *at today's price level.* What happens to the real-wage rate if the inflation rate exceeds the expected rate of 4 percent? If actual inflation during the next 12 months is 8 percent, for example, the real-wage rate one year from now will fall to $9.63 at current prices. The higher the actual inflation rate is, the lower the real wages of the employees. Unanticipated inflation tends to reduce the real-wage rates of employees whose money wages are fixed by long-term contracts. At the lower real-wage rate, firms will hire more workers and employment will expand.

There is a second reason why underestimation of the inflation rate will tend to expand employment. Misled by inflation, some job seekers will quickly accept job offers on the basis of a mistaken belief that the offers are particularly good ones in relation to the market for their labor services. When people underestimate the extent to which inflation has increased both prices and money wages, many job seekers will fail to recognize how much nominal wages have increased in their skill category. Unaware of just how much their money-wage opportunities have improved, they will tend to accept offers that are not as good as they think they are (relative to jobs that could be found with additional search). Unemployed workers thus shorten their search time, which lowers the unemployment rate.

To summarize, unanticipated (or underestimated) inflation reduces the real-wage rate of workers whose money wages are determined by long-term contracts and reduces the search time of job seekers. Both of these factors will expand employment and reduce the unemployment rate below its natural rate.

With adaptive expectations, though, decision makers will eventually anticipate a higher inflation rate after it has been present for a period of time. They will build the higher expected inflation rate into their decision making. Eventually, workers and their union representatives will demand and employers will agree to money-wage increases that fully reflect the higher current and expected future inflation rate. Similarly, job seekers will become fully aware of the extent that inflation has increased (and continues to increase) their money-wage alternatives. As they do so, their search time will return to normal. *Once decision makers fully anticipate the higher rate of inflation and reflect it in their choices, the inflation rate will neither depress real-wage rates nor reduce the search time of job seekers. As this happens, employment and real output will return to their natural (long-run) rates.*

Exhibit 14–4 uses our aggregate-demand/aggregate-supply (*AD/AS*) model to illustrate the implications of adaptive expectations with regard to the Phillips curve analysis. Beginning from a position of stable prices and long-run equilibrium (point *A*), part a of Exhibit 14–4 illustrates the impact of an unanticipated increase in aggregate demand. As we previously discussed, initially the demand stimulus will increase output (to Y_2) and employment. The unemployment rate will recede below the economy's natural rate. The strong demand and tight resource markets will place upward pressure on resource prices. *For a time,* the economy will experience both rising prices and an output beyond full employment capacity (point *B*). This high level of output, however, will not be long-lasting. With adaptive expectations, people will eventually anticipate the rising prices. When this happens, resource prices and costs will rise (from their

EXHIBIT 14–4

AD/AS MODEL, ADAPTIVE EXPECTATIONS, AND PHILLIPS CURVE

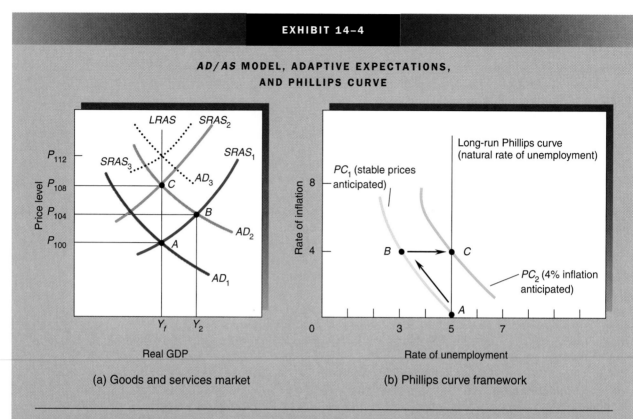

(a) Goods and services market

(b) Phillips curve framework

When stable prices are observed and anticipated, both full-employment output and the natural rate of unemployment will be present (A in both panels). With adaptive expectations, a shift to a more expansionary policy will increase prices, expand output beyond its full-employment potential, and reduce the unemployment rate below its natural level (move from A to B in both panels). Decision makers, though, will eventually anticipate the rising prices and incorporate them into their decision making. When this happens, the SRAS curve shifts to the left, output recedes to

the economy's full-employment potential, and unemployment returns to the natural rate (move from B to C in both panels). As the inflationary policy continues and decision makers anticipate it, both the AD and SRAS curves will continually shift upward (dotted AD and SRAS curves in panel a) without leading to an increase in output and employment. Inflation fails to expand output and reduce the unemployment rate when it is anticipated. Thus, the long-run Phillips curve is vertical at the natural rate of unemployment.

temporary low levels) relative to product prices, causing the *SRAS* curve to shift to the left. As the previous relationship between resource prices and product prices is restored, output will recede to the economy's full employment level (point *C*). If the rising prices continue at the same rate, they will be anticipated by decision makers. When this is the case, both the *AD* and *SRAS* curves will continually shift upward (the dotted curves of part a). The price level will steadily increase, but output and employment will remain at the full employment level.

Part b of Exhibit 14–4 illustrates the same case within the Phillips curve framework. Because initially stable prices are present and the economy is in long-run equilibrium, unemployment is equal to its natural rate (point *A*). We assume that the economy's natural rate of unemployment is 5 percent. The condition of long-run equilibrium implies that the stable prices are both anticipated and observed. Under adaptive expectations, an unanticipated shift to a more expansionary policy will temporarily increase output and reduce unemployment. It will also place upward pressure on prices. Suppose that demand-stimulus policies lead to 4 percent inflation and a reduction in the unemployment rate from 5 percent to 3 percent (moving from A to B along the short-run Phillips curve PC_1). Although point B is attainable, it will not be sustainable. After an extended period of 4 percent inflation, decision makers will begin to anticipate the higher rate of inflation. Workers and their union representatives will take the higher expected rate of inflation into account in their job search and collective bargaining decision making. Once the 4 percent rate of inflation is fully anticipated, the economy will confront a new, higher short-run Phillips curve (PC_2). The rate of unemployment will return to the long-run natural rate of 5 percent, even though prices will continue to rise at an annual rate of 4 percent (point C).

The moves from point A to point B in both panels of Exhibit 14–4 are simply alternative ways of representing the same phenomenon—a temporary increase in output and reduction in unemployment as the result of an unanticipated increase in aggregate demand. Similarly, the moves from point B to point C in the two panels both represent the return of output to its long-run potential and unemployment to its natural rate, once decision makers fully anticipate the observed rate of inflation.

What would happen if the macroplanners attempted to keep the unemployment rate low (below its natural rate) by shifting to a still more expansionary policy? As **Exhibit 14–5** illustrates, this course of action would accelerate the inflation rate to still higher levels. Under adaptive expectations, once the 4 percent inflation rate is anticipated, the rate of unemployment can, for a time, be reduced to 3 percent only if the macroplanners are willing to tolerate 8 percent

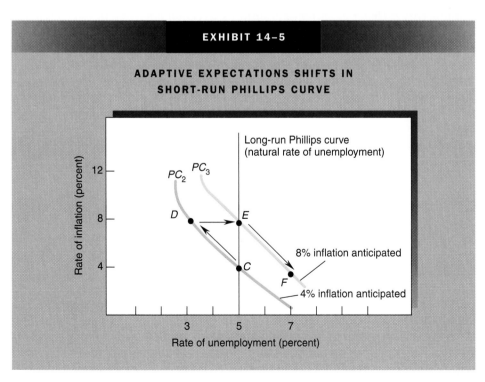

EXHIBIT 14–5

ADAPTIVE EXPECTATIONS SHIFTS IN SHORT-RUN PHILLIPS CURVE

Continuing with the example of Exhibit 14–4, part b, point C illustrates an economy experiencing 4 percent inflation that was anticipated by decision makers. Since the inflation was anticipated, the natural rate of unemployment is present. With adaptive expectations, demand-stimulus policies that result in a still higher rate of inflation (8 percent, for example) would once again temporarily reduce the unemployment rate below its long-run, normal level (move from C to D along PC_2). After a time, however, decision makers would come to anticipate the higher inflation rate, and the short-run Phillips curve would shift still farther to the right to PC_3 (move from D to E). Once the higher rate is anticipated, if macroplanners try to decelerate the rate of inflation, unemployment will temporarily rise above its long-run natural rate (for example, move from E to F).

inflation (movement from *C* to *D*). Of course, once the 8 percent rate has persisted for a while, it, too, will be fully anticipated. The short-run Phillips curve will again shift to the right (to *PC₃*), unemployment will return to its long-run natural rate, and inflation will continue at a rate of 8 percent (point *E*).

Once decision makers anticipate a higher rate of inflation (for example, the 8 percent rate), what will happen if macroplanners shift to a more restrictive policy designed to reduce the rate of inflation? When the inflation rate is declining, decision makers will systematically overestimate the future inflation rate under the adaptive-expectations hypothesis. Suppose that wage rates are based on agreements that anticipated a continuation of the 8 percent inflation rate (point *E* of Exhibit 14–5). If the actual inflation rate falls to 4 percent when 8 percent inflation was expected, the real wages of workers will exceed the real wage present when the actual and expected rates of inflation were equal at 8 percent. The more the actual inflation rate falls short of the expected rate, the higher the real wages of workers will be. Similarly, the search time of job seekers will increase when they overestimate the impact of inflation on money-wage rates. Unaware that the attractive money-wage offers they seek are unavailable, job hunters will lengthen their job search. In the short run, rising unemployment will be a side effect of the higher real wages and more lengthy job searches.

As Exhibit 14–5 illustrates, with adaptive expectations, once a high (8 percent) inflation rate is anticipated by decision makers, a shift to a more restrictive policy designed to decelerate the inflation rate will cause abnormally high unemployment (the move from *E* to *F* along *PC₃*) and economic recession. The abnormally high unemployment rate will continue until a lower rate of inflation convinces decision makers to alter their inflationary expectations downward and revise long-term contracts accordingly.

We can now summarize the implications of adaptive expectations for the Phillips curve. *Under adaptive expectations, decision makers will underestimate the future inflation rate when the rate is rising and overestimate it when the inflation rate is falling. As the result of this systematic pattern, a shift to a more expansionary policy will temporarily reduce the unemployment rate, while a move to a more restrictive policy will temporarily increase the unemployment rate. As an inflation rate persists over time, decision makers will eventually anticipate it, and unemployment will return to its natural rate. There is no long-run (permanent) trade-off between inflation and unemployment under adaptive expectations.* Like the *LRAS* curve, the long-run Phillips curve is vertical at the natural rate of unemployment.

RATIONAL EXPECTATIONS AND THE PHILLIPS CURVE

How would the Phillips curve analysis be altered if the rational-expectations hypothesis is correct? In a world of rational expectations, people quickly anticipate the effects of policy changes and adjust their actions accordingly. For example, if people see a surge in the money supply or a tax cut coming, they will adjust their expectations in light of the shift toward more expansionary policy. Anticipating the strong future demand, workers and union representatives immediately press for higher wages and/or inclusion of cost-of-living provisions to prevent the erosion of their real wages by inflation. Business firms, also anticipating the increase in demand, consent to the demands of labor, but they will also raise prices. By the time the demand stimulus arrives, it will have already been counteracted by higher money wages, costs, and product prices.[5]

If decision makers accurately anticipate the inflationary effects of a more expansionary macroeconomic policy, then the demand stimulus will merely increase the price level (inflation rate) without altering output or employment. Exhibit 14–1 (part b) illustrates this case within the framework of our *AD/AS* model. **Exhibit 14–6** provides parallel analysis for the Phillips curve framework. Suppose an economy is initially at point *A*, where a 4 percent inflation rate is both observed and expected. Because the actual and expected inflation rates are equal, the long-run natural rate of unemployment (U_n) is initially observed. Now, suppose policymakers shift to a more expansionary policy—a demand-stimulus policy consistent with an 8 percent rate of inflation. With rational expectations, the Phillips curve will immediately shift upward as decision makers anticipate an acceleration in the inflation rate due to the more expansionary macropolicy. If decision makers correctly forecast the rise in the inflation rate (to 8 percent), a short-run Phillips curve PC_2 will result. Even though the inflation rate increases to 8 percent, unemployment remains at its long-run natural rate (shifting from *A* to *B*).

As explained earlier, the rational-expectations hypothesis does not imply that decision makers are always right. People may either underestimate or

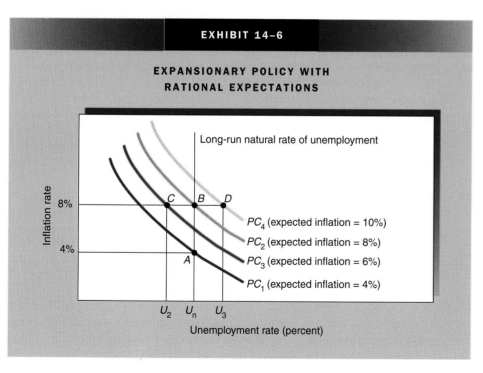

EXHIBIT 14–6

EXPANSIONARY POLICY WITH RATIONAL EXPECTATIONS

Long-run natural rate of unemployment

PC_4 (expected inflation = 10%)
PC_2 (expected inflation = 8%)
PC_3 (expected inflation = 6%)
PC_1 (expected inflation = 4%)

Inflation rate

8%

4%

U_2 U_n U_3

Unemployment rate (percent)

Suppose that when the actual and expected rates of inflation are 4 percent (point A), policy makers try to reduce unemployment by shifting to a more expansionary macropolicy consistent with an 8 percent inflationary rate. Proponents of rational expectations argue that the outcome is unpredictable. If people accurately anticipate the inflationary impact of the more expansionary course, the inflation rate will rise while unemployment remains unchanged (shift from A to B). On the other hand, if people underestimate the future inflation, unemployment will temporarily fall (as illustrated by the shift from A to C). In contrast, if individuals overestimate the actual increase in the inflation rate, unemployment will rise temporarily above its long-run natural rate (shift from A to D).

---

[5]As we discussed in the preceding chapter, expansionary monetary policy will also increase the expected rate of inflation and lead to a higher money interest rate in the loanable funds market. The rational-expectations hypothesis also implies that money interest rates will rise quickly in response to expansionary monetary policy.

overestimate the inflationary effects of the demand stimulus. When they underestimate the inflationary effects, the actual inflation rate will temporarily exceed the expected rate. Suppose that even though the actual inflation rate rises to 8 percent, decision makers anticipate an increase to only 6 percent. In this case, the short-run Phillips curve (PC_3 in Exhibit 14–6) will shift outward by a lesser amount than if the increase in inflation had been accurately forecast. Since individuals do not fully build the higher (8 percent) inflation rate into their decision making, the current unemployment rate declines to U_2 in the short run (moving from point A to point C).

In contrast, when individuals overestimate the increase in inflation, the current unemployment rate will temporarily increase. For example, if decision makers expect the inflation rate to rise to 10 percent while the expansionary policies generate an increase to only 8 percent, the short-run Phillips curve will shift by a larger amount (PC_4 in Exhibit 14–6) than if the increase in inflation had been correctly forecast. In the short run, unemployment will rise above its long-run normal rate (moving from point A to point D).

How can policymakers know whether rational decision makers will over- or underestimate the effects of a policy change? According to the proponents of rational expectations, they cannot. If the errors of decision makers are random, as the rational-expectations theory implies, people will be as likely to overestimate as to underestimate. *Under the rational-expectations hypothesis, then, the impact of expansionary policy on real output and employment is unpredictable, even in the short run. If decision makers accurately anticipate the inflationary impact of expansionary policy, the unemployment rate will remain unchanged even though the inflation rate accelerates. However, if they underestimate the future inflation impact, the unemployment rate will temporarily decline. Conversely, the unemployment rate will temporarily rise if they overestimate the inflationary impact of the policy.*

The rational-expectations hypothesis suggests it is extremely difficult for policymakers to use demand-stimulus policies to reduce the unemployment rate. Such a strategy is effective only when it catches people by surprise, and then only temporarily. If policymakers follow a systematic strategy, such as persistent demand stimulus or even countercyclical demand stimulus, rational human beings will catch on to the pattern, and the policy moves will fail to exert the intended effect.

RATIONAL EXPECTATIONS, MACROECONOMIC POLICY, AND THE INGREDIENTS OF A SUCCESSFUL ANTI-INFLATION STRATEGY

The policy implications of rational expectations are clear. The best policies are preannounced, stable policies (for example, a monetary policy that stabilized the price level). Macroeconomic policy should be directed toward long-term objectives, and changes should be weighed very carefully. Policy should not attempt to "fine tune" the economy. Efforts to do so will only contribute to economic uncertainty.

On the positive side, the rational-expectations hypothesis indicates that a move from inflation to stable prices can be achieved more easily than the adaptive-expectations hypothesis implies. If policymakers announce that they are going to shift to a more restrictive course and provide the public with credible assurances that they will stick with the policy until stable prices are achieved, the rational-expectations hypothesis indicates that expectations will change quickly. When this is the case, the inflation rate can be reduced without the economy going through a severe prolonged recession and high unemployment—a situation that is implied by the adaptive-expectations hypothesis.

The key to a successful anti-inflation policy is credibility.[6] If the policy is credible and the public is convinced that the monetary authorities really mean business, the expected rate of inflation will decline quickly (shifting the short-run Phillips curve down, and toward the origin). As the expectation of inflation declines, money-wage rates will be correspondingly scaled back. Money interest rates will fall. These adjustments will facilitate the reduction in the inflation rate and permit it to be achieved at a minimal cost in terms of reductions in employment and output.

In contrast, if market participants lack confidence in the long-term anti-inflationary commitment of policymakers, they will reduce their expectations for the future rate of inflation slowly even if current policy is restrictive. When policymakers have a past history of policy reversals and of saying one thing while doing another, it will be difficult for them to establish credibility. Proponents of rational expectations are thus not surprised that restrictive policies have often led to recession and abnormally high unemployment.

EXPECTATIONS AND THE MODERN VIEW OF THE PHILLIPS CURVE

Expectations substantially alter the naive Phillips curve view of the 1960s. Three major points follow from the modern view that integrates expectations into our analysis.

1. Demand stimulus will lead to inflation without permanently reducing unemployment below the natural rate. Once people fully anticipate the inflationary side effects of expansionary policies, resource prices will rise, profit margins will return to normal levels, and unemployment will return to its natural rate. Under adaptive expectations, this will happen only after the higher inflation rates have been observed for a period of time—say, a year or so. Under rational expectations, the adjustment process will occur more rapidly. If people accurately anticipate the inflationary effects, the demand-stimulus policies may fail to reduce, even temporarily, the unemployment rate when expectations are rational. *In the long run,* though, the implications of adaptive and rational expectations are identical—persistent expansionary policy will lead to inflation without permanently reducing the unemployment rate.

---

[6]For evidence that even hyperinflations can be brought under control quickly (with little loss of output) when credibility is present, see Thomas Sargent, "The Ends of Four Big Inflations," in *Inflation: Causes and Effects,* ed. Robert E. Hall (Chicago: University of Chicago Press for the National Bureau of Economic Research, 1982), pp. 41–98.

2. When inflation is greater than anticipated, unemployment falls below the natural rate. Conversely, when inflation is less than expected, unemployment will rise above the natural rate. It is the *difference* between the actual and expected rates of inflation that influences unemployment, not the magnitude of inflation, as some economists previously thought. **Exhibit 14–7** illustrates this point by recasting the Phillips curve within the expectations framework. When people underestimate the actual rate of inflation, abnormally low unemployment will occur. Conversely, when decision makers expect a higher rate of inflation than what actually occurs—when they overestimate the inflation rate—unemployment will rise above its natural rate. Equal changes in the actual and expected inflation rates, though, will fail to reduce the unemployment rate. If actual inflation rates of 5 percent, 10 percent, 20 percent, or even higher are accurately anticipated, they will fail to reduce unemployment below its natural rate.[7]

3. When the inflation rate is steady—when it is neither rising nor falling—the actual rate of unemployment will equal the economy's natural rate of unemployment. If the inflation rate of an economy is constant (or approximately so), decision makers will come to anticipate the rate. This rate will be reflected in

It is the difference between the actual and expected rates of inflation that influences the unemployment rate, not merely the size of the inflation rate, as the earlier, naive Phillips curve analysis implied. When inflation is greater than anticipated (people underestimate it), unemployment will fall below the natural rate. In contrast, when inflation is less than people anticipate, unemployment will rise above the natural rate. If the inflation rate is correctly anticipated by decision makers, the natural rate of unemployment will result.

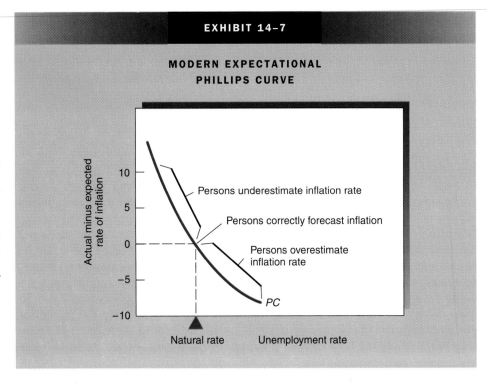

EXHIBIT 14–7

MODERN EXPECTATIONAL PHILLIPS CURVE

---

[7]Empirically, higher rates of inflation are generally associated with greater variability in the inflation rate. Erratic variability increases economic uncertainty. It is likely to inhibit business activity, reduce the volume of mutually advantageous exchange, and cause the level of employment to fall. Thus, higher, more variable inflation rates may actually increase the rate of unemployment.

THE NATURAL RATE OF UNEMPLOYMENT IN EUROPE, CANADA, JAPAN, AND THE UNITED STATES

Our analysis indicates that when the inflation rate of a country is steady (when it is neither rising nor falling) for an extended period of time, people will anticipate the rate, and unemployment will gravitate toward the economy's natural rate of unemployment. Interestingly, the inflation rates in the United States, Canada, Europe, and Japan were quite steady—they fluctuated within a narrow band—during 1986–1990.

Given these steady rates of inflation in the late 1980s, the actual unemployment rates during the latter part of the period should approximate the natural rate of unemployment for each of these economies. The following chart presents the unemployment rates in 1989 and 1990 and the average for the 1991–1995 period for each of these areas.

Rate of Unemployment

	1989	1990	1991–1995 AVERAGE
United States	5.3	5.5	6.5
Europe (11 EC countries)	7.3	7.0	9.1
Canada	7.5	8.1	10.6
Japan	2.3	2.1	2.5

The unemployment rate during 1989 and 1990 was approximately 5.5 percent in the United States, 7 percent in Europe, 8 percent in Canada, and 2 percent in Japan. These numbers imply that, compared to the United States, the natural rate of unemployment in the late 1980s was higher in Europe and Canada, but lower in Japan. The average unemployment rates for 1991–1995 are also consistent with this view.

Compared to the United States, why might the natural rate of unemployment be higher in Europe and Canada but lower in Japan? There are two major reasons. First, wages tend to be more flexible in Japan than in the United States, but less flexible in Europe and Canada.

Unions in Japan are almost exclusively of the "company union" variety. They seldom set wages for an entire industry, and they are much more likely than their U.S. counterparts to accept wage cuts during a period of declining demand for the products that they produce. In contrast, wages tend to be less flexible in Europe and Canada than in the United States. The unionization rate—that is, the percent of the nonagricultural labor force that is unionized—in Canada, the United Kingdom, Italy, and Germany is between two and three times the comparable figure for the United States.[1] To the extent that strong unions in Europe and Canada push wages above the market level and reduce wage flexibility, they tend to increase the natural rate of unemployment. In addition, many of the governments in Europe set wages—often at or above equilibrium rates—in various occupations and industries. This, too, contributes to wage rigidity and tends to push the natural rate of unemployment up.

Second, the unemployment-compensation system is generally more lucrative (and less restrictive with regard to eligibility) in Europe and Canada than in the United States.[2] This encourages more lengthy periods of job search and thereby pushes up the natural rate of unemployment in Europe and Canada. In contrast, unemployment compensation and other income-transfer programs are less lucrative in Japan than in the United States. This, too, contributes to the low natural rate of unemployment in Japan.

[1]Richard B. Freeman, "Contraction and Expansion: The Divergence of Private and Public Sector Unionism in the United States," *Journal of Economic Perspectives* (spring 1988): pp. 63–88.

[2]See Vivek Moorthy, "Unemployment in Canada and the United States: The Role of Unemployment Insurance Benefits," *Federal Reserve Bank of New York: Quarterly Review* (winter 1990): pp. 48–61.

both long-term contracts and the job search of workers. Once this happens, unemployment will return to its natural rate. In fact, the natural rate of unemployment is sometimes defined as the unemployment rate present when the inflation rate is neither rising nor falling (see the accompanying Measures of Economic Activity box).

EXPECTATIONS, INFLATION, AND UNEMPLOYMENT: THE EMPIRICAL EVIDENCE

Integration of expectations into our analysis helps clarify the U.S. data on inflation and unemployment during the last several decades. After nearly 20 years of low inflation (and moderate monetary and fiscal policy) following the Second World War, decision makers, accustomed to relative price stability, expected low rates of inflation. As a result, the shift toward expansionary policies in the mid-1960s caught people by surprise.[8] Therefore, as Exhibit 14–3 shows, these policies initially reduced the unemployment rate.

Contrary to the popular view of the 1960s, though, the abnormally low unemployment rate could not be sustained. **Exhibit 14–8,** which is an updated version of Exhibit 14–3, makes this point clear. Just as our theory predicts, the inflation-unemployment conditions worsened substantially as the expansionary

While the 1961–1969 unemployment-inflation data mapped Phillips curve PC$_1$ (see Exhibit 14–3), as demand-stimulus policies led to higher inflation rates, the Phillips curve shifted outward to PC$_2$ (for the 1970–1973 period) and PC$_3$ (for the 1974–1983 period). Just as our theories of expectations indicate, the high rates of inflation fail to permanently reduce the rate of employment. Similarly, as lower rates of inflation were achieved and eventually anticipated, the Phillips curve shifted inward (see 1984–1995 data).

Source: See *Economic Report of the President, 1982,* p. 51.

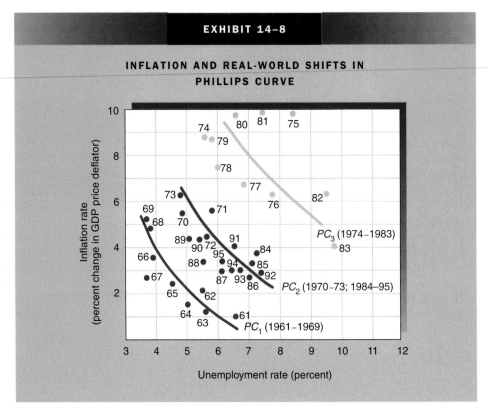

EXHIBIT 14-8

INFLATION AND REAL-WORLD SHIFTS IN PHILLIPS CURVE

[8]The following data are indicative of the shift toward more expansionary macroeconomic policies beginning in the mid-1960s. Between 1965 and 1980, the M1 money supply grew at an annual rate of 6.3 percent, compared to only 2.5 percent during the previous 15 years. Similarly, perpetual federal deficits replaced balanced budgets. During the 1950–1965 period, there were eight budget deficits and seven surpluses. On average, the federal budget was approximately in balance during the 15-year period. During the 1965–1980 period, however, there was only one year of budget surplus, and annual deficits averaged 1.5 percent of GDP.

policy persisted. The Phillips curve, consistent with the 1970–1973 data (PC_2), was well to the right of PC_1. During the 1974–1983 period, still higher rates of inflation were observed. As inflation rates in the 6 percent to 10 percent range became commonplace in the latter half of the 1970s, the Phillips curve once again shifted upward, to PC_3.

As monetary policy tightened in 1981–1983 and the Reagan administration promised to bring inflation under control, the inflation rate decelerated sharply. Just as our theory predicts, initially the unemployment rate soared, to 9.7 percent in 1982 and 9.6 percent in 1983 (see Exhibit 14–8), when macroeconomic policy shifted toward restraint. However, as the restraint continued, people scaled their expectations for the inflation rate downward, and the Phillips curve shifted inward. As Exhibit 14–8 indicates, during the 1984–1995 period, the inflation rate declined from the high rates of the late 1970s to the 2.5 percent to 4.5 percent range. Soon after the decline in inflation, people began to anticipate the lower rates, and the Phillips curve shifted inward (from PC_3 to PC_2).

Exhibit 14–9 presents the 1961–1993 inflation-unemployment data in a form that provides a still better test of our theory. Our analysis indicates that, when the actual inflation rate is higher than people anticipate, unemployment will fall short of the natural rate. On the other hand, if the inflation rate is less than was anticipated, unemployment will exceed its natural rate. Of course, we cannot directly observe the expected inflation rate. However, we would expect that it will be influenced by recent experiences.

In Exhibit 14–9, for each year shown, the average inflation rate during the previous three years is used as a proxy for the expected rate of inflation. The exhibit illustrates that, when the inflation rate was higher than anticipated (higher than the average of the last three years), unemployment was generally less than the natural rate. For example, as the inflation rate rose in the late 1960s, the actual inflation rate was approximately 2 percent higher than anticipated during 1966, 1968, and 1969. Just as our theory implies, unemployment was well below the natural rate during each of these years.

Conversely, when the inflation rate was less than anticipated, unemployment rose above the natural rate. Look at the dots for the years 1976, 1977, 1982–1985, 1991, and 1992. During each of these years, the actual inflation rate was significantly less than the anticipated rate. And during each of these years, unemployment well above the natural rate was observed.

While the data of Exhibit 14–9 show an obvious negative relationship between unanticipated inflation and unemployment, the observations for five years (1974–1975 and 1979–1981) do not fit as well as the others. Interestingly, these five years encompass periods of soaring oil prices. Oil prices quadrupled (from $2.50 to $10.00 per barrel) between 1973 and 1975, and more than tripled (from $12.00 to $40.00 per barrel) between 1978 and 1981. As we previously discussed (see Chapter 9, Exhibit 9–7), supply shocks of this type tend to push the price level up. Predictably, they lead to dislocations and adjustments that weaken the normal relationship between inflation and unemployment.

The modern view indicates that it is the difference between the actual and expected rates of inflation that will influence the rate of unemployment. Abrupt changes in the inflation rate are less likely to be correctly anticipated. **Exhibit 14–10** presents data on changes in the annual rate (12-month moving average) of inflation and the rate of unemployment. As the graph shows, there were sharp

Here we show the relationship between unanticipated inflation and actual unemployment compared to the natural rate for the period of 1961–1995. When the inflation rate is greater than anticipated, unemployment tends to fall below the natural rate. Conversely, when the inflation rate is less than anticipated, the unemployment rate is generally above the natural rate.

Source: *Economic Report of the President, 1996;* and Robert J. Gordon, *Macroeconomics* (Boston: Little Brown, 1993). The natural rate of unemployment data are from Gordon. The average inflation rate for the previous three years was used as a proxy for the anticipated inflation rate for each year.

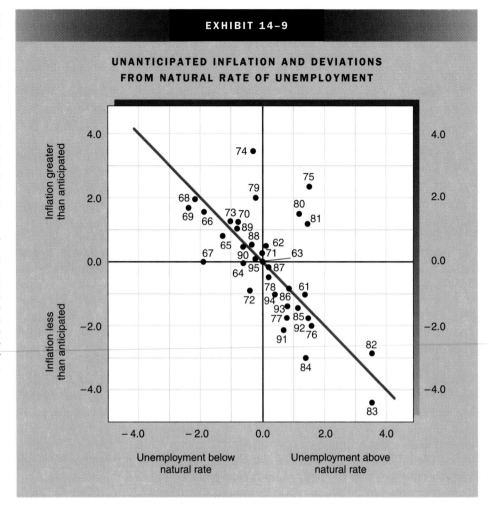

EXHIBIT 14-9

UNANTICIPATED INFLATION AND DEVIATIONS FROM NATURAL RATE OF UNEMPLOYMENT

reductions in the rate of inflation during 1975, 1981–1982, and 1991. For example, the inflation rate fell from 12.4 percent in 1974 to 6.9 percent in 1975, a drop of more than 5 percentage points. Decision makers are unlikely to foresee sharp reductions in the inflation rate. Certainly this will be true under adaptive expectations, but even rational decision makers are likely to underestimate the magnitude of sharp declines in the rate of inflation. When this is the case, the actual rate of inflation will be less than the expected rate. Under these circumstances, our analysis indicates that unemployment will rise above its natural rate. As Exhibit 14–10 shows, the unemployment rate rose substantially in response to the steep declines in the rate of inflation during 1975, 1981–1982, and again in 1991. These results can also be viewed within the framework of our familiar *AD/AS* model. Prices in the goods and services market tend to be lower than what people expect when there is a sharp decline in the rate of inflation. Given the lower-than-expected prices, profit margins are squeezed, businesses cut back on output and employment, and the unemployment rate increases.

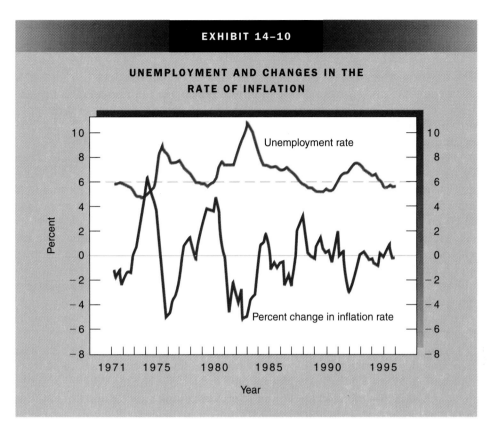

EXHIBIT 14–10

UNEMPLOYMENT AND CHANGES IN THE RATE OF INFLATION

Here we illustrate the relationship between changes in the rate of inflation (this year's inflation rate minus the rate during the prior year) and the rate of unemployment. Note how the sharp reductions in the rate of inflation during 1975, 1981–1982, and 1991 were associated with recession and substantial increases in the unemployment rate.

MICROECONOMICS AND THE NATURAL RATE OF UNEMPLOYMENT

The integration of expectations into our analysis indicates that monetary and fiscal policies are unable to reduce, at least not for long, unemployment below its natural rate. Can other methods be used to reduce the unemployment rate? In recent years, economists have turned to microeconomics as a means of addressing the traditional macroeconomic problem of high unemployment. The microeconomics approach to employment focuses on how the economy's natural rate of unemployment might be reduced and *LRAS* increased. Remember, the natural rate of unemployment is not immutable. Among other things, it reflects the incentive structure emanating from the economy's institutional arrangements. If changes in that incentive structure could improve the efficiency of job search and remove barriers to employment, the economy's natural rate of unemployment would decline.

What kinds of institutional changes would be most likely to reduce the natural rate of unemployment? We will consider three changes that have been widely discussed.

REVISING THE UNEMPLOYMENT-COMPENSATION SYSTEM

The unemployment-compensation system was designed to reduce the hardships of unemployment. As desirable as this program is from a humanitarian standpoint, it diminishes the opportunity cost of job search, leisure, nonproductive activities, and continued unemployment. The conflict between high benefit levels and low rates of unemployment should therefore not be surprising.

There are two major reasons why the current unemployment-compensation system increases the natural rate of unemployment. First, it reduces, and in some cases virtually eliminates, the personal cost of unemployment. The benefits in most states provide covered unemployed workers with payments of 50 percent to 60 percent of their previous gross earnings. Unemployment benefits are not subject to payroll taxes (and, in some cases, income taxes). In addition, unemployed workers may also qualify for other transfer benefits, such as food stamps and Medicaid. It is not unusual, then, for the benefit package of a covered unemployed worker to replace 75 percent or more of previous net earnings. Clearly, benefit levels in this range substantially reduce the incentive of individuals to search quickly and diligently for jobs and to accept employment at marginally lower wages prior to the exhaustion of their benefits.

Second, unemployment compensation acts as a subsidy to employers who offer unstable or seasonal employment opportunities. Employees would be more reluctant to work for such employers (for example, northern contractors who generally lay off workers in the winter) were it not for the fact that these employees can supplement their earnings with unemployment-compensation benefits during their layoffs. The system makes seasonal, temporary, and casual employment opportunities more attractive than would otherwise be the case. In essence, it encourages employers to adopt production methods and work rules that rely extensively on temporary employees and supplementary layoff benefits.

There is little doubt that the current unemployment-compensation system increases the natural rate of unemployment. Most researchers in the area believe that the long-run rate of unemployment is between 0.5 percent and 1.0 percent higher than it would be if the negative employment effects of the system could be eliminated.[9] In effect, unemployment benefits subsidize job search. There is one positive element accompanying this subsidy—the additional job search emanating from this subsidy may improve the match between the skills of unemployed workers and the requirements of potential jobs. To the extent this is true, the average productivity of workers is higher.

How can the unemployment-compensation system be reformed without undercutting its original humanitarian objectives? Several policy alternatives exist. Firms that regularly terminate and lay off a high percentage of their work force might be charged a payroll tax that more accurately reflects the cost of employment instability. (The current system performs this function imperfectly.) In addition, after a specified period of time, three months for example, unem-

---

[9]See David A. Green and Craig Riddell, "The Economic Effects of Unemployment Insurance in Canada: An Empirical Analysis of UI Disentitlement," *Journal of Labor Economics* (January 1993); Ray Thorne, *The Unemployment Compensation System: Paying People Not to Work* (Dallas: National Center for Policy Analysis, 1988); and Bruce Meyer, *Unemployment Insurance and Unemployment Spells* (Cambridge: National Bureau of Economic Research, 1988) for additional detail on this topic.

ployment-compensation recipients might be required to accept available jobs (including public-sector employment) that provide wage rates equal to their unemployment-compensation benefits. Alternatively, recipients' benefits might be gradually reduced as they engaged in more lengthy periods of job search and unemployment. This would reduce the incentive of individuals to wait until their benefits run out (generally 26 weeks) before accepting employment. Each of these proposals would increase the incentive of employers to offer stable employment and job searchers to seek out and accept employment more quickly.

REFORMING THE MINIMUM WAGE

Despite good intentions, minimum wage laws reduce the employment prospects of low-skilled, inexperienced workers. Many youthful workers fall into this category. As in the case of other price floors, the minimum wage leads to an excess supply. By mandating artificially high wage rates for jobs requiring few skills, the minimum wage reduces the employment opportunities available to low-skill workers.[10]

The adverse impact of the minimum wage on the on-the-job training opportunities available to low-skill workers is also important. The legislation often makes it unfeasible for an employer to (1) provide training to inexperienced workers and (2) pay the legal minimum wage at the same time. Thus, there are few low-paying jobs offering a combination of informal (or formal) training and skill-building experience. This makes it difficult for low-skill workers to acquire the training and experience necessary to move up to better, higher-paying jobs.

Several proposals have been suggested to minimize these negative effects. Some economists favor abolition of the minimum wage. Others would exempt teenagers from the legislation's coverage. Still others would exempt long-term unemployed workers from the legislation. In each case, the advocates argue that the wages of low-skill workers would settle at a market equilibrium, and the long-run employment and training opportunities available to such workers would improve.

PROVIDING TRAINING OPPORTUNITIES

Unemployment may result from mismatches between the requirements of available jobs and the skills of potential workers. Many economists believe that programs designed to improve the basic skills of workers and facilitate the development of new skills could reduce the natural rate of unemployment. Of course, improvement in our elementary and secondary educational system would be a step in that direction. Others believe that a vocational-training-loan program, similar in design to present college-loan programs, would assist low- and middle-income youths in developing technical skills. Martin Feldstein, former chairman of the Council of Economic Advisers, suggested that training subsidies (scholarships) be provided for youthful workers (for example, persons under 25

---

[10]For additional information on this topic, see John Kennan, "The Elusive Effects of Minimum Wage," *Journal of Economic Literature* 33 (December 1995): pp. 1949–1965; and Richard Vedder and Lowell Gallaway, *Should the Federal Minimum Wage Be Raised?* (Dallas: National Center for Policy Analysis, 1995).

years of age) who maintain jobs, but do not attend college. These wage supplements might be limited to employment that provided the youthful workers significant amounts of on-the-job technical training. Such a plan would reward youthful workers for both continuous employment and the acquisition of craft, clerical, operative, and perhaps even managerial skills. The long-run goal of such training programs is to improve the quality and flexibility of the labor force. Accomplishment of this objective would lead to a lower natural rate of unemployment because it would reduce the frequency and duration of unemployment.

DEMOGRAPHICS AND THE NATURAL RATE OF UNEMPLOYMENT

Compared to their elders, youthful workers are more likely to switch back and forth between the labor force and school. And even after they permanently enter the labor force, they are more likely to switch jobs as they search for a career path. Because of this, younger workers historically experience higher unemployment rates. In fact, the unemployment rate of persons under age 25 has typically run three times or more the rate for workers age 35 and over. For people age 25–34, the unemployment rate has generally been approximately one and one-half times the rate for their older counterparts (see **Exhibit 14–11, part b**).

Given the less stable employment pattern of youthful workers, the natural rate of unemployment rises as they make up a larger share of the labor force. As Exhibit 14–11, part a, shows, this is precisely what happened during the 1958–1980 period. As those born during the "baby boom" following the Second World War entered the work force during the 1960s and 1970s, the labor force grew rapidly and became progressively younger. In 1958 workers age 16–24 constituted only 15.6 percent of the labor force. By 1980 nearly one out of every four (23.7 percent) labor-force participants was in this age group. Similarly, young adults age 25–34 also increased as a proportion of the work force between 1958 and 1980. In contrast, workers over age 35 were a shrinking proportion of the labor force during the 1958–1980 period. As the youthful segments of the labor force grew rapidly, the natural rate of unemployment rose. Research in this area indicates that the natural rate of unemployment was between 0.5 percent and 1.5 percent higher in 1980 than in 1958 as a result of this factor. Obviously, it has contributed to the high unemployment rates of the 1970s and 1980s.

However, this adverse demographic factor has now reversed itself. By the year 2000, people age 16–24 are projected to compose 16.3 percent of the work force, substantially lower than the 1980 figure. Conversely, projections indicate that workers age 35 and over will compose 60.9 percent of the labor force in 2000, up from 49 percent in 1980 (see part a of Exhibit 14–11). Economic theory indicates that this maturing of the U.S. work force is currently reducing the natural rate of unemployment.

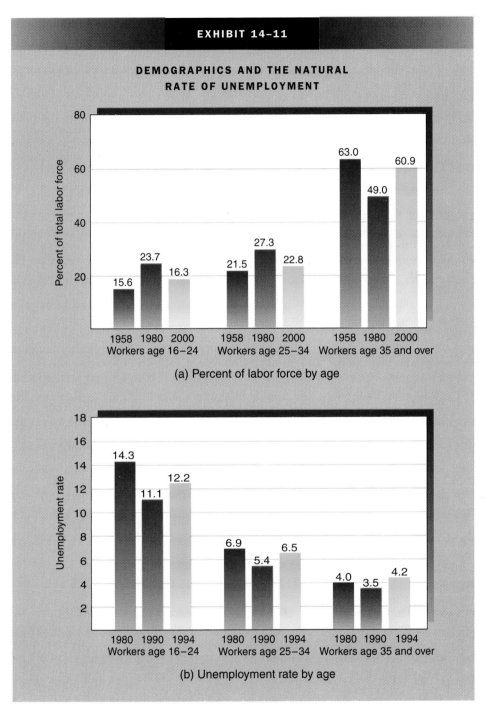

EXHIBIT 14–11

DEMOGRAPHICS AND THE NATURAL RATE OF UNEMPLOYMENT

(a) Percent of labor force by age

(b) Unemployment rate by age

Because younger workers have less stable employment patterns (part b), the natural rate of unemployment rises when they compose a larger share of the labor force. This was the case during the 1958–1980 period (part a). However, youthful workers are now becoming a smaller proportion of the labor force. This is currently reducing the natural rate of unemployment.

LOOKING AHEAD

Now that we have integrated expectations into our analysis, we are prepared to take a closer look at the potential of macroeconomic policy as a stabilization tool. The next chapter focuses on stabilization policy and related issues.

CHAPTER SUMMARY

1. The impact of demand-stimulus policies is dependent on whether the effects are anticipated. When the effects are unanticipated, an increase in aggregate demand will temporarily expand real GDP beyond the economy's long-run output potential. In contrast, when decision makers correctly anticipate the effects of expansionary policy, real output will remain unchanged even though the price level increases.

2. There are two major theories as to how expectations are formed: the adaptive-expectations hypothesis and the rational-expectations hypothesis.

3. According to the adaptive-expectations hypothesis, individuals base their expectations for the future on observations of the recent past. Expectations for the future will lag behind observed changes.

4. The rational-expectations hypothesis assumes that people use all pertinent information, including data on the conduct of current policy, in forming their expectations about the future. Although decision makers make forecasting errors under rational expectations, the errors are not systematic. Decision makers are as likely to overestimate as to underestimate the future change in an economic variable.

5. The Phillips curve indicates the relationship between the unemployment rate and inflation rate. Prior to the 1970s it was widely believed that higher inflation would lower the rate of unemployment.

6. Integrating expectations into macroeconomics makes it clear that any trade-off between unemployment and inflation will be short-lived. With adaptive expectations, expansionary policies will lead to a short-run trade-off of lower unemployment for an acceleration in the inflation rate. Individuals, though, will eventually come to expect the higher inflation rate and alter their decisions accordingly. This will cause unemployment to return to the natural rate.

7. With rational expectations, there is no consistent unemployment-inflation trade-off in either the short run or the long run. In fact, the short run impact of expansionary macropolicy is unpredictable. If decision makers accurately forecast the inflationary effects, expansionary policies will cause inflation while leaving the unemployment rate un-

changed. However, if expansionary policy leads to an increase in inflation that exceeds (is less than) the expected increase, unemployment will temporarily fall below (rise above) its long-run normal level.

8. Contrary to the expectations of the 1960s, expansionary policy during the post-1965 period did not consistently reduce the unemployment rate. There is no evidence that in the long run inflationary policies can reduce the unemployment rate—that inflation can be "traded off" for unemployment. Both adaptive- and rational-expectations theories imply that the long-run Phillips curve is vertical at the natural rate of unemployment.

9. The modern view of the Phillips curve integrates the effect of expectations. When the inflation rate is greater than anticipated, unemployment will tend to fall below the natural rate. Conversely, when the inflation rate is less than anticipated, unemployment will rise above its natural rate. Even high rates of inflation will fail to reduce unemployment once they are anticipated by decision makers.

10. In recent years, economists have given increased attention to the importance of incentives in the determination of the natural rate of unemployment. Many economists believe that the unemployment-compensation system, minimum wage legislation, and inadequate educational and training programs contribute to the high current rate of unemployment. Reform in these areas could lower the natural rate of unemployment.

11. During the 1960s and 1970s, rapid growth in the number of youthful labor-force participants increased the natural rate of unemployment. This demographic factor has now been reversed. The number of youthful workers as a share of the labor force has been declining in recent years. This trend is currently reducing the natural rate of unemployment.

CRITICAL ANALYSIS QUESTIONS

1. Suppose the monetary authorities accelerate the annual growth rate of the money supply from a long-term trend of 5 percent to 10 percent. If decision makers do not anticipate the effects of this policy change, how will it influence output, employment, and prices in the short run? If the effects are anticipated, how will the expansionary policy influence output, employment, and prices in the short run?

2. State in your own words the adaptive-expectations hypothesis. Explain why adaptive expectations imply that a shift to a more expansionary macroeconomic policy will only temporarily reduce the rate of unemployment.

3. Compare and contrast the rational-expectations hypothesis and the adaptive-expectations hypothesis. Are the

implications of the rational- and adaptive-expectations theories different with regard to the *short-run* impact of a shift to a more expansionary monetary policy? Do they differ with regard to the *long-run* effects of a more expansionary policy?

*4. How does the microeconomic approach to the problems of unemployment and economic growth differ from the traditional monetary and fiscal policy approach to these problems? Is the microeconomic approach a substitute for traditional monetary and fiscal policy? Explain.

5. After a period of persistent inflation, such as was experienced in the United States during the 1974–1981 period, most economists believe that a shift to a restrictive anti-inflation monetary policy will cause a recession. Why? If expectations are formed "rationally" rather than "adaptively," will it be easier or more difficult to decelerate the inflation rate? Explain. How could the monetary authorities minimize the negative effects of a more restrictive monetary policy?

*6. Prior to the mid-1970s, many economists thought a higher rate of unemployment would reduce the inflation rate. Why? How does the modern view of the Phillips curve differ from the earlier view?

7. Why do most economists think the natural rate of unemployment rose during the 1960s and 1970s? Why do these same economists think the natural rate will fall during the next decade?

8. Throughout the 1960s, many economists believed that expansionary macroeconomic policy would result in both more inflation and less unemployment. How would acceptance of this theory influence policymakers? Did the theory exert any impact on policy? Cite supportive evidence.

*9. Modern analysis rejects the view that inflationary policies reduce the long-term unemployment rate. How does this theory influence macroeconomic policy? Explain.

10. The proponents of rational expectations argue that the cost of decelerating the inflation rate and moving to price stability will be reduced if people believe that the monetary authorities are really going to achieve and maintain stable prices. Why is this credibility important? How might the monetary authorities enhance the credibility of their policies?

11. How would you expect the actual unemployment rate to compare with the natural unemployment rate in the following cases?

   a. Prices are stable and have been stable for the last four years.

   b. The current inflation rate is 3 percent, and this rate was widely anticipated more than a year ago.

   c. Expansionary policies lead to an unexpected increase in the inflation rate from 3 percent to 7 percent.

   d. There is an unexpected reduction in the inflation rate from 7 percent to 2 percent.

*12. Suppose that, after 10 weeks of drawing unemployment compensation, a worker's benefits were reduced weekly until they were phased out after 26 weeks. How might this policy influence the natural rate of unemployment? Discuss the pros and cons of such a policy.

*13. Explain what happens to real wages, the job-search time of workers, and the unemployment rate when there is unanticipated inflation. What happens when the inflation is anticipated?

*14. Several European countries provide weekly unemployment benefits to persons for as long as they remain unemployed. Can you think of problems that are likely to accompany a program of this type? What impact will it have on the rate of unemployment?

---

*Asterisk denotes questions for which answers are given in Appendix B.

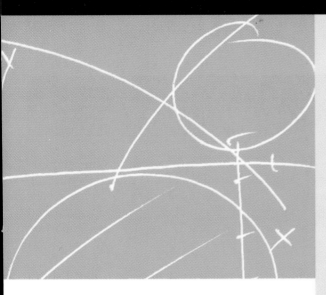

Unfortunately, policymakers cannot act as if the economy is an automobile that can quickly be steered back and forth. Rather, the procedure of changing aggregate demand is much closer to that of a captain navigating a giant super-tanker. Even if he gives a signal for a hard turn, it takes a mile before he can see a change, and ten miles before the ship makes the turn.

ROBERT J. GORDON[1]

---

[1]Robert J. Gordon, *Macroeconomics* (Boston: Little, Brown, 1978), p. 334.

CHAPTER FOCUS

■ Historically, how much has real output fluctuated? Are economic fluctuations becoming more or less severe?

■ Can discretionary macroeconomic policy moderate the business cycle? Would we have more or less stability if policymakers were bound by rules?

■ Why is proper timing of changes in macroeconomic policy both crucially important and difficult to achieve?

■ Did perverse macroeconomic policy cause the Great Depression?

■ Can structural reforms help promote a more stable economic environment?

D uring the 1960s, many economists were highly confident that macroeconomic policy could neutralize the economic ups and downs of the business cycle. Some even thought that the business cycle would soon be banished to the pages of history. Subsequent events have tempered this optimism. We now know that proper timing of macroeconomic policy is far more difficult than was perceived a few decades ago. Although we have already discussed the effects of monetary and fiscal policy, we have generally glossed over the problem of proper timing and the importance of the institutional structures. In this chapter, we will focus on the tools that enhance and the factors that limit the achievement of a stable economic environment. We will begin by taking a look at the historical record.

ECONOMIC FLUCTUATIONS— THE HISTORICAL RECORD

Wide fluctuations in the general level of business activity—in income, employment, and the price level—make personal economic planning extremely difficult. Such changes can cause even well-devised investment plans to go awry. The tragic stories of unemployed workers begging for food and newly impoverished investors jumping out of windows during the Great Depression vividly portray the enormous personal and social costs of economic instability and the uncertainty that it generates.

Historically, substantial fluctuations in real output have occurred. **Exhibit 15–1** illustrates the growth record of real GDP in the United States during the past 85 years. Prior to the Second World War, double-digit swings in real GDP during a single year were not uncommon. Real GDP rose by more than 10 percent annually during the First World War, during an economic boom in 1922, during a mid-1930s recovery, and again during the Second World War. In contrast, output fell at an annual rate of 5 percent or more during the 1920–1921 recession, in the Depression years 1930, 1931, 1932, and 1938, and again following the Second World War. Since 1950, economic ups and downs have been more moderate. Nevertheless, substantial fluctuations are still observable.

ACTIVISM VERSUS NONACTIVISM— AN OVERVIEW

There is widespread agreement concerning the goals of macroeconomic policy. Economists of almost all persuasions believe that the performance of a market economy would be improved if economic fluctuations were minimal, prices were stable, and employment were at a high level (unemployment at the nat-

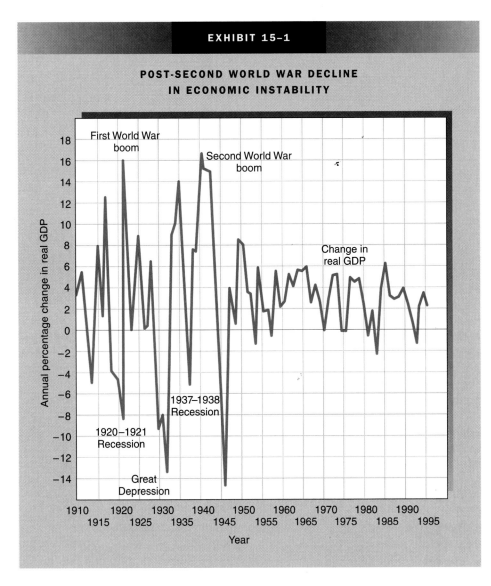

EXHIBIT 15–1

POST-SECOND WORLD WAR DECLINE
IN ECONOMIC INSTABILITY

Prior to the conclusion of the Second World War, the United States experienced double-digit increases in real GDP in 1918, 1922, 1935–1936, 1941–1943. In contrast, real output fell by 5 percent or more in 1920–1921, 1930–1932, 1938, and 1946. As illustrated here, fluctuations in real GDP have moderated during the last four decades. Most economists believe that more appropriate macropolicy— particularly monetary policy— deserves much of the credit (see Exhibit 15–2).

Sources: *Historical Statistics of the United States*, p. 224 and *Economic Report of the President, 1996.*

ural rate). How to achieve these goals is, however, a hot topic of debate among macroeconomists. In some respects, the current debate is an extension of earlier disagreements between Keynesians and monetarists. The Keynesian-monetarist debate of the 1960s and 1970s led to a consensus in several areas—the potency of money and the transmission path of monetary policy, for example. But this has not been the case with regard to the conduct of stabilization policy.

Most macroeconomists of Keynesian persuasion favor an **activist strategy.** Activists believe that the economy's self-corrective mechanism works slowly, if at all. Therefore, when economic shocks, such as poor harvests or a drastic change in oil prices, disrupt markets and throw an economy into a recession, the

Activist strategy
Deliberate changes in monetary and fiscal policy in order to inject demand stimulus during a recession and apply restraint during an inflationary boom and thereby, it is hoped, minimize economic instability.

restoration of full employment via lower real wages and interest rates is likely to be a lengthy process according to the activist view.

If the economy's self-corrective mechanism works slowly, it is reasonable to expect that policymakers will be able to inject demand stimulus during a recession and thereby minimize both the length and severity of a business downturn. Similarly, policymakers should be able to restrain aggregate demand and thereby retard inflation during an economic boom. *Activists are confident that discretionary monetary and fiscal policy can be used successfully to speed the adjustment process and reduce the swings in real GDP.*

Nonactivist strategy

The maintenance of the same monetary and fiscal policy— that is, no change in money growth, tax rates, or expenditures—during all phases of the business cycle.

In contrast with activist strategy, **nonactivist strategy** is based on the idea that we can best moderate the business cycle by adopting rules and guidelines (for example, a constant growth rate in the money supply and a balanced budget over the business cycle) that provide for stable monetary and fiscal policy, independent of current economic conditions. Furthermore, nonactivists argue that discretionary use of monetary and fiscal policy in response to changing economic conditions is likely to do more damage than good. They charge that erratic policy, particularly the instability of monetary policy, is a major source of economic fluctuations.

According to the nonactivist view, the self-corrective mechanism of a market economy works quite well. If not stifled by perverse macroeconomic policy, nonactivists believe that the economy's self-correcting mechanism will prevent prolonged periods of economic decline and high unemployment. Nonactivists note that the really serious cases of economic instability, such as the Great Depression and the inflation of the 1970s, were primarily the result of policy errors, not an inherent instability of markets.

Activists and nonactivists agree that in the past, policy errors contributed to economic instability. Prior to the Keynesian revolution, governments often raised taxes to balance the budget as revenue declined during a recession. Of course, modern analysis implies that such a policy would add to the severity of the recession. Correspondingly, as **Exhibit 15–2** illustrates, extreme gyrations in the money supply characterized monetary policy prior to the Second World War. Prior to 1947, sharp contractions in the money supply often accompanied major recessions. For example, the M2 money supply declined at an annual rate of 6 percent during the 1920–1921 recession, and by more than 10 percent annually as the United States entered into the Great Depression; it dipped again during the 1937–1938 relapse of the economy. In contrast, double-digit growth rates in the money supply were observed during the inflationary periods of the First and Second World Wars. One need not be a monetarist (or nonactivist) to recognize that the erratic changes in the money supply contributed to instability prior to the Second World War.

Although monetary fluctuations have continued since the post–Second World War period, they have been much less erratic. As Exhibit 15–2 illustrates, during the past four decades, the annual growth rate of the M2 money supply has generally been within the 3 percent to 9 percent range. Correspondingly, modern governments seldom raise taxes during a business recession. As Exhibit 15–1 shows, more moderate swings in real output have accompanied the increased stability of monetary and fiscal policy during the postwar era. Activists and nonactivists agree that the link between the more stable macroeconomic policy and moderation of the business cycle is no coincidence.

EXHIBIT 15–2

POST–SECOND WORLD WAR DECLINE IN MONETARY INSTABILITY

Prior to 1950, monetary policy was characterized by wide swings. Huge increases (15 percent or more) in the supply of money (M2) for a year or two were often followed by sharp contractions. Since the end of the Second World War, the fluctuations in the supply of money have declined, as the monetary authorities followed a more stable course.

Source: *Economic Report of the President, 1996;* and Robert J. Gordon, *Macroeconomics* (Glenview, Ill.: Scott Foresman, 1990).

ACTIVIST STABILIZATION POLICY

Macroeconomic policy reduces instability only if it injects stimulus and applies restraint at the proper phase of the business cycle. Proper timing is the key to effective stabilization policy. But how can policymakers know whether they should be stimulating aggregate demand or applying the economic brake?

Of course, economic indicators such as the growth of real GDP and rate of unemployment provide policymakers with information on the current state of the economy. However, this is not exactly what policymakers need. *Because it takes time for macroeconomic policy to work, policymakers really need to know about the future—where the economy is going to be 6 to 12 months from now. They need to know whether a business recession or an inflationary boom is around the corner. If they do not know where the economy is going, a policy change may fail to exert its primary impact quickly enough to offset a downturn or restrain future inflation.*

How can policymakers find out where the economy is going in the future and when a turn in the macroeconomic road is about to occur? The two most widely used sources of information on the future direction of the economy are the index of leading economic indicators and economic forecasting models.

INDEX OF LEADING INDICATORS

Index of leading indicators
An index of economic variables that historically has tended to turn down prior to the beginning of a recession and turn up prior to the beginning of a business expansion.

The **index of leading indicators** is a composite statistic based on 11 key variables that generally turn down prior to a recession and turn up before the beginning of a business expansion (see Measures of Economic Activity: Index of Leading Indicators). **Exhibit 15–3** illustrates the path of the index during the 1950–1995 period. Two or three consecutive monthly declines in the index are considered a warning that the economy is about to dip into a recession. This index has forecast each of the eight recessions since 1950. On four occasions, the downturn occurred eight to eleven months prior to a recession, providing policymakers with sufficient lead time to modify policy, particularly monetary policy. There has been significant variability, however, in the lead time of the index. Sometimes it is exceedingly short—the index declined just five months prior to the recession of 1954. In other instances it has been quite lengthy, as when it turned down 30 months prior to the recession of 1957–1958 and 18 months prior to the 1990–1991 recession.

A downturn in the index is not always an accurate indicator of the future. On five occasions (1950–1951, 1962, 1966, 1984, and 1987), a decline in the index

EXHIBIT 15–3

INDEX OF LEADING INDICATORS

The shaded periods represent business recessions. The index of leading indicators forecast each of the eight recessions during the 1950–1993 period. As the arrows show, however, the time lag between when the index turned down and when the economy fell into a recession varied. In addition, on five

occasions (1950–1951, 1962, 1966, 1984, and 1987) the index forecast a recession that did not occur.

[a]The arrows indicate the number of months that the downturn in the index preceded a recession. An asterisk (*) indicates a false signal of a recession.

MEASURES OF ECONOMIC ACTIVITY

INDEX OF LEADING INDICATORS

History indicates that no single indicator is able to accurately forecast the future direction of the economy. However, several economic variables do tend to reach a high or low prior to the peak of a business expansion or the trough of an economic recession. Such variables are called *leading economic indicators.*

To provide more reliable information on the future direction of the economy, economists have devised an index of 11 such indicators:

1. Length of the average workweek in hours
2. Initial weekly claims for unemployment compensation
3. New orders placed with manufacturers
4. Percent of companies receiving slower deliveries from suppliers
5. Contracts and orders for new plants and equipment
6. Permits for new housing starts
7. Change in unfilled orders for durable goods
8. Change in sensitive materials prices
9. Change in the index of stock prices (500 common stocks)
10. Change in money supply (M2)
11. Index of consumer expectations

The variables included in the index were chosen both because of their tendency to lead (or predict) turns in the business cycle and because they are available frequently and promptly. In some cases, it is easy to see why a change in an economic indicator precedes a change in general economic activity. Consider the indicator of "new orders placed with manufacturers" (measured in constant dollars). Manufacturers are usually quite willing to expand output in response to new orders. Thus, an expansion in the volume of orders is generally followed by an expansion in manufacturing output. Similarly, manufacturers will tend to scale back their future production when a decline in new orders signals the probability of weak future demand for their products. The index of leading indicators is calculated monthly by the Bureau of Economic Analysis of the Department of Commerce and published in the *Survey of Current Business.*

of leading indicators forecast a future recession that did not materialize. This has given rise to the quip that the index has accurately forecast thirteen of the last eight recessions.

FORECASTING MODELS

Economists have developed highly complex econometric (statistical) models to improve the accuracy of macroeconomic forecasts. In essence, these models use past data on economic interrelationships to project how currently observed changes will influence the future path of key economic variables, such as real GDP, employment, and the price level. The most elaborate of these models use hundreds of variables and equations to simulate the various sectors and macroeconomic markets. Powerful, high-speed computers are employed to analyze the effects of various policy alternatives and attempt to predict the future.

To date, the record of computer forecasting models is mixed. When economic conditions are relatively stable (for example, when the growth of real GDP and the inflation rate are relatively steady), the models have generally provided accurate forecasts for both aggregate economic variables and important subcomponents of the economy. Unfortunately, however, they have generally missed the major turns in the economic road. For example, none of the major computer models forecast either the 1982 recession or the sharp decline in the inflation rate during 1982–1984.

Many economists, particularly those of rational-expectations persuasion, maintain that accurate forecasts are beyond the reach of economics. Two major factors underlie this view. First, business cycle conditions often reflect economic shocks and unforeseen events—for example, an unexpected policy change, discovery of a new resource or technology, abnormal weather, or political upheaval in an important oil-exporting nation. There is no reason to believe that economists or anyone else will be able to predict such changes accurately and consistently. Thus, while economic theory helps to predict the implications of unforeseen events, it cannot foretell what those events will be and when they might occur. Second, the critics of forecasting models argue that the future will differ from the past because people will often make different choices as the result of what they learned from previous events. Thus, the past is an imperfect indicator of the future. Correspondingly, forecasting models based on past relationships—including elaborate computer models—will never be able to fully capture future economic relationships and consistently generate accurate predictions.

MARKET SIGNALS AND DISCRETIONARY MONETARY POLICY

Some economists believe that information supplied by certain markets can also provide policymakers with an early warning of the need to institute a change in policy. For example, since they fluctuate daily and are determined in auction markets, changes in commodity prices often foretell future changes in the general price level. An increase in a broad index of commodity prices implies that money is plentiful (relative to demand). This suggests the Fed should shift toward a more restrictive policy in order to offset future inflation. In contrast, falling commodity prices indicate that deflation is a potential future danger, in which case the Fed might want to shift toward a more expansionary policy.

Exchange rates also provide policymakers with information about the relative scarcity of money and fear of inflation. Because exchange rates, to a degree, reflect the willingness of foreigners to hold U.S. dollars, a decline in the exchange-rate value of the dollar (the value of the dollar relative to other currencies) often implies a fear of higher inflation and a reluctance to hold dollars. This would signal the need to shift to a more restrictive policy. Conversely, an increase in the exchange-rate value of the dollar is a strong vote of confidence in the future purchasing power of the dollar. This provides the Fed with some leeway to move toward a more expansionary policy.

Commodity prices, exchange rates, and other market signals can help us judge the early effects and likely future impact of current policies. They are best used as a supplement to, rather than as a substitute for, other economic indicators and forecasting devices.

ACTIVIST VIEW OF DISCRETIONARY POLICY

Activists recognize that it is difficult to institute countercyclical macroeconomic policy. However, they believe that the index of leading indicators, forecasting models, sensitive market variables, and other economic indicators provide policymakers with an early warning system. Thus, they are able to alter policy in a manner that will smooth business ups and downs. Responding to the early signals, policymakers can initially institute moderate changes. With the passage of time, more substantial changes can be instituted if more comprehensive information indicates they are needed.

The following scenario outlines the essentials of the activists' view. Suppose the economy were about to dip into a recession. Prior to the recession, the index of leading indicators would almost surely alert policymakers to the possibility of a downturn. This would permit them to shift toward macroeconomic stimulus, expanding the money supply more rapidly. Initially, the shift toward macroeconomic stimulus could be applied in moderate doses. It could then be easily offset with future action. On the other hand, if the signs of a downturn became more pronounced and current business conditions actually weakened, additional stimulus could be injected. Perhaps a tax reduction or a speedup in government expenditures might be used to supplement the more expansionary monetary policy.

Policymakers can constantly monitor the situation, adjusting their actions as additional information becomes available. If the weakness persists, the expansionary policy can be continued. Conversely, when the signs point to a strong recovery, policymakers can move toward restraint and thereby head off potential inflationary pressure. *According to the activist's view, policymakers are more likely to keep the economy on track when they are free to apply stimulus or restraint based on forecasting devices and current economic indicators.*

THE NONACTIVIST CASE

Nonactivists argue that economic and political factors undermine the potential effectiveness of discretionary macroeconomic policy. There are three major reasons why nonactivists believe discretionary policy will be ineffective as a stabilization tool.

LAGS AND THE PROBLEM OF TIMING

Discretionary changes in both monetary and fiscal policy must be timed properly if they are going to exert a stabilizing influence on the economy, and nonactivists believe that three time lags hinder proper timing. First, there is the **recognition lag,** the time period between a change in economic conditions and recognition by policymakers of the change. It can take months to gather and tabulate reliable information on the performance of the economy in the recent past in order to determine whether it has dipped into a recession or whether the inflation rate has accelerated, and so forth.

Second, even after the need for a policy change is recognized, there is generally an additional time period before the policy change is instituted. Economists refer to this delay as **administrative lag.** In the case of monetary policy, the administrative lag is generally quite short. The Federal Open Market Committee meets monthly and is at least potentially capable of instituting a change in monetary policy quickly. This is a major advantage of monetary policy. For discretionary fiscal policy, the administrative lag is likely to be much longer. Congressional

Recognition lag
The time period after a policy change is needed from a stabilization standpoint but before the need is recognized by policymakers.

Administrative lag
The time period after the need for a policy change is recognized but before the policy is actually implemented.

committees must meet. Legislation must be proposed and debated. Congress must act, and the president must consent. Each of these steps takes time.

Impact lag
The time period after a policy change is implemented but before the change begins to exert its primary effects.

Finally, there is the **impact lag,** the time period between the implementation of a macropolicy change and when the change exerts its primary impact on the economy. Although the impact of a change in tax rates is generally felt quickly, the expansionary effects of an increase in government expenditures are usually much less rapid. It will take time for the submission of competitive bids and the letting of new contracts. Several months may pass before work on a new project actually begins. The impact lag in the case of monetary policy is likely to be even longer. The time period between a shift in monetary policy, a change in interest rates, and, in turn, a change in the level of spending may be quite lengthy.

Economists who have studied this topic, including Milton Friedman and Robert Gordon, conclude that the *combined duration* of these time lags is generally 12 to 18 months in the case of monetary policy, and even longer in the case of fiscal policy. This means that, if a policy is going to exert the desired effect at the proper time, policymakers cannot wait until a problem develops before they act. Rather, they must act before there is a contraction in real GDP or an observable increase in the rate of inflation. It will be necessary for them to correctly forecast turns in the economy if they are going to properly time changes in policy. Nonactivists argue this is highly unrealistic. Rhetoric aside, economic forecasters usually cannot predict such turns, nor can we expect them to do so in the foreseeable future. Furthermore, even if forecasting were a more perfect science, the time lags accompanying changes in monetary and fiscal policies are so long and variable, it is highly unlikely that the primary effects of a policy change would come at the proper time. Therefore, nonactivists believe that discretionary policy is likely to be destabilizing rather than stabilizing.

Exhibit 15–4 presents a graphic illustration of the difference between the views of the activists and nonactivists. When the economy begins to dip into a recession, activists argue that policymakers can reasonably be expected to recognize the danger and shift to a more expansionary policy at point *B*. If the demand-stimulus effects are felt quickly (before the economy gets to point *C*), the shift to the more expansionary macropolicy will help to minimize the decline in output accompanying the business downturn.

In contrast, nonactivists believe that policymakers are unlikely to act so quickly, and, even if they did, the time lags accompanying changes in monetary and fiscal policies are likely to make their actions ineffective. The shift to the more expansionary policy will not come until point *C*, according to this reasoning, and its effects will not be significant until point *D*. In this case, the expansionary policy will contribute to the severity of the inflationary boom (beyond point *D*). Similarly, a subsequent shift to an anti-inflationary policy may begin to exert its major impact at point *F*, just in time to make an oncoming recession worse (beyond point *F*). Therefore, nonactivists believe that discretionary policy shifts are likely to be destabilizing rather than stabilizing.

POLITICS AND THE TIMING OF POLICY CHANGES

Public-choice analysis has led to an increased awareness of an additional pitfall of discretionary policy-making—macropolicy might be used to pursue political

EXHIBIT 15-4

TIME LAGS AND EFFECTS OF DISCRETIONARY POLICY

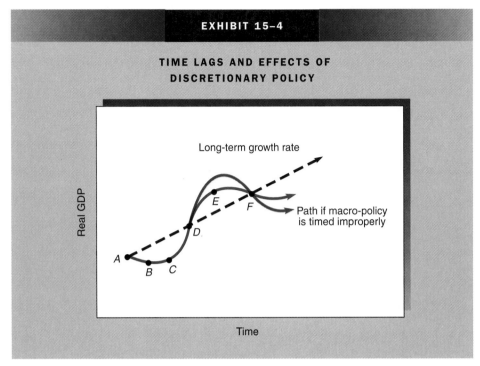

Beginning with A, we illustrate the path of a hypothetical business cycle. If a forthcoming recession can be recognized quickly and a more expansionary policy instituted at point B, the policy may add stimulus at point C and help to minimize the magnitude of the downturn. Activists believe that discretionary policy is likely to achieve this outcome. However, if delays result in the adoption of the expansionary policy at C and if it does not exert its major impact until D, the demand stimulus will exacerbate the inflationary boom. In turn, an anti-inflationary strategy instituted at E may exert its primary effects at F, just in time to increase the severity of a recession beyond F. Nonactivists fear that improper timing of discretionary macro-policy will exert such destabilizing effects.

objectives rather than stabilization. In a democracy, macropolicy will be designed by elected representatives, an elected president, and officials (such as the Board of Governors of the Federal Reserve) who are appointed by the elected president. Like other policy choices, macropolicy provides political entrepreneurs with a potential tool for furthering their political objectives. Predictably, discretionary macropolicy choices will be influenced by political considerations. It is naive to expect otherwise.

The nature of the political process, particularly the shortsightedness effect, provides politicians with little incentive to look beyond the next election. If the adaptive-expectations view is correct, expansionary policies 12 to 18 months prior to an election would stimulate output and employment, getting the economy in great shape by election day. Because demand-stimulus policies generally affect output before they begin to exert a major impact on the price level, the inflationary effects of such a policy would be most observable after the election. To the extent that politicians use macroeconomic policy to stimulate demand and output prior to a major election, they reduce its effectiveness as a stabilization weapon.

Is there evidence that politicians have sought to use macropolicy for political gain? Political scientist Edward Tufte has conducted extensive research on this issue. While reviewing evidence from 90 elections in 27 different countries, Tufte found that real disposable income accelerated in 77 percent of the election years compared to only 46 percent of the years without an election.[2] This suggests that there is at least a moderate tendency to follow more expansionary policies prior to major elections.

---

[2]Edward R. Tufte, *Political Control of the Economy* (Princeton: Princeton University Press, 1978).

RATIONAL EXPECTATIONS AND POLICY INEFFECTIVENESS

The theory of rational expectations suggests that predictable changes in macro-policy will fail to promote economic stability. Unlike a machine, the moving parts of our economy are living, breathing human beings capable of modifying their choices when the situation changes. As they learn from prior experience, their future response to a policy change may differ from their past responses.

As we have already discussed, the impact of macropolicy varies depending on whether it is anticipated by decision makers (see Chapter 14, Exhibit 14–1). The proponents of rational expectations believe that, sooner or later, the public will figure out any systematic policy, including countercyclical stabilization policy. And once a policy is widely anticipated and individuals adjust their decision making in light of its expected effects (for example, rising prices or higher interest rates), the policy no longer exerts its intended impact on real output and employment. Economists refer to this phenomenon as the **policy-ineffectiveness theorem.**

Policy-ineffectiveness theorem

The proposition that any systematic policy will be rendered ineffective once decision makers figure out the policy pattern and adjust their decision making in light of its expected effects. The theorem is a corollary of the theory of rational expectations.

Perhaps an example will illustrate why rational-expectations economists have little confidence that even properly timed macropolicy will be effective. Suppose it is widely anticipated that the government will employ expansionary macropolicy in response to a recession. As the signs of an economic slowdown appear, the public anticipates that policymakers will increase the growth of the money supply and cut taxes (perhaps by allowing a more attractive depreciation allowance or an investment tax credit) to spur business investment. It makes sense, once this strategy is anticipated, for investors to delay investment projects and wait for the expected lower interest rates and investment tax incentives. This delay, though, only increases the severity of the current downturn and leads to pent-up investment demand. Then, once the anticipated expansionary policy is instituted, investment expenditures will tend to grow more rapidly than past experience indicated would be the case (and more rapidly than is desirable from a stabilization viewpoint). In essence, once decision makers adjust their choices in light of the anticipated countercyclical policy, the policy fails to exert the desired stabilizing effects.

The logic of the analysis applies symmetrically to an economic boom. If the public anticipates that slower money growth, higher interest rates, and higher taxes will be used to restrain an economic boom, they will spend and invest more prior to the expected restrictive policy. In turn, the increase in spending will contribute to the development of an economic boom.

The message of rational-expectations theory to stabilization policymakers is clear. Human decision makers will foil your good intentions. Countercyclical macropolicy will fail because, once people expect your systematic response to recessions and booms, their personal interests will cause them to respond in a manner that undermines the policy.

NONACTIVIST STABILIZATION POLICY

Although the underlying logic of the monetarists, public choice economists, and proponents of rational expectations differs, the three groups arrive at the same two conclusions: (1) discretionary policy is an important source of instability, and (2) greater stability would result if stable, predictable policies based on predetermined rules were followed.

Exhibit 15–5 illustrates empirical data that nonactivists cite in their criticism of discretionary policy. Since 1960 the U.S. economy has experienced six recessions (indicated by shaded areas), periods of at least two consecutive quarters of declining real GDP. If the effects of monetary policy are going to speed recovery, monetary policy must be expansionary prior to and during the recession. Nonactivists stress that discretionary policy has failed to achieve this outcome. In fact, the growth rate of the money supply has generally declined prior to and/or during the early stages of recent recessions. Far from offsetting recessionary forces, monetary policy has often contributed to the downturns and slowed the recovery process, according to the nonactivists.

Given the obstacles to the proper timing of policy changes, how can errors be minimized? Nonactivists recommend that policymakers choose a long-run policy path (for example, a low, stable rate of inflation and no change in tax rates or real government expenditures) and inform the public of this choice. This course should then be pursued regardless of cyclical ups and downs. As policymakers stay on course, they will gain credibility. The public will develop confidence in the future stability of the policy. Uncertainty will be reduced, thereby increasing the efficiency of private decision making. Nonactivists are confident this strategy would result both in less instability and in more rapid growth than Western economies have experienced in the past.

NONACTIVIST MONETARY POLICY

Suppose we are going to adopt a nonactivist strategy. What rules or guidelines would we choose? Nonactivists believe that monetary policy should utilize one of the following: (1) a monetary growth rule, (2) a nominal income growth rule, or (3) a price level rule.

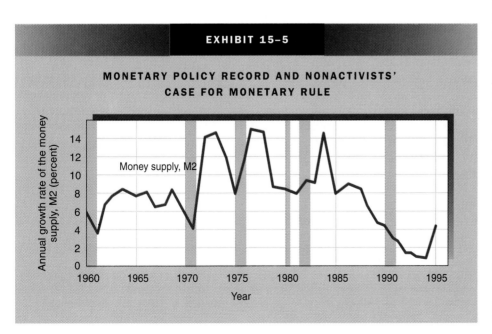

EXHIBIT 15–5

**MONETARY POLICY RECORD AND NONACTIVISTS'
CASE FOR MONETARY RULE**

Annual growth rate of the money supply, M2 (percent)

Money supply, M2

Although monetary instability has declined in recent decades (see Exhibit 15–2), instability and poor timing persist. Here we show the annual growth rate of the M2 money supply for each year from 1960 to 1995. The graph also indicates the years of recession (shaded areas). Note that the money supply was decelerating during or immediately prior to most of the recessions. This is the opposite *of the desired pattern. Nonactivists argue that a steady growth of the money supply or some other key aggregate variable (for example, nominal income) would lead to greater stability.*

Source: *Economic Report of the President, 1996.*

MONETARY RULE. The most widely advocated nonactivist monetary policy is the constant-money-growth rate long championed by Milton Friedman. Under this plan, the money supply would be expanded continuously at an annual rate (3 percent, for example) that approximates the long-run growth of the U.S. economy. When real output is growing rapidly (for example, 5 percent annually), the supply of money would decline relative to real GDP. Thus, monetary policy would automatically exert a restraining influence during a period of rapid growth. In contrast, during a recession, the constant-money-growth rate would exceed the growth of real output, offsetting any tendency toward a downward spiral.

Nonactivists, particularly those with monetarist leanings, believe that steady growth of the money supply would eliminate instability arising from stop-and-go policies on the part of the Fed. They point out that monetary planners have often expanded the money supply more rapidly than the economy's long-term growth rate, and thereby caused inflation. Then, responding to an acceleration in the inflation rate, the monetary authorities have often stepped on the monetary brakes and thrown the economy into a recession (see Exhibit 15–5). The nonactivists believe that monetary instability is the major source of economic instability. Rather than responding to forecasts and current economic indicators, the Fed, they say, would be more of a stabilizing force if it simply increased the supply of money, month after month, at a low (noninflationary) constant annual rate.

The experience of the 1980s has reduced the attractiveness of the monetary rule approach. In a dynamic economy the nature of money is constantly changing. As a result, even steady money growth may not yield a steady monetary policy. The introduction of interest-earning checking deposits drastically changed the nature of the M1 money supply during the 1980s. As the interest-earning checking accounts were legalized and more people began using them, the M1 money supply grew rapidly and fluctuated substantially during the 1980s. But this growth was not indicative of a highly expansionary monetary policy. The inflation rate declined sharply during the early 1980s and was relatively constant during the remainder of the decade.

As people shift their savings among financial instruments, the growth of the various money supply figures can send conflicting signals. For example, the M1 money supply expanded at a 12 percent annual rate during 1992 and 1993, suggesting that monetary policy was highly expansionary. In contrast, the annual growth of the M2 money supply was only 1.5 percent during this period, indicating that monetary policy was quite restrictive. Technological developments in the financial sector have substantially reduced the usefulness of the money supply figures as an indicator of monetary policy. Furthermore, changes in this area are almost sure to continue. (See pages 318–321 on measurement problems and the future of money.)[3]

---

[3]In recent years, economists have generally placed more confidence in the M2 money supply figures. But there are no assurances that future financial innovations will not also alter the nature of the M2 and undermine its use as a gauge of monetary policy. In fact, evidence of such changes is already present. In response to recent reductions in the start-up cost of stock and bond mutual funds, many individuals shifted funds from various savings instruments which are part of the M2 money supply to the mutual funds which are not. These shifts reduced both the growth rate of the M2 money supply during 1994–1995 and the reliability of these figures as an indicator of monetary policy.

NOMINAL INCOME RULE.   As the result of the measurement problems presented by the changing nature of money, many nonactivists now favor a nominal income rule. Under this rule, the monetary authorities would seek to follow a policy that would lead to steady growth of nominal income at a rate equal to the economy's long-run real growth of output (approximately 3 percent in the U.S. case). This rule would also provide long-run price stability because a stable price level is implied when nominal and real income expand at the same rate. In essence, this rule is a modified monetary rule, long advocated by Allan Meltzer of Carnegie Mellon University. Rather than expanding the supply of money by a constant amount, under this rule the supply of money would be increased by the economy's long-run growth rate (approximately 3 percent) *minus* the change in the velocity of money. If the velocity of money declined, as was the case for M1 during the 1980s, the money supply would grow more rapidly than real income. Alternatively, if velocity rose as was the case in 1994–1995, the money supply would be slowed accordingly. In effect, the policy would adjust the monetary-growth rate to offset fluctuations in velocity (the demand for money).

PRICE LEVEL RULE.   A growing number of nonactivists now believe that it would be better if the monetary authorities directly targeted a broad price index such as the GDP deflator or consumer price index. The advocates of this approach argue that, in the long run, monetary policy cannot determine real output, employment, interest rates, or other real variables. What it can and does determine is the level of prices. Therefore, why not require that the monetary authorities maintain a persistently low rate of inflation and hold them accountable for their actions? Under this plan, if the general price index were rising, the monetary authorities would have an incentive to institute more restraint. Conversely, if the price level were falling, a move toward expansion would be in order. The proponents of this rule argue that it would reduce both instability arising from monetary sources and the uncertainty of time-dimension transactions (for example, loan agreements and other long-term contracts).

New Zealand has recently adopted this approach. Although the central bank of New Zealand is fully responsible for monetary policy, it is legally required to maintain the inflation rate within a narrow range, currently between zero and 2 percent. If the central bank fails to meet this target, the bank's governor is subject to dismissal. Clearly, this approach requires the central bank to focus on a well-defined target (a low rate of inflation) that is achievable with monetary policy and holds it accountable for failure to meet the objective. To date, the policy has been highly successful. Prior to the adoption of this approach in 1990, New Zealand had the highest and most variable inflation rate among the high-income industrial nations. In contrast, its rate of inflation has been low (consistently less than 2 percent) since the legislation took effect. Similar reforms are now under consideration in several other countries.

NONACTIVIST FISCAL POLICY

In the area of fiscal policy, the simplest rule would require that the budget be balanced annually. Because revenues and expenditures fluctuate over the business cycle, however, a balanced budget rule would require tax increases and/or expenditure reductions during a recession. The opposite changes would be required during a period of rapid growth. Such changes are inconsistent with the nonactivist pursuit of stable (unchanged) policies.

In theory, the proper nonactivist fiscal strategy is a balanced budget *over the business cycle*. Under this plan, the same tax rates and expenditure policies would remain in effect during both booms and recessions. Surpluses would result during periods of prosperity, while deficits would accrue during recessions. The problem with this strategy is that it fails to provide a precise indicator revealing how well the policymakers are adhering to the steady course. Thus, nonactivists, particularly those with a public-choice background, recognize that a "balance the budget over the business cycle" rule is unlikely to impose a steady course on policymakers.

Some nonactivists believe that a constitutional amendment limiting both government spending and budget deficits is a necessary ingredient for stable fiscal policy. These nonactivists argue that pressure from special interest groups and the short time horizon of political officials elected for limited terms bias the political process toward expansionary fiscal policy (expanding debt and spending increases). Because of this, they favor a constitutional amendment that would require supramajority (for example, 60 percent) congressional approval for either (1) deficit-financed government spending or (2) rapid increases (more rapid than the growth of national income) in federal spending.

It is one thing to favor a general strategy and another to develop a practical, workable policy to implement the strategy. Clearly, the nonactivists have not yet arrived at a detailed fiscal policy program that would command wide acceptance among even the proponents of nonactivism.

EMERGING CONSENSUS VIEW

The accompanying Thumbnail Sketch summarizes the differences between activists and nonactivists. From a policy viewpoint, the central focus of disagreement between the two groups centers on the merits of policy-making flexibility. Activists fear that, if strictly followed, inflexible rules would prevent an appropriate response to uncertain future economic changes. In their view, failure to respond to a major shock, perhaps stemming from war, another oil-price run, or a collapse of investment, might well result in a major economic disaster.

On the other hand, the nonactivists fear that discretion will consistently be abused, that politicians will use policy to pursue either unattainable objectives or political goals. According to the nonactivists, unless you tie the hands of policymakers, they will inevitably pursue an activist's strategy that will magnify instability and result in inflation.

Although it is important to understand the fundamental differences between the activists' and nonactivists' viewpoints, we must not forget that most economists take a hybrid view, influenced by the analysis of alternative schools of thought. *Furthermore, activists and nonactivists actually share a great deal of common ground. Both recognize that the wrong use of policy is a potential source of economic instability. Both are highly sensitive to the potential*

WHAT ARE THE MAJOR DIFFERENCES BETWEEN ACTIVISTS AND NONACTIVISTS?

AREA OF DIFFERENCE	ACTIVISTS	NONACTIVISTS
1. **Speed of Self-Correcting Mechanism**	Self-correcting mechanism works slowly and ineffectually.	Self-correcting mechanism works with reasonable speed if it is not stifled by perverse macroeconomic policy.
2. **Proper Timing of Discretionary Policy**	Even though timing is difficult, discretionary policy can promote stability and has done so.	Given time lags, forecasting deficiencies, and the political incentive structure, discretionary policy is an ineffective stabilization tool.
3. **Impact of Monetary and Fiscal Rules**	Inflexible rules would prevent policymakers from responding to unanticipated shocks; thus, they would increase instability.	Rules providing for stable monetary and fiscal policy would reduce instability.

destructiveness of policy swings like those that were followed during the 1930s (see the Applications in Economics box on the macroeconomic policy of the 1930s). Similarly, both generally favor structural changes that will make the conduct of policy more transparent and provide information that will help us better judge the performance of policymakers.

WOULD INDEXED BONDS IMPROVE THE PERFORMANCE OF THE FED?

Historically, the U.S. Treasury has only issued bonds that pay interest in nominal terms. The interest rate on these conventional bonds is unchanged regardless of the inflation rate during the period the bond is outstanding. During the summer of 1996, the Treasury Department of the Clinton administration announced that it would also soon begin offering **indexed bonds.**

An indexed bond pays a market-determined real interest rate plus a premium equal to the actual rate of inflation that occurs (measured by a price index

Indexed bonds
Bonds that pay a market-determined real interest rate plus an inflationary premium equal to the actual rate of inflation that occurs during the period. When the bond is redeemed, the principal is also adjusted for the rate of inflation during the period the bond was outstanding.

PERVERSE MACROECONOMIC POLICY AND THE GREAT DEPRESSION

As we previously discussed, the Great Depression exerted an enormous impact both on economic thought and on economic institutions. **Chart 1** presents data that illustrate both the severity and length of the economic contraction. For four successive years (1930–1933), real output fell. Unemployment soared to nearly one-quarter of the work force in 1932 and 1933. Although recovery did take place during 1934–1937, the economy again fell into the depth of depression in 1938.

Ten years after the catastrophe began, real GDP was virtually the same as it had been in 1929.[1]

Armed with knowledge of how monetary and fiscal policies work, it is now clear that at least the severity of the Great Depression was the result of perverse macroeconomic policy. Three important factors contributed to the economic collapse of the 1930s.

1. A sharp reduction in the supply of money during 1930–1933 reduced aggregate demand and real output. The supply of money expanded slowly but steadily

---

CHART 1

THE ECONOMIC RECORD OF THE GREAT DEPRESSION

YEAR	REAL GDP IN 1989 DOLLARS (BILLIONS)	IMPLICIT GDP DEFLATOR (1929 = 100)	UNEMPLOYMENT RATE	CHANGES IN THE MONEY SUPPLY (M1)
1929	821.8	100.0	3.2	+1.0
1930	748.9	96.8	8.7	−6.9
1931	691.3	88.0	15.9	−10.9
1932	599.7	77.6	23.6	−4.7
1933	587.1	76.0	24.9	−2.9
1934	632.6	82.4	21.7	+10.0
1935	681.3	84.8	20.1	+18.2
1936	777.9	84.8	16.9	+13.9
1937	811.4	89.6	14.3	+4.7
1938	778.9	87.2	19.0	−1.3
1939	840.7	86.4	17.2	+12.1

Source: *Economic Report of the President: 1993* (Washington, D.C.: U.S. Government Printing Office, 1993); and Bureau of the Census, *The Statistical History of the United States from Colonial Times to Present* (New York: Basic Books, 1976).

---

like the GDP deflator or the CPI). When the bond matures, the principal is also adjusted to offset any loss of purchasing power during the period the bond was outstanding. Because the variable component (the component tied to the inflation rate) compensates financial investors for changes in the general level of prices, the market-determined fixed component of the interest rate on indexed throughout the 1920s.[2] As Chart 1 shows, monetary policy suddenly shifted in 1930. The supply of money declined by 6.9 percent during 1930, by 10.9 percent in 1931, and by 4.7 percent in 1932. Banks failed, and the Fed also failed to act as a lender of last resort to head off the huge decline in the supply of money. From 1929 to 1933, the quantity of money in circulation declined by 27 percent! Our analysis indicates that a shift to a restrictive monetary policy will reduce both aggregate demand and real output. A drastic reduction in the supply of money such as that of the early 1930s is likely to result in a drastic reduction in output. This is precisely what happened. Real output plunged. By 1933, real GDP was 29 percent lower than the 1929 level.

2. A large tax increase in the midst of a severe recession made a bad situation worse. Prior to the Keynesian revolution, the dominant view was that the federal budget should be balanced. Reflecting the ongoing economic downturn, the federal budget ran a deficit in 1931, and an even larger deficit was shaping up for 1932. Assisted by the newly elected Democratic majority in the House of Representatives, the Republican Hoover administration passed the largest peacetime tax-rate increase in the history of the United States. At the bottom of the income scale, marginal tax rates were raised from 1.5 percent to 4 percent in 1932. At the top of the scale, tax rates were raised from 25 percent to 63 percent. As our prior analysis of fiscal policy suggests, a huge tax increase in the midst of a severe recession will further reduce aggregate demand and the incentive to earn. Exhibit 1 shows the degree to which this happened. As tax rates were increased in 1932, real GDP fell by 13.3 percent. Unemployment rose from 15.9 percent in 1931 to 23.6 percent in 1932.

3. Tariff increases retarded international exchange. Concern about low agricultural prices, an influx of imports, rising unemployment, and declining tax revenues generated public sentiment for trade restraints. Responding to this pressure, political officials pushed for a substantial increase in tariffs (taxes on imported goods) on a wide range of products in early 1930. The tariff legislation took effect in June of 1930.[3] Other countries promptly responded by increasing their tariffs, further reducing the volume of trade between nations. As the flow of trade diminished, so too did the mutual gains trading partners derive from specialization and exchange.

When discussing the Great Depression, historians often stress the role of the 1929 stock market crash. Since the stock market crash diminished the wealth of many, it was a contributing factor to the reduction in aggregate demand and output. However, the severity of the Great Depression was the result of disastrous macroeconomic policy, not an inevitable consequence of a stock market crash. The experience following the October 1987 crash illustrates this point. In just a few days, the stock market lost a third of its value in 1987, just as it did in 1929. But that is where the parallel ends. In contrast with the crash of 1929, in 1987 the Fed moved quickly to supply reserves to the banking system. The money supply did not fall. Tax rates were not increased. And even though there was a lot of political rhetoric about "the need to protect American businesses," trade barriers were not raised. In short, sensible policies were followed subsequent to the crash of 1987. Continued growth and stability were the result. Inadvertently, perverse macroeconomic policies were followed subsequent to the crash of 1929. Economic disaster was the result.

---

[1]See Robert J. Samuelson, "Great Depression," in *The Fortune Encyclopedia of Economics,* ed. David R. Henderson (New York: Warner Books, 1993), for an interesting and informative commentary on this time period.

[2]From 1921 through 1929, the money stock expanded at an annual rate of 2.7 percent, slightly less rapidly than the growth in the output of goods and services. Thus, the 1920s were a decade of price stability, even of slight deflation.

[3]The high-tariff policy was ineffective as a revenue measure. Even though the taxes on imported goods were increased by approximately 50 percent, imports declined so sharply that tariff revenues fell from $602 million in 1929 to $328 million in 1932.

bonds reflects only the real rate of interest. Clearly, indexed bonds reduce risk and provide individuals and financial institutions with a convenient instrument to hedge against unexpected changes in the rate of inflation. Recognizing these advantages, several countries, including Australia, Canada, United Kingdom, Sweden, and New Zealand, have offered indexed bonds for several years.

As we previously explained, expansionary monetary policy cannot—at least not for long—affect real variables such as output, employment, and the real rate of interest. However, monetary policy can keep the inflation rate low and highly stable so that investors and other decision makers will be able to more easily and more accurately predict what the price level will be in the future.

Minimizing disturbances arising from monetary surprises is the central ingredient of sound monetary policy. When the monetary authorities follow policies that keep the expected rate of inflation low (some would argue that it should be zero) and stable, they are doing their part to promote economic stability and growth.

The introduction of indexed bonds should make it easier for the Fed to maintain a low and stable rate of inflation. *The interest-rate differential between the "regular bonds" paying a nominal interest rate and the real interest rate of the indexed bonds is equal to the expected rate of inflation.* For example, the interest-rate differential between the regular and indexed 12-month Treasury bills provides an estimate of the expected rate of inflation during the next 12 months. With indexed bonds, policy makers can directly observe changes in the expected rate of inflation. If there is an increase in the expected future rate of inflation, the Fed could quickly shift to a more restrictive policy. Correspondingly, the Fed could move toward a more expansionary policy if the expected rate of inflation fell or became negative. The information on the expected rate of inflation will help the Fed avoid policy swings and maintain a more stable price level.

Furthermore, indexed bonds will also supply "Fed watchers" with continuous, up-to-date information on the performance of monetary policy. A stable interest-rate *differential* between the regular and indexed bonds would indicate that the Fed was doing a good job—that it was establishing a stable economic environment. For example, if the interest-rate differential between the nominal interest rate bonds and the indexed bonds was approximately 2 percent over a long period of time, this would indicate that the Fed was following policies that resulted in a stable and therefore more predictable rate of inflation. In contrast, if the *expected* rate of inflation was constantly fluctuating—if it was 7 percent this year, 2 percent a year ago, and 5 percent the year before that, this would indicate that unstable Fed policies were generating uncertainty. With indexed bonds, it will be easier to evaluate the performance of the Fed and hold it more accountable for its actions. Thus, most economists believe that the introduction of the bonds is a positive development.

MONETARY STABILITY AND INSTITUTIONAL STRUCTURES AROUND THE WORLD

As we noted in Chapter 13, monetary instability and inflationary policies have plagued many countries around the world. Responding to this situation, there has been considerable recent interest in institutional reform. Do institutions influence monetary stability? What types of structural reforms are most likely to promote greater stability?

DOES THE INDEPENDENCE OF THE CENTRAL BANK MATTER?

As we discussed in Chapter 12, the central bank of the United States has several features designed to insulate it from political pressures. Most important, these include the lengthy (14-year) terms of the Fed governors and the presence of ample revenues for operating costs from a source (interest on the bonds held by the Fed) other than congressional appropriations.

Is this independence wise? There is good reason to believe that it is. In many countries the governing officials of the central bank are highly dependent on political officials. In some cases, they serve at the discretion of the president (or equivalent) or the legislature. Under these circumstances, if the political officials do not like what the monetary policymakers are doing, they simply replace them. When under the domination of political officials—even officials who are democratically elected—central banks have often been used to finance government expenditures with "printing-press" money. Monetary instability and inflation are the inevitable results.

Recent studies of this issue indicate that there is a linkage between price stability and the independence of monetary policymakers from political pressures. The industrial countries with the most independent central banks—Germany, Switzerland, Japan, and the United States—had the lowest average inflation rates during the 1973–1988 period, while the least independent central banks—those of Spain, Italy, and New Zealand (prior to 1990)—had the highest rates of inflation. This, coupled with the inflationary history of the politicized central banks of Latin America—and more recently, the politicized banks of the newly democratic countries of Eastern Europe and the former Soviet Union—indicates that subjecting monetary policy to the day-to-day pressures of politicians is not a good idea.[4]

CAN EXCHANGE RATE TARGETING PROVIDE MONETARY DISCIPLINE?

Several countries have sought to enhance the credibility of their currency by linking it at a fixed exchange rate to other stronger, more stable currencies. For example, several African nations (Benin, Cameroon, Central African Republic, Chad, Congo People's Republic, Ivory Coast, Gabon, Niger, Senegal, and Togo) have pledged to follow a monetary policy that will maintain a constant exchange rate with the French franc. During the 1988–1994 period, Mexico linked the exchange rate value of the peso to the U.S. dollar.

If such policies are going to be effective, the nation linking its currency with another country's currency must give up the independence of its monetary policy. The fixed exchange rate (or range of the rate) can be maintained only if the country follows a monetary policy that closely parallels that of the country with the stronger currency. A country will be unable to maintain the fixed exchange

---

[4]See Alberto Alesina and Lawrence H. Summers, "Central Bank Independence and Macroeconomic Performance: Some Comparative Evidence," *Journal of Money, Credit, and Banking* (May 1993): pp. 151–162; Patricia S. Pollard, "Central Bank Independence and Economic Performance," *Federal Reserve Bank of St. Louis Review* (July/August 1993): pp. 21–36; and Alex Cuklerman, *Central Bank Strategy, Credibility, and Independence: Theory and Evidence* (Cambridge: MIT Press, 1992).

rate if its monetary policy is more inflationary than that of the country to which its currency is tied. If it attempts to follow an inflationary policy, people will shift from its currency to that of the country with the more stable currency. When a lot of people do so, the country will run out of foreign exchange reserves and therefore be unable to maintain the fixed rate with the more stable currency. This is precisely what happened in Mexico. During 1989–1994, Mexico's money supply increased at an average annual rate of 45 percent, more than four times the rate of the United States. During the same period, the annual rate of inflation in Mexico was 17 percent, compared to only 4 percent in the United States. Responding to the different inflation rates, more and more people shifted away from the Mexican peso and toward the dollar until the foreign exchange reserves of Mexico fell to a level that could no longer maintain the fixed exchange rate with the dollar. Mexico devalued its currency in December 1994, triggering a crisis that affected several other countries following similar policies.

Unless a country is willing to apply monetary restraint to maintain the fixed exchange rate, this strategy is destined to fail. A few countries have adopted currency boards in an effort to assure decision makers that they will apply monetary discipline and maintain the fixed rate. A **currency board** does two things. First, it issues domestic currency at a fixed rate in exchange for a designated foreign currency. Second, the foreign currency is then invested in bonds denominated in that currency. This means that the money issued by the currency board is 100 percent backed by the foreign currency. Thus the holders of the money issued by the currency board know that they will always be able to exchange it for the widely accepted currency at a fixed rate.

Currency board
An entity that (a) issues a currency with a fixed designated value relative to a widely accepted currency (for example, the U.S. dollar), (b) promises to continue to redeem the issued currency at the fixed rate, and (c) maintains bonds and other liquid assets denominated in the other currency that provide 100 percent backing for all currency issued.

Hong Kong has used a currency board to tie its currency to the U.S. dollar for a number of years. The Hong Kong currency board issues HK dollars in exchange for U.S. dollars at a fixed rate of 7.7 Hong Kong dollars = $1 U.S. The HK dollars issued by the currency board are fully convertible and backed 100 percent with U.S. dollars and U.S. bonds denominated in dollars. If people want more Hong Kong dollars, they can obtain them by providing the currency board with U.S. dollars (at the fixed rate), which the board then invests in U.S. government bonds. Other countries have also followed this approach. Singapore has tied its currency to a bundle of foreign currencies. Recently, Argentina—a country long plagued with monetary expansion and inflation—established a currency board and tied its currency to the U.S. dollar.

Of course, countries that use the currency board approach, in essence, accept the monetary policy of the nation to which their currency is tied. If that currency has a stable international value, the currency board approach will provide monetary stability. Countries with a history of monetary instability may find this approach particularly attractive.

COMPETITION AMONG CURRENCIES

Currency boards are a structural change designed to improve the likelihood that the monetary authorities will not inflate or renege on their promises. Competition among currencies can provide similar assurance. During the past decade there has been a dramatic increase in the number of countries where citizens are free to use and maintain bank accounts in any currency they choose, including those issued by other governments. In most areas of the world, the U.S. dollar is the preferred foreign currency. As we noted in Chapter 12, more than half the currency issued by the Federal Reserve circulates in other countries. The use of the dollar as both a medium of exchange and a store of value is particularly widespread in those areas—Eastern Europe and Latin America, for example— recently plagued with monetary instability.

The legalization of foreign currencies is an important structural change. The availability of competitive currencies reduces the incentive of the domestic monetary authorities to inflate. If they do, more and more people will shift to the dollar and other more stable currencies. In essence, the use of a foreign currency provides citizens with an alternative to the uncertainties accompanying an unstable domestic monetary regime.

LOOKING AHEAD

Many people are concerned that the growing national debt of the United States and other countries might be a major source of economic instability. The following chapter will focus on this issue.

CHAPTER SUMMARY

1. Historically, the United States has experienced substantial swings in real output. Prior to the Second World War, year-to-year changes in real GDP of 5 percent to 10 percent were experienced on several occasions. Since the Second World War, the fluctuations in real output have been more moderate.

2. Macropolicy activists believe that a market economy is inherently unstable—that is, that the market's self-corrective process works too slowly to be effective. They are confident that discretionary monetary and fiscal policy can be used effectively to promote economic stability.

3. Nonactivists believe that a market economy's self-correcting tendencies work quite well in a stable policy environment. They argue that policymakers would make fewer errors if they merely instituted stable monetary and fiscal policies, rather than modifying policy in response to current economic conditions.

4. The index of leading indicators and other forecasting devices warn policymakers when a turn in the economic road is just ahead. While recognizing that forecasting devices sometimes give false signals, activists argue that policymakers can initially respond cautiously to signals indicating the need for a policy change and then act more aggressively if the situation requires it. Activists thus believe that discretionary macroeconomic policy can effectively restrain the economy during an inflationary boom and stimulate output during a business recession.

5. Nonactivists stress that inability to accurately forecast the future and quickly modify macroeconomic policy, along with uncertainty as to when a policy change will exert its primary impact, substantially reduces the effectiveness of discretionary policy as a stabilization tool.

6. Public-choice theory suggests that politicians have a strong incentive to follow an expansionary course prior to major elections. Such political use of macropolicy reduces its effectiveness as a stabilization tool.

7. The theory of rational expectations argues that even properly timed countercyclical policy will fail to reduce instability once decision makers figure out the systematic pattern and adjust their choices in light of the expected effects.

8. Nonactivists believe that stability would be enhanced if policymakers simply pursued stable, predictable policies rather than attempting countercyclical policies. In the area of monetary policy, nonactivists recommend that decision makers target one of the following: (a) slow, steady growth of the money supply, (b) growth of nominal GDP at a rate equal to the economy's long-run real growth rate, or (c) a constant price level. With regard to fiscal policy, nonactivists favor the maintenance of a stable tax and expenditure policy based on long-run considerations rather than on current cyclical conditions.

9. The major disagreement between activists and nonactivists involves the merits of a policy response to changing circumstances. Activists fear that strict adherence to a policy such as the constant (fixed) money growth rule will prevent policymakers from responding correctly to major recessions and inflations. Correspondingly, nonactivists fear that policymaker discretion will result in destabilizing policies.

10. Despite their differences, activists and nonactivists agree that (a) it is more difficult to properly time stabilization policy than was generally perceived during the 1960s, (b) past errors have contributed to economic instability,

and (c) structural changes that increase the transparency of stabilization policies are desirable.

11. Analysis of the Great Depression indicates that the severity and length of the economic plunge, if not its onset, was the result of perverse macroeconomic policy. A sharp contraction in the money supply, a huge tax increase, and a sharp rise in tariff rates were major contributing factors to the economic collapse of the 1930s.

12. Institutions influence economic stability. Both theory and empirical analysis indicate that central banks subject to intense political pressure are more likely to follow inflationary policies than are those with greater independence. In recent years, several countries with records of monetary instability have turned to currency boards in an effort to achieve a more stable monetary environment. Others have legalized the domestic use of more stable foreign currencies, such as the U.S. dollar and German mark.

CRITICAL ANALYSIS QUESTIONS

1. Compare the views of activists and nonactivists with regard to the following points:
   a. The self-stabilizing characteristics of a market economy
   b. The ability of policymakers to forecast the future
   c. The validity of the rational-expectations hypothesis
   d. The use of rules versus discretion in the institution of monetary and fiscal policy

2. What is the index of leading indicators? Evaluate its potential usefulness to policymakers.

3. Evaluate the effectiveness of monetary and fiscal policy during the past three years. Has it helped to promote stable prices, rapid growth, and high employment? Do you think policymakers have made mistakes during this period? If so, indicate why.

*4. How does economic instability during the past four decades compare with instability prior to the Second World War? Is there any evidence that stabilization policy has either increased or decreased economic stability during the post–Second World War period?

*5. Why do most nonactivists favor a monetary rule such as expansion of the money supply at a constant annual rate? What are some of the potential problems with a monetary rule? Do you think a monetary rule could be devised that would reduce economic instability? Why or why not?

6. The chair of the Council of Economic Advisers has requested that you write a short paper indicating how economic policy can be used to stabilize the economy and achieve a high level of economic growth during the next five years. Be sure to make specific proposals. Indicate why your recommendations will work. You may submit your paper to your instructor.

7. What are some of the problems that would arise if the monetary authorities sought to maintain a constant price level? Is this a desirable objective? Do you think the Fed could achieve it? Why or why not?

8. "The Great Depression indicates that the self-correcting mechanism of a market economy is weak and unreliable." Evaluate this statement.

*9. Suppose that the Fed tried to peg the real interest rate below the market level. How would it do so, and what would be the result of this policy?

10. If the Treasury issued indexed bonds, do you think this would result in a more stable monetary policy? Why or why not? How would the issuance of indexed bonds affect the ability of the federal government to gain at the expense of bondholders if a more expansionary monetary policy were followed? How would this influence the incentive of government officials to follow more inflationary policies? Do you think this is good or bad? Why?

11. What is a currency board? Do you think a currency board is a good method for a nation with a history of monetary instability and inflation to achieve a more stable monetary environment? Why or why not?

*12. Suppose that the Federal Reserve were a government agency under the direct control of Congress. Thus, the discount rate, open market policy, and growth rate of the money supply would be determined by Congress. How do you think this would affect the inflation rate and economic stability of the nation?

---

*Asterisk denotes questions for which answers are given in Appendix B.

▪ How large is the national debt? Will the debt have to be paid off?

▪ Are we mortgaging the future of our children and grandchildren? How do budget deficits affect future generations?

▪ Have the budget deficits of recent years pushed the debt to a dangerous level?

▪ How does the budget deficit of the United States compare with deficits of other countries?

▪ Are the large budget deficits of recent years an aberration, or do they reflect a fundamental problem with the budget process?

The attractiveness of financing spending by debt issue to the elected politicians should be obvious. Borrowing allows spending to be made that will yield immediate political payoffs without the incurring of any immediate political cost.

JAMES BUCHANAN[1]

---

[1]James Buchanan, *The Deficit and American Democracy* (Memphis: P. K. Steidman Foundation, 1984).

Deficit spending and the national debt were hot topics during the 1940s and 1950s, as Keynesian economists challenged the reigning orthodoxy—the view that the federal budget should be balanced annually. By the 1960s the Keynesians had clearly won the debate in both the academic and political arenas. Thus, no one paid much attention as the federal government incurred a string of budget deficits during the 1960s and 1970s. These deficits were assumed to be temporary and the result of scientifically determined demand-management policies.

As larger and larger deficits were incurred during the 1970s and 1980s, there was also a change in the attitude of the general public. News commentators, business leaders, and political officials often told us that the "monstrous" deficits were the most critical problem facing America. Is this really true? If so, what is the nature of the problem? What can be done to deal with it? This chapter focuses on these topics and related issues.

EXPENDITURES, REVENUES, BUDGET DEFICITS, AND THE NATIONAL DEBT

Exhibit 16–1 illustrates the path of federal expenditures and revenues during the past four decades. Of course, revenues have fluctuated with economic conditions. They have, however, generally remained within a narrow band between 18 percent and 20 percent of GDP since the 1950s. There is a modest upward trend. During the 1990–1995 period, federal revenues averaged 18.6 percent of GDP, only slightly higher than the 17.5 percent figure for the last half of the 1950s.

Compared to federal revenues, federal expenditures have risen more rapidly. *As a share of GDP*, federal expenditures persistently increased between 1955 and 1985 before leveling off and receding slightly during the past decade. In the early 1990s federal expenditures averaged 23 percent of GDP, up from 18 percent during the late 1950s. In recent years, there has been a persistent, sizable gap between federal expenditures and revenues. Thus, the government has had to borrow heavily in order to cover its expenditures.

When the federal government uses debt rather than taxes and user charges to pay for its expenditures, the U.S. Treasury fills this gap by borrowing in the loanable funds market. When borrowing funds, the Treasury generally issues interest-bearing bonds. These bonds compose the **national debt.** In effect, the national debt consists of outstanding loans from financial investors to the general fund of the U.S. Treasury.

National debt

The sum of the indebtedness of the federal government in the form of outstanding interest-earning bonds. It reflects the cumulative impact of budget deficits and surpluses.

The federal budget deficit and the national debt are directly related. The deficit is a "flow" concept (like water running into a bathtub), while the national debt is a "stock" figure (like the amount of water in the tub at a point in time). *In essence, the national debt represents the cumulative effect of all the prior budget deficits and surpluses.* A budget deficit increases the size of the national debt by the amount of the deficit. Conversely, a budget surplus allows the federal government to pay off bondholders and thereby reduce the size of the national debt.

EXHIBIT 16–1

FEDERAL EXPENDITURES AND REVENUES AS A PERCENT OF GDP

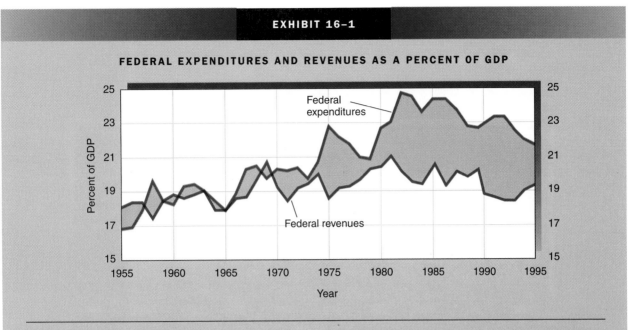

Here we illustrate the path of both federal revenues and expenditures as a percent of GDP. Federal revenues averaged 18.6 percent of GDP during the 1990–1995 period, only slightly more than the 17.5 percent figure of the late 1950s. Federal expenditures, however, have increased even more rapidly, rising from approximately 18 percent of GDP in the late 1950s to approximately 23 percent of GDP during the early 1990s.

The creditworthiness of an organization is dependent upon the size of its debt relative to its income base. Therefore, when analyzing the significance of budget deficits and the national debt, it is important to consider their size relative to the entire economy. **Exhibit 16–2** presents data for the 1950–1995 period for both the federal budget deficit and the national debt as a percent of GDP. Since the defense effort during the Second World War was financed substantially with debt rather than with taxes, the national debt was quite large at the end of the war. Following the war, the combination of economic growth and small budget deficits reduced the size of the national debt as a percent of GDP. During the 1950–1974 period, budget deficits averaged less than 1 percent of GDP. Historically, real output in the United States has grown at an annual rate of approximately 3 percent. When the budget deficit as a percent of GDP is less than the growth of real output, the federal debt will decline relative to the size of the economy. This is precisely what happened during the 1950–1974 period. Budget deficits were present, and they pushed up the *nominal* national debt (from $256.7 billion at year-end 1950 to $492.7 billion at the end of 1974). But GDP grew even more rapidly. By 1974 the national debt had fallen to 34 percent of GDP, down from 89 percent in 1950 (and 127 percent in 1946).

This situation was reversed in the mid-1970s. Since 1974, federal budget deficits have been much larger, averaging nearly 4 percent of GDP (part a of Exhibit 16–2). When the budget deficit as a percent of GDP exceeds the growth of real GDP, the national debt will increase relative to the size of the economy.

EXHIBIT 16-2

BUDGET DEFICITS AND THE NATIONAL DEBT AS A PERCENT OF GDP

(a) Federal budget deficit or surplus as a percent of GDP

(b) Gross and net federal debt as a percent of GDP

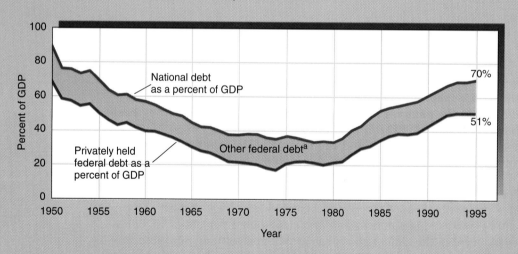

Throughout most of the 1950s and 1960s, federal budget deficits were small as a percent of GDP, and occasionally the government ran a budget surplus (a). During this period, the national debt declined as a proportion of GDP (b). Since 1974, however, the budget deficits have been quite large, *larger (as a percent of GDP) than the growth of real GDP. As a result, the national debt has increased as a percent of GDP in recent years.*

ªFederal debt held by U.S. government agencies and Federal Reserve banks.

As Exhibit 16–2 (part b) illustrates, this has clearly been the case since 1980. Pushed along by the large budget deficits of the 1980s and early 1990s, the national debt expanded to 70 percent of GDP in 1995, up from 34 percent in 1974.

A CLOSER LOOK AT THE NATIONAL DEBT

Who owns the national debt? As **Exhibit 16–3** illustrates, 26.1 percent of the national debt is held by agencies of the federal government. For example, social security trust funds are often used to purchase U.S. bonds. When the debt is owned by a government agency, it is little more than an accounting transaction indicating that one government agency (for example, the Social Security Administration) is making a loan to another (the U.S. Treasury). Even the interest payments, in this case, represent little more than an internal government transfer.

Another 7.8 percent of the public debt is held by the Federal Reserve System. As we have previously discussed, when the Fed purchases U.S. securities, it creates money. The bonds held by the Fed, therefore, are indicative of prior government expenditures that have been paid for with "printing-press" money—money created by the central bank. As in the case of the securities held by government agencies, the interest on the bonds held by the Fed is returned to the Treasury after the Fed has covered its costs of operation.

Only two-thirds of the national debt is held by private investors—individuals and institutional investors, such as insurance companies and commercial banks. This **privately held government debt** represents obligations of the federal government to another party. Most of this privately held debt is owned by

Privately held government debt
The portion of the national debt owed to domestic and foreign investors. It does not include bonds held by agencies of the federal government or the Federal Reserve.

Source: *Federal Reserve Bulletin,* July 1996.

EXHIBIT 16–3

OWNERSHIP OF THE NATIONAL DEBT
(DECEMBER 1995)

OWNERSHIP OF U.S. SECURITIES	DOLLAR VALUE (BILLIONS)	PERCENT OF NATIONAL DEBT
TOTAL NATIONAL DEBT	4,988.7	100.0
U.S. government agencies	1,304.5	26.1
Federal Reserve Banks	391.0	7.8
Privately held federal debt	3,294.9	66.0
Domestic investors	2,433.1	48.8
Foreign investors	861.8	17.3

domestic citizens. Thus, the largest component of the national debt (48.8 percent in 1995) is owned by domestic financial investors. Foreigners hold approximately one-sixth (17 percent) of the total national debt and one-fourth of the privately held government debt. The portion owned by foreigners is sometimes referred to as **external debt.**

External debt
The portion of the national debt owed to foreign investors.

It is important to distinguish between (1) the total national debt and (2) the privately held government debt. Only the latter imposes a net interest burden on the federal government. In the case of the privately held debt—that is, the bonds held by domestic and foreign investors—the federal government will have to impose taxes to meet the future interest payments on these bonds. In contrast, the government both pays and receives the interest on the bonds held by government agencies and the Federal Reserve (minus Fed expenses). Thus, these bonds do not represent a net interest obligation.

Part b of Exhibit 16–2 presents data on the size of the privately held federal debt as a percent of GDP for the 1950–1995 period. Like the overall national debt, the privately held federal debt as a share of GDP declined sharply during the 1950s and moderately during the 1960–1974 period. However, since 1974, it too has been rising as a percent of GDP. In 1995, the privately held federal debt stood at 51 percent of GDP, up from 20 percent in 1974.

CONCERNS ABOUT THE NATIONAL DEBT

Are large, persistent budget deficits harmful to the health of the U.S. economy? Persons who answer this question in the affirmative generally argue that the deficits (1) are harmful to the welfare of future generations, (2) result in a dangerous dependency on foreign capital, and (3) generate a large interest liability that threatens the financial stability of the federal government. Let us consider each of these concerns in some detail.

DEBT FINANCING AND FUTURE GENERATIONS

Lay people, politicians, and economists have debated about the burden of the national debt for many years.[2] One side argues that we are mortgaging the future of our children and grandchildren—that debt financing permits us to consume today, then send the bill to future generations. The other side, noting that most of the national debt is held by domestic citizens (see Exhibit 16–3), retorts, "We owe it to ourselves."

When considering our ability to shift the cost of government onto future generations, two points must be kept in mind. First, in the case of domestically held debt, our children and grandchildren will indeed pay the taxes to service the

---

[2]See Richard H. Fink and Jack High, eds., *A Nation in Debt: Economists Debate the Federal Budget Deficit* (Frederick: University Publications of America, 1987), for an excellent set of readings summarizing this debate.

debt, but they will also receive the interest payments. Admittedly, those paying the taxes and receiving the interest payments will not always be the same people. Some will gain and others will lose. But both those who gain and those who lose will be members of the future generation.

Second, debt financing of a government activity cannot push the opportunity cost of the resources used by government onto future generations. If current GDP is $7 trillion and the federal government spends $1.6 trillion on goods and services, then only $5.4 trillion will be available for consumption and investment by individuals, businesses, and state and local governments. This will be true regardless of whether the federal government finances its expenditures with taxes or debt. When the government builds a highway, constructs an antimissile defense system, or provides police protection, it draws resources with alternative uses away from the private sector. This cost is incurred in the present; it cannot be avoided through debt financing.

If the opportunity cost of resources occurs during the current period, does this mean that there is little reason to be concerned about an adverse impact of deficits on future generations? Not necessarily. Debt financing influences future generations primarily through its potential impact on saving and capital formation. If lots of factories, machines, houses, technical knowledge, and other productive assets are available to future generations, then their productive potential will be high. Alternatively, if fewer productive assets are passed along to the next generation, then their productive capability will be less. *Thus, the true measure of how government debt influences future generations involves knowledge of its impact on capital formation.*

When excess capacity is present, a deficit may stimulate aggregate demand and bring otherwise idle resources into the production of houses and factories, as well as consumption goods. Under such circumstances, budget deficits enlarge the stock of capital available to future generations and thereby enhance their well-being.

The impact of budget deficits on capital formation during normal times is a complex issue. Consider an economy operating at its normal productive capacity. Holding government expenditures constant, how would the substitution of debt financing for current taxation influence capital formation? As our discussion of fiscal-policy models implies, economists differ in their responses to this question. We will consider two alternative theories: the traditional view that budget deficits reduce future capital stock and the opposing new classical view that such deficits exert no significant future impact.

TRADITIONAL VIEW: BUDGET DEFICITS REDUCE FUTURE CAPITAL STOCK. Most economists embrace the traditional view that budget deficits will retard private investment and thereby reduce the welfare of future generations. Suppose that the government substitutes borrowing for current taxation. For example, consider what would happen if the government cut the *current* taxes of each household by $100 and borrowed the funds to replace the lost revenues. As a result, the after-tax income of each household increases by $100. Of course, the households may save some of the $100 addition to their disposable income, but they are also likely to spend some of it on consumption goods according to the traditional view. If they do not save all of the $100, the additional government borrowing will increase the demand for loanable funds relative to the supply and thereby push real interest rates upward.[3] In turn, the higher real interest rates will retard private investment, which will reduce the physical capital available to future generations. To the extent future generations work with less capital (fewer productivity-enhancing tools and machines), their productivity and wages will be lower than would have been the case had the budget deficits not crowded out private investment.

In addition, the higher interest rates will attract foreign investors. But investments in the United States will require dollars. As foreigners increase their investments in the United States, they will demand dollars in the foreign exchange market. This strong demand will cause the dollar to appreciate relative to other currencies. In turn, the appreciation in the exchange-rate value of the dollar will make U.S. exports more expensive to foreigners and foreign goods cheaper for Americans. These relative price changes will retard exports and stimulate imports. Predictably, net exports will decline.

The inflow of capital from abroad will dampen both the increase in interest rates and the reduction in domestic investment. However, it will also increase the asset holdings of foreigners in the United States. The returns to these assets will generate income for foreigners rather than Americans. Therefore, compared to the situation where government was financed with current taxation, future generations of Americans will inherit both a smaller stock of physical capital and less income from that capital (since the share owned by foreigners has increased). Succeeding generations will be less well-off as a result.

In summary, the traditional view argues that the substitution of debt financing for current taxation will increase current consumption, push up real interest rates, and retard private investment. In addition, the higher real interest rates will lead to an increase in net foreign investment, appreciation in the exchange-rate value of the dollar, and a decline in net exports (imports will increase relative to exports). According to the traditional view, budget deficits will retard the growth rate of capital formation, particularly that owned by Americans, and reduce national income and future living standards of Americans.

NEW CLASSICAL VIEW: BUDGET DEFICITS EXERT LITTLE IMPACT ON FUTURE CAPITAL STOCK. Not all economists accept the traditional view of budget deficits. An alternative theory, most closely associated with Robert Barro of Harvard University, encompasses the new classical perspective of fiscal policy.[4] This new classical view stresses that additional debt implies an equivalent amount of future taxes. If, as the new classical model assumes, individuals fully anticipate the added future tax liability accompanying the debt, current consumption will

---

[3]Alternatively, one could approach this topic from the viewpoint of how households value the government bonds relative to the future tax liability implied by the bonds. If bondholders recognize the asset value of the government bonds while taxpayers fail to recognize fully the accompanying tax liability, then the general populace will have an exaggerated view of its true wealth position. Wealth is an important determinant of consumption. When people think they are wealthier, they will consume more and save less than they would if they had fully recognized their future tax liability. Of course, the increase in consumption and reduction in savings would place upward pressure on the real rate of interest. This is simply an alternative way of viewing the substitution of government debt for current taxation.

[4]See Robert Barro, "Are Government Bonds Net Wealth?" *Journal of Political Economy* 82 (November–December 1974): pp. 1095–1117; and "The Ricardian Approach to Budget Deficits," *Journal of Economic Perspectives* 2 (spring 1989).

be unaffected when governments substitute debt for taxes. According to this view, when future taxes (debt) are substituted for current taxes, people will save the reduction in current taxes so that they will have the required income to pay the higher future taxes implied by the additional debt. Continuing with our prior example, the new classical theory implies that households receiving a $100 reduction in current taxes financed by issuing bonds (that imply higher future taxes) will save all of the $100 increase in their current disposable income. *This increase in saving, triggered by the anticipation of the higher future taxes, allows the additional government debt to be financed without an increase in the real rate of interest. Since there is no increase in interest rates, private investment is unaffected. Neither is there an influx of foreign capital. Under these circumstances, the substitution of debt for taxes exerts little or no impact on either capital formation or the welfare of future generations.*

EMPIRICAL EVIDENCE ON THE IMPACT OF THE DEFICIT.   What does the empirical evidence indicate with regard to the validity of the two theories? Studies focusing on the period prior to the 1980s have found only a weak relationship, if any, between year-to-year changes in the budget deficit and real interest rates. New classical economists argue that these findings are supportive of their theory.

However, the experience with the large budget deficits subsequent to 1980 would appear to be supportive of the traditional theory. **Exhibit 16–4** compares

---

EXHIBIT 16–4

BUDGET DEFICITS AND CHANGES IN PERSONAL CONSUMPTION, INVESTMENT, AND NET EXPORTS AS A SHARE OF GDP

	COMPONENT AS A PERCENT OF GDP					
TIME PERIOD	FEDERAL DEFICIT	PERSONAL CONSUMPTION	GROSS PRIVATE INVESTMENT	NET FOREIGN INVESTMENT	GROSS INVESTMENT LESS NET FOREIGN INVESTMENT	NET EXPORTS
1976–1980	2.9	62.3	17.5	0.0	17.5	−0.8
1983–1987	5.1	65.0	16.7	2.6	14.1	−2.6
DIFFERENTIAL[a]	+2.2	+2.2	−0.8	+2.6	−3.4	−1.8
1960–1974	0.9	62.0	15.7	−0.5	16.2	0.2
1981–1994	4.0	65.8	15.3	1.6	13.7	−1.6
DIFFERENTIAL[a]	+3.1	+3.8	−0.4	+2.1	−2.5	−1.8

[a]Later period minus earlier period. As the data of the first column indicate, the federal deficits were larger during the later period.

Source: Derived from the *Economic Report of the President, 1996*, Tables B-1 and B-28.

consumption, investment, and net exports as a share of GDP during the five years following the recession of 1982 with the five years subsequent to the recession of 1974–1975. Because the budget deficits averaged 5.1 percent of GDP during 1983–1987, compared with 2.9 percent during the 1976–1980 period, a comparison of the two periods sheds light on how larger budget deficits affect the economy. During the 1983–1987 period of larger budget deficits, personal consumption as a percent of GDP rose to 65.0, up from 62.3 during the 1976–1980 period. Gross investment as a percent of GDP declined from 17.5 percent in 1976–1980 to 16.7 percent during 1983–1987. At the same time, there was a substantial increase in the inflow of foreign capital. Net foreign investment rose from zero during the earlier period to 2.6 percent of GDP during 1983–1987. Look at what happened to the investment spending of Americans. The investment expenditures of Americans (gross investment less net foreign investment) fell from 17.5 percent of GDP in 1976–1980 to 14.1 percent in 1983–1987. Net exports also declined sharply.

Thus, as the size of the budget deficit increased substantially during the 1983–1987 period, Americans increased their current consumption expenditures and substantially reduced their *domestically financed* capital formation. Simultaneously, there was an inflow of net foreign investment and a reduction in net exports (imports increased relative to exports). This pattern is precisely what the traditional theory predicts will happen when debt financing is substituted for current taxation.

Exhibit 16–4 also presents data for the 1960–1974 and 1981–1994 periods. During the earlier period, federal budget deficits averaged slightly less than 1 percent of GDP, compared to 4.0 percent of GDP during the latter period. The pattern of the results for these two more lengthy periods was similar to that presented earlier. During the period when the budget deficits were larger, current consumption was higher and private investment lower. Once again, there was a substantial increase in net foreign investment and a reduction in net exports during the period when the deficits were large.

Nominal data were used to derive the gross investment/GDP ratio presented in Exhibit 16–4. Professor Barro and other leading new classical economists have argued that calculation of the figures in real terms and making other adjustments leads to a somewhat different picture. Clearly, this is an area of continuing research. Nonetheless, the evidence at this point appears to be more consistent with the traditional view.

DEPENDENCE ON FOREIGN INVESTORS

In recent years, a significant portion—approximately a tenth—of the domestic investment of the United States has been financed by foreigners. Studies indicate that foreigners own approximately 5 percent of the domestic capital assets of the United States.

How does foreign investment affect the U.S. economy? When considering a possible burden emanating from foreign investment, it is important to keep an eye on both sides of the transaction. The inflow of foreign capital leads to lower interest rates and a higher level of investment than would take place in its absence. An increase in machines, structures, and other capital assets, even if financed by foreign investment, will increase the productivity and wages of

American workers. Of course, the inflow of investment funds also enlarges the future profit and interest claims of foreigners. However, if the funds are invested wisely, the projects will generate returns (future income) that provide an offset against the future income claims of foreigners. On the other hand, if the funds are squandered on low-return projects, the wealth of investors will be reduced. But this would be equally true for projects financed solely with domestic funds.

Doesn't this inflow of capital from abroad make the United States more dependent on foreign creditors? When considering this issue, it is important to keep the nature of the foreign investment in mind. Substantial portions of the funds supplied by foreigners during the 1980s were in the form of risk capital—investments in stocks, land, physical structures, and business ventures. Such investments do not involve a contractual repayment commitment. Others are invested in bonds, both corporate and government. These investments are almost entirely fixed-interest-rate obligations. As long as the investment project is profitable, U.S. citizens as well as foreigners will gain as the result of undertaking the project.

What would happen if foreigners suddenly decided to take their "money" home and quit financing investments in the United States? It is not obvious why literally tens of thousands of foreign investors would be any more likely to suddenly "sell out" than tens of thousands of domestic investors. But, even if they did, market adjustments would exert a stabilizing effect. Remember, the "money" of foreigners is in the form of stocks, bonds, and physical assets. If foreigners suddenly tried to sell these assets, falling prices would create some real bargains for domestic investors. Domestic investors would gain and foreign investors would lose. Similarly, if foreigners cut back their financial investments in the United States, real interest rates would rise. But the higher real interest rates would make U.S. investments more attractive and thereby help deter any outflow of funds.

Finally, the vulnerability accompanying foreign investment almost certainly lies with the foreign investor rather than with the recipient country. It is much easier for a government to expropriate the property of a foreigner than it is for an investor to exercise much control over the policies of a foreign government. History illustrates the vulnerability of the foreign investor. The United States expropriated the property of Germans and Japanese during the Second World War. Several Middle Eastern countries expropriated the property of foreign investors when they nationalized their domestic oil industries in the 1950s and 1960s. Under Fidel Castro, the Cuban government expropriated the assets of foreigners. Foreign investment is a hostage to the domestic policies of the recipient country. A major reason why investment in the United States is attractive to foreigners is the confidence they have that the U.S. government will not abuse its superior position.

COULD BUDGET DEFICITS CAUSE ECONOMIC COLLAPSE?

Some people fear that economic collapse is imminent if the size of the budget deficit is not reduced. When considering this issue, it is important to recognize that borrowing is a standard method of doing business. Many large and profitable corporations continually have debt outstanding. As long as the net income of a business firm is large relative to its interest liability, the outstanding debt poses little problem.

So it is with the federal government. *As long as people have confidence that it can raise the tax revenue necessary to meet its debt obligations, the federal government will have no trouble financing and refinancing its outstanding debt. And it can do so in perpetuity. There is no date in the future at which the federal debt must be paid off.*

Thus, the key to creditworthiness is expected future income relative to interest liability. This is true for individuals, private businesses, and governments. What is happening to the creditworthiness of the U.S. federal government? In the late 1940s approximately 10 percent of U.S. federal revenues went to pay the interest on the national debt. As **Exhibit 16–5** illustrates, *net* interest costs were approximately 7 percent of federal revenues throughout the 1951–1974 period. During the 1980s, interest costs as a share of federal revenues rose sharply, soaring to 10 percent in 1980, 14 percent in 1983, and 16 percent in 1990. Since 1990, these costs have leveled off as a share of federal revenue.

An upward trend in interest costs as a share of federal revenue (or the size of the economy) cannot continue, at least not without serious consequences. Why not? If the interest costs continue to rise relative to federal revenues, the growing interest costs will make it increasingly difficult to cut spending, and people will become more and more fearful that the government will resort to printing-press money in an effort to escape its loan obligations. This combination of forces—heavy government borrowing to finance and refinance its debt and the fear of rapid money growth and inflation—would push interest rates up and make it even more difficult for the government to meet its debt obligations. If sufficiently intense, the fear of inflation alone could seriously disrupt the long-term capital market, not only for the federal government, but for other borrowers as well. And if the government did resort to printing-press money in order

During the period from 1950 to 1975, the net interest costs of the federal government consumed approximately 7 percent of federal revenues. By 1980 the ratio had jumped to 10 percent, and by the early 1990s it had risen to 16 percent. Obviously, interest costs cannot continue to increase as a share of federal revenue.

[a]The net interest costs include only the interest paid to private investors. The interest on debt held by federal government agencies and Federal Reserve banks is omitted.

Source: *Economic Report of the President*, various issues.

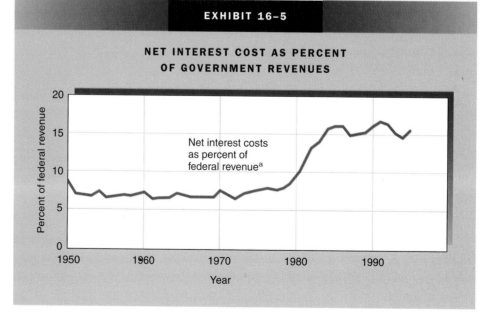

EXHIBIT 16–5

NET INTEREST COST AS PERCENT OF GOVERNMENT REVENUES

Net interest costs as percent of federal revenue[a]

to pay off its debt, hyperinflation and a breakdown in the exchange system would result. The economy would be severely crippled.

Excessive debt has led to financial crises elsewhere. The economies of several countries, including Bolivia, Argentina, Chile, Brazil, and Israel, have been ravaged in recent years by excessive debt, money creation, and runaway inflation. Most economists are confident that in the United States constructive action will be taken well before such a crisis develops. However, the United States is not immune to the laws of economics. Persistent increases in interest costs as a share of federal revenues would clearly lead to severe adverse economic consequences.

IS THE SIZE OF THE DEBT EXAGGERATED?

Some economists believe that the magnitude of the "deficit problem" has been exaggerated due to (1) lack of recognition that state and local governments are running sizable surpluses; (2) the failure of the federal accounting procedures to make the appropriate allowance for capital expenditures; and (3) the impact of inflation on the nominal budget deficit. Let us consider each of these points.

OFFSETTING EFFECT OF STATE AND LOCAL SURPLUSES

While the federal government has been running large budget deficits, state and local governments have been experiencing sizable surpluses. Therefore, the aggregate deficit of all government units is less than the federal data indicate.

Exhibit 16–6 presents the data on the deficit, including state and local governments. During the past 25 years, the combined budgets of state and local governments have run persistent surpluses equal to approximately 2 percent of GDP. Taken together, the deficits of all levels of government—federal, state, and local—have averaged approximately 2 percent of GDP since 1980. During this period, the *surpluses* of state and local governments have been approximately one-half the size of the federal deficits. Pointing to these figures, many economists argue that reliance on the federal data alone exaggerates the size of the government deficit.

ADJUSTMENT FOR CAPITAL EXPENDITURES

In private affairs, we recognize that it makes a difference whether borrowing is for long-lasting assets or current consumption. Borrowing to purchase a new home expected to last 30 years is one thing; borrowing to finance a weekend caper in Las Vegas is quite another. Businesses establish capital and current expense budgets in order to distinguish between expenditures for long-lasting assets and resources used during the current period. When undertaking a major capital expenditure, borrowing is a perfectly acceptable method of doing business.

EXHIBIT 16-6

INCLUSION OF STATE AND LOCAL GOVERNMENT FINANCE INTO THE BUDGET CALCULATION

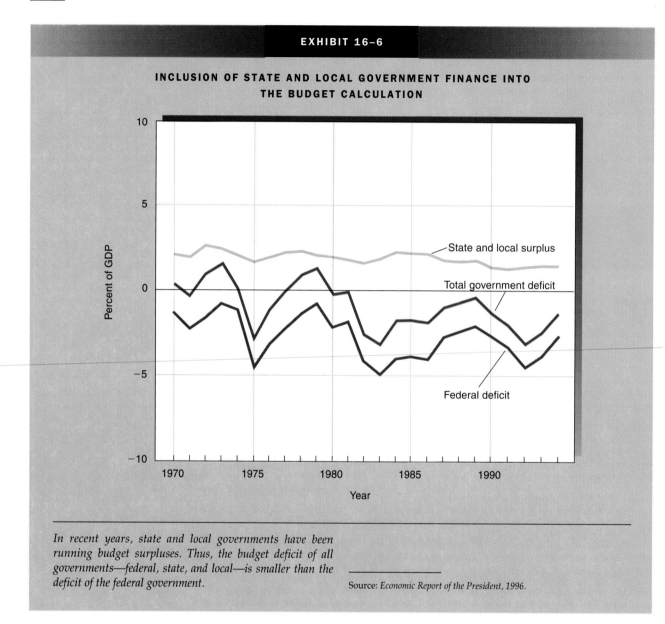

In recent years, state and local governments have been running budget surpluses. Thus, the budget deficit of all governments—federal, state, and local—is smaller than the deficit of the federal government.

Source: *Economic Report of the President, 1996.*

In contrast, the federal government makes no distinction between expenditures for a new highway or aircraft and expenditures for current services or transfer payments. To the extent the budget deficit is used to finance long-lasting assets, future taxpayers will receive a stream of services as an offset to the tax liability. For example, suppose the federal government spends $100 million to provide office space that is currently rented for $12 million. If the expenditure is debt financed at an annual interest rate of 12 percent, then $100 million is added to the national debt. But there is no change in the government's current expenditures; rent expense goes down by $12 million, and interest expense increases by $12 million.

Many economists believe that the government's inclusion of capital investment as a current expenditure exaggerates the magnitude of the deficit problem. Although it is difficult to determine the precise magnitude of the federal government's net capital expenditures, it is clear that they are substantial. Recent research on the topic indicates that such expenditures amounted to more than $20 billion in the mid-1980s.[5]

INFLATION DISTORTS THE BUDGET DEFICIT

By now you should be well aware that inflation affects nominal interest rates. Once people come to expect a given rate of inflation, it gets built into the nominal rate of interest.

When the rate of inflation accelerates to a higher level, the expected future inflation rate and nominal interest rates on *newly issued* bonds will also tend to rise. The interest rates applicable to previously issued bonds, however, will be unchanged until their maturity. Therefore, when there is an increase in the rate of inflation, the government's interest costs will lag behind the general growth of revenues and expenditures. As a result, the current budget deficit will, for a time, understate the longer-term liability accompanying the government's outstanding debt. Eventually, the "old bonds" will have to be refinanced at the higher nominal interest rates. When this happens, both the government's interest costs and its budget deficit will rise. Currently, the average maturity length on government debt is about six years. Thus, the time lag during which the relative size of the budget deficit is understated can be substantial.

The bias is in the opposite direction when there is a reduction in the rate of inflation. While a lower actual and expected rate of inflation will reduce the nominal interest rate on newly issued bonds, the interest payments on the bonds that were previously issued at the higher nominal rates will be unchanged. Thus, the reduction in the nominal amount of the government's interest costs will decline more slowly than other expenditures and revenues due to the lower rate of inflation. Under these circumstances, the budget deficit will temporarily be larger than will be true in the future (if the government's real outstanding debt remains constant).

Inflation also distorts the size of the budget deficit for another reason. Once persistent inflation is in place and nominal interest rates rise as a result, the inflation both (1) increases the nominal cost of financing the debt and (2) erodes the real liability accompanying the bonds that are outstanding. These two items are offsetting, but only the higher interest costs will show up in the government's budget.

Consider the following situation. Suppose the government has a net public debt of $3 trillion, approximately the net federal debt of the United States in the mid-1990s. As the result of a persistent inflation rate of 4 percent, nominal interest rates are 4 percent higher than would otherwise be the case if the general price level were stable. This 4 percent increase in nominal interest rates pushes the government's interest costs up by $120 billion (4 percent of $3 trillion). This increase in interest expense shows up in the budget. The 4 percent inflation also

---

[5]Robert Eisner, "Which Budget Deficit? Some Issues of Measurement and Their Implications," *American Economic Review* 74 (May 1988): pp. 138–143.

erodes the real burden of the $3 trillion of outstanding debt by $120 billion. This is a real capital gain (a decline in the liability of the government), but it does not appear in the budget. Therefore, even though the $120 billion of additional interest and $120 billion reduction in the government's real liability on outstanding debt are offsetting items resulting from the 4 percent inflation rate, only the additional nominal interest cost affects the budget. As a result, the budget deficit is overstated by $120 billion, about 2 percent of GDP in the case of the United States.

What are the implications of this analysis for the U.S. budget deficit? First, it indicates that as the inflation rate accelerated upward during the 1970s and then decelerated during the early 1980s, these forces initially resulted in an understatement in the size of the deficit during the 1970s and overstatement during the early 1980s because the change in interest expense tends to lag behind the rate of inflation. Second, the increases in the budget deficit/GDP ratio (see Exhibit 16–2) and the interest cost as a percent of federal revenue (see Exhibit 16–5) during the past 25 years are at least partially the result of the higher inflation rates of the 1970s and 1980s compared to the 25-year period following the Second World War.

THE SOCIAL SECURITY SYSTEM AND THE NATIONAL DEBT

As conventionally measured, the budget deficit includes the revenues and expenditures of government trust funds, including the social security trust fund. Until recently, the *net* revenue flowing into these funds was small relative to the size of the budget. Therefore, it really did not make much difference whether these funds were included in or excluded from budget deficit calculations.

All this began to change during the latter half of the 1980s. Under legislation passed in 1983, the social security trust fund is scheduled to run huge budget surpluses throughout the 1990s and into the next century. Now the size of the federal budget deficit differs substantially depending on whether the expenditures and revenues of the social security program are included in the deficit calculation. For example, if the $60 billion surplus of the social security system had not been included in the 1995 deficit calculation, the fiscal-year federal deficit would have been $225 billion rather than $165 billion. By the late 1990s, estimates indicate that inclusion of the social security surpluses in the budget calculations will reduce the size of the perceived budget deficit *annually* by $100 billion.

More is at stake here than just a definitional issue. There is a reason for the planned social security surpluses. During the 15 years following the Second World War, there was a huge group of people born in the United States (see Illustrated Exhibit I–E, page 3). When this "baby-boom" generation is in the retirement phase of their life during 2020 to 2050, enormous strain will be placed on the social security system. *Unless funds are set aside to finance the retirement benefits of the baby boomers, the solvency of the social security system will be endangered. Hence the planned social security surpluses are intended to increase the national saving rate and stimulate additional investment, and thereby help to finance the retirement benefits of the baby-boom generation. Using the trust funds to finance current government expenditures completely undermines this strategy.*

Given the future demands of the social security system, many economists argue that it will not be enough for the federal government to just balance its budget in the decade ahead. They argue that the government should be running a budget surplus that is at least equal to the annual surplus of the social security system.

DEBT FINANCING IN OTHER COUNTRIES

The United States has not been alone in its reliance on deficit financing. As **Exhibit 16–7** shows, all the major industrial countries ran budget deficits during the early 1990s. Among the major industrial countries, only Japan ran a smaller average deficit than the United States during the 1991–1995 period. The government deficits of Germany, France, the United Kingdom, and Canada

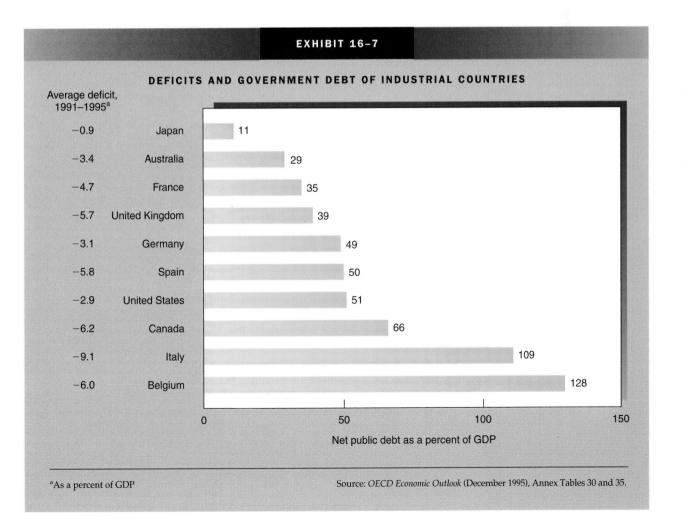

EXHIBIT 16–7

DEFICITS AND GOVERNMENT DEBT OF INDUSTRIAL COUNTRIES

Average deficit, 1991–1995[a]

Average deficit	Country	Net public debt as a percent of GDP
−0.9	Japan	11
−3.4	Australia	29
−4.7	France	35
−5.7	United Kingdom	39
−3.1	Germany	49
−5.8	Spain	50
−2.9	United States	51
−6.2	Canada	66
−9.1	Italy	109
−6.0	Belgium	128

Net public debt as a percent of GDP

[a]As a percent of GDP

Source: *OECD Economic Outlook* (December 1995), Annex Tables 30 and 35.

averaged between 3.1 percent and 6.2 percent of GDP during this period. Italy has consistently run larger budget deficits than the other large industrial economies. During 1991–1995, the budget deficits of the Italian government averaged 9.1 percent of GDP.

Exhibit 16–7 also provides data on the net public debt relative to the GDP. Among the industrial nations, the net public debt/GDP ratio in 1995 was lowest, 11 percent, for Japan. The net debt/GDP ratio of France and the United Kingdom was slightly lower than the figure for Germany and the United States at year-end 1995. The size of the net public debt as a share of GDP was quite large in Canada (66 percent) and Italy (109 percent). The net public debt of Belgium is the highest of any industrial country, 128 percent of GDP at year-end 1995.

The Belgium case sheds light on what is in store for countries that persistently run large budget deficits and expand their outstanding debt more rapidly than the growth of real GDP. Interest payments on the public debt of Belgium now compose approximately 30 percent of the government's budget and 15 percent of national income. Thus, the government of Belgium now has to tax away 15 percent of the income generated by its citizens just to make the interest payments on its outstanding debt.

As the size of a nation's outstanding debt gets larger and larger, eventually global credit markets will apply some discipline. Countries with large debt/GDP ratios will have to pay higher real interest rates in order to induce investors to purchase their bonds. At some point, countries will be more or less forced to bring spending into line with revenues in order to maintain the confidence of investors. This is what happened to Belgium in 1994. Loss of investor confidence led to a sharp decline in the foreign exchange value of the Belgian franc. In order to maintain creditworthiness, the Belgian government was forced to take some drastic steps. Spending on social programs—including social security, health care, and child benefits—was substantially reduced. Continuing discipline will be required if Belgium is going to fully regain the confidence of investors.

POLITICS AND BUDGET DEFICITS

Why has the federal government run a string of deficits during the past three decades? Why is deficit spending so widespread around the world? Many public choice economists, including the 1986 Nobel laureate James Buchanan, charge that politicians like to spend money in order to buy the favor of various interest groups and voting blocs, but they dislike taxes that impose visible costs on voting constituents.

However, government expenditures must be financed in some manner. Borrowing provides an alternative to current taxation. Because they push the taxes into the future, deficits are less visible to people than current taxation. As a result, people imagine that government services cost less than is really the case. Thus, borrowing allows politicians to supply voters with immediate benefits without having to impose a parallel visible cost in the form of higher taxes or user charges.

Prior to the Keynesian revolution, almost everyone—including the leading figures of both political parties—thought that the government should balance its budget except during times of war. In essence, until approximately 1960, there was widespread implicit agreement—much like a constitutional rule—that the federal budget should be balanced. The Keynesian analysis changed opinions, first among economists and later among others, including political officials. In essence, the Keynesian view eroded the discipline that emanated from the implicit balanced-budget concept. Released from that constraint, since the early 1960s politicians have consistently spent more than they have been willing to tax.[6] And as we have noted, the deficits have gotten larger and larger. On several occasions, Congress has passed legislation pledging to balance the budget at some designated time in the future. As the day approaches, however, the pledge is modified and the balancing of the budget delayed.

Despite all the talk about balancing the budget, why is accomplishing the task so difficult? Public-choice analysis sheds light on this question. Each political representative has a strong incentive to fight hard for expenditures beneficial to his or her constituents and little incentive to oppose spending by others. A legislator who is a spending "watchdog" will incur the wrath of colleagues favoring special programs for their districts. More important, the benefits (for example, tax reductions and lower interest rates) of spending cuts and deficit reductions will be spread thinly among the voters in all districts. Thus, the legislator's constituents will reap only a small part of these benefits.

It is as if 535 families go out to dinner knowing that after the meal each will receive a bill for 1/535th of the cost. No family feels compelled to order less, because their restraint will exert little impact on the total bill. Why not order shrimp for an appetizer, entrees of steak and lobster, and a large piece of cheesecake for dessert? After all, the extra spending will add only a few pennies to each family's share of the total bill. However, when everybody follows this course of action, many items are purchased that are valued less than their cost.[7]

So it is with congressional decision making. Representatives have a strong incentive to push for "desserts" helpful to their own districts, particularly when each recognizes that other legislators are doing the same. Then, after the spending decisions are made, Congress sums up the total and tries to figure out how to pay for it. Given this process, the presence of budget deficits should not come as a surprise.

STRUCTURAL CHANGE AND DEFICITS

Public-choice analysis indicates that budget deficits are an expected result of ordinary politics in the post-Keynesian era. According to this view, the deficits are a natural outgrowth of the current political structure. If we want a different

---

[6]See James M. Buchanan and Richard Wagner, *Democracy in Deficit: The Political Legacy of Lord Keynes* (New York: Academic Press, 1977), for a detailed account of the changes wrought by the Keynesian revolution.

[7]As E. C. Pasour, Jr., of North Carolina State University, has pointed out to the authors, the federal "dinner check" analogy can be carried one step further. Suppose the check is to be divided evenly among the large group, but the ordering will be done by committee so there will be separate committees for drinks, appetizers, entrees, salads, and desserts. Since each person can serve on the committee of his or her choice, lushes end up on the drinks committee, vegetarians on the salad committee, sweet tooths on the dessert committee, and so on. This arrangement further exacerbates the tendency toward overordering and overspending. The arrangement just described closely resembles the committee structure of the U.S. Congress.

outcome, we will have to change the incentive structure confronted by legislators. Most public choice economists believe that effective restraint on deficit spending would require constitutional action, making it difficult for political officials to spend more than they are willing to tax. The simplest approach would be a constitutional amendment mandating that the federal government balance its budget. Proposed amendments of this type would allow only a supramajority (for example, two-thirds or three-fourths) of Congress to override the restriction. In essence, this approach calls for an explicit constitutional restraint that its backers hope would reapply the kind of discipline that was present prior to the Keynesian revolution.

Is the balanced-budget requirement a good idea? Two criticisms are generally levied against it. First, some charge that it would reduce the effectiveness of fiscal policy as a stabilization tool. According to this view, Congress might feel compelled to raise taxes in the midst of a recession. Of course, the supramajority override provision would reduce the likelihood of this occurrence. Nonetheless, some critics fear that limitations on budget deficits might reduce the effectiveness of fiscal policy and exert a destabilizing influence on the economy.

A second group of critics argues that a balanced-budget requirement would be easily evaded and largely ineffective. According to this view, Congress would use things like off-budget expenditures, mandated spending, and unrealistic budget projections in order to escape the proposed discipline.

There are other ways that fundamental rule changes might retard the deficit spending tendencies of Congress. Many believe that recent legislation providing the president with a *line-item veto*—the authority to eliminate spending on specific line items without having to veto an entire bill—will help reduce pork-barrel spending and retard the power of special interests. William Niskanen, a member of the President's Council of Economic Advisers in the 1980s, has proposed that the Constitution be amended to require the approval of two-thirds of the members of both houses for an increase in either debt or taxes. Without eliminating the use of deficit financing, this proposal would stiffen the federal budget constraint. Others have proposed that Congress be required to adopt an aggregate spending constraint well before (six months, for example) the beginning of each fiscal year. Once the constraint was adopted, approval of any budget expenditure beyond the constraint would require a three-fourths majority.

Finally, Dwight Lee and Richard McKenzie have proposed that congressional salaries be inversely linked to the size of the deficit.[8] For example, congressional salaries might be reduced by 10 percent for each 1 percent increase in the deficit/GDP ratio. Therefore, if the budget deficit was 4 percent of GDP, as was the case in the early 1990s, congressional salaries would be cut by 40 percent! The same pay scale could also be applied to the president and all cabinet officials. This proposal would not only let Congress and the president know that they were expected to balance the budget, it would provide them with an incentive to do so.

---

[8]Dwight R. Lee and Richard B. McKenzie, *Regulating Government: A Preface to Constitutional Economics* (Lexington: Lexington Books, 1987), pp. 149–163.

CONCLUDING THOUGHTS

The topic of the budget deficit is both interesting and complex. It encompasses both economic and political dimensions. It is a topic about which the popular media are constantly disseminating false information and half-truths, usually because so many do not understand the issue.

Our analysis indicates that the recent growth of the federal debt is troublesome, but not catastrophic. It is troublesome because debt financing may be misleading Americans in regard to their true wealth position and thereby causing them to save and invest less than would otherwise be the case. It is also troublesome because the deficit may be partially hiding the true cost of government and thereby contributing to the inefficient use of resources. But these effects imply a gradual slowdown in economic growth, not a future "day of reckoning."

If action is taken now to reduce the growth of the debt relative to GDP, there is no reason why a combination of expenditure cuts, revenue increases, and economic growth cannot return the ratio of debt to GDP to the downward path of the three decades following the Second World War. However, there is reason to doubt that this will happen in the current political environment. Given the political pressures, a quick resolution is unlikely. The "deficit issue" will almost surely be with us in the foreseeable future.

CHAPTER SUMMARY

1. The national debt is the sum of the outstanding bonds of the U.S. Treasury. Budget deficits increase the national debt. In fact, the national debt reflects the cumulative effect of all prior budget deficits and surpluses.

2. Approximately one-third of the national debt is owned by U.S. government agencies and Federal Reserve banks. For this portion of the debt, the government both pays and receives the interest (except for the expenses of the Fed). Therefore, only the privately held federal debt—the portion of the national debt owned by domestic and foreign investors—generates a net interest liability for the government. Approximately three-fourths of the privately held federal debt is owed to domestic investors.

3. When considering the impact of the national debt on future generations, it is important to keep two points in mind. First, the future generations that pay the tax liability accompanying the debt will also receive the interest income implied by the debt. Second, the opportunity cost of using scarce resources to produce goods and services through the public sector is the decline in current private-sector output. This opportunity cost is incurred during the current period regardless of how the government activity is financed.

4. Budget deficits affect future generations through their impact on capital formation.

5. According to the traditional view, the substitution of debt financing for taxes during normal times will increase real interest rates, which will retard private investment. In addition, the higher interest rates will attract an inflow of foreign capital, which will lead to an appreciation in the dollar and decline in net exports. Thus, the traditional view implies that budget deficits will reduce the rate of capital formation—particularly capital owned by Americans—and thereby adversely affect the future incomes of Americans.

6. In contrast with the traditional view, the new classical theory argues that households will anticipate fully the added future tax liability implied by debt financing and increase their savings in order to meet the higher future taxes. This increase in saving offsets the increase in demand for loanable funds emanating from the debt. In the new classical model, the substitution of debt for taxes leaves interest rates, consumption, and investment unaffected.

7. Compared to earlier periods when budget deficits were smaller, the recent periods of large budget deficits have been characterized by a higher level of consumption, lower rates of investment (particularly domestically financed investment), and a decline in net exports. These changes are consistent with the traditional view regarding the impact of budget deficits.

8. As long as the interest liability accompanying the debt grows less rapidly than national income, the relative burden imposed on the economy by the debt is declining. The increase in net interest cost relative to GDP during the past 20 years is a worrisome trend.

9. Because the increase in interest costs will tend to lag behind other expenditures and revenues, an increase in the rate of inflation will *initially* tend to result in a smaller deficit/GDP ratio than the ratio that will emerge in the long run. In contrast, a reduction in inflation will *initially* increase the deficit/GDP ratio. Persistent inflation both increases the nominal interest payments on the debt and erodes the real value of the debt. Even though these two factors offset each other, only the higher nominal interest payments affect the budget.

10. In recent years, state and local governments have been running budget surpluses. Thus, the overall deficit of government is smaller than the federal deficit. On the other hand, the social security trust fund is currently running a sizable surplus, which reduces the federal debt as currently measured. Predictably, the current operating surplus of the social security system will dissipate and turn to a deficit as the baby-boom generation moves into the retirement phase of life around 2015.

11. Many public choice economists believe that the current budget process is structurally unsound. They argue

that it encourages deficit financing and fails to confront Congress with a firm budget constraint. These economists believe that constitutional changes are necessary to deal with the "budget problem."

CRITICAL ANALYSIS QUESTIONS

*1. Does the national debt have to be paid off at some time in the future? What will happen if it is not?

2. Do we owe the national debt to ourselves? Does this mean the size of the national debt is of little concern? Why or why not?

3. "The national debt is a mortgage against the future of our children and grandchildren. We are forcing them to pay for our current consumption of goods and services." Evaluate this statement.

*4. When government bonds are held by foreigners, the interest income from the bonds goes to foreigners rather than to Americans. Would Americans be better off if we prohibited the sale of bonds to foreigners?

*5. If citizen-taxpayers fail to anticipate the future tax liability accompanying debt finance, what does this imply about their perception of the cost of government? How do you think this affects the political popularity of debt financing relative to taxes?

*6. Even if it were unable or unwilling to raise taxes in order to meet the interest payments on outstanding debt, the federal government would be unlikely to default on its outstanding bonds. Why? What would happen in the event of such a crisis?

7. Is the federal government more or less likely than state and local governments to default on outstanding bonds? Why?

*8. When there is a budget deficit, what happens to the nominal national debt? Could the real outstanding government debt decline even though a budget deficit is present?

9. "We must start paying for what we get from government. A government worth having is worth paying for!" Evaluate this statement. Can we get things from government without paying for them?

*10. Does an increase in the national debt increase the supply of money (M1)? Can the money supply increase when the U.S. Treasury is running a budget surplus?

11. "If the government is spending $20 billion to maintain and improve highways, these costs are incurred during the current period regardless of whether they are financed with taxes or debt." Evaluate this statement.

12. When government expenditures are paid for with debt rather than with taxes, what is the likely impact on the growth of the U.S. economy? Explain.

13. Are the large deficits of the federal government a threat to our economy? Why or why not? Would our economy be healthier if taxes were raised sufficiently to generate a substantial budget surplus? Why or why not?

*14. Would you predict that government expenditures would be higher or lower if taxes (and user charges) were required for the finance of all expenditures? Why? Do you think the government would spend funds more or less efficiently if it could not issue debt? Why?

15. What are the implications of the shortsightedness effect with regard to the comparative attractiveness of tax and debt financing?

16. In most cases the credibility of governments in Eastern Europe and the former Soviet Union is very low with potential financial investors. Private investors are unwilling to purchase bonds issued by these governments. Under these circumstances, if the government runs a budget deficit, how must that deficit be financed? How will this method of finance influence the inflation rate?

17. Consider the following hypothetical information (dollar figures are in billions):

Budget receipts in 1993	$1,150
Budget expenditures in 1993	$1,300
Annual growth rate of GDP	6 percent

a. Complete the following table (some information has already been provided):

	BUDGET DEFICIT	NATIONAL DEBT (END OF PERIOD)	GDP	BUDGET DEFICIT AS SHARE OF GDP	NATIONAL DEBT AS SHARE OF GDP (END OF PERIOD)
1992	$145	$4,200	$6,000	____	____
1993	____	____	____	____	____

b. Why did the national debt fall as a share of GDP in 1993 even though the budget deficit rose?

---

*Asterisk denotes questions for which answers are given in Appendix B.

Changes in income levels, relative prices, and other factors influence spending patterns on consumption goods and services. Compared to 1963, Americans spent a smaller amount of the family budget on food, and a substantially larger share on medical services (including insurance) and recreation in 1993.

SOURCE: Herbert Stein and Murray Foss, *The New Illustrated Guide to the American Economy*, 2d ed. (Washington, D.C.: AEI Press, 1995), p. 23.

EXHIBIT III–A

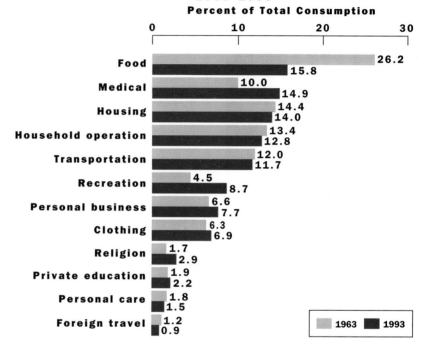

THE DISTRIBUTION OF CONSUMPTION EXPENDITURES: 1963–1993
Percent of Total Consumption

Most firms are small. In 1992, 87 percent of all business firms employed less than 20 workers. As illustrated here, these small firms employed 26.9 percent of those directly employed by a business firm. At the other end of the spectrum, firms with 500 or more workers employed 20 percent of the total. Between 1980 and 1992, there was a slight decline in the number of Americans working for large firms.

SOURCE: *Statistical Abstract of the United States, 1995,* Table 857.

EXHIBIT III–B

VARIATION IN THE SIZE OF FIRMS IN THE UNITED STATES

EXHIBIT III-C

The accounting profit rate of manufacturing firms has averaged less than 5 cents per dollar of sales and approximately 12 cents per dollar of stockholder equity invested in the firm. The profit rates of nonmanufacturing firms are generally smaller than the rates shown here.

SOURCE: *Economic Report of the President, 1996,* Table B-90.

AFTER-TAX PROFITS OF MANUFACTURING FIRMS AS A PERCENT OF SALES AND STOCKHOLDER EQUITY

The U.S. economy is highly dynamic. In recent years, newly incorporated businesses composed approximately 10 percent of the total, while business failures (bankruptcies) were approximately 1 percent of the total. In addition, many businesses closed their doors or sold their assets to other, more successful (or optimistic) operators, before they were forced into bankruptcy.

Source: *Statistical Abstract of the United States, 1995,* Table 860; and *Economic Report of the President, 1996,* Table B-92.

EXHIBIT III-D

NEW BUSINESS CORPORATIONS AND BUSINESS BANKRUPTCIES AS A PERCENT OF ALL BUSINESS CORPORATIONS: 1984-1994

EXHIBIT III–E

Here we illustrate the gross sales of four leading retailers. Sears, the number 1 retailer throughout most of this period, experienced substantial growth of sales between 1960 and 1990, prior to its recent decline. The sales of Montgomery Ward, the third leading retailer in 1960, grew during the 1960s, but they have declined sharply since that time. The sales of Kmart grew rapidly during the 1970s and 1980s, but have declined a bit in recent years. Wal-Mart, which had negligible sales in 1970, is now the largest merchandise retailer in the United States. Its 1995 sales of $61.4 billion (measured in 1985 dollars) constituted 30 percent of the merchandise retail sales market in 1995.

[a]Data are for S.S. Kresge's, which was eventually renamed Kmart.
[b]Was not established at the time.

DYNAMIC COMPETITION IN THE RETAIL BUSINESS: THE EXPERIENCE OF FOUR MAJOR FIRMS DURING 1960–1995

Sales (in billions of 1982–1984 dollars)

Montgomery Ward

Year	Sales
1960	4.2
1970	7.2
1980	6.7
1990	4.3
1995	4.6

Kmart

Year	Sales
1960	0.4[a]
1970	6.7[a]
1980	17.2
1990	24.5
1995	22.7

Sears Roebuck

Year	Sales
1960	14.0
1970	23.9
1980	30.6
1990	42.8
1994	36.8

Wal-Mart

Year	Sales
1960[b]	
1970	0.1
1980	2.0
1990	24.9
1995	61.4

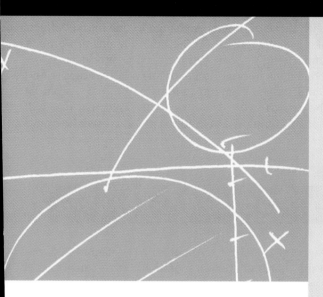

The most famous law in economics, and the one economists are most sure of, is the law of demand. On this law is built almost the whole edifice of economics.

DAVID R. HENDERSON[1]

A thing is worth whatever a buyer will pay for it.

PUBLILIUS SYRUS, FIRST CENTURY, B.C.[2]

---

[1]David R. Henderson, "Demand," in *The Fortune Encyclopedia of Economics,* ed. David R. Henderson (New York: Warner Books, Inc., 1993), p. 7.

[2]Quoted in Michael Jackman, ed., *Macmillan Book of Business and Economic Quotations* (New York: Macmillan, 1984), p. 150.

T he statement of David Henderson highlights the central position of the law of demand in economics. As Publilius Syrus noted more than 2,000 years ago, demand reflects the willingness of individuals to pay for what is offered in the market. In this section, we begin our examination of microeconomic markets for specific products with an analysis of the demand side of those markets.

Microeconomics focuses on how changes in *relative* prices influence consumer decisions. As we stressed in Chapter 3, the price system guides individuals in their production and consumption decisions.[3] Prices coordinate the vast array of individual economic activities. They signal relative wants and needs, and they provide incentives to all market participants to bring their own choices (and actions) into harmony with those of others. A change in one market affects others. In this chapter, we take a closer look at (1) the interrelationships among markets and (2) the factors underlying the demand for specific products.

The market price of a good signals information about its relative scarcity and value to all potential buyers and sellers. Demand (willingness to pay) is one of the critical determinants of the market price. The other critical element that will affect market price—the cost of supplying the item to the market—will be examined in the next chapter.

CHOICE AND INDIVIDUAL DEMAND

Illustrated Exhibit III–A on page 431 compares the shares of 12 categories of consumer spending in 1993 with the shares of spending on those same categories in 1963. Personal consumption expenditures, corrected for inflation, rose 157 percent between 1963 and 1993. The composition of purchases also changed significantly. As a share of the total, spending on food (including beverages and tobacco) fell from 26.2 percent in 1963 to 15.8 percent in 1993. In contrast, medical expenditures rose from 10 percent of the total to 14.9 percent during the same period. Why did consumers make these changes? The following principles shed light on this question and enhance our understanding of consumer behavior.

1. Limited income necessitates choice.   Scarcity results in limited incomes, which force each of us to make choices. When more of one good or service is purchased, less of some others can be obtained. That is precisely the meaning of "cost."

2. Consumers make decisions purposefully.   The goals that drive a consumer decision can usually be met in many different ways, so careful consideration of alternatives is useful. Consumers try to avoid a lesser valued alternative if another of equal cost but greater projected benefit is available.

3. One good can be substituted for another.   Consumers have many goals, so no single good is so precious that some of it will not be given up in exchange

---

[3]You may want to review Chapter 3 before proceeding with this chapter.

for a large enough quantity of other goods. For example, consumers will give up some fried chicken to have more pizza, hamburgers, and other foods. Sometimes a recreational activity may partially substitute for food, as when a hamburger and a movie replace a more elaborate four–course dinner. The buyer wants utility—satisfaction—from the substitute goods, not necessarily the same services. There are many alternative ways to satisfy the individual's wants and needs.

We have been discussing "wants," but how about our "need" for basic commodities such as water or energy? The need of a person for an item is closely related to its cost—what must be given up to obtain the item. Southern California residents need water from the north, but when water becomes more expensive, individual residents faced with a high water bill, will plant cactus instead of grass, pay a plumber to fix leaking faucets, and use flow constrictors on shower heads. The need for water thus depends on its cost to the user. People living in Montana, where household electricity costs nearly twice as much as in nearby Washington, use about half as much electricity per household. Montanans reduce their "need" for electricity by substituting gas, fuel oil, insulation, and wool sweaters for the relatively more expensive electricity. Each of the things we purchase has substitutes.

4. Consumers must make decisions without perfect information, but knowledge and past experience will help. No human being has perfect foresight. Consumers will not always correctly anticipate the consequences of their choices. They will, however, have a good chance of doing so in areas of common knowledge and experience. Consumer choices are not made in a vacuum. You have a pretty good idea of what to expect when you buy a cup of coffee, five gallons of gasoline, or a box of your favorite cereal. Why? Because you have learned from experience—your own and that of others—what to expect. Your expectations may not always be fulfilled precisely (for example, the coffee may be stronger than expected or the gasoline may make your car's engine knock), but even then, you will gain valuable information that will help you project the outcome of future choices more accurately.

5. The law of diminishing marginal utility applies: As the rate of consumption increases, the utility derived from consuming additional units of a good will decline. As explained earlier, *utility* is a term economists use to describe the subjective personal benefits that result from an action. The **law of diminishing marginal utility** states that the **marginal** (or additional) **utility** derived from consuming successive units of a product will eventually decline as the rate of utilization increases. For example, the law says that, even though you might like ice cream, your marginal satisfaction from additional ice cream will eventually decline. Ice cream at lunchtime might be great. An additional helping for dinner might be even better. However, after you have had it for evening dessert and a midnight snack, ice cream for breakfast will have lost some attraction. The law of diminishing marginal utility will have set in, and thus the marginal utility derived from the consumption of additional units of ice cream will decline. Consumers would be unlikely to stop purchasing a good if an additional unit yielded more satisfaction than the previous one. Failure to purchase an additional unit indicates that the buyer has reached the point where additional units

Law of diminishing marginal utility
The basic economic principle that, as the consumption of a commodity increases, the marginal utility derived from consuming more of the commodity (per unit of time) will eventually decline. Marginal utility may decline even though total utility continues to increase, but at a reduced rate.

Marginal utility
The additional utility received by a person from the consumption of an additional unit of a good within a given time period.

provide less and less marginal utility. Utility-seeking buyers will not operate in the range of increasing marginal utility, but in the range where their marginal utility is declining.

MARGINAL UTILITY AND CONSUMER CHOICE

Consumer choices, like other decisions, are influenced by changes in benefits and costs. If the cost of purchasing an item falls, or the benefits of buying it rise, then consumers who want more satisfaction can be expected to buy more of it. How much more? As a greater quantity of a good is consumed per unit of time, the law of diminishing marginal utility states that the consumer's marginal benefit will decline. A consumer will gain by purchasing more of the newly cheaper product as long as the benefit, or marginal utility (*MU*), derived from the consumption of an additional unit of this good exceeds the cost of the unit. The cost of this good, of course, is the marginal utility expected from the highest valued consumption alternative that could be purchased instead, for the same price. As expenditures are diverted to the lower–priced good, and away from other goods, the marginal utility of the other goods will rise with their declining quantity. A specific reduction in the price of one good will have a positive, but limited, effect on the amount purchased.

Given a fixed income and specified prices for the commodities to be purchased, consumers will maximize their satisfaction (or total utility) by ensuring that the last dollar spent on each commodity purchased yields an equal degree of marginal utility. If consumers are to get the most for their money, the last dollar spent on Product A must yield the same utility as the last dollar spent on Product B (or any other product). That is, the ratio of MU_A/P_A must equal the MU_B/P_B for any goods A and B.[4] After all, if tickets for an extra football game, for example, yielded less marginal utility *per dollar* than did extra movie tickets, the consumer could gain by spending less on football games and allocating those funds for movie tickets instead. If people really attempt to spend their money in a way that yields the greatest amount of satisfaction, the usefulness of the consumer decision-making theory outlined here is difficult to question.

---

[4]Mathematically, this implies that the consumer's total utility is at a maximum when limited income is spent on products such that

$$\frac{MU_A}{P_A} = \frac{MU_B}{P_B} = \cdots \frac{MU_n}{P_n}$$

where *MU* represents the marginal utility derived from the last unit of a product, and P represents the price of the good. The subscripts A, B, . . . , n indicate the different products available to the consumer. In the continuous case, this expression implies that the consumer will get the most for her money when the consumption of each product is increased only to the point at which the marginal utility from one more unit of the good is equal to the marginal utility obtainable from the best alternative purchase that must now be forgone. For more advanced students, this proposition is developed in an alternative, more formal manner in the addendum to this chapter on indifference curves.

PRICE CHANGES AND CONSUMER CHOICE

The demand curve or schedule shows the amount of a product that consumers would be willing to purchase at alternative prices during a specific time period. The first law of demand states that the amount of a product purchased is inversely related to its price. Why? First, as the price of a product declines, the lower opportunity cost will induce consumers to buy more of it—and, by implication, less of other, more highly priced products. Economists refer to this tendency to substitute a product that has become relatively cheaper for goods that are now more expensive as the **substitution effect.** What will happen to the marginal utility derived from the product, though, as the rate of consumption is increased? It will fall. Each additional unit consumed adds less to total utility. Thus, as more of the product is consumed, a point is reached where the benefits (marginal utility) derived from the consumption of still more units will again be less than the cost. Purposeful decision makers will not choose such units. A price reduction, then, will induce consumers to purchase more of a product, but the response will be limited because of the law of diminishing marginal utility.

Second, since the money income of consumers is constant, a reduction in the price of a product will increase real income—the amount of goods and services consumers are able to purchase. Typically, consumers will respond by purchasing more of the cheaper product (as well as other products) because they can now better afford to do so. This factor is referred to as the **income effect.** (Both the income and substitution effects are derived graphically in the addendum to this chapter, titled "Consumer Choice and Indifference Curves.")

Of course, the substitution and income effects will generally induce consumers to purchase less of a good if its price rises. The rising opportunity cost of consuming the product makes it a less attractive buy. However, as consumption is reduced, remaining units have a higher marginal utility—that is, they will be more highly valued by the consumer. If the price increase is not so great as to drive the consumer out of the market completely, consumption of the item will fall until the product's marginal utility is high enough to again equal its new, higher opportunity cost. With moderate increases in price, the consumer's reduction in consumption will be limited. We must also bear in mind that if the consumer's money income is constant, and other prices have not fallen, the price increase reduces the individual's real income. A reduction in real income will tend to result in a reduction in the consumption of many goods, generally including the good that has increased in price.

Exhibit 17–1 illustrates the adjustment of consumers to a change in price. During 1985–1986, gasoline prices fell rapidly in the United States. As demand theory would predict, consumers increased their rate of consumption. As per-gallon gasoline prices fell from $1.20 to $.80, Jones's average weekly consumption rose from 16 gallons to 20 gallons. The lower fuel price caused him to postpone a costly tuneup on his car, which would have saved some fuel. After the reduction in price, he went to the grocery store a little more often, rather than waiting to combine shopping trips with other business near the shopping center. He and his family took a vacation by car, which would have been much more expensive at the 1985 price of gasoline. At the higher rate of use, the marginal utility of gasoline fell, bringing it into line with the lower price. Further price declines would have created even greater increases in consumption, but the price stabilized near

Substitution effect
That part of an increase (decrease) in amount consumed that is the result of a good being cheaper (more expensive) in relation to other goods because of a reduction (increase) in price.

Income effect
That part of an increase (decrease) in amount consumed that is the result of the consumer's real income (the consumption possibilities available to the consumer) being expanded (contracted) by a reduction (rise) in the price of a good.

An individual, Jones in this case, will increase his rate of consumption of a product as long as his MU exceeds his opportunity cost (principally the price of the good). Lower prices will induce him to consume more, but the increase in consumption will be limited because the MU of the product will fall as consumption is expanded.

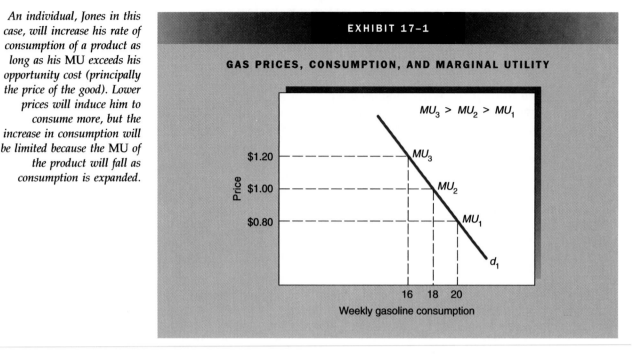

EXHIBIT 17–1

GAS PRICES, CONSUMPTION, AND MARGINAL UTILITY

its 1986 level for about four years. In late 1990 the price of gasoline jumped back up roughly to the 1985 level, partly as a result of higher gasoline taxes, and the price remained near that level into early 1996. Responding to the higher price, consumers such as Jones once again began decreasing their consumption.

TIME COST AND CONSUMER CHOICE

The monetary price of a good is not always a complete measure of its cost to the consumer. Consumption of most goods requires time as well as money; and time, like money, is scarce to the consumer. So a lower time cost, like a lower money price, will make a product more attractive.[5] Indeed, some commodities are demanded primarily because of their ability to save valuable time for consumers. People are often willing to pay relatively high money prices for such goods. The popularity of automatic dishwashers, prepared foods, air travel, and taxi service is based partly on the time savings they offer.

Time costs, unlike money prices, differ among individuals. They are higher for persons with greater earning power. Other things being equal, high-wage consumers choose fewer time-intensive (and more time-saving) commodities than persons with a lower time cost. High-wage consumers are overrepresented among air and taxicab passengers but underrepresented among television watchers, chess

---

[5]For a technical treatment of the importance of time as a component of cost from the vantage point of the consumer, see Gary Becker, "A Theory of the Allocation of Time," *Economic Journal* (September 1965): pp. 493–517.

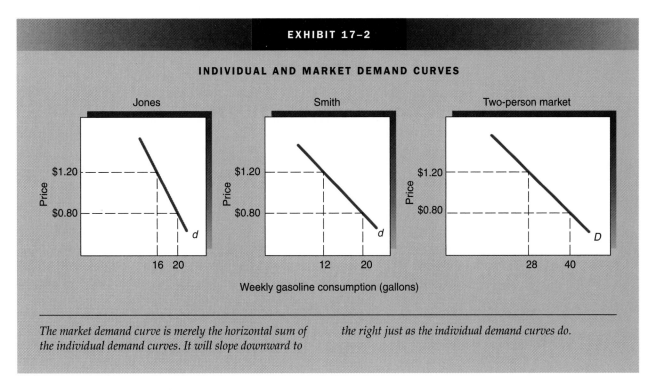

EXHIBIT 17–2

INDIVIDUAL AND MARKET DEMAND CURVES

Jones | Smith | Two-person market

Weekly gasoline consumption (gallons)

The market demand curve is merely the horizontal sum of the individual demand curves. It will slope downward to the right just as the individual demand curves do.

players, and long-distance bus travelers. Can you explain why? You can, if you understand how both money and time cost influence the choices of consumers.

MARKET DEMAND REFLECTS THE DEMAND OF INDIVIDUAL CONSUMERS

The market demand schedule is the relationship between the amount demanded by all the individuals in the market area, and the market price. Because individual consumers purchase less at higher prices, the amount demanded in a market area is also inversely related to price.

Exhibit 17–2 illustrates the relationship between individual demand and market demand for a hypothetical two-person market. The individual demand curves for both Jones and Smith are shown. Jones and Smith each consume 20 gallons of gasoline weekly at 80 cents per gallon. The amount demanded in the two-person market is 40 gallons. If the price rises to $1.20 per gallon, the amount demanded in the market will fall to 28 gallons, 16 demanded by Jones and 12 by Smith. *The market demand is simply the horizontal sum of the individual demand curves.*

Market demand reflects individual demand. Individuals buy less as price increases. Therefore, the total amount demanded in the market declines as price increases.

CONSUMER SURPLUS

The demand curve reveals how many units consumers will purchase at various prices. In so doing, it reveals consumers' evaluation of units of a good. *The height of the demand curve indicates how much consumers value an added unit.* The difference between the amount that consumers would be willing to pay and the amount they actually pay for a good is called **consumer surplus.** As **Exhibit 17–3** illustrates, it is measured by the area under the demand curve but above the market price.

Consumer surplus
The difference between the maximum amount a consumer would be willing to pay for a unit of a good, and the payment that is actually made.

Previously, we indicated that voluntary exchange is advantageous to buyer and seller alike. Consumer surplus is a measure of the net gain to the buyer/consumer. Consumer surplus also reflects the law of diminishing marginal utility. Consumers will continue to purchase additional units of a good, each yielding less marginal utility than the previous unit, until the marginal utility is just enough to justify paying the market price. Up to that point, however, consumption of each unit generates a surplus for the consumer, since the value of the unit exceeds the market price. In aggregate, the total value (utility) to consumers of a good may be far greater than the amount they pay.

The size of the consumer surplus is affected by the market price. A reduction in the market price will lead to an expansion in quantity purchased and a larger consumer surplus. Conversely, a higher market price will reduce the amount purchased and shrink the surplus (net gain) for consumers.

As the shaded area indicates, the difference between the largest amount consumers would be willing to pay for each unit and the price they actually pay for the unit is the consumer surplus.

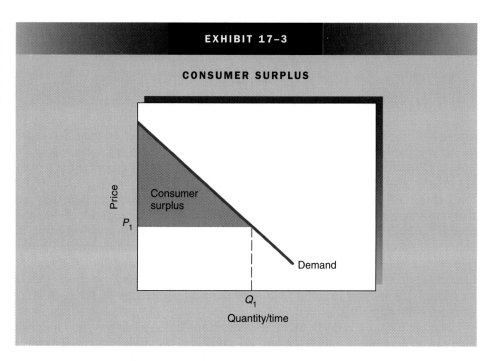

EXHIBIT 17–3

CONSUMER SURPLUS

CONSUMER SURPLUS AND TOTAL VALUE

Nothing is more useful than water; but it will purchase scarce anything. . . . A diamond, on the contrary, has scarce any value in use; but a very great quantity of other goods may frequently be had in exchange for it.

ADAM SMITH[6]

The classical economists, including Adam Smith, were puzzled that water, which is necessary for life, sells so cheaply, while diamonds have a far greater price. A century after Smith's time, economists discovered the importance of the marginal analysis we used in our discussions in the preceding sections. The willingness to pay for additional units depends on one's valuation of the *marginal* unit, not the value of all units taken together. When additional units are available at a low cost, they will be consumed until their marginal value is also low. Price is determined by the cost and value of marginal units, not average units. Thus, marginal value may be quite low, even though the total value is exceedingly high. This is the case for water and other commodities when they are plentiful. The total value (and average value) of a good includes consumer surplus; thus, the *total* value and the *average* value of goods like water can be quite large even though their price is low. These factors provide the explanation for why market price has so little to do with the total contribution that a good makes to the welfare of users.

WHAT CAUSES THE DEMAND CURVE TO SHIFT?

The demand schedule isolates the impact of price on the amount purchased, *assuming other factors are held constant.* Changes in these "other factors" will cause the entire demand schedule to shift. If a change in the other factors increases demand, the demand schedule will shift to the right. **Exhibit 17–4** illustrates an increase in demand, a rightward shift in the demand schedule. Of course, a change in "other factors" that reduces demand—the amount purchased at several different prices—will shift the demand schedule to the left. What are these "other factors" that (a) are held constant when a demand curve is constructed and (b) cause the entire demand schedule to shift when they change?

1. Changes in Income. The demand for most products is positively related to income. As their income expands, individuals will spend more on most goods (there are a few exceptions). Thus, the demand curve for most products shifts to the right (like the shift from D_1 to D_2 in Exhibit 17–4) as the income of consumers increases. Of course, the increase in expenditures will differ for specific goods. For example, as their income grows, consumers may spend a little more on food and

---

[6]Adam Smith, *An Inquiry into the Nature and Causes of the Wealth of Nations,* 1776, ed. Edwin Cannan (Chicago: University of Chicago Press, 1976), p. 33.

Other things constant, the demand schedule will slope downward to the right. However, changes in income and its distribution, in the prices of closely related products, in consumer preferences, in population (market demographics), and expectations about future prices will also influence consumer decisions. Changes in these factors will cause the entire demand curve to shift (for example, increase from D_1 to D_2).

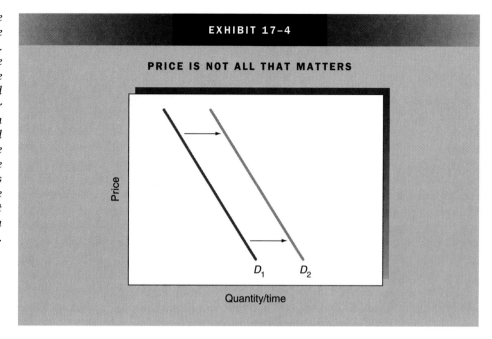

EXHIBIT 17–4

PRICE IS NOT ALL THAT MATTERS

D_1 D_2

Price

Quantity/time

clothing, and far more on automobiles, VCRs, and real butter; in the case of a few commodities (navy beans and bus travel, for example), purchases may fall. A reduction in income can cause the opposite effects on demand for various products.

2. Changes in the Distribution of Income.   Spending in the market for any product will vary both with the number of potential consumers in the market and with the income level of each consuming unit. When either of these two factors changes, the distribution of income is altered among consumers, thus altering spending in various product markets. In other words, the demand curve for certain products shifts when there is a change in distribution of income.

For example, from 1986 to 1991, an increase in the number of households headed by individuals aged 35–44 pushed the total income of consumers in that group up so that their total spending rose by 31 percent.[7] Meanwhile, the number of households headed by individuals aged 25–34 fell, reducing that group's total income, so that spending by them fell by more than 9 percent. These changes were felt strongly in the markets for beer and wine. Beer purchases peak in the 25–34 age group, while wine purchases peak in the 35–44 group. The strong shift in income distribution between these two groups was a major reason why the demand for wine increased (sales rose 12 percent) between 1986 and 1991, while the demand for beer declined (sales fell 24 percent.)

3. Changes in the Price of a Related Good.   Related goods may be either substitutes or complements. When two products perform similar functions or fulfill sim-

---

[7]These data are from the *Consumer Expenditure Survey* of the U.S. Department of Labor, as reported in *American Spending* (Ithaca, N.Y.: American Demographics, 1993), pp. 21–23.

ilar needs, they are generally **substitutes.** Economists define goods as substitutes when there is a direct relationship between the price of one and the demand for the other. Thus, an increase in the price of one increases demand for the other. For example, margarine is a substitute for butter. A supply problem that raises butter prices, or causes a butter shortage, will increase the demand for margarine. Consumers substitute margarine for the more expensive butter. Similarly, higher coffee prices will increase the demand for such substitutes as cocoa and tea. On the other hand, if technology, good weather, or some other factor reduces the price of a good, then the demand for its substitutes will decline. A substitute relationship exists between beef and pork, pencils and pens, apples and oranges, and so forth.

Other closely related products are consumed jointly, so the demands for them are linked together in a positive way. Examples of goods that "go together," so to speak, could be ham and eggs, or tents and other camping equipment. For these combinations of goods, called **complements,** a decrease in the price of one will not only increase the quantity demanded of it, but will also increase the demand for the other. With complements, there is an inverse relationship between the price of one and the demand for the other. For example, lower prices for videocassette players during the 1980s increased the demand for videocassette tapes. Similarly, declining prices for compact discs raised the demand for compact disc players.

4. Changes in Market Demographics.
The demand for many products is strongly influenced by the *demographics* of the market—the number and the characteristics of consumers in that market. Changes in population and its composition can have a large influence in markets. For example, young people age 15 to 24 are a major part of the U.S. market for jeans. When the population in that group fell by more than 5 million during the 1980s, fewer jeans were demanded. Sales, which had topped 500 million pairs in 1980, fell to less than 400 million pairs in 1989.[8] The decline in the number of young people reduced the demand for jeans—the demand schedule shifted to the left. An increase in the number of elderly people in the same time period increased the demand for medical care, retirement housing, and vacation travel, shifting the demand for these goods to the right.

5. Changes in Consumer Preferences.
Why do preferences change? Preferences change because people learn and change. Consider how consumers responded in the 1980s to new medical information linking certain fats and oils to heart disease. They purchased less of such products as whole milk, butter, and beef, which were thought to be dangerous, and increased their demand for such goods as olive oil and canola oil, thought to be much more "heart-healthy." Sales of olive oil doubled between 1984 and 1989, while canola oil sales doubled between 1988 and 1990. Consumption of butterfat fell at the same time. By 1995, Americans ate 25 percent less beef than they had in 1970. As consumers became more aware of the health implications of their diet, their preferences changed, shifting the demand for various foods.

Substitutes
Products that are related such that an increase in the price of one will cause an increase in demand for the other (for example, butter and margarine, Chevrolets and Fords).

Complements
Products that are usually consumed jointly (for example, coffee and nondairy creamer), so that a decrease in the price of one will cause a rise in demand for the other.

---

[8]These figures are from Suzanne Tregarthen, "Market for Jeans Shrinks," *The Margin* 6, no. 3 (January–February 1991), p. 28.

THUMBNAIL SKETCH

A CHANGE IN THIS FACTOR WILL CAUSE THE *QUANTITY DEMANDED* (BUT NOT *DEMAND*) TO CHANGE:

1. The current price of the product

CHANGES IN THESE FACTORS WILL CAUSE THE ENTIRE *DEMAND* CURVE TO SHIFT:

1. Consumer income
2. Distribution of consumer income
3. Price of related products (substitutes and complements)
4. Market demographics (population in the market)
5. Consumer preferences
6. Expectations about the future price of a product

---

6. Changes in the Expected Future Price of a Good. When consumers expect the future price of a product to rise, their current demand for it will expand. "Buy now, before the price goes even higher" becomes the order of the day. When the price of coffee rose sharply in 1986, how did shoppers respond? Current sales increased as consumers hoarded the product because they expected its price to continue rising. The converse of this maxim would be consumers' delaying a purchase if they expected the item to decrease in price. Current demand would be lower as a result of such expectations.

The accompanying Thumbnail Sketch points out that *quantity demanded* (but not demand) will change in response to a change in the price of a product. It also summarizes the major factors that cause a change in *demand*—a shift of the entire demand schedule.

DETERMINANTS OF SPECIFIC PREFERENCES—WHY CONSUMERS BUY WHAT THEY BUY

Did you ever wonder why a friend spent hard-earned money on something that you would not want even if it were free? Tastes differ, and, as we have already shown, they influence demand. What determines preferences? Why do people like one thing but not another? Economists have not been able to explain very much about how preferences are determined. The best strategy has generally been to take preferences as given, using price and other demand-related factors to explain and predict human behavior. Still, two observations about what influences consumer preferences have been made:

1. The determining factors in consumer preferences are frequently complex. People looking for a house want far more than just a shelter: They want an attractive setting, a convenient location, higher quality public services, and a great many other things. Moreover, each person may evaluate the same housing attribute differently. For example, living near a school may be a high priority for a family with children but a nuisance to a retired couple.

2. Advertising is a strong influence on consumer preferences. Advertisers would not spend more than $100 billion in the United States each year if they did not get results. But exactly how does advertising affect consumers? Does it simply provide valuable information about product quality, price, and availability? Or, does it use repetition and misleading information to manipulate consumers? Economists are not of one opinion. Let us take a closer look at this important issue.

ADVERTISING—HOW USEFUL IS IT?

One might ask, how did the 1995 advertising expenditures of more than $160 billion in the United States benefit consumers? Advertising is often used as a sponsoring medium, reducing the purchase price of newspapers, magazines, and television viewing. But since the consumers of the advertised products indirectly pay for these benefits, advertising cannot be defended solely on the basis of its sponsorship role.

Advertising does convey information about product price, quality, and availability. New firms or those with new products, new hours, new locations, or new services can use advertising to keep consumers informed, thus facilitating trade and increasing efficiency. After all, people who do not know the advantages of the newly available product or service, or the details of its availability, are not likely to become customers. But what about those repetitious television commercials that offer little or no new information? Critics charge that this type of advertising is wasteful, misleading, and manipulative. Let us look at each of these charges.

IS ADVERTISING WASTEFUL? A great deal of media advertising simply seems to say, "We are better," without providing supportive evidence. An advertiser may wish to take customers from a competitor or establish a brand name for a product. A multimillion-dollar media campaign by a soap, cigarette, or automobile manufacturer designed to capture a larger market share may largely be offset by a similar campaign waged by a competitor. The consumers of these products end up paying the costs of these battles for their attention and their dollars. We must remember, though, that consumers are under no obligation to purchase advertised products. If advertising results in higher prices with no compensating benefits, consumers can turn to cheaper, unadvertised products. And this fact leads to another question: How can brand names, especially when they are created by competing advertising campaigns, possibly benefit consumers?

A brand name in which people have confidence, even if it has been established by advertising, has a function beyond gaining the attention of consumers. It is an asset at risk for the seller. People value buying from sellers in whom they have confidence, and will pay a premium to do so. That premium makes a brand name valuable. If something happens to damage the reputation of a brand name, the willingness of consumers to purchase the product falls. In a very real sense, the brand name is hostage to consumer satisfaction.

When brand names are not allowed, as in the case of alcoholic beverages during Prohibition, consumers often suffer. For example, with no brand name reputations to protect, anonymous moonshiners sometimes were careless and allowed dangerous impurities into the brew. Some consumers were blinded, and others died. Today the situation is different. Those who buy Johnnie Walker scotch know that the distiller has an enormous sum of money tied up in the brand. In fact, *Financial World* magazine estimated that, in 1992, the Johnnie Walker Red brand name was worth $2.6 billion.[9] The Guinness Corporation, owner of the brand, would spend a large amount of money to avoid even one death from an impure batch. And this brand's value is dwarfed by many others. The Marlboro brand had an estimated value of $31.2 billion at one time, and Coca-Cola's brand value has been estimated at $24.4 billion. Is a brand name, promoted by costly advertising, worthwhile to the customer? In a market, each customer decides whether to pay the premium for the brand name.

IS ADVERTISING MISLEADING? Unfair and deceptive advertising—including false promises, whether spoken by a seller or packaged by an advertising agency—is illegal under the Federal Trade Commission Act. The fact that a publicly advertised false claim is easier to establish and prosecute than the same words spoken in private is an argument for freedom in advertising. But what about general, unsupported claims that a product is superior to the alternatives or that it will help a person enjoy life more? Some believe that such noninformational advertising should be prohibited. They would establish a government agency to evaluate the "informativeness" of advertising. But if consumers are misled by slick advertisers to part with their money without good reason, might they also be misled by a slick media campaign to support politicians and regulatory policies that are not in their interest? Yet, no one suggests outlawing "noninformational" political campaigns. Why should we expect consumers to make poor decisions under the influence of advertising when they make market choices, but wise decisions when they act in the political (and regulatory) arena, where advertising is also important? Clearly, additional regulation is not a cure-all. Like freedom in advertising, it has some defects.

DOES ADVERTISING MANIPULATE CONSUMERS? The demand for some products would surely be much lower without advertising. Some people's preferences may, in fact, be shaped by advertising. However, in evaluating the manipulative effect of advertising, we must keep two things in mind. First, business decision makers are likely to choose the simplest route to economic gain. Generally, it is easier for business firms to cater to the actual desires of consumers than to attempt to reshape their preferences or persuade them to purchase an undesired product. Second, even if advertising does influence preferences, does

---

[9]This and 41 additional *Financial World* estimates of brand-name values were reported in *USA Today*, August 12, 1992, p. 7B.

it follow that this is bad? College classes in music and art appreciation, for example, may also change preferences for various forms of art and music. Does this make them bad? Economic theory is neutral. It neither condemns nor defends advertising—or college classes—as they try to change the tastes of target audiences.

ELASTICITY OF DEMAND

In Chapter 3, we discussed how buyers and sellers respond when price changes. Buyers will predictably demand fewer units when the price rises, while sellers will predictably be willing to sell more. But these responses might be large or small, depending on such factors as the availability of substitutes for buyers and the cost of production for sellers, as well as the time available for adjustments. How responsive will consumers be to a specific change in the price of a good? How many more units will producers supply if the price of a good increases? If a tax is levied on the sale of an item, how much will the price rise as a result? The answers to these questions are important for predicting the changes in a market when circumstances change. To find answers, we must estimate the responses of buyers and sellers to the change that is being examined.

To quantify the responsiveness of consumers and producers to a change in price, economists have developed a concept called *elasticity*. In fact, the term *elasticity* means "responsiveness." If consumers are highly responsive to a change in price—for example, if the amount purchased by consumers declines sharply in response to a price increase—demand is said to be elastic. In contrast, if a substantial increase in price results only in a small reduction in quantity demanded, the demand is inelastic.

Price elasticity of demand is defined as

$$\frac{\text{Percent change in quantity demanded}}{\text{Percent change in price}}$$

Price elasticity of demand
The percent change in the quantity of a product demanded divided by the percent change in the price causing the change in quantity. Price elasticity of demand indicates the degree of consumer response to variation in price.

This ratio is called the *elasticity coefficient*. (Although the sign of the coefficient for price elasticity of demand is often ignored, it is always negative, since a change in price causes the quantity demanded to change in the opposite direction.) To calculate the elasticity coefficient, we begin with a price change, say from P_0 to P_1, which causes a change in quantity demanded, from Q_0 to Q_1. The change in quantity demanded is $Q_0 - Q_1$. Therefore, the *percent* change in quantity demanded, using the average of the two quantities as a basis,[10] is

$$\frac{Q_0 - Q_1}{(Q_0 + Q_1)/2} \times 100.$$

---

[10]This formula uses the average of the starting point and the ending point of the change so that it will give the same result whether we start from the lower or the higher price. This *arc* elasticity formula is not the only way to calculate elasticity, but it is the most frequently used.

Similarly, when the change in price is $P_0 - P_1$, the *percent* change in price is

$$\frac{P_0 - P_1}{(P_0 + P_1)/2} \times 100.$$

Dividing the percent change in quantity by the percent change in price gives us

$$\frac{(Q_0 - Q_1)/(Q_0 + Q_1)}{(P_0 - P_1)/(P_0 + P_1)}$$

(Note that, since each term within brackets is multiplied by 100 and the denominator of each term contains a 2, these factors offset each other and we can ignore them.)

A numerical example may help to illustrate the use of this formula to calculate price elasticity of demand. Suppose that Trina's Cakes can sell 50 specialty cakes per week at $7 each, or 70 of the cakes at $6 each. The elasticity coefficient for these cakes is

$$\frac{[(50 - 70)/(50 + 70)]}{[(7 - 6)/(7 + 6)]} = \frac{-20/120}{1/13} = \frac{-1/6}{1/13} = \frac{-13}{6} = -2.17$$

indicating that the percentage change in quantity is more than twice the percentage change in price.

The elasticity coefficient permits us to make a precise distinction between elastic and inelastic. When the elasticity coefficient is greater than 1 (ignoring the sign), as it was for the demand for Trina's Cakes, demand is elastic. When it is less than 1, demand is inelastic. *Unitary elasticity* is the term used to denote a price elasticity of 1.

GRAPHIC REPRESENTATION OF PRICE ELASTICITY OF DEMAND

Exhibit 17–5 presents demand curves of varying elasticity. A demand curve that is completely vertical is termed *perfectly inelastic*. In the real world, such a demand is nonexistent. Since any good has substitutes that become more attractive as the price of that good rises, and since the income effect is also present, we should expect that a higher price will always reduce quantity demanded, other things the same. Still, the (mythical) perfectly inelastic demand curve is shown in part a of Exhibit 17–5.

The more inelastic the demand, the steeper the demand curve *over any specific price range*. Inspection of the demand for cigarettes (part b of Exhibit 17–5), which is highly inelastic, and the demand for apples (part d), which is relatively elastic, indicates that the inelastic curve tends to be steeper. When demand elasticity is unitary, as part c illustrates, a demand curve that is convex to the origin will result. When a demand curve is completely horizontal, an economist would say that it is *perfectly elastic*. Demand for the wheat of a single wheat farmer, for example, would approximate perfect elasticity (part e).

Because elasticity is a relative concept, the elasticity of a straight-line demand curve will differ at each point along the line. As **Exhibit 17–6** illustrates, the elas-

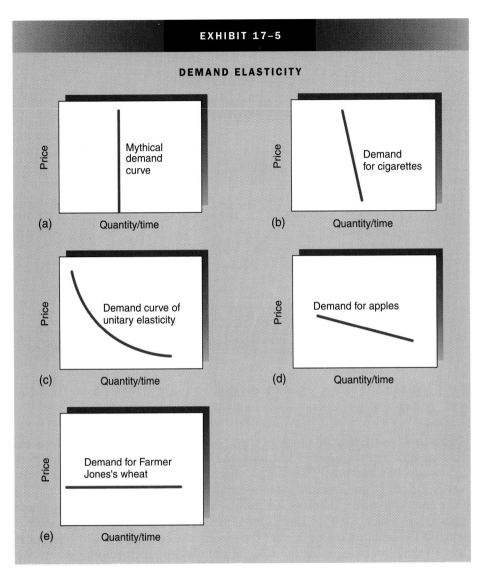

EXHIBIT 17–5

DEMAND ELASTICITY

(a) Price / Quantity/time — Mythical demand curve

(b) Price / Quantity/time — Demand for cigarettes

(c) Price / Quantity/time — Demand curve of unitary elasticity

(d) Price / Quantity/time — Demand for apples

(e) Price / Quantity/time — Demand for Farmer Jones's wheat

(a) *Perfectly inelastic:* Despite an increase in price, consumers still purchase the same amount. In fact, the substitution and income effects prevent this from happening in the real world.
(b) *Relatively inelastic:* A percent increase in price results in a smaller percent reduction in sales. The demand for cigarettes has been estimated to be highly inelastic.
(c) *Unitary elasticity:* The percent change in quantity demanded is equal to the percent change in price. A curve of decreasing slope results. Sales revenue (price times quantity sold) is constant.
(d) *Relatively elastic:* A percent increase in price leads to a larger percent reduction in purchases. When good substitutes are available for a product (as in the case of apples), the amount purchased will be highly sensitive to a change in price.
(e) *Perfectly elastic:* Consumers will buy all of Farmer Jone's wheat at the market price, but none will be sold above the market price.

ticity of a straight-line demand curve (one with a constant slope) will range from highly elastic to highly inelastic. Here, when the price rises from $10 to $11, sales decline from 20 to 10. According to the *arc elasticity formula,* the price elasticity of demand is –7.0. Demand is very elastic in this region. In contrast, demand is quite inelastic in the $1 to $2 price range. As the price increases from $1 to $2, the amount demanded declines from 110 to 100. The arc elasticity of demand in this range is only –0.14; demand is highly inelastic.

Why do we bother with elasticity? Why not talk only about the slope of a demand curve? We use elasticities because they are independent of the units of measure. Whether we talk about dollars per gallon or cents per liter, the elasticities, given in percentages, remain the same. This is appropriate because people do not care what units of measurement are used; their response depends on the actual terms of exchange.

With this straight-line (constant-slope) demand curve, demand is more elastic in the high-price range. The formula for arc elasticity shows that, when price rises from $1 to $2 and quantity falls from 110 to 100, demand is inelastic. A price rise of the same magnitude (but of a smaller percentage), from $10 to $11, leads to a decline in quantity of the same size (but of a larger percentage), so that elasticity is much greater. (Price elasticities are negative, but we typically ignore the sign and look only at the absolute value.)

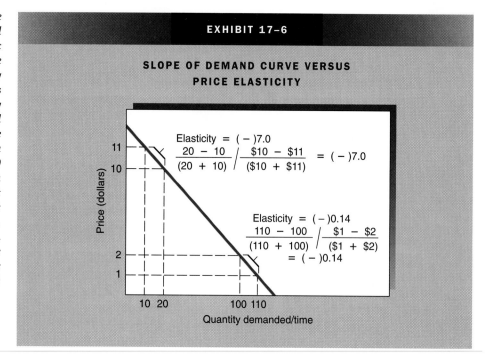

EXHIBIT 17–6

SLOPE OF DEMAND CURVE VERSUS PRICE ELASTICITY

Elasticity $= (-)7.0$

$$\frac{20 - 10}{(20 + 10)} \bigg/ \frac{\$10 - \$11}{(\$10 + \$11)} = (-)7.0$$

Elasticity $= (-)0.14$

$$\frac{110 - 100}{(110 + 100)} \bigg/ \frac{\$1 - \$2}{(\$1 + \$2)} = (-)0.14$$

DETERMINANTS OF PRICE ELASTICITY OF DEMAND

Economists have estimated the price elasticity of demand for many products. As the estimates of **Exhibit 17–7** illustrate, the elasticity of demand among products varies substantially. The demand for several products—salt, toothpicks, matches, light bulbs, and newspapers, for example—is highly inelastic. On the other hand, the demand curves for fresh tomatoes, Chevrolet automobiles, and fresh green peas are highly elastic. What factors explain this variation? Why is demand for some products, but not for others, highly responsive to changes in price? The answer lies primarily in the availability of good substitutes and also to some extent on the share of the typical consumer's total budget expended on a product.

AVAILABILITY OF SUBSTITUTES. *The most important determinant of the price elasticity of demand is the availability of substitutes. When good substitutes for a product are available, a price rise induces many consumers to switch to other products. Demand is elastic.* For example, if the price of felt-tip pens increased, many consumers would simply switch to pencils or ballpoint pens. If the price of apples increased, consumers would substitute oranges, bananas, peaches, pears, and several other products for the more expensive apples.

When good substitutes are unavailable, the demand for a product tends to be inelastic. Medical services are an example. When we are sick, most of us find witch doctors, faith healers, palm readers, and cod-liver oil to be highly imperfect substitutes for the services of a physician. Not surprisingly, the demand for physician services is inelastic.

Sources: Hendrick S. Houthakker and Lester D. Taylor, *Consumer Demand in the United States, 1929–1970* (Cambridge: Harvard University Press, 1966, 1970); Douglas R. Bohi, *Analyzing Demand Behavior* (Baltimore: Johns Hopkins University Press, 1981); Hsaing-tai Cheng and Oral Capps, Jr., "Demand for Fish," *American Journal of Agricultural Economics*, August 1988; and U.S. Department of Agriculture.

EXHIBIT 17–7

ESTIMATED PRICE ELASTICITY OF DEMAND FOR SELECTED PRODUCTS

INELASTIC		APPROXIMATELY UNITARY ELASTICITY	
Salt	0.1	Movies	0.9
Matches	0.1	Housing, owner occupied, long run	1.2
Toothpicks	0.1		
Airline travel, short run	0.1	Shellfish, consumed at home	0.9
Gasoline, short run	0.2		
Gasoline, long run	0.7	Oysters, consumed at home	1.1
Residential natural gas, short run	0.1		
		Private education	1.1
Residential natural gas, long run	0.5	Tires, short run	0.9
		Tires, long run	1.2
Coffee	0.25	Radio and television receivers	1.2
Fish (cod), consumed at home	0.5		
Tobacco products, short run	0.45	**ELASTIC**	
		Restaurant meals	2.3
Legal services, short run	0.4	Foreign travel, long run	4.0
Physician services	0.6	Airline travel, long run	2.4
Taxi, short run	0.6	Fresh green peas	2.8
Automobiles, long run	0.2	Automobiles, short run	1.2–1.5
		Chevrolet automobiles	4.0
		Fresh tomatoes	4.6

The availability of substitutes increases as the product class becomes more specific, thus increasing price elasticity. For example, as Exhibit 17–7 shows, the price elasticity of Chevrolets, a narrow product class, exceeds that of the broad class of automobiles in general. If the price of Chevrolets alone rises, many substitute cars are available. But if the prices of all automobiles rise together, consumers have fewer good substitutes.

SHARE OF TOTAL BUDGET EXPENDED ON PRODUCT. If the expenditures on a product are quite small relative to the consumer's budget, the income effect will be small even if there is a substantial increase in the price of the product. This will make demand less elastic. Compared to one's total budget, expenditures on some commodities are almost inconsequential. Matches, toothpicks, and salt are good examples. Most consumers spend only $1 or $2 per year on each of these items. A doubling of their price would exert little influence on the family budget. Therefore, even if the price of such a product were to rise sharply, consumers would still not find it in their interest to spend much time and effort looking for substitutes.

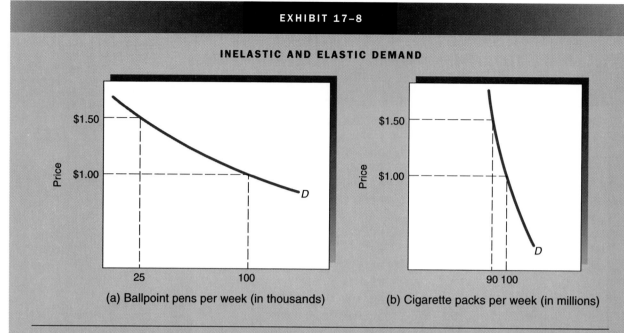

EXHIBIT 17–8

INELASTIC AND ELASTIC DEMAND

(a) Ballpoint pens per week (in thousands)

(b) Cigarette packs per week (in millions)

As the price of ballpoint pens (a) rose from $1.00 to $1.50, the quantity purchased plunged from 100,000 to 25,000. The percent reduction in quantity is larger than the percent increase in price. Thus, the demand for the pens is elastic. In contrast, an increase in the price of cigarettes from $1.00 to $1.50 results in only a small reduction in the number purchased (b). Reflecting the inelasticity of demand for cigarettes, the percent reduction in quantity is smaller than the percent increase in price.

Exhibit 17–8 provides a graphic illustration for both elastic and inelastic demand curves. In part a the demand curve for ballpoint pens is elastic, because there are good substitutes—for example, pencils and felt-tip pens. Therefore, when the price of the pens increases by 50 percent from $1.00 to $1.50, the quantity purchased declines sharply from 100,000 to only 25,000. The price elasticity coefficient calculated by the *arc elasticity method* will equal −3.0. The fact that the absolute value of the coefficient is greater than 1 confirms that the demand for ballpoint pens is elastic over the price range illustrated. Part b of Exhibit 17–8 illustrates the demand curve for cigarettes. Because most consumers do not find other products to be a good substitute, the demand for cigarettes is highly inelastic. In the case of cigarettes, a substantial (from $1.00 to $1.50) increase in price leads to only a small reduction in quantity demanded. The price elasticity coefficient is .26, substantially less than 1, confirming that the demand for cigarettes is inelastic.

TIME AND DEMAND ELASTICITY

As changing market conditions raise or lower the price of a product, both consumers and producers will respond. However, their response will not be instantaneous, and it is likely to become larger over time. *In general, when the price of a product increases, consumers will reduce their consumption by a larger amount in the long run than in the short run. Thus, the demand for most products will be more elastic in the long run than in the short run. This relationship between the elasticity coefficient and the length of the adjustment time period is often referred to as the second law of demand.*

The first law of demand says that buyers will respond predictably to a price change, purchasing more when the price is lower than when the price is higher, if other things remain the same. The second law of demand says that the buyers' response will be greater after they have had time to adjust more fully to a price change.

TOTAL EXPENDITURES AND DEMAND ELASTICITY

Price elasticity determines the relationship between a change in price and the resulting change in total expenditure on the product. Expenditures (which are revenues, from the sellers' point of view) amount to the price paid, multiplied by the quantity purchased.

When demand is inelastic, the percent change in unit sales is less than the percent change in price. Under these circumstances, the price change will have a greater impact on total expenditures than the quantity change. As a result, total expenditures will change in the same direction as price, when demand is inelastic. The inelastic market demand curve for cigarettes shown in Exhibit 17–8b can be used to illustrate this point. The increase in cigarette price leads to an increase in expenditures on the product from $100 million ($1 × 100 million packs) to $135 million ($1.50 × 90 million packs). Reflecting the inelastic demand for cigarettes, the price increase causes expenditures to change in the same direction.

When demand is elastic, the percent change in quantity purchased exceeds the percent change in price. Thus, the larger relative change in quantity will dominate, causing total expenditures to move in the opposite direction from the change in price. The elastic demand for ballpoint pens, shown in panel a of Exhibit 17–8, illustrates this point. Notice the price increase ($1 to $1.50) leads to a much larger percentage decline in quantity purchased (from 100,000 to 25,000). Reflecting the elastic demand, the price increase reduces revenue from $100,000 ($1 × 100,000 pens) to only $37,500 ($1.50 × 25,000 pens).

Exhibit 17–9 summarizes the relationship between changes in price and total expenditures, for demand curves of varying elasticity. *When demand is inelastic, a change in price will cause total expenditures to change in the same direction. If demand is elastic, price and total expenditures will change in opposite directions. For unitary elasticity, total expenditures will remain constant as price changes.*

INCOME ELASTICITY

As we previously discussed, increases in income will increase the demand for most goods. **Income elasticity** indicates the responsiveness of the demand for a product to a change in income. It is defined as:

Income elasticity
The percent change in the quantity of a product demanded divided by the percent change in consumer income causing the change in quantity demanded. It measures the responsiveness of the demand for a good to a change in income. The sign of the elasticity coefficient is usually positive.

[a]The sign of the elasticity coefficient is negative.

EXHIBIT 17-9

DEMAND ELASTICITY, CHANGE IN PRICE, AND CHANGE IN TOTAL EXPENDITURES

PRICE ELASTICITY OF DEMAND	NUMERICAL ELASTICITY COEFFICIENT[a]	IMPACT OF CHANGE IN PRICE ON TOTAL EXPENDITURES
Elastic	1 to ∞	Price and total expenditures change in opposite directions.
Unitary	1	Total expenditures remain constant as price changes.
Inelastic	0 to 1	Price and total expenditures change in the same direction.

$$\frac{\text{Percent change in quantity demanded}}{\text{Percent change in income}}$$

As **Exhibit 17–10** shows, although the income elasticity coefficients for products vary from one good to another, they are normally positive. In fact, the term **normal good** refers to any good with a positive income elasticity of demand. Some normal goods have lower income elasticities than others. In general, goods that people regard as "necessities" will have low income elasticities. Significant quantities are purchased even at low incomes, and, as income increases, spending on these items will increase by less than a proportional amount. It is understandable that such items as fuel, electricity, bread, tobacco, economy clothing, and potatoes have a low income elasticity. Interestingly, jewelry falls into this

Normal good
A good that has a positive income elasticity, so that, as consumer incomes rises, demand for that good rises also.

Sources: Hendrik S. Houthakker and Lester D. Taylor, *Consumer Demand in the United States, 1929–1970* (Cambridge: Harvard University Press, 1966); L. Taylor, "The Demand for Electricity: A Survey," *Bell Journal of Economics* (spring 1975); and F. W. Bell, "The Pope and the Price of Fish," *American Economic Review* 58 (December 1968).

EXHIBIT 17-10

ESTIMATED INCOME ELASTICITY OF DEMAND FOR SELECTED PRODUCTS

LOW INCOME ELASTICITY		HIGH INCOME ELASTICITY	
Margarine	−0.20	Private education	2.46
Fuel	0.38	New cars	2.45
Electricity	0.20	Recreation and amusements	1.57
Fish (haddock)	0.46	Alcohol	1.54
Food	0.51		
Tobacco	0.64		
Hospital care	0.69		

category, at least in the United States. The Consumer Expenditure Survey of the U.S. Department of Labor reports that the poorest fifth of all households reporting income in 1991 spent $536 (4 percent) of their $13,464 total expenditures on jewelry, while jewelry purchases claimed only 2 percent ($1,133) of the $57,597 spent on average by the richest fifth.

Goods that consumers regard as "luxuries" generally have a high (greater than 1) income elasticity. For example, private education, new automobiles, recreational activities, donations to environmental groups, swimming pools, and air travel are all highly income elastic. As income increases, the demand for these goods thus expands even more rapidly.

A few commodities, such as margarine, low-quality meat cuts, and bus travel, actually have a negative income elasticity. Economists refer to goods with a negative income elasticity as **inferior goods.** As income expands, the demand for inferior goods will decline.

Inferior good
A good that has a negative income elasticity, so that, as consumer incomes rise, the demand for that good falls.

USING THE CONCEPT OF ELASTICITY—THE BURDEN OF A TAX

When a tax is placed on the sale of a good, who pays it? How much does the price rise? How much is paid by the seller (in the form of accepting a lower amount, net of tax), rather than being passed on to the customer through a price increase? When the price of a good rises, we have seen that the effect on revenue and sales depends on the price elasticity of demand. In determining the relative burden of a tax, price elasticity again plays a major role.

Sellers would like to pass the entire tax on to buyers, raising the price by the full amount of the tax, rather than paying any part of it themselves. However, as the price rises, customers respond by purchasing less. Sales decline, and sellers must then lower their price toward its pretax level, accepting part of the tax burden themselves by receiving less revenue. In Chapter 5 we learned that, when taxes raise the amount paid by consumers and reduce the *net* (after-tax) price received by sellers, both buyer and seller share in the tax burden. Using the concept of elasticity, we can now say more about how the burden is divided and the size of the deadweight loss associated with the tax. (Now would be a good time for the reader to review the Issues of Efficiency and Equity section, pages 122–125.)

Exhibits 17–11 through 17–13 illustrate the results of a new tax on gasoline. **Exhibit 17–11** shows the results in the short run, when the price elasticity of demand is only 0.2. **Exhibit 17–12** shows the results in the long run, when demand elasticity is 0.7. In order to demonstrate what happens when demand elasticity changes but supply is the same, in Exhibit 17–12 we temporarily assume the same supply curve applies in the long run as in the short run.

In Exhibit 17–11 the equilibrium price of gasoline before the new tax is $1 per gallon. The $.20 tax shifts the supply upward by the amount of the tax. Because they must turn over $.20 to the government for each gallon sold, sellers must receive the old price plus $.20 per gallon in order to maintain their prior incentive to produce. This is precisely what happens when the pretax supply curve is shifted vertically by the $.20 tax.

When a $.20 gasoline tax is imposed, the supply curve shifts vertically by the amount of the tax. Since consumers will buy less as the price increases, sellers will not be able to pass all of the tax along to consumers. The new short-run equilibrium will be at a price of $1.15. As the result of the tax, consumers pay $.15 more and sellers receive $.05 less.

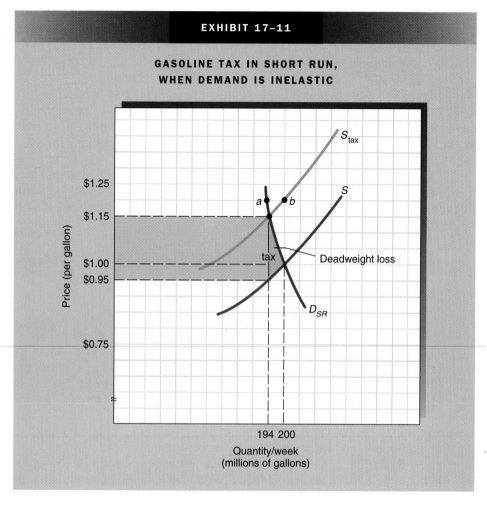

EXHIBIT 17–11

GASOLINE TAX IN SHORT RUN, WHEN DEMAND IS INELASTIC

Of course, sellers would like to raise prices to $1.20 and pass the entire amount of the tax on to motorists. However, they will be unable to do so, since motorists will reduce their purchases in response to higher prices. If the price of gasoline rose to $1.20, then an excess supply (*ab* in Exhibit 17–11) would result. Only at a lower price will the market clear, so sellers are able to increase the price to only $1.15, where they are able to sell 194 million gallons, 6 million fewer than before the tax was imposed. *Short-run equilibrium* is present at that price ($1.15) and output (194 million). In the short run, the buyers pay $.15 more, and the seller receives $.05 less per gallon.

There are relatively few ways that buyers can substitute away from the more expensive gasoline in the short run. Because their responsiveness—the price elasticity of their demand—is relatively small in the short run, consumers shoulder most of the tax burden.

In the long run, though, consumers will shift to smaller cars and find other ways to economize on the more expensive gasoline. As consumer purchases decline by a larger amount, sellers must further decrease the price they will accept (reducing the quantity they will supply). As Exhibit 17–12 illustrates, in the long run the equilibrium price will decline to $1.10, and quantity exchanged

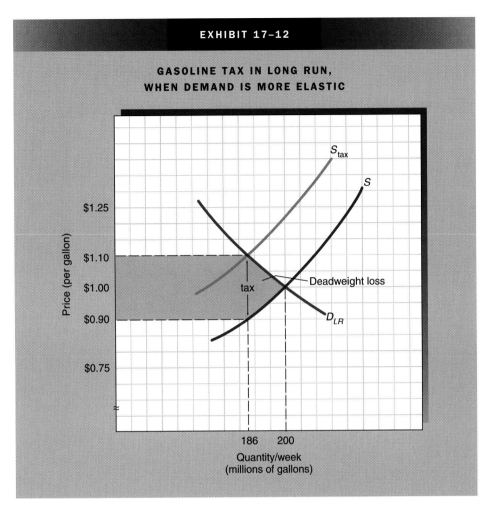

EXHIBIT 17–12

**GASOLINE TAX IN LONG RUN,
WHEN DEMAND IS MORE ELASTIC**

When demand is more elastic, consumers reduce their purchases by greater amounts. As a result, sellers must reduce price further [to $1.10 in this case, compared with $1.15 in Exhibit 17–11], and the tax burden falls more heavily on sellers, due to the greater demand elasticity. Here we assume that supply is unchanged.

will fall to 186 million gallons per week. In this case, buyers and sellers divide the burden of the $.20 tax equally. *Comparing Exhibit 17–11 with Exhibit 17–12 where supply is the same but the elasticities of demand differ, we can see that, when demand is more elastic, ceteris paribus, buyers pay a smaller share of the tax burden.* This makes good intuitive sense. When consumers find more ways to economize—when they reduce their purchases more in response to the higher price—in the long run, they put more pressure on sellers to lower the price they will accept.

Exhibit 17–13 introduces the other factor determining the burden of a tax: the **elasticity of supply,** which is the percent change in quantity supplied, divided by the percent change in the price causing the supplier response. Since this measures the responsiveness of sellers to a change in price, it is analogous to the price elasticity of demand. The elasticity of supply, however, is positive. When the price at which they can sell a product rises, suppliers will be willing and able to purchase more resources and to supply more of the product. A fall in price will bring the opposite response, as some sellers find better uses for their resources at a lower product price. As in the case of demand elasticity, time plays a role. Supply elasticities will be greater when suppliers have a longer time to

Elasticity of supply
The percent change in quantity supplied, divided by the percent change in the price causing that change in quantity supplied.

Supply is more elastic when resources have other good alternative uses, so that suppliers are less willing to reduce the price they receive in response to a tax. Instead, quantity supplied is reduced by a greater amount. The price to consumers rises from $1.00 to $1.15. Compared with Exhibit 17–12, where demand is the same as that shown here, the greater supply elasticity here causes less of the tax burden to be placed on suppliers.

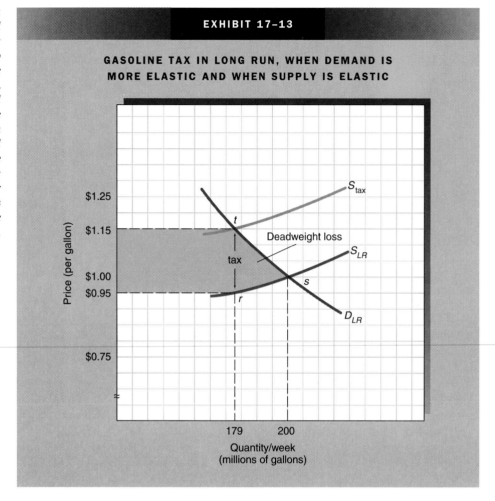

EXHIBIT 17-13

GASOLINE TAX IN LONG RUN, WHEN DEMAND IS MORE ELASTIC AND WHEN SUPPLY IS ELASTIC

respond to a price change. In the next two chapters we will discuss more fully the factors that determine supply elasticity. For now, it is important simply to recognize the concept of supply elasticity and the fact that suppliers (like buyers) will be more responsive to a price change when they have had more time to adjust to it.

Earlier, in going from Exhibit 17–11 to Exhibit 17–12, we allowed demand to become more elastic, since Exhibit 17–12 represented the long run. However, we unrealistically assumed that the elasticity of supply was the same in the long run as in the short run in order to isolate what would happen if only demand changed. Exhibit 17–13 shows the more realistic case in which supply, like demand, is more elastic in the long run. By comparing Exhibits 17–12 and 17–13, we can see that when supply elasticity is greater (and demand is the same), a smaller share of the tax burden is borne by suppliers. Here, supply is drawn so the gasoline price, tax included, happens to rise to $1.15, just as it did in the short-run case. That would not necessarily be the case in the real world. **In general, however, when supply is more elastic, ceteris paribus, suppliers will bear a smaller part of the tax burden.**

ELASTICITY AND THE DEADWEIGHT LOSS CAUSED BY A TAX

We have seen that elasticity of supply and demand plays an important part in determining how the burden of a tax is distributed between buyer and seller. Exhibits 17–11 through 17–13 also illustrate how these elasticities influence the size of the excess burden, or *deadweight loss,* caused by the tax. As we saw in Chapter 5 (Exhibit 5–7, page 124), reducing trade by taxing it not only transfers revenue (amount of the tax per unit, multiplied by the number of units sold after the tax) from buyers and sellers to the government, but it also reduces the gains from trade for both buyers and sellers by the transferred amount, plus somewhat more. Trades that would have taken place in the absence of the tax are eliminated. When either demand or supply is inelastic, meaning that few trades are discouraged by imposition of the tax, the excess burden is smaller. Exhibit 17–11 illustrates this point in the case of a highly inelastic demand. Since demand is highly inelastic, the quantity of gasoline traded declines by only 6 million gallons as the result of the $.20 tax.

In contrast, when both demand and supply are elastic, as in Exhibit 17–13, more trades are prevented by the tax. Given the more elastic demand and supply curves of Exhibit 17–13, the quantity of gasoline produced and sold declines by 21 million gallons (from 200 million to 179 million). As the triangle *rst* illustrates, the excess burden of a tax increases as the higher tax cuts off more exchanges. Therefore, the burden of excise taxes will be less if they are levied on goods and services for which either demand or supply is highly inelastic.

LOOKING AHEAD

In this chapter, we outlined the mechanism by which consumers' wants and tastes are communicated to producers. Consumer choices underlie the market demand curve. The market demand indicates how strongly consumers desire each good or service. In the following chapter, we turn to costs of production that arise because resources have alternative uses. In fact, the cost of producing a good tells the producer how badly the resources are desired in other areas. An understanding of these two topics—consumer demand and cost of production—is essential if we are to understand how markets allocate goods and resources.

CHAPTER SUMMARY

1. The demand schedule indicates the amount of a good that consumers would be willing to buy at each po-tential price. The *first law of demand* states that the quantity of a product demanded is inversely related to its price. A reduction in the price of a product reduces the opportunity cost of consuming it. At the lower price, many consumers will substitute the now cheaper good for other products. In contrast, a higher price will induce consumers to buy less as they turn to substitutes that are now *relatively* cheaper.

2. The market demand curve reflects the demand of individuals. It is simply the horizontal sum of the demand curves of individuals in that particular market. The market price is a marginal valuation, not an average valuation of the item.

3. Time, like money, is scarce for consumers. Consumers consider both time and money costs when they make decisions. Other things constant, a reduction in the time cost of consuming a good will induce consumers to purchase more of the good.

4. Consumers usually gain from the purchase of a good. The difference between the largest amount that

consumers would be willing to pay for each unit of a good and the amount they actually pay is the consumer surplus. It is measured by the area under the demand curve but above the market price.

5. In addition to price, the demand for a product is influenced (shifted) by the (a) level of consumer income, (b) distribution of income among consumers, (c) cost of obtaining related products (substitutes and complements), (d) size and composition of the population in the market, (e) preferences of consumers, and (f) consumer expectations about the future price of the product. Changes in any of these six factors will cause the *demand* for the product to change (the entire curve to shift).

6. Both functional and subjective factors influence the demand for a product, including advertising. The effect of advertising on consumer decisions is difficult to quantify. The advertising budgets of profit-seeking business firms are strong evidence, though, that advertising significantly influences consumer decisions. Advertising can reduce the search time of consumers, help them make more informed choices, and provide assurances with regard to quality (through brand names). However, a sizable share of all advertising expenditures is for messages with little informational content. It is clearly much easier to point out the shortcomings of advertising than to devise an alternative that would not have similar imperfections.

7. Price elasticity reveals the responsiveness of the amount purchased to a change in price. When there are good substitutes available and the item forms a sizable component of the consumer's budget, its demand will tend to be more elastic. Typically, the price elasticity of a product will increase as more time is allowed for consumers to adjust to the price change. This direct relationship between size of the elasticity coefficient and the length of the adjustment time period is often referred to as the *second law of demand*.

8. The concept of elasticity is useful in explaining the effects of a policy change, such as the imposition of a sales tax. When demand is more elastic, buyers bear less of the tax burden; when supply is more elastic, sellers bear less of the burden. When either is inelastic, the excess burden, or deadweight loss, of the tax is smaller.

CRITICAL ANALYSIS QUESTIONS

*1. What impact did the substantially lower gasoline prices of the mid-1980s have on the following?
   a. The demand for big cars
   b. The demand for small cars
   c. The incentive to experiment and to develop electric and other non-gas-powered cars
   d. The demand for gasoline (*be careful*)
   e. The demand for vacations by automobile in Florida

2. "As the price of beef rises, the demand of consumers will begin to decline. Economists estimate that a 5 percent rise in beef prices will cause demand to decline by 1 percent." Indicate the two errors in this statement.

*3. The accompanying chart presents data on the price of fuel oil, the amount of it demanded, and the demand for insulation.
   a. Calculate the price elasticity of demand for fuel oil as its price rises from 30 cents to 50 cents; from 50 cents to 70 cents.
   b. Are fuel oil and insulation substitutes or complements? How can you tell from the figures alone?

| | FUEL OIL | | INSULATION |
PRICE PER GALLON (CENTS)	QUANTITY DEMANDED (MILLIONS OF GALLONS)		QUANTITY DEMANDED (MILLIONS OF TONS)
30	100		30
50	90		35
70	60		40

4. Indicate five factors that would generally cause the demand schedule for beefsteak to increase. In each case, briefly explain why.

5. Residential electricity in the state of Washington costs about half as much as in nearby Montana. A study showed that in Washington, the average household used about 1200 kilowatt-hours per month, whereas Montanans used about half that much per household. Do these data provide us with two points on the average household's demand curve for residential electricity in this region? Why or why not?

*6. *What's wrong with this way of thinking?* "Economics is unable to explain the value of goods in a sensible manner. A quart of water is much cheaper than a quart of oil. Yet water is essential to both animal and plant life. Without it, we could not survive. How can oil be more valuable than water? Yet economics says that it is."

*7. The wealthy are widely believed to have more leisure time than the poor. However, even though we are a good deal wealthier today than our great-grandparents were 100 years ago, we appear to live more hectic lives and have less free time. Can you explain why?

8. What are the major determinants of a product's price elasticity of demand? Studies indicate that the demand for Florida oranges, Bayer aspirin, watermelons, and airfares to Europe are elastic. Why?

9. Most systems of medical insurance substantially reduce the costs to the consumer of using additional units of physician services and hospitalization. Some reduce these costs to zero. How does this method of payment affect the consumption levels of medical services? Might this method

of organization result in "too much" consumption of medical services? Discuss.

*10. Are the following statements true or false? Explain your answers.

    a. A 10 percent reduction in price that leads to a 15 percent increase in amount purchased indicates a price elasticity of more than 1.

    b. A 10 percent reduction in price that leads to a 2 percent increase in total expenditures indicates a price elasticity of more than 1.

    c. If the percent change in price is less than the resultant percent change in quantity demanded, demand is elastic.

*11. Respond to the following questions: If you really like pizza, should you try to consume as much pizza as possible? If you want to succeed, should you try to make the highest possible grade in your economics class?

*12. Sue loves ice cream but cannot stand frozen yogurt desserts. In contrast, Carole cannot tell the difference between ice cream and frozen yogurt desserts. Who will have the more elastic demand for yogurt?

*13. "If all the farmers reduced their output to one-half the current rate, farm incomes would increase, the total utility derived from farm output would rise, and the nation would be better off." Is this statement true or false? Explain your answer.

14. Can you think of any circumstances under which an increase in price might temporarily lead to an increase in amount purchased?

15. Can you think of any reason why the prices of shares of stock of a specific company, gold, and other commodities for which the supply is (approximately) fixed will fluctuate more than the prices of goods that are reproduceable at a constant cost?

*16. "Market competition encourages deceitful advertising and dishonesty." Is this statement true or false? Explain your answer.

*17. What is the nature of the deadweight loss accompanying sales taxes? Why is it often referred to as an "excess burden" of the tax?

18. The demand and supply curves for unskilled labor in a market are given in the accompanying table.

a. Find the equilibrium wage and number of workers hired.

b. What is the elasticity of the demand for workers at wages between $6.00 and $6.50 per hour? Is this in the elastic or inelastic portion of the demand curve?

c. What does this imply about what will happen to this firm's labor costs as wages increase from $6.00 to $6.50 per hour?

d. What is the elasticity of demand for workers at wages between $4.00 and $4.50 per hour? Is this in the elastic or inelastic portion of the demand curve?

e. What does this imply about what will happen to this firm's labor costs as wages increase from $4.00 to $4.50 per hour?

f. What happens to the elasticity of demand for workers as wages increase?

Suppose that a new law is passed requiring employers to pay an unemployment insurance tax of $1.50 per hour for every employee.

g. What happens to the equilibrium wage rate and number of workers hired?

h. How is this tax burden distributed between employers and workers?

Now suppose that, rather than being paid by the employers, the tax must be paid by workers.

i. How does this affect the equilibrium wage rate and number of workers hired?

j. How is this tax burden distributed between employers and workers?

k. Does it matter who pays the tax?

DEMAND		SUPPLY	
WAGE	QUANTITY DEMANDED	WAGE	QUANTITY SUPPLIED
$6.50	1,000	$6.50	1,900
$6.00	1,200	$6.00	1,800
$5.50	1,400	$5.50	1,700
$5.00	1,600	$5.00	1,600
$4.50	1,800	$4.50	1,500
$4.00	2,000	$4.00	1,400

_____

*Asterisk denotes questions for which answers are given in Appendix B.

ADDENDUM: CONSUMER CHOICE AND INDIFFERENCE CURVES

Indifference curve
A curve, convex from below, that separates the consumption bundles that are more preferred by an individual from those that are less preferred. The points on the curve represent combinations of goods that are equally preferred by the individual.

In the text of this chapter, we used marginal utility analysis to develop the demand curve of an individual. In developing the theory of consumer choice, economists usually rely on a more formal technique—**indifference curve** analysis. Since this technique is widely used at a more advanced level, many instructors like to include it in their introductory course. In this addendum, we use indifference curve analysis to develop the theory of demand in a more formal— some would say more elegant—manner.

WHAT ARE INDIFFERENCE CURVES?

There are two elements in every choice: (1) preferences (the desirability of various goods) and (2) opportunities (the attainability of various goods). The indifference curve relates to the former: preferences. It separates better (more preferred) bundles of goods from inferior (less preferred) bundles, providing a diagrammatic picture of how an individual ranks alternative consumption bundles.

In **Exhibit 17A–1,** we assume that Robinson Crusoe is initially consuming 8 fish and 8 breadfruit per week (point *A*). This initial bundle provides him with a certain level of satisfaction (utility). He would, however, be willing to trade this initial bundle for certain other consumption alternatives if the opportunity presented itself. Since he likes both fish and breadfruit, he would especially like to obtain bundles to the northeast of point *A,* since they represent more of both goods. However, he would also be willing to give up some breadfruit if in return he received a compensatory amount of fish. Similarly, if the terms of trade were right, he would be willing to exchange fish for breadfruit. The trade-offs he is just willing to make—those that would make him no better and no worse off— lie *along* the indifference curve. Of course, he is happy to move to any bundle on a higher indifference curve.

Starting from point *A* (8 fish and 8 breadfruit), we ask Crusoe if he is willing to trade that bundle for various other bundles. He answers "Yes" (*Y*), "No" (*N*), or "I do not care" (*i*). Exhibit 17A–1 illustrates the pattern of his responses. Crusoe's "I do not care" answers indicate that the original bundle (point *A*) and each alternative indicated by an *i* are valued equally by Crusoe. These *i* points, when connected, form the indifference curve. This line separates the preferred bundles of fish and breadfruit from the less valued combinations. Note that such a curve is likely to be entirely different for any two people. The preferences of individuals vary widely.

We can establish a new indifference curve by starting from any point not on the original curve and following the same procedure. If we start with a point (a consumption bundle) to the northeast of the original indifference curve, all points on the new curve will have a higher level of satisfaction for Crusoe than any on the old curve. The new curve will probably have about the same shape as the original.

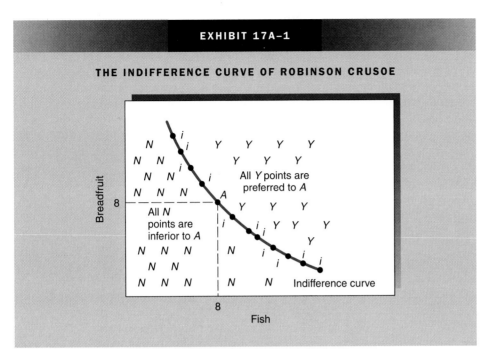

EXHIBIT 17A–1

THE INDIFFERENCE CURVE OF ROBINSON CRUSOE

The curve generated by connecting Crusoe's "I do not care" answers separates the combinations of fish and breadfruit that he prefers to the bundle A from those that he judges to be inferior to A. The i points map out an indifference curve.

CHARACTERISTICS OF INDIFFERENCE CURVES

In developing consumer theory, economists assume that the preferences of consumers exhibit certain properties. These properties enable us to make statements about the general pattern of indifference curves. What are these properties, and what do they imply about the characteristics of indifference curves?

1. More goods are preferable to fewer goods—thus, bundles on indifference curves lying farthest to the northeast of a diagram are always preferred. Assuming the consumption of only two commodities that are both desired, the individual will always prefer a bundle with more of one good (without loss of the other) to the original bundle. This means that combinations to the northeast of a point on the diagram will always be preferred to points lying to the southwest.

2. Goods are substitutable—therefore, indifference curves slope downward to the right. As we indicated in the text of this chapter, individuals are willing to substitute one good for another. Crusoe will be willing to give up some breadfruit if he is compensated with enough fish. Stated another way, there will be some amount of additional fish such that Crusoe will stay on the same indifference curve, even though his consumption of breadfruit has declined. However, in order to remain on the same indifference curve, Crusoe must always acquire more of one good to compensate for the loss of the other. The indifference curve for goods thus will always slope downward to the right (run northwest to southeast).

Marginal rate of substitution
The change in the consumption level of one good that is just sufficient to offset a unit change in the consumption of another good without causing a shift to another indifference curve. At any point on an indifference curve, it will be equal to the slope of the curve at that point.

3. The valuation of a good declines as it is consumed more intensively—therefore, indifference curves are always convex when viewed from below. The slope of the indifference curve represents the willingness of the individual to substitute one good for the other. Economists refer to the amount of one good that is just sufficient to compensate the consumer for the loss of a unit of the other good as the **marginal rate of substitution.** It is equal to the slope of the indifference curve. Reflecting the principle of diminishing marginal utility, the marginal rate of substitution of a good will decline as the good is consumed more intensively relative to other goods. Suppose Crusoe remains on the same indifference curve while continuing to expand his consumption of fish relative to breadfruit. As his consumption of fish increases (and his consumption of breadfruit declines), his valuation of fish relative to breadfruit will decline. It will take more and more units of fish to compensate for the loss of still another unit of breadfruit. The indifference curve will become flatter, reflecting the decline in the marginal rate of substitution of fish for breadfruit as Crusoe consumes more fish relative to breadfruit.

Of course, just the opposite will happen if Crusoe's consumption of breadfruit increases relative to that of fish—if he moves northwest along the same indifference curve. In this case, as breadfruit is consumed more intensively, Crusoe's valuation of it will decline relative to that of fish, and the marginal rate of substitution of fish for breadfruit will rise (the indifference curve will become steeper and steeper). Therefore, since the valuation of each good declines as it is consumed more intensively, indifference curves must be convex when viewed from the origin.

4. Indifference curves are everywhere dense. We can draw an indifference curve through any point on the diagram. This simply means that any two bundles of goods can be compared by the individual.

5. Indifference curves cannot cross—if they did, rational ordering would be violated. If indifference curves crossed, our postulate that more goods are better than fewer goods would be violated. **Exhibit 17A–2** illustrates this point. The crossing of the indifference curves implies that points Y and Z are equally preferred, since they both are on the same indifference curve as X. Consumption bundle Y, though, represents more of both fish and breadfruit than bundle Z, so Y must be preferred to Z. Whenever indifference curves cross, this type of internal inconsistency (irrational ranking) will arise. So, the indifference curves of an individual must not cross.

THE CONSUMER'S PREFERRED BUNDLE

Consumption-opportunity constraint
The constraint that separates consumption bundles that are attainable from those that are unattainable. In a money-income economy, this is usually a budget constraint.

Together with the opportunity constraint of the individual, indifference curves can be used to indicate the most preferred consumption alternatives available to an individual. The **consumption-opportunity constraint** separates consumption bundles that are attainable from those that are unattainable.

Assuming that Crusoe could produce only for himself, his consumption-opportunity constraint would look like the production-possibilities curves discussed in Chapter 2. What would happen if natives from another island visited Crusoe and offered to make exchanges with him? If a barter market existed that permitted Crusoe to exchange fish for breadfruit at a specified exchange rate, his

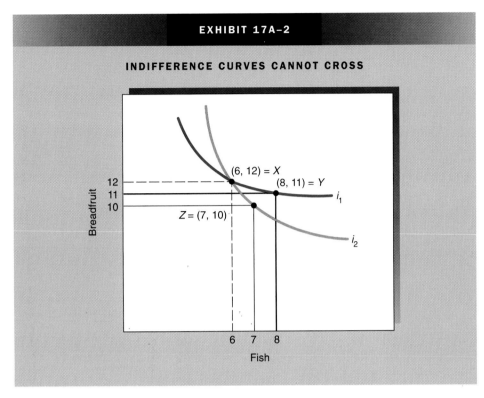

EXHIBIT 17A–2

INDIFFERENCE CURVES CANNOT CROSS

$(6, 12) = X$
$(8, 11) = Y$
i_1
$Z = (7, 10)$
i_2

Breadfruit

12
11
10

6 7 8

Fish

If the indifference curves of an individual crossed, it would lead to the inconsistency pictured here. Points X and Y must be equally valued, since they are both on the same indifference curve (i_1). Similarly, points X and Z must be equally preferred, since they are both on the indifference curve (i_2). If this is true, Y and Z must also be equally preferred, since they are both equally preferred to X. However, point Y represents more of both goods than Z, so Y has to be preferred to Z. When indifference curves cross, this type of internal inconsistency always arises.

options would resemble those of the market constraint illustrated by **Exhibit 17A–3.** First, let us consider the case where Crusoe inhabits a barter economy in which the current market exchange rate is 2 fish to 1 breadfruit. Suppose as a result of his expertise as a fisherman, Crusoe specializes in this activity and is able to bring 16 fish to the market per week. What consumption alternatives will be open to him? Since 2 fish can be bartered in the market for 1 breadfruit, Crusoe will be able to consume 16 fish, or 8 breadfruit, or any combination on the market constraint indicated by the line between these two points. For example, if he trades 2 of his 16 fish for 1 breadfruit, he will be able to consume a bundle consisting of 14 fish and 1 breadfruit. Assuming that the set of indifference curves of Exhibit 17A–3 outlines Crusoe's preferences, he will choose to consume 8 fish and 4 breadfruit. Of course, it will be possible for Crusoe to choose many other combinations of breadfruit and fish, but none of the other attainable combinations would enable him to reach as high a level of satisfaction. Because he is able to bring only 16 fish to the market, it would be impossible for him to attain an indifference curve higher than i_2.

Crusoe's indifference curve and the market-constraint curve will coincide (they will be tangent) at the point at which his attainable level of satisfaction is maximized. At that point (8 fish and 4 breadfruit), the rate at which Crusoe is willing to exchange fish for breadfruit (as indicated by the slope of the indifference curve) will be just equal to the rate at which the market will *permit* him to exchange the two (the slope of the market constraint). If the two slopes differ at a point, Crusoe will always be able to find an attainable combination that will permit him to reach a *higher* indifference curve. He will always move down the

Suppose that the set of indifference curves shown here outlines Crusoe's preferences. The slope of the market (or budget) constraint indicates that 2 fish trade for 1 breadfruit in this barter economy. If Crusoe produces 16 fish per week, he will trade 8 fish for 4 breadfruit in order to move to the consumption bundle (8 fish and 4 breadfruit) that maximizes his level of satisfaction.

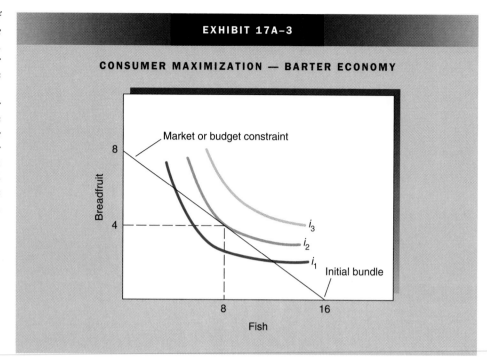

EXHIBIT 17A–3

CONSUMER MAXIMIZATION — BARTER ECONOMY

market constraint when it is flatter than his indifference curve, and up if the market constraint is steeper.

CRUSOE IN A MONEY ECONOMY

As far as the condition for maximization of consumer satisfaction is concerned, moving from a barter economy to a money income economy changes little. **Exhibit 17A–4** illustrates this point. Initially, the price of fish is $1, and the price of breadfruit is $2. The market therefore permits an exchange of 2 fish for 1 breadfruit, just as was the case in Exhibit 17A–3. In Exhibit 17A–4, we assume that Crusoe has a fixed money income of $16. At this level of income, he confronts the same market constraint (usually called a **budget constraint** in an economy with money) as in Exhibit 17A–3. Given the product prices and his income, Crusoe can choose to consume 16 fish, or 8 breadfruit, or any combination indicated by a line (the budget constraint) connecting these two points. Given his preferences, Crusoe will again choose the combination of 8 fish and 4 breadfruit if he wishes to maximize his level of satisfaction. As was true for the barter economy, when Crusoe maximizes his satisfaction (moves to the highest attainable indifference curve), the rate at which he is willing to exchange fish for breadfruit will just equal the rate at which the market will permit him to exchange the two goods. Stated in more technical terms, when his level of satisfaction is at a maximum, Crusoe's marginal rate of substitution of fish for breadfruit, as indicated by the slope of the indifference curve at E_1, will just equal the price ratio (P_f/P_b, which is also the slope of the budget constraint).

Budget constraint
The constraint that separates the bundles of goods that the consumer can purchase from those that cannot be purchased, given a limited income and the prices of the products.

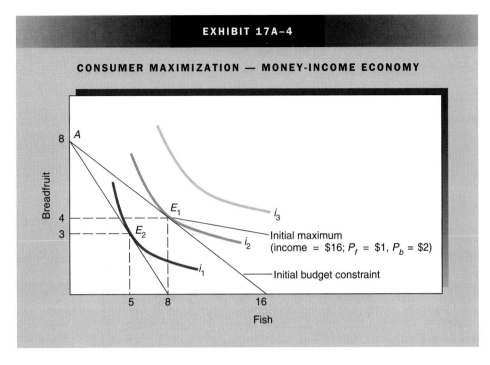

EXHIBIT 17A-4

CONSUMER MAXIMIZATION — MONEY-INCOME ECONOMY

Initial maximum
(income = $16; P_f = $1, P_b = $2)

Initial budget constraint

Suppose that Crusoe's income is $16 per day, the price of fish (P_f) is $1, and the price of breadfruit (P_b) is $2. Thus, Crusoe confronts exactly the same price ratio and budget constraint as in Exhibit 17A–3. Assuming that his preferences are unchanged, he will again maximize his satisfaction by choosing to consume 8 fish and 4 breadfruit. What will happen if the price of fish rises to $2? Crusoe's consumption opportunities will be reduced. His budget constraint will turn clockwise around point A, reflecting the higher price of fish. His fish consumption will decline to 5 units. (Note: Because Crusoe's real income has been reduced, his consumption of breadfruit will also decline.)

What will happen if the price of fish increases? Exhibit 17A–4 also answers this question. Since the price of breadfruit and Crusoe's *money* income are constant, a higher fish price will have two effects. First, it will make Crusoe poorer, even though his money income will be unchanged. His budget constraint will turn clockwise around point *A*, illustrating that his consumption options are now more limited—that is, his real income has declined. Second, the budget line will be steeper, indicating that a larger number of breadfruit must now be sacrificed to obtain an additional unit of fish. It will no longer be possible for Crusoe to attain indifference curve i_2. The best he can do is indifference curve i_1, which he can attain by choosing the bundle of 5 fish and 3 breadfruit.

Using the information supplied by Exhibit 17A–4, we can now locate two points on Crusoe's demand curve for fish. When the price of fish was $1, Crusoe chose 8 fish; when the price rose to $2, Crusoe reduced his consumption to 5 (see **Exhibit 17A–5**). Of course, other points on Crusoe's demand curve could also be located if we considered other prices for fish.

The demand curve of Exhibit 17A–5 is constructed on the assumption that the price of breadfruit remains $2 and that Crusoe's money income remains constant at $16. If either of these factors were to change, the entire demand curve for fish, illustrated by Exhibit 17A–5, would shift.

The indifference curve is a useful way to illustrate how a person with a fixed budget chooses between two goods. In the real world, of course, people have hundreds, or even thousands, of goods to choose from, and the doubling of only one price usually has a small impact on a person's overall consumption and satisfaction possibilities. In our simple example, the twofold increase in the price of fish makes Crusoe much worse off, because he spends a large portion of his budget on the item.

As Exhibit 17A–4 illustrates, when the price of fish is $1, Crusoe chooses 8 units. When the price of fish increases to $2, he reduces his consumption to 5 units. This gives us two points on Crusoe's demand curve for fish. Other points on the demand curve could be derived by confronting Crusoe with still other prices of fish. (Note: Crusoe's money income [$16] and the price of breadfruit [$2] are unchanged in this analysis.)

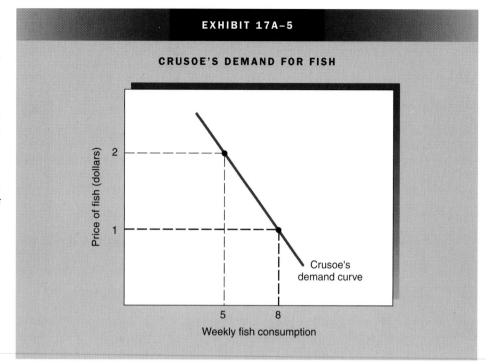

EXHIBIT 17A–5

CRUSOE'S DEMAND FOR FISH

THE INCOME AND SUBSTITUTION EFFECTS

In the text, we indicated that, when the price of a product rises, the amount consumed will change as a result of both an *income effect* and a *substitution effect*. Indifference curve analysis can be used to separate these two effects. **Exhibit 17A–6** is similar to Exhibit 17A–4. Both exhibits illustrate Crusoe's response to an increase in the price of fish from $1 to $2 when money income ($16) and the price of breadfruit ($2) are held constant. Exhibit 17A–6, however, breaks down his total response into the substitution effect and the income effect. The reduction in the consumption of fish solely because of the substitution (price) effect, holding Crusoe's real income (level of utility) constant, can be found by constructing a line tangent to Crusoe's original indifference curve (i_2), and having a slope indicating the higher price of fish. This line (the broken line in Exhibit 17A–6), which is parallel to Crusoe's actual budget constraint (the line containing point E_2), reflects the higher price of fish. It is tangent to the original indifference curve i_2, so Crusoe's real income is held constant. As this line indicates, Crusoe's consumption of fish would fall from 8 to 7, due strictly to the fact that fish are now more expensive. This move from E_1 to F is a pure substitution effect.

Real income, though, has actually been reduced. As a result, Crusoe will be unable to attain point F on indifference curve i_2. The best he can attain is point E_2, which decreases his consumption of fish by another 2 units to 5. Since the broken line containing F and the budget constraint containing E_2 are parallel, the relative price of fish and breadfruit is held constant as Crusoe moves from F to E_2. This move from F to E_2 is thus a pure income effect. (Note: Because the con-

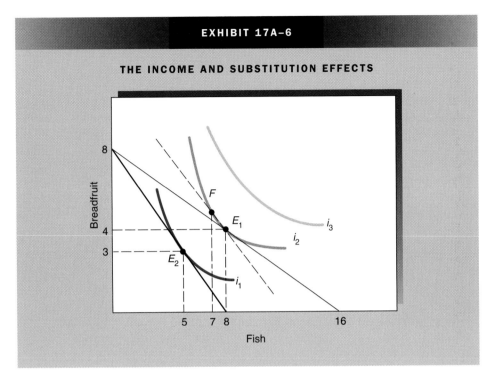

EXHIBIT 17A–6

THE INCOME AND SUBSTITUTION EFFECTS

Here we break down Crusoe's response to the rise in the price of fish from $1 to $2 (see Exhibit 17A–4) into the substitution and income effects. The move from E_1 to F illustrates the substitution effect, whereas the move from F to E_2 reflects the income effect.

sumption of both goods drops in this move, when income falls but the prices do not change, both goods must be normal goods.) This reduction in the consumption of fish (and breadfruit) in the move from F to E_2 is due entirely to the decline in Crusoe's real income.

Indifference curve analysis highlights the assumptions and considerations that enter into consumer decisions. The logic of the proof that there is an inverse relationship between the price and the amount demanded is both elegant and reassuring. It is elegant because of the internal consistency of the logic and the precision of the analysis. It is reassuring because it conforms with our expectations, which are based on the central postulate of economics—that incentives matter in a predictable way.

■ Why are business firms used by societies everywhere to organize production?

■ How are firms organized in market economies?

■ What are explicit and implicit costs, and how do they guide the behavior of the firm?

■ How does economic profit differ from accounting profit, and what role does it play?

■ How do short-run costs differ from long-run costs, and what factors shift the firm's cost curves?

[A] supply curve traces out the quantity of a good that sellers will produce at various prices. As the price falls, so does the number of units supplied.

AL EHRBAR[1]

Opportunity cost is the value of the best alternative that must be sacrificed in order to engage in an activity. This is the only relevant cost in economic analysis. . . . The supply curve of any commodity or service consequently reflects opportunity costs which are determined indirectly by consumers clamoring for a myriad of goods.

MARSHALL COLBERG[2]

---

[1]Al Ehrbar, "Supply," in *The Fortune Encyclopedia of Economics* (New York: Warner Books, 1993), p. 87.

[2]Marshall R. Colberg, Dascomb R. Forbush, and Gilbert R. Whitaker, *Business Economics* (Homewood, Ill.: Irwin, 1980), p. 12.

Demand and supply interact to determine the market price of a product. In the preceding chapter, we illustrated that the demand for a product reflects the strength of consumer desire for that product. In this chapter, we focus on costs of producing such a product. The resources needed for production could be used to produce other goods instead. As Professor Colberg points out in the second quote opening this chapter, the cost of resources to produce one product reflects consumer demands for the other products that could be produced instead, with the same resources. If the cost of producing a good exceeds its price, the market is signaling that, though the good may be desired, other goods that could be produced with the same resources are more urgently desired. The signal also carries an incentive. In a market economy, producers who receive the signal and anticipate suffering a loss if they continue production are unlikely to do so. Thus, supply and cost of production are closely linked. For example, a producer who faces a cost of $900 to produce a large-screen TV set is unlikely to continue supplying the sets for very long if the market price is $600. In the long run, sets that cost $900 will be supplied only if they can command a price of at least $900.

In this chapter, we lay the foundation for a detailed investigation of the link between costs and market supply. What do economists mean by costs? Why are costs so important? What is the function of costs in a market economy? We discuss these and related questions in this chapter.

ORGANIZATION OF THE BUSINESS FIRM

The business firm is an entity designed to organize raw materials, labor, and machines with the goal of producing goods and/or services. Firms (1) purchase productive resources from households and other firms, (2) transform them into a different commodity, and (3) sell the transformed product or service to consumers.

Economies differ in the amount of freedom they allow business decision makers. They differ also in the incentive structure used to stimulate and guide business activity. Nevertheless, every society relies on business firms to organize resources and transform them into products. In market economies, most business firms choose their own price, output level, and methods of production. They reap the benefits of sales revenues, but they are also fully responsible for their costs. In socialist countries, government policy often establishes the selling price and constrains the actions of business firms in various other ways. Firms typically are not expected to pay all their bills from their revenues, and they are often not allowed to keep the proceeds if revenues exceed costs. In any case, however, the central position of the business firm as the organized productive unit is universal to capitalist and socialist economies alike. In this chapter we focus on the organization and behavior of firms in a market economy.

INCENTIVES, COOPERATION, AND THE NATURE OF THE FIRM[3]

Most firms are privately owned in capitalist countries. The owners, who may or may not act as entrepreneurs, are the individuals who risk their wealth on the success of the business. If the firm is successful and makes profits, these financial gains go to the owners. Conversely, if the firm suffers losses, the owners must bear the consequences. Because the owners receive what remains after the revenue of the firm is used to pay the contractual costs, they are called **residual claimants.**

In a market economy, the property right of owners to the residual income of the firm plays a very important role: It provides owners with a strong incentive to organize and structure their business in a manner that will keep their cost of producing output low (relative to the value of the output). The wealth of these residual claimants is directly influenced by the success or failure of the firm. Thus, they have a strong incentive to see that resources under their direction are used efficiently.

There are two ways of organizing productive activity: contracting and **team production,** in which workers are hired by a firm to work together under the supervision of the owner, or the owner's representative. Most business firms use both contracting and team production.

In principle, all production could be accomplished solely through individual contracting. For example, a builder might have a house built by contracting with one person to pour the concrete for the floor, another to construct the wooden part of the house, a third to install the roofing, a fourth to do the electrical wiring, and so on. No employees would have to be involved in such a project. More commonly though, goods and services are produced with some combination of contracting and the use of team production by employees of a firm.

Why do firms use team production? If contracting alone is used to produce something, the producer must, for each project, (1) determine what is required to produce the desired result in the best way, given the circumstances and the current technology and prices, (2) search out reliable suppliers, and (3) negotiate and enforce the contracts. The entrepreneur who wants to produce by this method must have specialized knowledge in a variety of areas and must devote a great deal of time and effort to the planning and contracting processes. Not many people have the expertise or the time to take care of all these tasks by themselves except on a small scale. Team production for certain tasks may be more practical and less costly.

Accordingly, a builder is likely to hire knowledgeable, experienced workers to plan the construction process, to purchase materials, and to build such structures as houses and office buildings. The firm itself will then contract with others to obtain materials and specialized labor services.

A firm, then, is a business organization that may use team production to reduce many of the transaction costs associated with contracting. Team production, however, raises another set of problems. Team members—that is, the

Residual claimants
Individuals who personally receive the excess, if any, of revenues over costs. Residual claimants gain if the firm's costs are reduced or revenues increased.

Team production
A process of production wherein employees work together under the supervision of the owner or the owner's representative.

---

[3]A classic article on this topic is Ronald Coase, "The Nature of the Firm," *Economica* (1937): pp. 386–405. See also Armen Alchian and Harold Demsetz, "Production, Information Costs, and Economic Organization," *American Economic Review* (December 1972): pp. 777–795.

Shirking
Working at less than a normal rate of productivity, thus reducing output. Shirking is more likely when workers are not monitored, so that the cost of lower output falls on others than themselves.

Principal-agent problem
The incentive problem arising when the purchaser of services (the principal) lacks full information about the circumstances faced by the seller (the agent) and thus cannot know how well the agent performs the purchased services. The agent may to some extent work toward objectives other than those sought by the principal paying for the service.

employees working for the firm—must be monitored and provided with an incentive system that discourages **shirking** or working at less than a normal rate of productivity. Taking long work breaks, paying more attention to their own convenience than to work results, and wasting time when diligence is called for are examples of shirking. A worker will shirk more when the costs of doing so are shifted to other team members, including the owners of the firm. Hired managers, even including those at the top, must be monitored and provided with the incentive to avoid shirking.

When team production is utilized, the problem of imperfect monitoring and imperfect incentives is always present. It is part of a larger class of problems called, in general, the **principal-agent problem** (see the Applications in Economics feature on this subject). Any person who has taken a car to an auto mechanic has experienced such a problem. The mechanic wants to get the job done quickly and to make as much money on it as possible. The car owner wants to get the job done quickly also, but in a way that permanently fixes the problem, at the lowest possible cost. Because the mechanic typically knows far more about the job than the customer, it is hard for the customer to monitor the mechanic's work. There is a possibility, therefore, that the mechanic may charge a large amount for a "quick fix" that will not last.

The owner of a firm is in a similar situation. It is often difficult to monitor the performance of individual employees and provide them with an incentive structure that will encourage high productivity. Nonetheless, the ability of the firm to use resources effectively, and to succeed in a competitive market,

APPLICATIONS IN ECONOMICS

THE PRINCIPAL-AGENT PROBLEM

In recent years, economists have focused a great deal of attention on a class of problems in which one individual is hired to act on behalf of another. This *principal-agent problem* arises when the purchaser of services (the principal) lacks full information about the circumstances faced by the seller (the agent), and thus cannot know how well the agent performs the purchased services. As a result, the agent may to some extent work toward objectives other than those sought by the principal, who is paying for the services. Because agents exercise their own judgment in performing the work and cannot be completely monitored, they have opportunities to shirk, and, in general, to serve their own ends rather than those of the principal.

We all run into the principal-agent problem when we pay a dentist, a mechanic, or a lawyer to perform services for us. These agents we hire know more than we do about their work and about the circumstances of the specific job we pay them to do. We cannot be sure

that they are doing the best possible job for us. The owner of a business firm faces similar incentive problems with every employee hired. A large firm has many managers who spend a good deal of time monitoring the work of employees and providing them with the incentive to work efficiently. But they cannot monitor perfectly and, in any case, who will monitor the monitors?

Even top-level executives hired to manage a firm do not have the same objectives as owners—primarily profit maximization—unless, of course, the managers are the owners. So the judgments of executives, too, are influenced by what is in their personal best interests. They want perks, personal job security, and other benefits that may not be consistent with profit maximization for the firm. The problem is more serious as firms grow larger and acquire more managers and employees. Ultimately it is the job of the owners, as residual claimants, to develop an incentive structure that minimizes the principal-agent problem. For the owner, the saying "the buck stops here" always applies.

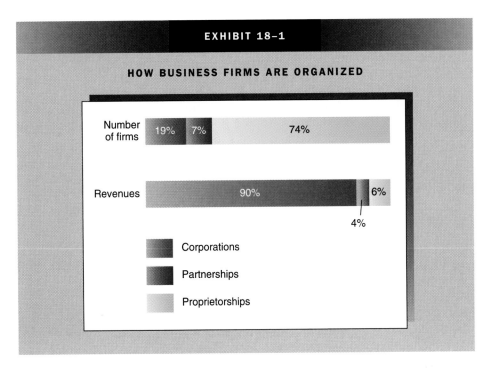

EXHIBIT 18-1

HOW BUSINESS FIRMS ARE ORGANIZED

Number of firms: 19% | 7% | 74%

Revenues: 90% | 4% | 6%

- Corporations
- Partnerships
- Proprietorships

Nearly three out of every four firms are proprietorships, but only 6 percent of all business revenue is generated by proprietorships. Corporations account for only one out of every five firms, but generate 90 percent of all revenues.

Source: *Statistical Abstract of the United States, 1995*, Table 847. (Data are for 1991.)

depends crucially upon resolving these problems. If a firm is going to keep costs low and the value of output high, it must discover and use an incentive structure that motivates managers and workers, and discourages shirking.

THREE TYPES OF BUSINESS FIRMS

Business firms can be organized in one of three ways: as a proprietorship, a partnership, or a corporation. The structure chosen determines how the owners share the risks and liabilities of the firm and how they participate in the making of decisions.

A **proprietorship** is a business firm that is owned by a single individual who is fully liable for the debts of the firm. In addition to assuming the responsibilities of ownership, the proprietor often works directly for the firm, providing managerial and other labor services. Many small businesses, including neighborhood grocery stores, barbershops, and farms, are business proprietorships. As **Exhibit 18-1** shows, proprietorships composed 74 percent of all business firms in 1991. Because most proprietorships are small, however, they generated only 6 percent of all business receipts for that year.

A **partnership** consists of two or more persons acting as co-owners of a business firm. The partners share risks and responsibilities in some prearranged manner. There is no difference between a proprietorship and a partnership in terms of owner liability. In both cases, the owners are fully liable for all business debts incurred by the firm. Many law, medical, and accounting firms are organized along partnership lines. This form of business structure accounts for only 7 percent of the total number of firms and 4 percent of all business receipts.

Proprietorship
A business firm owned by an individual who possesses the ownership right to the firm's profits and is personally liable for the firm's debts.

Partnership
A business firm owned by two or more individuals who possess ownership rights to the firm's profits and are personally liable for the debts of the firm.

Corporation
A business firm owned by shareholders who possess ownership rights to the firm's profits, but whose liability is limited to the amount of their investment in the firm.

Even though **corporations** composed less than 20 percent of all business firms in 1991, they accounted for 90 percent of all business receipts. One might ask, then, what accounts for the attractiveness of the corporate structure?

First, the stockholders of the corporation are the legal owners of the firm. Any profits of the firm belong to them. Their liability, however, is limited to the extent of their explicit investment. If a corporation owes you money, you cannot directly sue the stockholders. You can, of course, sue the corporation—but what if it goes bankrupt? You and others to whom the firm owes money will simply be out of luck.

This limited liability makes it possible for corporations to attract investment funds from a large number of "owners" who do not participate in the day-to-day management of the firm. The stockholders of many large corporations simply hire managers to operate the firm. Corporations are thus often characterized by a separation of ownership and operational management.

Another advantage of the corporate structure is that ownership can easily be transferred. The shares, or ownership rights, of an owner who dies can be sold by the heirs to another owner without disrupting the business firm. Because of this, the corporation is an ongoing concern. Similarly, stockholders who become unhappy with the way a corporation is run can bail out merely by selling their stock.

The corporate form of ownership is flexible enough to adjust easily to a different location or to many locations. Multinational corporations can do business wherever comparative advantage dictates, so many businesses operate in this way. In 1990 U.S. multinational firms had nearly $5 trillion in assets, while their foreign affiliates had assets of $1.6 trillion. They exported $108 billion worth of goods to their foreign affiliates, while importing $102 billion from them. IBM, for example, is an American corporation, but 55 percent of its employees were in foreign countries in 1990, and that percentage was growing. IBM Japan had more than 18,000 Japanese employees and annual sales of more than $6 billion, making it one of Japan's largest exporters of computers.[4] Corporations seeking lower production costs and higher-valued outputs are quite flexible in both hiring and location decisions.

The managers of a large corporation might be thought of as trained experts hired by the stockholders to run the firm. The decisions of stockholders to buy and sell shares of stock mirror the confidence of investors in the management of the firm. If enough current and prospective stockholders alike come to believe that the managers will do a good job, the demand for the firm's stock will increase. Rising stock prices will reflect this increase in demand.

Conversely, when investors are dissatisfied with a corporation's management, the stock's price will tumble. In turn, falling stock prices will often lead to a shake-up in the management of the firm. A constructive management change can bring significant change in the price of a corporation's stock. Consider Eastman Kodak Company's decision in August 1993 to search for a new chairman and chief executive, who would be allowed to bring in a new management team. Investors had been demanding stringent measures to cut costs, and the chief executive and

---

[4]Aggregate figures are from the *Statistical Abstract of the United States, 1993* (Washington, D.C.: U.S. Government Printing Office, 1993), Table 895, while the IBM data are from Robert Reich, "Does Corporate Nationality Matter?" *Issues in Science and Technology* (winter 1990–1991), pp. 40–44.

COSTS, SENSITIVITY TO CONSUMERS, AND THE STRUCTURE OF MODERN CORPORATIONS

Will business firms operate efficiently and respond to the interests of customers? In the case of owner-managed firms, clearly there is a strong incentive for efficient management, cost-effective production, and sensitivity to the interests of consumers. Offering consumers value at a low cost is the ticket to profitability. Because owner-managers are residual-income claimants, they have a strong incentive to manage firms wisely.

However, for a large corporation with millions of stockholders, the situation is complex. Although the stockholders hold the legal claim to residual income, professional managers direct the operation of the firm. The objectives of managers may conflict with those of stockholders. For example, managers may prefer high salaries, large offices, and first-class travel. They may also prefer the power and prestige of business expansion, even if it reduces profitability.

Can the stockholders control the actions of managers and direct them toward the pursuit of profitability? For large corporations, *direct* control is unlikely. Many large corporations are owned by shareholders, none of whom owns more than a tiny fraction of the firm's outstanding stock. Although they elect a board of directors, which in turn appoints high-level managers, few individual stockholders have the incentive or the information to exercise direct control. Most find it too expensive even to attend the annual shareholder's meeting.

Despite this problem, there are three major factors that promote cost efficiency and limit the power of corporate managers. Let us consider each.

COMPETITION FOR INVESTMENT FUNDS AND CUSTOMERS
Even without the ability to exercise control of the corporation, stockholders have an incentive to monitor management in order to anticipate problems or constructive innovations. Investors who are the first to spot a good, new management strategy can buy stock early, before others realize the opportunity and bid the price up. Stockholders who are the first to spot a problem can "bail out" by selling their stock before others see the problem and dump their stock, thus depressing the price. So managers get constant feedback via the stock price, which can be just as important as current profits to stockholders and boards of directors.

Similarly, consumers have an incentive to monitor the quality and price of the firm's output. No one forces them to buy the corporation's product; so, if other firms supply superior products or offer a lower price, consumers can take their business to rival firms.

The corporation's need to meet the competition limits the ability of managers to pursue their personal objectives at the expense of either stockholders or customers.

COMPENSATION AND MANAGEMENT INCENTIVES
The compensation of managers can be structured in a manner that will bring the interests of managers into harmony with those of shareholders. Market determination of managerial salaries will help achieve this objective. Those managers who establish a track record of business profitability and rising stock prices will command higher-paying positions in the job market. The demand for managers associated with losing enterprises and business failures will be weak. And internally, corporate firms can, and often do, tie the compensation of managers to the market success of the business. Salary increases and bonuses may be directly related to the firm's profitability, or managers may be required to buy and hold the company's stock. Senior managers may be paid in part with shares of corporate stock. Many firms have designed stock option-to-buy plans available to management that are extremely valuable if the market value of the firm's shares rises but worthless if it falls. Each of these corporate policies will encourage managers to follow policies that maximize the wealth holdings of all shareholders, reducing the conflict between the interests of managers and shareholders.[1]

THREAT OF CORPORATE TAKEOVER
Managers who do not serve the interests of their shareholders are vulnerable to a *takeover*, a move by an outside person or group to gain control of the firm. As we previously noted, shareholders who lose confidence in management can "fire" management by selling their shares. When a significant number of shareholders follow this course of action, the market value of the firm's stock will decline. This will increase the attractiveness of the firm to takeover specialists shopping for a poorly run business, the value of which could be substantially increased by a new management team.[2]

(continued)

Consider a firm currently earning $1.50 per share. Reflecting current earnings that are expected to continue, the market value of the firm's stock might be $15 per share (assuming a 10 percent interest rate). If the earnings of the firm are reduced because the current management team is pursuing its own objectives at the expense of profitability, then a corporate takeover could lead to substantial gain. Suppose some outside persons believe that they could restructure the firm, improve the management, and thereby increase the firm's earnings to $3 per share. Therefore, they tender a takeover bid—an offer to buy shares of the firm's stock—for $20 per share. If the takeover team is correct and it increases the firm's earnings to $3 per share, then the stock value of the firm will rise accordingly (to $30 per share).

Of course, the current management has an incentive to resist the takeover. After all, the current operating plans are their own, and the jobs they now hold are the best available to them. The outsiders who say that the current management is wrong and should be replaced will seldom be welcomed with open arms. Still, the presence of large inefficiencies is a powerful attraction for an effective takeover. Managers who pursue their own interests at the expense of stockholders make themselves vulnerable. The mere potential of the takeover reduces the likelihood that managers will stray too far from the profit-maximization strategy.

CONCLUDING THOUGHT   How efficient is the corporate business structure? Perhaps history provides the best answer. If the corporate structure were not an efficient form of business organization, it would not have continued to survive, nor would it be so prevalent. Rival forms of business organization, including proprietorships, partnerships, consumer cooperatives, employee ownership, and mutually owned companies can and do compete in the marketplace for investment funds. In certain industries, some of these alternative forms of business organization are dominant. Nonetheless, in most industries, the corporate structure is the dominant form of business organization (see Exhibit 18–1). This is strong evidence that, despite its defects, it is generally a cost-efficient, consumer-sensitive form of organization.

[1]A number of articles covering executive compensation and the effects of various plans appeared in a special section on "Executive Pay" in *The Wall Street Journal*, April 12, 1995, pp. R1–R14.

[2]For a discussion of corporate takeovers from various points of view, see Hal R. Varian et al., "Symposium on Takeovers," *The Journal of Economic Perspectives* 2, no. 1 (winter 1988): pp. 3–81. See also John R. Coffee, Jr., et al., "Corporate Takeovers: Who Wins: Who Loses; Who Should Regulate?" *Regulation* 12, no. 1 (1988), p. 23.

chairman had not taken such measures. The announcement apparently made investors optimistic. According to *The Wall Street Journal,* "Kodak stock surged $3.25, or 5.9 percent, on the news."[5] The capital market provides one of several forms of discipline placed on corporate management in a market economy. (See the Applications in Economics box on modern corporate structure.)

ECONOMIC ROLE OF COSTS

Consumers would like to have more economic goods, but resources to produce them are scarce. We cannot produce as much of all goods as we would like, because the use of resources to make one commodity takes resources from the production of other desired goods. The desire for a given product must be balanced against the desire for other items that must be sacrificed to produce it.

[5]Joan E. Rigdon and Joann S. Lublin, "Kodak Seeks Outsider to Be Chairman, CEO," *The Wall Street Journal,* August 8, 1993, p. A3.

Every economic system must make these balancing judgments. When decisions are made in the political arena, the budget process performs this balancing function. Congress (or the central committee, or the king) decides which goods will be purchased or produced by government agencies and which will be forgone. Taxes and budgets are set accordingly.

In a market economy, consumer demand and cost of production are central to the performance of this balancing function. The desire of consumers for a specific good must be balanced against the desire for other goods that could be produced with the resources. Production of one good necessitates a reduction in the output of other goods. The most highly valued opportunity forgone when a good is produced is the opportunity cost of the good—its costs of production. The owner of a resource employed in the production of one good must be paid at least as much as the resource would be worth if employed elsewhere. The production cost of a good reveals the value of the resources used to produce it, in terms of other opportunities forgone.

The demand for a product can be thought of as the voice of consumers instructing firms to produce a good. On the other hand, costs of production represent the voice of consumers saying that other items that could be produced with the resources are also desired. The demand for a product indicates the intensity of consumers' desires for the item. The cost of producing a product indicates the desire of consumers for other goods that must now be forgone because the necessary resources have been employed in the production of the first item. A profit seeking firm will try to produce only those units of output for which buyers are willing to pay the full cost.

CALCULATING ECONOMIC COSTS AND PROFITS

Business firms, regardless of their size, are primarily concerned with profit. Profit, of course, is the firm's total revenue minus the sum of its costs. But to state profit correctly, it is imperative that costs be measured properly. Most people, including some who are in business, think of costs as amounts paid for raw materials, labor, machines, and similar inputs. However, this concept of cost, which stems from accounting procedures, may exclude some of the firm's costs. When cost is miscalculated, profit is also misstated, and uneconomic decisions may result.

The key to understanding the economist's concept of profit is the oft-discussed *opportunity cost*. The firm incurs a cost whenever it uses a resource, thereby requiring the resource owner to forgo the highest valued alternative. These costs may either be explicit or implicit. **Explicit costs** result when the firm makes a monetary payment to resource owners. Money wages, interest, and rental payments are a measure of what the firm gives up to employ the services of labor and capital resources. Firms may also incur **implicit costs**—those associated with the use of resources owned by the firm. Since implicit costs do not involve a direct money or contractual payment, they are sometimes excluded from accounting statements. For example, the owners of small proprietorships often supply labor services to their businesses. There is an opportunity cost associated with the use of this resource; other opportunities for the owner's time have to be given up because of the time spent in the operation of the business. The highest valued alternative forgone is the opportunity cost of the labor service

Explicit costs
Payments by a firm to purchase the services of productive resources.

Implicit costs
The opportunity costs associated with a firm's use of resources that it owns. These costs do not involve a direct money payment. Examples include wage income and interest forgone by the owner of a firm who also provides labor services and equity capital to the firm.

Total cost

The costs, both explicit and implicit, of all the resources used by the firm. Total cost includes an imputed normal rate of return for the firm's equity capital.

provided by the owner. The **total cost** of production is the sum of the explicit and implicit costs incurred by the employment of all resources involved in the production process.

Accounting statements generally omit the implicit cost of equity capital—the cost of funds supplied by owners. If a firm borrows financial capital from a bank or other private source, it will have to pay interest. Accountants properly record this interest expense as a cost. In contrast, when the firm acquires financial capital through the issuance of stock, accountants make no allowance for the cost of this financial capital. Regardless of whether it is acquired by borrowing or stock (equity capital), the use of financial capital involves an opportunity cost. Persons who supply equity capital to a firm expect to earn a normal rate of return—a return comparable to what they could earn if they chose other investment opportunities (including bonds). If they do not earn this normal rate of return, investors will not continue to supply financial capital to the business.

Opportunity cost of equity capital

The implicit rate of return that must be earned by investors to induce them to continue to supply financial capital to the firm.

When calculating costs, economists use the normal return on financial capital as a basis for determining the implicit **opportunity cost of equity capital.** If the normal rate of return on financial capital is 10 percent, equity investors will refuse funds to firms that persistently fail to earn a 10 percent rate of return on capital assets. As a result, earning the normal rate of return—that is, covering the opportunity cost of all of its capital—is vital to the survival of a business firm.

ACCOUNTING PROFIT AND ECONOMIC PROFIT

Economic profit

The difference between the firm's total revenues and total costs.

Because economists seek to measure the opportunities lost due to the production of a good or service, they include both explicit and implicit costs in total cost. **Economic profit** is equal to total revenues minus total costs, including both the explicit and implicit cost components. Economic profits will be present only if the earnings of the business exceed the opportunity cost of all resources used by the firm, *including the opportunity cost of the assets owned by the firm.* Economic losses result when the earnings of the firm are insufficient to cover explicit and implicit costs. When the firm's revenues are just equal to its costs, both explicit and implicit, economic profits will be zero.

Remember that zero economic profits do not imply that the firm is about to go out of business. On the contrary, they indicate that the owners are receiving exactly the market (normal) rate of return on their investment (assets owned by the firm).

Accounting profits

The sales revenues minus the expenses of a firm over a designated time period, usually one year. Accounting profits typically make allowances for changes in the firm's inventories and depreciation of its assets. No allowance is made, however, for the opportunity cost of the equity capital of the firm's owners, or other implicit costs.

Because accounting procedures often omit implicit costs, such as those associated with owner-provided labor services or capital assets, the accounting costs of the firm generally understate the opportunity costs of production. This understatement of cost leads to an overstatement of economic profits. Therefore, the **accounting profits** of a firm are generally greater than the firm's economic profits (see the Applications in Economics box on accounting costs). When the omission of the costs of owner-provided services is unimportant, as is the case for most large corporations, accounting profits approximate the returns to the firm's equity capital. High accounting profits (measured as a rate of return on a firm's assets), relative to the average for other firms, suggest that a firm is earning an economic profit. Correspondingly, a low rate of accounting profit implies economic losses.

APPLICATIONS IN ECONOMICS

ECONOMIC AND ACCOUNTING COSTS—A HYPOTHETICAL EXAMPLE

The revenue-cost statement for a corner grocery store owned and operated by Terry Smith is presented here.

Terry works full-time as the manager, chief cashier, and janitor. Terry has $30,000 worth of refrigeration and other equipment invested in the store. Last year, Terry's total sales were $85,000; suppliers and employees were paid $50,000. Terry's revenues exceeded explicit costs by $35,000. Did Terry make a profit last year? The accounting statement for the store will probably show a net profit of $35,000. However, if Terry did not have a $30,000 personal investment in equipment, these funds could be collecting 10 percent interest. Thus, Terry is forgoing $3,000 of interest each year. Similarly, if the building that Terry owns were not being used as a grocery store, it could be rented to someone else for $500 per month. Rental income thus forgone is $6,000 per year. In addition, since Terry is tied up working in the grocery store, a $28,000 managerial position with the local Safeway is forgone. Considering the interest, rental, and salary income that Terry had to forgo in order to operate the grocery store last year, Terry's implicit costs were $37,000. The total costs were $87,000. The total revenue of Terry's grocery store was less than the opportunity cost of the resources utilized. Terry incurred an economic loss of $2,000, despite the accounting profit of $35,000.

TOTAL REVENUE	
Sales (groceries)	**$85,000**
COSTS (EXPLICIT)	
Groceries, wholesale	$38,000
Utilities	2,000
Taxes	3,000
Advertising	1,000
Labor services (employees)	6,000
TOTAL (EXPLICIT) COSTS	$50,000
NET (ACCOUNTING) PROFIT	$35,000
ADDITIONAL (IMPLICIT) COSTS	
Interest (personal investment)	$ 3,000
Rent (Terry's building)	6,000
Salary (Terry's labor)	$28,000
Total (implicit) costs	$37,000
TOTAL EXPLICIT AND IMPLICIT COSTS	**$87,000**
ECONOMIC PROFIT (TOTAL REVENUE MINUS EXPLICIT AND IMPLICIT COSTS)	**−$2,000**

SHORT RUN AND LONG RUN

A firm cannot instantaneously adjust its output. Time plays an important role in the production process. All of a firm's resources can be expanded (contracted) over time, but for specialized or heavy equipment, expanding (contracting) availability quickly may be very expensive or even impossible. Economists often speak of the **short run** as a time period so short that the firm is unable to alter its present plant size. In the short run, the firm is "stuck" with its existing plant and heavy equipment. They are "fixed" for a given time period. The firm can alter output, however, by applying larger or smaller amounts of variable resources, such as labor and raw materials. Existing plant capacity can thus be used more or less intensively in the short run.

In sum, we can say that the short run is that period of time during which at least one factor of production, usually the size of the firm's plant, cannot be varied. How long is the short run? The length varies from industry to industry. In some industries, substantial changes in plant size can be accomplished in a few months. In other industries, particularly those that use assembly lines and

Short run (in production)
A time period so short that a firm is unable to vary some of its factors of production. The firm's plant size typically cannot be altered in the short run.

mass production techniques (for example, aircraft and automobiles), the short run might be a year or even several years.

The **long run** is a time period of sufficient length to allow a firm the opportunity to alter its plant size and capacity and all other factors of production. All resources of the firm are variable in the long run. In the long run, from the viewpoint of an entire industry, new firms may be established and enter the industry; other firms may dissolve and leave the industry.

Perhaps an example will help to clarify the distinction between the short- and long-run time periods. If a battery manufacturer hired 200 additional workers and ordered more raw materials to squeeze a larger output from the existing plant, this would be a short-run adjustment. In contrast, if the manufacturer built an additional plant (or expanded the size of its current facility) and installed additional heavy equipment, this would be a long-run adjustment.

Long run (in production)
A time period long enough to allow the firm to vary all factors of production.

OUTPUT AND COSTS IN THE SHORT RUN

We turn now to definitions of various aspects of the firm's costs and to what we can say about the relationship of those costs to the level of output, even without detailed knowledge of the production process. We have emphasized that in the short run some of a firm's factors of production, such as the size of the plant, will be fixed. Other productive resources will be variable. In the short run, then, we can break the firm's costs into these two categories—fixed and variable. Examining how each category of costs behaves, and seeing that behavior graphically, will illustrate characteristics of the profit-maximizing level of output for a firm.

Each of the firm's fixed costs, and their sum, its **total fixed cost** *(TFC)*, will remain unchanged even though output is altered. For example, a firm's insurance premiums, its property taxes, and, most significantly, the opportunity cost of using its fixed assets will be present whether the firm produces a large or small rate of output. These costs will not vary with output. They are "fixed" as long as the firm remains in business. Fixed costs will be present at all levels of output, including zero. They can be avoided only if the firm goes out of business.

Total fixed cost
The sum of the costs that do not vary with output. They will be incurred as long as a firm continues in business and the assets have alternative uses.

Average fixed cost
Total fixed cost divided by the number of units produced. It always declines as output increases.

What will happen to **average fixed cost** *(AFC)* as output expands? Remember that the firm's fixed cost will be the same whether output is 1, 100, or 1,000. The *AFC* is simply fixed cost divided by output. As output increases, *AFC* declines because the fixed cost will be spread over more and more units (see part a of **Exhibit 18–2**).

Some costs vary with output. For example, additional output can usually be produced by hiring more workers and buying more raw materials. The sum of those and other costs that rise as output increases comprise the firm's **total variable cost** *(TVC)*. At any given level of output, the firm's **average variable cost** is the total variable cost divided by output.

Total variable cost
The sum of those costs that rise as output increases. Examples of variable costs are wages paid to workers and payments for raw materials

Average variable cost
The total variable cost divided by the number of

We have noted that total cost *(TC)* includes explicit and implicit costs. The total cost of producing a good is also the sum of the fixed and variable costs at

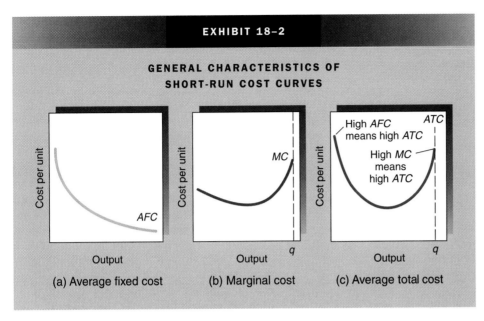

EXHIBIT 18-2

GENERAL CHARACTERISTICS OF SHORT-RUN COST CURVES

(a) Average fixed cost

(b) Marginal cost

(c) Average total cost

Average fixed costs (a) will be high for small rates of output, but they will always decline as output expands. Marginal cost (b) will rise sharply as the plant's production capacity q is approached. As graph (c) illustrates, ATC will be a U-shaped curve, since AFC will be high for small rates of output and MC will be high as the plant's production capacity is approached.

each output level. At zero output, total cost will equal total fixed cost. As output expands from zero, variable cost and fixed cost must be added to obtain total cost. **Average total cost** *(ATC),* sometimes referred to as *unit cost,* can be found by dividing total cost by the total number of units produced. *ATC* is also equal to the sum of the average fixed and average variable costs. It indicates the amount per unit of output that must be gained in revenue if total cost is to be covered.

The economic way of thinking emphasizes the importance of what happens "at the margin." How much does it cost to produce an additional unit? **Marginal cost** *(MC)* is the change in total cost that results from the production of one additional unit. The profit-conscious decision maker recognizes *MC* as the addition to cost that must be covered by additional revenue if producing the marginal unit is to be profitable. In the short run, as illustrated by Exhibit 18–2b, *MC* will generally decline if output is increased, then eventually reach a minimum, and then increase. The rising *MC* simply reflects the fact that it becomes increasingly difficult to squeeze additional output from a plant as the facility's maximum capacity (the dotted line of part b of Exhibit 18–2) is approached. The accompanying Thumbnail Sketch summarizes the interrelationships among a firm's various costs.

As a firm alters its rate of output in the short run, how will unit cost be affected? First, let us look at this question intuitively. In the short run, the firm can vary output by using its fixed plant size more (or less) intensively. As Exhibit 18–2 illustrates, there are two extreme situations that will result in a high unit cost of output. First, when the output rate of a plant is small relative to its capacity, it is obviously being underutilized. Under these circumstances, *AFC* will be high, and therefore *ATC* will also be high. It will be costly and inefficient to operate a large plant substantially below its production capacity. At the other

Average total cost
Total cost divided by the number of units produced. It is sometimes called per unit cost.

Marginal cost
The change in total cost required to produce an additional unit of output.

THUMBNAIL SKETCH

COMPACT GLOSSARY ON COST

TERM	SYMBOL	EQUATION	DEFINITION
Fixed cost			Cost that is independent of the output level
Variable cost			Cost that varies with the output level
Total fixed cost	TFC		Cost of the fixed inputs (equals sum of quantity times unit price for each fixed input)
Total variable cost	TVC		Cost of the variable inputs (equals sum of quantity times unit price for each variable input)
Total cost	TC	$TC = TFC + TVC$	Cost of all inputs (equals fixed costs plus variable costs)
Marginal cost	MC	$MC = \Delta TC \div \Delta q$	Change in total cost resulting from a one-unit rise in output (q) [equals the *change* in total cost divided by the *change* in output]
Average fixed cost	AFC	$AFC = TFC \div q$	Total fixed cost per unit of output (equals total fixed cost divided by total output)
Average variable cost	AVC	$AVC = TVC \div q$	Total variable cost per unit of output (equals total variable cost divided by total output)
Average total cost	ATC	$ATC = AFC + AVC$	Total cost per unit of output (equals average fixed cost plus average variable cost)

extreme, overutilization can also result in high unit cost. An overutilized plant will mean congestion, time spent by workers waiting for machines, and similar costly delays. As output approaches the maximum capacity of a plant, overutilization will lead to high *MC* and therefore to high *ATC*.

*Thus, the **ATC** curve will be **U**-shaped, as pictured in part c of Exhibit 18–2.* **ATC** *will be high for both an underutilized plant (because **AFC** is high) and an overutilized plant (because **MC** is high).*

DIMINISHING RETURNS AND PRODUCTION IN THE SHORT RUN

Our analysis of the changes in unit cost as the output rate rises is consistent with a long-established economic law. This **law of diminishing returns** states that, as more and more units of a variable factor are applied to a fixed amount of other resources, output will eventually increase by smaller and smaller amounts. Therefore, in terms of their impact on output, the returns to the variable factor will diminish. The impact on costs is clear: When the returns to the variable factor are rising, marginal costs (the additions to total variable cost from adding a unit of output) are falling. Similarly, when the returns to the variable factor are falling, marginal cost is increasing.

The law of diminishing returns is as famous in economics as the law of gravity is in physics. It is based on common sense and real-life observation. Have you ever noticed that, as you apply a single resource more intensively, the resource eventually tends to accomplish less and less? Consider a farmer who applies fertilizer (a resource) more and more intensively to an acre of land (a fixed factor). At some point, the application of additional 100-pound units of fertilizer will expand the wheat yield by successively smaller amounts.

Essentially, the law of diminishing returns is a constraint imposed by nature. If it were not valid, it would be possible to raise all the world's food on an acre of land, or even in a flowerpot. Logically, then, there would be no point in cultivating any of the less fertile land. We would be able to increase output simply by applying another unit of labor and fertilizer to the world's most fertile flowerpot! In the real world, of course, this is not the case; the law of diminishing returns is valid and it restricts our options.

Exhibit 18–3 illustrates the law of diminishing returns numerically. Column 1 indicates the quantity of the variable resource, labor in this example, that is combined with a specified amount of the fixed resource. Column 2 shows the **total product** that will result as the utilization rate of labor increases. Column 3 provides data on the **marginal product,** the change in total output associated with each additional unit of labor. Without the application of labor, output would be zero. As additional units of labor are applied, total product (output) expands. As the first three units of labor are applied, total product increases by successively larger amounts (8, then 12, then 14). Beginning with the fourth unit, however, diminishing returns are confronted. When the fourth unit is added, marginal product—the change in the total product—declines to 12 (down from 14, when the third unit was applied). As additional units of labor are applied, marginal product continues to decline. It is increasingly difficult to squeeze a larger total product from the fixed resources (for example, plant size and equipment). Eventually, marginal product becomes negative (beginning with the tenth unit).

Column 4 of Exhibit 18–3 provides data for the **average product** of labor, which is simply the total product divided by the units of labor applied. Note the average product increases as long as the marginal product is greater than the average product. Whenever the marginal unit's contribution is greater than the average, it must cause the average to rise. Here, this is true through the first four units. The marginal product of the fifth unit of labor, though, is 10, less than the average product for the first four units of labor (11.5). Therefore, beginning with the fifth unit, the average product declines as additional labor is applied. When marginal productivity is below the average, it brings down the average product.

Law of diminishing returns
The postulate that, as more and more units of a variable resource are combined with a fixed amount of other resources, employment of additional units of the variable resource will eventually increase output only at a decreasing rate. Once diminishing returns are reached, it will take successively larger amounts of the variable factor to expand output by one unit.

Total product
The total output of a good that is associated with alternative utilization rates of a variable input.

Marginal product
The increase in the total product resulting from a unit increase in the employment of a variable input. Mathematically, it is the ratio of the change in total product to the change in the quantity of the variable input.

Average product
The total product (output) divided by the number of units of the variable input required to produce that output level.

EXHIBIT 18-3

LAW OF DIMINISHING RETURNS
(HYPOTHETICAL DATA)

(1) UNITS OF THE VARIABLE RESOURCE, LABOR (PER DAY)	(2) TOTAL PRODUCT (OUTPUT)	(3) MARGINAL PRODUCT	(4) AVERAGE PRODUCT
0	0		—
		8	
1	8		8.0
		12	
2	20		10.0
		14	
3	34		11.3
		12	
4	46		11.5
		10	
5	56		11.2
		8	
6	64		10.7
		6	
7	70		10.0
		4	
8	74		9.3
		1	
9	75		8.3
		-2	
10	73		7.3

Using the data from Exhibit 18–3, **Exhibit 18–4** illustrates the law of diminishing returns graphically. Initially, the total product curve (part a) increases quite rapidly. As diminishing marginal returns are confronted (beginning with the fourth unit of labor), total product increases more slowly. Eventually, a maximum output (75) is reached with the application of the ninth unit of labor. The marginal product curve (part b) reflects the total product curve. Geometrically, marginal product is the slope—the rate of increase—of the total product curve. That slope, the marginal product, reaches its maximum with the application of three units of labor. Beyond three units, diminishing returns are present. Eventually, at ten units of labor, the marginal product becomes negative. When marginal product becomes negative, total product is necessarily declining. The average product curve rises as long as the marginal product curve is above it, since each added unit of labor is raising the average. The average product reaches its maximum at four units of labor. Beyond that, each additional unit of labor brings down the average product, and the curve declines.

DIMINISHING RETURNS AND COST CURVES

What impact will diminishing returns have on a firm's costs? Once a firm confronts diminishing returns, larger and larger additions of the variable factor are required to expand output by one unit. This will cause marginal costs (MC) to

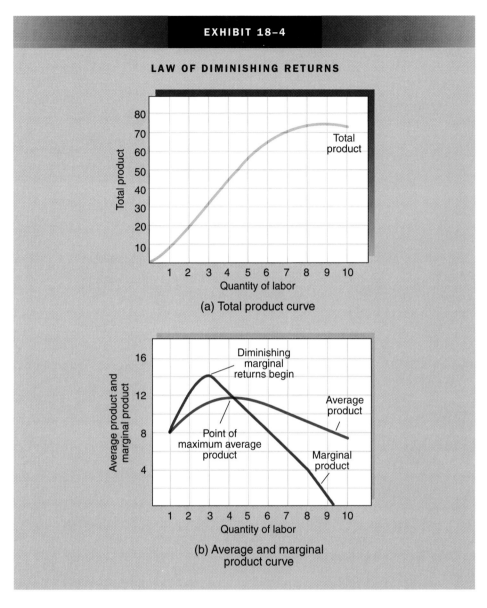

EXHIBIT 18–4

LAW OF DIMINISHING RETURNS

(a) Total product curve

(b) Average and marginal product curve

As units of the variable input (labor) are added to a fixed input, total product will increase, first at an increasing rate and then at a declining rate (a). This will cause both the marginal and average product curves (b) to rise at first and then decline. Note that the marginal product curve intersects the average product curve at its maximum (when 4 units of labor are used). The smooth curves indicate that labor can be increased by amounts of less than a single unit.

rise. As **MC** *continues to increase, eventually it will exceed average total cost. Until that point,* **MC** *is below* **ATC,** *bringing* **ATC** *down. When* **MC** *is greater than* **ATC,** *the additional units cost more than the average, and* **ATC** *must increase.* To make the point clear, consider a similar case in another setting. What happens when an above average student is added to a class? The class average goes up. What happens if a unit of above average cost is added to output? Average total cost rises. The firm's *MC* curve therefore crosses the *ATC* curve at the *ATC*'s lowest point. For output rates beyond the minimum *ATC,* the rising *MC* causes *ATC* to increase. Again, the *ATC* curve is U-shaped.

Exhibit 18–5 numerically illustrates the implications of the law of diminishing returns for a firm's short-run cost curve. Here, we assume that Royal Roller Blades, Inc., combines units of a variable input with a fixed factor to produce units of output (pairs of the popular inline skates). Columns 2, 3, and 4

EXHIBIT 18–5

NUMERICAL SHORT-RUN COST SCHEDULES OF
ROYAL ROLLER BLADES, INC.

	TOTAL COST DATA (PER DAY)				AVERAGE/MARGINAL COST DATA (PER DAY)			
(1)	(2)	(3)	(4)		(5)	(6)	(7)	(8)
OUTPUT			TC		AFC	AVC	ATC	MC
PER DAY	TFC	TVC	(2) + (3)		(2) ÷ (1)	(3) ÷ (1)	(4) ÷ (1)	$\Delta(4) \div \Delta(1)$
0	$50	$ 0	$ 50		—	—	—	—
1	50	15	65		$50.00	$15.00	$65.00	$15
2	50	25	75		25.00	12.50	37.50	10
3	50	34	84		16.67	11.33	28.00	9
4	50	42	92		12.50	10.50	23.00	8
5	50	52	102		10.00	10.40	20.40	10
6	50	64	114		8.33	10.67	19.00	12
7	50	79	129		7.14	11.29	18.43	15
8	50	98	148		6.25	12.25	18.50	19
9	50	122	172		5.56	13.56	19.11	24
10	50	152	202		5.00	15.20	20.20	30
11	50	202	252		4.55	18.36	22.91	50

indicate how the total cost schedules vary as output is expanded. Total fixed costs (TFC), representing the opportunity cost of the fixed factors of production, are $50 per day. For the first four units of output, total variable costs (TVC) increase at a *decreasing rate*. Why? In this range, there are increasing returns to the variable input. Beginning with the fifth unit of output, however, diminishing marginal returns are present. From this point on, TVC and TC increase by successively larger amounts as output is expanded.

Columns 5 through 8 of Exhibit 18–5 reveal the general pattern of the average and marginal cost schedules. For small output rates, the ATC of producing roller blades is high, primarily because of the high AFC. Initially, MC is less than ATC. When diminishing returns set in for output rates beginning with five units, however, MC rises. Beginning with the sixth unit of output, MC exceeds AVC, causing AVC to rise. Beginning with the eighth unit of output, MC exceeds ATC, causing it also to rise. ATC thus reaches a minimum at seven units of output. Look carefully at the data of Exhibit 18–5 to be sure that you fully understand the relationships among the various cost curves.

Using the numeric data of Exhibit 18–5, **Exhibit 18–6** graphically illustrates both the total and the average (and marginal) cost curves. Note that the MC curve intersects both the AVC and ATC curves at the minimum points (part b). As MC continues to rise above ATC, unit costs rise higher and higher as output increases beyond seven units.

In sum, the firm's short-run cost curves reflect the law of diminishing marginal returns. Assuming that the price of the variable resource is constant, MC

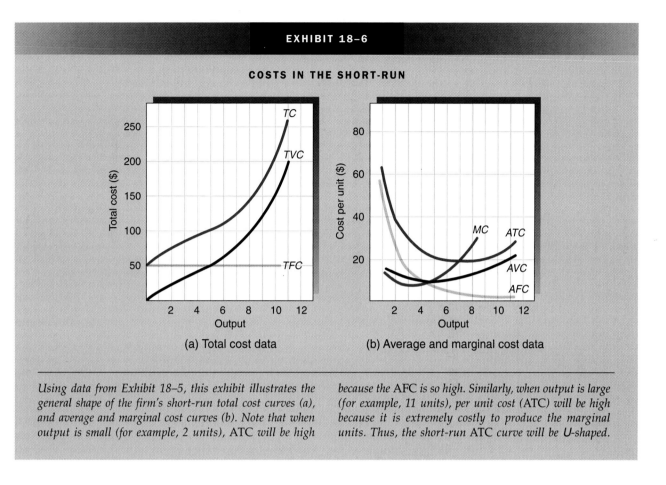

EXHIBIT 18–6

COSTS IN THE SHORT-RUN

(a) Total cost data

(b) Average and marginal cost data

Using data from Exhibit 18–5, this exhibit illustrates the general shape of the firm's short-run total cost curves (a), and average and marginal cost curves (b). Note that when output is small (for example, 2 units), ATC will be high because the AFC is so high. Similarly, when output is large (for example, 11 units), per unit cost (ATC) will be high because it is extremely costly to produce the marginal units. Thus, the short-run ATC curve will be U-shaped.

declines so long as the marginal product of the variable input is rising. This results because, in this range, smaller and smaller additions of the variable input are required to produce each extra unit of output. The situation is reversed, however, when diminishing returns are confronted. Once diminishing returns set in, more and more units of the variable factor are required to generate each additional unit of output. *MC* will rise, because the marginal product of the variable resource is declining. Eventually, *MC* exceeds *AVC* and *ATC*, causing these costs also to rise. A U-shaped short-run average total cost curve results.

OUTPUT AND COSTS IN THE LONG RUN

The short-run analysis relates costs to output *for a specific size of plant*. Firms, though, are not committed forever to their existing plant. In the long run, a firm can alter its plant size and all other factors of production. All resources used by the firm are variable in the long run.

How will the firm's choice of plant size affect production costs? **Exhibit 18–7** illustrates the short-run *ATC* curves for three plant sizes, ranging from small to

The short-run average total cost curves are shown for three alternative plant sizes. If these three were the only possible plant sizes, the long-run average total cost curve would be ABCD.

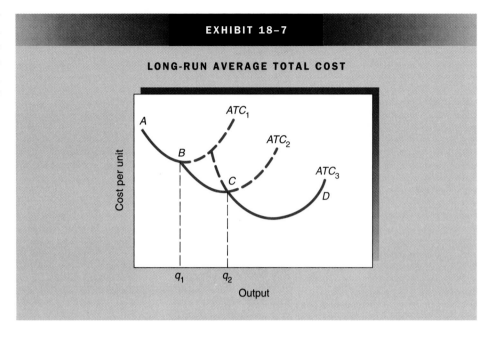

EXHIBIT 18–7

LONG-RUN AVERAGE TOTAL COST

large. If these three plant sizes were the only possible choices, which one would be best? The answer depends on the rate of output the firm expects to produce. The smallest plant would have the lowest cost if an output rate of less than q_1 were produced. The medium-sized plant would provide the least-cost method of producing output rates between q_1 and q_2. For any output level greater than q_2, the largest plant would be the most cost-efficient.

The long-run ATC curve shows the minimum average cost of producing each output level when the firm is free to choose among all possible plant sizes. It can best be thought of as a planning curve, because it reflects the expected per unit cost of producing alternative rates of output while plants are still in the blueprint stage.

Exhibit 18–7 illustrates the long-run *ATC* curve when only three plant sizes are possible, and the planning curve *ABCD* is thus mapped out. But, of course, given sufficient time, firms can usually choose among many plants of various sizes. **Exhibit 18–8** presents the long-run planning curve under these circumstances. It is a smooth curve, with each short-run *ATC* curve tangent to it.[6]

*It is important to keep in mind that no single plant size could produce the alternative output rates at the costs indicated by the planning curve **LRATC** in Exhibit 18–8.** Any of the planning-curve options are available before a plant size is chosen and the plant is built, but, although the firm can plan for the long run, choosing among many options, it can *operate* only in the short run. The *LRATC* curve outlines the possibilities available in the planning stage, indicating the expected average total costs of production for each of a large number of plants, which differ in size.

---

[6]The tangency, though, will occur at the least-cost output level for the short run only when the long-run curve is parallel to the *x*-axis, as in q_n, Exhibit 18–8.

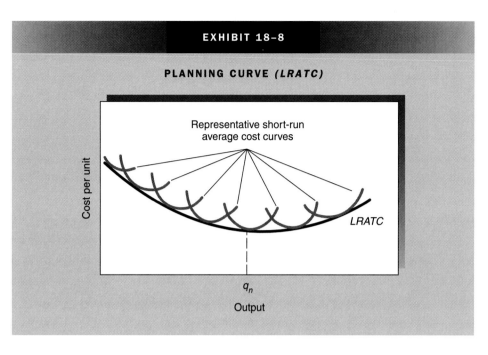

EXHIBIT 18–8

PLANNING CURVE (LRATC)

Representative short-run
average cost curves

Cost per unit

LRATC

q_n

Output

When many alternative plant sizes are possible, the long-run average total cost curve (LRATC) is mapped out.

SIZE OF FIRM AND UNIT COST IN THE LONG RUN

Do larger firms have lower minimum unit costs than smaller ones? The answer to this question depends on which industries are being considered. There is a sound basis, though, for expecting some initial reductions in per unit cost from large-scale production methods. Why? Large firms typically produce a large total volume of output.[7] Volume of output denotes the total number of units of a product that the firm expects to produce.[8] There are three major reasons why planning a larger volume generally reduces, at least initially, unit costs: (1) mass production, (2) specialization, and (3) improvements in production as a result of experience, or "learning by doing." Let us consider each of these factors.

Mass-production techniques usually are economical only when large volumes of output are planned, since they tend to involve large development and setup costs. Once the production methods are established, though, marginal

---

[7]Throughout this section, we assume that firms with larger plants necessarily plan a larger volume of output than do their smaller counterparts. Reality approximates these conditions. Firms choose large plants because they are planning to produce a large volume.

[8]Note the distinction between rate and volume of output. Rate of output is the number of units produced during a specific period (for example, the next six months). Volume is the total number of units produced during all time periods. For example, Boeing might produce two 767 airplanes per month (rate of output) while planning to produce a volume of two hundred 767s during the expected life of the model. Increasing the rate (reducing the time period during which a given output is produced) tends to raise costs, whereas increasing the volume (total amount produced) tends to lower costs. For additional information on production and costs, see Armen Alchian, "Costs," in *International Encyclopedia of the Social Sciences* (New York: Macmillan, 1968), pp. 404–415; and Jack Hirshleifer, "The Firm's Cost Function: A Successful Reconstruction," *Journal of Business* (July 1962): pp. 235–255.

costs are low. For example, the use of molds, dies, and assembly-line production methods reduce the per unit cost of automobiles only when the planned volume is in the millions. High-volume methods, although cheaper to use for high rates of output and high volumes, will typically require high fixed costs, and therefore will cause unit costs to be far higher for low volumes of production.

Large-scale operation also permits specialized use of labor and machines. Adam Smith noted 200 years ago that the output of a pin factory is much greater when one worker draws the wire, another straightens it, a third cuts it, a fourth grinds the point, a fifth makes the head of the pin, and so on.[9] In economics, the whole can sometimes be greater than the sum of the parts. Specialization provides the opportunity for people to become exceptionally proficient at performing small but essential functions. The result is more output per unit of labor.

Workers and managers in a firm that has made more units have probably learned more from their experience than their counterparts in smaller firms that have produced less output. Improvements in the production process result. Baseball players improve by playing baseball, and pianists by playing the piano. Similarly, the employees of a firm improve their skills as they "practice" productive techniques. This factor of "learning by doing" has been found to be tremendously important in the aircraft and automobile industries, among others. As managers and workers learn and develop skills producing the first 50 airplanes, for example, they are able to use these resources to produce the next batch of 50 airplanes more economically. Thus, firms that produce a large volume of output are able to achieve lower per unit costs because of their prior production experience.

ECONOMIES AND DISECONOMIES OF SCALE

Economies of scale
Reductions in the firm's per unit costs that are associated with the use of large plants to produce a large volume of output.

Economic theory suggests that, at least initially, larger firms have lower unit costs than comparable smaller firms. When unit costs decline as output expands, **economies of scale** are present over the initial range of outputs. The long-run *ATC* curve is falling.

Are *diseconomies of scale* possible—that is, are there ever situations in which the long-run average total costs are greater for larger firms than they are for smaller ones? The economic justification for diseconomies of scale is less obvious (and less tenable) than that for economies of scale. However, as a firm gets bigger and bigger, bureaucratic inefficiencies *may* result. Code-book procedures tend to replace managerial genius. Motivating the work force and carrying out managerial directives are also more complex when the firm is larger and principal-agent problems grow as there are more employees and more levels of monitoring to be done. Coordinating more people and conveying information to them is more difficult. These factors combine to cause rising long-run average total costs in some, though certainly not all, industries.

---

[9]Smith went on to state, "I have seen a small manufactory of this kind where ten men only were employed, and where some of them consequently performed two or three distinct operations. Those ten persons, therefore, could make among them upwards of forty-eight thousand pins in a day. But if they had all wrought separately and independently, and without any of them having been educated to this particular business, they certainly could not each of them have made twenty, perhaps not one pin in a day," Adam Smith, *An Inquiry into the Nature and Causes of the Wealth of Nations,* 1776, ed. Edwin Cannan (Chicago Press, 1976), pp. 8–9.

Economies and diseconomies of scale stem from different sources than do increasing and diminishing returns, because the former are long-run concepts. They relate to conditions of production when all factors are variable. In contrast, increasing and diminishing returns are short-run concepts, applicable only when the firm has a fixed factor of production.

Exhibit 18–9 outlines three different long-run average total cost (*LRATC*) curves that describe real-world conditions in differing industries. For part a, both economies and diseconomies of scale are present. Higher per unit costs will result if the firm chooses a plant size other than the one that minimizes the cost of producing output *q*. If each firm in an industry faces the same cost conditions, we can generalize and say that any plants that are larger or smaller than this ideal size will experience higher unit costs. A very narrow range of plant sizes would be expected in industries with the *LRATC* depicted by part a. Some lines of retail sales and agriculture might approximate these conditions.

Part b demonstrates the general shape of the *LRATC* that economists believe is present in most industries. Initially, economies of scale exist, but once a minimum efficient scale is reached, wide variation in firm size is possible. Firms smaller than the minimum efficient size would have higher per unit costs, but firms larger than that would not gain a cost advantage. **Constant returns to scale** are present for a broad range of output rates (between q_1 and q_2). This situation is consistent with real-world conditions in many industries. For example, small firms can be as efficient as larger ones in such industries as apparel, lumber, shoes, and publishing, and in many lines of retailing.

In part c of Exhibit 18–9, economies of scale exist for all relevant output levels. The larger the firm size, the lower the per unit cost. The *LRATC* in the local telephone service industry may approximate the curve shown here.

Constant returns to scale
Unit costs that are constant as the scale of the firm is altered. Neither economies nor diseconomies of scale are present.

WHAT FACTORS CAUSE COST CURVES TO SHIFT?

In outlining the general shapes of a firm's cost curves in both the long run and short run, we assumed that certain other factors—resource prices, taxes, and technology—remained constant as the firm altered its rate of output. Let us now consider how these other factors would affect production costs if they did not remain constant.

PRICES OF RESOURCES

If the price of resources used should rise, the firm's cost curves will shift upward, as **Exhibit 18–10** illustrates. Higher resource prices will increase the cost of producing each alternative output level. For example, what happens to the cost of producing automobiles when the price of steel rises? The cost of producing automobiles also rises. Conversely, lower resource prices will result in cost reductions. Thus, the cost curves for any specific plant size will shift downward.

For one type of LRATC curve, economies of scale are present for output levels less than q, but immediately beyond q, diseconomies of scale dominate (a). In another instance, economies of scale are important until some minimum output level (q_1) is attained. Once the minimum has been attained, there is a wide range of output levels (q_1 to q_2) that are consistent with the minimum ATC for the industry (b). In a third situation, economies of scale exist for all relevant output levels (c). As we will see later, this type of LRATC curve has important implications for the structure of the industry.

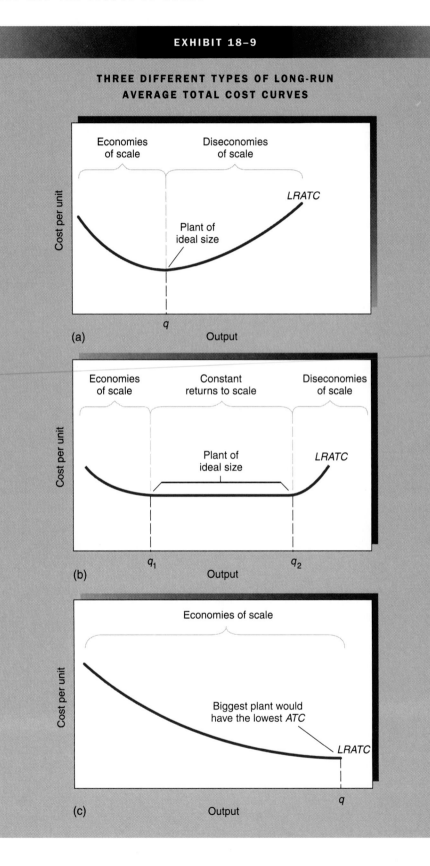

EXHIBIT 18-9

THREE DIFFERENT TYPES OF LONG-RUN AVERAGE TOTAL COST CURVES

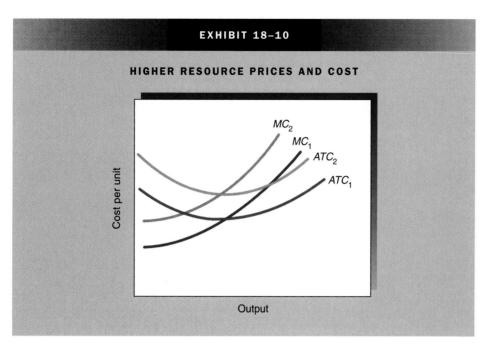

EXHIBIT 18–10

HIGHER RESOURCE PRICES AND COST

An increase in resource prices will cause the firm's cost curves to shift upward.

TAXES

Taxes are a component of a firm's cost. Suppose that an excise tax of 20 cents were levied on each gallon of gasoline sold by a service station. What would happen to the seller's costs? They would increase, just as they did in Exhibit 18–10. The firm's average total and marginal cost curves would shift upward by the amount of the tax. If the tax were an annual business license fee instead, it would raise the average cost, but not the variable cost.

TECHNOLOGY

Technological improvements often make it possible to produce a specific output with fewer resources. For example, the printing press drastically reduced the number of labor-hours required to print newspapers and books. The spinning wheel reduced the labor-hours necessary to weave cotton into cloth. More recently, computers and robots have reduced costs in many industries. As **Exhibit 18–11** shows, a technological improvement will shift the firm's cost curves downward, reflecting the reduction in the amount of resources used to produce alternative levels of output.

ECONOMIC WAY OF THINKING ABOUT COSTS

When analyzing the firm's costs, economists often present a highly mechanical— some would say unrealistic—view. The role of personal choice in uncertain circumstances tends to be glossed over.

Suppose that an egg producer discovers (or develops) a "super" mineral water that makes it possible to get more eggs from the same number of chickens. Because of this technological improvement, various output levels of eggs can now be produced with less feed, space, water, and labor. Costs will be reduced. The egg producer's ATC and MC curves will shift downward.

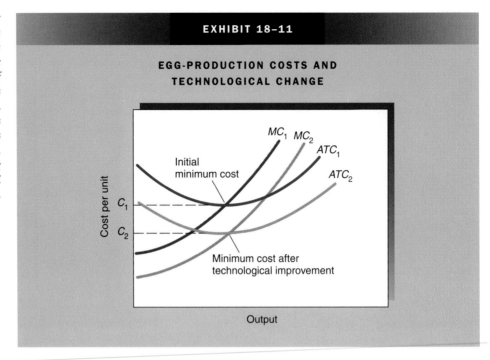

EXHIBIT 18–11

EGG-PRODUCTION COSTS AND TECHNOLOGICAL CHANGE

It is important to keep in mind that costs are incurred when choices are made. When business decision makers choose to purchase raw materials, hire new employees, or renew the lease on a plant, they incur costs. All these decisions, like other choices, must be made under conditions of uncertainty. Of course, past experience acts as a useful guide, yielding valuable information. Because of this, business decision makers will have a good idea of the costs that will be associated with alternative decisions.

Opportunity costs are usually expected costs—they represent the highest valued option that the decision maker expects to give up as the result of a choice. Think for a moment of what the cost curves developed in this chapter really mean. The firm's short-run *MC* curve represents the opportunity cost of expanding output, *given the firm's current plant size.* The firm's long-run *ATC* curve represents the opportunity cost per unit of output associated with varying plant sizes and rates of output, *given that the alternative plants are still on the drawing boards.* Opportunity costs look forward, reflecting expectations—often based on the past record—as to what will be forgone as a result of current decisions. At the time decisions must be made, neither the short-run *MC* nor the long-run *ATC* can be determined from accounting records, since accounting costs look backward. Accounting figures yield valuable information about historical costs, but, as the following discussion will show, they must be interpreted carefully when forecasting future costs.

SUNK COSTS

Sunk costs

Costs that have already been incurred as a result of past decisions. They are sometimes referred to as historical costs.

Historical costs associated with past decisions that cannot be reversed—economists call them **sunk costs**—will provide knowledge relevant to current decisions, but the specific costs themselves are no longer relevant. When past choices cannot be reversed, money that has been spent is gone for good. Current choices must be based on the costs and benefits expected in relation to *current and future* market conditions, if mistakes are to be avoided (see the Myths of Economics box).

If they are to minimize costs, business decision makers must recognize the irrelevance of sunk costs. Let us consider a simple example that emphasizes this point. Suppose that the firm of Exhibit 18–5 pays $100,000 to purchase and install a roller blade–producing machine. The machine is expected to last ten years. The company's books record the cost of the machine as $10,000 each year under the heading of depreciation. The machine can be used only to make roller blades. Since dismantling and reinstallation costs are high, it cannot be leased or sold to another firm. Also, it has no scrap value. In other words, there are no alternative uses for the machine. The machine's annual production of roller blades will generate $50,000 of revenues for the firm when it is employed with raw materials and other factors of production that cost $46,000.

Should the firm continue to use the machine? Its annual depreciation cost suggests that the firm loses $6,000 annually on its output. The depreciation cost, however, is a sunk cost. It was incurred when the machine was installed. The current opportunity cost of the machine is precisely zero. The firm is not giving up anything by continuing to use it. Since operating the machine generates $4,000 of additional net revenue, the firm can gain by continuing the operation of the machine. Of course, if current market conditions are not expected to improve, the firm will not purchase a similar machine or replace the machine when it wears

MYTHS OF ECONOMICS

"A GOOD BUSINESS DECISION MAKER WILL NEVER SELL A PRODUCT FOR LESS THAN ITS PRODUCTION COSTS."

This statement contains a grain of truth. A profit-seeking entrepreneur would not *undertake* a project knowing that the costs could not be covered. However, this view fails to emphasize (1) the time dimension of the production process and (2) the uncertainty associated with business decisions. The production process takes time. Raw materials must be purchased, employees hired, and plants equipped. Retailers must contract with suppliers. As these decisions are made, costs result. Many of the firm's costs of production are incurred long before the product is ready for marketing.

Even a good business decision maker is not always able to predict the future. Market conditions may change in an unexpected manner. At the time the product is ready for sale, buyers may be unwilling to pay a price that will cover the seller's past costs of production. These past costs, however, are now sunk costs and no longer relevant. Current decisions must be made on the basis of current cost and revenue considerations.

Should a grocer refuse to sell oranges that are about to spoil because their wholesale cost cannot be covered?

The grocer's current opportunity cost of selling the oranges may be nearly zero. The alternative may be to throw them in the garbage next week. Almost any price, even one far below past costs, would be better than letting the oranges spoil.

Consider another example. Suppose a couple who own a house plan to relocate temporarily. Should they refuse to rent their house for $400 (if this is the best offer available) because their monthly house payment is $600? Of course not. The house payment will go on, regardless of whether they rent the house. If the homeowners can cover their opportunity costs (perhaps wear and tear plus a $60 monthly fee for a property management service), they will gain by renting rather than leaving the house vacant.

Past mistakes provide useful lessons for the future, but they cannot be reversed. Bygones are bygones, even if they resulted in business loss. Only current revenue and cost considerations are relevant to current decisions about prices and profitability. There is no need to fret over spilt milk, burnt toast, or yesterday's business losses.

out, but this should not influence the decision of whether to continue operating the current one. The irrelevance of sunk costs helps explain why it often makes sense to continue operating older equipment (it has a low opportunity cost), even though it may not be wise to purchase similar equipment again.

COST AND SUPPLY

Economists are interested in cost because they seek to explain the supply decisions of firms. A strictly profit-maximizing firm will compare the expected revenues derived from a decision or a course of action with the expected costs. If the expected revenues exceed costs, the course of action will be chosen because it will expand profits (or reduce losses).

In the short run, when making supply decisions, the marginal cost of producing additional units is the relevant cost consideration. A profit-maximizing decision maker will compare the expected marginal costs with the expected additional revenue from larger sales. If the latter exceeds the former, output (the quantity supplied) will be expanded.

Whereas marginal costs are central to the choice of short-run output, the expected average total cost is vital to a firm's long-run supply decision. Before entering an industry (or purchasing capital assets for expansion or replacement), a profit-maximizing decision maker will compare the expected market price with the expected long-run average total cost. Profit-seeking potential entrants will supply the product if, and only if, they expect the market price to exceed their long-run average total cost. Similarly, existing firms will continue to supply a product only if they expect that the market price will enable them at least to cover their long-run average total cost.

LOOKING AHEAD

In this chapter, we outlined several basic principles that affect costs for business firms. We will use these basic principles when we analyze the price and output decisions of firms under alternative market structures in the chapters that follow.

CHAPTER SUMMARY

1. The business firm is used to organize productive resources and transform them into goods and services. There are three major business structures—proprietorships, partnerships, and corporations. Proprietorships are the most numerous, but most of the nation's business activity is conducted through corporations. To solve the principal-agent problem, which tends to reduce worker efficiency in team production, every firm must provide work incentives and monitoring. The business structure chosen can influence the cost of those provisions and ultimately, of course, the cost of the product.

2. The demand for a product indicates the intensity of consumers' desires for the item. The (opportunity) cost of producing the item indicates the desire of consumers for other goods that must be given up because the necessary resources are being used in the production of the item. In a market economy, these two forces—demand and costs of production—balance the desire of consumers for more of a good against the reality of scarce resources, which requires that other goods be forgone in order to supply more of any specific item.

3. Economists employ the opportunity-cost concept when figuring a firm's costs. Therefore, total cost includes not only explicit payments for resources employed by the firm, but also the implicit costs associated with the use of productive resources owned by the firm.

4. When accounting procedures omit the opportunity cost of the firm's equity capital or owner-provided services, accounting costs understate the opportunity cost of producing a good. As a result of these omissions, the accounting profits of a firm are generally larger than the firm's economic profits.

5. Economic profit (loss) results when a firm's sales revenues exceed (are less than) its total costs, both explicit and implicit. Firms that are making the market rate of return on their assets will therefore make zero economic profit. Firms that transform resources into products of greater value than the opportunity cost of the resources used will make an economic profit. On the other hand, if the opportunity cost of the resources used exceeds the value of the product, losses will result.

6. The firm's short-run average total cost (ATC) curve will tend to be U-shaped. When output is small (relative to plant size), average fixed cost (AFC)—and therefore ATC—will be high. As output expands, however, AFC—and initially ATC—will fall. As the firm attempts to produce a larger and larger rate of output with its fixed plant size, diminishing returns will eventually set in, and marginal cost (MC) will rise quite rapidly as the plant's maximum capacity is approached. Thus, the short-run ATC will also be high because MC is high when the existing size of the plant is overutilized.

7. The law of diminishing returns explains why a firm's short-run marginal and average total costs will eventually rise. When diminishing marginal returns are present, successively larger amounts of the variable input will be required to increase output by one more unit. Thus, marginal costs will eventually rise as output expands. Eventually, MC will exceed ATC, causing the latter to rise also.

8. The ability to plan a larger volume of output often leads to cost reductions. These cost reductions associated with the scale of one's operation result from (a) a greater opportunity to employ mass production methods, (b) specialized use of resources, and (c) learning by doing.

9. The long-run ATC (LRATC) reflects the costs of production for plants of various sizes. When economies of scale are present (that is, when larger plants have lower minimum per unit costs of production), LRATC will decline. When constant returns to scale are experienced, LRATC will be constant. A rising LRATC is also possible. Bureaucratic decision making and other diseconomies of scale may in some cases cause LRATC to rise.

10. In analyzing the general shapes of a firm's cost curves, we assumed that the following factors were constant: (a) resource prices, (b) technology, and (c) taxes. Changes in any of these factors would cause the cost curves of a firm to shift.

11. In any analysis of business decision making, it is important to keep the opportunity-cost principle in mind. Economists are interested in costs primarily because costs affect the decisions of suppliers. Short-run MC represents the supplier's opportunity cost of producing additional units with the existing plant facilities of the firm. The LRATC represents the opportunity cost of supplying alternative rates of output, given sufficient time to vary all factors, including plant size.

12. Sunk costs are costs that have already been incurred and cannot be recovered. They should not exert a direct influence on current business choices. However, they may provide information that will be useful in making current decisions.

CRITICAL ANALYSIS QUESTIONS

*1. What is economic profit? How might it differ from accounting profit? Explain why firms that are making zero economic profit are likely to continue in business.

*2. Which of the following statements do you think reflect sound economic thinking? Explain your answer.
   a. "I paid $200 for this economics course. Therefore, I'm going to attend the lectures even if they are useless and boring."
   b. "Because we own rather than rent, and the house is paid for, housing doesn't cost us anything."
   c. "I own 100 shares of stock that I can't afford to sell until the price goes up enough for me to get back at least my original investment."
   d. "It costs to produce private education, whereas public schooling is free."

3. Suppose a firm produces bicycles. Will the firm's accounting statement reflect the opportunity cost of producing bicycles? Why or why not? What costs would an accounting statement reveal? Should current decisions be based on accounting costs? Explain.

4. What is the principal-agent problem? When will the principal-agent problem be most severe? Why might there be a principal-agent problem between the stockholder-owners and the managers of a large corporation?

5. Suppose that Ajax, Inc., is the target of a takeover attempt by the management of Beta Corporation, which is offering to buy stock from any Ajax stockholder who wants to sell at 20 percent above the current price. Explain how the resistance of Ajax management to the takeover attempt might illustrate the principal-agent problem. Is it possible that the Beta Corporation management's action is itself an illustration of the principal-agent problem? Explain.

6. What are some of the advantages of the corporate business structure of ownership for large business firms? What are some of the disadvantages? Is the corporate form of business ownership cost-efficient? In a market economy, how would you tell whether the corporate structural form was efficient?

*7. Explain the factors that cause a firm's short-run average total costs to decline initially, but eventually to increase as the rate of output rises.

8. Which of the following are relevant to a firm's decision to increase output: (a) short-run average total cost, (b) short-run marginal cost, (c) long-run average total cost? Justify your answer.

9. Economics students often confuse (a) diminishing returns to the variable factor and (b) diseconomies of scale. Explain the difference between the two, and give one example of each.

10. "Firms that make a profit have increased the value of the resources they used; their actions created wealth. In contrast, the actions of firms that make losses reduce wealth. The discovery and undertaking of profit-making opportunities are key ingredients of economic progress." Evaluate the statement.

*11. Is profit maximization consistent with the self-interest of corporate owners? Is it consistent with the self-interest of corporate managers? Is there a conflict between the self-interest of owners and of managers?

*12. What is the opportunity cost of (a) borrowed funds and (b) equity capital? Under current tax law, firms can take the opportunity cost of borrowed funds, but not equity capital, as an expense. How does this tax feature affect the debt/equity ratio of business firms?

*13. "If a firm maximizes profit, it must minimize the cost of producing the profit-maximum output." Is this statement true or false? Explain your answer.

14. Why do economists consider normal returns to capital as a cost? How does economic profit differ from normal returns (or "normal profit")?

*15. Draw a U-shaped short-run *ATC* curve for a firm. Construct the accompanying *MC* and *AVC* curves.

16. What is shirking? If the managers of a firm are attempting to maximize the profits of the firm, will they have an incentive to limit shirking? How might they go about doing so?

17. What are implicit costs? Do implicit costs contribute to the opportunity cost of production? Should an implicit cost be counted as cost? Give three examples of implicit costs. Does the firm's accounting statement take implicit costs into account? Why or why not?

*18. Consider a machine purchased one year ago for $12,000. The machine is being depreciated $4,000 per year over a three-year period. Its current market value is $5,000, and the expected market value of the machine one year from now is $3,000. If the interest rate is 10 percent, what is the expected cost of holding the machine during the next year?

*19. Investors seeking to take over a firm often bid a positive price for the business even though it is currently experiencing losses. Why would anyone ever bid a positive price for a firm operating at a loss?

20. Fill in the blanks in the following table:

---

*Asterisk denotes questions for which answers are given in Appendix B.

Units of Variable Input	Total Product	Marginal Product	Average Product	Price of Input	Total Variable Cost	Average Variable Cost	Total Fixed Cost	Total Cost	Average Total Cost	Marginal Cost
0	0	____	____	$1	____	____	$2	____	____	____
1	6	____	____	$1	____	____	$2	____	____	____
2	15	____	____	$1	____	____	$2	____	____	____
3	27	____	____	$1	____	____	$2	____	____	____
4	37	____	____	$1	____	____	$2	____	____	____
5	45	____	____	$1	____	____	$2	____	____	____
6	50	____	____	$1	____	____	$2	____	____	____
7	52	____	____	$1	____	____	$2	____	____	____
8	50	____	____	$1	____	____	$2	____	____	____

a. What happens to total product when marginal product is negative?

b. What happens to average product when marginal product is greater than average product?

c. What happens to average product when marginal product is less than average product?

d. At what point does marginal product begin to decrease?

e. At what point does marginal cost begin to increase?

f. Summarize the relationship between marginal product and marginal cost.

g. What happens to marginal costs when total product begins to fall?

h. What is happening to average variable costs when they equal marginal costs?

i. Marginal costs equal average variable costs between what output levels?

j. What is happening to average total costs when they equal marginal costs?

k. Marginal costs equal average total costs between what output levels?

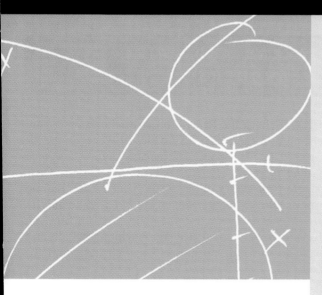

CHAPTER FOCUS

- What is the difference between firms that are price takers and those that are price searchers?
- What determines the output of a price taker?
- How do price takers change their output when price changes in the short run? In the long run?
- What is the role of time in determining the elasticity of supply?
- What must firms do in order to make profits? How do profits and losses influence the supply and market price of a product?
- How does competition influence the incentive of self-interested producers to supply goods that consumers want at an economical cost?

Competition means decentralized planning by many separate persons.

FRIEDRICH A. VON HAYEK[1]

Competition is conducive to the continuous improvements of industrial efficiency. It leads some producers to eliminate wastes and cut costs so that they may undersell others. It compels others to adopt similar measures in order that they may survive. It weeds out those whose costs remain high and thus operates to concentrate production in the hands of those whose costs are low.

CLAIR WILCOX[2]

---

[1]F. A. Hayek, "The Use of Knowledge in Society," *American Economic Review* 35 (September 1945): 519–550.

[2]Clair Wilcox, *Competition and Monopoly in American Industry*, Monograph no. 21, Temporary National Economic Committee, Investigation of Concentration of Economic Power, 76th Congress, 3d session (Washington, D.C.: U.S. Government Printing Office, 1940).

I n the previous chapters we saw how firms make production decisions, and how costs affect those decisions. In this and the next two chapters, we take a closer look at how the product prices and profit levels that emerge from market trading will influence production. How much will be produced in a given market? What determines the profitability of firms, and how does the level of profit influence market supply over time? When goods and services are allocated by markets, will resources be allocated efficiently? Is there any reason to believe that there will be a linkage between market allocation and economic prosperity? These are the major questions that we will address in the next several chapters.

PRICE TAKERS AND PRICE SEARCHERS

Price takers

Sellers who must take the market price in order to sell their product. Because each price taker's output is small relative to the total market, price takers can sell all their output at the market price, but they are unable to sell any of their output at a price higher than the market price.

This chapter will focus on markets where the firms are **price takers:** They simply take the price that is determined in the market. *In a price-taker market, the firms all produce identical products (for example, wheat, eggs, or regular unleaded gasoline) and each seller is small relative to the total market. Thus, the output supplied by any single firm exerts little or no effect on the market price. Each firm can sell all its output at the market price, but it is unable to sell any of its output at a price higher than the market price.* When a firm is a price taker, there is no price decision to be made. Price takers will merely attempt to choose the output level that will maximize profit, given their costs and the price determined by the market.

In the real world, most firms are not price takers. There is generally an inverse relationship between the price charged by the firm and the number of units the firm is able to sell. If the firm lowers its price, it will generally attract additional customers. Correspondingly, firms are usually able to increase their price, at least a little, without losing all their customers. For example, if Nike increased the price of its athletic shoes by 10 percent, the number of shoes sold would decline (although it would not fall to zero). Firms like Nike are **price searchers:** They can choose what price they will charge for their product, but the quantity that they are able to sell is very much related to their price. As price searchers seek maximum profit, they must not only decide how much to produce, but also what price to charge. We will examine markets where the firms are price searchers in the following two chapters.

Price searchers

Firms that face a downward sloping demand curve for their product. The amount that the firm is able to sell is inversely related to the price that it charges.

Competition as a dynamic process

A term that denotes rivalry or competitiveness between or among parties (for example, producers or input suppliers), each of which seeks to deliver a better deal to buyers when quality, price, and product information are all considered. Competition implies a lack of collusion among sellers.

If most real-world firms are price searchers rather than price takers, why take the time to analyze the latter? There are several reasons to do so. First, although most firms are not price takers, there are a number of important markets, particularly in agriculture, where the firms do essentially take the price determined in the market. Second, the price-taker model helps clarify the relationship between the decision making of individual firms and market supply in both price-taker and price-searcher markets. Finally, and perhaps most important, the study of markets where firms are price takers enhances our knowledge of **competition as a dynamic process.** Understanding how the competitive process works when firms are price takers will also contribute to our understanding of the process as it applies to many price searchers.

Historically, almost all economists have referred to markets where firms are price takers as **purely competitive markets.** Increasingly, however, these markets are referred to as price-taker markets because this expression is more descriptive. Furthermore, it avoids the implication that competitive forces are necessarily less pure or less intense in price-searcher markets. Clearly, this is not always the case. In fact, price searchers often use a broad array of competitive weapons—for example, quality of product, style, convenient location, advertising, and price—all in an effort to attract consumers. When **barriers to entry** are low, the competitive process is just as important in price-searcher markets as it is when the firms are price takers.

Nonetheless, it should be noted that price-taker markets and purely competitive markets are merely alternative names for the same thing. Thus, if you hear someone speak of pure competition or a purely competitive market, the person is referring to markets that have characteristics like those analyzed in this chapter.

Purely competitive markets
Markets characterized by a large number of small firms producing an identical product in an industry (market area) that permits complete freedom of entry and exit. Also called price-taker markets.

Barriers to entry
Obstacles that limit the freedom of potential rivals to enter and compete in an industry or market.

MARKETS WHEN FIRMS ARE PRICE TAKERS

Consider the situation of Les Parrot, a Texas cattle rancher. As Parrot consults the financial pages of the local newspaper, he finds that the current market price of quality steers is 88 cents per pound. Even if his ranch is quite large, there is little that Parrot can do to change the market price of beef cattle. After all, there are tens of thousands of farmers who raise cattle. Thus, Parrot supplies only a small portion of the total cattle market. The amount that he sells will exert little or no impact on the market price of cattle. Parrot is a price taker.

The firms in a market will be price takers when the following four conditions are met:

1. All the firms in the market are producing an identical product (for example, beef cattle of a given grade).
2. A large number of firms exist in the market.
3. Each firm supplies only a very small portion of the total amount supplied to the market.
4. No barriers limit the entry or exit of firms in the market.

When these conditions are met, the firms in the market must accept the market price. This is why they are called price takers. **Exhibit 19–1** illustrates the relationship between the market forces (frame b) and the demand curve facing the price-taking firm (frame a). If the firm sets a price above the market level, consumers will simply buy from other sellers. Why pay the higher price when the identical good is available elsewhere at a lower price? For example, if the price of wheat were $5.00 per bushel, a farmer would be unable to find buyers for wheat at $5.50 per bushel. A firm could set its price below the market level. However, since it is small relative to the total market, the firm can already sell as much as it wants at the market price. A price reduction would merely reduce revenues. A firm that is a price taker thus confronts a perfectly elastic demand for its product. (Note that a lower case "d" is used to denote the demand curve faced by the *firm* while a capital "D" indicates the *market* demand curve.)

The market forces of supply and demand determine price (b). Price takers have no control over price. Thus, the demand for the product of the firm is perfectly elastic (a).

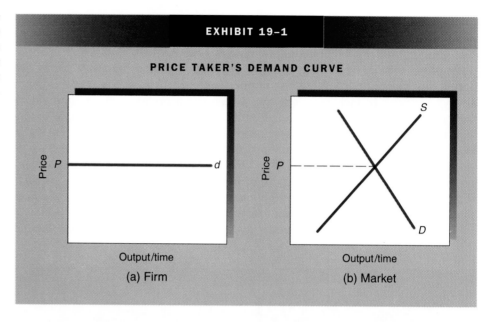

EXHIBIT 19-1

PRICE TAKER'S DEMAND CURVE

(a) Firm

(b) Market

OUTPUT IN THE SHORT RUN

The firm's output decision is based on comparison of benefits with costs. If a firm produces at all, it will continue expanding output as long as the benefits (additional revenues) from the production and sales of the additional units exceed their marginal costs.

How will changes in output influence the firm's costs? In the preceding chapter, we discovered that the firm's short-run marginal costs will eventually increase as the firm expands its output by working its fixed plant facilities more intensively. The law of diminishing marginal returns assures us that this will be the case. Eventually, both the firm's short-run marginal and average total cost curves will turn upward.

Marginal revenue (MR)
The incremental change in total revenue derived from the sale of one additional unit of a product.

What about the benefits or additional revenues from output expansion? **Marginal revenue (MR)** is the change in the firm's total revenue per unit of output. It is the additional revenue derived from the sale of an additional unit of output. Mathematically,

$$MR = \text{Change in total revenue/Change in output}$$

The price taker sells all units at the same price; therefore, its marginal revenue will be equal to the market price.

In the short run, the price taker will expand output until marginal revenue (its price) is just equal to marginal cost. This decision-making rule will maximize the firm's profits (or minimize its losses).

Exhibit 19–2 helps explain why. Since the firm can sell as many units as it would like at the market price, the sale of one additional unit will increase revenue by the price of the product. Does the firm gain by producing an extra unit? The answer is yes, as long as the marginal revenue (selling price, for the price taker) is greater than or equal to the marginal cost of that unit. Profit is simply the difference between total revenue and total cost. Profit will increase as long

The price taker would maximize profits by producing the output level q, *where* P = MC.

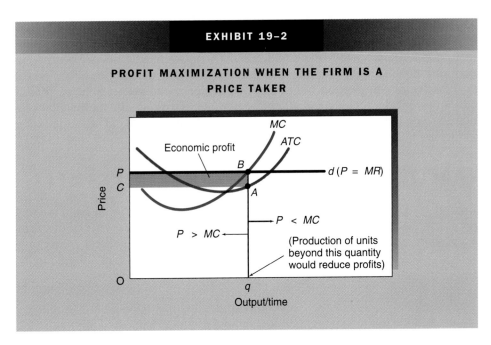

EXHIBIT 19–2

PROFIT MAXIMIZATION WHEN THE FIRM IS A PRICE TAKER

as production and sale of a unit add more to revenue than to cost. Thus, the firm will gain from an increase in output as long as marginal revenue exceeds marginal cost. Eventually, however, as the firm produces a larger and larger quantity from its fixed size of plant, marginal costs will rise and exceed price and marginal revenue. When production of an additional unit adds more to cost than it adds to revenue, profit will be reduced if the unit is produced. Thus, the profit of the price taker is maximized at the output rate where $P = MR = MC$. In Exhibit 19–2, this occurs at output level q.

A profit-maximizing firm with the cost curves indicated by Exhibit 19–2 would produce exactly q. The total revenue of the firm would be the sales price P multiplied by output sold q. Geometrically, the firm's total revenues would be $POqB$. The firm's total cost would be found by multiplying the average total cost by the output level. Geometrically, total costs are represented by $COqA$. The firm's total revenues exceed total costs, and the firm is making short-run economic profit (the shaded area).

In the real world, of course, decisions are not made by entrepreneurs who sit around drawing demand and marginal cost curves. Many have not even heard of these concepts. A business decision maker who has never heard of the $P = MC$ rule for profit maximization, however, probably has another rule that yields approximately the same outcome. For example, the rule might be to produce those units, and only those units, that add more to revenue than to cost. This ensures maximum profit (or minimum loss). It also takes the firm to the point at which $P = MC$. Why? To stop short of that point would mean not producing some profitable units—units that would add more to revenue than to cost. Similarly, the decision maker would not go beyond that point because production of such units would add more to costs than to revenues. This commonsense rule thus leads to the same outcome as our model, even when the decision maker knows none of the technical jargon of economics. No wonder economics is sometimes thought of as "organized common sense."

Just how accurate is the price taker's competitive model in predicting behavior in real markets? Do other models, which assume that sellers collude to eliminate competition, yield better predictions? Direct scientific evidence bearing on such questions is highly desirable. As the Applications in Economics box on the significance of competition indicates, such evidence has been produced repeatedly in recent decades by the relatively new subdiscipline of experimental economics. The evidence indicates that the general implications of the price-taker model are valid under a variety of circumstances.

PROFIT MAXIMIZING — A NUMERIC EXAMPLE

Exhibit 19–3 uses numeric data to illustrate profit-maximizing decision making for a firm that is a price taker. Put yourself in the place of the owner of this firm. Your short-run total and marginal cost schedules have the general characteris-

---

EXHIBIT 19–3

PROFIT MAXIMIZATION FOR A PRICE TAKER: A NUMERIC ILLUSTRATION

(1) Output (per day)	(2) Total Revenue (TR)	(3) Total Cost (TC)	(4) Marginal Revenue (MR)	(5) Marginal Cost (MC)	(6) Profit (TR − TC)
0	$ 0.00	$ 25.00	$0.00	$ 0.00	$−25.00
1	5.00	29.80	5.00	4.80	−24.80
2	10.00	33.75	5.00	3.95	−23.75
3	15.00	37.25	5.00	3.50	−22.25
4	20.00	40.25	5.00	3.00	−20.25
5	25.00	42.75	5.00	2.50	−17.75
6	30.00	44.75	5.00	2.00	−14.75
7	35.00	46.50	5.00	1.75	−11.50
8	40.00	48.00	5.00	1.50	− 8.00
9	45.00	49.25	5.00	1.25	− 4.25
10	50.00 .	50.25	5.00	1.00	− 0.25
11	55.00	51.50	5.00	1.25	3.50
12	60.00	53.25	5.00	1.75	6.75
13	65.00	55.75	5.00	2.50	9.25
14	70.00	59.25	5.00	3.50	10.75
15	75.00	64.00	5.00	4.75	11.00
16	80.00	70.00	5.00	6.00	10.00
17	85.00	77.25	5.00	7.25	7.75
18	90.00	85.50	5.00	8.25	4.50
19	95.00	95.00	5.00	9.50	0.00
20	100.00	108.00	5.00	13.00	− 8.00
21	105.00	125.00	5.00	17.00	−20.00

EXPERIMENTAL ECONOMICS—THE SIGNIFICANCE OF COMPETITION

Do individual decision makers, without any economics training, behave as if they understand marginal costs? Do they act as price takers, even though not all the assumptions of that model are satisfied? Or, when there are only a few sellers, do they collude successfully so as to raise price above marginal cost?

Verifying economic principles and comparing alternative economic models by scientific testing is not an easy task. Simply observing people to see whether they behave as economic principles suggest is not completely satisfactory. A normal economic event that we can observe may be the result of more than one cause; therefore, the economist trying to isolate the impact of one causal factor must try to be sure that other factors influencing the outcome do not vary, or else try to take them into account in the analysis. To isolate the impact of a change in the price of a product on consumer behavior, for example, the economist must somehow account for the impact of all other price changes, income changes, and so on, that may have occurred. In other disciplines, scientists use experiments in the laboratory, with all factors controlled, to tackle a problem. They test the principles on which their science is built, using carefully detailed methods, so that other scientists can replicate the experiment.

Beginning about the middle of the twentieth century, economists also began to conduct laboratory experiments. A good many experiments have been conducted to investigate the predictive power of the price-taker model. In one of the earliest, conducted in 1956 by leading experimental economist Vernon Smith of the University of Arizona, individuals were brought into a laboratory setting and arbitrarily assigned roles as buyers and sellers, in a game-like setting. Each buyer was given a different "limit price" (that is, a maximum price he or she was allowed to pay) for a paper asset. If the buyer could purchase the paper commodity for less than the limit price, he or she received a cash payment equal to the difference between the limit price and the amount actually paid. Therefore, as in other markets, each buyer gained financially by purchasing at lower prices. The sellers were treated in a parallel fashion. Each had a "limit price" (a minimum selling price) and received in cash any extra revenue above that price.

Buyers and sellers were free to make verbal offers to buy or sell. How did markets develop? Did the outcomes resemble a market where sellers compete, or did sellers collude, controlling the market price for their own benefit and controlling entry into the market?

The price-taker model predicts that all mutually advantageous trades among buyers and sellers will occur and that there will be a tendency for the price of the good to converge toward a single price—the market price. Prior to the work in experimental economics, many economists thought this model was relevant only under highly restrictive conditions. By changing the number of sellers, the type of trading rules, and so on, experimental researchers have generated similar results under a wide variety of conditions. Their findings suggest that outcomes approximating those of the price-taker model tend to emerge under a wide variety of circumstances. For example, experimental work indicates that outcomes similar to those predicted by the price-taker model generally hold even when there is a relatively small number of sellers, say, ten or more.

Vernon Smith and Arlington Williams, two of the leading researchers in this area, summarize the findings of their work in the following manner:

Experimental market research has provided an empirical foundation for tenets of economic theory that were already well established, and it has also yielded insight into the details of how particular rules affect the outcome of the trading process. Thirty years of experiments have also brought good news: under most circumstances, markets are extremely efficient in facilitating the movement of goods from the lowest-cost producers to the consumers who place the highest value on them. Organized exchange thus effectively advances human welfare.[1]

---

[1]Vernon L. Smith and Arlington W. Williams, "Experimental Market Economics," *Scientific American* (December 1992), pp. 116–121. For additional background, see Charles R. Plott, "Will Economics Become an Experimental Science?" *Southern Economic Journal* (April 1991).

tics we discussed in the previous chapter. Since the firm confronts a market price of $5 per unit, its marginal revenue is $5. Total revenue thus increases by $5 per additional unit of output. You will maximize your profit when you supply an output of 15 units.

There are two ways of viewing this profit-maximizing output rate. First, profit is equal to the difference between total revenue and total cost. Thus, profit will be maximized at the output rate at which this difference (*TR* minus *TC*) is greatest. Column 6 of Exhibit 19–3 provides this information. For small output rates (less than 11), you and your firm would actually experience losses. But at 15 units of output, an $11 profit is earned ($75 total revenue minus $64 total cost). A look at the profit figures of column 6 indicates that it would be impossible to earn a profit larger than $11 at any other rate of output.

Exhibit 19–4a presents the total revenue and total cost approach in graph form. (However, the curves are drawn smoothly, as though output could be increased by tiny amounts, not just in whole-unit increments as shown in Exhibit 19–3.) Profits will be greatest when the total revenue line exceeds the total cost curve by the largest vertical amount. That takes place, of course, at 15 units of output.

You can also use the marginal approach to determine the profit-maximizing rate of output for this competitive firm. Remember, as long as price (marginal revenue) exceeds marginal cost, production and sale of additional units will add to the firm's profit (or reduce its losses). A look at columns 4 and 5 of Exhibit 19–3 reveals that *MR* is greater than *MC* for the first 15 units of output. Producing these units will expand the firm's profit. In contrast, producing any unit beyond 15 adds more to cost than to revenue. Profit will therefore decline if you expand output beyond 15 units. Given the firm's cost and revenue schedule, you will maximize profit by producing 15, and only 15, units per day.

Exhibit 19–4b graphically illustrates the marginal approach. Note here that the output rate (15 units) at which the marginal cost and marginal revenue curves intersect coincides with the output rate in Exhibit 19–4a at which the total revenue curve exceeds the total cost curve by the largest amount.

LOSSES AND GOING OUT OF BUSINESS

Suppose changes take place in the market that depress the price below a firm's average total cost. How will a profit-maximizer (or loss-minimizer) respond to this situation? The answer to this question depends on both the firm's current sales revenues relative to its variable cost and its expectations about the future. The firm's owner has three options: (1) continue to operate in the short run, (2) shut down temporarily, or (3) go out of business.

If the firm anticipates that the lower market price is temporary, it may want to continue operating in the short run as long as it can cover its variable cost.[3]

---

[3]In thinking about this issue, we must keep in mind the opportunity-cost concept. The firm's fixed costs are *opportunity costs* that do not vary with the level of output. They can be avoided if, and only if, the firm goes out of business. To specify fixed costs, we need to know (1) how much the firm's fixed assets would bring if they were sold or rented to others and (2) any other costs, such as operating license fees and debts, that could be avoided if the firm declared bankruptcy and/or went out of business. Since fixed costs can be avoided if the firm goes out of business, the firm should not operate even in the short run if it does not expect conditions to improve. See Marshall Colberg and James King, "Theory of Production Abandonment," *Revista Internazionale di Scienze Ecnomiche e Commerciali* 20 (1973): 961–1072.

Using the data of Exhibit 19–3, here we provide two ways of viewing profit maximization. In the first, the profits of the price taker are maximized at the output level at which total revenue exceeds total cost by the maximum amount (a). In the second, the maximum-profit output is identified by comparing marginal revenue and marginal cost (b).

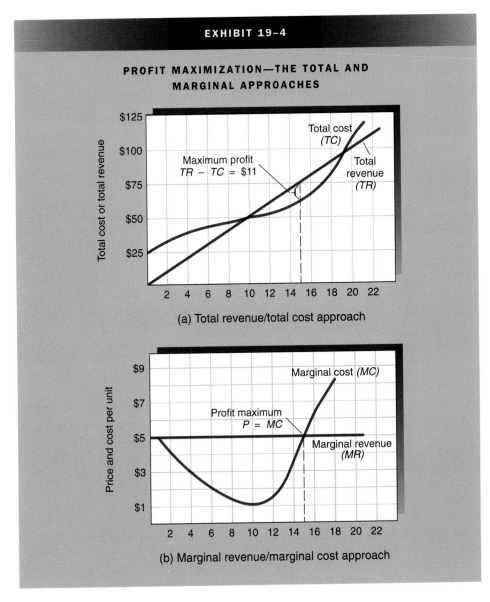

EXHIBIT 19–4

PROFIT MAXIMIZATION—THE TOTAL AND MARGINAL APPROACHES

(a) Total revenue/total cost approach

(b) Marginal revenue/marginal cost approach

Exhibit 19–5 illustrates why. The firm shown in this exhibit would minimize its loss at output level q, where $P = MC$. But at q, total revenues ($OqBP_1$) are less than total costs ($OqAC$). The firm faces short-run economic losses. Even if it shuts down completely, it will still incur fixed costs, *unless the firm goes out of business*. If it anticipates that the market price will increase enough that the firm will be able to cover its average total costs in the future, it may not want to sell its assets and terminate operations. It may choose to produce q units in the short run, even though losses are incurred. At price P_1, production of output q is clearly more advantageous than shutting down, because the firm is able to cover its variable costs and pay some of its fixed costs. If it were to shut down, *but not sell out*, the firm would lose the entire amount of its fixed cost.

What if the market price declines below the firm's average variable cost (for example, P_2)? Under these circumstances, a temporary **shutdown** is preferable

Shutdown
A temporary halt in the operation of a business in which the firm anticipates a return to operation in the future and therefore does not sell its assets. The firm's variable cost is eliminated for the duration of the shutdown, but its fixed costs continue.

A firm making losses will operate in the short run if it (1) can cover its variable costs now and (2) expects price to be high enough in the future to cover all its costs.

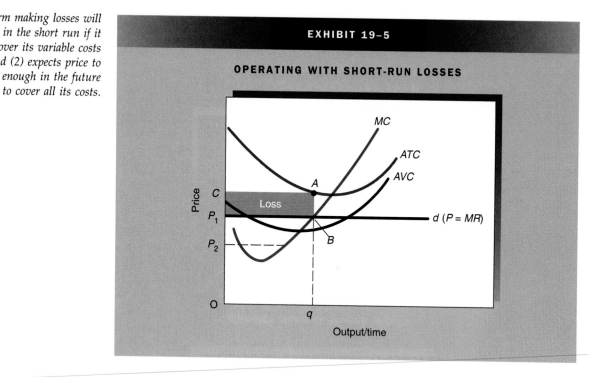

EXHIBIT 19–5

OPERATING WITH SHORT-RUN LOSSES

to short-run operation. If the firm continues to operate in the short run, operating losses merely add to losses resulting from the firm's fixed costs. Therefore, even if the firm's owner expects the market price to increase, enabling it to survive and prosper in the future, shutting down in the short run when the market price falls below its average variable cost will reduce losses. Temporary shutdowns are actually planned on a regular basis in some markets. For example, restaurants and motels in some areas shut down in slow seasons, operating only when tourists or other seasonal purchasers provide enough demand. The price-taker model predicts that these firms will operate only when they expect to cover their variable costs. (See photo on page 514.)

The firm's third option is **going out of business** immediately. After all, even the losses resulting from the firm's fixed costs (remember that if they are costs of doing business, they must be avoidable by not doing business) can be avoided if the firm sells out. If market conditions are not expected to change for the better, then going out of business is the preferred option.

Going out of business
The sale of a firm's assets and its permanent exit from the market. By going out of business, a firm is able to avoid fixed costs, which would continue during a shutdown.

FIRM'S SHORT-RUN SUPPLY CURVE

The price taker that intends to stay in business will maximize profits (or minimize losses) when it produces the output level at which P = MC and variable costs are covered. Therefore, the portion of the firm's short-run marginal cost curve that lies above its average variable cost is the short-run supply curve of the firm.

Exhibit 19–6 illustrates that, as the market price increases, the firm will expand output along its *MC* curve. If the market price were less than P_1, the firm

EXHIBIT 19-6

SUPPLY CURVE FOR THE FIRM AND THE MARKET

(a) Representative firm

(b) Market

When resource prices are constant, the short-run market supply of the firm (a) is merely the sum of the supply produced by all the firms in the market area (b).

would shut down immediately because it would be unable to cover even its variable costs. If the market price is P_1, however, a price equal to the firm's average variable cost, the firm may supply output q_1 in the short run. Economic losses will result, but the firm would incur similar losses if it shut down completely. As the market price increases to P_2, the firm will happily expand output along its MC curve to q_2. At P_2, price is also equal to average total costs. The firm is making a "normal rate of return," or zero economic profits. Higher prices will result in a still larger short-run output. The firm will supply q_3 units at market price P_3. At this price, economic profits will result. At still higher prices, output will be expanded even more. As long as price exceeds average variable cost, higher prices will cause the firm to expand output along its MC curve, which therefore becomes the firm's short-run supply curve.

SHORT-RUN MARKET SUPPLY CURVE

The short-run market supply curve corresponds to the total amount supplied by all the firms in the industry. *When the firms are price takers, the short-run market supply curve is the horizontal summation of the marginal cost curves (above the level of average variable cost) for all firms in the industry. Since individual firms will supply a larger amount at a higher price, the short-run market supply curve will slope upward to the right.*

Exhibit 19–6 illustrates this relationship. As the price of the product rises from P_1 to P_2 to P_3, the individual firms expand their output along their marginal cost curves. Since the individual firms supply a larger output as the market price increases, the total amount supplied to the market also expands.

Our construction of the short-run market supply curve assumes that the prices of the resources used by the industry are constant. When the entire

This ice cream store in Morgantown, West Virginia, closes for several months each winter and reopens in the summer. During these short-run shutdowns, the store still pays fixed costs, such as rent, taxes, and insurance. Only variable costs are avoided during the winter months.

industry (rather than just a single firm) expands output, resource prices may rise. If so, the short-run market supply curve (reflecting the higher prices of purchased inputs) will be slightly more inelastic (steeper) than the sum of the supply curves of the individual firms.

The short-run market supply curve, together with the demand curve for the industry's product, will determine the market price. At the short-run equilibrium market price, each firm will have expanded output until marginal costs have risen to the market price. Firms will have no desire to change output, *given their current size of plant.*

OUTPUT ADJUSTMENTS IN THE LONG RUN

In the long run, firms have the opportunity to alter their plant size and enter or exit an industry. As long-run adjustments are made, output in the whole industry may either expand or contract.

LONG-RUN EQUILIBRIUM

In addition to the balance between quantity supplied and quantity demanded necessary for short-run equilibrium, firms that are price takers must earn the normal rate of return, and only the normal rate, before long-run equilibrium can be attained. *If economic profit is present, new firms will enter the industry, and the current producers will have an incentive to expand the scale of their operations. This will lead to an increase in supply, placing downward pressure on prices. In contrast, if firms in the industry are suffering economic losses, they will leave the market. Supply will decline, placing upward pressure on prices.*

Therefore, as **Exhibit 19–7** illustrates, when a price-taker market is in long-run equilibrium (1) the quantity supplied and the quantity demanded will be equal at the market price, and (2) the firms in the industry will be earning normal (zero) economic profit (that is, their minimum *ATC* will just equal the market price).

ADJUSTING TO EXPANSION IN DEMAND

Suppose a price-taker market is in equilibrium. What will happen if there is an increase in demand? **Exhibit 19–8** presents an example. An entrepreneur introduces a fantastic new candy product. Consumers go wild over it. However, since it sticks to one's teeth, the market demand for toothpicks increases from D_1 to D_2. The price of toothpicks rises from P_1 to P_2. What impact will the higher market price have on the output level of toothpick-producing firms? It will increase (from q_1 to q_2 in part a of the exhibit) as the firms expand output along their *MC* curves. In the short run, the toothpick producers will make economic profits. The profits will attract new toothpick producers to the industry and cause the existing firms to expand the scale of their plants. Hence, the market supply will

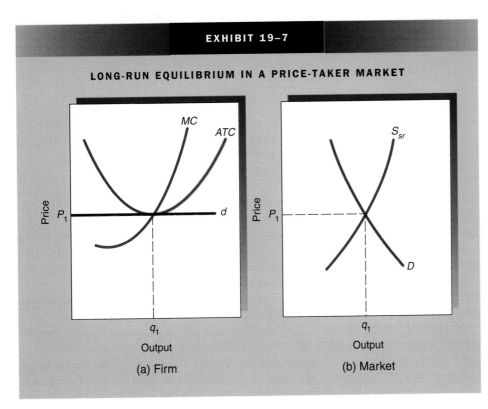

EXHIBIT 19–7

LONG-RUN EQUILIBRIUM IN A PRICE-TAKER MARKET

(a) Firm

(b) Market

The two conditions necessary for equilibrium in a price-taker market are depicted here. First, quantity supplied and quantity demanded must be equal in the market (b). Second, the firms in the industry must earn zero economic profit (that is, the "normal rate of return") at the established market price (a).

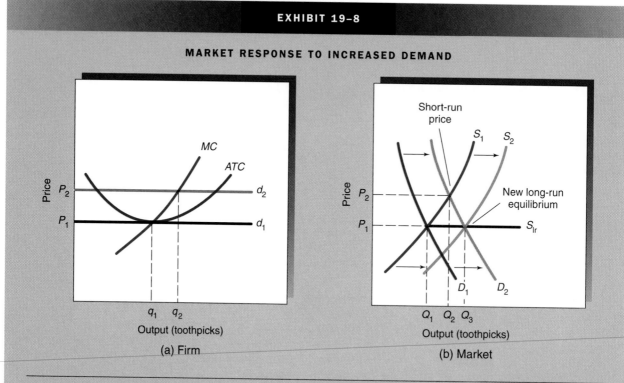

EXHIBIT 19–8

MARKET RESPONSE TO INCREASED DEMAND

(a) Firm

(b) Market

The introduction of a new candy product that sticks to one's teeth causes the demand for toothpicks to increase to D_2 (b). Toothpick prices rise to P_2, inducing firms to expand output. Toothpick firms make short-run profits (a), which draw new competitors into the industry. Thus, the toothpick supply expands (shifts from S_1 to S_2). If cost conditions are unchanged, the expansion in supply will continue until the market price of toothpicks has declined to its initial level of P_1.

increase (shift from S_1 to S_2) and eventually eliminate the short-run profits. If cost conditions are unchanged in the industry, the market price for toothpicks will return to its initial level, even though output has expanded to Q_3.

ADJUSTING TO DECLINE IN DEMAND

Economic profits attract new firms to an industry. In contrast, economic losses (when they are expected to continue) encourage capital and entrepreneurship to move out of the industry and into other areas where the profitability potential is more favorable. Economic losses mean that the owners of capital in the industry are earning less than the market rate of return. The opportunity cost of continuing in the industry exceeds the gain.

Exhibit 19–9 illustrates how market forces react to economic losses. Initially, an equilibrium price exists in the industry. The firms are able to cover their average costs of production. Now suppose there is a reduction in consumer income, causing the market demand for the product to decrease and the market price to

EXHIBIT 19-9

IMPACT OF DECLINE IN DEMAND

(a) Firm

(b) Market

A reduction in market demand will cause price to fall and short-run losses to occur. The losses will cause some firms to go out of business and others to reduce their scale. In the long run, the market supply will fall, causing the market price to rise. The supply will continue to decline and price will continue to rise until the short-run losses have been eliminated (S_2).

decline. At the new, lower price, firms in the industry will not be able to cover their costs of production. In the short run, they will reduce output along their MC curve. This reduction in output by the individual firms results in a reduction in the quantity supplied in the market. For an illustration of demand reduction from a different source, see the Applications in Economics boxed feature on a shift in demand.

In the face of short-run losses, the inflow of capital will decline and the industry's capital assets will shrink as firms fail to replace equipment when it wears out. Some firms will leave the industry as their fixed costs become variable and they are no longer able to cover their variable costs at the prevailing price. Others will reduce the scale of their operations, producing only those units for which the new, lower revenues can still justify the production costs. These factors will cause the industry supply to decline, to shift from S_1 to S_2. What impact will this have on price? It will rise. In the long run, the short-run market supply curve will decline until the price rises sufficiently to permit the firms remaining in the industry to once again earn "normal profits."

LONG-RUN SUPPLY

The *long-run market supply curve* indicates the minimum price at which firms will supply various market output levels, given sufficient time both to adjust plant size (or other fixed factors) and to enter or exit from the industry. The shape of the curve depends on what happens to the cost of production as the *industry's* output is altered. Three possibilities emerge, although one is far more likely than the other two.

A SHIFT IN DEMAND—IMPACT OF A PAPAL DECREE ON THE PRICE OF FISH

Sometimes changes in institutions, legal restrictions, or regulatory policies influence the demand for a product. The 1966 papal decree lifting the Roman Catholic church's ban on the eating of meat on Fridays provides an interesting illustration of this point. Before the ban was lifted, most of the nearly 600 million Roman Catholics consumed fish on Fridays. After the decree, many shifted to substitute goods such as beef, pork, and chicken. The demand for fish therefore declined. As our analysis indicates, a decline in demand will lead to a lower market price in the short run.

Economist Frederick Bell of Florida State University estimated the impact of the reduction in demand on the market price of fish in the Northeastern United States, an area where Catholics compose a large proportion of the total population.[1] As we discussed earlier, changes in personal income and the price of related commodities (beef, pork, and poultry in this case) will influence the demand for a good. Bell utilized statistical techniques to adjust for these factors. This permitted him to isolate the independent effect of the papal decree on the demand for and price of fish.

The prices of seven different species of fish were considered. As the accompanying exhibit illustrates, Bell's analysis showed that the price of each variety fell. In the case of large haddock, it was 21 percent lower after the papal decree than for the previous ten years. In other instances, the decline in price was smaller. On average,

Bell estimated, the price of fish in the Northeastern United States fell by 12.5 percent as a result of the pope's edict. Just as economic theory indicates, a reduction in demand for a product leads to a lower price in the short run (see Exhibit 19–9).

THE PAPAL DECREE AND THE PRICE OF FISH

SPECIES	PERCENT CHANGE IN PRICE OF FISH AFTER PAPAL DECREE
Sea scallops	−17
Yellowtail flounder	−14
Large haddock	−21
Small haddock (scrod)	−2
Cod	−16
Ocean perch	−10
Whiting	−20
All species (average)	−12.5

[1]Frederick W. Bell, "The Pope and the Price of Fish," *American Economic Review* 58 (December 1968): 1346–1350.

Constant-cost industry

An industry for which factor prices and costs of production remain constant as market output is expanded. Thus, the long-run market supply curve is horizontal.

CONSTANT-COST INDUSTRIES.   If factor prices remain unchanged, the long-run market supply curve will be perfectly elastic. In terms of economics, this describes a **constant-cost industry.** Exhibits 19–8 and 19–9 both picture constant-cost industries. As Exhibit 19–8 illustrates, an expansion in demand causes prices to increase *temporarily*. The high prices and profits stimulate additional production. The short-run market supply continues to expand (the entire schedule shifts to the right) until the market price returns to its initial level and profits return to their normal level. In the long run, the larger supply will not require a permanent price increase. The *long-run supply curve* (S_{lr}) is thus perfectly elastic. Exhibit 19–9 illustrates the impact of a decline in demand in a constant-cost industry. Again, the long-run supply curve is perfectly elastic, reflecting the basically unchanged cost at the lower rate of industry output.

A constant-cost industry is most likely to arise when the industry's demand for resource inputs is quite small relative to the total demand for these resources.

For example, the demand of the matches industry for wood, chemicals, and labor is very small relative to the total demand for these resources; therefore, doubling the output of matches would exert only a negligible impact on the price of the resources used by the industry. Matches therefore approximate a constant-cost industry.

INCREASING-COST INDUSTRIES. In most industries, an increase in market demand and *industry* output will lead to higher per unit production costs for the firms in the industry. Economists refer to these as **increasing-cost industries.** When the output of an industry expands, the demand for resources used by the industry increases. This usually results in higher prices for at least some resources, causing the firms' cost curves to shift upward. For example, an increase in demand for housing places upward pressure on the prices of lumber, roofing, window frames, and construction labor, causing the cost of housing to rise. Similarly, an increase in demand (and market output) for beef may cause the prices of feed grains, hay, and grazing land to rise. Thus, the production costs of beef rise as more of it is produced.

In some industries, additional demand may lead to industrial congestion, which will reduce the efficiency of the industry and cause costs to rise, even though resource prices are constant. For example, as the demand for lobster increases, additional fishermen are attracted to the industry. However, the increase in the number of fishermen combing lobster beds typically leads to congestion, which reduces the catch per hour of individual fishermen. The lobster beds themselves may be unpriced, but the production cost in the lobster industry rises as output per labor hour declines.

For an increasing-cost industry, an expansion in market demand will bid up resource prices and/or lead to industrial congestion, causing the per unit cost of the firms to rise. As a result, a larger market output will be forthcoming only at a higher price. The long-run market supply curve for the product will therefore slope upward.

Exhibit 19–10 depicts an increasing-cost industry. An expansion in demand causes higher prices and a larger market output. The presence of short-run profit attracts new competitors to the industry, expanding the market output even more. *As the industry expands,* factor prices rise and congestion costs increase. What happens to the firm's cost curves? Both the average and marginal cost curves rise (shift to ATC_2 and MC_2). This increase in production cost necessitates a higher long-run price (P_2). Hence, the long-run supply curve slopes upward to the right.

DECREASING-COST INDUSTRIES. Sometimes, factor prices will decline if the market output of a product is expanded. A reduction in factor prices will lead to a lower long-run competitive market price for the product, so economists refer to such industries as **decreasing-cost industries.** The long-run (but not the short-run) market supply curve for a decreasing cost industry will slope downward to the right. For example, as the electronics industry expands, suppliers of certain components may be able to adopt large-scale techniques that will lead to lower component prices. If this occurs, the cost curves of the electronics firms may shift downward, causing the industry supply curve for electronics products to slope downward to the right (at least temporarily). However, since expansion of an industry is far more likely to cause rising rather than falling input prices, decreasing-cost industries are atypical.

Increasing-cost industries
An industry for which costs of production rise as output is expanded. Thus, even in the long run, higher market prices will be required to induce the firms to expand the total output in such industries. The long-run market supply curve in such industries will slope upward to the right.

Decreasing-cost industries
Industries for which costs of production decline as the industry expands. The market supply is therefore inversely related to price. Such industries are atypical.

EXHIBIT 19–10

INCREASING COSTS AND LONG-RUN SUPPLY

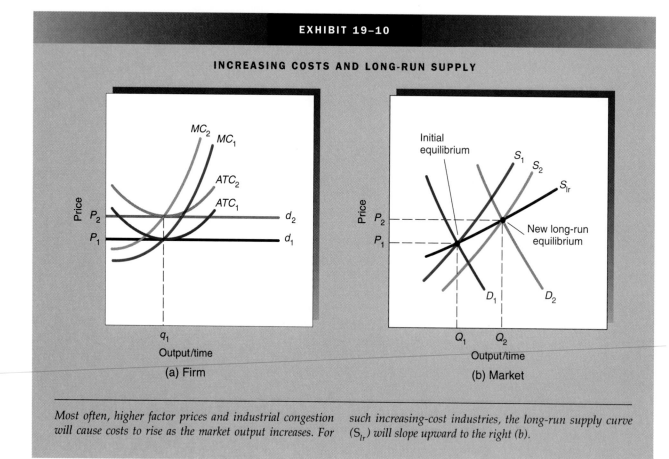

(a) Firm

(b) Market

Most often, higher factor prices and industrial congestion will cause costs to rise as the market output increases. For *such increasing-cost industries, the long-run supply curve (S_{lr}) will slope upward to the right (b).*

SUPPLY ELASTICITY AND THE ROLE OF TIME

It takes time for firms to adjust to a change in the price of a product. In the short run, firms are stuck with the existing size of their plant. If price increases in the short run, they can expand output only by utilizing their existing plant more intensely. Thus, their output response will be limited. In the long run, however, they will have time to build new plants. This will allow them to expand output by a larger amount in response to an increase in price. Thus, the market supply curve will be more elastic in the long run than in the short run.

The short- and long-run distinction offers a convenient two-stage analysis, but in the real world there are many intermediate production "runs." Some factors that could not be easily varied in a one-week time period can be varied over a two-week period. Expansion of other factors might require a month, and still others, six months. To be more precise, the cost penalty for quicker availability is greater for some production factors than for others. In any case, a faster expansion usually means that greater cost penalties are necessary to provide for an earlier availability of productive factors.

When a firm has a longer time period to plan output and adjust all of its productive inputs to the desired utilization levels, it will be able to produce any specific rate of output at a lower cost. *Because it is less costly to expand output slowly in response to a demand increase, the expansion of output by firms will increase with time, as long as price exceeds cost. Therefore, the elasticity of the market supply curve will be greater when more time is allowed for firms to adjust output.*

Exhibit 19–11 illustrates the impact of time on the response by producers to an increase in price resulting from an expansion in demand. When the price of a product increases from P_1 to P_2, the immediate supply response of the firms is small because it is costly to expand output hastily. After one week, firms are willing to expand output only from Q_1 to Q_2. After one month, because of cost reductions made possible by the longer production planning period, firms are willing to offer Q_3 units at the price P_2. After three months, the rate of output expands to Q_4. In the long run, when it is possible to adjust all inputs to the desired utilization levels (after a six-month time period, for example), firms are willing to supply Q_5 units of output at the market price of P_2. *The supply curve for products is typically more elastic over a longer time period than for a shorter period.*

ROLE OF PROFITS AND LOSSES

The price-taker model highlights the role of profits and losses: They are signals sent to producers by consumers. Economic profits will be largest in those areas in which consumer wants at the margin are greatest relative to costs of production. Profit-seeking entrepreneurs will guide additional resources into these

EXHIBIT 19–11

TIME AND ELASTICITY OF SUPPLY

t_1 = one week
t_2 = one month
t_3 = three months
t_{lr} = six months

The elasticity of the market supply curve usually increases as more time is allowed for adjustment to a change in price.

areas. Supply will increase, driving prices down and eliminating the profits. Free entry and the competitive process will protect the consumer from arbitrarily high prices. In the long run, competitive prices will reflect costs of production.

Economic profits result because a firm or entrepreneur increases the value of resources. Business firms purchase resources and use them to produce a product or service that is sold to consumers. Costs are incurred as the business pays workers and other resource owners for their services. If the sales of the business firm exceed the costs of employing all the resources required to produce the firm's output, then the firm will make a profit. *In essence, profit is a reward that business owners will earn if they produce a good that consumers value more (as measured by their willingness to pay) than the resources required for the good's production (as measured by the cost of bidding the resources away from their alternative employment possibilities).*

For example, suppose that it costs a shirt manufacturer $20,000 per month to lease a building, rent the required machines, and purchase the labor, cloth, buttons, and other materials necessary to produce and market 1,000 shirts per month. Thus, the average cost of the shirts is $20 (the $20,000 monthly cost divided by the 1,000 monthly output). If the manufacturer sells the 1,000 shirts for $22 each, its actions create wealth. Consumers value the shirts more than they value the resources required for their production. The manufacturer's $2 profit per shirt is a reward received for increasing the value of the resources.

In contrast, losses are a penalty imposed on businesses that reduce the value of resources. The value of the resources used (as measured by their cost) by such unsuccessful firms exceeds the price consumers are willing to pay for their product. Losses to the firms, along with bankruptcies, are the market's way of bringing such wasteful activities to a halt.

We live in a world of changing tastes and technology, imperfect knowledge, and uncertainty. Business decision makers cannot be sure of either future market prices or costs of production. Their decisions must be based on expectations. Nonetheless, the reward-penalty structure of a market economy is clear. *Firms that produce efficiently and anticipate correctly the products and services for which future demand will be most urgent (relative to production cost) will make economic profits. Those that are inefficient and allocate resources incorrectly into areas of weak future demand (relative to cost) will be penalized with losses.*

A look at the market for videotape rental provides a vivid illustration of the role played by profits and losses when entry barriers are low.[4] In 1982 videotape rental stores were new, and there were only an estimated 5,000 stores in the United States. They could charge $5 and more per 24-hour rental. The availability of rentals and the falling prices of home video players meant that profits could at times reach 80 percent of rental revenues. More important, expected profits were very high. This optimism led to the rapid entry of many new stores, which increased competition and forced prices down. By 1990 there were about 25,000 stores. Prices had fallen dramatically. Even new releases were typically renting for $1.99, and most videos rented for even less. At times, video rental supply expanded faster than the demand for rentals, and some of the firms had

---

[4]The facts in this example are taken from Tim Tregarthen, "Supply, Demand, and Videotape," *The Margin* 6 (September–October 1990): 29.

to leave the business. Even for those who were efficient and stayed in the business, profits were slim. Consumers, however, benefited tremendously from the highly competitive nature of the video rental business.

PRICE TAKERS, COMPETITION, AND PROSPERITY

Our analysis indicates that market forces provide price takers with a strong incentive to use resources wisely. Each firm will have a strong tendency to produce its output as cheaply as possible. Holding quality constant, the price taker can maximize profits only by minimizing the cost of production—using the least valued set of resources needed to produce the desired output.

Firms have a strong incentive to produce goods that are valued more highly than the resources required for their production. Thus, resources are drawn to those uses where they are most productive, as judged by the consumers' willingness to pay for the various goods produced. The ability of firms freely to expand or contract their businesses, and to enter or exit the market, means that resources that could be more valuable elsewhere will not be trapped unproductively in a particular industry. Resource owners can move them to where they are most highly valued in production.

The price-taker model highlights the more general importance of the competitive process. As the chapter opening quotation from Professor Wilcox indicates, competition places pressure on producers to operate efficiently and to avoid waste. It weeds out the inefficient—those who fail to provide consumers with quality goods at low prices. Competition also keeps producers on their toes in other areas. The production techniques and product offerings that lead to success today will not necessarily pass the competitive market test tomorrow. Producers who survive in a competitive environment cannot be complacent. They must be forward-looking and innovative. They must be willing to experiment and quick to adopt improved methods.

In competitive markets, business firms must serve the interests of consumers. As Adam Smith noted more than 200 years ago, competition harnesses personal self-interest and puts it to work, elevating our standard of living and directing

OUTSTANDING ECONOMIST

FRIEDRICH A. VON HAYEK (1899–1992)
Remarkably the writings of this 1974 Nobel Prize recipient spanned seven decades. His work on knowledge and markets both enhanced our understanding of the competitive process and highlighted the fatal defect of central planning. He also made major contributions in areas as diverse as monetary theory, law and economics, business cycles, and capital theory.

our resources toward the production of those goods that we desire most intensely relative to their cost. Smith stated:

> *It is not from the benevolence of the butcher, the brewer, or the baker, that we expect our dinner, but from their regard to their own self-interest. We address ourselves, not to their humanity but to their self-love, and never talk to them of our own necessities, but of their advantages.*[5]

In a competitive environment, even self-interested individuals and profit-seeking business firms have a strong incentive to recognize and serve the interests of others, and to supply products that are valued more highly than the resources required for their production. This is the path to greater income and larger profits. Paradoxical as it may seem, personal self-interest—a characteristic many view as less than admirable—is a powerful source of economic progress when it is directed by competition.

---

[5]Adam Smith, *An Inquiry into the Nature and Causes of the Wealth of Nations* (1776; Cannan's ed., Chicago: University of Chicago Press, 1976), p. 18.

LOOKING AHEAD

In the real world, consumers often seek variety in product design, style, durability, service, and location. As a result, the products of one firm are not perfect substitutes for those of another. In such cases, not all consumers switch to other suppliers when the price of one firm's output changes. Most firms are price searchers rather than price takers. In addition, barriers to entry sometimes limit competition. In the next two chapters, we will examine markets where the firms are price searchers and will consider the importance of entry barriers into such markets.

CHAPTER SUMMARY

1. Firms producing identical products in markets where they have to accept the market price are called price takers. A price taker confronts a perfectly elastic demand for its product. Firms that are able to raise their price without losing all their customers (and which must lower their price in order to sell more units) are called price searchers.

2. A price taker will maximize profit by expanding output as long as the additional output adds more to revenues than to costs. Therefore, the profit-maximizing price taker will produce the output level at which marginal revenue (and price) equals marginal cost.

3. The firm's short-run marginal cost curve (above its average variable cost) is its supply curve. The short-run market supply curve is the horizontal summation of the marginal cost curves (the portions where *MC* is above *AVC*) for all firms in the industry.

4. If a firm is covering its average variable cost and anticipates that the price is only temporarily below average total cost, it may operate in the short run even though it is experiencing a loss. However, even if it anticipates more favorable market conditions in the future, loss minimization will require the firm to shut down if it is unable to cover its average variable cost. If the firm does not anticipate that it will be able to cover its average total cost even in the long run, loss minimization requires that it immediately go out of business (even if it is covering its average variable cost) so that it can at least avoid its fixed cost.

5. When price exceeds average total cost, a firm will make economic profits. When no entry barriers exist, profits will attract new firms into the industry and stimulate the existing firms to expand. The market supply will increase, pushing price down to the level of average total cost. Firms will be unable to make long-run economic profits.

6. Losses exist when the market price is less than the firm's average total cost. Losses imply that the resources could be used to produce more value elsewhere. They will cause firms either to leave the industry or to reduce the scale of their operations. Market supply will decline, pushing the market price upward until the firms remaining in the industry are able to earn normal (that is, zero economic) profits.

7. As the output of an industry expands, marginal costs will increase in the short run, causing the short-run market supply curve to slope upward to the right. If the

prices of resources purchased by the industry remain unchanged, as the market output is expanded, the long-run supply curve will be perfectly elastic. However, as the output of an industry expands, rising factor prices will normally cause the firm's costs to increase. Therefore, the long-run market supply curve for most products will slope upward to the right.

8. In the short run, "fixed" resources like the size of the firm's plant will limit the ability of firms to expand output quickly. In the long run, the firms in a market will have time to alter the size of their plants and other resources that are fixed in the short run. As a result, the market supply curve will generally be more elastic as more time is allowed for firms to adjust their fixed factors in response to a price change.

9. Firms will earn economic profit if they produce a product that they can sell for more than the cost of the resources required for its production. In essence, profit is a reward derived from actions that increase the value of resources. Conversely, losses are a penalty imposed on those who reduce the value of resources.

10. Firms that produce efficiently and anticipate correctly the goods for which the future demand will be most urgent, relative to costs of production, will make profits. Firms that produce inefficiently and that incorrectly use resources to produce goods for which future demand turns out to be weak will be penalized with losses. Over time, entry and exit of resources and firms will eliminate economic profits and losses.

11. The competitive process places producers under strong pressure to operate efficiently and heed the views of consumers. As Adam Smith recognized long ago, self-interest is a strong motivator of human beings. If it is bridled by competition and the market process, self-interest leads producers to search for and undertake wealth-creating activities.

CRITICAL ANALYSIS QUESTIONS

*1. Farmers are often heard to complain about the high costs of machinery, labor, and fertilizer, suggesting that these costs drive down their profit rate. Does it follow that if, for example, the price of fertilizer fell by 10 percent, farming (a highly competitive industry with low barriers to entry) would be more profitable? Explain.

*2. If the firms in a price-taker market are making short-run profits, what will happen to the market price in the long run? Explain.

3. "In a price-taker market, if a business operator produces efficiently—that is, if the cost of producing the good is minimized—the operator will be able to make at least a normal profit." True or false?

4. Suppose that the government of a large city levies a 5 percent sales tax on hotel rooms. How will the tax affect (a) prices of hotel rooms, (b) the profits of hotel owners, and (c) gross (including the tax) expenditures on hotel rooms?

*5. Within the framework of the price-taker model, how will an unanticipated increase in demand for a product affect each of the following in a market that was initially in long-run equilibrium?
   a. the short-run market price of the product
   b. industry output in the short run
   c. profitability in the short run
   d. the long-run market price in the industry
   e. industry output in the long run
   f. profitability in the long run

*6. Suppose that the development of a new drought-resistant hybrid seed corn leads to a 50 percent increase in the average yield per acre without increasing the cost to the farmers who use the new technology. If the producers in the corn production industry are price takers, what will happen to the following:
   a. the price of corn
   b. the profitability of corn farmers who quickly adopt the new technology
   c. the profitability of corn farmers who are slow to adopt the new technology
   d. the price of soybeans, a substitute product for corn

7. "When the firms in the industry are just able to cover their cost of production, economic profit is zero. Therefore, if there is a reduction in demand causing prices to go down even a little bit, all of the firms in the industry will be driven out of business." True or false? Explain.

8. Why does the short-run market supply curve for a product slope upward to the right? Why does the long-run market supply curve generally slope upward to the right? Why is the long-run market supply curve generally more elastic than the short-run supply curve?

9. How does competition among firms affect the incentive of each firm to (a) operate efficiently (produce at a low per unit cost) and (b) produce goods that consumers value? What happens to firms that fail to do these two things?

10. Will firms in a price-taker market be able to earn profits in the long run? Why or why not? What are the major determinants of profitability for a firm? Discuss.

*11. During the summer of 1988, drought conditions throughout much of the United States substantially reduced the size of the corn, wheat, and soybean crops, three commodities for which demand is inelastic. Use the price-taker model to determine how the drought affected (a) grain prices, (b) revenue from the three crops, and (c) the profitability of farming.

12. Explain why the market supply curve is slightly less elastic than the summation of the marginal cost curves for the firms in a competitive industry.

*13. The accompanying table presents the expected cost

and revenue data for the Tucker Tomato Farm. The Tuckers produce tomatoes in a greenhouse and sell them wholesale in a price-taker market.

a. Fill in the firm's marginal cost, average variable cost, average total cost, and profit schedules.

b. If the Tuckers are profit maximizers, how many tomatoes should they produce when the market price is $500 per ton? Indicate their profits.

c. Indicate the firm's output level and maximum profit if the market price of tomatoes increases to $550 per ton.

d. How many units would the Tucker Tomato Farm produce if the price of tomatoes declined to $450? Indicate the firm's profits. Should the firm continue in business? Explain.

14. In the accompanying table, you are given information about two firms that compete in a price-taker market. Assume that fixed costs for each firm are $20.

a. Complete the table.

b. What is the lowest price at which Firm A will produce?

c. How many units of output will it produce at that price? (Assume that it cannot produce fractional units.)

d. What is the lowest price at which Firm B will produce?

e. How many units of output will it produce?

f. How many units will Firm A produce if the market price is $20?

g. How many units will Firm B produce at the $20

COST AND REVENUE SCHEDULES—TUCKER TOMATO FARM, INC.

OUTPUT (TONS PER MONTH)	TOTAL COST	PRICE PER TON	MARGINAL COST	AVERAGE VARIABLE COST	AVERAGE TOTAL COST	PROFITS (MONTHLY)
0	$1,000	$500	—	—	—	—
1	1,200	500	——	——	——	——
2	1,350	500	——	——	——	——
3	1,550	500	——	——	——	——
4	1,900	500	——	——	——	——
5	2,300	500	——	——	——	——
6	2,750	500	——	——	——	——
7	3,250	500	——	——	——	——
8	3,800	500	——	——	——	——
9	4,400	500	——	——	——	——
10	5,150	500	——	——	——	——

FIRM A

QUANTITY	TOTAL VARIABLE COST	MARGINAL COST	AVERAGE VARIABLE COST
1	$ 24	——	——
2	30	——	——
3	38	——	——
4	48	——	——
5	62	——	——
6	82	——	——
7	110	——	——

FIRM B

QUANTITY	TOTAL VARIABLE COST	MARGINAL COST	AVERAGE VARIABLE COST
1	$ 8	——	——
2	10	——	——
3	16	——	——
4	24	——	——
5	36	——	——
6	56	——	——
7	86	——	——

price? (Assume it cannot produce fractional units.)

h. If each firm's total fixed costs are $20 and the price of output is $20, which firm would be receiving a higher net profit or smaller loss?

i. How much would that net profit or loss be?

*15. Emma is a landscape architect for a large design firm. She earns a salary of $50,000 per year, but is considering quitting to start her own business. She talks to her accountant, who helps her draw up the accompanying chart with their best predictions about costs and revenues.

	PREDICTED ANNUAL COSTS	PREDICTED ANNUAL REVENUES
Basic wage (Emma)	$22,000	Sales $80,000
Rent of space	10,000	
Rent of equipment	6,000	
Plants	14,000	
Utilities	2,000	
Miscellaneous	5,000	

The accountant admits that the basic wage seems low, but she tells Emma to keep in mind that since she will own her business, Emma will get to keep any profit she earns. From an economist's point of view, is the accountant's list of costs complete? From the accountant's perspective, what are Emma's expected profits? From an economist's perspective, what are Emma's expected profits?

---

*Asterisk denotes questions for which answers are given in Appendix B.

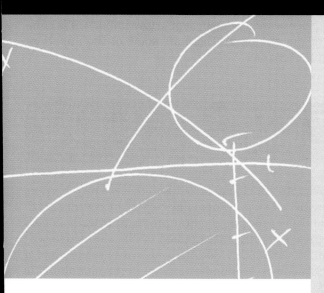

CHAPTER FOCUS

■ Why do firms engage in competitive advertising and price cutting?

■ How do price searchers act when entry barriers are low? How do consumers fare in such markets?

■ What do entrepreneurs do? Why is the important role of the entrepreneur left out of economic models?

■ What are contestable markets? Can contestable markets be competitive when there is room for only one or two rival firms?

■ Why do some economists criticize price-searcher behavior when entry barriers are low, while others like the results?

■ Why is competition critical to a prosperous, innovative economy?

[T]he price to the price-searcher is not determined for him as if by some impersonal market mechanism. Instead he must search out the optimal (wealth-maximizing) price. And, not knowing the demand schedule exactly, he will have to resort to retrial-and-error search processes.

ARMEN A. ALCHIAN
AND WILLIAM R. ALLEN[1]

---

[1]Armen A. Alchian and William R. Allen, *University Economics,* 2d ed. (Belmont, Calif.: Wadsworth Publishing Co., 1967), p. 113.

Competitive price-searcher market
A market where the firms have a downward-sloping demand curve, and entry into and exit from the market are relatively easy.

I n the previous chapter we learned that price takers must accept the market price. They merely adjust their output, choosing to supply more units as long as the cost of the additional units is less than the market price. Price searchers have a more complex set of decisions to make in their search for profit. (See the chapter opening quotation from Professors Alchian and Allen.) In this chapter we consider the choices facing price searchers in markets where entry barriers are low. Low entry barriers are the key to competitive markets. When the restraints limiting entry are minimal, opportunity for profit will attract competitors. Thus, we will refer to these markets where firms can alter their price but where the entry barriers are low as **competitive price-searcher markets**.

How do firms that are price searchers choose price and output combinations? Are the business practices of price searchers inefficient? How important is competition to the performance of the economy? These are some of the important questions we will examine in this chapter.

COMPETITIVE PRICE-SEARCHER MARKETS

Differentiated products
Products distinguished from similar products by such characteristics as quality, design, location, and method of promotion.

Monopolistic competition
Term often used by economists to describe markets characterized by a large number of sellers that supply differentiated products to a market with low barriers to entry. Essentially, it is an alternative term for competitive price-searcher markets.

Competitive price-searcher markets are characterized by (1) low entry barriers and (2) *firms* that face a downward-sloping demand curve.[2] In contrast with price-taker markets where the firms produce identical products, price searchers produce **differentiated products.** The products supplied by the alternative sellers may differ in their design, dependability, location, ease of purchase, and a multitude of other factors. Sometimes economists use the term **monopolistic competition** to describe markets quite similar to those of the competitive price-searcher model. Since there is nothing "monopolistic" about these markets, we believe that this term is misleading. *Competitive price searcher* is much more descriptive of the conditions present in these markets. However, students should be aware that the expression "monopolistic competition" refers to the situation where the firm faces a downward-sloping demand curve but the entry barriers into the market are low.

Product differentiation explains why firms in price-searcher markets confront a downward-sloping demand curve. Since some consumers are willing to pay more in order to get the distinctive product, the *firm* will not lose all its customers to rivals if it raises its price. Rival firms, however, supply products that are quite similar to that supplied by the price searcher, so if the firm raises its price too much, many of its consumers will switch to the substitutes. *Thus, the demand curve faced by the firm in a competitive price-searcher market will be highly elastic, because good substitutes for its output are readily available from other suppliers.*

The price searcher must choose between low prices with large quantities sold, and higher prices with smaller sales. *Although a price searcher can set the price for its products, market forces will determine the quantity sold at alternative prices.* In trying to find the profit-maximizing price and quantity combi-

---

[2]Note that the *firm* faces a downward-sloping demand curve in a price-searcher market. In price-taker markets, the *firm* will confront a perfectly elastic demand. Of course, the *market* demand curve will be downward sloping in a price-taker market.

nation, therefore, price searchers must try to estimate not just one market price, but how buyers will respond to the various prices that might be charged. In effect, price searchers must estimate the relationship between price and quantity demanded for their product. And the complexity does not stop there.

Demand is not simply a given for a price searcher. The firm, by changing product quality, location, and service (among many other factors), and by advertising, can alter the demand for its products. It can increase demand by drawing customers from rivals if it can convince consumers that its products provide more value. When an airline adopts a more generous frequent-flier program or a soap manufacturer provides "cents-off" coupons, each is trying to make its product a little more attractive than rival products. The precise effects of such decisions cannot easily be predicted, but they can make the difference between profit and loss for the firm. In the real world, most firms occupy this complex and risky territory of the price searcher.

Sellers in competitive price-searcher markets face competition both from firms already producing in the market and from potential new entrants into the market. If profits are present, firms can expect that new rivals will be attracted. Because of the low entry barriers, competitive forces will be strong in price-searcher markets.

PRICE AND OUTPUT IN COMPETITIVE PRICE-SEARCHER MARKETS

How does a price searcher decide what price to charge and what level of output to produce? As the price searcher reduces price in order to expand output and sales, there will be two conflicting influences on total revenue. As **Exhibit 20–1** illustrates, the increase in sales (from q_1 to q_2) due to the lower price will, by itself, add to the revenue of the price searcher. The price reduction, however, also applies to units *that would otherwise have been sold at a higher price* (P_1, rather than the lower price, P_2). This factor by itself will cause a reduction in total revenue. As price is reduced in order to sell additional units, these two conflicting forces will result in marginal revenue—that is, change in total revenue—that is less than the sales price of the additional units. Since the price of units that could have been sold at the higher price must also be reduced, the price searcher's marginal revenue will be less than price. As Exhibit 20–1 shows, the marginal revenue curve of the price searcher will always lie below the firm's demand curve.[3] (Remember, the lower case "d" is used when the reference is to the *firm's* demand curve.)

Any firm can increase profits by expanding output as long as marginal revenue exceeds marginal cost. Therefore, a price searcher will lower price and expand output until marginal revenue is equal to marginal cost.

Exhibit 20–2 illustrates the profit-maximizing price and output. The price searcher will increase profit by expanding output to q, where marginal revenue is equal to marginal cost and price P can be charged. Beyond q, the price

---

[3]For a straight-line demand curve, the marginal revenue curve will bisect any line parallel to the *x*-axis. For example, the *MR* curve will divide the line P_2F into two equal parts, P_2E and EF.

When a firm faces a downward-sloping demand curve, a price reduction that increases sales will exert two conflicting influences on total revenue. First, total revenue will rise because of an increase in the number of units sold (from q_1 to q_2). However, revenue losses from the lower price (P_2) on units that could have been sold at a higher price (P_1) will at least partially offset the additional revenues from increased sales. Therefore, the marginal revenue curve will lie inside the firm's demand curve.

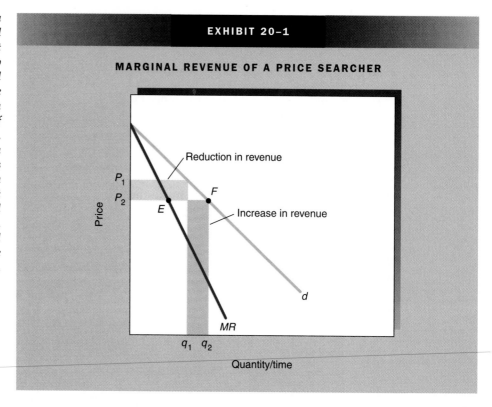

EXHIBIT 20–1

MARGINAL REVENUE OF A PRICE SEARCHER

reduction required for the sale of additional output would reduce the firm's profit. For any output level less than q (for example, R), a price reduction and sales expansion will add more to total revenues than to total costs. At output R, marginal revenues exceed marginal costs. Thus, profits will be greater if price is reduced so output can be expanded. On the other hand, if output exceeds q (for example, S), sale of additional units beyond q will add more to costs (MC) than to revenues (MR). The firm will therefore gain by raising the price to P, even though the price rise will result in the loss of some customers. Profits will be maximized by charging price P and producing the output level q, where $MC = MR$.

The firm pictured in Exhibit 20–2 is making an economic profit. Total revenues $PAqO$ exceed the firm's total costs $CBqO$ at the profit-maximizing output level. Since barriers to entry are low, profits will attract rival competitors. If this is a typical firm, other firms will enter the market and attempt to produce a similar product (or service).

What impact will the entry of new rivals have on the demand for the products of the firms already in the market? These new rivals will draw customers away from existing firms. As long as new entrants expect to make economic profits, additional competitors will be attracted to the market. This pressure will continue until the competition among rivals has shifted the demand curve of the typical price searcher inward far enough to eliminate economic profits. In the long run, as illustrated by **Exhibit 20–3**, a price searcher in a market with low entry barriers will just be able to cover its production costs. It will

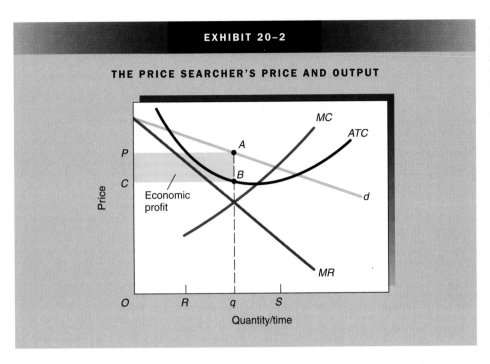

EXHIBIT 20-2

THE PRICE SEARCHER'S PRICE AND OUTPUT

A price searcher maximizes profits by producing output q, for which MR = MC, and charging price P. The firm is making economic profits. What impact will they have, if this is a typical firm?

produce to the *MR = MC* output level, but for the typical firm, the entry of new competition will force the price down to the average per unit cost. Once economic profit has been eliminated for a firm so that all its costs are just equaled by its revenue, potential competitors are likely to seek other, greener pastures.

If losses are present in a specific market, with time, some of the firms in the market will go out of business. Losses are the market's way of saying that some of the resources currently being used by a firm are more valuable in other uses. (See Applications in Economics: The Positive Side of Business Failure.) As firms leave, some of their previous customers will buy from other firms. The demand curve facing the remaining firms in the industry will be shifted outward by this process until the economic losses are eliminated and the long-run, zero-profit equilibrium illustrated by Exhibit 20–3 is restored.

Whenever firms can freely enter and exit a market, profits and losses play an important role in determining the size of the industry. Economic profits will attract new competitors to the market. The increased availability of the product (and similar products) will drive the price down until the profits are eliminated. Conversely, economic losses will cause competitors to exit from the market. The decline in the availability of the product (supply) will allow the price to rise until firms are once again able to cover their average total costs.

In the short run, a price searcher may make either economic profits or losses, depending on market conditions. After long-run adjustments have been made, however, only a normal profit (that is, zero economic profit) will be possible because of the competitive conditions caused by freedom of entry. As we will see in the following section, price adjustments are sometimes made even before entry occurs, in order to prevent that entry.

Since entry and exit are free, competition will eventually drive prices down to the level of average total cost for the representative price searcher.

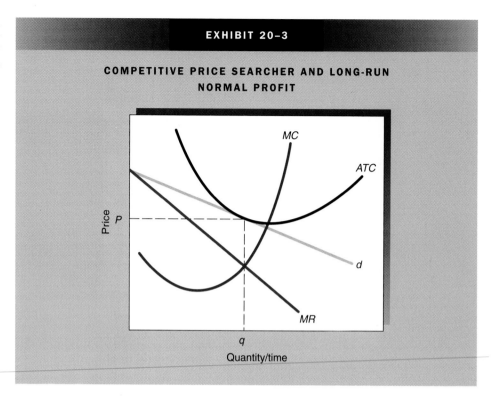

EXHIBIT 20-3

COMPETITIVE PRICE SEARCHER AND LONG-RUN NORMAL PROFIT

CONTESTABLE MARKETS AND THE COMPETITIVE PROCESS

Markets with few sellers are sometimes more competitive than they seem. Consider the case of the airline route between Salt Lake City, Utah, and Albuquerque, New Mexico. Only two airlines serve this route directly, since it has so little traffic. Further, there would seem to be high barriers to entry, since it takes multimillion-dollar airplanes to compete, as well as facilities for reservations, ticketing, baggage handling, and so on. The two airlines are well aware of the rivalry (with or without competition) between them, and they both charge a similar price. One might expect the price to be high, substantially above the cost of the service. But there is reason to believe that the two airlines, much as they would like to collude and drive up the price, will not be able to do so, as long as other airlines are free to enter this market.

To compete on an airline route may require millions of dollars in equipment, but if there is no problem with renting access to airport facilities, then the barriers to entry are much lower than equipment costs suggest. The Salt Lake City–Albuquerque market, for example, can be entered simply by shifting aircraft, personnel, and equipment from other locations. The aircraft can even be rented or leased. By the same token, if a new entrant (or an established firm) wants to leave that market, nearly all the invested capital values can be recov-

APPLICATIONS IN ECONOMICS

THE POSITIVE SIDE OF BUSINESS FAILURE

Each year, new businesses start up and others expand. At the same time, still other businesses will be contracting and some of them will be forced out of business and into bankruptcy. (See Illustrated Exhibits III-D and III-E on pages 432–433 for evidence of this dynamic process.) Business successes bring about the improved quality, price reductions, and the increased product availability that are the core ingredients of economic progress. Each success, however, means failure elsewhere as buyers switch their purchases and resources are bid away from established businesses. So economic progress brings not only business success, but also business failure.

Economists Dwight Lee and Richard McKenzie point out that, in a progressive market economy, business failure is inevitable.[1] More than that, they say, business failure is a blessing in disguise. Losses—and bankruptcy in extreme cases—provide both the information and the incentives to move resources to more highly valued, more productive uses. However, because business failure is painful for the investors, managers, and employees involved, there is constant political pressure to subsidize firms on the verge of bankruptcy, particularly if they are large.

Lee and McKenzie point out, though, that because it is the new, low-cost, and highly productive enterprises that force the failure of less-efficient firms, government support for a firm using highly valued resources to produce less highly valued output promotes wasteful activity. The resources have higher alternative uses elsewhere. The failure of an inefficient firm provides its employees and other suppliers with the signal and the incentive to search for the higher-valued uses for their resources, including their talents.

Only when inefficient, high-cost businesses are allowed to fail, and workers and other resource owners feel the lack of income (relative to market opportunities) pushing them to seek alternative employment, are the customers, workers, and capital of resource-wasting firms made available to more efficient, low-cost producers. And only when the more-efficient enterprises gain the resources and the business, will the economy produce more at a lower cost.

[1]Dwight R. Lee and Richard B. McKenzie, *Failure and Progress: The Bright Side of the Dismal Science* (Washington, D.C.: Cato Institute, 1993).

---

ered, through shifting the aircraft and other capital equipment to other routes, or leasing them to other firms.

When there are no legal barriers restricting entry, an airline route is a classic case of a **contestable market:** The costs of entry and exit are low, so a firm risks little by entering.[4] If entry is later judged to be a mistake, exit is relatively easy because large components of the capital costs are not sunk costs, but they are instead recoverable. Entry into a contestable market may require the use of large amounts of capital, but so long as the capital is recoverable, and not a sunk cost, the large capital requirement is not a high barrier to entry.

In a contestable market, potential competition, as well as actual entry, can discipline firms selling in the market. When entry and exit are not expensive, even a single seller in a market faces the serious prospect of competition. Contestable markets yield two important results: (1) prices will not for long be higher than the level necessary to achieve zero economic profits, and (2) minimum cost of production will occur. This is true because both prices above costs and

Contestable market
A market in which the costs of entry and exit are low, so a firm risks little by entering. Efficient production and zero economic profits should prevail in a contestable market. A market can be contestable even if capital requirements are high.

---

[4]The classic article on this topic is William J. Baumol's "Contestable Markets: An Uprising in the Theory of Industry Structure," *American Economic Review* 72 (March 1982): 1–15.

inefficiency in production present a profitable opportunity to new entrants. Potential competitors who see an opportunity for economic profit can be expected to enter and drive the price down to the level of per unit costs.

These results do have a policy implication: If policymakers are concerned that a market is not sufficiently competitive, they should consider what might be done to make the market in question contestable. Much of the enthusiasm of economists for deregulation can be traced to the fact that regulation often is the primary restraint to entry. Many economists believe that deregulation permitting new entry can make many markets contestable, achieving lower prices and more efficiency than can direct regulation of producers. We will have more to say about this in the next chapter.

Our model of price and output for price-searcher markets with low entry barriers is, of course, a very much simplified view of the real world. The market process is complex, and competition is an ongoing, dynamic process. It is important to recognize that since this ongoing competitive process is at work, the experience of a specific market participant may differ considerably from that of the "typical firm" being discussed. We turn now to a brief discussion of the important variable not found in economic models: entrepreneurship.

THE LEFT-OUT VARIABLE: ENTREPRENEURSHIP

To help us understand facts and make predictions, a scientific model must simplify what it describes, and draw attention to the most important relationships. Economic models are no exception. Our model of decision making in business firms is designed to highlight the decision-making elements common to all firms, and it performs this job quite well. But it leaves out some important elements of the business decision-making process. Furthermore, it glosses over the complexity of many decisions that must be made by real-world entrepreneurs.

Would profits increase if prices were raised, or would lower prices lead to larger profits? Real-world decision makers cannot go into the back room and look at their demand-cost diagram to answer these questions. They must search for clues, experiment with actual price changes, and interpret what they see, often using a great deal of "seat-of-the-pants" judgment. The successful entrepreneur will search and find (or at least approximate) the profit-maximizing price—the $MR = MC$ price-and-output combination that our model shows so simply.

Our models indicate how entrepreneurs will react to profit and loss in a specific market and explain why their reactions will tend to direct markets toward equilibrium. They do not, however, explain how and when new products will be developed or new production techniques applied. Decisions in these areas involve entrepreneurial judgment and discovery in an uncertain world. How will consumers react to a potential new product? Can it be produced profitably? How can the necessary finances for additional capital assets or a new business venture be obtained? Would adoption of a new production process or alternative technology reduce cost? Could per unit costs be reduced if the firm offered a different combination of products and services? Could a successful business activity in one area be expanded to other locations? If so, what would be the best way to expand? All these questions and many more require entrepreneurial judgment.

Entrepreneurial judgment is necessary when there is no decision rule that can be applied using only information that is freely available. For this reason, we are unable to incorporate fully the function of the entrepreneur into economic models. There simply is no way to model these complex decisions that involve uncertainty, discovery, and business judgment. All we can do is note the importance of entrepreneurial judgment and recognize that our models are limited because they are unable to capture this critical element of both business success and economic progress.

THE ENTREPRENEUR: A JOB DESCRIPTION

If we cannot put entrepreneurship into our models, what can we say about its function? One way to answer this question is to consider a generalized job description for an entrepreneurial position. An investor who lacks the desire, or perhaps the skill, to be an entrepreneur, but nonetheless wants to be in business, may seek someone to act as the business entrepreneur, while the investor provides some of the capital. A newspaper ad to find such a person (though perhaps not the usual way for the investor to search) might read as follows:

> *Wanted: Entrepreneur.* Must have many qualities. Must be (1) alert to new business opportunities and to new problems before they become obvious; (2) willing to back judgments with investments of hard work and creative effort before others recognize correctness of judgments; (3) able to make correct decisions and to convince others of their validity, so as to attract additional financial backing; and (4) able to recognize own inevitable mistakes and to back away from incorrect decisions without wasting additional resources. Exciting, exhausting, high-risk position. Pay will be very good for success, and very poor for failure.

Entrepreneurship is not for the faint-hearted or the lazy. Entrepreneurs are at the center of the action in the real world, even if they do not have a place in most economic models.[5]

AN EVALUATION OF COMPETITIVE PRICE-SEARCHER MARKETS

As we saw earlier, determination of price and output for price searchers is in some ways very similar to that for price takers. Also, since the long-run, equilibrium conditions in price-taker markets are consistent with ideal economic efficiency, it is useful to compare and contrast them with conditions in

---

[5]For a more complete overview of entrepreneurship, and references on the topic, see Mark Crosson, "Entrepreneurship," in *The New Palgrave: A Dictionary of Economics,* ed. John Eatwell, et al. (New York: Stockton Press, 1987), pp. 151–153.

FOUR ENTREPRENEURS WHO HAVE CHANGED OUR LIVES

Unlike movie stars and athletes, business entrepreneurs seldom command great respect in our society. Often, their contributions are either overlooked or misunderstood. In a competitive economy, entrepreneurs get ahead by discovering better ways of doing things, such as new production techniques that reduce cost or new products that are highly valued (relative to their cost). An interesting aspect of entrepreneurship is that it often comes from unusual sources—people who have an ability to think about and institute unconventional ideas.

Of course, highly successful entrepreneurs make a lot of money. Remember, however, that trade helps both the buyer and the seller. To be successful, entrepreneurs must provide their customers with value—a better deal than they can get elsewhere. Thus, they are an important source of economic progress. Highly successful entrepreneurs often exert enormous impact on our lives, far more than most of us realize. Consider how four key entrepreneurs of our age have affected our lives.[1]

SAMUEL M. WALTON (1917–1992) Sam Walton worked his way through the University of Missouri with odd jobs, including delivering newspapers, waiting tables, and life guarding. After college, he first became a management trainee with JCPenney department stores, the second-largest retailer in the United States at the time. He stayed with Penney's for less than two years. After two years in the military, Walton purchased a Ben Franklin department store franchise in Arkansas. Over the next decade, he was able to open several new stores. Because each Ben Franklin store was an independently owned franchise, Walton had little influence on the overall direction of the company.

Frustrated with some of the corporate policies, he opened up his own store called Discount City in 1962. The business was not even incorporated until 1969. Soon the name was changed to Wal-Mart and, beginning with two stores in Arkansas, Sam Walton developed it into the largest retail chain in America. Today there are almost

2,000 Wal-Mart stores, and the company is No. 4 on the *Fortune* 500 list. In 1995, its sales were almost three times those of its closest competitor, Sears, Roebuck.

What accounts for the success of Wal-Mart? The primary ingredients of Walton's business strategy were warehouse stores, inventory control, name-brand goods at low prices, and the targeting of small- and medium-sized towns without a major retailer. Initially, Walton did not attempt to compete with the big stores, such as Sears or Montgomery Ward. Instead, he focused on smaller towns without a major department store. His cost-saving distribution warehouse centers allowed Walton to provide consumers with brand-name goods at prices below those of his competitors. Low cost, volume sales, great prices, and convenience of location—Walton used this recipe to provide consumers with more value than they could get elsewhere. It made Walton one of the richest men in America and Wal-Mart the nation's leading retailer.

RAY A. KROC (1902–1984) In 1954 Ray Kroc was an unlikely source of entrepreneurial genius. Already in his late 50s, he had worked for radio stations, sold paper cups, and was currently selling milk shake machines. One day he called on a little hamburger shop in San Bernardino, California. Kroc was amazed at how well this business was doing. After several days of negotiations, he was able to convince the owners of the restaurant, Maurice and Richard McDonald, to allow him to sell franchises in other areas. Each of these franchise stores would be independently owned, but would use the McDonald's name and food menu.

Kroc was careful to whom he sold the franchises. Owners were required to undertake extensive training and work full time in the restaurant. Locations had to be approved before a franchise could be obtained. The food preparation was carefully standardized, with rules on the size of buns, the amount of certain condiments that could be used, and so on. Eventually, all franchise owners were required to complete a comprehensive training program at a Chicago center that was often referred to as "hamburger university."

Within six years, Kroc had sold 200 McDonald's

franchises. He borrowed funds and used his earnings from the franchise sales to buy the entire business from the McDonald brothers. McDonald's provides customers with fast service and economical meals served in a pleasant environment. The restaurant chain changed the way many Americans eat and, in essence, established a new industry, the fast-food business. Who would have thought that a middle-aged milk shake machine salesman could have exerted such an impact on our lives?

TED TURNER (1938–) Born in Cincinnati, Ted Turner moved with his family to Georgia when he was nine. He attended Brown University, where after enrolling as a humanities major, he eventually shifted to economics. Debate, sailing, and partying occupied most of his time at Brown. He was both vice-president of the Debating Union and commodore of the Yacht Club. His partying resulted in a number of problems with both his fraternity, Kappa Sigma, and university authorities.

After leaving college, Turner worked in his father's billboard advertising business and eventually took over the company. In 1970 he risked his assets in outdoor advertising to acquire an unprofitable TV station, WTCG, in Atlanta. He renamed the station WTBS, the "Superstation," and managed to get it on many of the local cable systems around the country. The station offered mostly movies and major league baseball after Turner purchased the Atlanta Braves.

In 1980, Turner risked all of his assets and arranged for additional financing through the "junk bond" market in order to launch a 24-hour news network, a network that is now known to the world as CNN (Cable News Network). Most experts in the TV industry predicted the venture would fail. Prior to his final decision to start CNN, Turner's own employees gave him the following message: "Please, Ted! Don't do this to us! If you commit to a venture of this size you'll sink the whole company!"

Of course, risk taking is an integral part of entrepreneurship. Few, however, have risked so much on ideas that were so widely viewed as long shots. Propelled by Turner's determination and confidence concerning what Americans wanted to watch on television, the market verified his judgment. By 1991 Turner's cable TV operations (WTBS, CNN, TNT, and Headline News) attracted one-third of the cable TV audience. Turner's news stations are now widely viewed around the world. Who would have predicted that an enthusiast who obtained his initial business experience in billboard advertising would change the way the world watches television?

WILLIAM "BILL" GATES III (1955–) Even as a child, Bill Gates loved computers. At the early age of 15 he earned $20,000 by writing a computer program to help manage traffic. He entered Harvard at the age of 17, and while still an undergraduate, developed BASIC for the first microcomputer, the MITS Altair. Convinced that eventually most offices and homes would have a microcomputer, Gates, along with his friend Paul Allen, created Microsoft in 1975. The focus of the business was the development of software designed to make microcomputers both more useful and more user friendly.

Gates quickly earned a reputation as a programming genius. When IBM decided to enter the personal computer (PC) market in 1980, they contracted with Gates to provide the basic operating software for their computers, a system now known as MS-DOS. Gates reserved the rights to sell his MS-DOS software to other firms. As IBM (and IBM clones) grew to dominate the PC market during the 1980s, Gates's fortune rose as well. Microsoft developed into the dominant firm in the computer software industry. Gates's MS-DOS program is now used to run more than 90 percent of the world's computers. Gates's MS-DOS–based software programs, Windows and Windows 95, are among the most popular in the world.

Gates attributes his success to his workaholic nature. He continues to work long hours and is still actively involved in the operation and strategic decision making of Microsoft. If you have ever used a computer, you have almost certainly benefited from programs that Gates created. His remarkable programming genius has changed the way we use personal computers both at home and in the workplace.

---

[1]See Gene N. Landrum, *Profiles of Genius* (Buffalo: Prometheus Books, 1993), and Robert F. Hartley, *Management Mistakes and Successes* (New York: John Wiley and Sons, Inc., 1994), for additional information on entrepreneurship and the personalities of this feature.

price-searcher markets when entry barriers are low. There are both similarities and differences.

Neither price takers nor price searchers in markets with low entry barriers will be able to earn long-run economic profit. In the long run, competition will drive the price of competing firms down to the level of average total cost. In each case, entrepreneurs have a strong incentive to manage and operate their businesses efficiently. Inefficient operation will lead to losses and forced exit from the market. Price takers and competitive price searchers alike will be motivated to develop and adopt new cost-reducing procedures and techniques because lower costs will mean higher short-run profits (or at least smaller losses).

The response to changing demand conditions of price takers and price searchers in markets with low entry barriers is similar. In both cases, an increase in market demand leads to higher prices, short-run profits, expansion of the existing producers, and the entry of new firms. With the entry of new producers, and the concurrent expansion of existing firms, the market supply will increase, placing downward pressure on price. The process will continue until the market price falls to the level of average total cost, squeezing out all economic profit.

Similarly, a reduction in demand will lead to lower prices and short-run losses, causing output to fall and some firms to exit. As the market supply declines, prices will rise and eventually the short-run losses will be eliminated and the firms remaining in the industry will once again be able to cover their costs. Regardless of whether the firms are price takers or price searchers, profits and losses will direct their output decisions when barriers to entry are low.

As **Exhibit 20–4** illustrates, while the price taker confronts a horizontal demand curve, the demand curve faced by a price searcher is downward sloping. This is important because it means that the marginal revenue of the price searcher will be less than, rather than equal to, price. So, when the profit-maximizing price searcher expands output until $MR = MC$, price will still exceed marginal cost (panel b). In contrast, the price charged by a profit-maximizing price taker will equal marginal cost (panel a). In addition, when a price searcher is in long-run equilibrium, the firm's output rate will be less than the rate that would minimize average total cost. The price searcher would have a lower per unit cost (97 cents rather than $1) if a larger output were produced.

ALLOCATIVE EFFICIENCY IN PRICE-SEARCHER MARKETS WITH LOW ENTRY BARRIERS

The efficiency of price searchers in markets with low entry barriers has been the subject of debate among economists for years. At one time, the dominant view seemed to be that allocative inefficiency results because price searchers fail to operate at an output level that minimizes their long-run average total cost. As a result of the proliferation in the number of firms, the sales of each competitor fall short of their least-cost capacity level. The potential social gain associated with the expansion of production to the $P = MC$ output rate is therefore lost. The advocates of this view argue that if there were fewer producers, each would be able to operate at the minimum-cost output rate. They see inefficiency resulting from costly duplication—too many producers each operating below their

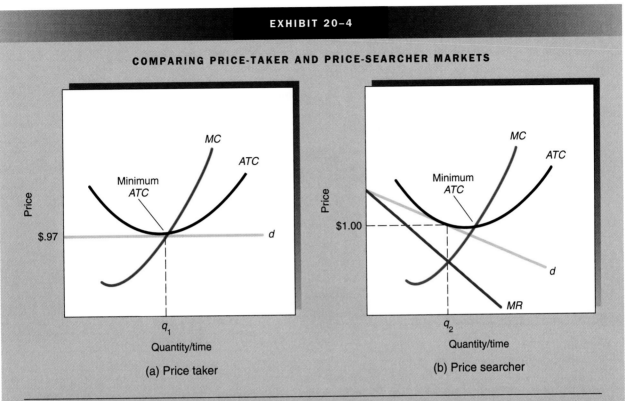

EXHIBIT 20–4

COMPARING PRICE-TAKER AND PRICE-SEARCHER MARKETS

(a) Price taker

(b) Price searcher

Here we illustrate the long-run equilibrium conditions of a price taker and a price searcher when entry barriers are low. In both cases, price is equal to average total cost, and economic profit is zero. However, since the price searcher confronts a downward-sloping demand curve for its product, its profit-maximizing price exceeds marginal cost, and output is not large enough to minimize average total cost when the market is in long-run equilibrium. For identical cost conditions, *the price of the product in a price-searcher market will be slightly higher than in a price-taker market. This slightly higher price is considered by some to be indicative of inefficiency, while others perceive it to be the premium a society pays for variety and convenience (product differentiation).*

minimum-cost output capacity. Two or more filling stations, restaurants, grocery stores, or similar establishments operating side by side are given as examples of the economic waste generated by price-searcher markets.

In addition, the various price searchers' efforts to inform and convince consumers that their differentiated products are better than others also bring criticism. Their competitive advertising campaigns are charged with being self-defeating and wasteful. Firms have an incentive, critics say, to use advertising to promote artificial distinctions between similar products, and firms that do not engage in such advertising can expect their sales to decline. Advertising, though, results in higher prices for consumers and thus it is costly from society's point of view.

In recent years, this traditional view has been seriously challenged. Many economists now believe that it is mechanistic and fails to take into account the significance of dynamic competition. Most important, the traditional view assumes that consumers place no value on the wider variety of qualities and styles that result. Prices might very well be slightly lower if there were fewer gasoline stations, if they were located farther apart, and if they offered a more limited variety of service and credit plan options. Similarly, the prices of groceries might very well be slightly lower if there were fewer supermarkets, each a bit more congested and located less conveniently for some customers. However, since customers value convenience and product diversity as well as lower prices, some argue that consumers are served quite well by price-searcher markets. According to this view, the higher prices (and costs) are simply the premium consumers pay for ease of purchase and variety.

When consumers receive utility from differentiated products, one cannot conclude that uniform products with a lower price, but less variety from which to select, would be preferable to products of greater diversity with somewhat higher prices. In fact, consumers often pay more for various unique products, rather than all flocking to a single, cheaper version even when they know the latter is available at a lower price. For example, many consumers purchase designer jeans and specialty shirts even when they are aware that equally durable, more standardized versions are available at a lower price.

The defenders of product diversity also deny that price-searcher markets lead to excessive, wasteful advertising. They point out that advertising often reduces the consumer's search time and provides valuable information about prices, new products, and new firms entering the market. Furthermore, if advertising results in higher prices with no compensating benefits, people can turn to cheaper, nonadvertised products. After all, consumers are under no obligation to purchase advertised products. In fact, some price searchers use higher-quality service and lower prices to compete with rivals who advertise heavily. When consumers really prefer lower prices and less advertising, firms offering that combination do quite well.

A SPECIAL CASE: PRICE DISCRIMINATION

Thus far, we have assumed that all sellers of a product will charge each customer the same price. Sometimes, though, price searchers can increase their revenues (and profits) by charging different prices to different groups of consumers. Such businesses as hotels, fast-food restaurants, and drugstores often charge senior citizens less than other customers; students and children are often given discounts at movie theaters and athletic events. Sometimes bars and sports teams charge women lower prices than men. This practice is called **price discrimination**. *To gain from this practice, price searchers must be able to do two things: (1) identify and separate at least two groups with differing elasticities of demand, and (2) prevent those who buy at the low price from reselling to the customers charged higher prices.*

Price discrimination
A practice whereby a seller charges different consumers different prices for the same product or service.

Let us take a closer look at why sellers may find price discrimination advantageous. Suppose that a seller has two groups of customers: one with an inelastic demand for its product and the other with an elastic demand. An increase in the price charged the first group will increase the total revenue derived from that group. On the other hand, a reduction in price will increase revenues derived from the latter. Thus, the seller may be able to increase its total revenue and profit by charging the first group a higher price than the second.

The pricing of airline tickets illustrates the potential of price discrimination. The airline industry has found that the demand of business fliers is substantially more inelastic than the demand of vacationers, students, and other travelers. Thus, airlines usually charge high fares to persons who are unwilling to stay over a weekend, who spend only a day or two at their destination, and who make reservations a short time before their flight. These high fares fall primarily on business travelers who are less sensitive to price. In contrast, discount fares are offered to fliers willing to make reservations well in advance, travel during off-peak hours, and stay at their destinations over a weekend before returning home. Such travelers are likely to be vacationers and students, who are highly sensitive to price.

Exhibit 20–5 illustrates the logic of this policy. Panel a shows what would happen if a single price were charged to all customers. Given the demand, the profit-maximizing firm expands output to 100, where *MR* equals *MC*. The profit-

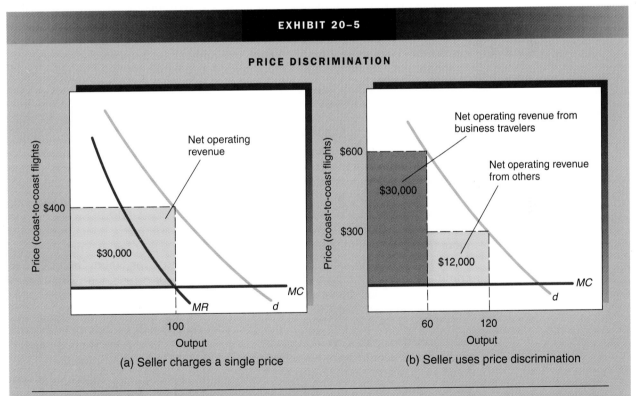

EXHIBIT 20–5

PRICE DISCRIMINATION

(a) Seller charges a single price

(b) Seller uses price discrimination

As panel a illustrates, a $400 ticket price will maximize profits on coast-to-coast flights if an airline charges a single price. However, the airline can do still better if it raises the price to $600 for passengers (business travelers) with a highly inelastic demand and reduces the price to $300 for travelers (for example, students and vacationers) with a more elastic demand. When sellers can segment their market, they can gain by (a) charging a higher price to consumers with a less elastic demand and (b) offering discounts to customers whose demand is more elastic.

maximizing price on coast-to-coast flights is $400, which generates $40,000 of revenue per flight. Since the marginal cost per passenger is $100, this provides the airline with net operating revenue of $30,000 with which to cover other costs.

However, as panel b shows, although the market demand schedule is unchanged, the airline can do even better if it uses price discrimination. When it charges business travelers $600, most of these passengers continue to travel since their demand is highly inelastic. On the other hand, a $100 price cut generates substantial additional ticket sales from vacationers, students, and others whose demands are more elastic. Therefore, with price discrimination, the airline can sell 60 tickets (primarily to business travelers) at $600 and 60 additional tickets to others at $300. Total revenue jumps to $54,000 and leaves the airline with $42,000 ($54,000 minus 120 times the $100 marginal cost per passenger) of revenue in excess of variable cost. Compared to the single-price outcome (panel a), the price discrimination strategy expands profit by $12,000.

When sellers can segment their market (at a low cost) into groups with differing price elasticities of demand, price discrimination can increase profits. *For each group,* the seller will maximize profit by equating marginal cost and marginal revenue. This rule will lead to higher prices for groups with the most inelastic demand and lower prices for the groups with the most elastic demand. Compared to the single-price situation, price discrimination increases profitability because a higher price increases the net revenue from groups with an inelastic demand, while a lower price increases the net revenue from price-sensitive customers. With price discrimination, the number of units sold also increases (compare panel a with panel b) because the discounts provided to price-sensitive groups increase the quantity sold more than the higher prices charged the less price-sensitive groups reduce sales.

Sometimes price discrimination is subtle. Colleges engage in price discrimination by charging a high standard tuition to get additional revenue from high-income students with a more inelastic demand, while providing low-income students with scholarships based on need (tuition "discounts"). The partial tuition scholarships given to students whose parents are less wealthy enables the college to attract students who have a more elastic demand. Low-income students thus are not priced out of their market by the high standard tuition.

How do buyers fare when a seller can price discriminate? Some buyers pay more than they would if a single intermediate price were offered. They purchase fewer units, and they are worse off. In contrast, those for whom the price discrimination process lowers the price are better off. Of course, with some products, such as airline transportation, a single buyer might be better off with some purchases and worse off with others.

On balance, however, we can expect that output will be greater with price discrimination than it would be with a single price. The market is not as understocked as it would have been in the absence of the price discrimination. Thus, from an allocative standpoint, price discrimination gets high marks; it reduces the allocative inefficiency due to price being set above marginal cost. Some of the gains that would accrue to consumers with an inelastic demand are transferred to the price searcher as increased revenue, but additional gains from trade are created by the increased output of goods that would be lost if the price searcher did not (or could not) price discriminate.

In some markets, there is an additional gain emanating from price discrimination: Production may occur that would be lost if only a single price were charged. With price discrimination, some otherwise unprofitable firms may be able to generate enough additional revenue to operate successfully in the marketplace. For example, some small towns in Montana might not provide enough revenue at a single price to enable a local physician to cover her opportunity costs. However, if she is able to discriminate on the basis of income, charging higher-income patients more than normal rates and lower-income patients less, the resulting revenues from practice in the small town may enable the physician to stay in the community. In this case, all residents of the town may be better off as the result of the price discrimination, since it provides them with access to a local physician. After all, even those being charged the highest prices are not disadvantaged if the price discrimination keeps the physician in town. They are just as able to seek physician services elsewhere as they would have been in the absence of the price-discriminating local doctor. With or without price discrimination, access to competing sellers (or buyers) protects market participants from unfair treatment.

In summary, if potential customers can be segmented into groups with different elasticities of demand and retrading can be controlled at a low cost, sellers can often gain by charging higher prices to those with the more inelastic demand (and lower prices to those with an elastic demand). Price discrimination can also increase the total gains from trade and thereby reduce allocative inefficiency. Sometimes it even allows production where none would have otherwise occurred.

COMPETITION AMONG FIRMS: HOW IT INCREASES PROSPERITY

When barriers to entry are low, businesses must compete for the loyalty of customers. This is true for price takers and price searchers alike, for small-scale or large-scale firms, in local, regional, national, or even global markets. There are three major reasons why firms operating in a competitive environment will be a force promoting economic progress.

1. Competition places pressure on producers to operate efficiently and cater to the preferences of customers.
2. Competition provides firms with a strong incentive to develop improved products and discover lower-cost methods of production.
3. Competition causes firms to discover the type of business structure and size that can best keep the per unit costs of production low.

EFFICIENT OPERATION AND CONSUMER SATISFACTION

First, competition weeds out the inefficient. An efficient firm will seek ways to cut costs by adopting lower-cost production techniques or figuring out how to produce a given output with fewer resources. In some cases, this will involve "downsizing," to use the terminology of the news media. Firms that fail to provide consumers with quality goods at competitive prices will experience losses and eventually be driven out of business, making available to other firms the labor and capital they had employed. Successful competitors have to outperform rival firms. They may do so through a variety of methods—quality of product, style, service, convenience of location, advertising, and price—but they must consistently offer consumers as much or more value than they can get elsewhere.

What keeps McDonald's, Wal-Mart, General Motors, or any other business firm from raising prices, selling shoddy products, and providing lousy service? Competition is the answer. If McDonald's fails to provide an attractively priced, tasty sandwich with a smile, people will turn to Burger King, Wendy's, Dairy Queen, and other rivals. If Wal-Mart does not provide convenience and value, people will turn to Sears, Kmart, and other retailers. Similarly, as recent experience has shown, even a firm as large as General Motors will lose customers to Ford, Honda, Toyota, Chrysler, Volkswagen, Mazda, and other automobile manufacturers if it fails to please the customer as much as rival suppliers.

INCENTIVE FOR INNOVATION

When markets are competitive, suppliers have a strong incentive to be innovative. An entrepreneur who figures out how to produce a good more efficiently

Competition is the disciplining force of a market economy. The presence of alternative sellers more or less forces business firms to cater to the wishes of consumers.

or who develops a new product that is highly valued relative to its cost gains an advantage over rivals. Such producers will earn larger profits.

Think of the new products that have been introduced during the last 50 years: microwave ovens, videocassette recorders, color television sets, personal computers, compact disc players, fax and telephone answering machines, non-wrinkle clothes, fast-food restaurants, and coronary artery bypass devices come to mind. New, improved products are constantly upgrading the way that we live and work.

Since no one knows precisely what products consumers will want next or which production techniques will minimize per unit costs, competition is necessary to motivate an attempt to discover the answers. Is that new visionary idea the greatest thing since the development of the fast-food chain? Or is it simply another dream that will soon turn to vapor? Entrepreneurs need only win the support of investors willing to finance the potentially successful new product or production technology. Competition demands that a firm make such discoveries before its rivals do. Yet, at the same time, competition holds entrepreneurs and the investors who support them accountable; their ideas must face a "reality check" imposed by consumers. Consumers must value the innovative idea enough to cover its cost. When competition is present, consumers are the ultimate judge and jury of business innovation and performance.

Since today's successful product may not pass tomorrow's competitive test, businesses in a competitive market must be good at anticipating, identifying, and quickly adopting improved ideas, whether their own or others'. Again, the ongoing, dynamic characteristic of competition must continually be considered.

APPROPRIATE STRUCTURE AND SIZE

Competition also demands that a firm discover the type and size of business structure that best keeps the per unit cost of its product or service low. Unlike other economic systems, a market economy does not mandate or limit the types of firms that are permitted to compete. Any form of business organization is permissible. An owner-operated firm, partnership, corporation, employee-owned firm, consumer cooperative, commune, or any other form of business is free to enter the market. In order to be successful, however, a business structure must be cost-effective. A form of business organization that results in high per unit cost will be driven from a competitive market.

The same is true for the size of a firm. For some products, a business must be quite large to take full advantage of economies of scale. When per unit costs decline as output increases, small businesses tend to have higher production costs (and therefore higher prices) than their larger counterparts. When this is the case, consumers interested in maximum value for their money will tend to buy from the lower-priced larger firm. Consequently, only large firms, generally organized as corporations, are able to survive in such markets. The auto and airplane manufacturing industries provide examples.

In other instances, small firms, often organized as individual proprietorships or partnerships, will be more cost-effective. When personalized service and individualized products are valued highly by consumers, it may be difficult for large firms to compete. Under these circumstances, mostly small firms will survive. For example, this is generally true for law and medical practices, printing shops, and hair-styling salons. A market economy permits cost considerations and the interaction between producers and consumers to determine the type and size of firm in each market.

When large-scale enterprises have lower costs, it will be particularly important that nations do not either limit competition from foreign suppliers or prevent domestic firms from selling abroad. This point is vitally important for small countries. For example, since the domestic market of a country like South Korea is small, a Korean automobile manufacturer would have extremely high costs per unit if it could not sell automobiles abroad. Similarly, domestic consumers in small countries would have to pay an exceedingly high price for automobiles if they were prohibited from buying from large-scale, lower-cost foreign producers.

In essence, competition harnesses personal self-interest—an undeniably powerful motivator—and puts it to work elevating our standard of living. Rival firms struggle for the dollar votes of consumers. When entry barriers are low, attracting buyers means providing them with at least as good a deal as is available elsewhere. In order to earn a profit, businesses have to figure out better ways of doing things and supply goods that consumers value highly relative to their cost. As they do so, they create wealth, increase the value of resources, and promote economic progress.

LOOKING AHEAD

In this chapter we have analyzed the choices facing price searchers, and their behavior when barriers to entry are low. Next, we will see how barriers to entry might be formed, how price searchers react, and how the results differ when entry barriers are high rather than low.

CHAPTER SUMMARY

1. In price-searcher markets with low barriers to entry, the firms face a downward-sloping demand curve and they are free to set the prices for the products that they sell. However, because of the low entry barriers, they face strong competitive pressure from both direct and potential rivals. Correspondingly, even though the firm chooses the prices charged for its products, market forces will determine the quantities sold at alternative prices.

2. The distinguishing characteristic of the price-searcher market with low barriers to entry is product differentiation. Each price searcher in such a market faces a gently downward-sloping demand curve. Price searchers use product quality, style, convenience of location, advertising, and price as competitive weapons. Since all rivals within the market are free to duplicate one another's prod-

ucts (or services), the demand for the product of any one firm is highly elastic.

3. A profit-maximizing firm will expand output as long as marginal revenue exceeds marginal cost. Thus, a price searcher will lower its price so that output can be expanded until $MR = MC$. The price charged by the profit-maximizing price searcher will be greater than its marginal cost.

4. If firms in a price-searcher market with low barriers to entry are making economic profits, rival firms will be induced to enter the market. They will expand the supply of the product (and similar products), enticing some customers away from established firms. The demand curve faced by an individual firm will fall (shift inward) until the economic profits have been eliminated.

5. Economic losses will cause price searchers to exit from the market. The demand for the products of each remaining firm will rise (shift outward) until the losses have been eliminated.

6. When barriers to entry are low, firms in a market will make only normal profits in the long run. In the short run, they may make either economic profits or losses, depending on market conditions.

7. Competition can come from potential as well as actual rivals. If entry and exit are not expensive, and if there are no legal barriers to entry, the theory of contestable mar-

kets indicates that competitive results may occur even if there are only a few firms actually in the market.

8. Although standard economic models do not include the central role of entrepreneurial decision making in a world of uncertainty, economists recognize its importance. Entrepreneurs who discover and introduce lower-cost production methods and new products that are highly valued relative to cost are an important source of economic progress.

9. Traditional economic theory has emphasized that price-searcher markets with low barriers to entry are inefficient because (a) price exceeds marginal cost at the profit-maximizing output level; (b) long-run average cost is not minimized; and (c) excessive advertising is sometimes encouraged. However, other economists have argued more recently that this criticism is misdirected. According to the newer view, when barriers to entry are low, price searchers have an incentive to (a) produce efficiently; (b) undertake production if and only if their actions will increase the value of resources used; and (c) be innovative in offering new product options.

10. When a price searcher can (a) identify groups of customers that have different price elasticities of demand and (b) prevent customers from retrading the product, price discrimination may emerge. The seller may be able to gain by charging higher prices to groups with a more inelastic demand and lower prices to those with a more elastic demand. The practice generally leads to a larger output and more gains from trade than would otherwise occur.

11. When barriers to entry are low, competition is an important disciplinary force in a market. In a competitive environment, even profit-seeking business firms have a strong incentive to (a) operate efficiently and cater to the preferences of consumers, (b) improve products and discover lower-cost methods of production, and (c) discover the type of business structure and size of firm that can best keep the per unit cost of a product or service low. These factors are important elements of economic progress.

CRITICAL ANALYSIS QUESTIONS

1. Street-corner vendors using pushcarts have sometimes engaged in price wars at popular locations within Washington, D.C. Explain why a strategy of cutting price below cost in order to drive out other vendors from a given location would not make sense if there were no legal barriers to entry.

2. Price searchers can set the price of their product. Does this mean that price searchers will charge the highest possible price for their product? What price will maximize the profits of a price searcher? How will the firm's marginal cost compare with price at the profit-maximum output?

*3. What determines the *variety* of styles, designs, and sizes of different products? Why do you think there are only a few different varieties of toothpicks but lots of different types of napkins on the market?

*4. How would the imposition of a fixed, per unit tax of $2,000 on new automobiles affect the average *quality* of automobiles, if the proceeds of the tax were used to subsidize a government-operated lottery?

5. What is the primary function of the entrepreneur? Some economists have charged that the major market-structure models of economic theory assume away the function of the entrepreneur. In what sense is this true? Is the function of the entrepreneur important? Discuss.

6. Is quality and style competition as important as price competition? Would you like to live in a country where government regulation restricted the use of quality and style competition? Why or why not? Do you think you would get more or less for your consumer dollar if quality and style competition were restricted? Discuss.

*7. Suppose that a price searcher is currently charging a price that maximizes the firm's total revenue. Will this price also maximize the firm's profit? Why or why not? Explain.

8. Since price searchers can set their prices, does this mean that their prices are unaffected by market conditions? In price-searcher markets with low barriers to entry, will the firms be able to make economic profit in the long run? Why or why not? What do competitive price searchers have to do in order to make economic profit?

*9. Suppose that a group of investors wants to start a business operated out of a popular Utah ski area, and the group is considering either building a new hotel complex or starting a new local airline serving that market. Each new business would require about the same amount of capital and personnel hiring. The group believes each to have the same profit potential. Which is the safer (less likely to result in a substantial capital loss) investment? Why? Is there an offsetting advantage to the other investment?

10. "Really tough competition is deadly to innovation. Producers have no profits to plow back into innovation." Evaluate. (Hint: Investments are made in search of future profit.)

*11. "When competition is really severe, only the big firms survive. The little guy has no chance." True or false? Explain.

12. Is price discrimination harmful to the economy? How does price discrimination affect the total amount of gains from exchange? Explain. Why do colleges often charge students different prices, based on their family income?

13. What is the primary requirement for a market to be competitive? Is competition necessary for markets to work well? Why or why not? How does competition influence

the following: (a) the cost efficiency of producers, (b) the quality of products, and (c) the discovery and development of new products? Explain your answers.

14. The accompanying graph shows the short-run demand and cost situation for a price searcher in a market with low barriers to entry.
   a. What level of output will maximize the firm's profit level?
   b. What price will the firm charge?
   c. How much revenue will the firm receive in this situation? How much is total cost? Total profit?
   d. How will this situation change with the passage of time?

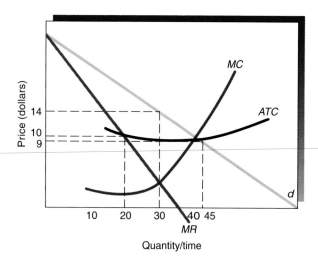

*15. Rod N. Reel owns a dealership that sells fishing boats in an open price-searcher market. In developing his pricing strategy, Rod hired an economist to estimate his demand curve. Columns (1) and (2) of the following chart provide the data for the expected weekly quantity demanded for Rod's fishing boats at alternative prices.

Rod's marginal (and average) cost of supplying each boat is constant at $5,000 per boat no matter how many boats he sells per week in this range. This cost includes all opportunity costs and represents the economic cost per boat.
   a. Find Rod's economic profits at each alternative price by calculating the difference between total revenue and total cost.
   b. Find Rod's marginal revenue and marginal cost from the sale of each additional boat.
   c. If Rod wants to maximize his profits, what price should he charge per boat?
   d. How many boats will Rod sell per week at the profit-maximizing price?
   e. What will Rod's profits be per week at this price and sales volume?
   f. At the price and sales level where profits are maximized, has Rod sold all boats that have higher marginal revenue than marginal cost?
   g. If Rod's profits are typical of all firms in the boat sales business, what might be expected to happen in the future? Will more boat dealers open in the area or will some of the existing ones go out of business? What will happen to the profitability of the boat dealers in the future once the entry/exit has occurred?
   h. *Challenge Question:* Recall the relationship between elasticity of demand, price changes, and their impact on total revenues. As Rod lowers his price from $9,000 down to $5,000, his total revenues keep increasing. Is demand in this price range elastic, inelastic, or unitary elastic? When Rod lowers his price from $5,000 to $4,000, his total revenues stay the same. Is demand in this price range elastic, inelastic, or unitary elastic? Can you guess what might happen at prices below $4,000? Explain.

*Asterisk denotes questions for which answers are given in Appendix B.

PRICE OF FISHING BOATS (1)	NUMBER OF FISHING BOATS SOLD PER WEEK (2)	TOTAL REVENUES PER WEEK (3)	TOTAL COST PER WEEK (4)	ECONOMIC PROFIT PER WEEK (5)	MARGINAL REVENUE (6)	MARGINAL COST (7)
$9,000	0	_____	_____	_____	—	—
8,000	1	_____	_____	_____	_____	_____
7,000	2	_____	_____	_____	_____	_____
6,000	3	_____	_____	_____	_____	_____
5,000	4	_____	_____	_____	_____	_____
4,000	5	_____	_____	_____	_____	_____

If there are economies of scale throughout the region of possible industry outputs, only one or a few firms may be able to exist in the industry.

GEORGE STIGLER[1]

---

[1]George J. Stigler, *The Theory of Price* (New York: Macmillan, 1987), p. 204.

■ What are the barriers to entry that protect some firms against competition from potential market entrants?

■ What is a monopoly? Does it guarantee the ability to make a profit?

■ What is an oligopoly? When are oligopolists likely to collude? Why is it impossible to construct a general theory of output and price for an oligopolist?

■ Why are economists critical of high barriers to entry?

■ What policy alternatives do economists suggest to reduce the problems associated with high barriers to entry?

■ Is competition able to discipline large firms in markets with high barriers to entry?

n the previous two chapters, we analyzed the way firms behave in competitive markets, characterized by low barriers to entry. We now turn to the analysis of firm behavior when entry barriers are high and there are few, if any, rival firms offering the same or similar products. This chapter focuses on factors that increase the difficulty of entry into a market and analyzes how they influence the ability of markets to discipline business firms. The potential of various policy alternatives that might improve the efficiency of resource allocation in these markets will also be considered.

WHY ARE ENTRY BARRIERS SOMETIMES HIGH?

What makes it difficult for potential competitors to enter a market? Four factors can be important: economies of scale, government licensing, patents, and control over an essential resource.

ECONOMIES OF SCALE

In some industries, firms experience declining average total costs over the full range of output that consumers are willing to buy. When this is the case, the larger firm will always have lower unit costs. Since smaller firms have higher per unit costs, it will be difficult for them to enter the market, build a reputation, and compete effectively with larger firms. Under these circumstances, a single firm will tend to emerge from the competitive process in the industry, and the cost advantage resulting from its size will provide the firm with protection from potential rivals.

GOVERNMENT LICENSING

Legal barriers are the oldest and most effective method of protecting a business firm from potential competitors. Kings once granted exclusive business rights to favored citizens or groups. Today, governments continue to establish barriers, restricting the right to buy and sell goods. To compete in certain parts of the communications industry in the United States (for example, to operate a radio or television station), one must obtain a government franchise. Similarly, local governments often grant exclusive franchises for the operation of cable television systems.

Licensing, a process by which one obtains permission from the government to enter a specific occupation or business, often limits entry. In many states, a person must obtain a license before operating a liquor store, barbershop, taxicab, funeral home, or drugstore. Sometimes these licenses cost little and are designed to ensure certain minimum standards. In other cases, they are expensive and designed primarily to limit competition.

PATENTS

Most countries have established patent laws designed to provide inventors with a property right to their inventions. Patent laws grant the owner the exclusive legal right to the commercial use of a newly invented product or process for a limited period of time, 17 years in the United States. Once a patent is granted, other persons are prevented from producing the product or using the procedure unless they obtain permission from the patent holder. Costs, as well as benefits, accompany a patent system. As we will soon illustrate, the barrier to entry created by the grant of a patent generally leads to higher prices for consumers of already existing products. On the positive side, however, patents increase the potential returns to inventive activity, thus encouraging scientific research and technological improvements. Without patents, the pace of technological development would be slowed.

CONTROL OVER ESSENTIAL RESOURCE

If a single firm has sole control over a resource essential for entry into an industry, it can eliminate potential competitors. An example often cited is the Aluminum Company of America, which before the Second World War controlled the known supply of bauxite conveniently available to American firms. Without this critical raw material, potential competitors could not produce aluminum. With time, however, other supplies of bauxite were found, and this source of monopoly was lost to the company.

New technology, mineral exploration, and other ways to exploit profitable price situations are always sought. Over time, they are usually found. Barriers to entry are often temporary, but they do exist. Let us move on to see what happens when, at least temporarily, there is a barrier to entry high enough to limit the market to only one seller.

THE CASE OF MONOPOLY

The word *monopoly*, derived from two Greek words, means "single seller." We will define **monopoly** as a market characterized by (1) high barriers to entry and (2) a single seller of a well-defined product for which there are no good substitutes. Even this definition is ambiguous, because "high barriers" and "good substitutes" are both relative terms. Are the barriers to entry into the automobile or steel industries high? Many observers would argue that they are. After all, economies of scale are important in these industries and it would take a great deal of financial capital to operate at the least-cost scale of output. However, there are no *legal* restraints that prevent an entrepreneur from producing automobiles or steel. If price is well above cost and profit potential is present in these industries, it should not be too difficult to find the necessary investment capital. Thus, some would argue that entry barriers into these industries are not particularly high.

Monopoly
A market structure characterized by (1) a single seller of a well-defined product for which there are no good substitutes and (2) high barriers to the entry of any other firms into the market for that product.

"Good substitute" is also a subjective term. There is always some substitutability among products, even those produced by a single seller. Is a letter a good substitute for telephone communication? For some purposes—correspondence between law firms, for example—a letter delivered by mail is a very good substitute. In other cases, when the speed of communication and immediacy of response are important, telephone communication can have a tremendous advantage over letter writing. Are there any good substitutes for electricity? Most of the known substitutes for electric lighting (candles, oil lamps, and battery lights, for example) are inferior to electric lights in most uses. Natural gas, fuel oil, and wood, though, are often excellent substitutes for electric heating.

Monopoly, then, is always a matter of degree. Only a small fraction of all markets are served by only one seller. Nevertheless, there are two reasons why it is important to understand how such markets work. First, the monopoly model will help us understand markets in which there are few sellers and little active rivalry. When there are only two or three producers in a market, rather than competing with each other firms may seek to collude and thus together behave like a monopoly. Second, in a few important industries there is by law often only a single producer in each market. Local telephone and electricity services are examples. The monopoly model will illuminate the operation of such markets.

PRICE AND OUTPUT UNDER MONOPOLY

Suppose you invent, patent, and produce a microwave device that locks the hammer of any firearm in the immediate area. This fabulous invention can be used to immobilize potential robbers or hijackers. Since you own the exclusive patent right to the firearm lock device, you are not concerned about a competitive supplier in the foreseeable future. Although other products are competitive with your invention, they are poor substitutes. In short, you are a monopolist.

What price should you charge for your product? Since you are the only seller of this device, the demand for your product is also the market demand curve. It will be downward sloping because consumers will cut back on their purchases as the price of the firearm lock increases. Like other price searchers, you will have to search to determine the most profitable price to charge. An expansion in output will increase profit as long as the production and sale of additional units adds more to revenue than cost. *Like other price searchers, the monopolist will expand output until marginal revenue equals marginal cost. This profit maximizing output rate can be sold at a price along the firm's demand curve.*

Exhibit 21–1 provides a graphic illustration of profit maximization for a price searcher—in this case a monopolist.[2] The firm will continue to expand output as long as marginal revenue exceeds marginal cost. Therefore, output will be expanded to Q, where $MR = MC$. The monopolist will be able to sell the profit-maximizing output Q at price P, the height of the demand curve at Q. At any output less than Q, the benefits (marginal revenue) of producing the *additional* units will exceed their costs. In this range, the monopolist will gain by

---

[2]In this chapter we assume that firms are unable to use price discrimination to increase their revenues. If they could, the analysis of price discrimination from the previous chapter would help to describe their decisions.

EXHIBIT 21–1

SHORT-RUN PRICE AND OUTPUT OF MONOPOLIST

The monopolist will reduce price and expand output as long as MR exceeds MC. Output Q will result. When price exceeds average total cost at any output level, profit will accrue at that output level.

reducing price and expanding output toward Q. For any output greater than Q, the monopolist's costs of producing additional units will be greater than the benefits (marginal revenue). Production of such units would reduce profits. Thus, output rate Q and price P will maximize the firm's profit.

Exhibit 21–1 also depicts the profits of a monopolist. At output Q and price P the firm's total revenue is equal to $PAQO$, the price times the number of units sold. The firm's total cost would be $CBQO$, the average per unit cost multiplied by the number of units sold. The firm's profits are merely total revenue less total cost, the shaded area of Exhibit 21–1.

Exhibit 21–2 provides a numeric illustration of profit-maximizing decision making. At low output rates, marginal revenue exceeds marginal cost. The monopolist will continue expanding output as long as MR is greater than MC. Thus, an output rate of eight units per day will be chosen. Given the demand for the product, the monopolist can sell eight units at a price of $17.25 each. Total revenue will be $138, compared to a total cost of $108.50. The monopolist will make a profit of $29.50. The profit rate will be smaller at all other output rates. For example, if the monopolist reduces the price to $16 in order to sell nine units per day, revenue will increase by $6. However, the marginal cost of producing the ninth unit is $6.25. Since the cost of producing the ninth unit is greater than the revenue it brings in, profits will decline.

When high barriers to entry are present, they will insulate the monopolist from direct competition with rival firms producing a similar product. In markets with high entry barriers, monopoly profits will not attract—at least not quickly—rivals who will expand supply, cut prices, and spoil the seller's market. Protected by high entry barriers, therefore, a monopolist may be able to continue earning a profit, even in the long run. Does this mean that monopolists can charge as high a price as they want? Monopolists are often accused of price

EXHIBIT 21-2

PROFIT MAXIMIZATION FOR A MONOPOLIST

RATE OF OUTPUT (PER DAY) (1)	PRICE (PER UNIT) (2)	TOTAL REVENUE (1) × (2) (3)	TOTAL COST (PER DAY) (4)	PROFIT (3) − (4) (5)	MARGINAL COST (6)	MARGINAL REVENUE (7)
0	—	—	$ 50.00	$−50.00	—	—
1	$25.00	$ 25.00	60.00	−35.00	$10.00	$25.00
2	24.00	48.00	69.00	−21.00	9.00	23.00
3	23.00	69.00	77.00	−8.00	8.00	21.00
4	22.00	88.00	84.00	4.00	7.00	19.00
5	21.00	105.00	90.50	14.50	6.50	17.00
6	19.75	118.50	96.75	21.75	6.25	13.50
7	18.50	129.50	102.75	26.75	6.00	11.00
8	17.25	138.00	108.50	29.50	5.75	8.50
9	16.00	144.00	114.75	29.25	6.25	6.00
10	14.75	147.50	121.25	26.25	6.50	3.50
11	13.50	148.50	128.00	20.50	6.75	1.00
12	12.25	147.00	135.00	12.00	7.00	−1.50
13	11.00	143.00	142.25	.75	7.25	−4.00

gouging. In evaluating this charge, however, it is important to recognize that, like other sellers, monopolists will seek to maximize *profit*, not *price*. Consumers will buy less as price increases. Thus, a higher price is not always best for monopolists. Exhibit 21–2 illustrates this point. What would happen to the profit of the monopolist if price were increased from $17.25 to $18.50? At the higher price, only seven units would be sold, and total revenue would equal $129.50. The cost of producing seven units would be $102.75. Thus, when price is $18.50 and output seven units, profit is only $26.75, less than could be attained at the lower price ($17.25) and larger output (eight units). The highest price is not always the best price for the monopolist. Sometimes a price reduction will increase the firm's total revenue more than its total cost.

Will a monopolist always be able to make an economic profit? The profitability of a monopolist is limited by the demand for the product that it produces. In some cases, a monopolist—even one protected by high barriers to entry—may be unable to sell for a profit. For example, there are thousands of clever, patented items that are never produced because demand-cost conditions are not favorable. **Exhibit 21–3** illustrates this possibility. When the average total cost curve of a monopolist is above its demand curve at every level of output, economic losses will result. Even a monopolist will not want to operate for long under these conditions. A monopolist in this market would operate only if it could cover its variable costs. It would produce output Q (at which $MR = MC$) and charge price P, *operating in the short run* as long as variable cost could be

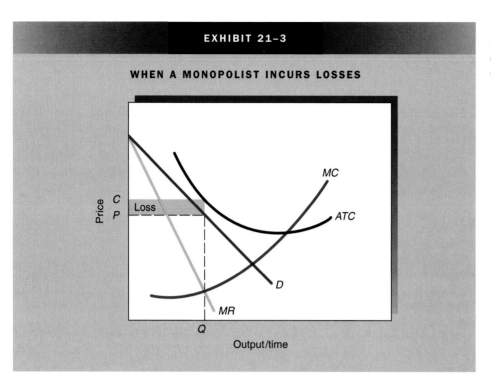

EXHIBIT 21–3

WHEN A MONOPOLIST INCURS LOSSES

Even a monopolist will incur short-run losses if the average total cost curve lies above the demand curve.

covered. If the loss-producing conditions persisted, however, the monopolist would discontinue production when fixed costs became variable, and the higher variable costs could no longer be covered.

THE MONOPOLY MODEL AND DECISION MAKING IN THE REAL WORLD

Until now, we have proceeded as if monopolists always knew exactly what their revenue and cost curves looked like. Of course, this is not true in the real world. Like other price searchers, a monopolist cannot be sure of the demand conditions for a product. Demand curves frequently shift, and choices must be made without the benefit of perfect knowledge. How many sales will be lost if the price is raised? How many sales will be added if the price is lowered? Like other price searchers, monopolists often experiment with price changes, attempting to find the price at which profit will be maximized. Price will be set on the basis of what the price searching monopolist *expects* to happen when price is changed. Thus, the revenue and cost data illustrated in Exhibits 21–1, 21–2, and 21–3 might be thought of as representing *expected* revenues and costs associated with various output levels. To complicate matters further in real life, quality changes of various sorts can be undertaken by the monopolist searching for additional profits. Buyer reactions to potential quality changes, and resulting shifts in demand and revenue, also must be considered by the price searcher–monopolist.

A monopolist, like other business decision makers, seldom calculates what we have called demand, marginal revenue, and cost curves. Given imperfect information, the profit-maximizing price may only be approximated. Like other price searchers, however, the monopolist has a strong incentive to find the profit maximizing price and output rate and, when it does, the outcome will be *as if* *MR* and *MC* had been used to maximize profit.

It is difficult for a monopolist to predict the demand conditions it will face, and thus consumer response to alternative prices (and quality changes). But life is even more complex for the next class of price searchers we consider: large firms with few rivals in a market protected by high barriers to entry.

CHARACTERISTICS OF OLIGOPOLY

Oligopoly

A market situation in which a small number of sellers compose the entire industry. It is competition among the few.

In the United States, the great majority of output in such industries as automobiles, steel, cigarettes, and aircraft is produced by five or fewer dominant firms. These industries are characterized by **oligopoly.** *Oligopoly* means "few sellers." *The distinguishing characteristics of an oligopolistic market are (1) a small number of rival firms, (2) interdependence among the sellers because each is large relative to the size of the market, (3) substantial economies of scale, and (4) high entry barriers into the market.*

INTERDEPENDENCE AMONG OLIGOPOLISTIC FIRMS

Since the number of sellers in an oligopolistic industry is small, the decisions of a firm often influence the demand, price, and profit of rivals. This adds to the complexity of the firm's decision making. When a firm is deciding what price to charge, output to produce, or quality of product to offer, the potential reactions of rivals must be taken into account. The business decisions of the firms are interrelated. Thus, the welfare of each seller is dependent on the policies followed by its major rivals.

SUBSTANTIAL ECONOMIES OF SCALE

In an oligopolistic industry, large-scale production (relative to the total market) is generally required to achieve minimum per unit cost. Economies of scale are significant. When the firms operate at the least-cost rate of output, a small number of large-scale firms will be able to produce the entire market demand for the product. Using the automobile industry as an example, **Exhibit 21–4** illustrates the importance of economies of scale as a source of oligopoly. It has been estimated that each firm must produce approximately 1 million automobiles annually before its per unit cost of production is minimized. However, when the selling price of automobiles is barely sufficient for firms to cover their costs, the total quantity demanded from these producers is only 6 million. To minimize costs, then, each firm must produce at least one-sixth (1 million of the 6 million) of the output demanded. In other words, the industry can support no more than five or six domestic firms of cost-efficient size.

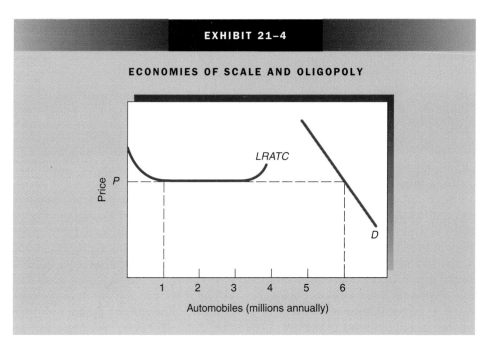

EXHIBIT 21–4

ECONOMIES OF SCALE AND OLIGOPOLY

Oligopoly exists in the automobile industry because firms do not fully realize the cost reductions from large-scale output until they produce approximately one-sixth of the total market.

SIGNIFICANT BARRIERS TO ENTRY

As with monopoly, barriers to entry limit the ability of new firms to compete effectively in oligopolistic industries. Economies of scale are probably the most significant entry barrier protecting firms in an oligopolistic industry.[3] A potential competitor may be unable to start out small and gradually grow to the optimal size, since it must gain a large share of the market before it can minimize per unit cost. The manufacture of refrigerators and diesel engines, as well as automobile production, seems to fall into this category. Other factors, including patent rights, control over an essential resource, and government-imposed entry restraints, may also prevent new competitors from entering profitable oligopolistic industries. The presence of high entry barriers is what distinguishes oligopoly from a competitive price-searcher market.

PRODUCTS MAY BE EITHER IDENTICAL OR DIFFERENTIATED

The products of sellers in an oligopolistic industry may be either similar or differentiated. When firms produce identical products, such as milk or gasoline, there is less opportunity for nonprice competition. On the other hand, rival firms

---

[3]Economies of scale will not be a barrier to entry in the industry, of course, if resources can be freely moved into and out of the industry at a low cost. Such resource mobility would render the market contestable, as we learned in the previous chapter, removing scale economies as a barrier to entry in this special case.

producing differentiated products are more likely to use style, quality, and advertising as competitive weapons.

PRICE AND OUTPUT IN THE CASE OF OLIGOPOLY

Unlike a monopolist or a price taker, an oligopolist cannot determine the product price that will deliver maximum profit simply by estimating market demand and cost conditions. A key factor in determining the demand facing an oligopolistic firm is the pricing behavior of close rivals. Thus, an oligopolist must predict not only how consumers will react to options, but also how rival firms (that is, the rest of the industry) will react to alternative price (and quality) adjustments that it is considering. Each oligopolist confronts this complex problem, and since economics cannot specify the reaction of each to the action of the others, it is impossible to determine the precise price and output policy that will emerge in oligopolistic industries. Economics does, however, indicate a potential range of prices, and the factors that will determine whether prices in the industry will be high or low relative to costs of production.

Consider an oligopolistic industry in which seven or eight rival firms produce the entire market output. Substantial economies of scale are present. The firms produce identical products and have similar costs of production. **Exhibit 21–5** depicts the market demand conditions and long-run costs of production of the individual firms for such an industry.

What price will prevail? We can answer this question for two extreme cases. First, suppose that each firm sets its price independently of the other firms. There is no collusion, and each competitive firm acts independently, seeking to maximize profits by offering consumers a better deal than its rivals. Under these conditions, the market price would be driven down to P_c. Firms would be just able to cover their per unit costs of production. What would happen if a single firm raised its price? Its customers would switch to rival firms, which would now expand to accommodate the new customers. The firm that raised its price would lose out. It would be self-defeating for any one firm to raise its price if the other firms did not raise theirs.

What happens if supply conditions are such that the current market price was greater than P_c? Any *individual firm* that reduces its price slightly, by 1 or 2 percent, for example, will gain numerous customers if the other firms maintain the higher price. The price-cutting firm will attract some new buyers to the market, but more important, it will also lure many buyers away from rival firms charging higher prices. Thus, if the rival sellers act independently, each will have a strong incentive to reduce price in order to increase sales and gain a larger share of the total market. But what happens when each firm attempts to undercut its rivals? Price is driven down to P_c, and the economic profit of the firms is eliminated.

When rival oligopolists compete (on the basis of price) with one another, they drive the market price down to the level of costs of production. They do

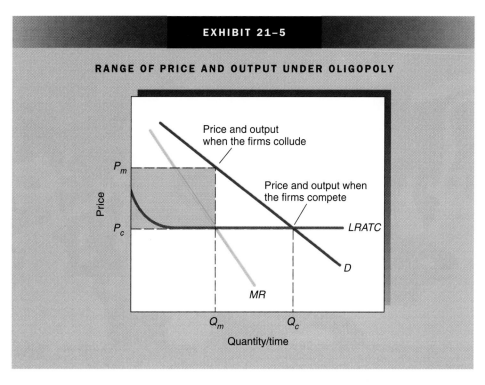

EXHIBIT 21–5

RANGE OF PRICE AND OUTPUT UNDER OLIGOPOLY

Price and output when the firms collude

Price and output when the firms compete

LRATC

P_m

P_c

Price

MR

D

Q_m Q_c

Quantity/time

If oligopolists competed with one another, price cutting would drive price down to P_c. In contrast, perfect cooperation among firms would lead to a higher price of P_m and a smaller output (Q_m rather than Q_c). The shaded area shows profit if firms collude. Demand here is the market demand.

not always compete, however. There is a strong incentive for oligopolists to collude, raise price, and restrict output.

Suppose the oligopolists, recognizing their interdependence, acted cooperatively to maximize their joint profit. They might form a **cartel,** such as the Organization of Petroleum Exporting Countries (OPEC), to accomplish this objective. Alternatively, they might collude without the aid of a formal organization. Under federal antitrust laws in the United States, collusive action to raise price and expand the joint profit of the firms would, of course, be illegal. Nevertheless, let us see what would happen if oligopolists followed this course. Exhibit 21–5 shows the marginal revenue curve that would accompany the market demand D for the product. Under perfect cooperation, the oligopolists would refuse to produce units for which marginal revenue was less than marginal cost. Thus, they would restrict joint output to Q_m where $MR = MC$. Market price would rise to P_m. With collusion, substantial joint profits (the shaded area of Exhibit 21–5) could thus be attained. The case of perfect cooperation would be identical with the outcome under monopoly.

In the real world, however, the outcome is likely to fall between the extremes of price competition and perfect cooperation. Oligopolists generally recognize their interdependence and try to avoid vigorous price competition, which would drive price down to the level of per unit costs. But there are also obstacles to collusion, which is why prices in oligopolistic industries do not rise to the monopoly level. Oligopolistic prices are typically above marginal cost but below those a monopolist would set.

Cartel

An organization of sellers designed to coordinate supply decisions so that the joint profits of the members will be maximized. A cartel will seek to create a monopoly in the market.

Collusive agreements among oligopolists and cartels like OPEC are difficult to maintain because each cartel member would be better off if it could cheat on the agreement and charge a slightly lower price.

OBSTACLES TO COLLUSION

Collusion

Agreement among firms to avoid various competitive practices, particularly price reductions. It may involve either formal agreements or merely tacit recognition that competitive practices will be self-defeating in the long run. Tacit collusion is difficult to detect. In the United States, antitrust laws prohibit collusion and conspiracies to restrain trade.

Collusion is the opposite of competition. It involves cooperative actions by sellers to turn the terms of trade in favor of the group, and against buyers. Since oligopolists can profit by colluding to restrict output and raise price, economic theory suggests that they will have a strong incentive to do so. To accomplish this, however, the firms must also agree on production shares for each firm, or a division of the market so that production is limited to the level that will be purchased at the chosen cartel price.

Each individual oligopolist, though, also has an incentive to cheat on collusive agreements. **Exhibit 21–6** will help us understand why. An undetected price cut will enable a firm to attract (1) customers who would not buy from any firm at the higher price *and* (2) those who would normally buy from other firms. Thus, the demand facing each *individual firm* will be considerably more elastic than the market demand curve. As Exhibit 21–6 shows, the price P_i that maximizes the industry's profits will be higher than the price P_f that is best for a single oligopolist when the others hold firm to the higher price. If a firm can find a way to undercut the price set by the collusive agreement, while other sellers maintain the higher price, expanded sales, beyond the level agreed upon by the cartel, will more than make up for the reduction in per unit profit margin.

In oligopolistic industries, there are two conflicting tendencies. An oligopolistic firm has a strong incentive to cooperate with its rivals so that joint profit can be maximized. However, it also has a strong incentive to cheat secretly on any collusive agreement in order to increase its share of the joint profit. Oligopolistic agreements therefore tend to be unstable. This instability exists whether the cooperative behavior is formal, as in the case of a cartel, or informal.

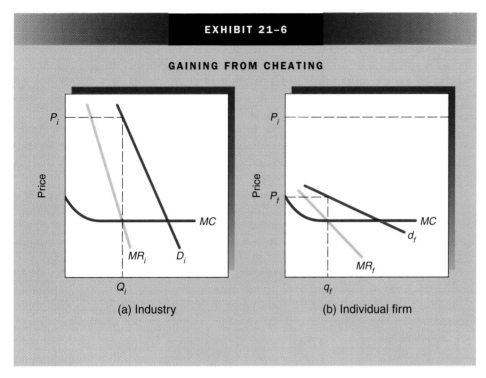

EXHIBIT 21–6

GAINING FROM CHEATING

(a) Industry

(b) Individual firm

The industry demand (D_i) and marginal revenue (MR_i) curves show that the joint profits of oligopolists would be maximized at Q_i where $MR_i = MC$. Price P_i would be best for the industry as a whole (a). However, the demand curve (d_f) facing each firm (under the assumption that no other firms cheat) would be much more elastic than D_i. Given the greater elasticity of its demand curve, an individual firm (b) would maximize its profit by cutting its price to P_f and expanding output to q_f, where $MR_f = MC$. Thus, individual oligopolists could gain by secretly shaving price and cheating on the collusive agreement.

There are certain situations in which it is difficult for oligopolists to collude. Five major obstacles limit collusive behavior.

1. As the number of firms in an oligopolistic market increases, the likelihood of effective collusion declines. Other things constant, an increase in the number of major firms in an industry will make it more difficult for the oligopolists to communicate, negotiate, and enforce agreements among themselves. In addition, the greater the number of firms, the more likely it is that the objectives of individual firms will conflict with those of the industry. Each firm will want a bigger slice of the pie. Opinions about the best collusive price arrangement will differ because marginal costs, unused plant capacity, and estimates of market demand elasticity are likely to differ among firms. Aggressive, less mature firms may be especially interested in expanding their share of total output. These conflicting interests contribute to the breakdown of collusive agreements.

2. When it is difficult to detect and eliminate price cuts, collusion is less attractive. Unless a firm has a way of policing the pricing activities of its rivals, it may be the "sucker" in a collusive agreement. Firms that secretly cut prices may gain a larger share of the market, while others maintain their higher prices and lose customers and profits. Price cutting can sometimes be accomplished in ways that are difficult for the other firms to identify. For example, a firm might provide better credit terms, faster delivery, and other related services "free" to improve slightly the package offered to the buyer.

When firms sell a differentiated product, improvements in quality and style can be used as competitive weapons. "Price cuts" like this are particularly attractive to an oligopolist because they cannot be easily and quickly duplicated by rivals. Competitors can quickly match a reduction in money price, but it will take time for them to match an improvement in quality. When firms can freely use improvements in quality to gain a larger share of the market, collusive agreements on price are of limited value. When cheating (price-cutting) is profitable and difficult for rivals to police, it is a good bet that oligopolistic rivals will be induced to cheat.

3. Low entry barriers are an obstacle to collusion. Unless potential new rivals can be excluded, oligopolists will be unable to make unusually large profits. Successful collusion will merely attract competitors into the industry, which will eliminate the profits. Even with collusion, long-run profits will not be possible unless entry into the industry can be blocked.

Local markets are sometimes dominated by a few firms. For example, many communities have only a small number of ready-mix concrete producers, bowling alleys, accounting firms, and furniture stores. In the absence of government restrictions, however, entry barriers into these markets are generally low. The threat of potential rivals reduces the gains from collusive behavior under these conditions. Even if the number of rival firms is small, the firms will be unable to maintain above-normal profit rates when entry barriers are low. Under these circumstances, the competitive price searcher model, rather than oligopoly, is most applicable.

4. Unstable demand conditions are an obstacle to collusion. Demand instability tends to increase the honest differences of opinion among oligopolists about what is best for the industry. One firm may want to expand because it anticipates a sharp increase in future demand, while a more pessimistic rival may want to hold the line on existing industrial capacity. The larger the differences in expectations about future demand, the greater the potential for conflict among oligopolistic firms. Successful collusion is more likely when demand is relatively stable.

5. Vigorous antitrust action increases the cost of collusion. Under existing antitrust laws, collusive behavior is prohibited. Secret agreements are, of course, possible. Simple informal cooperation might be conducted without discussions or collusive agreements. However, like other illegal behavior, such agreements are not legally enforceable by any firm. Vigorous antitrust action can discourage firms from making such illegal agreements. As the threat of getting caught increases, participants will be less likely to attempt collusive behavior.

UNCERTAINTY AND OLIGOPOLY

Market power
The ability of a firm that is not a pure monopolist to earn unusually large profits, indicating that it has some monopoly power. Because the firm has few (or weak) competitors, it has a degree of freedom from the discipline of vigorous competition.

Uncertainty and imprecision characterize the theory of oligopoly. We know that firms will gain if they successfully restrict output and raise price. However, collusion is fraught with conflicts and difficulties. In some industries, these difficulties are so great that the **market power** of the oligopolists is relatively small. In other industries, oligopolistic cooperation, although not perfect, may raise prices significantly, indicating a higher degree of market power, which is, in effect, a degree of monopoly power. Analysis of the costs and benefits of collusive behavior, under varying degrees of cooperation and conflict, has become an important part of economics over the last two decades. (See the Applications in Economics

THE PRISONER'S DILEMMA AND GAME THEORY

In an oligopoly, a few firms compete by selling into the same market, and the actions of each influence the demand faced by rival sellers. Because they sell similar products and compete for the same customers, the interests of each firm are in conflict with the interests of the others. One firm can gain customers, at the expense of the others, by reducing its price or increasing its advertising. But if the other firms react competitively by doing the same, then all the firms may lose. Yet if rivals cut price or take other steps to offer consumers a better deal, firms that fail to follow suit will lose customers to their more aggressive competitors. Thus, each firm finds itself on the horns of a dilemma—in this case a variant of the classic "prisoner's dilemma."

Economists have increasingly used game theory, as in the analysis of the prisoner's dilemma, to analyze strategic choices made by competitors in a conflict situation, such as members of an oligopoly. Such choices depend on the anticipated actions of others.

To understand the prisoner's dilemma, consider the hypothetical case of Al and Bob, two touring Americans who just met at a train station in a small foreign country. They are taken prisoner and hauled into the local police station to be questioned separately. They are suspected of being the two men who robbed a local merchant, and each is told that if he makes the job of the police easier by confessing immediately, he will get only a 6-month sentence. But each is also told that if he says nothing while the other confesses, then the one who did not confess immediately will get a 12-month sentence. If neither confesses, both will be held for 3 months while the investigation continues. Al and Bob will not be allowed to communicate with each other. Will they confess?

To analyze such situations, the game theorist begins by laying out the alternative outcomes and showing how they are related to choices made by the players of the game, as we do in **Exhibit 21–7.** For each man individually, in this version of the dilemma, the box reveals that the best choice depends on what the other does. If Al confesses, then Bob can save 6 months of jail time by also confessing. The same holds for Al, if he thinks Bob will confess. But if neither confesses, both serve only three months in jail.[1] The proper strategy for each prisoner depends heavily on his estimate of the likelihood that the other will confess. The problem becomes more complex if we consider prisoners who face a series of

such decisions over time, each prisoner learning the other's previous choice before the next set of choices must be made.

Firms in an oligopoly must make decisions somewhat like those of the prisoners: Should a firm cut its price, luring more customers, some from competitors, or should it keep its price high and risk losing customers to competitors who cut prices? If all firms keep the price high, then as a group they will reap more profit. If all cut prices, then as a group they will reap less profit. But the firm that fails to cut price when others do so will lose many customers to the other competing firms. The decision about whether to spend large amounts on advertising has similar characteristics.

For example, consider the pricing policy or advertising strategy of large automakers, such as Ford, General Motors, and Chrysler. Suppose the profit rate of each

(continued)

EXHIBIT 21–7

THE PRISONER'S DILEMMA

		Al's Choice	
		Confess	Not Confess
Bob's Choice	Confess	6 months each	Al: 12 months Bob: 6 months
	Not Confess	Al: 6 months Bob: 12 months	3 months each

Al and Bob must each decide, without communicating with each other, whether to confess. Al knows that if Bob does not confess, then Al can either confess and spend 6 months in jail, or not confess and spend 3 months. But if Bob does confess, then Al's failure to confess would cost him an additional 6 months in jail. Bob is in a similar situation, facing the same options under the same assumptions about whether Al confesses. Each has the incentive to confess if he thinks the other one will, but to not confess if he thinks the other will also remain silent.

would be 15 percent if all the major automobile producers raised their prices (or cut their advertising expenditures) by a similar amount. In contrast, each would have a profit rate of only 10 percent if intense competition leads to lower prices and/or larger advertising expenditures. Industry profits are highest when all firms decide to charge high prices. However, if one automaker reduces its price or advertises more heavily, it will be able to win customers away from rivals and increase its profit rate to 20 percent. Thus, if the firm thinks its rivals will continue to charge higher prices (or fail to match its advertising expenditures), it will be able to gain from cutting its prices (and increasing its advertising). If the other firms follow a similar course, however, this strategy will backfire and the profit rate of all the firms in the industry will be less than the level that would have been achieved had they all charged higher prices (or spent less on advertising).

While our simplified analysis highlights the interdependence among the firms and the importance of probability estimates concerning the strategy of rivals, the real world is much more complex. The choices of the rival firms will be repeated over and over again, although often in modified forms. A prior strategy may be modified in light of previous reactions on the part of rivals. The attractiveness of a strategy will be influenced by the likelihood it will be detected by rivals and the speed with which they might be able to react effectively. In addition, the strategies of oligopolistic firms will be influenced by market conditions and the threat of foreign competition, factors that change with the passage of time. Within the framework of game theory models, additional assumptions must be made in order to account for these and other complex factors—factors that often change in the real world. In turn, if the assumptions incorporated into game theory models are not consistent with real-world conditions, the implications of the game theory analysis may well be invalid.

Economists have used game theory extensively to show how results change when the "rules of the game" change for the firms in an oligopolistic market, as well as for auction-bidding markets and other business decision-

making situations. When the rules of the game are carefully defined and enforced, as in the case of economic experiments in laboratories, game theory has yielded interesting and important testable conclusions. But in open markets in the real world, empirical work using game theory has been less successful. The use of models is always difficult when the problem to be solved is complex, and human expectations about the changing strategy choices of other human beings must be taken into account. There is no question, however, that game theory can be useful for scholars and business practitioners alike, in helping them to frame the issues involved in strategic decision making.[2]

---

[1]If the numbers were sightly different from those in the accompanying chart, both Al and Bob would have an incentive to confess regardless of what they thought the other would do. For example, if each were told that he would get only a 1-month sentence if he confessed and the other party did not, then confession would become the dominant strategy for both Bob and Al. Under these circumstances, if Bob thought Al would remain silent, then Bob would spend only 1 month in jail if he confessed (compared to 3 months if he also remained silent). Al would also be in a similar situation if he believed Bob would remain silent. On the other hand, if Bob thought Al would confess, then Bob's best option would be to also confess since confession would lead to only a 6-month sentence while silence would result in a 12-month jail term. The same would also be true for Al if he thought Bob would confess. Thus, in this classic prisoner's dilemma case, both have an incentive to confess even though confession leads to more jail time for both of them—6 months rather than 3 months. What is best for the individual (or firm) does not always lead to the best outcome from the viewpoint of the group (or industry).

[2]For a further explanation of game theory and the prisoner's dilemma, see Avinash Dixit and Barry Nalebuff, "Game Theory," in *The Fortune Encyclopedia of Economics* (New York: Warner Books, 1993), pp. 640–643.

Game theory
Analyzes the strategic choices made by competitors in a conflict situation, such as decisions made by members of an oligopoly.

feature on **game theory**.) Although this developing field of economics does not yield precise predictions on oligopoly pricing, at least it allows us to determine when discipline by competitive pressures is more likely to exist for an oligopolist.

MARKET POWER AND PROFIT—THE EARLY BIRD CATCHES THE WORM

Our analysis of both monopoly and oligopoly indicates that because entry barriers into these markets are often high, firms may be able to earn economic profit over lengthy periods of time. Suppose a well-established firm, such as Exxon or IBM, is able to use its market power to persistently earn above-normal returns. Do the current stockholders gain? Surprisingly, the answer is no. The ownership value of a share of corporate stock for such corporations long ago began to reflect their market power and expected future profitability. Many of the present stockholders paid high prices for their stock because they expected these firms to be highly profitable. In other words, they paid for the above-normal economic profits that the firm was expected to earn because of its market power.

Do not expect to get rich buying the stock of monopolistic or oligopolistic firms known to be highly profitable. You are already too late. The early bird catches the worm. Those who owned the stock when these firms initially developed their market position have already captured the gain. The value of their stock increased at that time. After a firm's future prospects are widely recognized, subsequent stockholders fail to gain a higher-than-normal rate of return on their financial investment.

DEFECTS OF MARKETS WITH HIGH ENTRY BARRIERS

Monopolists, by keeping the market constantly understocked, by never fully supplying the effectual demand, sell their commodities much above the natural price, and raise their emoluments, whether they consist of wages or profit, greatly above their natural rate.

ADAM SMITH[4]

What types of problems arise when competition is restricted by barriers to entry—a protected monopoly composing the extreme case? Can public policy improve resource allocation in markets having high entry barriers?

From Adam Smith's time to the present, economists have generally considered monopoly a necessary evil at best. The attitude toward markets with only a few sellers and high entry barriers is only slightly more tolerant. Open competition, unfettered by high barriers to entry, has been recognized as a key form of market discipline restraining the behavior of producers and encouraging innovation. There are four major reasons for this view.

---

[4]Adam Smith, *An Inquiry into the Nature and Causes of the Wealth of Nations* (1776; Cannan's ed., Chicago: University of Chicago Press, 1976), p. 69.

"Last year, as in previous years, your company had to contend with spiralling labor costs, exorbitant interest rates, and unconscionable government interference, management was able once more, through a combination of deceptive marketing practices, false advertising, and price fixing, to show a profit which, in all modesty, can only be called excessive."

1. A reduction in the competitiveness of a market limits the options available to consumers. If you do not like the food at a local restaurant, you can go to another restaurant. If you do not like the wares of a local department store, you can buy good substitutes from other retailers. The competition of rivals, both existing and potential, protects the consumer from the arbitrary behavior of any seller. But consider your alternatives if you do not like the local telephone service. The entry of competitors is typically forbidden in that market. What can you do when the service is bad? You can complain to the company or your legislative representative, but you have no option other than sacrificing your phone service if your complaints are ignored. When consumers do not have options—when they must either take what the seller offers or do without—their ability to discipline sellers is greatly reduced.

2. Reduced competition results in allocative inefficiency. Allocative efficiency requires that additional units be produced when they are valued more highly than what it costs to produce them. When barriers to entry are low, production of each good will be expanded until its price is driven down to the level of per unit costs. With high barriers to entry, however, this will not generally be the case. A monopolist or cartel that does not have to worry about rivals entering the market can often gain by restricting output and raising price. That is, output may not be produced even though consumers value it more than its costs of production. Prices may exceed not only marginal costs, but also average total cost for a long period of time when entry barriers into a market are high. As Adam Smith noted more than 200 years ago, monopolists (and cartels) will understock the market and charge a higher price than would prevail if the producers were disciplined by independent rivals and the threat of new entrants.

3. When barriers to entry are high, consumers are less able to direct producers to serve their interests. With low barriers to entry, producers have little choice but to serve the interests of consumers. Producers that do not operate efficiently will lose out to lower-cost rivals. Firms that fail to produce goods that consumers value highly relative to their costs will experience losses. Thus, if producers want to make profits when entry barriers are low, they will have to provide consumers what they want at an attractive price.

In contrast, when entry barriers are high and there are few, if any, alternative suppliers, the discipline of market forces is weakened. Protected from potential new competitors, inefficient firms may be able to earn a normal return or even a profit.

4. Government grants of monopoly power will encourage rent seeking; resources will be wasted by firms attempting to secure and maintain grants of market protection. Grants of special favor by the government will lead to costly activities seeking those favors. As we noted in Chapter 4, economists refer to such activities as *rent seeking*. When government licenses or the imposition of other entry barriers increase profitability and provide protection from the rigors of market competition, people will expend scarce resources attempting to secure and maintain these political favors. From an efficiency standpoint, such rent-seeking activities are wasteful; they consume valuable resources without contributing to output. In aggregate, output is reduced as the result of these wasteful activities. Inefficiency emanating from such grants of monopoly power will supplement the welfare losses resulting from the allocative inefficiency.

By way of illustration, suppose the government issues a license providing a seller with the exclusive right to sell liquor in a specific market. If this grant of monopoly power permits the licensee to earn monopoly profit, potential suppliers will expend resources trying to convince government officials that they should be granted the license. The potential monopolists will lobby government officials, make political contributions, hire representatives to do consulting studies, and undertake other actions designed to convince politicians and their appointees that they can best "serve the public interest" as a monopoly supplier. Any firm that expects its rent-seeking activities to be successful will be willing to spend up to the present value of the future expected monopoly profits, if necessary, to obtain the monopoly protection. Other suppliers, of course, may also be willing to invest in rent-seeking activities. When several suppliers believe they can win, the total expenditures of all firms on rent-seeking activities may actually consume resources worth more than the economic profit expected from the monopoly enterprise.

POLICY ALTERNATIVES WHEN ENTRY BARRIERS ARE HIGH

What government policies might be used to counteract the problems that result from high barriers to entry? Economists suggest four policy options:

1. Restructure the industry in order to increase the number of rival firms.

2. Reduce tariffs and other artificial barriers that limit competition.
3. Regulate the price and output of firms in the market.
4. Supply the market with goods produced by a government firm.

Each of these policies has been used to either reduce entry barriers or to counteract their negative results. We will briefly discuss each in turn.

RESTRUCTURE EXISTING FIRMS

The most serious problems raised by a monopoly would be avoided if the monopolist faced the threat of rivals producing the same product or even close substitutes. The presence of competitors limits the ability of firms to restrict output and raise prices.

When monopoly is present, why not divide the monopolist up into a number of smaller firms? If it were not for economies of scale, this might be a very good strategy. If economies of scale are important, however, larger firms will have a lower per unit cost than smaller rivals. Sometimes economies of scale can be so important that the per unit cost of production will be lowest when the entire output of the industry is produced by a few firms (an oligopoly) or even a single firm (a monopoly). In the latter case, without government intervention, the "natural" tendency will then be toward monopoly—a **natural monopoly**—in which a single firm, large enough to have the lowest attainable cost in this situation, produces the entire output demanded in the market.

When natural monopoly (or oligopoly) exists, smaller firms will have higher per unit costs. Therefore, if the large firm(s) is subdivided into several smaller rivals, the newly created firms will be too small to fully realize the economies of scale in the industry. Since their costs are higher, the price charged by the smaller firms may even exceed that of a monopolist. Furthermore, it will be difficult to maintain the larger number of rivals because the firms will have a strong incentive to grow and/or merge in order to achieve the lower per unit costs accompanying the larger scale of operation. Thus, restructuring an industry in an attempt to increase the number of firms is not an attractive option when the industry is a natural monopoly.

Natural monopoly
A market situation in which the average costs of production continually decline with increased output. Therefore, average costs of production will be lowest when a single large firm produces the entire output demanded.

REDUCE ARTIFICIAL BARRIERS TO TRADE

A second strategy would be to reduce tariffs, quotas, licensing requirements, and other restraints that limit the entry in a market. Government-imposed entry restraints are often the source of monopoly power. When this is the case, removal of these restraints is the most effective way to strengthen the forces of competition.

When a few firms dominate a domestic market, competition from foreign suppliers can help keep the domestic firms on their toes. The foreign competition will help assure that the domestic firms seek to improve quality and keep their costs low. For example, most observers believe that foreign competition in the U.S. automobile industry has played precisely this role.

Not all goods are traded in international markets. Thus, competition from abroad is not always a realistic alternative. In addition, political obstacles often undermine this option. Trade restraints protecting an industry against competition from abroad are generally a special interest issue. The beneficiaries of the

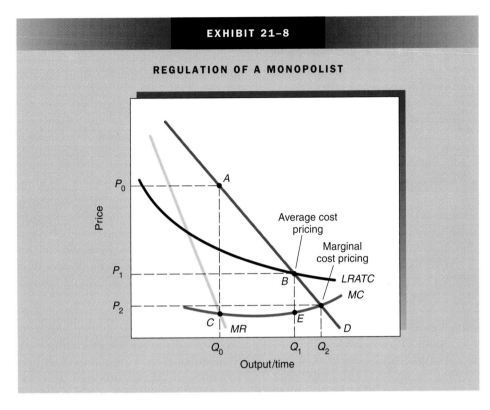

EXHIBIT 21-8

REGULATION OF A MONOPOLIST

If unregulated, a profit-maximizing monopolist with the costs indicated here would produce Q_0 units and charge P_0. If a regulatory agency forced the monopolist to reduce price to P_1, the monopolist would expand output to Q_1. Ideally, we would like output to be expanded to Q_2, where P = MC, but regulatory agencies usually do not attempt to keep prices as low as P_2. Can you explain why?

restraints—primarily the owners, managers, and workers in the protected industries—are highly concentrated and generally well organized. In contrast, the costs of the restraints are nearly always thinly spread among poorly organized consumers. The better organized, concentrated interests are likely to prevail. Therefore, even when lower trade barriers are needed to increase the competitiveness of an industry, political factors may reduce the likelihood they will be adopted.

REGULATE THE PROTECTED PRODUCER

Can government regulation improve the allocative efficiency of a monopoly or an oligopoly? In theory, the answer to this question is clearly yes. **Exhibit 21–8** illustrates why ideal government price regulation, in the case of a monopolist, would improve resource allocation. The profit-maximizing monopolist sets price at P_0 and produces output Q_0, where $MR = MC$. Consumers, however, would value additional units more than the opportunity cost. There are steps that the regulatory agency can take to improve resource allocation in the presence of a monopoly.

AVERAGE COST PRICING.   If a regulatory agency forces the firm in Exhibit 21–8 to reduce price to P_1, at which the ATC curve intersects with the market (and firm) demand curve, the firm will expand output to Q_1. Since it cannot charge a price above P_1, the firm cannot increase revenues by selling a smaller output at a higher price. Once the price ceiling is instituted, the firm can increase revenues by P_1, and by only P_1, for each unit it sells. The regulated firm's MR is constant at P_1 for all units sold until output is increased to Q_1. Since the firm's MC is less than P_1 (and therefore less than MR), the profit-maximizing regulated firm shown here will expand output from Q_0 to Q_1. The benefits from the consumption of these units (ABQ_1Q_0) clearly exceed their costs (CEQ_1Q_0). Social welfare has improved as a result of the regulatory action (we will ignore the impact on the distribution of income). At that output level, revenues are sufficient to cover costs. The firm is making zero economic profit (or "normal" accounting profit).

MARGINAL COST PRICING. Ideally, since even at the Q_1 output level, marginal cost is still less than price, additional welfare gains are possible if output is increased to Q_2. However, if a regulatory agency forced the monopolist to reduce price to P_2 (so that price would equal marginal cost at the output level Q_2), economic losses would result. Even a monopolist, unless subsidized, would not undertake production if the regulatory agency set the price at P_2 or any price below P_1. Usually, problems associated with determining and allocating the necessary subsidy would make this option unfeasible.

PROBLEMS WITH REGULATION. Even though government regulation of monopoly seems capable of improving market results, as in the preceding average cost pricing example, economic analysis suggests that regulation will usually not be an ideal solution. Why? Three factors tend to reduce both the effectiveness of regulation and the probability that the regulators will act on behalf of all citizens to control monopoly. Let us look at each of these factors.

1. LACK OF INFORMATION. In discussing ideal regulation, we assumed that we knew what the firm's ATC, MC, and demand curves looked like. In reality, of course, this would not be the case. The firms themselves have difficulty knowing their costs, and especially their demand curves, with any precision.

Because estimates of demand and marginal costs are difficult to obtain, regulatory agencies usually use profits (or rate of return) as a gauge to determine whether the regulated price is too high or too low. The regulatory agency, guarding the public interest, seeks to impose a "fair" or "normal" rate of return on the firm. If the firm is making profits (that is, an abnormally high rate of return), the price must be higher than P_1 and should be lowered. If the firm is incurring losses (less than the fair or normal rate of return), the regulated price must be less than P_1, and the firm should be allowed to increase price.

The actual existence of profits, though, is not easily identified. Accounting profit, even allowing for a normal rate of profit, is not the same as economic profit. In addition, regulated firms have a strong incentive to adopt reporting techniques and accounting methods that conceal profits. This will make it difficult for a regulatory agency to identify and impose the price consistent with allocative efficiency.

2. COST SHIFTING. As long as demand is sufficient, the owners of the regulated firm can expect the long-run rate of profit to be essentially fixed, regardless of whether efficient management reduces costs or inefficient management allows costs to increase. If costs decrease, the "fair return" rule imposed by the regulatory agency will force a price reduction; if costs increase, the "fair return" rule will allow a price increase. Thus, the owners of the regulated firm have less incentive to be concerned about costs than the owners of unregulated firms. Managers, therefore, will have a freer hand to pursue personal objectives. They will be more likely to fly first-class, entertain lavishly on an expense account, give their relatives and friends good jobs, grant unwarranted wage increases, and in general make decisions that yield personal benefits and increase company costs. Since monopoly means that buyers do not have a close substitute to turn to, consumers will bear the burden of managerial inefficiency. Normally, wasteful activities would be policed by the owners, but since the firm's rate of return is set by the regulatory agency, the owners have little incentive to be concerned.

3. SPECIAL-INTEREST INFLUENCE.   The difficulties of government regulation discussed thus far are practical limitations that a regulatory agency would confront in seeking to perform its duties efficiently. But, in the political arena, regulatory authorities cannot necessarily be expected to pursue only efficiency. Regulated firms have a strong incentive to see that "friendly," "reasonable" people serve as regulators, and they will invest political and economic resources to this end. Just as rent-seeking activities designed to gain monopoly privileges can be expected, so can activities to influence regulatory decisions.

Consumer interests, in contrast to those of industry, are widely dispersed and disorganized. Ordinarily, consumers cannot be expected to invest time, resources, votes, and political contributions to ensure that a particular regulatory commission represents their views. The firms that are regulated can, however, be expected to make such investments. Even though the initial stimulus for a regulating agency might come from consumer interests, economic theory suggests that such agencies will eventually reflect the views of the business and labor interests they are supposed to regulate.

SUPPLY MARKET WITH GOVERNMENT PRODUCTION

Government-operated firms—socialized firms such as the U.S. Postal Service, the Tennessee Valley Authority, and many local public utilities—present an alternative to both private monopoly and regulation. However, both theory and experience indicate that socialized firms will fail to counteract fully the problems that stem from high barriers to entry. The same perverse managerial incentives—incentives to ignore efficiency and pursue personal or professional objectives at the firm's expense—that regulated firms confront also tend to plague the government-operated firm. And since the "owners" of a socialized firm (voters) are typically uninformed about how well a socialized firm is run, or how it might be run better, they are unable to police management inefficiency. This is especially true when the firm has no direct competitors against which the firm's performance can be easily compared. Voters tend to be ignorant, quite rationally, about matters on which, as individuals, they have no decisive vote. This is in sharp contrast with individual stockholders in a firm, each of whom can personally either "bail out" (sell his or her stock) upon learning about approaching trouble from the firm's decisions or buy more stock upon seeing promising management initiatives.

Government-operated firms do not provide an environment that rewards efficient management and reductions in cost. Unlike investors in the private sector, no small group of voters normally is in a position to gain substantial wealth by taking over the socialized firm and improving its management. Even more than with monopoly or oligopoly in the private sector, customers of the socialized monopoly (voter-taxpayers) cannot easily switch their business to other sellers. Even those voter-taxpayers who do not consume the product often have to pay taxes to support the socialized firm. The result is that when the government operates a business—particularly one with monopoly power—there is typically less investor scrutiny, less reward for efficiency, and less penalty for inefficiency. Higher costs are an expected result.

Government ownership, like unregulated monopoly and government regulation, is a less than ideal solution. Thus, it should not be surprising that those who denounce monopoly in, for instance, the telephone industry seldom point to a government-operated monopoly—such as the postal service—as an example of how an industry should be run.

PULLING IT TOGETHER

The policy implications that can legitimately be drawn from an analysis of high barriers to entry are less than fully satisfying. We may not like the reduction in competition or its effects, but economic analysis suggests important qualifications to the "solutions" usually put forth.

Most of the policy alternatives are not terribly attractive. Economies of scale reduce the benefits from breaking up existing firms to provide additional competitors. Since smaller firms have higher per unit costs, restructuring the industry to increase the number of firms may be costly and difficult to maintain. Government measures such as tariff reductions and removal of entry barriers into markets are perhaps the surest recommendation for increasing competition in a market. Such policies, however, will certainly face political opposition, primarily from owners and workers in protected industries.

We have pointed out that regulation is a less than ideal solution. Regulators do not possess the information necessary to impose an efficient outcome, and they may be susceptible to manipulation by industrial and labor interests. Moreover, since public-sector managers are likely to pursue political objectives at the expense of economic efficiency, public ownership is also a less than ideal solution. Thus, economic theory indicates that there are no ideal solutions when substantial economies of scale are present. Choices must be made among alternatives, all of which are imperfect.

THE COMPETITIVE PROCESS IN THE REAL WORLD

How competitive are markets? This question is difficult to answer. In a very real sense, every firm competes with every other firm for the consumer's additional dollar of spending. Competition is everywhere; the seller of compact discs, for

MYTHS OF ECONOMICS

"THE PRICES OF MOST GOODS ARE UNNECESSARILY INFLATED BY AT LEAST 25 PERCENT AS A RESULT OF THE HIGH PROFIT RATE OF PRODUCERS."

Profits are about as popular with consumers as failing grades are with students at the end of a term. When food prices rise, the profits of farmers, meat processors, and food store chains are heavily publicized by the news media. If gasoline prices jump, many people believe that they are being pushed up by greedy profiteering on the part of the major oil companies. The casual observer might easily be left with the impression that large profits are the major source of the high cost of living.

This issue is clouded by the fact that both the size of profits and their function are largely misunderstood by most people. Surveys show that young people believe the after-tax profits of corporations compose between 25 percent and 30 percent of sales. A national sample poll of adults conducted by Opinion Research of Princeton found that the average person thought profits composed 29 cents of every dollar of sales in manufacturing. In reality, the after-tax accounting profits of manufacturing corporations are about 4 cents to 5 cents per dollar of sales. (See Illustrated Exhibit III-C on page 432.) The public believes that the rate of profit as a percentage of sales is nearly six times as great as the actual figure! In recent years, after-tax corporate profits have averaged about 12 percent of the equity stockholders have invested in the firm.

Why are people so misinformed on this issue? The popular media are one source of confusion. They nearly always report the accounting profits of firms in dollar terms, comparing them to profits in the previous period, instead of comparing them to sales, stockholder equity, or the value of the firms' assets. Unless we know whether profits were high, normal, or low during the previous period, this type of statement tells little or nothing about the firm's earnings rate on its capital assets. For example, suppose a corporation with $100 million of assets earned a profit of $2 million last year, a 2 percent rate of return on its capital assets. Now, suppose the firm's earnings this year are $4 million, generating only a 4 percent rate of return. It would not be unusual for the popular media to report, "The profits of corporation X soared to $4 million, a 100 percent increase over last year." What this statement conceals is that the profits of the firm as a percentage of its capital assets were less than one could earn on a savings account.

Most people do not understand the important economic function of profits. Many believe that if profits were eliminated, our economy would continue to operate as if nothing had happened. This is an erroneous view. Accounting profits are primarily a monetary return to those who have invested in machines, buildings, and nonhuman productive resources. Investment in physical capital involves both risk and the forgoing of current consumption. If profits were eliminated, the incentive of persons to invest and provide the tools that make the American worker the most productive in the world would be destroyed.

There is also often misunderstanding concerning what entrepreneurs must do in order to earn profit. In order to make economic profit (or an above-average accounting profit), entrepreneurs must increase the value of resources. Put another way, they must produce something that consumers value more than the resources required for its production. Investors and business decision makers who allocate resources to a venture producing outputs that consumers value less than the venture's opportunity cost will experience economic losses (below-average accounting profits). Without this reward-penalty system, individuals (and firms) would have neither the information nor the incentives to use resources wisely and produce the goods that consumers desire most, relative to their opportunity costs.

example, competes with the bookstore and the local restaurant for our entertainment budgets. The sellers of swimming pools compete with airlines, hotels, casinos, and automobile rental companies for the vacation and leisure time expenditures of consumers.

Moreover, price competition is only one element of the competitive process. Even though they are difficult for our models to capture fully, nonprice factors like quality, design, convenience, and terms of credit are important competitive weapons firms use as they seek to increase profitability and market share. These nonprice competitive weapons are generally more important in concentrated industries because, unlike a reduction in price, it is more difficult for rivals to quickly duplicate improvements in these areas. Like price reductions, however, improvements in the various dimensions of product quality provide consumers with more value per dollar of expenditure. Furthermore, competition of this type makes collusion more difficult and erodes profits even in industries with few rival firms. Perhaps this helps explain why profit levels, even in manufacturing industries, are considerably lower than is generally thought to be the case (see the Myths of Economics feature on prices and profits on page 575).

Over time, technological change and the development of new products is also an integral part of the competitive process. No firm can be assured that customers will continue to purchase its product or service. Dynamic change can threaten the market position of even well-entrenched firms with monopoly power. For example, the development of fax machines and growth of e-mail pose a substantial threat to the market power of the U.S. Postal Service, a legally protected monopoly. Profitability and high prices will hasten the development of substitutes. The high price of natural rubber spurred the development of synthetic rubber. High rail-shipping rates accelerated the development of long-distance trucking. More recently, the strong exercise of monopoly power by the Organization of Petroleum Exporting Countries (OPEC) subjected oil to vastly intensified competition from coal, solar energy, and other nonpetroleum energy sources, as well as from greatly expanded exploration efforts in non-OPEC nations. The result was a long tumble in the price the OPEC cartel was able to charge for its oil. What seemed to be a secure monopoly position for OPEC in the 1970s turned out to be something very different during the 1980s.

The patent system is based on the premise that the expectation of monopoly profit for a period of time will stimulate technological change and the discovery of new, improved products. This is why new products or production methods are granted a patent—that is, a monopoly—for a period of 17 years. Others are prohibited from copying the product or technique. If this "reward" of temporary monopoly power and profit did not exist, businesses would be less inclined to undertake research designed to reduce costs and improve product quality. Of course, dynamic competitive forces may operate slowly in response to price changes. Nonetheless, they are often able to erode the dominant market position of even giant firms.

The dynamic nature of competitiveness in the U.S. economy is shown by the fact that the firms composing the largest 100 or 200 corporations are different from one another and are constantly changing. As successful management and the vagaries of business fortune exert their influences, some firms are pushed out of the top group and others enter. Following the fate of various firms over time is not easy, since mergers occur and names change, but historical research indicates that, of the largest 100 manufacturing corporations in 1909, only 36 remained on the list in 1948. Of the 50 largest in 1947, only 25 remained on the list in 1972, and 5 failed to make even the top 200. Of the firms on the *Fortune* 500 list in 1980, only about half were able to make the list in 1990. With time, in an economy as competitive as that in the United States, even giants tumble and fall, as technology, leadership, and consumer preferences change.

LOOKING AHEAD

The competitiveness of markets is complex and difficult to measure. However, economists generally agree that the U.S. economy has become more competitive over the past several decades. Better communications, reductions in transportation costs, increased competition from imports, and deregulation of several key markets have all tended to enhance the competitiveness of markets. The following chapter will focus on the competitiveness of the U.S. economy and how it is influenced by public policy.

CHAPTER SUMMARY

1. The four major barriers to entry into a market are economies of scale, government licensing, patents, and control of an essential resource. Any gains to the firm from establishing such barriers to entry will accrue to those who own the firm at the time that barriers are established.

2. A monopoly is characterized by (a) high barriers to entry and (b) a single seller of a well-defined product for which there are no good substitutes.

3. Analysis of pure monopoly is important for two reasons. First, the monopoly model will help us understand the operation of markets dominated by a few firms. Second, in a few important industries, such as local telephone services and utilities, there is often only a single producer in a market area. The monopoly model will help us understand these markets.

4. The monopolist's demand curve is the market demand curve. As a price searcher, a profit-maximizing monopolist will lower price and expand output as long as marginal revenue exceeds marginal cost. At the maximum-profit output, *MR* will equal *MC*. The monopolist will charge the price on its demand curve corresponding to that rate of sales.

5. If losses occur in the long run, a monopolist will go out of business. If profit results, high barriers to entry will shield a monopolist from competitive pressures. Therefore, monopolists can sometimes earn long-run economic profits.

6. An oligopolistic market is characterized by high barriers to entry, including substantial economies of scale that result in only a small number of interdependent firms in the industry.

7. There is no general theory of price, output, and equilibrium for oligopolistic markets. If rival oligopolists acted totally independently of their competitors, they would drive price down to the level of cost of production. Alternatively, if they used collusion to obtain perfect coop-

eration, price would rise to the level that a monopolist would charge. The actual outcome will generally fall between these two extremes.

8. Collusion is the opposite of competition. Oligopolists have a strong incentive to collude and raise their prices. However, the interests of individual firms will conflict with those of the industry as a whole. Since the demand curve faced by individual firms is far more elastic than the industry demand curve, each firm could gain by cutting its price (or raising product quality) by a small amount so that it could attract customers from rivals. If several firms tried to do this, however, the collusive agreement would break down.

9. Oligopolistic firms are less likely to collude successfully against the interests of consumers if (a) the number of rival firms is large; (b) it is costly to prohibit competitors from offering secret price cuts (or quality improvements) to customers; (c) entry barriers are low; (d) market demand conditions tend to be unstable; and/or (e) the threat of antitrust action is present.

10. Economists are critical of markets with high barriers to entry because (a) the ability of consumers to discipline producers is weakened; (b) the unregulated monopolist or oligopolist can often gain by restricting output and raising price; (c) profits are less able to stimulate new entry, which would expand the supply of the product until price declines to the level of average production costs; and (d) legal barriers to entry will encourage firms to "invest" resources in seeking additional protective barriers and the maintenance of existing ones.

11. A natural monopoly exists when long-run average total costs continue to decline as firm size increases, over the entire range of market demand. Thus, a larger firm always has lower costs. When natural monopoly is present, costs of production will be lowest when a single firm generates the entire output of the industry.

12. Economists suggest four kinds of policy alternatives to reduce the problems stemming from high barriers to entry: (a) breaking up firms in the industry into additional, more competitive firms—an option that is not attractive when economies of scale are important; (b) reduction of artificial barriers to trade, such as tariffs and import restrictions—an economically sound option that will generate strong political opposition from owners and workers in protected industries; (c) government regulation of firms—an option hampered by regulators' incomplete ability to control aspects of quality and their lack of knowledge about the firm's cost curves and market demand conditions; and (d) provision of output by government firms, which is also made unattractive by the inability of voters and consumers to properly monitor and discipline government-owned firms.

13. Competitive forces are widespread, even having influence in markets with high barriers to entry. Quality competition is an important element of the competitive process. Profitability and high prices encourage technological change and the development of substitute products.

CRITICAL ANALYSIS QUESTIONS

*1. "Barriers to entry are crucial to the existence of long-run profits, but they cannot guarantee the existence of profits." Evaluate.

2. "Monopoly is good for producers but bad for consumers. The gains of the former offset the losses of the latter. On balance, there is no reason to think that monopoly is bad for the economy." Evaluate.

*3. Do monopolists charge the highest prices for which they can sell their products? Do they maximize their average profit per sale? Are monopolistic firms always profitable? Why or why not?

4. The retail liquor industry is potentially a competitive industry. However, the liquor retailers of a southern state organized a trade association that sets prices for all firms. For all practical purposes, the trade association transformed a competitive industry into a monopoly. Compare the price and output policy for a purely competitive industry with the policy that would be established by a profit-maximizing monopolist or trade association. Who benefits and who is hurt by the formation of the monopoly?

5. Does economic theory indicate that a monopoly forced by an ideal regulatory agency to set prices according to either marginal or average cost would be more efficient than an unregulated monopoly? Explain. Does economic theory suggest that a regulatory agency will in fact follow a proper regulation policy? What are some of the factors that complicate the regulatory function?

6. Is a monopolist subject to any competitive pressures? Explain. Would an unregulated monopolist have an incentive to operate and produce efficiently? If so, why?

7. How will high entry barriers into a market influence (a) the long-run profitability of the firms, (b) the cost efficiency of the firms in the industry, (c) the likelihood that some inefficient (high cost) firms will survive, and (d) the incentive of entrepreneurs to develop substitutes for the product supplied by the firms? Are competitive pressures present in markets with high barriers to entry? Discuss.

*8. Why is oligopolistic collusion more difficult when there is product variation than when the products of all firms are identical?

9. In large cities, taxi fares are often set above the market equilibrium rate. Sometimes the number of licenses is limited in order to maintain the above-market price. Other times licenses are automatically granted to anyone wanting to operate a taxi. When taxi fares are set above market equilibrium, compare and contrast resource allocation under the restricted license system (assume the licenses are tradable) and the free-entry system. In which case will it be easier for customers to get a taxi? In which case will the amount of capital required to enter the taxi business be greater?

10. Which of the following are monopolists: (a) your local newspaper, (b) the Boston Celtics, (c) General Motors, (d) the U.S. Postal Service, (e) Jay Leno, (f) the American Medical Association? Is the definition of an industry or market area important in the determination of a seller's monopoly position? Explain.

*11. Historically, the real cost of transporting both goods and people has declined substantially. What impact does a reduction in transportation cost have on the market power of individual producers? Do you think the U.S. economy is more or less competitive today than it was 100 years ago? Explain.

12. We have a theory to explain the equilibrium price and output for monopoly, but not for oligopoly. Why? What role can game theory play in helping us to understand decisions made by oligopolists?

*13. Gouge-em Cable Company is the only cable television service company licensed to operate in Backwater County. Most of its costs are access fees and maintenance expenses. These fixed costs total $640,000 monthly. The marginal cost of adding another subscriber to its system is constant at $2 per month. Gouge-em's demand curve can be determined from the data in the accompanying table.

SUBSCRIPTION PRICE (PER MONTH)	NUMBER OF SUBSCRIBERS
$25	20,000
20	40,000
15	60,000
10	80,000
5	100,000
1	150,000

a. What price will Gouge-em charge for its cable services? What are its profits at this price?

b. Now suppose the Backwater County Public Utility Commission has the data and feels that cable subscription rates in the county are too expensive and that Gouge-em's profits are unfairly high. What regulated price will it set so that Gouge-em makes only a normal rate of return on its investment?

*14. "My uncle just bought 1,000 shares of Mammoth Manufacturing, one of the largest and most profitable companies in the United States. Given the high profit rate of this company, he will make a bundle from this purchase." Evaluate this statement. Is it necessarily true? Explain.

*15. The American Honeymakers Association has 1,000 members. Each member firm faces essentially the same cost structure. The demand for honey and the supply curve of one typical producer can be determined from the data in the accompanying table.

MARKET PRICE	DEMAND QUANTITY (QUARTS)	FIRM'S PRICE	SUPPLY QUANTITY (QUARTS)
$10	10,000	$10	60
9	15,000	9	55
8	20,000	8	50
7	25,000	7	45
6	30,000	6	40
5	35,000	5	35
4	40,000	4	30

a. If all the members of the Honeymakers Association agree to collude to maximize industry profits, what is the profit-maximizing price? How many quarts of honey will be sold at this price? How many quarts of honey will each firm produce to sustain this price?

b. If the cartel charges the price computed in part a, how many quarts would an individual firm like to produce?

c. Suppose all the firms cheat and the market becomes competitive. What is the new market-clearing price and quantity?

16. Suppose that you produce and sell children's tables in a localized market. Past experience permits you to estimate your demand and marginal cost schedules. This information is presented in the accompanying table.

a. Fill in the missing revenue and cost schedules.

b. Assuming you are currently charging $55 per table set, what should you do if you want to maximize profits?

c. Given your demand and cost estimates, what price should you charge if you want to maximize weekly profit? What output should you produce? What is your maximum weekly profit?

17. The diagram below shows demand and long-run cost conditions in an industry.

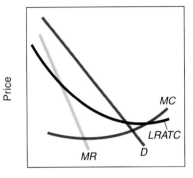

a. Explain why the industry is likely to be monopolized.

b. Indicate the price that a profit-maximizing monopolist would charge, and label it P.

c. Indicate the monopolist's output level, and label it Q.

d. Indicate the maximum profits of the monopolist.

e. Will the profits attract competitors to the industry? Why or why not? Explain.

_____

*Asterisk denotes questions for which answers are given in Appendix B.

PRICE	QUANTITY DEMANDED (PER WEEK)	MARGINAL COST	TOTAL REVENUE	MARGINAL REVENUE	FIXED COST	TOTAL COST
$60	1	$50	___	___	$40	___
55	2	20	___	___	___	___
50	3	24	___	___	___	___
45	4	29	___	___	___	___
40	5	35	___	___	___	___
35	6	45	___	___	___	___

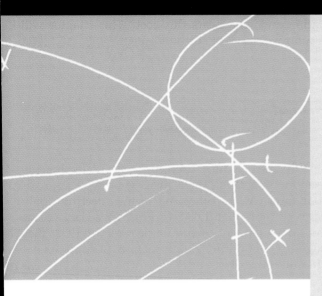

CHAPTER FOCUS

■ How has the structure of the U.S. economy changed during the last 100 years? How competitive is the U.S. economy?

■ What are the objectives of antitrust policy? How do these laws affect industrial structure?

■ How effective has antitrust policy been? What new directions has it taken during the last two decades?

■ How does regulation of business activities influence our lives? Who bears the cost of regulation?

■ How does the regulation of health and safety compare to traditional economic regulation? What can we say about its costs and benefits?

■ What does public choice analysis imply with regard to the motivation for and effectiveness of regulatory activities?

People of the same trade seldom meet together, even for merriment and diversion, but the conversation ends in a conspiracy against the public, or in some contrivance to raise prices.

ADAM SMITH (1776)[1]

[I]t is competition that drives down costs and prices, induces firms to produce the goods consumers want, and spurs innovation and the expansion of new markets abroad. . . . In stark contrast . . . are the inefficiencies that result from monopoly. . . . The disadvantages of monopoly are sufficient to warrant government action to ensure competition or regulate the conduct of monopolies.

COUNCIL OF ECONOMIC ADVISERS (1996)[2]

---

[1]See Adam Smith, *An Inquiry into the Nature and Causes of the Wealth of Nations* (1776; Cannan's ed., Chicago: University of Chicago Press, 1976), p. 144.

[2]President's Council of Economic Advisers, *Economic Report of the President, 1996* (Washington, D.C.: U.S. Government Printing Office, 1996), p. 155.

B eginning with Adam Smith, economists have stressed the role of competition. Competition forces producers to operate efficiently and to supply consumers with goods that have the qualities they desire most (relative to costs). Similarly, competition for resources forces each producer to treat workers and other resource suppliers fairly, offering them pay rates and work environments that are attractive relative to those available elsewhere.

As the chapter opening quotation indicates, Adam Smith was also keenly aware of forces that will sometimes undermine competition. How can public policy promote competitive markets? Has government action in this area been effective? Can government regulation improve the outcomes of the marketplace? Does regulation protect the interests of consumers and promote workplace safety? How costly is regulation and who bears this cost? This chapter will address these issues and the controversies that surround them.

STRUCTURE OF THE U.S. ECONOMY

The U.S. economy is extremely diverse. About 87 percent of all establishments hire fewer than 20 employees. In 1992, these small firms employed approximately 25 percent of the labor force. At the other end of the spectrum, only one establishment in 1,000 employs more than 1,000 workers. These large firms provided employment for about 13 percent of the work force in 1992. (See Illustrated Exhibit III-B on page 431 for additional information on employment by size of firm.) More than 10 million workers, or one worker in 12, were self-employed in 1994.

The structure of the U.S. economy has changed significantly over the years. As **Exhibit 22–1** illustrates, 38 percent of all workers were employed in agriculture in 1900. With the passage of time, fewer and fewer Americans derived their living from the agriculture sector. By 1970, only 4.4 percent of the work force was employed in agriculture and the figure continued to decline to 2.8 percent in 1994.

In contrast, employment in services, wholesale and retail trade, finance, insurance, and real estate has steadily increased in this century.[3] These areas now account for 62.4 percent of total employment, up from 23.1 percent in 1900. Employment in manufacturing rose during the first half of the twentieth century, reaching a peak of 28 percent of the work force in the 1950s. In 1970, manufacturing accounted for 26.4 percent of the total employment and since that time the figure has declined sharply, plunging to 16.4 percent in 1994. Productivity has risen faster in manufacturing than in other sectors of the economy. As a result, manufacturing *output* has fallen by a lesser amount than the reduction in employment.

---

[3]The service category includes employment in advertising, education, health care, legal services, protective services, and personal services, including persons employed by hotels and lodges.

EXHIBIT 22–1

THE INDUSTRIAL STRUCTURE OF THE U.S. ECONOMY: 1900–1994

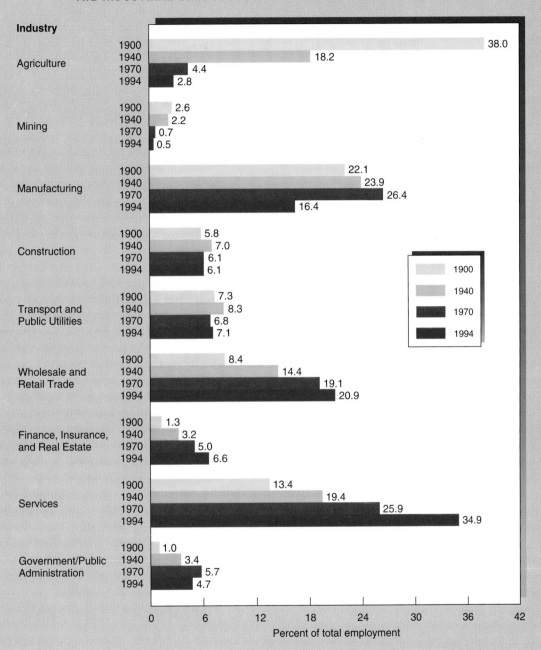

Industry

Agriculture
- 1900: 38.0
- 1940: 18.2
- 1970: 4.4
- 1994: 2.8

Mining
- 1900: 2.6
- 1940: 2.2
- 1970: 0.7
- 1994: 0.5

Manufacturing
- 1900: 22.1
- 1940: 23.9
- 1970: 26.4
- 1994: 16.4

Construction
- 1900: 5.8
- 1940: 7.0
- 1970: 6.1
- 1994: 6.1

Transport and Public Utilities
- 1900: 7.3
- 1940: 8.3
- 1970: 6.8
- 1994: 7.1

Wholesale and Retail Trade
- 1900: 8.4
- 1940: 14.4
- 1970: 19.1
- 1994: 20.9

Finance, Insurance, and Real Estate
- 1900: 1.3
- 1940: 3.2
- 1970: 5.0
- 1994: 6.6

Services
- 1900: 13.4
- 1940: 19.4
- 1970: 25.9
- 1994: 34.9

Government/Public Administration
- 1900: 1.0
- 1940: 3.4
- 1970: 5.7
- 1994: 4.7

Legend: 1900, 1940, 1970, 1994

X-axis: Percent of total employment (0, 6, 12, 18, 24, 30, 36, 42)

Source: *Statistical Abstract of the United States, 1995,* Table 653; and *The Statistical History of the United States,* Table D-152-166.

COMPETITIVENESS IN THE U.S. ECONOMY

Concentration ratio

The total sales of the four (or sometimes eight) largest firms in an industry as a percentage of the total sales of the industry. The higher the ratio, the greater the market dominance of a small number of firms. The ratio can be seen as a measure of the potential for oligopolistic power.

How competitive is the U.S. economy? How important are markets characterized by oligopoly and monopoly? In the past, economists have traditionally used a tool, the concentration ratio, to help answer these questions. The **concentration ratio** is the percentage of total industry sales made by the four (or sometimes eight) largest firms of an industry. This ratio can vary from nearly zero to 100, with 100 indicating that the sales of the four largest firms compose those of the entire industry.

The concentration ratio can be thought of as a broad indicator of competitiveness. In general, the higher the concentration ratio, the more likely that the firms of the industry will be able to successfully collude against the interests of consumers. This ratio, though, is by no means a perfect measure of competitiveness. Since the sales of foreign producers are excluded, it overstates the degree of concentration in industries in which foreign firms compete. It is also unable to measure the difficulty of entry into an industry or a market. As contestable market analysis reveals, even markets with only a few suppliers can be quite competitive when entry barriers are low. Neither does the concentration ratio reveal the elasticity of demand for products, even though concentration is a smaller problem when better substitutes for a product are available. For example, the market power of aluminum producers is partially limited by competition from steel, plastics, copper, and similar products. Similarly, the monopoly power of commercial airlines is substantially reduced by the availability of automobiles, buses, chartered private flights, and even conference telephone calls.

Despite these deficiencies, data on concentration supplemented with other information on the presence of rival firms can be used to analyze the competitiveness of markets. Economist William G. Shepherd examined the structure of the U.S. economy in depth, using four categories based in part on concentration ratios, to classify the structure of various industries. He estimated the amount of national income produced by firms in each category, and how those percentages changed during the 1939–1980 period. As **Exhibit 22–2** shows, he found that the share of output produced in "effectively competitive" markets rose only slightly between 1939 and 1958. *However, during the 1958–1980 period, there was a sharp increase in the competitiveness of the U.S. economy according to Shepherd. Correspondingly, there was a substantial decline in the share of national income produced in markets characterized by monopoly, a single dominant firm, and tight oligopoly. In 1980, Shepherd estimated that more than three-fourths of national income was produced in effectively competitive markets.* Shepherd attributed the sharp increase in competition to antitrust policy, increased import competition, and deregulation. Other economists also point to reductions in transportation costs as a contributing factor to the increase in competition.

MERGERS, COMPETITIVENESS, AND THE STRUCTURE OF THE ECONOMY

Horizontal merger

The combining of the assets of two or more firms engaged in the production of similar products into a single firm.

Mergers have exerted a substantial influence on the structure of the U.S. economy. A **horizontal merger** combines the assets of two or more firms under the same ownership. The desire of oligopolistic firms to merge is not surprising. Horizontal mergers may provide firms in oligopolistic markets with an alternative to both the insecurity of collusion and the discipline of competition. However, combining firms may also improve efficiency. For example, most observers

EXHIBIT 22-2

THE INCREASING COMPETITIVENESS OF THE U.S. ECONOMY, 1939-1980

MARKET-STRUCTURE CATEGORY	PERCENTAGE SHARES OF NATIONAL INCOME PRODUCED IN EACH CATEGORY		
	1939	1958	1980
1. Pure Monopoly	6.2	3.1	2.5
2. Single Dominant Firm	5.0	5.0	2.8
3. Tight Oligopoly	36.4	35.6	18.0
4. Effectively Competitive	52.4	56.3	76.7
Total	100.0	100.0	100.0

This chart presents the findings of a study by William Shepherd, an industrial organization economist from the University of Michigan. Shepherd found that the share of national income produced by the competitive sectors of the U.S. economy has been rising for several decades, while the share produced in less competitive markets has been falling. The "single dominant firm" here is one with more than a 50 percent market share in a market with high barriers to entry. A "tight oligopoly" means a four-firm concentration ratio above 60 percent or government-regulated firms with the ability to strongly influence the regulated prices.

Source: William G. Shepherd, "Causes of Increased Competition in the U.S. Economy, 1939–1980," *Review of Economics and Statistics,* November 1982, p. 618.

believe that the merger of Piedmont Airlines and USAir improved both the integration of routes and the convenience of flight schedules. Lower cost and better customer service resulted.

Another type of merger, the **vertical merger,** joins a supplier and a buyer—for example, an automobile maker and a steel producer. A vertical merger might simplify the long-range planning process for both firms and reduce the need for costly legal contracting between the two. Even though vertical mergers generally do not increase concentration within industries, some economists are concerned that such mergers may reduce competition if either the buyer or the supplier grants a market advantage to the other.

A **conglomerate merger** combines two firms in unrelated industries. The stated intent is usually to introduce new and superior management into the firm being absorbed, or to strengthen the two firms by combining their different strengths. This type of merger results in increased size but not necessarily in reduced competition.

Vertical merger
The creation of a single firm from two firms, one of which was a supplier or customer of the other—for example, a merger of a lumber company with a furniture manufacturer.

Conglomerate merger
The combining under one ownership of two or more firms that produce unrelated products.

ANTITRUST LEGISLATION— THE POLICY OBJECTIVES

Economists generally believe that monopolies and other restraints of trade are bad because they usually have the effect of reducing total output and, therefore, aggregate economic welfare.

FRED S. MCCHESNEY[4]

---

[4]Fred S. McChesney, "Antitrust," in *The Fortune Encyclopedia of Economics,* ed. David R. Henderson (New York: Warner Books, 1993), p. 385. In this section we utilize the content of McChesney's essay, which provides a fascinating overview of the rationale for, and history of, antitrust policy.

As American manufacturing developed during the latter part of the last century, a wave of horizontal mergers exerted an important influence on the structure of markets. Several producers in the oil, railroad, sugar, and tobacco industries, among others, merged and formed giant corporations during this period. Many businesses whose names are now household words—U.S. Steel, General Electric, Standard Oil, General Foods, General Mills, and American Can, for example— were formed by these mergers. In some cases, a trust was formed to control the assets of the firms. A **trust** places the assets of several firms under the custody of trustees who manage the trust for the benefit of the owners. Concern about the economic and political power created by the mergers and the formation of trusts led to adoption of antitrust legislation.

Trust

In American history, an arrangement in which the assets of several firms were placed in the custody of trustees who managed the trust for the benefit of the owners. Trusts were used to form cartels in the United States in the late 1800s.

MAJOR ANTITRUST LEGISLATION

The United States, to a greater degree than most Western countries, has adopted antitrust legislation designed to promote competitive markets. Three major legislative acts—the Sherman Act, the Clayton Act, and the Federal Trade Commission Act—form the foundation of antitrust policy in the United States.

SHERMAN ACT. Passed in 1890, the Sherman Act was the first response to the demands for antitrust measures. Its most important provisions are

> *Section 1: Every contract, combination in the form of trust or otherwise, or conspiracy, in restraint of trade or commerce among the several states or with foreign nations, is hereby declared illegal.*
> *Section 2: Every person who shall monopolize, or conspire with any other person or persons to monopolize, any part of the trade or commerce among the several states, or with foreign nations, shall be guilty of a misdemeanor.*

The language of the Sherman Act is vague and subject to interpretation. What does it mean to attempt to "monopolize" or "conspire to monopolize" with another person? Initially, the courts were hesitant to apply the act to manufacturing corporations. In 1911, however, the Supreme Court ruled that Standard Oil and American Tobacco had used "unreasonable" tactics to restrain trade. At the time, the Standard Oil trust controlled 90 percent of the country's refinery capacity. American Tobacco controlled three-fourths of the tobacco manufacturing market. Both firms were broken up into several smaller rival firms.

The Supreme Court, however, did not prohibit monopoly per se. In fact, passage of the Sherman Act was followed by a second wave of mergers, which, between 1898 and 1902 alone, involved perhaps half of the U.S. manufacturing capacity. Firms that could not conspire, could merge. It was "unfair or unethical" business practices that the courts would not condone. Since the Sherman Act did not clearly define unfair or unethical business practices, additional legislation was required. In 1914 Congress passed two other antitrust laws to remedy the situation.

CLAYTON ACT. The Clayton Act was an effort to spell out and prohibit specific business practices. The following are prohibited by the Clayton Act when they "substantially lessen competition or tend to create a monopoly":

1. *Price discrimination*—charging purchasers in different markets different prices that are unrelated to transportation or other costs.

2. *Tying contracts*—a practice whereby the seller requires the buyer to purchase another item.
3. *Exclusive dealings*—an agreement between a manufacturer and retail distributor that prohibits the distributor from handling the products of firms that are competitors of the manufacturer.
4. *Interlocking stockholding*—one firm purchasing the stock of a competing firm.
5. *Interlocking directorates*—the same individual(s) serving on the boards of directors of competing firms.

Although somewhat more specific than the Sherman Act, the Clayton Act is still vague. At what point do the prohibited actions actually become illegal? Under what circumstances do these actions "substantially lessen competition"? The task of interpreting this ambiguous phrase still remains with the courts.

FEDERAL TRADE COMMISSION ACT. The Federal Trade Commission Act declared unlawful all "unfair methods of competition in commerce." The Federal Trade Commission (FTC), composed of five members appointed by the president to seven-year terms, was established to determine the exact meaning of "unfair methods." However, a 1919 Supreme Court decision held that the courts, not the FTC, had the ultimate responsibility for interpreting the law. Today the FTC is concerned primarily with (1) enforcing consumer protection legislation, (2) prohibiting deceptive advertising, a power it acquired in 1938, and (3) preventing overt collusion.

When a complaint is filed with the FTC, usually by a third party, the commission investigates. If there is a violation, the FTC initially attempts to settle the dispute by negotiation between the parties. If the attempts to negotiate a settlement fail, a hearing is conducted before one of the commission's examiners. The decision of the hearing examiner may be appealed to the U.S. Court of Appeals. The great majority of cases brought before the FTC are now settled by mutual consent of the parties involved.

OTHER ANTITRUST LEGISLATION

Additional antitrust legislation was passed in the 1930s. The Robinson-Patman Act of 1936 prohibits selling "at unreasonably low prices" when such practices reduce competition. The section of the Clayton Act dealing with price discrimination was aimed at eliminating **predatory pricing,** a practice whereby a firm temporarily reduces its price below cost in certain market areas in order to damage or eliminate weaker rivals. Once the rivals have been eliminated, the firm may then be able to use its monopoly power to raise prices above costs. The Robinson-Patman Act went beyond this. It was intended to protect competitors not just from stronger rivals who might temporarily sell below cost, but also from more efficient rivals who were actually producing at a lower cost. Chain stores and mass distributors were the initial targets of the legislation. Economists have often been critical of the Robinson-Patman Act, since it has tended to reduce price competition and thereby protect inefficient producers.

In 1938 Congress passed the Wheeler-Lea Act, which was designed to strengthen sections of the Federal Trade Commission Act that had been weakened by restrictive court decisions. Before the passage of the act, the courts were reluctant to prohibit unfair business practices, such as false and deceptive advertising,

Predatory pricing
The practice in which a dominant firm in an industry temporarily reduces prices to damage or eliminate weaker rivals, so that prices can be raised above the level of costs at a later time.

unless there was proof of damages to either consumers or rival firms. The Wheeler-Lea Act removed this limitation and gave the FTC extended powers to prosecute and ban false or deceptive advertising.

In 1950 Congress passed the Celler-Kefauver Act (sometimes referred to as the antimerger act), which prohibits a firm from acquiring the assets of a competitor if the transaction substantially lessens competition. The Clayton Act, though it prohibits mergers through stock acquisition, proved unable to prevent business combinations from being formed by sale of assets. The Celler-Kefauver Act closed this loophole, further limiting the ability of firms to combine in order to escape competitive pressures.

Since the intent of the Celler-Kefauver Act is to maintain industrial competition, its applicability to mergers between large firms in the same industry is obvious. The act also prohibits vertical mergers between large firms if competition is reduced by such mergers. For example, the merger of a publishing company with a paper producer is illegal if the courts find that it lessens competition. However, few vertical merger cases have been brought under this act since the early 1970s, when antitrust policy began to focus more on consumer welfare and less directly on the structure of industries.

CURRENT ANTITRUST POLICY

An important trend over the past two decades has been the increased weight given by antitrust policymakers to consumer welfare. In recent years, the Justice Department has been less likely to oppose mergers, including those increasing a firm's market share, if the merger is expected to reduce the prices paid by buyers of the industry's output. The Justice Department's 1982 Merger Guidelines stressed this position. They called for challenges only to proposed mergers deemed likely to harm consumers.

Herfindahl index
A measure of industry concentration, calculated by squaring the percentage share of each firm in the industry, then summing the squares. The index can range from zero to 10,000. It is a more sophisticated measure of concentration than the traditional concentration ratio, and is used by the Justice Department in antitrust policy.

The guidelines also highlighted the importance of the **Herfindahl index,** a relatively new measure of market concentration. (See the Measures of Economic Activity boxed feature.) If a merger results in a Herfindahl index of less than 1,000, this indicates that the market is relatively competitive and therefore the Justice Department is unlikely to challenge such mergers. If the index would be above 1,000 after the merger, and the merger would add at least 100 points to the index, then a challenge is likely. A 50-point rise triggers agency concern if the merger raises the index above 1,800.

Other factors also are considered under the guidelines, especially in borderline cases. A merger is less likely to be challenged if:

1. Foreign firms are an important source of competition in the industry.
2. One of the firms involved in the merger would otherwise be likely to go out of business.
3. The firms in the industry do not produce a homogeneous product (thus, quality competition is more likely).
4. New competitors are likely to enter the industry if the current producers increase their prices.

In general, the purpose of the new guidelines is to bring a challenge against only those mergers likely to harm consumers by significantly increasing the market power of affected firms.

MEASURES OF ECONOMIC ACTIVITY

THE HERFINDAHL INDEX

The Herfindahl index measures market concentration in a way that gives a great deal of weight to the share of the largest one or two firms in the market. It does so by squaring the percentage each firm has in the market, and summing the squares. If there are n firms in the market, then H, the Herfindahl index, is:

$$H = S_1^2 + S_2^2 + S_3^2 + \ldots + S_n^2$$

where S_1 in the formula is the percentage share of the largest firm in the market, S_2 is the percentage share of the second largest firm, and so on. Each S can vary from 100 (a pure monopoly, with only one firm in the market) down to almost zero. For a pure monopoly,

$$H = (100)^2 = 10,000$$

This is the largest possible value for the Herfindahl in-dex. By contrast, if there are 100 firms in a market, each with an equal 1 percent share, then

$$H = (1)^2 + (1)^2 + (1)^2 + \ldots + (1)^2 = 100$$

The Herfindahl index is a more sophisticated tool for measuring market power than is the traditional concentration ratio, which treats a market with four firms of equal size the same as a market with four firms, one of which has 70 percent of the market and three that have 10 percent each. The Herfindahl index would assign the equal-shares market an index of 2,500 (4×25^2) and the unequal-shares market an index of 5,200 ($70^2 + 10^2 + 10^2 + 10^2$), indicating the larger potential for market power when one firm has a 70 percent share of the market. Only the shares of the larger firms are needed to approximate the index, since firms with small shares add little to the Herfindahl index.

LIMITING ANTICOMPETITIVE PRACTICES

The modern approach to antitrust policy also seeks to prohibit business practices that tend to stifle competition. However, this presents a problem: It is often difficult to know when observed behavior is really anticompetitive. The same practices that some regard as anticompetitive may merely reflect lower cost and efforts to provide consumers with more dependable service.

Consider predatory pricing. Price cutting by a more efficient firm in an industry will tend to drive less efficient firms out of business, but this is not considered "predatory" unless the pricing is below cost. How can anyone know whether the price is truly below the cost of production and delivery without knowing intimate details about how the firm's costs vary with the season, the territory, the provision of other complementary products, and so on? Investigating many cases of alleged predatory pricing over the years, economists have found that the evidence often failed to support the charges. A price cutter's competitors may be unhappy, but that may simply reflect vigorous competition rather than the presence of anticompetitive behavior.

Exclusive contracts, or dealerships, provide another example. This practice is prohibited under the Clayton Act when it substantially lessens competition or creates a monopoly. A manufacturer of a line of products may seek exclusive dealings—that is, a contract that would prevent retailers from selling rival products—in order to lessen competition or limit the entry of rival firms. However, firms may also seek such arrangements in order to protect advertising expenditures and assure quality maintenance service. Suppose that A-OK and X-tra Good are both manufacturers of lawn mowers. The A-OK company decides to spend $20 million on a massive advertising campaign in order to inform consumers and stimulate

Exclusive contract
An agreement between a manufacturer and retailer that prohibits the retailer from carrying the product lines of firms that are rivals of the manufacturer. Such contracts are illegal under the Clayton Act when they "lessen competition."

THUMBNAIL SKETCH

WHAT DOES ANTITRUST LEGISLATION PROHIBIT?

Antitrust laws prohibit the following practices:

1. Collusion—contracts and conspiracies to restrain trade (Sherman Act, Sec. 1)
2. Monopoly and attempts to monopolize any part of trade or commerce among the several states (Sherman Act, Sec. 2)
3. Persons serving on the boards of directors of competing firms with more than $1 million of assets (Clayton Act, Sec. 8)
4. Unfair and deceptive advertising (Federal Trade Commission Act as amended by Wheeler-Lea Act)
5. Price discrimination if the intent is to injure a competitor (Robinson-Patman Act)

Antitrust laws prohibit the following practices when they substantially lessen competition or tend to create a monopoly:

1. Tying contracts (Clayton Act, Sec. 3)
2. Exclusive dealings (Clayton Act, Sec. 3)
3. Interlocking stockholdings and horizontal mergers (Clayton Act, Sec. 7, as amended by Celler-Kefauver Act)
4. Interlocking directorates (Clayton Act, Sec. 8)

---

interest in their product. Customers, drawn by the campaign, flock to Marty's Mower Mart, where X-tra Good mowers are also sold, and they are able to make price and performance comparisons between the two brands. Obviously, without spending a penny on advertising, X-tra Good will benefit from the expensive campaign of its competitor, and since its advertising costs are lower, it may be able to sell at a lower price. Similarly, if A-OK trains Marty's personnel in service methods that could be used for both products, X-tra Good also gets a free ride on the service offered. A-OK could avoid these undesirable spillover effects of its advertising campaign and its training program if it could require that Marty's Mower Mart carry only the A-OK brand. If it cannot so require, it may forgo its desired activities, and consumers will lose the potential benefits.

Unfortunately, it is often difficult to identify and separate anticompetitive behavior from competitive actions that cut the costs of marketing and product service. Thus, formulating and administering a set of antitrust laws that consistently promote competition in the marketplace is not an easy task.

ANTITRUST POLICY—DISSENTING VIEWS

The accompanying Thumbnail sketch summarizes the central elements of the antitrust policy of the United States. For the reasons just given and for others as well, economists have often been critical of antitrust policy. People in business also are critical, often arguing that current legislation is so vague that it is difficult to determine whether a proposed action is in compliance. In addition to the need for greater clarity, some analysts believe that there is a need for stronger laws and more vigorous enforcement. Another school of thought holds that antitrust policy does more harm than good and actually is unnecessary. Let us look briefly at each of these positions.

ANTITRUST POLICIES SHOULD BE STRONGER AND MORE VIGOROUSLY ENFORCED.   The proponents of this position argue that greater effort is required to ensure the existence of competitive markets. They often point out that antitrust policy has functioned primarily as a holding action. That is, it prevents large firms from increasing their market share, but it is ineffective as a means for reducing industrial concentration. Policy can end up working against its own objectives. For example, an established firm controlling 50 percent or 60 percent of a market is generally left untouched, whereas two smaller firms with a combined market share of as little as 10 percent may be prohibited from merging. Current policy, therefore, often protects strong, established firms while weakening their smaller rivals. Those who view current policy as self-defeating typically favor an antitrust policy that would more thoroughly restructure concentrated industries, dividing large firms into smaller, independent units.

ANTITRUST POLICY IS UNNECESSARY AND OFTEN HARMFUL.   The advocates of this position argue that antitrust legislation places too much emphasis on the number of competitors without recognizing the positive role of dynamic competition. They believe an antitrust policy that limits business concentration will often promote inefficient business organization and will therefore encourage higher prices. They reject the notion that pure competition is a proper standard of economic efficiency.[5] As Joseph Schumpeter, an early proponent of this view of competition and regulation, emphasized more than four decades ago, "It... is a mistake to base the theory of government regulation of industry on the principle that big business should be made to work as the respective industry-would work in perfect competition."[6]

Like Schumpeter, current advocates of this position believe innovative activity is at the heart of competition. An ingenious innovator may forge ahead of competitors, but competition from other innovators will always be present. The competitor facing such innovation may seek shelter by demanding agency enforcement of antitrust laws against its successful competitors, or it may file suit itself. In fact, for every antitrust case brought by government, 20 are brought by private parties. Competition, according to this view, is a perpetual game of leapfrog, not a process that is dependent on the number of firms in an industry. Bigness is a natural outgrowth of efficiency and successful innovation. One of the leading proponents of this position, John McGee, a long-time professor of economics at the University of Washington, argues that concentration is neither inefficient nor indicative of a lack of competition:

> *Take an industry of many independent producers, each of which is efficiently using small scale and simple methods to make the same product.... Suppose that a revolution in technology or management techniques now occurs, so that there is room in the market for only one firm using the new and most efficient methods. Whether it occurs*

---

[5]See Dominick T. Armentano, *Antitrust and Monopoly: Anatomy of a Policy Failure* (New York: John Wiley, 1982), for an excellent presentation of this viewpoint.

[6]Joseph Schumpeter, *Capitalism, Socialism and Democracy* (New York: Harper Torchbooks, 1950), p. 106.

TAXIS AND REGULATORY ENTRY RESTRAINTS

Occupational and business licensing by state and local governments often restricts entry and reduces the competitiveness of markets. The taxicab business illustrates this point and highlights some potentially important recent developments in this area.

A 1983 survey found that 87 percent of the cities (population 50,000 or more) imposed regulations limiting entry into the taxi business. Some impose an absolute ban on the entry of new firms; others restrict the availability of operating licenses. For example, New York City's infamous medallion system restricts the number of taxi licenses to 12,200. These licenses are tradable and in the mid-1990s they sold for $175,000, a figure high enough to discourage many aspiring entrepreneurs, particularly those with limited capital. Taxicabs are also heavily regulated and entry severely limited in other cities, including Los Angeles, Chicago, Miami, Houston, and San Francisco. Of course, the primary effect of such regulations is less competition and higher fare prices.

Despite the presence of only three taxicab companies, the Colorado Public Utilities Commission (PUC) denied numerous requests and prohibited the entry of new firms into the Denver taxicab market for almost 50 years. Potential new entrants requesting a license were required to prove that (a) the existing service was inadequate and (b) the firms currently in the market were un-

able to handle the volume of traffic. Every time a potential rival sought a license, the three existing companies argued they were quite capable of handling the current demand and the PUC denied the request. In effect, the regulations imposed a three-firm oligopoly on the Denver taxicab market.

Leroy Jones, Ani Ebong, and Girma Molalegne requested a license to start Quick Pick Cabs in 1993. When their request was denied by the PUC, the entrepreneurs along with the Institute for Justice, a public interest legal firm located in Washington, D.C., filed a suit challenging the regulations. The plaintiffs argued that the regulations limiting entry were arbitrary, excessive, and in conflict with the privileges or immunities clause of the U.S. Constitution. Thus, they asserted that their right to pursue a business and earn a living was being violated. The case attracted the attention of CBS News, *The Wall Street Journal*, and other national media. Eventually, the regulatory commission backed down and the law was changed, permitting entry except in cases where the existing firms could prove that a new rival would cause their business to fail. Obviously, this shifted the burden of proof and made it much more difficult for the existing firms to restrain entry. Subsequently, Jones, Ebong, and Molalegne started Freedom Cabs, which became Denver's first new taxicab company since 1947. By 1996, the company had grown into a thriving business with approximately 100 employees (see accompanying picture).

quickly through merger or gradually through bankruptcy, an atomistic industry is transformed into a "monopoly," albeit one selling the same product at a lower price than before. If expected long-run price should rise, resort can still be had to the old and less efficient ways, which were compatible with . . . small firms. It would be incomplete and misleading to describe that process as a "decline of competition."[7]

Some observers point out that where other forces, such as foreign competition, protect consumers by offering additional options, antitrust measures that may reduce efficiency can harm competitiveness and disadvantage domestic producers. MIT economist Lester Thurow writes that "in markets where international trade exists or could exist, national antitrust laws no longer make sense. If they do anything, they only serve to hinder U.S. competitors who must live by a code that their foreign competitors can ignore."[8]

GOVERNMENT IS OFTEN THE SOURCE OF MONOPOLY. The critics of antitrust policy also argue that government action is often the source of market

---

[7]John S. McGee, *In Defense of Industrial Concentration* (New York: Praeger, 1971), pp. 21–22.

[8]Lester Thurow, *The Zero Sum Society* (New York: Basic Books, 1980), p. 146.

The Denver case is having an impact in other areas. Both Indianapolis and Cincinnati revised their regulations liberalizing entry into the taxi business. The Institute for Justice promises to assist plaintiffs in other areas and occupations, seeking to challenge restraints limiting economic freedom. It will be interesting to see if future challenges to government regulations limiting entry and restraining trade are an effective means of promoting competition.[1]

---

[1]For additional information on this topic, see Gail Diane Cox, "Tackling Taxis: First Step?", *The National Law Journal*, July 26, 1993; and Institute for Justice, *Challenging Denver's Taxicab Monopoly*, Litigation Backgrounder, 1993.

Girma Molalegne, Leroy Jones, and Ani Ebong (left to right) challenged regulations limiting entry into the taxicab market and eventually started Denver's first new cab company in almost 50 years.

power and monopoly. For example, government licensing in various forms has restricted entry and/or established monopolies in the markets for local cable television and telephone service, broadcasting, airports, and taxi service (see Applications in Economics: Taxis and Regulatory Entry Restraints). When government itself is the source of the monopoly, antitrust policy is unlikely to be an effective weapon with which to preserve competition.

REGULATION OF BUSINESS

Antitrust policy seeks to establish a competitive business environment and then allow the forces of competition to protect the interests of market participants. Regulation of business takes a more direct approach; it often dictates prices, establishes criteria for entry, and mandates procedures and production methods that must be followed.

Regulatory activity in the United States has expanded substantially in the past two decades. As **Exhibit 22–3** shows, federal regulatory spending and

Source: Center for the Study of American Business, Washington University. Derived from the *Budget of the United States Government* and related documents, various fiscal years.

EXHIBIT 22-3

TRENDS IN REGULATORY SPENDING AND STAFFING BY FEDERAL GOVERNMENT, 1970–1996

Trends in Regulatory Spending

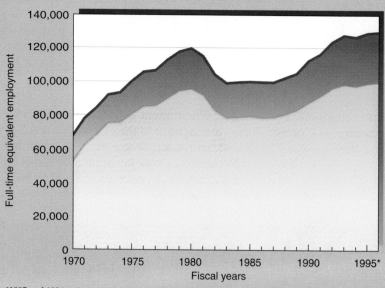

Federal Regulatory Staffing Trends

*1995 and 1996 estimates

Economic regulation   Social regulation

staffing levels increased rapidly in the 1970s, dropped in the early 1980s, then resumed their expansion in the late 1980s, through at least 1996. Budgeted 1996 federal spending (estimated) for economic regulation was $3.3 billion, while the figure for health and safety regulation expenditures was $12.4 billion. Compliance costs are much larger. For example, while the budgeted federal expenditures on environmental regulation for 1996 were $6 billion, the estimated private and public expenditures to meet the objectives of environmental regulation brought the national spending total to more than $120 billion.

TRADITIONAL ECONOMIC REGULATION

Regulation of business activity is not a new development. In 1887 Congress established the Interstate Commerce Commission (ICC), providing it with the authority to regulate the railroad industry. In 1935 the trucking industry was also brought under the ICC's regulatory jurisdiction. State regulatory commissions began to oversee local delivery of electricity, natural gas, and telephone services as early as 1907. Little was done at the federal level to expand regulation beyond the railroads until the 1930s, when commissions were formed during the Roosevelt administration to regulate interstate telephone service, broadcasting, airlines, natural gas pipelines, and other industries. These activities focus on **economic regulation** and usually control the product price or the structure of a particular industry rather than specifying the production processes used by the regulated firm.

    It was usually argued that economic regulation of entry and price was necessary to protect consumers in markets characterized by natural monopoly or to preserve orderly competition in markets characterized by high fixed cost, but low variable cost. Railroad transport provides an example of the latter. Regardless of why they were initially established, regulations that fix prices and restrict entry stifle the competitive process. With time, such regulation will end up protecting inefficient producers and limiting the options of consumers. High costs and production inefficiencies generated widespread dissatisfaction with the traditional economic regulation of several industries during the 1970s. Major steps toward deregulation were taken in the ground and air transportation industries as a result. Consumers benefited substantially from that change, confirming much of the criticism that many economists and others had leveled at the regulatory process.

    Regulatory reform continues in several markets. Deregulation in the market for electricity has begun. The Energy Policy Act of 1992, for example, requires that utilities give consumers access to other utilities and to the growing number of independent power producers.[9] As President Clinton's Council of Economic Advisers said in their *Economic Report of the President, 1996*, "Regulatory reform enjoys broad support, but disagreement exists over how best to make the transition from regulated monopoly to competition, and over the role of government once that transition is complete." (p. 156)

Economic regulation
Regulation of product price or industrial structure, usually imposed on a specific industry. By and large, the production processes used by the regulated firms are unaffected by this type of regulation.

---

[9]An excellent summary of the history, the problems, and the prospects for improvement through deregulation in this market is Vernon L. Smith, "Regulatory Reform in the Electric Power Industry," *Regulation* 19, no. 1 (1996): pp. 33–46.

RECENT HEALTH AND SAFETY REGULATION OF BUSINESS

Health and safety regulation

Legislation designed to improve the health, safety, and environmental conditions available to workers and/or consumers. The legislation usually mandates production procedures, minimum standards, and/or product characteristics to be met by producers and employers.

Along with movement toward deregulation of industrial structure and prices, there has been a sharp increase in **health and safety regulation.** In the late 1960s and early 1970s, people had great faith in the ability of government to improve the quality of life. The economy was prospering, and people turned their attention more toward policies to reduce health hazards, preserve environmental quality, and reduce risks and negative impacts of new technologies and the booming economy. For a wealthier nation, reducing air and water pollution and other externalities became more feasible and more desirable. Added regulation to protect individuals against risks from occupational hazards as well as risks from newly developed drugs and other consumer products was also demanded by activist groups.

The new health and safety regulation resulted from these demands. Agencies such as the Occupational Safety and Health Administration (OSHA), Consumer Product Safety Commission (CPSC), Food and Drug Administration (FDA), and Environmental Protection Agency (EPA) have grown rapidly. As Exhibit 22–3 indicates, both the expenditures and employment of these and other health and safety regulatory agencies have increased substantially since 1970. As a group, these agencies are now far larger than the older agencies that focus on economic regulation. Moreover, their regulatory authority cuts across industries and involves them more in the actual operation of individual firms. In contrast with economic regulation, the health and safety regulatory agencies frequently specify in detail the engineering processes to be followed by regulated firms and industries.

The major cost of health and safety regulation is generally felt in the form of higher production costs and thus higher prices. As producers obey regulators' orders to make workplaces accessible to handicapped workers, to emit less pollution, or to reduce noise levels, for example, costs rise. And of course the process of regulation itself is costly: Employment and operating costs of regulatory agencies must be met, which means higher taxes. These costs can be substantial. EPA, for example, estimated that when it hired contractors to clean up Superfund hazardous waste sites in 1988, the indirect costs within EPA itself— the cost of activities such as formulating and enforcing the rules for cleanups— amounted to more than $328 for every hour spent by a worker actually involved in cleaning any site, not counting the costs paid to the contracting firm and its workers.[10]

The primary cost of health and safety regulation, however, comes in the form of higher operating costs of firms striving to meet the new standards. In effect, these higher costs are like a tax. As **Exhibit 22–4** illustrates, the higher cost shifts the supply curve to the left for a good affected by the regulation. Higher prices and a decline in the output of the good result. Who pays the cost? As with any tax, the burden is shared by buyers and sellers according to the elasticity of supply and demand. When consumers have more options to the taxed good, so that their demand is more elastic, they will pay a small portion of the tax. In Exhibit

---

[10]The statement by EPA appeared in the *Federal Register* 57, no. 152 (August 6, 1992). Corrected for inflation to 1996, the indirect cost per hour of work would be $435.

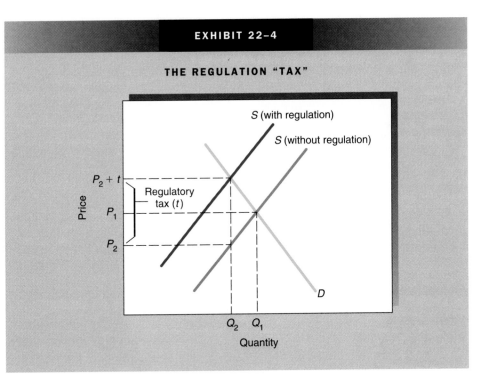

EXHIBIT 22–4

THE REGULATION "TAX"

S (with regulation)

S (without regulation)

$P_2 + t$

Regulatory tax (t)

P_1

P_2

Price

Q_2 Q_1

Quantity

D

Regulation that requires businesses to adopt more costly production techniques is similar to a tax. If the regulation increases per unit costs by t, the supply curve shifts upward by that amount. Higher prices and a smaller output result.

22–4, the new price ($P_2 + t$) will be closer to P_1 when demand is more elastic. On the other hand, sellers will pay a smaller portion when the supply curve is more elastic, meaning that they have other options besides production of this regulated good. The burden on sellers is passed on in reduced profits to investors, and to workers in reduced demand for labor. In the short run, sellers may have few options for the use of capital already committed to the production process. Therefore, the short-run supply is likely to be inelastic. In the long run, of course, capital and labor are quite mobile among users, and supply in the taxed market should be more elastic.

Sometimes the opportunity cost of health and safety regulation is exceedingly difficult to calculate. For example, the FDA often bans the sale of a new drug until years of tests costing millions of dollars are completed. Two important opportunity costs of this regulation, if the drug finally proves (or would have proven) to be safe, are (1) some drugs are never developed because of the expensive tests and delays, and (2) people who could have been helped by a drug, had it been approved, have to forgo it for several years. Deaths often result from these delays. Other regulations that seek to promote health and safety can also have increased risk as an unintended consequence (see Applications in Economics: Buying Fuel Conservation—Expensively). These opportunity costs are large, but they do not show up as expenditures so they are hard to measure. So, too, are the benefits of these regulations hard to measure.

An important characteristic of most activities covered by health and safety regulations is a lack of information about their effects. This is not a coincidence. In most cases, the lack of information contributes directly to the demand for the regulation. For example, if consumers knew exactly what the effects of a particular

BUYING FUEL CONSERVATION—EXPENSIVELY

Fear of global warming—which some scientists think could be caused by rising levels of carbon dioxide in the air—has led to louder calls for more fuel-efficient cars, since cars that burn less fuel emit less carbon dioxide. In 1991 U.S. Senator Richard Bryan introduced a bill into Congress that would require automakers to boost their average mileage per gallon (mpg) from 27.5 mpg to 40 mpg.

Would such mandatory fuel economy reduce fuel usage significantly? And if so, at what cost? We have some answers to these questions because Congress has been mandating fuel-economy standards since 1975. Experience with these standards reveals some severe problems and indicates that large sacrifices will be required if standards are further tightened. The problems also illustrate the complex effects of government regulations.

Congress mandated Corporate Average Fuel Economy (CAFE) standards in 1975 after the price of oil went up dramatically. Supporters said that the standards would conserve energy and make the United States less dependent on foreign oil. However, if Congress had simply allowed gasoline prices to rise, the higher prices would have encouraged people to adjust their habits in ways that suited them individually and minimized their personal cost. Some consumers would have simply driven less; others would have saved on gasoline by buying smaller cars or having more tune-ups. Some people who lived far from their workplaces might have bought larger cars and carpooled; others might have chosen to live in places where they could walk to work.

Indeed, before the CAFE standards had an impact, people began to respond to higher gasoline prices by purchasing fuel-efficient cars. According to the *1986 Economic Report of the President*, average fuel economy in the United States increased by 43 percent between 1973 and 1979, as consumers responded to higher fuel prices. By the time the fuel-efficiency standards influenced the design of cars, which probably occurred with model year 1986, much fuel economy had already been achieved and the price of gasoline was going down.

By that time, some consumers wanted larger cars, but the CAFE standards forced automakers to offer smaller cars. Although they could make some reductions in fuel usage by such steps as redesigning transmissions or fuel-injection systems, car companies had to reduce vehicle weight to meet the standards. Robert W. Crandall of the Brookings Institution and John Graham of the Har-

vard School of Public Health estimate that model year 1989 cars were on average 500 pounds lighter than they would have been without the CAFE standards.[1]

A serious problem with lighter cars is that they are less safe than larger cars in crashes. Crandall and Graham estimated that 2,200 to 3,900 lives would be lost over a 10-year period as a result of the application of the CAFE standards to the cars of the 1989 model year, with similar numbers of lives likely to be lost with each succeeding model year. These findings led Jerry Ralph Curry, administrator of the National Highway Traffic Safety Administration, to oppose tighter standards in 1991. "The bottom line is drastically smaller cars and more injuries and deaths," he wrote in *The Washington Post*.

The CAFE standards have had other unwanted effects. To sell enough small cars to raise the fuel-economy average, domestic automakers reduced small-car prices and raised prices for large cars. Buying decisions were distorted, and consumers paid more on balance for their cars.

Because Congress required the car companies to calculate average fuel economy separately for their domestic-manufactured cars and their imports, they cannot use their smaller, more fuel-efficient imports to bring down their domestic fleets' average. This has encouraged small-car production in the United States, even though production might be cheaper overseas, and has led the Ford Motor Company to move some of its large-car production out of the country.

Another outcome of the CAFE regulations was to set in motion a big lobbying effort in Washington, D.C.—taking creative skills and energy away from productive activity. General Motors and Ford have lobbied to keep the government from tightening the standards. In contrast, Chrysler Corporation, which specializes in small cars, has a vested interest in keeping the standards tight, because the standards increase the costs of their rivals.

Were the CAFE standards effective in reducing fuel use? Not very. According to the Federal Highway Administration, even though fuel usage per vehicle has fallen since 1969, total fuel consumption has been rising since 1982. With new large cars more expensive as a result of the standards, some people probably kept their old cars longer, increasing gas consumption (and pollution). The lower prices of small cars probably increased the total number of cars purchased. More cars on the road meant greater fuel consumption because the marginal cost of driving in a small car is lower than in a large car, and because smaller car sizes lead people to share

APPLICATIONS IN ECONOMICS *(continued)*

fewer rides. Robert A. Leone of Boston University estimates that a 2- or 3-cent tax on gasoline beginning in 1984 would have saved as much fuel as the CAFE standards did, at much less cost to society. In sum, the evidence suggests that the standards did not accomplish what was intended and placed costly burdens on society.

Source: Jane S. Shaw, Senior Associate at the Political Economy Research Center, Bozeman, Montana.

[1]Robert W. Crandall and John D. Graham, "The Effect of Fuel Economy Standards on Automobile Safety," *Journal of Law and Economics* 32, no. 1 (April 1989): pp. 97–118.

drug would be, there would be little need for the FDA to regulate its availability. Many people, though, are unaware of the precise effects of drugs, air pollution, or workplace hazards. Even when the information is available to experts, consumers may never receive it because of the cost of communicating information, particularly highly technical information. A case can be made, therefore, that we should let the experts decide which drugs, how much air pollution, and what forms of workplace safety should be sought.

Ironically, choosing regulation to protect citizens who do not understand the danger introduces a related problem: When regulators make the decisions, most of the incentive for individuals to learn about comparative risks is removed. And it is these individuals who vote and who can apply political pressure on regulators. (See Applications in Economics: Alar on Apples: Give Consumers a Choice?)

Although the lack of information generates much of the demand for health and safety regulation, it also makes it difficult to evaluate the effectiveness of the regulatory activity. The current system of health and safety regulation in the United States produces high costs as well as large benefits, but these costs and benefits of regulations can only be crudely estimated. When Robert Hahn and John Hird estimated the sum of the costs and benefits from health and safety regulations, they could not even state with confidence whether the benefits exceeded the costs. They concluded that the annual costs of these regulations in the late 1980s may have exceeded the benefits by as much as $65 billion, or that alternatively, benefits may have exceeded costs by as much as $104 billion. They suggest that the benefits of health and safety regulation are probably larger than the costs, but only by a small amount.[11]

THE POLITICAL ECONOMY OF REGULATION

Regulation involves a complex set of forces, political as well as economic. Public choice analysis provides us with some insight regarding political support of regulation and how we would expect the regulatory process to work. Four factors are particularly important.

1. The demand for regulation often stems from special-interest effects and redistribution considerations rather than from the pursuit of economic efficiency.

---

[11]Data are from Robert W. Hahn and John A. Hird, "The Costs and Benefits of Regulation: Review and Synthesis," *Yale Journal on Regulation* 8 (winter 1991): pp. 233–278.

ALAR ON APPLES: GIVE CONSUMERS A CHOICE?

In the 1980s, growers of certain apple varieties sprayed the chemical Alar on their apples to reduce apple spoilage in the orchard and to improve the color and the shelf life of the apples, thus reducing the cost and improving the appearance of the apples. But some scientists were concerned that the traces of Alar left on the apples might increase slightly the risk of cancer for children eating them. Scientists also knew, however, that if forbidding the use of Alar led to even small increases in cost or decrease in attractiveness of apples, and decreased apple consumption resulted, then some protection against cancer would be lost as a result of the change in the diets of consumers.

The problem of whether to ban the use of chemicals such as Alar is more general across many fruits and many chemicals. With treated fruit available, buyers could choose either organic fruits, advertised to be grown without such chemicals, or the standard supermarket fruits. In order to choose more wisely for themselves and their families, they had an incentive to read consumer magazines and news articles, comparing the contrasting opinions on both sides of the issue, as more

was learned by scientists. But once regulators stepped in to make such a decision for consumers, no consumer had that personal choice, and the personal benefit to learning more about the legally forbidden option disappeared.

In the case of Alar, citizens alarmed by the publicity campaign of an activist organization caused EPA to consider banning the chemical, and it was removed from the market. Most citizens, who could no longer buy products treated with Alar, were unaware that the EPA's Scientific Advisory Panel did not believe that it was dangerous and therefore they had repeatedly refused to recommend a ban on its use. Dr. Richard Adamson, director of the Division of Cancer Biology at the National Cancer Institute, stated that "the risk posed by Alar was no greater than eating a peanut butter sandwich."[1] This episode illustrated one of the major problems with regulation: The regulators are often more responsive to political pressure than to science.

---

[1]Elizabeth Whelan, "The Carcinogen or Toxin of the Week Phenomenon: The Facts Behind the Scares," in *The State of Humanity*, ed. Julian L. Simon (Cambridge: Blackwell Publishers, 1995), p. 596.

The wealth of an individual (or business firm) can be increased by an improvement in efficiency and an expansion in production. Regulation introduces another possibility. Sellers can gain from regulatory policies that either reduce competition in their market or increase the costs of rival firms. Buyers can gain, at least in the short run, if a legal requirement forcing producers to supply goods below cost is passed. Regulation opens up an additional avenue whereby those most able to bend the political process to their advantage can increase their wealth.

Public choice analysis (see Chapter 4) indicates that special-interest groups, such as well-organized, concentrated groups of buyers or sellers, can be expected to exert a disproportionate influence on the political process. Furthermore, the regulators themselves often compose a politically powerful interest group. Regulatory bureaucrats are key figures in the process. Their cooperation is important to those who are regulated. These factors suggest that there will be demand for economic regulation even if it contributes to economic inefficiency.

2. With the passage of time, regulatory agencies will often adopt the views of the business interests they are supposed to regulate. Once again, the special interest effect indicates why this is an expected result, even if the regulation initially was designed to police the actions of a business group. The personal payoff derived by *individual* consumers (and taxpayers) from regulatory actions is likely to be small. Often they are lulled into thinking that since there is a regulatory agency, the "public interest" is served. In contrast, firms (and employees) in regulated industries are vitally interested in the structure and composition of regulatory commissions and agencies. Favorable actions by these regulatory bodies could result in larger profits, higher-paying jobs, and insulation from the uncertainties of competition. Thus, firms and employee groups, recognizing their potential gain, will invest both economic and political resources to influence the actions of regulatory agencies. In return for their organized political support, political officials will have a strong incentive to support their position when setting policy and making appointments to regulatory agencies.

3. Regulation is inflexible. It often fails to adjust to changing market conditions. Dynamic change often makes regulatory procedures obsolete. The introduction of trucking vastly changed the competitiveness of the ground transportation industry (previously dominated by railroad interests). Nevertheless, the regulation of price, entry, and routes continued for years after competitive forces had eliminated the monopoly power of firms in this industry. Similarly, city building codes that may have been appropriate when adopted have become obsolete and now retard the introduction of new, more efficient materials and procedures. In many cities regulatory procedures have prevented builders from introducing such cost-saving materials as plastic pipes, preconstructed septic tanks, and prefabricated housing units.

4. When approval has to be obtained from regulators, it will be difficult to introduce new products, including those that might potentially save lives. The activities and management of a regulatory agency, the Food and Drug Administration for example, will come under severe scrutiny if they inadvertently permit a dangerous product on the market. In contrast, they face few problems if they keep a highly beneficial product—including one that would save lives—off the market.

"OF COURSE YOU MAY REGISTER A COMPLAINT ABOUT ALL THE GOVERNMENT PAPERWORK, SIR... BUT IT HAS TO BE IN WRITING."

Thus, the cost to the regulatory agency of the former error is much greater than the latter. As a result, regulatory agencies will predictably apply tests that are too restrictive from the viewpoint of economic efficiency and consumer welfare.

FUTURE DIRECTIONS FOR REGULATORY POLICY

Most people concede that regulation, both economic and social, is like a two-edged sword. Regulations can be beneficial, but they tend to be costly and can also be counterproductive. Some regulations are far more costly than others, even when their major goals are similar. **Exhibit 22–5** demonstrates this point. Research on several hundred regulations that save lives, in several agencies, were analyzed by a group of well-known risk researchers who estimated their cost, per year of life saved. Some of their cost estimates, summarized by agency, are listed here. The researchers estimated that the median cost of Federal Aviation Administration (FAA) regulations *per life year* saved was $23,000. In contrast, that of the Environmental Protection Agency was $7,600,000, or 330 times that of the FAA.

The cost varied widely among the rules within each agency also. The researchers suggest that if the least costly methods to save lives were chosen, the same expenditures could save tens of thousands of additional lives per year, or alternatively, the same number of lives could be saved while expenditures could be reduced by tens of billions of dollars per year.

How can the regulations that generate large gains relative to cost be separated from those that generate few, if any, net benefits? Large gains could be realized if we could retain and expand the former, while modifying or eliminating the latter. Even though there is strong support for the continuation and expansion of social regulatory activities, the voices favoring regulatory reform, and even deregulation, are growing louder. Improved empirical evidence on the effectiveness of specific regulatory policies will continue to emerge and, in some cases, it will alter the direction of regulatory activities.

Source: T. O. Tengs et al., "Five Hundred Life-Saving Interventions and Their Cost-Effectiveness," *Risk Analysis* 15 (1995): pp. 369–390.

EXHIBIT 22–5

REGULATIONS AND DIFFERENCES IN THE COST OF SAVING LIVES

AGENCY	MEDIAN COST PER LIFE YEAR SAVED
Federal Aviation Administration	$23,000
Consumer Product Safety Commission	$68,000
National Highway Transportation Safety Administration	$78,000
Occupational Safety and Health Administration	$88,000
Environmental Protection Agency	$7,600,000

LOOKING AHEAD

In later chapters, we will discuss both environmental regulation and related political economy issues in more detail. The following chapter will focus on the resource market and the employment decisions of both business firms and resource suppliers.

CHAPTER SUMMARY

1. For more than a century, the structure of the U.S. economy has been changing. The relative size of the agricultural sector has declined, while the service and trade sectors have expanded. The size of the manufacturing sector increased as a share of the economy during the first half of this century, but it has declined in recent decades.

2. Competitiveness in an industry is difficult to measure. The traditional measure of competitiveness is the concentration ratio, which measures the share of industry output produced by a small number—usually four—of the largest firms in the industry.

3. An analysis of industrial concentration (and other measures of competitiveness) indicates that the U.S. economy has become more competitive over the past several decades, probably due to antitrust policy, rising import competition, and deregulation.

4. Antitrust legislation seeks to (a) maintain a competitive structure in the unregulated private sector and (b) prohibit business practices that are thought to stifle competition.

5. The Sherman, Clayton, and Federal Trade Commission acts form the foundation of antitrust policy in the United States. The Sherman Act prohibits conspiracies to restrain trade and/or monopolize an industry. The Clayton Act prohibits specific business practices, such as price discrimination, tying contracts, exclusive dealings, and mergers and acquisitions (as amended), when they "substantially lessen competition or tend to create a monopoly." As it has evolved through the years, the Federal Trade Commission is concerned primarily with enforcing consumer protection legislation, prohibiting deceptive advertising, and investigating industrial structure.

6. Compared to earlier periods, antitrust policy has given more weight to consumer welfare. If a merger is expected to result in lower prices for consumers, it is more likely to be approved by antitrust policymakers. A relatively new way to measure concentration, the Herfindahl index, is now used to measure concentration and guide antitrust policy.

7. Antitrust policy is made more difficult by the fact that it is not always easy to determine when a business practice is being used to further competition, and when it

will have an anticompetitive result. Most economists believe that antitrust policy in the United States has promoted competition and reduced industrial concentration, but not to a dramatic extent. On the other hand, government licensing and other legal barriers to entry have sometimes protected firms from the discipline of competition.

8. While antitrust policy seeks to establish a competitive environment, regulation takes a more direct approach; it often dictates prices, establishes criteria for entry, and mandates procedures and production methods that must be followed.

9. Traditional economic regulation has generally sought to fix prices and/or influence industrial structure. During the 1970s, changing market conditions and empirical studies generated widespread dissatisfaction with economic regulation. Significant moves toward deregulation have been made since that time, beginning with the trucking and airline industries. New entry, intense competition, and discount prices have accompanied the deregulation of these industries.

10. While economic regulation has been relaxed in recent years, health and safety regulation has expanded rapidly. Health and safety regulation seeks to provide a cleaner, safer, healthier environment for workers and consumers. Pursuit of this objective is costly, bringing about higher product prices and higher taxes, as well as unintended safety problems. Since the costs, and particularly the benefits, are often difficult to measure and evaluate, the efficiency of social regulatory programs is a controversial topic, and the subject of much current research.

11. Regulation involves a complex set of economic and political forces. Public choice provides some insight regarding how the regulatory process will work. The following four points are particularly important:

a. The demand for regulation often stems from special-interest and redistribution considerations.

b. With the passage of time, regulatory agencies are likely to adopt the views of the interest groups they are supposed to regulate.

c. Regulation is inflexible; it will be slow to adjust to changing conditions.

d. Since introduction of a harmful product causes more obvious damage and causes more trouble for the regulators than exclusion of a beneficial one, the agency approving new products (for example, medical drugs) will predictably apply tests that are too restrictive from the viewpoint of consumer welfare.

CRITICAL ANALYSIS QUESTIONS

1. How competitive is the U.S. economy? Has it become more or less competitive during the last three or four decades? Does the fact that a firm is large indicate that it

does not face important competition? What factors influence the competitiveness of markets?

2. "Big business is taking over the U.S. economy. Giant firms decide what we can buy, and even what government does." Evaluate this statement.

3. How is competitiveness measured? Is the concentration ratio a good measure of competitiveness? Why or why not? How does the Herfindahl index differ from the concentration ratio? Which is the better measure of competitiveness?

*4. "Any merger that reduces competition hurts consumers and clearly should be stopped." Evaluate this statement.

5. "Efficiency requires large-scale production. Yet big businesses mean monopoly power, high prices, and market inefficiency. We must choose between production efficiency and monopoly." Evaluate this statement.

*6. Legislation mandating stronger side and door panels to protect drivers and passengers against side collisions presumably makes cars both safer and more expensive. The same could be said for air bags. Are laws like these necessary for auto safety? Do they save lives and make auto travel safer? Why or why not?

7. "Without legal safety requirements, products such as lawn mowers would be unsafe." Evaluate this statement.

*8. Will health and safety legislation mandating workplace and product safety standards reduce the profitability of the regulated firms? Who bears the cost and who gains the benefits of such legislation?

*9. If tariff and quota barriers for foreign imports are lifted, making imports easier to obtain, does this strengthen or weaken the case for strict antitrust legislation and enforcement?

10. In large cities, taxi fares are often set above the market equilibrium rate. Sometimes the number of licenses is limited in order to maintain the above-market price. In other cases, licenses are automatically granted to anyone wanting to operate a taxi. When taxi fares are set above market equilibrium, compare and contrast resource allocation under the restricted license system (assume the licenses are tradable) and the free-entry system. In which case will it be easier for customers to get a taxi? In which case will the amount of capital required to enter the taxi business be greater?

11. "Regulations on the introduction of new drugs should be strengthened. Fewer people would die if more research were required prior to the introduction of new drugs. Only an economist could possibly disagree. Sure, it would cost more, but saving even one life would be worth more than whatever it costs." Evaluate this statement.

*12. "People cannot be expected to make good decisions on their own regarding auto safety. Only experts know enough to make such decisions." Evaluate this statement.

13. "Safety regulation is not an economic question. Where lives and health are at stake, economics has no place." Evaluate this statement.

14. "We owe it to our coal miners to see that mines become much safer. Regulations can accomplish this, and the mine owners will pay. Since users of coal have many sources of supply, they will not pay for these regulations. Workers will clearly be better off." Explain the logic here, and show what additional assumptions must be made about mine owners, and about mine workers, before the statement can be true.

*15. "If we force increased safety measures in the workplace by regulation, business may bear the cost in the short run, but capital will receive the market rate of return in the long run." Evaluate this statement, and explain your reasoning.

---

*Asterisk denotes questions for which answers are given in Appendix B.

Note how the mean earnings of both men and women increase with additional education. Even though these data are for year-round, full-time workers, the earnings of women are only about two-thirds those of men with similar education.

SOURCE: Department of Commerce, Current Population Reports, P-60 Series, *Income, Poverty, and Valuation of Non-cash Benefits, 1994,* Table 7.

EDUCATION LEADS TO HIGHER EARNINGS

Mean Earnings of Year-Round Full-Time Workers, 1994

Thousands of Dollars

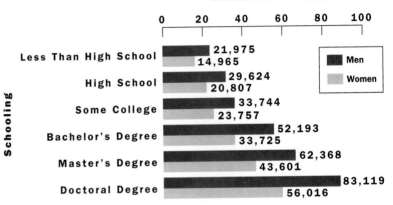

The educational level of persons in the labor force has been increasing. In 1994, only 12.2 percent of the labor force participants failed to complete high school, compared to 36.1 percent in 1970. Correspondingly, 25 percent of the labor force participants in 1994 had 4 or more years of college, compared to only 14.1 percent in 1970.

SOURCE: *Statistical Abstract of the United States, 1995,* Table 629; and Department of Commerce, P-60 Series 60-189, Current Population Reports, *Income, Poverty, and Valuation of Non-cash Benefits, 1994,* Table 7.

THE INCREASING EDUCATIONAL ATTAINMENT OF LABOR FORCE PARTICIPANTS

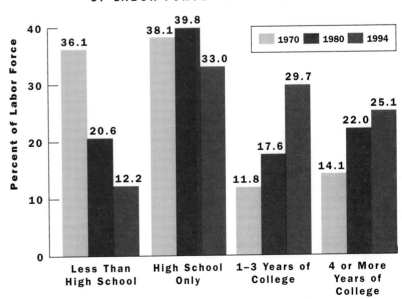

Here we illustrate the amount of private business capital per hour worked (1950 = 100). The amount of capital per hour of work has steadily increased, but note how it has risen at a slower rate beginning in the 1970s.

How will this slower increase in capital per unit of labor influence the growth of labor productivity?

EXHIBIT IV-C

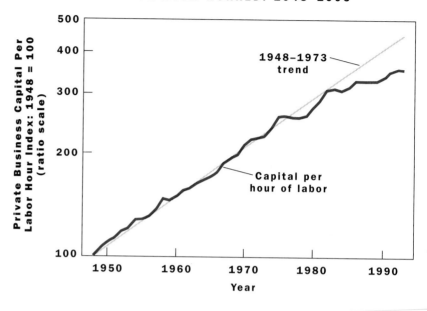

PRIVATE BUSINESS CAPITAL PER LABOR HOUR WORKED: 1948–1993

Here we present the growth rates of real per capita GDP for the 1955–1973 and 1974–1995 periods for industrial economies. In every case, the growth of real GDP during the more recent period was substantially less than growth during the earlier period.

What factors account for this slowdown in growth? This question will be addressed in Part IV.

Source: Stanley Fischer, "Symposium on the Slowdown in Productivity Growth," *Journal of Economic Perspectives* (Fall 1988), Table 1. Data from the *Economic Report of the President, 1996,* were used to update the figures.

EXHIBIT IV-D

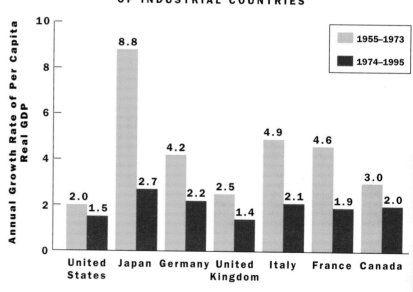

THE POST-1973 DECLINE IN THE GROWTH RATES OF INDUSTRIAL COUNTRIES

EXHIBIT IV-E

Employee compensation and the income of self-employed workers account for approximately 80 percent of national income. These earnings are primarily a return to human capital. Rents, interest, and corporate profits—which reflect returns to physical capital—receive approximately 20 percent of the national income. This division of national income—approximately four-fifths to human capital and one-fifth to physical capital—has been relatively constant over several decades.

Between 1960 and 1980, there was a sharp increase in youthful workers (teenagers and persons age 20 to 24 years) as a share of the labor force, while the representation of men age 25 years and over declined. The representation of women rose from 26.7 percent in 1960 to 38.2 percent in 1994.

What impact would this changing composition of the labor force have on the overall productivity of labor, income inequality, and the earnings of women relative to men?

SOURCE: *Statistical Abstract of the United States, 1995,* Table 631.

THE INCOME SHARES OF HUMAN AND PHYSICAL CAPITAL

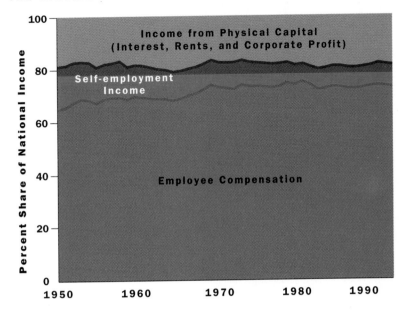

EXHIBIT IV-F

CHANGES IN THE COMPOSITION OF THE LABOR FORCE

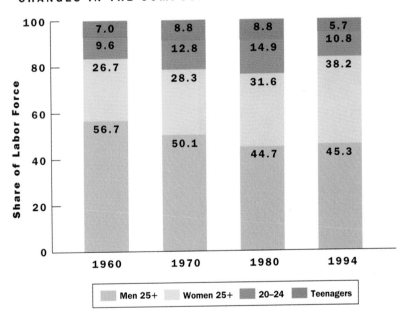

Typically both younger, less experienced workers and older workers (as they move toward the retirement phase of life) will have lower earnings than workers in prime working-age (35–54 years) groups. This pattern is illustrated here.

How does the pattern of earnings over a lifetime influence earnings (and income) inequality at a point in time?

SOURCE: U.S. Department of Commerce, *Income, Poverty, and Valuation of Non-Cash Benefits: 1994,* Series P60-189 (April 1996).

EXHIBIT IV–G

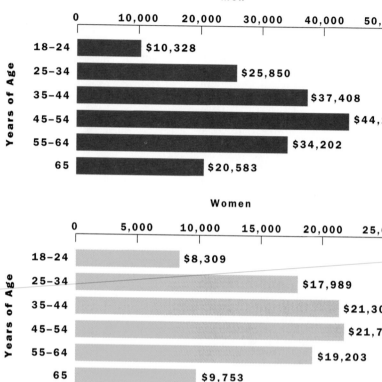

THE PATTERN OF LIFETIME EARNINGS

1994 Mean Earnings

Men

Years of Age	Earnings
18–24	$10,328
25–34	$25,850
35–44	$37,408
45–54	$44,
55–64	$34,202
65	$20,583

Women

Years of Age	Earnings
18–24	$8,309
25–34	$17,989
35–44	$21,30
45–54	$21,7
55–64	$19,203
65	$9,753

CHAPTER FOCUS

■ Why do business firms demand labor, machines, and other resources?
■ Why is the demand for a productive resource inversely related to its price?
■ How do business firms decide how many skilled laborers, unskilled laborers, machines, and other factors of production to employ?
■ How is the quantity supplied of a resource related to its price in the short run? In the long run?
■ What determines the market price in resource markets?

It is . . . necessary to attach price tags to the various factors of production . . . in order to guide those who have the day-to-day decisions to make as to what is plentiful and what is scarce.

PROFESSOR JAMES MEADE[1]

---

[1]James E. Meade, "Economic Efficiency and Distributional Justice," in *Contemporary Issues in Economics*, ed. Robert W. Crandall and Richard S. Eckaus (Boston: Little, Brown, 1972), p. 319.

Resource markets

Markets in which business firms demand factors of production (for example, labor, capital, and natural resources) from household suppliers. The resources are then used to produce goods and services. These markets are sometimes called factor markets *or* input markets.

I n previous chapters we focused on product markets in which consumers purchase products that are supplied by business firms. To produce these products, firms must hire productive resources, such as machines and workers. How do businesses decide which resources to employ and the quantity of each that will be used? What encourages them to conserve on their use of scarce resources? What factors influence the availability of resources both now and in the future? Analysis of **resource markets** will help us answer these questions and related issues. (Note: Because resources are also referred to as *factors,* or *inputs,* these markets are also known as *factor markets* or *input markets.*)

Just as in product markets, the forces of supply and demand combine to determine price in resource markets. The buyers and sellers in resource markets are just the reverse of what they are in product markets. In resource markets, business firms are the purchasers; they demand resources that are used to produce goods and services. Households are the sellers; they supply resources in exchange for income. The income derived from supplying productive resources, such as the wages received from selling our labor services, provides the major source of income for most of us. Prices in resource markets coordinate the choices of buyers and sellers and bring the amount of each resource demanded into harmony with the amount supplied. Resource prices also help to allocate factors of production efficiently and channel them into the areas in which they are most productive. This enables us to have higher incomes and a larger supply of consumer goods than would otherwise be the case.

As the circular flow diagram of **Exhibit 23–1** illustrates, there is a close relationship between product and resource markets. Households earn income by selling factors of production—for example, the services of their labor and capital—to business firms. Their offers to sell form the supply curve in resource markets (bottom loop). In turn, the income households derive from the sale of resources provides them with the buying power required to purchase goods and services in product markets. These household expenditures for products generate revenues that provide business firms with the incentive to produce goods and services (top loop). In turn, the business firms demand resources because they contribute to the production of goods and services that can be sold in product markets.

HUMAN AND NONHUMAN RESOURCES

Nonhuman resources

The durable, nonhuman inputs that can be used to produce both current and future output. Machines, buildings, land, and raw materials are examples. Investment can increase the supply of nonhuman resources. Economists often use the term physical capital *when referring to nonhuman resources.*

Broadly speaking, there are two different types of productive inputs—nonhuman and human. **Nonhuman resources** can be further broken down into the categories of physical capital, land, and natural resources. *Physical capital* consists of human-made goods, such as tools, machines, and buildings, that are used to produce other things.

Net investment can increase the supply of nonhuman resources. Investment, however, involves a cost. Resources that are used to produce machines, upgrade the quality of land, or discover natural resources could be used directly to produce goods and services for current consumption. Why take the roundabout

EXHIBIT 23–1

THE MARKET FOR RESOURCES

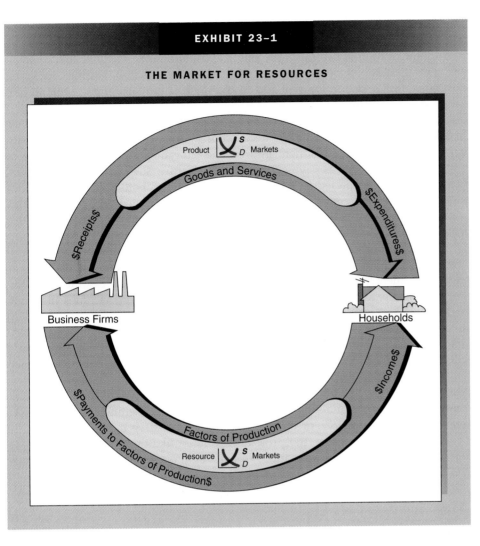

Until now, we have focused on product markets, where households demand goods and services that are supplied by firms (upper loop). We now turn to resource markets, where firms demand factors of production—human capital (for example, skills and knowledge of workers) and physical capital (for example, machines, buildings, and land), which are supplied by households in exchange for income (bottom loop). In resource markets, firms are buyers and households are sellers, just the reverse of the case for product markets.

path? The answer is that sometimes indirect methods of producing goods are less costly in the long run. For example, Robinson Crusoe found he could catch more fish by taking some time off from hand-fishing to build a net. Even though his initial investment in the net reduced his current catch, once the net was completed he was able to more than make up for his earlier loss of output. Benefits and costs will influence investment choices ranging from fishing nets to complex machines. These investments will only be undertaken when decision makers expect the benefits of a larger future output to more than offset the current reduction in the production of consumption goods.

Just as the supply of machines can be increased, so, too, can wise land development and soil-conservation practices be used to upgrade both the quantity and quality of land. Similarly, the supply of natural resources can be increased (within limits) by the application of more resources to discovery and development.

Human resources are composed of the skills and knowledge of workers. Sometimes people act as if these resources were strictly the result of inheritance or chance. This is not the case. Investment in such things as education, training,

Human resources
The abilities, skills, and health of human beings that can contribute to the production of both current and future output. Investment in training and education can increase the supply of human resources.

Investment in human capital
Expenditures on training, education, skill development, and health designed to increase the productivity of an individual.

health, and experience can enhance the skill, ability, and ingenuity of individuals, and thereby increase their productivity. Economists refer to such activities as **investment in human capital.**[2] Like physical capital, human capital also depreciates (as the skills of a person decline with age or lack of use). During any given year, education and training will add to the stock of human capital while depreciation detracts from it.

Decisions to invest in human capital involve all the basic ingredients of other investment decisions. Consider the decision of whether to go to college. As many of you will testify, an investment in a college education requires the sacrifice of current earnings as well as payments for direct expenses, such as tuition and books. The investment is expected to lead to a better job (when both monetary and nonmonetary aspects are considered) and other benefits associated with a college education. The rational investor will weigh the current costs against the expected future benefits. College will be chosen only if the latter are greater than the former.

Human resources differ from nonhuman resources in two important respects. First, human capital is embodied in the individual. Individuals cannot be separated from their knowledge, skills, and health conditions in the same way that they can be separated from physical capital like buildings or machines that they might own. As a result, choices concerning the use of human resources are vitally affected by working conditions, location, job prestige, and similar nonpecuniary factors. Although monetary factors influence human-capital decisions, individuals will often choose to trade off some money income for better working conditions.

Second, human resources cannot be bought and sold in nonslave societies. Workers sell only the *services* of their labor, not the ownership to the human resource itself. Individuals have the option of quitting, selling their labor services to another employer, or using them in an alternative manner.

In competitive markets, the price of resources, like the price of products, is determined by supply and demand. We will begin our analysis of resource markets by focusing on the demand for resources, both human and nonhuman.

---

[2]The contributions of T. W. Schultz and Gary Becker to the literature on human capital have been particularly significant. See Daniel S. Hamermesh and Albert Rees, *The Economics of Work and Pay* (New York: Harper & Row, 1988), Chapter 3, for additional detail on human-capital theory.

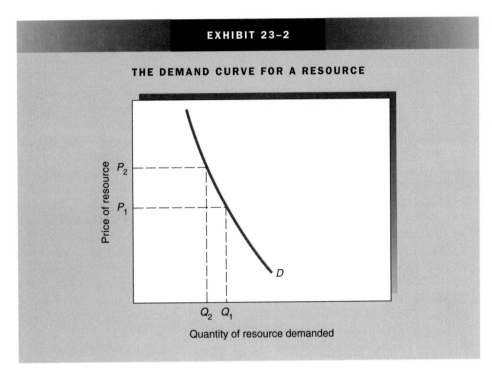

EXHIBIT 23–2

THE DEMAND CURVE FOR A RESOURCE

As the price of a resource increases, producers that use the resource intensely will (1) turn to substitute resources and (2) face higher costs, which will lead to higher prices and reduction in output. At the lower rate of output, producers will use less of the resource that increased in price. Both of these factors contribute to the inverse relationship between the price and amount demanded of a resource.

DEMAND FOR RESOURCES

Profit-seeking producers employ laborers, machines, raw materials, and other resources because they help produce goods and services. *The demand for a resource exists because there is a demand for goods that the resource helps to produce. The demand for each resource is thus a **derived demand**; it is derived from the demand of consumers for products.*

For example, a service station hires mechanics because customers demand repair service, not because the service station owner receives benefits simply from having mechanics around. If customers did not demand repair service, mechanics would not be employed for long. Similarly, the demand for such inputs as carpenters, plumbers, lumber, and glass windows is derived from the demand of consumers for houses and other consumer products these resources help to make. Most resources contribute to the production of numerous goods. For example, glass is used to produce windows, ornaments, dishes, light bulbs, and mirrors, among other things. The total demand for a resource is the sum of the derived demand for it in each of its uses.

The demand curve for a resource shows the amount of the resource that will be used at different prices. As **Exhibit 23–2** illustrates, there will be an inverse relationship between the price of a resource and the amount demanded of it. There are two major reasons why less of a resource will be demanded as its price increases: (1) producers will turn to substitute resources and (2) consumers will buy less of goods that become more expensive as the result of higher resource costs. Let us take a closer look at each of these factors.

Derived demand
Demand for an item based on the demand for products the item helps to produce. The demand for resources is a derived demand.

SUBSTITUTION IN PRODUCTION. *Firms will use the input combination that minimizes their cost. When the price of a resource goes up, cost-conscious firms will turn to lower-cost substitutes and cut back on their use of the more expensive resource.*

Typically, there are many ways producers can reduce their use of a more expensive resource. For example, if the price of oak lumber increases, furniture manufacturers will use other wood varieties, metals, and plastics more intensely. Similarly, if the price of copper tubing increases, construction firms and plumbers will substitute plastic pipe for the more expensive tubing. Sometimes producers will alter the style and dimensions of a product in order to conserve on the use of a more expensive resource. In other cases, a shift in location may play a role in the substitution process. For example, if prices of office space and land increase in the downtown area of a large city, firms may move to the suburbs in order to cut back on their use of the more expensive resource.

The degree to which firms will be able to reduce their use of a more expensive resource will vary. The easier it is to turn to substitute factors, the more elastic the demand for a resource. *Other things constant, the more (and better) substitute resources that are available, the more elastic the demand for the resource.*

SUBSTITUTION IN CONSUMPTION. An increase in the price of a resource will lead to higher costs of production and thus higher prices for the products that the input helps to produce. Faced with these higher prices, *consumers* will turn to substitutes and cut back on their purchases of the more expensive products. In turn, a smaller quantity of resources (including less of the one that rose in price) will be required to produce the smaller amount demanded by consumers at the higher price.

The experience of the American automobile industry in the early 1980s illustrates the importance of this substitution-in-consumption effect. Throughout much of the 1970s, wages in the domestic auto industry increased quite rapidly. The higher wages placed upward pressure on the prices of American-made automobiles. However, as auto prices rose, many consumers switched to substitute products, particularly foreign-produced automobiles. American auto sales declined, causing a reduction in the quantity of labor demanded (and employment) in the automobile industry.

Other things constant, the more elastic the demand for the product, the more elastic the demand for the resource. This relationship stems from the derived nature of resource demand. An increase in the price of a product for which the demand is highly elastic will cause a sharp reduction in the sales of the good. There will thus also be a relatively sharp decline in the demand for the resources used to produce the good.

TIME AND THE DEMAND FOR RESOURCES

It takes time for producers to adjust fully to a change in the price of a resource. Typically, a producer will be unable to alter a production process or the design of a product immediately to conserve on the use of a more expensive input or to use more efficiently an input whose price has declined. Consumers may also

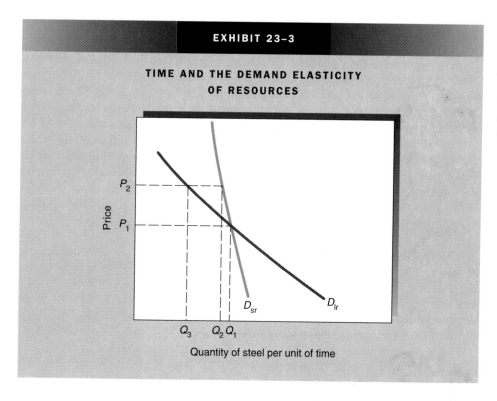

EXHIBIT 23-3

TIME AND THE DEMAND ELASTICITY OF RESOURCES

An increase in the price of steel will lead to a much larger reduction in consumption in the long run than in the short run. Typically, the demand for resources will be more inelastic in the short run.

find it difficult to alter their consumption patterns quickly in response to price changes. Thus, the short-run demand for resources is typically less elastic than the demand in the long run.

Using steel as an example, **Exhibit 23-3** illustrates the relationship between time and the demand for resources. Initially, higher steel prices may lead to only a small reduction in usage. If the high price of steel persists, however, automobile manufacturers will alter their designs, moving toward lighter-weight cars that require less steel. Architectural firms will design buildings that permit more substitution of plastics, wood, aluminum, glass, and other resources for steel. Products made with steel will increase in price, which will encourage consumers to find more and more ways to cut back on their use. These and numerous similar adjustments will help conserve on the use of the more expensive steel. It will take time, however, for decision makers to carry out many of these adjustments. Therefore, the demand for steel, like that for most other resources, will be more inelastic in the short run (D_{sr}) than in the long run (D_{lr}).

SHIFTS IN THE DEMAND FOR RESOURCES

The entire demand curve for a resource, like that for a product, may shift, for one of three reasons.

1. A change in the demand for a product will cause a similar change in the demand for the resources used to make the product. Anything that increases the demand for a consumer good simultaneously increases the demand for resources required to make it. Conversely, a decline in product demand will reduce the demand for resources embodied in the product.

Changes in the auto industry provide a good example of the linkage between product and resource demand. During the 1970s the demand for small automobiles increased sharply, primarily because of higher gasoline prices. This increase in demand for small cars led to an increase in demand for workers to produce them. Employment at plants producing small cars expanded during the 1970s, even while autoworkers were being laid off at plants producing large cars. Falling gasoline prices in the mid-1980s reversed this situation. Propelled by the lower gasoline prices, the demand for larger automobiles increased, while the demand for small cars declined. Reflecting the demand in product markets, employment at automobile plants making full-size cars expanded, while employment at plants producing small cars fell.

2. Changes in the productivity of a resource will alter the demand for the resource. The higher the productivity of a resource, the greater will be the demand for it. Several factors combine to determine the productivity of a resource. First, the **marginal product (MP)** of any resource will depend on the amount of other resources with which it is working. In general, additional capital will tend to increase the productivity of labor. For example, someone with a lawn mower can cut more grass than the same person with a pair of scissors. A student working with a textbook, class notes, and tutor can learn more economics during a semester than the same student without these tools. The quantity and quality of the tools with which we work significantly affect our productivity.

> **Marginal product (MP)**
> *The change in total output that results from the employment of one additional unit of a factor of production—one workday of skilled labor, for example.*

Second, technological advances can improve the productivity of resources, including labor. Advances in the computer industry illustrate this point. Working with computer technology, an accountant and a data-entry person can maintain business records and create bookkeeping reports that previously would have required 10 to 15 workers. Improvements in word-processing equipment have vastly increased the productivity of typists, journalists, lawyers, and writers. Similarly, computers have substantially increased the productivity of typesetters, telephone operators, quality-control technicians, and workers in many other occupations.

Third, improvements in the quality (skill level) of a resource will increase productivity and therefore the demand for the resource. As workers obtain valuable new knowledge and/or upgrade their skills, they enhance their productivity. In essence, such workers move into a different skill category, one where demand is greater.

All these factors help explain why wage rates in the United States, Canada, Western Europe, and Japan are higher than in most other areas of the world. Given the skill level of workers, the technology, and the capital equipment with which they work, individuals in these countries produce more goods and services per hour of labor. The demand for labor (relative to supply) is greater because of the high labor productivity. Essentially, the workers' greater productivity leads to higher wage rates.

3. A change in the price of a related resource will affect the demand for the original resource. A rise in the price of the resource will cause the demand for *substitute* resources to expand. For example, when the price of lumber increases, the demand for bricks will increase as home builders switch to building more brick homes and fewer wood homes. Conversely, an increase in the price of a resource that is a complement to a given resource will decrease the demand for the given resource. Thus, higher prices for lumber would most likely cause the demand for nails, which are used to hold wood in place, to fall.

MARGINAL PRODUCTIVITY AND THE FIRM'S HIRING DECISION

How does a producer decide whether to employ additional units of a resource? We noted previously that the marginal product of a resource is the increase in output that results when the employment of that resource is expanded by one unit. The resource's marginal product multiplied by the marginal revenue of the product being produced yields what is known as the **marginal revenue product (MRP).** The *MRP* is simply the change in the firm's total revenue brought about by the employment of one extra unit of a resource. Thus, the *MRP* reveals how much is added to the firm's revenue by the employment of the additional unit of the resource.

Marginal revenue product (MRP)
The change in the total revenue of a firm that results from the employment of one additional unit of a factor of production. The marginal-revenue product of an input is equal to its marginal product multiplied by the marginal revenue (price) of the good or service produced.

EMPLOYMENT OF A VARIABLE RESOURCE WITH A FIXED RESOURCE

A profit-maximizing firm will, of course, continue to expand output as long as marginal cost is less than marginal revenue. This rule can be generalized to include the firm's employment of resources. Since firms are usually *price takers* (meaning they are too small to affect the market price) when they buy resources, the marginal cost of the resource is its price. Firms maximize profits by hiring units of a resource so long as the employment of each additional unit adds more to the firm's revenues than it adds to the firm's cost. *Thus, profit maximizing firms will expand their employment of each variable resource until the **MRP** of the resource (the firm's additional revenue generated by the resource) is just equal to the price of the resource (the firm's marginal cost). This profit-maximization rule applies to all firms, price takers and price searchers alike.*

The marginal product of a resource multiplied by the selling price of the product yields the resource's **value marginal product (VMP).** When a firm sells its product in a purely competitive market, the selling price and the marginal revenue of the product are equal. Under pure competition, therefore, the *MRP* of a resource is equal to its *VMP*. What if the firm is not a perfect competitor? When the firm confronts a downward-sloping demand curve for its product, the marginal revenue of the product will be less than its price. When this is the case, the *MRP* of a resource will be less than its *VMP*.

Exhibit 23–4 illustrates how a firm decides how much of a resource to employ. Compute-Accounting, Inc., uses computer equipment and data-entry operators to supply clients with monthly accounting statements. The firm is a

Value marginal product (VMP)
The marginal product of a resource multiplied by the selling price of the product it helps to produce. Under pure competition, a firm's marginal revenue product (MRP) will be equal to the value marginal product (VMP).

EXHIBIT 23–4

SHORT-RUN DEMAND SCHEDULE OF A FIRM

UNITS OF VARIABLE FACTOR (DATA-ENTRY OPERATORS) (1)	TOTAL OUTPUT (ACCOUNTING STATEMENTS PROCESSED PER WEEK) (2)	MARGINAL PRODUCT (CHANGE IN COLUMN 2 DIVIDED BY CHANGE IN COLUMN 1) (3)	SALES PRICE PER STATEMENT (4)	TOTAL REVENUE (2) × (4) (5)	MRP (3) × (4) (6)
0	0.0	—	$200	$ 0	—
1	5.0	5.0	200	1,000	1,000
2	9.0	4.0	200	1,800	800
3	12.0	3.0	200	2,400	600
4	14.0	2.0	200	2,800	400
5	15.5	1.5	200	3,100	300
6	16.5	1.0	200	3,300	200
7	17.0	0.5	200	3,400	100

Compute-Accounting, Inc., uses computer technology and data-entry operators to provide accounting services in a competitive market. For each accounting statement processed, the firm receives a $200 fee (column 4). Given the firm's current fixed capital, column 2 shows how total output changes as additional data-entry operators are hired. The marginal revenue product (MRP) schedule (column 6) indicates how hiring an additional operator affects the total revenue of the firm. Since a profit-maximizing firm will hire an additional employee if, and only if, the employee adds more to revenues than to costs, the marginal revenue product curve is the firm's short-run demand curve for the resource (see Exhibit 23–5).

price taker: it sells its service in a competitive market for $200 per statement. Given the fixed quantity of computer equipment owned by Compute-Accounting, column 2 relates the employment of data-entry operators to the expected total output (quantity of accounting statements). One data-entry operator can process five statements per week. When two operators are employed, nine statements can be completed. Column 2 indicates how total output is expected to change as additional data-entry operators are employed. Column 3 presents the marginal product schedule for data-entry operators. Column 6, the *MRP* schedule, shows how the employment of each additional operator affects total revenue.

Since Compute-Accounting is a price taker, the marginal revenue product and the value marginal product of labor are equal. Thus, the marginal revenue product of labor (column 6) can be calculated by multiplying the marginal product (column 3) times the sales price of an accounting statement (column 4).

How does Compute-Accounting decide how many operators to employ? As additional operators are employed, the output of processed statements (column 2) will increase, which will expand total revenue (column 5). Employment of

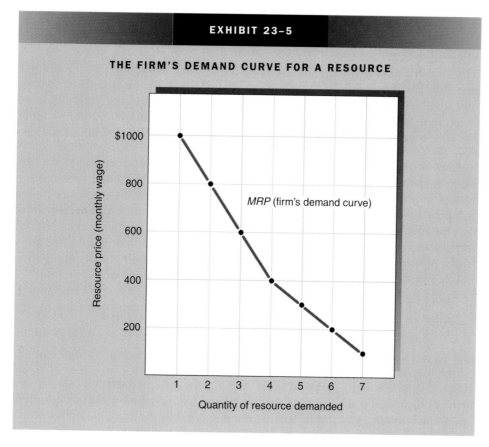

EXHIBIT 23–5

THE FIRM'S DEMAND CURVE FOR A RESOURCE

MRP (firm's demand curve)

Resource price (monthly wage)

Quantity of resource demanded

The firm's demand curve for a resource will reflect the marginal revenue product (MRP) of the resource. In the short run, it will slope downward because the marginal product of the resource will fall as more of it is used with a fixed amount of other resources. The location of the MRP curve will depend on (1) the price of the product, (2) the productivity of the resource, and (3) the quantity of other factors working with the resource.

additional operators, though, will also add to production costs because the operators must be paid. Applying the profit-maximization rule, Compute-Accounting will hire additional operators as long as their employment adds more to revenues than to costs. This will be the case as long as the *MRP* (Exhibit 23–4, column 6) of the data-entry operators exceeds their wage rate. Thus, as **Exhibit 23–5** illustrates, the *MRP* curve of operators is also the firm's short-run demand curve for the resource.[3] At a weekly wage of $1,000, Compute-Accounting would hire only one operator. If the weekly wage dropped to $800, two operators would be hired. At still lower wage rates, additional operators would be hired.

The location of the firm's *MRP* curve depends on (1) the price of the product, (2) the productivity of the resource, and (3) the amount of other resources with which the resource is working. Changes in any one of these three factors will cause the *MRP* curve to shift. For example, if Compute-Accounting obtained additional computer equipment that made it possible for the operators to complete more statements each week, the *MRP* curve for labor would increase. This increase in the quantity of the other resources working with labor would increase labor's productivity.

---

[3]Strictly speaking, this is true only for a variable resource that is employed with a fixed amount of another factor.

EMPLOYMENT LEVELS WHEN THERE ARE NUMEROUS FACTORS OF PRODUCTION

Thus far, we have analyzed the firm's hiring decision assuming that it employed one variable resource (labor) and one fixed resource. Production, though, usually involves the use of many resources. How should these resources be combined to produce the product? We can answer this question by considering either the conditions for profit maximization or the conditions for cost minimization.

PROFIT MAXIMIZATION WHEN MULTIPLE RESOURCES ARE EMPLOYED. The same decision-making considerations apply when the firm employs several factors of production. The profit-maximizing firm will expand its employment of a resource as long as the *MRP* of the resource exceeds its employment cost. If we assume that resources are perfectly divisible, the profit-maximizing decision rule implies that, in equilibrium, the *MRP* of each resource will be equal to the price of the resource. Therefore, the following conditions will exist for the profit-maximizing firm:

MRP of skilled labor $= P_{SL}$ (wage rate of skilled labor)
MRP of unskilled labor $= P_{UL}$ (wage rate of unskilled labor)
MRP of machine A $= P_M$ (explicit or implicit rental price of machine A)

and so on, for all other factors.

COST MINIMIZATION WHEN MULTIPLE RESOURCES ARE EMPLOYED. If the firm is maximizing profits, clearly it must produce the profit-maximizing output at the least possible cost. If the firm is minimizing costs, the marginal dollar expenditure for each resource will have the same impact on output as every other marginal resource expenditure. *Factors of production will be employed such that the marginal product per last dollar spent on each factor is the same for all factors.*

To see why, consider a situation in which a dollar expenditure on labor caused output to rise by ten units, whereas an additional dollar expenditure on machines generated only a five-unit expansion in output. Under these circumstances, five more units of output (at no added cost) would result if the firm spent $1 less on machines and $1 more on labor. The firm's *per unit* cost would be reduced if it substituted labor for machines.

If the marginal dollar spent on one resource increases output by a larger amount than a dollar expenditure on other resources, costs can always be reduced by substituting resources with a high marginal product per dollar expenditure for those with a low one. This substitution continues to reduce unit costs (and add profit) until the marginal product per dollar expenditure is equalized—that is, until the resource combination that minimizes cost is attained. This equality will eventually be achieved through this substitution because as additional units of a resource are hired, its marginal product will fall. When this condition is true, the proportional relationship between the price of each resource and its marginal product will be equal for all resources.

Therefore, the following condition exists when per unit costs are minimized:

$$\frac{MP \text{ of skilled labor}}{Price \text{ of skilled labor}} = \frac{MP \text{ of unskilled labor}}{Price \text{ of unskilled labor}} = \frac{MP \text{ of machine A}}{Price \text{ (rental value) of machine A}}$$

and so on, for the other factors.

This relation, which will be present if a firm is minimizing its per unit cost of production, indicates why wage differences across skill categories will tend to reflect productivity differences. If skilled workers are twice as productive as unskilled workers, their wage rates will tend toward twice the wage rates of unskilled workers. For example, suppose that a construction firm hiring workers to hang doors is choosing among skilled and unskilled workers. If skilled door hangers can complete four doors per hour, while unskilled workers can hang only two doors per hour, a cost-minimizing firm would hire only skilled workers—as long as their wages are less than twice the wages of unskilled workers. On the other hand, only unskilled workers would be hired if the wages of skilled workers are more than twice that of unskilled workers. With competition, wages across skill categories will tend to mirror productivity differences. (See Addendum on page 957 for a graphic presentation of the relationship between resource use and cost minimization.)

Low wages do not necessarily mean low cost; it is not always cheaper to hire the lowest wage workers. Our marginal productivity theory explains why this is true. It is not just wages, but rather wages *relative to productivity* that matter. If the wages of skilled workers are twice those of unskilled workers, it will still be cheaper to hire additional skilled workers if their marginal productivity (output per hour) is more than twice that of the unskilled workers.

THE CENTRAL PROPOSITION OF THE MARGINAL PRODUCTIVITY THEORY OF EMPLOYMENT

The central proposition of the marginal productivity theory of resource employment is that firms minimize their per unit costs of production when they hire additional units of each resource as long as the units' marginal productivity generates revenues in excess of costs. Firms that minimize per unit costs and maximize profit will never pay more for a unit of input, whether it is skilled labor, a machine, or an acre of land, than the input is worth to them. The worth of a unit of input to the firm is determined by how much additional revenue (marginal revenue product) is expected when the unit is used.

In the real world, it is sometimes difficult to measure the marginal product of a factor. And, as we have indicated, the marginal product of a resource is influenced by the other factors with which it is employed. Production is a team effort involving joint and interdependent use of resources. We do not mean to imply that business decision makers will necessarily think in terms of equating the marginal product/price ratio (MP_i/P_i) for each factor of production. Their thought process may well be something like, "Can we reduce costs by using more of one resource and less of another?" Real-world business decision makers may use experience, trial and error, and intuitive rules as they seek to minimize costs.

Regardless of the methods and procedures used, however, when a firm maximizes profits and minimizes costs, the marginal product/price ratio will be equal for all factors of production. The results will be as if the firms had followed the cost-minimization decision-making rules presented earlier. Furthermore, competitive forces will more or less force firms to approximate these minimum cost conditions. Firms that fail to do so will be unable to compete successfully with rivals achieving lower per unit costs.

The marginal-productivity theory explains the conditions underlying the demand for resources. Of course, resource prices will also be influenced by the supply of resources. We now turn to that topic.

SUPPLY OF RESOURCES

In essence, our analysis of resource demand concludes that employers will hire a resource so long as they can gain by doing so. The same basic postulate also applies to resource suppliers. Resource owners will supply their services to an employer only if they perceive that the benefits of doing so exceed their costs (the value of the other things they could do with their time or resources). Thus, in order to attract factors of production, employers must offer resource owners at least as good a deal as they can get elsewhere. For example, if an employer does not offer a potential employee a package of income payments and working conditions that is as good as or better than the employee can get elsewhere, the employer will be unable to attract the employee.

Resource owners will supply their services to those who offer them the best employment alternative, all factors considered. Other things constant, as the price of a specific resource (for example, engineering services, craft labor, or wheat farmland) increases, the incentive of potential suppliers to provide the resource increases.

An increase in the price of a resource will attract potential resource suppliers into the market. A decrease will cause them to shift into other activities. Therefore, as **Exhibit 23–6** illustrates, the supply curve for a specific resource will slope upward to the right.

SHORT-RUN SUPPLY

As in the case of demand, the supply response in resource markets may vary between the short run and long run. In the short run, there is insufficient time to alter the availability of a resource through investment in human and physical capital. In contrast, in the long run, resource suppliers have time to fully adjust their investment choices to a change in resource prices. Let us begin by considering the supply response in the short run.

Most resources have alternative uses; they can be used to perform a variety of functions. Those that can be easily transferred from one use to another in response to changing price incentives are said to have high **resource mobility.** The supply of such factors to any specific use will be highly elastic. Factors that have few alternative uses are said to be immobile and will have a relatively inelastic short-run supply.

Consider the mobility of labor. When labor skills can be transferred easily and quickly, human capital is highly mobile. Within a skill category (for example, plumber, store manager, accountant, or secretary), labor will be highly mobile within the same geographic area. Movements between geographic areas and from one skill category to another are more costly to accomplish. Labor will thus be less mobile for movements of this variety.

What about the mobility of land? Land is highly mobile among uses when location does not matter. For example, the same land can often be used to raise

Resource mobility
A term that refers to the ease with which factors of production are able to move among alternative uses. Resources that can easily be transferred to a different use or location are said to be highly mobile. In contrast, when a resource has few alternative uses, it is immobile. For example, the skills of a trained rodeo rider would be highly immobile, since they cannot be easily transferred to other lines of work.

EXHIBIT 23-6

THE SUPPLY OF A RESOURCE

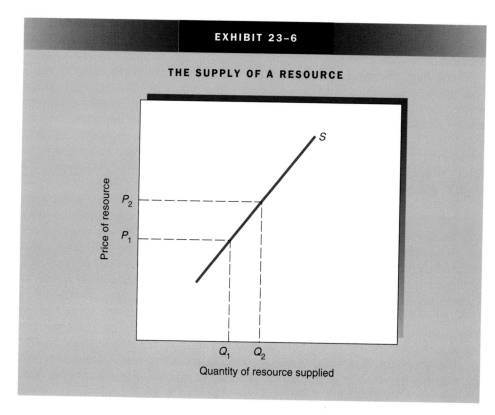

As the price of a resource increases, individuals have a greater incentive to supply it. Therefore, a direct relationship will exist between the price of a resource and the quantity supplied.

corn, wheat, soybeans, or oats. Thus, the supply of land allocated to production of each of these commodities will be highly responsive to changes in their relative prices. Undeveloped land on the outskirts of cities is particularly mobile among uses. In addition to its value in agriculture, such land might be quickly subdivided and used for a housing development or a shopping center. Because land is totally immobile physically, one might think that its supply is unresponsive to changes in price that reflect the desirability of a location. This is true; however, by building multiple-story buildings, the supply of usable area can be expanded, even in a specific location.

Machines are typically not very mobile among uses. A machine developed to produce airplane wings is seldom of much use in the production of automobiles, appliances, or other products. Steel mills cannot easily be converted to produce aluminum. There are, of course, some exceptions. Trucks can typically be used to haul a variety of products. Building space can often be converted from one use to another. In the short run, however, immobility and inelasticity of supply characterize much of our physical capital.

LONG-RUN SUPPLY

In the long run, the supply of resources can change substantially. Machines wear out, human skills depreciate, and even the fertility of land declines with use and erosion. These factors reduce the supply of resources. On the other hand, investment can expand the supply of productive resources. Additional resources can be used to expand the stock of machines, buildings, and durable assets.

Correspondingly, current resources can be used to train, educate, and develop the skills of future labor-force participants. The supply of both physical and human resources in the long run is determined primarily by investment and depreciation.

Price incentives will, of course, influence the investment decisions of firms and individuals. Considering both monetary and nonmonetary factors, investors will choose those alternatives they believe to be most advantageous. Higher resource prices will induce utility-maximizing individuals to undertake investments that will permit them to supply more of the resource. In contrast, lower resource prices will reduce the incentive of individuals to invest and expand the future supply of those resources. Thus, there is a direct relationship between the price of a resource and quantity supplied in the long run.

The theory of long-run resource supply is general. The expected payoff from an investment alternative will influence the decisions of investors in human as well as physical capital. For example, the higher salaries of physical and space scientists employed in the expanding space program during the early 1960s induced an increasing number of college students to enter these fields. Similarly, attractive earning opportunities in accounting and law led to an increase in investment and quantity supplied in these areas during the period from 1965 to 1975. More recently, as the computer revolution spread throughout our economy, high salaries for programmers, systems analysts, and computer technicians led to an expansion in the number of students training for jobs in these areas.

The long run, of course, is not a specified length of time. Investment can increase the availability of some resources fairly quickly. For example, it does not take very long to train additional over-the-road truck drivers. Thus, in the absence of barriers to entry, the quantity of truck drivers supplied will expand rapidly in response to higher wages. However, the period between expansion in investment and an increase in quantity supplied is substantially longer for some resources. It takes a long time to train physicians, dentists, lawyers, and pharmacists. Higher earnings in these occupations may have only a small impact on their current availability. Additional investment will go into these areas, but it will typically be several years before there is a substantial increase in the quantity supplied in response to higher earnings for these resources.

Given time, investment in physical and human capital can substantially expand the availability of a resource. Therefore, the supply of a resource will be much more elastic in the long run than in the short run. This is particularly true when there is a lengthy gestation period between an increase in investment and an actual increase in the availability of the resource.

Using engineering services as an example, **Exhibit 23–7** illustrates the relationship between the short- and long-run supply of resources. An increase in the price of engineering services (the wage rate of engineers) will result in some immediate increase in quantity supplied. Persons currently employed as engineers may choose to work more hours. In addition, the higher wage may induce workers with engineering skills currently employed in mathematics, physics, or similar fields to switch to engineering. Although these adjustments are important, they may fail to substantially increase the quantity supplied in the short run. With time, however, the more attractive earning opportunities in engineering will raise the level of investment in human capital in this area. More students will enter engineering programs. Because it takes time to acquire an engineering degree, several years may pass before the additional degrees exert a major impact on supply. Nevertheless, the expanded human capital investments

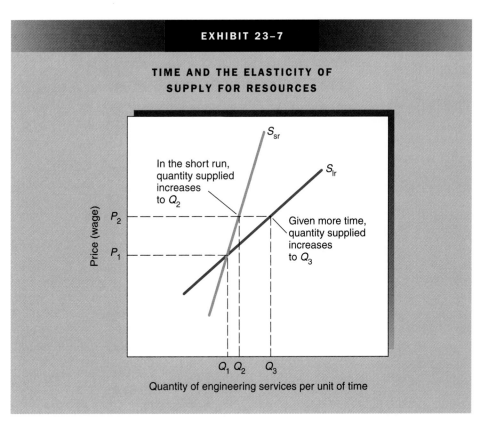

EXHIBIT 23-7

**TIME AND THE ELASTICITY OF
SUPPLY FOR RESOURCES**

S_{sr}

In the short run,
quantity supplied
increases
to Q_2

S_{lr}

Price (wage)

P_2

P_1

Given more time,
quantity supplied
increases
to Q_3

Q_1 Q_2 Q_3

Quantity of engineering services per unit of time

*The supply of engineering
services (and other resources
that require a substantial
period of time between current
investment and expansion in
the future quantity supplied)
will be more elastic in
the long run than in the
short run.*

will eventually exert important effects. Thus, in the long run, the supply of engineering services may be quite elastic, even though supply is highly inelastic in the short run.

SUPPLY, DEMAND, AND RESOURCE PRICES

In a market economy, resource prices will be determined by the forces of supply and demand. When factor prices are free to vary, resource prices will bring the choices of buyers and sellers into line with each other. Continuing with our example of engineers, **Exhibit 23–8** illustrates how the forces of supply and demand push the market price toward equilibrium, where quantity demanded and quantity supplied are equal. Equilibrium is achieved when the price (wage rate) for engineering services is P_1. Given the market conditions illustrated by Exhibit 23–8, an excess supply is present if the price of engineering services exceeds P_1. Some engineers will be unable to find jobs at the above-equilibrium wage. This excess supply of engineers will cause the wage rate for engineers to fall, thereby pushing the market toward equilibrium. In contrast, if the resource price is less than P_1, excess demand is present. Employers are unable to obtain the desired amount of engineering services at a below-equilibrium resource

The market demand for a resource, such as engineering services, is a downward-sloping curve, reflecting the declining MRP of the resource. The market supply curve slopes upward since higher resource prices (wage rates) will induce individuals to supply more of the resource. Resource price P₁ brings the choices of buyers and sellers into harmony. At the equilibrium price (P₁), the quantity demanded will just equal the quantity supplied.

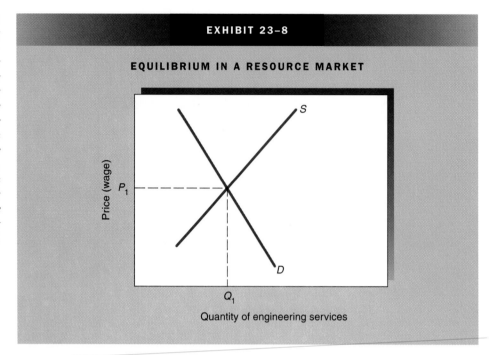

EXHIBIT 23–8

EQUILIBRIUM IN A RESOURCE MARKET

price. Rather than doing without the resource, employers will attempt to hire engineers away from other firms by bidding the price up to P_1 and thereby eliminating the excess demand.

How will a resource market adjust to an unexpected change in market conditions? Suppose that there is a sharp increase in the demand for houses, apartments, and office buildings. The increase in demand for these products will also increase the demand for resources required for their construction. Thus, the demand for resources like steel, lumber, brick, and the labor services of carpenters, architects, and construction engineers will increase. **Exhibit 23–9** provides a graphic illustration of both the increase in demand for new houses and buildings (frame a) and the accompanying increase in demand for construction engineers. The market demand for the services of construction engineers increases from D_1 to D_2 (frame b) and initially there is a sharp rise in their wages (price increase from P_1 to P_2). The higher wages will induce additional people to undertake the education and training necessary to become a construction engineer. With the passage of time, the entry of the newly trained construction engineers will increase the elasticity of the resource supply curve. As these new construction engineers eventually enter the occupation, the supply curve will become more elastic (S_{lr} rather than S_{sr}), which will place downward pressure on wages in the occupation (the move from b to c). Therefore, as Exhibit 23–9b illustrates, the long-run price increase (to P_3) will be less than the short-run increase (to P_2).

The supply response and market adjustment for other resources—physical as well as human—will be similar. For example, an unexpected construction boom will generally cause sharp initial increases in the prices of lumber, bricks, and other building materials. With time, however, additional investment will increase the availability of these resources and moderate the increase in their

EXHIBIT 23–9

ADJUSTING TO DYNAMIC CHANGE

(a) Product market—new houses and commercial buildings

(b) Resource market—services of construction engineers

An increase in demand for housing and commercial buildings (frame a) will lead to an increase in demand for the services of construction engineers (frame b) and other resources used in the construction industry. Initially, the increase in the resource price will be substantial (move from a to b), particularly if the supply of the resource is highly *inelastic in the short run. The higher resource price will attract additional human capital investment and, with time, the re-source supply curve will become more elastic, which will moderate the price (or wage) increase of the resource (move from b to c).*

price, just as additional investment in human capital eventually moderated the wage increases of the construction engineers.

The market adjustment to an unexpected reduction in demand for a resource is the same. The price falls farther in the short run than in the long run. At the lower price, some resource suppliers will use their talents in other areas, and the incentive for potential new suppliers to offer the resource will be reduced. Thus, with time, the quantity of the resource supplied will decline, making the decline in price more moderate. Those with the poorest alternatives (that is, lowest opportunity cost) will continue to provide the resource at the lower prices. Those with better alternatives will move to other areas.

Pulling things together, our analysis indicates that prices in resource markets play a vitally important role. These prices coordinate the actions of the firms demanding factors of production and the households supplying them. Resource prices provide users with both information on scarcity and the incentive to economize on resource use when producing output. They also provide suppliers with an incentive to train for and provide resources—particularly

APPLICATIONS IN ECONOMICS

THE IMPORTANCE OF FACTOR MARKETS: THE CASE OF ENERGY

Our analysis indicates that resource markets encourage conservation and direct users away from more expensive resources. Could these functions be accomplished as well without the use of price incentives? Examination of energy use under central planning indicates that it would be difficult to achieve a similar response without the information and incentives generated by prices in markets.

Economist Mikhail Bernstam, in a book written for London's Institute of Economic Affairs, examined the efficiency of energy use under both central planning and market allocation. He used data from the 1980s, before the fall of socialist regimes in Europe, and the results of his research are striking. The centrally planned socialist economies used nearly three times as much energy per unit of GDP as economies employing factor markets. The comparison holds also for countries that are similar except for their use of markets. Centrally planned North Korea used three times as much energy per unit of GDP

as South Korea, where factor markets and resource prices distributed energy. And centrally planned East Germany consumed 3.5 times as much energy per unit of output as West Germany.[1]

Energy prices rose sharply during the 1973–1980 period. Bernstam found that in North America and Europe, per capita energy consumption (which had been increasing) began to decline during the period following the price increases of the 1970s. Resource markets in these areas directed users toward substitutes and away from the more expensive energy resources during the post-1973 period. In contrast, there was no evidence of a similar response on the part of central planners in the former Soviet Union. Per capita energy consumption continued to rise in the former Soviet Union throughout the 1970s and 1980s.

---

[1]Mikhail S. Bernstam, *The Wealth of Nations and the Environment* (London: Institute of Economic Affairs, 1991).

those that are intensely demanded by users. Without the use of resource markets and the price incentives they provide, efficient use and wise conservation of resources is unlikely. (See the Applications in Economics feature for evidence on this point.)

LOOKING AHEAD

In this chapter we presented the theoretical underpinnings of factor markets. This analysis can be applied to a broad range of economic issues. The next chapter will focus on the labor market and the determination of wage rates. Later, we will focus on the capital market and the allocation of resources over time. The operation of these two markets plays an important role in determining the distribution of income, a topic that will also be analyzed in detail in a subsequent chapter.

CHAPTER SUMMARY

1. Factor markets, where productive resources and services are bought and sold, help to determine what is produced, how it is produced, and how the distribution of

income (output) is accomplished. Two broad classes of productive resources exist—nonhuman capital and human capital. Both are durable in the sense that they will last into the future, thereby enhancing future productive capabilities. Both yield income to their owners. Investment can expand the future supply of both.

2. The demand for resources is derived from the demand for products that the resources help to produce. The quantity of a resource demanded is inversely related to its price. Two reasons explain why, if the price of a resource increases, less of it will be used. First, producers will substitute other resources for the now more expensive input (substitution in production). Second, the higher resource price will lead to higher costs for products that the resource helps to make. In turn, the higher costs will lead to higher prices and a reduction in the purchases of these goods (substitution in consumption).

3. The short-run market demand curve will be more inelastic than the long-run curve. It will take time for producers to adjust their production process to use more of the resources that have become cheaper and less of the ones that are more expensive.

4. The demand curve for a resource, like the demand for a product, may shift. The major factors that can increase the demand for a resource are (a) an increase in demand for products that use the resource, (b) an increase in the productivity of the resource, and (c) an increase in the price of substitute resources.

5. Profit-maximizing firms will hire additional units of a resource as long as the marginal revenue product (MRP) of the resource exceeds its hiring cost, usually the price of the resource. If resources are perfectly divisible, firms will expand their usage of each resource until the MRP of each resource is just equal to its price.

6. When a firm is minimizing its costs, it will employ each factor of production up to the point at which the marginal product per last dollar spent on the factor is equal for all factors. This condition implies that the marginal product of labor divided by the price of labor must equal the marginal product of capital (machines) divided by the price of capital, and that this ratio (MP_i/P_i) must be the same for all other inputs used by the firm. When real-world decision makers minimize per unit costs, the outcome will be as if they had followed these mathematical procedures, even though they may not consciously do so.

7. Resource owners will use their factors of production in the manner that they consider most personally advantageous. Many resources will be relatively immobile in the short run. The less mobile a resource is, the more inelastic its short-run supply. There will be a positive relationship, however, between amount supplied and resource price, even in the short run.

8. In the long run, investment and depreciation will alter the availability of resources. Resource owners will shift factors of production toward areas in which resource prices have risen and away from areas in which resource prices have fallen. Thus, the long-run supply will be more elastic than the short-run supply.

9. The prices of resources will be determined by both supply and demand. The demand for a resource will reflect the demand for products that it helps to produce. The supply of resources will reflect the human and physical capital investment decisions of individuals and firms.

10. Changing resource prices will influence the decisions of users and suppliers alike. Higher resource prices give users a greater incentive to turn to substitutes and suppliers a greater incentive to provide more of the resource. Since these adjustments take time, when the demand for a resource expands, the price will usually rise more in the short run than in the long run. Similarly, when there is a fall in resource demand, price will decline more in the short run than in the long run.

CRITICAL ANALYSIS QUESTIONS

1. What is the meaning of the expression "invest in human capital"? In what sense is the decision to invest in human capital like the decision to invest in physical capital? Is human capital investment risky? Explain.

2. "The demand for resources is a derived demand." What is meant by that statement? Why is the employment of a resource inversely related to its price?

*3. Use the information of Exhibit 23–4 to answer the following:
   a. How many employees (operators) would Compute-Accounting hire at a weekly wage of $250 if it were attempting to maximize profits?
   b. What would the firm's maximum profit be if its fixed costs were $1,500 per week?
   c. Suppose there was a decline in demand for accounting services, reducing the market price per monthly statement to $150. At this demand level, how many employees would Compute-Accounting hire at $250 per week in the short run? Would Compute-Accounting be able to stay in business at the lower market price? Explain.

*4. Are productivity gains the major source of higher wages? If so, how does one account for the rising real wages of barbers, who by and large have used the same technique for a half-century? (Hint: Do not forget opportunity cost and supply.)

5. Are the following statements both correct? Are they inconsistent with each other? Explain.
   a. "Firms will hire a resource only if they can make money by doing so."
   b. "In a market economy, each resource will tend to be paid according to its marginal product. Highly productive resources will command high prices, whereas less productive resources will command lower prices."

6. "However desirable they might be from an equity viewpoint, programs designed to reduce wage differentials will necessarily reduce the incentive of people to act efficiently and use their productive abilities in those areas where demand is greatest relative to supply." Do you agree or disagree? Why?

7. Suppose that you were the manager of a large retail store that was currently experiencing a shoplifting problem. Every hour, approximately $15 worth of merchandise was being stolen from your store. Suppose that a security guard would completely eliminate the shoplifting in your store. If you were interested in maximizing your profits, should you hire a security guard if the wage rate of security guards was $20 per hour? Why or why not?

*8. A dressmaker uses labor and capital (sewing machines) to produce dresses in a competitive market. Suppose the last unit of labor hired cost $1,000 per month and increased output by 100 dresses. The last unit of capital hired (rented) cost $500 per month and increased output by 80 dresses. Is the dressmaker minimizing cost? If not, what changes need to be made?

9. Suppose that the wages of workers in an industry in Mexico are one-fifth of the wages of workers in that same industry in the United States. Does this mean that the Mexican firms in that industry will have lower costs than firms producing in the United States?

*10. "The earnings of engineers, doctors, and lawyers are high because lots of education is necessary to practice in these fields." Evaluate this statement.

11. Other things constant, what impact will a highly elastic demand for a product have on the elasticity of demand for the resources used to produce the product? Explain.

*12. The following chart provides information on a firm that hires labor competitively and sells its product in a competitive market:

UNITS OF LABOR	TOTAL OUTPUT	MARGINAL PRODUCT	PRODUCT PRICE	TOTAL REVENUE	MRP
1	14	___	$5	___	___
2	26	___	$5	___	___
3	37	___	$5	___	___
4	46	___	$5	___	___
5	53	___	$5	___	___
6	58	___	$5	___	___
7	62	___	$5	___	___

a. Fill in the missing columns.
b. How many units of labor would be employed if the market wage rate was $40? Why?
c. What would happen to employment if the wage rate rose to $50? Explain.

13. Leisure Times, Inc., employs skilled workers and capital to install hot tubs. The capital includes the tools and equipment that the workers use to construct and install the tubs. The installation services are sold in a competitive market for $1,200 per hot tub. Leisure Times is able to hire workers for $2,200 per month, including the cost of wages, fringe benefits, and employment taxes. As additional workers are hired, the increase in the number of hot tubs installed is indicated in the table.

NUMBER OF WORKERS EMPLOYED	NUMBER OF HOT TUBS INSTALLED (PER MONTH)
1	5
2	12
3	18
4	23
5	27
6	30
7	32
8	33
9	34

a. Indicate the marginal product and MRP schedules of the workers.
b. What quantity of workers should Leisure Times employ if it is maximizing profit?
c. If a construction boom pushes the wages of skilled workers up to $2,500 per month, how many workers would Leisure Times employ if it is maximizing profit?
d. Suppose that strong demand for hot tubs pushes the price of installation services up to $1,500 per month. How would this affect employment of the skilled workers if the wage rate of the workers remained at $2,500 per month?

14. A recent flyer on a university campus stated that consumers should boycott sugar due to the low wages earned by laborers on sugar cane farms in Florida. Using the notion of derived demand, what impact would a boycott on sugar have on the wages of the farm laborers in the short run? In the long run?

---

*Asterisk denotes questions for which answers are given in Appendix B.

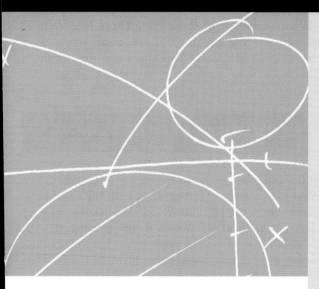

A fair day's-wages for a fair day's-work; it is as just a demand as governed men ever made of governing. It is the everlasting right of man.

THOMAS CARLYLE[1]

---

[1]Thomas Carlyle, *Past and Present*, Book 1, Chapter 3 (Boston: Little and Brown, 1843).

CHAPTER FOCUS

- Why do some people earn more than others?
- Are earnings differences according to race and gender the result of employment discrimination?
- Who pays for fringe benefits? Do government-mandated fringe benefits increase employee compensation?
- Why are wages higher in the United States than in India or China?
- Why do wages increase? Why has the growth of wages and income per capita slowed during the past 25 years?
- Does automation destroy jobs?
- Can we legislate higher wages?

T he earnings of workers reflect the availability of tools (physical capital) and the skills and abilities of individual workers (human capital). Approximately four-fifths of the national income in the United States is earned by employees and self-employed workers. The earnings in these two categories primarily reflect a return to human capital. The other one-fifth—income in the form of interest, rents, and corporate profits—reflects mostly returns to physical capital. These shares to human and physical capital have been relatively constant for several decades (see Illustrated Exhibit IV-E on page 607).

The earnings of U.S. workers are among the highest in the world. However, they vary widely. An unskilled laborer may earn $5.50 per hour, or even less. Lawyers and physicians often earn $100 per hour. Dentists and even economists might receive $60 per hour. What accounts for these differences in earnings? Compared to other countries, why are the earnings of American workers so high? How have earnings changed in recent years? This chapter addresses these topics and related issues.

WHY DO EARNINGS DIFFER?

The earnings of individuals in the same occupation or with the same amount of education often differ substantially. The earnings of persons with the same family background also vary widely. For example, one researcher found that the average earnings differential between brothers was $24,485, compared with $27,120 (figures are in 1995 dollars) for men paired randomly.[2] In addition, the earnings of persons with the same intelligence quotient, level of training, or amount of experience typically differ. How do economists explain these variations? Several factors combine to determine the earning power of an individual. Some seem to be the result of good or bad fortune. Others are clearly the result of conscious decisions made by individuals. In the previous chapter, we analyzed how the market forces of supply and demand operate to determine resource prices. The subject of earnings differentials can be usefully approached within the framework of this model.

If (1) all individuals were homogeneous, (2) all jobs were equally attractive, and (3) workers were perfectly mobile among jobs, the earnings of all employees in a competitive economy would be equal. If, given these conditions, higher wages existed in any area of the economy, the supply of workers to that area would expand until the wage differential was eliminated. Similarly, low wages in any area would cause workers to exit until wages in that area returned to parity. However, the conditions necessary for earnings equality do not exist in the real world. Thus, earnings differentials are present.

EARNINGS DIFFERENTIALS FROM NONHOMOGENEOUS LABOR

Workers differ in several important respects that influence both the supply of and demand for their services.

---

[2]Christopher Jencks, *Inequality* (New York: Basic Books, 1972), p. 220.

EXHIBIT 24-1

DEMAND, SUPPLY, AND WAGE RATES FOR SKILLED AND UNSKILLED WORKERS

(a) Demand for skilled and unskilled labor

(b) Supply of skilled and unskilled labor

(c) Wages of skilled and unskilled labor

The productivity—and therefore marginal product (MP)—of skilled workers is greater than that of unskilled workers. Therefore, as part a illustrates, the demand for skilled workers (D_s) will exceed the demand for unskilled workers (D_u). Education and training generally enhance skills. Since upgrading skills through investments in human capital is costly, the supply of skilled workers (S_s) is smaller than the supply of unskilled workers (part b). As part c illustrates, the wages of skilled workers are high relative to unskilled workers due to the strong demand and small supply of skilled workers relative to unskilled workers. (Note: The quantity of skilled labor employed may be far smaller, far larger, or by accident equal to the quantity of unskilled labor hired.)

WORKER PRODUCTIVITY AND SPECIALIZED SKILLS. The demand for employees who are highly productive is greater than the demand for those who are less productive. Persons who can operate a machine more skillfully, hit a baseball more consistently, or sell life insurance policies with greater regularity will be more valuable to employers. Such employees will have a higher marginal revenue product (*MRP*) than their less-skillful counterparts. As a result, the labor services of the more skillful will command a higher wage in the marketplace.

Worker productivity is the result of a combination of factors, including native ability, parental training, hard work, and investment in human capital. The link between higher productivity and higher earnings provides individuals with the incentive to invest in themselves and thereby upgrade their knowledge and skills. If additional worker productivity did not lead to higher earnings, individuals would have little incentive to incur the direct and indirect cost of productivity-enhancing educational and training programs.

Exhibit 24–1 illustrates the impact of worker productivity and the cost of investment in human capital on the wages of skilled and unskilled workers. Since the productivity of skilled workers exceeds the productivity of unskilled workers, the demand for skilled workers (D_s) exceeds the demand for unskilled workers (D_u). The vertical distance between the two demand curves reflects the higher marginal product (*MP*) of skilled workers relative to the unskilled workers (part a). Since investments in human capital (for example, education or training) are costly, the supply of skilled workers (S_s) will be smaller than the supply of unskilled workers (S_u). The vertical distance between the two supply curves indicates the wage differential that is necessary to compensate workers for the costs incurred in the acquisition of their skills (part b). Wages are determined by demand relative to supply (part c). Since the demand for skilled workers is large, while their supply is small, the equilibrium wage of skilled workers will be high ($20 per hour). In contrast, since the supply of unskilled workers is large relative to the demand, the wages of unskilled workers will be substantially lower ($6 per hour). (Note that, although economic logic tells us why the wages will differ, it does not tell us how many workers will be in each group.)

Of course, native ability and motivation will influence the rate at which an individual can transform education and training into greater productivity. Individuals differ in the amount of valuable skills they develop from a year of education, vocational school, or on-the-job training. We should not expect, therefore, a rigid relationship to exist between years of training (or education) and skill level.

Nevertheless, detailed empirical studies indicate that investment in human capital leads to higher earnings once the person enters the labor force full time. (See Illustrated Exhibit IV-A on page 605 at the beginning of this part for evidence on this point.) In 1994 the mean annual earnings of males age 25 and over, working full time, year-round was $52,193 for those with a college degree, compared to $29,624 for high school graduates. The parallel figure for women college graduates was $33,725 compared to $20,807 for those who only graduated from high school. Some of the additional earnings of college graduates may reflect native ability, intelligence, and motivation. Research, however, indicates that a large proportion of the additional earnings also reflects knowledge and skills acquired as the result of investment in additional education. Economic research has also shown that on-the-job training enhances the earnings of workers.

Investment in human capital and development of specialized skills can protect high-wage workers from the competition of others willing to offer their services at a lower price. Few persons could develop the specialized skills of a Whitney Houston or a Tom Hanks. Similarly, the supply of heart surgeons, trial lawyers, engineers, business entrepreneurs, and many other specialized workers is limited in occupations where specific skills, knowledge, and human-capital investments contribute to job performance. (See the Applications in Economics feature on tournament pay.)

Other things constant, a skilled specialist will command a higher wage than one with less skill, but high skill will not guarantee high wages in the absence of demand. For example, expert harness makers and blacksmiths typically command low wages today.

WORKER PREFERENCES. An important source of earnings differentials that is sometimes overlooked is worker preferences. People have different objectives in life. Some want to make a great deal of money. Many are willing to work long hours, undergo agonizing training and many years of education, and sacrifice social and family life to make money. Others may be "workaholics" because they enjoy their jobs. Still others may be satisfied with enough money to get by on, preferring to spend more time with their family, the Boy Scouts, television, or the local tavern keeper.

Economics does not indicate that one set of worker preferences is more desirable than another, any more than it suggests that people should eat more spinach

TOURNAMENT PAY: EARNINGS IN A WINNER-TAKE-ALL ENVIRONMENT

Star athletes, such as Shaquille O'Neal and Michael Jordan, and entertainers, such as Michael Jackson and Sylvester Stallone, earn $20 million and up per year. Star lawyers, doctors, and business executives also command huge earnings. What factors account for the earnings of these superstars?

THE MARGINAL PRODUCTIVITY THEORY EXPLANATION Marginal productivity theory suggests that a worker's pay is related to his or her marginal revenue product. Do star players and entertainers really generate such huge revenues? When a team signs a major star, the team's ticket sales rise, their television contracts may increase, sales of items containing the team's logo (such as clothes) may rise, and, finally, the team's chances of making it into the playoffs (which yields additional revenues) will improve. Economic studies have found that, in fact, professional sports players have marginal revenue products that are very close to their salaries.[1]

What is the marginal revenue product of a superstar entertainer, such as Arnold Schwarzenegger? How many more people will go see a movie in which Arnold is the star compared to the number who would attend if the lead actor was lesser known and lesser talented? If an additional two or three million people spend five dollars to attend a movie, this would generate $10 million or $15 million of additional revenue. It is easy to see how a star "box office" attraction would provide the company producing the movie with substantial additional revenues. In turn, competitive labor markets will ensure that big stars get paid their marginal revenue product.

What about the large salaries received by CEOs of major corporations? Decisions made by the CEOs of major corporations can and do exert a huge financial impact on the company. If a CEO can substantially reduce a company's losses, or increase its profits, he or she will be rewarded for this productivity in the form of higher earnings. A CEO may be particularly valuable when a company is in trouble, faces new competition, or confronts a changing technological or regulatory environment.

THE TOURNAMENT PAY EXPLANATION There may also be another factor contributing to the huge salaries superstars are able to command. The earnings in some markets resemble tournaments. Only the top-ranked person receives the big payoff, while those who finish second receive much less. This type of compensation is called *tournament pay*.[2] This name refers to reward systems structured like golf tournaments, in which a slight difference in productivity (perhaps one or two shots) is associated with a difference in pay of several hundred thousand dollars.

In this type of environment, workers basically subject themselves to a lottery where the winner (the person with the highest productivity) receives compensation higher than his or her marginal revenue product, while the losers receive less than their marginal revenue product. There are some constraints against how low the compensation of the losers can be, however, because they could find alternative jobs that would pay a salary equal to their marginal revenue product.

Because there is such a large bonus associated with having higher productivity than others in the field, the tournament pay environment creates a strong incentive for potential superstars to expend considerable effort attempting to become the best (or one of only a few top performers). As a result, many people spend long hours developing skills that will increase their chances of becoming a "star" in athletics, entertainment, professions, and business. Is this good or bad? Economics does not answer that question; it merely explains how these markets work.

[1]Paul M. Sommers and Noel Quinton, "Pay and Performance in Major League Baseball: The Case of the First Family of Free Agents," *Journal of Human Resources* (summer 1982): 426–435.

[2]Edward Lazear and Sherwin Rosen, "Rank Order Tournaments as an Optimum Labor Contract," *Journal of Political Economy* 89 (October 1981): 841–864, and Robert Frank and Phillip Cook, *The Winner-Take-All Society* (New York: The Free Press, 1995).

and less pastrami. Economics does indicate, however, that these factors contribute to differences in wages and earnings. Other things constant, persons who are more highly motivated by monetary objectives will be more likely to do the things necessary to command higher wage rates.

Employment discrimination

Unequal treatment of persons on the basis of their race, sex, or religion, restricting their employment and earnings opportunities compared to others of similar productivity. Employment discrimination may stem from the prejudices of employers, consumers, and/or fellow employees.

RACE AND GENDER.   Discrimination on the basis of race or gender contributes to earnings differences among individuals. **Employment discrimination** may directly limit the earnings opportunities of minorities and women. Employment discrimination exists when minority or women employees are treated in a manner different from similarly productive whites or men. Of course, the earnings of minorities or women may differ from those of whites or men, respectively, for reasons other than employment discrimination. Nonemployment discrimination may limit the opportunity of minority groups and women to acquire human capital (for example, access to high-quality education or specialized training) that would enhance both productivity and earnings. Limited opportunities as the result of growing up in a low-income or a single-parent family may also influence skill development and educational achievement. Thus, factors other than employment discrimination will influence earnings differences among individuals according to race or ethnic status. The following section will analyze the impact of employment discrimination in some detail.

EARNINGS DIFFERENTIALS FROM NONHOMOGENEOUS JOBS

Nonpecuniary job characteristics

Working conditions, prestige, variety, location, employee freedom and responsibilities, and other nonwage characteristics of a job that influence how employees evaluate the job.

Compensating wage differentials

Wage differences that compensate workers for risk, unpleasant working conditions, and other undesirable nonpecuniary aspects of a job.

When individuals evaluate employment alternatives, they consider working conditions as well as wage rates. Is a job dangerous? Does it offer the opportunity to acquire the experience and training that will enhance future earnings? Is the work strenuous and nerve-racking? Are the working hours, job location, and means of transportation convenient? These factors are what economists call **nonpecuniary job characteristics.** People will accept jobs with unpleasant working conditions if the wages are high enough (compared to potential job alternatives with better working conditions) to compensate for the undesirable nonpecuniary job characteristics. Since the higher wages, in essence, compensate workers for the unpleasant nonpecuniary attributes of a job, economists refer to wage differences stemming from this source as **compensating wage differentials.**

Examples of higher wages that compensate various workers for less attractive working conditions abound. Because of the dangers involved, aerial window washers (those who hang from windows 20 stories up) earn higher wages than other window washers. Sales jobs involving a great deal of out-of-town travel typically pay more than similar jobs without such inconvenience. Coal miners and sewer workers accept these jobs because they generally pay more than the alternatives available to low-skill workers. Compensating factors even influence the earnings of economists. When economists work for colleges or universities, they generally enjoy a more independent work environment and stimulating intellectual climate than when they are employed in the business sector. Unsurprisingly, the earnings of economists in academia are typically lower than those of economists in business.

EARNINGS DIFFERENTIALS FROM IMMOBILITY OF LABOR

It is costly to move to a new location or train for a new occupation in order to obtain a job. Such movements do not take place instantaneously. In the real world, labor, like other resources, does not possess perfect mobility. Some wage differentials thus result from an incomplete adjustment to change.

Since the demand for labor resources is a derived demand, it is affected by changes in product markets. An expansion in the demand for a product causes a rise in the demand for specialized labor to produce the product. Since resources are often highly immobile (that is, the supply is inelastic) in the short run, the expansion in demand may cause the wages of the specialized laborers to rise sharply. This happened in the oil-drilling industry in the late 1970s. An expansion in demand triggered a rapid increase in the earnings of petroleum engineers, oil rig operators, and other specialized personnel. Falling oil prices triggered the opposite effect in the mid-1980s. The demand for and employment opportunities of specialized resources declined substantially as output in the oil industry fell during 1985–1986. Demand shifts in the product market favor those in expanding industries but work against those in contracting industries.

Institutional barriers may also limit the mobility of labor. Licensing requirements, for example, limit the mobility of labor into many occupations—medicine, taxicab driving, architecture, and mortuary science among them. Unions may also follow policies that limit labor mobility and alter the free-market forces of supply and demand. Minimum wage rates may retard the ability of low-skill workers to obtain employment in certain sectors of the economy. These restrictions on labor mobility will influence the size of wage differentials among workers.

SUMMARY OF WAGE DIFFERENTIALS

As the Thumbnail Sketch shows, wage differentials stem from many sources, which can be categorized in three main ways: differences in workers, differences in jobs, and immobility of resources. Many of these factors play an important

---

THUMBNAIL SKETCH

WHAT ARE THE SOURCES OF EARNINGS DIFFERENTIALS?

DIFFERENCES IN WORKERS
1. Productivity and specialized skills (reflects native ability, parental training, and investment in human capital).
2. Worker preferences (trade-off between money earnings and other things).
3. Race and gender discrimination.

DIFFERENCES IN JOBS
1. Location of job.
2. Working conditions (for example, job safety, likelihood of temporary layoffs, and comfort of work environment).
3. Opportunity for training and skill-enhancement work experience.

IMMOBILITY OF RESOURCES
1. Temporary disequilibrium resulting from dynamic change.
2. Institutional restrictions (for example, occupational licensing and union-imposed restraints).

allocative role, compensating people for (1) human-capital investments that increase their productivity or (2) unfavorable working conditions. Other wage differentials reflect, at least partially, locational preferences or the desires of individuals for higher money income rather than nonmonetary benefits. Still other differentials, such as those related to discrimination and occupational restrictions, are unrelated to worker preferences and are not required to promote efficient production.

THE ECONOMICS OF EMPLOYMENT DISCRIMINATION

How does employment discrimination affect the job opportunities available to women and minorities? Do employers gain from discrimination? Economics sheds light on both these questions. There are two outlets for labor-market discrimination: wage rates and employment restrictions. **Exhibit 24–2** illustrates the impact of wage discrimination. When majority employees are preferred to minority workers (or men to women workers), the demand for the latter groups is reduced. Consequently, the wages of minorities and women decline relative to those of white men.

Essentially, there is a dual labor market—one market for the favored group and another for the group against which the discrimination is directed. The favored group, such as whites, is preferred, but the less-expensive labor of minority workers is a substitute productive resource. Both white and minority employees are employed, but the whites are paid a higher wage rate.

If there is employment discrimination against minorities or women, the demand for their services will decline, and their wage rate will fall from W_w to W_m.

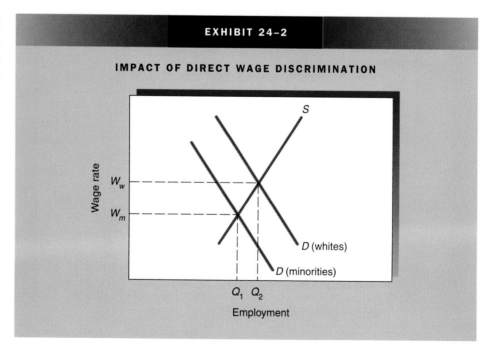

EXHIBIT 24–2

IMPACT OF DIRECT WAGE DISCRIMINATION

Exclusionary practices may also be an outlet for employment discrimination. Either in response to outside pressure or because of their own views, employers may primarily hire whites and males for certain types of jobs. When minority and female workers are excluded from a large number of occupations, they are crowded into a smaller number of remaining jobs and occupations. If entry restraints prevent people from becoming supervisors, plumbers, electricians, and truck drivers, they will be forced to accept alternatives. When the supply of labor in the unrestricted occupations increases, wage rates fall. The exclusionary practices thus result in higher wages for white males holding jobs from which minorities and females are excluded.

Although employment discrimination undoubtedly influences earning opportunities available to minorities and women, economic theory indicates that discrimination is costly to employers when they are merely reflecting their own prejudices. *If employers can hire equally productive minority employees (or women) at a lower wage than whites (or men), the profit motive gives them a strong incentive to do so. Hiring the higher-wage whites when similar minority employees are available will increase the costs of firms that discriminate.* Employers who hire employees regardless of their race or gender will have lower costs and higher profits than rival firms who try to fill positions with (mostly) white males. Thus, competitive forces tend to reduce the profitability of firms that discriminate.

Discriminatory hiring practices can be the result of factors other than employer prejudices, however. If either the firm's employees or its customers have discriminatory preferences, these might cause discriminatory hiring by the firm. The fact that adult nightclubs mainly hire young, attractive women, and that Chinese restaurants mainly hire Chinese employees are examples of this phenomenon.

EMPLOYMENT DISCRIMINATION AND THE EARNINGS OF MINORITIES

Earnings may differ among groups for reasons other than employment discrimination. If we want to isolate the impact of employment discrimination, we must (1) adjust for differences between groups in education, experience, and other productivity-related factors and (2) then make comparisons between similarly qualified groups of employees who differ only with regard to race (or gender).

How do the earnings of minorities compare with those of similarly productive whites? **Exhibit 24–3** presents data on this topic.[3] Both the actual wages of minorities relative to whites and the "productivity-adjusted" minority/white wage ratio are presented. In essence, the adjusted ratio is an estimate of how the wages of minorities would compare with those of whites if the two groups had the same productivity characteristics (schooling, work experience, marital status, regional location, and union and industry status). The actual wages of black men were 78 percent of the wages of white men in 1993–1995. However, when the work-force

---

[3]See Leonard A. Carlson and Caroline Swartz, "The Earnings of Women and Ethnic Minorities, 1959–1979," *Industrial and Labor Relations Review* 41 (July 1988), for a more detailed study based on earlier data that analyzes the impact of productivity characteristics on the earnings of minorities relative to whites. June O'Neill, "The Role of Human Capital in Earnings Differences between Black and White Men," *Journal of Economic Perspectives* (fall 1990): 25–45, provides additional information on earnings differences between white and black men.

[a]Primarily Chinese Americans and Japanese Americans.

Source: These data were supplied to the author by David Macpherson. They were derived from the 1993–1995 Current Population Surveys. The data were adjusted for years of schooling, work experience, region, industry, sector of employment, union status, and marital status.

EXHIBIT 24–3

THE ACTUAL AND PRODUCTIVITY-ADJUSTED WAGES OF MINORITIES COMPARED TO WHITES: 1993–1995

	MEN		WOMEN	
	ACTUAL	ADJUSTED	ACTUAL	ADJUSTED
White	100	100	100	100
African-American	78	85	91	93
American Indian	83	94	89	96
Asian-American[a]	99	92	106	97
Mexican-American	67	92	77	96
Other Hispanic	79	92	88	97

characteristics of black men were taken into account, the adjusted hourly earnings of black men rose to 85 percent of the white male earnings. This implies that productivity-related factors accounted for one-quarter of the wage differential between the two groups. A 15 percent differential, that may well be the result of employment discrimination, remained after adjustment for the productivity characteristics.[4]

Mexican Americans constitute the second-largest minority group in the United States. Even though the actual wages of Mexican-American men were only 67 percent of the wages of white men, their "adjusted" earnings were equal to 92 percent of the white wages. These data were not adjusted for language—inability to speak English. Adjustment for this factor would almost certainly further narrow the differential. This suggests that when Mexican-American men possess the same worker characteristics as white men, their earnings are pretty close to parity with their white counterparts.

The actual and corrected earnings for other minority groups are also presented in Exhibit 24–3. Interestingly, adjustment for productivity factors reduces the wages of Asian Americans relative to whites. This occurs because the productivity characteristics—particularly the average level of education—of Asian Americans are higher than those of whites.

Turning to the data for women, the productivity-adjusted wage rates of minority women relative to white women are between 93 percent and 97 percent for each of the groups included in Exhibit 24–3. This implies that the independent effect of racial discrimination is relatively small. The accompanying Applications in Economics feature presents data on the earnings of women relative to men and analyzes the impact of employment discrimination on the basis of gender.

---

[4]For a detailed explanation of how the adjusted ratios of Exhibit 24–3 were derived and information on the significance of productivity differences and employment discrimination on the basis of gender, see Barry T. Hirsch and David A. Macpherson, "Wages and Gender Composition: Why Do Women's Jobs Pay Less?" *Journal of Labor Economics* (July 1985).

EMPLOYMENT DISCRIMINATION AND THE EARNINGS OF WOMEN

Since the Second World War, there has been a dramatic shift in the household/work-force role of women, particularly married women. In 1994, 59.3 percent of women were in the labor force, compared with 33.2 percent in 1949, and 37.6 percent in 1960 (see **Chart 1**). Married women accounted for most of this dramatic increase; their labor-force participation rate soared from 32 percent in 1960 to 60 percent in 1994.

As Chart 1 shows, the female-male (F/M) earnings ratio for full-time workers was approximately 60 percent throughout the 1950–1980 period. Since 1980, the earnings of women have increased relative to those of men. Nevertheless, women working full time earned only 73.6 percent as much as their male counterparts in 1994. (Note: Women employed full time still work approxi-

mately 10 percent fewer hours than men who are employed full time. Therefore, the hourly earnings of full-time working women were approximately 80 percent as high as their male counterparts in 1994.)

EMPLOYMENT DISCRIMINATION AND FAMILY SPECIALIZATION Why are the earnings of women so low compared to those of men? Most people blame employment discrimination. There is substantial evidence that appears to support this view. In contrast with minorities relative to whites, the age, education, marital status, language, and regional locational characteristics of men and women are similar. Thus, correcting for these factors does little to reduce the earnings differential between men and women. Occupational data are consistent with the view that women are crowded into a few low-paying jobs. Until recently, more than half of

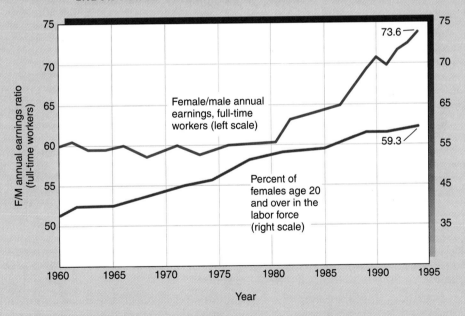

CHART 1

LABOR-FORCE EXPERIENCE OF WOMEN, 1960–1994

Between 1960 and 1994, the labor-force participation of females rose from 37.6 to 59.3 percent. However, the F/M earning ratio fluctuated around 60 percent during the 1960–1980 period, before climbing throughout the 1980s. By 1994, the F/M earnings ratio had risen to 73.6 percent.

all women were employed in just four occupations—clerical workers, teachers, nurses, and food-service workers.

Despite this evidence, the case that employment discrimination is the sole or even the major source of the earnings differential between men and women is less than airtight. First, the size of even the adjusted differential should cause one to pause. If an employer could really hire women who are willing and able to do the same work as men for 25 percent less, the profit motive would provide the employer with a strong incentive to do so. If an employer could really cut labor costs 25 percent merely by hiring women (primarily) rather than men, surely many less "sexist" employers (both men and women) would jump at the chance. Of course, as more and more employers substituted women for men workers, the earnings ratio of women to men would move toward parity.[1]

Second, it is important to recognize that married men and women have different areas of traditional specialization within the family. Historically, married men typically pursued paid employment aggressively because they were expected to be the family's primary breadwinner. Given this traditional responsibility for monetary earnings, men were more likely to (1) have continuous labor-force participation, (2) move in order to get a higher paying job, and (3) accept jobs with long hours, uncertain schedules, and out-of-town travel.

In contrast, married women traditionally had the primary responsibility for operating the household and caring for children. Given these areas of specialization, historically many women sought jobs with less out-of-town travel, more flexible hours, and other characteristics complementary with household responsibilities.[2] Viewed in this light, it is not particularly surprising that women found nursing, teaching, secretarial, and other jobs with more flexible work schedules and easily transportable skills and credentials highly attractive.

How important are gender differences in specialization within the family? Since preferences cannot be directly observed, the family specialization theory is difficult to test. However, **Chart 2** sheds some light on its importance. Here we illustrate the median annual earnings of women relative to men, according to marital status. Clearly, married women earn substantially less than married men. Even when working full time, year-round, married women earn only 66 percent as much as men. However, the earnings gap between men and women is substantially less for singles, the group least influenced

by actual and potential differences in specialization within the traditional family. In fact, in 1994 the female/male annual earnings ratio for full-time, full-year workers was 92 percent for singles. Thus, the earnings of single women were only 8 percent less than those of single men. This pattern of earnings differences according to

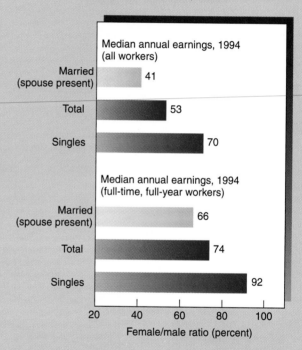

CHART 2

FEMALE-MALE EARNINGS ACCORDING TO MARITAL STATUS, 1994

Median annual earnings, 1994 (all workers)

- Married (spouse present): 41
- Total: 53
- Singles: 70

Median annual earnings, 1994 (full-time, full-year workers)

- Married (spouse present): 66
- Total: 74
- Singles: 92

Female/male ratio (percent)

Although the female/male earnings ratio varies considerably according to marital status and time worked, the earnings of single women relative to the earnings of single men are much higher than the earnings of women in other marital status groupings.

Source: U.S. Department of Commerce, "Income, Poverty, and Valuation of Noncash Benefits: 1994," *Current Population Reports*, Series P-60, 189.

marital status implies that, although employment discrimination may well be a contributing factor, family specialization is also an important determinant of the overall earnings differential between men and women.

THE FUTURE What can we say about the future direction of earnings according to gender? Although the career objectives of men and women have often differed substantially in the past, the differences have narrowed substantially in recent years. In 1968 a national sample of women 14 to 24 years of age found that only 27 percent expected to be working at age 35. In contrast, a similar sample of young women in 1979 found that 72 percent expected to be working at that age.[3] These figures indicate that there has been a dramatic increase in the proportion of young women who are preparing for a career and planning for a lifetime of labor-force participation.

The dramatic change in the career plans of women is also reflected in their educational choices. In the past, women were less likely than men to study mathematics, engineering, medicine, law, and similar fields leading to high-paying professional jobs. As **Chart 3** illustrates, more and more women are now preparing for the professions—such fields as accounting, veterinary medicine, dentistry, medicine, law, architecture, pharmacy, and economics. The dramatic increase during the last two decades in the number of women earning degrees in these fields reflects the changing career objectives of women.

In recent years, the education plans and career objectives of women and men have become more and more similar.[4] This factor was the moving force underlying the growth of the F/M earnings ratio in the 1980s and it will almost surely continue to erode earnings differences according to gender in the future.

CHART 3

WOMEN AS A PROPORTION OF PERSONS EARNING SELECTED PROFESSIONAL DEGREES, 1970–71 AND 1992–93

FIELD OF STUDY	1970–71	1992–93
Engineering	0.8	15.8
Dentistry	1.2	33.9
Optometry	2.4	49.1
Law	7.3	42.5
Veterinary Medicine	7.8	62.8
Medicine	9.2	37.7
Accounting	10.1	54.2
Economics	11.2	29.8
Architecture	12.0	35.2
Pharmacy	25.2	64.6

Source: Commission of Professionals in Science and Technology, *Professional Women and Minorities* (Washington, D.C.: CPST, 1987); and U.S. Department of Education, *Digest of Education Statistics, 1995* (Washington, D.C.: U.S. Government Printing Office), Tables 241 and 252.

---

[1]The employment and earnings data of self-employed workers are also inconsistent with the employment-discrimination hypothesis. One would expect that many women would shift to self-employment in order to escape the effects of discrimination, resulting in an overrepresentation of women and a higher female/male earnings ratio in self-employment occupations. In fact, the opposite results occur. See Robert L. Moore, "Employer Discrimination: Evidence from Self-Employed Workers," *Review of Economics and Statistics* 65 (August 1983).

[2]For an analysis of how family specialization influences the employment and earnings of women, see Solomon Polachek, "Discontinuous Labor Force Participation and Its Effect on Women's Market Earnings," in *Sex Discrimination and the Division of Labor*, ed. Cynthia B. Lloyd (New York: Columbia University Press, 1975); and James Gwartney and Richard Stroup, "Measurement of Employment Discrimination According to Sex," *Southern Economic Journal* (April 1973).

[3]See Chapter 7 of the *Economic Report of the President, 1987*. The numbers presented here are from Table 7–3 of the report.

[4]For additional details on this topic, see James P. Smith and Michael P. Ward, "Women in the Labor Market and in the Family," *Journal of Economic Perspectives* (winter 1989): 9–23; and Claudia Goldin, "Gender Gap," *Fortune Encyclopedia of Economics*, ed. David R. Henderson (New York: Warner Books, 1993).

THE ECONOMICS OF FRINGE AND MANDATED BENEFITS

When referring to wages or compensation, we have proceeded as if employees were compensated only with money payments. Of course, this is an oversimplification. There are generally two components of employee compensation: (1) money wages and (2) **fringe benefits,** which include such items as health-care insurance, layoff benefits, pension benefits, on-the-job training, on-the-premises child-care services, severance benefits, use of an automobile, discounts on life and auto insurance, parental-leave benefits, and paid time off for sickness, personal business, vacation, jury duty, and holidays.

As **Exhibit 24–4** illustrates, fringe benefits compose a sizable and increasing share of employee compensation. In 1994, fringe benefits accounted for approximately 29 percent of the total compensation of employees in the United States. In the manufacturing sector, the fringe benefit component was even larger; it accounted for just over one-third of total employee compensation.

Like money wages, provision of fringe benefits is costly to employers. When deciding whether to employ a worker, the employer must consider the total cost of the compensation package. Employment will be expanded as long as the employee's *MRP* exceeds the cost of the employee's total compensation package,

Fringe benefits
Benefits other than normal money wages that are supplied to employees in exchange for their labor services.

Fringe benefits are an increasingly important component of employee compensation. These benefits accounted for 29 percent ($4.94 out of the $17.08 total) of employee compensation per hour in 1994, up from 24 percent in 1980.

Source: *Statistical Abstract of the United States,* various issues.

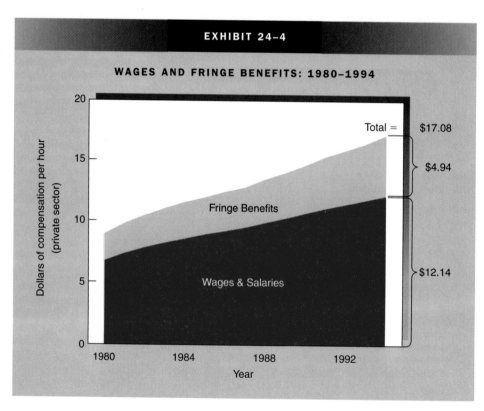

EXHIBIT 24–4

WAGES AND FRINGE BENEFITS: 1980–1994

Total = $17.08

$4.94

$12.14

Fringe Benefits

Wages & Salaries

Dollars of compensation per hour (private sector)

Year

including the cost of the fringe benefits. Conversely, workers will not be hired if their employment adds more to cost than to revenue.

In a competitive situation, employers will have to pay a compensation package equal to that prevailing in the market for workers in each skill category. If they do not, they will lose employees to rival firms. *Fringe benefits are nothing more than a component of the market-determined compensation package. Employers who offer more attractive fringe benefits will be able to attract workers with a lower money wage.* Those who offer little in the way of fringe benefits will have to pay higher wages. In essence, employees pay for fringe benefits in the form of lower money wages. Contrary to the view of some, fringe benefits are not a "gift" from the employer. Rather, they are earned by the employees as a component of their total compensation package.

Why might employers and employees find a compensation package that includes fringe benefits mutually advantageous? There are two major reasons. First, it may be cheaper for the employees of a firm to purchase certain benefits as a group rather than separately as individuals. When this is the case, employees may prefer the group-purchased benefit rather than additional money wages of equal cost. Health-care insurance is an example. It is often cheaper for an insurance company to provide a single policy covering 100 employees (and their families) than it would be for workers to buy 100 separate policies. Therefore, group-purchased health insurance is often cheaper than the same coverage purchased as an individual.

Second, compensation in the form of fringe benefits may lead to a tax savings. For example, employer-provided health insurance, child-care services or use of company-purchased football tickets generate "income" to the employee, but such in-kind benefits are usually not taxable. Therefore, compensation in this form may increase the employee's after-tax compensation more than an equivalent amount of money earnings. Thus, current tax law often makes it more attractive for employees to obtain these benefits through their employers.

The cost of providing fringe benefits will vary among employers. Large firms may be able to provide some fringe benefits—health-care insurance and child-care services, for example—much more cheaply than small firms. Moreover, employees will vary in their personal valuation of various fringe benefits. For example, parental-leave benefits or child-care services may be a highly valued benefit to one employee while yielding little or no utility to another.

In the absence of legislation, agreements between employers and employees (and their representatives) determine the proportion of money wages and fringe benefits in the total compensation package. *Employers and employees have an incentive to structure the compensation package so that it will transfer the maximum amount of value to employees for any given cost to the employer. Compensation packages of this type will attract employees and thereby minimize the employer's labor costs.*

It will cost an employer the same to pay an employee $1,000 per month as it will to pay $800 per month plus a fringe-benefit package that costs $200 per month. In both cases, the employer's monthly cost is $1,000. When the employer's cost of providing a fringe benefit is low (relative to its cost if purchased directly by the employee) and the employee's valuation of the benefit is high, employers and employees will find it mutually advantageous to substitute the fringe benefits for higher money wages. Conversely, when there is little or no advantage derived from employer-coordinated group provision, or when employees value a fringe benefit less than its cost, employees will prefer higher money wages rather than the fringe benefit. *In fact, failure to include a fringe benefit in a wage package is strong evidence that it costs more than the value it provides to employees (or that the employee could purchase the benefit just as cheaply without assistance from the employer).*

IMPACT OF MANDATED BENEFITS

Mandated benefits

Fringe benefits that the government forces employers to include in their total compensation package paid to employees.

In recent years several states, and in some cases the federal government, have mandated that employers supply their employees with various fringe benefits, including health-care insurance, parental leave, and child-care services. Proponents of **mandated benefits** argue that they provide protection for employees who work for employers who are unwilling to provide various fringe benefits. Critics charge that mandated benefits are not worth their price—by pushing up labor costs, they reduce employment.

In analyzing the full impact of mandated benefits, there are three key points to keep in mind. First, a mandated benefit is only one component of the total compensation package. Increasing a single component of the package will not necessarily increase the size of the overall package. The parties will adjust. As they adjust, money wages and other fringe benefits will be reduced below what they would have been in the absence of the mandated benefits. Legislation mandating benefits thus reduces flexibility. It forces employers and employees to include a specific item in the total compensation package even when the parties would have preferred to structure the compensation package differently. In many cases, employer-provision of a benefit—particularly provision by small firms—will cost more than the benefit is valued by employees. When this is the case, mandated benefits will increase labor costs without providing a proportional increase in value to employees.

Second, employees earn and ultimately pay for all components of their compensation package—including any benefits mandated by government. Workers will not be hired if their employment adds more to costs than to revenues. The view that fringe benefits are a gift from the employer, and that the size of the benefits package can be increased by requiring employers to include various government-mandated benefits, is purely and simply wrong.

Third, fringe benefits are often an inefficient form of compensating employees. When neither savings from group purchase nor tax advantages exist, employees will prefer money wages to in-kind benefits. When in-kind compensation is efficient—when employees value a fringe benefit more than the additional money that it costs—an employer has a strong incentive to adopt (and employees have a strong incentive to bargain for) this form of compensation. Failure of a fringe benefit to emerge in a given employment setting is strong evidence that it is inefficient—that employees would prefer additional money wages rather than the fringe benefit (given its cost of provision).

How do mandated benefits affect the welfare of workers? Our analysis indicates that adjustments in other dimensions of employment contracts will erode much of their impact. Even when they alter the structure of compensation, mandated benefits are unlikely to increase the overall level of employee compensation. In cases where employees would prefer additional money wages rather than the benefits, forcing the mandated benefits into the compensation package will reduce the welfare of employees because, as labor markets adjust, losses from reductions in other components of the compensation package will more than offset the gains derived from the mandated benefits. Even if specific employees value the benefits more than their costs, lower money wages will partially offset the positive effects of the mandated benefits. Thus, any positive impact of mandated benefits on the total compensation of employees will generally be substantially less than the proponents believe. Similarly, the negative impact on labor costs and employment will generally be substantially less than the critics charge.

PRODUCTIVITY AND EARNINGS

Output and income are closely linked. In fact, they are opposite sides of the same coin. Output is the value of the goods and services produced as measured by the amount purchasers pay for these items. Income is the payments to the resource suppliers, including the profits and losses of the entrepreneurs, who generated the output. This, too, is equal to the amount purchasers pay for the goods and services produced.

Productivity—that is, output per worker—and wages are also closely linked. When workers are more productive, the demand for their services will be higher and therefore they will be able to command higher wage rates. High productivity is the source of high wages. When the output per hour of workers is high, the real wages of the workers will also be high.

Differences in output per worker are the major source of variations in earnings across countries. For example, the earnings per worker are vastly greater in the United States than they are in India or China, because the output of U.S. workers is much greater than the output of their counterparts in those countries. The average worker in the United States is better educated, works with more productive machines, and benefits from more efficient economic organization than the average person in India or China. Thus, the value of the output produced by the average U.S. worker is approximately 15 times that produced by the average worker in India or China. American workers earn more because they produce more. If they did not produce more, they would not be able to earn more.

The *growth* of productivity provides the source for the growth of real earnings. Average real earnings (total compensation) per hour in the United States in 1995 were approximately double the earnings of U.S. workers 40 years earlier. Similarly, the output of goods and services per hour of U.S. workers in 1995 was approximately twice the level of the mid-1950s. Earnings rose because productivity increased. If productivity had not increased, the increase in earnings would not have been possible.

Increased availability of physical capital, improvements in the skill level of the labor force, and advances in technology provide the impetus for the growth of both productivity and earnings. For several decades, the educational level of members of the work force in the United States (representing investment in human capital) has steadily increased. Simultaneously, the physical capital per

"AUTOMATION IS THE MAJOR CAUSE OF UNEMPLOYMENT. IF WE KEEP ALLOWING MACHINES TO REPLACE PEOPLE, WE ARE GOING TO RUN OUT OF JOBS."

Machines are substituted for people if, and only if, the machines reduce costs of production. Why has the automatic elevator replaced the operator, the tractor replaced the horse, and the power shovel replaced the ditch digger? Because each is a cheaper method of accomplishing a task.

When automation and technological improvements reduce the cost of producing a good, they allow us to obtain each unit of the product with fewer resources. If the demand for the product is inelastic, consumers will spend less on the good and therefore have more of their income available for spending on other things.

Consider the following example. Suppose that someone develops a new toothpaste that really prevents cavities and sells it for half the price of the current brands. If the demand for toothpaste is inelastic, at the lower price, consumers will spend less on this product than was previously the case. Furthermore, the decline in cavities will reduce the demand for and expenditures on dental services. Lower dental care expenditures, however, will increase the income available for consumers to spend on other goods and services. As a result, they will spend more on clothes, recreation, vacations, swimming pools, education, and many other items. This additional spending, which would not have taken place if dental costs had not been reduced, will generate additional demand and employment in these sectors.

When the demand for a product is elastic, a cost-saving invention can even generate an increase in employment in the industry affected by the invention. This was essentially what happened in the automobile industry when Henry Ford's mass-production techniques reduced the cost (and price) of cars. When the price of automobiles fell 50 percent, consumers bought three times as many cars. Even though the worker-hours per car fell by 25 percent between 1920 and 1930, employment in the industry increased by approximately 50 percent during the decade.

Of course, technological advances may diminish the earnings of specific individuals or groups. Home appliances, such as automatic washers and dryers, dishwashers, and microwave ovens, reduced the job opportunities of maids. Computer technology has reduced the demand for telephone operators. In the future, videotaped lectures may even reduce the job opportunities available to college professors. It is understandable why those groups directly affected this way by automation fear and oppose it.

Focusing on the loss of specific jobs, though, conceals the overall impact of technological improvements. Cost-reducing improvements in technology release scarce resources for the expansion of output and employment in other areas. As a result, we are able to produce more and achieve a higher standard of living than would have otherwise been possible.

Furthermore, running out of jobs is not a problem. Jobs represent obstacles, tasks that must be accomplished if we desire to loosen the bonds of scarcity. As long as our ability to produce goods and services falls short of our consumption desires, there will be jobs. A society running out of jobs would be in an enviable position: It would be nearing the impossible goal—victory over scarcity.

---

worker has expanded (See Illustrated Exhibits IV-B and IV-C on pages 605–606 for evidence on recent increases in both the educational level of the labor force and physical capital per worker.)

Automation
A production technique that reduces the amount of labor required to produce a good or service. It is beneficial to adopt the new labor-saving technology only if it reduces the cost of production.

Technological advances can also enhance productivity, and thereby contribute to the growth of output and income. Some observers argue that technology and **automation** adversely affect workers (see accompanying Myth). In fact, just the opposite is true. *Once you recognize that expansion in output is the source of higher earnings, the positive impact of improvements in technology is apparent: Better technology makes it possible for workers to produce more and thus to earn more.* For example, accountants can handle more business accounts using microcomputers rather than a pencil and calculator. A secretary can prepare more letters when working with a word processor rather than a typewriter.

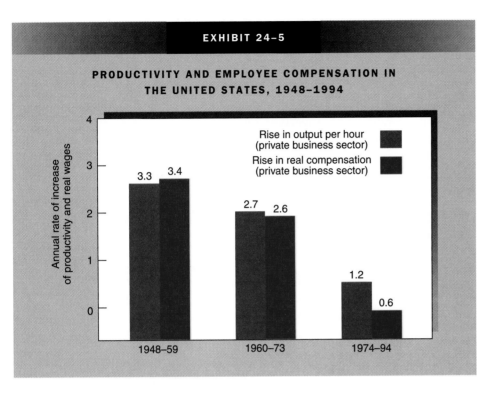

EXHIBIT 24-5

PRODUCTIVITY AND EMPLOYEE COMPENSATION IN THE UNITED STATES, 1948–1994

Legend:
- Rise in output per hour (private business sector)
- Rise in real compensation (private business sector)

Period	Rise in output per hour	Rise in real compensation
1948–59	3.3	3.4
1960–73	2.7	2.6
1974–94	1.2	0.6

(Y-axis: Annual rate of increase of productivity and real wages)

As illustrated in the graph, worker productivity and employee compensation per hour are closely linked. Since 1973, however, growth of both productivity and real compensation per hour has slowed substantially compared to the growth figures achieved during the 1948–1973 period.

Source: *The Economic Report of the President, 1996*, Table B-46.

THE GREAT PRODUCTIVITY SLOWDOWN

What has happened to productivity in recent decades? **Exhibit 24–5** sheds light on this question. For 25 years following the Second World War, the output per worker in the United States increased at an annual rate of approximately 3 percent. Real compensation per hour grew at a similar rate. However, since 1973 the growth of both productivity and real hourly compensation has sagged badly. During the 1973–1994 period, the annual growth of hourly worker productivity fell to 1.2 percent. Real compensation per hour grew at an annual rate of only 0.6 percent during this period.

The per capita GDP reflects this slowdown in the growth of output and income. Between 1955 and 1973, the per capita GDP of the United States increased at an annual rate of 2.5 percent. Since 1973, the growth of per capita GDP of the United States has fallen to 1.5 percent. The United States is not alone with regard to this slowdown. If anything, the reductions in the growth rates of the other major industrial economies have been even greater than that of the United States. For example, the growth rate of per capita GDP of Japan fell from 8.8 percent during 1955–1973 to 2.7 percent during 1974–1995. In Germany, growth of per capita real GDP declined from 4.2 percent during the earlier period to 2.2 percent during the later period. France's growth rate fell from 4.6 percent during 1955–1973 to 1.9 percent during 1974–1995. Italy, Canada, and the United Kingdom have also experienced substantial reductions in growth during the last two decades. (See Illustrated Exhibit IV-D on page 606 at the beginning of this part for the growth data for the seven major industrial economies.)

What accounts for this decline in the growth of the major industrial economies during the last two decades? Researchers in this area believe that at least four major factors contributed to the slowdown in productivity.

1. A slowdown in the rate of capital formation has retarded the growth of productivity.   As we have previously noted, more and better equipment and tools enhance the productivity of workers. Other things constant, workers are able to produce more when they are working with more physical capital. When the supply of productivity-enhancing capital assets grows more slowly, the growth of labor productivity also tends to slow. This is precisely what has happened. **Exhibit 24–6** presents the figures for investment as a share of GDP for the most recent decade and the decade prior to 1973. In every case, the investment rate of the major industrial countries during the more recent period was lower than that for the period prior to 1973.

2. Both sharply higher energy prices and an increase in environmental regulations have reduced the productivity of capital during the last two decades.   The sharply higher oil prices of the 1973–1981 period substantially reduced the efficiency of vast amounts of capital. Machines and structures designed for cost effectiveness at pre-1973 energy prices were suddenly rendered obsolete. They were too costly to operate at the higher level of energy prices. At the same time, regulations designed to improve the environment and reduce the level of pollution also reduced the effectiveness of capital. Many firms were forced either to terminate their use of various equipment or to undertake costly modifications in order to meet the more rigid regulatory standards of the 1970s and 1980s.[5] As Robert Solow, the 1987 recipient of the Nobel Prize in Economics, notes,

> *Since the 1970s a substantial fraction of all investment has gone into pollution control and environmental improvement. That may be very valuable, but it doesn't contribute to the output we measure for the economy.*[6]

3. During the 1970s and 1980s, youthful, less-experienced workers composed a large share of the U.S. labor force.   Beginning in the latter half of the 1960s, the United States experienced a sharp influx of less-experienced workers into the work force as the labor-force participation of women increased and the children of the post–Second World War baby boom came of working age. Economics indicates that a rapid growth of the labor force—particularly the growth of inexperienced and less-skilled workers—will reduce productivity.

4. A reduction in the average achievement level of the new labor-force entrants may have retarded growth.[7]   As we have previously noted, educational levels as measured by years of school have increased throughout the post–Second

---

[5]See Edward F. Denison, *Trends in American Economic Growth, 1929–1982* (Washington, D.C.: Brookings Institution, 1985); and the articles in *The Journal of Economic Perspectives* (fall 1988) for additional details on this topic.

[6]Robert Solow, quoted in Timothy Tregarthen, "Explaining the Great Slowdown," *The Margin* (November–December 1988).

[7]See John H. Bishop, "Is the Test Score Decline Responsible for the Productivity Decline?" *American Economic Review* (March 1989): 178–197.

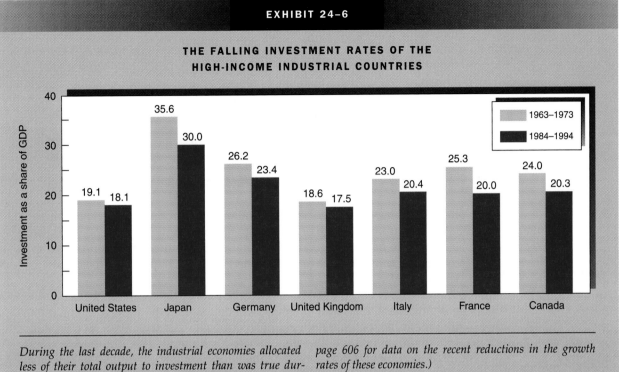

EXHIBIT 24–6

**THE FALLING INVESTMENT RATES OF THE
HIGH-INCOME INDUSTRIAL COUNTRIES**

Legend: 1963–1973, 1984–1994

- United States: 19.1, 18.1
- Japan: 35.6, 30.0
- Germany: 26.2, 23.4
- United Kingdom: 18.6, 17.5
- Italy: 23.0, 20.4
- France: 25.3, 20.0
- Canada: 24.0, 20.3

(Y-axis: Investment as a share of GDP)

During the last decade, the industrial economies allocated less of their total output to investment than was true during the 1963–1973 period. This reduction in the rate of capital formation is one reason why the growth rates of these economies have declined. (See Illustrated Exhibit IV-D on page 606 for data on the recent reductions in the growth rates of these economies.)

Source: Derived from International Monetary Fund, *International Financial Statistics Yearbook: 1995*, p. 170–173.

World War period. However, additional schooling may not necessarily mean a more knowledgeable and skillful work force. The SAT scores of high school graduates and other measures of basic skills declined during the 1970s and have failed to rebound to their previous highs. Prior to that time, these basic-skills test scores had been improving for at least 50 years. Thus, compared with the 1950s and 1960s, the improvement in the quality of the labor force may have slowed during the last two decades. Furthermore, the amount of human capital possessed by the more recent labor-force entrants may be less than the schooling figures imply.

PERSPECTIVE ON THE PRODUCTIVITY ISSUE

Clearly, the lagging growth rate of productivity is a serious matter. Unless it is reversed, the future growth of income will be quite slow compared with the 25 years following World War II. Some of the unfavorable factors—for example, the oil price increases and the rapid growth of inexperienced workers—have reversed. Perhaps these changes will lead to an increase in the growth rate in the near future. In addition, some would argue that the recent growth figures should be viewed in a longer-term historical context. Perhaps the 1948–1973 period was an aberration. Most researchers place the annual per capita growth rate of the United States, Germany, France, and the United Kingdom at approximately 1 percent throughout most of the century prior to 1950. Maybe this is the proper benchmark against which the growth of the last two decades should be measured.[8]

CAN HIGHER WAGES BE LEGISLATED?

Minimum wage

Legislation requiring that workers be paid at least the stated minimum hourly rate of pay.

In 1938 Congress passed the Fair Labor Standards Act, which provided for a national **minimum wage** of 25 cents per hour. During the past 50 years, the minimum wage has been increased several times. Under legislation passed in 1996, the federal minimum wage was pushed up to $5.15 per hour (beginning in September 1997).

Minimum wage legislation is intended to help the working poor. There is good reason to question, however, whether it actually does so. Economic theory indicates that the quantity demanded of labor, particularly a specific skill category of labor, will be inversely related to its wage rate. If a higher minimum wage increases the wage rates of unskilled workers above the level that would be established by market forces, the quantity of unskilled workers employed will fall. The minimum wage will price the services of the least productive (and therefore lowest-wage) workers out of the market.

Exhibit 24–7 provides a graphic illustration of the direct effect of a $5.15 minimum wage on the employment opportunities of a group of low-skill workers. Without a minimum wage, the supply of and demand for these low-skill workers would be in balance at a wage rate of $4.00. Since the minimum wage makes low-skill labor service more expensive, employers will substitute machines and highly skilled workers (whose wages have not been raised by the minimum) for the now more expensive low-productivity employees. Jobs in which low-skill employees are unable to produce a marginal revenue product equal to or greater than the minimum wage will be eliminated. In addition, as the cost (and price) of goods and services produced by low-skill employees rises, consumers will rely more heavily on substitute goods produced by highly skilled labor or in foreign markets. The net effect of these substitutions will be a reduction in the quantity demanded of low-skill labor.[9]

---

[8]See Claudia Goldin, *Labor Markets in the Twentieth Century*, National Bureau of Economic Research Historical Working Paper No. 58 (June 1994), for evidence on the long-term growth rate of labor productivity.

[9]The impact of minimum wage legislation could differ from the theoretical results we have outlined if labor markets were dominated by a single buyer. Economists refer to this situation as *monopsony*. We choose not to present the monopsony model here because (1) in a modern society, where labor is highly mobile, the major assumptions of the model are seldom met, and (2) the bulk of the empirical evidence in this area is consistent with the competitive model.

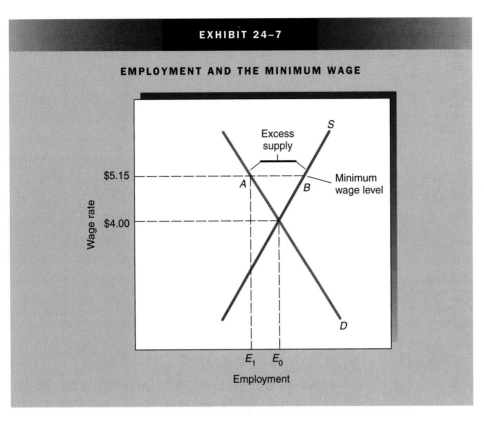

EXHIBIT 24–7

EMPLOYMENT AND THE MINIMUM WAGE

If the market wage of a group of employees were $4.00 per hour, a $5.15-per-hour minimum wage would increase the earnings of persons who were able to maintain employment but would reduce the employment of others (E_0 to E_1), pushing them onto the unemployment rolls or into less-preferred jobs.

INDIRECT EFFECTS OF THE MINIMUM WAGE

When analyzing the effects of the minimum wage, we must not forget that money wages are only one dimension of the exchange. Other aspects of the labor-service exchange will be affected by the imposition of the minimum wage. When a minimum wage rate pushes wages of low-skill workers above the market level, employers will have no trouble hiring workers. Therefore, they have little incentive to offer workers training, convenient working hours, continuous employment, fringe benefits, and other nonwage components of the total compensation package. Predictably, a higher minimum wage will lead to an erosion in the quality of the nonwage components of minimum wage jobs.[10] As we discussed previously, higher mandated benefits do not necessarily increase total compensation. Neither does a higher mandated money wage—at least not by the amount of the increase in the money wage.

---

[10]Our treatment here is parallel to that for rent controls in Chapter 3. There we noted that, in response to a below-market price and accompanying excess demand, the quality of rental housing deteriorates because sellers (landlords) have little incentive to maintain quality in order to attract buyers (renters). Correspondingly, in response to an above-equilibrium price and accompanying excess supply, the nonwage characteristics of jobs deteriorate because buyers (employers) have little incentive to maintain the quality of working conditions and fringe benefits in order to attract sellers (workers). It is hard to repeal the laws of supply and demand.

Of the nonwage elements adversely affected by minimum wage legislation, the decline in training opportunities is particularly important. Many inexperienced workers face a dilemma: They cannot find a job without experience (or skills), but they cannot obtain experience without a job. This is particularly true for younger workers. Employment experience obtained at an early age, even on seemingly menial tasks, can help one acquire work habits (for example, promptness and self-confidence), skills, and attitudes that will enhance one's value to employers in the future. Since minimum wage legislation prohibits the payment of even a temporarily low wage, it is often too costly for employers to offer low-skill workers jobs with training. In effect, the minimum wage acts as an institutional barrier limiting on-the-job training opportunities. In a comprehensive study of this issue, Masanori Hashimoto estimated that a 28 percent increase in the minimum wage reduced the value of on-the-job training available to the affected low-skill workers by 2.7 percent to 15 percent.[11] As a result, opportunities for on-the-job training are limited and low-skill workers can be pushed into dead-end jobs—positions with little opportunity for future advancement.

ESTIMATED IMPACT ON EMPLOYMENT

In recent years, the minimum wage has varied between 35 percent and 45 percent of the average wage of all workers. In this range, empirical studies suggest that a 10 percent increase in the minimum wage would reduce the employment of low-skill workers by 1 percent to 3 percent.[12] Given the expected adverse impact of the minimum wage on other forms of compensation, this relatively small decline in employment is not surprising. Proponents of a higher minimum wage argue that the higher wages for low-skill workers are worth these relatively small reductions in employment.

Of course, workers who are able to maintain employment—most likely these will be the better qualified among those with low skill levels—gain when the minimum wage is increased. Other low-skill workers, particularly those with the lowest pre-legislation wage rates and skill levels, will find it more difficult to find employment. Some will be pushed into the ranks of the unemployed or out of the labor force and onto welfare rolls. Youthful blacks and Hispanic Americans are likely to be overrepresented among those who are adversely affected by increases in the minimum wage.

---

[11]Masanori Hashimoto, "Minimum Wage Effects on Training on the Job," *American Economic Review* 72 (December 1982): 1070–1087; and Charles Brown, "Minimum Wage Laws: Are They Overrated?" *Journal of Economic Perspectives* (summer 1988): 133–145.

[12]See Jacob Mincer, "Unemployment Effects of Minimum Wages," *Journal of Political Economy* 84 (August 1976); James Ragan, "Minimum Wages and the Youth Labor Market," *Review of Economics and Statistics* 59 (May 1977); Finis Welch, *Minimum Wages: Issues and Evidence* (Washington, D.C.: American Enterprise Institute, 1978); Charles L. Betsey and Bruce H. Dunson, "Federal Minimum Wage Laws and the Employment of Minority Youth," *American Economic Review* 71 (May 1981); and Charles Brown, Curtis Gilroy, and Andrew Kohen, "The Effect of the Minimum Wage on Employment and Unemployment," *Journal of Economic Literature* 20 (June 1982). For an alternative view, see David Card and Alan B. Krueger, *Myth and Measurement: The New Economics of the Minimum Wage* (Princeton: Princeton University Press, 1995). The authors argue that an increase in the minimum wage would exert little or no adverse impact on employment. This book has generated considerable debate and is the subject of continuing controversy among economists.

WOULD A HIGHER MINIMUM WAGE HELP THE POOR?

The proponents of a higher minimum wage argue that the current minimum wage will not provide the head of a family with enough income to keep the family out of poverty. This is true. When considering the relevance of this fact, however, it is important to keep two points in mind. First, the minimum wage does not assure one a job. A minimum wage high enough for a worker to support a family of three or four at an above-poverty income level will reduce the employment of low-skill workers, including some who are supporting families. Second, and perhaps more important, most minimum wage workers are not supporting a family. In 1994 less than 12 percent of the workers earning the minimum wage were heads of families with incomes below the poverty level. Perhaps surprising to some, more than half of all the minimum wage workers were members of a family with an income above the median. Most (63 percent) of the minimum wage workers were employed only part-time. Approximately one-third (31 percent) were teenagers.

The typical minimum wage worker is a spouse or a teenage member of a household with an income well above the poverty level. Therefore, even if the adverse impact of a higher minimum wage on both employment and nonwage forms of compensation is small, a higher minimum wage would exert little impact on the income of the poor. This is precisely the conclusion reached in a recent study by William R. Johnson and Edgar K. Browning. Johnson and Browning estimated that a 22 percent increase in the minimum wage would add less than one-half of one percent to the income of households in the bottom 30 percent of the income distribution *even if there were no reductions in employment.*[13] Given the composition of the minimum wage workers, a higher minimum wage will not be a very effective means of either helping families living in poverty or reducing the degree of income inequality.

---

[13]William R. Johnson and Edgar K. Browning, "The Distributional and Efficiency Effects of Increasing the Minimum Wage: A Simulation," *American Economic Review* 73 (March 1983): 204–211.

LOOKING AHEAD

While this chapter focused on the labor market, the following chapter will analyze the capital market. The real income and output of a nation are strongly influenced by the amount of both the physical and human capital with which people work. The next chapter analyzes the factors that underlie the availability of capital and the investment choices of decision makers.

CHAPTER SUMMARY

1. Three major sources of wage differentials exist among individuals: differences in workers, differences in jobs, and degree of labor mobility. Individual workers differ with respect to productivity (skills, human capital, motivation, native ability, and so on), specialized skills, employment preferences, race, and gender. Each of these factors contributes to wage and earning differences among individuals. In addition, differences in nonpecuniary job characteristics, changes in product markets, and institutional restrictions that limit labor mobility also contribute to variations in wages among workers.

2. Both employment discrimination and differences in employability characteristics (the quality and quantity of schooling, skill level, prior job experience, and other human-capital factors) contribute to earnings differentials among groups. Economic research indicates that approximately half of the earnings disparity between whites and blacks is due to differences in employability (productivity) characteristics rather than employment discrimination.

3. In 1994, women working full time, year-round earned only about 74 percent as much as men. Some of this differential may emanate from discrimination in the labor market. However, differences between men and women in other areas that influence earnings—particularly differences in their attachment to the labor force and historical roles within the family—also contribute to earnings differences according to gender. Differences between men and women in these areas have been shrinking. Increasingly, women are continuously in the labor force and acquiring education suitable for professional careers. These developments have pushed the female/male earnings ratio upward since 1980 and they will almost surely continue to do so in the future.

4. Fringe benefits are a component of employee compensation. When the employer's cost of providing a fringe benefit is low, and the employee's personal valuation of the benefit is high, employers and employees will find it mutually advantageous to substitute fringe benefits for money wages in the total compensation package. Conversely, when these conditions are absent, money wages are the more efficient form of compensation.

5. Other forms of compensation will be scaled back as markets adjust to legislation mandating various fringe benefits. These adjustments will largely erode both the positive effects of the mandated benefits on employee compensation and the adverse effects of the benefits on labor costs and employment.

6. Productivity is the ultimate source of high wages and earnings. Workers in the United States (and other high-income industrial countries) earn high wages because their output per hour is high as the result of (a) worker knowledge and skills (human capital) and (b) the use of modern machinery (physical capital).

7. During the last 25 years, the growth of productivity in the United States and other major industrial nations has lagged well below the growth rate achieved during the 25 years following the Second World War. A slowdown in the growth of capital per worker, higher energy prices, environmental regulations, an influx of inexperienced younger workers, and a decline in the basic skill levels of new labor-force entrants contributed to the slowdown in productivity in the United States. If the slowdown in productivity continues, future improvements in our standard of living will come about more slowly.

8. Automated methods of production will be adopted only if they reduce costs. Although automation might reduce employment in a specific industry, it also releases resources that can be employed in other areas. Improved technology permits us to achieve larger output and income levels than would otherwise be possible.

9. Minimum wage legislation increases the earnings of some low-skill workers, but others are forced to accept inferior employment opportunities, join the ranks of the unemployed, or drop out of the labor force. The direct effects, however, will be moderated by an erosion in the quality of the nonwage components in response to the minimum rate. These adjustments will moderate both (a) the increase in total compensation and (b) the adverse employment effects emanating from the minimum wage. Part-time and youthful workers compose the bulk of those employed at the minimum wage. Only a small share (less than 12 percent) of the minimum wage workers are heads of families with incomes below the poverty level.

CRITICAL ANALYSIS QUESTIONS

1. What are the major reasons for the differences in earnings among individuals? Why are wages in some occupations higher than in others? How do wage differentials influence the allocation of resources? Explain.

*2. Why are real wages in the United States higher than in other countries? Is the labor force itself responsible for the higher wages of American workers? Explain.

3. What are the major factors that would normally explain earnings differences between (a) a lawyer and a minister, (b) an accountant and an elementary school teacher, (c) a business executive and a social worker, (d) a country lawyer and a Wall Street lawyer, (e) an experienced, skilled craftsperson and a 20-year-old high school dropout, and (f) an upper-story and a ground-floor window washer?

4. Is employment discrimination the only important cause of earnings differences between whites and blacks? Carefully justify your answer.

5. During the last three decades, the labor-force participation of married females approximately doubled. What impact did this influx of married workers into the labor force have on (a) the average years of work experience of women relative to men, (b) the mean hours of work time of women relative to men, and (c) the female/male earnings ratio?

*6. "Jobs are the key to economic progress. Unless we create more jobs, our standard of living will fall." Is this statement true or false? Explain.

7. If Jones has a skill that is highly valued, she will be able to achieve high market earnings. In contrast, Smith may work just as hard or even harder, and still earn only a low income.
   a. Does hard work necessarily lead to a high income?
   b. Why are the incomes of some workers high and others low?
   c. Do you think the market system of wage determination is fair? Why or why not?
   d. Can you think of a more equitable system? If so, explain why it is more equitable.

*8. People who have invested heavily in human capital (for example, lawyers, doctors, and even college professors) generally have higher wages, but they also generally work more hours than other workers. Can you explain why?

*9. Analyze the impact of an increase in the minimum wage from the current level to $7.00 per hour. How would the following be affected?

    a. Employment in skill categories previously earning less than $7 per hour.

    b. The unemployment rate of teenagers.

    c. The availability of on-the-job training for low-skill workers.

    d. The demand for high-skill workers who provide good substitutes for the labor services offered by low-skill workers, assuming the low-skill workers are paid higher wage rates due to the increase in the minimum wage.

*10. "If individuals had identical abilities and opportunities, earnings would be equal." Is this statement true or false?

11. "If it were not for employment discrimination against women, the average earnings of men and women would be equal." Is this statement true or false?

*12. Other things being constant, how will the following factors influence hourly earnings?

    a. The employee must work the midnight to 8:00 A.M. shift.

    b. The job involves broken intervals (work 3 hours, off 2 hours, work 3 additional hours, and so on) of employment during the day.

    c. The employer provides low-cost child-care services on the premises.

    d. The job is widely viewed as prestigious.

    e. The job requires employees to move often from city to city.

    f. The job requires substantial amounts of out-of-town travel.

*13. In addition to money-wage compensation, some employers provide employees with health-care benefits; paid time off for sickness, vacation, and jury duty; on-the-premises child-care services; and severance benefits in case of termination.

    a. How do these benefits affect the employer's cost of employment? Do you think employers offering the benefits would be willing to pay higher wages if the benefits were not offered?

    b. Would you be willing to work for an employer who did not offer any of these benefits if the money-wage payments were high enough?

    c. Are these benefits "gifts" from employers offering them? Who really pays for the benefits?

14. Does it sometimes make sense for employers to pay workers with in-kind benefits (health-care insurance, child-care services, termination payments, and the like) rather than higher money wages? Why? Discuss.

*15. Consider two occupations (A and B) that employ persons with the same skill and ability. When employed, workers in the two occupations work the same number of hours per day. In occupation A, employment is stable throughout the year, while employment in B is characterized by seasonal layoffs. In which occupation will the hourly wage rate be highest? Why? In which occupation will the annual wage be highest? Why?

*16. Recognizing that one cannot support a large family at the current minimum wage, suppose that Congress passes legislation requiring that businesses employing workers with three or more children pay these employees at least $7.50 per hour. How would this legislation affect the employment level of low-skill workers with three or more children? Do you think some workers with large families might attempt to conceal the fact? Why?

17. Part-time jobs held by college students rarely provide fringe benefits such as health insurance. Do you think the typical college student would prefer a job that paid $6.00 per hour with no health insurance benefits or a job that paid $5.00 per hour with health insurance benefits? Suppose the government were to mandate that all employers must provide health-care benefits. What impact would this have on the welfare of college students who hold part-time jobs?

*18. In 1994 the median earnings of single men working full time, year-round were only 75 percent of their married counterparts. Does this indicate that employment discrimination existed against single men and in favor of married men?

---

*Asterisk denotes questions for which answers are given in Appendix B.

■ Why do people invest? Why are capital resources often used to produce consumer goods?

■ Why are investors willing to pay interest to acquire loanable funds? Why are lenders willing to loan funds?

■ What is the interest rate? How is the nominal interest rate influenced by the inflation rate and the riskiness of a loan?

■ Why is the interest rate so important when evaluating costs and revenues across time periods?

■ When is an investment profitable? How do profitable and unprofitable investments influence the wealth of nations?

■ How important are investment and the efficient use of capital to the wealth of a nation?

To produce capital, people must forgo the opportunity to produce goods for current consumption. People can choose whether to spend their time picking apples or planting apple trees. In the first case there are more apples today; in the second, more apples tomorrow.

STEVEN LANDSBURG[1]

[1]Steven E. Landsburg, *Price Theory and Applications* (Fort Worth: The Dryden Press, 1992), p. 581.

n the previous chapter we noted that the income of both individuals and nations is closely related to their productivity—their ability to supply goods and services that are highly valued by others. In turn, productivity is influenced by investment choices. Consider such choices as whether to construct an office building, purchase a harvesting machine, or go to law school. The returns derived from investments such as these are generally spread over several years (or even decades). In some cases, the costs of investments may also be incurred over a lengthy time period. How can people compare the benefits and costs of an activity when they are spread across lengthy periods of time? What factors determine whether an investment project should be undertaken? How can investment funds be channeled toward projects that will increase the wealth of people and nations? This chapter will address these questions and related issues.

WHY PEOPLE INVEST

Capital

Resources that enhance our ability to produce output in the future.

Investment

The purchase, construction, or development of capital resources, including both physical capital and human capital. Investments increase the supply of capital.

Saving

Current income that is not spent on consumption goods.

Capital is a term used by economists to describe long-lasting resources that are valued because they can help us produce goods and services in the future. As we previously discussed, there are two broad categories of capital: (1) *physical capital*—nonhuman resources such as buildings, machines, tools, and natural resources—and (2) *human capital*—human resources, that is, the knowledge and skills of people. **Investment** is the purchase, construction, or development of a capital resource. Thus, investment expands the availability of capital resources.

Saving is income not spent on current consumption. *Investment and saving are closely linked. In fact, the two words describe different aspects of the capital-formation process. Saving applies to the nonconsumption of income, while investment applies to the use of the unconsumed income to produce a capital resource.* Sometimes saving and investment are conducted by the same person, as when a farmer saves current income (refrains from spending it on consumption goods) in order to purchase a new tractor (an investment good).

It is important to recognize that saving is required for investment. Someone must save—refrain from consumption—in order to provide the resources for investment. When investors finance a project with their own funds, they are also saving (refraining from current consumption). Investors, however, do not always use their own funds to finance investments. Sometimes they will borrow funds from others. When this is the case, it is the lender rather than the investor who is doing the saving.

The alternative use of resources also highlights the linkage between investment and saving. Resources used to produce capital will be unavailable for the direct production of consumption goods. If we invest more and use more of our resources to produce capital resources today, fewer current resources will be available to produce consumption goods. Thus, if we invest more, we will have to reduce our current consumption.

Why would anyone want to delay consumption in order to undertake an investment? Consumption is the ultimate objective of all production. However, we can sometimes magnify our production of consumption goods by first using resources to produce capital resources and then applying these resources to the production of the desired consumer goods. The use of capital to produce consumption goods makes sense only when the capital enhances our total production of consumption goods.

Perhaps a simple illustration will help clarify the major considerations involved in the use of capital to produce consumption goods. Suppose that Robinson Crusoe could catch fish by either (1) combining his labor with natural resources (direct production) or (2) constructing a net and eventually combining his labor with this capital resource (indirect production). Let us assume that Crusoe could catch 2 fish per day by hand-fishing, but could catch 3 fish per day if he constructed and used a net that would last for 310 days. Suppose it would take Crusoe 55 days to build the net. The opportunity cost of constructing the net would be 110 fish (2 per day for each of the 55 days Crusoe spent building the net). As the accompanying chart indicates, if Crusoe invested in the capital resource (the net), his output during the next year (including the 55 days required to build the net) would be 930 fish (3 per day for 310 days). Alternatively, hand-fishing during the year would lead to an output of only 730 (2 fish per day for 365 days).

NUMBER OF FISH CAUGHT

	WITHOUT NET	WITH NET
Per day	2	3
Annual	730	930

Crusoe's investment in the net will enhance his productivity. With the net, his total output during the year will increase by 200 fish. In the short term, however, investing in the net will impose a sacrifice. During the 55 days it takes to construct the net, Crusoe's production of consumption goods will decline.

How can Crusoe or any other investor know if the value of the larger future output is worth the short-term cost? Most of us have a preference for goods now rather than later. For example, if you are typical, you would prefer a sleek new sports car now rather than the same car ten years from now. On average, individuals possess a **positive rate of time preference.** By this we mean that people subjectively value goods obtained in the immediate or near future (including the present) more highly than goods obtained in the distant future.

When only Crusoe is involved, the attractiveness of the investment in the fishing net is dependent upon his time preference. If he places a high value on a couple of fish per day during the next 55 days, as indeed he may if he is on the verge of starvation, the cost of the investment may well exceed the value of the larger future output. If Crusoe could find someone who would loan him fish while he built the net, however, this would open up an additional option. In this case, the attractiveness of the investment would be influenced by the price of borrowing fish, or, more broadly, by the interest rate.

Positive rate of time preference
The desire of consumers for goods now rather than in the future.

INTEREST RATES

In making decisions across time periods, the interest rate is of central importance because it links the future to the present. *The interest rate allows individuals to place a current valuation on future income and costs. In essence, it is the price of earlier availability.* From the viewpoint of a potential borrower, the interest rate is the premium that must be paid if you want to acquire goods now rather than later. From the lender's viewpoint, it is a reward for waiting—a return received if you are willing to delay consumption into the future.

In a modern economy, people often borrow funds in order to finance current investments and consumption. Because of this, the interest rate is often defined as the price of loanable funds. This definition is proper. But we should remember that it is the earlier availability of goods and services purchased, not the money itself, that is desired by the borrower.

DETERMINATION OF INTEREST RATES

Interest rates are determined by the demand for and supply of loanable funds. Investors demand funds in order to finance capital assets that they believe will increase output and generate profit. Simultaneously, consumers demand loanable funds because they have a positive rate of time preference; they prefer earlier availability.

The demand of investors for loanable funds stems from the productivity of capital. Investors are willing to borrow in order to finance the use of capital in production because they expect that an expansion in future output will provide them with at least resources to repay both the principal and interest on the loan. Our prior example of Robinson Crusoe illustrates this point. Remember, Crusoe could increase his output by 200 fish this year if he could take off 55 days to build a net. Crusoe's fish production, however, would decline (by 2 fish per day) while he was constructing the net. Suppose a fishing crew from a neighboring island visited Crusoe and offered to lend him 110 fish so that he could undertake the capital investment project (building the net). If Crusoe could borrow the 110 fish (the principal) in exchange for, say, 165 fish a year later (110 to repay the principal and 55 as interest on the loan), the investment project would be highly profitable. Crusoe could repay the funds borrowed, plus the 50 percent interest rate, and still have 145 additional fish (the 200 additional fish caught minus the 55 fish paid in interest).

Crusoe's demand for loanable fish—and, more generally, the demand of investors for loanable funds—stems directly from the productivity of the capital investment. Crusoe can gain by borrowing to finance the construction of a fishing net only because the net enables him to expand his total output during the year. Similarly, investors can gain by borrowing funds to undertake investment projects only when the capital assets purchased permit them to expand output (or reduce costs).

As **Exhibit 25–1** illustrates, the interest rate brings the choices of investors and consumers wanting to borrow funds into harmony with the choices of lenders willing to supply funds. Higher interest rates make it more costly for investors to undertake capital spending projects and for consumers to buy now rather than later. Both investors and consumers will therefore curtail their borrowing as the interest rate rises. Investors will borrow less because some investment projects that would be profitable at a low interest rate will be unprofitable at higher rates. Some consumers, rather than pay the high interest premium, will reduce their current consumption when the interest rate increases. Therefore, the amount of funds demanded by borrowers is inversely related to the interest rate.

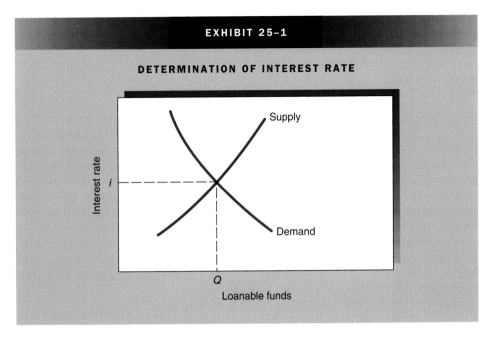

EXHIBIT 25-1

DETERMINATION OF INTEREST RATE

The demand for loanable funds stems from the consumer's desire for earlier availability and the productivity of capital. As the interest rate rises, current goods become more expensive in comparison with future goods. Therefore, borrowers will demand less loanable funds. On the other hand, higher interest rates will stimulate lenders to supply additional funds to the market.

The interest rate also provides a reward to persons (lenders) willing to reduce their current consumption in order to provide loanable funds to others. If some individuals are going to borrow in order to undertake an investment project (or consume more than their current income), others must curtail their current consumption by an equal amount. In essence, the interest rate provides lenders with the incentive to reduce their current consumption so that borrowers can either invest or consume beyond their current income. Higher interest rates provide persons willing to save (willing to supply loanable funds) with the ability to purchase more goods in the future, in exchange for the sacrifice of current consumption. Even though people have a positive rate of time preference, they will give up current consumption to supply funds to the loanable funds market if the price is right—that is, if the interest rate is attractive enough. Therefore, as the interest rate rises, the quantity of funds supplied to the loanable funds market expands.

The interest rate will bring the quantity of funds demanded into balance with the quantity supplied. *At the equilibrium interest rate, the quantity of funds borrowers demand for investment and consumption now (rather than later) will just equal the quantity of funds lenders save. So the interest rate brings the choices of borrowers and lenders into harmony.*

MONEY RATE VERSUS REAL RATE OF INTEREST

We have emphasized that the interest rate is a premium paid by borrowers for earlier availability and a reward received by lenders for delaying consumption. However, during a period of inflation—a general increase in prices—the nominal, or **money rate of interest,** is a misleading indicator of how much borrowers

Money rate of interest
The rate of interest in monetary terms that borrowers pay for borrowed funds. During periods when borrowers and lenders expect inflation, the money rate of interest exceeds the real rate of intertest.

are paying and lenders are receiving. Inflation reduces the purchasing power of a loan's principal. When the principal is repaid in the future, it will not purchase as much as it would have when the funds were initially loaned.

Recognizing the decline in the purchasing power of the dollars with which they will be repaid, lenders reduce the amount of loanable funds supplied unless they are compensated for the anticipated rate of inflation. When borrowers are aware that they will be paying back their loans with dollars of less purchasing power, they are, of course, willing to pay this **inflationary premium,** an additional amount that reflects the expected rate of future price increases. If borrowers and lenders fully anticipate a 5 percent rate of inflation, for example, they will be just as willing to agree on a 10 percent interest rate as they were to agree on a 5 percent interest rate when both anticipated stable prices. The advantage to borrowers is that they can purchase goods and services before they become even more expensive in the future.

Compared to the situation when the general price level is stable, the supply of loanable funds will decline (the curve will shift to the left) and the demand will increase (the curve will shift to the right) once decision makers anticipate future inflation. The money interest rate thus rises, overstating the "true" cost of borrowing and yield from lending. This true cost is the **real rate of interest,** which is equal to the money rate of interest minus the inflationary premium. It reflects the real burden to borrowers and payoff to lenders in terms of command over goods and services.

Our analysis indicates that high rates of inflation will push up the money rate of interest. The real world is consistent with this view. Money interest rates rose to historical highs in the United States as inflation soared to double-digit rates during the 1970s. Cross-country comparisons also illustrate the linkage between inflation and high interest rates. The lowest money interest rates in the world are found in Germany, Switzerland, and, in recent years, Japan. All are countries with low rates of inflation. In contrast, the highest money interest rates are observed in Brazil, Mexico, Turkey, and other countries with high rates of inflation.

INTEREST RATES AND RISK

We have proceeded as though there were only a single interest rate present in the loanable funds market. In the real world, of course, there are many interest rates. There is the mortgage rate, the prime interest rate (the rate charged to business firms with strong credit ratings), the consumer loan rate, and the credit card rate, to name only a few.

Interest rates in the loanable funds market will differ primarily as the result of differences in the risk associated with the loan. It is riskier to loan funds to an unemployed worker than to a well-established business with substantial assets. Similarly, extending an unsecured loan like that accompanying purchases on a credit card is riskier than extending a loan that is secured by an asset, such as a mortgage loan on a house. The risk also increases with the duration of the loan. The longer the time period, the more likely that the financial standing of the borrower will deteriorate or that market conditions will change unfavorably.

As **Exhibit 25–2** shows, the money rate of interest on a loan has three components. The pure-interest component is the real price one must pay for earlier

Inflationary premium
A component of the money interest rate that reflects compensation to the lender for the expected decrease, due to inflation, in the purchasing power of the principal and interest during the course of the loan. It is determined by the expected rate of future inflation.

Real rate of interest
The money rate of interest minus the expected rate of inflation. The real rate of interest indicates the interest premium, in terms of real goods and services, that one must pay for earlier availability.

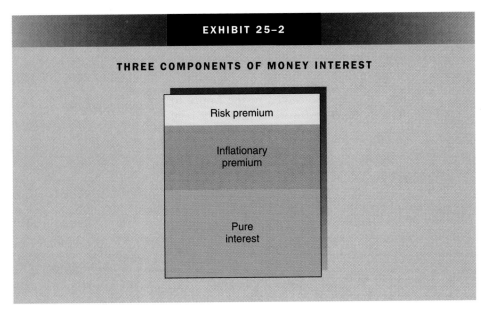

EXHIBIT 25–2

THREE COMPONENTS OF MONEY INTEREST

Risk premium

Inflationary premium

Pure interest

The money interest rate reflects three components: pure interest, inflationary premium, and risk premium. When decision makers expect a high rate of inflation during the period in which the loan is outstanding, the inflationary premium will be substantial. Similarly, the risk premium will be large when the probability of default by the borrower is substantial.

availability. The inflationary-premium component reflects the expectation that the loan will be repaid with dollars of less purchasing power as the result of inflation. The risk-premium component reflects the probability of default—the risk imposed on the lender by the possibility that the borrower may be unable to repay the loan.

PRESENT VALUE OF FUTURE INCOME AND COSTS

If you deposited $100 today in a savings account earning 6 percent interest, you would have $106 one year from now. Therefore, the present value of $100 one year from now is equal to the amount that you would have to invest today in order to have that amount at that time. The interest rate allows us to make this calculation. *The interest rate connects the value of dollars (and capital assets) today with the value of dollars (and expected receipts) in the future. It is used to discount the value of a dollar in the future so that its present worth can be determined today.*

The **present value (PV)** of a payment received one year from now can be expressed as follows:

$$PV = \frac{\text{receipts one year from now}}{1 + \text{interest rate}}$$

If the interest rate is 6 percent, the current value of the $100 to be received one year from now is

$$PV = \frac{\$100}{1.06} = \$94.34$$

Present value (PV)
The current worth of future income after it is discounted to reflect the fact that revenues in the future are valued less highly than revenues now.

If you placed $94.34 in a savings account yielding 6 percent interest, during the year the account would earn $5.66 interest (6 percent of $94.34) and therefore grow to $100 one year from now. Thus, the present value of $100 a year from now is $94.34.

Discounting

The procedure used to calculate the present value of future income, which is inversely related to both the interest rate and the amount of time that passes before the funds are received.

Economists use the term **discounting** to describe this procedure of reducing the value of a dollar to be received in the future to its present worth. Clearly, the value of a dollar in the future is inversely related to the interest rate. For example, if the interest rate is 10 percent, the present value of $100 received one year from now would be only $90.91 ($100 divided by 1.10).

The present value of $100 received two years from now is

$$PV = \frac{\$100}{(1 + \text{interest rate})^2}$$

If the interest rate is 6 percent, $100 received two years from now would be equal to $89 today ($100 divided by 1.06^2). In other words, $89 invested today would yield $100 two years from now.

The present-value procedure can be used to determine the current value of any future income (or cost) stream. If R represents receipts received at the end of various years in the future (indicated by the subscripts) and i represents the interest rate, the present value of the future income stream[2] is

$$PV = \frac{R_1}{(1 + i)} + \frac{R_2}{(1 + i)^2} + \cdots + \frac{R_n}{(1 + i)^n}$$

Exhibit 25–3 shows the present value of $100 received at various times in the future at several different discount rates. The chart clearly illustrates two points. First, the present value of income received at a date in the future declines with the interest rate. The present value of the $100 received one year from now, when discounted at a 4 percent interest rate, is $96.15, compared to $98.04 when a 2 percent discount rate is applied. Second, the present value of the $100 also declines as the date of its receipt is set further into the future. If the applicable discount rate is 6 percent, the present value of $100 received one year from now is $94.34, compared to $89 if the $100 is received two years from now. If the $100 is received five years from now, its current worth is only $74.73. *So the present value of a future dollar payment is inversely related to both the interest rate and to how far in the future the payment will be received.*

PRESENT VALUE, PROFITABILITY, AND INVESTMENT

Investment decisions involve an up-front cost of acquiring a machine, skill, or other asset that is expected to generate additional output and revenue in the future. How can an investor know if the expected future revenues will be suffi-

---

[2]For a specific annual income stream in perpetuity, the present value is equal simply to R/i, where R is the annual revenue stream and i the interest rate. For example, if the interest rate is 10 percent, the PV of a $100 annual income stream in perpetuity is equal to $100/0.10 or $1,000.

The columns indicate the present value of $100 to be received a designated number of years in the future for alternative interest rates. For example, at a discount rate of 2 percent, the present value of $100 to be received five years from now is $90.57. Note that the present value of the $100 declines as either the interest rate or the number of years in the future increases.

EXHIBIT 25–3

PRESENT VALUE OF $100 TO BE RECEIVED IN THE FUTURE

PRESENT VALUE OF $100 TO BE RECEIVED
A DESIGNATED NUMBER OF YEARS
IN THE FUTURE FOR ALTERNATIVE INTEREST RATES

YEARS IN THE FUTURE	2 PERCENT	4 PERCENT	6 PERCENT	8 PERCENT	12 PERCENT	20 PERCENT
1	98.04	96.15	94.34	92.59	89.29	83.33
2	96.12	92.46	89.00	85.73	79.72	69.44
3	94.23	88.90	83.96	79.38	71.18	57.87
4	92.39	85.48	79.21	73.50	63.55	48.23
5	90.57	82.19	74.73	68.06	56.74	40.19
6	88.80	79.03	70.50	63.02	50.66	33.49
7	87.06	75.99	66.51	58.35	45.23	27.08
8	85.35	73.07	62.74	54.03	40.39	23.26
9	83.68	70.26	59.19	50.02	36.06	19.38
10	82.03	67.56	55.84	46.32	32.20	16.15
15	74.30	55.53	41.73	31.52	18.27	6.49
20	67.30	45.64	31.18	21.45	10.37	2.61
30	55.21	30.83	17.41	9.94	3.34	0.42
50	37.15	14.07	5.43	2.13	0.35	0.01

cient to cover the costs? The discounting procedure helps provide the answer, since it permits the investor to place both the costs and the expected future revenues of an investment project into present-value terms. If the present value of the revenue derived from the investment exceeds the present value of the cost, it makes sense to undertake the investment. If revenues and costs of such an investment turn out as expected, the investor will reap economic profit. In turn, profitable investments will increase the value of resources, and thereby create wealth.

On the other hand, if the cost of the project exceeds the discounted value of the future receipts, losses will result. The losses indicate that the resources used to undertake the investment were more valuable than the future revenues generated by the investment. Thus, investments that result in losses reduce the value of resources and thereby diminish wealth. Such investments are counterproductive.

Suppose a truck rental firm is contemplating the purchase of a new $40,000 truck. Past experience indicates that, after making allowances for operational and maintenance expenses, the firm can rent out the truck for net revenues of $12,000 per year (received at the end of each year) for the next four years, the expected life of the vehicle.[3] Since the firm can borrow and lend funds at an interest rate

---

[3]For the sake of simplicity, we assume that the truck has no scrap value at the end of four years.

of 8 percent, we will discount the future expected income at an 8 percent rate. **Exhibit 25–4** illustrates the calculation. Column 4 shows how much $12,000, available at year-end for each of the next four years, is worth today. In total, the present value of the expected rental receipts is $39,744—less than the purchase price of the truck. Therefore, the project should not be undertaken.

If the interest rate in our example had been 6 percent, the present value of the future rental income would have been $41,580.[4] Since it pays to purchase a capital good whenever the present value of the income generated exceeds the purchase price of the capital good, the project would have been profitable at the lower interest rate.

EXPECTED FUTURE EARNINGS AND ASSET VALUES

The present value of the expected revenue minus cost of an investment reveals whether the project should be undertaken. However, *once an investment project has been completed*, the present value of the expected future net earnings will determine the market value of the asset. If the present value of the expected net earnings rises (falls), so too will the value of the asset.

The value of an asset is equal to the present value of the expected net revenues that can be earned by the asset. If the asset is expected to generate a constant annual net income each year in the future, its value would be equal to:

$$\text{Asset value} = \frac{\text{Annual net income from the asset}}{\text{Interest rate}}$$

How much would a tract of land be worth that was expected to generate $1,000 of rental income net of costs each year indefinitely in the future? If the market interest rate is 10 percent, investors would be willing to pay $10,000 for the land. When purchased at this price, the land would provide an investor with the 10 percent market rate of return. Correspondingly, if an asset generates $2,500 of net earnings annually and the market interest rate is 10 percent, the asset would be worth $25,000. There is a direct relationship between the expected future earnings generated by an asset and the asset's market value. *As the present value of the future earnings derived from the ownership of an asset increases, so too does the market value of the asset.*

This linkage between expected future earnings and the price of an asset provides a strong incentive for the owners of business assets to make sure that the assets are being used wisely. Some entrepreneurial investors are particularly

---

[4]The derivation of this figure is shown in the following tabulation:

YEAR	EXPECTED FUTURE INCOME	DISCOUNTED VALUE PER DOLLAR (6 PERCENT RATE)	PRESENT VALUE OF INCOME
1	$12,000	0.943	$11,316
2	12,000	0.890	10,680
3	12,000	0.840	10,080
4	12,000	0.792	9,504
			$41,580

EXHIBIT 25–4

DISCOUNTED PRESENT VALUE OF $12,000 OF TRUCK RENTAL FOR FOUR YEARS (INTEREST RATE = 8 PERCENT)

YEAR (1)	EXPECTED FUTURE INCOME RECEIVED AT YEAR-END (2)	DISCOUNTED VALUE (8 PERCENT RATE) (3)	PRESENT VALUE OF INCOME (4)
1	$12,000	0.926	$11,112
2	12,000	0.857	10,284
3	12,000	0.794	9,528
4	12,000	0.735	8,820
			$39,744

good at (1) identifying a business that is poorly operated, (2) purchasing the business at a depressed price, (3) improving the operational efficiency of the firm, and (4) then reselling the business at a handsome profit. Suppose that a poorly run business currently has net earnings of $1 million per year. What is the market value of the business? If the firm is expected to continue earning $1 million per year, the market value of the firm would be $10 million if the interest rate is 10 percent. Suppose that an alert entrepreneur buys the business for $10 million, hires new management, and improves the operational efficiency of the firm. As the result of these changes, the annual net earnings of the firm increase to $2 million per year. Now how much is the firm worth? If the $2 million annual earnings are expected to continue into the future, the net present value of the firm would rise to $20 million. Thus, the entrepreneur who improved the performance of the firm would be able to sell the firm for a very substantial profit.

In a competitive environment, there is a strong incentive for business managers and asset owners to use the resources under their control efficiently. If they do not, the value of the assets will decline, and the business will be vulnerable to a takeover by alert entrepreneurs capable of operating the firm more efficiently and using the assets more profitably.

INVESTORS AND CORPORATE INVESTMENTS

In modern market economies, investors typically are not entrepreneurs who personally decide which factories to expand, which machine tools to build, and which research investments to undertake. Instead, corporate officers, under the scrutiny of corporate boards of directors, make the entrepreneurial capital investment choices. Nevertheless, individual investors (buyers and sellers of stock)

Changes in stock values provide immediate feedback on what investors think about business strategy and management decisions.

influence that process through the stock market itself. Stock-market investors who believe that a corporation is making sound investment decisions that are likely to yield future profits will buy more of the corporation's stock, driving up its price. Similarly, stockholders who believe that the corporation's current investment decisions will not prove to be profitable have an incentive to "bail out" by selling their stock holdings. Either way, the stock-market price of a corporation's stock gives corporate officers very fast feedback on how market investors evaluate their investment decisions. The choices of individual buyers (and nonbuyers) of the firm's product provide the ultimate judgments on business performance. However, the choices of investors provide early forecasts on the expected success of business ventures.

INVESTING IN HUMAN CAPITAL

In principle, investments in human capital—a choice about continuing in school, for example—involve all the ingredients of other investment decisions. And, because the returns and some of the costs normally accrue in the future, the discounting procedure is as helpful here as in decisions about physical capital.

Exhibit 25–5 is a simplified illustration of the human-capital decision confronting Susan, an 18-year-old high school graduate contemplating the pursuit of a bachelor's degree in business administration. Just as an investment in a truck involves a cost in order to generate a future income, so, too, does a degree in business administration. If Susan does not go to college, she will be able to begin work immediately at annual earnings of E_1. Alternatively, if she goes to college, she will

EXHIBIT 25–5

INVESTING IN HUMAN CAPITAL

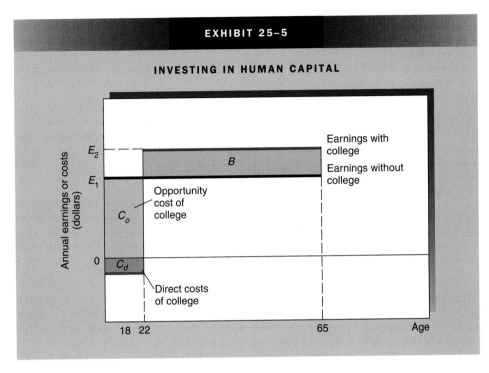

Here we provide a simplified illustration of the human-capital investment decision confronting Susan, an 18-year-old who just finished high school. If Susan goes to college and majors in business administration, she will incur the direct cost (C_d) of the college education (tuition, books, transportation, and so on) plus the opportunity cost (C_o) of earnings forgone while in college. However, with a business degree, she can expect additions to future earnings (B) during her career. If the discounted present value of the additional future earnings exceeds the discounted value of the direct and indirect cost of a college education, the business degree will be a profitable investment for Susan.

incur direct costs (C_d) in the form of tuition, books, transportation, and related expenses. She will also bear the opportunity cost (C_o) of lower earnings while in college. However, the study of business will expand Susan's knowledge and skills, and thereby enable her to earn a higher future income (E_2 rather than E_1).

Will the higher future income be worth the cost? To answer this question, Susan must discount each year's additional income stemming from completion of the business degree and compare that with the discounted value of the cost, including the opportunity cost of earnings lost during the period of study. If the discounted present value of the additional future income exceeds the discounted present value of the cost, acquiring the degree is a worthwhile human-capital investment.

Of course, nonmonetary considerations may also be important, particularly for human-capital investment decisions, since human capital is embodied in the individual. For example, Susan's preferences might be such that she would really prefer working as a college graduate in the business world (rather than in the jobs available to high school graduates) even if she did not make more money. Thus, the nonmonetary attractiveness of business may induce her to pursue the business degree even if the monetary rate of return is low (or even negative).

Although nonmonetary factors are more important in human-capital decision making, opportunity cost and the pursuit of profit influence human-capital investors just as they do physical-capital investors. As with choosing to purchase a new machine, choosing a human-capital investment project such as Susan's degree involves cost, the possibility of profit, and uncertainty. The same principles apply to both types of decisions. Giving due consideration to nonmonetary factors as a potential "benefit," human-capital investors, like physical-capital investors, seek to undertake only those projects that they anticipate will yield benefits in excess of costs.

PROFIT, ENTREPRENEURSHIP, AND PROSPERITY

As we previously discussed, firms and individual investors may be able to earn persistent economic profit—a return in excess of the opportunity cost of funds—if they are able to restrict entry into various industries and occupations. Economic profit, however, may also be present in competitive markets. In a competitive market economy, there are two sources of economic profit: uncertainty and entrepreneurship.

While investment places people in a position to earn a handsome return, it also exposes them to additional uncertainty. We live in a world of uncertainty, imperfect information, and dynamic change. No one knows precisely what will happen in the future. In a sense, investing resembles a game of chance. Unanticipated changes, changes that no one could have foreseen, create winners and losers. If people did not care whether their income experienced substantial variability or not, the uncertainty accompanying investment projects would not affect the average rate of return. Most people, though, dislike uncertainty. They prefer the certain receipt of $1,000 to a fifty-fifty chance of receiving either nothing or $2,000. Therefore, people must be paid a premium—an economic profit—if they are going to willingly accept the uncertainty that necessarily accompanies investments.

Alertness to potential opportunities to combine resources in a manner that increases their value provides a second source of economic profit in a competitive setting. Some individuals are better than others at identifying potentially profitable opportunities. *At any given time, there is virtually an infinite number of potential investment projects. Some will increase the value of resources and therefore lead to a handsome rate of return on capital. Others will reduce the value of resources, generating economic losses. Entrepreneurship involves the ability to recognize and undertake economically beneficial projects that have gone unnoticed by others.* Originality, quickness to act, and imagination are important aspects of entrepreneurship. Successful entrepreneurship involves leadership; most profits will be gone by the time the imitators arrive on the scene. But, of course, there is usually risk involved. Frequently, the entrepreneur's vision turns out to have been a mirage. What appeared to be a profitable opportunity turns out to have been an expensive illusion.

The great Harvard economist Joseph Schumpeter believed that entrepreneurship and innovative behavior were the moving forces behind capitalism. According to Schumpeter, this entrepreneurial discovery of new, improved ways of doing things is a central engine of economic progress and improvements in living standards. As Schumpeter put it:

> *The fundamental impulse that sets the capitalist engine in motion comes from the new consumer's goods, the new methods of production or transportation, and new markets, and the new forms of industrial organization that capitalist enterprise creates.*[5]

---

[5]Joseph A. Schumpeter, *Capitalism, Socialism, and Democracy* (New York: Harper Torchbooks, 1950), p. 83.

JOSEPH SCHUMPETER (1883–1950)

Born in Austria, Schumpeter was a long-time professor of economics at Harvard University. Generally recognized as one of the top five economists of this century, he is perhaps best known for his views on entrepreneurship and the future of capitalism. He believed that the creative and innovative behavior of business entrepreneurs was the primary fuel of economic progress under capitalism.

Potential entrepreneurs are confined to using their own wealth and that of coventurers, in addition to whatever can be borrowed. Entrepreneurs with a past record of success will be able to attract funds more readily for investment projects. Therefore, in a market economy, previously successful entrepreneurs will exert a disproportionate influence over decisions as to which projects will be undertaken and which will not.

THE CAPITAL MARKET AND THE WEALTH OF NATIONS

Both interest and profit perform important allocative functions.[6] Interest induces people to give up current consumption, a sacrifice that is a necessary ingredient for capital formation. Economic profit provides both human- and physical-capital decision makers with the incentive to (1) undertake investments yielding an uncertain return and (2) discover and develop beneficial and productive investment opportunities.

If a nation is going to realize its potential, it must have a mechanism capable of attracting savings and channeling them into investment projects that create wealth. In a market economy, the capital market performs this function. This highly diverse market includes markets for stocks, real estate, and businesses, as well as the loanable funds market.

---

[6]In addition to wages, interest, and profits, economists often discuss rent as a return to a factor of production, the supply of which is perfectly inelastic. We have not included this discussion for two reasons. First, one can legitimately argue that the supply of all factors of production has some elasticity. After all, even the supply of usable land can be expanded through drainage, clearing, and conservation. Therefore, rent is always a matter of degree. Second, the term *rent* is used in a variety of ways, even by economists. The macroeconomic usage differs substantially from the usage in microeconomics. The term is sometimes used to define the returns to a specialized resource, such as an actor's talent, even though training plays an integral part in the supply of the resource. Rent is also sometimes applied to a factor the supply of which is temporarily fixed, even though it can clearly be expanded in the future. Since the returns to capital can be adequately discussed without introducing rent, we concluded that the cost of the ambiguity of the term exceeded the benefits of an extended discussion.

The capital market brings together people who are willing to save with those willing to invest. Some people save and supply funds to the capital market in exchange for a fixed rate of return. People who purchase bonds and maintain savings deposits are examples. Other people supply funds in exchange for an uncertain return linked to the success or failure of a business or investment project. Stockholders and partnership investors fall into this category. Still others supply funds to the capital market when they use their own funds to purchase a business or acquire additional schooling.

The key attribute of the capital market is its ability to direct funds toward wealth-creating projects. When investment in a capital asset generates additional output (and revenue) that is valued more highly than the value of the resources required for its production, the investment will create wealth. When property rights are securely defined and enforced, wealth-creating investments will also be profitable.

Private ownership and a competitive capital market provide investors with a strong incentive to evaluate potential projects carefully and search for profitable projects. In an uncertain world, however, private investors will sometimes make mistakes, undertaking projects that prove unprofitable. If investors were unwilling to take such chances, many new ideas would go untested and many worthwhile but risky projects would not be undertaken. Thus, mistaken investments are a necessary price paid for fruitful innovations in new technologies and products. The capital market will at least assure that the mistakes are self-correcting. Losses will signal investors to terminate unprofitable and unproductive projects.

Without a private capital market, it is virtually impossible to attract funds and consistently channel them into wealth-creating projects. When investment funds are allocated by the government rather than the market, an entirely different set of criteria comes into play. Political clout replaces market return as the basis for allocating the funds. As a result, investment projects that reduce wealth rather than enhance it become more likely.

The experience of Eastern Europe and the former Soviet Union illustrates this point. The investment rates of these countries were among the highest in the world. The central planners of these countries channeled approximately one-third of the national output into investment. But even these high rates of investment did little to improve the standard of living. Political rather than economic considerations determined which investment projects would be undertaken. Therefore, investment funds were often wasted on political boondoggles and high-visibility projects favored by important political leaders.

INVESTMENT AND GROWTH: EMPIRICAL EVIDENCE

Economic analysis indicates that investment in both physical and human capital is an important source of productivity and income growth. Other things constant, countries that invest more and channel more of their investments into productive projects today will tend to have a higher income tomorrow.

EXHIBIT 25-6

INVESTMENT AND ECONOMIC GROWTH:
CROSS-COUNTRY COMPARISONS

	INVESTMENT AS A SHARE OF GDP		ANNUAL GROWTH RATE	PER CAPITA GDP (IN 1985 U.S. DOLLARS)	
	1975–84	1985–94	1980–94	1970	1994
HIGH-INVESTMENT AND HIGH-GROWTH COUNTRIES					
Hong Kong	30.1	27.1	5.0	4,502	17,834
South Korea	29.9	33.6	7.4	1,680	8,565
Thailand	27.8	34.1	6.1	1,526	4,450
Singapore	43.4	39.3	5.3	3,017	14,415
Indonesia	23.6	32.9	4.1	715	2,310
Malaysia	33.9	30.6	4.1	2,154	6,510
HIGH-INCOME INDUSTRIAL COUNTRIES					
Japan	30.8	30.2	2.9	7,303	15,105
United States	19.9	17.8	1.6	12,963	18,850
Canada	22.8	20.3	1.3	10,124	11,510
United Kingdom	17.9	17.5	1.9	8,537	13,430
Germany	22.3	23.5	1.8	9,425	15,005
LATIN AMERICAN COUNTRIES					
Argentina	23.8	17.3	0.1	5,637	6,025
Chile	15.4	24.0	2.8	3,605	5,250
Brazil	21.3	21.8	0.1	2,434	4,118
Mexico	24.5	19.0	−0.1	3,987	6,260
Bolivia	17.5	12.7	−1.5	1,661	1,730
Peru	23.0	19.3	−1.3	2,736	2,390

Source: International Monetary Fund, *International Financial Statistics Yearbook*; and Robert Summers and Alan Heston, *Penn World Tables* (Cambridge: National Bureau of Economic Research, 1994). The 1992 per capita income data from the latter source were updated to 1994 by the authors.

Exhibit 25–6 presents data on investment in physical capital, growth, and per capita GDP for several countries. Look at the investment rates of Hong Kong, South Korea, Thailand, Singapore, Indonesia, and Malaysia. Throughout most of the last two decades, these countries have persistently channeled 30 percent or more of their GDP into investment. In contrast, the investment rates of both the high-income industrial and Latin American countries have been much lower. Among the latter two groups, only Japan invested anything close to the amounts of the high-growth Asian economies.

Propelled by high rates of investment, the Asian economies of Exhibit 25–6 have achieved the world's highest growth rates during the last 25 years. In 1970, the per capita incomes of even the two wealthiest less developed Asian nations—Hong Kong and Singapore—were only a fraction of the income levels of the industrial countries. In general, the 1970 per capita incomes of the Asian countries were less than those of the major countries of Latin America. Twenty-five years of growth, however, have made a dramatic difference. Except for the two poorest (Indonesia and Thailand), the per capita GDP of the high-investment, high-growth Asian economies now exceeds that of all Latin American countries. Even more impressive, the per capita GDP of Hong Kong and Singapore is now greater than that of the United Kingdom. Hong Kong's per capita income is now the second highest in the world, behind only the United States. Since 1980, the high-investment Asian nations have achieved annual growth rates ranging from the 4.1 percent of Malaysia and Indonesia to the 7.4 percent rate of South Korea, substantially higher than the rates of both the industrial and Latin American countries.

In addition to high investment rates, other factors have contributed to the impressive growth rates of the Asian economies. Since these countries had low incomes at the beginning of the period, they were in a position to borrow, emulate, and adopt successful technologies and business ideas from more advanced countries. Studies have shown that education—particularly strong elementary and secondary schooling—has led to a substantial improvement in the human capital of labor force participants in the high-growth Asian nations.[7] Furthermore, investment does not just happen. A legal system that protects property rights and a tax system that encourages saving an investment also play a role. Economic theory indicates that several factors influence the growth of nations. Capital formation and investment directed into wealth-creating projects is one of the most important. The data of Exhibit 25–6 illustrate its significance as a source of growth.

---

[7]See World Bank, *The East Asian Miracle* (Washington, D.C.: The World Bank, 1993) for additional information on this topic.

LOOKING AHEAD

As the preceding two chapters have stressed, investment in physical and human capital will influence the wealth and income of both individuals and nations. Differences among individuals in these factors will also contribute to income inequality. After analyzing the importance of unions in the labor market, we will consider the issue of income inequality in some detail.

CHAPTER SUMMARY

1. We can often produce more consumption goods by first using our resources to produce physical- and human-capital resources and then using those capital resources to produce the desired consumption goods. Resources used to produce capital goods will be unavailable for the direct production of consumption goods. Therefore, someone must save—refrain from current consumption—in order to release the resources required for investment.

2. People have a positive rate of time preference; they generally value present consumption more highly than future consumption.

3. The interest rate is the price of earlier availability. From the viewpoint of a potential borrower, interest is the premium that must be paid if you want to acquire goods now rather than later. From the lender's viewpoint, it is a reward for waiting.

4. Interest provides lenders with an incentive to curtail current consumption and to supply loanable funds to others. The demand for loanable funds stems from the pro-

ductivity of capital resources and the positive rate of time preference of consumers. The market interest rate will bring the quantity of funds demanded by borrowers (to undertake current investments and to consume beyond their current income) into balance with the supply of funds provided by lenders willing to forgo current consumption in exchange for the interest premium.

5. During inflationary times, the money rate of interest incorporates an inflationary premium reflecting the expected future increase in the price level. Under these circumstances, the money rate of interest exceeds the real rate of interest.

6. The money rate of interest on a specific loan reflects three basic factors—the pure interest rate, an inflationary premium, and a risk premium that is directly related to the probability of default by the borrower.

7. In decisions made across time periods, the interest rate is of central importance because it allows individuals to place a current valuation on future revenues and costs. Since a dollar in the future is valued less than a dollar today, the value of future receipts must be discounted to calculate their current worth. The discounting procedure can be used to calculate the present value of an expected net income stream from a potential investment project. If the present value of the expected revenues exceeds the present value of the expected costs, the project will be profitable when things turn out as expected.

8. The present value of expected future net earnings will determine the market value of existing assets. An increase (decline) in the expected future earnings derived from an asset will increase (reduce) the market value of the asset.

9. Economic profit plays a central role in the allocation of capital and the determination of which investment projects will be undertaken. In a competitive environment, economic profit reflects both uncertainty and entrepreneurial alertness. Entrepreneurship involves the ability to recognize and undertake profitable projects that have gone unnoticed by others.

10. If a nation is to grow and prosper, it must have a mechanism that will attract savings and channel them into investment projects that create wealth. The capital market performs this function in a market economy. When the value of the output (and revenue) derived from an investment exceeds its costs (the value of the resources required for the production of the capital good), the investment will be productive. When property rights are defined and securely enforced, productive investments will also be profitable and the profit motive will give private investors the incentive to undertake wealth-creating projects.

11. Investment in both physical and human capital is an important source of productivity growth. The economies of countries that invest more and channel their investment funds into more productive projects generally grow more rapidly.

12. The empirical evidence confirms the importance of investment. High-growth economies like Hong Kong, Singapore, and South Korea have high investment rates.

CRITICAL ANALYSIS QUESTIONS

*1. How would the following changes influence the rate of interest in the United States?
   a. an increase in the positive time preference of lenders
   b. an increase in the positive time preference of borrowers
   c. an increase in domestic inflation
   d. increased uncertainty about a nuclear war
   e. improved investment opportunities in Europe

2. "Any return to capital above the pure-interest yield is unnecessary. The pure-interest yield is sufficient to provide capitalists with the earnings necessary to replace their assets and to compensate for their sacrifice of current consumption. Any return above that is pure gravy; it is excess profit." Do you agree with this view? Why or why not?

3. How are human- and physical-capital investment decisions similar? How do they differ? What determines the profitability of a physical-capital investment? Do human-capital investors make profits? If so, what is the source of the profit? Explain.

*4. A lender made the following statement to a borrower: "You are borrowing $1,000, which is to be repaid in 12 monthly installments of $100 each. Your total interest charge is $200, which means your interest rate is 20 percent." Is the effective interest rate on the loan really 20 percent? Explain.

5. In a market economy, investors have a strong incentive to undertake profitable investments. What makes an investment profitable? Do profitable investments create wealth? Why or why not? Do all investments create wealth? Discuss.

*6. Over long periods of time, the rate of return of an average investment in the stock market has exceeded the return on high-quality bonds. Is the higher return on stocks surprising? Why or why not?

7. The interest rates charged on outstanding credit card balances are generally higher than the interest rate that banks charge customers with a good credit rating. Why do you think the credit card rate is so high? Should the government impose an interest rate ceiling of, say, 4 percent above the prime lending rate (the rate banks charge customers with a good credit rating) on credit card loans? If it did, who would be hurt and who would be helped? Discuss.

*8. If the money rate of interest on a low-risk government bond is 10 percent and the inflation rate for the last several years has been steady at 4 percent, what is the estimated real rate of interest?

9. Suppose you are contemplating the purchase of a personal computer at a cost of $1,000. The expected lifetime of the asset is three years. You expect to lease the asset to a business for $400 annually (payable at the end of each year) for three years. If you can borrow (and lend) money at an interest rate of 8 percent, will the investment be a profitable undertaking? Is the project profitable at an interest rate of 12 percent? Provide calculations in support of your answer.

10. The data presented in Exhibit 25–6 indicate that countries investing more of their total output grow more rapidly. Explain in your own words why this is true. Do you think the government should adopt policies designed to increase the saving and investment rates of citizens? Why or why not? Discuss.

*11. Alicia's philosophy of life is summed up by the proverb "A penny saved is a penny earned." She plans and saves for the future. In contrast, Mike's view is "Life is uncertain; eat dessert first." Mike wants as much as possible now.

    a. Who has the highest rate of time preference?

    b. Do people like Alicia benefit from the presence of people like Mike?

    c. Do people like Mike benefit from the presence of people like Alicia? Explain.

*12. Some countries with very low incomes per capita are unable to save very much. Are people in these countries helped or hurt by people in high-income countries with much higher rates of saving?

*13. According to a news item, the owner of a lottery ticket paying $3 million over 20 years is offering to sell the ticket for $1.2 million cash now. "Who knows?" the ticket owner explained, "We might not even be here in 20 years, and I do not want to leave it to the dinosaurs."

    a. Assuming that the ticket pays $150,000 per year at the end of each year for the next 20 years, what is the present value of the ticket if the appropriate rate for discounting the future income is thought to be 10 percent?

    b. Assuming the discount rate is in the 10 percent range, is the offer price of $1.2 million reasonable?

    c. Can you think of any disadvantages of buying the lottery earnings rather than a bond?

14. Suppose you decide to rent an apartment for five years. Further suppose that the owner offers to provide you with a used refrigerator for free and promises to maintain and repair the refrigerator during the next five years. You also have the option of buying a new energy-efficient refrigerator (with a five-year free maintenance agreement) for $700. The new refrigerator will reduce your electric bill by $150 per year and will have a market value of $200 after five years. If necessary, you can borrow money from the bank at an 8 percent rate of interest. Which option should you choose?

*15. Suppose that you are considering whether to enroll in a summer computer training program that costs $2,500. If you take the program, you will have to give up $1,500 of earnings from your summer job. You figure that the program will increase your earnings by $500 per year for each of the next 10 years. Beyond that, it is not expected to affect your earnings. If you take the program, you will have to borrow the funds at an 8 percent rate of interest. From strictly a monetary viewpoint, should you enroll in the program?

---

*Asterisk denotes questions for which answers are given in Appendix B.

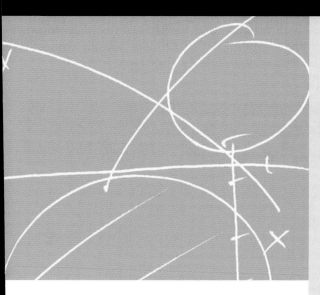

Analysts who have attributed national economic problems ranging from unemployment to wage inflation to low productivity to unions will have to find a new culprit to blame: unless there is a remarkable renaissance in unionism, critics won't have unions to kick around any more.

RICHARD B. FREEMAN[1]

---

[1]Richard B. Freeman, "Contraction and Expansion: The Divergence of Private Sector and Public Sector Unionism in the United States," *Journal of Economic Perspectives* 2 (spring 1988), p. 86.

CHAPTER FOCUS

■ How much of the U.S. work force is unionized?

■ How does the collective-bargaining process work?

■ How important is the strike in the bargaining process?

■ Can unions increase the wages of their members? What makes a union strong? What factors limit the power of a union?

■ Can unions increase the share of income going to labor?

■ How important are unions in other countries?

■ What impact have unions had on the legal structure of worker-management relations?

Labor union

A collective organization of employees who bargain as a unit with employers.

In an earlier chapter, we mentioned that labor unions may be able to influence wage rates. We are now prepared to examine the labor-market effects of unions. A **labor union** is an organization of employees, usually working either in the same occupation or same industry, who have consented to joint bargaining with employers concerning wages, working conditions, grievance procedures, and other elements of employment. The primary objective of a labor union is to improve the welfare of its members.

Unions have historically been controversial. Some see them as a necessary shield protecting workers from employer greed. Others charge that unions are monopolies seeking to provide their members with benefits at the expense of other workers, consumers, and economic efficiency. Still others argue that the economic influence of unions—both for good and for bad—is vastly overrated. This chapter will enhance our understanding of labor unions and the economic factors that influence their ability to achieve desired objectives.

UNION MEMBERSHIP AS SHARE OF WORK FORCE

Historically, the proportion of the U.S. labor force belonging to a labor union has fluctuated substantially. In 1910 approximately 10 percent of the nonfarm employees belonged to a union. As **Exhibit 26–1** shows, this figure rose to 18 percent in 1920. In the aftermath of the First World War, union membership declined, falling to 12 percent of the nonfarm work force by 1929. Favorable legislation adopted during the Great Depression of the 1930s encouraged unions, and union membership as a share of the nonfarm labor force rose from 13.5 percent in 1935 to 30.4 percent by 1945. By 1954 one-third of the nonfarm work force in the United States was unionized.

Since the mid-1950s, however, union membership has waned. As Exhibit 26–1 illustrates, it declined as a share of the labor force slowly during 1955–1970, and then quite rapidly since 1980. By 1995 only 14.9 percent of wage and salary workers were union members, down from 24 percent in 1979 (and 32 percent in 1954).

Several factors have contributed to this decline. First, much of the recent growth in employment has been with relatively small firms (less than 100 employees) in service and high-tech industries. Small firms are costly for unions to organize, and unions have traditionally been weak in service and high-tech industries. Second, competition has eroded union strength in several important industries. Foreign producers have increased their market share in steel, mining, automobiles, and other heavy-manufacturing industries. Employment has thus been shrinking in these areas of traditional union strength. Deregulation in transportation and communication industries has further reduced the effectiveness of unions. As these industries have become more competitive, unionized firms have faced increased competition from nonunion producers. Finally, even regional growth patterns have adversely affected union strength. During the 1960s and 1970s, population and employment grew rapidly in the Sunbelt, while stagnating in the Northeast and upper Middle West. Since the former is an area of union weakness and the latter an area of strength, this pattern also retarded the growth of union membership.

EXHIBIT 26–1

UNION MEMBERSHIP AS SHARE
OF NONAGRICULTURAL EMPLOYMENT

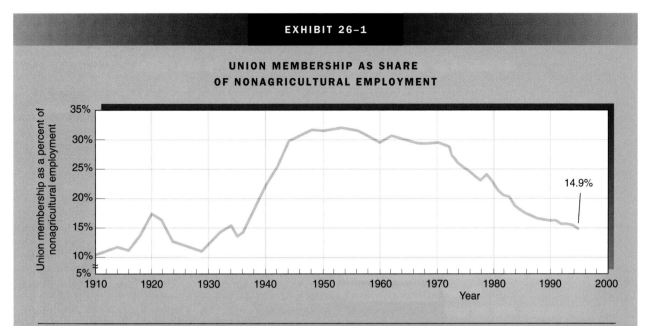

Between 1910 and 1935, union membership fluctuated between 12 percent and 18 percent of nonagricultural employment. During the 1935–1945 period, union membership
increased sharply to approximately one-third of the nonfarm
work force. Since the mid-1950s, union membership has declined as a percent of nonfarm employment, and the decline
has been particularly sharp since 1979.

Source: Leo Troy and Neil Sheflin, *Union Source Book: Membership,
Structure, Finance, Directory* (West Orange, N.J.: Industrial Relations
and Information Services, 1985); and Barry T. Hirsch and David A.
Macpherson, *Union Membership and Earnings Data Book* (Washington,
D.C.: Bureau of National Affairs, 1996). The post-1973 data are for all
wage and salary workers.

All these factors, of course, have to some extent been caused by union success in raising union wages. Business investment and employment will tend to
move toward geographic areas, industries, and classes of firms where wages are
lower *relative to productivity*. Therefore, when unions increase the wages of their
members *relative to nonunion workers of similar productivity*, they also retard the
growth of employment in unionized sectors.

As **Exhibit 26–2** shows, there is substantial variation in the incidence of
union membership across gender, racial, and occupational groups. Men are more
likely than women to belong to a union. In 1995, 17.2 percent of employed men
were union members compared with only 12.3 percent of employed women. The
incidence of unionization among blacks (19.9 percent) was higher than for whites
(14.2 percent) and Hispanics (13.0 percent). There is substantial variation in
unionization according to occupation. Less than 10 percent of the workers in
technical, sales, clerical, and service occupations were unionized in 1995. In contrast, 23 percent of the workers in craft, operative, and laborer occupations
belonged to a union.

*The biggest difference in unionization is found when comparing the pri-
vate and public sectors. While only 10.4 percent of the private wage and salary
workers are unionized, 37.8 percent of the government employees belong to a
union.* And while the share of the private work force belonging to a union has
been shrinking, unionization has been increasing in the public sector. During

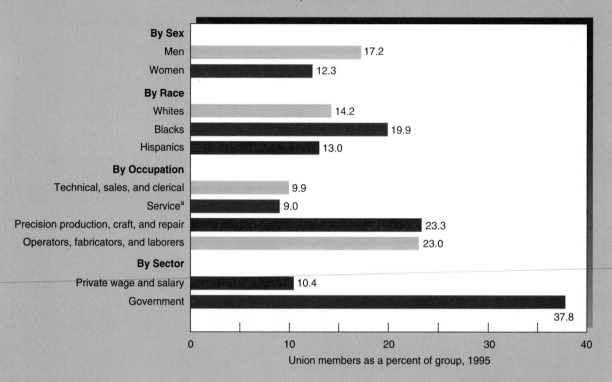

EXHIBIT 26–2

INCIDENCE OF UNION MEMBERSHIP ACCORDING TO SEX, RACE, OCCUPATION, AND SECTOR

By Sex
Men — 17.2
Women — 12.3

By Race
Whites — 14.2
Blacks — 19.9
Hispanics — 13.0

By Occupation
Technical, sales, and clerical — 9.9
Service[a] — 9.0
Precision production, craft, and repair — 23.3
Operators, fabricators, and laborers — 23.0

By Sector
Private wage and salary — 10.4
Government — 37.8

Union members as a percent of group, 1995

The incidence of unionism is higher among (a) men than women and (b) blacks than whites and Hispanics. Technical, sales, clerical, and service workers are far less likely to be unionized than craft, operator, and repair workers. As a share of the work force, unionization among government em- *ployees is nearly four times that of private sector workers.*

[a]Excluding protective service workers.

Source: U.S. Department of Labor, Employment and Earnings (January 1996).

the last 35 years, the proportion of government employees belonging to a union has more than tripled, rising from 11 percent in 1960 to 37.8 percent in 1995.

There is also substantial variation in the rate of unionization among states. **Exhibit 26–3** indicates the share of wage and salary employees that is unionized for the ten states with the lowest and highest unionization rates. Except for South Dakota, southern states compose the group of ten with the lowest incidence of union membership. Less than 7 percent of the employees are unionized in South Carolina, North Carolina, Mississippi, Texas, Virginia, and Georgia. Heading the list of states with highest rate of unionization are New York, Hawaii, Michigan, Alaska, and New Jersey. The rate of unionization tends to be high in the industrial states of the Northeast and upper Midwest.

*Indicates state has a right-to-work law.

Source: Barry T. Hirsch and David A. Macpherson, *Union Membership and Earnings Data Book* (Washington, D.C.: Bureau of National Affairs, 1996), Table 8.

EXHIBIT 26–3

TEN STATES WITH THE HIGHEST AND LOWEST INCIDENCE OF UNION MEMBERS AS A PERCENT OF ALL WAGE AND SALARY EMPLOYEES

TEN LOWEST	UNION MEMBERS AS A PERCENT OF WAGE AND SALARY EMPLOYEES	TEN HIGHEST	UNION MEMBERS AS A PERCENT OF WAGE AND SALARY EMPLOYEES
*South Carolina	3.3	New York	27.7
*North Carolina	4.2	Hawaii	24.6
*Mississippi	5.2	Michigan	23.7
*Texas	6.5	Alaska	23.1
*Virginia	6.7	New Jersey	21.9
*Georgia	6.8	Washington	21.0
*Louisiana	7.0	Minnesota	20.3
*Florida	7.3	Illinois	20.2
*South Dakota	7.7	Connecticut	20.2
*Arkansas	7.8	*Nevada	20.2

THE COLLECTIVE BARGAINING PROCESS

Each year, **collective bargaining contracts** covering wages and working conditions for 6 million to 9 million workers are negotiated. These are union-management agreements prescribing the conditions of employment. Union negotiators, acting as agents for a group of employees, bargain with management about the provisions of a labor contract. If the union representatives are able to obtain a contract they consider acceptable, they will typically submit it to a vote of the union members. If approved by the members, the contract establishes in detail wage rates, fringe benefits, and working conditions for a future time interval, usually the next two or three years. During that time interval, union and management alike must abide by the conditions of the contract. Although the labor contract is between management and union, it also applies to the nonunion bargaining unit members who are employed by the firm in positions covered by the agreement.

Some labor-management contracts contain a **union-shop provision** requiring all workers to join the union after a specified length of employment, usually 30 days. Proponents of this provision argue that since all workers in the bargaining

Collective bargaining contract
A detailed contract between a group of employees (a labor union) and their employer.

Union-shop provision
The requirement that all employees join the recognized union and pay dues to it within a specified length of time (usually 30 days) after their employment with the firm begins.

unit enjoy the benefits of collective bargaining, all should be required to join and pay dues.

Opponents of the union shop argue that all employees are not helped by a union. Some unions lack the necessary power to obtain wage increases. Some employees may feel that they would be better off if they could bargain for themselves. In addition, unions often engage in political activities that may run counter to the views of individual employees. Why should an employee be forced, as a condition of employment, to support activities he or she does not approve? In 1947 Congress passed the Taft-Hartley Act; Section 14-B allows states to enact **right-to-work laws** prohibiting union-shop contracts. Thus, when a state has a right-to-work statute, a union-management contract cannot require a worker to join a union as a condition of employment. Right-to-work legislation is currently present in 21 states, most of them in the Sunbelt. Union membership tends to be lower in states with right-to-work laws. Indeed, it has been states with relatively few union members that have been most likely to adopt right-to-work laws. As Exhibit 26–3 illustrates, all the ten states with the lowest incidence of unionization were right-to-work states. In contrast, only one (Nevada) of the ten states with the highest rate of union membership had a right-to-work law.

Right-to-work laws
Laws that prohibit the union shop—the requirement that employees must join a union as a condition of employment. Each state has the option to adopt (or reject) right-to-work legislation.

THE STRIKE AND COLLECTIVE BARGAINING

Typically, management and labor negotiators begin the bargaining process for a new labor contract several months, or even a year, before the termination of the current agreement. The new contract is usually approved before the old contract is terminated. However, at the termination of the old labor-management agreement, if the bargaining process has broken down and there is no agreement on a new contract, either side may use its economic power to try to bring the other to terms. Employers can withhold employment from workers at the expiration of the old contract. However, since employers can unilaterally announce their terms for continued employment, they seldom discontinue operations.

Strike
An action of unionized employees in which they (1) discontinue working for the employer and (2) take steps to prevent other potential workers from offering their services to the employer.

The major source of work stoppage is the **strike**, which consists of two major actions by a union: (1) employees, particularly union employees, refuse to work, and (2) steps are taken to prevent other employees from working for the employer. Both conditions are essential to a strike. Unless other employees, often referred to as scabs or strike-breakers, are prevented from accepting jobs with the employer, the strike becomes merely a mass resignation. A strike also involves picketing to restrict and discourage the hiring of other workers, actions to prevent free entry and exit from a plant, and perhaps even violence or the threat of violence against workers willing to cross the picket lines.

The purpose of a strike is to impose economic costs on an employer so that the terms proposed by the union will be accepted. When the strike can be used to disrupt the production process and interfere with the employer's ability to sell goods and services to customers, it is a very powerful weapon. Under such conditions, the employer may submit to the wage demands of the union as a means of avoiding the costs of the strike.

Given the nature of the strike, it is not surprising that the "right to strike" has had an uneven history. At times, striking was prohibited because it was thought to interfere with the rights of nonunion workers. Before the passage of legislation in the early 1900s clearly establishing the right to strike, courts were sometimes willing to intervene and limit certain types of strikes. The role of law enforcement in strikes also has had a mixed history. In some areas, the police have given nonstrikers (employees who desire to continue working) protection to and from their jobs. In other cases, they have permitted pickets to block entry and have turned their backs on violence between strikers and nonstrikers. Even today, the protection a nonstriker can expect from the police varies from location to location.

The United States has established some limitations on the right to strike. The use of the strike by government employees—the single area of union growth—is substantially restricted. Most states limit the right of public employees to strike. When strikes are prohibited, states and municipalities typically provide provisions for binding arbitration in the event the parties cannot reach an agreement. Prohibitions against strikes by police officers and firefighters are particularly commonplace. Strikes by federal employees are also prohibited by law. When the federally employed air-traffic controllers called a strike during the summer of 1981, striking workers who refused to return to work were fired and eventually replaced. Although used infrequently, the Taft-Hartley Act allows the president to seek a court injunction prohibiting a private-sector strike for 80 days when it is believed that the strike would create a "national emergency." During the 80-day period, work continues under the conditions of the old contract. If a settlement is not reached during this "cooling-off" period, however, employees again have the option of using the strike as a weapon.

COST OF A STRIKE

A strike can be costly to both union and management. From the firm's viewpoint, a work stoppage may mean that it will be unable to meet the current demand for its product. It may lose customers, and they may be difficult to win back once they have turned to competitors during the strike. A strike will be more costly to the firm when (1) demand for its product is strong, (2) it is unable to stockpile its product, and (3) its fixed costs are high even during the strike. If the firm can stockpile its product in anticipation of a strike, a work stoppage may not have much impact on current sales. For example, automobile producers, particularly during slack times, often have an inventory of new cars that allows them to meet current demand during a 60- or even 90-day strike. In contrast, the shipping revenues of a trucking firm may be completely eliminated by a truckers' strike. The firm is unable to deliver its service because of the strike, and potential customers therefore turn to rail, air, postal, and other forms of shipping. The firm suffers a permanent loss of sales.

Careful timing can also magnify the cost of a strike. Agricultural unions can threaten farmers with the loss of an entire year's income by striking at harvest time. Similarly, baseball players and umpires can strengthen their position by threatening a strike shortly before or during the playoffs and World Series.

The nature of the product, the level of current demand, and the ability of the firm to continue to meet the requests of its customers during a strike all influence the effectiveness of the strike as a weapon. The more costly a work stoppage would be to a firm, the greater the pressure on it to yield to the demands of the union.

Strikes, particularly if they are long, are also quite costly to employees. Although a carnival attitude often prevails during the early days of a strike, a few weeks without a paycheck imposes an extreme hardship on most families. Strike funds are usually inadequate to deal with a prolonged strike. Some workers may be able to arrange for a temporary job to help pay the bills, but such employment will generally be much less attractive than their regular jobs. Therefore, as a strike continues, pressures build on the union to arrive at a settlement.

Strikes sometimes exert a substantial impact on secondary parties who are unable to influence union-management relations. For example, a prolonged strike in the steel industry might cause a loss of work time in automobile, construction, and other industries. A teachers' strike might force a working parent to quit his or her job to care for the children. A public transit strike in New York can paralyze Fun City. Should third parties be protected when strikes involve the public interest? Many would answer this question in the affirmative. But how can the public be protected without interfering with the bargaining process? These questions have not yet been fully answered.

KEEPING WORK STOPPAGES IN PERSPECTIVE

Because a strike is news, work stoppages receive considerable media exposure. Nevertheless, work stoppages due to strikes must be placed in proper perspective. The strike, or the threat of it, forces both management and labor to bargain seriously. Both have a strong incentive to settle without a work stoppage. This is usually what happens. Each year an estimated 120,000 labor-and-management bargaining teams sit across the bargaining table from each other. They deal with the important issues of wages, fringe benefits, grievance procedures, and conditions of employment. More than 99 percent of the time, labor-management contracts are agreed to without the use of strikes. One seldom hears about these contracts because peaceful settlements are back-page news at best. It is the strikes that rate the headlines.

As **Exhibit 26–4** illustrates, very little work time is lost as the result of strikes. During the last three decades, the number of worker-hours lost because of strikes was less than one-tenth of 1 percent of the total working time—and the proportion has been falling. The amount of work time lost due to strikes is substantially less than the work time lost because of absenteeism.

HOW CAN UNIONS INFLUENCE WAGES?

The collective bargaining process often gives the impression that wages are established primarily by the talents of the union and management representatives who sit at the bargaining table. It might appear that market forces play a

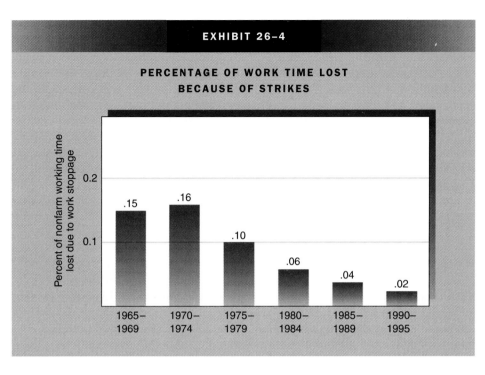

EXHIBIT 26-4

**PERCENTAGE OF WORK TIME LOST
BECAUSE OF STRIKES**

Percent of nonfarm working time lost due to work stoppage

- 1965–1969: .15
- 1970–1974: .16
- 1975–1979: .10
- 1980–1984: .06
- 1985–1989: .04
- 1990–1995: .02

Since 1965, less than one-tenth of 1 percent of nonfarm working time has been lost due to labor disputes, and the annual figure has been declining. These data are for work stoppages involving 1,000 or more workers.

Source: *Statistical Abstract of the United States* (annual) and *Monthly Labor Review* (various issues).

relatively minor role. However, as both union and management are well aware, market forces provide the setting in which the bargaining process is conducted. They often tip the balance of power one way or the other.

High wages increase the firm's costs. When union employers face stiff competition from nonunion producers or foreign competitors, they will be less able to pass along higher wage costs to their customers. Competition in the product market thus limits the bargaining power of a union. Changing market conditions also influence the balance of power between union and management. When the demand for a product is strong, the demand for labor will be high, and the firm will be much more willing to consent to a significant wage increase. When demand is weak, however, the product inventory level of the firm (or industry) is more likely to be high. Under these circumstances, the firm will be much less vulnerable to a work stoppage and wage increases will be much more difficult to obtain. (Note: When we speak of wage rates, we are referring to the total compensation package, including both fringe benefits and money wages.)

A union can use three basic strategies to increase the wages of its members: supply restrictions, bargaining power, and increased demand for union labor. We will examine each of these in turn.

SUPPLY RESTRICTIONS

If a union can successfully reduce the supply of competitive labor, higher wage rates will automatically result. Licensing requirements, long apprenticeship programs, immigration barriers, high initiation fees, refusal to admit new members to the union, and prohibition of nonunion workers from holding jobs are all practices that unions have used to limit the supply of labor to various occupations and jobs. Craft unions, in particular, have been able to restrict supply into various occupations and boost the wages of union members.

Part a of **Exhibit 26–5** illustrates the impact of supply restrictions on wage rates. Successful exclusionary tactics will reduce supply, shifting the supply curve from S_0 to S_1. Facing the supply curve S_1, employers will consent to the wage rate W_1. Compared to a free-entry market equilibrium, the wage rate has increased from W_0 to W_1, but employment has declined from E_0 to E_1. At the higher wage rate, W_1, an excess supply of labor, AB, will result. The restrictive practices will prevent this excess supply from undercutting the above-equilibrium wage rate. Because of the exclusionary practices, the union will be able to obtain higher wages for E_1 employees. Other employees who would be willing to accept work even at wage rate W_0 will now be forced into other areas of employment.

BARGAINING POWER

Must unions restrict entry? Why can they not simply use their bargaining power, enhanced by the strike threat, as a vehicle for raising wages? If they have enough economic power, this will be possible. A strike by even a small percentage of vital employees can sometimes halt the flow of production. For example, a work stoppage by airline mechanics can force major airlines to cancel their flights. Because the mechanics perform an essential function, an airline cannot operate

The impact of higher wages obtained by restricting supply is very similar to that obtained through bargaining power. As illustrated by part a, when union policies reduce the supply of one type of labor, higher wages result. Similarly, when bargaining power is used in order to obtain higher wages (part b), employment declines and an excess supply of labor results.

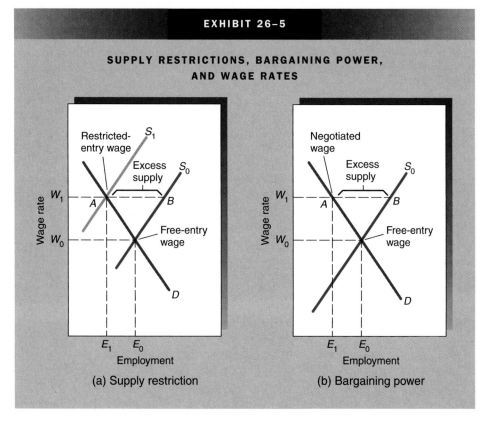

EXHIBIT 26–5

SUPPLY RESTRICTIONS, BARGAINING POWER, AND WAGE RATES

(a) Supply restriction

(b) Bargaining power

without their services, even though they constitute only 10 percent of all airline employees.

If the union is able to obtain an above-free-entry wage rate, the impact on employment will be similar to a reduction in supply. As part b of Exhibit 26–5 illustrates, employers will hire fewer workers at the higher wage rate obtained through bargaining power. Employment will decline below the free-entry level (from E_0 to E_1) as a result of the rise in wages. An excess supply of labor, AB, will exist, at least temporarily. More employees will seek the high-wage union jobs than employers will choose to hire. Nonwage methods of rationing jobs will become more important.

INCREASED DEMAND

Unions may attempt to increase the demand for union labor by appealing to consumers to buy only union-produced goods. Union-sponsored promotional campaigns instructing consumers to "look for the union label" or "buy American" are generally designed to increase the demand for union-made products.

Most people, however, are primarily interested in getting the most for their consumer dollar. Thus, the demand for union labor is usually determined primarily by factors outside the union's direct control, such as the availability of substitute inputs and the demand for the product. Unions, though, can sometimes use their political power to increase the demand for their services. They may be able to induce legislators to pass laws requiring the employment of certain types or amounts of labor for a task (for example, unneeded firemen on trains, allegedly for safety reasons, or a certain number of stage engineers). Unions often seek import restrictions as a means of increasing the demand for domestic labor. For example, automobile workers generally support restrictions limiting the sale of foreign-made automobiles in the United States. Garment workers have used their political muscle to raise tariffs and reduce import quotas for clothing goods produced abroad. Such practices increase the demand for domestic automobiles and clothing, thereby increasing the demand for domestic auto and garment workers. It is not surprising that the management and union representatives of a specific industry often join hands in support of trade restrictions limiting foreign competition. As **Exhibit 26–6** illustrates, successful union actions to increase demand for the services of union members result in both higher wages and an expansion in employment, usually at the expense of consumers.

A union in a strong bargaining position may shift the firm off its demand curve. This can happen if the union offers an "all-or-none" settlement in which the union specifies both wage and the quantity of labor (or restrictive work rules). To get any labor at all in this case, the firm must hire more labor at the union wage than it wants. For example, the International Typographical Union sometimes stipulated that advertisements printed from molded mats supplied by advertisers must be set, proofread, and corrected in the newspaper's composing room. This "bogus type" was then discarded. But the newspaper was nevertheless required to either pay its typesetters to produce the unneeded "bogus" work or make other bargaining concessions to induce the union to withdraw the rule. This type of "make-work rule" is another way in which a union may be able to loosen the connection between higher wages and lower levels of employment.

If a union is able to institute policies that increase the demand for its service, wages will automatically rise.

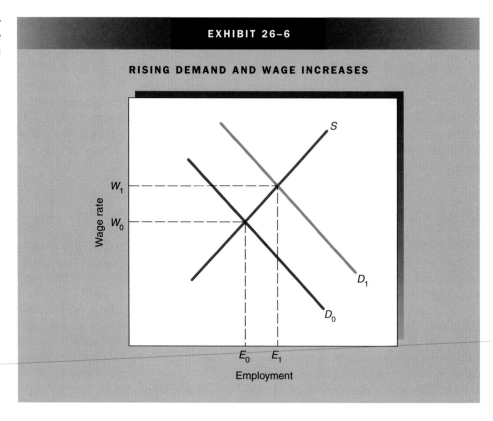

EXHIBIT 26-6

RISING DEMAND AND WAGE INCREASES

UNION POWER, EMPLOYMENT, AND MONOPSONY

Is unionization necessary to protect employees from the power of employers? The answer may be yes or no depending on the circumstances. When a large number of employers exists in a market, the interests of employees will be protected by competition among employers. Under these circumstances, each employer must pay the market wage to employees to keep them from shifting to higher-paying alternative employers. In a modern society, labor is highly mobile. Most employees work in a labor market in which there are many employers. However, a few workers may confront a situation in which there is only a single employer, at least for the specific skill category of labor supplied by the workers. For example, if a single large employer—perhaps a textile manufacturer or lumber mill—dominates the labor market of a small town, local workers who are unwilling to move may have few alternative employment opportunities.

Monopsony
A market in which there is only one buyer. The monopsonist confronts the market supply curve for the resource (or product) bought.

    Monopsony refers to this type of market situation in which there is a single buyer for a specific resource—for example, a specific skill category of labor. As we previously discussed, when the seller has a monopoly, the seller can profit by restricting output and charging a price above the marginal cost of produc-

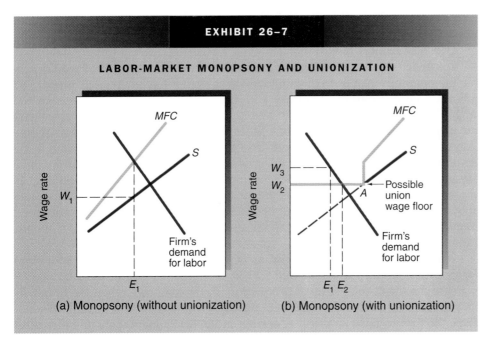

EXHIBIT 26–7

LABOR-MARKET MONOPSONY AND UNIONIZATION

(a) Monopsony (without unionization)

(b) Monopsony (with unionization)

As part a illustrates, the monopsonist's supply curve for labor will slope upward to the right. The marginal factor cost (MFC) curve for labor will be steeper than the labor supply curve (S). The monopsonist will hire E_1 units of labor and pay a wage rate W_1, along its labor supply curve. If a union establishes a wage floor, W_2 of part b, for example, the monopsonist may hire additional workers (E_2 rather than E_1) at the higher wage rate.

tion. Under monopsony, the buyer has a monopoly. Since the alternatives available to sellers are limited, the monopsonist-buyer will be able to profit by restricting the purchase of the resource and paying a price (wage rate) that is less than the marginal revenue generated by the resource.

Exhibit 26–7 illustrates the impact of monopsony in the labor market. Because the monopsonist is the only employer (purchaser of labor), the supply curve for the resource it purchases will coincide with the market supply curve for that resource. The supply curve for the resource will slope upward to the right because higher wages are necessary to attract the additional workers desired. For now, we will assume that both the old and new employees will be paid the higher wage rates if employment is expanded. The **marginal factor cost (MFC)** curve indicates the marginal cost of labor to the monopsonist. This cost of labor will exceed the wage rate because the higher wages necessary to attract each additional worker must be paid to all employees. As illustrated by Exhibit 26–7, the monopsonist's *MFC* curve will therefore be steeper than the labor supply curve.

How many workers should a profit-maximizing monopsony employ? The monopsonist's demand curve for labor indicates how much each additional worker adds to the firm's total revenue. The monopsonist will continue to expand employment as long as hiring additional workers adds more to total revenues than to total costs. This means that the monopsonist will choose employment level E_1, where the firm's demand curve, reflecting the marginal revenue product of labor, is just equal to the marginal factor cost of labor. A wage rate of W_1 will be sufficient to attract E_1 employees. For employment levels beyond E_1, it would cost the monopsonist more to hire an additional worker *(MFC)* than that worker would add to total revenue. As the result of this cost, the monopsonist

Marginal factor cost (MFC)
The cost of employing an additional unit of a resource. When the employer is small relative to the total market, the marginal factor cost is simply the price of the resource. In contrast, under monopsony, marginal factor cost will exceed the price of the resource, since the monopsonist faces an upward-sloping supply curve for the resource because to hire another worker, wages must be raised for all workers.

firm will hire fewer employees than it would if it were not the only buyer in the labor market.

Part b of Exhibit 26–7 illustrates what would happen if a union established a wage floor—W_2, for example—for a monopsonist. The wage floor would prohibit the monopsonist from paying low wages even if employment dropped. The union would confront the employer with the supply curve W_2AS. In essence, the wage floor would become the firm's MFC curve until the wage floor intersected the labor supply curve at A. As long as the MFC of additional units of labor was less than the firm's demand curve, additional workers would continue to be employed. Thus, if a union imposed wage rate W_2, the monopsonist would expand employment to E_2. In this case unionization would result in both higher wages and an expansion in employment. If the union expanded the wage rate above W_3, employment would fall below E_1, the level employed by a nonunion monopsonist. But for any wage floor less than W_3, the monopsonist would expand employment beyond E_1.

Although this analysis is sound as far as it goes, there are three additional factors that should be considered.[2] First, a higher wage rate will obviously increase the firm's total costs of production. In the long run, when the firm sells its product in a competitive market, higher per unit costs will almost certainly force the firm to raise its price. A decline in the firm's market share and output is a likely result. As the firm's market share declines, employment of all factors of production, including labor, will fall.

Second, a monopsonist will often be able to confine the higher wage rates to new employees only. When this is the case, the MFC curve of the monopsonist will not differ from its labor supply curve. Rather than restricting employment to keep wages low, the firm may simply expand employment along its supply curve, offering new employees (but not old ones) higher job classifications and more attractive employment conditions to obtain their services.

Third, given the speed of transportation, employers often draw workers from 30 to 50 miles away. In addition, many employees (particularly skilled workers, professionals, and managers) compete in a much broader labor market, a national labor market in some cases. Over a period of time, such workers will flow into and away from local labor markets. Given the mobility of labor, then, most employers will be small relative to their labor market, and their decisions to expand or contract their work force will not exert much impact on the market wage rate. Under these circumstances, MFC will be the same (or nearly the same) as the wage rate in the competitive-market model. A rise in the wage rate will therefore almost certainly reduce employment.

All these factors reduce the relevance of the monopsony model in most labor markets. When economic researchers have compared the predictive power of the monopsony model with the competitive model, unsurprisingly the latter has generally performed better. Empirical evidence indicates that unions normally operate in labor markets characterized by competition rather than monopsony.

---

[2]See Armen Alchian and William Allen, *Exchange and Production: Competition, Coordination, and Control* (Belmont, Calif.: Wadsworth, 1983), pp. 334–339, for additional theoretical analysis of monopsony.

WHAT GIVES A UNION STRENGTH?

Not all unions are able to raise the wages of their workers. What are the factors that make a union strong? Simply stated, if a union is to be strong, the demand for its labor must be inelastic. This will enable the union to obtain large wage increases while suffering only modest reductions in employment. In contrast, with an elastic demand for union labor, a substantial rise in wages will mean a large loss in jobs.

There are four major determinants of the demand elasticity for a factor of production: (1) the availability of substitutes, (2) the elasticity of product demand, (3) the share of the input as a proportion of total cost, and (4) the supply elasticity of substitute inputs.[3] We now turn to the importance of each of these conditions as a determinant of union strength.

AVAILABILITY OF GOOD SUBSTITUTE INPUTS

When it is difficult to substitute other inputs for unionized labor in the production of a good, the union is strengthened. The demand for union labor is then more inelastic, and reductions in employment tend to be small if the union is able to use its bargaining power and the threat of a strike to push wages up. In contrast, when there are good substitutes for union labor, employers will turn to the substitutes and cut back on their use of union labor as it becomes more expensive. Under these circumstances, higher union wages will price the union workers out of the market and lead to a sharp reduction in their employment.

Some employers may be able to automate various production operations—in effect, substituting machines for union workers if their wages increase. When machines are a good substitute for union labor, the demand for union labor will be fairly elastic. An elastic demand for union labor will substantially reduce the ability of the union to gain above-market wages.

The best substitute for union labor is generally nonunion labor. Thus, the power of unions to gain more for their members will be directly related to their ability to insulate themselves from competition with nonunion labor. When employers are in a position to substitute nonunion labor for unionized workers, it will be difficult for a union to push wages above the market level.

Within a given plant, a union will negotiate the wages and employment conditions for all workers, both union and nonunion. However, as union wages rise, it may be economical for unionized firms to contract with nonunion firms to handle specific operations or supply various components used in production. Thus, contracting out often permits employers to indirectly substitute nonunion for union workers. In addition, many large firms in automobile, textile, and other manufacturing industries operate both union and nonunion plants. They may be able to substitute nonunion for union labor by shifting more and more of their

---

[3]Alfred Marshall, *Principles of Economics,* 8th ed. (New York: Macmillan, 1920).

production to their nonunion plants, including those located overseas or in right-to-work states where unions are generally weaker.

ELASTICITY OF DEMAND FOR PRODUCTS OF UNIONIZED FIRMS

Wages are a component of costs. An increase in the wages of union members will almost surely lead to higher prices for goods produced with union labor. Unless the demand for the good produced by union labor is inelastic, the output and employment of unionized firms will decline if the union pushes up wages (and costs). If a union is going to have a significant impact on wages (without undermining employment opportunities), its workers must produce a good for which the demand is inelastic.

Our analysis implies that a union will be unable to significantly increase wages above the free market rate when producing a good that competes with similar (or identical) goods produced by nonunion labor or foreign producers. The demand for the good produced by union labor will almost surely be highly elastic when the same product is available from nonunion and foreign producers. Thus, if the union pushes up wages and costs, the market share of unionized firms will shrink and their employment will fall substantially.

Both past history and recent events are consistent with this view. In the 1920s the United Mine Workers obtained big wage gains in unionized coal fields. The union, however, was unable to halt the growth of nonunion mining, particularly in the strip mines of the West. The unionized mines soon lost the major share of their market to nonunionized fields, leading to a sharp reduction in the employment of unionized miners.

More recently, the strength of the Teamsters' union was substantially eroded when deregulation subjected the unionized segment of the trucking industry to much more intense competition from nonunion firms in the early 1980s. With deregulation, nonunion firms with lower labor costs entered the industry. Given their labor-cost advantage, many of the new entrants cut prices to gain a larger share of the market. The market share of the unionized firms declined. More than 100,000 Teamsters lost their jobs. Given the sharp reduction in the employment of their members, the Teamsters eventually agreed to wage concessions and a reduction in their fringe-benefit package.[4]

Unions sometimes negotiate substantial wage increases, even though they may eventually result in significant reductions in employment. This appears to be the case in both the steel and automobile industries. The hourly earnings of production workers in these two industries rose sharply compared with other workers in the private sector during the 1970s. By 1982 the average hourly earnings of steel workers were 74 percent greater than for all private-sector workers, up from a 19 percent premium in 1969. The parallel wage premium in the auto-

---

[4]A study on the deregulation of the trucking industry found that the wage premium of unionized truckers fell by approximately 30 percent in the regulated sector of the industry. More drivers were employed, but the employment of union members in the regulated sector fell to roughly half the level prior to deregulation. See Barry Hirsch, "Trucking Regulation, Unionization, and Labor Earnings," *Journal of Human Resources* 23 (summer 1988): pp. 296–319.

mobile industry was 51 percent in 1982, up from 21 percent in 1969. These substantial wage increases during the 1970s pushed up the costs of American steel and automobile producers relative to their foreign competitors. Foreign producers were able to capture a larger share of the U.S. market and, as a result, the employment of unionized labor in both the steel and automobile industries declined sharply. Between 1978 and 1982, membership in the United Steel Workers Union fell by 45 percent. The United Automobile Workers (UAW) lost 142,000 members, approximately 16 percent of their total, in the late 1970s and early 1980s. The experience of workers in both the steel and automobile industries provides vivid evidence that higher wages at unionized firms will mean less employment when the unionized firms compete with nonunion and foreign competitors.

UNION LABOR AS SHARE OF COST OF PRODUCTION

If the unionized labor input composes only a small share of total production cost, demand for that labor typically will be relatively inelastic. For example, since the wages of plumbers and pilots compose only a small share of the total cost of production in the housing and air travel industries, respectively, a doubling or even tripling of their wages would result in only a 1 percent or 2 percent increase in the cost of housing or air travel. A large increase in the price of such inputs would have little impact on product price, output, and employment. This factor has sometimes been called "the importance of being unimportant," because it is important to the strength of the union.

SUPPLY ELASTICITY OF SUBSTITUTE INPUTS

We have just explained that if wage rates in the unionized sector are pushed upward, firms will look for substitute inputs, and the demand for these substitutes will increase. If the supply of these substitutes (such as nonunion labor) is inelastic, however, their price will rise sharply in response to an increase in demand. The higher price will reduce the attractiveness of the substitutes. An inelastic supply of substitutes will thus strengthen the union by making the demand for union labor more inelastic.

WAGES OF UNION AND NONUNION EMPLOYEES

The precise impact of unions on the wages of their members is not easy to determine. In order to isolate the union effect, differences in other factors must be eliminated. Comparisons must be made between union and nonunion workers who have similar productivity (skills) and who are working on similar jobs.

Most studies indicate that the wages of union workers have been between 10 percent and 20 percent higher than those of similar nonunion workers during the past several decades. The union-nonunion wage differential widened during the 1970s. On average, union workers earned approximately 18 percent more than similar nonunion workers during the 1990s.

Sources: H. Gregg Lewis, *Unionism and Relative Wages in the United States: An Empirical Inquiry* (Chicago: University of Chicago Press, 1963), p. 222; and H. Gregg Lewis, *Union Relative Wage Effects: A Survey* (Chicago: University of Chicago Press, 1986), p. 9. The 1983–1989 and 1990–1995 figures are from Barry T. Hirsch and David A. Macpherson, *Union Membership and Earnings Data Book* (Washington, D.C.: The Bureau of National Affairs, 1996).

EXHIBIT 26-8

WAGE PREMIUM OF UNION WORKERS, 1950–1995

Percent higher wages of union workers relative to similar nonunion workers

1950–1954	1955–1958	1967–1970	1971–1975	1976–1979	1980–1982	1983–1989	1990–1995
11%	15%	12%	15%	18%	20%	19%	18%

Numerous studies have examined the effect of unions on wages. The pioneering work in this area was a 1963 study by H. Gregg Lewis of the University of Chicago.[5] Lewis estimated that, on average, union workers during the 1950s received wages between 10 percent and 15 percent higher than those of nonunion workers *with similar productivity characteristics*. The findings of other researchers using data from the 1950s and 1960s are generally consistent with the early work of Lewis.[6]

In a 1986 work, Lewis reviewed the evidence from nearly 200 studies on this topic and used more recent data to develop estimates of the union wage premium for the 1960s and 1970s.[7] **Exhibit 26–8** summarizes Lewis's findings and provides similar estimates for more recent periods. Research in this area indicates that the union-nonunion wage differential widened during the 1970s.[8] Lewis estimates that union workers received an 18 percent premium compared with similar nonunion workers during the 1976–1979 period, up from a 12 percent premium during 1967–1970. Labor economists Barry Hirsch and David Macpherson of Florida State University have used data from the annual *Current*

---

[5]H. Gregg Lewis, *Unionism and Relative Wages in the United States* (Chicago: University of Chicago Press, 1963).

[6]See Albert Rees, *The Economics of Trade Unions* (Chicago: University of Chicago Press, 1967); and Michael J. Boskin, "Unions and Relative Wages," *American Economic Review* 62 (June 1972): pp. 466–472.

[7]H. Gregg Lewis, *Union Relative Wage Effects: A Survey* (Chicago: University of Chicago Press, 1986).

[8]See William J. Moore and John Raision, "The Level and Growth of Union/Nonunion Relative Wage Effects, 1967–1977," *Journal of Labor Research* 4 (winter 1983): pp. 65–79; Richard B. Freeman and James L. Medoff, *What Do Unions Do?* (New York: Basic Bllks, 1984); and Barry T. Hirsch and John T. Addison, *The Economic Analysis of Unions: New Approaches and Evidence* (Boston: Allen and Unwin, 1986), for evidence on this point.

Population Survey to estimate the adjusted union-nonunion wage differential during the 1980s and 1990s.[9] Their work indicates that, on average, union workers earned 18 percent to 19 percent more than *similar* nonunion employees during the past decade.[10] *Like other research in this area, this suggests that the average union-nonunion wage differential has been between 15 percent to 20 percent in recent years.*

Our theory indicates that some unions will be much stronger than others—that is, better able to achieve higher wages for their members. In some occupations, the size of the union-nonunion differential will be well above the average, while in other occupations, unions will exert little impact on wages.

Lewis estimated that strong unions, such as those of the electricians, plumbers, tool and die makers, metal craft workers, truckers (prior to the moves toward deregulation), and commercial airline pilots were able to raise the wages of their members substantially more than the average for all unions. Other economists have found that the earnings of unionized merchant seamen, postal workers, and rail, auto, and steel workers exceed the wages of similarly skilled nonunion workers by 25 percent or more.

Unionization appears to have had the least impact on the earnings of cotton-textile, footwear, furniture, hosiery, clothing, and retail sales workers. In these areas, the power of the union has been considerably limited by the existence of a substantial number of nonunion firms in these industries. The demands of union workers in these industries are moderated by the fear of placing unionized employers at a competitive disadvantage in relation to the nonunion employers of the industry.

UNIONS, PROFITABILITY, AND EMPLOYMENT IN THE UNIONIZED SECTOR

If unions increase the wages of unionized firms above the competitive market level, the costs of those firms will rise unless (as seems unlikely) there is a corresponding increase in productivity. In the short run, the higher costs will reduce the profitability of the unionized firm. Recent research indicates that this was true during the 1970s. Barry Hirsch found that as the union-nonunion wage premium increased during the 1970s, the profitability of unionized firms lagged behind the profitability of other firms.[11]

---

[9]Barry T. Hirsch and David A. Macpherson, *Union Membership and Earnings Data Book* (Washington, D.C.: The Bureau of National Affairs, 1996).

[10]The studies referred to in the text compared the wages of similarly productive union and nonunion workers at a point in time. Another approach would be to compare the change in the wages of the same worker in cases where the worker moves from a union to a nonunion job and vice versa. Research using this approach has generally placed the union wage premium in the 10 percent range, somewhat smaller than the estimates derived from cross-section studies. For evidence provided by studies using this methodology, see Wesley Mellow, "Unionism and Wages: A Longitudinal Analysis," *Review of Economics and Statistics* 63 (February 1981): pp. 43–52; and Richard B. Freeman, "Longitudinal Analysis and Trade Union Effects," *Journal of Labor Economics* 2 (January 1984): pp. 1–26.

[11]Barry Hirsch, *Labor Unions and the Economic Performance of Firms* (Kalamazoo, Mich.: Upjohn Institute for Employment Research, 1991). Also see Freeman and Medoff, *What Do Unions Do?* Chapter 12, for evidence that unions exert a negative impact on the profits of unionized firms.

If unions are able to transfer profits from unionized firms to union workers, clearly this is a two-edged sword. For a time, workers enjoy higher wages. In the long run, however, investment will move away from areas of low profitability. Like other mobile resources, capital may be exploited in the short run, but this will not be the case in the long run. Therefore, to the extent that the profits of unionized firms are lower, investment expenditures on fixed structures, research, and development will flow into the nonunion sector and away from unionized firms. As a result, the growth of both productivity and employment will tend to lag in the unionized sector. Investment, production, and employment will all shift away from unionized operations and toward nonunion firms.

The larger the wage premium of unionized firms, the greater the incentive will be to shift production toward nonunion operations. The findings of Linneman, Wachter, and Carter are highly supportive of this view.[12] They found that industries with the largest union wage premiums were precisely the industries with the largest declines in the employment of unionized workers. On the other hand, union employment tended to be either constant or increasing in those industries with only a small union wage premium. Viewed from this perspective, the sharp decline in union membership during recent years (see Exhibit 26–1) is at least partially the result of the union wage premium—and the increase in the size of that premium in important industries during the 1970s (see Exhibit 26–8).

IMPACT OF UNIONS ON WAGES OF ALL WORKERS

Although unions have increased the average wages of their members, there is no reason to believe that they have increased the average overall compensation of workers—both union and nonunion. At first glance, this may seem paradoxical. However, the economic way of thinking enhances our understanding of this issue. As unions push wages up in the unionized sector, employers in this sector will hire fewer workers. Unable to find jobs in the high-wage union sector, some employees will shift to the nonunion sector. This increase in labor supply will depress the wages of nonunion workers. Thus, higher wages for union members do not necessarily mean higher wages for all workers. (See the accompanying Myths of Economics feature for additional detail on this subject.)

With regard to the impact of unions on the overall level of wages, it is important to keep one other key point in mind. The general level of wages is dependent upon productivity—output of goods and services that people value. Income is simply the flip side of output. Increases in the general level of wages are dependent upon increases in productivity per hour. Of course, improvements in (1) technology, (2) the machines and tools available to workers (physical capital), (3) worker skills (human capital), and (4) the efficiency of economic organi-

---

[12]Peter D. Linneman, Michael L. Wachter, and William Carter, "Evaluating the Evidence on Union Employment and Wages," *Industrial and Labor Relations Review* 44 (October 1990). Linneman, Wachter, and Carter estimate that increases in the union wage premium were responsible for up to 64 percent of the decline in the union share of employment during the last two decades.

"UNIONS HAVE INCREASED THE WAGES OF WORKERS AND THEREBY EXPANDED THE SHARE OF INCOME GOING TO LABOR."

It is one thing for unions to increase the wages of union members. It is quite another for them to increase the wages of all workers, both nonunion and union. Neither economic theory nor empirical evidence indicates unions are able to increase the general level of wages. To the extent unions increase the wages of union members, there is good reason to believe they do so primarily at the expense of nonunion workers. Higher union wages (and costs) will lead to a reduction in the output of products that intensively use union labor. This factor will cause employment in the unionized sectors to fall. What will happen to employees who are unable to find jobs in the unionized sector? They will compete for nonunion jobs, increasing supply and depressing nonunion wages. Thus, the real wages of nonunion workers will be slightly lower than they would be in the absence of unionism.

If labor unions increased the wages of all workers and therefore the share of income going to labor, we would expect labor's share of income to be directly related to union membership. This has not been the case. Union membership rose sharply as a share of the labor force during the 1930s and moderately during the 1940s. In contrast, it declined slowly during the 1960s and 1970s and rapidly during the 1980s (see Exhibit 26–1). Nonetheless, the distribution of income between labor and capital remained amazingly constant throughout this entire period. The share of national income allocated to physical capital in the form of corporate profits, interest, and rents has varied between 19 percent and 20 percent, while the share allocated to labor or human capital (employee compensation plus self-employment income) has been approximately 80 percent for the last several decades (see Illustrated Exhibit IV-E on page 607). There was no tendency for the share of national income going to labor to rise as union membership grew as a proportion of the labor force during the 1935–1955 period. Neither has it fallen as union membership has declined since 1955.

If unions were the primary source of high wages, the real wages of workers would be higher in highly unionized countries, such as Australia and the United Kingdom, than they are in the United States. But this is not what we observe. For example, real wages are at least 40 percent lower in the United Kingdom than they are in the United States, even though almost 40 percent of the work force is unionized in the United Kingdom compared to 15 percent in the United States (see Exhibit 26–9).

The real source of high wages is high productivity, not labor unions. In turn, high productivity depends on abundant physical capital, the knowledge and skill of the work force, and institutional arrangements that encourage the creation of wealth.

zation provide the essential ingredients for higher levels of productivity. *Higher real wages can be achieved only if the production of goods and services is expanded. Although unions can increase the wages of union workers, they cannot increase the wages of all workers unless their activities increase the total productivity of labor.*

DO UNIONS CAUSE INFLATION?

Labor unions are often accused of pushing up wages and thereby triggering price increases that cause inflation. Inspection of this view, however, indicates that it suffers from a major defect: It fails to incorporate the secondary effects of higher union wages. Let us consider this issue in more detail.

Suppose an economy were initially experiencing stable prices and the normal (natural) rate of unemployment. What would happen if a major union, that of the automobile workers, for example, used its economic power and the threat of a strike to obtain a very substantial increase in wages? The higher wages would trigger both direct and secondary effects. The increased labor costs would push up the prices of automobiles, trucks, and buses, particularly if imports could also be restrained. The direct effect of the higher automobile prices would be an increase in the consumer price index.

However, there would also be important secondary effects that are often overlooked. Confronting the higher automobile prices, consumers must either (1) purchase significantly fewer automobiles (quality-constant units) or (2) increase their expenditures on automobiles. To the extent that consumers purchased fewer (or less expensive) automobiles, the amount of labor services required by the automobile industry would decline. Automotive employment would fall (or at least expand by an abnormally small amount). Some workers who would have been able to find jobs in the automobile industry will now be forced into other lines of employment. The labor supply in these alternative employment areas would increase, placing downward pressure on wages and costs in these sectors.

On the other hand, if the higher auto prices cause consumers to spend more on automobiles, they would have less income to spend on other things. Consumers would be forced to cut back their spending in other areas. The demand for other products, the consumption of which must now be forgone as a result of the increase in expenditures on automobiles, would decline. Market adjustments would place downward pressure on prices in these areas.

Clearly, neither of these secondary effects would trigger an inflationary spiral. In fact, quite the opposite is true. Both (purchasing fewer automobiles and increasing expenditures on automobiles) would place downward pressure on costs and prices outside of the automobile industry, which would, at least partially, offset the impact of higher automobile prices on the general price level. Once we consider the secondary effects, there is no reason to expect that an increase in the wages of automobile or other unionized workers would trigger a sustained increase in the general price level.[13]

UNIONISM IN OTHER COUNTRIES

Exhibit 26–9 presents data on the level of unionism for several industrial economies. The data illustrate that union workers compose a larger share of the labor force in other major industrial countries than they do in the United States. Furthermore, collective bargaining agreements in other countries, particularly those in Europe, often apply to all employees and employers in a sector or region, regardless of whether they belong to a union or participate in the collective bargaining process. Thus, the percent of workers who are covered by and whose wages are set by collective bargaining is often substantially greater than union membership as a share of the work force. For example, while only one-third of the wage and salary workers in Germany belong to a labor union, the

---

[13]For an in-depth analysis of the impact of unions on inflation, see Daniel J. Mitchell, *Unions, Wages, and Inflation* (Washington, D.C.: Brookings Institution, 1980).

EXHIBIT 26-9

UNIONIZATION: AN INTERNATIONAL COMPARISON

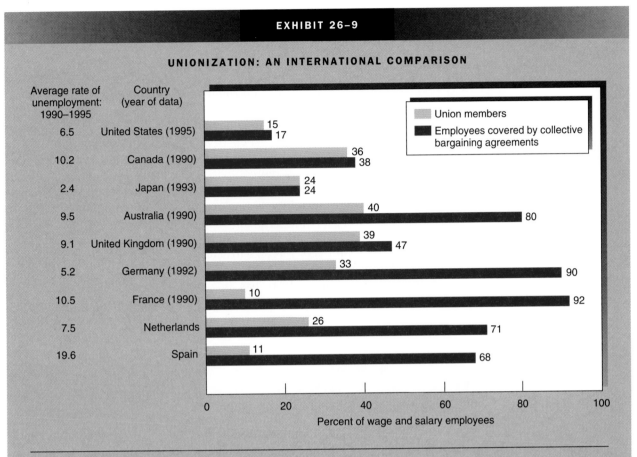

Average rate of unemployment: 1990–1995	Country (year of data)	Union members	Employees covered by collective bargaining agreements
6.5	United States (1995)	15	17
10.2	Canada (1990)	36	38
2.4	Japan (1993)	24	24
9.5	Australia (1990)	40	80
9.1	United Kingdom (1990)	39	47
5.2	Germany (1992)	33	90
10.5	France (1990)	10	92
7.5	Netherlands	26	71
19.6	Spain	11	68

Percent of wage and salary employees

Here we present the share of wage and salary workers belonging to a union and covered by collective bargaining agreements for various countries. Both the unionization rate and proportion of employees covered are lower in the United States and Japan than in other industrial countries. The proportion of employees whose wages are set by collective bargaining agreements is particularly high in France, Germany, Australia, Netherlands, and Spain.

Source: *OECD Employment Outlook*, July 1994 (chapter 5); and U.S. Department of Labor, Bureau of Labor Statistics, *Union Membership in Twelve Countries, 1955–1993* (October 1994).

wages and employment conditions for 90 percent of the workers are determined by collective bargaining agreements. In France, only 10 percent of the workers belong to a union, but 92 percent of the employees are covered by the collective bargaining process. In Spain, Netherlands, and Australia, more than two-thirds of the wage and salary workers are covered by collective bargaining even though union membership is much lower. In contrast, union members constitute only 15 percent of employment in the United States and collective bargaining agreements set the wages for only 17 percent of the wage and salary workers.

Both union membership and the proportion of employees covered by collective bargaining in Canada and the United Kingdom are more than twice the rates for the United States. Japan is the only one of the industrial nations with union representation and coverage rates somewhat similar to those of the United

States. Less than one-quarter of Japanese wage and salary workers belong to a union. Since most of the unions in Japan are organized at the company or enterprise level, collective bargaining agreements do not apply to nonunion workers. Thus, the union membership and coverage rates in Japan are virtually identical.

The data on union membership and coverage of collective bargaining suggest that, compared to other industrial countries, unions are less significant and wages more flexible in Japan and the United States. Widespread determination of wage rates by collective bargaining will result in less variation in wages across firms and within job categories. When coverage of an agreement applies to nonunion as well as union workers, there is less opportunity to substitute away from union labor that becomes more expensive. As a result, wages tend to be less flexible as coverage becomes more widespread. Many economists believe that this lack of wage flexibility is one reason why unemployment rates in Europe, Canada, and Australia are considerably higher than in Japan and the United States, where wages are more flexible.[14] Among the more highly unionized countries, only Germany was able to achieve an average unemployment rate of less than 7 percent during the 1990–1995 period. As Exhibit 26–9 shows, the rate of unemployment in the 1990s has averaged 9 percent or more in Canada, Australia, the United Kingdom, France, and Spain—countries with high unionization rates and/or widespread coverage of collective bargaining agreements.

UNIONS AND THE NATURE OF THE WORKPLACE

If one talks to any worker long enough, and candidly enough, one discovers that his loyalty to the union is not simply economic. One may even be able to show him that, on a strictly cost-benefit analysis, measuring income lost from strikes and jobs lost as a result of contract terms, the cumulative economic benefits are delusions. It won't matter. In the end, he will tell you, the union is the only institution that ensures and protects his "dignity" as a worker.

IRVING KRISTOL[15]

Economists generally focus on wages and employment when discussing the impact of unions. However, unions also exert important effects on the operation of the workplace and the structure of compensation. When evaluating the overall contribution and significance of unions, the following points should also be considered.

1. Unions have played a central role in the development of contractual or formal rules and procedures that govern promotions, raises, layoffs, termina-

---

[14]In addition to wage flexibility, economic theory indicates that the attractiveness of the benefit package available to unemployed workers will also exert a major impact on the rate of unemployment. These benefits are also generally higher in European countries than in the United States and Japan.

[15]Irving Kristol, "Understanding Trade Unionism," *The Wall Street Journal*, October 23, 1978. Reprinted with permission of *The Wall Street Journal*.

tions, and other aspects of the relationship between employers and employees. In essence, unions have established a system of "industrial jurisprudence" that protects workers against arbitrary actions by a supervisor or management representative. Labor contracts define a worker's rights and provide the worker with a means of appeal. Specifically, a worker cannot be fired without good cause, which must be proved to the satisfaction of his or her union representative. Actions the worker considers arbitrary or unfair can be taken to a shop steward, appealed through labor-management channels, and eventually brought to an objective arbitrator. Production at multimillion-dollar plants has been brought to a halt because a single worker's rights, as specified by the collective bargaining agreement, were violated. In addition, these contractual procedures provide employers with a strong incentive to pay attention to the complaints of workers and to treat them with dignity.

The contribution of unions in this area may also enhance employer-employee relations in a nonunion setting. Many employers are anxious to avoid the time-consuming procedures and inflexible rules that often accompany collective bargaining agreements. One of the best ways of doing that is to establish a positive work environment and open lines of communication with employees. Put another way, concern about possible unionization provides nonunion employers with a strong incentive to treat their employees right.

2. Unions tend to elevate the importance of seniority. In a union setting, employees with more seniority generally have more job security and protection than similar employees in a nonunion setting. Senior employees are also more likely to receive favorable treatment with regard to promotion. As a result of this emphasis on seniority, the managers of unionized firms generally have less opportunity for the subjective evaluation of employees than their nonunion counterparts. The greater weight given to seniority in the determination of wages in a union environment tends to reduce wage variation among workers. Consequently, the dispersion of wages among workers in union plants is generally less than the dispersion in nonunion plants.

3. In unionized firms, fringe benefits usually compose a larger component of the total compensation package than is true for nonunion firms. Studies indicate that the fringe benefits of union employees—particularly deferred benefits for pensions and life, accident, and health insurance—exceed the benefits of nonunion employees with similar pay rates. Senior union members are often more active and in positions of greater influence within the union than their younger counterparts. The higher pension and health benefits and greater protection against layoffs will also be particularly attractive to union members with substantial amounts of seniority.

4. Unions tend to reduce the turnover rate of employees. Union employees are less likely to quit than their nonunion counterparts. This may partially reflect the union wage premium. But it may also reflect other factors. Freeman and Medoff argue that unions provide employees with a "collective voice" through which they can communicate their problems and grievances to management.[16] This collective voice provides employees an alternative to quitting as a way of sending a message to management. The closer relationship between seniority and employee benefits (for example, pension benefits and job protection) in the

---

[16]Freeman and Medoff, *What Do Unions Do?*

unionized sector also reduces the incentive of employees to quit. These factors increase the work-force stability of unionized firms relative to their nonunion counterparts. In turn, the greater stability reduces the firm's recruitment, hiring, and training costs. However, the more rigid system may also reduce the firm's ability to establish a close relationship between employee productivity and wage rates. Therefore, on balance, it is difficult to determine the impact of the unionized wage structure on the firm's costs.

Unions have played a central role in the shaping of the current work environment in both the union and nonunion sectors. Their role in the establishment of the governance system between employers and employees has been particularly important. In fact, many would argue that these nonwage effects of unions are even more important than their role in the determination of wage rates.

LOOKING AHEAD

In the last four chapters we have analyzed markets for human and physical resources. Wages, prices, and employment levels in these markets determine our personal incomes. The next chapter will focus on the distribution of income among individuals.

CHAPTER SUMMARY

1. Union membership as a share of the nonagricultural labor force has fluctuated substantially during the last 80 years. During the 1910–1935 period, union workers composed between 12 percent and 18 percent of the nonfarm labor force. Unionization increased rapidly during the 1935–1945 period, soaring to one-third of the nonfarm work force. Since the mid-1950s, union membership has waned. In 1995 only 15 percent of employees in the United States belonged to a labor union.

2. The strike is a major source of union power. A strike can cause the employer to lose sales while incurring continuing fixed costs. The threat of a strike, particularly when inventories are low, is an inducement for the employer to consent to the union's terms.

3. A strike is also costly to employees. Strike funds are usually inadequate to deal with a prolonged strike. The loss of just a few paychecks can impose extreme hardship on most families. The potential cost of a strike to both union and management provides each with an incentive to bargain seriously to avoid a work stoppage.

4. Agreement on most collective bargaining contracts is reached without a work stoppage. During the last three decades, the number of hours lost due to strikes was less than one-tenth of one percent of the total work time—and the proportion of work time lost due to strikes has been declining.

5. There are three basic methods a union can use to increase the wages of its members: (a) restrict the supply of competitive inputs, including nonunion workers; (b) apply bargaining power enforced by a strike or threat of one; and (c) increase the demand for the labor service of union members.

6. When a large number of employers compete in the market for labor services, each employer will have to pay the market wage rate to keep employees from shifting to higher-wage alternatives. However, when monopsony is present, the single purchaser of labor may be able to profit by restricting employment and paying a wage rate that is less than the marginal revenue generated by the labor. Under these unusual circumstances, a wage floor established by a union might result in both higher wages and increased employment.

7. If a union is going to increase the wages of its members without experiencing a significant reduction in employment, the demand for union labor must be inelastic. The strength of a union is enhanced if (a) there is an absence of good substitutes for the services of union employees, (b) the demand for the product produced by the union labor is highly inelastic, (c) the union labor input is a small share of the total cost of production, and/or (d) the supply of available substitutes is highly inelastic. An absence of these conditions weakens the power of the union.

8. Studies suggest that the wage premium of union members relative to similar nonunion workers increased during the 1970s. Research indicates that the union-nonunion wage differential has been between 15 percent and 20 percent throughout the 1980s and 1990s.

9. Recent research indicates that the profitability of unionized firms is lower than the profitability of nonunion firms. Responding to the lower profitability rates, investment expenditures for fixed structures, research, and development have tended to flow into the nonunion sector and away from the unionized sector. As a result, employ-

ment in the unionized sector has declined, particularly in industries where the union wage premium is large.

10. Union membership and collective bargaining agreements cover a substantially larger proportion of the work force in other industrial countries than in the United States. Among the industrial nations, only Japan has unionization and coverage rates even close to those of the United States. Because coverage of collective bargaining is less widespread in the United States and Japan, wages tend to be more flexible than in more highly unionized countries.

11. Even though unions have increased the average wage of their members, there is no indication that they have either increased the average wage of all workers or increased the share of national income going to labor (human capital rather than physical capital). The real wages of workers are a reflection of their productivity rather than the share of the work force that is unionized. Although union membership as a percent of the labor force has fluctuated substantially during this century, the share of national income going to labor (human capital) has been virtually unchanged.

12. An increase in the wages of union members will either reduce expenditures on goods produced by nonunion labor or increase the supply of nonunion labor. In either case, the secondary effects of higher union wages will tend to reduce prices in the nonunion sector. Thus, there is no reason to believe that unions cause sustained increases in the general price level (inflation).

13. Unions have played a central role in the development of the current system of industrial jurisprudence, which governs the relationship between employers and employees. Many think that the positive role of unions in this area is as important, if not more important, than their role in the determination of wage rates.

CRITICAL ANALYSIS QUESTIONS

1. Assume that the primary objective of a union is to raise wages.
   a. Discuss the conditions that will help the union achieve this objective.
   b. Why might a union be unable to meet its goal?

*2. Suppose that Florida migrant workers are effectively unionized. What will be the impact of the unionization on (a) the price of Florida oranges, (b) the profits of Florida fruit growers in the short run and in the long run, (c) the mechanization of the fruit-picking industry, and (d) the employment of migrant farm workers?

*3. Unions in the North have been vigorously involved in efforts to organize lower-wage workers in the South. Union leaders often express their compassion for the low-money-wage Southern workers. Can you think of a reason, other than compassion, for Northern union leaders' (and workers') interest in having the higher union scale extended to the South? Explain.

4. "Unions cannot repeal the law of demand; they cannot have both high wages and high employment. The more successful they are at raising wages above competitive levels, the smaller the number of unionized employees."
   a. Evaluate this view.
   b. Does the success of unions at enlarging their wage premium tend to undermine their growth? Why or why not?

5. Evaluate the following statements.
   a. "An increase in the price of steel will be passed along to consumers in the form of higher prices for automobiles, homes, appliances, and other products made with steel." Do you agree or disagree?
   b. "An increase in the price of craft-union labor will be passed along to consumers in the form of higher prices of homes, repair and installation services, appliances, and other products that require craft-union labor." Do you agree or disagree?
   c. Are the interests of labor unions in conflict primarily with the interests of union employers? Explain.

6. "The purpose of unions is to push the wage rate above the competitive level. By their very nature, they are monopolists. Therefore, they will necessarily cause resources to be misallocated." Do you agree or disagree? Explain.

*7. "If a union is unable to organize all the major firms in an industry, it is unlikely to exert a major impact on the wages of union members." Indicate why you either agree or disagree.

8. The Retail Clerks Union has organized approximately one-third of the department stores in a large metropolitan area. Do you think the union will be able to significantly increase the wages of its members? Explain.

*9. "When an industry is highly unionized, higher labor costs will reduce industry profitability. Unions benefit workers at the expense of capitalists." True or false?

*10. "Unions provide the only protection available to working men and women. Without unions, employers would be able to pay workers whatever they wanted." True or false?

11. Suppose that the United Automobile Workers (UAW) substantially increases wages in the auto industry. What impact will the higher wages in the auto industry have on the following?
   a. wages of nonunion workers outside the automobile industry
   b. price of automobiles made by the UAW
   c. demand for foreign-produced automobiles
   d. profitability of U.S. automobile manufacturers

*12. Even though the wage scale of union members is substantially greater than the minimum wage, unions have generally been at the forefront of those lobbying for higher minimum rates. Why do you think unions fight so hard for a higher minimum wage?

*13. Suppose that Congress was considering the following revenue measures: (a) a 10-cent-per-gallon increase in the gasoline tax or (b) an increase in the tariff (tax) on imported automobiles that would raise an equivalent amount of revenue. Which of the two options would the United Auto Workers be most likely to favor? Which would American automobile manufacturers be most likely to favor? Explain.

14. "Unions provide workers with protection against the greed of employers." Evaluate this statement. Be sure to consider the following questions:

a. With whom do union workers compete?

b. When union workers restrict entry into a market, whom are they trying to keep out?

*15. A survey of firms in your local labor market reveals that the average hourly wage rate of unionized production workers is $1.50 higher than the average wage rate of nonunion production workers. Does this indicate that unionization increases the wage rates of workers in your area by $1.50? Why or why not?

16. Are the wages of union members determined by the bargaining skill of union officials? Do market conditions influence the wages of unionized employees? Discuss.

17. What are the major forces that influence the ability of a union to increase the wages of the employees it represents? Why are some unions able to attain higher wages for members than others? Explain.

_____

*Asterisk denotes questions for which answers are given in Appendix B.

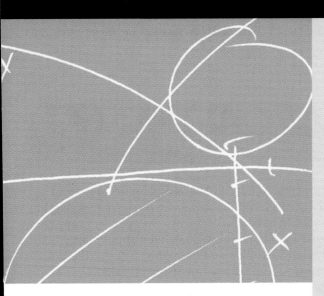

All animals are equal, but some animals are more equal than others.

GEORGE ORWELL[1]

---

[1]George Orwell, *Animal Farm* (New York: Harcourt Brace and Company, 1946), p. 112.

CHAPTER FOCUS

■ Why do incomes vary? Do income differences influence the incentive of people to develop resources and use them productively?

■ How much income inequality is there in the United States?

■ How has income inequality changed in the United States in recent years?

■ How does the degree of income inequality in the United States compare with that of other countries?

■ How much income mobility is there in the United States—do the rich remain rich while the poor remain poor?

■ What are the characteristics of the poor? Have they changed in recent decades?

■ Have income transfers reduced the poverty rate?

I n a market economy, resource prices both reflect relative scarcity and play an important role in determining the distribution of income. Differences in resource prices and the productivity of individuals will cause market incomes to vary substantially. Of course, economic inequality is present in all societies. Substituting politics and central planning for markets does not eliminate inequality. Nonetheless, most of us are troubled by the extremes of inequality—extravagant luxury on the one hand and grinding poverty on the other. How much inequality is there in a market economy such as the United States? Do the same families continually enjoy high incomes, while those in poverty are unable to escape that condition? How have income-transfer programs designed to reduce poverty influenced the distribution of income and the welfare of the poor? This chapter focuses on these questions and related issues.

THE INCENTIVE EFFECTS OF INCOME DIFFERENCES

Incomes not only determine how much individuals can spend on goods and services, they also affect the individual's incentive to supply the resources required to produce goods and services. Market participants prosper by supplying resources that are highly valued by others. Individuals who supply large quantities of human and physical resources others value highly will be able to earn large incomes. Others who are less able or less successful at supplying highly valued resources will have lesser incomes. The close link between personal prosperity and provision of productive resources provides market participants with a strong incentive to develop resources others value, use them wisely, and find better (more productive) ways of doing things.

Returns to work effort are by far the largest contributor to income—more than 80 percent of national income in the United States, for example, comes in return for work performed (see Illustrated Exhibit IV-E on page 607). But people differ with regard to their productive abilities, opportunities, preferences, and intestinal fortitude. Some will be able to hit a baseball, perform a rock concert, design a computer, or operate a restaurant so effectively that people will pay millions to consume the product or service that they supply. There will be others with disabilities and/or few skills who may be unable even to support themselves. Income from physical capital is less than 20 percent of total income. Like the capability for work, however, ownership of physical capital and income derived from it are unequally distributed.

A market economy does not have a central distributing agency that carves up the economic pie and allocates slices to various individuals. Rather, the distribution of income is determined by the quantity and value of the resources supplied by the various individuals. Differences in market incomes simultaneously: (1) reflect the relative scarcity of resources, (2) provide the incentive for individuals to use their talent and energy to supply those resources that are highly valued by others, and (3) determine the distribution of income among the market participants. All of these functions are important; changes in any one of the three will alter the other two. Therefore, while focusing on the distribution of income, we must not forget the role that income differences play in the allocation of resources.[2]

INCOME INEQUALITY IN THE UNITED STATES

Money income is only one component of economic well-being. Such factors as leisure, noncash transfer benefits, the nonpecuniary advantages and disadvantages of a job, and the expected stability of future income are also determinants of economic welfare. Nevertheless, since money income represents command over market goods and services, it is highly significant. Moreover, it is readily observable. Consequently, it is the most widely used measure of economic well-being and the degree of inequality prevailing in society.

Exhibit 27–1 presents data on the allocation of income. First, consider the data on the share of *before-tax* annual money income received by quintile—that is, each fifth of families—ranked from the lowest to the highest. If there were total equality of annual income, each quintile of the population would receive 20 percent of the aggregate income. Given the differences in educational levels, skill, ability, work effort, and numerous other factors, clearly we would not expect this to be the case. It is, however, informative to observe the shares of income received by each of the quintiles. In 1994 the bottom 20 percent of family income recipients received 4.2 percent of the total before-tax money income. At the other end of the spectrum, the 20 percent of families with the highest annual incomes received 46.7 percent of the before-tax income in 1994. The top quintile of income recipients thus received approximately eleven times as much of the before-tax money income as the bottom quintile.

As Exhibit 27–1 illustrates, there was a reduction in before-tax income inequality throughout the 1950s and 1960s. In 1970 the top quintile of recipients received 40.9 percent of the aggregate money income, down from 42.7 percent in 1950. During the same period, the share of income received by the lowest quintile of income recipients rose from 4.5 percent in 1950 to 5.4 percent in 1970. Thus, between 1950 and 1970 the income share received by the top quintile of earners declined, while that received by the bottom quintile rose.

The earlier trend toward less income inequality reversed during the 1970s. The income share of the lowest quintile of income recipients fell to 4.2 percent in 1994, well below the 1970 figure. Simultaneously, the income share received by the top quintile of families rose from 40.9 percent in 1970 to 43.5 percent in 1985 and 46.7 percent in 1994. While the income share received by the highest quintile of earners rose between 1970 and 1993, the income share received by the other four quintile groups fell.

---

[2]Public policy often focuses on issues of income inequality and the distribution of income. Chapter 31 analyzes several policy issues—including social security, welfare reform, and the potential of public policy to reduce income inequality—that are closely related to this chapter. Thus, some readers and instructors may want to consider some of the issue debates in Chapter 31 in conjunction with this chapter.

EXHIBIT 27–1

INEQUALITY IN MONEY INCOME DURING SELECTED YEARS, 1950–1994

	LOWEST 20 PERCENT OF RECIPIENTS	SECOND QUINTILE	THIRD QUINTILE	FOURTH QUINTILE	TOP 20 PERCENT OF RECIPIENTS
FAMILY INCOME BEFORE TAXES					
1950	4.5	12.0	17.4	23.4	42.7
1960	4.8	12.2	17.8	24.0	41.3
1970	5.4	12.2	17.6	23.8	40.9
1980	5.1	11.6	17.5	24.3	41.6
1985	4.7	10.9	16.8	24.1	43.5
1990	4.6	10.8	16.6	23.8	44.3
1992	4.3	10.5	16.5	24.0	44.7
1994	4.2	10.0	15.7	23.3	46.7
FAMILY INCOME AFTER TAXES AND TRANSFERS					
1979	6.4	12.6	17.8	24.2	39.0
1992	5.5	11.3	17.0	24.2	42.0
HOUSEHOLD EXPENDITURES					
1961	7.1	13.2	18.2	24.1	37.4
1972	7.1	12.9	18.0	23.9	38.1
1980	6.8	12.8	18.1	24.1	38.2
1991	7.0	12.5	17.4	23.4	39.7

Sources: Bureau of the Census, *Current Population Reports*, Series P-60; *Statistical Abstract of the United States: 1995*, Table 733; Congressional Budget Office, *1994 Green Book*, p. 1191; and Daniel T. Slesnick, "Consumption, Needs, and Inequality," *International Economic Review*, August 1994.

It is also possible to obtain data on income shares *after taxes and transfers* for the post-1979 period. Low-income households are the primary beneficiaries of noncash transfer programs that provide people with food (food stamps), health care, and housing. Correspondingly, under a system of progressive taxation, taxes take a larger share of income as one's income increases. Therefore, one would expect the *after tax and transfer* income to be less unequally allocated than before-tax income. Indeed, this is the case. After taxes and transfers, the bottom quintile of families received 5.5 percent of the total income in 1992, compared to 4.3 percent of the before-tax income. At the same time, the after tax and transfer share of the top quintile of families was 42.0 percent in 1992, down from 44.7 percent before taxes. Thus, taxes and transfers increased the income share of the bottom quintile, while reducing that of the top group.

Like the before-tax figures, the income data after taxes and transfers suggest that there has been an increase in income inequality in recent years. Note that after taxes and transfers, the income share received by the bottom quintile fell between 1979 and 1992, while that of the top group rose.

A CLOSER LOOK AT FACTORS INFLUENCING INCOME DISTRIBUTION

How meaningful are the data of Exhibit 27–1? If all families were similar except in the amount of income received, the use of annual income data as an index of inequality would be more defensible. However, the fact is that the aggregate data lump together (1) small and large families, (2) prime-age earners and elderly retirees, (3) multi-earner families and families without any current earners, and (4) husband-wife families and single-parent families.

Consider just one factor: the impact of age and the pattern of lifetime income. Typically, the annual income of young people is low, particularly if they are going to school or acquiring training. Many persons under 25 years of age studying to be lawyers, doctors, engineers, and economists will have a low annual income during this phase of their life. But this does not mean they are poor, at least not in the usual sense. After completing their formal education and acquiring work experience, such individuals move into their prime working years, when annual income is generally quite high, particularly for families in which both husband and wife work. Remember, though, that this is also a time period when families are purchasing houses and providing for children. Consequently, all things considered, annual income during the prime working years may overstate the economic well-being of most households. Finally, there is the retirement phase, characterized by less work, more leisure, and smaller family size. Even families who are quite well-off tend to experience income well below the average for the entire population during the retirement phase. Given the life cycle of income, lumping together families of different ages (phases of their life-cycle earnings) would result in substantial inequality in the annual income figures even if incomes over a lifetime were approximately equal. (See Illustrated Exhibit IV-G on page 608 for information on the pattern of income by age.)

Exhibit 27–2 highlights major differences between high- and low-income families that underlie the distributional data of Exhibit 27–1. The typical high-income family (top 20 percent) is headed by a well-educated person in the prime working-age phase of life whose income is supplemented with the earnings of other family members, particularly working spouses. In contrast, persons with little education, nonworking retirees, younger workers (under age 35), and single-parent families are substantially over-represented among low-income families (bottom 20 percent of income recipients). In 1994, 37 percent of the householders in the lowest income quintile failed to complete high school, compared to only 4 percent for the highest income quintile. While only 5 percent of the household heads in the bottom quintile completed college, more than half (54 percent) of the householders in the top group did so. Seventy-nine percent of the high-income families had household heads in the prime working-age category (age 35 to 64), compared with only 41 percent of the low-income families. Only one parent was present in 51 percent of the low-income families, whereas 95 percent of the high-income group were husband-wife families. Contrary to the views of some, high-income families are larger than low-income families. In 1994 there were 3.4 persons per family in the top income quintile, compared to only 2.9 family members among the bottom quintile of income recipients.

There was a striking difference in the work time between low- and high-income families. No doubt, much of this difference reflected factors such as family size, age, working spouses, and the incidence of husband-wife families. In high-income families, the average number of workers per family was 2.27,

Sources: U.S. Department of Commerce, *Income, Poverty, and Valuation of Noncash Benefits: 1994* (Washington, D.C.: Government Printing Office, 1995); and *Statistical Abstract of the United States, 1995.*

EXHIBIT 27–2

DIFFERING CHARACTERISTICS OF HIGH- AND LOW-INCOME FAMILIES, 1994

	BOTTOM 20 PERCENT OF INCOME RECIPIENTS	TOP 20 PERCENT OF INCOME RECIPIENTS
EDUCATION OF HOUSEHOLDER		
Percent with less than high school	37	4
Percent with college degree or more	5	54
AGE OF HOUSEHOLDER (PERCENT DISTRIBUTION)		
Under 35	37	13
35–64	41	79
65 and over	22	8
FAMILY STATUS		
Married-couple family (percent of total)	49	95
Single-parent family (percent of total)	51	5
PERSONS PER FAMILY	2.9	3.4
EARNERS PER FAMILY	0.74	2.3
PERCENT OF TOTAL WEEKS WORKED SUPPLIED BY GROUP	7	32

compared with .74 for low-income families. The top 20 percent of income recipients contributed 32 percent of the total number of weeks worked, while the low-income group contributed only 7 percent of the total work time. Thus, high-income families worked 4.6 times as many weeks as low-income families and earned almost 10 times as much income. This implies that the earnings per week worked of the top income recipients were only slightly greater than twice the earnings per week worked of the low-income recipients. Clearly, differences in the amount of time worked were a major factor contributing to the income inequality of Exhibit 27–1.

In summary, Exhibit 27–2 sheds substantial light on the distributional data of Exhibit 27–1. *Those with high incomes are far more likely to be well-educated, husband-wife families with dual-earners in their prime working years. In contrast, those with low incomes are often single-parent families headed by a poorly educated adult who is either youthful or elderly. The household heads of those families with little income are often either out of the labor force or working only part of the time. Given these factors, it is not surprising that the top 20 percent of recipients have substantially higher incomes, both before and after taxes, than the bottom quintile of family income recipients.*

WHY HAS INCOME
INEQUALITY INCREASED?

Exhibit 27–1 indicates that there has been an increase in income inequality in the United States during the last couple of decades. Why has the gap between the rich and the poor been growing? The answer to this question is a point of controversy among social scientists. No single factor can be isolated. Research in this area, however, indicates that at least three factors contributed substantially to the recent shift toward greater inequality.

1. The increasing proportion of single-parent and dual-earner families has contributed to the increase in the inequality of family income. The nature of the family and the allocation of work responsibilities within the family have changed dramatically in recent decades. In 1994 slightly more than one-fifth (22 percent) of all families were headed by a single parent, double the figure of the mid-1960s. At the same time, the labor-force participation rate of married women increased from 40 percent in 1970 to 61 percent in 1994.

By way of comparison with the late 1960s and early 1970s, we now have both more single-parent families and more dual-earner families. Both of these changes tend to promote income inequality. Perhaps an example will illustrate why. Consider two hypothetical families, the Smiths and the Browns. In 1970 both were middle-income families with two children and one market worker earning $30,000 (in 1996 dollars). Now consider their 1996 counterparts. The Smiths of 1996 are divorced and one of them, probably Mrs. Smith, is trying to work part-time and take care of the two children. The probability is very high that the single-parent Smith family of 1996 will be in the low-, rather than the middle-, income category. They may well be in the bottom quintile of the income distribution. In contrast, the Browns of 1996 both work outside the home, and each earns $30,000 annually. Given their dual incomes, the Browns are now a high-, rather than a middle-, income family. Along with many other dual-income families (see Exhibit 27–2), the Browns' 1996 family income will probably place them in the top quintile of income recipients.

Even if there were no changes in earnings between skilled and less-skilled workers, the recent changes within the family would enhance income inequality among families and households. More single-parent families like the Smiths increase the number of families with low incomes, while more dual-earner families like the Browns increase the number of high-income families. Both will promote income inequality.

2. Earnings differentials between skilled and less-skilled workers have increased in recent years, further magnifying income inequality. In 1970 workers with little education who were willing to work hard, often in a hot and sweaty environment, were able to command high wages. This is less true today. Throughout the 1950s and 1960s, guidance counselors told high school students that a college education was essential for economic success. For a long time, it appeared that they were wrong. In 1974 the annual earnings of men who graduated from college were only 27 percent higher than the earnings of male high school graduates, hardly a huge payoff for the time and cost of a college degree. Since 1974, however, things have changed dramatically. By the mid-1980s, the earnings premium of male college graduates relative to male high school grads had risen to the 50–60 percent range, approximately twice the premium of 1974. By 1993, the income premium of male college graduates relative to high school graduates had risen to 72 percent. Similarly, the earnings of women college graduates have increased sharply during the last two decades relative to women with only a high school education.

Why have the earnings of persons with more education (and skill) risen relative to those with less education (and skill)? Deregulation of the transport industry and the waning power of unions may have reduced the number of high-wage, blue-collar jobs available to workers with little education. No doubt, international competition has also played an important role here. Increasingly, American workers compete in a global economy. Recent innovations and cost reductions in both communications and transportation provide firms with greater flexibility with regard to location. Firms producing goods that require substantial amounts of low-skill labor are now better able to move to places such as Korea, Taiwan, and Mexico, where low-skill labor is cheaper. As firms using lots of low-skill labor move overseas, both the demand for and earnings of Americans with few skills and little education will decline. In an international setting, the United States will be far more attractive to firms requiring substantial amounts of high-skill, well-educated workers. Thus, the globalization of our economy tends to expand the earnings differences across skill categories in the United States. (In contrast, globalization reduces income inequality *worldwide*.)

3. As marginal tax rates were reduced during the 1980s, the observed incomes of high-income Americans increased sharply because they had more incentive to earn and less incentive to engage in tax-shelter activities. Prior to 1981, high-income Americans confronted top marginal tax rates of up to 70 percent (50 percent on earnings). Such high marginal tax rates encouraged high-income earners to undertake investments and structure their business affairs in a manner that sheltered much of their income from the Internal Revenue Service. As we indicated in Chapter 5 (see Exhibit 5–9), the taxable incomes of the top 10 percent of earners expanded sharply when the top marginal tax rates were reduced to the 30 percent range during the 1980s. Some of this increase in income reflected greater work effort due to the increased incentive to earn. Much of it, however, merely reflected a reduction in tax-shelter activities in response to the lower marginal tax rates. The flip side of the reduction in tax-shelter activities accompanying the lower marginal tax rates of the 1980s was an increase in the visible income of the rich. In essence, after the rate cuts, the earnings of the rich were more readily observable. To the extent this factor contributed to the increase in the measured income of wealthy Americans, the increase in income inequality was more imaginary than real.

4. Reductions in communication and transportation costs may have increased the number of markets characterized by a few people at the top with very high earnings. As we noted in Chapter 24, the market compensation of star entertainers and athletes, the most talented professionals, and top business executives is often like that of winner-take-all tournaments. At any point in time, a few people at the top command huge earnings, while most others in these areas have modest or even low incomes. As transport and communications costs have declined, markets have increasingly become national and even global, rather than local. This increases the incomes of a few people at the top, but it also increases the degrees of income inequality.

EXHIBIT 27–3

INCOME INEQUALITY AROUND THE WORLD

COUNTRY	YEAR	PERCENT SHARE OF HOUSEHOLD INCOME RECEIVED BY:		
		BOTTOM 20 PERCENT	MIDDLE THREE QUINTILES	TOP 20 PERCENT
DEVELOPING NATIONS				
Indonesia	1990	8.7	49.0	42.3
India	1989–1990	8.8	49.9	41.3
Jamaica	1990	6.0	45.6	49.4
Venezuela	1989	4.8	45.7	49.5
Costa Rica	1989	4.0	45.2	50.8
Malaysia	1989	4.6	41.7	53.7
Colombia	1991	3.6	40.8	55.6
Nicaragua	1993	4.2	40.5	55.3
Mexico	1984	4.1	40.0	55.9
Chile	1992	3.3	36.4	60.4
Kenya	1992	3.4	34.8	61.8
Brazil	1989	2.1	30.4	67.5
DEVELOPED NATIONS				
France	1989	5.6	52.5	41.9
Italy	1986	6.8	52.2	41.0
Germany	1984	6.8	54.5	38.7
Spain	1988	8.3	55.1	36.6
Canada	1987	5.7	54.1	40.2
Australia	1985	4.4	53.4	42.2
United Kingdom	1988	4.6	51.1	44.3
United States	1994	3.6	49.3	49.1

Sources: The World Bank, *World Development Report 1995*, Table 30; and Peter Saunders, Helen Stott, and Garry Hobbes, "Income Inequality in Australia and New Zealand: International Comparisons and Recent Trends," *Review of Income and Wealth*, March 1991, pp. 63–79.

INCOME INEQUALITY IN OTHER COUNTRIES

How does income inequality in the United States compare with that in other nations? **Exhibit 27–3** presents a summary of household income data compiled by the World Bank. These data indicate that the degree of income inequality in the United States exceeds that of the other large industrial economies. For example, the bottom quintile of income recipients receive a larger share (and the top quintile a smaller share) of the total income in Spain, France, Italy, and Germany than is the case for the United States. The lesser degree of inequality in these countries is not surprising. Compared to the United States, the other large industrial economies are characterized by a more homogeneous population—that is, uniformity with respect to race and ethnicity—and more extensive use of income transfer policies.

The share of income going to the wealthy is usually greater in less developed countries. According to the World Bank study, the top 20 percent of income recipients received 67.5 percent of the aggregate income in Brazil, 61.8 percent in Kenya, 60.4 percent in Chile, and approximately 55 percent in Mexico, Nicaragua, and Colombia. Among the developing nations of Exhibit 27–3, only Indonesia and India were marked by a degree of inequality similar to that of most developed countries.[3]

INCOME MOBILITY AND INEQUALITY IN ECONOMIC STATUS

Income mobility
Movement of individuals and families either up or down income-distribution rankings when comparisons are made at two different points in time. When substantial income mobility is present, one's current position will not be a very good indicator as to what one's position will be a few years in the future.

Statistics on the distribution of annual income fail to reveal **income mobility—** the degree of movement across income groupings—and thus they may be misleading. Consider two countries with identical distributions of annual income.[4] In both cases, the annual income of the top quintile of income recipients is eight times greater than the bottom quintile. Now, suppose that in the first country— we will refer to it as Static—the same people are at the top of the income distribution, year after year. Similarly, the poor people of Static remain poor year after year. Static is characterized by an absence of income mobility. In contrast, earners in the second country, which we will call Dynamic, are constantly changing places. Indeed, during every five-year period, each family spends one year in the upper-income quintile, one year in each of the three middle-income quintiles, and one year in the bottom-income quintile. In Dynamic, no one is rich for more than one year (out of each five), and no one is poor for more than a year. Obviously, the degree of economic inequality in Static is vastly different from that in Dynamic. You would not know it, though, by looking at their identical annual income distributions.

The contrast between Static and Dynamic indicates why it is important to consider income mobility when addressing the issue of economic inequality. Until recently, detailed data on income mobility were sparse. Fortunately, this is no longer the case. Both the University of Michigan's Survey Research Center

---

[3]The data of Exhibit 27–3 are not adjusted for either differences across countries in size of households or the demographic composition of the population. In addition, procedures used to make the estimates and the reliability of the data vary across countries. Thus, these data should be interpreted with a degree of caution.

[4]The authors are indebted to Mark Lilla, from whom this illustrative method was drawn. See Mark Lilla, "Why the 'Income Distribution' Is So Misleading," *The Public Interest* 77 (fall 1984), pp. 63–76.

EXHIBIT 27–4

INCOME MOBILITY—INCOME RANKING, 1979 AND 1988

INCOME STATUS OF TAXPAYER IN 1979	INCOME STATUS OF TAXPAYER IN 1988				
	TOP-PAID QUINTILE	NEXT-HIGHEST- PAID QUINTILE	MIDDLE QUINTILE	NEXT-LOWEST- PAID QUINTILE	LOWEST-PAID QUINTILE
Top-Paid Quintile	64.7	20.3	9.4	4.4	1.1
Next-Highest-Paid Quintile	35.4	37.5	14.8	9.3	3.1
Middle Quintile	15.0	32.3	33.0	14.0	5.7
Next-Lowest-Paid Quintile	11.1	19.5	29.6	29.0	10.9
Lowest-Paid Quintile	14.7	25.3	25.0	20.7	14.2

Note: Only persons with income in both 1979 and 1988 are included.   Source: Department of the Treasury, Office of Tax Analysis.

and the U.S. Department of the Treasury now collect data for a representative sample of individuals and track them each year.[5] With these data, researchers are now able to see how income and other indicators of economic status change over lengthy periods of time.

Exhibit 27–4 summarizes the Treasury Department's findings on income mobility. These data were derived from a representative sample of tax returns during 1979–1988. Only taxpayers with income during each year of the 1979–1988 period were included in the analysis. As Exhibit 27–4 illustrates, after grouping taxpayers by their income in 1979, the Treasury study derives the relative income position of the *same taxpayers* nine years later in 1988. For example, the first row of the exhibit indicates the relative income position in 1988 of taxpayers who were in the top quintile of income recipients in 1979. Almost two-thirds (64.7 percent) of those with incomes in the top quintile were able to maintain this lofty position nine years later. One-fifth of the top earners in 1979 fell to the second quintile, while the incomes of another 15 percent placed them in one of the bottom three quintiles of the 1988 income distribution. This suggests that once households are able to achieve high-income status, dramatic reductions that push them back to a low level of income are rare.

The bottom row of Exhibit 27–4 tracks the experience of individuals in the lowest-income quintile in 1979. Surprisingly, only 14.2 percent of the taxpayers with incomes in the lowest quintile in 1979 remained in that quintile in

---

[5]Greg J. Duncan et al., *Years of Poverty, Years of Plenty: The Changing Fortunes of American Workers and Families* (Ann Arbor: Institute for Social Research, University of Michigan, 1984). Also see Bradley R. Schiller, "Relative Earnings Mobility in the United States," *American Economic Review* 67, no. 5 (1977): pp. 926–939, for an earlier pioneer study of income mobility.

1988. Among those with incomes in the bottom quintile in 1979, 86 percent of them had moved to a higher income quintile by 1988. Two-fifths (40 percent) of those with the lowest incomes in 1979 were in either the highest or the next-to-highest income quintile by 1988. Among those in the next-to-lowest income quintile in 1979, three-fifths moved up to a higher income grouping nine years later, while only 10.9 percent fell into the bottom quintile.

The income mobility data highlight a point that is concealed by the annual figures: Many households with low incomes are not permanently poor. Often, current income is low because the household is young and inexperienced or going to school while working part-time. In other cases, the low current income status is the result of a job loss or business setback during the year. In still other cases, it reflects an accident or temporary health problem. The distribution of income in the United States is dynamic. With time, most of those with low incomes *at a point in time* move up the income ladder only to be replaced by others who are youthful, inexperienced, or victims of current misfortune.[6]

Given the pattern of lifetime income and the mobility up and down the income ladder, many economists argue that differences in household *expenditures* are a more accurate indicator of economic status than income. When the current income of an individual or household understates either their future earning prospects or their income level during an earlier period, current expenditures generally exceed current income. On the other hand, if current income is high relative to one's prior or expected future income, more will be saved, causing expenditures to fall short of current income. To a large degree, current expenditures reflect long-term economic status, or what economists call *permanent income.*

What do expenditures indicate with regard to the degree of inequality in the United States? Daniel Slesnick of the University of Texas has studied this issue extensively. In addition to the income data, Exhibit 27–1 also presents Slesnick's calculations on share of household expenditures by quintile. In 1991, the 20 percent of households with the smallest consumer expenditure levels composed 7 percent of the total. On the other hand, the expenditures of the top quintile summed to 39.7 percent of the total. The expenditures of the top group were 5.7 times those of the bottom group. Thus, the expenditure share of the bottom quintile relative to the top group is significantly greater than the income share both before and after taxes.

In contrast with the annual income data, the distribution of household consumption expenditures does not indicate that there has been a major change in economic inequality in the United States during recent decades. Throughout the 1961–1991 period, the expenditures of the bottom quintile were approximately 7 percent of the total, while those of the top quintile were slightly less than 40 percent. This suggests that the increase in inequality as measured by the annual income data is more a reflection of dynamic change and temporary fluctuations in annual income rather than an increase in economic inequality.

---

[6]See Isabel Sawhill and Mark Condon, "Is U.S. Income Inequality Really Growing?" *Policy Bites* (Washington, D.C.: Urban Institute, June 1992); and Federal Reserve Bank of Dallas, *By Our Own Bootstraps: Economic Opportunity and Dynamics of Income Distribution,* Annual Report 1995, for additional information on income mobility. Even though they use different databases and cover different time periods, the findings of these studies concerning income mobility are similar to those of the Treasury Department presented in Exhibit 27–4.

Sources: Bureau of the Census, *Current Population Reports*, Series P60-189, *Income, Poverty, and Valuation of Noncash Benefits: 1994*, Tables B-5 and B-7; and *Economic Report of the President 1964*, Table 7.

EXHIBIT 27–5

POVERTY RATE OF PERSONS AND FAMILIES IN THE UNITED STATES, 1947–1994

| | POVERTY RATE (PERCENT) | |
YEAR	PERSONS	FAMILIES
1947	n.a.	32.0
1960	22.2	18.1
1970	12.6	10.1
1980	13.0	10.3
1985	14.0	11.4
1990	13.5	10.7
1992	14.8	11.9
1994	14.5	11.6

POVERTY IN THE UNITED STATES

In an affluent society such as the United States, income inequality and poverty are related issues. Poverty could be defined in strictly relative terms—the bottom one-fifth of all income recipients, for example. However, this definition would not be very helpful, since it would mean that poverty could never decline.

The official definition of poverty in the United States is based on the perceived minimum income necessary to provide food, clothing, shelter, and basic necessities economically for a family. This **poverty threshold income level** varies with family size and composition, and it is adjusted annually for changes in prices. For purposes of determining whether income is above the poverty threshold, the official poverty rate considers only money income. (See the Measures of Economic Activity feature for additional details on how the poverty rate is measured.)

How many people are poor? According to the official definition of poverty, there were 38 million poor people and 8.1 million poor families in 1994. As **Exhibit 27–5** indicates, 14.5 percent of the population and 11.6 percent of the families were officially classified as poor in 1994. During the 1950s and 1960s, the poverty rate declined substantially. By 1970 the official poverty rate for families had fallen to 10.1 percent, down from 18.1 percent in 1960 and 32.0 percent in 1947. During the 1970s this rate changed little. In fact, it was slightly higher in 1980 than it was in 1970. During the early 1980s, the poverty rate rose. Most commentators point to the stagnating economy during 1979–1982 and to

Poverty threshold income level
The level of money income below which a family is considered to be poor. It differs according to family characteristics (for example, number of family members) and is adjusted when consumer prices change.

Sources: U.S. Department of Commerce, *Characteristics of the Population Below the Poverty Level: 1982*, Table 5; and *Income, Poverty, and Valuation of Noncash Benefits: 1994*, Tables B-5, B-6, and B-7.

EXHIBIT 27–6

CHANGING COMPOSITION OF POOR AND POVERTY RATE OF SELECTED GROUPS: 1959, 1976, AND 1994

	1959	1976	1994
Number of Poor Families (in millions)	8.3	5.3	8.1
Percent of Poor Families Headed by a:			
Female	23	48	53
Black	26	30	27
Elderly person (age 65 and over)	22	14	9
Person who worked at least some during the year	70	55	49
Poverty Rate			
All families	18.5	10.1	11.6
Married-couple families	15.8	7.2	6.1
Female-headed families	42.6	32.5	34.6
Whites	18.1	9.1	11.7
Blacks	55.1	31.1	30.6
Children (under age 18)	27.3	16.0	21.8

cutbacks in transfer programs as the sources of the rising poverty rates in the late 1970s and early 1980s.

In recent years, the composition of the poverty population has changed substantially. As **Exhibit 27–6** indicates, elderly persons and the working poor formed the core of the poverty population in 1959. Twenty-two percent of the poor families were headed by an elderly person in 1959. Most poor people (70 percent) worked at least some hours during the year. In 1994 the picture is dramatically different: Only 9 percent of the poor families were headed by an elderly person and less than half of the heads of poor households worked at all during the year.

There has also been a substantial growth in the proportion of female-headed families and an accompanying decline in the proportion of husband-wife families. Since the poverty rate of female-headed families is several times higher than the rate for husband-wife families (34.6 percent compared with 6.1 percent in 1994), an increase in family instability tends to push the poverty rate upward. In 1994 more than half (53 percent) of the poor families were headed by a female, compared with only 23 percent in 1959.

The poverty rate of blacks in 1994 was 30.6 percent, compared to 11.7 percent for whites. Nonetheless, two-thirds of the poor people in the United States

MEASURES OF ECONOMIC ACTIVITY

DETERMINING THE POVERTY RATE

Families and individuals are classified as poor or non-poor based on the poverty threshold income level originally developed by the Social Security Administration (SSA) in 1964. Since consumption survey data indicated that low- and median-income families of three or more persons spent approximately one-third of their income on food, the SSA established the poverty threshold income level at three times the cost of an economical, nutritionally adequate food plan. A slightly larger multiple was used for smaller families and individuals living alone. The poverty threshold figure varies according to family size, because the food costs vary by family size and composition. It is adjusted annually to account for rising prices. The following chart illustrates how the poverty threshold for a family of four has increased as prices have risen from 1959 to 1995:

1959	$ 2,973
1970	3,968
1980	8,414
1990	13,359
1992	14,343
1993	14,773
1994	15,141
1995	15,570

Even though the poverty threshold income level is adjusted for prices, it is actually an absolute measure of economic status. As real income increases, the poverty threshold declines relative to the income of the general populace.

The official poverty rate is the number of persons or families living in households with a money income below the poverty threshold as a proportion of the total. *When determining a person's or family's income, the official poverty rate considers only money income.* Income received in the form of noncash benefits, such as food stamps, medical care, and housing subsidies, is completely ignored in the calculation of the official poverty rate.

Since noncash benefits targeted for low-income households have grown rapidly since the late 1960s, the failure of the official poverty rate to count this "income" reduces its accuracy as a measurement tool. To remedy this deficiency, the Bureau of the Census has developed several alternative measures of poverty that count the estimated value of noncash benefits as income. In addition to the official poverty rate, the bureau now publishes annual data for the "adjusted" poverty rates that include a valuation for various noncash benefits (for example, food stamps, medical care, school lunch, and housing benefits). Of course, inclusion of these benefits reduces the poverty rate. For example, while the official poverty rate for persons was 14.5 percent in 1994, the adjusted poverty rate that included the value of the noncash food, housing, and medical benefits was only 11.1 percent.

The poverty rate is calculated each year based on a current population survey of nearly 60,000 households designed to reflect the population of the United States. The most comprehensive source for detailed data on this topic is the Bureau of the Census annual publication, *Income, Poverty, and Valuation of Noncash Benefits.*

---

were white. Perhaps the most tragic consequence of poverty is its impact on children. During the last two decades, the poverty rate among children has increased substantially. In 1994, 21.8 percent of the children in the United States lived in poverty, up from 16.0 percent in 1976.

TRANSFER PAYMENTS AND THE POVERTY RATE

In the mid-1960s, it was widely believed that an increase in income transfers directed toward the poor would substantially reduce, if not eliminate, the incidence of poverty. The *1964 Economic Report of the President* (see page 77 of the report) argued that poverty could be virtually eliminated if the federal government increased its expenditures by approximately 2 percent of aggregate income. Following the declaration of the "War on Poverty" by the Johnson administration, expenditures on transfer programs increased rapidly. Overall transfers, including those directed toward the elderly, approximately doubled as a proportion of personal income between 1965 and 1975. Including both cash and noncash benefits, the transfers directed toward the poor also grew rapidly. Measured in 1982–1984 dollars, **means-tested income transfers**—those limited to people with incomes below a certain cutoff point—tripled, expanding from $24 billion in 1965 to $70 billion in 1975. *As a proportion of personal income,* means-tested transfers jumped from 1.5 percent in 1965 to 3.0 percent in 1975. During the 1975–1990 period both total transfers and means-tested transfers continued to increase as a percent of personal income, although at a much slower rate than during the decade following the 1964 declaration of the War on Poverty. By 1992, means-tested transfers had risen to 4.3 percent of personal income.[7]

Did the expansion in government income transfers reduce the poverty rate as the *1964 Economic Report of the President* anticipated? Antipoverty programs provide both cash and noncash benefits. **Exhibit 27–7** shows the poverty rate with and without the benefits of noncash transfer programs counted as income. Continuing the trend of the post–Second World War era, the official poverty rate fell throughout the 1960s. During the 1970s, however, the rate leveled off. By 1980 it was 10.3 percent, virtually unchanged from the 1968 rate. By 1994, as we reported earlier, the rate had drifted up to 11.6 percent.

Aggregate poverty-rate data as presented in Exhibit 27–7 conceal an important difference between the experience of the elderly and nonelderly that has largely gone unnoticed. **Exhibit 27–8** highlights this point. The poverty rate for the elderly continued to decline throughout the 1970s. By 1990, the official poverty rate of the elderly had fallen to 6.3 percent, down from 17.0 percent in 1968 and 30.0 percent in 1959 (see part a of Exhibit 27–8). The experience of working-age Americans, however, was vastly different. After falling for several

Means-tested income transfers

Transfers that are limited to persons or families with an income below a certain cutoff point. Eligibility is thus dependent on low-income status.

---

[7]The following chart indicates the expenditures on both total income transfers and means-tested transfers as a percent of personal income for 1965, 1975, 1985, and 1992. Both cash and in-kind benefits are included in the figures.

PERCENT OF PERSONAL INCOME

YEAR	TOTAL TRANSFER PAYMENTS	MEANS-TESTED TRANSFER PAYMENTS
1965	8.5	1.5
1975	17.4	3.0
1985	18.8	3.4
1992	21.0	4.3

The means-tested noncash transfers included food (food stamps, school lunch subsidies, and WIC program), housing, and energy assistance benefits, plus Medicaid payments. In addition to these benefits, Medicare payments were also included in the total transfer figures. Expenditures on job training and educational subsidies are not included. See *Statistical Abstract of the United States: 1995,* Tables 584 and 589.

EXHIBIT 27-7

POVERTY RATE, 1947–1994

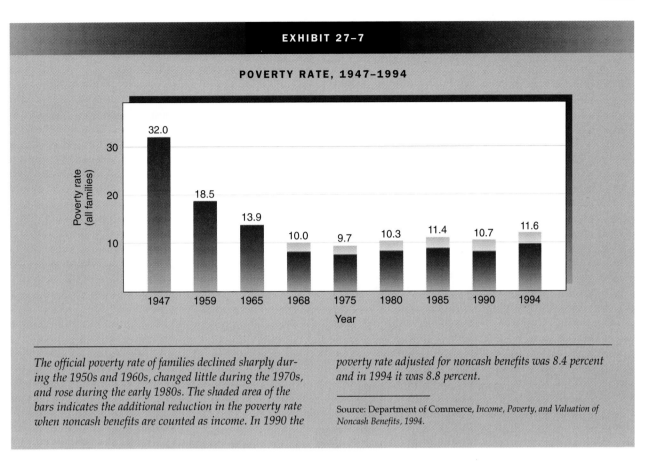

The official poverty rate of families declined sharply during the 1950s and 1960s, changed little during the 1970s, and rose during the early 1980s. The shaded area of the bars indicates the additional reduction in the poverty rate when noncash benefits are counted as income. In 1990 the poverty rate adjusted for noncash benefits was 8.4 percent and in 1994 it was 8.8 percent.

Source: Department of Commerce, *Income, Poverty, and Valuation of Noncash Benefits, 1994.*

decades, the official poverty rate of nonelderly families bottomed in 1968 and rose throughout the 1970s and early 1980s (part b). In 1994 the official poverty rate of nonelderly families was 12.6 percent, compared with 9.0 percent in 1968 (and 10.9 percent in 1965, just prior to the increase in expenditures on transfer programs accompanying the War on Poverty). Even after adjustment for the non-cash benefits (part c), the poverty rate of the nonelderly in the late 1980s and early 1990s was approximately the same as it had been in the 1960s prior to the War on Poverty programs.

THE LIMITATIONS OF INCOME TRANSFER PROGRAMS

Why weren't the income-transfer programs more effective? Clearly, a slowdown in economic growth has retarded progress against poverty. As we previously discussed, the growth rate of all the major industrial economies has slowed since the early 1970s (see Illustrated Exhibit IV-D on page 606). Social changes have also slowed progress against poverty. The divorce rate, the proportion of births

[a] Adjusted for food, medical, and housing benefits.

Sources: Derived from Department of Commerce, *Income, Poverty, and Valuation of Noncash Benefits: 1994; Poverty in the United States, 1990;* and *Measuring the Effects of Benefits and Taxes on Income and Poverty, 1990 and 1992.* See also James Gwartney and Thomas S. McCaleb, "Have Antipoverty Programs Increased Poverty?" *The Cato Journal* (spring/summer, 1985)

EXHIBIT 27-8

CHANGING POVERTY RATES FOR ELDERLY VERSUS NONELDERLY, 1959–1994

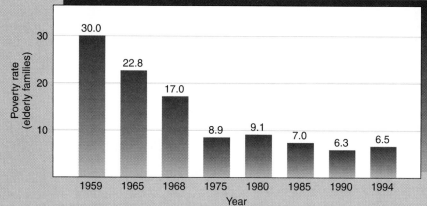

(a) The official poverty rate for elderly families has declined sharply since 1959.

(b) In contrast, the official poverty rate for nonelderly families has been rising since the late 1960s.

(c) Adjusting for noncash transfers reduces the poverty rate of the nonelderly but it does not alter the basic pattern.

to unwed mothers, and the incidence of female-headed households have all increased significantly in recent years, pushing the poverty rate upward.[8]

Nonetheless, the results achieved have been disappointing. After all, per capita income adjusted for inflation in the United States was more than 50 percent greater in 1994 than 1965. Why hasn't this growth of income significantly reduced the poverty rate?

There are various reasons why people have poverty level incomes. Some individuals are in poverty because they are victims of debilitating disease, or physical, mental, or emotional disability. For others, however, periods of poverty reflect factors such as divorce, premature termination of schooling (or training), having a child while young and unmarried, or choice of a high-risk lifestyle. Still others have low current incomes because they are in school or just starting in the labor force. The diversity among those with low incomes makes it difficult to design government programs that will help the poor without generating unintended side effects that increase the incidence of poverty.

Means-tested income transfers generate two major side effects that reduce their effectiveness as an antipoverty weapon. *First, transfer programs that significantly reduce the adversities of poverty will also reduce the opportunity cost of choices that often lead to poverty.* This factor is sometimes called the **Samaritan's dilemma**. To the extent that antipoverty programs reduce the negative side effects of, for example, births by unmarried mothers, abandonment of children by fathers, dependence on drugs or alcohol, or dropping out of school, they inadvertently encourage people to make choices that result in these conditions. Of course, this is not the intent of the transfers, but nonetheless it is one of their side effects. In the short run, these secondary effects may not be very important. Over the longer term, however, their negative consequences may be substantial.

Second, income-linked transfers reduce the incentive of low-income individuals to help themselves. When the size of transfer benefits is linked to income, an increase in transfers tends to increase the **implicit marginal tax rate** of the poor— the percentage of additional earnings that must be paid explicitly in taxes or implicitly in the form of a reduction in income supplements. Therefore, as the income of a poor family increases, the family qualifies for fewer (and smaller) benefits. Once this reduction in transfers is taken into consideration, the *net* income many low-income families derive from work is extremely low. In some cases, it may even be negative—that is, work and additional earnings may actually reduce the family's economic status. Because the high implicit marginal tax rates reduce the incentive of poor families to work and earn, to a degree, the transfers merely replace income that would have otherwise been earned.

INCOME TRANSFERS AND THE NEGATIVE INCOME TAX

The adverse side effects of income transfers can be viewed within the framework of a simple **negative income tax.** This concept, which has been widely discussed

Samaritan's dilemma
General assistance to those with low incomes reduces the opportunity cost of choices that lead to poverty. Thus, there is a conflict between providing income transfers to the poor and discouragement of behavior that increases the incidence of poverty.

Implicit marginal tax rate
The amount of additional (marginal) earnings that must be paid explicitly in taxes or implicitly in the form of a reduction in income supplements. Since the marginal tax rate establishes the fraction of an additional dollar earned that an individual is permitted to keep, it is an important determinant of the incentive to work.

Negative income tax
A system of transferring income to the poor whereby a minimum base level of income is guaranteed to an individual or a family. If nothing is earned, the base income is received in the form of transfers. As additional income is earned, the base income transfer is reduced by some fraction (less than 1) of the additional earnings. An increase in earnings, thus, would always cause disposable income to rise.

---

[8]For additional analysis of why antipoverty income transfers have not been more effective, see Lawrence M. Mead, *The New Politics of Poverty: The Nonworking Poor in America* (New York: Basic Books, 1990); and Robert Rector, "Why Congress Must Reform Welfare," *Heritage Foundation Backgrounder,* No. 1063, December 1995.

for several decades, incorporates both (1) a guaranteed minimum or base income supplement and (2) an implicit marginal tax rate. Most plans call for a larger guaranteed income level for larger families. Under a negative income tax, the size of the income supplement is reduced by a fraction of the additional earnings as the family's non-transfer income expands. This fraction is the implicit marginal tax rate of the plan.

Exhibit 27–9 illustrates the mechanics of a negative income tax. Under the plan represented here, the guaranteed minimum income for a family of four is $6,000 and the marginal tax rate is 33 percent. As outside income expands, the family's disposable income increases by two-thirds of the amount earned. For example, initial earnings of $1,500 would increase their disposable income by $1,000, from $6,000 to $7,000. The family would receive more in supplementary income than it would pay in taxes until their earnings expand to $18,000, the **break-even point.** At the break-even point, the family's tax bill is just equal to the income supplement; beyond the break-even point, the family faces a positive tax bill.

The mechanics of the negative income tax illustrate the problems generated by transfers. A guaranteed income level of $6,000 would leave families with little additional income in poverty. Thus, many would argue for a higher base income level. However, holding the implicit marginal tax rate constant, an increase in the minimum guaranteed income would extend the break-even point to higher income brackets, and thereby substantially expand both the number of people receiving the transfers and the cost of the program. For example, assuming an implicit marginal tax rate of 33 percent, if the minimum income level were increased from $6,000 to $12,000, this would increase the break-even income level to $36,000 (rather than $18,000). At the higher break-even income level, lower-middle and middle-income families (rather than just the poor) would qualify for the income supplements. This would cause the cost of the program to skyrocket. In addition, the higher guaranteed income would reduce both (a) the cost of activities that often lead to low incomes and (b) the payoff derived from investments in human capital and other activities that lead to higher incomes. With time, more people will end up drawing the income supplements and fewer will earn the higher incomes required to generate the taxes to pay for the transfers.

Alternatively, the marginal tax rate might be increased in order to better target the transfer toward the poor. For example, the guaranteed income could be increased to $12,000 and the marginal tax rate raised to 66.7 percent. This would keep the break-even income level at $18,000.[9] But look how this affects the incentive of the poor to earn. Under this plan, the net income of poor families would rise by only $1 for every $3 of additional earnings. Because poor families would get to keep only a small part of their additional earnings, their incentive to earn would be seriously retarded.

The mechanics of the negative income tax highlight the inherent conflict between aid to the poor and improvement in their net income. Income supplements that substantially increase the economic status of people with little or

Break-even point
Under a negative income tax plan, the income level at which the reduction in transfers that accompany additional earnings is equal to the base income. Thus, the individual neither pays taxes nor receives supplementary income transfers.

---

[9] A family that earned $18,000 would have its income supplement reduced by two-thirds (the 66.7 percent implicit marginal tax rate) of its earnings. Thus, the $12,000 income supplement would be fully eliminated when the family's income rose to $18,000.

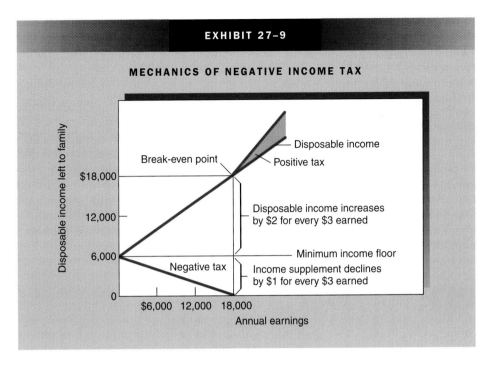

EXHIBIT 27-9

MECHANICS OF NEGATIVE INCOME TAX

The graph illustrates how a negative income tax with a 33 percent marginal tax rate and a minimum income of $6,000 for a family of four would work. If the family had zero earnings during the year, it would receive a $6,000 annual subsidy. As earnings rose, the family's after-tax income would increase by 67 cents (and the subsidy would decline by 33 cents) for every dollar of income earned, until the break-even income level of $18,000 was attained.

no earnings will either (a) be extremely costly because much of the aid will go to middle-income recipients and the transfers will encourage behavior that leads to poverty and/or (b) the high marginal tax rate will substantially reduce the incentive of the poor to help themselves.

Many economists believe that the adverse side effects of the current welfare system are worse than our analysis of the negative income tax implies. Under the current system, poor families often confront "notches" where, over a range of income, additional earnings will make them worse off because, at the higher income level, they will completely lose certain benefits (for example, medical aid or school lunch benefits).

ESTIMATING COSTS OF REDISTRIBUTION

Economics indicates that the use of income transfers to upgrade the status of those with low incomes is like trying to transfer water with a "leaky bucket." The increase in the marginal tax rates (either explicit or implicit) confronted by both the taxpayer-donor and the transfer recipient adversely affect work incentives and reduce the size of the economic pie. Thus, the cost of the transfers in terms of loss of output exceeds the amount of income transferred. Furthermore, much of the income received by recipients merely replaces income that they otherwise would have earned.

A study by Edgar Browning and William Johnson sought to measure the loss of output due to the reduction in the supply of labor associated with the rise in marginal tax rates accompanying income transfers.[10] Browning and Johnson estimated that it would cost $3.49 in terms of lost output to transfer an additional $1 from the top 60 percent to the bottom 40 percent of recipients under a negative income tax plan.

So transferring income from producers to nonproducers is an expensive undertaking. Are redistribution programs worth the cost? Economics cannot answer that question. It can only help identify and quantify the cost (in terms of lost output) and expected effectiveness of alternative programs. Hopefully, better information in these areas will help voters and policymakers to make wiser decisions.

---

[10]See Edgar K. Browning and William Johnson, "The Trade-off between Equality and Efficiency," *Journal of Political Economy* (April 1984).

LOOKING AHEAD

Income transfers are the focal point of many current policy issues. Demographic changes are causing policymakers to consider the future structure of social security, which is, by far, the largest single income transfer program. There is also considerable concern and controversy about the recent increases in income inequality and the potential of public policy to deal with this issue. Possible reform of the current welfare system is also an important and hotly debated current policy issue. All these debates are discussed in Chapter 31, which focuses on several of today's major policy issues.

CHAPTER SUMMARY

1. In a market economy, resource prices reflect scarcity and provide individuals with a strong incentive to work, develop productive resources, and discover better ways of doing things. Individuals prosper by supplying resources that are highly valued by others. The distribution of income is determined by quantity and value of resources supplied by the various individuals. There is no central distributing agency that carves up the economic pie and allocates slices to various individuals when markets are used to allocate resources.

2. Prior to taxes and transfers, the bottom 20 percent of families received 4.2 percent of the aggregate income in 1994, while the top 20 percent received approximately eleven times that amount (46.7 percent). *After taxes and transfers*, the bottom quintile of recipients received 5.5 percent of the total income in 1992, compared to 42 percent for the top group. Thus, taxes and transfers reduce the degree of income inequality.

3. During the 1950s and 1960s, there was a reduction in income inequality in the United States. Since 1970, the earlier trend has reversed; there has been an increase in income inequality as measured by the annual income data during the last two decades. This was true for both the before- and after-tax distribution of income.

4. A substantial percentage of the inequality in the annual income distribution reflects differences in age, education, family status, number of earners in the family, and time worked. Young, inexperienced workers, students, and retirees are overrepresented among those with low incomes. Persons in their prime working years are overrepresented among high-income recipients. Persons with high incomes have substantially more schooling. Married-couple families with multi-earners are overrepresented among the high-income recipients, while youthful and single-parent families with few earners make up a large share of the low-income recipients.

5. Differences in time worked contributed substantially to the inequality of annual income. The number of weeks worked by members of the top quintile of families was 4.6 times the weeks worked by families in the bottom quintile of income recipients.

6. No single factor can explain the shift toward greater measured income inequality during the last two decades. However, the following four factors contributed to this shift: (a) the increasing number of single-parent and dual-earner families, (b) an increase in earnings differentials between high- and low-skill (and high- and low-education) groups, (c) reduced tax-shelter activities due to the sharp reduction in marginal tax rates during the 1980s, and (d) the increase in national and global "winner-take-all" markets characterized by a few people at the top with huge earnings.

7. Among the large industrial nations, there is less income inequality in Spain, France, Italy, Germany, and Canada than in the United States. In general, income is distributed more equally in the advanced industrial countries than in less developed nations.

8. In interpreting the significance of the annual income distribution, it is important to recognize that the data camouflage the movement of persons up and down the distribution over time. The distribution of income in the United States is dynamic rather than static. The tracking of household and personal income over time indicates that many with low incomes at a point in time soon move up the income ladder and achieve substantially higher incomes in the future.

9. According to the official data, 14.5 percent of the population and 11.6 percent of the families in the United States were officially classified as poor in 1994. Those living in poverty were generally younger, less educated, less likely to be working, and more likely to be living in families headed by a single parent than those who were not poor.

10. During the 1965–1975 period, transfer payments—including means-tested transfers—increased quite rapidly in both real dollars and as a share of personal income. As income transfers expanded, the poverty rate of the elderly continued to decline. However, beginning in the late 1960s, the poverty rate for working-age Americans began to rise. Even after adjustment for in-kind food, housing, and medical benefits, the poverty rate of working-age Americans has been rising gradually since the late 1960s.

11. Income supplements large enough to significantly increase the economic status of poor people will (a) encourage behavior that increases the risk of poverty and/or (b) create high implicit marginal tax rates that reduce the recipient's incentive to earn. Thus, the relative ineffectiveness of transfers—particularly those received by the non-elderly—is not surprising.

CRITICAL ANALYSIS QUESTIONS

1. Do you think the current distribution of income in the United States is too unequal? Why or why not? What criteria do you think should be used to judge the fairness of the distribution of income?

*2. Is annual money income a good measure of economic status? Is a family with a $50,000 annual income able to purchase twice the quantity of goods and services as a family with $25,000 of annual income? Is the standard of living of the $50,000 family twice as high as that of the $25,000 family? Discuss.

3. What is income mobility? If there is substantial income mobility in a society, how does this influence the importance of income distribution data?

*4. Consider a table such as Exhibit 27–4 in which the family income of parents is grouped by quintiles down the rows, and that of their offspring is grouped by quintiles across the columns. If there were no intergenerational mobility in this country, what pattern of numbers would be present in the table? If the nation had attained complete equality of opportunity, what pattern of numbers would emerge? Explain.

5. Do individuals have a property right to income they acquire from market transactions? Is it a proper function of government to tax some people in order to provide benefits to others? Why or why not? Should there be some constitutional limitations on the use of the political process to take income from some in order to provide benefits to others? Discuss.

*6. Since income transfers to the poor typically increase the marginal tax rate confronted by the poor, does a $1,000 additional transfer payment necessarily cause the income of poor recipients to rise by $1,000? Why or why not?

*7. Sue is a single parent with two children. She is considering a job that pays $800 per month ($5 per hour). She is currently drawing monthly cash benefits of $300, plus food-stamp benefits of $100, and Medicaid benefits valued at $80. If she accepts the job, she will be liable for employment taxes of $56 per month and lose all transfer benefits. What is Sue's implicit marginal tax rate for this job?

8. Between 1965 and 1975, there was a substantial increase in transfer payments, both in real dollars and as a share of total income. What impact did the government's expanded tax-transfer role have on the distribution of income and the poverty rate? Discuss.

9. Some argue that taxes exert little effect on people's incentive to earn income. In considering this issue, suppose you were required to pay a tax rate of 50 percent on all money income you earn while in school. Would this affect your employment? How might you minimize the personal effects of this tax?

*10. Transfer payments targeted at the poor make up only a small portion of the total government income transfers. Large income transfers are targeted toward the elderly, farmers, and the unemployed, regardless of their economic condition. Why do you think this is so? Does an expansion in the size of tax-transfer activities reduce income inequality?

11. "Welfare is a classic case of conflicting goals. Low welfare payments continue to leave people in poverty, but high welfare payments attract people to welfare rolls, reduce work incentives, and cause higher rates of unemployment" (quoted from the *There Is No Free Lunch* newsletter).

    a. Evaluate this statement. (Hint: Apply the opportunity cost concept.)

    b. Can you think of a plan to resolve the dilemma? Is the dilemma resolvable? Why or why not?

12. What groups are overrepresented among those with relatively low incomes? Do the poor in the United States generally stay poor? Why or why not?

13. "Means-tested transfer payments reduce the current poverty rate. However, they also create an incentive structure that discourages self-provision and self improvement. Thus, they tend to increase the future poverty rate. Welfare programs essentially purchase a lower poverty rate today in exchange for a higher poverty rate in the future." Evaluate this statement.

*14. Under legislation passed in 1983, after-tax social security benefits are reduced as income increases for recipients with incomes above $25,000. Recently, some have ad-

vocated that social security benefits be completely eliminated for elderly persons with high incomes. Do you think this is a good idea? Why or why not? If social security benefits are reduced (and perhaps eliminated in some cases) as income increases, how will this influence the incentive of the elderly to save and provide income support for their own retirement? How will the number of low-income elderly be affected?

_____

*Asterisk denotes questions for which answers are given in Appendix B.

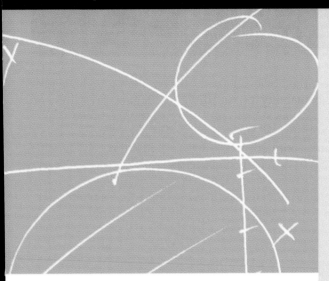

CHAPTER FOCUS

■ What does the economic way of thinking have to say about resource markets and environmental decision making?
■ Are we in danger of running out of vital natural resources in the future?
■ Is economic growth harmful to the environment?
■ How do private ownership and competitive markets affect the quality of the environment?
■ Can government regulation help protect the quality of the environment?

In nearly every case, environmental problems stem from insecure, unenforceable, or nonexistent property rights.

JANE S. SHAW[1]

---

[1]Jane S. Shaw, "Private Property Rights: Hope for the Environment," *Liberty* 2, no. 2 (November 1988): p. 55.

N atural resource and environmental issues have become increasingly important, especially over the past 30 years. Will there be enough minerals, water, and other natural resources for future generations? Will pollution increase as capital formation and technological improvements lead to greater production of goods and services? What does economics have to say about protecting the environment and using natural resources wisely? This chapter will focus on these questions and related topics.

RESOURCE MARKETS AND THE ENVIRONMENT

As we have previously stressed, the price of a good or service influences the production, quantity used, and availability of substitutes. A higher price for one good makes others more attractive as substitutes. If, for example, movie tickets rise in price, then a host of substitutes, such as cable television subscriptions, books, and live concerts become more attractive options for entertainment. The price increase causes fewer movie tickets to be purchased. Similar forces are at work on the supply side, since investors and workers have options as well. For example, if the price of television sets increases, those manufacturers will be able to bid more capital and labor away from other uses, and will supply more TV sets at the higher price.

THE CASE OF RESOURCE MARKETS

Are the demand and supply of natural resources shaped by similar influences? For something so basic as water, for example, are good substitutes readily available? Water is used for drinking, cleaning, irrigating crops, and for industrial processes and other purposes as well. In each use, we can substitute reduced activity (to use less with no other changes), more care (to spill less, for example), different methods of conducting the activity (drip irrigation rather than sprinklers, perhaps), or equipment to recycle the water we use. **Exhibit 28–1** illustrates how several industries adjusted their water use during the California drought of the late 1980s. Firms in that area had already seen water costs rise, and many conservation measures had already been taken. During the drought they came to anticipate further cost increases as well as possible supply interruptions. Their response was to install recycling facilities and to alter their production processes in order to conserve more water. Thus, these industrial users sharply reduced their use of water per unit of output between 1985 and 1989. Other studies have shown that agricultural users and households respond to price increases in a similar manner.

When economists examine markets for water, petroleum products, access to wilderness recreation, and other natural resources, they find that the sensitivity of decision makers to price and cost is similar to that found for other goods and services. Substitutes, it seems, are everywhere. For example, when the price of gasoline rises, users find many ways to use less of it: smaller cars, less distant vacation destinations, fewer shopping trips, and the use of public transportation

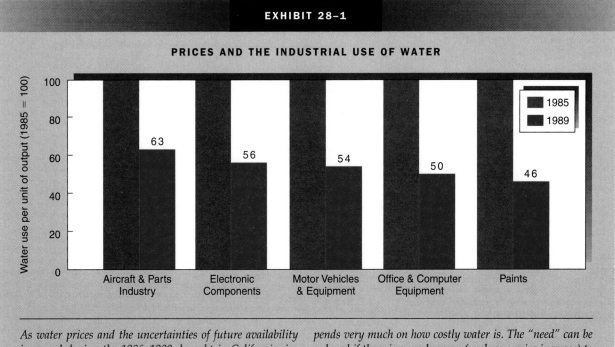

EXHIBIT 28-1

PRICES AND THE INDUSTRIAL USE OF WATER

Water use per unit of output (1985 = 100)

- 1985
- 1989

| Aircraft & Parts Industry | Electronic Components | Motor Vehicles & Equipment | Office & Computer Equipment | Paints |
| 63 | 56 | 54 | 50 | 46 |

As water prices and the uncertainties of future availability increased during the 1986–1989 drought in California, industrial users cut back on their usage. As illustrated here, the amount of water used per unit of output declined by almost 50 percent in several key industries. When the use of water is expensive, people find ways to use less of it. How much water is needed to generate a gallon of paint? That de-pends very much on how costly water is. The "need" can be reduced if there is a good reason (such as a price increase) to do so.

Source: *Cost of Industrial Water Shortages*, California Urban Water Agencies, 1991; Executive Summary, Table 1-1.

or carpooling, to name just a few. **Users always seem to find ways to achieve their goals while using less of a resource whose price has risen. Like other goods and services, the amount demanded of a natural resource is negatively related to its price.**

Higher prices will also induce suppliers to search for and recover more deposits of the resource. For example, when oil prices increase, wildcatters will search new territories, drillers will dig deeper, and water flooding and other techniques will be used to recover more oil from existing wells. **Thus, the quantity supplied of oil—or any other resource—is positively related to its price.** Similarly, as incomes grow and the demand for access to fly fishing, attractive wooded homesites, and hiking trails in relatively undisturbed natural areas increases, owners of such land will work to preserve those characteristics that make the land more valuable. When lands are owned or controlled by government, political pressures will tend to move in the same directions as market pressures, although the decision-making process is different. Have markets and government action led to responses great enough to allow people to prosper, even as they use up some of Earth's resources? Or are we running out of natural resources? The Myths of Economics feature addresses that question.

As in other markets, the responsiveness of producers and users will vary with time. The longer a sharp rise or fall in price persists, the stronger the

"WE ARE RUNNING OUT OF ENERGY, MINERALS, TIMBER, AND OTHER NATURAL RESOURCES. DOOMSDAY IS JUST AROUND THE CORNER."

For centuries, various social commentators have argued that the world is about to run out of trees, vital minerals, or various sources of energy. In sixteenth-century England, fear arose that the supply of wood would soon be exhausted as that resource was widely used as a source of energy. As the forests around urban areas receded, wood prices rose. People soon began substituting coal for charcoal, a wood derivative, in both personal and commercial uses. England's economic growth continued and the island nation still has forests.

In the middle of the nineteenth century, dire predictions arose that the United States was about to run out of whale oil, at that time the primary fuel for artificial lighting. As the demand for whale oil increased, many predicted that all the whales would soon be gone and that Americans would face long nights without light. Whale-oil prices rose sharply from 23 cents per gallon in 1820 to $1.42 per gallon in 1850.[1] Higher prices again motivated consumers and entrepreneurs to seek alternatives, including distilled vegetable oils, lard oil, and coal gas. By the early 1850s, coal oil (kerosene) had won out. And very soon thereafter, a new substitute for whale oil appeared: Petroleum replaced coal oil as the source of kerosene. As for whale oil, by 1896 its price had fallen to 40 cents per gallon, and even at that price few people used it. The whale-oil crisis had passed.

As people switched to petroleum, doomsday predictions about its exhaustion arose almost as soon as the resource was developed. In 1914 the Bureau of Mines reported that the total U.S. supply of oil was 6 million barrels, an amount less than the United States now produces every two years. In 1926 the Federal Oil Conservation Board informed people that the U.S. supply of oil would last only seven years. A couple of decades later the secretary of the interior forecast that the United States would run out of oil in just a few more years.

Dire predictions about our natural resource future became a fad during the 1970s. The "year of exhaustion" of important natural resources, especially crude oil, was a popular news item. The arithmetic of the doomsday calculations was unassailable. One simply found the current annual consumption rate (averaged over, say, the last two decades) and divided that number into the quantity of proved reserves of the resource. That provided the years of the resource remaining. Add that number to the current date, and you had the "year of exhaustion."

WHY HAVE DOOMSDAY PROJECTIONS BEEN WRONG?
There are two major reasons for their inaccuracy. First, "proved reserves" of a mineral resource are the verified quantity of the resource that producers have discovered and that they believe can be produced *at current prices and levels of technology*. Contrary to popular belief, such figures reveal little or nothing about the sufficiency of a mineral reserve for the future. Proved reserves are quite similar to inventories in manufacturing industries. Just as it is costly to produce and hold inventories of a manufactured good—for example, automobiles—so, too, it is costly to find and verify reserves of a mineral

response will be to the price change. The adjustment process will require time. Users will need time to alter their equipment, for example, in order to conserve on the use of a more expensive resource. Similarly, suppliers will need time to employ more capital and labor in order to expand their output of a resource that has increased in price. Product innovation and technological change are among the additional factors that have greater impact over time, both on quantities demanded and on those supplied, in response to a price change.

Economists have used statistical methods to analyze both the impact of price changes and the role of time in energy markets. **Exhibit 28–2** summarizes the findings of several studies on the price elasticities of demand for three major energy sources. For residential electricity, the estimated price elasticity of demand is 0.2 in the short run. This implies that a 10 percent rise in price would lead to a 2 percent short-run reduction in quantity demanded. The short run here means one year. When buyers have up to 10 years to respond, the long-run elasresource. Just as automobile dealers choose to hold only a two- or three-month inventory of cars, mineral producers commonly hold only a 10- to 15-year supply of mineral resources. And just as the current inventory of automobiles reveals little about their future availability, the size of current proved reserves reveals little about the absolute quantity of a mineral resource that can be supplied in the future.

Second, doomsday predictions have generally failed to consider the role of price changes. When a resource becomes more scarce, its price rises. This provides additional incentive for (1) resource users to cut back on their consumption, (2) suppliers to develop new methods of discovering and recovering larger quantities of the resource, and (3) both users and producers to search for and develop substitutes. To date, these forces have pushed "doomsday" further and further into the future.

In fact, the empirical evidence indicates that the relative scarcity of most resources is declining, and as a result, the relative price of most resources is falling. The classic study of Harold Barnett and Chandler Morse illustrates this point.[2] Using data from 1870 to 1963, Barnett and Morse found that the real price of resources declined during that long period. Updates and extensions of this work indicate that resource prices are continuing to decline. In 1980 economist Julian Simon bet doomsday environmentalist Paul Ehrlich that the inflation-adjusted price of any five natural resources of Ehrlich's choosing would decline during the 1980s. In fact, the prices of all five of the resources chosen by Ehrlich declined, and Simon won the highly publicized bet. A recent book edited by Simon, containing chapters written by a number of prominent economists and resource experts, provides a good deal of evidence that the availability of most resources continues to improve in the 1990s.[3]

THE FUTURE

Far from suggesting that doomsday is just around the corner, the price data paint a rather optimistic picture. Historical data on relative prices of key resources indicate that technology and the ever-increasing availability of substitutes tend to outrun our use of scarce natural resources. When price changes are allowed to reflect changing scarcities, constructive human responses to specific scarcities are a predictable occurrence. Just as they have been wrong in the past, future doomsday forecasts that fail to incorporate human response to relative price changes are likely to be wrong in the future.

.

[1]See J. Clayburn LaForce, *The Energy Crisis: The Moral Equivalent of Bamboozle* (Los Angeles: International Institute for Economic Research, 1978).

[2]Harold Barnett and Chandler Morse, *Scarcity of Growth: The Economics of Natural Resource Availability* (Baltimore: The Johns Hopkins University Press for Resources for the Future, 1963). For an update of this study, see Manuel H. Johnson, Fredrick W. Bell, and J. T. Bennett, "Natural Resource Scarcity: Empirical Evidence and Public Policy." *Journal of Environmental Economics and Management* 7 (September 1980): pp. 258–269.

[3]Julian L. Simon, *The State of Humanity* (Cambridge, Mass.: Blackwell Publishers, 1995), Part III, Natural Resources.

ticity indicates that the same 10 percent price rise would cause a 7 percent decline in residential use of electricity, other factors held constant.

The price elasticities of demand for natural gas and gasoline follow a similar pattern. In the short run, a change in price will lead to only a small change in amount demanded. With time, however, consumers will be able to adjust more fully and come up with more and better ways to reduce consumption. Thus, the demand for both natural gas and gasoline is also substantially more elastic in the long run than in the short run.

Price elasticities are useful in predicting fuel usage as fuel prices change. However, other factors, such as income and the price of substitutes, will also influence consumption. In addition, we cannot expect the same reaction to a price change from people in different situations. Once auto manufacturers have spent years researching and developing techniques to save fuel, for example, even a return to the much lower gasoline prices of years past would not bring

[a]When income and other factors such as other fuel prices are held constant, the elasticities indicate the ratio of percent change in quantity to the percent change in price causing the quantity change. Each elasticity is actually a negative number, since price and quantity demanded move in opposite directions.

Source: Douglas R. Bohi, *Analyzing Demand Behavior* (Baltimore: Johns Hopkins University Press, 1981), p. 159.

EXHIBIT 28–2

PRICE RESPONSIVENESS OF ENERGY FORMS: ESTIMATED PRICE ELASTICITIES OF DEMAND

FUEL	ESTIMATED ELASTICITY[a]	
	SHORT RUN	LONG RUN
Residential electricity	0.2	0.7
Residential natural gas	0.1	0.5
Gasoline	0.2	0.7

back the previous level of gas guzzling. Measured elasticities reflect history, but history can never be retraced exactly, even if the path of prices is somehow repeated. Estimated price elasticities are a rough but often useful guide to buyer behavior when prices of an important commodity such as energy change.

Both economic theory and statistical studies indicate that resource markets are quite similar to other markets. The quantity of a natural resource demanded will fall and the quantity supplied will rise when its price increases (other things constant). Higher resource prices will increase the incentive of users to conserve on their use of a resource and find substitutes for it. The higher price also brings forth extra production, providing additional supplies. Lower prices have the opposite effects, reducing the quantity supplied of the resource and increasing the quantity demanded.

ECONOMIC PRINCIPLES AND ENVIRONMENTAL DECISIONS

Markets coordinate the choices of people with regard to natural resource use. But what about environmental decisions, which often are made outside the markets, and thus without the benefit of fully priced goods and services? There are relatively few markets for clean air, pure water, and endangered species. As we have previously discussed, the absence of clearly defined and securely enforced property rights and the resulting lack of markets and decision-maker accountability are at the heart of pollution and other externality problems. Let us consider how the economic way of thinking enhances our understanding of environmental choices and problems.

1. Incentives matter. One economics professor demonstrated the importance of incentives in environmental decisions by walking into class with a lighted cigarette, taking a puff, then dropping the cigarette on the floor, and grinding it out with his shoe. Then he pointed out that he would never do such a thing in his own living room, where he personally would bear the cost of having to clean up the mess. In fact, he said, he probably would not do it if the building's janitor were watching and likely to voice strong disapproval of the behavior. Further, he said that he would be less likely to grind out the cigarette on a classroom floor if an ashtray were handy—in other words, if he were not required to go to the trouble of finding one. The professor's actions regarding the environment around him thus depended on the expected costs to him, of his actions.

Do incentives matter in the preservation of wildlife? Consider the case of African elephants, which are valuable for their meat and ivory, among other factors. Poachers like to kill the wild elephants illegally, to take the most valuable parts. Poaching is illegal, but the animals in central African nations are not owned by the local residents, who might most easily help prevent poaching. The local residents gain nothing from the presence of the elephants, yet they must endure the loss of crops and water, and even the danger to their children that elephants bring. Many local residents would therefore prefer fewer of them. The control of poaching is consequently weak, and the herds in Central Africa have been declining—almost to the point of extinction.[2]

In southern African nations, however, many elephants are owned privately. Even when the elephants are not owned privately, the residents of the villages near each herd are allowed to share the gains from the human use of elephants, whether from hunting or tourism. These partial private-ownership rights provide local residents with an incentive to help control poaching, and they have been quite effective in doing so. As a result, elephant herds thrive in southern African nations.

As these simple examples demonstrate, when people make decisions affecting the environment, their actions will be guided by expected benefits and opportunity costs, just as they are for other decisions.

2. The value of a good or service is subjective. The fact that values are subjective also bears on environmental decisions. How valuable is a tract of unroaded wilderness land, relative to the same land with roads and campgrounds added to enhance recreation, or the same land developed for high-quality residential use? Individuals will differ dramatically in their evaluations of those alternatives. Some believe that wilderness is the highest and best use for such a tract of land. Others prefer more intensive recreational use or tastefully planned residential development, where people can be in close contact with the beauty of nature.

Consider another, similar question: Will persons living near a river be willing to vote for sewage plant improvements to help clean up a half-mile stretch of the river, even though that will add an extra $12 per month to their water bill? Again, we can expect people to differ in how much value they place on making a stretch of river a little cleaner. Some will be quite happy to pay the fee, while others will probably object.

Environmental values, like all others, are subjective. Individuals will differ substantially in the value they place on various options for environmental management.

---

[2]See Randy Simmons and Urs Kreuter, "Herd Mentality: Banning Ivory Sales Is No Way to Save the Elephant," *Policy Review* (fall 1989): pp. 46–49.

THE ENDANGERED SPECIES ACT: HELPING LISTED SPECIES?

The intent of the Endangered Species Act (ESA), which the Congress passed in 1973, was to help save endangered species from extinction. To do that, the ESA gave to the U.S. Fish and Wildlife Service (FWS) the power to prohibit any land use by private owners (and government agencies) that might disturb the habitat of members of a species listed as endangered under the ESA. The majority of species that are listed, or are candidates for listing, are found on private lands. Farming, building, cutting trees, clearing brush, and even walking are activities that have been prohibited on private parcels of land where FWS biologists believe that such activities might harm a listed animal.

Colonies of many listed species have benefitted from this control. The affected landowners, however, have often been forced by ESA requirements to sacrifice highly productive activities. Although a public good—habitat provision for endangered species—is produced as a result of these sacrifices, no compensation is given to owners called on to make them. This generates problems.

Consider the sacrifice—the opportunity cost—required to set aside the southern pine forest habitat favored by the red cockaded woodpecker, a listed species found in southern pine forests from Virginia to Texas. Trees the birds normally use for nesting must be left standing for several decades beyond the time they would normally be harvested for wood. Many acres of forage must also be available around the nest. Ben Cone is one person affected by the woodpecker. He owns 7,200 acres in North Carolina. For decades he managed the land primarily for wildlife, clearcutting 50 acres of very old timber every 5 to 10 years, to gain revenue and to renew the forest. The red cockaded woodpecker loves the old trees. So in 1991 when he wanted to cut and sell some timber, the FWS said that he must set aside large parts of his land for the woodpecker. The wildlife biologists hired to analyze the situation told him that 1,560 acres could no longer be cut, and that the cost to him would be about $1.4 million. He told an interviewer for a story in *the Wall Street Journal*, "I cannot afford to let those woodpeckers take over the rest of the property. I'm going to start massive clear-cutting. I'm going to a 40-year rotation instead of a 75- to 80-year rotation."

The cost of protecting other species can be much lower or much higher, depending on the value of the land they need, and the restrictions judged necessary by the FWS biologists. Many landowners living in the range of a listed species, having heard about the costs they might face, dread the possibility that the species will be found on their land. What can they do? Some might risk severe punishment by taking the illegal step of killing an animal before the FWS learns about it, and trying to hide the fact that the animal was there. This is

---

3. Remember the secondary effects. As in other areas of human action, the secondary effects of environmental actions must be considered. For example, when citrus growers use chemical pesticides to protect their fruit against certain insects, the pesticides may impose some danger to consumers if they are not washed completely from the fruit. To avoid such danger to consumers, government agencies control the use of most pesticides and have banned the use of certain compounds. That was the case for DDT, which was banned by the U.S. Environmental Protection Agency in 1972 because it was believed to be a source of human health risk and damage to wild birds. Unfortunately, the ban had unwanted secondary effects. In place of DDT, some other pesticides were used that were more risky to the workers who applied them in the fields.

In other nations, the results were even more tragic when DDT was stopped. In Sri Lanka, for example, where mosquitoes had been controlled by DDT, the incidence of malaria had declined from 2.8 million cases in 1946 to only 110 cases in 1961. After the government of Sri Lanka stopped the use of DDT in the early sometimes referred to as the "shoot, shovel, and shut up" strategy.

More often, we suspect, the landowner learns from experts what the listed species desires for habitat, and adjusts land management in subtle ways to make that land unattractive to the listed species. Michael Bean is an environmental attorney who is informally credited with writing the Endangered Species Act. He still supports it, but recognizes the need for change. He says there is "increasing evidence that at least some private landowners are actively managing their land so as to avoid potential endangered species problems," and that such actions are "not the result of malice" but "fairly rational decisions, motivated by a desire to avoid potentially significant economic constraints." The result, nonetheless, is that the act has caused a serious reduction in habitat for listed and candidate species.

Prior to the ESA, landowners often were quite willing to help preserve declining wildlife. When fears of extinction for bluebirds arose, landowners allowed volunteers to place hundreds of thousands of nest boxes on their land and to monitor them. The bluebird has recovered and as a result never had to be listed. Many similar efforts, large and small, have been successful in gaining landowner cooperation with little or no payment in return.

Today, nest boxes for red cockaded woodpeckers would make it much less costly to provide habitat for them. With a suitable nest, their habitat can be young trees, managed for timber. New nests can be provided when the existing trees are ready for harvest, if the nest tree is not cut during the nesting season. But finding a landowner willing to cooperate under the current ESA is obviously difficult. No one wants to put himself in Ben Cone's shoes. So long as the ESA provides unlimited powers for the FWS to restrict the land used when a listed species is in the area, few landowners will welcome the species. In fact, many will not even welcome hikers who might discover it on the land. Property rights to the owner's land are placed in jeopardy by the ESA.

The ESA provides a clear example of a policy adopted with a noble goal—saving species from extinction—that has unwanted, and even tragic, secondary effects. This example shows once again the importance of enforceable property rights in bringing about cooperative behavior. Owners who did not fear the loss of rights usually cooperated at low cost. The example also shows why it is important for decision makers to be wary of unwanted secondary effects of their actions.

Sources: Thomas R. Bourland and Richard L. Stroup, "Rent Payments as Incentives: Making Endangered Species Welcome on Private Land," *Journal of Forestry* 94, no. 4 (April 1996): pp. 18–21; and Richard L. Stroup, *The Endangered Species Act: Making Innocent Species the Enemy*, PERC Policy Series, No. 3 (Bozeman, Mont.: PERC, April 1995).

1960s, however, the number of malaria cases jumped back up to 2.5 million in 1968–1969.

It is important that environmental decision makers, like those in other policy areas, be alert for secondary effects. (See the Applications in Economics feature on the Endangered Species Act.) This basic economic principle is just as important for environmental decision making as it is in other areas of human action.

We have seen that economic principles apply to the choices of people regarding natural resources and the environment just as they do to choices in other areas. But since markets and easily defended property rights are not always present, especially for air and water quality and other environmental services, observers often worry that as an economy grows, more resources will be used and additional waste will be imposed on the environment. Clearly, this is an extremely important concern. What can economists say about the effects of economic growth on environmental quality? We turn now to examine this important question.

IS ECONOMIC GROWTH HARMFUL TO THE ENVIRONMENT?

The need to choose between economic growth and environmental quality may seem obvious when economic activities affect the quality of our air or water. In the United States, the federal government has been asked to constrain polluters, and, historically, courts have protected the rights of those harmed by pollution, requiring polluters to pay damages and/or clean up their emissions, and sometimes ordering them to stop the polluting activities. As a result, certain economic activities are made more costly and specific economic outputs are reduced in order to maintain environmental quality. It is not surprising, then, that many people believe a choice must be made between economic growth on the one hand and environmental protection on the other. Yet data from around the world support a more optimistic view.

As we will see, many of the same forces that encourage economic growth, such as market institutions and improvements in technology, also help to reduce pressures on the environment. In addition, rising incomes foster the willingness and ability to pay for a cleaner, more pleasant environment. Although environmental protection often imposes some cost on economic activities, growth can still proceed when the controls are intelligently applied. And growth itself, properly controlled to avoid environmental harms, has important beneficial effects on the environment.

Once people have enough income so that they are not struggling to put food on the table, they become more willing and able to take actions to reduce (or avoid) environmental damage and improve the quality of the environment. For example, as incomes have risen in North America, Europe, and other parts of the world, private actions to maintain nature preserves have proliferated. Individuals, firms, and nonprofit groups have established areas for the protection of plant and animal habitats.[3] Profit-seeking firms, such as Big Sky of Montana, find it profitable to buy large tracts of mountainous land, far more than they plan to develop, then sell some of the tracts with environmentally protective restrictions. By guaranteeing the pristine quality of the resort and its surroundings, with legal restrictions on what every owner can do, they increase the value of the property they sell.

Economic growth generally leads to environmental improvements because people with higher incomes are willing to pay more for environmental quality. Economist Donald Coursey has studied this topic extensively. He finds that in the United States and in other industrial nations, citizens' support for measures to improve environmental quality is highly sensitive to income changes.[4] In economic terms, willingness to pay for environmental measures, such as costly envi-

---

[3]Chapter 9 of *Environmental Quality* (1984) the annual report of the President's Council on Environmental Quality, describes a representative sample of these private projects, some of which date back to the last century, to benefit the environment.

[4]Donald Coursey discussed this topic in "The Demand for Environmental Quality," a paper presented in January 1993 at the annual meeting of the American Economic Association in Anaheim, California.

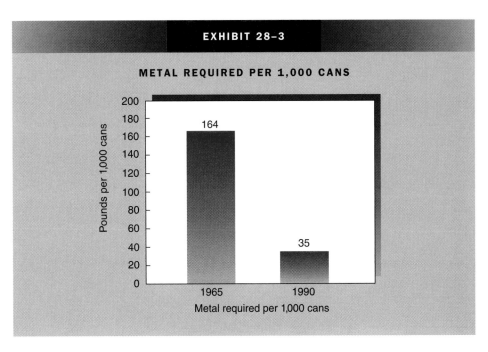

EXHIBIT 28-3

METAL REQUIRED PER 1,000 CANS

Pounds per 1,000 cans

164

35

1965   1990

Metal required per 1,000 cans

By improving their engineering techniques and switching to a thinner can made of lightweight aluminum, producers reduced their use of metal per can by almost 80 percent between 1965 and 1990.

Source: Lynn Scarlett, "Make Your Environment Dirtier—Recycle," *The Wall Street Journal,* January 14, 1991.

ronmental regulations, is highly elastic with respect to income. He estimates that in industrial nations the income elasticity of demand for environmental quality is 2.5. Thus, a 10 percent increase in income leads to a 25 percent increase in citizens' willingness to pay for environmental measures. Similarly, a 10 percent decline in a community's income leads to a 25 percent decline in that community's support for costly environmental measures. According to Coursey, the demand for environmental quality has approximately the same income elasticity as the demand for luxury automobiles like the BMW and Mercedes-Benz.

Technological change is another factor that generally improves the environment. Economic growth and technological change generally accompany each other. The same market processes that encourage growth also encourage technological advances. In the United States, advancing technology was itself cleaning the environment well before major environmental laws were passed.

In a market system, producers using advanced technology can profit by getting a given performance from a smaller amount of a costly resource. **Exhibit 28–3** illustrates this process for producers and users of soft-drink and beer cans. As they sought greater profits, producers found ways to reduce the amount of metal used per can, and also switched to lightweight, easily recycled aluminum. As a result, less ore was dug and processed, and less energy was needed to transport both the raw materials and the filled cans, reducing pollution from the use of the cans. Because this search for lower-cost means of producing each marketed service is going on constantly in a market economy, the result is a continuing series of reductions in the emissions of polluting wastes. Partially offsetting this, of course, is the increased quantity of goods and services produced, which, in turn, can also mean more resource use and more pollution, depending on the amount of resource-saving technical progress that accompanies income growth.

Note: Estimates are based on cross-country regression analysis of data from the 1980s.

Source: World Bank, *World Development Report*, 1992, p. 11.

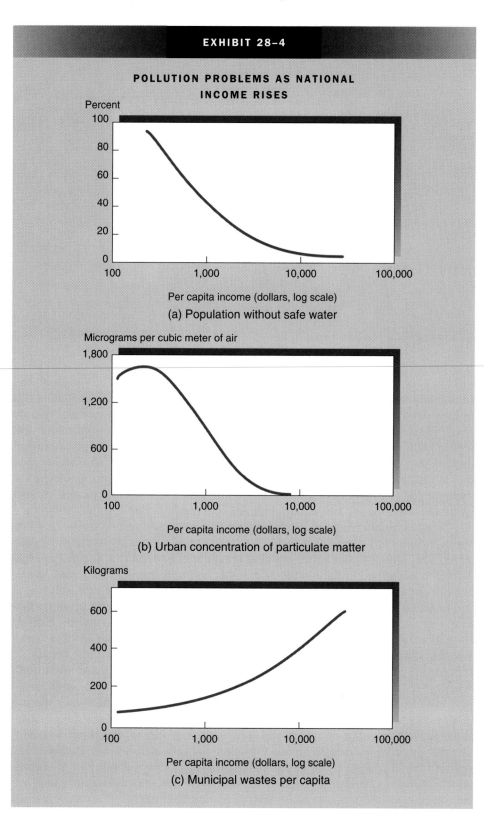

EXHIBIT 28-4

POLLUTION PROBLEMS AS NATIONAL INCOME RISES

Percent

Per capita income (dollars, log scale)
(a) Population without safe water

Micrograms per cubic meter of air

Per capita income (dollars, log scale)
(b) Urban concentration of particulate matter

Kilograms

Per capita income (dollars, log scale)
(c) Municipal wastes per capita

Exhibit 28–4 illustrates the general relationship between three types of environmental problems and per capita income, showing that some problems are ameliorated with higher income, others are worsened, and still others are worsened only up to a point, and then improve with still higher levels of economic development. Problems such as a lack of safe drinking water (part a) are steadily reduced as income rises. As people become richer, they are more able to reduce waterborne diseases by installing sewers to handle human waste, and by reducing water contamination by animals. Certain pollutants, however, such as particulates in the air (part b), tend initially to become worse as incomes increase from extremely low levels. But as income levels continue to rise, heavily used roads are paved and industrial processes become more efficient, emitting smaller amounts of waste. As a result, particulate air pollution will eventually fall as per capita income continues to increase. Especially among developed countries, economic growth most often brings cleaner air and water, along with improvements in several other aspects of environmental quality.

Unfortunately, the amount of solid waste generated normally increases steadily with economic development (part c). But proper disposal facilities can minimize the negative effects of this problem. On balance, richer seems to be environmentally better.[5] One reason lies in the fact that markets and property rights allow citizens to achieve both growth and environmental protection from identifiable polluters. Without enforceable rights to resources, both goals are more difficult to reach. We turn now to a discussion of how property rights have helped the environment in several nations around the world.

PROPERTY RIGHTS AND THE ENVIRONMENT

When people have open access to forests, pastureland, or fishing grounds, they tend to overuse them. Providing land titles to farmers in Thailand has helped reduce damage to forests. The assignment of property titles to slum dwellers in Bandung, Indonesia, has tripled household investment in sanitation facilities. Providing security of tenure to hill farmers in Kenya has reduced soil erosion. Formalizing community rights to land in Burkina Faso is sharply improving land management. And allocating transferable rights to fishery resources has checked the tendency to overfish in New Zealand.

WORLD BANK[6]

Income growth helps to increase the demand for environmental quality, while technological advances help to lower the cost of reducing resource use. Yet incomes above the poverty level and an understanding of technology are not enough to protect the environment. The recent opening up of Eastern European

---

[5]The *World Development Report*, 1992 (New York: World Bank), especially Chapters 2 and 3, provides a detailed look at the connection between economic development and environmental quality.

[6]The quoted passage is from *World Development Report*, 1992 (New York: World Bank), p. 12.

nations and the Soviet Union exposed widespread environmental disasters. These disasters occurred despite the presence of good technical capabilities and above-average per capita incomes in those nations.

Why did these relatively advanced nations not take better care of their environments? The answer appears to lie in the fact that property rights and market exchange were largely missing. Property rights are an important factor influencing environmental quality (see quotation on previous page). The former Soviet Union and the Eastern European nations, in the decades during which they were controlled by socialist governments, refused to allow most resources to be privately owned and declared that most market exchanges were criminal acts. Most types of entrepreneurship were prohibited by law. Production instead was centrally planned. Land and other resources were owned by the state, rather than by individuals.

In a competitive market, the profit motive provides clear incentives to reduce resource usage and waste products. When a firm is privately owned, the personal wealth of the owners is enhanced by effective economizing behavior. For government-operated enterprises, this is much less true. There is no owner (or group of owners) whose wealth is directly affected by economizing behavior (or the lack of it) on the part of the managers of government enterprises. Thus, government-owned firms are less likely than their market counterparts to minimize cost and resource use.

One index of resource conservation is energy use per unit of output. In modern economies, energy constitutes more than half of all the resources utilized. Mikhail Bernstam has compiled data to compare the energy use in the largest 12 industrialized market economies with its use in the Eastern European socialist countries (plus North Korea). The market-based economies used only 37 percent as much energy per $1,000 of output as the socialist nations in 1986. The figure had fallen from 44 percent in 1980.

The same sort of comparison applies to the use of steel. Socialist economies used more than three times as much steel per unit of output as market economies did.[7] The data gathered by Bernstam show that, across a variety of socialist economies, resource use is far greater per unit of output than across a variety of market-oriented economies. All these nations had the capability of using advanced technologies, but without a market process in which producers and consumers individually choose among competing options, and individually pay for what they choose, there was little incentive to conserve resources effectively. And a less efficient economy tends to be a less clean economy.

After the fall of rigidly socialist regimes in the Soviet Union and Eastern Europe, leaders in several of these countries are now seeking ways to increase private ownership and the role of markets. What, exactly, is important about private ownership of resources? Four functions of property rights are especially important to the economy and to the environment:

1. Private property rights provide owners with the incentive to share (sell to others) resource access, while resource prices provide users with the incentive to conserve. As we have previously discussed, markets do not function well when sellers are denied the right to sell their assets, if they wish, to potential

---

[7]The facts in this paragraph are from Mikhail Bernstam, *The Wealth of Nations and the Environment* (London: Institute of Economic Affairs, 1991), pp. 1–28.

buyers in the marketplace. The right to sell forces each owner to confront the opportunity cost accompanying alternative uses of the resource, including uses that improve environmental quality and conserve resources for future use. Furthermore, when resources are privately owned, producers will have a strong incentive to reduce costs by conserving on their use of resources. In essence, private ownership encourages less resource usage per unit of value produced. Business firms pursuing profits have a strong incentive to implement new technologies that conserve on the use of resources. Thus, it should not be surprising that resource-saving changes tend to occur earlier in a market setting than under socialism. The experience of Eastern Europe and the former Soviet Union under socialism is consistent with this view.

2. A resource owner has a strong incentive to exercise good stewardship. Private ownership of property provides owners with an incentive to take good care of things, an incentive that is generally absent under government ownership and control. If the resource is well cared for, it will be more valuable and add more to the personal wealth of its owner. If the owner allows the resource to deteriorate or be harmed by pollution, he or she personally bears the cost of that negligence in the form of a decline in the value of the resource. The value of the property right to the resource is, in a very real sense, a hostage to good care of that resource.

3. A resource owner has legal rights against anyone who would harm the resource. A private owner of a resource has more than just the incentive to preserve the value of that resource. Private property rights also provide the owner with legal rights against anyone (usually including a government agency) who invades—physically or by pollution—and harms the resource. Much environmental damage is prevented this way. The private owner of a forest or a farm will not sit idly by if someone is cutting down trees or invading the property with hazardous pollutants. Lawsuits can be used to protect those rights. For example, owners of copper and lead smelters in the United States have been forced to compensate owners of agricultural crops and homes for damage from sulfur dioxide emissions. Once such a company has been successfully sued, the decision sets a legal precedent that effectively discourages further pollution.

Before they closed it down, the owners of a smelter near Tacoma, Washington, had been sued in such a manner. After the court found the firm liable and forced it to pay damages, measures were taken to reduce future pollution. Moreover, whenever unusual weather conditions nonetheless caused sulfur dioxide from its smokestack to damage the foliage or the homes of downwind households, the company routinely made direct payments of compensation to avoid the cost of further lawsuits.

When resources are not privately owned, no individual will receive large personal rewards for bringing suit against polluters, even when the source of the pollution is clear. In the United States, fish in a river might be damaged by pollution, but they are not owned by anyone whose personal wealth depends on their safety. Political and bureaucratic authorities must be counted on to protect the resource. In England, by contrast, where fishing rights on a stream are privately owned, the owners guard jealously the quality of the water. (See the Applications in Economics feature on property rights and water quality.)

4. Changes in the value of a privately owned resource bring all of the anticipated future benefits and costs of today's resource decisions immediately to

PROPERTY RIGHTS AND WATER QUALITY

Could property rights help protect water quality in rivers and streams? Private ownership of fishing rights in England illustrates what happens when private ownership is present. In England the adjacent landowner has title to fishing rights out to the middle of the stream. The fishing right can be rented, leased, or sold. Fishing clubs and owners of country inns are among those who have purchased those rights. Club members and guests of the inns may then have access to fishing in this area.

Some clubs are exclusive and expensive. The Houghton Club, with fewer than 25 members, owns fishing rights on 17 miles of the Test River, estimated in 1988 to be worth more than $35 million. But fishing rights on an adjacent stretch of the same river, a few hundred yards long, are owned by the Greyhound Inn bed and breakfast. The owner allows two guests (at about $55 each, in 1988), to fish each day. "Rough fishing" (non-trout fishing) is available from clubs organized at local pubs, for perhaps $50 per year. In all cases, access is strictly controlled to eliminate crowding, and the stream banks are generally kept cleared of brush and are well protected against cattle and other potential sources of pollution that might disturb the fish.

Historically, as trout fishing became more popular and the rights became more valuable over the years, fishing-rights owners became more serious about protecting their rights. In 1948, long before the first Earth Day in 1970 and 20 years before the government established authorities to control water pollution, the Anglers' Cooperative Association (ACA) was formed to help clubs and anglers obtain damage awards or court orders forcing intruders to cease polluting activities. The ACA won its first major case in 1951 against two chemical companies and the city of Derby for pumping untreated sewage, hot water, and tar products into the River Derwent. Through the years, it won several other cases, including a 1987 case against the Thames Water Authority for fouling the Thames River. It has established enough court precedents that it seldom has to go to court now.

In the United States, fishing rights on most streams are owned by state governments, which might in principle sue to protect their rights just as the ACA does in England. However, without their own wealth at stake, bureaucratic decision makers seem less inclined to aggressively protect the fish or the water quality. Instead, control of water pollution in streams is typically left up to environmental regulators. England, however, has demonstrated what seems to be a more sure and far less expensive way—private ownership of fishing rights—to protect waters that are valuable for fishing.

Source: This feature is based on Jane S. Shaw and Richard L. Stroup, "Gone Fishin'," *Reason* 20, no. 4 (August 1988): pp. 34–37.

bear on the resource owner. An additional benefit of private property rights is their ability to bring expected future effects of current decisions to bear now. Property rights provide long-term incentives for maximizing the value of a resource, even for owners whose personal outlook is short term. If using a tract of land for the construction of a toxic waste dump reduces its future productivity, its value today falls, and the decline in the land's value reduces the owner's wealth. That happens because land's current worth reflects the net present value of its future services—the revenue from production or services received directly from the land, minus the costs (including amounts that must be paid to anyone harmed by escaping wastes) required to generate the revenues.

Thus, fewer services from a privately owned resource, or greater costs associated with it in the future, mean lower value (and less wealth for the owner) now. In fact, as soon as an appraiser or potential buyer can see future problems, the wealth of the owner declines by the amount of the reduction in potential buyers' willingness to pay for the resource. Not only does using land to store hazardous waste reduce future options for the land's productivity, but the value also may be reduced by the risk of future lawsuits if the wastes leak and cause damage to other people or property.

This is true even if the owner of the resource is a corporation, and the corporate officers, rather than the owner-stockholders, are in control. Corporate officers may be concerned mainly about the short term, not expecting to be present when future problems arise. However, property rights hold such decision makers accountable. If a current action causes the expectation of future problems, or if current expenditures promise future benefits, those who buy and sell stock will push the stock price up or down accordingly, capturing the reduction or the increase in future net benefits. Corporate officers are concerned with current profits, but must be equally concerned with current changes in the value of the corporation's stock.

Of course, the average owner of stock is not a pollution expert, but anyone can gain the necessary knowledge by reading the published reports of business journalists or stock analysts who are tuned in to all phases of the industry they cover. Watchdog environmental groups also spread the word about suspected problems. It is in the stockholder's interest to keep an "ear to the ground" because correctly anticipating how the market will react can allow the discerning investor to buy before good news is fully captured in the stock price, or to sell before bad news is fully reflected in a falling stock price. Such self-interested scrutiny and the resultant decisions of investors provide a continual assessment of corporate strategies.

GOVERNMENT REGULATION AND THE ENVIRONMENT

Substantial contributions to environmental quality are made through the normal operation of property rights and a market system. However, certain kinds of environmental problems cannot be solved merely by the enforcement of individual property rights. Only when pollution is local, affecting strongly a few people who can enforce their rights in court, can property rights deal effectively with the problem. Most pollutants capable of doing proven and serious damage are of this sort. But others of potentially great harm are not. If the effects of an emitted substance are both serious and widespread over a large population, or if the substance has many sources, then government regulation may be more efficient.

Government regulation is an alternative method of seeking to protect and preserve the quality of the environment. (Note: The following chapter explains in more detail why regulation may be called for, and how regulators might best reduce environmental problems with the use of a variety of policy tools.) Regulation, however, seldom leads to ideal outcomes, and it can be enormously expensive. The Environmental Protection Agency has estimated that in 1994 environmental regulation in the United States cost about $150 billion. Regulation is seldom based on market signals, and so it is subject to all the problems caused by lack of information and lack of incentives that have plagued the socialist nations. It can be very wasteful.[8] Scientific uncertainty is often great in cases where regulation is demanded, and the stakes can be very high.

Consider the issue of global warming. Emissions of carbon dioxide from the efficient burning of all fuels cause no harm where they are emitted. No one's rights are being violated by the invasion of a harmful pollutant. Yet these emissions have been building up in the atmosphere. They may in the future require regulation if the buildup acts as an invisible blanket and causes the earth to warm, as some scientists claim that it will. Such warming could change weather patterns, making hurricanes and other storms more intense, and might even result in rising sea levels around the globe. If the "worst-case scenarios" suggested by scientists were to materialize, some communities would face flooding of their lands, serious ecological disruptions, and other problems.

Some scientists and many environmental groups argue that the threat of global warming is so serious that despite high costs, the nations of the world must impose strong regulations quickly. Government limits of some sort, they point out, are the only way that carbon dioxide emissions can be controlled. Other scientists, and many policy analysts, believe that imposing strong regulation at this time would be a mistake. They point out that the science of global warming is filled with uncertainties. For example:

1. We do not know whether changes in the earth's cloud cover will enhance the warming effects of carbon dioxide or offset them. Water vapor and clouds in the atmosphere account for more than 98 percent of the total warming we now experience, so even small changes in where that water is in the atmosphere, and the form it takes, could easily overcome the impact of the buildup in carbon dioxide. All scientists agree that the atmospheric models used to predict global warming do not accurately incorporate the effects of atmospheric water vapor.

2. It is true that in the past, over thousands of years, added carbon dioxide has been associated with warming. But does this association mean that the carbon dioxide caused the warming? Studies of ice cores drilled deep into Antarctica and Greenland allow scientists to measure the levels of carbon dioxide in the atmosphere during earlier years. The evidence indicates that the warming often preceded, rather than followed, the buildup of carbon dioxide. In such cases, how could the buildup cause the warming, when the warming came first?

3. If warming does occur, will sea levels rise or fall? Warming would cause glaciers and ice caps to melt and shrink at the edges. However, warmer air carries more moisture, and the added precipitation would build up snow and ice in the still-frigid centers of the polar ice caps, increasing their thickness. Whether the net effect on the sea level would be positive or negative is unknown.

These questions and many more are in dispute. We cannot even be sure whether the buildup and a warmer world would, on balance, be better or worse. Some people would gain from a warmer, wetter world. Also, the direct effects of added carbon dioxide are helpful to plants. Owners of greenhouses routinely

---

[8]For a more thorough explanation of why environmental regulation is often inefficient, and some quantitative estimates of how costly it is, see Robert Crandall, *Why Is the Cost of Environmental Regulation So High?* Policy Study No. 110 (St. Louis: Center for the Study of American Business, February 1992).

purchase carbon dioxide to enrich the enclosed atmosphere and enhance plant growth.

The cost of such policies is another consideration. One large study estimates that in the United States alone, the cost of merely stabilizing emissions at their current levels, with no net reduction, would be $95 billion in the first year, with larger costs after that. These facts and the many scientific uncertainties combine to make many economists unwilling to endorse strong regulations to force reductions in the emissions of carbon dioxide. As economist William Nordhaus suggested in an article about global warming, "The best investment today may be in learning about climatic change, rather than in preventing it."[9]

In sum, environmental regulation is a powerful tool, capable of providing important improvements in environmental quality, but it tends to be very costly, and its unintended consequences can be serious also. The results of regulations banning DDT proved that point, as we described earlier, especially in the tragic case of Sri Lanka.

Policymakers and analysts considering environmental regulations should recognize that environmental quality is an economic good. Like food, clothing, and shelter, it is something that people are willing to pay for, though not in unlimited amounts. In addition, policymakers should recognize that the linkage between environmental quality and economic prosperity is important. Environmental regulations can exert a powerful influence on both, for good or for ill. Finally, they should not forget that enforceable property rights were for many years our main form of regulating environmental pollution and allowing far-sighted individuals and groups to exercise their visions of preserved natural areas. Overall, property rights continue to play a positive role in the preservation of a quality environment.

PULLING IT ALL TOGETHER

We have seen that in matters of natural resources and the environment, as in other matters, economic principles can help us to understand and predict the actions that individuals will take. Providing for resource conservation and the prevention of harmful pollution can often be accomplished through the use of property rights, market exchange, and the resulting signals and incentives that emanate from market prices. The market for capital assets even provides a voice for future resource users. As Jane S. Shaw pointed out in the opening quote, it is when property rights are not properly applied, or cannot be, that problems occur. Property rights and market prices are not a panacea, because property rights cannot always be specified and enforced. As in other economic issues, government regulation may provide improvements when markets fail. But here, as elsewhere, government is not an automatic corrective device.

---

[9]William Nordhaus, "Global Warming: Slowing the Greenhouse Express," in *Setting National Priorities: Policies for the Nineties,* ed. Henry J. Aaron (Washington, D.C.: The Brookings Institution, 1990), p. 207.

LOOKING AHEAD

The following section on public choice analyzes more fully the conditions that strengthen the case of government action and provides insight concerning the workings of political decision making and its potential as a mechanism to promote more efficient use of resources.

CHAPTER SUMMARY

1. In resource markets, as in other markets, incentives matter. Both the quantity demanded of a resource and the quantity supplied depend on the resource price. Substitutes can be found everywhere. Both the demand and the supply curves will be more elastic when buyers and sellers have more time in which to respond to a price change.

2. Neither economic analysis nor empirical evidence is supportive of the view that the world is about to run out of key natural resources. When private property rights are present, increased scarcity (relative to demand) of a natural resource will increase the price of the resource and thereby encourage (a) conservation, (b) the use of substitutes, and (c) the development of new technologies capable of both enhancing the supply of the resource and reducing our reliance on it. The fact that the real prices of most natural resources have declined during the last century is inconsistent with the doomsday view of resource scarcity.

3. Even though environmental decisions are often made outside a market context, the basic principles of economics still apply. Purposeful choices, influenced by prices and other incentives, are made without full knowledge. Values are subjective, and the secondary effects of decisions are often important.

4. Environmental quality and economic growth tend to go together. People living in poverty are hard on the environment. Market prices provide potential users with an incentive to conserve on their use of resources. Technological improvements enhance economic growth and reduce resource waste. The demand for environmental quality is positively and strongly linked to income levels.

5. Resources are better protected and more efficiently allocated, producing less waste and pollution, when property rights are protected and markets are utilized to allocate resources. The stronger economic and environmental performance of market economies relative to socialist economies confirms this point.

6. Private resource ownership is important to environmental quality and resource conservation because it (a) is necessary for the wide, but controlled, access encouraged by the market process, (b) provides an incentive for resource

stewardship, (c) gives owners legal standing against those who would overuse or harm the resource, and (d) through asset value, gives future users a voice in today's markets.

7. Environmental policy is implicit in property rights and a market system. Enforceable property rights cannot always be put into place, however. Government regulation is an alternative mechanism that might be used to promote wise use of resources and the environment. Since regulatory choices are not based on information and incentives from market prices, however, regulation has the same potential for inefficiency and ineffectiveness faced by the socialist governments whose citizens have suffered many environmental harms. Environmental regulations cost the U.S. economy about $150 billion per year. Benefits are mostly unmeasured, but potentially large.

CRITICAL ANALYSIS QUESTIONS

*1. Does a resource that is not owned, and therefore is not priced, have a zero opportunity cost? Might it be treated as if it did? Explain.

2. Why is the price elasticity of demand for resources, such as water and natural gas, greater in the long run than the short run? What examples of responses to price changes can you think of that are more complete after one year than after one week?

*3. "Steel production typically requires 40,000 gallons of water per finished ton of steel. Steel is important to U.S. industry and our national defense. As water becomes more scarce in the nation, it is imperative that the required amounts of water be reserved for the steel industry." Evaluate this statement.

4. "The federal government should do a complete survey of mineral availability in the nation. It is inexcusable that we do not know how much oil, for example, the country can ultimately produce." Evaluate this statement.

*5. Why will more oil in total be produced from an oil well when the price of crude oil is higher?

6. "Unlike in a marketplace, where pollution is profitable, government control of resources and pollution can take into account the desires of all the people." What does economic thinking have to say about this statement?

*7. "Private ownership of a natural resource, such as a lake in the woods, is tantamount to setting aside that resource for the personal, selfish enjoyment of one owner. Society will be better off if it is recognized that such a resource was provided by nature, for all to enjoy." Evaluate this statement.

8. Will the world ever run out of any mineral resource? In your answer, be sure to consider the role played

by rising extraction costs and by the existence of property rights to minerals. Does a negative answer to the question imply that increasing resource scarcity will never be a problem?

*9. "Corporations should not be allowed to own forests. Corporate managers are just too shortsighted. Their philosophy is to make a profit now, regardless of the future consequences. For example, trees may be cut after growing 30 years to get revenue now, even though another 20 years' growth would yield a very high rate of return. The long-run health of our forests is too important to entrust them to this sort of management." Evaluate this statement.

10. "Since our national forests are owned by all the people, their resources will be conserved for the benefit of all, rather than exploited in a shortsighted way, to produce benefits only for the owners." Evaluate this statement.

---

*Asterisk denotes questions for which answers are given in Appendix B.

During the last three decades, government expenditures have increased substantially as a share of the economy in the industrial democracies. Between 1960 and 1995, government expenditures *as a share of GDP* more than doubled in Denmark, Greece, Spain, and Sweden. These expenditures are now 45% or more of GDP in Germany, France, Italy, Canada, Belgium, Denmark, Greece, Netherlands, and Sweden. In the United States, government expenditures currently sum to approximately one-third the economy. Both the size and growth of government in the United States are smaller than for other high-income democracies. The increasing role of government around the world makes it vitally important that we understand the benefits and limitations of government intervention and how the political process works. This will be the focus of the chapters in this part.

EXHIBIT V-A

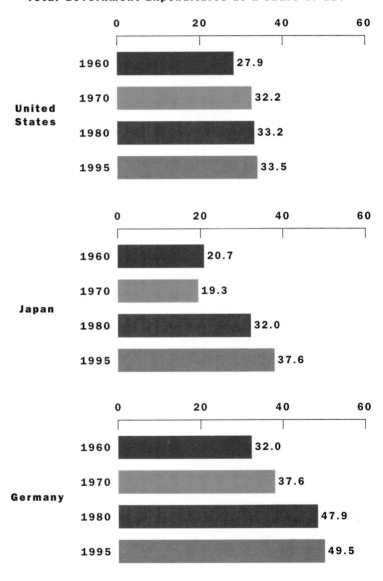

THE GROWTH OF DEMOCRATIC GOVERNMENTS

Total Government Expenditures as a Share of GDP

United States

Year	Value
1960	27.9
1970	32.2
1980	33.2
1995	33.5

Japan

Year	Value
1960	20.7
1970	19.3
1980	32.0
1995	37.6

Germany

Year	Value
1960	32.0
1970	37.6
1980	47.9
1995	49.5

EXHIBIT V-A

THE GROWTH OF DEMOCRATIC GOVERNMENTS (continued)

Total Government Expenditures as a Share of GDP

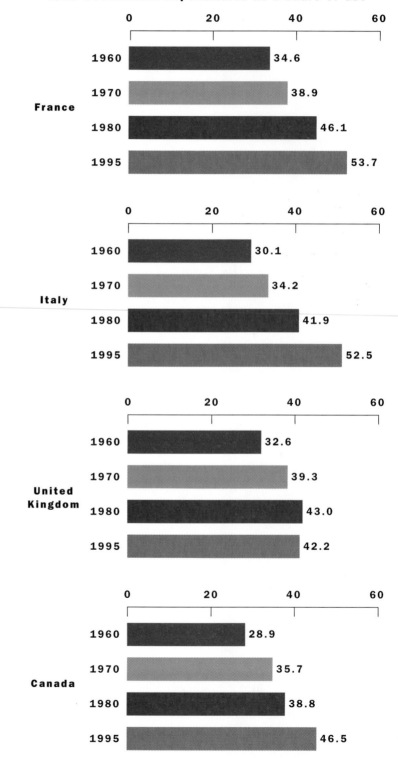

EXHIBIT V-A

THE GROWTH OF DEMOCRATIC GOVERNMENTS (continued)

Total Government Expenditures as a Share of GDP

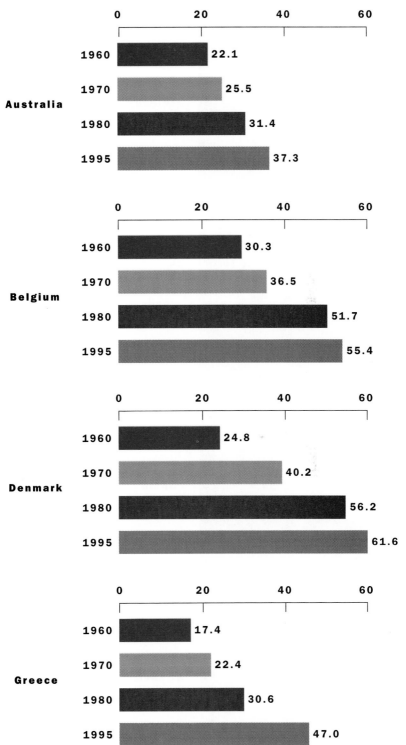

Australia

1960	22.1
1970	25.5
1980	31.4
1995	37.3

Belgium

1960	30.3
1970	36.5
1980	51.7
1995	55.4

Denmark

1960	24.8
1970	40.2
1980	56.2
1995	61.6

Greece

1960	17.4
1970	22.4
1980	30.6
1995	47.0

755

EXHIBIT V-A

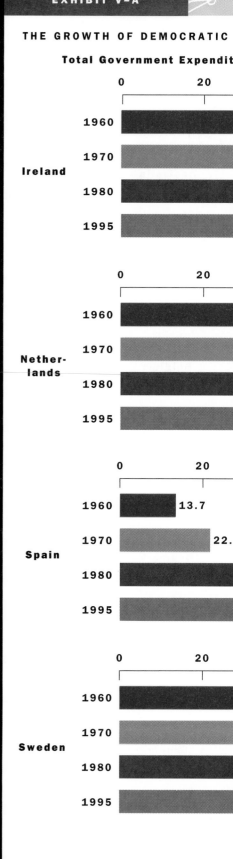

THE GROWTH OF DEMOCRATIC

Total Government Expendit

Ireland

	0	20
1960		
1970		
1980		
1995		

Nether-lands

	0	20
1960		
1970		
1980		
1995		

Spain

	0	20
1960		13.7
1970		22.
1980		
1995		

Sweden

	0	20
1960		
1970		
1980		
1995		

The principal justification for public policy intervention lies in the frequent and numerous shortcomings of market outcomes.

CHARLES WOLF [1]

---

[1] Charles Wolf, Jr., *Markets or Government* (Cambridge: MIT Press, 1988), p. 17.

CHAPTER FOCUS

■ Why do market decision makers face inappropriate incentives when an externality is present?

■ What role do imperfect information and imperfect property rights play in causing externalities?

■ What can we learn from the theory of external effects about pollution problems and alternative solutions? Why are some solutions to pollution problems less effective than others?

■ What is the "free rider" problem? What kinds of goods are likely to be susceptible to this problem?

■ What can we say about buyers' and sellers' lack of knowledge in the market, and when is this problem likely to be most serious? What market innovations have entrepreneurs used to reduce this problem?

We have seen how a properly functioning market system uses prices to coordinate the decisions of buyers and sellers. Market prices give each decision maker the information needed to make intelligent production and consumption decisions, weighing the relative desires of others. Each individual has the incentive to use that information to reduce the costs to others (reflected in the market cost of the resources used) and to increase the value of goods made available to others (reflected in prices of the goods sold). Even when they seek to serve only themselves, decision makers facing appropriate prices have the incentive to act as if they care about others. For example, resource owners are rewarded for moving their resources to uses which others value more highly. Owning the right to use or let others use a resource provides one with an incentive to think creatively about how others might benefit from using that resource.

Efficiency in production is encouraged by properly working markets, which reward producers for getting the most highly valued production from the bundle of resources they use, and for minimizing the cost (the value to others) of those resource inputs. Buyers are rewarded if they economize on their consumption of each good and service in order to get as much satisfaction as possible from their limited budgets.

In short, the "invisible hand" of Adam Smith provides each decision maker in the market economy with the information and incentive to act efficiently, and to consider the needs of others. Individuals will spend their income on the goods and services they value most. Therefore, those who are providing the goods and services must consider the needs—and wants—of buyers if they wish to stay in business. This arrangement is efficient in that no production will pay for itself if the buyer does not expect to value its benefits more than competing uses of the valuable resources needed for the production of the good.

Even when the market is working with ideal efficiency, observers may object. Some may reject market outcomes because in their view insufficient income is allocated to various individuals or groups. Positive economics has little to say about which income distribution is best. It does, however, indicate that (1) replacing a well-functioning market with other arrangements will normally reduce economic efficiency, and (2) impediments to trade, such as restrictions, taxes, and subsidies, will often fail to achieve the intended distributional results after individuals adjust to them. Even when these factors are recognized, economics cannot tell us whether a well-functioning market should be replaced or modified in order to change the income distribution. This is a normative question, one of values and priorities, not just economics.

Market failure
The failure of the market system to attain hypothetically ideal allocative efficiency. This means that potential gain exists that has not been captured. However, the cost of establishing a mechanism that could potentially capture the gain may exceed the benefits. Therefore, it is not always possible to improve the situation.

Does economics tell us that markets always function well? To the contrary: As we pointed out in Chapter 4, the invisible hand will sometimes slip. (At this point, you might wish to review Chapter 4.) Market prices will not always reflect the full range of costs and benefits produced by an action. There are several potential causes of such **market failure**—that is, economic activity that results in allocative inefficiency relative to the hypothetical ideal of economists. These causes can be grouped into four general classes: (1) externalities, (2) public goods, (3) poorly informed buyers or sellers, and (4) monopoly. Because the impact of monopoly in the product and factor markets has already been investigated in detail, this chapter will emphasize the other three categories of market failure. We will also explore possible responses, especially government responses.

Keep in mind that market failure is merely a failure to attain conditions of ideal efficiency. Alternative forms of economic organization may also have defects. Even though the government can sometimes improve the situation, this will not always be the case; sometimes it may even be counterproductive. After analyzing market failure in this chapter, we will focus on the operation of the public sector and its problems in the next.

MARKET FAILURE AND PROPERTY RIGHTS

Most economic arguments for government intervention are based on the idea that the marketplace cannot provide public goods or handle externalities.

TYLER COWEN[2]

As Tyler Cowen points out, problems that arise as the result of external effects and public goods are the central elements of the economic case against market allocation. Both of these problems are a reflection of insecure property rights. A resource that is not under the effective protection of a private owner, whose wealth is at stake in the resource, is more likely to be wasted or abused. As we explained in Chapter 2, private property rights give owners the exclusive right to control and benefit from their resources as long as their actions do not harm others. It is important to notice the last part of that definition. For example, private property rights do not grant the owners of rocks the right to throw them randomly at automobiles.

An important function of property rights is to provide legal protection against damage, abuse, or theft. Property rights are often associated with self-ishness on the part of owners, since owners have the option of doing as they wish with what they own. But selfishness requires that an owner reject even the most attractive offers to buy or rent. Private ownership permits owners (including corporate owners) to protect their property against unauthorized use or harm by others. However, owners will, if adequately compensated, often allow others to use their assets, even though it is costly for them to do so. Rental car firms sell individuals the right to use their automobiles despite the reduction in the resale value of the car. Housing is often rented, even though normal use by the renter imposes a maintenance and upkeep cost on the home-owner. *When property rights are clearly defined and enforceable, the market exchange system induces people who use the property (including the owner, whose wealth is tied up in the value of the property) to fully consider the costs of their actions. This will not be the case, however, when property rights are not clearly defined, or are not fully enforceable. Problems will arise under these circumstances.*

[2]Tyler Cowen, "Public Goods and Externalities," *Fortune Encyclopedia of Economics* (Ithaca, N.Y.: Warner, 1993), p. 74.

ENFORCEABLE PROPERTY RIGHTS AND INFORMATION

To legally enforce property rights, the owner must be able to show in court that those rights have in fact been violated. If John runs into Mary's car, the case is often fairly simple, and the parties may not even have to go to court. When John knows that Mary can prove him at fault and quantify the damages, he (or his insurance company) will simply compensate Mary for the damage done. (If John was insured, his rates will likely rise.) Such actions may also be brought to protect the rights of individuals against polluters. In the United States, many lawsuits have been successfully filed against smelters and other polluting sources. In England, where rights to fish for trout and salmon are privately owned (but not the water or the fish themselves), fishing-rights owners have successfully sued polluters of streams on the basis of pollution interfering with the value of fishing. All these legal actions to protect the rights of individuals have been brought under the traditional English *common law*, sometimes called *private law*, because individuals have the rights, and they individually can bring actions to protect themselves. Government, however, provides the courts and the enforcement of court orders.

Enforcement of property rights under private law is not automatic. To collect damages from pollution, or to stop polluting activities before serious damage occurs, the court must be convinced that the weight of the evidence is that pollution in fact has done (or would do) the damage claimed. That is, the court will take action against the polluter only if it is convinced that the claim of damage, whether past or expected, is more likely true than false.

The party asking the court to control the actions of a polluter, for example, must prove that the pollution caused the suspected damage. But the important facts are not always easy to know or to demonstrate. Consider the case of Mr. Steel, the factory owner whose smoke fouls the air at Mary's home. Mary has a right not to be harmed by Mr. Steel's smoke, but to receive compensation, she must show in court that significant harm was caused by the smoke from Mr. Steel's factory. Such lawsuits are not uncommon, and have been successful. But some types of possible damage are difficult to prove. When Mary's claim is not supported by the weight of the evidence, then her property rights may not be enforceable. Is her health damaged by long-term exposure to the smoke? If damage is done but cannot be shown, then Mary's property rights are unenforced,

External costs
Harmful effects of an individual's or a group's action on the welfare of a nonconsenting secondary party, not accounted for in market prices.

resulting in **external cost,** defined as the harmful effects of an individual's or group's action on the welfare of a nonconsenting secondary party, not accounted for in market prices. We will discuss this point at greater length later in this chapter.

Courts take the position that mere suspicion of harm done is not enough to justify siding with one citizen against another. Pollution cases are especially difficult for a system of private law to handle efficiently when they involve a large number of parties as well as uncertainty of information about sources of pollution and the magnitude of damages. As a result, government often steps in to protect individuals against possible damage, using pollution-control regulation.

It is the high cost (or the unavailability) of information that can make property rights unenforceable, and bring about market failure. Unfortunately, turning the problem over to government regulators does not produce the information needed for efficient resource allocation. Whoever is in charge of controlling pollution needs the same information to connect pollution emissions with resulting harms that courts need to enforce property rights. If the harm from emitting a specified amount of a pollutant at a specified time and place cannot be estimated well enough to say whether it causes a rights violation, then a rational evaluation of the problem is unlikely. It is important to bear in mind that if harm cannot be shown, there are two very different possible reasons. One possibility is that the harm is present even though the evidence is not. But the other possibility is that the harm does not exist. When a claim of pollution damage cannot be shown to be more likely true than false, courts will refuse to act. Regulators might act on the basis of suspicion, to avoid possible pollution problems, but costly mistakes are likely with that approach also. Protecting citizens by taking away the rights of other citizens who own factories— or cars—that are thought (but not shown) to cause harm by pollution is like protecting them by taking away the rights of other citizens who are thought (but not shown) to commit traffic violations. Citizens may or may not be safer, but they face a greater risk of penalties based on false suspicions acted upon by government authorities. The information problem for the pollution control agency is as difficult as that for the courts.

COMMON-PROPERTY RESOURCES AND EFFICIENCY

Property rights sometimes are not enforced in a market setting because they are held in common. A **common-property resource** is one for which rights are held in common by a group of individuals, none of whom has a transferable ownership interest. Access to a common-property resource may be unrestricted, as in the case of air, or may be controlled politically, as wildlife is controlled by state governments in the United States.

If access to the resource is unrestricted, it is an **open-access resource.** When there is more of it than people wish to use, then the open-access resource is not scarce and there is no problem. However, trouble arises when such a resource becomes scarce. (See the Applications in Economics box on common and private property rights.) Without either the establishment of private rights or some form of political control to replace the ownership functions of controlling access and caring for or maintaining the resource, external costs are almost guaranteed. For example, when people who live in a large city are harmed when their view of the mountains disappears due to air pollution, but cannot sue for damages because there are too many polluters (drivers of cars, for example), then external costs due to pollution are present. The polluters (who do not individually own the air or the view of the mountains from the city) have little incentive to curtail the activities that are causing the pollution. *Air and other resources are much more likely to be abused when they are treated as open-access resources. We have established environmental control agencies in order to deal with the problems that arise when there is open access to a resource.*

Common-property resource
A resource for which rights are held in common by a group of individuals, none of whom has a transferable ownership interest. Access to the resource may be open (unrestricted), or may be controlled politically.

Open-access resource
A resource to which access is unrestricted. No one has the right to exclude others from using the resource. Overuse and abuse of such a resource is typical.

IMPORTANCE OF COMMON AND PRIVATE PROPERTY RIGHTS

What is common to many is taken least care of, for all men have greater regard for what is their own than for what they possess in common with others.

ARISTOTLE[1]

The point made by Aristotle more than 2,000 years ago is as true now as it was then. It is as important in primitive cultures as it is in developed ones. When resources are held in common and access is unrestricted, the resource typically is abused and endangered. In contrast, when the rights are held by an individual, a family, or a small group, conservation and wise utilization generally result. The following examples from sixteenth-century England, nineteenth-century native-American culture, present-day Africa, and ocean fisheries illustrate the point.

CATTLE GRAZING ON THE ENGLISH COMMONS. Many English villages in the sixteenth century had *commons,* or commonly held pastures, that were available to any villagers who wanted to graze their animals. Because the benefits of grazing an additional animal accrued fully to the individual, whereas the cost of overgrazing was an external one, the pastures were grazed extensively. Because the pastures were communal property, there was little incentive for any individual to conserve grass in the present so that it would be more abundant in the future. When everyone used the pasture extensively, there was not enough grass at the end of the grazing season to provide a good base for next year's growth. What was good for the individual was bad for the village as a whole. To preserve the grass, pastures were fenced in the Enclosure Movement. After the Enclosure Movement established private property rights, owners and managers saw to it that overgrazing no longer occurred.

PROPERTY RIGHTS OF NATIVE AMERICANS. Among native-American tribes, common ownership of the hunting grounds was the rule. Because the number of native Americans was small and their hunting technology was not highly developed, hunted animals seldom faced extinction. However, there were at least two exceptions.

One was the beaver hunted by the Montagnais Indians of the Labrador Peninsula. When the French fur traders came to the area in the early 1600s, the beaver increased in value and therefore became increasingly scarce. Recognizing the depletion of the beaver population and the animal's possible extinction, the Montagnais began to institute private property rights. Each beaver-trapping area on a stream was assigned to a family, and conservation practices were adopted. The last remaining pair of beavers was never trapped, since the taker would only be hurting his own family the following year. For a time, the supply of beavers was no longer in jeopardy. However, when a new wave of European trappers invaded the area, the native Americans, because they were unable to enforce their property rights, abandoned conservation to take the pelts while they could.[2] Individual ownership was destroyed, and conservation disappeared with it.

PROPERTY RIGHTS AND AFRICAN ELEPHANTS. The excessive exploitation of wildlife can be linked to an absence of property rights. Because herds of Great Plains buffalo were available for everyone to use, allowing individuals to kill animals without facing the costs of herd depletion, the buffalo suffered near-extinction during the nineteenth century.[3] Today we see contrasting approaches to such a problem with the African elephant. In Kenya, elephants roam unowned on unfenced terrain. The Kenyan government tries to protect them from poachers seeking valuable ivory by banning all commercial use of the elephant except tourism. In the first decade that this policy was in effect, the Kenyan elephant population fell from 65,000 to 19,000. In other East and Central African countries that have followed the Kenyan approach, the collective elephant popula-

---

[1]Aristotle, as quoted by Will Durant in *The Life of Greece* (New York: Simon and Schuster, 1993), p. 536.

[2]For an economic analysis of the Montagnais management of the beaver, together with historical references, see Harold Demsetz, "Toward a Theory of Property Rights," *American Economic Review* (May 1967): pp. 347–359.

[3]See Francis Haines, *The Buffalo* (New York: Crowell, 1970).

tions dropped from 1,044,050 to 429,520 between 1979 and 1989.[4]

In Zimbabwe, by contrast, shops openly sell ivory and hides, and legislation was passed giving the local people on whose land the elephant roam the right to hunt the elephants. This encourages the people to preserve elephants and to permit only controlled hunting. Since assigning property rights in elephants, Zimbabwe has seen its elephant population grow from 30,000 to 43,000. Elephant populations in the countries adopting a similar approach—Botswana, South Africa, Malawi, and Namibia—are increasing at a rate of 5 percent a year.

PROPERTY RIGHTS AND OCEAN FISHERIES. Once, the waters off the northeastern United States teemed with Atlantic cod, haddock, flounder, and pollock—fish that many people love to eat, and many fishermen love to catch. But fish populations have fallen sharply in recent years due to overfishing, a problem for wild fisheries all over the world.[5] Wild fisheries of the oceans are open-access resources. The only way to claim ownership of fish is to catch them. In addition, there is no individual incentive to leave some fish for next year's catch; other fishermen will probably catch them. Without an authority, such as an owner, in place to control access, the fish population faces possible extinction.

When demand for the fish is high, and new people enter the fishing occupation as a result, overfishing occurs. As the population of fish falls, costs rise because the sparser population of fish requires that a more intensive effort be made to find them. The smaller catch may reduce supply enough to raise the price of fish, but entry of new fishermen will occur until there is no profit; and if the population is falling, profit is likely to turn negative. Yet, in the short run, fishermen will continue to fish so long as they can cover their variable costs, keep the fishing pressure intense, and further reduce the number of fish and the available breeding stock.

Compare this open-access fishery with one where the fish population or its territory is owned by a person or group who can control the rate of take, practicing conservation to protect next year's profits, which, after all, belong to the owner. We would expect that more conservation would be practiced, and overfishing would not occur. As a result, the income of fishermen would be higher. Richard J. Agnello and Lawrence P. Donnelley found just such results when they compared open-access and private-property oyster beds.[6] Using data from Maryland, Virginia, Louisiana, and Mississippi, they found that from 1945 to 1970 the ratio of harvest in the earlier part of the season to the later part was 1.35 for open-access oyster beds and 1.01 for the private-property beds. In the open-access beds, each fisherman tried to catch as many fish as possible, as quickly as possible, just as our logic predicts. Too much fishing effort was expended all season, relative to the more efficient allocation of fishing effort under the private-property regime. Fishermen in the private-property state of Louisiana earned $3,207, while their counterparts in the open-access state of Mississippi earned $807. Such a finding supports the expectation of higher incomes and larger harvests over the years under the private-property regime. By solving the open-access problem, private property rights help conserve a fishery resource and encourage more efficient management of it.

Could property rights be established for fisheries on the high seas? Such a scheme is not costless, and both federal and state governments have held that private rights there would violate antitrust laws. Informal unions of fishermen have tried to limit entry, but they have had limited success, since any agreement is difficult to maintain without an authority to enforce it.[7] Although private ownership of fishing grounds appears to be the solution to overfishing, this solution also appears unlikely to be instituted without further innovations in technology.

[4]The facts used in this section were provided by Randy Simmons and Urs Kreuter, "Herd Mentality: Banning Ivory Sales Is No Way To Save the Elephant," *Policy Review* (fall 1989): pp. 46–49.

[5]See Jennifer A. Kingston, "Northeast Fishermen Catch Everything, and That's a Problem," *The New York Times*, November 13, 1988.

[6]Richard J. Agnello and Lawrence P. Donnelley, "Prices and Property Rights in the Fisheries," *Southern Economic Journal* 42 (October 1979): pp. 253–262.

[7]Ronald N. Johnson and Gary D. Libecap, "Contracting Problems and Regulation: The Case of the Fishery," *American Economic Review* (December 1982): pp. 1005–1022.

Source: Donald Leal, Senior Research Associate, Political Economy Research Center, Bozeman, Montana.

As we will see in more detail in the next chapter, political control of a common-property resource, such as the air or a river, has its own problems. Typically, no one person or small group has a large stake in seeing to it that decision makers protect the resource and allocate its use efficiently. Would private ownership, then, be more efficient? Not necessarily. It is costly to establish and defend property rights to certain resources.[3] Exclusive ownership can easily be defined and defended for such commodities as apples, cabbages, waterbeds, cars, and airline tickets, but how would one establish and defend property rights to an oil pool that is located on the property of hundreds of different landowners? Similarly, who owns salmon or whales, which travel thousands of miles each year? In the absence of clearly assigned property rights, spillover costs and overutilization are inevitable.

Certain whales have been on the verge of extinction because no single individual (or small group) has the ability to protect the whales, nor even an incen-

APPLICATIONS IN ECONOMICS

CREATING PROPERTY RIGHTS WHEN RESOURCE VALUES INCREASE

The creation and protection of property rights is not always easy, and is never free. When the payoff for better protection and more careful management of a resource rises, however, the incentive to protect and manage it well rises also. Economic historians Terry Anderson and P. J. Hill have shown how, as a resource becomes more valuable, entrepreneurs, using technological inventions or legal innovations, often have been able to come up with new ways to create wealth by establishing property rights and defending them.[1] Technology enabled the establishment of property rights in the case of the grazing lands in the Great Plains of the United States as entrepreneurial individuals used newly invented barbed wire to fence and thus effectively privatize grazing areas. In England, polluters of trout and salmon streams found themselves the targets of legal actions by owners of the fishing rights, forcing them to "clean up their act" on the grounds that their polluting actions were damaging the fishing rights, even though damage to the water itself was not grounds for action as no one had property rights to the actual water. Once legal precedents were set, future trips to court were seldom needed. Potential polluters got the message.[2]

Texas state government found a property-rights solution to the problem of too many wells drilled into common oil pools by multiple-surface landowners. Too many wells can harm the oil field and reduce the total amount of oil obtained. By "unitizing" the oil field, the state government forced surface owners (potential drillers for the oil in a pool) to join an owners' association authorized to regulate oil production from that pool.

Other common-pool problems have yet to be solved, and salmon and whales in the ocean are more difficult cases for the establishment of private rights since they move from one ocean area to another, but the preceding examples give reason for optimism. Technical and institutional entrepreneurship may again find solutions, as the value of certain resources continues to rise.

---

[1]See Terry L. Anderson and Donald R. Leal, with Timothy Iijima, *Free Market Environmentalism* (San Francisco: Pacific Research Institute, 1991) pp. 37–50.

[2]On this topic, see Jane S. Shaw and Richard L. Stroup, "Gone Fishin'," *Reason* (August–September 1988), pp. 34–37.

---

[3]The problems entailed in defining and enforcing private, transferable property rights are discussed in Terry L. Anderson and P. J. Hill, "Privatizing the Commons: An Improvement?" *Southern Economic Journal* 50, no. 2 (October 1983).

WIZARD OF ID   BY BRANT PARKER & JOHNNY HART

Reprinted by permission of Johnny Hart and Creators Syndicate, Inc.

The problem of pollution emanates from external costs that arise when property rights are ambiguously defined or poorly enforced.

tive to reduce its own current catch so that the future catch will be larger. Each tries to catch as many whales as possible now; someone else will catch those whales, the argument goes, if the first person (or group) does not. The same principle applies to oil-pool rights when many well owners can draw from the pool and no single owner can control the rate of withdrawal. In the absence of regulation, each oil-well operator has an incentive to draw the *oil from a common pool* as rapidly as possible. When all operators do so, though, the commonly owned oil is drawn out too rapidly, and the total amount that can be withdrawn falls.

We shall not be too quick to despair about such property rights problems, however. The common-pool problem in oil and similar areas has been addressed by government creation of joint operating rights, and other such solutions, so the creation of a new property-rights arrangement may also be possible. (See the Application in Economics box on creating property rights.)

EXTERNAL EFFECTS AND THE MARKET

The genius of a market exchange system lies in its ability to bring personal and social welfare into harmony. When two parties trade, and only they are affected, production and voluntary exchange also promote the social welfare. When externalities are present, however, production and exchange can impose costs or confer benefits on nonconsenting parties. Externalities are likely to occur when property rights are not assigned (as in the case of open-access resources) or are not readily enforceable (as when pollution damages exist but cannot be proven).

External costs are present when the actions of a party spill over and harm non-consenting parties. The steel mill pouring pollution into the air imposes an external cost on surrounding residents. A junkyard creates an eyesore, making an area less pleasant for passersby. Similarly, litterbugs, drunk drivers, muggers, and robbers impose unwanted costs on others. But spillover effects can also be positive. If the external effects enhance the welfare of secondary

External benefits

Beneficial effects of group or individual action on the welfare of nonpaying secondary parties.

parties, they are called **external benefits.** A beautiful rose garden provides external benefits for the neighbors of the gardener. A golf course often provides spillover benefits to owners of surrounding property since it raises the market value of that property. Scientific research often produces knowledge that benefits others in addition to those who financed the research. The broadcast of a television program over the air is typically available to all in the area, including those who have not contributed to the cost of its production. *When external costs and external benefits are present, market prices will not send the proper signals to producers and consumers. This situation results in market failure.*

EXTERNAL COSTS

Social costs

The sum of (1) the private costs incurred by a decision maker and (2) any external costs imposed on nonconsenting secondary parties. If there are no external costs, private and social costs will be equal.

From the viewpoint of economic efficiency, an action should be undertaken only if it generates benefits in excess of its **social costs,** which are (1) the private costs borne by the consenting parties and (2) external costs imposed on nonconsenting secondary parties. When external costs are present, market prices understate the social cost generated by the use of resources or consumption of products. Decision makers are not forced to fully bear the cost to others generated by their actions. Motivated by self-interest, they may undertake actions that generate a net loss to the community. The harm done to nonconsenting parties may exceed the net private gain. When this happens, private interest and economic efficiency are in conflict.

EXTERNAL BENEFITS

Sometimes the actions of an individual (or firm) generate external benefits: gains that accrue to nonparticipating (and nonpaying) secondary parties. As in the case of external costs, external benefits occur when property rights are undefined or unenforceable. Because of this, it is costly—or impossible—to withhold these benefits from nonconsenting parties and retain them for oneself at the same time. The producer of a motion picture has rights to the film and can collect a fee from anyone who sees or rents it. In contrast, the production of rose gardens, golf courses, scientific research, and television broadcasts, as mentioned above, will often produce benefits for individuals who do not pay for them. Of course, when those benefits are large, entrepreneurs will seek ways to capture the benefits. Rose gardens are often planted by landlords who can then charge higher rents in their apartments, or planted at community expense in condominium communities, for example. Developers of golf courses in recent years typically purchase the land around the planned course before it is built, in order to resell it at a higher price reflecting the benefits produced when the golf course is completed. Television broadcasters sometimes scramble their signals, so they will be accessible only to those who pay a fee for a descrambler. But ingenious as their efforts may be, entrepreneurs cannot always capture all the benefits of their output; some benefits remain external to the producer.

When external benefits are present, the market demand understates the social gains of conducting the beneficial activity. Social gains from potentially valuable projects may go unrealized because no potential producer can fully appropriate or capture the projects' gains.

PUBLIC-SECTOR RESPONSES TO EXTERNALITIES

What can the government do to improve the efficiency of resource allocation when externalities are present? Sometimes private property rights can be more clearly defined and more strictly enforced. The granting by government of property rights to ranchers and homesteaders minimized the threat of overgrazing and improved the efficiency of land use in the Old West, once barbed wire made enforcement of land rights economical. More recently, the establishment of enforceable property rights to the oyster beds of the Chesapeake Bay improved the efficiency of oyster farming in the area. The granting to inventors of government-enforced patents or sole rights to use (or license the use of) their new inventions encourages productive research and development of technology. Thus, government action can sometimes bring market incentives more in line with society's interests. In many instances, however, it is difficult to delineate boundaries for a resource, determine who owns what portion, and enforce those rights. In those cases, externalities result.

Why not simply prohibit activities that result in external cost? After all, why should we allow nonconsenting parties to be harmed? This idea has an initial appeal, but closer inspection reveals its flaw. The activities that impose costs also usually provide benefits. Buses that pour out exhaust fumes that impose external costs on pedestrians and bicyclists also provide public transportation. Dogs that are notorious for using neighborhood lawns for bone burying and relief purposes also are often someone's beloved pets. Motorboats are noisy and frighten fish, much to the disgust of fishermen, but also provide enjoyment to boaters. Few people would argue that we should do away with buses, dogs, and motorboats. *From a social viewpoint, prohibition is often a less desirable alternative than tolerating some external costs. Tolerance has its limits, however, so activities that generate external costs are often regulated in an attempt to keep the costs within those limits.* The gains from the activity must be weighed against the costs imposed on those who are harmed, as well as against practical problems associated with controlling the activity.

Apart from establishing and enforcing property rights, there are four general approaches that government might take in controlling such resources as air and water:

1. A government agency might act as a resource manager, charging the users of the resource a fee.
2. A regulatory agency might establish a maximum pollution-emission standard and require that polluters attain at least that standard.

3. The agency might establish a maximum level of total emissions, assign each polluter a certain share of those emissions, and then allow the polluters to trade emission quotas.
4. The agency might specify exactly what pollution-control steps each polluter must take.

POLLUTION-TAX APPROACH

Some economists favor a user's charge, which we will call a pollution tax. **Exhibit 29–1** uses actual cost estimates from a copper smelter (which subsequently was dismantled) to illustrate the economics of this approach. The copper-producing firm has minimum costs of production when it spends nothing on pollution control. The marginal control-cost curve reveals the cost savings (control costs avoided) that accrue to the firm when it pollutes. The marginal damage-cost curve shows the estimated cost ($32.50 per ton) imposed on parties downwind from the smelter. Without any tax or legal restraints, the smelter would emit 190,000 tons of sulfur dioxide into the air per year, causing $6.2 million in damage. A tax equal to the marginal damage cost of $32.50 per ton emitted would cause the firm to reduce its emissions to 17,100 tons per year and thus would reduce pollution damage from $6.2 million to about $0.6 million per year. The control cost of reducing emissions to this level would be about $2.9 million per year. Total social costs each year would fall from $6.2 million (all borne by

The marginal control-cost curve shows that the firm, if it pays no damage costs itself, will emit 190,000 tons per year while spending nothing on control costs. However, if taxed according to the marginal damages it imposes ($32.50 per ton), it will voluntarily cut back its emissions to 17,100 per year, which is the socially efficient level. Further control would cost more than its social benefits.

Source: Richard L. Stroup, "The Economics of Air Pollution Control"(Ph.D. diss., University of Washington, 1970).

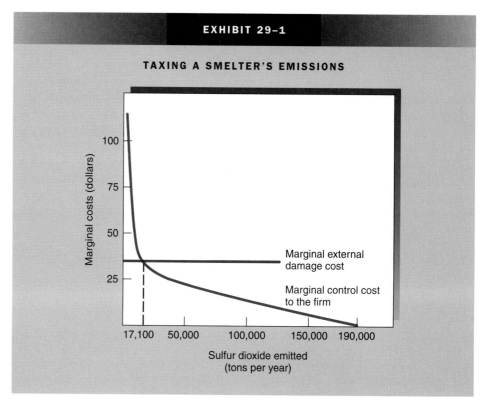

EXHIBIT 29–1

TAXING A SMELTER'S EMISSIONS

those suffering pollution damage) to $3.5 million (combined costs of pollution damage and control, paid entirely by the firm and its customers). The net social gain would be $2.7 million.

The tax approach would promote efficient resource allocation by altering several economic incentives in a highly desirable way. First, the pollution tax would increase the cost of producing pollution-intensive goods, causing the supply in these industries to decline. A properly set tax would approximate the true cost of emissions, internalizing the cost of pollution. The revenues generated by the tax could be used to compensate secondary parties harmed by the pollutants; the pollution authority would in effect be acting as a court, recognizing the rights of those harmed by pollution, and awarding them compensation for damages suffered. Alternatively, the revenues could be used to finance a wide range of projects, including applied research on alternative methods of improving air quality.

Second, a pollution tax would give firms an economic incentive to use methods of production (and control technology) that would create less pollution. A firm finding it cheaper to control harmful emissions than to pay the emission fee (tax) would opt for control. Third, since firms would be able to lower their tax bills by controlling pollution, the market for innovative emission-control devices would be strengthened. Entrepreneurs would be induced to develop low-cost control devices and market them to firms that would now have a strong and continuing incentive to reduce their levels of emissions.

The pollution tax has several advantages, but observers often cite four problems with the tax approach:

1. It allows some pollution harms to continue. Even if those who suffer the harms are compensated, some would object that polluters should have no right to knowingly cause harm and then "buy their way out." That, they say, is like allowing a thief to take a car without the owner's consent, and then be responsible only for paying a reasonable rent.
2. To be efficient, the tax must be based on damage costs of the emissions, and it is difficult to estimate these costs (which is why property rights are difficult to enforce). Of course, this same lack of knowledge hinders any strategy that might be intended to be efficient.
3. Emissions would have to be monitored, because, again, any efficient approach would require knowledge of who is polluting and how much.
4. Very large tax payments required of polluters would mean that whole industries could be shaken up, and some firms put out of business. Lobbyists for polluters have successfully prevented such taxes up to this point.

Given the damage and control costs estimates of Exhibit 29–1, the pollution-tax approach does not fully eliminate damages from pollution emissions. Should it? For a person to whom only zero harm is morally acceptable, the answer is yes. But if the goal is to minimize the total costs of pollution, including the cost of controlling it, the answer clearly is no. At pollution-emission levels of less than 17,100 tons per year, the marginal costs of pollution control would exceed the marginal benefits of the control. In cases such as that illustrated by the exhibit, substantial improvement can be made at a modest cost. At some point, however, it will become extremely costly to make additional improvements. As in the case of noise abatement, airplane and highway safety measures, and other health and safety matters, most of us are willing to tolerate small harms and risks to gain freedoms and benefits, including reasonably priced goods and services.

The pollution-tax approach recognizes that cleaning up the environment is like squeezing water from a wet towel. Initially, a great deal of water can be squeezed from the towel with very little effort, but it becomes increasingly difficult to squeeze out still more. So it is with reducing environmental pollution. At some point, the marginal benefit of a cleaner environment declines to the level where the additional clean-up efforts (or reductions in emissions) are simply not worth the cost. Thus, the optimal level of pollution is seldom zero.

People want clean air and water, but they want other things as well. *Those entrusted with the authority to regulate pollution should ask themselves two critical questions: How many other goods and services are we willing to give up to fight each of the many battles against pollution? And how much would the public like us to spend, from its own pockets, to achieve additional freedom from pollution?* Since we all want to obtain the maximum benefit from expenditures on pollution control, it is important that these questions be answered carefully, no matter which control strategy we adopt.

MAXIMUM-EMISSION-STANDARD APPROACH

Maximum emission standard

The maximum amount of pollution that a polluter is permitted to emit, established by the government or a regulatory authority. Fines are generally imposed on those who are unwilling or unable to comply.

Although economics suggests that the pollution-tax approach would be much more efficient, a **maximum emission standard** is often imposed. In this case, the regulatory agency forces all producers to reduce their emissions to a designated level. The level may be chosen to produce a tolerable level of total pollution. Producers who are unable to meet the standard are required to pay a fine or even to terminate production.

One problem with this approach is that the costs of eliminating pollution emissions generally vary widely among polluters. Some can control pollution much more cheaply than others, but the maximum emission standard fails to use this fact to get more control per dollar of expenditure in control costs, or to minimize the costs of achieving a given level of total pollution. It thus results in less pollution control per dollar than, for example, the pollution-tax strategy.

Exhibit 29–2 illustrates why the maximum emission standard is an inefficient method of reducing the pollution level. Estimated minimum costs of added control by three particulate pollution emitters are listed. Suppose the regulatory agency wants to reduce the total particulate emissions from the three firms by 3 tons. The emission-standards approach might accomplish this simply by requiring each firm to reduce its particulate emissions by 1 ton. The cost of these equal reductions will differ substantially among the firms; it will cost the electric utility $80, the steel plant $990, and the petroleum refiner $573. If this method is adopted, it will cost society $1,643 in control costs to meet the new maximum pollution standard, which is 3 tons below the previous level of emissions.

Alternatively, the regulatory agency might levy a pollution tax and eliminate the same amount of pollution for much less. If we assume that a 3-ton reduction is small for each producer, so that each additional ton of pollution reduction raises control costs by only one dollar, then a tax of just $82.50 per ton

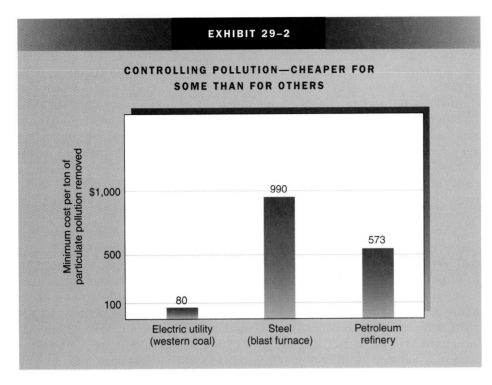

EXHIBIT 29–2

CONTROLLING POLLUTION—CHEAPER FOR SOME THAN FOR OTHERS

Minimum cost per ton of particulate pollution removed

$1,000

500

100

80 — Electric utility (western coal)

990 — Steel (blast furnace)

573 — Petroleum refinery

Some polluters face much higher costs than others. If the authorities' control strategy does not properly take this into account, control may be needlessly expensive and opposition to control needlessly strong. If each polluter were required to reduce particulate pollution by one ton, total control costs for that change would be $80 + $990 + $573 = $1,643. But, if a pollution tax of $82.50 were levied, the steel and petroleum plants would pay it, while the electric utility would find it cheaper to control some of its particulate pollution, and a reduction of 3 tons of emissions would cost roughly $240 instead of more than $1,640.

Source: EPA reports, summarized by Robert Crandall in *Controlling Industrial Pollution* (Washington D.C.: The Brookings Institution, 1983) p. 36.

would cause the electric utility to reduce particulate emissions by 3 tons, at a total cost of $243 ($80 + $81 + $82 = $243). That would allow the utility to escape 3 × $82.50 = $247.50 in added tax. The other polluters would not cut back emissions, but would choose to pay the tax, which is cheaper for them than the control costs. With the tax approach, which causes the cheapest control to take place, society buys the 3-ton reduction in pollution for $243, about one-seventh the cost incurred in the elimination of the same amount of pollution under the maximum-emission control strategy.

TRANSFERABLE EMISSION RIGHTS

A much more efficient form of the maximum-emission strategy is to require the same 1-ton reduction of each firm, but allow the remaining rights to pollute (their original pollution rate, minus 1 ton each) to be traded among the three. In this case, the electric utility would sell 2 tons of its rights-to-pollute, one to each of the other two firms. Why? It can profit by reducing its pollution by 3 tons for $243, then selling its "excess" pollution rights to the other two firms, saving the steel firm $990 and the refinery $573. The amount paid by the two firms to the utility for its service (added pollution control, beyond its own requirement) would be more than $80 per ton, but no higher than the $990 plus $573 saved by the other two. The net savings to society in getting the full 3-ton reduction in pollution is again the same as in the pollution-tax case. The emission-rights-trading strategy also has an important political advantage: No large payments (or small ones either) have to be made by the firms to the tax collector.

Because each polluter has a different control-cost schedule, either the pollution-tax strategy or the emission-rights-trading strategy, properly applied with the use of good information, would result in the most pollution control per control dollar spent, and reach any desired pollution level at the lowest possible price. Some people object to the emissions-trading strategy because pollution emitted at one location may cause more damage or less damage than the same pollution at another place. This is true, but any efficient strategy would have to make adjustments to recognize this fact. The emissions-trading strategy might allow polluters in densely populated areas to exchange their pollution rights with polluters in a sparsely populated area with a bonus. Two tons of pollution rights in Manhattan might trade for 3 tons on a sparsely populated part of the coast, where the winds usually blow the particulates out to sea with much less damage.

The emissions-trading strategy was incorporated, in a limited way, into the Clean Air Act amendments of 1990. Beginning in 1995, power plants fueled by coal were required to scale back their emissions of sulfur dioxide by more than half from 1980 levels. Firms that control more than required, however, can save their "allowances" (the amount they are allowed by the new law to emit) for future use or sell them to other power plants. In 1994 Southern California implemented a regional emissions-trading market, called the Regional Clean Air Incentives Market, or RECLAIM, for nitrogen oxides. Other areas are in the process of developing their own nitrogen oxide trading programs.

SPECIFIC-PRESCRIPTION APPROACH

We have shown how the emissions-standard approach (without emissions trading) is less efficient than the pollution tax. Even less efficient, in general, is a policy that specifies the technology that must be used by polluters to reduce their emissions. That was the approach taken, for example, when Congress required the Environmental Protection Agency (EPA) to implement the Clean Air Act of 1970 for coal-burning electric-power plants. Instead of setting emission standards, Congress ordered the EPA to require that new plants use a specific kind of pollution-control apparatus—giant "scrubbers" to clean exhaust gases from new coal-burning electric-power plants. Even though cheaper and more reliable means are frequently available to produce electricity with the same or less pollution, especially the use of clean coal, the far more expensive scrubbers were mandated. This rule favored certain regions of the country over others, and delayed the construction of newer, cleaner power plants, so that the air was dirtier than it would have been with the cheaper control methods. As ironic and as well known as this situation was,[4] more efficient approaches were not politically feasible until 1990, when the Clean Air Act amendments began to focus on emis-

---

[4]See Robert Crandall, *Controlling Industrial Pollution: The Economics and Politics of Clean Air* (Washington: The Brookings Institution, 1983); and Bruce Yandle, *The Political Limits of Environmental Regulation: Tracking the Unicorn* (New York: Quorum Books, 1989), for fascinating accounts of the politics and economics of this situation. Eastern coal-mine owners and the United Mine Workers Union, who wanted less mining of the cleaner western coal, joined forces with environmental interests in the West to push through the requirement that costly scrubbers be used instead of allowing power plants to switch to cleaner western coal.

sion standards. For reasons that we will explore more fully in the next chapter, the government solution to market failure is often inefficient.

SHOULD GOVERNMENT ALWAYS TRY TO CONTROL EXTERNALITIES?

When an externality is present, ideal efficiency of resource allocation may not be attained. It does not follow, though, that the government can always improve the situation and bring the economy closer to its ideal allocation level. In evaluating the case for a public-sector response to externalities, one should keep in mind the following three points:

1. Sometimes the economic inefficiency resulting from externalities is small; therefore, given the cost of public-sector action, net gain from intervention is unlikely.   The behavior of individuals often influences the welfare of others. The length of hair, choice of clothing, and personal hygiene of some individuals may affect the welfare of secondary parties. Should an agency in charge of personal appearance and hygiene be established to deal with externalities in these areas? Persons who value personal freedom would answer with a resounding no. And from the standpoint of economic efficiency, their view is correct. The effects of externalities in these and similar areas are small. The costs of correcting externalities of this type would often be greater than the benefit.

Government intervention requires the use of scarce resources. Regulatory agencies must be established and experts, clerks, managers, and lawyers hired. Transportation and office costs must be paid, along with many other costs. These actions require the use of scarce and costly resources. The EPA has estimated that its overhead costs were more than $425 (in 1996 dollars) for every hour of work performed by an individual working on an EPA-ordered cleanup of a site contaminated by hazardous wastes.[5] That amount does not include any direct cost of the cleanup, but only the cost to EPA of carrying out its regulatory functions in ordering and enforcing the cleanups. Unlike market decision makers using priced inputs to produce priced outputs, public-sector decision makers normally lack the information necessary to determine which activities should be taxed or restricted, and which should be subsidized or ordered done. Administrative problems such as these greatly reduce the attractiveness of public-sector action. When the external effects are small, the cost of government intervention is likely to exceed the loss due to market inefficiency, *relative to the hypothetical ideal.* Under these circumstances, the best approach is usually to do nothing.

2. Entrepreneurs in the market often find reasonably efficient means of dealing with externalities.   The existence of externalities implies the presence of potential gain. When external effects are significant, market participants have an incentive to find a way to organize economic activity that will enable them to capture the potential gain. If the number of parties affected by the externality is small, they may be able to arrive at a multi-party bargain that will at least partially negate the inefficiency and loss resulting from the externality.

---

[5]The estimate is an average of 1988 costs (updated to 1996 dollars) reported in the *Federal Register* 57, no. 152 (August 6, 1992), p. 34775, for work done under EPA's Superfund program.

Some entrepreneurs have devised ingenious schemes to capture benefits that were previously external to private parties. We mentioned earlier that private developers of country clubs and golf courses often capture the benefits of these amenities by placing them on large tracts of land. The purchasers of lots and houses will benefit from trees, gardens, manicured lawns, and so on. When consumers are willing to pay for these amenities, tract developers who provide them benefit in the form of higher prices on the sale of surrounding lots.[6] The greater the potential gains, the greater the incentive to find answers to these kinds of problems. Thus, market participants will often devise efficient arrangements for dealing with external effects when those effects become large.

3. Government action may also impose an external cost on secondary parties. Government intervention designed to correct the inefficiencies created by externalities is costly. When the costs of public-sector intervention exceed the benefits, efficiency requires that intervention should be rejected. In addition, we should recognize that even democratic public-sector action may impose an externality—as when political winners impose an external cost on those opposed to the action. Just as an individual may carry an activity too far when some of the costs are borne by others, a winning political coalition may also carry an action beyond the point of ideal efficiency. The gains that accrue to the political winners may be less than the costs imposed on others. (Limits to the effectiveness of government action will be discussed more fully in the next chapter.)

MARKET FAILURE: PUBLIC GOODS

Public goods compose the extreme case of external benefits. They are nonexcludable, so producers cannot exclude those who do not pay. In addition, they are nonrival in consumption, meaning that consumption by one person does not reduce the good's availability to others. It is important to note that only goods with these two characteristics qualify as public goods in an economic sense. Goods provided in the public sector, ranging from medical services and education to trash collection, are not necessarily public goods. Examples of pure public goods are rare. National defense is one. The defense system that protects you provides similar protection to all other citizens. Keeping the air in a city clear enough for citizens to enjoy the view of surrounding mountains might also be classified as a public good.

---

[6]The development of Walt Disney World in Florida is an interesting case of how entrepreneurial ingenuity made it possible to capture external benefits more fully. When Walt Disney developed Disneyland in California, the market value of the land in the immediate area soared as a result of the increase in demand for services (food, lodging, gasoline, and so on). Because the land in the areas was owned by others, the developers of Disneyland were unable to capture these external benefits. However, when Walt Disney World was developed near Orlando, Florida, the owners purchased an enormous plot of land, far more than was needed for the amusement park. As was the case with Disneyland in California, the operation of Walt Disney World caused land values in the immediate area to rise sharply. Because the developers of Walt Disney World had initially purchased that land, they were able to capture the external benefits by selling it to hotels, restaurants, and other businesses desiring a nearby location.

The Dutch boy has his finger in the dike, to prevent the leak from becoming a torrent and breaking the dike. Will the man help out with a donation, or will he be a free rider?

THE FREE-RIDER PROBLEM

Because nonpaying consumers cannot be excluded (at a reasonable cost), the market mechanism may not provide a sufficient amount of public goods. This result is likely because each of us has an incentive to become a **free rider,** one who receives the benefits of a good without paying toward its costs. Why contribute to the cost of supplying clean air, pure water, national defense, or legal justice when your contribution will have a negligible impact? The sensible path will lead you to do nothing. As long as you travel that path alone, or in minimal company, you will ride along, free and easy. If enough others join you, however, the aggregate lack of action will lead to an insufficient quantity of public goods.

Suppose national defense were provided entirely through the market. Would you voluntarily help to pay for it? Your contribution would have little impact on the total supply of defense available to each of us, even if you made a large personal contribution. Many citizens, even though they might value defense highly, would become free riders, and few funds would be available to finance the necessary supply. If the military-industrial complex were dependent on market forces alone, it would be small indeed!

The harmony between private and social interests tends to break down for public goods. The amount of a public good available to an individual (and others) will be virtually unaltered by whether or not the individual pays for it. Each individual thus has an incentive to become a free rider. When numerous individuals become free riders, however, less than the ideal amount of the public

Free rider
One who receives the benefit of a good without contributing to its costs. Public goods and commodities that generate external benefits offer people the opportunity to become free riders.

APPLICATIONS IN ECONOMICS

PRIVATE PROVISION OF PUBLIC GOODS

An excellent example of a public good is the preservation of wildlife. Hawks, sea lions, and wild geese belong to no one, but their survival keeps ecosystems in balance and intact. We all benefit when habitats are kept available to ensure that such species do not become extinct. The fact is that each of us can be a free rider if others make the effort and sacrifice needed to bring about such preservation, and successful voluntary efforts in the private sector have done just that: Thousands of organizations, each defying the free-rider problem, have for many decades led the conservation movement, privately establishing successful conservation projects.

Some of these groups are very large. The Nature Conservancy owns and manages a national system of nearly 800 sanctuaries and has preserved some 2.4 million acres since 1951. The National Audubon Society has a sanctuary system of over 63 units totaling over 250,000 acres. Others are small—a local garden club might own and manage two acres to preserve a particular wildflower.

Private groups have often been leaders in educating the public, and have been well ahead of government in providing their particular public good. Two examples involve hawks and sea lions.

THE HAWK MOUNTAIN SANCTUARY In the 1930s hawks were considered a nuisance or worse, because they killed certain other birds, including domestic chickens. There was often a bounty on them—the government would pay people who killed hawks. Conservationists, however, had begun to worry about the declining numbers of hawks, pointing out that, among other things, hawks ate rodents, keeping down the grain losses experienced by farmers. The environmental movement was still very weak, however, and the slaughter of hawks continued.

In one area in particular, Hawk Mountain of eastern Pennsylvania, thousands of hawks were killed on certain days each year. So upset was Rosalie Edge, an early conservationist (and leading suffragist), that when reasoning with government authorities failed, she organized a small group of conservationists who simply bought Hawk Mountain for $3,500. They prevented further shooting from that critical spot and established a nonprofit educational and conservation group—the Hawk Mountain Sanctuary Association. Seven thousand members from all over the nation, in addition to admission fees paid by 50,000 visitors per year, support a visitor and education center at the mountain where previously the hawks were slaughtered by the thousands each year.

SEA LION CAVES, INC. Like hawks, sea lions on the Oregon coast were formerly hunted, and bounties were paid to those who killed them. Sea lions feed on fish, and during the 1920s the state of Oregon paid $5 per sea lion killed. Several bounty hunters made their living in this fashion. The intent was to reduce sea lion consumption of coastal salmon. Earlier, commercial fishing interests had hired professional hunters to exterminate the sea lion. However, one important area of the sea lion's Oregon habitat was privately owned and used as a tourist attraction—Sea Lion Caves, where the animals could be viewed up close, in a natural setting. The owners of the caves had to spend a good deal of time driving off bounty hunters. By 1931 conservation legislation was passed to protect sea lions in most areas of the Oregon coast. Nevertheless, while the extermination pressure was on, the profit-seeking Sea Lion Cave operation played an important part in the survival of the sea-going mammals. The sea lions themselves are not owned, and their survival is largely a public good. But private ownership of the habitat had concentrated enough of the benefits in the hands of a tourist-based business to help guarantee the survival of the endangered animals at a critical time.

Can private clubs and businesses eliminate the public-goods problem? Not necessarily, since there is no guarantee that the optimal amount of public goods will be provided. However, these private-sector philanthropic and entrepreneurial solutions to certain public-goods problems remind us that, whenever the will exists to solve such problems, government action is not the only possible way. The same sort of informed and determined efforts needed to convince government to do the right thing can frequently find private solutions even more quickly and cheaply.

good is likely to be produced. (It should be noted that markets will sometimes supply public goods. See the Applications in Economics box on private provision of public goods.)

NEAR PUBLIC GOODS

Few commodities are pure public goods, but a much larger set of goods are jointly consumed even though nonpaying customers can be excluded. For example, such goods as radio and television broadcasts, national parks, interstate highways, movies, and football games may be jointly consumed. Until congestion sets in, additional consumption of these "near public goods," once they are produced, is costless to society.

Should nonpaying customers be excluded when the marginal cost of providing the good to them is zero? Many economists argue that such near public goods as highways, national parks, and television programming should be provided free to consumers, at the expense of the taxpayers. Why exclude people from the consumption of these near public goods when their use of the goods does not add to the costs? The argument has a certain appeal.

We must be careful, however. Television programs, highways, parks, and other public goods are scarce. The consumption of other products must be sacrificed to produce such goods. If a zero price is charged, how does one determine whether consumers value additional units enough to cover their opportunity cost? How can an intensely concerned minority communicate its views as to the types of near public goods that should be produced? If some users become dissatisfied, will the government-funded producer have an incentive to consider change, as happens when users reduce their patronage of market establishments? Taxes will be necessary to cover the costs of making near public goods freely available. Will such taxes lead to inefficiency? These factors reduce the attractiveness of public-sector provision of jointly consumed commodities, especially when exclusion of nonpaying consumers is possible.

MARKET FAILURE: POOR INFORMATION

In the real world, market choices, like other decisions, are made with incomplete information. Consumers do not have perfect knowledge about the quality of a product, the price of alternative products, or side effects that may result from a product. They may make incorrect decisions, decisions they will later regret, because they do not possess good information.

The reality of imperfect knowledge is not, of course, the fault of the market. In fact, the market provides consumers with a strong incentive to acquire information. Because consumers must bear the consequences of their mistakes, they certainly will seek to avoid the deliberate purchase of "lemon" products.

GETTING YOUR MONEY'S WORTH

The consumer's information problem is minimal if the item is purchased regularly. Consider the purchase of soap. There is little cost associated with trying alternative brands. Since soap is a regularly purchased product, trial and error is an economical means of determining which brand is most suitable to one's

Repeat-purchase item
An item purchased often by the same buyer.

needs. Soap, like toothpaste, most food products, lawn service, and gasoline, is a **repeat-purchase item.** The consumer can use past experience to good advantage when buying such items.

What incentive does the producer have to supply accurate information that will help the consumer make a satisfying long-run choice? Is there a conflict between consumer and producer interests? The answers to these questions are critically affected by the seller's dependence on return customers.

If dissatisfaction on the part of *current* customers is expected to have a strong adverse effect on *future* sales, a business entrepreneur will attempt to provide accurate information to help customers make wise choices. The future success of business entrepreneurs who sell repeat-purchase products is highly dependent on the future purchases of currently satisfied customers. There is a harmony of interest because buyer and seller alike will be better off if the customer is satisfied with the product purchased.

LET THE BUYER BEWARE

Major problems of conflicting interests, inadequate information, and unhappy customers arise when goods either (1) are difficult to evaluate on inspection and are seldom repeatedly purchased from the same producer or (2) are potentially capable of serious and lasting harmful side effects that cannot be predicted by a

Brand names and franchises provide consumers with valuable information that helps them make more informed choices.

layperson. Under these conditions, human nature being what it is, we would expect some unscrupulous producers to sell low-quality, defective, and even harmful goods.

When customers are unable to distinguish between high-quality and low-quality goods, their ability to police quality and price is weakened. When this is the case, business entrepreneurs have a strong incentive to cut costs by reducing quality. Consumers get less for their dollars. Since sellers in this situation are not dependent on repeat customers, those who cut cost by cutting quality may survive and even prosper in the marketplace. *The probability of customer dissatisfaction is thus increased by the presence of inadequate information. Accordingly, the case for an unhampered market mechanism is weakened.*

Consider the consumer's information problem when an automobile is purchased. Are most consumers capable of properly evaluating the safety equipment? Except for a handful of experts, most people are not. Some consumers might individually seek expert advice. It may be more efficient, though, to prevent market failure by having the government regulate automobile safety and require certain safety equipment.

As another example of the problem of inadequate consumer information, consider the case of a drug manufacturer's exaggerated claims for a new product. Until consumers have had experience with the drug or have listened to others' experiences, they might make wasteful purchases. Government regulation might benefit consumers by forcing the manufacturer to modify its claims.

ENTREPRENEURS AND INFORMATION

Consumers have the incentive to seek good information, even though it is costly. Entrepreneurial publishers and other providers of information help consumers find what they seek by providing expert evaluations of the special characteristics built into complex products. For car buyers and computer buyers, for example, publishers market dozens of specialized magazines containing expert analyses and opinions from almost any point of view. Laboratory test results and detailed product evaluations on a wide variety of goods are provided by *Consumer Reports, Consumer Research,* and other publications.

Entrepreneurial sellers, when they are in fact providing good value, have an incentive to bridge the information gap, and to let consumers know it. Comparative advertising is utilized to illustrate for potential buyers the advantage of one product or service relative to rivals. Consumers who will soon have to choose among the products being compared, and will be required to pay for their choice, will tend to be especially receptive to comparative advertising.

Franchises are another way that entrepreneurs have responded to the consumer need for more information, as we pointed out in Chapter 2. The tourist traveling through an area for the first time—and very possibly the last—may find that eating at a franchised food outlet and sleeping at a franchised motel is the cheapest way to avoid annoying and costly mistakes. The franchiser sets the standards for all firms in the chain and establishes procedures, including continuous inspection, designed to maintain the standards. Franchisers have a strong incentive to maintain their reputation for quality, because if it declines, their ability to sell new franchises is hurt. Even though the tourist may visit a particular establishment only once, the franchise turns that visit into a "repeat purchase," since the reputation of the entire national franchise operation is at stake.

Similarly, the advertising of a brand name nationally develops a reputation that is at stake when purchases are made. How much would the Coca-Cola Company pay to avoid a dangerous bottle of Coke being sold? Surely, it would be a large sum. The company's brand name is worth an estimated $24 billion, and that good name is a hostage to quality control. Because it is a household name worldwide, any serious quality-control problem would be broadcast worldwide, and do enormous financial damage to the firm. Advertising investments play a part too, helping to build a reputation that consumers know is at stake. The reputation built with the help of advertising is threatened if the firm cheats customers.

Source Perrier's experience with its Perrier mineral water is a concrete example of how far a company is willing to go to protect a brand name. On February 2, 1990, Source Perrier learned that tiny traces of benzene, a cancer-causing chemical, had been discovered in a few bottles of Perrier mineral water. The U.S. Food and Drug Administration announced that the amounts of benzene were so small—less than 20 parts per billion—that there was no danger even to steady drinkers of the water, unless the contamination problem persisted for many years. Nevertheless, the company announced on February 8 that it was not only shutting down until it found and corrected the problem, but that it was also recalling all 100 million bottles from store shelves in 120 countries. To protect its reputation for product purity, the company set aside 835 million French francs, or about $152 million, to finance the dramatic recall. In the end, Source Perrier spent an estimated $80 million to assure consumers that its product was safe and pure.

Enterprising entrepreneurs have found ways to assure buyers that products meet high standards of quality, even when the producer is small and not so well known. Consider the case of Best Western Motels.[7] Best Western owns no motels, but building on the franchise idea, it publishes rules and standards that motel owners must comply with if they are to use the Best Western brand name and the reservation service that the company also operates. In order to protect its brand name, Best Western sends out inspectors to see that each Best Western motel in fact meets the standards. Every disappointed customer reduces the value of the Best Western name, and reduces the willingness of motel owners to pay for use of the name. The standards are designed to keep customers satisfied. Even though each motel owner has only a relatively small operation, renting the Best Western name provides the small operator with the kind of international reputation formerly available only to large firms. In effect, Best Western acts as a regulator of all motels bearing its name. It does so to the benefit of consumers and producers, and the entire operation is a voluntary, market solution to the information problem.

Another kind of private regulator is Underwriters Laboratories, or UL. It establishes its own standards for safety in electrical equipment. Manufacturers voluntarily submit their equipment to UL and pay the firm to test the product. They do so because if UL certifies that the product meets UL standards, that fact

---

[7]This section draws from Randall G. Holcombe and Lora P. Holcombe, "The Market for Regulation," *Journal of Institutional and Theoretical Economics* 142, no. 4 (1986): pp. 684–696.

can be advertised, and consumers, knowing the UL reputation, will be more willing to buy the product. Again, the certifying firm, UL in this case, has a strong incentive to certify only those electrical products that do indeed meet their safety standards, because the value of the UL name is at stake. That value depends entirely on the effectiveness of its claims that UL-certified products are safe to use.

As these examples indicate, entrepreneurial measures such as assuring the quality of a firm or franchise, or otherwise protecting a brand name, can be both expensive and effective. They cannot, however, guarantee that customers will never be cheated or disappointed after a transaction. Despite the best efforts of entrepreneurs, the lack of consumer information will continue to assure that the market will remain imperfect relative to the economists' ideal, and that government will have a potential role to play in improving on the market's results.

ONE-SIDED INFORMATION

As useful and important as the published evaluations of experts, franchise operations, advertising, brand-name reputations, and private regulatory firms are, they cannot solve a kind of information problem that has little to do with product design or manufacture. This is called the **asymmetric-information problem,** and it can make markets themselves, for some products, difficult to operate effectively. *The problem of asymmetric information arises when either the potential buyer or potential seller has important information that the other side does not have.*

Think for a moment about buyers trying to avoid "lemons" in the used car market. Sellers know which cars are above average quality and which are below average. Buyers on the other hand, cannot tell which is which simply by looking at and test-driving them. Thus buyers will be willing to pay no more than what they believe is the average value of all cars on the market. But if better-than-average cars cannot bring better-than-average prices, then fewer of them will be sold in the market, and if below-average cars bring average prices, then more of the below-average cars will be offered. Buyers understand this, so they expect the average car in such a market to be below the average of all existing cars of that age and type. Owners of better cars are reluctant to sell at the low market price and it is hard to make a market for cars of above-average quality when buyers cannot be convinced that they actually are better than average.

Can anything be done to reduce this kind of asymmetric-information problem? Sellers of the better cars have an incentive to provide additional information in order to get a higher price for their superior goods. But how is this done? How can they support their claims about their product being better? The answers differ according to whether the seller is a private owner or a dealership. Car owners can present their records of oil changes and lubrications to show that these services, important to the long-run durability of a car, have been performed on schedule. Dealers, whose mechanics inspect the cars before they are offered for sale, may offer money-back guarantees, or warranties that promise free repairs if needed within a specified time, on the most reliable cars they sell. The other cars they sell will be sold "as is" with no warranty. Sellers of products can even give price guarantees, as some stores do when they advertise that, if the buyer finds a lower price for the same product within a specified period of time, the seller will refund the difference. By offering to bear such risks, sellers

Asymmetric-information problem
A problem arising when either buyers or sellers have important information about the product that is not possessed by the other side in potential transactions.

provide credibility to their claims about better products and prices. In other words, they improve the quality of the information offered and reduce the problem of asymmetric information.

The problem of asymmetric information also arises when buyers know more than sellers. Consider the market for health insurance. Buyers know their own health problems better than insurance companies. Those whose health history and lifestyles threaten greater potential health costs may pay the same as others but later collect more from the insurance company. In contrast, the same insurance at the same price is less attractive to the healthiest people, and fewer of them will buy it. When the company is unable to identify those with the greatest potential health costs and charge them more, it will have to charge its healthier customers a rate that exceeds their expected future insurance claims. But this would drive away even more of the healthier potential buyers, making the situation even worse. As in the case of used cars, asymmetric information reduces the effectiveness of the market. Just as the best used cars may be hard to sell, so, too, may the healthiest individuals be hard to insure when asymmetric information is present.

What can be done about asymmetric information when buyers have information but sellers do not? Buyers, like sellers, are willing to provide information when it is to their advantage to do so. In the case of insurance buyers, those buyers with the best health record, who are therefore least likely to have future insurance claims, can often get lower insurance rates by opening their private medical records to the insurance company. Sellers who otherwise have no right to see that information may find it gladly offered by the healthiest buyers when buyers know they will be offered lower insurance prices in return.

Another strategy sellers use to deal with the insurance problem is to offer "bundle purchases." Knowing that some employees in any sizable firm are likely to have good health and some bad health, insurance companies find it economical to offer a "group rate" policy covering all the employees of the firm. By screening out only the easily identified bad risks, so that they can save the cost of carefully screening every employee's medical history, they can offer moderate rates.

We have discussed many ways in which market participants can reduce the problems they face due to the scarcity and cost of information. These are not totally effective, however, and poor information remains a problem that keeps markets from reaching their hypothetical ideal.

LOOKING AHEAD

In this chapter we focused on the failures of the market. In the next chapter, we will use economic analysis to come to a better understanding of the workings of the public sector. We will also discuss some of the expected shortcomings of public-sector action. Awareness of both the strengths and weaknesses of alternative forms of economic organization will help us to make more intelligent choices in this important area.

CHAPTER SUMMARY

1. The sources of market failure can be grouped into four major categories: externalities, public goods, poor information, and monopoly. Externality and public-goods problems are present when property rights are undefined or poorly enforced.

2. When externalities are present, the market may fail to confront decision makers with the proper incentives. When decision makers are not forced to consider external

cost, they may find it personally advantageous to undertake an economic activity even though it generates a net loss to the community. In contrast, when external benefits are present, decision makers may fail to undertake economic action that would generate a net social gain.

3. When external costs originate from the activities of a business firm, the firm's costs will understate the social cost of producing the good. If production of the good generates external costs, the price of the product under competitive conditions will be too low and the output too large to meet the ideal requirements of economic efficiency.

4. Clearly established private property rights enable owners to prohibit others from using or abusing their property. In contrast, common property rights with open access will normally result in overutilization, since most of the cost of overutilization (and misuse) is imposed on others.

5. When external benefits are present, market demand will understate the social gains of conducting the activity. The consumption and production of goods that generate external benefits will tend to be lower than the socially ideal levels.

6. The efficient use of air and water resources is particularly troublesome for the market because the resources themselves are usually not owned, and it is often difficult to know what damages are done when pollution is released into them at a particular time and place, and who released the pollution. This lack of information means that the property rights of those harmed may not be protected. Government regulation will not produce the needed information, but may improve the situation. A system of emission charges or of transferable emission rights might induce individuals to make wiser use of these resources. Either strategy will (a) increase the cost of releasing pollution, (b) grant firms an incentive to use methods of production that create less pollution, and (c) provide producers with an incentive to seek effective and innovative control devices.

7. When the control costs of firms vary, the emission-charge (pollution-tax) approach will permit society to reduce pollution by a given amount at a lower cost than will the maximum-emission-standard method that is currently widely used. The marginal cost of attaining a cleaner environment will rise as the pollution level is reduced. At some point, the economic benefits of a still cleaner environment will be less than the costs.

8. When the marginal benefits (for example, cleaner air) derived from ending pollution are less than the social gains associated with a pollution-generating activity, prohibition of the activity that results in pollution (or other external cost) is not an ideal solution.

9. In evaluating the case for government intervention in situations involving externalities, one must consider the following factors: (a) the magnitude of the external effects relative to the cost of government action; (b) the ability of the market to devise means of dealing with the problem

without intervention; and (c) the possibility that the political majority may carry the government intervention too far if the external costs imposed on the minority are not fully considered.

10. When it is costly or impossible to withhold a public good from persons who do not or will not help pay for it, the market system breaks down because everyone has an incentive to become a free rider. When this happens, production of the public good will be lower than the socially ideal level.

11. The market provides an incentive for buyers and sellers to acquire information. When a business is dependent on repeat customers, it has a strong incentive to promote customer satisfaction. However, when goods are either (a) difficult to evaluate on inspection and seldom purchased repeatedly from the same producer or (b) have potentially serious and lasting harmful effects, consumer trial and error may be an unsatisfactory means of determining quality. Franchising, brand names, and voluntary regulatory schemes often communicate reliable information on product quality to consumers and thereby reduce the likelihood that consumers will be cheated or misled, even in cases when the specific item is not purchased regularly. Asymmetric information provides an additional challenge to market participants.

CRITICAL ANALYSIS QUESTIONS

*1. When cattle grazed on the English commons open-access pastures, overgrazing took place. Eventually, many of the pastures became private property. What other option might have solved the open-access problem?

2. Why might businesses that are causing pollution problems prefer transferable emission rights to the pollution-tax approach? When might they not?

3. "Elementary education is obviously a public good. After all, it is provided by government." Evaluate this statement.

*4. Why is it difficult to determine the proper output of a pure public good?

5. "Since free riders can enjoy public goods, there is no way those goods will be provided privately." Evaluate this statement.

*6. Are people more likely to take better care of an item they own jointly (communally) or one they own privately? Why? Does the presence of private property rights affect the behavior of persons in noncapitalist nations? Why or why not?

*7. What's wrong with this way of thinking? "Corporations are the major beneficiaries of our lax pollution control policy. Their costs are reduced because we permit them free use of valuable resources—clean water and air—in order to produce goods. These lower costs are simply added to the profits of the polluting firms."

8. What's wrong with this way of thinking? "Private property rights are a gamble. What if the owner doesn't take good care of what she or he owns? Communal property rights are better because there are more people to take care of what they own together. Surely someone will exercise the needed care." (Hint: What was Aristotle's position on the issue?)

*9. Can you think of any public goods, or near public goods, that are supplied privately? Do such examples show that there is no such thing as a free-rider problem?

*10. What factor limits the private supply of public goods?

*11. "Corporations in America are being persecuted unfairly by environmental legislation such as air-pollution-control laws. Corporate leadership is responsible and would work for cleaner air without all this legal hassle." Evaluate this statement using the economic way of thinking.

*12. In a small town located next to an interstate highway are two prospering family restaurants. Both are locally owned, but one is franchised, part of a nationally advertised chain of such restaurants. The other does not advertise. Assuming that highway travelers and local residents have seen equal amounts of advertising from the chain, in which restaurant would you expect to find more highway travelers? Why?

13. Many consumers are willing to pay more for brand-name products (for example, Bayer aspirin or Minute Maid orange juice) than for generic versions of the same products. Is this irrational? Do consumers get anything for their additional expense? Explain.

---

*Asterisk denotes questions for which answers are given in Appendix B.

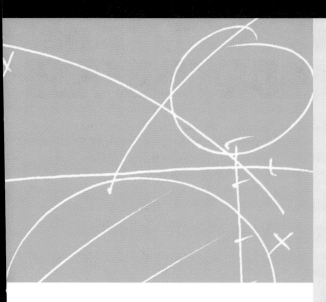

It does not follow that whenever laissez faire falls short government interference is expedient; since the inevitable drawbacks of the latter may, in any particular case, be worse than the shortcomings of private enterprise.

HARRY SIDGWICK, 1887[1]

---

[1]Quoted in Charles Wolf, Jr., *Markets or Government* (Cambridge: MIT Press, 1988), p. 17.

CHAPTER FOCUS

- What is government? Which of its functions provide its most important benefits?
- What are the major forces that determine outcomes under representative democracy?
- Can government action be mutually advantageous to all citizens? Does it sometimes reduce the economic welfare of citizens?
- Will government action sometimes be more efficient than market exchange? When is it likely to be less efficient?
- Why does representative democracy often tax some people in order to provide benefits to others? What types of income transfers are attractive to politicians?
- Can constitutional rules influence political outcomes? What types of constitutional rules and restraints make sense?

About two-fifths of U.S. national income is channeled through various government departments and agencies. As we pointed out in Chapter 5, that figure has been growing for several decades. In addition, about two-fifths of the nation's land is owned by the government, and the legal framework set by the government establishes many of the "rules of the game" for the market sector. Government regulation of prices, of the use of land, water, and air, along with labor relations and business practices, exerts a major impact on the operation of the economy. Given the size and influence of government, understanding how it works is a crucial issue. In this chapter, building on materials presented in Chapters 4 and 29, we will examine further the workings of government.

WHAT IS GOVERNMENT?

At the most basic level, the distinguishing characteristic of government is its monopoly on the use of coercive force to modify the actions of adults. Most societies allow parents to use force to influence the actions of their children. But with regard to adults, governments possess the exclusive right to use force. No individual has a right to use violence in order to take your wealth. Neither can a business firm, no matter how large or powerful, levy a "tax" on your income or force you to buy its product. The legitimate use of force to tax and control the behavior of adults is reserved for government.

How large should the scope of government action be? From an economic viewpoint, what are the proper functions of government? Philosophers, economists, and other scholars have disputed these issues for centuries. General agreement exists, however, that there are two legitimate economic functions of government: (1) protection against invasions by others and (2) provision of goods that cannot easily be provided through markets. These two functions correspond to what Nobel laureate James Buchanan conceptualizes as the protective and productive functions of government.

PROTECTIVE FUNCTION

As philosopher John Locke wrote more than three centuries ago, individuals are constantly threatened by "the invasions of others." Therefore, each individual "is willing to join in society with others, who are already united, or have a mind to unite, for the mutual preservation of their lives, liberties, and estates."[2]

The protective function of government involves the maintenance of a framework of security and order; an infrastructure of rules within which people can interact peacefully with one another. It entails the enforcement of rules against theft, fraud, physical harm to one's person and property, and the like. It also

---

[2]John Locke, *Treatise of Civil Government*, 1690, ed. Charles Sherman (New York: Appleton-Century-Crofts, 1937), p. 82.

involves provision of national defense designed to protect domestic residents against invasion from a foreign power.

It is easy to see the economic importance of this function. Without the assurance that the wealth they create will not be taken from them by others, individuals will have little incentive to produce. When the protective function is performed well, the property of citizens is secure and they are provided with the assurance that if they sow (produce), they will be permitted to reap. When individuals are protected in this way, their resources will be directed toward productive activities that benefit the society as a whole. When protection and property rights are not secure, problems of external costs and benefits arise, as we discussed in the previous chapter.

PRODUCTIVE FUNCTION

Governments may also enhance the wealth of people by undertaking productive activities that cannot easily be organized through market transactions. The production of public goods, such as national defense, a monetary system that provides price stability, a system of legal justice, flood-control projects, and insect-abatement programs, are examples of productive activities that markets are likely to undersupply, increasing the likelihood that government might provide them to the advantage of its citizens. It is easy to see why markets have difficulty supplying the services. In each case, there are strong elements of nonexcludability and nonrival consumption—the two conditions that define public goods.

Although pure public goods are rare, several goods generate spillover benefits that accrue to persons other than the primary consumer. Consider the example of education. Clearly education is not a pure public good. As the presence of private schools illustrates, consumption of schooling can be linked to payment by the consumer. Nonetheless, many believe that consumption of schooling promotes better citizenship, reduces crime, and in many other ways generates spillover benefits for persons other than the students going to school. When spillover benefits are present, market allocation is expected to produce less than the ideal quantity of such goods. Some government provision or subsidy of private provision may be productive in that case.

For still other near public goods, it may be costly to administer a market collection system linking consumption and payment. Consider the case of streets and highways. It would be costly to set up a tollbooth to charge for the use of streets in heavily congested urban areas. New technology shows some promise of lowering these costs dramatically. Up to now, however, given the resources required to establish the payment-consumption link, it has been generally more efficient to have the government supply highways and streets for the use of all. When these roads are financed with taxes on gasoline and tires, the system may even roughly approximate the outcome that would result if people were required to pay directly for their use of the roads.

Finally, a productive government will also promote competitive markets. In this area, the first guideline might be borrowed from the medical profession: Do no harm. A productive government will refrain from the imposition of licenses, discriminatory taxes, price controls, tariffs, quotas, and other entry and trade restraints that lessen the intensity of competition. When there are only a few firms in an industry, and competition from new firms (including rival foreign firms) can be restricted, market participants may collude in an effort to rig the market. Government rejection of the inevitable political demands for trade restraints, together with legislation prohibiting collusion and price-fixing agreements, can help promote competition in such markets.

We repeat: *When there is good reason to expect markets to fall short of optimal provision of goods and services, it is possible—but not always the case—that government might act productively to improve the situation.*

ECONOMICS OF REPRESENTATIVE DEMOCRACY

Government is controlled by the political process. During the past three decades, public-choice economists have studied democratic politics, greatly enhancing our knowledge of that topic and providing us with insight on how we might better design the rules of politics. As we proceed in this chapter, we will consider this issue. Most political decisions in Western countries are made legislatively. Therefore, we will focus our analysis on a democratic system of representative government. Let us see what the tools of economics reveal about the political process.

DEMAND FOR GOVERNMENT

Public-choice theory indicates that there are two general forces underlying political action: (1) the correction of market failure and (2) *rent seeking,* which is the pursuit of private gain at public expense. Citizens can reap gains from government action that reduces market inefficiency emanating from externalities, public goods, an absence of competition, and poor information. However, the political process is merely an alternative form of economic organization, not an automatic corrective device. It is not a pinch hitter we can count on to supply a base hit whenever we fear the market might strike out. (See Myths of Economics.)

Government failure
Failure of government action to meet the criteria of ideal economic efficiency.

As with markets, there are categories of activity that economic theory indicates even democratic governments will do poorly. As we discussed briefly in previous chapters, there is government failure, as well as market failure. **Government failure** is present when the political process leads to economic inefficiency and the waste of scarce resources.

In modern representative democracies, voters elect representatives to direct the actions of governments. In turn, the representatives establish agencies and hire bureaucrats to conduct day-to-day government affairs. Voters, politicians, and bureaucrats are the major players in the democratic political process. Under representative democracy, government action is the result of a complex set of interrelationships among the members of these three groups. Like consumers in the market, voters use their electoral support, money, and other political resources to express their demand for legislation. Like business entrepreneurs, politicians are suppliers: They design and shape legislation. Finally, just as man-

"WHENEVER MARKETS FAIL TO ALLOCATE RESOURCES EFFICIENTLY, GOVERNMENT ACTION WILL IMPROVE THE SITUATION."

Sometimes there is a tendency to think of government, particularly democratically elected government, as a tool that can be used to solve all types of problems ranging from inadequate health care to the high cost of housing. Even some economists act as if government were a corrective device available to cure the economic ills of the world. If there is a problem of monopoly, government regulation can set the "optimal price." In the case of externalities, government can levy the "optimal tax." Some even argue that government can use income transfers to achieve the "optimal distribution of income."

It is, of course, important to understand alternative actions that might *potentially* lead to outcomes that are more consistent with economic efficiency and prosperity. But it is also important to recognize that government is merely an alternative method of social organization—an institutional process through which individuals collectively make choices and carry out activities. It is in no way an entity that can always be counted on to correct the deficiencies of the market or make decisions in the "public interest," however that nebulous expression might be defined.

Collective outcomes, including those that are determined by democratic political procedures, reflect the choices of the participants and the incentive structure that influences those choices. No matter how lofty the rhetoric of political officials, the people (for example, voters, legislators, lobbyists, and bureau managers) who make the choices that determine political outcomes are ordinary mortals, persons with ethical standards and personal motivations very much like those present in the market sector.

Since the incentive structure emanating from the political process generally differs from that of the market, collective outcomes will often differ from market outcomes. For some categories of economic activity, there are reasons to believe that democratic political procedures will generate outcomes consistent with economic efficiency. But this will not always be the case. Furthermore, in certain cases (for example, when a policy generates substantial benefits for well-organized interest groups at the expense of a disorganized majority), there is good reason to expect that democratic-representative government will lead to the adoption of policies that conflict with economic efficiency. There is "government failure" just as there is "market failure." Recognition of this point is important because it challenges us to think more seriously about both how the political process works and how procedures and constitutional rules might be designed to make it work better.

agers and employees are assigned the details of the production process in the market, bureaucrats perform this task in the public sector.[3]

Economists use the self-interest postulate to better understand decisions made by consumers, business decision makers, and resource suppliers. Likewise, public-choice economists apply the self-interest postulate to political decision making. They assume that, just as people are motivated by personal wealth, power, and prestige in the market sector, so, too, will these factors influence them when they make decisions in the political arena.

Closely related to self-interest as a motivator for politicians and bureaucrats are the concepts of survival and expansion. In the private sector, even if there are some managers not primarily seeking profits, it will be the profit-making firms that are most likely to survive, prosper, and expand; and they are the firms that will be imitated. Similarly, in the public sector, politicians and the

---

[3]For a more comprehensive view of public-choice theory and the operation of democratic governments, see James Gwartney and Richard Wagner, eds., *Public Choice and Constitutional Economics* (Greenwich: JAI Press, 1988). Our analysis borrows from this work.

bureaucrats they hire must often act in the narrow self-interest of their constituents (and thus in their own career self-interests) if they hope to survive. Those who cooperate most closely with powerful constituency groups will obtain more political clout and have the opportunity to lead larger government agencies.

THE VOTER-CONSUMER

How do voters decide whom to support? No doubt, many factors influence their decisions. Which candidate is the most persuasive, and which presents the best television image? Who appears to be honest, sincere, and competent? However, the self-interest postulate indicates that voters, like market consumers, will also ask, "What can you do for me, and how much will it cost me?" The greater the voter's perceived net personal gain from a particular candidate's platform, the more likely it is that the voter will favor that candidate. In contrast, the greater the perceived net economic cost imposed on the voter by the positions of a candidate, the less inclined the voter will be to support the candidate. Other things equal, voters will tend to support those candidates whom they believe will provide them the most political goods, services, and transfer benefits, net of personal costs. Unfortunately, rational voters frequently lack the detailed information needed to cast their ballots in a truly knowledgeable fashion.

As we discussed in Chapter 4, collective decisions break the direct link between the individual voter's choice and the outcome of the issue. The choice of a single voter is seldom decisive when the decision-making group is large. Recognizing that the outcome will not depend on one vote, the individual voter has little incentive to seek information (which is costly) on issues and candidates in order to cast a more informed vote. Economists refer to this phenomenon as the *rational-ignorance effect* (see Chapter 4, pages 102–103).[4] The rational-ignorance effect explains why the majority of individuals of voting age cannot accurately identify their congressional representatives, much less identify and understand those representatives' positions on such issues as minimum wage legislation, tariffs, and agricultural price supports. *The fact that voters acquire scanty information merely indicates that they are responding rationally to economic incentives.*

To see in a more personal way why citizens are likely to make better informed decisions as consumers than as voters, imagine that you are planning to buy a car next week and also to vote for one of two Senate candidates. You have narrowed your car choice to either a Ford or a Honda. In the voting booth, you will choose between candidates Smith and Jones. Both the car purchase and the Senate vote involve complex trade-offs for you. The two cars come with many options, and you must choose among dozens of different combinations; the winning Senate candidate will represent you on hundreds of issues, although you are limited to voting for one of the two choices.

Which decision will command more of your scarce time for research and thinking about the best choice? Because your car choice is decisive, and you must

---

[4]The concept of rational ignorance among voters was initially developed by Anthony Downs. See Downs, *An Economic Theory of Democracy* (New York: Harper and Row, 1957).

pay for what you choose, an uninformed car purchase could be very costly for you. But if you mistakenly vote for the wrong candidate out of ignorance, the probability is virtually zero that your vote will be decisive. Because your vote will not swing the election, a mistake or poorly informed choice will have little consequence. It would not be surprising, then, if you spent substantial time considering the car purchase and very little time becoming informed about either the candidates or the political issues at election time.

Car choices are not perfectly informed decisions, but the buyer is certain to benefit from giving careful consideration to the alternatives. As a result, car companies may well be guided by better-informed votes (dollar votes) than the U.S. Senate, even though Senate activities are far more important than cars to the voters as a group.

The fact that one's vote is unlikely to be decisive explains more than lack of information on the part of voters. It also helps to explain why many citizens fail to vote. Even in a presidential election, only about half of all voting-age Americans take the time to register and vote. Given the low probability that one's vote will be decisive, this low voter turnout should not be surprising. The rationality of voters is further indicated by the fact that, when voters perceive that the election is close, voter turnout is larger.[5] A vote in a close election has a greater chance of actually making a difference.

THE POLITICIAN-SUPPLIER

Public-choice theory postulates that pursuit of votes is the primary stimulus shaping the behavior of political suppliers. In varying degrees, such factors as pursuit of the public interest, compassion for the poor, and the achievement of fame, wealth, and power may influence the behavior of politicians. But regardless of ultimate motivation, the ability of politicians to achieve their objectives is sorely dependent upon their ability to get elected and reelected.

Rationally uninformed voters often must be convinced to "want" a candidate. Voter perceptions may be based on realities, but it is always perceptions, not the realities themselves, that influence decisions. This is true regardless of whether the decisions are private or political. As a result, a candidate's positive attributes must be brought to the attention of the rationally ignorant voter, who may well be more interested in the local sports teams (which are probably more entertaining) than in seeking out detailed knowledge about the attributes of the various candidates. An expert staff, polls to ferret out which issues and which positions will be favored by voters, high-quality advertising to present the candidate's image and favored positions, and other forms of political resources are of great value in politics. Thus, political campaigns are costly. For example, in the 1994 campaign, the top two candidates for the U.S. Senate from California spent a combined total of more than $44 million. The losing candidate, Michael Huffington, spent nearly $30 million, while incumbent Dianne Feinstein spent

---

[5]This and other results consistent with the rational actions of voters have long been observed by economists. An early exposition can be found in Yoram Barzel and Eugene Silberberg, "Is the Act of Voting Rational?" *Public Choice* 16 (fall 1973): pp. 51–58.

more than $14 million to be reelected. There were 32 additional Senate seats contested that year, and at least 13 Senate candidates in other states spent more than $5 million each.[6]

Are we implying that politicians are selfish, caring only for their pocketbooks and reelection chances? The answer is no. When people act in the political sphere, they may genuinely want to help their fellow citizens. Factors other than personal political gain, narrowly defined, influence the actions of many political suppliers. On certain issues, one may feel strongly that one's position is best for the nation, even though it may not be currently popular. The national interest as perceived by the political supplier may conflict with the position that would be most favorable to reelection prospects. Some politicians may opt for the national interest even when it means political defeat. None of this is inconsistent with an economic view of political choice.

However, the existence of political suicide does not change the fact that most politicians who win elections are those who prefer political survival. There is a strong incentive for political suppliers to stake out positions that will increase their vote total in the next election. In fact, competition more or less forces politicians to make decisions in light of political considerations. *Regardless of ultimate motivation, the ability of politicians to achieve their objectives depends on their ability to get elected and reelected. Just as profits are the lifeblood of the market entrepreneur, votes are the lifeblood of the politician.* Many factors undoubtedly influence political suppliers. Political competition, however, limits their options. In the same way that neglect of economic profit is the route to market oblivion, neglect of potential votes is the route to political oblivion.

WHEN VOTING WORKS WELL

We have shown how the theory of market failure highlights the potential for protective and productive governmental action—action that generates benefits in excess of costs. Will voting and representative government provide support for productive projects while rejecting unproductive projects? People have a tendency to believe that support by a majority makes a political action productive or legitimate. Perhaps surprising to some, if a government project is really productive, it will always be possible to allocate the project's cost so that *all* voters will gain. **Exhibit 30–1** illustrates this point. Column 1 presents hypothetical data on the distribution of benefits from a government road-construction project. These benefits sum to $40, which exceeds the $25 cost of the road. Since voter benefits exceed costs, the project is indeed productive. If the project's $25 cost were allocated equally among the voters (Plan A), Adams and Brown gain substantially, but Green, Jones, and Smith will lose. The value of the project to the

---

[6]Candidate Huffington spent more than $28 million of his own money. Data are from Michael Barone and Grant Ujifusa, *The Almanac of American Politics–1996* (Washington: National Journal, 1995), p. 1511.

EXHIBIT 30–1

BENEFITS DERIVED BY VOTERS FROM HYPOTHETICAL ROAD CONSTRUCTION PROJECT

VOTER	BENEFITS RECEIVED (1)	TAX PAYMENT PLAN A (2)	PLAN B (3)
Adams	$20	$ 5	$12.50
Brown	12	5	7.50
Green	4	5	2.50
Jones	2	5	1.25
Smith	2	5	1.25
Total	$40	$25	$25.00

latter three voters is less than their $5 cost. If the fate of the project were decided by majority vote, the project would be defeated by the "no" votes of Green, Jones, and Smith.

In contrast, look what happens if the cost of the project is allocated among voters in proportion to the benefits that they receive (Plan B). Under this arrangement, Adams would pay half ($12.50) of the $25 cost, since she receives half ($20) of the total benefits ($40). The other voters would all pay in proportion to their benefits received. Under this finance plan, all voters would gain from the proposal. Even though the proposal could not muster a majority when the costs were allocated equally among voters, it would be favored by all five voters when they are taxed in proportion to the benefits that they receive (Plan B).

This simple illustration highlights an extremely important point about voting and productive projects. *When voters pay in proportion to benefits received*, all voters will gain if the government action is productive (and all will lose if it is unproductive).[7] When the benefits and costs of voters are directly related, productive government actions will be favored by almost all voters. Correspondingly, if a project is counterproductive—if the costs exceed the benefits generated for voters—it will be opposed by almost all voters. *Therefore, when voters pay in proportion to benefits received, there is a harmony between good politics and sound economics.*

---

[7]The principle that productive projects generate the potential for political unanimity was initially articulated by Swedish economist Knut Wicksell in 1896. See Wicksell, "A New Principle of Just Taxation," in *Public Choice and Constitutional Economics*, Gwartney and Wagner. Nobel laureate James Buchanan has stated that Wicksell's work provided him with the insights that led to his large role in the development of modern public-choice theory.

With public-sector action, however, the link between receipt of and payment for a good can be broken in that the beneficiaries of a proposal may not bear its cost. Public-choice theory indicates that the pattern of benefits and costs among voters will influence the workings of the political process. The benefits from a government action may be either widespread among the general populace or concentrated among a small subgroup (for example, farmers, students, business interests, or members of a labor union). Similarly, the costs may be either widespread or highly concentrated among voters. As **Exhibit 30–2** illustrates, there are four possible patterns of voter benefits and costs: (1) widespread benefits and widespread costs, (2) concentrated benefits and widespread costs, (3) concentrated benefits and concentrated costs, and (4) widespread benefits and concentrated costs.

When both the benefits and costs are widespread among voters (Type 1), essentially everyone benefits and everyone pays. Although the costs of Type 1 measures may not be precisely proportional to benefits, there will be a rough relationship. When Type 1 measures are productive, almost everyone gains more than they pay. There will be little opposition, and political representatives have a strong incentive to support such proposals. In contrast, when Type 1 proposals generate costs in excess of benefits, almost everyone loses, and representatives will confront pressure to oppose such issues. Thus, for Type 1 projects, the political process tends to be consistent with economic efficiency.

It is useful to visualize four possible combinations for the distribution of benefits and costs among voters and to consider how the alternative distributions affect the operation of representative government. When the distribution of benefits and costs are both widespread among voters (1) or both concentrated among voters (3), representative government will tend to undertake projects that are productive and reject those that are unproductive. In contrast, when the benefits are concentrated and the costs are widespread (2), representative government is biased toward adoption of counterproductive activity. Finally, when benefits are widespread but the costs concentrated (4), the political process may reject projects that are productive.

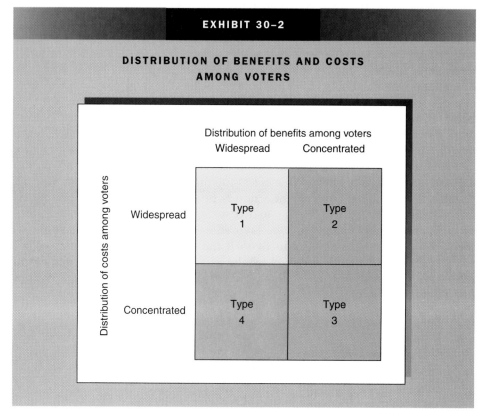

EXHIBIT 30–2

DISTRIBUTION OF BENEFITS AND COSTS AMONG VOTERS

	Distribution of benefits among voters	
	Widespread	Concentrated
Distribution of costs among voters — Widespread	Type 1	Type 2
Distribution of costs among voters — Concentrated	Type 4	Type 3

Interestingly, the provision of traditional public goods—for example, national defense, a legal system for the protection of persons and property and enforcement of contracts, and a monetary system to oil the wheels of exchange—best fits Type 1. Nearly everyone pays and nearly everyone benefits from public-sector action of this type.

Similarly, there is reason to believe that the political process will work pretty well for Type 3 measures—those for which both benefits and costs are concentrated on one or more small subgroups. In some cases, the concentrated beneficiaries may pay for the government to provide services. This would be the case when user charges finance public services (for example, air safety or garbage collection) benefiting subgroups of the populace. Under these circumstances, voter support will provide politicians with an incentive to provide public services that generate value in excess of cost.

Of course, the subgroup of beneficiaries might differ from the subgroup footing the bill. But even in this case, if the benefits exceed the costs, the concentrated group of beneficiaries will have an incentive to expend more resources supportive of the measure than those harmed by it will expend opposing it. Thus, productive measures will tend to be adopted. Similarly, unproductive measures will tend to be rejected when both the benefits and costs are concentrated.

WHEN VOTING CONFLICTS WITH ECONOMIC EFFICIENCY

Although the political process works well when there is a close relationship between receipt of benefits and payment of cost, the harmony between good politics and sound economics sometimes breaks down. There are four major reasons why unrestrained majority-rule voting may conflict with economic prosperity. (Note: Several of the concepts analyzed here were briefly introduced in Chapter 4.)

SPECIAL-INTEREST EFFECT

Public-choice analysis indicates that problems will arise when an issue generates substantial personal benefits for a small number of constituents while imposing a small individual cost on a large number of other voters (Type 2 in Exhibit 30–2). Measures of this type are special-interest issues. A number of factors combine to make special-interest groups far more powerful in a representative democracy than their numbers would indicate.

It is easy to see how politicians can improve their election prospects by catering to the views of special interests. Since their personal stake is large, members of the interest group (and lobbyists representing their interests) have a strong incentive to inform themselves and their allies and to let legislators know how strongly they feel about an issue of special importance. Many of them will vote for or against candidates strictly on the basis of whether they support their specific interests. In addition, such interest groups are generally an attractive source of campaign resources, including financial contributions. In contrast, most other voters will care little about a special-interest issue. For the non-special-interest voter, opportunity cost of the time and energy necessary to examine the issue will generally exceed any possible personal gain from a preferred resolution of any specific special-interest issue. Of course, there are many such issues, but each would have to be considered separately, so most non-special-interest voters will simply ignore such issues.

If you were a vote-seeking politician, what would you do? Clearly, little gain would be derived from supporting the interest of the largely uninformed and uninterested majority. In contrast, support for the interests of easily identifiable, well-organized groups would generate vocal supporters, campaign workers, and, most important, campaign contributors. Predictably, politicians will be led as if by an invisible hand to support legislation that provides concentrated benefits to interest groups at the expense of disorganized groups (such as taxpayers and consumers), even if such policies waste resources.

The "rational ignorance" of voters strengthens the power of special interests. Since the cost imposed on individual voters for each specific issue is small, and since the individual is unable to avoid the cost even by becoming informed, voters bearing the cost of special-interest legislation tend to be uninformed on the issue. This will be particularly true if the complexity of the issue makes it difficult for voters to think through how an issue affects their personal welfare. Thus, politicians often make special-interest legislation complex in order to hide the cost imposed on the typical voter.

The ability of the voter to punish politicians for supporting special-interest legislation is further hindered by the fact that many issues are bundled together when the voter chooses between one candidate and another. Even if the voter knows and dislikes the politician's stand on one or a few issues, the bundling of hundreds of future issues into one candidate choice severely limits the voter's ability to take a stand at the ballot box for or against any particular issue.

Bureaucratic interests can be an additional factor favoring special-interest programs. The interests of bureaucrats are often complementary with those of interest groups. The bureaucrats who staff an agency usually want to see their department's goals furthered, whether the goals are to protect more wilderness, build more roads, or provide additional subsidized irrigation projects. To accomplish these things requires larger budgets, which—not so incidentally—are

Logrolling
The exchange between politicians of political support on one issue for political support on another issue.

Pork-barrel legislation
A package of spending projects benefiting local areas at federal expense. The projects typically have costs that exceed benefits, but are intensely desired by the residents of the district getting the benefits without having to pay much of the costs.

likely to provide the bureaucrats with expanded career opportunities while helping to satisfy their professional aspirations as well. Bureaus, therefore, are usually happy to work to expand their programs to deliver benefits to special-interest groups, who, in turn, work with politicians to expand their bureau budgets and programs.

Yet another force that strengthens the political clout of special-interest groups is **logrolling**, the practice of trading votes by a representative in order to pass intensely desired legislation. Representative A promises to vote for measures favored by other representatives in exchange for their support of a measure that A strongly favors. With logrolling, legislative bodies often pass a bundle of proposals, each of which would be rejected if voted on separately.

Pork-barrel legislation is a variant of logrolling. This type of legislation bundles together a set of projects to benefit regional interests (for example, water projects, dredging of harbors, or expenditures on military bases) at the expense of the general taxpayer. As in the case of logrolling, the bundle of pork-barrel projects can often gain approval even if the items by themselves would be seen as counterproductive and would individually be rejected by the legislative assembly.

Exhibit 30–3 provides a numeric illustration of the forces underlying logrolling and pork-barrel legislation. Here we consider the operation of a five-member legislative assembly considering three projects: construction of a post office in District A, dredging of a harbor in District B, and expenditures on a military base in District C. In each case, the project is inefficient—the net cost of the project exceeds the net benefit (by a 12-to-10 ratio). If the projects were voted on separately, and the representatives reflected the views of their constituents, each project would lose by a 4-to-1 vote. However, when the projects are bundled together through either logrolling or pork-barrel legislation, Representatives A, B, and C will vote yes. The legislative bundle will pass 3 to 2 even though it is counterproductive (on average, the projects, as a bundle, reduce the wealth of constituents by $6).[8]

Legislation providing subsidies to electricity consumers in California, Nevada, and Arizona illustrates the relevance of logrolling and pork-barrel legislation. Under legislation passed in 1937, electricity generated by Hoover Dam has been sold to residents in the three surrounding states at rates ranging between 10 percent and 25 percent of the market price. The law providing for the subsidized rates was scheduled to expire in 1987. However, before it did,

---

EXHIBIT 30–3

VOTE TRADING AND PASSING
COUNTERPRODUCTIVE LEGISLATION

	NET BENEFITS (+) OR COSTS (−) TO EACH VOTER IN DISTRICT			
VOTERS OF DISTRICT[a]	CONSTRUCTION OF POST OFFICE IN A	DREDGING HARBOR IN B	CONSTRUCTION OF MILITARY BASE IN C	TOTAL
A	+$10	−$ 3	−$ 3	+$4
B	−$ 3	+$10	−$ 3	+$4
C	−$ 3	−$ 3	+$10	+$4
D	−$ 3	−$ 3	−$ 3	−$9
E	−$ 3	−$ 3	−$ 3	−$9
Total	−$ 2	−$ 2	−$ 2	−$6

[a]We assume the districts are of equal size.

---

[8]Logrolling and pork-barrel policies can lead to the adoption of productive measures. However, if a project is productive, there would always be a pattern of finance that would lead to its adoption even if logrolling were absent. Thus, the tendency for logrolling and pork-barrel policies to result in the adoption of inefficient projects is the more significant point.

Congress extended the subsidies for another 30 years. The residents of many western states are the recipients of federally subsidized electricity. Every senator west of Missouri voted to continue the subsidized rates for electricity generated by Hoover Dam. In turn, they can expect senators and representatives from California, Arizona, and Nevada to support subsidized electricity rates in their states. In contrast, residents of other states will pay higher taxes so that many residents in western states can enjoy cheap electricity.

Why don't representatives oppose measures that force their constituents to pay for projects that benefit others? There is some incentive to do so, but the constituents of any one elected representative can capture only a small portion of the benefits of tax savings from improved efficiency, since they would be spread nationwide among all taxpayers. Just as we do not expect a corporation's president to devote the firm's resources to projects not primarily benefiting stockholders, we should not expect an elected representative to devote political resources to projects such as defeating pork-barrel programs, when the benefits of greater efficiency would not go primarily to that representative's constituents. Instead, each representative has a strong incentive to work for programs whose benefits are concentrated among his or her constituents—especially the organized interest groups who can help the representative be reelected. Heeding such incentives is a survival (reelection) characteristic.

The bottom line is clear: Public-choice analysis indicates that majority voting and representative democracy do not work so well when concentrated interests benefit at the expense of widely dispersed interests. This special-interest bias of the political process helps to explain the presence of many programs that reduce the size of the economic pie. For example, the agricultural price-support programs of the United States and Western Europe promote inefficient methods of production (such as the use of too much fertilizer relative to land), protect high-cost producers, and result in higher food prices. Approximately 1 percent of the populace (primarily large farmers) individually gain a lot at the expense of consumers and taxpayers, each of whom pay somewhat higher food prices and taxes than they otherwise would. Given their substantial personal gain, the agricultural interests feel strongly about the price-support programs, while most others are uninformed and largely uninterested in the issue. Therefore, politicians find it advantageous to support the programs even though they waste resources and reduce the general standard of living. (An example of an agricultural price-support program is given in the Applications in Economics box.)

The analysis is symmetrical. When the benefits of a government action are widespread and the costs highly concentrated (Type 4 of Exhibit 30–2), the concentrated interests will strongly oppose the proposal. Most others will be largely uninformed and uninterested. Once again, politicians will have an incentive to respond to the views of the concentrated interests. Projects of this type will tend to be rejected even when they are productive—that is, when they would generate larger benefits than costs.

SHORTSIGHTEDNESS EFFECT

Voters find it difficult to identify the effects of complex issues over time, so they tend to rely primarily on current economic conditions when evaluating the performance of political incumbents. Unfortunately, policies that look good around

APPLICATIONS IN ECONOMICS

THE POWER OF SPECIAL INTERESTS: THE CASE OF RICE FARMERS

There are roughly 33,000 rice farmers in the United States. In essence, the government guarantees them an above-market price for rice by paying them to grow less rice so the artificially high price can be maintained. The program reduces output, pushes up the price of rice, and requires higher taxes. As a nation, we are worse off as a result.

Nonetheless, Congress continues to support the program. The rice farmers gain more than $800 million in gross income, approximately $25,000 per rice farm. More than 60 percent of these subsidies go to rice farmers re-ceiving payments of $50,000 or more. Given the sizable impact on their personal wealth, it is perfectly sensible for rice farmers to inform themselves and use their votes, contributions, and political influence to help politicians who support their interests. In contrast, it makes no sense for the average voter to investigate this issue or give it any significant weight when deciding for whom to vote. In fact, most Americans are unaware that they pay ap-proximately $4 more per year to help rice growers, most of which goes to wealthy farmers. As a result, politicians can generally gain more by continuing to support the rice farmers, even though the subsidy program wastes re-sources and reduces the wealth of the nation.

election day may have substantial negative side effects after the election. On the other hand, policies that generate costs before the election in order to provide long-term gains that emerge only after the next election reduce the reelection prospects of incumbents. As a result, the political process is biased toward the adoption of shortsighted policies and against the selection of sound long-range policies that involve observable costs prior to the next election. As we noted in Chapter 4, this bias is called the *shortsightedness effect*.

Consider one example of the relative shortsightedness of governmental man-agement. Economist Brian Cromwell, in a study of municipal bus systems around the United States, observed the maintenance practices of owners of tran-sit buses. He found that private companies spend more on maintenance than do government bus systems. As a result, privately owned transit buses have longer in-service lives and hold their value better than public buses.[9] Of 645 buses sold by city bus systems in 1987 and 1988, those that were privately owned and main-tained had far more value, as indicated in **Exhibit 30–4.** The difference in resale prices supports the claim that private owners, who personally pay for current upkeep expenditures, but also personally capture the future benefits, are willing to spend more in producing and protecting those benefits than are public offi-cials, who hear the complaints about current costs, but may not be there later to get credit for future benefits.

This bias toward shortsighted decisions, inherent in the collective decision-making process, is another problem made worse by the rational ignorance of vot-ers. It is unlikely that many voters in the cities where the public bus systems are located would know that their government bus system was investing less in maintenance than private systems, or that it would prove costly to the system over time.

---

[9]Brian Cromwell, "Capital Subsidies and the Infrastructure Crisis: Evidence from the Local Mass-Transit Industry," Federal Reserve Bank of Cleveland, *Economic Review* 25, no. 2 (1989).

EXHIBIT 30-4

AVERAGE RESALE PRICE OF VEHICLES

DATE OF MANUFACTURE	PUBLICLY OWNED VEHICLES	PRIVATELY OWNED VEHICLES
1961–1970	$ 571	$ 5,045
1971–1975	$1,648	$ 7,500
1976–1980	$8,863	$18,000

The shortsightedness effect is also compounded by the lack of tradeable property rights—the lack of a capital market—in government enterprises. For comparison, consider the problem of choosing programs and strategies for a large corporation such as General Motors. Its stockholders elect a board of directors to set policy and select professional management leadership. The corporation, like a government, faces complex choices of programs that are difficult for the individual stockholder to fully understand and evaluate. However, when evaluating the business programs and strategy of the corporation, the stockholder has an incentive very different from that of a voter. Why? Any stockholder who senses trouble before others do can sell out before the stock price falls. Similarly, the stockholder (or other observer) who recognizes a good program choice by a firm before others do can profit individually by buying stock in the firm. These choices of stockholders will be registered and passed on almost instantly. Stockholder decisions to buy or sell stock causes the stock price to rise or fall, signaling whether trouble or a winning program is forecast by those stock buyers and sellers who are most attentive. A strategy choice, or a new program that investors like, will quickly be signaled by a rising share price that rewards management choices well ahead of actual changes in profits and losses. No such advanced market signals exist in the collective decision-making processes of government. The result is the restriction of the planning horizon of elected officials.

As a result of the shortsightedness effect, politicians have a strong incentive to promote programs providing easily observable benefits prior to the next election, even when the true cost of these programs outweigh the benefits. Similarly, they have an incentive to oppose and delay productive actions that generate observable costs prior to the next election. This shortsighted nature of the political process leads to economic inefficiency, even when political decisions are made democratically.

It is easy to think of instances where positive short-term effects have increased the political attractiveness of policies that exert a long-term detrimental impact. For example, budget deficits allow politicians to finance current projects with future taxes. This strategy has political attractiveness even though it will probably result in higher interest rates and less capital formation. Rent controls that reduce the current price of rental housing provide another example. The short-term results will be far more positive than the effects in the long run (housing shortages, black markets, and deterioration in the quality of housing).

RENT SEEKING

There are two ways individuals can acquire wealth: production and plunder. When they produce goods or services and exchange them for income, they not only enrich themselves but they also enhance the wealth of the society. Sometimes the rules also allow people to get ahead by plundering what others have produced, a method that enriches one at the expense of another, often after a strenuous political effort that consumes additional resources, thereby reducing the wealth of the society.

Rent seeking is the term describing actions taken by individuals and groups seeking to use the political process to plunder the wealth of others. The incentive to engage in rent-seeking activities is directly proportional to the ease with which the political process can be used for personal (or interest group) gain at the expense of others. When the effective law of the land makes it difficult to take the property of others or force others to pay for projects favored by you and your interest group, rent seeking is unattractive. Under such circumstances, its benefits are relatively low, and few resources flow into rent-seeking activities. In contrast, when government fails to levy user fees or similar forms of financing to allocate the cost of its projects to the primary beneficiaries, or when it becomes heavily involved in tax-transfer activities, the payoff for rent seeking expands.

Rent seeking will also increase when governments, including democratic governments, become more heavily involved in erecting trade barriers, mandating employment benefits, providing subsidies, fixing prices, and levying discriminatory taxes (taxes unrelated to the provision of public services to the taxpayer).

When a government, rather than acting as a neutral force protecting property rights and enforcing contracts, attempts to favor some at the expense of others, counterproductive activities will expand while positive-sum productive activities will shrink. People will spend more time organizing and lobbying politicians and less time producing goods and services. Since fewer resources will be utilized to create wealth (and more utilized in rent-seeking activities), economic progress will be retarded.

INEFFICIENCY OF GOVERNMENT OPERATIONS

Will government goods and services be produced efficiently? Professional pride, and pride in doing a job well, are likely to be present in the public sector as well as the private. However the incentive to operate efficiently differs in the two sectors. In the private sector, there is a strong incentive to produce efficiently because lower costs mean higher profits. This index of performance (profit rate) is unavailable in the public sector. Direct competition in the form of other firms trying to take an agency's customers is generally absent in the public sector.

While bankruptcy weeds out inefficiency in the private sector, there is no parallel mechanism to eliminate inefficiency in the public sector. In fact, poor performance and failure to achieve objectives are often used as an argument for *increased* funding in the public sector. Furthermore, public-sector managers are seldom in a position to gain personally from measures that reduce costs. The opposite is often true. If an agency fails to spend this year's allocation, its case for a larger budget next year is weakened. Agencies typically go on a spending spree at the end of the budget period if they discover that they have failed to spend all the current year's appropriation.

It is important to note that the argument of internal inefficiency is not based on the assumption that employees of a bureaucratic government are necessarily lazy or incapable. Rather, the emphasis is on the information and incentives under which managers and other workers toil. No individual or relatively small group of individuals has much incentive to ensure economic efficiency. Their performances cannot readily be judged, and, without private ownership, their personal wealth cannot be significantly altered by changes in the level of efficiency. Because public officials and bureau managers spend other people's money, they are likely to be less conscious of cost than they would be with their own resources. Without a need to compare sales revenues to costs, there is no test with which to define economic inefficiency or measure it accurately, much less to eliminate it. The perverse incentive structure of a bureaucracy is bound to have an impact on its internal efficiency.

The empirical evidence is consistent with this view. Economies dominated by government control, like those of Eastern Europe, the former Soviet Union, and Latin America, have a poor economic record. The level of output per unit of resource input in those economies is low.[10] Similarly, when private firms are compared with government agencies providing the same goods or services, the private firms generally have been shown to provide them more economically.

PUBLIC SECTOR VERSUS THE MARKET: A SUMMARY

Throughout this text, we have argued that theory can explain why both market forces and public-sector action sometimes break down—that is, why they sometimes fail to meet the criteria for ideal efficiency. The deficiencies of one or the other sector will often be more or less decisive depending on the type of

---

[10]For an overall comparison of the efficiency of resource utilization in socialist nations compared to market economies, see Mikhail Bernstam, *The Wealth of Nations and the Environment* (London: Institute of Economic Affairs, 1991).

economic activity. Nobel laureate Paul Samuelson has stated, "There are not rules concerning the proper role of government that can be established by *a priori* reasoning."[11] This does not mean, however, that economics has nothing to say about the *strength* of the case for either the market or the public sector in terms of specific classes of activities. Nor does it mean that social scientists have nothing to say about institutional arrangements for conducting economic activity. It merely indicates that each issue and type of activity must be considered individually.

The case for government intervention is obviously stronger for some activities than for others. For example, if an activity involves substantial external effects, market arrangements often result in economic inefficiency, and public-sector action may allow for greater efficiency. Similarly, when competitive pressures are weak and when there is reason to expect consumers to be poorly informed, market failure may result, and again government action may be called for. (See the Thumbnail Sketch for a summary of factors that influence the case for market or for public-sector action.)

The identical analysis holds for the public sector. When there is a good reason to believe that special-interest influence will be strong, the case for government action to correct market failures is weakened. Similarly, the lack of a means to identify and weed out public-sector inefficiency weakens the case for government action. More often than not, the choice of proper institutions may be a choice among evils. For example, we might expect private-sector monopoly if an activity is left to the market, or perverse regulation due to the special-interest effect if we turn to the public sector. Understanding the shortcomings of both the market and the public sectors is important if we are to improve our current economic institutions.

THUMBNAIL SKETCH

WHAT WEAKENS THE CASE FOR MARKET-SECTOR ALLOCATION VERSUS PUBLIC-SECTOR INTERVENTION, AND VICE VERSA?

These factors weaken the case for market-sector allocation:

1. External costs and benefits
2. Public goods
3. Monopoly
4. Uninformed consumers

These factors weaken the case for public-sector intervention:

1. The power of special interests
2. The shortsightedness effect
3. Rent seeking
4. Little incentive for operational efficiency

---

[11]Paul A. Samuelson, "The Economic Role of Private Activity," in *The Collected Scientific Papers of Paul A. Samuelson*, vol. 2, ed. J. E. Stiglitz (Cambridge: MIT Press, 1966), p. 1423.

ECONOMICS, POLITICS, AND THE TRANSFER SOCIETY

As **Exhibit 30–5** illustrates, direct income transfers through the public sector have increased sharply during the past six decades. In 1929 cash income transfers accounted for only 1.8 percent of national income; by 1994 the figure had risen to 17.3 percent. If in-kind benefits such as food stamps, medical care, and housing were included, the size of the transfer sector would have constituted well over 20 percent of national income.

As in other areas, both the market failure and rent-seeking models of government underlie public-sector income transfers. Sometimes income transfers reflect the public-good characteristics of antipoverty efforts. Because the number of poor people is largely independent of one's personal contribution, individuals motivated by the desire to reduce poverty in general may simply become *free riders*. When a large number of people become free riders, though, less than the desired amount of antipoverty effort will be voluntarily supplied. If everyone is required to contribute through the tax system, then the free-rider problem can

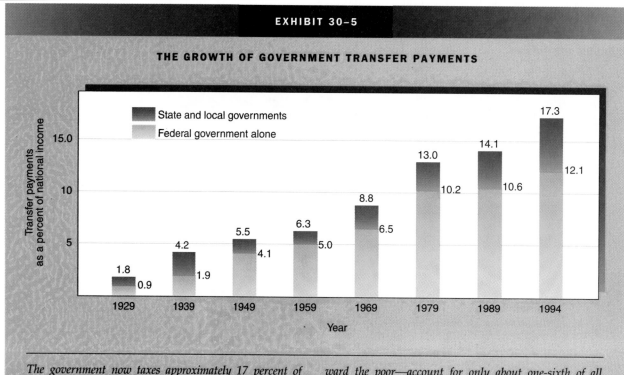

EXHIBIT 30–5

THE GROWTH OF GOVERNMENT TRANSFER PAYMENTS

The government now taxes approximately 17 percent of national income away from some people and transfers it to others. Means-tested income transfers—those directed toward the poor—account for only about one-sixth of all income transfers.

Source: *Economic Report of the President, 1994.* Tables B-25, B-82, B83.

be overcome. Under these circumstances, transfers directed to the poor may be consistent with economic efficiency.

However, in the United States, *means-tested transfers*, those directed toward the poor, constitute only about one-sixth of all income transfers. No income test is applied to the other five-sixths, and they are generally directed toward groups that are either well organized or easily identifiable. The recipients of these transfers often have incomes well above the average. This suggests that the rent-seeking model of government also plays an important role in the allocation of income transfers.

Within the framework of public-choice analysis, the relatively small portion of income transfers directed toward the poor is not surprising. There is little reason to believe that transfers to the poor will be particularly attractive to vote-seeking politicians. After all, in the United States, the poor are less likely to vote than middle- and upper-income recipients. They are less likely than others to be well informed on political issues and candidates. They are not united. Neither are they a significant source of financial resources that exert a powerful influence on the political process.

Before leaving the topic of transfers, one final point should be stressed. Market adjustments and competition for the transfers will erode much of the long-run gain of the intended beneficiaries. This point follows from a standard proposition of economic theory: Competitors will be attracted to activities that yield abnormally high rates of return until the abnormally high profit is eroded. Application of this proposition to politics indicates that, whenever the government establishes criteria (as it must in a world of scarce resources) that must be met in order to qualify for transfers or other political favors, competition to meet the standard will erode the opportunity for profit. Unanticipated changes in public policy will impose temporary gains and losses on various groups. Paradoxical as it may appear, it is extremely difficult to bestow favors upon a class of recipients in a manner that will *permanently* improve their well-being.

As people and markets adjust to a new transfer program, any abnormally high returns derived by recipients of government subsidies will be dissipated. Generally, government transfer programs require recipients to either own something (for example, land with an acreage allotment eligible for farm subsidies), do something, or be something in order to qualify for the transfer. When one considers all that is required to qualify as a beneficiary, it is clear that the net gain of the recipients is substantially less than the size of the transfers. In the case of the poor, high implicit marginal tax rates accompanying income-tested transfers severely retard the incentive of the poor to earn. Thus, the net increase in income of the poor is much less than the dollars transferred. To a large extent, the transfers merely replace income that would have been earned in their absence. The high implicit tax rates often induce the poor to drop out of the work force. When this happens, the skills of the poor depreciate, further reducing their ability to support themselves and escape poverty. Government involvement in antipoverty transfers crowds out private charitable efforts by families, individuals, churches, and civic organizations. When taxes are levied to do more, predictably, private individuals and groups will adjust and do less. When the effects of these adjustments are considered, it is not at all clear that the poor benefit very much from transfers, particularly in the long run.

If transfer programs fail to provide significant benefits to recipients beyond the windfall gains at the time the programs are instituted or unexpectedly expanded, what accounts for the continued political support for such programs?

Gordon Tullock's work on the transitional gains trap provides the answer.[12] Elimination of the programs would be costly for recipients who have adjusted to or "bought into" the programs. Even though the programs do little to improve their welfare, the current beneficiaries would be harmed by the elimination or unexpected reduction in the programs. Thus, they form a vocal lobby supportive of the programs.

CONSTITUTIONAL ORGANIZATION AND GETTING MORE FROM GOVERNMENT

The role of government is central to the achievement of economic progress. When government performs its protective function well, it will improve the efficiency of markets. Similarly, government's production of public goods can create wealth and help promote prosperity. Public-choice analysis, however, indicates that unconstrained democratic governments will often enact programs that waste resources and impair the general standard of living of citizens. How can we reap the benefits available from government while minimizing its unwanted, counterproductive activities?

An efficient political organization does not emerge naturally. It must be shaped by the legal environment. The Founding Fathers of the United States recognized this point. They sought to establish a constitutional order that would limit the misuse of the ordinary political process, while allowing government to undertake activities important to the welfare of citizens. With time, many of the safeguards embodied in the U.S. Constitution have either eroded or been modified. Nonetheless, the general idea was a sound one.

What would a constitutional structure consistent with economic efficiency look like? Interestingly, public-choice analysis indicates that it would include a number of the ideas incorporated into the U.S. Constitution. First, it would seek to constrain government from taking rights and wealth from some in order to bestow them on others. The U.S. Constitution contains provisions designed to prevent such takings. The Fifth Amendment states "nor shall private property be taken for public use without just compensation."[13] Article I, Section 10, mandates, "No state shall . . . pass any . . . law impairing the obligations of contracts." These provisions might be strengthened and supplemented with prohibitions against the use of government to fix prices and to bar entry into the production of otherwise legal goods, both of which restrain trade and are indirect forms of taking property without compensation. With regard to income-transfer programs, federal transfer activities might be restricted to those directed toward the poor (means-tested programs).

---

[12]Gordon Tullock, "The Transitional Gains Trap," *Bell Journal of Economics* 6 (autumn 1975).

[13]For a detailed analysis of the importance of this clause from a law and economics viewpoint, see Richard A. Epstein, *Takings: Private Property and the Power of Eminent Domain* (Cambridge: Harvard University Press, 1985).

Second, the efficiency of the political process would be enhanced if the primary beneficiaries of government activities were required to foot the bill for their cost. Again, there is evidence that this is what the Founding Fathers had in mind. The U.S. Constitution, Article I, Section 8, states, "The Congress shall have power to lay and collect taxes, duties, imports and excises to . . . provide for the common defense and general welfare of the United States, but all duties, imports and excises shall be uniform throughout the United States." This constitutional provision indicates that it was the intent of the Founders that, at the federal level, uniformly levied taxes would be used only for the finance of expenditures yielding general benefits—the common defense and general welfare (Type I issues in Exhibit 30–2). In order to strengthen this substantive provision, tax and spending proposals at the federal level could be required to secure the approval of a supra-majority (for example, three-fourths) of the legislative members. Such a provision would reduce the power of interest groups and the viability of pork-barrel spending projects. Projects that truly provided benefits for most people, however, should receive the required level of approval.

Finally, if we want efficiency in government, the constitutional structure could strengthen independent state and local governments. One reason to expand the role of lower levels of government is that higher levels, such as the federal government, have a greater ability to spread costs for projects that provide benefits to only a few. Another reason is to promote competition. In *The Federalist Papers*, James Madison argues that competition among state and local governments will help check abusive and counterproductive government action.[14] Public-choice analysis indicates that Madison's perception was correct.

How might the constitutional order promote competition among governments? One way would be to require more inclusive majorities in the higher levels of government. For example, local legislative bodies (city commissions, county commissions, regional authorities, and so on) might continue to act with the approval of only a simple majority, while a three-fifths majority might be required for legislative action at the state level, and a three-fourths majority at the federal level. The increasing majorities required for legislative action at higher levels of government would help remedy a deficiency of the current system—the tendency of federal and state governments to get involved with issues that are best dealt with at lower levels of government. Decentralization in government would permit states and localities to adopt different government environments. Those that people like best—the ones that supply public-sector goods highly valued relative to their tax cost—would grow and prosper relative to those that people appreciate less. This structure would allow individuals and businesses to "vote with their feet" as well as with their ballots.

Of course, public-choice theorists are continuing to investigate the operation of alternative forms of political organization. The challenge is to develop political institutions capable of bringing, to the fullest extent possible, the self-interest of politicians, bureaucrats, and voters into harmony with the general welfare of society.

---

[14]See Charles Tiebout, "A Pure Theory of Local Expenditures," *Journal of Political Economy* (October 1956); Vincent Ostrom, *The Political Theory of a Compound Republic* (Fairfax: Center for Study of Public Choice, George Mason University, 1971); and Robert Bish, "Federalism: A Market-Economics Perspective," in *Public Choice and Constitutional Economics*, ed. Gwartney and Wagner for additional information on the importance of competition among government units.

LOOKING AHEAD

Democratic governments are a creation of the interactions of human beings. Public-choice analysis helps us better understand these interactions and the constitutional rules capable of improving the results achieved from government. As we consider trade among nations, how economies develop, and alternative forms of economic organization, public-choice analysis will again prove helpful to our understanding.

CHAPTER SUMMARY

1. It is fruitful to analyze the public sector in the same way we analyze the private sector. The public sector is an alternative to the market—it provides an alternative means of organizing production and/or distributing output.

2. Voters cast ballots, make political contributions, lobby, and adopt other political strategies to demand public-sector action. Other things constant, voters have a strong incentive to support the candidate who offers them the greatest gain relative to personal costs. Obtaining information is costly. Because group decision making breaks the link between the choice of the individual and the outcome of the issue, it is rational for voters to remain uninformed on many issues. Candidates are generally evaluated on the basis of a small subset of issues that are of the greatest personal importance to individual voters.

3. Under a democratic system, politicians have a strong incentive to follow a strategy that will enhance their chances of getting elected (and reelected). Political competition more or less forces politicians to focus on how their actions influence their support among voters.

4. Market failure presents government with an opportunity to undertake action that will result in additional benefits relative to costs. Other things constant, the greater the social loss resulting from the market failure, the stronger is the incentive for public-sector action. Ultimately, though, it is votes, not efficiency, that will determine political outcomes.

5. The distribution of the benefits and costs among voters influences how the political process works. When voters pay in proportion to the benefits they receive from a public-sector project, democratic decision making works quite well. Productive projects tend to be approved and counterproductive ones rejected. However, problems arise when the pattern of benefits among voters differs from the pattern of costs.

6. There is a strong incentive for political entrepreneurs to support special-interest issues and to make the issues difficult for the unorganized, largely uninformed majority to understand. Special-interest groups supply both financial and direct elective support to the politician. Constitutional rules are one way to limit the power of special interests to use the political process to achieve their interests at the expense of the group as a whole.

7. In government, where decision makers normally do not hold private property rights to the resources they control, the shortsightedness effect is another potential source of conflict between good politics and sound economics. Both voters and politicians tend to support projects that promise substantial current benefits at the expense of difficult-to-identify future costs. There is also a bias against legislation that involves immediate and easily identifiable costs but complex future benefits.

8. The economic incentive for operational efficiency is small for public-sector action. No individual or relatively small group of individuals can capture the gains derived from improved operational efficiency. There is no force analogous to the threat of bankruptcy in the private sector that will bring inefficient behavior to a halt. Since public-sector resources, including tax funds, are communally owned, their users are less likely than private resource owners to be cost-conscious.

9. A growing portion of public-sector activity involves income redistribution. Economic analysis indicates two potential sources of pressure for income redistribution: (a) the public-good nature of antipoverty efforts and (b) rent seeking. From the viewpoint of a vote-maximizing politician, there is incentive to support redistribution from unorganized to well-organized groups. Considerable income redistribution in the United States is of this type.

10. Keeping government from engaging in counterproductive activities while encouraging it to undertake things that it does well is difficult. Properly designed constitutional rules and restraints can help us achieve that objective.

CRITICAL ANALYSIS QUESTIONS

*1. "Voters should simply ignore political candidates who play ball with special-interest groups, and vote instead for candidates who will represent all the people when they are elected. Government will work far better when this happens." Evaluate this view.

*2. "Government can afford to take a long view when it needs to, while a private firm has a short-term outlook. Corporate officers, for example, typically care about the next three to six months, not the next 50 to 100 years. Government, not private firms, should own things like forests, that take decades to develop." Evaluate this view.

3. Suppose that you are part of a group of nature enthusiasts that has discovered a bog it would like to pre-

serve, although the site might soon be transferred to another use. Your group has some cash and could spend it several ways: It could buy the land or lease it, obtaining the right to manage it as it wishes. Alternatively, it could lobby the local authorities to regulate the land's use, preventing the current owner from changing the bog's condition or use. Using economic thinking, what analysis of the options could you provide to the group? The group wants to get the most for its money in the long run, and it prefers cooperation to conflict.

4. Do you think that advertising exerts more influence on the type of car chosen by a consumer than on the type of politician chosen by the same person? Explain your answer.

5. Do you think that the political process works to the advantage of the poor? Explain your answer. Are the poor well organized? Do they make substantial campaign contributions to candidates? Are they likely to be well informed? Is it surprising that only about one-sixth of the approximately $900 billion of cash income-transfer payments in the United States is directed toward the poor? Explain.

6. Which of the following public-sector actions are designed primarily to correct "market failure": (a) laws against fraud, (b) truth-in-lending legislation, (c) rate regulation in the telephone industry, (d) legislation setting emission-control standards, (e) subsidies for pure research, and (f) operation of the post office? Explain your answer.

*7. "When an economic function is turned over to the government, social cooperation replaces personal self-interest." Is this statement true? Why or why not?

*8. The liquor industry contributes a large share of the political funds to political contests on the state level. Yet its contributions to candidates for national office are minimal. Why do you think this is true? (Hint: Who regulates the liquor industry?)

9. One explanation for the shortsightedness effect in the public sector is that future voters cannot vote now to represent their future interests. Are the interests of future generations represented in market decisions? For example, if the price of chromium were expected to rise rapidly over the next 30 years due to increased scarcity, how could speculators grow rich while providing the next generation with more chromium at the expense of current consumers?

*10. What's wrong with this way of thinking? "Public policy is necessary to protect the average citizen from the power of vested interest groups. In the absence of government intervention, regulated industries, such as airlines, railroads, and trucking, would charge excessive prices, products would be unsafe, and the rich would oppress the poor. Government curbs the power of special-interest groups."

11. Are shoppers making decisions in the local supermarket likely to make better-informed choices than voters making choices in political races? Why or why not?

12. Why might members of Congress who work for special-interest and pork-barrel legislation under an unconstrained system of representative democracy nonetheless favor constitutional restraints limiting such spending?

13. "Since government-operated firms do not have to make a profit, they can usually produce at a lower cost and charge a lower price than privately owned enterprises." Evaluate this view.

14. "Governments can promote economic growth by using taxes and subsidies to direct investment funds toward high-tech, heavy manufacturing, and other growth industries that will enhance the future income of the nation." Evaluate this view.

*Asterisk denotes questions for which answers are given in Appendix B.

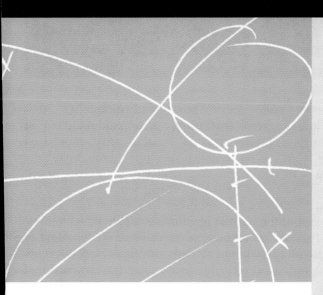

When alternatives are possible, social efficiency will be gained by channeling man's self-interest toward mutually compatible goals.

JAMES M. BUCHANAN[1]

---

[1]*What Should Economists Do?* (Indianapolis, Ind.: Liberty Press, 1979), p. 207.

CHAPTER FOCUS

■ What impact will the retirement of the baby-boom generation have on the social security system? Should current workers be offered a private investment option?

■ How has income inequality changed in recent years? Should the government take action to reduce inequality?

■ Why have health-care costs risen so much in recent years? What needs to be done to improve efficiency in the delivery of health-care services?

■ Should the United States adopt a flat tax system?

■ What were the major factors underlying the recent welfare reforms? Will these reforms work?

Five key policy issues are currently being widely discussed and debated in the United States. Background material and the nature of the policy debate is presented in this chapter for each of the issues. We anticipate that many instructors will focus on these issues while covering other text material, so the Critical Analysis Questions appear following each issue rather than at the end of the chapter. Additional readings on the topics are also provided. Because the focus is on economic policy, the usual summary at the conclusion of the chapter is omitted.

SOCIAL SECURITY: THE APPROACHING CRISIS AND WHAT SHOULD BE DONE ABOUT IT

Social security—officially known as Old Age and Survivors Insurance (OASI)—offers protection against the loss of income that usually accompanies old age or the death of a breadwinner. In spite of its official title, social security is not based on principles of insurance. Private insurance and pension programs invest the current premiums of customers in stocks and bonds, which finance the development of real assets. In turn, the assets generate income, which increases the value of the pension funds and provides the resources with which the pension fund (or insurance company) fulfills the future obligations made to its customers.

Social security does not follow this saving-and-investment model. Most of the funds flowing into the system are paid out to current retirees and survivors under the program. In essence, the social security system is an intergenerational income-transfer program. Taxes are collected from the present generation of workers and, for the most part, paid out to current beneficiaries.

The social security program is financed by a payroll tax of 5.26 percent levied on both the employee and the employer. (Additional payroll taxes finance Medicare and disability programs, which are sometimes considered part of the social security program.) Therefore, the total tax for the social security retirement program is equal to 10.52 percent of employee earnings. In 1995 the tax applied to all employee earnings up to $61,200. Thus, employees earning $61,200 or more paid $6,438 (counting both employee and employer payments) in social security taxes to finance the OASI retirement program.

When the program was initiated in 1935, the nation had lots of workers and few eligible retirees. As the number of workers per social security recipient declined through the years, higher and higher taxes per worker have been required just to maintain a constant level of benefits. Benefits for retirees have been raised several times, however, making the financial burden even larger.

Today's retirees paid lower tax rates for most of their working years, but are receiving the higher benefits. They typically are receiving real benefits of four or five times the amount they paid into the system, equivalent to a rate of return of more than 25 percent—far better than they could have done had they invested the funds privately.

In contrast, studies indicate the workers now paying for these large benefits will not do nearly as well. For example, those now at age 35 can expect to earn a real rate of return of only 2 or 3 percent on their social security tax dollars, less than what they could earn from personal investments. For two-earner couples just entering the labor force, the expected return from social security taxes is negative.

In summary, social security has been a good deal for current and past retirees. It is not, however, a very good deal for younger workers. Workers now entering the labor force would be better off if they could invest their tax dollars privately.

THE APPROACHING CRISIS

During the 15 years following the Second World War, the birthrate in the United States was very high. The baby boomers are now in their prime working years and their large numbers are an important factor explaining why the revenues from the social security tax currently exceed the expenditures. However, when these baby boomers move into the retirement phase of their life, the situation is going to change dramatically. As **Exhibit 31–1a** shows, the number of persons age 70 and over is expected to double between 1995 and 2030. The increase in the number of elderly will be particularly sharp following 2010. As **Exhibit 31–1b** illustrates, the number of workers per beneficiary is expected to decline from 3.2 in 1995 to only 2.0 by 2030.

Exhibit 31–2 shows how these demographic factors will influence the expenditures and tax revenues of the current pay-as-you-go system. With so few workers *per beneficiary*, the annual deficits of the social security system will become larger and larger during the period following 2010.

Large surpluses are planned for the system through 2010. These surpluses reduce the size of overall budget deficit and, *if other federal spending were constant,* they would reduce interest rates and increase private sector investment. Critics, however, argue that the surpluses conceal the true size of the deficit and reduce the pressure on Congress to hold the line on spending. To the extent the surpluses are spent on other things, they will fail to reduce interest rates and spur additional private investment that would help provide real income (and future tax revenue) to support the retirement benefits of the baby-boomer.

When the social security system enters its deficit years (beginning about 2010) and the bonds held in the trust funds are drawn down, the U.S. Treasury will have to raise taxes (or borrow more funds) in order to redeem these bonds. If the current real social security benefit levels are going to be maintained, a huge increase in taxes—both payroll and other taxes—will be required.

What might be done to reduce the burden accompanying the retirement of the baby-boom generation? A number of economists suggest that workers be allowed to opt out of the social security system, and instead use most or all of their social security tax contributions to purchase mutual fund shares, private annuities, and insurance funds backed with real assets. The individual's right to future social security system payments would be reduced accordingly. Several countries, facing crises much like ours, have allowed workers to choose this option.

MAKING PRIVATE SOCIAL SECURITY AN OPTION

The most widely discussed national program allowing workers to choose a private option was adopted in 1981 by the government of Chile. Workers in Chile could continue with the government social security program or contribute a

As part a illustrates, the number of persons over age 70 is expected to double between 1995 and 2030. As a result, the number of workers per beneficiary will decline from 3.2 in 1995 to 2.0 in 2030 (part b). Under a pay-as-you-go system, these trends will require either a sharp increase in taxes or a reduction in benefits (or both).

Sources: Bipartisan Commission on Entitlement and Tax Reform, *Final Report to the President* (Washington, D.C.: Government Printing Office, 1995), p. 13; and *1995 Annual Report of the Board of Trustees of the Federal Old Age and Survivors Insurance and Disability Insurance Trust Funds*, p. 21.

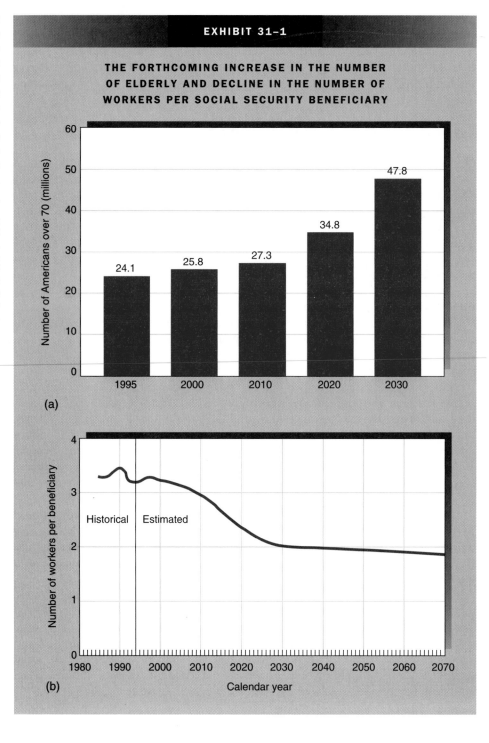

EXHIBIT 31–1

THE FORTHCOMING INCREASE IN THE NUMBER OF ELDERLY AND DECLINE IN THE NUMBER OF WORKERS PER SOCIAL SECURITY BENEFICIARY

minimum of 10 percent of their wages (up to 20 percent if they want earlier retirement or greater retirement benefits) to any of several private investment funds that would contract to deliver retirement and insurance benefits in place of the social security program. By 1995 workers could choose among 21 com-

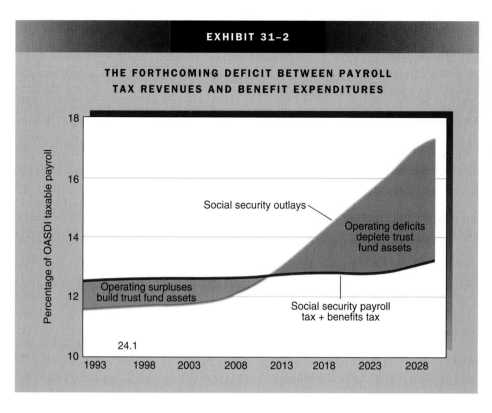

EXHIBIT 31–2

THE FORTHCOMING DEFICIT BETWEEN PAYROLL TAX REVENUES AND BENEFIT EXPENDITURES

Percentage of OASDI taxable payroll

Social security outlays

Operating deficits deplete trust fund assets

Operating surpluses build trust fund assets

Social security payroll tax + benefits tax

24.1

Given current payroll taxes and retirement benefit levels, the system will run larger and larger deficits during the 2010–2030 period.

Source: Bipartisan Commisson on Entitlement and Tax Reform, *Final Report to the President* (Washington, D.C.: Government Printing Office, 1995), p. 22.

peting "Pension Fund Administration" companies, or AFPs. Each AFP is a management firm with investment and operating policies regulated by the government. Each is a separate legal entity from the portfolio of stocks and bonds it manages. It receives a management fee, but has no claim on the portfolio that it manages. So if an AFP were to go bankrupt—although none has since the plan began—the holdings would remain to finance the future benefits to workers.

Prior to the start of the new system in 1981, the government of Chile had a large obligation to fund future worker retirement payments, just as the U.S. government now has. Worker and employer contributions totaled more than 20 percent of wages, but that was not enough. In 1980, general revenues (in addition to worker and employer contributions) paid 28 percent of the Chilean social security system's benefits. Ninety percent of all workers chose to leave the government system even though they had paid into it for years. They were issued "recognition bonds" that reflected the value of their previous contributions. The government pledged to buy back these bonds, with interest, from each worker upon retirement. Workers may either spend this supplemental money in retirement or use it to purchase annuities that pay a fixed amount until death. To finance the temporary, but costly transition to the new system, the government is selling off government-owned enterprises and real estate, both to increase their productivity and to raise revenue. The rest of the burden is spread over time and across the population through increased borrowing and higher general taxes.

Employers paid more than half in the old Chilean system, but the new system requires no contribution from them. Instead, they were required in 1981 to provide an 18 percent raise to workers, from which workers then paid their own contributions.

In the first 14 years of Chile's privatized pension plan, the economy has grown enough that, without subsidies from the government, the benefits provided (by the income and value of stocks and bonds purchased by the fund managers) are expected to be roughly 50 percent to 70 percent larger than under the old, subsidized program. The general retirement age is 65 for men and 60 for women, but a worker whose plan has accumulated enough assets may retire earlier and begin to draw on those assets. Early retirement funds are not available until the worker's fund has enough assets to pay at least 50 percent of the worker's average earnings over the previous ten years and 100 percent of the minimum wage. In addition to the private fund, the government also guarantees a minimum pension benefit to all workers under the new system, supplementing the worker's private benefits if necessary. This minimum benefit is 85 percent of the minimum wage, rising to 90 percent for retirees age 70 and over.

The new plan in Chile is one that forces workers to save, rather than forcing current workers to pay for the pensions of current retirees. In contrast with a pay-as-you-go system like that of the United States, Chilean workers have a property right to the funds paid into their new system.

The Chilean plan does not redistribute funds from one group to another, and thus it is less subject to political manipulation to help some favored groups at the expense of others. Importantly, from the workers' point of view, the benefits represent earnings and an investment backed by private assets, rather than a political favor to be lobbied from politicians and paid for by current workers and employers. The pension of the typical participating worker exceeds the value of that worker's house. As part-owners of the private economy, workers have an incentive to oppose inefficient regulations or excessive taxes placed on "business" that would hurt the economy and reduce their retirement funding. The change has helped to depoliticize the economy, as well as the pension system.

The forced savings plan provides added capital for the economy, as the management firms buy stocks and bonds to fund workers' future retirement benefits. The mandatory contributions, together with voluntary additions by workers seeking earlier retirement or larger benefits, have helped boost Chile's savings rate up to 26 percent of GDP, compared to less than 20 percent prior to adoption of the plan. Stimulated in part by the higher saving and investment, Chile's per capita GDP increased by 4.8 percent during the 1985–1994 period, one of the highest growth rates in the world.

The privatized plan that replaced a governmental social security program for more than 90 percent of Chile's workers has worked very well. It is not free of criticism, of course. Even its supporters recognize that it can only do as much for workers as the assets purchased by the funds allow. If the economy becomes depressed and the stocks and bonds earn little, or fall in value, then the retirement payments will be smaller. In fact, government regulations are being relaxed to allow funds to purchase some foreign assets to reduce that risk. Of course, under the old system, a failing economy would bring the same problem, because worker earnings and tax payments to the government would fall. And over the past 14 years, the new plan has built up so much value that one or two bad years would not cause significant problems for future retirees.

The new plan has also been criticized because its administration cost is larger than that for a single, monopoly plan like the old social security system. Despite that fact, the returns to the mostly private assets purchased by the fund managers have greatly outweighed the increased cost, and it seems clear that workers will receive far more for their dollars under the new plan.

Given the record of the Chilean experience, and the problems facing the social security system in the United States, it is no wonder that there are serious discussions today about changing our system to one that resembles the plan chosen voluntarily by most of the workers in Chile.

CRITICAL ANALYSIS QUESTIONS

1. Is the social security system based on the same principles as private insurance? Why or why not?

2. Why does the social security system face a crisis? Will the surplus that is currently being built up in the Social Security Trust Fund help to avert higher future taxes and/or benefit reductions when the baby boomers retire? Why or why not?

3. Do you think workers should be permitted to invest all or part of their social security contribution in private investment funds? What are the advantages and disadvantages of a private option system? If given the opportunity, would you choose the private option or stay with the current system? Why?

ADDITIONAL READINGS ON THIS TOPIC

Board of Trustees of the Federal Old-Age and Survivors Insurance and Disability Insurance Trust Funds, *1995 Annual Report.*

Ferrara, Peter. "Social Security and Medicare." In *Cato Handbook for Congress.* Washington: Cato Institute, 1995.

Piñera, José. "The Success of Chile's Privatized Social Security." *Cato Policy Report* 17 (July–August, 1995).

Robertson, A. Haeworth. "Social Security's Uncertain Future." In *Market Liberalism,* ed. David Boaz and Edward H. Crane. Washington: Cato Institute, 1993.

Steuerle, C. Eugene, and Jon M. Bakija. *Retooling Social Security for the 21st Century.* Washington: Urban Institute, 1994.

INCOME INEQUALITY: HOW HAS IT CHANGED AND WHAT MIGHT BE DONE TO REDUCE IT?

Various factors—including education, skill level, attitude, work effort, ambition, and luck—influence personal income and earnings. In turn, earnings differentials influence the efficiency of resource use and the incentive of individuals to develop their talents. Most people recognize that some differences in earnings are both fair and vitally important for economic progress.

Differences in family incomes also reflect the characteristics of families. Compared to low-income families, upper-income families are, on average, both larger in size and better educated. In the upper-income groups, it is more likely that (a) both parents are present, (b) the adults in the family are of prime working age (between 30 and 55 years old), and (c) more than one family member is working.

CHANGES IN INEQUALITY SINCE THE EARLY 1970s

Concern about inequality is likely to be more intense when it is increasing and when many believe that it is becoming more and more difficult for those with less education and fewer skills to earn a decent living. What has been happening to income inequality in the United States?

Exhibit 31–3 presents data on the proportion of total family income after taxes and income transfers (including in-kind food and housing benefits) received by each quintile of recipients arranged from low to high. The data are also adjusted for size of family. These data indicate that the degree of income inequality has been increasing. Look at the income share received by the top 20 percent of families. It was persistently higher in 1989, 1991, and 1992 than in 1979. Just the opposite was true for families in the bottom three quintiles. In every case, families in the bottom three quintiles had lower income shares in the late 1980s and early 1990s than in 1979.

Data like those of Exhibit 31–3 are unavailable prior to 1979. However, the *before-tax* figures suggest that the trend toward greater inequality started in the early 1970s. Economists have also analyzed hourly and monthly earnings figures. These also suggest that the degree of income inequality has increased significantly during the past 25 years, particularly during the 1980s.

The annual income figures of both families and individuals fluctuate considerably from year to year. In contrast, consumption expenditures are more stable as families borrow more (or save less) when their income is temporarily low. Correspondingly, they increase their saving rate when their income is temporarily high. As a result, some economists argue that consumption expenditures provide a better measure of long-term income than do annual income and wage data.

Exhibit 31–4 presents the household *expenditure* figures by quintile for 1972, 1981, and 1991. In contrast with the income figures, these data suggest that the increase in inequality during the past two decades has been quite small. The household expenditures of the top quintile were only slightly higher in 1991 than in 1972 (39.7 percent compared to 38.1 percent). Correspondingly, the share of total expenditures of the bottom quintile was virtually unchanged between 1972 and 1991. (Note: The expenditure data are not adjusted for family size, which increases with both income and expenditure level.)

Exhibit 31–5 presents the median income figures for college graduates and persons with post-college education compared to those for high school graduates. These data indicate that the earnings of the two higher-educated groups have increased considerably during the past two decades relative to those with only a high school education. Other studies have also shown that the incomes of those with more education and higher skill levels have grown more rapidly during the past two decades than have the incomes of their counterparts with less education and skill.

Although the precise magnitude of the change is a continuing subject of debate, the weight of the evidence indicates that there has been an increase in

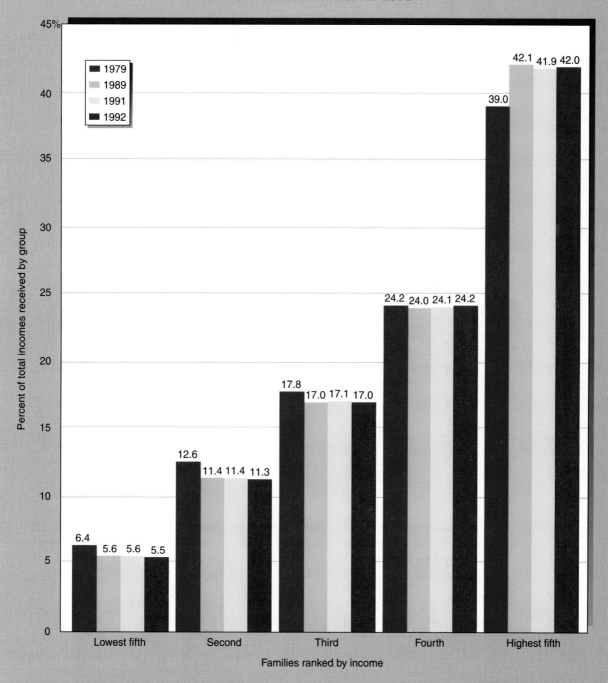

EXHIBIT 31–3

**SHARE OF TOTAL INCOME OF ALL FAMILIES AFTER
TAXES AND BENEFITS: 1979–1992**

Legend:
- 1979
- 1989
- 1991
- 1992

Y-axis: Percent of total incomes received by group

X-axis: Families ranked by income

	Lowest fifth	Second	Third	Fourth	Highest fifth
1979	6.4	12.6	17.8	24.2	39.0
1989	5.6	11.4	17.0	24.0	42.1
1991	5.6	11.4	17.1	24.1	41.9
1992	5.5	11.3	17.0	24.2	42.0

Here we show the share of family income after taxes and benefits (including in-kind food and housing benefits) by quintile. The data are adjusted for size of family. They indicate that the income share received by the top quintile rose during the 1980s, while the share received by each of the *bottom three quintiles declined.*

Source: Herbert Stein and Murray Foss, *The New Illustrated Guide to the American Economy*, Washington, D. C.: AEI Press, 1995, p. 109. The graphic was based on data from the U. S. Congressional Budget Office.

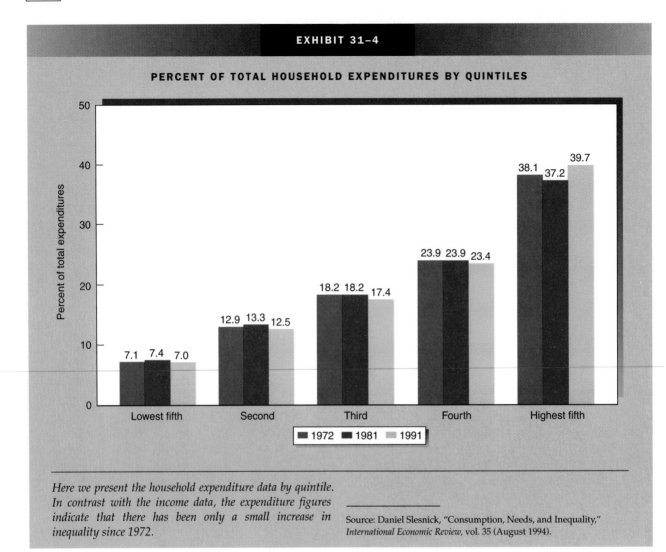

EXHIBIT 31-4

PERCENT OF TOTAL HOUSEHOLD EXPENDITURES BY QUINTILES

Here we present the household expenditure data by quintile. In contrast with the income data, the expenditure figures indicate that there has been only a small increase in inequality since 1972.

Source: Daniel Slesnick, "Consumption, Needs, and Inequality," *International Economic Review,* vol. 35 (August 1994).

economic inequality during the past two decades. Should the government attempt to do something to reverse this trend? Let us consider pro and con views of this question.

THE CASE FOR GOVERNMENT ACTION TO REDUCE INCOME INEQUALITY

The proponents of government action argue that the recent increase in economic inequality is unhealthy, unnecessary, and dangerous to the social stability of the nation. They generally believe that several factors have contributed to the increase in inequality. The list of culprits usually includes increased globalization of the economy, immigration, the reduction in the clout of labor unions, a decline in the real value of the minimum wage, and technological change. Thus, the agenda of those seeking to reduce inequality includes several, if not all, of the following proposals.

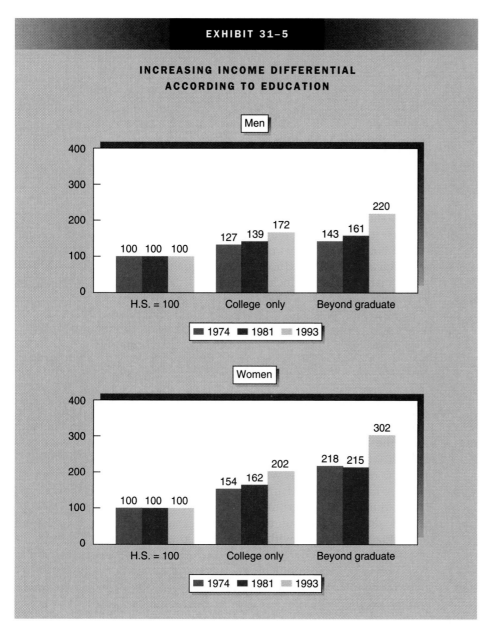

EXHIBIT 31–5

INCREASING INCOME DIFFERENTIAL ACCORDING TO EDUCATION

Men

400
300
200
100
0

| H.S. = 100 | College only | Beyond graduate |

100 100 100 · 127 139 172 · 143 161 220

■ 1974 ■ 1981 ▨ 1993

Women

400
300
200
100
0

| H.S. = 100 | College only | Beyond graduate |

100 100 100 · 154 162 202 · 218 215 302

■ 1974 ■ 1981 ▨ 1993

Here we show the annual income figures for college graduates and persons with post-graduate schooling compared to those with only a high school education. The income of the latter group is assigned a value of 100. Note how during the last two decades the incomes of those with more education have risen sharply compared to the incomes of the high school graduates. This was true for both men and women.

Sources: U.S. Department of Commerce, *Survey of Current Population, Series P-60*, "Trends in Income by Selected Characteristic, 1947–1988," and "Income, Poverty, and Valuation of Noncash Benefits: 1993."

1. *Erect trade barriers to protect American industries and prevent American firms from moving abroad.* American workers cannot compete with workers in India, China, and other less-developed countries making one or two dollars per day. Trade with such countries will merely drive our wages down to their levels. Neither can we stand idly by and allow American firms to move their plants to low-wage countries. Legislation should be adopted making it more difficult for firms to move abroad and restricting the import of goods from low-wage countries.

2. *Restrict immigration.* The entry of low-skill workers from less-developed countries like Mexico reduces employment opportunities and drives down the wages of Americans, particularly those with few skills. To keep this from happening, we need more restrictive immigration laws and stricter enforcement of existing laws prohibiting the employment of illegal immigrants.

3. *Promote unions.* Historically, unions have reduced the inequality of wages and salaries within firms. This compression of wage differentials helps to reduce the general level of income inequality. In recent years, union membership has declined as a share of the labor force. This trend needs to be reversed. Legislation making it easier for unions to organize and more difficult for firms to resist unionization should be adopted.

4. *Increase the minimum wage.* An increase in the minimum wage would boost the earnings of those at the bottom of the income distribution and thereby reduce income inequality. Studies indicate that the demand for labor, including low-skill labor, is highly inelastic. Therefore, the reduction in employment accompanying the wage increase would be small.

THE CASE AGAINST GOVERNMENT ACTION

In response, the opponents generally raise the following three points:

1. *The underlying forces are beyond the reach of government.* Consider the impact of technology. Even if it is true that new technologies have reduced the demand for blue collar production workers relative to those with computer, math, and communication skills, what is the government going to do about it? Does anyone really think that government could devise a sensible plan that would slow the rate of technological change or make it more advantageous to those with few skills? Do we really want to freeze technology and live in a time capsule? Improvements in technology help us get more out of resources and generate a larger output that helps both the rich and the poor. Any attempt to slow this process would be a big mistake.

2. *The proposed solutions will retard economic growth and reduce income levels across the board.* Trade restrictions, a higher minimum wage, and labor union monopolies all distort competitive markets and promote the inefficient use of resources. Let us consider each of them. Trade restraints will not only reduce our imports, they will also reduce exports. When foreigners sell less to us (because of import restrictions), they will acquire fewer of the dollars needed to buy from us. Thus, our exports will also fall. There will not be any increase in employment—jobs "saved" by the import restrictions will be offset with jobs lost in export industries. The primary result will be greater use of our resources to produce things that we do poorly as reflected by our inability to compete in international mar-

kets. A higher minimum wage will simply make it more difficult for inexperienced, low-skilled workers to get a start up the job ladder. Similarly, legislation promoting unions will generally reduce the job opportunities available to the least skilled workers.

3. *The pattern of economic outcomes is not nearly so important as the process that generates the outcomes.* The distribution of income reflects the choices and mutually advantageous exchanges between responsible adults. In a market economy, people who earn exceedingly high incomes do so because they supply goods, services, and resources that others value highly. Invariably, their actions improve the welfare of others. What is unfair about this process? If the process is fair, why should government try to change the outcomes?

CRITICAL ANALYSIS QUESTIONS

1. Can you think of alternatives other than the preceding ones that might reduce income inequality? What impact would these alternatives have on efficiency?

2. Indicate the pro and con points with which you agree. Explain why you agree with these points.

3. Prior to 1981, high-income Americans confronted top marginal tax rates of up to 70 percent. These high marginal tax rates were reduced sharply during the 1980s. What impact would these reductions have on the observed income of high-income Americans?

4. If people with more education now have higher incomes relative to those with less education, how will this affect the incentive to invest in education (human capital)? With time, might an increase in the supply of highly educated workers moderate or even reverse this trend? Why or why not?

ADDITIONAL READINGS ON THIS TOPIC

Borjas, George J. and Valerie A. Ramey. "Time-Series Evidence on the Source of Trends in Wage Inequality." *American Economic Review* 84 (May 1994), pp. 10–16.

Freeman, Richard B. "Are Your Wages Set in Beijing?" *The Journal of Economic Perspectives* 9, no. 3 (summer 1995).

Levy, Frank, and Richard J. Murnane, "U.S. Earnings Levels and Earnings Inequality: A Review of Recent Trends and Proposed Explanations." *Journal of Economic Literature* 30 (September 1992).

Richardson, J. David, "Income Inequality and Trade: How to Think, What to Conclude?" *The Journal of Economic Perspectives* 9, no. 3 (summer 1995).

Wood, Adrian, "How Trade Hurts Unskilled Workers." *The Journal of Economic Perspectives* 9, no. 3 (summer 1995).

HEALTH CARE: WHY IS IT A PROBLEM AND WHAT CAN BE DONE TO IMPROVE THE SITUATION?

The current debate about health care in the United States is driven by two factors: (1) rapidly rising costs and (2) people without health-care insurance. **Exhibit 31–6** presents data on medical care prices compared with all consumer prices for the 1960–1995 period. This ratio is set equal to 1.0 in 1960. If medical prices had risen at the same rate as other prices, this ratio would remain at 1.0. Obviously,

Here we show the price index for medical services divided by the overall consumer price index (CPI). This ratio was set equal to 1.0 in 1960. A ratio exceeding 1.0 indicates that medical care prices have risen more than the overall consumer price index. Since 1960, medical care prices have risen almost twice as much as the overall consumer price index.

Source: *Economic Report of the President*, various years.

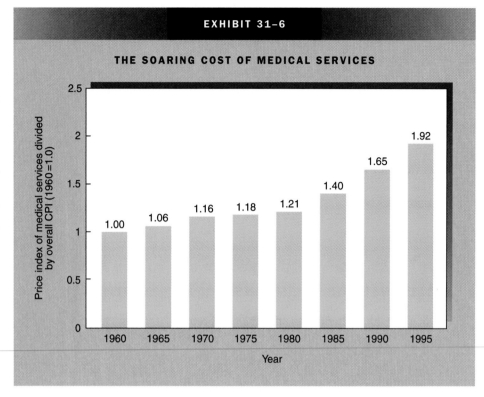

EXHIBIT 31-6

THE SOARING COST OF MEDICAL SERVICES

this has not been the case. The prices of medical services have increased far more rapidly than other prices, particularly since 1980. By 1995, the ratio of medical care prices to overall consumer prices was 1.92. This indicates that between 1960 and 1995, medical care prices rose almost twice as much as overall consumer prices.

No doubt propelled by the rising prices, spending on health care has also soared. As **Exhibit 31–7** illustrates, the total real (adjusted for inflation) expenditures on health-care services and supplies doubled between 1980 and 1993, after tripling between 1960 and 1980. *As a share of GDP, expenditures on health care rose from 4.5 percent in 1960 to 9.0 percent in 1980 and 13.5 percent in 1993. This indicates that Americans now spend three times as much of their total aggregate income on health care as was the case in 1960.*

A second major issue exists concerning the current health-care system: Approximately one out of every six Americans is without health-care insurance of any kind. In 1993, 70.2 percent of the U.S. population was covered by private health insurance, while another 14.5 percent was covered by government health insurance (Medicare and Medicaid). The remaining 15.3 percent of the U.S. population was not covered by any health insurance. Most of the uninsured remain that way for only a short period of time, however. As we will see in a moment, health insurance is much cheaper if purchased through an employer. Thus, many of those without health-care insurance are temporarily uninsured because they are changing jobs.

THE SOURCES OF HEALTH-CARE PAYMENTS

Health-care expenditures can be broken down by the three major sources of payment: (1) individual health-care consumer, (2) private insurance, or (3) government (mostly Medicare and Medicaid). Payments made by insurance companies and the government are called *third-party payments,* because they are made by someone other than the consumer (or the provider) of health care.

Exhibit 31–7 provides data on the share of health-care expenditures funded directly by the consumer as well as those funded through third-party payments. In 1960, almost half (49.4 percent) of all health-care expenditures were paid directly "out-of-pocket" by the consumers of health care. By 1993 this figure had declined to only 17.8 percent. During this same period, the share of health-care costs funded by both private insurance and the government increased sharply. In 1993, the government paid for 41.9 percent of all health-care spending, up from 20 percent in 1965. *Thus, a rather dramatic increase in third-party payments for health-care and an accompanying reduction in the share paid for directly by the individual consumer have occurred during the last three decades.*

Of course, individuals also pay for the health care funded by the government through taxes, and for the spending by insurance companies through insurance premiums. These payment forms, however, do not carry the same incentives as does out-of-pocket spending. In fact, many economists argue that this growth of third-party payments is a major source of the current problems in the health-care market.

EXHIBIT 31–7

NATIONAL HEALTH-CARE EXPENDITURES

	TOTAL HEALTH-CARE SPENDING		BY PAYMENT SOURCE (PERCENT OF TOTAL)		
YEAR	BILLIONS OF 1982–1984 DOLLARS	PERCENT OF GDP	PRIVATE OUT-OF-POCKET	PRIVATE INSURANCE	GOVERNMENT
1960	91.6	4.5	49.4	23.6	21.0
1965	132.1	5.8	45.7	26.2	20.0
1970	191.5	7.2	34.2	25.0	33.6
1975	246.5	8.1	29.5	26.4	37.9
1980	304.7	9.0	24.4	31.9	39.1
1985	403.8	10.4	22.7	35.5	38.0
1990	533.0	12.1	19.9	37.5	39.1
1993	611.9	13.5	17.8	37.0	41.9

Source: *Statistical Abstract of the United States,* 1995.

THE CURRENT STRUCTURE OF PRIVATE HEALTH INSURANCE

Why do people purchase health-care insurance? Health insurance provides protection against unforeseen major medical expenses. Health insurance companies charge premiums to their customers, and use the money to cover medical claims. Basically, individuals and families covered by health insurance pay premiums that reflect the average expenditures by all members of the group. Health insurance companies often charge some individuals higher (or lower) premiums based upon personal characteristics that reflect the person's health, such as the person's age or whether the person is a smoker. The important point to understand is this: The more medical claims filed by members, the higher the premiums the company must charge to all members.

Like automobile and life insurance, health insurance can be purchased directly from insurance companies. Most people who have private medical insurance, however, purchase it through their employer. Why is this the case? The government's tax treatment of medical insurance payments provides a major part of the answer. Under the current tax code, when employees use some of their wages to purchase medical insurance, these wages are not subject to income tax. In contrast, if employees were to take all their income in wages and purchase their health insurance directly from the insurance company of their choice, the income spent on health insurance would be taxable. Since income used to purchase health insurance is untaxed if the plan is purchased through an employer, but taxed if purchased as an individual, it is cheaper for employees to purchase health insurance through their employers.

When individuals purchase health insurance through their employer, a job change is accompanied by a temporary loss of insurance. The current tax code increases the number of people who experience these temporary periods without insurance because it encourages individuals to purchase insurance through their employer. Changing the tax code so that health insurance expenses were treated the same, whether purchased through an employer or as an individual, would eliminate this distortion. This could be accomplished either by making health-care insurance purchased by individuals tax deductible or by eliminating the current deductibility of the policies purchased through an employer.

ADVERSE INCENTIVES OF THIRD-PARTY PAYMENTS AND THE GROWTH OF HEALTH-CARE EXPENDITURES

When an individual is covered by health insurance (either private or funded by the government), a visit to a doctor costs the person very little in out-of-pocket expenses. Thus, the incentive for individuals to conserve on their purchases of health care is weakened by the presence of insurance. Because the consumers do not directly pay for the full cost of the service, they will have a tendency to overconsume health care. For example, assume a new treatment is invented that alleviates the symptoms of the common cold and costs $800. Would you be willing to pay $800 out-of-pocket for this procedure? Most people would not. Now, suppose that your insurance covered this new treatment so that you could obtain it free (or for a small fee of $5 or $10). Would you choose to get this new treatment now that it is covered by your insurance? Most of us probably would.

Furthermore, health-care providers get paid based on services performed. The more services they provide, the higher their income. Thus, your doctor would have every incentive to recommend that you have the $800 treatment to ease the symptoms of your cold. If you chose to have the treatment, the doctor would get paid for providing it. Thus, from both the provider and consumer standpoints, there is currently little incentive to conserve on the purchase of health-care services.

The current system that relies extensively on third-party payments and rewards suppliers on a fee-for-services basis leads to overconsumption of health-care services. This system increases the demand for health care, pushing prices upward, and leads to higher costs for both private health insurance and government health-care programs than would prevail under a system in which users shouldered a larger share of the cost.

OTHER FACTORS CONTRIBUTING TO RISING HEALTH-CARE COSTS

The growth in third-party payments and the accompanying increase in demand provide one explanation for the increasing health-care prices and expenditures of recent decades. Several other factors, however, have also contributed to the growth in health-care costs.

Technological change has perhaps been more rapid in the health-care industry than in any other area of our economy. Diseases that could not be treated just a decade ago can now be cured. Sophisticated equipment can now diagnose problems much more accurately than in the past. This increased technology has meant that the quality of health care has been rising rapidly. Part of the rapid increase in health-care prices (see Exhibit 31–6) reflects improvements in quality brought about by modern technology.

The aging of the U.S. population has also contributed to the rising health-care costs and expenditures of recent decades. The elderly purchase substantially more health care than persons in other age groups. Over the past 50 years the percentage of the population over age 65 has doubled. The increase in demand for medical care associated with this change has led to increasing health-care prices and expenditures. Unfortunately, this problem will continue to get worse as the baby-boom generation moves into the retirement phase of life in the near future (see the discussion of social security earlier in this chapter).

WHAT CAN BE DONE TO IMPROVE THE CURRENT SYSTEM?

The health-care issue has been a focal point of political debate during the 1990s. To date, however, only modest changes have been instituted. Several alternatives have been widely discussed.

HEALTH-CARE PRICE CONTROLS. Several reform proposals have espoused the use of health-care price controls as a means of controlling the rising costs. As we noted in Chapter 3, when the price of a good is fixed below market equilibrium, consumers will want to purchase more than suppliers are willing to provide. Shortages and a deterioration in the quality of the good or service are the predictable side effects. There is no reason to believe that health care is an exception. Price controls on health-care services will lead to waiting lines and other forms of non-price rationing. A government bureaucracy would then have to be established to monitor quality and determine who would receive treatment now and who would have to wait.

Canada has a government-operated system that uses price controls as a means of controlling costs. The results are consistent with economic theory. For example, there are often long waiting lists for major surgeries that require specialists (such as open heart surgery). As a result, Canadians often come to the United States to have procedures of this type performed.

PROVIDING OPTIONS TO STANDARD MEDICAL INSURANCE. As we have discussed, the standard insurance plan provides little incentive for either the consumer or provider to economize. Health maintenance organizations (HMOs) provide one option to these standard plans. The use of HMOs has been growing rapidly and the number of persons enrolled in HMOs has doubled over the past decade. The idea behind an HMO is to give the doctor an incentive to conserve on medical treatments. A doctor participating in an HMO gets a fixed sum of money for each person enrolled with the HMO, no matter how much medical care the patient consumes. Because the doctor gets a fixed fee, she or he presumably has an incentive to provide any specific treatment in the most efficient manner possible.

This concentration on cost reduction has led many people to fear that doctors, trying to save money, may fail to give necessary treatments. Incentives exist, however, to prevent HMOs from cutting necessary treatments. First, if a doctor fails to sufficiently treat a person for an illness, that illness may become more severe and the HMO will incur all the resulting higher medical costs. This is one reason that HMOs usually cover many types of preventive care expenses. If an HMO can spend money in a way that prevents a member from having a major medical illness, the HMO will save money in the long run. A second incentive to prevent HMOs from cutting necessary treatments is the competition for members between HMOs. If an HMO provides its members with inadequate care, they will tend to shift to other health-care providers, including other HMOs.

Most economists believe that the health-care market would work better if consumers could more easily shift among potential providers (and alternative insurers) and if they had more incentive to shop and economize on the use of health care. As we previously mentioned, removing the current tax-favored treatment of insurance purchased through employers would increase the consumer's ability to shift among insurers and providers, including HMOs. However, as long as individual consumers pay only a small fraction of their medical costs, competitive pressure will be relatively weak and the incentive to overconsume will be strong. The following reform is designed to help correct this problem.

MEDICAL SAVINGS ACCOUNTS (MSAs). This reform would increase the incentive of consumers to shop and shift toward those providers offering them the most value for their health-care dollar. The idea behind MSAs is quite simple. Individuals would purchase what is called a *catastrophic insurance plan*—one that covers only medical expenses above a high cutoff level—say, those above $2,000 during a year. Because the cost of this insurance would be much less, the savings in insurance premiums could be put into a savings account that the person could use to pay for minor medical expenses. Any money left in this account at the end of the year could either be taken in cash, or rolled over into the account for next year.

Because any money spent out of this account would reduce the amount that could be taken in cash at the end of the year, individual consumers would have a strong incentive to conserve on medical expenses. Thus, they would "shop" among alternative providers. In turn, this shopping would increase the intensity of competition among suppliers, which would tend to reduce the cost of medical care for everyone. In addition, since fewer individuals would waste money on unnecessary treatments (such as the $800 common cold treatment), the demand for medical care would decline, placing downward pressure on prices. Furthermore, the lower prices would tend to reduce medical insurance premiums.

CONCLUDING THOUGHTS

The baby boomers are moving toward retirement. As they do so, the demand for medical care will increase, making reform of the current system and modification of its perverse incentives even more imperative. The main problems that must be dealt with are the weak incentives for providers to control cost and for consumers to conserve on their use of medical care. This issue is sure to remain a focal point of public policy debates in the future.

CRITICAL ANALYSIS QUESTIONS

1. *As a share of GDP,* the United States now spends almost twice as much on medical care as was true in 1970. Why have health-care expenditures risen so rapidly? What has happened to the amount of "third-party" medical payments as a share of total spending on medical care during this period? Do you think the size of the third-party payments influences medical expenditures? Why or why not?

2. Exhibit 31–1a indicates that there will be a big increase in the number of elderly people between now and 2030. How will this increase influence expenditures on medical care?

3. Explain how medical savings accounts would work. How would they alter the consumer's incentive to conserve on the use of health-care services? What impact would they have on the competitiveness of the health-care market? Do you think they are a good idea? Why or why not?

ADDITIONAL READINGS ON THIS TOPIC

Baker, L. C. and K. S. Corts. "The Effects of HMOs on Conventional Insurance Premiums: Theory and Evidence." National Bureau of Economic Research Working Paper No. 5356 (November 1995).

Dilulio, John J., Donald F. Kettl, and Richard P. Nathan. "Making Health Reform Work: the View from the States." *The Brookings Review* (summer 1994).

Feldstein, M. and J. Gruber. "A Major Risk Approach to Health Insurance Reform." In *Tax Policy and the Economy* 9, ed. J. M. Poterba Cambridge, MIT Press, 1995.

Gruber, J. and B. C. Madrian. "Non-employment and Health Insurance Coverage." National Bureau of Economic Research Working Paper No. 5228 (August 1995).

Goodman, John C. and Gerald L. Musgrave. *Patient Power: Solving's America's Health Care Crisis.* Washington, D. C.: Cato Institute, 1992.

Litow, Mark. "Saving the Medicare System with Medical Savings Accounts." *Policy Briefing No. 199.* Dallas, Texas: National Center for Policy Analysis, September, 1995.

THE FLAT TAX: IS IT AN IDEA WHOSE TIME HAS COME?

The replacement of the current federal individual income tax with a "flat tax" has recently become a major issue of debate. It has been the central focus of several recent political campaigns. Various flat tax proposals have been widely discussed in the media. This section describes the basic structure of a flat tax and discusses the arguments for and against this major reform of the federal income tax structure.

THE STRUCTURE OF TAX RATES UNDER A FLAT TAX

The most commonly cited plan for the structure of a flat tax is that of Robert Hall and Alvin Rabushka.[2] Their plan would allow a family of four to earn up to $25,500 per year without owing any income tax. All income above this amount would be taxed at a flat rate of 19 percent. Although the *marginal tax rate* of 19 percent would be the same whether a person makes $250,000 or $35,000, the *average tax rate* would still increase with income because of the $25,500 exemption. Recall from Chapter 5 that the marginal tax rate is the percent of an *additional* dollar of income that must be paid in taxes, while the average tax rate is the percent of all income paid in taxes. The marginal and average tax rates associated with Hall and Rabushka's plan for a family of four are shown graphically in **Exhibit 31–8**.

As an example, consider the computation of the income tax for a family of four making $250,000. The family would have taxable income of $224,500 after

With a personal exemption, the average tax rate would increase with income (see dotted line) for a flat tax.

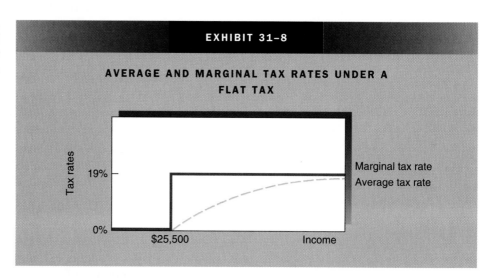

EXHIBIT 31–8

AVERAGE AND MARGINAL TAX RATES UNDER A FLAT TAX

Tax rates

19%

0%

$25,500   Income

Marginal tax rate
Average tax rate

---

[2]Robert E. Hall and Alvin Rabushka, *The Flat Tax*, 2d ed. (Stanford, Calif.: The Hoover Institution Press, 1995).

subtracting the $25,500 exemption. The $224,500 of taxable income would be taxed at a marginal rate of 19 percent, making the family's income tax payment $42,655. The family's average tax rate is calculated as the total tax of $42,655 divided by total family income of $250,000. This amounts to an average tax rate of just over 17 percent. Contrast this with a family of four making $35,000 in income. This family would have taxable income of $9,500 after subtracting the $25,500 exemption. The total tax due for this family would be 19 percent of taxable income, or $1,805. This family's average tax rate would be just over 5 percent. *Although the flat tax has a constant marginal tax rate, the average tax rate rises with income because of the standard exemption. Therefore, like the current tax system, the structure of the flat tax is progressive.*

COMPARISON OF TAX RATES AND TAX REVENUES WITH CURRENT INCOME TAX

As recently as the early 1960s, the top marginal income tax rate was as high as 91 percent. During the 1960s, the top marginal income tax rate fell to 70 percent, and, during the tax reforms of the 1980s, the top marginal income tax rate was reduced as low as 28 percent. The rates began to rise again in the 1990s, and the top marginal rate is now back up to 39.6 percent. The top marginal tax rates are applicable in the highest tax bracket. As of 1995, the lowest marginal tax rate (15 percent) for a family of four started at an income of $16,550. As taxable income rises, marginal tax rates of 28 percent, 31 percent, and 36 percent are applied in the middle tax brackets. With a flat tax rate of 19 percent, most Americans would face a lower marginal tax rate than under the current system, but the tax structure would be less progressive than is currently the case.

Although the marginal tax rate of 19 percent is lower than the rate currently paid by most people, the flat tax reform proposal is designed to generate the same amount of tax revenue. The flat rate can be lower than existing income tax rates because the flat tax reform also includes the removal of most tax deductions. As the result of the deductions and exemptions, less than half of all personal income in the United States is taxed under current law. Under the flat tax, items such as charitable contributions, medical expenses, moving expenses, and mortgage interest payments would no longer be deductible for tax purposes. Because the removal of these tax deductions would increase the taxable income base, a lower tax rate can be used to raise the same amount of revenue.

THE ELIMINATION OF DOUBLE TAXATION

The flat tax reform also proposes changes in the tax code to eliminate the double taxation of savings, investment, and business income present under the current system. In the current tax system, when a corporation makes a profit, that profit is taxed under the corporation income tax at a rate of approximately 35 percent. The profits (less taxes) are then either paid out as dividends to stockholders or reinvested by the company. The amount paid out in dividends is counted as personal income that is then taxed again under the individual income tax at rates as high as 39.6 percent. The amount the company keeps and reinvests will tend to increase the value of the company (and its stock price). The rising stock prices must be reported by shareholders as capital gains that are also taxed under the personal income tax. As the result of this double taxation, many taxpayers pay combined federal tax rates of approximately 60 percent on income generated by business activities. Since many states also tax personal and corporate income, the aggregate marginal rates are even higher.

Interest income (such as that from a savings account) is also subject to double taxation under the current tax system. Income saved by an individual is taxed when it is earned and then, if it is saved, the interest on the savings is taxed again as interest income. In contrast, when the initial income is spent on consumption, it is taxed only once.

The flat tax would eliminate this double taxation since income from dividends, capital gains, and interest would not be subject to the personal income tax. Business income would be taxed only once, when it is generated as business or corporate income. At the personal level, taxable income would consist only of wage, salary, and pension income. In turn, this would make it possible to simplify the personal income tax return greatly and substantially reduce the administrative and compliance cost of the system.

THE CASE FOR THE FLAT TAX

Proponents of the flat tax cite several advantages over the current system. First, the flat tax would be much simpler to pay and collect. It would eliminate the pages of tax forms that individuals must now fill out and replace them with something much like a postcard. This simplification results from the removal of loopholes, deductions, and the double taxation of the current tax code. With no tax deductions, no need to document income from interest, dividends, and capital gains, and a flat tax rate of 19 percent, an individual tax return could be as short as 12 lines! Compared with the current system, the taxpayers' savings of both time and money would be huge—something between $20 billion and $30 billion.

Removal of the deductions would reduce the distortions in consumption patterns of the current system. When an item is tax deductible, it becomes cheaper for a taxpayer to purchase relative to goods that are not deductible. For example, consider a person in the 28 percent marginal tax bracket who purchases a $100 business dinner that is tax deductible. This person's *after-tax* earnings fall by only $72 for spending this $100. In other words, if the person had not purchased the $100 business dinner, his or her take-home pay would have been only $72 larger. Because tax-deductible items are less expensive relative to items that are not deductible, people purchase more tax-deductible items than is efficient.

Proponents argue that adoption of a flat tax would stimulate economic activity. Both reductions in the top marginal tax rates and the elimination of the double taxation of corporate income would increase the incentive to work and invest. In addition, a flat tax would lower interest rates and stimulate investment. Elimination of the home mortgage interest deduction would reduce the demand for loanable funds, while the exemption of interest income from the personal income tax would increase the supply of savings. This would place downward pressure on interest rates. In turn, the lower interest rates would reduce the cost of loanable funds and thereby encourage investment.

Proponents of the flat tax also believe that the elimination of the double taxation on business income, coupled with the removal of the many personal deductions, would make the tax system fairer. Because the amount of dollars taken in tax deductions usually increases with income, high-income families gain more from these deductions than do those with lower incomes. For example, a poor family that does not own a home receives no benefits from the home mortgage interest deduction. According to the proponents of the flat tax, removal of these exemptions would increase the fairness of the tax code because it would eliminate these preferential tax breaks that are most beneficial to high-income taxpayers.

THE CASE AGAINST THE FLAT TAX

Two major groups oppose the flat tax. The first is composed of those who believe that it would be less progressive and therefore less fair than the current system. Clearly, high-income taxpayers would pay lower *marginal rates.* No doubt, many would also pay lower average tax rates. Perhaps even more significant, many opponents argue that the exclusion of interest and dividends from personal income taxation would mean that wealthy "coupon clippers" would pay lower personal income tax rates than many low- and middle-income taxpayers. If one does not consider the business taxes, some would avoid taxes entirely. Opponents ask: "How can a system with this characteristic be fair?"

The second group that opposes the flat tax is composed of those individuals who would be hurt by the removal of loopholes and deductions. Many lower- and middle-income recipients with large deductible expenditures under the current system would pay more under a flat tax system. For example, consider a person with a large home mortgage and substantial charitable contributions. The value of these deductions under the current system might well more than offset the larger personal exemptions of a flat rate system. Furthermore, charitable contributions would probably decline. This would hurt organizations dependent on these contributions and those benefiting from their support. Finally, there are those who benefit from the complexity of the current system. Many tax accountants and lobbyists, for example, might lose their jobs or experience a substantial reduction in income if the flat tax were adopted.

CONCLUSIONS ABOUT THE FLAT TAX

With regard to the positive issues, general agreement exists that a flat tax would simplify the tax system and substantially reduce the paperwork, compliance, and administrative costs. Most economists also believe that it would lower interest rates and stimulate economic activity. There is also general agreement that, while elimination of the double taxation would reduce distortions, it would also make the tax system less progressive. Are the benefits of greater simplicity and growth worth the cost of less progressivity? This is a central issue Americans will continue to debate in the years ahead.

CRITICAL ANALYSIS QUESTIONS

1. With a flat tax, people with high incomes would clearly pay lower marginal tax rates. Does this necessarily mean that less tax revenue would be collected from them? Why or why not?

2. Do you think the double taxation of business income—once when it is earned by a corporation and again when it is paid to stockholders as dividends—is fair? Do businesses (in contrast with individuals) really pay taxes? Who really bears the burden of taxes imposed on businesses?

3. Do you think the flat tax is a good idea? Why or why not? What do you think is the major advantage of a flat tax system? What is the major disadvantage?

ADDITIONAL READINGS ON THIS TOPIC

Ballentine, J. Gregory. "The Structure of the Tax System versus the Level of Taxation: An Evaluation of the 1986 Act." *The Journal of Economic Perspectives* 6, no. 1 (winter 1992).

Blum, Walter J., and Harry Kalven. *The Uneasy Case for Progressive Taxation.* Chicago: University of Chicago Press, 1953.

Bosworth, Barry, and Gary Burtless. "Effects of Tax Reform on Labor Supply, Investment, and Saving." *The Journal of Economic Perspectives* 6, no. 1 (winter 1992).

Hall, Robert E., and Alvin Rabushka. *The Flat Tax.* Stanford, Calif.: Hoover Institution Press, 1995.

National Commission of Economic Growth and Tax Reform. *"Unleashing America's Potential."* January 1996.

WELFARE REFORM: CAN WE HELP THE POOR WITHOUT GENERATING SUBSTANTIAL ADVERSE SIDE EFFECTS?

Three decades ago considerable optimism existed that increased spending on income transfer programs would substantially reduce, if not eliminate, poverty. *As a share of GDP,* expenditures on *means-tested* transfer benefits jumped from 1.5 percent in 1965 to 3.0 percent in 1975. (Note: Only those with low incomes qualify for means-tested transfers.) Since 1975, expenditures on means-tested benefits have continued upward, reaching 4 percent of GDP in 1992. Despite this increase in spending, poverty continues at a high rate. There has been little change in the overall official poverty rate since 1970. In fact, the poverty rate of the nonelderly has actually increased slightly during the past 25 years.

Alarmingly, the poverty rate of children has been moving higher. As **Exhibit 31–9** *indicates, the official poverty rate of children rose from 14.9 percent in 1970 to 21.8 percent in 1994.* Even after adjustment for the valuation of food, housing, medical, and other noncash benefits, the poverty rate of children was 15.6 percent in 1994. This indicates that, even when the value of in-kind benefits is counted as income, approximately one out of every six children in America was living in poverty in 1994.

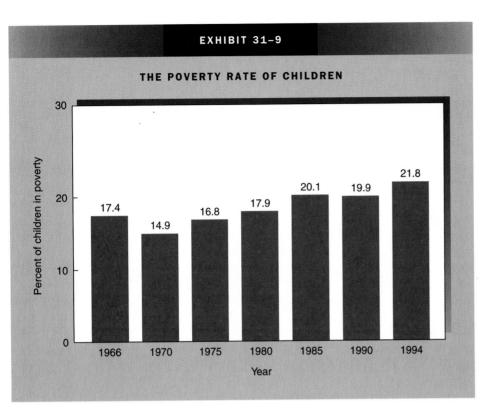

EXHIBIT 31-9

THE POVERTY RATE OF CHILDREN

The poverty rate of children rose from 14.9 percent in 1970 to 21.8 percent in 1994.

Source: *Statistical Abstract of the United States,* various years.

WHY HAVE THE CURRENT PROGRAMS BEEN INEFFECTIVE?

Several factors have contributed to the ineffectiveness of the current welfare system. *First, the high implicit marginal tax rates that accompany the current transfer system make it very difficult for low-income families to increase their earnings and thereby escape poverty.* If a poor family earns more, their transfer benefits are reduced. Thus, additional earnings do not increase the family's spendable income by very much. **Exhibit 31-10** uses the actual data for a single mother in Pennsylvania to illustrate this point. If the mother does not work, the family qualifies for $7,548 of benefits in the form of cash transfers, food stamps, housing, and medical benefits. If family earnings were to increase from $2,000 to $4,000, disposable income (after taxes and transfers) would increase by only $367 (from $8,923 to $9,290). In this income range, the family faces an implicit marginal tax rate of 81.7 percent. This situation continues up the income scale. In fact, if the family earned $15,000 rather than zero, its disposable income would increase by only $5,058 (from $7,548 to $12,606) after the additional taxes (primarily the payroll tax) and the reduction in transfers are taken into account. On average, the family confronts an implicit marginal tax rate of 66 percent. If the mother got a full-time job at $7.50 per hour and worked all year to earn $15,000, she would get to keep only one-third of additional earnings. In the mid-1990s the situation was quite similar in other states. Given this incentive structure,

---

EXHIBIT 31–10

EARNINGS AND DISPOSABLE INCOME FOR A SINGLE MOTHER WITH TWO CHILDREN IN PENNSYLVANIA

ANNUAL EARNINGS	DISPOSABLE INCOME	IMPLICIT MARGINAL TAX RATE	AVERAGE TAX RATE ON EARNINGS	SHARE OF EARNINGS INDIVIDUAL GETS TO KEEP
$ 0	$ 7,548	—	—	—
2,000	8,923	31.2	31.2	68.8
4,000	9,290	81.7	57.4	42.6
5,000	9,473	81.7	61.5	38.5
6,000	9,657	81.6	64.8	35.2
7,000	9,840	81.7	67.3	32.7
8,000	9,956	88.4	69.9	30.1
9,000	10,523	43.3	66.9	33.1
10,000	10,937	58.6	66.1	33.9
15,000	12,606	66.6	66.3	33.7

Source: Congressional Research Service, as published in the 1994 Green Book, p. 335.

even able-bodied adults in welfare families—particularly those headed by a single parent—often found it unattractive to work.[3]

Second, when the poor opt out of the labor force because of the high implicit marginal tax rates, declining skills further limit their ability to escape poverty. Failure to participate in the labor force exerts a secondary effect: One's skills and work habits deteriorate. Individuals who do not use their skills for extended periods of time will find it difficult to compete with otherwise similar individuals with continuous labor-force participation. The long-term consequence of an incentive structure that encourages nonwork is highly destructive. With the passage of time, welfare recipients—even those with substantial potential—become less and less able to support themselves.

Third, the collapse of the two-parent family has substantially increased the poverty rate in recent decades. In 1994, the poverty rate of single-parent families was five times higher than the rate for husband-wife families (38.6 percent compared to 7.4 percent). Children born to a single mother are seven times more likely to be poor than those born into a husband-wife family. Some argue that the current welfare system encourages family dissolution. The evidence on this topic is mixed. This issue aside, however, there is no doubt that the rising incidence of divorce, single-parent families, and births to unmarried mothers has contributed to the increase in poverty of recent years.

---

[3]In 1994, the household head did not work at all during the year in three-fourths of the single-parent families with poverty level incomes.

REFORM PROPOSALS

What can be done to make the system work more effectively? Several alternatives have been put forth to deal with the situation. In 1996, legislation was passed instituting some of these reforms and providing states with the flexibility to enact others.

STRICT WORK REQUIREMENT.   This reform would require all able-bodied people, including mothers with small children, to work as a condition for the receipt of government-financed benefits. When the welfare system was initiated, most mothers stayed home with the children, particularly if they were preschoolers. This is no longer true. More than half of the mothers with small children are now in the labor force. Thus, proponents of a strict work requirement ask: "How can we ask families with working mothers to pay taxes to support welfare benefits without also requiring the recipients to work?"

A work requirement would greatly reduce some of the worst side effects of the current system. With a work requirement, recipients would no longer have the option of staying home and drawing benefits. This would make welfare less attractive relative to work, and thereby reduce the average length of time recipients are likely to spend on welfare. A work requirement would also increase the incentive of recipients to search for marginally more attractive jobs and move up the job ladder. If you have to work in order to receive the benefits, you might as well work at the most attractive job you can obtain. Thus, the tendency for basic workplace skills to deteriorate from nonuse would be minimized.

Two major objections are generally raised against a strict work requirement: (1) finding jobs for workers, most of whom have few skills, and (2) provision of child care. When recipients cannot find private sector employment at market wage rates, it will be necessary to provide them with training, wage subsidies, and/or government jobs. Mothers with small children will be unable to work unless child care is available. The proponents argue that these two obstacles can be overcome simultaneously. Beneficiaries of welfare programs can be required to work in child care centers—either those provided by the government or operated by private suppliers. This will both increase the availability of child care and employ the welfare recipients.

In the short term, a successful workfare program may actually require additional government expenditures. Since it would have fewer negative side effects, however, one would expect cost to decline with the passage of time.

HOLD FATHERS MORE ACCOUNTABLE.   Several states are now making a more intense effort to hold fathers, including those never married to the child's mother, more responsible for the support of their children. In the past, fathers often escaped child support payments by moving to another state. The federal government now helps track down delinquent fathers in other states and uses other legal channels to obtain court-mandated child support payments. Some would like to see more done in this area. A special tax (for example, a 5 percent payroll tax) could be levied on fathers of children receiving welfare benefits. Alternatively, they could be required to work for free at public service jobs. Proponents of this view argue that just as we impose taxes on polluters who impose costs on society, we should do the same to irresponsible fathers who foist the cost of their actions onto society.

Of course, there are limits to this approach. Many of those who abandon their children or father a child out of wedlock have little or no earnings. This is not always the case, however. Proponents of strong action in this area argue that it will remove some of the glamour from macho behavior and thereby help to reduce the incidence of births to unmarried mothers in the future.

TIME LIMIT FOR WELFARE RECIPIENTS. Many believe that welfare to able-bodied adults should be temporary—that is, short-term assistance to bridge the gap while recipients get their lives turned around. In 1994, almost half (48 percent) of the welfare recipients had been receiving the benefits for five years or more. Limitations on the length of time recipients can draw benefits was a central component of welfare reform legislation adopted in 1996. The legislation prohibits able-bodied adults from drawing benefits for more than five years over the course of their lifetime. It also requires most heads of families drawing benefits to begin work within two years. Failure to do so would lead to the loss of benefits. Able-bodied adults with no dependents must work at least 20 hours per week in order to remain eligible for food stamps for more than three months (during any three-year period).

CONCLUDING THOUGHTS

In addition to imposing various time limitations and work requirements, the 1996 legislation also provides states with block grants while increasing their leeway for experimentation. It will be interesting to follow the implementation of this act. States are likely to institute additional reforms and, at least for a time, move in vastly different policy directions.

In economics, the results of a change often differ between the short run and the long run. This is likely to be the case with welfare reform. It would not be surprising to observe an initial increase in the poverty rate if strict work requirements and time limitations for program benefits are enforced. With time, however, the results are likely to be more positive. One thing is for sure: Analysis of alternative approaches will be an important area of future research as we continue to search for more effective policy alternatives in this area.

CRITICAL ANALYSIS QUESTIONS

1. Which reforms do you think would be most effective at reducing the poverty rate? Why? Can you think of additional reforms that would be effective in this area? Explain.

2. If two unmarried teenagers have a child, who should be responsible for the child's support? Is it fair to expect the taxpayer to shoulder these costs?

3. Why is the implicit marginal tax rate confronted by low-income welfare recipients so high? How will the work requirements of the 1996 welfare reform legislation affect the marginal tax rates confronted by low-income welfare recipients?

ADDITIONAL READINGS ON THIS TOPIC

Burtless, Gary. "Paychecks or Welfare Checks: Can AFDC Recipients Support Themselves?" *The Brookings Review* (fall 1994).

Haveman, Robert, and Barbara Wolfe. "Children's Prospects and Children's Policy." *The Journal of Economic Perspectives* 7, no. 4 (fall 1993).

Lerman, Robert I. "Child Support Policies." *The Journal of Economic Perspectives* 7, no. 1 (winter 1993).

Nightingale, Demetra, and Robert Haveman, eds. *The Work Alternative: Welfare Reform and the Realities of the Job Market.* Washington, D.C.: Urban Institute, 1995.

EXHIBIT VI–A

Here we illustrate the size of the trade sector as a share of the economy for various countries grouped by size. Note that the trade sector is generally larger for smaller (less populous) countries. The trade sectors of Singapore, Hong Kong, Thailand, Philippines, South Korea, and Indonesia are large compared to countries of similar size.

[a]Population more than 120 million.
[b]Population between 40 and 65 million.
[c]Population less than 10 million.

SOURCE: World Bank, *World Development Report, 1995*, Table 9, and International Monetary Fund, *Monthly International Financial Statistics* (December, 1995).

SIZE OF TRADE SECTOR OF SELECTED COUNTRIES: 1970 AND 1994

Large Countries[a]
Exports as Percent of Total Output

Mid-size Countries[b]

Small Countries[c]

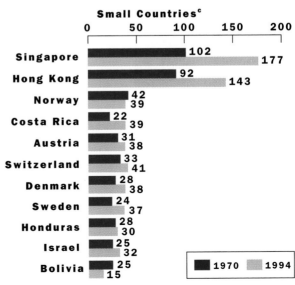

Between 1980 and 1994, the growth rates of per capita GDP of China, South Korea, Thailand, Taiwan, Singapore, Hong Kong, Malaysia, and Indonesia were the highest in the world. The performance of these Asian countries is a success story of economic development. In contrast, the growth rates of Argentina, Brazil, Mexico, Venezuela, and Nigeria have been a major disappointment.

Why did the former group grow rapidly while the latter stagnated?

SOURCE: Derived from World Bank, *World Tables, 1995.*

EXHIBIT VI-B

THE GROWTH RATE OF PER CAPITA REAL GDP DURING 1980–1994 FOR SELECTED HIGH AND LOW GROWTH RATE COUNTRIES

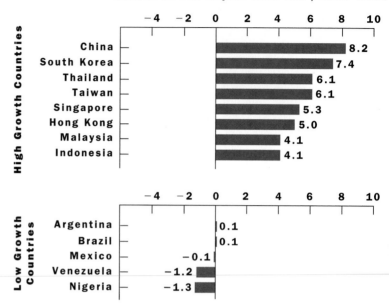

Growth of Per Capita Real GDP, 1980–1994

This exhibit presents data on investment as a share of GDP. Since capital formation is an important source of growth, economic theory predicts that the investment rate of the high growth countries will be larger. As the graph indicates, this is indeed the case.

SOURCE: Derived from International Monetary Fund, *International Financial Statistics Yearbook, 1995.*

EXHIBIT VI-C

INVESTMENT AS A SHARE OF GDP (1980–1994) FOR THE HIGH AND LOW GROWTH COUNTRIES

Investment as a Percent of GDP: 1980–1994

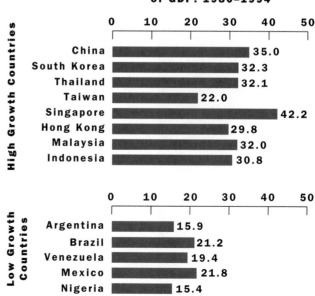

EXHIBIT VI–D

Here we compare the inflation rates of the high and low growth countries of Exhibit VI-B. Clearly, the high-growth countries followed monetary policies that were far more consistent with price stability.

SOURCE: Derived from International Monetary Fund, *International Financial Statistics Yearbook, 1995.*

THE AVERAGE ANNUAL INFLATION RATE (1980–1994) OF THE HIGH AND LOW GROWTH COUNTRIES

Average Annual Rate of Inflation, 1980–1994

High Growth Countries

China	8.8
South Korea	7.3
Thailand	4.4
Taiwan	3.2
Singapore	2.6
Hong Kong	6.2
Malaysia	4.0
Indonesia	8.5

Low Growth Countries

Argentina	349.6
Brazil	575.1
Venezuela	26.4
Mexico	54.5
Nigeria	27.3

EXHIBIT VI–E

Economic theory indicates that gains from specialization and trade are an important potential source of growth. Thus, one would expect the higher growth economies to generally have fewer trade restraints and therefore larger trade sectors. This is precisely the case.

SOURCE: The size of the trade sector is equal to exports plus imports divided by 2 as a share of GDP. Derived from International Monetary Fund, *International Financial Statistics Yearbook, 1995.*

THE SIZE OF THE INTERNATIONAL TRADE SECTOR AS A SHARE OF GDP A COMPARISON OF THE HIGH AND LOW GROWTH COUNTRIES

Size of Trade Sector

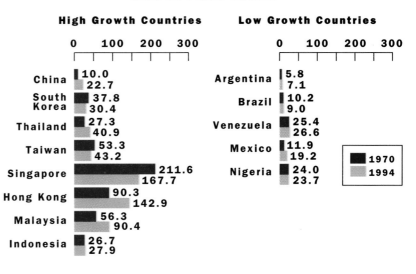

High Growth Countries

	1970	1994
China	10.0	22.7
South Korea	37.8	30.4
Thailand	27.3	40.9
Taiwan	53.3	43.2
Singapore	211.6	167.7
Hong Kong	90.3	142.9
Malaysia	56.3	90.4
Indonesia	26.7	27.9

Low Growth Countries

	1970	1994
Argentina	5.8	7.1
Brazil	10.2	9.0
Venezuela	25.4	26.6
Mexico	11.9	19.2
Nigeria	24.0	23.7

- ■ 1970
- ▨ 1994

■ How does the size of the international trade sector vary across countries?

■ What are the major import and export products of the United States? Which countries are the major trading partners of the United States?

■ Under what conditions can a nation gain from international trade?

■ What impact do trade restrictions have on an economy?

■ Do trade restrictions create jobs? Does trade with low-wage countries depress wage rates in high-wage countries like the United States?

■ Why do nations adopt trade restrictions?

■ How does the economic record of countries that impose trade restrictions compare with that of countries following free-trade policies?

Free trade consists simply in letting people buy and sell as they want to buy and sell. It is protection [trade restrictions] that requires force, for it consists in preventing people from doing what they want to do. Protective tariffs are as much applications of force as are blockading squadrons, and their objective is the same—to prevent trade. The difference between the two is that blockading squadrons are a means whereby nations seek to prevent their enemies from trading; protective tariffs are a means whereby nations attempt to prevent their own people from trading.

HENRY GEORGE, 1886[1]

---

[1]Henry George, *Protection or Free Trade* (1886; reprint, New York: Robert Schalkenbach Foundation, 1980), p. 47.

W e live in a shrinking world. The breakfast of many Americans includes bananas from Honduras, coffee from Brazil, or hot chocolate made from Nigerian cocoa beans. Americans often drive a car produced by a Japanese or European manufacturer that consumes gasoline refined from petroleum extracted in Saudi Arabia or Venezuela. Similarly, many work for companies that sell a substantial amount of their products to foreigners. Trade statistics reflect these factors. The volume of international trade, enhanced by improved transportation and communications, has grown rapidly in recent years. Approximately 21 percent of the world's total output is now sold in a country other than that in which it was produced—double the figure of three decades ago.

Perhaps surprising to some, most international trade is not between the governments of the nations involved but rather between individuals (or business firms) that happen to be located in different countries. International trade, like other voluntary exchange, results because both the buyer and the seller expect to gain and generally do. If both parties did not expect to gain, they would not agree to the exchange.

SIZE OF THE TRADE SECTOR

The size of the trade sector varies substantially among nations. Some of the difference is due to size of country. For industries in which economies of scale are important, the domestic market of a less-populated country may not be large enough to support cost-efficient firms. Therefore, in small countries, firms in such industries will tend to export a larger share of their output, and consumers will be more likely to purchase goods produced abroad. As a result, the size of the trade sector as a share of the economy tends to be inversely related to the population of the country.

Even among countries of similar size, there is considerable variation in the size of the trade sector. (See Illustrated Exhibit VI–A at the beginning of this section.) Among the countries with a large population (120 million or more), the trade sector is largest in Indonesia. In 1994 exports accounted for 26 percent of the Indonesian output, more than twice the figure for the United States, India, and Japan. The trade sector of the latter three constitutes approximately 10 percent of their total output. The trade sector of Brazil is the smallest among the large countries. Exports summed to only 9 percent of the Brazilian GDP in 1994.

Among the mid-size countries (population between 40 million and 65 million), the trade sectors of Thailand, the Philippines, and South Korea are larger than those of Egypt, the United Kingdom, France, Italy, and Turkey. As a share of domestic output, Singapore and Hong Kong have the largest international trade sectors in the world. Both of these small countries import large quantities of raw materials and unfinished goods and manufacture them into products that are often exported abroad. Therefore, the gross exports of these two vibrant trade centers actually exceed their gross domestic product.

THE TRADE SECTOR OF THE UNITED STATES

Exhibit 32–1 summarizes the leading products that the United States imports and exports. The United States both imports and exports a substantial quantity of food and agricultural products. The major imported products, however, are

EXHIBIT 32–1

MAJOR MERCHANDISE EXPORT AND IMPORT PRODUCTS OF THE UNITED STATES BY CATEGORIES, 1994

EXPORTS	VALUE (IN BILLIONS)	PERCENT OF TOTAL EXPORTS	IMPORTS	VALUE (IN BILLIONS)	PERCENT OF TOTAL IMPORTS
FOOD AND AGRICULTURAL PRODUCTS			FOOD AND AGRICULTURAL PRODUCTS		
Vegetables and fruits	$ 6.8	1.3%	Fish products	$ 6.6	1.0%
Cigarettes and tobacco	6.3	1.2	Vegetables and fruits	6.1	0.9
Meat products	5.2	1.0	Meat products	2.6	0.4
Soybeans	4.4	0.8	Coffee	2.2	0.3
Corn	4.2	0.8	Alcoholic beverages	1.8	0.3
Wheat	4.1	0.8	MINERALS AND RAW MATERIALS		
MINERALS AND RAW MATERIALS			Oil and petroleum	48.7	7.3
Organic chemicals	12.8	2.5	Organic chemicals	10.8	1.6
Plastics	12.5	2.4	Cork, wood, and lumber	6.7	1.0
Coal	3.0	0.6	MANUFACTURED GOODS		
MANUFACTURED GOODS			Automobiles (incl. trucks)	71.0	10.7
Electrical machinery	44.3	8.6	Electrical machinery	57.7	8.7
Industrial machinery	41.5	8.1	Office machinery	52.1	7.9
Office machinery	30.9	6.0	Industrial machinery	38.1	5.7
Airplanes and parts	28.7	5.6	Clothing	36.7	5.5
Automobile parts	21.2	4.1	Telecommunications equipment		
Power-generating machinery	20.3	4.0	(incl. TV sets)	32.5	4.9
Automobiles			Automobile parts	19.6	3.0
(incl. trucks)	19.6	3.8	Power-generating machinery	19.6	2.9
Scientific instruments	16.5	3.2	Footwear (shoes)	11.7	1.8
Telecommunications equipment	15.8	3.1	Paper	9.1	1.4
TOTAL	$512.5	100.0	TOTAL	$663.8	100.0

Source: *Statistical Abstract of the United States, 1995*, Table 1342.

generally quite different from primary products that are exported. Reflecting the temperate climate and fertile agricultural lands of the United States, vegetables and fruits, corn, soybeans, and wheat are the primary food and agricultural exports. In contrast, the primary imported food products include fish, coffee, and alcoholic beverages. The mineral and raw material products exported are also quite different from those that are imported. In this category, chemicals, plastics, and coal compose the primary export goods, while crude oil, petroleum, and wood products are the major imports. In the manufacturing area, automobiles and machines are major items among both imports and exports. The markets for automobiles, computer equipment, televisions, and telephone equipment are worldwide. Therefore, in these markets U.S. producers sell substantial quantities abroad, while, at the same time, many U.S. consumers purchase these goods from foreign manufacturers.

Clearly, international trade exerts a different impact on some industries than on others. In some industries, domestic producers find it very difficult to compete with their rivals abroad. For example, approximately 90 percent of the shoes purchased by Americans and nearly two-thirds of the radio and television sets, watches, and motorcycles are produced abroad. Imports also supply a high percentage of the clothing and textile products, paper, and toys consumed in the United States. On the other hand, a large proportion of the aircraft, power-generating equipment, scientific instruments, construction equipment, and fertilizers produced in the United States is exported to purchasers abroad.

With which countries does the United States trade the most? As **Exhibit 32–2** illustrates, Canada and Japan head the list. In 1994 approximately one-third of U.S. exports were sold to purchasers in Canada and Japan. Almost 40 percent of U.S. imports were produced in those two countries. Mexico, the nations of the European Union (particularly Germany, the United Kingdom, France, and Italy), China, and the four "Asian tigers" (Taiwan, South Korea, Hong Kong, and Singapore) were also among the leading trading partners of the United States. During the 1970s, U.S. trade with petroleum-exporting countries such as Saudi Arabia and Venezuela grew rapidly. However, the volume of trade with these nations declined as the price of crude oil fell in the 1980s.

GAINS FROM SPECIALIZATION AND TRADE

If a foreign country can supply us with a commodity cheaper than we ourselves can make it, [we had] better buy it of them with some part of our own industry, employed in a way in which we have some advantage.

ADAM SMITH[2]

Comparative advantage
The ability to produce a good at a lower opportunity cost than others can produce it. Relative costs determine comparative advantage.

As we discussed in Chapter 2, the law of **comparative advantage** explains why a group of individuals, regions, or nations can gain from specialization and

---

[2]Adam Smith, *An Inquiry into the Nature and Causes of the Wealth of Nations* (1776; Cannan's ed., Chicago: University of Chicago Press, 1976), pp. 478–479.

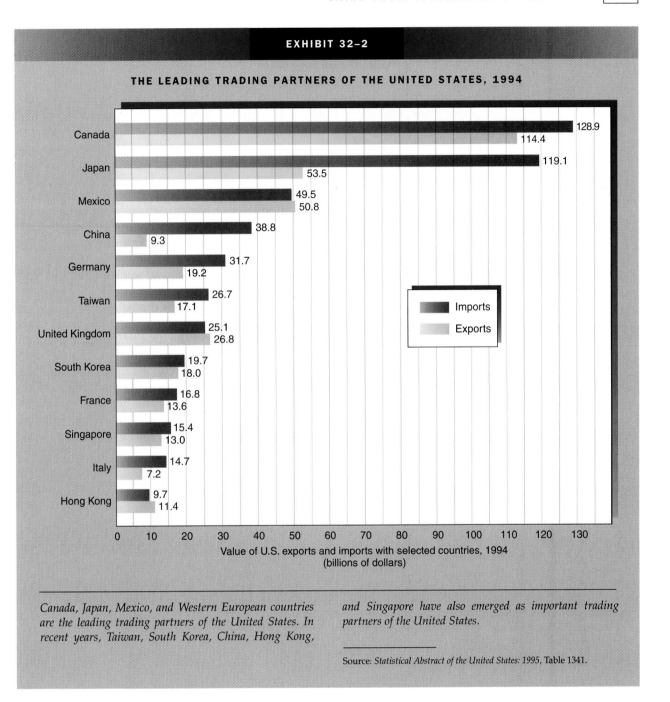

EXHIBIT 32–2

THE LEADING TRADING PARTNERS OF THE UNITED STATES, 1994

Country	Imports	Exports
Canada	128.9	114.4
Japan	119.1	53.5
Mexico	49.5	50.8
China	38.8	9.3
Germany	31.7	19.2
Taiwan	26.7	17.1
United Kingdom	25.1	26.8
South Korea	19.7	18.0
France	16.8	13.6
Singapore	15.4	13.0
Italy	14.7	7.2
Hong Kong	9.7	11.4

Value of U.S. exports and imports with selected countries, 1994
(billions of dollars)

Canada, Japan, Mexico, and Western European countries are the leading trading partners of the United States. In recent years, Taiwan, South Korea, China, Hong Kong, and Singapore have also emerged as important trading partners of the United States.

Source: *Statistical Abstract of the United States: 1995*, Table 1341.

exchange. Trading partners can gain if each specializes in the production of the goods for which it is a low-opportunity-cost producer and trades for those goods for which it is a high-opportunity-cost producer. Specialization in the area of one's comparative advantage minimizes the cost of production and leads to maximum joint output.

International trade leads to mutual gain because it allows each country to specialize more fully in the production of those things that it does best. Labor-force skills and resource endowments differ substantially across countries. These differences influence costs. Therefore, a good that is quite costly to produce in one country may be economically produced in another country. For example, the warm, moist climate of Brazil and Colombia enhances the economical production of coffee. Countries like Saudi Arabia and Venezuela with rich oil fields can produce petroleum cheaply. Countries with an abundance of fertile land, like Canada and Australia, are able to produce products like wheat, feed grains, and beef at a low cost. In contrast, land is scarce in Japan, a nation with a highly skilled labor force. The Japanese, therefore, specialize in manufacturing, using their comparative advantage to produce cameras, automobiles, and electronic products for export. With international trade, each country can gain by specializing in the production of goods that it can produce economically and using the proceeds to import goods that would be expensive to produce domestically.

It is easy to see why trade and specialization expand joint output and lead to mutual gain when the resource bases of regions differ substantially. However, even when resource differences among nations are less dramatic, mutual gain is possible. Since failure to comprehend the principle of mutual gains from trade is often a source of "fuzzy thinking," we will take the time to illustrate the principle in detail.

To keep things simple, we will consider a case involving only two countries, the United States and Japan, and two products, food and clothing. Furthermore, we will assume that labor is the only resource used to produce these products. In addition, since we want to illustrate that gains from trade are nearly always possible, we are going to assume that Japan has an **absolute advantage**—that the Japanese workers are more efficient than the Americans—in the production of both commodities. **Exhibit 32–3** illustrates this situation. Perhaps due to their prior experience or higher skill level, Japanese workers can produce three units

Absolute advantage

A situation in which a nation, as the result of its previous experience and/or natural endowments, can produce more of a good (with the same amount of resources) than another nation.

Columns 1 and 2 indicate the daily output of either food or clothing of each worker in the United States and Japan. If the United States moves 3 workers from the clothing industry to the food industry, it can produce 6 more units of food and 3 fewer units of clothing. Similarly, if Japan moves 1 worker from food to clothing, clothing output will increase by 9 units while food output will decline by 3 units. With this reallocation of labor, the United States and Japan are able to increase their aggregate output of both food (3 additional units) and clothing (6 additional units).

EXHIBIT 32–3

GAINS FROM SPECIALIZATION AND TRADE

COUNTRY	OUTPUT PER WORKER DAY		POTENTIAL CHANGE IN OUTPUT[a]	
	FOOD (1)	CLOTHING (2)	FOOD (3)	CLOTHING (4)
United States	2	1	+6	−3
Japan	3	9	−3	+9
Change in Total Output			+3	+6

[a]Change in output if the United States shifts three workers from the clothing to the food industry and if Japan shifts one worker from the food to the clothing industry.

of food per day, compared with only two units per day for U.S. workers. Similarly, Japanese workers are able to produce nine units of clothing per day, compared to one unit of clothing per day for U.S. workers.

Let us consider the following question: Can two countries gain from trade if one of them can produce both goods with fewer resources? Perhaps surprising to some, the answer is yes. As long as *relative* production costs of the two goods differ between Japan and the United States, gains from trade will be possible. Consider what would happen if the United States shifted three workers from the clothing industry to the food industry. This reallocation of labor would allow the United States to expand its food output by six units (two units per worker), while clothing output would decline by three units (one unit per worker). Suppose Japan reallocates labor in the opposite direction. When Japan moves one worker from the food industry to the clothing industry, Japanese clothing production expands by nine units while food output declines by three units. The exhibit shows that this reallocation of labor *within* the two countries has increased their joint output by three units of food and six units of clothing.

The source of this increase in output is straightforward: Aggregate output expands because the reallocation of labor permits each country to specialize more fully in the production of those goods that it can produce at a *relatively* low cost. Our old friend, the opportunity-cost concept, reveals the low-cost producer of each good. If Japanese workers produce one additional unit of food, they sacrifice the production of three units of clothing. Therefore, in Japan the opportunity cost of one unit of food is three units of clothing. On the other hand, one unit of food in the United States can be produced at an opportunity cost of only one-half unit of clothing. American workers are therefore the low-opportunity-cost producers of food, even though they cannot produce as much food per day as the Japanese workers. Simultaneously, Japan is the low-opportunity-cost producer of clothing. The opportunity cost of producing a unit of clothing in Japan is only one-third unit of food, compared to two units of food in the United States. The reallocation of labor illustrated in Exhibit 32–3 expanded joint output because it moved resources in both countries toward areas where they had a comparative advantage.

As long as the relative costs of producing the two goods differ in the two countries, gains from specialization and trade will be possible. When this is the case, each country will find it cheaper to trade for goods that can be produced only at a high opportunity cost. For example, both countries can gain if the United States trades food to Japan for clothing at a trading ratio greater than one unit of food equals one-half unit of clothing (the U.S. opportunity cost of food) but less than one unit of food equals three units of clothing (the Japanese opportunity cost of food). Any trading ratio between these two extremes will permit the United States to acquire clothing more cheaply than it could be produced within the country and simultaneously permit Japan to acquire food more cheaply than it could be produced domestically.

HOW TRADE EXPANDS CONSUMPTION POSSIBILITIES

Since trade permits nations to expand their joint output, it also allows each nation to expand its consumption possibilities. The production-possibilities concept can be used to illustrate this point. Suppose that there were 200 million workers in the United States and 50 million in Japan. Given these figures and the productivity of workers indicated in Exhibit 32–3, the production-possibilities curves for the two countries are presented in **Exhibit 32–4.** If the United States used all of its 200 million workers in the food industry, it could produce 400 million units of food per day (two units per worker) and zero units of clothing. Alternatively, if the United States used all its workers to produce clothing, daily output would be 200 million units of clothing and no food. Intermediate output combinations along the production-possibilities line (*MN*) intersecting these two extreme points also could be achievable. For example, the United States could produce 150 million units of clothing and 100 million units of food (point *US₁*).

Part b of Exhibit 32–4 illustrates the production possibilities of the 50 million Japanese workers. Japan could produce 450 million units of clothing and no food (*R*), 150 million units of food and no clothing (*S*), or various intermediate combinations, like 225 million units of clothing and 75 million units of food (*J₁*). The slope of the production-possibilities constraint reflects the opportunity cost of food relative to clothing. Since Japan is the high-opportunity-cost producer of food, its production-possibilities constraint is steeper than the constraint for the United States.

In the absence of trade, the consumption of each country is constrained by the country's production possibilities. Trade, however, expands the consumption possibilities of both. As we previously indicated, both countries can gain from specialization if the United States trades food to Japan at a price greater than one unit of food equals one-half unit of clothing but less than one unit of food equals three units of clothing. Suppose that they agree on an intermediate price of one unit of food equals one unit of clothing. As part a of **Exhibit 32–5** illus-

Here we illustrate the daily production possibilities of a U.S. labor force of 200 million workers and a Japanese labor force of 50 million workers, given the cost of producing food and clothing presented in Exhibit 32–3. In the absence of trade, consumption possibilities will be restricted to points such as US₁ in the United States and J₁ in Japan along the production possibilities curve of each country.

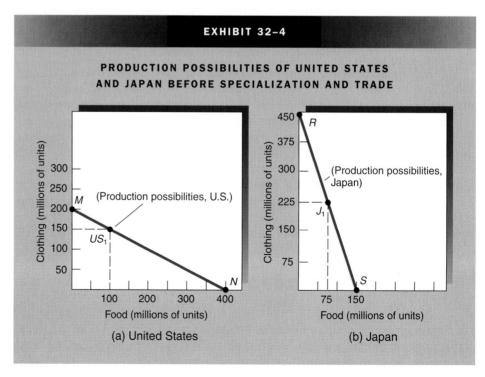

EXHIBIT 32–4

PRODUCTION POSSIBILITIES OF UNITED STATES AND JAPAN BEFORE SPECIALIZATION AND TRADE

(a) United States

(b) Japan

EXHIBIT 32–5

CONSUMPTION POSSIBILITIES WITH TRADE

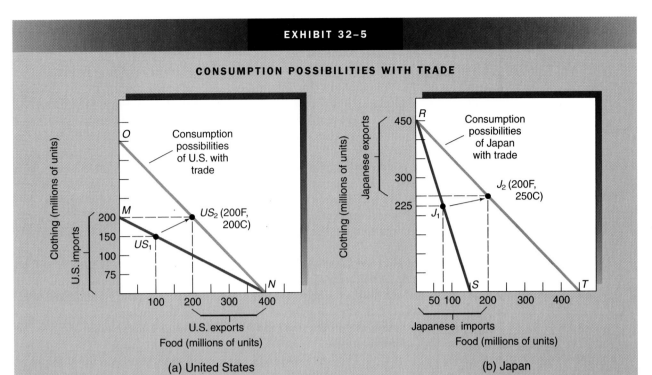

(a) United States

(b) Japan

With specialization and trade, the consumption possibilities of a country can be expanded. If the United States can trade one unit of clothing for one unit of food, it can specialize in the production of food and consume along the ON line (rather than its original production-possibilities constraint, MN). Similarly, when Japan is able to trade one unit of clothing for one unit of food, it can specialize in the production of clothing and consume any combination along the line RT. For example, with specialization and trade, the United States could increase its consumption from US_1 to US_2, gaining 50 million units of clothing and 100 million units of food. Simultaneously, Japan could increase consumption from J_1 to J_2, a gain of 125 million units of food and 25 million units of clothing.

trates, when the United States specializes in the production of food (where it has a comparative advantage) and trades food for clothing (at the price ratio where one unit of food equals one unit of clothing), it can consume along the line ON. If the United States insisted on self-sufficiency, it would be restricted to consumption possibilities like US_1 (100 million units of food and 150 million units of clothing) along its production-possibilities constraint of MN. With trade, however, the United States can achieve combinations such as US_2 (200 million units of food and 200 million units of clothing) along the line ON. Trade permits the United States to expand its consumption of both goods.

Simultaneously, Japan is also able to expand its consumption of both goods when it is able to trade clothing for food at the one-to-one price ratio. As part b of Exhibit 32–5 illustrates, Japan can specialize in the production of clothing and consume along the constraint RT when it can trade one unit of clothing for one unit of food. Without trade, consumption in Japan would be limited to points like J_1 (75 million units of food and 225 million units of clothing) along the line

RS. With trade, however, it is able to consume combinations like J_2 (200 million units of food and 250 million units of clothing) along the constraint *RT.*

Look what happens when Japan specializes in clothing and the United States specializes in food. Japan can produce 450 million units of clothing, export 200 million to the United States (for 200 million units of food), and still have 250 million units of clothing remaining for domestic consumption. Simultaneously, the United States can produce 400 million units of food, export 200 million to Japan (for 200 million units of clothing), and still have 200 million units of food left for domestic consumption. After specialization and trade, the United States is able to consume at the point of US_2 and Japan at point J_2, consumption levels that would otherwise be unattainable. Specialization and exchange permit the two countries to expand their joint output, and, as a result, both countries can increase their consumption of both commodities.

The implications of the law of comparative advantage are clear: Trade between nations will lead to an expansion in total output and mutual gain for each trading partner when each country specializes in the production of goods it can produce at a relatively low cost and uses the proceeds to buy goods that it could produce only at a high cost. It is comparative advantage that matters. As long as there is some variation in the relative opportunity cost of goods across countries, each country will always have a comparative advantage in the production of some goods.

SOME REAL WORLD CONSIDERATIONS

In order to keep things simple, we ignored the potential importance of transportation costs, which, of course, reduce the potential gains from trade. Sometimes transportation and other transaction costs, both real and artificially imposed, exceed the potential for mutual gain. In this case, exchange does not occur.

We also assumed that the cost of producing each good was constant in each country. This is seldom the case. Beyond some level of production, the opportunity cost of producing a good will often increase as a country produces more and more of it. Rising marginal costs as the output of a good expands will limit the degree to which a country will specialize in the production of a good. This situation would be depicted by a production-possibilities curve that was convex, or bowed out from the origin. In cases of increasing cost there will still be gains from trade but there need not be complete specialization.

ADDITIONAL SOURCES OF GAIN FROM INTERNATIONAL TRADE

In addition to the gains derived from specialization in areas of comparative advantage, there are two other important sources of gains from international trade.

GAINS FROM ECONOMIES OF SCALE AND EXPANSION IN THE SIZE OF THE MARKET. *International trade allows both domestic producers and consumers to gain from reductions in per-unit costs that often accompany large-scale production, marketing, and distribution.* Trade expands the potential size of the market available to both domestic and foreign firms. When economies of scale are important in an industry, successful domestic firms will be able to produce larger outputs and achieve lower costs than would be possible if they were unable to sell abroad. This point is particularly important for small countries. For example, textile manufacturers in Hong Kong, Taiwan, and South Korea would have much higher costs if they could not sell abroad. The domestic textile markets of these countries are too small to support large, low-cost firms in this industry. With international trade, however, textile firms in these countries operate at a large scale and compete quite effectively in the world market.

International trade also benefits domestic consumers by permitting them to purchase from large-scale producers abroad. The aircraft industry provides a vivid illustration of this point. Given the huge design and engineering costs, the domestic market of almost all countries would be substantially less than the quantity required for the efficient production of jet planes. With international trade, however, consumers around the world are able to purchase planes economically from a large-scale producer, such as Boeing or McDonnell Douglas.

GAINS FROM MORE COMPETITIVE MARKETS. *International trade promotes competition in domestic markets and allows consumers to purchase a wide variety of goods at economical prices.* Competition from abroad helps keep domestic producers on their toes. It forces them to improve the quality of their products and keep costs low. At the same time, the variety of goods that are available from abroad provides consumers with a much broader array of choices than would be available in the absence of international trade.

The recent experience of the U.S. automobile industry illustrates this point. Faced with stiff competition from Japanese firms, U.S. automobile manufacturers worked hard to improve the quality of their vehicles. As a result, the reliability of the automobiles and light trucks available to American consumers—including those vehicles produced by domestic manufacturers—is almost certainly higher than would have been the case in the absence of competition from abroad.

EXPORT-IMPORT LINK

Doubts about the merits of international trade often result from a failure to consider all the consequences. Why are other nations willing to export their goods to the United States? So they can obtain dollars. Yes, but why do they want dollars? Would foreigners be willing to continue exporting oil, radios, watches, cameras, automobiles, and thousands of other valuable products to Americans in exchange for pieces of paper? If so, Americans could all be semiretired, spending only an occasional workday at the dollar printing-press office! Of course, foreigners are not so naive. They trade goods for dollars so they can use the dollars to import goods and purchase ownership rights to U.S. assets.

Exports, broadly perceived to include goods, services, and assets, provide the buying power that makes it possible for a nation to import. If a nation did not export goods, it would not have the foreign currency that is required for the purchase of imports. Similarly, if a nation did not import goods, foreigners would not have the purchasing power to buy that nation's export products. Therefore, if imports decline, so will the demand for the nation's exports. Exports and imports are closely linked.

SUPPLY, DEMAND, AND INTERNATIONAL TRADE

How does international trade affect prices and output levels in domestic markets? Supply and demand analysis will help us answer this question. Given our modern transportation and communication networks, the market for many commodities is worldwide. When a product can be transported long distances at a low cost (relative to its value), the domestic price of the product is in effect determined by the forces of supply and demand in the worldwide market.

Using soybeans as an example, **Exhibit 32–6** illustrates this relationship between the domestic and world markets for an internationally traded commodity. Worldwide market conditions determine the price of soybeans. In an open economy, domestic producers are free to sell and domestic consumers are free to buy the product at the world market price (P_W). At this price, U.S. producers will supply Q_p, while U.S. consumers will purchase Q_c. Reflecting their comparative advantage, U.S. soybean producers will export $Q_p - Q_c$ units at the world market price.

The price of soybeans and other internationally traded commodities is determined by the forces of supply and demand in the world market (b). If U.S. soybean producers were prohibited from selling to foreigners, the domestic price would be P_n (a). Free trade permits the U.S. soybean producers to sell Q_p units at the higher world price (P_W). The quantity $Q_p - Q_c$ is exported abroad. Compared to the no-trade situation, the producers' gain from the higher price (P_WbcP_n) exceeds the cost imposed on domestic consumers (P_WacP_n) by the triangle abc.

EXHIBIT 32–6

PRODUCER BENEFITS FROM EXPORTS

(a) U.S. market for soybeans

(b) World market for soybeans

Let us compare the open-economy outcome with the situation in the absence of trade. If U.S. producers were not allowed to export soybeans, the domestic price would be determined by the domestic supply (S_d) and demand (D_d) only. A lower "no-trade" price (P_n) would emerge. Who are the winners and losers as the result of free trade in soybeans? Clearly, soybean producers gain. Free trade allows domestic producers to sell a larger quantity (Q_p rather than Q_n). As a result, the net revenues of soybean producers will rise by P_WbcP_n. On the other hand, domestic consumers of soybeans will have to pay a higher price under free trade. Consumers will lose (1) because they have to pay P_W rather than P_n for the Q_c units they purchase, and (2) because they lose the consumer surplus on the $Q_n - Q_c$ units now purchased at the higher price. Thus, free trade imposes a net cost of P_WacP_n on consumers. As can be seen in Exhibit 32–6, however, the gains of producers outweigh the losses to consumers by the triangle abc. Free trade leads to a net welfare gain.

When one focuses only on an export product, it appears that free trade benefits producers relative to consumers—but this ignores the secondary effects. How will foreigners generate the dollars they need to purchase the export products of the United States? If foreigners do not sell goods to us, they will not have the purchasing power necessary to purchase goods from us. U.S. imports—that is, the purchase of goods from low-cost foreign producers—provide foreigners with the dollar purchasing power necessary to buy U.S. exports. In turn, the lower prices in the import-competitive markets will benefit the U.S. consumers who appeared at first glance to be harmed by the higher prices (compared to the no-trade situation) in export markets.

Exhibit 32–7 illustrates the impact of imports, using shoes as an example. In the absence of trade, the price of shoes in the domestic market would be P_n,

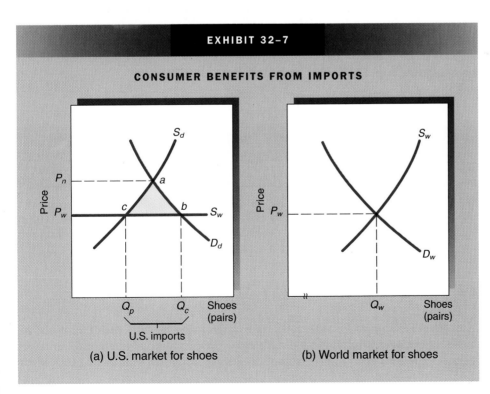

EXHIBIT 32–7

CONSUMER BENEFITS FROM IMPORTS

(a) U.S. market for shoes

(b) World market for shoes

In the absence of trade, the domestic price of shoes would be P_n. Since many foreign producers have a comparative advantage in the production of shoes, international trade leads to lower prices. At the world price P_W, U.S. consumers will demand Q_c units, of which $Q_c - Q_p$ are imported. Compared to the no-trade situation, consumers gain P_nabP_W, while domestic producers lose P_nacP_W. A net gain of abc results.

the intersection of the domestic supply and demand curves. However, the world price of shoes is P_W. In an open economy, many U.S. consumers would take advantage of the low shoe prices available from foreign producers. At the lower world price, U.S. consumers would purchase Q_c units of shoes, importing $Q_c - Q_p$ from foreign producers.

Compared to the no-trade situation, free trade in shoes results in lower prices and an expansion in domestic consumption. The lower prices lead to a net consumer gain of $P_n ab P_W$. Domestic producers lose $P_n ac P_W$ in the form of lower sales prices and reductions in output. However, the net gain of consumers exceeds the net loss of producers by abc.

For an open economy, international competition directs the resources of a nation toward the areas of competitive advantage. When domestic producers have a comparative advantage in the production of a good, they will be able to compete effectively in the world market and profit from the export of goods to foreigners. In turn, the exports will generate the purchasing power necessary to buy goods that foreigners can supply more economically.

International trade and specialization result in lower prices (and higher domestic consumption) for imported products and higher prices (and lower domestic consumption) for exported products. More important, trade permits the producers of each nation to concentrate on the things they do best (produce at a low cost), while trading for those they do least well. The result is an expansion in both output and consumption compared to what could be achieved in the absence of trade.

The pattern of U.S. exports and imports is consistent with this view. The United States is a nation with a technically skilled labor force, fertile farmland, and substantial capital formation. Thus, we export computers, aircraft, power-generating equipment, scientific instruments, and land-intensive agricultural products—items we are able to produce at a comparatively low cost. Simultaneously, we import substantial amounts of petroleum, textile (clothing) products, shoes, coffee, and diamonds—goods costly for us to produce. Clearly, trade permits us to gain by specializing in those areas in which our comparative advantage is greatest.

ECONOMICS OF TRADE RESTRICTIONS

Despite the potential benefits from free trade, almost all nations have erected trade barriers. Tariffs, quotas, and exchange-rate controls are the most commonly used trade-restricting devices. Let us consider the impact of each.

ECONOMICS OF TARIFFS

Tariff
A tax levied on goods imported into a country.

A **tariff** is nothing more than a tax on foreign imports. As **Exhibit 32–8** shows, tariffs of between 30 percent and 50 percent of product value were often levied prior to the 1940s. During the past 50 years, however, the tariff rates of the

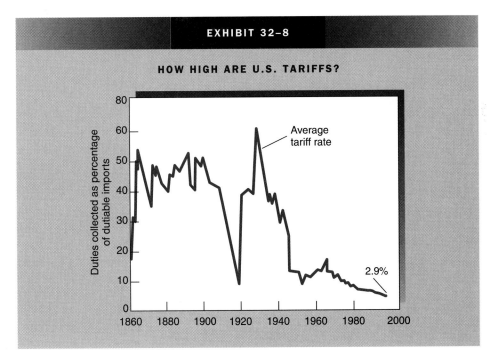

EXHIBIT 32–8

HOW HIGH ARE U.S. TARIFFS?

(chart: y-axis "Duties collected as percentage of dutiable imports" from 0 to 80; x-axis years 1860 to 2000; labeled "Average tariff rate" with endpoint "2.9%")

Tariff rates in the United States fell sharply during the period from 1930 to 1950. Subsequently, after rising slightly during the 1950s, they have trended downward since 1960. In 1994, the average tariff rate on merchandise imports was 2.9 percent.

United States have declined substantially. In 1994 the average tariff rate on imported goods was only 2.9 percent.

Exhibit 32–9 illustrates the impact of a tariff on automobiles. In the absence of a tariff, the world market price of P_W would prevail in the domestic market. At that price, U.S. consumers purchase Q_1 units. Domestic producers supply Q_{d1}, while foreigners supply $Q_1 - Q_{d1}$ units to the U.S. market. When the United States levies a tariff, t, on automobiles, Americans can no longer buy cars at the world price. U.S. consumers have to pay $P_W + t$ to purchase an automobile from foreigners. The domestic market price thus rises to $P_W + t$. At that price, domestic consumers demand Q_2 units (Q_{d2} supplied by domestic producers and $Q_2 - Q_{d2}$ supplied by foreigners). The tariff results in a higher price and lower level of domestic consumption.

The tariff benefits domestic producers and the government at the expense of consumers. Since they do not pay the tariff, domestic producers will expand their output in response to the higher (protected) market price. In effect, the tariff acts as a subsidy to domestic producers. Domestic producers gain the area S (Exhibit 32–9) in the form of additional net revenues. The tariff raises revenues equal to the area T for the government. The areas U and V represent costs imposed on consumers that do not benefit either producers or the government. Simply put, U and V represent a *deadweight loss* (loss of efficiency).

As a result of the tariff, resources that could have been used to produce goods that U.S. firms produce efficiently (compared to producers abroad) are diverted into the production of automobiles. Thus, we end up producing less in areas where we have a comparative advantage and more in areas where we are a high-cost producer. Potential gains from specialization and trade go unrealized.

Here we illustrate the impact of a tariff on automobiles. In the absence of the tariff, the world price of automobiles is P_W: U.S. consumers purchase Q_1 units (Q_{d1} from domestic producers plus $Q_1 - Q_{d1}$ from foreign producers). The tariff makes it more costly for Americans to purchase automobiles from foreigners. Imports decline and the domestic price increases. Consumers lose the sum of the areas S + U + T + V in the form of higher prices and a reduction in consumer surplus. Producers gain the area S and the tariff generates T tax revenues for the government. The areas U and V are deadweight losses due to a reduction in allocative efficiency.

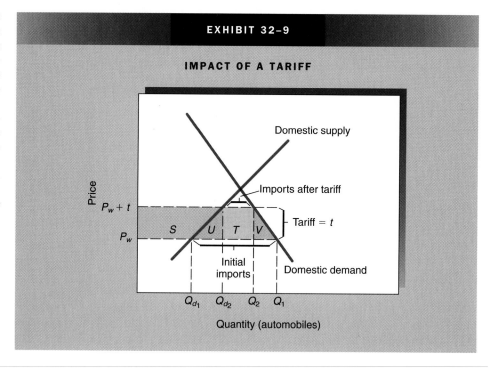

EXHIBIT 32-9

IMPACT OF A TARIFF

ECONOMICS OF QUOTAS

Import quota

A specific quantity (or value) of a good permitted to be imported into a country during a given period.

An **import quota,** like a tariff, is designed to restrict foreign goods and protect domestic industries. A quota places a ceiling on the amount of a product that can be imported during a given period (typically a year).

The United States imposes quotas on several products, including brooms, steel, shoes, sugar, dairy products, and peanuts. As in the case of tariffs, the primary purpose of quotas is to protect domestic industries from foreign competition.

Since 1953 the United States has imposed a quota to limit the importation of peanuts to 1.7 million pounds per year, approximately two peanuts per American. Using peanuts as an example, **Exhibit 32–10** illustrates the impact of a quota. If there were no trade restraints, the domestic price of peanuts would be equal to the world market price (P_W). Under those circumstances, Americans would purchase Q_1 units. At the price P_W, domestic producers would supply Q_{d1}, and the amount $Q_1 - Q_{d1}$ would be imported from foreign producers.

Now consider what happens when a quota limits imports to $Q_2 - Q_{d2}$, a quantity well below the free-trade level of imports. Since the quota reduces the foreign supply of peanuts to the domestic market, the price of the quota-protected product increases (to P_2). At the higher price, U.S. consumers will reduce their purchases to Q_2, and domestic producers will happily expand their production to Q_{d2}. With regard to the welfare of consumers, the impact of a quota is similar to that of a tariff. Consumers lose the area $S + U + T + V$ in the form of higher prices and the loss of consumer surplus. Similarly, domestic producers gain the area S, while the areas U and V represent deadweight losses from allocative inefficiency.

EXHIBIT 32–10

IMPACT OF A QUOTA

Here we illustrate the impact of a quota such as the one the United States imposes on peanuts. The world market price of peanuts is P_W. If there were no trade restraints, the domestic price would also be P_W, and the domestic consumption would be Q_1. Domestic producers would supply Q_{d1} units, while $Q_1 - Q_{d1}$ would be imported. A quota limiting imports to $Q_2 - Q_{d2}$ would push up the domestic price to P_2. At the higher price, the amount supplied by domestic producers increases to Q_{d2}. Consumers lose the sum of the areas $S + U + T + V$, while domestic producers gain the area S. In contrast with tariffs, quotas generate no revenue for the government. The area T goes to foreign producers who are granted permission to sell in the U.S. market.

However, there is a big difference between tariffs and quotas with regard to the area T. Under a tariff, the U.S. government would collect revenues equal to T, representing the tariff rate multiplied by the number of units imported. With a quota, however, these revenues will go to the foreign producers, who are granted import permits to sell in the U.S. market. Clearly, this right to sell at a premium price (since the domestic price exceeds the world market price) is extremely valuable. Thus, foreign producers will compete for the permits. They will hire lobbyists, make political contributions, and engage in other rent-seeking activities in an effort to secure the right to sell at a premium price in the U.S. market.

In many ways, quotas are more harmful than tariffs. With a quota, foreign producers are prohibited from selling additional units regardless of how much lower their costs are relative to those of domestic producers. In contrast with a tariff, a quota brings in no revenue for the government. While a tariff transfers revenue from U.S. consumers to the Treasury, quotas transfer these revenues to foreign producers. Obviously, this politically granted privilege creates a strong incentive for foreign producers to engage in wasteful rent-seeking activities. Thus, by rewarding both domestic producers with higher prices and foreign producers with valuable import permits, quotas generate two strong interest groups supportive of their continuation. As a result, removal of a quota is often even more difficult to achieve than a tariff reduction.

OTHER NONTARIFF BARRIERS TO TRADE

In order to avoid the imposition of other types of trade barriers such as tariffs and quotas, foreign firms will sometimes agree to limit their exports to a country. Even

Voluntary export restraint (VER)

An agreement by foreign firms to limit their own exports.

though they are almost always the result of political pressure, agreements of this type are called **voluntary export restraints (VERs)**. Japanese auto manufacturers have agreed to a VER on exports to the United States. The economic impact of a VER is similar to that of a quota. The higher selling price of the product that is caused by the VER creates a gain for both foreign and domestic producers, but hurts domestic consumers by more than an offsetting amount.

Other types of barriers, such as licensing requirements and product quality standards, are also used by governments to restrict trade. These barriers make it difficult and more costly for firms to import products into the country. Again these policies hurt domestic consumers but benefit domestic producers.

EXCHANGE-RATE CONTROLS AS A TRADE RESTRICTION

Many countries, particularly less-developed countries, fix the exchange-rate value of their currency above the market rate. At the official (artificially high) exchange rate, the country's export goods will be extremely expensive to foreigners. As a result, foreigners will purchase goods elsewhere, and the country's exports will be small. In turn, the low level of exports will make it extremely difficult for domestic residents to obtain the foreign currency required for the purchase of imports. Such exchange-rate controls both reduce the volume of trade and lead to black-market currency exchanges. Indeed, a large black-market premium indicates that the country's exchange-rate policy is substantially limiting the ability of its citizens to trade with foreigners. The greater the black-market premium, the larger the expected decline in the size of the country's international trade sector as the result of the exchange-rate controls.

WHY DO NATIONS ADOPT TRADE RESTRICTIONS?

Physical obstacles, like bad roads and stormy weather, that increase transaction costs will retard the gains from trade. Tariffs, quotas, exchange-rate controls, and other human-made trade restrictions have similar effects. Henry George compared trade restrictions to a blockade (see the chapter's opening quote). Both the blockade imposed by an enemy and a self-imposed blockade in the form of trade restrictions will retard the gains from specialization and exchange.

If trade restrictions promote inefficiency and reduce the potential gains from exchange, why do nations adopt them? Several factors play a role. First, there are some partially valid arguments for the protection of specific industries under certain circumstances. Second, economic illiteracy plays a role. Failing to comprehend the implications of the law of comparative advantage and the linkage between imports and exports, many people wrongly believe that trade restrictions increase employment and help keep the wages of Americans high. (See the accompanying Myths of Economics box on these topics.) Finally, and most important, trade restrictions reflect the political power of concentrated interests. We will now take a look at each of these factors.

"TRADE RESTRICTIONS THAT PROHIBIT FOREIGN PRODUCERS FROM SELLING THEIR GOODS AT LOWER PRICES THAN DOMESTIC PRODUCERS WILL INCREASE EMPLOYMENT AND PROTECT AMERICAN JOBS."

Many people sincerely believe that trade restrictions increase employment and "save American jobs." This fallacious belief stems from a failure to consider the secondary effects of import restrictions on export industries. Tariffs, quotas, exchange-rate controls, and other trade restrictions may result in more employment *in industries shielded by the restraints*, but they will *destroy jobs in other industries*.

Remember, the sales from foreigners to us (our imports) provide them with the purchasing power required to buy from us (our exports). If foreigners are unable to sell as much to Americans, then they will have fewer dollars with which to buy from Americans. Therefore, a secondary effect accompanies trade restrictions: The demand for American export goods declines. As a result, output and employment in export industries will be smaller, offsetting any jobs saved in protected industries. Most noneconomists fail to recognize the link between a decline in imports due to trade restrictions and a decline in exports because foreigners have acquired fewer dollars. Thus, it is easy to see why this myth is so widely believed.

When trade restraints are lowered (or there is discussion about lowering them), predictably many workers and business officials in import-competitive industries will charge that jobs will be lost to foreign competitors. In contrast, the additional jobs in the export industries do not yet exist. No one will be saying, "I will not be employed next year if the trade restraints are not lowered." Because the jobs (and employees) in the import-competitive industries are highly visible, while the future jobs in the exporting industries are invisible, reducing trade restraints is very difficult.

Actually, the focus on jobs is misleading. After all, it is income and high productivity, not jobs, that are the sources of prosperity. The shift from less to more productive jobs is not without cost, but is necessary if workers and the economy are to prosper. In essence, import

restraints direct resources away from areas where domestic producers have a comparative advantage and into areas where domestic producers are relatively inefficient. Since fewer of our resources are used to produce things that we are good at (as indicated by our ability to compete effectively) and more resources are squandered attempting to produce things that we do poorly (as evidenced by our inability to compete in the world market), the per capita output and income of Americans is lower than would be the case in the absence of the restraints.

Consider the following: If import restrictions are a good idea, why don't we use them to restrict trade among the 50 states? After all, think of all the jobs that are lost when, for example, Michigan "imports" oranges from Florida, apples from Washington, wheat from Kansas, and cotton from Georgia. All these products could be produced in Michigan. However, the residents of Michigan generally find it cheaper to "import" these commodities rather than produce them domestically. Michigan gains by using its resources to produce and "export" automobiles (and other goods it can produce economically) and then using the sales revenue to "import" goods that would be expensive to produce in Michigan.

Most people recognize that free trade among the 50 states is a major source of prosperity for each of the states. Similarly, most recognize that "imports" from other states do not destroy jobs—at least not for long. The source of gains from trade among nations is exactly the same as for trade among people in different states. Free trade among the 50 states promotes prosperity; so, too, does free trade among nations.

Of course, sudden removal of trade barriers might harm producers and workers in protected industries. It may be costly to quickly transfer the protected resources to other, more productive activities. Gradual removal of the barriers would minimize this shock effect and the accompanying cost of relocation.

PARTIALLY VALID ARGUMENTS FOR RESTRICTIONS

There are three major, at least partially valid, arguments for protecting certain domestic industries from foreign competitors: the national-defense, infant-industry, and anti-dumping arguments.

More than one-fifth of the world's output is produced in one country and sold in another. The gains from specialization, division of labor, and adoption of mass production methods that accompany international trade allow the trading partners to achieve a larger output and higher living standards than would otherwise be the case.

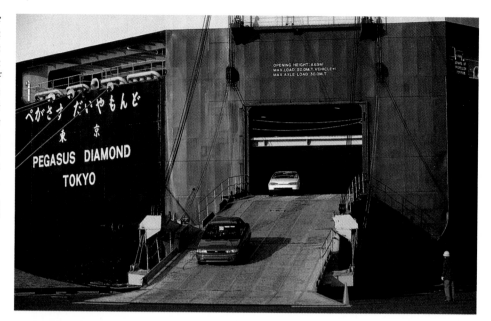

NATIONAL-DEFENSE ARGUMENT. According to the national-defense argument, certain industries—aircraft, petroleum, and weapons, for example—are vital to national defense and therefore should be protected from foreign competitors so that a domestic supply of necessary materials would be available in case of an international conflict. Would we want to be entirely dependent on Arabian or Russian petroleum? Would complete dependence on French aircraft be wise? Many Americans would answer no, even if trade restrictions were required to prevent such dependence by preserving domestic industries.

Although the national-defense argument has some validity, it is often abused. Relatively few industries are truly vital to our national defense. If a resource is important for national defense, often it would make more sense to stockpile the resource during peacetime rather than follow protectionist policies to preserve a domestic industry. Furthermore, it is important to recognize that a strong economy capable of producing large volumes of the goods necessary to sustain a large war effort, is itself part of a strong defense. Since the national-defense argument is often used by special interests to justify protection for their industry at the expense of the economy in general, the merits of each specific case must be carefully evaluated.

INFANT-INDUSTRY ARGUMENT. Advocates of the infant-industry argument hold that new domestic industries should be protected from older, established foreign competitors. As the new industry matures, it will be able to stand on its own feet and compete effectively with foreign producers, at which time protection can be removed.

The infant-industry argument has a long and often notorious history. Alexander Hamilton used it to argue for the protection of early U.S. manufacturing. Although it is an argument for only temporary protection, the protection, once granted, is generally difficult to remove. For example, a century ago, this argument was used to gain tariff protection for the newly emerging steel industry in the United States. With time, the steel industry developed and became very powerful, both politically and economically. Despite this maturity, the tariffs remained. To this day, legislation continues to provide the industry with various protections that limit competition from abroad.

ANTI-DUMPING ARGUMENT.   In some cases, **dumping,** the sale of goods abroad at a price below their cost (and below their price in the domestic market of the exporting nation), merely reflects the exporter's desire to penetrate a foreign market. In other instances, dumping may be prompted by export subsidies of foreign governments. At various times, it has been alleged that Argentina has dumped textiles, Korea has dumped steel, and Canada has dumped radial tires into the U.S. market. Dumping is illegal. The Trade Agreements Act of 1979 provides for special anti-dumping *duties* (tariffs) when a good is sold in the United States at a price lower than that found in the domestic market of the exporting nation.

Dumping
The sale of a good by a foreign supplier in another country at a price below that charged by the supplier in its home market.

As in the case of imports, dumping generally benefits domestic consumers and imposes costs on domestic producers of goods for which the imports are good substitutes. The lower prices of the "dumped" goods permit consumers to obtain the goods more economically than they are available from domestic producers. Simultaneously, the lower prices make it more difficult for domestic producers of the goods to compete. Predictably, domestic producers (and their employees) are the major source of the charge that dumping is unfair.

Economists generally emphasize two points with regard to dumping. First, dumping can, in a few instances, be used as a weapon to gain monopoly power. For example, if the foreign firm temporarily cuts its price below cost, it might eliminate domestic competition and later raise its price to a higher level after the domestic competitors have been driven from the market. However, this is usually not a feasible strategy. After all, domestic producers might reenter the market if the price rises in the future. In addition, alternative foreign suppliers limit the monopoly power of a producer attempting this strategy.

Second, the law of comparative advantage indicates that a country (as a whole) can gain from the purchase of foreign-produced goods when they are cheaper than domestic goods. This is true regardless of whether the low price of foreign goods reflects comparative advantage, subsidies by foreign governments, or poor business practices. Unless the foreign supplier is likely to monopolize the domestic market, there is little reason to believe that dumping harms the economy receiving the goods.

SPECIAL INTERESTS AND THE POLITICS OF TRADE RESTRICTIONS

Protectionism is a politician's delight because it delivers visible benefits to the protected parties while imposing the costs as a hidden tax on the public.

MURRAY L. WEIDENBAUM[3]

Although the support for trade restrictions arises from multiple sources, as Professor Weidenbaum points out, there is no question as to the primary reason for their adoption. *Trade restrictions provide highly invisible, concentrated benefits for a small group of people, while imposing on the general citizenry widely*

---

[3]Former chairman of the President's Council of Economic Advisers.

dispersed costs that are often difficult to identify. As we discussed in Chapter 4, politicians have a strong incentive to favor issues of this type, even if they conflict with economic efficiency.

Trade restrictions almost always benefit producers (and resource suppliers) at the expense of consumers. In general, the former group—investors and workers in a specific industry—are well organized, and the "jobs saved" and "high wages protected" in these industries are often highly visible (refer again to the Myths of Economics box on trade restrictions). Thus, organized interest groups that benefit from trade restrictions frequently provide contributions and other resources to politicians willing to support trade restrictions favorable to their industry. In contrast, consumers, who will pay higher prices for the products of a protected industry, are an unorganized group. Most of them will not associate the higher product prices with the trade restrictions. However, it has been estimated that the average U.S. family pays at least $1,000 more per year for the products it buys because of trade restrictions. Similarly, potential workers and investors in export industries harmed by the restrictions are often unaware of their impact. Thus, most of the people harmed by trade restrictions are likely to be uninformed and thus unconcerned about trade policy.

Predictably, well-organized special interests favoring trade restrictions will generally have more political clout than those harmed by the restrictions. As a result, politicians will often be able to gain more votes by supporting trade restrictions that benefit organized interest groups than they could gain from the support of consumers and exporters. In the case of trade restrictions, sound economics often conflicts with a winning political strategy.

EMPIRICAL EVIDENCE ON THE IMPACT OF TRADE RESTRICTIONS

Our analysis indicates that countries imposing trade barriers will fail to realize their full economic potential. There are various ways—tariffs, quotas, exchange-rate controls, and licensing requirements, for example—countries use to restrain international trade. It is not always easy to determine the extent to which various countries are restricting trade.

Taxes on international trade are generally substantially lower in high-income industrial nations than in less-developed countries (LDCs). Similarly, while exchange-rate controls are a negligible restrictive factor in developed countries, they are a major factor restricting trade in several less-developed countries. Among LDCs, considerable variation exists in the height of trade barriers. Some LDCs impose exceedingly high tariffs. Others impose exchange-rate controls. When a country both imposes high tariffs and fixes the value of its currency at unrealistic rates (relative to convertible currencies like the dollar and yen), its international trade will be retarded substantially.

Among 80 less-developed countries analyzed in a recent study, **Exhibit 32–11** presents data for the ten with the lowest trade barriers.[4] The trade sectors

---

[4]The empirical data presented in this section are part of a larger study undertaken by one of the authors. See James Gwartney, Robert Lawson, and Walter Block, *Economic Freedom of the World: 1975–1995* (Washington, D.C.: Cato Institute, 1996).

EXHIBIT 32-11

ECONOMIC GROWTH OF LESS-DEVELOPED COUNTRIES
WITH LOW AND HIGH TRADE RESTRICTIONS

	SIZE OF TRADE SECTOR AS A PERCENT OF GDP, 1993[a]	AVERAGE TAX RATE ON INTERNATIONAL TRADE		BLACK MARKET EXCHANGE-RATE PREMIUM		GROWTH OF PER CAPITA GDP, 1980–1994
		1980	1992	1980	1995	
LOW TRADE RESTRICTIONS[b]						
Singapore	170.4%	0.5	0.2	0	0	5.3
Hong Kong	142.9	0.5	0.3	0	0	5.1
Malaysia	77.1	7.7	2.8	0	0	4.1
Ireland	58.0	3.0	2.4	0	0	3.1
Taiwan	43.3	3.6	2.0	1	0	6.1
Portugal	33.8	2.1	0.5	2	0	2.1
Thailand	38.6	6.9	3.9	5	0	6.1
Greece	28.1	3.2	0.1	7	0	0.8
South Korea	30.8	4.1	2.2	5	0	7.4
Indonesia	27.9	2.9	1.9	2	2	4.1
AVERAGE	**65.1**	**3.5**	**1.6**	**2**	**0**	**4.4**
HIGH TRADE RESTRICTIONS[b]						
Uganda	12.6	3.1	—	360	12	0.5
Bangladesh	13.3	13.4	12.1	111	30	2.2
Rwanda	14.7	13.3	14.6	67	105	−1.7
Iran	15.6	17.0	8.7	164	156	−0.2
Burundi	19.6	18.1	22.9	45	42	1.0
Madagascar	20.6	8.5	8.7	51	30	−2.8
Cameroon	20.3	11.0	7.7	2	1	−2.3
Sierra Leone	25.2	13.3	8.3	62	1	−1.2
Syria	32.0	7.1	3.6	35	283	0.2
Nicaragua	32.6	8.7	8.0	91	4	−3.3
AVERAGE	**20.6**	**11.4**	**10.5**	**99**	**66**	**−0.8**

[a]The size of the trade sector is equal to one-half of exports plus imports as a percent of GDP. As Illustrated Exhibit VI-A on page 839 shows, the size of the trade sector tends to be inversely related to the population of a country. Given population, the trade sector is generally large in countries with low trade restrictions and small in countries with high trade restrictions.

[b]More than 100 countries were rated on the basis of three international trade factors: (1) tariff rates, (2) black-market exchange rate, and (3) the actual size of the trade sectors relative to the expected size given the country's population, geographic size, and location. The countries in this table are the ten highest and ten lowest rated in the area of international trade. See James Gwartney, Robert Lawson, and Walter Block, *Economic Freedom of the World: 1975–1995* (Washington, D.C.: Cato Institute, 1996).

Sources: Derived from World Bank, *World Tables, 1995*; International Monetary Fund, *Government Finance Yearbook, 1994*; and International Currency Analysis, *The World Currency Yearbook, 1989–90*.

of these ten countries are large, given the size of their population. Their tariff rates are low, and the exchange-rate value of their currencies is pretty much in line with market forces (a low black-market exchange-rate premium provides evidence on this point). Data are also provided for the ten LDCs that follow the most restrictive trade policies. For this latter group, the size of the trade sector is small (given the size of the country), tariffs are high, and the black-market exchange-rate premium for the conversion of the domestic currency is high. As we previously discussed, a high black-market premium indicates that the country has imposed tight exchange-rate controls.

The average size of the trade sector of the low-restriction countries (65.1 percent of GDP) was more than three times the average for the nations imposing substantial trade barriers. Compared to the low-restriction countries, the average tax (tariff) rate imposed on international trade was more than six times higher in 1993 (and three times higher in 1980) for the high-restriction countries. Similarly, the black-market exchange-rate premium for the domestic currency was substantially higher in the high-restriction countries in both 1980 and 1995.

Look at the growth of per capita GDP during the 1980–1994 period for the two groups. Singapore and Hong Kong, the two countries that most closely follow free-trade policies—their tariffs are negligible and their currencies are fully convertible—both achieved per capita GDP growth rates greater than 5 percent during the period. The average annual growth of per capita GDP in the low-restriction countries was 4.4 percent during 1980–1994. All the nations with low trade barriers achieved positive growth rates; except for Greece, all the low-restriction countries achieved an annual growth rate of per capita GDP of more than 2 percent. In contrast, the growth rate of the ten countries with high trade restrictions was *minus* 0.8 percent. Per capita GDP declined during 1980–1994 in six of the ten countries that imposed substantial restrictions on international trade. Only one of the countries with high trade restrictions—Bangladesh—was able to achieve a growth rate in excess of 1 percent. Just as our theory implies, these data indicate that trade barriers are harmful to the economic health of a country.[5]

RECENT REDUCTIONS IN TRADE RESTRICTIONS

ROLE OF GATT AND THE WORLD TRADE ORGANIZATION

Despite their vulnerability to special-interest politics, the potential gains from reductions in trade restrictions have not been ignored. Reacting to a wave of trade restrictions adopted during the 1930s, the major industrial nations estab-

---

[5]For additional evidence that trade restrictions retard economic growth, see Robert Barro, "Economic Growth in a Cross-Section of Countries," *Quarterly Journal of Economics* (May 1991): pp. 407–443; David M. Gould, Roy J. Ruffin, and Graeme L. Woodbridge, "The Theory and Practice of Free Trade," *Economic Review–Federal Reserve Bank of Dallas* (fourth quarter 1993): pp. 1–16; and Michael Michaely, Demetris Papageorgiou, and Armeane M. Choksi, eds., *Liberalizing Foreign Trade: Lessons of Experience in the Developing World* (Cambridge, Mass.: Basil Blackwell, 1991).

lished the multination **General Agreement on Tariffs and Trade (GATT)** organization shortly following the Second World War. For five decades, GATT played a central role in the multilateral tariff reductions and the relaxation (or elimination) of quotas. The average tariff rates of GATT members fell from approximately 40 percent in 1947 to less than 5 percent in 1994.

The most recent GATT session—the Uruguay Round—was finally completed at year-end 1993, after seven years of intense negotiations. This round primarily focused on nontariff issues, such as quotas and agricultural subsidies. As the result of the recent GATT proceedings, members agreed to (1) eliminate quotas (however, countries are permitted to maintain tariffs) on textile products, (2) accept uniform standards of evidence that will make it more difficult to take unilateral action against alleged dumping, (3) reduce tariffs on wood, paper, nonferrous metals, and some electronic products, (4) adopt standards that will make it easier to prosecute parties that violate intellectual property rights (copyrights, patents, and software and movie rights), and (5) reduce agricultural subsidies gradually during the next decade.

At the conclusion of these negotiations, GATT was given a new name: the **World Trade Organization.** This organization of 117 countries is now responsible for the monitoring and enforcement of the trade agreements developed through GATT.

NORTH AMERICAN FREE TRADE AGREEMENT (NAFTA)

In 1993, the United States, Canada, and Mexico adopted the North American Free Trade Agreement (NAFTA). As the result of NAFTA, tariffs on the shipment of most products among the three countries will be eliminated during the next ten years. The agreement will also remove limits on financial investments, liberalize trade in services such as banking, and establish uniform legal requirements for the protection of intellectual property.

Coming on the heels of the 1988 trade agreement between the United States and Canada, NAFTA will further expand the free movement of goods and investments among the countries of North America. Domestic producers in all three countries will have free access to a larger market. Many products will now be produced at a lower per unit cost because producers will be able to plan for and produce a larger volume of output. The economies of scale are likely to be particularly important for producers in Canada and Mexico. Elimination of trade barriers will also provide consumers with greater variety and an expanded choice among suppliers.

Although NAFTA is relatively new and has not had time to fully affect the North American economies, some evidence suggests that the agreement is already contributing to the growth of U.S. exports. During 1994, the first year that the agreement was in effect, U.S. exports to Canada and Mexico grew twice as fast as U.S. exports to the rest of the world, and total trade among all three nations expanded by 17 percent. Approximately half the increase in U.S. exports in 1994 was accounted for by Canada and Mexico.

Compared with the Canadian-American trade agreement, the free trade agreement with Mexico was—and continues to be—much more controversial. As we have discussed, trade flows among nations are determined by comparative advantage, not relative wage rates. Nonetheless, many Americans and

General Agreement on Tariffs and Trade (GATT)
An organization formed following the Second World War designed to set the rules for the conduct of international trade and reduce barriers to trade among nations.

World Trade Organization
The new name given to GATT in 1994; it is currently responsible for monitoring and enforcing the multilateral trade agreements among the 117 member countries.

Canadians fear that competition from low-wage workers will adversely affect their earnings (see the Myths of Economics box on free trade with low-wage countries). As in the case of the U.S.-Canada agreement, economics indicates that NAFTA will help all trading partners. It will tend to reduce the cost of labor-intensive goods to U.S. and Canadian consumers while simultaneously increasing the availability of high-tech manufactured goods for Mexican consumers. Adjustment will be required by suppliers and workers, leading to temporary unemployment for some. The benefit, however, is that all three countries can expect to gain by using their resources more fully in those areas where they have the greatest comparative advantage.

MYTHS OF ECONOMICS

"FREE TRADE WITH LOW-WAGE COUNTRIES SUCH AS CHINA AND INDIA WOULD CAUSE THE WAGES OF U.S. WORKERS TO FALL."

Many Americans believe that if it were not for trade restrictions, the wages of American workers would fall to the level of workers in less-developed countries. How can U.S. labor compete with workers in China or India who are willing to work for $1 per hour or less? The fallacy of this argument stems from a misunderstanding of the source of high wages and ignorance of the law of comparative advantage.

High hourly wages do not necessarily mean high per unit labor cost. Labor productivity must also be considered. For example, suppose a U.S. steel worker receives an hourly wage rate of $20 and a steel worker in India receives only $2 per hour. Given the skill level of the workers and the capital and production methods used in the two countries, however, the U.S. worker produces 20 times as many tons of steel per worker-hour as the Indian worker. Because of the higher productivity per worker-hour, labor cost per unit of output is actually lower in the United States than in India!

Labor in the United States possesses a high skill level and works with large amounts of capital equipment. These factors contribute to the high productivity per worker, which is the source of the high wages. Similarly, low productivity per worker-hour is the foundation of the low wages in such countries as India and China.

When analyzing the significance of wage and productivity differentials across countries, one must remember that gains from trade emanate from comparative advantage, not absolute advantage (see Exhibits 32–3, 32–4, and 32–5). The United States cannot produce everything cheaper than China or India merely because U.S. workers are more productive and work with more capital than workers in China and India. Neither can the Chinese and Indians produce everything cheaper merely because

their wage rates are low compared to those of U.S. workers. When resources are directed by relative prices and the principle of comparative advantage, both high-wage and low-wage countries gain from the opportunity to specialize in those activities that, relatively speaking, they do best.

The comparative advantage of low-wage countries is likely to be in the production of labor-intensive goods, such as wigs, rugs, toys, textiles, and assembled manufactured products. On the other hand, the comparative advantage of the United States lies in the production of high-technology-manufacturing products (computers, aircraft, and scientific instruments, for example) and land-intensive agricultural products (wheat, corn, and soybeans).

Trade permits both high- and low-wage countries to reallocate their resources away from productive activities in which they are inefficient (relative to foreign producers) toward activities in which they are highly efficient. The net result is an increase in output and consumption opportunities for both trading partners.

If foreigners, even low-wage foreigners, will sell us a product cheaper than we ourselves could produce it, we can gain by using our resources to produce other things. Perhaps an extreme example will illustrate the point. Suppose a foreign producer, perhaps a Santa Claus (who was able to hire workers at low wages) was willing to supply us with free winter coats. Would it make sense to enact a tariff barrier to keep out the free coats? Of course not. Resources that were previously used to produce coats could now be freed to produce other goods. Output and the availability of goods would expand. The real wage of U.S. workers would rise. It makes no more sense to erect trade barriers to keep out cheap foreign goods than to keep out the free coats of a friendly, foreign Santa Claus.

TOMATOES, TRADE RESTRICTIONS, AND NAFTA[a]

In 1995–1996, Florida tomato growers complained to the Clinton administration and Congress that the import of cheap tomatoes from Mexico was driving them out of business. Blaming the North American Free Trade Agreement (NAFTA) for their plight, they sought to have Congress declare "winter vegetables" a separate industry so they would qualify for greater protection. They also filed an anti-dumping suit with the Commerce Department seeking the imposition of higher tariffs on Mexican tomatoes.

When these strategies failed, the growers asked Congress to pass special package and labeling legislation. While the hard, unripe Florida tomatoes are shipped in solid-tray boxes, the Mexican tomatoes are ripened on the vine, hand-packaged, and shipped in cushioned cartons. At least some consumers believe that this procedure makes the tomatoes tastier. This issue aside, the Florida growers wanted legislation that would require all growers to use the hard-tray cartons. Of course, this would make it difficult for the riper Mexican tomatoes to be shipped without being battered or bruised.

Interestingly, the problems of the Florida growers had little to do with NAFTA. The pre-NAFTA tariffs on tomatoes were low and the initial reduction under NAFTA reduced their price by less than a penny per pound. The major factor contributing to the increased competitiveness of the Mexican-grown tomatoes was the sharp reduction in the exchange rate of the peso relative to the dollar during 1994–1995.

This case illustrates why it is so difficult to maintain freedom of exchange in international markets. Rather than simply argue for trade restraints, organized interest groups often support regulations that they say will be "safer," or "more convenient," or "facilitate inspection." Of course, such regulations also just happen to give the special-interest groups a competitive advantage over their rivals. This is true in all countries. Japan, in particular, has been charged with the use of such diversionary tactics.

Neither is Mexico blameless. For example, the Mexican government attempted to impose cumbersome labeling and inspection procedures in an effort to reduce the competitiveness of American tires in the Mexican market. Mexico continues to prohibit American express delivery firms such as United Parcel Service from using large trucks south of the border. Consumers are the losers when restrictions of this type are imposed. Unfortunately, since consumers are disorganized and generally unaware they are being harmed, support of well-organized interest groups is often politically attractive.

---

[a]This feature is based on an article by Helene Cooper and Bruce Ingersoll, "With Little Evidence, Florida Growers Blame Tomato Woes on NAFTA," *The Wall Street Journal*, April 3, 1996, p. 1.

FALLING TRADE BARRIERS IN OTHER COUNTRIES

In many ways the recent GATT and NAFTA agreements were merely a reflection of changes that were already taking place worldwide—particularly among LDCs. No doubt influenced by the economic success of relatively open economies like those of Hong Kong and Singapore, many LDCs unilaterally reduced their trade barriers during the late 1980s and early 1990s. Among Latin American countries, Chile began moving toward freer trade policies in the early 1980s. Spurred by the rapid economic growth of Chile during the latter half of the 1980s, other Latin American countries also reduced their trade barriers. Mexico cut its tariff rates by more than 50 percent during the late 1980s. In 1991 Argentina cut its average tariff level from 18 percent to 11 percent. Brazil, Bolivia, Colombia, Ecuador, Peru, and Venezuela have also made substantial cuts in their tariff rates and reduced other trade barriers in the 1990s.[6] Exchange-rate controls have also been relaxed or eliminated throughout much of Latin America during the past five years.

In other parts of the world, even some of the most "protectionist" countries—including Pakistan, the Philippines, and Turkey—have cut their tariffs and/or relaxed restrictive quotas in the 1990s. Perhaps the stage is now set for many of these countries to follow the path of Chile and the trade-oriented countries of Southeast Asia toward a more prosperous future.

---

[6]See Susan Hickok, "Recent Trade Liberalization in Developing Countries: The Effects of Global Trade and Output," *Quarterly Review: Federal Reserve Bank of New York* (autumn 1993): pp. 6–19.

LOOKING AHEAD

There are many similarities between trade within national borders and trade across national boundaries. However, there is also a major difference. In addition to the exchange of goods for money, trade across national borders generally involves the exchange of national currencies. The next chapter deals with the financial arrangements under which international trade is conducted.

CHAPTER SUMMARY

1. The volume of international trade has grown rapidly in recent decades. In the early 1990s approximately 21 percent of the world's output was sold in a country different from the one where it was produced. The size of the trade sector as a share of the economy varies substantially among countries. It is generally larger in countries with a smaller population.

2. The trade sector is approximately 10 percent of the U.S. GDP. More than half of all U.S. trade is with Canada, Japan, and the developed nations of Western Europe.

3. Comparative advantage rather than absolute advantage is the source of gains from trade. As long as the relative production costs of goods differ among nations, the nations will be able to gain from trade.

4. Mutual gains from trade accrue when each nation produces goods for which it is a low-opportunity-cost producer and trades for goods for which it is a high-opportunity-cost producer. This pattern of specialization and trade allows trading partners to maximize their joint output and expand their consumption possibilities.

5. Exports and imports are closely linked. The exports of a nation are the primary source of purchasing power used to import goods. When a nation restricts imports, it si-

multaneously limits the ability of foreigners to acquire the purchasing power necessary to buy the nation's exports.

6. International competition directs the resources of a nation toward the areas of its comparative advantage. In an open economy, when domestic producers have a comparative advantage in the production of a good, they will be able to export their product and compete effectively in the world market. On the other hand, for commodities in which foreign producers have the comparative advantage, a nation could import the goods more economically (at a lower opportunity cost) than it could produce them domestically.

7. Relative to the no-trade alternative, international exchange and specialization result in lower prices for products that are imported and higher domestic prices for products that are exported. However, the net effect is an expansion in the aggregate output and consumption possibilities available to a nation.

8. The application of a tariff, quota, or other import restriction to a product reduces the amount that foreigners supply to the domestic market. As a result of diminished supply, consumers face higher prices for the protected product. Essentially, import restrictions are subsidies to producers (and workers) in protected industries at the expense of (a) consumers and (b) producers (and workers) in export industries. Restrictions reduce the ability of domestic producers to specialize in those areas for which their comparative advantage is greatest.

9. National-defense, infant-industry, and anti-dumping arguments can be used to justify trade restrictions for specific industries under certain conditions. It is clear, though, that the power of special-interest groups and voter ignorance about the harmful effects of trade restrictions offer the major explanations for real-world protectionist public policies.

10. Trade restrictions are often attractive to politicians because they generate visible benefits to special interests—

particularly business and labor interests in protected industries—while imposing costs on consumers and taxpayers that are individually small and largely invisible.

11. Trade restrictions do not create jobs. Jobs protected by import restrictions are offset by jobs destroyed in export industries. Since this secondary effect of restrictions often goes unnoticed, their political popularity is understandable. Nevertheless, trade restrictions are inefficient, since they lead to the loss of potential gains from specialization and exchange.

12. Both high-wage and low-wage countries gain from the opportunity to specialize in the production of goods that they produce at a low opportunity cost. If a low-wage country can supply a good to the United States cheaper than the United States can produce it, the United States can gain by purchasing the good from the low-wage country and using U.S. resources to produce other goods for which the United States has a comparative advantage.

13. There is substantial variation among LDCs with regard to the imposition of trade restrictions. LDCs that have low tariff rates, a freely convertible currency, and large trade sectors (relative to the size of their population) grew rapidly during the 1980–1994 period, while the per capita GDP of countries following the most restrictive trade policies generally declined.

CRITICAL-ANALYSIS QUESTIONS

*1. "Trade restrictions limiting the sale of cheap foreign goods in the United States are necessary to protect the prosperity of Americans." Evaluate this statement made by an American politician.

2. Suppose at the time of the Civil War the United States had been divided into two countries, and that through the years no trade existed between the two. How might the standard of living in the "divided" United States have been affected? Explain.

*3. Can both of the following statements be true? Why or why not?
   a. "Tariffs and import quotas promote economic inefficiency and reduce the real income of a nation. Economic analysis suggests that nations can gain by eliminating trade restrictions."
   b. "Economic analysis suggests that there is good reason to expect trade restrictions to exist in the real world."

4. "Tariffs and quotas are necessary to protect the high wages of the American worker." Do you agree or disagree with this statement? Why or why not?

*5. "An increased scarcity of a product benefits producers and harms consumers. In effect, tariffs and other trade restrictions increase the domestic scarcity of products by reducing the supply from abroad. Such policies benefit domestic producers of the restricted product at the expense of domestic consumers." Evaluate this statement.

*6. The United States uses an import quota to maintain the domestic price of sugar well above the world price. Analyze the impact of the quota. Use supply-and-demand analysis to illustrate your answer. To whom do the gains and losses of this policy accrue? How does the quota affect the efficiency of resource allocation in the United States? Why do you think Congress is supportive of this policy?

7. Suppose that it costs American textile manufacturers $20 to produce a shirt, while foreign producers can supply the same shirt for $15.
   a. Would a tariff of $6 per shirt help American manufacturers compete with foreigners?
   b. Would a subsidy of $6 per shirt to domestic manufacturers help them compete?
   c. Is there any difference between the tariff and a direct subsidy to the domestic manufacturer?

*8. "Getting more Americans to realize that it pays to make things in the United States is the heart of the competitiveness issue." (This is a quote from an American business magazine.)
   a. Would Americans be better off if more of them paid higher prices in order to "buy American" rather than purchase from foreigners? Would U.S. employment be higher? Explain.
   b. Would Californians be better off if they bought only goods produced in California? Would the employment in California be higher? Explain.

*9. It is often alleged that Japanese producers receive subsidies from their government that permit them to sell their products at a low price in the U.S. market. Do you think we should erect trade barriers to keep out cheap Japanese goods if the source of their low price is governmental subsidies? Why or why not?

10. How do tariffs and quotas differ? Can you think of any reason why foreign producers might prefer a quota rather than a tariff? Explain your answer.

11. What's wrong with this economic experiment? A researcher hypothesizes that higher tariffs on imported automobiles would cause total employment in the United States to increase. Automobile tariffs are raised, and the following year employment in the U.S. auto industry increases by 50,000. The researcher concludes that the higher tariffs created 50,000 jobs.

*12. Does international trade cost American jobs? Does interstate trade cost your state jobs? What is the major effect of international and interstate trade?

13. "The United States is suffering from a huge excess of imports. Cheap foreign products are driving American firms out of business and leaving our economy in shambles." Evaluate this statement from an American politician.

14. Do you think the United States will benefit as trade barriers with Mexico are reduced? Will Mexico benefit?

Will trade with a low-wage country like Mexico push wages down in a high-wage country like the United States? Why or why not?

*15. Tariffs not only reduce the volume of imports, they also reduce the volume of exports. Is this statement true or false? Explain your answer.

16. If the workers in one country are substantially more productive because they are more skilled and work with more capital than the workers of another country, trade between the two countries will drive wages of the less-productive workers even lower than is currently the case. Is this statement true or false, or are you uncertain? Explain your answer.

17. a. Would the people of Europe be better off if there were dangerous rivers with no bridges that ran along the borders between countries? Why or why not?

b. Would the people of Europe be better off if there were sizable tariffs (taxes on imports), import quotas, and other regulations that limited foreigners from selling goods cheaply in the domestic market of another country? Why or why not?

c. If foreigners were "dumping" their goods—if they were selling below their production costs in another country—would your answer to part b have been different?

*18. When you travel abroad, you are permitted to bring a limited amount of goods into the United States duty-free. Will the presence of a U.S. tariff on a certain good affect the likelihood that you will find a bargain on the good while abroad?

19. **Special problem on the economics of trade:** Suppose that farmers in Ukraine can produce either 125 bushels of wheat or 50 bushels of corn on an acre of land. Farmers in the Czech Republic can produce either 50 bushels of wheat or 40 bushels of corn.

a. Measured in terms of corn, what is the opportunity cost of producing a bushel of wheat in Ukraine? What is the opportunity cost of raising a bushel of wheat in the Czech Republic?

b. Which country has a comparative advantage in the production of wheat?

c. Which has a comparative advantage in the production of corn?

d. Suppose the residents of the two countries are each currently consuming 10 million bushels of wheat and 6 million bushels of corn. If there is no trade between the two countries (or with any other country), how many acres of farmland will the two countries have to devote to the production of wheat and corn?

e. Suppose the people in the two countries begin trading with each other. Indicate the range of wheat prices (measured in terms of corn) that would permit the people in both countries to gain. (In order to simplify matters, assume that the transport cost of the grains is zero.)

f. Suppose that the midpoint of the range of potentially advantageous prices emerges as the market price. What is that midpoint? If the Czech Republic reallocates all of the land it previously used to produce wheat and corn to the production of the grain for which it has a comparative advantage, how much will it produce? If it trades half of that crop to Ukraine for the other grain at the market price, how much of the two grains will the Czech Republic be able to consume?

g. If Ukraine devotes all of the land it previously used to produce both wheat and corn to the crop for which it has a comparative advantage, how much of the two grains will Ukraine be able to consume after the trade for half the Czech output (of the grain that the Czechs are best at producing) at the market price?

h. Who gains and who loses from the trade?

---

*Asterisk denotes questions for which answers are given in Appendix B.

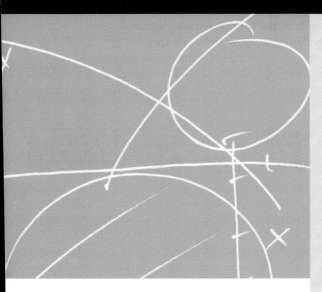

Currencies, like tomatoes and football tickets, have a price at which they are bought and sold. An exchange rate is the price of one currency in terms of another, such as the price of a French franc in U.S. dollars or German marks.

GARY SMITH[1]

---

[1]Gary Smith, *Macroeconomics* (New York: W. H. Freeman and Company, 1985), p. 514.

CHAPTER FOCUS

- What determines the exchange-rate value of the dollar relative to other currencies?
- What are the major factors that would cause the exchange-rate value of a currency to change?
- What information is included in the balance-of-payments accounts of a nation? Why are these accounts important?
- Will the balance-of-payments accounts of a country always be in balance? Will the balance of trade always be in balance?
- How do monetary and fiscal policies influence the exchange-rate value of a nation's currency?
- Will a healthy economy run a balance-of-trade surplus? Does a balance-of-trade deficit indicate that a nation is in financial trouble?
- What impact do restrictions on the convertibility of a currency have on people in the countries that impose them?

873

As we discussed in the preceding chapter, the volume of international trade has grown in recent decades. Trade across national boundaries is complicated by the fact that nations generally use different currencies to buy and sell goods in their respective domestic markets. Germans use marks, the British pounds, the Japanese yen, the Mexicans pesos, and so on.

When exchange is between people in different countries, it generally involves the conversion of one currency to another. For example, farmers in the United States want dollars, not some foreign currency, when they sell their wheat. Therefore, foreign purchasers must exchange their currency for dollars before they buy U.S. wheat. Similarly, French winemakers will prefer payment in francs, not dollars. Thus, U.S. importers will have to exchange dollars for francs (or, if they are paid in dollars, the French winemakers will want to change dollars for francs) when Americans purchase French wines.

In this chapter, we analyze how international currencies are linked and how the rates for their exchange are determined. We will also analyze the balance-of-payments accounting that is utilized to keep track of international transactions.

FOREIGN EXCHANGE MARKET

Foreign exchange market
The market in which the currencies of different countries are bought and sold.

The **foreign exchange market** is a widely dispersed, highly organized market in which the currencies of different countries are bought and sold. Commercial banks and currency brokers around the world are the primary organizers of the market.

Let's assume you own a shoe store in the United States and are preparing to place an order for sandals from a manufacturer. You can purchase the sandals from a domestic manufacturer and pay for them with dollars. Or you can buy them from a British manufacturer and pay for them in pounds. If you buy from the British firm, either you will have to change dollars into pounds at a bank and send them to the British producer, or the British manufacturer will have to go to a bank and change your dollar check into pounds. In either case, purchasing the British sandals will involve an exchange of dollars for pounds.

If the British producer sells sandals for 10 pounds per pair, how can you determine whether the price is high or low? To compare the price of the sandals produced by the British firm with the price of domestically produced sandals, you must know the exchange rate between the dollar and the pound. The **exchange rate** is simply the price of one national currency (the pound, for example) in terms of another national currency (such as the U.S. dollar). *The exchange rate is one of the most important prices of an economy because it enables consumers in one country to translate the prices of foreign goods into units of their own currency. Specifically, the dollar price of a foreign good is determined by multiplying the foreign product price by the exchange rate (the dollar price per unit of the foreign currency).* For example, if it takes $1.50 to obtain 1 pound, then the British sandals priced at 10 pounds would cost $15.00 (ten times the $1.50 price of the pound).

Exchange rate
The domestic price of one unit of foreign currency. For example, if it takes $1.50 to purchase one English pound, the dollar-pound exchange rate is 1.50.

Suppose the dollar-pound exchange rate is $1.50 = 1 pound and that you decide to buy 200 pairs of sandals from the British manufacturer at 10 pounds ($15) per pair. You will need 2,000 pounds in order to pay the British manufacturer. If you contact an American bank that handles exchange-rate transactions and write the bank a check for $3,000 (the $1.50 exchange rate multiplied by 2,000), it will supply the 2,000 pounds. The bank will typically charge a small fee for handling the transaction.

Where does the American bank get the pounds? The bank obtains the pounds from British importers who want dollars to buy things from Americans. *Note that the U.S. demand for foreign currencies (such as the pound) comes from the demand of Americans for things purchased from foreigners. On the other hand, the U.S. supply of foreign exchange comes from the demand of foreigners for things bought from Americans.*

Exhibit 33–1 presents data on the exchange rate between the dollar and selected foreign currencies during the 1973–1995 period, as well as an index of the exchange-rate value of the dollar against ten major currencies. Under the flexible-rate system (discussed in detail later in this chapter) present in most industrial countries, the exchange rate between currencies changes from day to

EXHIBIT 33–1

FOREIGN EXCHANGE RATES, 1973–1995

	U.S. CENTS PER UNIT OF FOREIGN CURRENCY					INDEX OF EXCHANGE-RATE VALUE OF THE DOLLAR (TEN CURRENCIES)[a]
YEAR	FRENCH FRANC	GERMAN MARK	JAPANESE YEN	BRITISH POUND	CANADIAN DOLLAR	
1973	22.5	37.8	0.369	245.10	99.9	99.1
1975	23.4	40.7	0.337	222.16	98.3	98.5
1977	20.3	43.1	0.373	174.49	94.1	103.4
1979	23.5	54.6	0.458	212.24	85.3	88.1
1981	18.4	44.4	0.453	202.43	83.4	103.4
1983	13.1	39.2	0.421	151.59	81.1	125.3
1985	11.1	34.0	0.419	129.74	73.2	143.0
1986	14.4	46.1	0.594	146.77	72.0	112.2
1987	16.6	55.6	0.691	163.98	75.4	96.9
1988	16.8	56.9	0.780	178.13	81.3	92.7
1989	15.7	53.2	0.724	163.82	84.4	98.6
1990	18.4	61.9	0.690	178.41	85.7	89.1
1991	17.7	60.2	0.743	176.74	87.3	89.3
1992	18.9	64.0	0.789	176.63	82.7	86.6
1993	17.6	60.4	0.900	150.16	77.5	93.2
1994	18.0	61.7	0.979	153.19	73.2	91.3
1995	20.1	69.8	1.064	157.85	72.9	84.2

[a]March 1973 = 100. In addition to the five currencies listed above, the index includes the Belgian franc, Italian lira, Netherlands guilder, Swedish krona, and Swiss franc.

Sources: Council of Economic Advisers, *Economic Report of the President* (Washington, D.C.: U.S. Government Printing Office, 1993); and *Federal Reserve Bulletin*, April 1996.

day and even from hour to hour. Thus, the annual exchange rate data given in Exhibit 33–1 are really averages for each year.

Between 1979 and 1985, the exchange-rate value of the dollar appreciated against the major foreign currencies. An **appreciation** in the value of a nation's currency means that fewer units of the currency are now required to purchase one unit of a foreign currency. For example, in 1985 only 34 cents were required to purchase a German mark, down from 54.6 cents in 1979.[2] *As the result of this appreciation in the value of the dollar relative to the mark, German goods became less expensive to Americans.* The direction of change in the prices that Germans paid for American goods was just the opposite. An appreciation of the U.S. dollar in terms of the mark is the same thing as a depreciation in the mark relative to the dollar.

A **depreciation** makes foreign goods more expensive, since it decreases the number of units of the foreign currency that can be purchased with a unit of domestic currency. As Exhibit 33–1 shows, the number of cents required to purchase a French franc, German mark, Japanese yen, British pound, or Canadian dollar rose substantially between 1985 and 1990. This depreciation of the dollar against these currencies increased the price of goods purchased by Americans from producers in these countries.

The ten-currency index of the dollar's exchange-rate value presented in Exhibit 33–1 provides evidence on what is happening to the dollar's general exchange-rate value.[3] An increase in the index implies an appreciation in the dollar, while a decline is indicative of a depreciation in the dollar. During the 1970s, the ten-currency index changed by only small amounts from year to year. However, between 1980 and 1985, the index indicates that the exchange-rate value of the dollar increased sharply each year. The dollar appreciated by more than 60 percent during the five-year period. In contrast, it depreciated by a similar amount during 1986–1990.

Appreciation
An increase in the value of a domestic currency relative to foreign currencies. An appreciation increases the purchasing power of the domestic currency for foreign goods.

Depreciation
A reduction in the value of a domestic currency relative to foreign currencies. A depreciation reduces the purchasing power of the domestic currency for foreign goods.

DETERMINANTS OF EXCHANGE RATE

Flexible exchange rates
Exchange rates that are determined by the market forces of supply and demand. They are sometimes called floating exchange rates.

What determines the exchange rate between two currencies? Under a system of **flexible exchange rates,** also called *floating exchange rates,* the value of currencies in the exchange-rate market is determined by market forces. Just as the forces of

---

[2]Because an appreciation means a lower price of foreign currencies, some may think it looks like a depreciation. Just remember that a lower price of the foreign currency means that one's domestic currency will buy more units of the foreign currency and thus more goods and services from foreigners. For example, if the dollar price of the pound falls, this means that a dollar will buy more pounds and thus more goods and services from the British. Therefore, a lower dollar price of the pound means the dollar has appreciated relative to the pound.

[3]In the construction of this index, the exchange rate of each currency relative to the dollar is weighted according to the proportion of U.S. trade with the country. For example, the index weights the U.S. dollar–Japanese yen exchange rate more heavily than the U.S. dollar–Swiss franc exchange rate because the volume of U.S. trade with Japan exceeds the volume of trade with Switzerland.

supply and demand determine other prices, so, too, they determine the exchange-rate value of currencies in the absence of government intervention.

The exchange-rate system in effect since 1973 might best be described as a managed flexible-rate system. It is flexible because all the major industrial countries allow the exchange-rate value of their currencies to float. Several small countries maintain **fixed exchange rates** against the dollar, the English pound, or some other major currency. Therefore, the exchange-rate value of these currencies rises and falls with the major currency to which they are tied. The system is "managed" because the major industrial nations have from time to time attempted to alter supply and demand in the exchange-rate market by buying and selling various currencies. Compared to the size of the exchange-rate market, however, these transactions have been relatively small. Thus, the exchange-rate value of major currencies like the U.S. dollar, British pound, German mark, Japanese yen, and French franc is determined primarily by market forces.

Fixed exchange rate
An exchange rate that is set at a fixed rate by government policy.

DEMAND, SUPPLY, AND EQUILIBRIUM PRICE IN THE FOREIGN EXCHANGE MARKET

To simplify our explanation of how the exchange-rate market works, let us assume that the United States and Great Britain are the only two countries in the world. When Americans buy and sell with each other, they use dollars. Therefore, American sellers will want to be paid in dollars. Similarly, when the British buy and sell with each other, they use pounds. As a result, British sellers will want to be paid in pounds.

If Americans want to buy from British sellers, they will need to acquire pounds. *In our two-country world, the demand for pounds in the exchange-rate market originates from the demand of Americans for British goods, services, and assets (either real or financial).* For example, when U.S. residents purchase men's suits from a British manufacturer, travel in the United Kingdom, or purchase the stocks, bonds, or physical assets of British business firms, they demand pounds from (and supply dollars to) the foreign exchange-rate market to pay for these items.

The supply of foreign exchange (pounds in our two-country case) originates from sales by Americans to foreigners. When Americans sell goods, services, or assets to the British, for example, the British buyers will supply pounds (and demand dollars) in the exchange-rate market in order to acquire the dollars required to pay for the items purchased from Americans.[4]

Exhibit 33–2 illustrates the demand and supply curves of Americans for foreign exchange—British pounds in our two-country case. The demand for pounds is downward sloping because a lower dollar price of the pound—meaning a dollar will buy more pounds—makes British goods cheaper for American importers. The goods produced by one country are generally good substitutes for the goods of another country. This means that when foreign (British) goods become cheaper,

---

[4]We analyze the foreign exchange market in terms of the demand and supply of foreign currencies. Alternatively, this analysis could be done in terms of the supply and demand of dollars. Since one currency is traded for another, the same actions that generate a demand for foreign exchange simultaneously generate a supply of dollars. Correspondingly, the same exchanges that create a supply of foreign currencies simultaneously generate a demand for dollars in the foreign exchange market.

The dollar price of the pound is measured on the vertical axis. The horizontal axis indicates the flow of pounds to the foreign exchange market. The equilibrium exchange rate is $1.50 = 1 pound. At the equilibrium price, the quantity demanded of pounds just equals the quantity supplied. A higher price of pounds such as $1.80 = 1 pound would lead to an excess supply of pounds, causing the dollar price of the pound to fall. On the other hand, a lower price—for example, $1.20 = 1 pound— would result in an excess demand for pounds, causing the pound to appreciate.

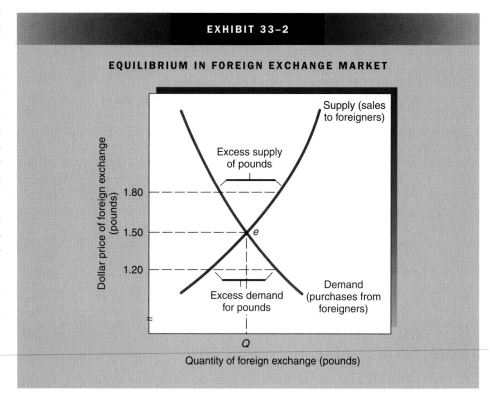

EXHIBIT 33–2

EQUILIBRIUM IN FOREIGN EXCHANGE MARKET

Americans will increase their expenditures on imports (and therefore the quantity of pounds demanded will increase). Thus, as the dollar price of the pound declines, Americans will both buy more of the lower-priced (in dollars) British goods and demand more pounds, which are required for the purchases.

Similarly, the supply curve for pounds is dependent on the sales by Americans to the British (that is, the purchase of American goods by the British.) An increase in the dollar price of the pound means that a pound will purchase more dollars and more goods priced in dollars. Thus, the price (in pounds) of American goods, services, and assets to British purchasers declines as the dollar price of the pound increases. The British will purchase more from Americans and therefore supply more pounds to the exchange-rate market as the dollar price of the pound rises. Because of this, the supply curve for pounds tends to slope upward to the right.

As Exhibit 33–2 shows, equilibrium is present at the dollar price of the pound that brings the quantity demanded and quantity supplied of pounds into balance, $1.50 = 1 pound in this case. The market-clearing price of $1.50 per pound not only equates demand and supply in the foreign exchange market, it also equates (1) the value of U.S. purchases of items supplied by the British with (2) the value of items sold by U.S. residents to the British. Demand and supply in the currency market are merely the mirror images of these two factors.

What would happen if the price of the pound were above equilibrium— $1.80 = 1 pound, for example? At the higher dollar price of the pound, British goods would be more expensive for Americans. Americans would cut back on their purchases of English shoes, glassware, textile products, financial assets, and other items supplied by the British. Reflecting this reduction, the quantity of pounds demanded by Americans would decline. Simultaneously, the higher dollar price of the pound would make U.S. exports cheaper for the British. For example, an $18,000 American automobile would cost British consumers 12,000 pounds when 1 pound trades for $1.50, but it would cost only 10,000 pounds when 1 pound exchanges for $1.80. If the price of the pound were $1.80, the British would tend to supply more pounds to the exchange-rate market to purchase the cheaper American goods. Thus, at the $1.80 = 1 pound price, the quantity of pounds demanded by Americans is lower, and the quantity supplied by the British is higher. As can be seen in Exhibit 33–2, an excess supply of pounds results, causing the dollar price of the pound to decline until equilibrium is restored at the $1.50 = 1 pound price.

At a below-equilibrium price such as $1.20 = 1 pound, an opposite set of forces would be present. The lower dollar price of the pound would make English goods cheaper for Americans and American goods more expensive for the British. The quantity demanded of British goods and pounds by Americans would increase. Simultaneously, the quantity of American goods demanded and pounds supplied by the British would decline. An excess demand for pounds would result at the $1.20 = 1 pound price. The excess demand would tend to cause the dollar price of the pound to rise until equilibrium was restored at $1.50 = 1 pound.

The implications of the analysis are general. In our multicountry and multicurrency world, the demand for foreign currencies in exchange for dollars reflects the purchases by Americans of goods, services, and assets from foreigners. The supply of foreign currencies in exchange for dollars reflects the sales by Americans of goods, services, and assets to foreigners. The equilibrium in the exchange rate market will bring the quantity of foreign exchange demanded by Americans into equality with the quantity supplied by foreigners. It will also bring the purchases by Americans from foreigners into equality with the sales by Americans to foreigners.

CHANGES IN EXCHANGE RATES

When exchange rates are free to fluctuate, the market value of a nation's currency will appreciate and depreciate in response to changing market conditions. Any change that alters the quantity of goods, services, or assets bought from foreigners relative to the quantity sold to foreigners will also alter the exchange rate. What types of change will alter the exchange-rate value of a currency?

CHANGES IN INCOME. An increase in domestic income will encourage the nation's residents to spend a portion of their additional income on imports. When the income of a nation grows rapidly, the nation's imports tend to rise rapidly as well. As **Exhibit 33–3** illustrates, an increase in imports also increases the demand for foreign exchange (the pound in our two-country case). As the demand for pounds increases, the dollar price of the pound rises (from $1.50 to $1.80). This depreciation of the dollar reduces the incentive of Americans to import British goods and services, while increasing the incentive of the British to purchase U.S. exports. These two forces will restore equilibrium in the foreign exchange market at a new, higher dollar price of the pound.

Other things constant, if incomes grow in the United States, U.S. imports will grow. The increase in the imports will increase the demand for pounds, causing the dollar price of the pound to rise (from $1.50 to $1.80).

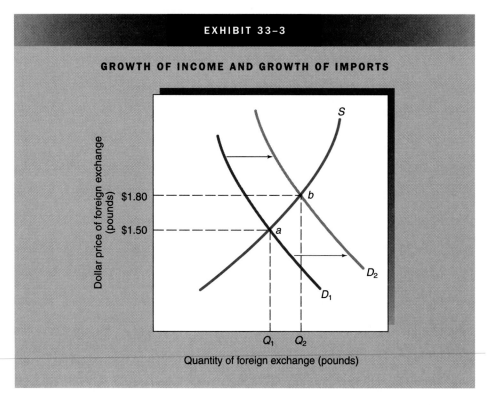

EXHIBIT 33–3

GROWTH OF INCOME AND GROWTH OF IMPORTS

Just the opposite takes place when the income of a trading partner (Great Britain in our example) increases. Rapid growth of income abroad will lead to an increase in U.S. exports, causing the demand for the dollar to rise. This will result in dollar appreciation—equilibrium at a new, lower dollar price of the pound.

What happens to the exchange rate if income increases in both countries? The key here is to identify the nation that is growing the fastest. For countries that are similar in size and propensity to import, the country that is growing the fastest will increase its demand for imports relatively more than its trading partner, resulting in a decrease in the value of the more rapidly growing nation's currency. *Paradoxical as it may seem, sluggish growth of income relative to one's trading partners tends to cause the slow-growth nation's currency to appreciate, since the nation's imports decline relative to exports.*

DIFFERENCES IN RATES OF INFLATION. *Other things constant, domestic inflation will cause the nation's currency to depreciate on the exchange market, whereas deflation will result in appreciation.* Suppose prices in the United States rise by 50 percent while our trading partners are experiencing stable prices. The domestic inflation will cause U.S. consumers to increase their demand for imported goods (and foreign currency). In turn, the inflated domestic prices will cause foreigners to reduce their purchases of U.S. goods, thereby reducing the supply of foreign currency to the exchange market. As **Exhibit 33–4** illustrates, the exchange rate will adjust to this set of circumstances. The dollar will depreciate relative to the pound.

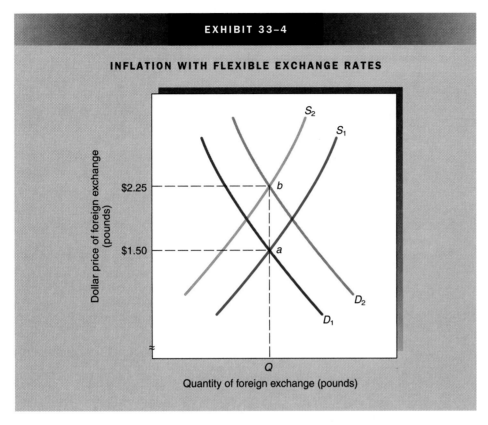

EXHIBIT 33–4

INFLATION WITH FLEXIBLE EXCHANGE RATES

If prices were stable in Britain while the price level increased 50 percent in the United States, the U.S. demand for British products (and pounds) would increase, whereas U.S. exports to Britain would decline, causing the supply of pounds to fall. These forces would cause the dollar to depreciate relative to the pound.

Exchange-rate adjustments permit nations with even high rates of inflation to engage in trade with countries experiencing relatively stable prices. A depreciation in a nation's currency in the foreign exchange market compensates for the nation's inflation rate. For example, if inflation increases the price level in the United States by 50 percent, and the value of the dollar in exchange for the pound depreciates (such that the value of the foreign currency increases 50 percent), then the prices of American goods measured in pounds are unchanged to British consumers. Thus, when the exchange-rate value of the dollar changes from $1.50 = 1 pound to $2.25 = 1 pound, the depreciation in the dollar restores the original prices of U.S. goods to British consumers even though the price level in the United States has increased by 50 percent.

What if prices in both England and the United States are rising at the same annual rate, say, 10 percent? The prices of imports (and exports) will remain unchanged relative to domestically produced goods. Equal rates of inflation in each country will not cause the value of exports to change relative to imports. Identical rates of inflation will not disturb an equilibrium in the exchange market. Inflation contributes to the depreciation of a nation's currency only when that country's rate of inflation is more rapid than that of its trading partners.

CHANGES IN INTEREST RATES. Financial investments will be quite sensitive to changes in real interest rates—that is, interest rates adjusted for the expected rate of inflation. International loanable funds will tend to move toward areas where the expected real rate of return (after compensation for differences in risk) is highest.

WHAT FACTORS CAUSE A NATION'S CURRENCY TO APPRECIATE OR DEPRECIATE?

THESE FACTORS WILL CAUSE A NATION'S CURRENCY TO APPRECIATE:
1. Slow growth of income (relative to trading partners) that causes imports to lag behind exports.
2. A rate of inflation that is lower than that of one's trading partners.
3. Domestic real interest rates that are greater than real interest rates abroad.

THESE FACTORS WILL CAUSE A NATION'S CURRENCY TO DEPRECIATE:
1. Rapid growth of income (relative to trading partners) that stimulates imports relative to exports.
2. A rate of inflation that is higher than that of one's trading partners.
3. Domestic real interest rates that are lower than real interest rates abroad.

Thus, high interest rates relative to a nation's trading partners will tend to cause that nation's currency to appreciate. For example, if real interest rates increase in the United States relative to Western Europe, investors in Britain, France, and Germany will demand dollars (and supply their currencies) in the exchange-rate market to purchase the high-yield American assets. The increase in demand for the dollar and supply of European currencies will cause the dollar to appreciate relative to the British pound, French franc, and German mark.

In contrast, when real interest rates in other countries are high relative to the United States, short-term financial investors will move to take advantage of the improved earnings opportunities abroad. As investment funds move from the United States to other countries, there will be an increase in the demand for foreign currencies and an increase in the supply of dollars in the foreign exchange market. A depreciation in the dollar relative to the currencies of countries experiencing the high real interest rates will be the result. The accompanying Thumbnail Sketch summarizes the major forces that cause a nation's currency to appreciate or depreciate when exchange rates are determined by market forces.

FIXED EXCHANGE RATES

Between 1944 and 1971, most of the world operated under a system of fixed exchange rates, where each nation "pegs" the price of its currency to another currency, such as the dollar (or gold), for long periods of time. Governments intervene in the foreign exchange market or alter their economic policies in an effort to maintain the fixed value of their currency.

Fixing the price of a currency in the exchange market, like fixing other prices, results in surpluses and shortages. As market conditions change, the exchange rate that equates the quantity supplied of each currency with the quantity demanded of that currency also changes. What happens when the fixed rate differs from the equilibrium rate? Building on the analysis of Exhibit 33–2, suppose the equilibrium exchange rate were $1.50 = 1 pound. If the price of the pound is fixed at $1.80 = 1 pound, an excess supply of pounds will result. At the $1.80 = 1 pound rate, the pound is overvalued (and the dollar undervalued). At the $1.80 per pound exchange rate, the United States will persistently export more goods, services, and assets to the British than it will import from the British. The central bank in the United States will have to continually increase its holdings of pounds—that is, buy the excess supply of pounds—to maintain the above-equilibrium price of the pound. In essence, this situation leads to a surplus of exports over imports for the United States in its trade with England.

What would happen if the dollar price of the pound were set below equilibrium, such as $1.20 = 1 pound (Exhibit 33–2)? The below-equilibrium price of the pound would lead to an excess demand for pounds. Since the pound is undervalued (and the dollar overvalued) at the $1.20-per-pound price, British imports are cheap to Americans (and U.S. exports expensive for the British). In its trade with the British, the United States would persistently buy (import) more than it sells (exports). To defend the $1.20-per-pound fixed rate, the U.S. central bank would have to draw down its holdings of pounds, balances that were perhaps built up during periods when the dollar-price of the pound was above equilibrium.

To make a fixed-rate system work, each country must maintain a reserve balance of other currencies that will permit it to weather temporary periods of excess demand relative to supply. When the fixed-rate system was put in place at the end of the Second World War, the **International Monetary Fund (IMF)** was established to perform this function. The IMF required each of its more than 100 member countries to deposit a specified amount of its currency into a reserve fund held by the IMF. Thus, it possessed substantial holdings of dollars, francs, pounds, marks, and other currencies of the participating nations. As the need arose, these reserves were loaned to nations experiencing difficulties with their balance of payments.

If both the fixed-rate system and freedom of international exchange are going to be maintained, countries must maintain monetary and fiscal policies that are consistent with the fixed rates. Put another way, maintenance of a fixed-rate system requires the countries to give up monetary and fiscal policy independence. Of course, countries may temporarily experience periods where purchases from foreigners exceed their sales to foreigners. During such periods, nations can draw down their reserve balance. However, nations that persistently buy (import) more than they sell (export) will have to take corrective action. During the 1944–1971 period, the IMF provided discipline to the system by encouraging—and in some cases requiring—member nations (as a condition for the receipt of loans) to adopt policies that would bring the nation's purchases from and sales to foreigners into balance.

What steps can a nation experiencing an excess of imports over exports take to remedy this situation under a fixed-rate system? Basically, there are three alternatives.

International Monetary Fund (IMF)
An international banking organization, with more than 100 member nations, designed to oversee the operation of the international monetary system. Although it does not control the world supply of money, it does hold currency reserves for member nations and makes currency loans to national central banks.

Devaluation
An official act that changes the level of the fixed exchange rate downward in terms of other currencies. In essence, it is a one-step depreciation of a currency under a fixed-exchange-rate system.

1. A nation can devalue its currency. **Devaluation** is a one-step reduction in the value of a nation's currency under a fixed-rate system. When a currency is overvalued, a devaluation can restore equilibrium between the demand and supply of the currency in the exchange market. For example, if there is an excess supply of dollars (excess demand for pounds) in the exchange market when the fixed exchange rate is $1.20 = 1 pound, a devaluation of the dollar (perhaps to $1.50 = 1 pound) could restore balance. A devaluation makes imports more expensive to domestic consumers, while encouraging exports. It thus tends to correct an excess of imports relative to exports.

2. A nation can heighten trade barriers, adopting tariffs and quotas in an effort to reduce imports and bring the value of its currency on the foreign exchange market into equilibrium. This strategy is in conflict with economic efficiency and the promotion of the free flow of trade between nations. Nevertheless, it was often adopted during the period of 1944–1971. Once a nation's exchange rate was established, it tended to become sacred. Politicians during that period, including many in the United States, frequently argued that, even though they did not like to impose trade restrictions, the barriers were necessary to avoid devaluation. The balance-of-payments issue was an excellent excuse to promote trade restrictions—which were advocated by special interests—against low-cost foreign goods.

3. A nation can follow restrictive macroeconomic policy designed to promote deflation (or at least retard inflation) and high interest rates. Policymakers might use restrictive monetary and fiscal policy to retard inflation and increase interest rates. A slower rate of inflation relative to one's trading partners would encourage exports and discourage imports. Higher domestic real interest rates would attract foreign investment and thereby increase the nation's supply of foreign exchange.

When a nation uses macroeconomic policy to restore balance in the exchange market, an important point emerges. This method of bringing about equilibrium in the exchange market attempts to manipulate the level of all other prices to maintain one price—the fixed exchange rate. In contrast, a flexible exchange rate system changes one price—the foreign exchange rate—to restore balance between what is bought from and what is sold to foreigners.

BALANCE OF PAYMENTS

Balance of payments
A summary of all economic transactions between a country and all other countries for a specific time period, usually a year. The balance-of-payments account reflects all payments and liabilities to foreigners (debits) and all payments and obligations received from foreigners (credits).

Just as countries calculate their gross domestic product (GDP) so that they have a general idea of their domestic level of production, most countries also calculate their balance of international payments in order to keep track of their transactions with other nations. The **balance of payments** summarizes the transactions of the country's citizens, businesses, and governments with foreigners. It provides information on the nation's exports, imports, earnings of domestic residents on assets located abroad, earnings on domestic assets owned by foreigners, international capital movements, and official transactions by central banks and governments.

Balance-of-payments accounts are kept according to the principles of basic bookkeeping. Any transaction that creates a demand for foreign currency (and a supply of the domestic currency) in the foreign exchange market is recorded as a debit, or minus, item. Imports are an example of a debit item. Transactions that create a supply of foreign currency (and demand for the domestic currency) on the foreign exchange market are recorded as a credit, or plus, item. Exports are an example of a credit item. Since the quantity demanded will equal the quantity supplied in the foreign exchange market, the total debits will equal the total credits.

Balance-of-payments transactions can be grouped into three basic categories: current account, capital account, and official reserve account. Let us take a look at each of these.

CURRENT-ACCOUNT TRANSACTIONS

All payments (and gifts) related to the purchase or sale of goods and services and income flows during the designated period are included in the **current account.** In general, there are four major types of current-account transactions: the exchange of merchandise goods, the exchange of services, income from investments, and unilateral transfers.

Current account
The record of all transactions with foreign nations that involve the exchange of merchandise goods and services, current income derived from investments, and unilateral gifts.

MERCHANDISE-TRADE TRANSACTIONS. The export and import of merchandise goods compose by far the largest portion of a nation's balance-of-payments account. When U.S. producers export their products, foreigners will supply their currency in exchange for dollars in order to pay for the U.S.-produced goods. Since U.S. exports generate a supply of foreign exchange and demand for dollars in the foreign exchange market, they are a credit (plus) item. In contrast, when Americans import goods, they will demand foreign currencies and supply dollars in the exchange-rate market. Thus, imports are a debit (minus) item.

As **Exhibit 33–5** shows, the United States exported $575 billion of merchandise goods in 1995, compared to imports of $749 billion. The difference between the value of a country's merchandise exports and the value of its merchandise imports is known as the **balance of merchandise trade** (or *balance of trade*). If the value of a country's merchandise exports falls short of the value of its merchandise imports, it is said to have a balance-of-trade deficit. In contrast, the situation where a nation exports more than it imports is referred to as trade surplus. In 1995 the United States ran a merchandise trade deficit of $174 billion.

Other things constant, a U.S. merchandise-trade deficit implies that Americans are supplying more dollars to the exchange market in order to purchase foreign-made goods than foreigners are demanding for the purchase of American goods. If the merchandise-trade deficit were the only factor influencing the value of the dollar on the exchange market, one could anticipate a decline in the foreign exchange value of the U.S. currency. However, several other factors also affect the supply of and demand for the dollar on the exchange market.

Balance of merchandise trade
The difference between the value of merchandise exports and the value of merchandise imports for a nation. The balance of merchandise trade is only one component of a nation's total balance of payments. Also called simply balance of trade *or* net exports.

SERVICE EXPORTS AND IMPORTS. The export and import of *invisible services,* as they are sometimes called, also exert an important influence on the foreign exchange market. The export of insurance, transportation, and banking services

Source: *Federal Reserve Bulletin,*
July 1996.

EXHIBIT 33-5

U.S. BALANCE OF PAYMENTS, 1995

	BILLIONS OF DOLLARS	
	AMOUNT	DEFICIT (−) OR SURPLUS (+)
CURRENT ACCOUNT		
1a. U.S. merchandise exports	+575	
1b. U.S. merchandise imports	−749	
Balance of merchandise trade		−174
2a. U.S. service exports	+212	
2b. U.S. service imports	−142	
Balance on goods and services		−104
3. Net investment income	−11	
4. Net transfers	−38	
Balance on current account		**−153**
CAPITAL ACCOUNT		
5. Private capital inflow to U.S.	+316	
6. Private outflow of U.S. capital	−270	
Balance on capital account		**+46**
CURRENT AND CAPITAL ACCOUNT BALANCE		−107
OFFICIAL RESERVE-ACCOUNT TRANSACTIONS		+107

generates a supply of foreign exchange and demand for dollars just as the export of merchandise does. A French business that is insured with an American company will supply francs and demand dollars with which to pay its premiums. Similarly, when foreigners travel in the United States or transport cargo on American ships, they will supply foreign exchange and demand dollars with which to pay for these services. These service exports are thus entered as credits on the current account.

On the other hand, the import of services from foreigners generates a demand for foreign currency and supply of dollars in the exchange market. Therefore, service imports are entered on the balance-of-payments account as debit items. Travel abroad by U.S. citizens, the shipment of goods on foreign carriers, and the purchase of other services from foreigners are all debit items, since they create a demand for foreign exchange.

These service transactions are substantial. As Exhibit 33–5 illustrates, in 1995 U.S. service exports were $212 billion, compared with service imports of $142 billion. Thus, the U.S. ran a $70 billion surplus on its service trade transactions.

When we add the balance of service exports and imports to the balance of merchandise trade, we obtain the **balance on goods and services.** In 1995 the

Balance on goods and services

The exports of goods (merchandise) and services of a nation minus its imports of goods and services.

United States ran a $104 billion deficit (the sum of the $174 billion merchandise trade deficit minus the $70 billion service surplus) in the goods and services account.

INCOME FROM INVESTMENTS.   In the past, Americans have made substantial investments in stocks, bonds, and real assets in other countries. As these investments abroad generate income, dollars will flow from foreigners to Americans. Since the income of Americans from their investments abroad supplies foreign currency (and creates a demand for dollars) in the foreign exchange market, it enters as a credit item on the current account.

Correspondingly, foreigners hold substantial investments in the United States. As these investments earn dividends, interest, and rents, they earn income for foreigners. This income of foreigners leads to an outflow of dollars. As foreigners convert their dollar earnings to their domestic currency, the demand for foreign currency (and supply of dollars) increases in the foreign exchange market. Thus, the income of foreigners from their investments in the United States is a debit item in the balance-of-payments accounts.

As Exhibit 33–5 shows, in 1995 Americans earned $11 billion less on their investments abroad than foreigners earned on their investments in the United States. Since these items resulted in a *net* flow of income to foreigners, the result is recorded as a debit.

UNILATERAL TRANSFERS.   Monetary gifts to foreigners, such as U.S. aid to a foreign government or private gifts from U.S. residents to their relatives abroad, generate a demand for foreign currencies and supply dollars in the exchange market. Thus, these gifts are debit items in the balance-of-payments accounts. Monetary gifts to Americans from foreigners are credit items. Gifts in kind are more complex. When products are given to foreigners, goods flow abroad, but there is no offsetting influx of foreign currency—that is, a demand for dollars. Balance-of-payments accountants handle such transactions as though the United States had demanded the foreign exchange and supplied the dollars with which to purchase the direct grants made to foreigners. So these items are also entered as debits. Because the U.S. government and private U.S. citizens made grants of $38 billion more to foreigners than we received from them, this net unilateral transfer was entered as a debit item on the current account in 1995.

BALANCE ON CURRENT ACCOUNT.   The difference between (1) the value of a country's current exports and earnings from investments abroad and (2) the value of its current imports and the earnings of foreigners on their domestic assets (plus net unilateral transfers to foreigners) is known as the **balance on current account.** Current-account transactions involve only current exchanges of goods and services and current income flows (and gifts). They do not involve changes in the ownership of either real or financial assets. The current-account balance provides a summary of all current-account transactions. As with the balance of trade, when the value of the current-account debit items (import-type transactions) exceeds the value of the credit items (export-type transactions), we say that the country is running a current-account deficit. Alternatively, if the credit items are greater than the debit items, the country is running a current-account surplus. In 1995 the United States ran a current-account deficit of $153 billion.

Balance on current account
The import-export balance of goods and services, plus net investment income earned abroad, plus net private and government transfers. If the value of the nation's export-type items exceeds (is less than) the value of the nation's import-type items (plus net unilateral transfers to foreigners), a current-account surplus (deficit) is present.

CAPITAL-ACCOUNT TRANSACTIONS

Capital account

Transactions with foreigners that involve either (1) the exchange of ownership rights to real or financial assets or (2) the extension of loans.

In contrast with current-account transactions, **capital-account** transactions focus on changes in the ownership of real and financial assets. These transactions are composed of (1) direct investments by Americans in real assets abroad (or by foreigners in the United States) and (2) loans to and from foreigners. When foreigners make investments in the United States—for example, by purchasing stocks, bonds, or real assets from Americans—their actions will supply foreign currency and generate a demand for dollars in the foreign exchange market. Thus, these capital-inflow transactions are a credit.

On the other hand, capital-outflow transactions are recorded as debits. For example, if a U.S. investor purchases a shoe factory in Mexico, the Mexican seller will want to be paid in pesos. The U.S. investor will supply dollars (and demand pesos) on the foreign exchange market. Since U.S. citizens will demand foreign currency (and supply dollars) when they invest in stocks, bonds, and real assets abroad, these transactions enter into the balance-of-payments accounts as a debit. In 1995 foreign investments in the United States (capital inflow) summed to $316 billion, while U.S. investments abroad (capital outflow) totaled $270 billion. Since the capital inflow exceeded the outflow, the United States ran a $46 billion capital-account surplus in 1995.

OFFICIAL RESERVE ACCOUNT

Special drawing rights (SDRs)

Supplementary reserves, in the form of accounting entries, established by the International Monetary Fund (also called paper gold). Like gold and foreign currency reserves, they can be used to make payments on international accounts.

Governments maintain official reserve balances in the form of foreign currencies, gold, and **special drawing rights (SDRs)** with the International Monetary Fund (IMF), which is, as explained earlier, a type of international central bank. Countries running a deficit on their current- and capital-account balances can draw on their reserves. Similarly, countries running a surplus can build up their reserves of foreign currencies and reserve balances with the IMF. Under the fixed-rate exchange system present during 1944–1971, these reserve transactions were highly significant. Countries experiencing balance-of-payments difficulties were forced to draw on their reserves to maintain their fixed exchange rate. Countries that were selling more to foreigners than foreigners were buying from them accumulated the currencies of other nations.

Under the current (primarily) flexible-rate system, changes in the official reserve account of nations are less significant. Changes in the exchange rate are generally relied on to balance the amount of goods, services, and assets purchased from foreigners and the amount sold to foreigners. However, sometimes nations have their central banks buy and sell currencies in an attempt to reduce sharp swings in the exchange rate. During some years, a nation might build up its holdings of foreign currencies, while in other years it might permit them to be drawn out.

Under the current system, these official reserve transactions are usually quite modest relative to the total of all international transactions. In comparison with recent years, the U.S. official reserve transactions in 1995 were abnormally large. The decline in U.S. holdings of foreign currencies plus the increase in foreign holdings of U.S. reserve assets summed to $107 billion in 1995. However, compared to the trade and capital flows of more than 1.1 trillion, the reserve transactions were still relatively small.

BALANCE OF PAYMENTS MUST BALANCE

The aggregated balance-of-payments accounts must balance. The following identity must hold:

$$\text{Current-account balance} + \text{Capital-account balance} + \text{Official reserve account balance} = 0$$

However, the specific components of the accounts need not balance. For example, the debit and credit items of the current account need not be equal. Specific components may run either a surplus or a deficit. Nevertheless, since the balance of payments as a whole must balance, a deficit in one area implies a surplus in another.

If a nation is experiencing a deficit on its current-account balance, it must experience an offsetting surplus on the sum of its capital-account and official-reserve-account balances. *Under a pure flexible-rate system, official reserve transactions are zero; therefore, a current-account deficit implies a capital-account surplus. Similarly, a current-account surplus implies a capital-account deficit.*

A current-account deficit means that, in aggregate, the citizens of a nation are buying more goods and services from foreigners than they are selling to foreigners. Under a pure flexible-rate system, this excess of expenditures relative to receipts is paid for by borrowing from and selling assets to foreigners.

Since countries, to some extent, engage in official reserve transactions, the current system is not a pure flexible-rate system. If it were, there would be no official reserve transactions. In 1995 the United States ran a $153 billion deficit on its current account and a $46 billion surplus on its capital account. This $107 billion combined deficit was exactly offset by a $107 billion surplus on the official-reserve-account transactions. Thus, the deficits and surpluses on current-account, capital-account, and official-reserve-account transactions summed to zero.

MACROECONOMIC POLICY IN AN OPEN ECONOMY

During the post–Second World War period, there has been a dramatic increase in international trade and in the flow of investment capital across national boundaries. This increasing mobility of both goods and capital influences the effects of macroeconomic policy, even in a country such as the United States with a relatively small trade sector. We now live in a global economy. No country can conduct its macroeconomic policy in isolation.

Throughout this text, we have focused on the impact of macroeconomic policy within the framework of an open economy. To date, however, we have paid little attention to the impact of macroeconomic policy on exchange rates and on the components of a nation's balance-of-payments accounts. We now turn to these issues.

MACROECONOMIC POLICY AND THE EXCHANGE RATE

Since monetary and fiscal policies exert an impact on income growth, inflation, and real interest rates, they will also influence exchange rates. Because these two major macropolicy tools differ with regard to their impact on the foreign exchange market, we will consider them separately.

MONETARY POLICY AND THE EXCHANGE RATE. Suppose the United States began to follow a more expansionary monetary policy. How would this policy influence the exchange-rate market? *When the effects are not fully anticipated,* expansionary monetary policy will lead to more rapid economic growth, an increase in the inflation rate, and lower real interest rates.[5] As we previously discussed, each of these factors will increase the demand for foreign exchange, causing the dollar to depreciate (see Thumbnail Sketch, page 882). The rapid growth of income will stimulate imports. Similarly, the increase in the U.S. inflation rate (relative to our trading partners) will make U.S. goods less competitive abroad, causing a decline in exports. Simultaneously, the lower real interest rate will encourage the flow of capital abroad. *The expected short-run effect of an unanticipated shift to a more expansionary monetary policy is a depreciation in the exchange-rate value of the dollar.*

The expected outcome of an unanticipated switch to a more restrictive monetary policy will be just the opposite. The restrictive monetary policy will retard economic growth, reduce the rate of inflation, and push real interest rates upward. Exports will grow relative to imports. Investment funds from abroad will be drawn by the high real interest rates in the United States. Foreigners will demand more dollars with which to purchase goods, services, and real assets in the United States. The increase in the supply of foreign currencies and strong demand for the dollar in the foreign exchange market will cause the dollar to appreciate.

FISCAL POLICY AND THE EXCHANGE RATE. Fiscal policy tends to generate conflicting influences on the foreign exchange market. Suppose the United States unexpectedly shifts toward a more restrictive fiscal policy, planning a budget surplus or at least a smaller deficit. Just as with restrictive monetary policy, the restrictive fiscal policy will tend to cause a reduction in aggregate demand, an economic slowdown, and a decline in the rate of inflation. These factors will discourage imports and stimulate exports, placing upward pressure on the exchange-rate value of the dollar. However, restrictive fiscal policy will also

---

[5]As we previously noted when considering monetary policy, the impact of a policy change is dependent on whether the effects of the change are anticipated or unanticipated. Neither growth nor the real interest rate will change if people fully anticipate the effects of the change in monetary policy on the price level. In this chapter, we assume for simplicity that the price-level effects of monetary policy are unanticipated. This clearly is more relevant in the short run than in the long run.

mean less government borrowing, which will reduce real interest rates in the United States. The lower real interest rates will cause financial capital to flow from the United States. This will increase the supply of dollars in the foreign exchange market, and thereby place downward pressure on the exchange-rate value of the U.S. dollar.

Which of these two effects is likely to dominate? When answering this question, it is important to consider the mobility of capital relative to trade flows. *Financial capital is highly mobile. Investors can and do quickly shift their funds from one country to another in response to changes in interest rates. In contrast, importers and exporters often enter into long-term contracts when buying and selling goods. Thus, they are likely to respond more slowly to changing market conditions. Consequently, to the extent that a more restrictive fiscal policy places downward pressure on interest rates, the outflow of capital is likely to dominate in the short run.* At least a temporary depreciation in the nation's currency is the most likely outcome.

The analysis of expansionary fiscal policy is symmetrical. To the extent that larger budget deficits stimulate aggregate demand and domestic inflation, they will encourage imports, which will place downward pressure on the exchange-rate value of a nation's currency. However, the increased borrowing to finance larger budget deficits will push real interest rates up and draw foreign investment to the United States, causing the dollar to appreciate. In the short run, the latter outcome is more likely.

MACROECONOMIC POLICY AND CURRENT ACCOUNT

How does macroeconomic policy affect a nation's balance on current account? When considering this question, it is important to remember that the current- and capital-account balances must sum to zero under a pure flexible-rate system. Thus, any deficit on current (capital) account must be exactly offset by a capital (current) account surplus of equal size. Since unanticipated shifts in macroeconomic policy influence both the demand for imports and real interest rates, then, clearly, they will exert an impact on both current account and capital account balances.

MONETARY POLICY AND CURRENT ACCOUNT. Suppose that the Federal Reserve suddenly increases the growth rate of the money supply. How will this shift to a more expansionary monetary policy influence the U.S. balance on current account? As we just indicated, the more rapid money growth will stimulate income, place upward pressure on the inflation rate, and reduce real interest rates. Think how this combination of factors will affect the current and capital accounts. The growth of income and higher domestic prices will stimulate imports, retard exports, and thus cause the current account to shift toward a larger deficit (or smaller surplus). At the same time, the lower domestic interest rates will encourage investors, both domestic and foreign, to shift funds from the United States to other countries where they can earn a higher rate of return. Predictably, this outflow of capital will cause a capital-account deficit and depreciation in the exchange-rate value of the dollar. In turn, the dollar depreciation will encourage exports, discourage imports, and act as a partial offset to the

THUMBNAIL SKETCH

HOW WILL MONETARY AND FISCAL POLICY AFFECT THE EXCHANGE-RATE AND BALANCE-OF-PAYMENTS COMPONENTS?

A. THE IMPACT OF UNANTICIPATED SHIFT IN MONETARY POLICY:

	EXPANSIONARY MONETARY POLICY	RESTRICTIVE MONETARY POLICY
Exchange rate[a]	Depreciates.	Appreciates.
Real interest rates	Decline.	Increase.
Flow of capital	Capital outflow.	Capital inflow.
Current account	Shifts toward a surplus.	Shifts toward a deficit.

B. IMPACT OF UNANTICIPATED SHIFT IN FISCAL POLICY:

	EXPANSIONARY FISCAL POLICY	RESTRICTIVE FISCAL POLICY
Exchange rate[a]	Uncertain, but the interest rate effect is likely to cause appreciation.	Uncertain, but the interest rate effect is likely to cause depreciation.
Real interest rates	Increase.	Decline.
Flow of capital	Capital inflow.	Capital outflow.
Current account	Shifts toward a deficit.	Shifts toward a surplus.

[a]Value of domestic currency

direct effects of the more rapid income growth. Since capital is far more mobile than goods in international markets, the outflow of capital effect will generally dominate in the short run. For a time, therefore, the shift to the expansionary monetary policy will tend to cause an outflow of capital that will shift the capital account toward a deficit (or smaller surplus) and the current account toward a surplus (or smaller deficit).

Now consider the impact of an unanticipated shift to a more restrictive monetary policy on a nation's current-account balance. The restrictive policy will tend to slow growth and inflation, which will reduce the demand for imports. However, it will also increase real interest rates, leading to an inflow of capital and appreciation in the nation's currency. In the short run, the inflow of capital will generally dominate. Thus, the expected result of the more restrictive monetary policy is higher interest rates, an inflow of capital, a shift toward a capital-account surplus (or smaller deficit), and a shift toward a current-account deficit in the short run.

FISCAL POLICY AND CURRENT ACCOUNT. What impact will large budget deficits have on a nation's current account? Expansionary fiscal policy will tend to stimulate aggregate demand and push domestic interest rates upward (the *crowding-out effect*). The increase in aggregate demand will encourage the purchase of imports, and thereby shift the current account toward a deficit (or smaller surplus). Simultaneously, the higher real interest rates will both attract foreign capital and help keep domestic capital at home. Predictably, there will be a net capital inflow, which will shift the capital account toward a surplus.

When fiscal policy is expansionary, both the increase in imports due to the demand stimulus and the increase in the net capital inflow as the result of the higher interest rates will shift the current account toward a deficit and the capital account toward a surplus. In this way, large budget deficits will also tend to result in large current-account deficits.

Once again, the analysis is symmetrical. A shift to a more restrictive fiscal policy—for example, a reduction in the size of a budget deficit—will retard demand and reduce interest rates. As the result of the decline in aggregate demand, imports will tend to fall, shifting a nation's current account toward a surplus (or smaller deficit). Simultaneously, the low interest rates will lead to a net capital outflow, which will shift the capital account toward a deficit. Thus, restrictive fiscal policy will tend to cause a current-account surplus and a capital-account deficit. The Thumbnail Sketch on page 892, summarizes the expected impacts of unanticipated shifts in monetary and fiscal policy.

MACROECONOMIC POLICY AND THE CURRENT-ACCOUNT DEFICITS OF THE 1980s AND 1990s

We are now in a position to analyze the impact of recent macroeconomic policy on the foreign exchange value of the dollar and the current account of the United States. Responding to the double-digit inflation rates of 1979–1980, the Federal Reserve shifted toward a more restrictive monetary policy in the early 1980s. The U.S. inflation rate plunged from the double-digit levels of 1979–1980 to 3.2 percent in 1983. At the same time, fiscal policy was shifted toward expansion. Increases in defense expenditures coupled with a reduction in tax rates led to a substantial increase in the federal budget deficit during the early 1980s.

Our analysis indicates that this combination of macroeconomic policy—a more restrictive monetary policy coupled with a more expansionary fiscal policy—will cause higher real interest rates, an inflow of capital, currency appreciation, and a current-account deficit (see Thumbnail Sketch). This is precisely what happened. In the early 1980s, real interest rates in the United States rose to historic highs. As part a of **Exhibit 33–6** illustrates, the dollar appreciated sharply beginning in 1981. Shortly thereafter, as part b of Exhibit 33–6 shows,

EXHIBIT 33-6

EXCHANGE-RATE VALUE OF THE DOLLAR AND THE CURRENT-ACCOUNT DEFICIT, 1973–1994

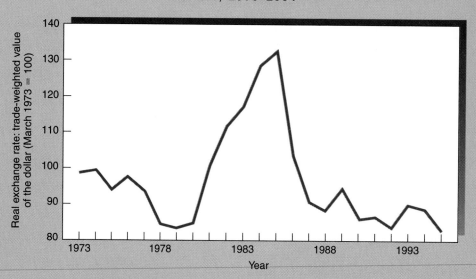

(a) Exchange-rate value of the dollar (compared with ten currencies)

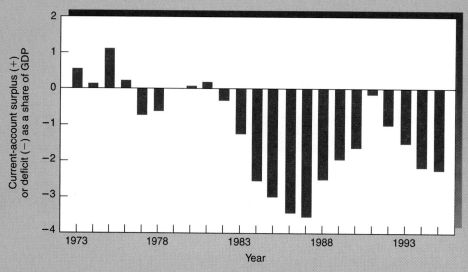

(b) Current account balance as a share of GDP

As the dollar appreciated during the early 1980s, the current-account deficit of the United States soared. In early 1985 the dollar reversed course and began to depreciate. The current-account deficit (b), however, continued to expand throughout 1986 and 1987. It was not until 1988, approximately three years after the dollar began to depreciate, that the current-account deficit began to shrink. Just as the J-curve analysis (discussed later in this chapter) indicates, there will be a substantial lag between a change in the exchange-rate value of a currency and the ultimate change in a nation's current-account balance.

the current account began to shift dramatically toward a deficit position. The annual current account of the United States shifted from a small surplus in 1981 to a deficit equal to 2.5 percent of GDP in 1984. It eventually climbed to 3.5 percent of GDP in 1987. As the dollar appreciated throughout 1981–1985, capital continued to flow into the United States and the current-account deficit continued to widen.

J-CURVE EFFECT

Beginning in early 1985, the situation again changed abruptly. As the low rate of inflation persisted, real interest rates declined. During 1985–1986, declining U.S. interest rates relative to other countries and concern about the size of the current-account deficit led to a sharp reduction in the exchange-rate value of the dollar during 1986–1987 (see Exhibit 33–6a). Nonetheless, the current-account deficit continued to expand in 1986 and 1987.

Why didn't the depreciation in the dollar in 1986 and 1987 reduce the current-account deficit during those years? It takes time for a depreciation in a nation's currency to turn around a current-account deficit, and, initially, the depreciation generally enlarges rather than shrinks the current-account deficit.

The impact of a currency depreciation on a current-account deficit can be broken down into a *price effect* and a *quantity effect*. A 10 percent depreciation in the dollar means that import prices increase by 10 percent in terms of dollars. Of course, this increase in the dollar price of imports will discourage purchases. However, the 10 percent depreciation also means that, *for a given quantity sold,* foreigners will earn 10 percent more dollars. Therefore, unless Americans reduce the *quantity* of their imports by more than 10 percent, their *expenditures* on imports will increase in response to a depreciation in the dollar. Similarly, the depreciation will make U.S. exports 10 percent cheaper to foreigners. Unless foreigners increase their *quantity* purchased by more than 10 percent, their demand for dollars in the exchange market will *decrease* as the result of the depreciation.

Since American and foreign-produced goods are excellent substitutes for one another, there is good reason to expect that both the U.S. demand for imports and foreign demand for U.S. exports will be highly elastic in the long run.[6] However, this may not be true in the short run. When the dollar depreciates, it will take time for American consumers to substitute away from the more expensive imports and for foreign consumers to adjust their consumption, purchasing more of the now cheaper American exports. The new suppliers (or new customers) must be contacted. New agreements must be completed. In some cases, these developments must await the expiration of prior contracts. Therefore, initially, the increase in the quantity of exports may be less than the 10 percent reduction in price. If this is the case, for a time the depreciation will actually cause the

---

[6]Students who have not yet studied microeconomics may be unfamiliar with the terms *elastic* and *inelastic. Elastic* simply means that the quantity purchased is highly responsive to a change in price. When this is true, a change in price will cause total expenditures to change in the opposite direction. Correspondingly, *inelastic* means that the quantity purchased will be relatively unresponsive to a change in price. When this is the case, an increase in price will cause total expenditures to change in the same direction.

current-account deficit to worsen—the dollar expenditures on imports will rise while the dollar sales of exports will decline. Eventually, this situation will reverse. With the passage of time, the U.S. demand for imports and foreign demand for U.S. exports will become more elastic. The quantity effects will dominate, and a depreciation will reduce the current-account deficit.

J-curve effect
The tendency of a nation's current-account deficit to widen initially before it shrinks in response to an exchange-rate depreciation. This tendency results because the short-run demand for both imports and exports is often inelastic, even though the long-run demand is almost always elastic.

Economists refer to this time path of adjustment as the **J-curve effect.** *A nation's current-account deficit will initially widen (slide down the hook of the "J") before it shrinks (moves up the stem of the "J") as the result of a currency depreciation. This occurs because the short-run domestic demand for imports and foreign demand for exports are inelastic. Thus, the depreciation initially increases import expenditures and export sales. However, in the long run, the demand for both imports and exports is elastic. Therefore, the depreciation of a nation's currency will eventually shrink the nation's current-account deficit.*[7]

Empirical studies are consistent with the J-curve analysis. There is often a lag of two or three years before a change in the exchange-rate value of a nation's currency will exert a major impact on current-account transactions. This lagged effect can be observed from the data of Exhibit 33–6. As part a illustrates, the exchange value of the dollar appreciated substantially (approximately 30 percent) during 1981 and 1982. Initially, however, there was only a small impact on current-account transactions. The size of the current-account deficit in 1981 and 1982 was not much different from the levels of 1978–1980. Beginning in 1983, two years after the dollar began to appreciate, the current-account deficit began to widen considerably. Clearly, the appreciation in the dollar during 1981–1985 reduced the price of imports (and increased the price of U.S. exports) and, with approximately a two-year lag, contributed to the sizable increase in the current-account deficit, during 1983–1987.

Beginning in mid-year 1985, the exchange-rate value of the dollar took a sharp plunge, and it declined by 40 percent during 1986 and 1987. Nonetheless, the current-account deficit continued to widen during that time. It was not until 1988, approximately two and a half years after the dollar began to depreciate, that the current-account deficit began to shrink. Just as the J-curve analysis implies, there was a lengthy lag between the depreciation of the dollar and the reversal in the direction of the nation's current-account deficit.

HOW DO CURRENT-ACCOUNT DEFICITS AFFECT AN ECONOMY?

There is a tendency to think that current account and trade surpluses are good and deficits bad. This is certainly understandable. The term *deficit* generally suggests something bad—things like excessive spending relative to income or an overdraft at the bank. In the balance-of-payments area, however, this is not always true.

---

[7]See Jeffrey A. Rosensweig and Paul D. Koch, "The U.S. Dollar and the 'Delayed J-Curve,'" *Federal Reserve Bank of Atlanta, Economic Review*, July–August 1988, pp. 2–15, for an interesting article on the J-curve effect as it applies to the trade imbalances of the United States during the 1980s.

WHAT PRECISELY IS A CURRENT ACCOUNT DEFICIT? The current account measures mainly trade in goods and services. The other two current-account categories—net income from investments abroad and unilateral transfers—are generally small. Since trade in goods and services dominates current-account transactions, trade deficits and current-account deficits are closely related. They generally go together—countries with large trade deficits almost always run substantial current-account deficits. Both of these deficits generally reflect that the country is importing more goods and services than it is exporting. In contrast, trade (and current-account) surpluses imply that sales of goods and services to foreigners (exports) exceed purchases from them (imports).

It is not obvious that a surplus is preferable to a deficit. After all, a nation that is running a deficit is getting more goods and services from others than it is supplying to them. What is so bad about that? Similarly, a trade surplus implies that a nation is producing more goods and services for foreigners to consume than it is receiving from foreigners. Is this something that people will want to continue to do?

A nation's trade deficit or surplus is an aggregation of the voluntary choices of businesses and individuals. In contrast with a budget deficit of an individual, business, or government, there is no legal entity that is responsible for the trade deficit. As Herbert Stein, a former chairman of the president's Council of Economic Advisers, once put it,

> *The trade deficit does not belong to any individual or institution. It is a pure statistical aggregate, like the number of eggs laid in the U.S. or the number of bald-headed men living here.*[8]

How long can a nation continue to run a current-account deficit? Perhaps surprising to some, the answer is a long time. A current-account deficit is not like business losses or an excess of household spending relative to income—conditions that eventually force decision makers to change their ways. The United States ran a current (trade) account deficit almost every year from 1800 to 1875. On the other hand, it consistently ran current-account surpluses from 1946 to 1976. The trade accounts of other countries have followed similar lengthy periods of both deficits and surpluses.

CURRENT ACCOUNT DEFICITS AND THE FLOW OF CAPITAL. A current-account (and trade) deficit must be financed. Under a pure flexible-rate system, a current-account deficit implies a capital-account surplus—that is, an inflow of investments and financial capital (loans) from abroad. Nations that import more than they export must fill the gap with loans from and the sale of capital assets to foreigners.

But it is equally true to say that a capital-account surplus—that is, an inflow of foreign capital—implies a current-account deficit. In a global economy where capital moves rather freely across borders, countries with the most attractive investment environments will experience an inflow of capital. If the investments of foreigners in a country exceed those of the domestic investors abroad, foreigners will have to fill this gap. Under a flexible-rate system, foreigners pay for their excess of capital purchases relative to capital sales with an excess of exports

---

[8]Herbert Stein, "Leave the Trade Deficit Alone," *The Wall Street Journal*, March 11, 1987.

relative to imports. Thus, countries that attract a net inflow of foreign capital also tend to run current-account deficits.

ARE CURRENT-ACCOUNT DEFICITS AND AN INFLOW OF FOREIGN CAPITAL BAD? The prudent answer is: It depends on why the capital inflow is occurring and how it is used. Low-income countries often find it difficult to finance even attractive investment opportunities from their current domestic saving. When this is the case, investment funds from abroad can help them increase both their rate of capital formation and economic growth. As long as the inflow of capital is channeled into profitable investment, it enhances the growth and prosperity of a nation. Examples of this abound. Prior to 1985, Singapore ran large current-account deficits financed with an inflow of capital. Propelled by a high investment rate, it has achieved rapid growth for more than two decades and it is now running a large current-account surplus. During the 1970s, South Korea ran huge current-account deficits and capital-account surpluses. Like Singapore, Korea used the inflow of capital to achieve high rates of both capital formation and growth. As **Exhibit 33–7** illustrates, Thailand, Malaysia, Chile, and Indonesia all used an inflow of capital (and current-account deficit) to enhance domestic investment during 1980–1994. They also achieved highly impressive growth rates during this period. Clearly, capital inflow can—if directed into profitable investments—play a positive role in the development of an economy.

Correspondingly, a current-account surplus is not always indicative of strength. For example, a country would run a current-account surplus and

---

EXHIBIT 33–7

**CURRENT ACCOUNT DEFICITS, INVESTMENT, AND
GROWTH OF GDP:
EVIDENCE FROM VARIOUS COUNTRIES**

	CURRENT-ACCOUNT DEFICIT AS A PERCENT OF GDP: 1980–1994	PRIVATE INVESTMENT AS A SHARE OF GDP: 1980–1994	ANNUAL GROWTH RATE OF PER CAPITA GDP: 1980–1994
HIGH INVESTMENT COUNTRIES			
Thailand	4.7	28.7	6.1
Malaysia	3.3	30.3	4.1
Chile	5.3	24.0[a]	4.8[a]
Indonesia	3.0	30.8	4.1
INDUSTRIAL COUNTRIES			
United States	2.0[b]	17.2	1.6
Australia	4.7	23.4	1.6
Canada	2.3[b]	20.6	1.3

[a]1985–1994
[b]1983–1994

Source: Derived from International Monetary Fund, *International Financial Statistics Yearbook, 1995.*

capital-account deficit if its profitable domestic investment alternatives were insufficient to absorb its current savings. Since domestic investors would be drawn to the more attractive investment opportunities abroad, such countries would experience an outflow of capital. In recent years, Japan has been in this position.

THE CURRENT-ACCOUNT DEFICIT OF THE UNITED STATES. The United States has a system of secure property rights, a stable monetary and political environment, and a rapidly growing labor force (compared with Europe and Japan). This makes it an attractive country in which to invest. On the other hand, the saving rate of the United States is low compared to our major trading partners. To a degree, the U.S. current-account deficit reflects this combination of factors—an attractive domestic investment environment and a low saving rate.

As Exhibit 33–6b illustrates, the United States has persistently run sizable current-account deficits since 1982. This widening of the current-account deficit has been associated with increases in the size of federal budget deficits, a reduction in investment, and increase in consumption *as a share of GDP*. This suggests that the inflow of funds from abroad is being used to finance current consumption rather than additional investment. This is a cause for concern. (As Exhibit 33–7 shows, the private investment rate *as a share of GDP* for the United States is much lower than that of the other countries running large current-account deficits.)

However, it is important to note that the problem is not the current-account deficit, but rather the large budget deficits. The deficits are consuming a large portion of the domestic savings and diverting it away from private investment.[9] Given this factor, the capital inflow (and accompanying current-account deficits) help to moderate the reduction in domestic investment. It would be a mistake to impose trade restrictions in an effort to reduce the current-account deficit. Clearly, the appropriate policy response would be a reduction in the size of the deficit as well as, perhaps, modifications that would encourage additional domestic saving.

IMPORTANCE OF CURRENCY CONVERTIBILITY

If the people of one country are going to trade with buyers and sellers in other countries, they must be able to convert their domestic currency into foreign currencies. For example, American sellers will not want to be paid in Iranian rials because the Iranian currency cannot be used to buy things in the United States. Neither is it freely convertible to U.S. dollars. Nonconvertibility of one's domestic currency is a major obstacle that will reduce the ability of people to realize gains from trade and specialization in areas where they have a comparative advantage.

---

[9]The reductions in private investment could be partially offset by increases in government investment. To a degree, this was the case in the United States during the 1980s. As a share of GDP, government investment rose from 2.9 percent in 1980 to 3.5 percent in 1987. Most of this increase in government investment was for defense-related equipment. In the 1990s government investment has receded to 3 percent of GDP, approximately the same rate as the late 1970s.

Of course, if a country has a flexible exchange rate—if it permits its currency to be freely and legally converted to other currencies in foreign exchange markets—currency convertibility is no problem. Many governments, however, fix the price of their currency and prohibit currency exchanges at other prices. Both a fixed exchange rate and free convertibility of a currency can be maintained if a country is willing to use its monetary policy to maintain the fixed exchange rate.

A country can either (1) follow an independent monetary policy and allow its exchange rate to fluctuate or (2) tie its monetary policy to the maintenance of the fixed exchange rate. It cannot, however, maintain convertibility if it is going to both fix the exchange-rate value of its currency and follow an independent monetary policy. It must either give up its monetary independence or allow its exchange rate to fluctuate if its currency is going to be fully convertible with other currencies.

Some countries, particularly small countries, have chosen to forgo monetary independence and tie the exchange-rate value of their domestic currency to a widely accepted currency, such as the U.S. dollar, the German mark, or the French franc. This is not a bad strategy. Worldwide, people already have confidence in such currencies as the dollar, mark, and franc. Thus, tying one's currency to those currencies increases its acceptability.

Currency board

An institution that issues a currency at a fixed rate in exchange for an equivalent amount of another designated currency that has greater acceptability. As the currency board receives the more widely accepted currency, it is invested in bonds and liquid assets that provide 100 percent backing for the currency units issued.

Hong Kong has followed this strategy. It does not have a central bank that conducts monetary policy. Instead it has a **currency board** that issues Hong Kong dollars in exchange for U.S. dollars at an exchange rate of 7.7 Hong Kong dollars = 1 U.S. dollar. When U.S. dollars are received in exchange for newly issued Hong Kong dollars, the U.S. dollars are invested in U.S. government bonds. Thus, the Hong Kong dollar is fully backed by the U.S. dollar (or U.S. bonds).[10] Recently, Argentina has adopted a similar approach as a means of controlling inflation and increasing the acceptability of its currency.

In contrast with countries like Hong Kong that give up their monetary independence in order to tie the exchange-rate value of their currency to another that is widely accepted, several countries have tried to both fix the exchange-rate value of their currency and maintain monetary independence, which is often used to follow a highly inflationary monetary policy. This strategy generally results in the exchange-rate value of the nation's currency being fixed above the market level.

When a country fixes the exchange-rate value of its currency above the market level, however, it is simultaneously fixing the price of foreign currencies below market level. This policy will make it extremely difficult for domestic residents to convert their domestic currency to foreign exchange. Since domestic citizens are less able to acquire foreign currencies, they will be less able to trade

---

[10]Under this currency board system, exchanges between the Hong Kong dollar and U.S. dollar will tend to keep the price levels of the two countries in line. If the general level of prices were to rise in Hong Kong relative to the United States, fewer people would want to use Hong Kong dollars and more would want to use U.S. dollars. Thus, people would ask the currency board to exchange Hong Kong dollars for U.S. dollars, which would have more purchasing power. In response, however, the supply of Hong Kong dollars would shrink, which would put a brake on inflation in Hong Kong. In contrast, if inflation in the United States were greater than that in Hong Kong, just the opposite would happen. People would exchange U.S. dollars for Hong Kong dollars. In turn, this would increase the supply of Hong Kong dollars and bring prices in Hong Kong back into line with prices in the United States.

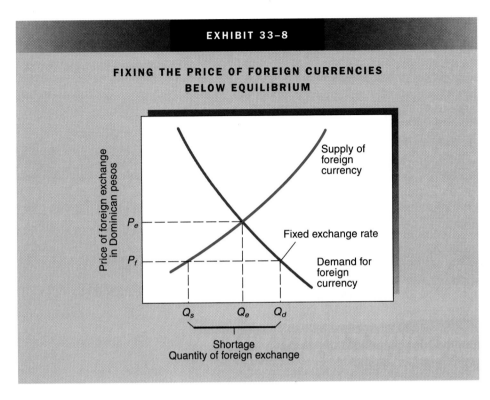

EXHIBIT 33–8

FIXING THE PRICE OF FOREIGN CURRENCIES BELOW EQUILIBRIUM

When the price of foreign currency in terms of a country's domestic currency is fixed below equilibrium, a shortage of foreign currency will emerge. Illegal black markets will develop as the citizens of the country seek more foreign currency so they can trade with people in other countries.

with foreigners. As a result, the volume of the country's international trade will decline.

Using the Dominican Republic as an example, **Exhibit 33–8** illustrates the impact of exchange-rate controls. When the Dominican Republic fixes the price of foreign exchange (in terms of the Dominican peso) below equilibrium, the quantity of foreign exchange demanded by Dominicans (so they can buy from foreigners) will exceed the quantity generated by Dominican exports. Under a flexible-rate system, this excess demand for foreign currency would be eliminated by a depreciation of the Dominican peso in the exchange-rate market. The price of foreign exchange would rise from P_f to P_e. With a fixed rate, however, this cannot happen. Instead, Dominican citizens will confront a shortage $(Q_d - Q_s)$ of foreign exchange. Since they are able to obtain only Q_s units of foreign exchange, the volume of their trade with foreigners will decline (from Q_e to Q_s). In other words, since Dominicans cannot, at least not legally, convert as much of their currency to foreign exchange as they would like, they will not be able to buy as much from foreigners as they would like.

Of course, when price controls—exchange-rate controls are a type of price control—lead to shortages, as they inevitably do, black markets develop. Currency markets are not an exception to this rule. If you have ever traveled in a country that imposes exchange-rate controls and been approached by someone offering to trade local currency at a premium for your foreign currency, you have observed the black market in foreign exchange. The greater the black-market premium, the more the fixed price of the country's currency is out of line with market conditions, thereby restricting the volume of trade with foreigners.

Our analysis illustrates that fixing exchange rates and limiting the convertibility of one's currency will retard international trade and reduce the ability of people to realize gains from specialization and adoption of mass-production methods. Like tariffs, quotas, and other trade restrictions, this limitation on international exchange will reduce both productivity and living standards.

Since 1985 there has been a sharp reduction in the number of countries imposing exchange-rate controls. In 1985 35 countries imposed controls such that the black-market premium exceeded 25 percent. By 1995, that figure had fallen to only 9.[11] **Exhibit 33–9** lists these 9 countries and indicates their growth rate during the last decade. On average, the per capita GDP of these countries declined at an annual rate of 1.0 percent during 1985–1994. Given the negative impact of exchange-rate controls on trade and prosperity, the poor economic performance of these countries is not surprising.

EXHIBIT 33–9

GROWTH RECORD OF COUNTRIES WITH HIGHEST BLACK-MARKET EXCHANGE-RATE PREMIUM IN 1995

	BLACK-MARKET EXCHANGE-RATE PREMIUM			ANNUAL GROWTH RATE OF PER CAPITA GDP, 1985–1994
COUNTRY/REGION	1985	1990	1995	
Haiti	60	2	224	−5.4%
Iran	533	2,197	156	−1.7
Syria	251	301	283	0.6
Bangladesh	168	165	30	1.9
Algeria	335	140	205	−2.3
Burundi	25	6	42	0.3
Madagascar	9	7	30	−1.9
Nigeria	270	23	277	1.1
Rwanda	49	28	105	−1.7
AVERAGE GROWTH RATE				−1.0

Source: The black-market exchange-rate data are from International Currency Analysis, *World Currency Yearbook* (various issues). The data on growth of per capita GDP are from the World Bank, *World Tables.*

These nine countries had the highest black-market exchange-rate premiums in 1995.

[11]These data are from James Gwartney, Robert Lawson, and Walter Block, *Economic Freedom of the World: 1975–1995* (Washington, D.C.: Cato Institute, 1996).

LOOKING AHEAD

International trade is only one of several factors influencing economic performance. The following chapter will consider additional factors as we analyze why some nations prosper and grow while others continue to experience economic stagnation.

CHAPTER SUMMARY

1. The foreign exchange market is a highly organized market in which currencies of different countries are bought and sold. The exchange rate is the price of one national currency in terms of another. The exchange rate permits consumers in one country to translate the prices of foreign goods into units of their own currency.

2. When international trade takes place, it is usually necessary for one party to convert its currency to the currency of its trading partner. Imports of goods, services, and assets (both real and financial) by the United States generate a demand for the foreign currency required to pay for these items. On the other hand, exports of goods, services, and assets supply foreign currency to the exchange market because foreigners exchange their currency for the dollars needed to purchase the export items.

3. The value of a nation's currency on the exchange market is in equilibrium when the supply of the currency generated by imports (that is, the sale of goods, services, and assets to foreigners) is just equal to the demand for the currency generated by exports (the purchases of goods, services, and assets from foreigners).

4. Under a flexible-rate system, if there is an excess supply of dollars (excess demand for foreign currencies) on the foreign exchange market, the value of the dollar will depreciate relative to other currencies. A depreciation will make foreign goods and assets more expensive to U.S. buyers and U.S. goods and assets cheaper for foreign purchasers, reducing the value of U.S. imports and increasing the value of its exports until equilibrium is restored. On the other hand, an excess demand for dollars (excess supply of foreign currencies) will cause the dollar to appreciate, stimulating imports and discouraging exports until equilibrium is restored.

5. With flexible exchange rates, a nation's currency tends to appreciate when (a) rapid economic growth abroad (relative to growth at home) stimulates exports relative to imports, (b) the rate of domestic inflation is below that of the nation's trading partners, and (c) domestic real interest rates increase relative to one's trading partners. The reverse of these conditions will cause a nation's currency to depreciate.

6. During the period of 1944–1971, most nations operated under a system of fixed exchange rates. Under this system, if the value of the goods, services, and capital assets exported to foreigners is less than the value of the items imported, there is an excess supply of the country's currency on the foreign exchange market. When this happens, the country must (a) devalue its currency, (b) take action to reduce imports (for example, heighten its trade barriers), or (c) pursue a restrictive macropolicy designed to increase interest rates and retard inflation. During the period when the fixed rates were in effect, corrective action taken to maintain the rates was often in conflict with free trade in international markets and the macropolicy objective of full employment.

7. The balance-of-payments accounts record the flow of payments between a country and other countries. Transactions that generate a demand for foreign currencies (and supply of the domestic currency) in the foreign exchange market (for example, imports) are recorded as debit items. Transactions that create a supply of foreign currencies (and demand for the domestic currency) in the foreign exchange market (for example, exports) are recorded as credit items.

8. In aggregate, the balance-of-payments accounts must balance. Thus, (a) the current-account balance plus (b) the capital-account balance plus (c) the official-reserve-account balance must equal zero. However, the individual components of the accounts need not be in balance. A deficit in one area implies an offsetting surplus in other areas.

9. Under a pure flexible-rate system, there will not be any official-reserve-account transactions. Under these circumstances, a current-account deficit implies a capital-account surplus (and vice versa).

10. An unanticipated shift to a more restrictive monetary policy will raise the real interest rate, reduce the rate of inflation, and, at least temporarily, reduce aggregate demand and the growth of income. These factors will in turn cause the nation's currency to appreciate on the foreign exchange market. In turn, the currency appreciation along with the inflow of capital will result in a current-account deficit. In contrast, the effects of a more expansionary monetary policy will be just the opposite: lower interest rates, an outflow of capital, currency depreciation, and a shift toward a current-account surplus.

11. An unanticipated shift to a more expansionary fiscal policy will tend to increase real interest rates, lead to an inflow of capital, and cause the nation's current account to shift toward a deficit. The effects of a shift to a more restrictive fiscal policy will be just the opposite: lower interest rates, an outflow of capital, and movement toward a current-account surplus.

12. Under a flexible-rate exchange system, a current-account deficit implies an inflow of capital. Correspondingly,

a current-account surplus implies an outflow of capital. Whether a country runs a current-account deficit or surplus is largely dependent upon the attractiveness of domestic investment opportunities relative to the nation's saving rate. Countries with more attractive investment opportunities and a low saving rate will tend to run capital-account surpluses and current-account deficits. On the other hand, countries with less attractive investment opportunities and a high saving rate will tend to experience capital outflow and current-account surpluses under a flexible-rate system.

13. The prudence of a current-account deficit and inflow of capital is dependent on the availability of profitable investment opportunities. An inflow of capital will often help low-income countries with attractive investment opportunities (but only a small supply of domestic savings) to achieve both a high rate of capital formation and rapid growth.

14. When a country fixes the exchange-rate value of its currency above the market level (and that of foreign currencies below the market level), a shortage of foreign exchange will result. Since residents of the country are less able to acquire foreign exchange, they are less able to engage in international trade. The decline in the volume of trade accompanying such exchange-rate controls will tend to reduce the productivity and income level of the country.

CRITICAL-ANALYSIS QUESTIONS

*1. If the dollar depreciates relative to the German mark, how will this affect your ability to purchase the BMW you have longed for? How will this change influence the quantity of BMWs purchased by Americans? How will it affect the dollar expenditures of Americans on BMWs?

2. How do flexible exchange rates bring about balance in the exchange-rate market? Do they lead to a balance between merchandise exports and imports? Explain.

3. "If a trade deficit means that we are getting more items from abroad than we are sending to foreigners, why is it considered a bad thing?" Answer this question.

*4. The accompanying chart indicates an actual newspaper quotation of the exchange rate of various currencies. On February 2, did the dollar appreciate or depreciate against the British pound? How did it fare against the French franc?

	U.S. DOLLAR EQUIVALENT	
	FEB. 1	FEB. 2
British pound	1.755	1.746
French franc	.1565	.1575

*5. Suppose the exchange rate between the United States and Mexico freely fluctuates in the open market. Indicate which of the following would cause the dollar to appreciate (or depreciate) relative to the peso.

a. An increase in the quantity of drilling equipment purchased in the United States by Pemex, the Mexican oil company, as a result of a Mexican oil discovery

b. An increase in the U.S. purchase of crude oil from Mexico as a result of the development of Mexican oil fields

c. Higher real interest rates in Mexico, inducing U.S. citizens to move their financial investments from U.S. to Mexican banks

d. Lower real interest rates in the United States, inducing Mexican investors to borrow dollars and then exchange them for pesos

e. Inflation in the United States and stable prices in Mexico

f. An increase in the inflation rate from 2 percent to 10 percent in both the United States and Mexico

g. An economic boom in Mexico, inducing Mexicans to buy more U.S.–made automobiles, trucks, electric appliances, and television sets

h. Attractive investment opportunities, inducing U.S. investors to buy stock in Mexican firms

6. Explain why a current-account balance and a capital-account balance must sum to zero under a pure flexible-rate system.

7. "A nation cannot continue to run a deficit on current account. A healthy, growing economy will not persistently expand its indebtedness to foreigners. Eventually, the trade deficits will lead to national bankruptcy." Evaluate this view.

8. In recent years, a substantial share of the domestic capital formation in the United States has been financed by foreign investors. Is this inflow of capital from abroad indicative that the U.S. economy is in poor health? How might the United States go about reducing its current-account deficit?

*9. Suppose that the United States were running a current-account deficit. How would each of the following changes influence the size of the current-account deficit?

a. A recession in the United States

b. A decline in the attractiveness of investment opportunities in the United States

c. An improvement in investment opportunities abroad

10. "Foreigners are flooding our markets with goods and using the proceeds to buy up America. Unless we do something to protect ourselves, the Japanese, Europeans, and Arabs are going to own America." Evaluate this recent statement by an American political figure.

*11. If foreigners have confidence in the U.S. economy and therefore move to expand their investments in the United States, how will the U.S. current-account balance be affected? How will the exchange-rate value of the dollar be affected?

12. Is a trade surplus indicative of a strong, healthy economy? Why or why not?

*13. During the early 1980s, the United States shifted toward a more restrictive monetary policy that sharply decelerated the domestic inflation rate. Simultaneously, the federal government was running a large budget deficit. Explain how this policy mix influenced the value of the dollar in the exchange-rate market and the on current-account balance.

14. What is the J-curve effect? According to the J-curve effect, how will a depreciation in a nation's currency affect its current-account balance?

*15. Changes in exchange rates will automatically direct a country to a current-account balance under a flexible-rate exchange system. Is this statement true or false?

16. Suppose that a country fixes the rate that its currency can legally be converted to foreign exchange (other currencies) above the market level. As a result, a black-market exchange rate emerges, and domestic citizens are willing to pay more than the legally fixed rate for foreign exchange.

    a. Measured in terms of the domestic currency, will imports be cheaper or more expensive at the legally fixed exchange rate?

    b. Will export goods be cheaper or more expensive at the legally fixed rate?

    c. How will this fixed-exchange-rate policy influence the country's volume of trade and level of investment?

    d. Do you think this policy will help promote economic growth and prosperity? Why or why not?

    e. Can you think of any reasons why people in politically powerful positions might favor the fixed-exchange-rate policy?

17. The newly independent country of Estonia recently tied the exchange-rate value of its currency to the German mark and pledged to conduct its monetary policy in a manner that would maintain the fixed exchange rate with the mark. Do you think this is a sound strategy? Why or why not? How will the policy affect the ability of the Estonian government to finance government programs with money creation? What impact do you think the policy will have on the level of investment and the operation of its capital market in Estonia?

*18. In recent years many American political figures have been highly critical of the fact that U.S. imports from Japan have consistently exceeded U.S. exports to Japan.

    a. Under a flexible exchange-rate system, is there any reason to expect that the imports from a given country will tend to equal the exports to that country?

    b. Can you think of any reason why the United States might persistently run a trade deficit with a country such as Japan?

    c. If Japan purchased substantially more American goods, would this significantly reduce the current-account deficit the United States has been running? Why or why not?

19. Recently, various plans have been put forward to reduce the federal budget deficit during the next several years. If the federal government moved toward a balanced budget, what is the expected impact on interest rates, the inflow of capital, the current-account deficit, and the foreign exchange value of the dollar? Explain the reasoning underlying your answer.

---

*Asterisk denotes questions for which answers are given in Appendix B.

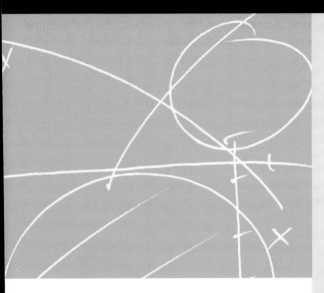

Certain fundamental principles—formulating sound monetary and fiscal policies, removing domestic price controls, opening the economy to international market forces, ensuring property rights and private property, creating competition, and reforming and limiting the role of government—are essential for a healthy market economy.

ECONOMIC REPORT OF THE PRESIDENT, 1991

CHAPTER FOCUS

▪ How is income measured across countries?
▪ How does per capita income vary among nations?
▪ How does sustained economic growth change income levels and the lives of people?
▪ Are the rich countries getting richer while the poor countries are getting poorer?
▪ What are the major sources of economic growth?
▪ What policies will help promote economic growth?
▪ What countries are "success stories" of economic development?

T hroughout history, most of the world's population has struggled 50, 60, and 70 hours per week just to obtain the basic necessities of life—food, clothing, and shelter. During the last two centuries, sustained economic growth has changed that situation for most people in North America, Europe, Oceania, and Japan. More recently, several countries of East Asia including South Korea, Thailand, Hong Kong, Singapore, and Malaysia have also experienced impressive growth rates. Subsistence levels of food, shelter, and clothing are now taken for granted, and the typical family in high-income industrial countries worries instead about financing summer vacations, purchasing new cars and nicer homes, and providing for the children's college educations.

Rising incomes and improvements in the standard of living have not always been present in Western countries. According to Phelps Brown, the real income of English building trade workers was virtually unchanged between 1215 and 1798, a period of nearly six centuries.[1] In other parts of Europe, workers experienced a similar stagnation of real earnings throughout much of this period.

Low incomes and widespread poverty are still the norm in most countries—particularly those of South and Central America, Africa, and South-Central Asia. Why have some countries that were poor just a few decades ago prospered in recent decades, while others have continued to stagnate? What can governments do to promote economic prosperity? At various points throughout this book, we have addressed these questions and related issues. We are now prepared to pull together the lessons of basic economics and address the topic of economic growth and sources of prosperity in a more comprehensive manner.

MEASUREMENT OF INCOME ACROSS COUNTRIES

The gross domestic product (GDP) of a country is a measurement of how much output (and income) is generated domestically by the residents of the nation. Per capita GDP is a measure of output per person, and therefore a broad indicator of the standard of living. However, when we use GDP to compare output and income across countries, there is an obvious problem. The GDP of each country is measured in units of the country's domestic currency. Mexico's GDP is measured in pesos, Japan's in yen, Germany's in marks, and so on. How, then, can these various measures of GDP be compared?

The simplest way is to convert the income figures to a common currency by the **exchange-rate conversion method.** Here the value of each nation's currency in the foreign exchange market is used to convert the nation's GDP (or GNP) to a common currency, such as the U.S. dollar. For example, if the British pound is worth 1.5 times as much as the U.S. dollar in the foreign exchange market, then the GDP of the United Kingdom is converted to dollars by multiplying the British GDP in pounds by 1.5.

Although income comparisons based on the exchange-rate conversion method are widely reported, they are sometimes highly misleading. The foreign

Exchange-rate conversion method

Method that uses the foreign exchange-rate value of a nation's currency to convert that nation's GDP (or GNP) to another monetary unit, such as the U.S. dollar.

---

[1]Phelps Brown, *A Century of Pay: The Course of Pay and Production in France, Germany, Sweden, the United Kingdom, and the United States* (London: Macmillan, 1968).

exchange value of a currency is influenced by only a limited number of goods and services that are traded internationally and by the purchase and sale of assets—particularly financial assets—across countries. In addition, some countries fix their exchange rates at a level that may differ substantially from the equilibrium rate. Thus, the exchange-rate value of a currency may not be a reliable indicator of the currency's purchasing power over the typical bundle of goods and services purchased by households in the domestic market. For example, merely because a British pound purchases 1.5 dollars in the foreign exchange market, it does not follow that it will purchase 1.5 times as much housing, recreation, child-care services, and similar items in the United Kingdom as a dollar will purchase in the United States. For this reason, income comparisons based on the exchange-rate conversion method are not highly regarded among economists.

Rather, economists favor the use of the purchasing-power parity method to make income comparisons across nations. The **purchasing-power parity (PPP) method** compares the cost of purchasing the typical bundle of goods and services consumed by households in the domestic market of various nations. Each category in the bundle is weighted according to its contribution to GDP. The cost of purchasing the typical bundle in each nation is then compared to the dollar cost of purchasing the same bundle in the United States. Once the purchasing power of each nation's currency (in terms of the typical bundle) is determined, this information is used to convert the GDP of each country to a common monetary unit (for example, the U.S. dollar).

Purchasing-power parity method
Method of comparing the outputs of different countries. The amount of each currency required to purchase a typical bundle of goods and services in domestic markets is used to determine the relative purchasing power of different currencies. This information is then used to convert the GDP (or GNP) of each nation to a common monetary unit.

INCOME DIFFERENCES AMONG COUNTRIES

In recent years, Robert Summers and Alan Heston of the University of Pennsylvania have spearheaded a project of the United Nations Statistical Office that has used the purchasing-power parity method to develop measures of output for approximately 150 countries.[2] **Exhibit 34–1** presents the 1994 per capita GDP data (measured in 1985 U.S. dollars) from this project. These data illustrate that there is wide variation in per capita GDP among countries. The estimated per capita annual GDP (measured in 1985 dollars) of the United States in 1994 was $18,850. The estimated 1994 per capita GDP of Hong Kong, Canada, Norway, Switzerland, Australia, Japan, and Germany was greater than $15,000. In contrast, the GDP per person of Zaire, Tanzania, Mali, Zambia, Haiti, Malawi, and Uganda was less than $600, only a tiny fraction of the U.S. figure.

Most of the poorest countries (annual GDP less than $1,200) were in Africa. On the other hand, with the exception of Australia, New Zealand, Japan, Hong Kong, Singapore, and Taiwan, the high-income countries were either European or North American. South and Central American countries and the other nations of Asia generally fell into the middle categories with annual per capita incomes in the $1,200 to $10,000 range.

---

[2]Robert Summers and Alan Heston, "The Penn World Tables (Mark 5): An Expanded Set of International Comparisons, 1950–1988," *Quarterly Journal of Economics* (May 1991): pp. 327–368.

EXHIBIT 34–1

THE 1994 PER CAPITA OUTPUT OF NATIONS MEASURED IN 1985 DOLLARS (DERIVED BY THE PURCHASING-POWER PARITY METHOD)

POOREST COUNTRIES (ANNUAL OUTPUT LESS THAN $1,200)		LOW-INCOME COUNTRIES (ANNUAL OUTPUT $1,200–$4,000)		MIDDLE-INCOME COUNTRIES (ANNUAL OUTPUT $4,000–$10,000)		HIGH-INCOME COUNTRIES (ANNUAL OUTPUT MORE THAN $10,000)	
COUNTRY	PER CAPITA GDP, 1994	COUNTRY	PER CAPITA GDP, 1994	COUNTRY	PER CAPITA GDP, 1994	COUNTRY	PER CAPITA GDP, 1994
Zaire	$ 300	India	$1,335	Brazil	$4,118	Taiwan	$10,152
Tanzania	470	Romania	1,400	Poland	4,150	Ireland	10,640
Mali	495	Pakistan	1,435	Russia	4,200	New Zealand	12,240
Zambia	525	Bangladesh	1,575	Syria	4,270	Italy	12,920
Haiti	534	Philippines	1,720	Thailand	4,450	Austria	13,250
Malawi	534	Bolivia	1,730	Hungary	4,720	United	
Uganda	570	China	1,865	Czech		Kingdom	13,430
Madagascar	605	Egypt	1,915	Republic	4,800	Netherlands	13,505
Somalia	653	Paraguay	2,209	Bulgaria	5,000	Belgium	13,735
Niger	726	Guatemala	2,303	Chile	5,250	France	13,910
Rwanda	762	Indonesia	2,310	Argentina	6,025	Sweden	13,930
Kenya	894	Dominican		Mexico	6,260	Singapore	14,415
Nigeria	960	Republic	2,322	Venezuela	6,395	Denmark	14,800
Cameroon	975	Peru	2,390	Malaysia	6,510	Germany	15,005
Ghana	975	Algeria	2,700	Greece	6,783	Japan	15,105
Nepal	1,005	Ecuador	2,860	Portugal	7,685	Australia	15,169
Côte d'Ivoire	1,065	South Africa	3,025	South Korea	8,565	Switzerland	15,980
Zimbabwe	1,162	Colombia	3,495	Israel	9,970	Norway	16,589
Nicaragua	1,165	Iran	3,650	Spain	9,990	Canada	17,510
		Turkey	3,665			Hong Kong	17,832
		Costa Rica	3,785			United States	18,850

Source: Robert Summers and Alan Heston, *Penn World Tables* (Cambridge: National Bureau of Economic Research, 1994). These data were through 1992. They were updated to 1994 by the authors.

Does it really make much difference whether income comparisons are based on purchasing-power parity (PPP) or the more widely cited exchange-rate conversion method? In recent years, the World Bank has used both methods to estimate the gross national product (GNP) of countries. **Exhibit 34–2** presents these data for several countries. A comparison of figures illustrates that the distortions produced by the exchange-rate method are often substantial. For example, the per capita income (GNP) of Switzerland is estimated to be approximately

Source: The World Bank, *World Development Report, 1995* (Tables 1 and 30).

EXHIBIT 34–2

COMPARISON OF PER CAPITA OUTPUT (GNP) OF VARIOUS COUNTRIES BY EXCHANGE-RATE CONVERSION VERSUS PURCHASING-POWER PARITY METHODS

| | 1993 PER CAPITA GNP | |
| | EXCHANGE-RATE | PURCHASING-POWER |
COUNTRY	CONVERSION	PARITY
India	$ 300	$ 1,220
China	490	2,330
Thailand	2,110	6,260
Brazil	2,930	5,370
Mexico	3,610	6,810
Argentina	7,220	8,250
Hong Kong	18,060	21,560
United Kingdom	19,300	17,210
France	22,490	19,900
Germany	23,560	16,800
United States	24,740	24,740
Japan	31,490	20,850
Switzerland	35,760	23,660

45 percent greater than that of the United States by the exchange-rate conversion method. In contrast, the PPP method indicates that the per capita income (GNP) of the United States is slightly (5 percent) greater than the figure for Switzerland. Similarly, the exchange-rate conversion method implies that the income of Japan is 27 percent *greater* than that of the United States, while the PPP method indicates that the Japanese figure is approximately 12 percent *less* than that of the United States.

The differences are particularly large when comparisons are made between **less-developed countries (LDCs)** and industrial countries. In general, the exchange-rate conversion method understates the per capita income figure for LDCs. For example, the per capita income estimate for India derived by the exchange-rate conversion method is less than one-fourth the income figure derived by the purchasing-power parity method ($300 compared with $1,220). The exchange-rate conversion method indicates that the per capita income of the United States is 82 times that of India; more realistically, the PPP estimates imply that the U.S. figure is 20 times that of India. In the case of China, the distortions are even greater. The per capita income of China derived by the exchange-rate conversion method is only about one-fifth of the estimate ($490 compared with $2,330) based on purchasing-power parity! The exchange-rate conversion

Less-developed countries (LDCs)
Low-income countries generally characterized by rapid population growth and an agriculture-household sector that dominates the economy. Sometimes these countries are referred to as developing countries.

method places the per capita income of the United States at 50 times the figure for China; the purchasing-power parity method at only 10.6 times.

For almost all LDCs, including Thailand, Brazil, Mexico, and Argentina, the per capita income estimates based on the PPP method are substantially greater than the parallel estimates derived by exchange-rate conversion. Since the informal economy—including production in the household sector—is undoubtedly a larger share of the total output in LDCs, even the purchasing-power parity method probably understates the standard of living in these countries relative to more highly developed market economies. At least, however, the PPP figures reflect the prices of a broader set of commodities than just the items traded in international markets. *Consequently, most economists believe that the purchasing-power parity estimates are a more accurate indicator of per capita income than the more widely circulated estimates based on exchange-rate conversions. This is particularly true with regard to comparisons of income and living standards in developed countries against those in LDCs.*[3]

ECONOMIC GROWTH AND DEVELOPMENT

Both economists and laypersons often use the term *economic development* when referring to low-income countries experiencing growth in income per capita. *When a nation's GDP is increasing more rapidly than its population, per capita GDP will also expand. Typically, increases in per capita GDP will upgrade other broad indicators of living standards, such as life expectancy, literacy, and health indicators.*

Specialists in the development area generally consider economic development to be a broader concept than economic growth. Development encompasses not only growth, but also distributional and structural changes that imply an improvement in the standard of living for most of the populace. Development requires not only growth in output per person but also an improvement in the availability of consumption goods for a wide spectrum of the populace, including those people in the bottom half of the income distribution.

Obviously, economic growth and development are closely related. Growth is necessary for development. Without sustained economic growth, continuous improvement in the economic opportunities and status of a nation's populace, including those at the bottom of the economic spectrum, will be impossible.

Increases in per capita GDP, on average, increase the availability of goods and services per person, and thus are generally associated with economic development—that is, an improvement in the standard of living throughout the populace. There are exceptions, however. For example, during the 1965–1980 period,

---

[3]For additional data on income differences across nations, see Stephen L. Parente and Edward C. Prescott, "Changes in the Wealth of Nations," *Quarterly Review: Federal Reserve Bank of Minneapolis,* spring 1993, pp. 3–16.

Brazil achieved substantial economic growth. The distribution of income in Brazil, however, was highly skewed. More than 60 percent of the aggregate income was allocated to the wealthiest 20 percent of the population. By way of comparison, the wealthiest one-fifth of the population earn between 40 percent and 45 percent of the aggregate income in the developed countries of Europe and North America. The economic growth of Brazil during the 1965–1980 period did little to improve the economic status of those in the bottom half of the income distribution. Thus, Brazil experienced growth but was unable to achieve economic development.

IMPACT OF SUSTAINED ECONOMIC GROWTH

With the passage of time, economic growth—increases in per capita GDP—can exert a substantial impact on incomes. When the income per person of a country grows at an annual rate of 3.5 percent, per capita income will double every 20 years. (Note: In order to approximate how many years it will take for income to double, you can simply divide 70 by the country's growth rate. In this case, 70 divided by 3.5 equals 20. This approximation method is sometimes called the simple 70 rule.) In contrast, if a country's growth rate of income per person is 1.75 percent, it would take 40 years for per capita income to double. Consider the case where two countries initially have the same level of income, but the annual growth rate of Country A is 3.5 percent while that of Country B is 1.75 percent. Even though the two started with the same income level, after 40 years the income of Country A would be twice that of Country B.

Differences in sustained growth rates over two or three decades will substantially alter relative income positions of countries. Nations that experience sustained periods of rapid economic growth will move up the income ladder and eventually achieve high-income status. On the other hand, nations that grow slowly or experience declines in real GDP per capita will slide down the economic ladder.

Using the actual income figures for Hong Kong, Japan, Argentina, and Venezuela, **Exhibit 34–3** vividly illustrates how sustained growth over a lengthy time period influences relative incomes. Look at the figures for 1960. *Measured in 1985 dollars*, the per capita GDP of Hong Kong was $2,247 in 1960, substantially less than the comparable figures of both Argentina ($4,462) and Venezuela ($6,338). Between 1960 and 1994, however, the per capita real GDP of Hong Kong expanded at a 6.3 percent annual rate, compared to rates of 1 percent for Argentina and 0.1 percent for Venezuela. Now look at the 1994 figures for these three countries. In 1994, per capita GDP of Hong Kong was $17,832—nearly three times the figures of Argentina and Venezuela.

The per capita income of Japan in 1960 was $2,954, well below the figure for Argentina. Between 1960 and 1994, the per capita growth rate of Japan was 5 percent. Look how this 4 percent differential altered the relative incomes of the two countries during the 34-year period. In 1960 the per capita GDP of Japan was 30 percent *less* than that of Argentina, but by 1994 the Japanese figure was 150 percent *more* than that of Argentina. Differences in growth rates exert a big impact when sustained over 15 or 20 years.

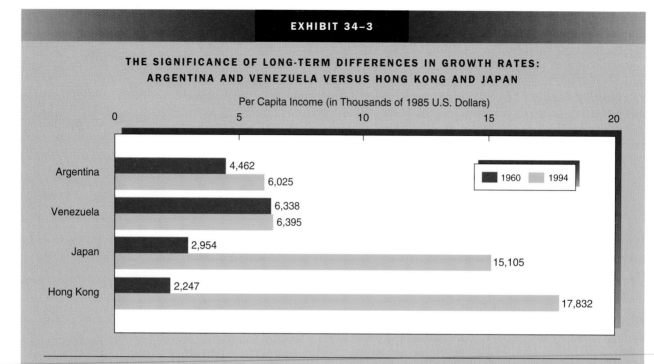

EXHIBIT 34-3

THE SIGNIFICANCE OF LONG-TERM DIFFERENCES IN GROWTH RATES: ARGENTINA AND VENEZUELA VERSUS HONG KONG AND JAPAN

Per Capita Income (in Thousands of 1985 U.S. Dollars)

The graph illustrates the 1960 and 1994 per capita GDP figures for Argentina, Venezuela, Japan, and Hong Kong. During the 1960–1994 period, the per capita growth rates of Hong Kong and Japan were 6.3 percent and 5 percent, respectively, compared to growth rates of 1 percent for Argentina and 0.1 percent for Venezuela. Note how the more rapid growth rates of the two Asian nations drastically altered their relative incomes compared to those of the two Latin American countries.

Source: Robert Summers and Alan Heston, *Penn World Tables* (Cambridge: National Bureau of Economic Research, 1994). These data were through 1992. They were updated to 1994 by the authors.

DIFFERENCES IN GROWTH RATES AMONG NATIONS

Observing the income differences between the wealthy industrial nations and LDCs, some have argued that the rich are consistently getting richer while the poor are getting poorer. Is this true? Which countries are growing most rapidly? Which are falling behind?

Exhibit 34–4 presents data on the growth of per capita GDP for (a) high-growth LDCs, (b) high-income industrial economies, and (c) LDCs with the worst growth records. Only eight countries with a population of 2 million or more were able to achieve a growth rate of real per capita GDP of 4 percent or more during 1980–1994. Interestingly, all eight of the high-growth economies were classified as LDCs at the beginning of the period, and they were all Asian

EXHIBIT 34–4

THE GROWTH OF PER CAPITA GDP (1980–1994) OF HIGH-INCOME INDUSTRIAL COUNTRIES, HIGH-GROWTH LDCs, AND LOW-GROWTH LDCs

HIGH-GROWTH LDCs[a]	GROWTH OF PER CAPITA GDP, 1980–1994	HIGH-INCOME INDUSTRIAL COUNTRIES	GROWTH OF PER CAPITA GDP, 1980–1994	LOW-GROWTH LDCs[b]	GROWTH OF PER CAPITA GDP, 1980–1994
China	8.2	Japan	2.9	Zaire	−5.3
South Korea	7.4	United Kingdom	1.9	Haiti	−4.5
Thailand	6.1	Germany	1.8	Togo	−4.2
Taiwan	6.1	Italy	1.7	Niger	−4.0
Singapore	5.3	United States	1.6	Côte d'Ivoire	−3.9
Hong Kong	5.0	Australia	1.6	Nicaragua	−3.3
Malaysia	4.1	France	1.4	Madagascar	−2.8
Indonesia	4.1	Canada	1.3	Cameroon	−2.3
		Netherlands	1.3	Romania	−2.3
		Switzerland	0.8	Zambia	−2.1

[a]LDCs with a growth rate of 4 percent or more during 1980–1994.
[b]LDCs with a negative growth rate of 2 percent or less during 1980–1994.

Source: Derived from World Bank, *World Tables, 1995*. Only countries with a population of 2 million or more are included in this table.

nations. China, South Korea, Thailand, Taiwan, Singapore, and Hong Kong head the list of the world's fastest growing economies. The growth of per capita GDP of these countries was 5 percent or more during 1980–1994. The growth rates of Malaysia and Indonesia were also highly impressive. In these high-growth economies, per capita income has increased sharply and living standards improved dramatically in recent decades. (See the Applications in Economics box, page 916, on how growth affects the lives of people.)

Among the high-income industrial economies, Japan had the highest annual growth rate during this period—2.9 percent. The growth rates of the other large economies in the G-7 group (the United States, Germany, France, the United Kingdom, Italy, and Canada) were bunched within a narrow range between 1.3 percent and 1.9 percent. Most of the smaller high-income economies also had growth rates within this same range. Thus, the per capita income of the high-growth economies was expanding at three or four times the rate of the typical high-income industrial economy.

Unfortunately, there is another group of LDCs that not only has failed to grow, but has regressed. Exhibit 34–4 presents the data for the countries that experienced declines in per capita GDP of 2 percent or more during 1980–1994. Per capita GDP fell at an annual rate of 4 percent or more in Zaire, Haiti, Togo,

HOW ECONOMIC GROWTH CHANGES LIVES

(Author's Note: It is easy to overlook the changes implied by income figures and growth data. The following feature, written by development economist James Cobbe of Florida State University, reminds us how rapid economic growth like that achieved in Malaysia brings dramatic change in the lifestyles of real people.)

I spent a year as a teacher at Saratok Secondary School in Sarawak, East Malaysia, in 1964–65. To get to the school one flew to Kuching, the capital of Sarawak, took a boat downriver to the coast, along the coast, and then up the Saratok river to Saratok town. Finally one took a Land-Rover four and a half miles up the mud jeep-track to the school. The whole journey took a minimum of 36 hours, and at wet times of year the last four and a half miles could take hours, the passengers getting out frequently to pull branches from trees to put under the wheels to stop them sinking to their axles in the mud, and to push the truck up the hills.

In the whole of the district (similar in size to a large U.S. county), there were six motor vehicles, all Land-Rovers, and no surfaced roads at all. Most of the students at the school, the first secondary school in the district, had never seen a tarred road or an ordinary car. Most of

them lived in wood longhouses, and their families grew rice and tapped a few rubber trees or had a small pepper garden. In Saratok town there were only three masonry buildings—the police station, the government district office, and the post office. There was a telephone at each of those buildings, at the secondary school, and in the health post, which was a two-room, wooden building staffed by one Senior Hospital Assistant who had rather less training than a registered nurse. There was no doctor and certainly no air-conditioning. At the school, we had electricity for a few hours each day so long as our generator was working and we had fuel.

In 1996, I did some work in Kuala Lumpur in West Malaysia, and had the opportunity to go back to Sarawak for a weekend. I flew into Kuching again, and rented a car—a Malaysian-manufactured Proton, with an AM-FM radio and air-conditioning. I drove the 350 kilometers to my old school, and then to Saratok town and various other places I had visited 30 years before, without ever leaving a blacktop road. The only buildings I recognized in Saratok were the government office and the police station; all the old wooden buildings were gone. There was now a large, modern, well-equipped hospital, with a large billboard outside warning of the dangers of AIDS. Where there had been two rows of wooden shop-houses facing each other,

and Niger. This implies that the per person income level of these countries in 1994 was only about half the income level of 1980. The per capita GDP of Côte d'Ivoire, Nicaragua, Madagascar, Cameroon, Romania, and Zambia also declined substantially between 1980 and 1994.

The growth picture of LDCs is clearly one of diversity. The fastest growing countries in the world are all LDCs. These rapidly growing countries are closing the income gap relative to their wealthier counterparts.[4] At the same time, other LDCs are doing very poorly and falling further and further behind.[5]

---

[4]In fact, the income levels of two of the high-growth countries—Hong Kong and Singapore—have risen so much that they are no longer classified as less developed.

[5]The diversity in the growth rates of LDCs is also true over a more lengthy time period. In a study of the 1960–1985 period, Stephen Parente of Northeastern University and Edward Prescott of the University of Minnesota also found that several LDCs had more rapid growth rates than the high-income industrial economies, while others fell further and further behind. As Parente and Prescott put it, "There have been development miracles and disasters." See Parente and Prescott, "Changes in the Wealth of Nations," *Quarterly Review: Federal Reserve Bank of Minneapolis*, spring 1993, pp. 3–16.

there were now three distinct shopping areas, all concrete or masonry, including one shop that was a computer center, and several video rental places. There were lots of private cars and trucks, taxis, minibus taxis, a large and well-organized bus station with regular services to many towns and villages, and several gas and service stations.

In 1964, only two or three towns in the whole of Sarawak had piped water supply; in 1996, in almost 800 kilometers of driving, every settlement, however small, had a water purification plant outside it. In 1964–65, the district around Saratok was almost all tree-covered, either secondary forest or small-holder rubber plantations, with the occasional dry rice field planted after burning off the brush. In 1996, there were almost no trees visible from the roads. Most of the land was planted to oil-palm, with the occasional pepper garden or rice field. Incomes in the district were obviously enormously higher than they had been before—solid houses, air-conditioning units, kids on bicycles (no child had a bicycle in the old days), young people with boomboxes, and CD-jukeboxes and Karaoke setups in the coffee shops and bars in town. In 1964–65, one coffee shop had a broken jukebox, there was no such thing as a bar, and you needed shortwave to get anything on the radio. In 1965, the one secondary school had fewer than 250 students; now, three secondary schools had over ten times as many. Of course, changes of this magnitude have not occurred everywhere. Away from major roads, conditions are often still quite primitive. Nevertheless, it is clear that growth has changed the lives of many people.

I met with a former pupil, Sia Jit Yong, whose father had owned one of the old wooden shop-houses. Jit Yong had never seen an ordinary car, used a phone, or seen a doctor before he graduated from secondary school. Now, he drove a Honda [and] had a prosperous business, a cellular phone, a daughter doing postgraduate medical study in the United States, and a son at the Polytechnic in Singapore. As we talked about his classmates of 30 years before, he automatically gave me their phone numbers—they all had phones.

If I had told Jit Yong in 1965 that 30 years later he would regularly get phone calls from a daughter in Washington, D.C., studying to be a medical specialist, or that he would ride in an air-conditioned car between his shop and houses similar to those in U.S. suburbs, he would have thought I was crazy. But those 30 years brought a thriving market for palm oil, roads, good communications, and readily available education. All the accessories of the consumer society followed naturally. I could hardly believe it myself.

SOURCES OF ECONOMIC GROWTH

Why have some countries grown rapidly, while others have experienced economic stagnation and even reductions in income? Laypersons often argue that natural resources are the key ingredient of economic growth. Of course, other things constant, countries with abundant natural resources do have an advantage. It is clear, though, that natural resources are neither a necessary nor sufficient condition for economic growth. Other than its harbor, Hong Kong has practically no natural resources. Japan likewise has few natural resources, and it imports almost all of its industrial energy supply. Nonetheless, as Exhibit 34–3 illustrates, both Hong Kong and Japan have grown rapidly during the past several decades and achieved high levels of income. In contrast, Argentina has a great deal of fertile land and several other natural resources, and Venezuela is one of the most oil-rich countries in the world. Yet these countries, along with other resource-rich countries like Ghana, Kenya, and Bolivia, are poor, and they have been growing slowly, if at all. Natural resources can help promote economic prosperity, but clearly they are not the primary determinant of growth.

Economic growth is a complex process. Several factors contribute to it, and they are often interrelated. Much as the performance of an athletic team reflects the joint output of the team members, economic growth is jointly determined by several factors. And just as one or two weak players can substantially reduce overall team performance, a counterproductive policy in one or two key areas can substantially harm the overall performance of an economy. Although economics cannot provide us with a precise recipe for economic growth, it does reveal the important sources of such growth: (1) investment in physical and human capital, (2) technological advances, and (3) improvement in economic organization.

INVESTMENT IN PHYSICAL AND HUMAN CAPITAL

Machines can have a substantial impact on a person's ability to produce. Even Robinson Crusoe on an uninhabited island can catch more fish with a net than he can with his hands. Farmers working with modern tractors and plows can cultivate many more acres than could their great-grandparents, who probably worked with hoes. Similarly, education and training that improve the knowledge and skills of workers can vastly improve their productivity. For example, a cabinetmaker, skilled after years of training and experience, can build cabinets far more rapidly and efficiently than a neophyte.

Investment in both physical capital (machines) and human capital (knowledge and skills) can expand the productive capacity of a worker. In turn, people that produce more goods and services valued by others will tend to have higher incomes. Economics suggests that, other things constant, countries using a larger share of their resources to produce tools, machines, and factories will tend to grow more rapidly. Allocation of more resources to education and training will also tend to enhance economic growth.

Of course, investment is not a free lunch; an opportunity cost is involved. When more resources are used to produce machines and factories and develop skills, fewer resources are available for production of current-consumption goods. Economics is about trade-offs. It does, however, indicate that people who save and invest more will be able to produce more in the future.

TECHNOLOGICAL PROGRESS

Technological advancement

The introduction of new techniques or methods of production that enable a greater output per unit of input.

Technological advancement—the adoption of new improved techniques or methods of production—enables workers to generate additional output with the same amount of resources. Such improvements reduce the cost of producing goods and services.

Clearly, improved technology—the result of using brainpower to discover economical new products and/or less costly methods of production—has substantially enhanced our production possibilities. During the last 250 years, the substitution of power-driven machines for human labor, the development of miracle grains, fertilizer, and new sources of energy, and improvements in transportation and communication have vastly improved living standards around the world. Technological improvements continue to change our lives. Consider the impact of compact disc players, microcomputers, word processors, microwave ovens, video cameras and cassette players, fax machines, and automobile air-conditioners. Development and improvement of these products during just the past couple of decades has vastly changed the way many people work and play.

Obviously, technological progress encompasses **invention,** the discovery of new products or processes. But, it also includes **innovation,** the practical and effective adoption of new techniques. Compared to scientific inventions, it is easy to overlook the highly significant role of innovators in the adoption and dissemination of technological improvements. Many innovators were not even involved in the invention of the products for which they are now famous. Henry Ford played a minor role in the invention and development of the automobile. His contribution was an innovative one—the adoption of mass-production techniques that enabled the low-cost production of reliable automobiles. Ray Kroc, the developer of the McDonald's fast-food chain, did not invent anything. In fact, he was not even involved in the operation of the first McDonald's restaurant. But he recognized a good idea when he saw it. Kroc was an innovator. He franchised the business, trained operators of McDonald's, and in the process changed the eating habits of a nation. Inventions are important, but without innovators, inventions are merely ideas waiting to be exploited.

Modern technology is available to all nations—rich and poor alike. Poor nations do not have to invest in research and development—they can emulate (or import at a low cost) the proven technologies of the developed countries. Thus, the opportunity to grow by adopting improved technology is greater for poor developing countries than it is in high-income developed nations. This factor helps explain why countries that were relatively poor just a few years ago generally dominate the list of the world's fastest growing economies (see Exhibit 34–4 for evidence on this point).

However, as in the case of natural resources, it is important to keep the contribution of technology in perspective. If technology were the primary factor limiting the creation of wealth, most low-income countries would be growing more rapidly than developed nations. This is not the case. Many poor countries continue to stagnate even though the proven technologies of high-income industrial countries are available to them freely (or at a low cost).

Invention
The discovery of a new product or process, often facilitated by the knowledge of engineering and scientific relationships.

Innovation
The successful introduction and adoption of a new product or process; the economic application of inventions.

EFFICIENT ECONOMIC ORGANIZATION

The efficiency with which the economic activity of a country is organized will influence the country's output and growth rate. If the economic organization of a nation encourages waste and fails to reward the creation of wealth, economic growth will be stunted.

Regardless of the form of economic organization present, certain basic conditions must be met if waste and inefficiency are to be avoided. The incentive structure must encourage production of the goods and services that are most desired by people (relative to their costs). **Allocative inefficiency** results when a nation's resources are used to produce the wrong products. For example, in a nation whose people need (intensely desire) more food and better housing, valuable resources might be used to produce unwanted national monuments and luxurious vacations for political leaders. In the same way, waste results when a nation ill-equipped to manufacture steel and automobiles insists on using

Allocative inefficiency
The use of an uneconomical combination of resources to produce goods and services, or the use of resources to produce goods that are not intensely desired relative to their opportunity cost.

resources that could be productive in other areas (for example, agriculture) to produce these prestige goods.

Efficient economic organization must also encourage producers to choose low-opportunity-cost methods of production. Regardless of whether an economy is centrally planned or market-directed, efficient production requires that the marginal productive contribution of each resource reflect its opportunity cost. Waste results when producers are discouraged from adopting the least-cost resource combination. For example, if unfavorable tax treatment or price control distorts prices and causes producers to choose higher-cost methods of production, the nation's production possibilities will be reduced.

The supply of public goods and goods that generate substantial external benefits is also an important ingredient of efficient economic organization. Broadly speaking, this issue relates to the provision of an economic **infrastructure**, a term used by economists to describe the economy's legal, monetary, educational, transportation, and communication structure. Providing an adequate infrastructure involves several factors, foremost among which are a legal system that clearly defines property rights, an educational system that encourages children of all social classes to develop their skills and abilities, and the development of highways, telephones, and power sources necessary to realize gains from specialization, division of labor, and mass-production methods. Although government often provides these networks, each has also been provided privately because users can be made to pay for the benefits they receive through tolls and user charges. However these factors are provided, a sound infrastructure is an integral part of efficient economic organization.

> **Infrastructure**
> *The provision of a legal, monetary, educational, transportation, and communication structure necessary for the efficient operation of an exchange economy.*

POLICIES THAT IMPROVE EFFICIENCY OF ECONOMIC ORGANIZATION

Policy can influence growth, either for good or ill, in many ways. The task is thus to try to exploit as many as possible of these avenues for good.

ARNOLD C. HARBERGER[6]

The efficiency of economic organization is not the result of happenstance or the forces of nature. It reflects political choices, institutional structures, and economic policies. Both economic theory and real-world experience suggest that the following six factors are important ingredients of efficient economic organization:

1. Security of property rights and political stability
2. Competitive markets
3. Stable money and prices
4. International trade and an open economy

---

[6]Arnold C. Harberger, *Economic Policy and Economic Growth* (San Francisco: International Center for Economic Growth, 1985), p. 8.

5. An open capital market
6. Avoidance of high marginal tax rates

Let us take a closer look at each of these factors.

SECURITY OF PROPERTY RIGHTS AND POLITICAL STABILITY

As we have previously discussed, private ownership provides legal protection against those who would use violence, theft, and fraud to take things that do not belong to them. Most important is the incentive structure that emanates from private ownership. *When the property rights of all citizens—including the vitally important property right to their labor—are clearly defined and securely enforced, trade replaces plunder as the means through which wealth is acquired. When property ownership rights are securely defined and enforced, people get ahead by helping and cooperating with others.* Employers, for example, have to provide prospective employees and other resource suppliers with at least as good a deal as they can get elsewhere. If business owners are to succeed, they will have to develop and provide potential customers with goods and services that they value highly (relative to cost). Moreover, private owners have an incentive to practice wise maintenance and conservation. If owners fail to maintain their assets properly, the value of those assets will fall and so, too, will the owner's wealth.

Throughout history, people have searched for and established other forms of ownership that they thought would be more humanitarian or more productive. These experiences have ranged from unsuccessful to disastrous. To date, we do not know of any alternative institutional arrangement that provides individuals with as much incentive to use resources productively and efficiently as private ownership.

A volatile political climate undermines the security of property rights. Historically, governments have confiscated physical and financial assets, imposed punitive taxes, and used regulations to punish those out of favor with the current political regime. Countries with a history of this type will find it difficult to restore confidence and reestablish the security of property rights.

Unfortunately, the political climate of many poor, less-developed countries is highly unstable. In some cases, prejudice, injustice, and highly unequal wealth status create a fertile environment for political upheaval. In other instances, political corruption and a history of favoritism to a ruling class provide the seeds for unrest. Regardless of its source, one thing is clear: Potential political upheaval and insecurity of property rights will repel capital investment and retard economic growth. In recent years, this factor has contributed to the dismal economic performance of several LDCs, including Zaire, Haiti, and Nicaragua (see Exhibit 34–4).

COMPETITIVE MARKETS

As Adam Smith stressed long ago, when competition is present, even self-interested individuals will tend to promote the general welfare. Conversely, when competition is weakened, business firms have more leeway to raise prices and pursue their own objectives and less incentive to innovate and develop better ways of doing things. Such policies as free entry into businesses and occupations, and freedom of exchange with foreigners, will enhance competition and thereby help to promote economic progress. In contrast, such policies as business subsidies, price controls, entry restraints, and trade restrictions stifle competition and conflict with economic progress.

Competition is a disciplining force for both buyers and sellers. In a competitive environment, producers must provide goods at a low cost and serve the interests of consumers since they will have to woo them away from other suppliers. Firms that develop improved products and figure out how to produce them at a low cost will succeed. Sellers that are unable to provide consumers with quality goods at competitive prices will be driven from the market. This process leads to improvement in both products and production methods, while directing resources toward projects where they are able to produce more value. It is a powerful stimulus for economic progress.

STABLE MONEY AND PRICES

A stable monetary environment provides the foundation for the efficient operation of a market economy. In contrast, monetary and price instability make both the price level and relative prices unpredictable, generate uncertainty, and undermine the security of contractual exchanges. When prices increase 20 percent one year, 50 percent the next year, 15 percent the year after that, and so on, individuals and businesses are unable to develop sensible long-term plans. The uncertainty will reduce the attractiveness of time-dimension exchanges, particularly investment decisions. Rather than deal with the uncertainties that accompany double- and triple-digit inflation rates, citizens will save less, while many investors and business decision makers will move their activities to countries with a more stable environment. Foreigners will invest elsewhere, and citizens will often go to great lengths to get their savings (potential funds for investment) out of the country. As a result, potential gains from capital formation and business activities will be lost.

INTERNATIONAL TRADE AND AN OPEN ECONOMY

In the absence of trade barriers, producers in various countries will be directed toward those areas where they have a comparative advantage, and the competition from abroad will help keep domestic producers on their toes. International trade allows the residents of each country to use more of their resources to produce and sell goods that they do well and use the proceeds to purchase goods that could be produced domestically only at a high cost. As a result, the trading partners are each able to produce a larger output and purchase a wider variety of products at more economical prices than would otherwise be possible.

Policies that retard international trade stifle this process and thereby retard economic progress. Obviously, tariffs and quotas fall into this category since they limit the ability of domestic citizens to trade with people in other countries. So, too, do exchange-rate controls. When a nation fixes the exchange-rate value of its currency above the market level, the country's export products will be unattractive to foreigners. But if domestic citizens sell less to foreigners, they will have less foreign currency with which to buy from foreigners. Thus, exchange-rate controls will reduce the volume of international trade and thereby retard economic progress.

OPEN CAPITAL MARKET

If investment is going to increase the wealth of a nation, capital must be channeled into productive projects. When the value of the additional output derived from an investment exceeds the cost of the investment, the project will increase the value of the resources, and thereby create wealth. In contrast, if the value of the additional output is less than the cost of the investment, undertaking the project will reduce the wealth of the nation. If a nation is going to realize its potential, it must have a mechanism capable of attracting savings and channeling them into wealth-creating projects. A competitive capital market performs this function.

When a nation's capital market is integrated with the world capital market, it will be able to attract savings (financial capital) from throughout the world at the cheapest possible price (interest rate). Similarly, its citizens will have access to the most attractive investment opportunities regardless of where they are located.

In a competitive capital market, private investors have a strong incentive to evaluate projects carefully and allocate their funds toward those projects expected to yield the highest rates of return. In turn, profitable projects will tend to increase the wealth not only of the investor but also of the nation.

When governments fix interest rates, they hamper the ability of the capital market to bring savers and investors together and channel funds into wealth-creating projects. Worse still, when the fixing of interest rates is combined with inflationary monetary policy, negative real interest rates will result. In turn, the negative rates will lead to capital flight as domestic investors seek positive returns abroad and foreign investors completely shun the country's potential investment projects. Such policies undermine capital markets, while retarding both investment and economic growth.

Without a capital market, it will be virtually impossible to attract funds and consistently allocate them into wealth-creating projects. If investment funds are allocated by governments rather than by the capital market, political clout rather than the expected rate of return will determine which investment projects are undertaken. And when politics replaces economic considerations, more unprofitable and counterproductive investment projects will predictably be undertaken.

The experience of Eastern Europe and the former Soviet Union highlights the importance of a capital market. For four decades (1950–1990), the investment rates (as a share of GDP) of these countries were among the highest in the world. The central planners of these countries channeled approximately one-third of GDP into investment. Even these high rates of investment, however, did little to improve living standards. Without the direction of a capital market, the investment funds were often channeled toward political and military projects favored by the planners rather than projects that would increase the future availability of consumer goods.

AVOIDANCE OF HIGH MARGINAL TAX RATES

When high marginal tax rates take a large share of the fruits generated by productive activities, the incentive of individuals to work and undertake business projects is reduced. High tax rates may also drive a nation's most productive citizens to other countries (where taxes are lower) and discourage foreigners from financing domestic investment projects. In short, economic theory indicates that high marginal tax rates will retard productive activity, capital formation, and economic growth.

The most detailed study of the impact of high marginal tax rates on the economic growth of LDCs has been conducted by Alvin Rabushka of Stanford University.[7] Rabushka undertook the tedious task of reconstructing the tax structure for 54 LDCs for a period of more than two decades. He found that some countries levied very high marginal tax rates, which took effect only at very high income thresholds. Others levied high marginal rates on even modest levels of income. A few countries imposed only low or medium tax rates.

Finally, Rabushka analyzed the relationship between the tax structure and economic growth. He found that the countries that kept marginal tax rates low (or applied higher marginal rates only to high income thresholds) generally experienced more rapid economic growth. He summarized his findings as follows:

> *Good economic policy, including tax policy, fosters economic growth and rising prosperity. In particular, low marginal income tax rates, or high thresholds for medium- and high-rate tax schedules, appear consistent with higher growth rates. The key in any system of direct taxation is to maintain low tax rates or high (income) thresholds.*[8]

High taxes on employment can also reduce economic efficiency. A large gap between the employer's cost of hiring a worker and the employee's receipts will reduce employment in the formal economy. Such policies tend to drive workers into the "informal," or underground, economy, where the legal structure is less certain and property rights less secure. Therefore, such policies reduce the gains from investment and trade, and thereby retard economic growth. Studies indicate that high employment taxes have been an important factor retarding the growth of several Latin American economies. For example, in Brazil the combination of payroll taxes, social contributions, and mandated holidays and termination benefits creates approximately a 100 percent tax wedge. That is, employment of a worker costs the employer twice the after-tax wage received by the

---

[7]See Alvin Rabushka, "Taxation, Economic Growth, and Liberty," *Cato Journal* (spring–summer 1987): pp. 121–148.

[8]Alvin Rabushka, "Taxation and Liberty in the Third World" (paper presented at conference on Taxation and Liberty, Santa Fe, New Mexico, September 26–27, 1985).

worker. Responding to this incentive structure, it is estimated that approximately one-third of the Brazilian labor force works in the underground economy.

A CLOSER LOOK AT THE SUCCESS STORIES

The accompanying Thumbnail Sketch summarizes the three major sources of economic growth and six key elements that influence the efficiency of resource use. If these factors really matter, a comparison between the high- and low-growth economies should reflect their importance.

Several of the illustrated exhibits introducing the international section presented data for the eight fastest growing economies in the world (China, South Korea, Thailand, Taiwan, Singapore, Hong Kong, Malaysia, and Indonesia) and five major economies (Argentina, Brazil, Mexico, Venezuela, and Nigeria) with disappointing growth records during the 1980–1994 period. Illustrated Exhibit VI–B shows the growth records of each country in both the high- and low-growth groups.

Illustrated Exhibit VI–C indicates the share of GDP that each of these countries allocated to investment. The investment/GDP ratio for the high-growth economies ranged from a low of 22 percent for Taiwan to a high of 41.3 percent for Singapore. The average investment rate of the eight high-growth economies was 31 percent of GDP. In contrast, the investment rate of the low-growth countries ranged from a low of 15.4 percent to a high of 21.8 percent. The average investment rate for the five low-growth countries was 19 percent, less than two-thirds the average for the high-growth economies. Like the low-growth economies, most countries allocate approximately 20 percent of their GDP to capital investment. Clearly, the high-growth economies invest a substantially larger

THUMBNAIL SKETCH

SOURCES OF ECONOMIC GROWTH
1. Investment in physical and human capital
2. Advancements in technology
3. Improvements in the efficiency of economic organization

KEY POLICIES THAT ENHANCE EFFICIENCY OF ECONOMIC ORGANIZATION
1. Private ownership
2. Competitive markets
3. Stable money and prices
4. Free trade
5. Open capital markets
6. Avoidance of high marginal tax rates

amount. Just as our theory indicates, these high investment rates help to propel growth.[9]

Illustrated Exhibit VI–D compares the inflation rates for the two groups. As we have previously shown, inflation is closely linked with monetary expansion. Countries experience high inflation rates because they finance government expenditures with printing-press money. The average annual inflation rate during 1980–1994 was less than 10 percent in each of the high-growth countries. In contrast, the lowest average annual inflation rate among the five low-growth economies was the 26.4 percent rate of Venezuela. Argentina and Brazil followed hyperinflationary policies throughout much of the period. Clearly, the monetary policies of the high-growth economies were considerably more stable than those of the low-growth group.

What about the openness of economies in the two groups? When comparisons are made between countries with similar population, the size of the trade sector provides insight on this topic. China, Indonesia, and Brazil all have populations in excess of 160 million. In 1994 the size of Brazil's trade sector (as a share of GDP) was less than half that of China and approximately one-third of the figure for Indonesia. Correspondingly, the populations of Taiwan, Malaysia, and Venezuela are quite similar, approximately 20 million. Once again the size of the trade sector of the two high-growth countries (Taiwan and Malaysia) was substantially larger than that of the low-growth country (Venezuela). This evidence, coupled with the fact that Hong Kong and Singapore have the largest trade sectors in the world, suggests that international trade is an important element of the success achieved by the high-growth economies.

Exhibit 34–5 provides additional evidence on the openness of the high-growth economies (except for China). The tariff rates of Hong Kong and Singapore were negligible, less than 0.5 percent of their trade volume in 1992. Compared to other LDCs, the tariff rates of all the high-growth economies were low, and they have been consistently reduced in recent years. As we discussed in the previous chapter, exchange-rate controls are another potential barrier restricting international exchange. Exchange-rate controls restrict trade because they make it more difficult for domestic citizens to obtain the foreign currencies required for trade with foreigners. Invariably, the controls lead to black markets. The more restrictive the exchange-rate controls, the larger the black-market premium they will generate (and the greater the negative impact on the volume of international trade). As Exhibit 34–5 shows, the high-growth Asian economies have all shunned exchange-rate controls since the mid-1980s. Their domestic currencies are all fully convertible in the foreign exchange market.

Finally, Exhibit 34–5 also shows that these high-growth economies persistently reduced marginal tax rates during the 1980–1994 period. Except for South Korea's 48 percent rate, the top marginal tax rates in all the high-growth economies is now 40 percent or less, quite low compared to other countries.

A general pattern emerges from an analysis of the policies of the high-growth countries. These successful economies have exceedingly high investment

---

[9]Some would argue that, given their high investment rates, the growth rates of the Asian success stories are not particularly impressive. See Paul Krugman, "The Myth of Asia's Miracle," *Foreign Affairs* 73 (1994): pp. 62–78, for a presentation of this view.

EXHIBIT 34-5

THE TAX, TRADE, AND CURRENCY POLICIES OF THE HIGH-GROWTH ASIAN ECONOMIES: 1980–1994

	AVERAGE TARIFF RATE[a]		WAS THE DOMESTIC CURRENCY FULLY CONVERTIBLE IN THE FOREIGN EXCHANGE MARKET?		TOP MARGINAL TAX RATE		
	1980	1992	1980	1994	1980	1990	1994
South Korea	4.1	2.2	No[b]	Yes	89	60	48
Thailand	6.9	3.9	No[c]	Yes	60	55	37
Taiwan	3.6	2.0	Yes	Yes	60	50	40
Singapore	0.5	0.2	Yes	Yes	55	33	30
Hong Kong	0.5	0.3	Yes	Yes	15	25	25
Malaysia	7.7	2.8	Yes	Yes	60	45	34
Indonesia	2.9	1.9	Yes	Yes	50	35	35

[a]Taxes on international trade as a percent of exports plus imports.
[b]The black-market exchange-rate premium for South Korea was 11 percent in 1980. The Korean won has been fully convertible since the mid-1980s.
[c]The black-market exchange-rate premium for Thailand was 5 percent in 1980. The Thai baht has been fully convertible since the mid-1980s.
Sources: Derived from Price Waterhouse, *Individual Tax Rates* (various issues); The International Monetary Fund, *Government Finance Statistics Yearbook, 1995;* and International Currency Analysis, *The World Currency Yearbook* (various issues).

rates. Their monetary policies have been relatively stable. Enhanced by low tariffs and fully convertible currencies, their trade sectors are large. Low taxes and integration into the world capital market have also contributed to their success. Economic analysis indicates that they have followed policies consistent with growth and prosperity.

CHINA: IS IT A SPECIAL CASE?

Some may be surprised to find China among the high-growth countries of Exhibit 34–4. After all, isn't China a centrally planned socialist economy that has generally followed policies inconsistent with growth and prosperity?

Following the 1978 Communist Party Congress, China began to introduce reforms that have dramatically changed the structure of the economy. *Today, there are essentially two Chinese economies: (1) agriculture, small businesses, and "special economic zones," and (2) the state enterprises. The first is now a relatively free economy, while the second continues to be centrally planned.*

Initially, China took several important steps toward economic liberalization of the agricultural sector. The collective farms were dismantled and replaced with what the Chinese refer to as a contract responsibility system. Under this organizational form, individual families are permitted to lease land for up to 15 years in exchange for supplying the state with a fixed amount of production at a designated price (which is generally below the market price). Amounts produced above the required quota belong to the individual farmers and may be either directly consumed or sold at a free market price.

Even though the legal ownership remains with the state, this system of long-term land leases provides farmers with something akin to a private property right. This is particularly true since renewal of the lengthy leases is now virtually automatic. Because the state quota is relatively low—approximately 15 percent—and the farmers are permitted to keep all production above the fixed quota, the effective marginal tax rate is zero. Clearly, this provides a strong incentive for farmers to expand output. Markets play a key role in the allocation of agricultural products. Currently, more than 85 percent of the grain (rice, wheat, and barley) output is produced privately and sold at market-determined prices.[10]

The success in agriculture encouraged reforms in other sectors. Restrictions on the operation of small-scale service and retail businesses were relaxed in the 1980s. Private restaurants, stores, and repair shops sprang up and began to compete with state-operated enterprises. By the mid-1980s, Chinese cities were teeming with sidewalk vendors, restaurants, small retail businesses, and hundreds of thousands of individuals providing personal services.

At the same time, China has established so-called "special economic zones." Approximately 15 percent of the Chinese labor force now works in these zones. In these areas, people are permitted to establish businesses, engage in trade with foreigners, maintain bank accounts in foreign currencies, and undertake investment without having to obtain government approval. Taxes in the special zones are generally quite low. During the past decade these zones attracted substantial investment from abroad, which has contributed to the growth of the Chinese investment rate. Economic activity in these regions has also made a sizable contribution to the growth of the trade sector. As Illustrated Exhibit VI–E shows, the size of China's international trade sector has more than doubled since 1980.[11]

---

[10]Other reforms also enhanced the development of markets in agricultural products. Restrictions on individual stock breeding, household sideline occupations, transport of agricultural goods, and trade fairs (marketplaces) were removed. Farmers were permitted to own tractors and trucks, and even hire laborers to work in their leased fields. Such economic activities were prohibited prior to 1978.

[11]Although the moves toward liberalization have contributed substantially to China's recent growth, there may also be a second factor at work: The growth-rate data of China may be significantly overstated. Clearly, this was the case for the former Soviet Union and the countries of Eastern Europe during the 1970s and 1980s. Since centrally planned economies do not rely on product prices to allocate goods and services, output is measured by the physical quantities of goods produced and inputs used. These factors may be a highly unreliable indicator of the value of what is actually being produced. As China has moved away from a command/barter economy in recent years toward greater reliance on markets, some productive activities that were not counted (or were counted only at a depressed level) are now being counted as part of GDP. This will tend to exaggerate the growth of GDP. Thus, the growth estimates of China should be interpreted with caution.

WINDS OF CHANGE IN LATIN AMERICA

Increasingly, opinion leaders around the world are taking a look at the policies of the high-growth Asian economies. This is particularly true in South and Central America. Like most other LDCs, Latin American countries have often substituted central planning and price controls for markets, established and protected government-operated enterprises, and erected barriers restricting international trade. In addition, Latin American governments have often financed their operations with "printing-press" money. As a result, the region has been plagued with hyperinflation. Economic theory indicates that policies of this type will undermine economic progress.

Indeed this has been the case. The 1980s were an economic disaster in Latin America. As **Exhibit 34–6** illustrates, except for Chile and Colombia, the per capita GDP of every country in South and Central America declined during the decade. Understandingly, Latin leaders are searching for an alternative strategy.

EXHIBIT 34–6

THE 1980S: THE LOST DECADE OF LATIN AMERICA

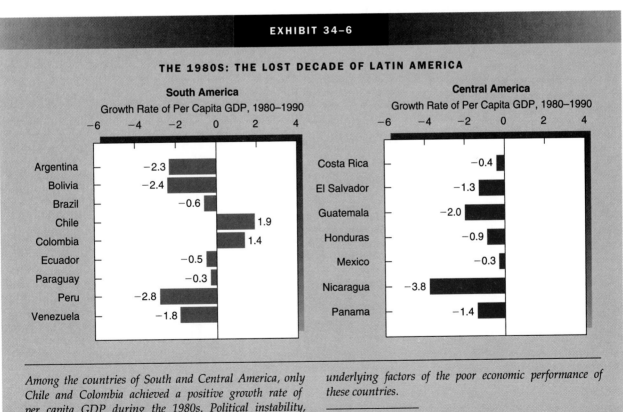

Among the countries of South and Central America, only Chile and Colombia achieved a positive growth rate of per capita GDP during the 1980s. Political instability, hyper-inflation, and perverse economic policies were the underlying factors of the poor economic performance of these countries.

Source: World Bank, *World Tables, 1995.*

THE EXPERIENCE OF CHILE AND PERU

In contrast with other Latin American countries, Chile began shifting away from policies of monetary expansion, price controls, and trade restrictions in the late 1970s and early 1980s. Chile's annual growth rate of the money supply, which averaged 150 percent during the 1970s, was reduced to around 20 percent in the 1980s. Predictably, the inflation receded to more respectable levels. Tariff rates were cut and exchange-rate controls relaxed. This has contributed to the growth in the size of the trade sector. Tax rates were reduced. The top marginal rate was cut from 80 percent in 1975 to 60 percent in 1980, 50 percent in 1990, and 48 percent in 1994. Interest rate controls were eliminated, and several state enterprises were privatized during the 1980s.

Spurred by these more liberal policies, Chile has become the growth economy of Latin America. Although Chile's GDP per capita was virtually unchanged during the 1970s, it increased at an annual rate of 1.9 percent during the 1980s. During the 1985–1995 period, Chile's annual growth rate of per capita GDP soared to 5 percent, one of the highest rates in the world.

More recently, Peru—one of the poorest countries in Latin America—also began instituting an economic liberalization plan. When the new president, Alberto Fujimori, took office in 1990, the Peruvian economy was in shambles. The inflation rate was running at an annual rate of 7,000 percent. (This means the general level of prices was 70 times higher at the end of the year than at the beginning.) Peru's high tariffs and restrictive quotas gave it perhaps the most protectionist trade policy in the world. Fueled by the economic decline, civil unrest was widespread.

Fujimori had an economic plan to deal with the situation. First, the rate of the monetary growth was sharply curtailed and the inflation rate gradually reduced. Second, trade policies were liberalized. Most tariffs were slashed from rates of 75 percent or more to a maximum rate of 15 percent. Quotas were abolished. Exchange-rate controls were relaxed and eventually eliminated. Finally, numerous state enterprises were privatized under a program designed to encourage participation by those with low incomes. Low-income households were permitted to purchase shares of profitable state enterprises on favorable terms and pay for them over a three-year period. By 1993, the Peruvian economy was on a positive growth path and its 13 percent real GDP increase in 1994 was the highest in the world.

MEXICO AND ARGENTINA

Beginning in the late 1980s, Mexico and Argentina also took significant steps toward economic liberalization. Both reduced tariffs sharply, relaxed exchange-rate controls, sliced high marginal tax rates, and began privatizing various government enterprises. The economies of both Mexico and Argentina grew during 1990–1994. However, the growth came to an abrupt halt in 1995, following Mexico's financial crisis.

Mexico had tied the peso to the U.S. dollar and pledged to follow a monetary policy that would maintain the peso's foreign exchange value within a relatively narrow band. As we noted in the preceding chapter, when a country pegs its currency to another, it must be willing to give up its monetary independence.

It cannot expand its domestic money supply at a rate that is out of line with that of the other currency. This is precisely what Mexico attempted to do. During the six years after the peso was pegged to the dollar, the money supply of Mexico increased fivefold. During this same period, the U.S. money supply increased by only 50 percent. This rapid growth of the money supply (and Mexico's higher rate of inflation) along with political unrest (two key political figures were assassinated during the 1994 presidential campaign) undermined the confidence of investors. As both domestic and foreign investors attempted to convert their pesos to dollars in late 1994, Mexico's foreign currency reserves fell to low levels. Eventually, Mexico allowed the peso to float and its foreign exchange value plummeted by approximately 60 percent in 1995.

Mexico's financial unrest produced fallout in other countries, including Argentina. Both Mexico and Argentina experienced an outflow of capital and a sharp decline in real GDP during 1995.

THE FUTURE

It is too early to assess fully the results of the changes in Latin America. LDCs in this region, as well as in other parts of the world, are continuing to institute changes and search for forms of economic organization more consistent with growth and prosperity. The dynamic forces of economic change will make the next decade an exciting time to study economic development.

LOOKING AHEAD

For more than four decades the economies of most countries in Eastern Europe were centrally planned. In the case of the countries of the former Soviet Union, central economic planning has an even longer history. In the next chapter, we will use economic tools to analyze centrally planned economies and consider the problems that arise when a socialist country attempts to move toward a market-directed economy.

CHAPTER SUMMARY

1. Most income comparisons across countries are derived by the exchange-rate conversion method. Since this method reflects the exchange-rate value of a currency rather than its purchasing power over a broad range of domestic goods and services, income comparisons derived by it are often unreliable.

2. The purchasing-power parity method uses data on the cost of purchasing a typical bundle of consumer goods and services to determine the relative purchasing power of each currency and estimate the GDP of each nation in terms of a common currency. Most economists believe that income comparisons derived by this method provide a more accurate measure of income levels and living standards across countries.

3. Most of the poorest countries—those with a per capita annual GDP of less than $1,200—are located in Africa. Most of the high-income countries are located in North America, Europe, Oceania, and East Asia (for example, Japan and Hong Kong).

4. Income comparisons based on the exchange-rate conversion method generally understate the income of less-developed countries relative to the income of industrial countries. As the cases of India and China indicate, oftentimes this understatement is substantial.

5. China, South Korea, Thailand, Taiwan, Singapore, and Hong Kong head the list of the world's fastest growing economies. All of these countries are Asian and all were classified as LDCs in 1980.

6. There is substantial variation in the growth record of LDCs. Per capita incomes in the high-growth Asian economies are increasing rapidly both in real terms and relative to the income level of the industrial nations. On the other hand, a sizable number of LDCs have experienced negative growth rates or economic stagnation. The latter

group continues to fall further behind their high-income counterparts.

7. Economic growth is a complex process. Economists stress the importance of three major sources of economic progress: (a) investment in physical and human capital, (b) development and implementation of technologically improved production methods and products, and (c) efficient economic organization. Contrary to a popular view, the availability of domestic natural resources is not the major determinant of growth. Countries such as Japan and Hong Kong have impressive growth rates without such resources, while many resource-rich nations continue to stagnate.

8. Economic policies influence the efficiency of economic organization. In general, secure property rights and political stability, competitive markets, monetary stability, international trade, integration into the world capital market, and avoidance of high taxes will enhance the efficiency of economic organization.

9. Countries that have grown rapidly in recent years have generally invested a large portion of their GDP, followed a stable monetary policy, imposed few restrictions on international trade, and relied on markets to allocate goods and services. In contrast, stagnating economies were characterized by rapid monetary expansion, high inflation rates, high tariffs, exchange- and interest-rate controls, and low rates of investment.

CRITICAL-ANALYSIS QUESTIONS

1. How do the exchange-rate conversion and purchasing-power parity methods differ as tools for comparing relative incomes among countries? Which is the most widely cited in the popular news media? Which is the most reliable? Why?

*2. It is often argued that the rich nations are getting richer and the poor ones are getting poorer. Is this view correct? Is it an oversimplification? Explain.

*3. "Without aid from the industrial nations, poor countries are caught in the poverty trap. Because they are poor, they are unable to save and invest; and, lacking investment, they remain poor." Evaluate this view.

4. Imagine you are an economic adviser to the president of an LDC. You have been asked to suggest policies to promote economic growth and a higher standard of living

for the citizens. Outline your suggestions, and discuss their rationale.

5. Evaluate each of the following policies in terms of its impact on the growth and prosperity of a nation.
   a. Adoption of a regulation that would limit foreign ownership of domestic businesses
   b. Imposition of a surtax on the corporate profits of foreign firms operating in the country
   c. A 50 percent increase in tariff rates
   d. Adoption of a minimum wage equal to 50 percent of the country's average hourly wage
   e. Legislation requiring employers to provide health care for all of their employees
   f. Legislation requiring employers to provide one year of severance pay to any employee who is dismissed from employment

6. Discuss the importance of the following as determinants of economic growth: (a) natural resources, (b) physical capital, (c) human capital, (d) technical knowledge, (e) size of the domestic market, and (f) economic policy.

*7. Do you think that the absence of international trade barriers would be more important for a small country like Costa Rica than for a larger country like Mexico? Explain.

8. "Since government-operated firms do not have to make a profit, they can usually produce at a lower cost and charge a lower price than privately owned enterprises." Evaluate this view.

9. "Governments can promote economic growth by using taxes and subsidies to direct investment funds toward high-tech, heavy manufacturing, and other growth industries that will enhance the future income of the nation." Evaluate this view.

10. What can government do to promote economic growth? Is it important to have a comprehensive plan? Why or why not?

11. More than 200 years ago, Adam Smith argued that the wealth of nations was dependent upon gains from (a) specialization and trade, (b) expansion in the size of the market, and (c) the discovery of better (more productive) ways of doing things. Explain why you either agree or disagree with Smith's view.

---

*Asterisk denotes questions for which answers are given in Appendix B.

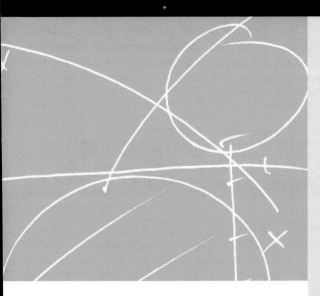

- What are the characteristics of a socialist economy?
- How did the central planning process work? Why did it fail?
- How are the former centrally planned economies doing?
- Why might the official output statistics during the transition period be misleading?
- Why is the transition from central planning to markets so difficult?
- How did the transitional strategy of the Czech Republic differ from that of Russia?

We know what doesn't work; now we are trying to figure out what will work.

RUSSIAN TOURIST GUIDE[1]

---

[1]This statement was made by a Russian tourist guide to one of the authors during a visit to St. Petersburg in August 1992.

More than 400 million people live in formerly Communist countries that were either part of or under the domination of the former Soviet Union. Until recently, these economies were characterized by central planning and government ownership of most physical assets. Fueled by poor economic performance, stability in this region began to unravel in the 1980s. The process culminated with the fall of the Berlin Wall in 1989 and the collapse of the Soviet Union in 1991. Currently, the economies of former Soviet bloc nations are in transition. Several have moved rapidly toward a market-oriented economy. Others are continuing to search for alternatives. This transitional period has not been easy.

The events in Eastern Europe and the former Soviet Union during the last decade raise several questions. Why did the central planning system collapse? Why has the transitional period been so difficult? What lies ahead for these countries? What do they need to do to achieve healthy economic growth in the future? This chapter will address these questions and analyze a number of the issues confronting these transitional economies.

PER CAPITA INCOME IN THE FORMER SOVIET BLOC COUNTRIES

Exhibit 35–1 provides data on the population and estimated per capita income in 1993 for the former Soviet bloc countries. The per capita incomes of these countries are well below the comparable figures for the United States and other major industrial countries. Compared to the rest of the world, however, these countries are not particularly poor. In most instances, their per capita incomes are between $4,000 and $8,000. Thus, the income levels of Eastern Europe are similar to those of Mexico, Brazil, and other Latin American countries.

Just a few decades ago, several of these countries were quite wealthy. For example, just prior to the Second World War, the average income level of Czechoslovakia (now the Czech and Slovak republics) was about the same as that of Germany, France, and Austria. In general, the skill levels and literacy rates of the people living in Eastern Europe are quite high. Thus, their potential for achievement of higher income levels should be quite good.

CHARACTERISTICS OF SOCIALIST ECONOMIES

One cannot understand the transitional problems of Eastern Europe without knowledge of socialism and the central planning processes that dominated these economies for such a long time. Two central factors underlie the differences between capitalist market economies and socialist centrally planned economies: (1) ownership of physical capital and (2) the mechanism used to allocate resources.

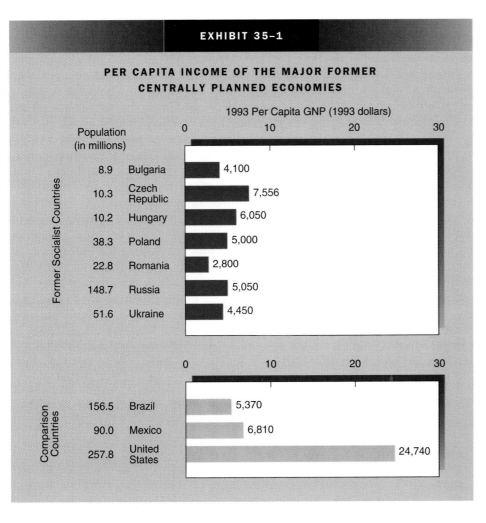

EXHIBIT 35-1

PER CAPITA INCOME OF THE MAJOR FORMER CENTRALLY PLANNED ECONOMIES

1993 Per Capita GNP (1993 dollars)

Former Socialist Countries

Population (in millions)	Country	1993 Per Capita GNP
8.9	Bulgaria	4,100
10.3	Czech Republic	7,556
10.2	Hungary	6,050
38.3	Poland	5,000
22.8	Romania	2,800
148.7	Russia	5,050
51.6	Ukraine	4,450

Comparison Countries

Population (in millions)	Country	1993 Per Capita GNP
156.5	Brazil	5,370
90.0	Mexico	6,810
257.8	United States	24,740

The per capita incomes of most of the former centrally planned countries are similar to those of Brazil and Mexico and approximately 25 percent as large as the figure for the United States.

Source: World Bank, *World Development Report, 1995* (Tables 1 and 30). The per capita GNP estimates were derived by the purchasing power parity method.

Capitalism is characterized by private ownership of physical assets and the use of market forces to coordinate the actions of buyers and sellers and thereby determine the allocation of goods and resources. This is not to say that everything is privately owned in a capitalist economy. Even in market economies, governments often operate public utilities, transportation systems, and other business enterprises. However, most things, including houses, farms, land, businesses, and even large manufacturing plants, are generally owned privately in market economies. Even more important, the legal structure respects and enforces the ownership rights of the private parties. Thus, we might say that a market economy is characterized by a private-ownership regime.

In contrast, under **socialism** most physical assets—particularly those that are used to produce goods and services—are owned by the state. Private parties are not permitted to own various classes of physical assets or operate most types of businesses. Thus, everyone (or almost everyone) in the labor force is employed by the government. Government ownership of physical assets and conduct of business activity is a dominant characteristic of a socialist economy.

With regard to resource allocation, market economies rely on the choices of consumers, private owners of the resources, and business entrepreneurs to direct

Capitalism
An economic system based on private ownership of productive resources and allocation of goods according to the price signals provided by free markets.

Socialism
A system of economic organization where (1) the ownership and control of the basic means of production rest with the state and (2) the allocation of resources and products is determined by centralized planning rather than by market forces.

activities. Their choices are coordinated by prices reflecting the forces of supply and demand, which determine what is going to be produced, how goods will be produced, and who will consume them. In contrast, under socialism, resources are used and allocated in accordance with the priorities of a centrally determined and administered plan. Economic decisions, such as what and how much will be produced, how resources will be used in production, and to whom the product will be distributed, are made by a central-planning authority (and the political officials that it represents). The central plan may also include decisions on quantities of raw materials and inputs, techniques of production, prices, wages, locations of firms and industries, and the employment of labor. Thus, socialist economic objectives generally reflect the preferences and value judgments of central planners and political authorities.

In a market economy, the interaction between savers and investors will determine the share of current income allocated to investment, and pursuit of profit will tend to direct funds toward those projects yielding the highest rate of return. Under central planning, the political process will determine both the share of current output allocated to investment and which projects will be undertaken. To the extent that the planners (and the political officials they represent) give priority to future income relative to current consumption, centrally planned economies will be able to achieve high rates of capital formation. The accompanying Thumbnail Sketch summarizes the distinctive characteristics of capitalist and socialist economic organization.

THUMBNAIL SKETCH

WHAT ECONOMIC CHARACTERISTICS DISTINGUISH CAPITALISM FROM SOCIALISM?

	CAPITALISM	SOCIALISM
PROPERTY RIGHTS	Nonhuman resources are owned by private parties (that is, individuals or corporations).	Nonhuman resources are owned by the government.
ALLOCATION OF GOODS AND RESOURCES	Determined by market forces	Determined by central planning
EMPLOYMENT	Workers are self-employed or employed by private firms.	Workers are employed by the government or government-controlled cooperatives.
INVESTMENT	Undertaken by private parties seeking profits and higher future incomes	Undertaken by the government in accordance with the objectives of the planners

THE CENTRAL PLANNING PROCESS

Organizationally, a centrally planned economy is similar to a huge vertically and horizontally integrated corporation. Government central planners establish economic policy objectives, allocate resources to business firms (enterprises), and provide the enterprises with directives that they are supposed to implement.

In turn, the government's central-planning agency acquires various types of information from the enterprises and drafts the basic plan for the entire economy. It has the responsibility of making sure that the plan is internally consistent—that, for example, all the inputs promised to the various enterprises will be available. The planning agency tells each enterprise what quantity of each commodity it is required to produce, the amounts of labor and raw materials that it will be allocated, what new machinery should be installed, what the timing of available credit will be, and other operational details. The task of the enterprise is to transform its allotted inputs into the target output. The operational targets of the annual plan are used to evaluate the performance of firms and reward them accordingly.

The central planners decide how much of each good will be produced and the quantity of resources, including intermediate goods, that will be supplied to the enterprises. Accordingly, the planners prepare a balance sheet of all available resource supplies and sources of resource demand. Labor, raw materials, minerals, imports, and so on, are all allocated this way—in the quantities believed necessary to produce each enterprise's target output. Obviously, central planning presents an enormous coordination problem. Since the output of one enterprise (steel, for example) is often the input of another enterprise (a tractor-producing firm, for example), each enterprise must be supplied with just the right amount of labor and materials at just the right time in order to keep things moving smoothly. If one firm fails to meet its output quota, perhaps as the result of equipment failure or bad weather, other firms will lack the resources required for the achievement of their production targets. Literally millions of output objectives must be both properly interfaced and achieved in a timely fashion for the system to work.

Consider the problems that arise if the target output for, say, trucks is increased by 20 percent. The planners must ensure that the truck-producing enterprises receive the additional required labor, capital equipment, component parts manufactured by other enterprises, and raw materials, such as steel, aluminum, glass, and copper. Suppliers of these inputs must either increase their output or cut back on the quantity provided to other producers so more can be supplied to the truck producers. If any input supplier fails to meet its increased quotas to the truck-manufacturing enterprises, the truck producers will be unable to produce the additional output.

Under central planning, prices play a secondary role. The supply of goods is determined by the objectives of planners rather than by prices relative to opportunity costs. When a good is in short supply, there is no assurance that more of it will be produced in the future. Prices are used as one means of rationing goods among consumers, but they reflect the preferences of planners rather than market forces.

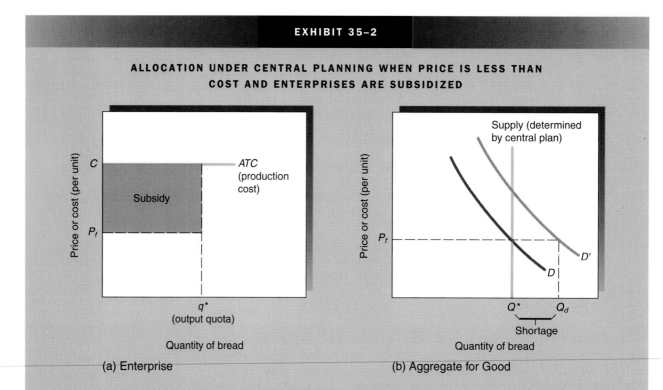

EXHIBIT 35-2

ALLOCATION UNDER CENTRAL PLANNING WHEN PRICE IS LESS THAN COST AND ENTERPRISES ARE SUBSIDIZED

(a) Enterprise

(b) Aggregate for Good

The central planners set both the quantity supplied and price for each good. Each enterprise producing the good, bread for example, will be given an output quota such as q* (part a). The aggregate quantity produced (Q* of part b) is the sum of the quantity produced by the bread-producing enterprises. This quantity reflects the priorities of the central planners. When the price set by the planners (P_f) is less than the per unit production cost, enterprises producing the good will have to be granted a subsidy by the state (shaded area of part a). If the demand for the good is D, the amount supplied and demanded will be in balance. On the other hand, if the demand is D', a shortage of the good will result. The planners of the former Soviet bloc countries often set prices such that an excess demand was present in the market. Shortages and waiting lines were the visible results.

Exhibits 35–2 and 35–3 illustrate the operation of the planning process within the framework of supply and demand. Because the aggregate supply of each good is determined by the priorities of the central plan, the supply curve for each good is vertical. Of course, the planners are constrained by resource scarcity, and if they choose to produce more of one good, they will have to reduce the output of other goods. This trade-off, however, reflects the choices of the planners rather than market prices relative to costs. The law of demand— the inverse relation between the price and amount purchased of a good—is just as relevant in socialist countries as it is in market economies. If the planners reduce the price of a good, consumers in centrally planned economies will buy a larger quantity. Thus, the demand curve for each good is the usual downward-sloping curve.

Since central planning rather than prices determines the amount of each good supplied, the prices of goods do not have to reflect per unit production cost. Often the planners of the former Soviet bloc nations set prices substantially

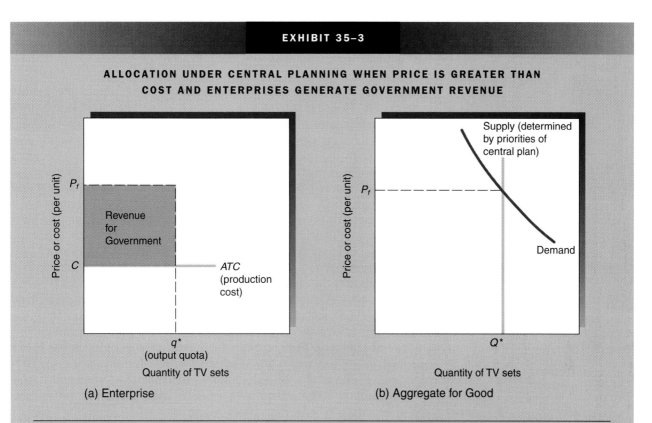

EXHIBIT 35–3

ALLOCATION UNDER CENTRAL PLANNING WHEN PRICE IS GREATER THAN COST AND ENTERPRISES GENERATE GOVERNMENT REVENUE

(a) Enterprise

(b) Aggregate for Good

Here we illustrate the case where the planners set the price for a good (television sets, for example) above the per unit cost of producing it. Once again, the enterprises producing the good are given a target output (q* in part a) and the aggregate amount produced by all suppliers is Q* (part b), the amount called for by the central plan. Since the price (P$_f$) set by the planners is above the per unit cost, production and sale of this good generates net revenue for

the government (shaded area of part a). The revenue derived from selling above cost need not equal the subsidies to firms selling below cost (the situation illustrated by Exhibit 35–2). When the subsidies exceed the state revenues, the people of the planned economy will have more income than will be required to purchase the output produced, given the prices and quantities of the goods that are available.

below cost of production. Exhibit 35–2 illustrates the planning process when prices are set below cost. Each enterprise producing the good, bread for example, is given a production quota (q^*). The sum of the amount produced by all the bread producers equals Q^*, the supply of bread called for by the central plan. Since the planners have set the price at P_f, which is below the cost of the labor and other inputs required to produce a unit of bread, the enterprises producing bread will have to be subsidized (the shaded area of Exhibit 35–2).

Sometimes the planners attempt to set the product price such that the amount demanded by consumers is approximately equal to the amount supplied under the central plan. If the demand schedule for bread was D (part b of Exhibit 35–2), the P_f price would bring the amount demanded into balance with the amount supplied. But this may not be the case. The demand for bread might be greater—for example, schedule D'. When this is true, the planners often choose to maintain the price at a low level, presumably so the good would be affordable to more people. When the price set by the planners is below equilibrium, consumers will want to buy a larger quantity than the amount available. For example, if the demand for bread was D', a shortage of Q_d minus Q^* would be present at the price P_f.

Of course, shortages and waiting lines were commonplace in the former socialist economies. Housing provides a well-known example. The rental price of government-owned (and highly subsidized) housing was generally set well below equilibrium. At the low price, however, the availability of housing was substantially less than the quantity demanded. Thus, families waited for years before an apartment was available.

Sometimes the central planners will set the price of a good substantially higher than its production cost. When this is the case, the government reaps a "profit"—an excess of revenues relative to cost—from the production and supply of the good. Using television sets as an example, Exhibit 35–3 illustrates the case where the planners fix price above per unit production cost. Once again, they provide each enterprise producing television sets with a quota (q^* of part a), and the sum of the output of the enterprises is equal to the quantity called for by the central plan (Q^* of part b). At the price P_f set by the planners, the revenues from the sales of the television sets are greater than their costs of production. Thus, the production and sale of televisions generates net revenue for the government.

Under central planning, there is often little relationship between the prices of products and the opportunity cost of their production. In some cases, the government supplies goods at a substantial "loss" (and therefore enterprises producing such goods have to be subsidized), while in other instances the government reaps a "profit."

Furthermore, there is no reason why the subsidies to the enterprises operating at a loss cannot exceed the revenues derived by the government from goods supplied at a profit. If prices were determined by market forces, inflation would result if the government created additional money in order to finance spending in excess of revenues. Under central planning, however, the prices of goods and services are fixed by the planners. *Thus, the excess of the subsidies relative to the revenues derived from "profitable" state enterprises will simply mean that, at current prices, the resource suppliers will have more than the required amount of income to purchase the quantity of goods produced. If this is the case, the demand for goods will persistently exceed the limited supply. As a result, non-price factors, such as waiting in line, favors, and bribes, will play a greater role in the allocation of goods and services among consumers.*

WHY DID SOCIALIST CENTRAL PLANNING FAIL?

The man of system . . . is apt to be very wise in his own conceit. . . . [H]e seems to imagine that he can arrange the different members of a great society with as much ease as the hand arranges the different pieces upon a chess-board; he does not consider that the pieces upon the chess-board have not another principle of motion besides that which the hand impresses upon them; but that, in the great chess-board of human society, every single piece has a principle of motion of its own, although different from that which the legisla-

ture might choose to impress upon it. If those two principles coincide and act in the same direction, the game of human society will go on easily and harmoniously, and is very likely to be happy and successful. If they are opposite or different, the game will go on miserably, and the society must be at all times in the highest degree of disorder.

ADAM SMITH[2]

Several factors contributed to the failure of the centrally planned economies of Eastern Europe and the former Soviet Union. Most of them, however, are a reflection of a single factor: The personal interests of various individuals—for example, regional planners, local enterprise managers, group leaders, and workers—often conflicted with the objectives of the central plan. As Adam Smith noted in a book that he wrote prior to *The Wealth of Nations*, when this happens problems are sure to arise. More specifically, centrally planned economies suffer from four major weaknesses that tend to undermine their effectiveness. Let us consider each of them.

1. Central planners will be unable to attain the vast amount of information required to develop a sensible central plan and induce local decision makers to carry it out. The diversity of wants and desires among consumers is both highly fragmented and incredibly complex. Similarly, the production process is highly complex and influenced by prior experience, learning by doing, and circumstances that are unique to the enterprise. There is no way that a central-planning agency can even begin to command the required knowledge of local circumstances and elements of timing that affect both costs of production and the consumer evaluation of goods. Furthermore, we live in a dynamic world. Changing demands and weather conditions, technological advances, development of new products and superior production processes, and the discovery of new resources are constantly altering the relative scarcity of both goods and resources.

Put simply, the inability of central planners to gather the widely dispersed but highly relevant information along with the constantly changing conditions make central planning infeasible. Without the constant feedback of market-clearing prices, it is unrealistic to expect that a central-planning authority will be able to acquire the necessary information, process and communicate it through the chain of command quickly, and provide local enterprise managers and workers with both the instructions and motivation to carry out the plan sensibly. The required information is too vast, the coordination problem is too complicated, and the central-planning process is too slow for the planners to keep up with a modern dynamic economy.

2. Under socialism, there is little incentive for enterprises to produce quality products that are highly valued by consumers, and to produce them in an economical manner. In a market economy, business owners have a property right to the residual income of the firm. This provides them with a strong incentive to produce goods and services that are highly valued by consumers—and to produce them at a low cost. Doing so will increase their income. In a centrally planned socialist economy, neither plant managers nor the central planners have

---

[2]Adam Smith, *The Theory of Moral Sentiments* (1759; New York: A. M. Kelley, 1966).

a property right to the net income of the enterprise. Thus, there is little incentive for them to keep cost down and quality up.

Predictably, enterprise managers will confront the central planners with the image of overworked managers and employees squeezing the maximum output from an unrealistically small quantity of resources. They will seek more resources in order to maintain or expand the quantity of output and provide benefits for themselves (for example, vacation houses in the countryside, better recreation and health facilities, and less work effort). From the viewpoint of an enterprise manager, the ideal plan is one that provides a quantity of resources such that the firm's output target can be easily achieved. Thus, enterprise officials have an incentive to provide the central planners with misleading and even false information with regard to the actual productive capability of the firm. Since high-level central planners have limited knowledge of the real output that a specific firm can achieve if it operated efficiently, they are in a weak position to contradict the enterprise managers.

In addition, the problem is complicated by the fact that, without market prices as a guide to value per unit, central-planning systems have to measure the output of enterprises in terms of quantity (rather than value). Enterprises are rewarded on the basis of the weight, surface area, or number of units produced (relative to the target). Whether consumers actually value the output has little impact on the income of producers. Variety and quality of products are, at best, secondary considerations. This focus on gross output leads to numerous anomalies and the wasteful use of resources. Consider the case of an enterprise that produces nails. If output is measured in terms of weight, the enterprise will produce mostly large nails. On the other hand, if output is measured in terms of number of nails, the enterprise will produce small nails (since they can be produced with a smaller quantity of inputs). When output is measured in physical units rather than value, predictably suppliers will be less responsive to the preferences of consumers.

3. Under central planning, the incentive to innovate and invest resources wisely is weak. Under the gross-output planning system, enterprise managers have little incentive to improve quality, to innovate, or to experiment with alternative production techniques. The potential gains to the managers associated with the discovery of better ways of doing things are small, while the risks are great if an innovative method proves to be a failure. In addition, resource combinations are supplied by the central-planning authority, which often limits the adoption of innovative production methods. As long as enterprise managers can get goods past the inspector, there is little incentive to try to improve the quality, reliability, or durability of the product.[3]

Similarly, there is little reason to expect that investment funds will be allocated efficiently under central planning. The link between the selection of prof-

---

[3]Under the openness of the Gorbachev era, the problem of shoddy product quality became well publicized. The Soviet magazine *Ogonek* reported that exploding TV sets caused 18,000 fires, 512 serious injuries, and 929 deaths between 1980 and 1986. The Soviet press reported that when independent quality-inspector groups were established at plants manufacturing consumer goods and machine tools, up to 30 percent of the output in these plants was initially rejected. Seventy percent of the shoes at a factory in Volgograd were rejected, and 40 percent of all products from plants in Ukraine were rejected.

itable projects and the personal wealth of the central planners will be weak. Even if a project is productive—if it increases wealth—the personal gain of planners, including those directing the project, is likely to be modest. Neither will an unproductive project exert any significant negative impact on the personal wealth of planners. In fact, the planner may be in a stronger position to reap personal gain from wasteful projects that channel subsidies and other benefits toward politically powerful groups.

It is interesting to compare the incentive structure confronting market investors with that facing the central planner. If a market investor is going to earn economic profit, he or she must discover and invest in projects that increase the value of resources. If the market investor makes a mistake—if the project turns out to be a loser—the private investor will bear the consequences directly. Given this incentive structure, there is strong justification for the belief that individuals risking their own money will make better investment choices than central planners using the funds of the general citizenry.

4. The priorities of the central plan will reflect the preferences of those with political power rather than those of consumers. Real-world central planners are not a group of altruistic saints seeking to serve the general interest. They are people with their own personal objectives and political ambitions. In some cases, their self-interest might be promoted by an expansion in the employment level of a firm or the regional development of a favored area. In other instances, catering to those willing to offer political and economic favors that enhance the power or wealth of planners in key positions may be personally advantageous. In still other cases, military expenditures that strengthen one's political hold or provide the resources for foreign expansionism may be a priority. All these factors will influence how those in charge of the planning process will dole out subsidies and allocate investment funds. Neither theory nor experience suggests that this politicized process will result in operational efficiency and lead to the production of goods and services that are highly valued by the general citizenry.

THE ECONOMIC PERFORMANCE OF THE ECONOMIES IN TRANSITION

The general nature of the transition problem is straightforward: How can resources be directed more consistently toward the production of goods and services that people value more highly relative to their costs? Under central planning, many goods were produced that had little value relative to their cost. Furthermore, many of the state-owned enterprises were grossly overstaffed. The amount of labor used by many of them was three or four times the quantity used by firms in market economies producing similar commodities.

Attempting to move toward a market economy, all the former socialist countries removed price controls on most commodities, relaxed regulations limiting the entry of private firms into markets, and, in varying degrees, privatized state enterprises. Later in this chapter, we will take a closer look at the transitional policies of two countries—the Czech Republic and Russia—that have chosen different strategies. Before we turn to that topic, let us take a look at the economic

Source: International Monetary Fund, *International Financial Statistics Yearbook, 1995,* and *Business Central Europe* (various issues).

EXHIBIT 35-4

GROWTH RATE OF REAL GDP FOR SELECTED COUNTRIES OF EASTERN EUROPE AND THE FORMER SOVIET UNION, 1990–1995

COUNTRY	1990	1991	1992	1993	1994	1995
Czech Republic	0.0%	−14.0%	−7.0%	−0.9%	+2.5%	+5.0%
Hungary	−4.0	−12.0	−4.0	−0.8	+2.0	+1.5
Poland	−12.0	−7.0	+1.0	+3.8	+5.1	+6.5
Bulgaria	−9.0	−12.0	−8.0	−2.4	+1.4	+2.8
Romania	−7.0	−13.0	−14.0	+1.0	+3.5	+3.8
Russia	−4.0	−5.0	−15.0	−8.7	−12.6	−4.0
Ukraine	—	−14.0	−14.0	−14.2	−23.0	−8.0

record of the transitional economies and consider some of the factors affecting their performance.

CHANGES IN REAL OUTPUT

As **Exhibit 35–4** illustrates, the real GDP of the transitional economies initially declined as they attempted to restructure their economies away from central planning and toward a market economy. As Poland removed price controls and moved toward markets, output fell by 12 percent in 1990 and 7 percent in 1991. In the Czech Republic (which was part of Czechoslovakia at the time) output declined by 14 percent in 1991 and 7 percent in 1992. Hungary, which had the most liberal of the Eastern European economies prior to 1990, moved more slowly toward markets and privatization. Nonetheless, there was a sharp reduction in Hungary's real GDP during 1990–1992. The real GDP of Bulgaria and Romania followed a similar path.

During 1993–1995, these five economies have shown signs of recovery. Poland achieved strong growth during this period. The real GDP of Poland increased by 3.8 percent in 1993, 5.1 percent in 1994, and 6.5 percent in 1995. These are impressive growth rates and, if they can be maintained over a lengthy time period, they will transform living standards. The Czech Republic also registered solid growth. Real GDP increased by 2.5 percent in 1994 and 5 percent in 1995. Although the growth rates of Hungary, Bulgaria, and Romania were less impressive, they suggest that these countries are now on the road to recovery.

In contrast, the economies of Russia and Ukraine continue to slide downward. Russia, which did not decontrol prices until 1992, has experienced six consecutive years of falling real GDP. In total, Russia's real GDP has declined by almost 40 percent since 1989. Ukraine's reduction in output has been even larger than that of Russia. As measured by the official statistics, Ukraine's 1995 real GDP was only about 50 percent of the level achieved in 1990.

Source: European Bank for
Reconstruction and Development,
Annual Economic Outlook,
September 1993, p. 97; and *Business
Central Europe* (various issues).

EXHIBIT 35-5

UNEMPLOYMENT RATE FOR SELECTED COUNTRIES OF EASTERN EUROPE AND THE FORMER SOVIET UNION, 1990–1995

	RATE OF UNEMPLOYMENT					
COUNTRY	1990	1991	1992	1993	1994	1995
Czech Republic	1.0%	4.0%	3.0%	3.5%	3.2%	2.8%
Hungary	3.0	8.0	12.0	12.6	10.9	10.0
Poland	6.0	12.0	14.0	16.4	16.0	14.9
Bulgaria	2.0	10.0	15.0	16.4	12.8	10.9
Romania	—	3.0	9.0	10.4	10.9	9.5
Russia	<1.0	<1.0	1.0	1.5	2.2	3.1
Ukraine	—	—	—	0.4	0.4	1.0

UNEMPLOYMENT AND INFLATION

Given the declines in the official GDP figures, substantial increases in the rate of unemployment would be expected. As **Exhibit 35–5** illustrates, the unemployment rates of Hungary, Poland, Bulgaria, and Romania increased sharply between 1990 and 1993. At year-end 1993, double-digit levels of unemployment were present in all of these countries. During the past two years, these high rates have leveled off and begun to decline. Among the major countries now experiencing economic growth, only the Czech Republic was able to achieve this objective without a sharp increase in unemployment.

Interestingly, even though the real GDP of Russia and Ukraine has declined sharply, unemployment has remained relatively low. This reflects the fact that the structural change of these two countries has been modest.

Exhibit 35–6 presents data on the rate of inflation in the former centrally planned economies. All the economies experienced a substantial jump in the annual rate of inflation when prices were decontrolled. For example, when prices were decontrolled in Poland at the beginning of 1990, the price level increased by 500 percent in three months. In Russia, a partial decontrol of prices led to a 250 percent increase in prices in one day.

After the decontrol of prices, the rate of inflation has persistently declined in the Czech Republic, Hungary, Poland, Bulgaria, and Romania. In varying degrees, these countries have resorted to "printing press" money to cover their budget deficits. However, they now appear to be moving toward lower, more stable rates of inflation.

The situation is somewhat different in Russia and Ukraine. These two countries have subsidized—and are continuing to subsidize—enterprises that are unable to cover their costs. Expenditures on these subsidies generate large budget deficits that are then financed with money creation. These policies have led

Source: International Monetary Fund, *International Financial Statistics Yearbook, 1995;* and *Business Central Europe Annual Report* (December 1995).

EXHIBIT 35-6

RATE OF INFLATION FOR THE MOST POPULOUS COUNTRIES OF EASTERN EUROPE AND THE FORMER SOVIET UNION, 1990–1995

COUNTRY	ANNUAL RATE OF INFLATION					
	1990	1991	1992	1993	1994	1995
Czech Republic	10%	58%	11%	21%	10%	10%
Hungary	29	34	23	23	19	29
Poland	555	77	45	37	33	25
Bulgaria	26	334	83	73	87	68
Romania	4	231	211	255	137	35
Russia	6	93	1,354	880	320	150
Ukraine	—	—	—	4,735	891	380

to hyperinflation in both Russia and Ukraine. (Note the inflation rates of these two countries during 1992–1995.)

DO THE OFFICIAL FIGURES OVERSTATE THE REDUCTION IN OUTPUT?

There is no question that the former centrally planned economies have experienced substantial reductions in output. The reductions have been particularly severe in Russia, Ukraine, Romania, and Bulgaria. However, three reasons exist to suspect that the official figures overstate the economic decline, particularly for countries like the Czech Republic, Poland, and Hungary where the private sectors have grown rapidly.

First, the income generated by small-business activities, such as construction renovation and the operation of retail shops and restaurants, is difficult for the authorities to measure accurately. This is particularly true when the income, if it is fully reported, is heavily taxed. Tax rates throughout Eastern Europe are exceedingly high. Payroll taxes are between 40 percent and 60 percent throughout the region. The top marginal tax rates on personal income are generally 40 percent and up, and they take effect at modest levels of income. In addition, most of these countries have a valued-added tax that is generally between 20 percent and 30 percent. Furthermore, enforcement of tax laws is exceedingly difficult since almost all transactions in this part of the world are conducted in cash. Given these conditions, it is a virtual certainty that a sizable portion of the income generated in the newly emerging private firms is unreported and therefore undetected by both the taxing authorities and the national-income accountants.

Second, there is a strong tendency for price indexes to overstate the magnitude of price increases during the transition phase. In turn, the use of these overstated indexes to adjust the nominal income figures results in an understatement of GDP. The problem here is one of failure to adjust fully to changes in availability and product quality. Prior to decontrol, the prices of many products were fixed below equilibrium, but the quality was poor and the availability uncertain. In the transitional economies that have managed to bring inflation under control, the queues have disappeared, the quality of goods has improved rapidly, and the diversity of products available has expanded by leaps and bounds. Price indexes do not pick up these qualitative factors. This measurement error leads to both an overstatement of the inflation rate and an understatement of output and its growth.

Finally, the official figures understate the growth of GDP because the earlier figures under central planning were grossly overstated. Several reasons explain why this was the case. When goods are produced in the government sector, their production costs add to GDP. It makes no difference whether consumers actually value the goods. For example, if it costs the equivalent of $500 to produce a 1950s style and quality refrigerator, production of that good adds $500 to GDP. In addition, under socialist planning, the enterprises had a strong incentive to overstate their output figures and ignore poor quality. Because the earlier output figures were systematically overstated, the growth figures following the transition are systematically understated.[4]

WHY IS THE TRANSITION FROM CENTRAL PLANNING TO MARKETS SO DIFFICULT?

The transition from socialism to markets has proven to be substantially more difficult than many people, including a good number of economists, thought would be the case. It is now abundantly clear that the initial conditions of the centrally planned economies complicated the process. In addition, political factors have proven to be major stumbling blocks. Let us consider the major factors that have slowed the transition process and, in a number of countries, led to policies that are undermining the development of a market economy.

1. The central-planning process left behind an aftermath of oversized enterprises and industrywide monopolies. Under socialism, the planning agency's control over and direction of the enterprises was easier when the number of firms

---

[4]Following the fall of communism, this prior overstatement of output became more obvious. For example, the best estimates now indicate that the per capita income level of East Germany was only about 40 percent of the figure for West Germany prior to 1989. Based on the accounting data available under central planning, it was previously thought that the average income of East Germans was between 60 percent and 70 percent of the comparable figure for West Germans. Similarly, the output figures for Russia were previously thought to be significantly higher than is now believed to be the case.

in each industry was small. Therefore, the industrial structure of these economies was characterized by a small number of very large enterprises in each industry. Many of these enterprises were substantially larger than the optimal size—that is, the size that would be consistent with minimum per unit costs of production. Furthermore, having only a few producers in each industry made it more difficult to privatize the enterprises in a manner consistent with competitive markets.

2. Because a huge portion of the enterprises were overstaffed and producing goods that had little value (relative to their cost), redirecting such a large share of the work force into productive activities proved to be a difficult and painful process. Markets use losses and bankruptcies to bring high-cost, inefficient business activities to a halt. In a healthy market economy, workers who lose jobs in declining industries and with inefficient firms will have reasonable alternatives with more efficient firms in expanding industries. Even in a healthy economy, however, this process is often painful for the workers and owners of the firms that fail. The situation in the former centrally planned economies is far more complex. Since so many of the firms are—at least initially—either inefficient or producing the wrong things, they will find it difficult to keep up in the new competitive environment. However, when many firms are laying off workers, the options available to the terminated workers will be extremely limited—particularly if they are employed by a dominant enterprise in an obscure location. Sharp increases in the rate of unemployment are the expected result. As Exhibit 35–5 shows, this is precisely what occurred in several of the transitional economies.

3. Ambiguous and difficult-to-enforce property rights led to opportunism, corruption, and the stripping of the assets of many newly privatized firms. In market economies, several factors—including compensation of management with stock options, competition for managerial services, and the threat of takeovers—bring the interest of managers into harmony with that of stockholders. Furthermore, evolutionary growth allows time for various checks on opportunistic behavior to be put in place. These factors were largely absent in the former socialist countries.

Regardless of how assets were privatized, it was difficult to keep managers from the misuse and even seizure of the firm's assets. If the ownership of the newly privatized firm was widely dispersed, managers would often have leeway—at least for a time—to use, lease, or sell the firm's assets at a fraction of their value in exchange for side payments or, perhaps more accurately, bribes. The incentive to follow this course was particularly strong if the managers anticipated that they would soon be replaced or that the firm would be unable to survive in the new environment. On the other hand, if insider managers became the majority stockholders of the firm—as was generally the case with the privatization in Russia—then they were in a position to channel net revenue generated by the firm to themselves in the form of managerial salaries and thereby cut out the ownership rights of the minority owners. Even though the opportunistic behavior and corrupt practices were a reflection of poorly defined and enforced property rights, many people associated them with a market economy. In several former socialist countries, this factor undermined the enthusiasm for the reform process and slowed the movement toward a market economy. Furthermore, the ambiguous relationship between ownership and control retarded investment.

4. Failure to reduce the subsidies to the enterprises led to large budget deficits, money creation, and hyperinflation.   If prices of goods are going to reflect their per unit opportunity cost, the subsidies granted to enterprises under the old socialist regime must be reduced. Politically, however, this was, and still is, very difficult to achieve. The subsidies are a special-interest issue. The managers and workers of the enterprises compose a concentrated interest group that can be expected to fight the subsidy reductions with all their might.[5]

On the other hand, if the subsidies are not reduced, their costs will have to be covered with higher taxes, borrowing, or the creation of money. Given the number of state-owned enterprises and the small size of the private sector, raising taxes on private firms to subsidize the state-operated firms was not a viable option. Neither was borrowing, given the political insecurity of the transitional governments. Lacking credibility in the financial credit market, the only way the state could continue to subsidize the government enterprises was through money creation. Predictably, the money creation led to hyperinflation. This is precisely what has happened in several former socialist countries, including Russia and Ukraine (see Exhibit 35–6).

5. Absence of a legal framework for the protection of private property and enforcement of contracts undermined private ownership.   Secure property rights and enforceable contracts are essential for the smooth operation of markets. Widely recognized legal codes—common law practices—and a system of courts to assist in the development and enforcement of these codes provide this infrastructure in market economies. Since the state owned all, or virtually all, physical capital under socialism, there was no need for institutions that would protect property rights and enforce contracts. In fact, since the official ideology of the state was hostile toward private ownership, the existing legal codes often limited and undermined the security of privately owned property. It takes time to develop this institutional structure that is vitally important for a market economy.[6]

---

[5]The structure of industries under socialism also made it difficult to reduce the subsidies. In many cases, the central planners located a dominant manufacturing enterprise and constructed high-rise apartment complexes in sparsely populated areas. Often small and medium-sized cities were developed around such firms. Since the dominant enterprise employs almost everyone in these cities, removal of the subsidies would lead to skyrocketing unemployment in the region.

In other instances, a firm may be a key supplier or purchaser for most of the output of another firm. Under these circumstances, the failure of one enterprise would cause several other enterprises to fail as well. Cascading unemployment throughout the economy as the result of these complex networks and interrelationships among monopoly and monopsony suppliers would result in sharp reductions in output, unacceptably high rates of unemployment, and social unrest.

[6]Some of the problems accompanying privatization in Poland illustrate the importance of this factor. Since Poland did not have a registry or any common record of either bankruptcies or mortgages, borrowers were able to obtain large business loans from state-operated banks even though they had recently taken bankruptcy. Sometimes this was done several times, and each time the "business operator" would then use the funds for private purposes (for example, payment of a large personal salary or the purchase of expensive automobiles). In other instances, the same property was used several times to arrange for mortgages from different lenders. Admittedly, arrangement of such "scam loans" also generally involved bribes to state banking officials and other corrupt practices. However, if there had been an easy way to check for recent bankruptcies and prior mortgages, practices of this type would have been both more risky and less widespread.

CONTRASTING POLICIES—THE CZECH REPUBLIC AND RUSSIA

A tendency sometimes exists to think that the countries of Eastern Europe and the former Soviet Union confront similar problems and have followed similar transition strategies. This is not the case. Comparing and contrasting the conditions and policies of the Czech Republic and Russia illustrates this point. The transition policies of these two countries differed substantially. We now turn to an explanation of these differences.

TRANSITION POLICIES OF THE CZECH REPUBLIC

Following the fall of communism in late 1989, the newly elected government of Czechoslovakia began laying the groundwork for the transition from central planning to a market economy. Monetary policy prior to and during the period of price decontrol was very tight. During 1990 and 1991 the supply of money grew very slowly. It was only slightly higher—about 4 percent—in 1991 than at year-end 1989. Therefore, when prices were decontrolled on approximately 85 percent of the goods in January 1991, the restrictive monetary policy helped reduce the magnitude of the jump in prices. Following price decontrol, there was a sharp increase in prices. Consumer prices rose 47 percent during the first six months of 1991. The inflation rate, however, soon became moderate. The annual rate of inflation in 1992 was 11 percent (see Exhibit 35–6).

Fiscal policy also played an important role in the stabilization of the economy. Except for two relatively small budget deficits in 1991 and 1992, the government has balanced its budget throughout the 1990s. Persistent reductions in the subsidies to enterprises contributed substantially to the tight budgetary policies of the Czech Republic (Czechoslovakia until January 1993). Of course, these enterprise subsidies were a central element of the prior socialist regime. In 1989, 37 percent of the government budget was channeled into enterprise subsidies. This figure was reduced to 27 percent (for Czechoslovakia) in 1990 and was subsequently pared to 11 percent (for the Czech Republic) in 1993. The Czech Republic followed monetary and fiscal policies designed to avoid the vicious cycle of continual enterprise subsidies, large budget deficits, rapid monetary growth, and hyperinflation.

The tight macropolicy was coupled with privatization and liberalization of trade. The establishment of new enterprises and the sale of enterprises previously owned by the state contributed to the growth of the private sector in the Czech Republic. By 1993, more than 1 million unregistered private enterprises were operating there. A large proportion of these enterprises were new small businesses that had sprung up since the fall of communism. (See the Applications in Economics box on the growth of the private retail sector in the Czech Republic and other Eastern European countries.)

Following the passage of legislation in 1990, privatization of small, state-owned enterprises began in earnest in 1991. Restitution and sales at public auc-

MARKET COMPETITION AND THE CHANGING RETAIL SECTOR OF EASTERN EUROPE

Under communism, shopping for Eastern Europeans was an ordeal. The state-operated stores were typically dark and dingy. Shopping hours were limited—almost all stores closed at 6:00 P.M. on weekdays and at 1:00 on Saturday afternoons. At grocery stores, as well as the various sections of a retail store, shoppers were required to have a basket or cart in order to enter. Usually there was a line to obtain the obligatory basket. Once inside a retail area the customer faced a line waiting to inspect the low-quality merchandise, which was tightly controlled by an unsmiling, unhelpful clerk. Having made a selection, the customer would have to take an order form to a cashier and then return to collect the purchase, being careful to maintain the appropriate position in each queue. Of course, the chances were always high that, once inside the store, customers would find the desired item was not even available.

As restrictions on private-sector business activities were relaxed in Poland, the former nation of Czechoslovakia, and other Eastern European countries, market competition began to change this situation. Because entry into retailing is relatively easy, privatization has moved forward rapidly in this sector. For example, in the Czech Republic, private-sector retail sales increased as a proportion of the total from 20 percent in 1991 to 68 percent in 1992 to 90 percent at year-end 1995.[1]

Initially, most of the new private retail firms were small shops, owned and operated by adventurous entrepreneurs. More recently, major retailers like Kmart and Hit, a German supermarket chain, have entered the market. Kmart purchased 13 formerly government-operated stores that were privatized by the Czechoslovakian government prior to the split into the Czech and Slovak republics. After spending millions of dollars on remodeling, several of the stores began operation under the Kmart logo in 1993–1994. Bright lighting and the colorful Kmart decor replaced the dingy gray, and clerks were retrained to be helpful and courteous and to smile. The initial advertising campaign emphasized that at Kmart you could enter without a basket. Goods were located conveniently for the customers' inspection. Evening and late Saturday afternoon shopping became commonplace. Bar-code pricing made the checkout process faster and more convenient.

Hit has exerted a similar impact in Warsaw. After renovating a 10,000-square-meter factory, Hit opened a giant one-stop shopping mart complete with parking for 600 cars, a wide variety of products, and economical prices kept low by purchasing in bulk directly from producers. Approximately 80 percent of the products offered in its Polish stores are produced in Poland. The nature of shopping in Prague, Bratislava, Warsaw, and other cities throughout Eastern Europe is rapidly changing, thanks to competition from both small entrepreneurs and larger established firms.

---

[1]Czech Statistical Office, *Monthly Statistics of the Czech Republic*, March 1996.

---

tions were the two primary methods used to privatize restaurants, shops, small buildings, and other small enterprises. When feasible, restitution was used to return previously seized assets to their owners. In addition, more than 20,000 small, state enterprises—mostly stores and companies providing services—were sold at public auctions during 1991 and 1992.

The centerpiece of the Czech privatization strategy was the use of a voucher plan to transfer the ownership of medium-sized and large-scale enterprises to the market sector. Under this plan, each Czech citizen was eligible to purchase voucher points for a nominal price (the equivalent of approximately $30). These points were then used to purchase shares in large-scale, state-owned enterprises that were thought to be suitable for operation in the private sector. Individuals could either use their voucher points to bid directly for enterprise shares, or invest them in mutual funds that would then use the vouchers to purchase shares. During the first wave of privatization in 1992, approximately 1,500 state

THE KEY CHARACTERISTICS OF PRIVATE ENTERPRISES AND WHY THEY ARE IMPORTANT

In a market economy, firms are dependent on sales to consumers for their revenues and are disciplined by the forces of competition. Owners of private firms have a strong incentive to produce efficiently—to keep costs per unit low and quality high—because lower costs and higher quality will increase the size of the owner's residual income.

For this process to work well, however, three conditions are vitally important. *First, the enterprises must confront a hard budget constraint—that is, they must be dependent on sales to customers rather than subsidies and favorable tax treatment for their revenues.* It is this dependence on sales revenues that provides enterprises with the incentive to produce efficiently and cater to the preferences of consumers. In contrast, government enterprises (and subsidized private firms) confront what Hungarian economist Janos Kornai calls a "soft budget constraint."[1] When the costs of public sector enterprises rise or their sales revenues fall, governments have a tendency to bail them out—to provide them with larger subsidies rather than forcing them to either operate more efficiently or go out of business. This soft budget constraint reduces operational efficiency and encourages the managers of the firm to engage in wasteful rent-seeking activities.

Second, the owners must be in a position to capture the residual income and buy and sell their ownership shares. Their property right to this residual income provides owners with the incentive to monitor the firm's managers and keep them on their toes.

Third, private firms must raise their investment funds in the capital market rather than seek the favor and approval of government planners. Firms thus have a strong incentive to be innovative—to seek better ways of doing things.

---

[1]Janos Kornai, "The Soft Budget Constraint," in *The Road to Capitalism,* ed. David Kennett and Marc Lieberman (Fort Worth: The Dryden Press, 1992).

Hard budget constraint
A situation in which the enterprise is fully dependent on revenues from sales to cover its costs. The constraint is "hard" because, if losses are present, they will have to be covered by enterprise owners; continuing losses will result in bankruptcy since government subsidies and special grants are unavailable.

enterprises, with an estimated value of between $5 billion and $10 billion, were privatized by the voucher method. This was followed by a slightly smaller second-wave voucher privatization plan in 1994. As the result of the privatization plans, it is now estimated that approximately 60 percent of the GDP of the Czech Republic is generated by the private sector, up from less than 4 percent in 1989.[7]

The Czech privatization plan both eliminated the subsidies and provided the new private owners with a clear property right to the net income generated by the firm, thus establishing a regime of private ownership. The newly privatized firms of the Czech Republic must derive their revenues from sales to customers. They now confront a **hard budget constraint.** They no longer receive subsidies and other types of government assistance if they are unable to cover their costs. (See the Applications in Economics box on the key characteristics of private enterprises.)

---

[7]For additional details on the privatization of state enterprises in the Czech Republic, Russia, and other countries of Eastern Europe, see John S. Earle, Roman Frydman, and Andrzej Rapaczynski, "Transition Policies and the Establishment of a Private Property Regime in Eastern Europe" (paper delivered at a meeting of Economic Policy: A European Forum, hosted by the National Bank of Belgium, Brussels, October 22–23, 1993); and Roman Frydman and Andrzej Rapaczynski, "Privatization in Eastern Europe: Is the State Withering Away?" *Finance and Development* (June 1993).

This is not to say that there have been no problems with privatization. As in other transitional economies, there have been cases where the new owners were unable to effectively enforce their legal property rights and, as a result, opportunistic managers have stripped valuable assets from the firms. However, there has been less of this than in most other countries and the process has been both open and transparent. It is difficult to move assets from the government to the private sector. The Czechs handled the difficulties quite well.

Finally, trade liberalization has also been an important component of the overall transition strategy of the Czech Republic. The tariff rates average about 5 percent, and there are few quota restrictions limiting the entry of foreign-produced goods. The liberal trade policies and the strong trade sector have helped to bring the relative prices of goods produced by both private and public sector enterprises into line with their opportunity cost.

Perhaps the most serious problem currently confronting the Czech Republic is the high rate of taxation. The payroll tax is 59 percent, one of the highest in the region. Personal income is taxed at marginal rates ranging from 15 percent to 44 percent. In addition, there is a flat rate corporate tax of 45 percent and a value-added tax of 23 percent. Given these tax rates and the current enforcement policies, tax evasion is thought to be widespread in the Czech Republic. Imposing high tax rates on honest citizens while driving large numbers of people into the underground economy is not a solid foundation for prosperity. Coupling substantial reductions in tax rates with the development of a system to improve tax compliance would help the economy of the Czech Republic.

The Czech Republic has not done everything right during the transition period. Nonetheless, its transition record is a good one. Given the difficulties involved, privatization was handled well. The Czechs avoided the large budget deficits and high rates of inflation that plagued most of the transitional economies. If the Czech Republic continues to follow its current policy path, most economists and investors are optimistic that its future will be bright.

TRANSITION POLICIES OF RUSSIA

As Boris Yeltsin assumed the presidency of Russia in 1991, both the Soviet Union and the Russian economy were in a state of collapse. There had been a lot of talk about reform and restructuring, but very little had in fact taken place. Output declined by 4 percent in 1990 and another 5 percent in 1991 (see Exhibit 35–4). In 1991 Russia's budget deficit was 21 percent of its GDP, and the money supply doubled during the year. Even though price controls remained in place on most goods, the annual rate of inflation in 1991 was 93 percent.

Against this background, the team assembled by President Yeltsin moved to decontrol prices in January 1992. In contrast with the situation a year earlier in Czechoslovakia, the monetary and fiscal policies of Russia prior to decontrol were highly expansionary. The results were predictable. Price controls were lifted on 90 percent of the tradeable goods on January 2, 1992, and by the next day prices rose by an average of 250 percent.

During the next six months, the new government tried valiantly to get the budget under control. To a degree it was successful; the budget deficit was reduced to 4 percent of GDP in 1992, down from more than 20 percent during the previous year. These efforts, however, were eventually undermined by the issuing of credits by the state enterprises that dominated the economy. Rather than restructure in order to cut costs, the state enterprises in Russia continued with operations as usual. Workers were paid with company credits—coupons or vouchers, or even ruble-like notes with the picture of the company manager—that could be used to purchase goods supplied by the company. Given the major role of enterprises in the provision of health care, education, housing, and the operation of stores, these credits had some value.

In addition, the intercompany debt of state enterprises soared in 1992 and eventually a powerful coalition of state-enterprise managers and employees convinced the Parliament to supply the enterprises with the rubles to pay for the credits. During the 12 months from midyear 1992 until midyear 1993, the domestic money supply of Russia increased approximately tenfold. Not surprisingly, prices followed suit, and Russia moved into hyperinflation (see Exhibit 35–6).

Even though the political climate for privatization of Russian state enterprises was exceedingly poor in 1992–1993, the Yeltsin administration decided that it had to move ahead with some type of plan. In order to make privatization more palatable to enterprise workers and managers, substantial accommodations were required. While a citizenwide voucher privatization plan was instituted, workers and managers of the privatized enterprises were allowed to choose whether they wanted to receive 25 percent of the enterprise shares free, or whether they would prefer to pay 1.7 times the nominal book value and purchase 51 percent of the shares. Since the latter option assured workers that they would retain control of the enterprise, and the inflation had drastically reduced the burden of the nominal payment, more than three-fourths of the enterprises chose this second option. Therefore, to a large extent, the Russian privatization plan simply made the managers of the enterprises the new majority owners. Because the minority owners could not easily buy and sell shares, those who purchased stock with vouchers had little opportunity to exert a significant impact on the direction of the firm.

Equally important, it is unclear whether the privatization in Russia has really changed the relationship between the enterprises and the central government. Many of the enterprises are still subsidized. Knowledge about how to get favors from the government is the primary strength of many of the new "insider owners." At least for a time, there is every reason to expect that enterprises will continue to spend a substantial amount of their time and resources seeking political favors. Since the "outside owners" are minority stockholders, who cannot easily buy and sell shares, the likelihood is extremely low that they will be able to play a constructive role in shaping the future direction of the firms.

In addition to the problems of inflation and privatization, the current legal environment in Russia and throughout most of the former Soviet Union is extremely hostile to the development and enforcement of secure private property rights. The activities of the so-called Russian Mafia—an underground network generally composed of criminals, former Communist party officials, and local government officials—are a major factor in this area. Essentially the Russian Mafia uses violence (car bombings, kidnapping of family members, and even murder) and the threat of violence as means of extorting "payments" from private businesses in exchange for "protection." In some cases, the Mafia is organized along industrial lines and protection of existing state enterprises from competition from newly established private firms appears to be an objective. In other instances, Mafia members are apparently only interested in raising funds through extortion. Regardless of the objectives, the atmosphere is undermining the development of the private sector in Russia and the legitimate government authorities are currently either too weak or unwilling to do much about it.

Given (a) the current inflation rate and monetary instability, (b) the insider control of state enterprises, and (c) the insecurity of private property rights, the prospects are dim for the development of business activity and a market economy in Russia and most of the former Soviet Union in the near future.

CONCLUDING THOUGHTS

The landscape of economics is constantly changing. Who would have predicted a few years ago that in the 1990s economists would be addressing the problems of how countries make the transition from socialism to an organizational structure capable of providing more opportunity and prosperity? This issue is sure to continue enlivening the study and research of economists in the decade ahead. What will be the next major issue? We cannot be sure, but whatever it is, the tools of economics will enhance our ability to understand and deal with it.

CHAPTER SUMMARY

1. Capitalist economies are characterized by private ownership of productive assets and the use of markets to allocate goods and resources. The distinguishing characteristics of socialist economies are government ownership of physical capital and resource allocation by central planning.

2. Under socialism, the central planners set the prices of all goods and provide the enterprises with directives concerning the resources that will be provided to them, new machines that are to be installed, the firm's target output, and other aspects of production. The task of the firm is to transform the resources into the output quota.

3. Under central planning, the supply of each good reflects the priorities of the planners and price plays a secondary role. Sometimes the planners attempt to set the price of a good such that the amount demanded will balance the amount supplied. But this is not generally the case. When the price of a good produced by an enterprise is set below the good's production cost, the enterprise has to be subsidized. On the other hand, when price exceeds opportunity cost, the state reaps a "profit."

4. When the subsidies to firms selling at prices below cost exceed the revenues derived from goods sold at prices above cost, the income payments to the resource suppliers will be greater than the amount required to purchase the available goods, at the prices fixed by the planners. This process leads to both queuing (waiting lines) and other nonprice forms of rationing.

5. Several factors contributed to the poor performance and eventual breakup of the central-planning regimes of Eastern Europe and the former Soviet Union. The most important of these were:
   a. The inability of a central-planning agency to acquire and react to widely dispersed but highly relevant information concerning local circumstances, elements of timing, and changing conditions.
   b. The weak incentive of enterprises to maintain quality, produce efficiently, and provide products highly valued by consumers.
   c. The weak incentive for central planners and enterprises to innovate and invest resources wisely.
   d. The misallocation of resources that results because the priorities of the plan inevitably reflect political factors and the views of the planners rather than economic considerations and the preferences of consumers.

6. The former centrally planned economies have decontrolled prices, reduced barriers limiting the development of private firms, and, in varying degrees, privatized state enterprises. The GDP data indicate that all transitional economies experienced sharp declines in output during the two or three years after central planning was abandoned. Several of the former centrally planned economies—particularly Poland and the Czech Republic—subsequently achieved solid growth.

7. The official GDP figures probably overstate the reductions in output during the transitional period because (a) they do not fully measure the new private-sector activities, (b) they fail to consider adequately the rapid changes in product quality and availability that have occurred during this period, and (c) the prior output figures under central planning were overstated.

8. The transition from socialism to a market-based economy is more difficult than was initially perceived because
   a. socialism left behind an aftermath of oversized firms and industrywide monopolies
   b. a large share of the centrally planned economy was unproductive
   c. ambiguous and difficult-to-enforce property rights have led to opportunism and corruption

d. continued subsidies led to large budget deficits, money creation, and hyperinflation

e. the legal framework for a market economy was initially absent

9. For privatization to work well, the privatized firms must (a) confront a hard budget constraint—that is, they must derive their revenues from customers rather than from government favors, and (b) the owners must have a clearly defined property right to the net income of the firm. The privatization of the Czech Republic was more consistent with these criteria than that of Russia.

CRITICAL ANALYSIS QUESTIONS

1. Compare and contrast the role of firm managers under socialism and capitalism. In which case would a manager have the greatest incentive to (a) operate the firm efficiently, (b) maximize the profits of a firm, and (c) adopt a new innovative production method or introduce a new product? Explain.

2. Are there economic functions that you think a centrally planned economy can accomplish more effectively than a market economy? Why or why not? What are the major disadvantages of a centrally planned economy? Discuss.

3. Under central planning, managers of state enterprises were generally told what resources to use, what price to charge, and how many units to produce. Why aren't instructions of this type given to owners and managers of firms in a market setting? Who controls the actions of firms in a market economy?

4. "Socialism means production for use, not for profit. Workers contribute according to their qualifications, and they are rewarded according to egalitarian principles. Socialism takes power from the business elite and grants it to the workers, who, after all, produce the goods." Analyze this point of view.

*5. When an economy is centrally planned, the subsidies paid to enterprises selling below cost may exceed the revenues the government derives from enterprises selling above cost. Why doesn't this lead to inflation? What are two major side effects of this strategy?

6. What are the major factors that make the transition from central planning to markets so difficult? In many parts of Eastern Europe, people associate a market economy with "insider deals" and corrupt practices. What factors contribute to this view? Is it justified? Why or why not?

7. How did the voucher plan used by the former Czechoslovakia (and later by the Czech Republic) differ from the voucher plan implemented in Russia? What are the advantages and disadvantages of the alternative plans? Which is most likely to result in an effective regime of private ownership? Explain.

8. Compare and contrast the transition policies and experiences of Russia and the Czech Republic. How did the policies of these two countries differ? How have these differences influenced the rate of inflation, growth of the private sector, and future economic prospects of the two countries?

9. Evaluate the economic record of the former centrally planned economies of Eastern Europe during the 1990s. Which economies are now growing? Which are continuing to stagnate or regress? Why have some of the transitional economies done much better than others?

*10. Socialists often claim that under capitalism resources are wasted producing luxury goods for the rich. Evaluate this charge.

11. Suppose you were hired as a consultant to develop a comprehensive economic reform plan for Russia. What specific reforms would you suggest? Indicate why you think they would be effective.

*12. "Capitalism is better at producing wealth; socialism is better at distributing it fairly." Evaluate this statement.

---

*Asterisk denotes questions for which answers are given in Appendix B.

PRODUCTION THEORY AND ISOQUANT ANALYSIS

hen analyzing production theory and input utilization, economists often rely on isoquant analysis. Since the technique is widely used at the intermediate level, some instructors explain the concept in their introductory course.

WHAT ARE ISOQUANTS?

Generally, several alternative input combinations can be used to produce a good. For example, 100 bushels of wheat might be produced with 2 acres of land, 5 bushels of seed, and 100 pounds of fertilizer. Alternatively, the wheat could be produced with more land and less fertilizer, or more seed and less land, or more fertilizer and less seed. Many input combinations could be used to produce 100 bushels of wheat.

Isoquant

A curve representing the technically efficient combinations of two inputs that can be used to produce a given level of output.

The word "isoquant" means "equal quantity." An **isoquant** is a curve that indicates the various combinations of two inputs that could be used to produce an equal quantity of output. **Exhibit 1** provides an illustration. The isoquant labeled "100 units of cloth" shows the various combinations of capital and labor that a technically efficient producer could use to produce 100 units of cloth. Every point on an isoquant is technically efficient. By that we mean that it would not be possible, given the current level of technology, to produce a larger output with the input combination. If a producer wanted to produce a larger output, 140 units of cloth, for example, it would be necessary to use more of at least one of the resources. Since larger output levels require additional resources, isoquants representing larger levels of output always lie to the northeast in an isoquant diagram.

An isoquant represents all input combinations that, if used efficiently, will generate a specific level of output. As illustrated here, 100 units of cloth could be produced with the input combinations L_1K_1 or L_2K_2 or any other combination of labor and capital that lies on the isoquant representing 100 units of cloth.

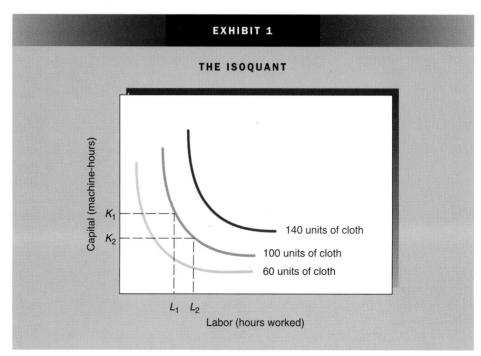

EXHIBIT 1

THE ISOQUANT

CHARACTERISTICS OF ISOQUANTS

Isoquant analysis must be consistent with the laws of production. What do the laws of production imply about the characteristics of isoquants?

1. Isoquants Slope Downward to the Right.   Within the relevant range of utilization, an increase in the usage level of an input makes it possible to expand output. If, for example, the use of the labor input is expanded, it is possible to produce the same output level (stay on the same isoquant) with a smaller quantity of capital. Since both labor and capital can be used to increase production, they can be substituted for each other. Constant output can be maintained either by (a) using more labor and less capital or (b) by using more capital and less labor. Thus, every isoquant runs from the northwest to the southeast, as illustrated by Exhibit 1.

2. Isoquants Are Convex When Viewed from the Origin.   The convexity of isoquants stems from the fact that as one continues to substitute labor for capital, larger and larger amounts of labor are required to maintain output at a constant level. As labor is used more intensively, it becomes increasingly difficult to substitute labor for each additional unit of capital. Since larger and larger amounts of labor are required to compensate for the loss of each additional unit of capital (and thus maintain the constant level of output), the isoquant becomes flatter as labor is used more intensively (see **Exhibit 2,** point *B*).

On the other hand, when capital is used more and more intensively, larger and larger amounts of capital are required to compensate for the loss of a unit of labor. Thus, an isoquant becomes steeper as capital (the *y* factor) is used more intensively (see Exhibit 2, point *A*). It is convex when viewed from the origin.

3. The Slope of the Isoquant Is the Marginal Product of Labor Divided by the Marginal Product of Capital.   The slope of the isoquant is determined by the

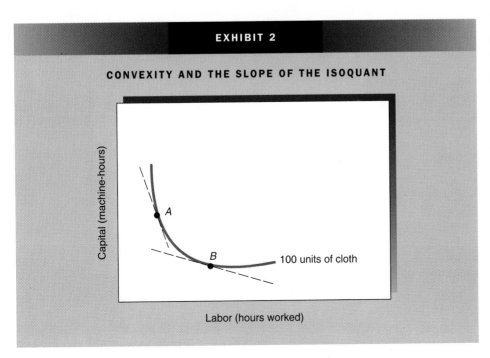

EXHIBIT 2

CONVEXITY AND THE SLOPE OF THE ISOQUANT

Capital (machine-hours)

A

B   100 units of cloth

Labor (hours worked)

When labor is used intensively relative to capital (point B), the slope of the isoquant is much flatter than it is when capital is used more intensively (point A). The slope of an isoquant is the ratio of the marginal products of the two factors (MP_L divided by MP_K). When labor is used more intensively relative to capital, its marginal product falls (and that of capital increases). Since the marginal product of labor is low (and the marginal product of capital is high) when labor is used intensively (as at point B), the isoquant is relatively flat.

amount of labor that must be added to maintain a constant level of output when one less unit of capital is used. This slope is dependent on the marginal productivity of labor relative to capital. When labor is used intensively relative to capital, its marginal product is low, relative to capital. Under these circumstances, as Exhibit 2 (point B) illustrates, the slope of the isoquant is small (the isoquant is relatively flat). In contrast, when capital is used intensively (Exhibit 2, point A), the marginal product of labor is high, relative to capital. The steepness of the isoquant reflects this fact. At any point on the isoquant, the slope of the isoquant is equal to MP_L/MP_K.

THE ISOCOST LINE

A set of isoquants outlines the technically efficient input combinations that could be used to produce alternative levels of output. Before we can determine the economically efficient input combinations for producing a level of output, we must also incorporate information about cost and resource prices.

Isocost line
A line representing the various combinations of two factors that can be purchased with a given money budget (cost).

Firms generally can purchase inputs at a fixed price per unit. The **isocost line** shows the alternative combinations of inputs that can be purchased with a given outlay of funds. As the term implies, the cost of purchasing an input combination on the isocost line is equal to the cost of purchasing any other input combination on the same line. To construct an isocost line, two pieces of information are required: (a) the prices of the resources and (b) the specific outlay of funds. **Exhibit 3** illustrates the construction of three different isocost lines, assuming that the price of labor is $5 per unit and that the price of capital is $10

The isocost line indicates the alternative combinations of the resources that can be purchased with a given outlay of funds. When the price of a unit of labor is $5 and that of a unit of capital is $10, the three isocost lines shown here represent the alternative combinations of labor and capital that could be purchased at costs of $500, $1,000 and $1,500. The slope of the isocost line is equal to P_L/P_K ($5/$10 = ½ in this case).

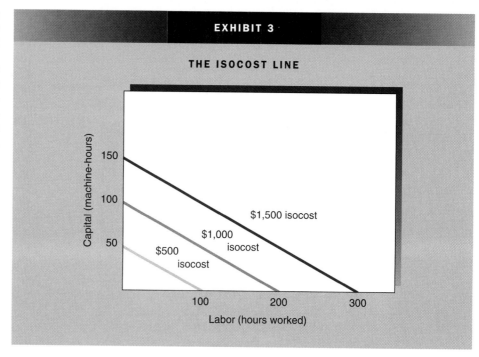

EXHIBIT 3

THE ISOCOST LINE

per unit. Consider the $500 isocost line. If all funds were spent on labor, 100 units of labor could be purchased. Alternatively, if the entire $500 were expended on capital, 50 units of capital could be purchased. It would be possible to purchase any input combination between these two extremes—for example, 80 units of labor and 10 units of capital—with the $500. The input combinations are represented by a line connecting the two extreme points, 100 units of labor on the x-axis and 50 units of capital on the y-axis. Note that the slope of the isocost line is merely the price of labor divided by the price of capital (P_L/P_K).

If the outlay of funds were to increase, it would be possible to purchase more of both labor and capital. Thus, as Exhibit 3 illustrates, the isocost lines move in a northeast direction as the size of the outlay of funds increases.

MINIMIZING THE COST OF PRODUCTION

A profit-seeking firm will want to choose the minimum-cost method of production. We can combine isoquant analysis and the isocost line to derive the minimum-cost input combination for producing a given output level. As **Exhibit 4** illustrates, the minimum-cost input combination for producing 100 units of cloth is represented by the point at which the lowest isocost line just touches (is tangent to) the isoquant for 100 units of cloth. At that point (*A* of Exhibit 4), the

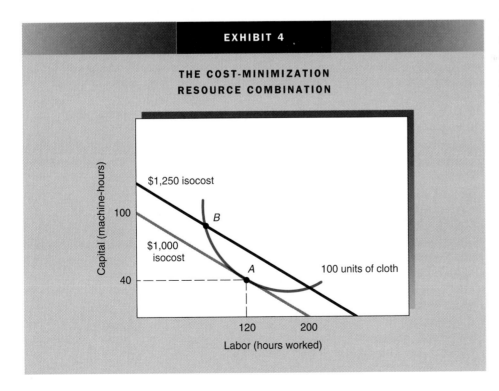

EXHIBIT 4

THE COST-MINIMIZATION RESOURCE COMBINATION

$1,250 isocost

$1,000 isocost

B

A

100 units of cloth

Capital (machine-hours)

100

40

120   200

Labor (hours worked)

When the cost of producing an output level (for example, 100 units of cloth) is minimized, the isoquant is tangent to the isocost line. At that point (A), $MP_L/MP_K = P_L/P_K$.

producer will be able to combine 120 units of labor purchased at a cost of $600 ($5 per unit) with 40 units of capital purchased at a cost of $400 ($10 per unit) to produce 100 units of cloth. The total cost of the 100 units is $1,000 ($10 per unit).

Of course, other input combinations could be used to produce the 100 units of cloth. However, they would be more costly, given the current prices of labor and capital. For example, if the input combination B were used to produce the 100 units, the total cost would be $1,250 ($12.50 per unit).

When costs are at a minimum, the isoquant is tangent to the isocost line. The slopes of the two are equal at that point. In other words, when the cost of producing a specific output is at a minimum, the MP_L/MP_K (the slope of the isoquant) will be equal to P_L/P_K (the slope of the isocost line). Since:

$$\frac{MP_L}{MP_K} = \frac{P_L}{P_K}$$

then:

$$\frac{MP_L}{P_L} = \frac{MP_K}{P_K}$$

The latter equation represents precisely the condition that our earlier analysis indicated would be present if the cost of production were at a minimum (See Chapter 23).

The isoquant analysis indicates that when a firm chooses the minimum-cost method of production, the ratio of the price of labor to the price of capital will equal the ratio of the marginal productivities of the factors. This makes good economic sense. It implies, for example, that if capital is twice as expensive per unit as labor, the firm will want to substitute the cheaper labor for capital until the marginal product of capital is twice that of labor.

COST MINIMIZATION AND CHANGES IN RESOURCE PRICES

The minimum-cost input combination is dependent on both (a) the technical relationship between the productive inputs and output, as illustrated by the isoquant, and (b) the price of the factors, represented by the isocost line. If the ratio of the price of labor to the price of capital changes, the minimum-cost input combination will be altered.

Exhibit 5 illustrates this point. Exhibit 4 shows that if the price of labor were $5 and the price of capital were $10, the minimum-cost input combination to produce 100 units of cloth would be 120 units of labor and 40 units of capital. The total cost of the 100 units would be $1,000. Exhibit 5 indicates what would happen if the price of labor increased from $5 to $10. At the higher price of labor, a $1,000 outlay of funds would now purchase only 100 units of labor (rather than 200). As a result of the increase in the price of labor, the isocost line would become steeper, as indicated by the change in isocost lines from MN to OP. The lowest isocost line that is tangent to the isoquant for 100 units would now be OP. The new minimum-cost input combination would be 90 units of labor and

EXHIBIT 5

THE IMPACT OF AN INCREASE
IN THE PRICE OF A RESOURCE

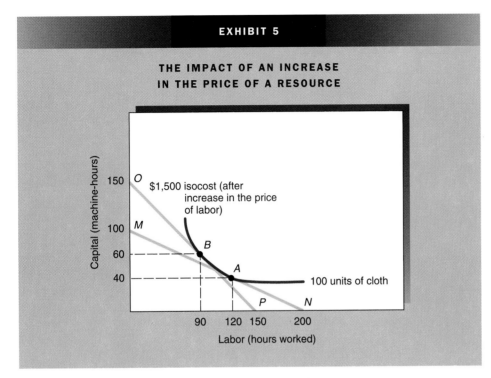

The slope of the isocost line increases as the price of a unit of labor rises from $5 to $10. As a result of the increase in the price of labor, (a) cost-minimizing producers substitute capital for the more expensive labor, and (b) the minimum cost of producing 100 units of cloth rises.

60 units of capital. Cost-minimizing producers would substitute capital for labor. The cost of producing the 100 units would rise (from $1,000 to $1,500).

THE SIGNIFICANCE OF ISOQUANT-ISOCOST ANALYSIS

Isoquant-isocost analysis is most applicable in the long run, when all factors are variable and the possibilities for substitution are greatest. It is a conceptual tool, more suitable for illustrating principles than for solving management problems. Few firms would try to design their production activities by drawing isoquants, although some managers might make mental use of the model when analyzing and developing alternative manufacturing processes designed to minimize costs. In any case, firms that do maximize profits behave as though they were using the analysis.

Isoquant-isocost analysis helps clarify the production conditions that must be met if a firm is to minimize its production cost and get the largest possible output from a specific outlay of funds.

GENERAL BUSINESS AND ECONOMIC INDICATORS

Note: The figures are in billions of current dollars.

Source: *Economic Report of the President*, 1996, Table B-1.

SECTION 1

GROSS DOMESTIC PRODUCT AND ITS COMPONENTS

YEAR	PERSONAL CONSUMPTION EXPENDITURES	GROSS PRIVATE DOMESTIC INVESTMENT	GOVERNMENT CONSUMPTION & GROSS INVESTMENT	NET EXPORTS	GROSS DOMESTIC PRODUCT (GDP)
1959	318.1	78.8	112.0	−1.7	507.2
1960	332.2	78.8	113.2	2.4	526.6
1961	342.6	77.9	120.9	3.4	544.8
1962	363.4	87.9	131.4	2.4	585.2
1963	383.0	93.4	137.7	3.3	617.4
1964	411.4	101.7	144.4	5.5	663.0
1965	444.3	118.0	153.0	3.9	719.1
1966	481.9	130.4	173.6	1.9	787.8
1967	509.5	128.0	194.6	1.4	833.6
1968	559.8	139.9	212.1	−1.3	910.6
1969	604.7	155.0	223.8	−1.2	982.2
1970	648.1	150.2	236.1	1.2	1,035.6
1971	702.5	176.0	249.9	−3.0	1,125.4
1972	770.7	205.6	268.9	−8.0	1,237.3
1973	851.6	242.9	287.6	0.6	1,382.6
1974	931.2	245.6	323.2	−3.1	1,496.9
1975	1,029.1	225.4	362.6	13.6	1,630.6
1976	1,148.8	286.6	385.9	−2.3	1,819.0
1977	1,277.1	356.6	416.9	−23.7	2,026.9
1978	1,428.8	430.8	457.9	−26.1	2,291.4
1979	1,593.5	480.9	507.1	−24.0	2,557.5
1980	1,760.4	465.9	572.8	−14.9	2,784.2
1981	1,941.3	556.2	633.4	−15.0	3,115.9
1982	2,076.8	501.1	684.8	−20.5	3,242.1
1983	2,283.4	547.1	735.7	−51.7	3,514.5
1984	2,492.3	715.6	796.6	−102.0	3,902.4
1985	2,704.8	715.1	875.0	−114.2	4,180.7
1986	2,892.7	722.5	938.5	−131.5	4,422.2
1987	3,094.5	747.2	992.8	−142.1	4,692.3
1988	3,349.7	773.9	1,032.0	−106.1	5,049.6
1989	3,594.8	829.2	1,095.1	−80.4	5,438.7
1990	3,839.3	799.7	1,176.1	−71.3	5,743.8
1991	3,975.1	716.2	1,225.9	−20.5	5,916.7
1992	4,219.8	790.4	1,263.8	−29.5	6,244.4
1993	4,454.1	871.1	1,289.9	−64.9	6,550.2
1994	4,698.7	1,014.4	1,314.7	−96.4	6,931.4
1995	4,924.3	1,065.3	1,358.5	−102.3	7,245.8

Source: *Economic Report of the President*, 1996, Tables B-2 and B-27.

SECTION 1 (continued)

REAL GROSS DOMESTIC PRODUCT

REAL GROSS DOMESTIC PRODUCT 1959–1995

YEAR	1992 PRICES (BILLIONS OF DOLLARS)	ANNUAL REAL RATE OF GROWTH	REAL GDP PER CAPITA (1992 DOLLARS)
1959	2,212.3	5.5	12,494
1960	2,261.7	2.2	12,512
1961	2,309.8	2.1	12,571
1962	2,449.1	6.0	13,125
1963	2,554.0	4.3	13,492
1964	2,702.9	5.8	14,083
1965	2,874.8	6.4	14,792
1966	3,060.2	6.4	15,565
1967	3,140.2	2.6	15,800
1968	3,288.6	4.7	16,382
1969	3,388.0	3.0	16,712
1970	3,388.2	0.0	16,520
1971	3,500.1	3.3	16,853
1972	3,690.3	5.4	17,579
1973	3,902.3	5.7	18,412
1974	3,888.2	−0.4	18,178
1975	3,865.1	−0.6	17,896
1976	4,081.1	5.6	18,713
1977	4,279.3	4.9	19,426
1978	4,493.7	5.0	20,185
1979	4,624.0	2.9	20,541
1980	4,611.9	−0.3	20,252
1981	4,724.9	2.5	20,542
1982	4,623.6	−2.1	19,911
1983	4,810.0	4.0	20,527
1984	5,138.2	6.8	21,736
1985	5,329.5	3.7	22,345
1986	5,489.9	3.0	22,810
1987	5,648.4	2.9	23,260
1988	5,862.9	3.8	23,924
1989	6,060.4	3.4	24,497
1990	6,138.7	1.3	24,559
1991	6,079.0	−1.0	24,058
1992	6,244.4	2.7	24,447
1993	6,383.8	2.2	24,728
1994	6,604.2	3.5	25,335
1995	6,739.0	2.1	25,615

Source: *Economic Report of the President*, 1996, Tables B-3 and B-58.

SECTION 2

PRICES AND INFLATION

PRICE INDEXES: 1959–1995

YEAR	GDP DEFLATOR INDEX (1992 = 100)	GDP DEFLATOR ANNUAL PERCENTAGE CHANGE	CONSUMER PRICE INDEX INDEX (1982–84 = 100)	CONSUMER PRICE INDEX PERCENTAGE CHANGE (DEC. TO DEC.)
1959	23.0	2.8	29.1	1.7
1960	23.3	1.4	29.6	1.4
1961	23.6	1.2	29.9	0.7
1962	23.9	1.3	30.2	1.3
1963	24.2	1.2	30.6	1.6
1964	24.6	1.5	31.0	1.0
1965	25.0	1.9	31.5	1.9
1966	25.7	2.8	32.4	3.5
1967	26.6	3.2	33.4	3.0
1968	27.7	4.4	34.8	4.7
1969	29.0	4.7	36.7	6.2
1970	30.6	5.3	38.8	5.6
1971	32.1	5.2	40.5	3.3
1972	33.5	4.2	41.8	3.4
1973	35.4	5.6	44.4	8.7
1974	38.5	8.9	49.3	12.3
1975	42.2	9.4	53.8	6.9
1976	44.6	5.8	56.9	4.9
1977	47.5	6.4	60.6	6.7
1978	50.9	7.3	65.2	9.0
1979	55.3	8.5	72.6	13.3
1980	60.4	9.3	82.4	12.5
1981	66.1	9.4	90.9	8.9
1982	70.2	6.3	96.5	3.8
1983	73.2	4.2	99.6	3.8
1984	75.9	3.8	103.9	3.9
1985	78.6	3.4	107.6	3.8
1986	80.6	2.6	109.6	1.1
1987	83.1	3.1	113.6	4.4
1988	86.1	3.7	118.3	4.4
1989	89.7	4.2	124.0	4.6
1990	93.6	4.4	130.7	6.1
1991	97.3	3.9	136.2	3.1
1992	100.0	2.8	140.3	2.9
1993	102.6	2.6	144.5	2.7
1994	105.0	2.3	148.2	2.7
1995	107.5	2.4	152.4	2.5

Source: *Economic Report of the President*, 1996, Table B-31.

SECTION 3

POPULATION AND EMPLOYMENT

POPULATION AND LABOR FORCE

Year	Civilian Noninstitutional Population Age 16 and Over (Millions)	Civilian Labor Force (Millions)	Civilian Labor Force Participation Rate (Percent)	Civilian Employment/ Population Ratio (Percent)
1959	115.3	68.4	59.3	56.0
1960	117.2	69.6	59.4	56.1
1961	118.8	70.5	59.3	55.4
1962	120.1	70.6	58.8	55.5
1963	122.4	71.8	58.7	55.4
1964	124.5	73.0	58.7	55.7
1965	126.5	74.5	58.9	56.2
1966	128.1	75.8	59.2	56.9
1967	130.0	77.3	59.6	57.3
1968	132.0	78.7	59.6	57.5
1969	134.3	80.7	60.1	58.0
1970	137.1	82.8	60.4	57.4
1971	140.2	84.4	60.2	56.6
1972	144.1	87.0	60.4	57.0
1973	147.1	89.4	60.8	57.8
1974	150.1	91.9	61.3	57.8
1975	153.2	93.8	61.2	56.1
1976	156.2	96.2	61.6	56.8
1977	159.0	99.0	62.3	57.9
1978	161.9	102.3	63.2	59.3
1979	164.9	105.0	63.7	59.9
1980	167.7	106.9	63.8	59.2
1981	170.1	108.7	63.9	59.0
1982	172.3	110.2	64.0	57.8
1983	174.2	111.6	64.0	57.9
1984	176.4	113.5	64.4	59.5
1985	178.2	115.5	64.8	60.1
1986	180.6	117.8	65.3	60.7
1987	182.8	119.9	65.6	61.5
1988	184.6	121.7	65.9	62.3
1989	186.4	123.9	66.5	63.0
1990	188.0	124.8	66.4	62.7
1991	189.8	125.3	66.0	61.6
1992	191.6	127.0	66.3	61.4
1993	193.6	128.0	66.2	61.6
1994	196.8	131.1	66.6	62.5
1995	198.6	132.3	66.6	62.9

Source: *Economic Report of the President*, 1996, Table B-38.

SECTION 3 (continued)

POPULATION AND EMPLOYMENT

UNEMPLOYMENT RATES

YEAR	ALL WORKERS	BOTH SEXES, AGE 16–19 YEARS	MEN AGE 20+	WOMEN AGE 20+
1959	5.5	14.6	4.7	5.2
1960	5.5	14.7	4.7	5.1
1961	6.7	16.8	5.7	6.3
1962	5.5	14.7	4.6	5.4
1963	5.7	17.2	4.5	5.4
1964	5.2	16.2	3.9	5.2
1965	4.5	14.8	3.2	4.5
1966	3.8	12.8	2.5	3.8
1967	3.8	12.9	2.3	4.2
1968	3.6	12.7	2.2	3.8
1969	3.5	12.2	2.1	3.7
1970	4.9	15.3	3.5	4.8
1971	5.9	16.9	4.4	5.7
1972	5.6	16.2	4.0	5.4
1973	4.9	14.5	3.3	4.9
1974	5.6	16.0	3.8	5.5
1975	8.5	19.9	6.8	8.0
1976	7.7	19.0	5.9	7.4
1977	7.1	17.8	5.2	7.0
1978	6.1	16.4	4.3	6.0
1979	5.8	16.1	4.2	5.7
1980	7.1	17.8	5.9	6.4
1981	7.6	19.6	6.3	6.8
1982	9.7	23.2	8.8	8.3
1983	9.6	22.4	8.9	8.1
1984	7.5	18.9	6.6	6.8
1985	7.2	18.6	6.2	6.6
1986	7.0	18.3	6.1	6.2
1987	6.2	16.9	5.4	5.4
1988	5.5	15.3	4.8	4.9
1989	5.3	15.0	4.5	4.7
1990	5.5	15.5	4.9	4.8
1991	6.7	18.6	6.3	5.7
1992	7.4	20.0	7.0	6.3
1993	6.8	19.0	6.4	5.9
1994	6.1	17.6	5.4	5.4
1995	5.6	17.3	4.8	4.9

Source: *Economic Report of the President*, 1996, Tables B-65 and B-69.

SECTION 4

MONEY SUPPLY, INTEREST RATES, AND FEDERAL FINANCES

Year	Money Supply M1 (Billions)	Annual Change in M1	Money Supply M2 (Billions)	Annual Change in M2	AAA Corporate Bonds
	Money Supply Data				Interest Rate
1959	140.0	—	297.8	—	4.38
1960	140.7	0.5	312.3	4.9	4.41
1961	145.2	3.2	335.5	7.4	4.35
1962	147.8	1.8	362.7	8.1	4.33
1963	153.3	3.7	393.2	8.4	4.26
1964	160.3	4.6	424.8	8.0	4.40
1965	167.9	4.7	459.3	8.1	4.49
1966	172.0	2.4	480.0	4.5	5.13
1967	183.3	6.6	524.3	9.2	5.51
1968	197.4	7.7	566.3	8.0	6.18
1969	203.9	3.3	589.5	4.1	7.03
1970	214.4	5.1	628.1	6.5	8.04
1971	228.3	6.5	712.7	13.5	7.39
1972	249.2	9.2	805.2	13.0	7.21
1973	262.8	5.5	861.0	6.9	7.44
1974	274.3	4.4	908.5	5.5	8.57
1975	287.4	4.8	1,023.2	12.6	8.83
1976	306.3	6.6	1,163.7	13.7	8.43
1977	331.1	8.1	1,286.5	10.6	8.02
1978	358.1	8.2	1,388.6	7.9	8.73
1979	382.4	6.8	1,496.9	7.8	9.63
1980	408.5	6.8	1,629.3	8.8	11.94
1981	436.3	6.8	1,793.3	10.1	14.17
1982	474.3	8.7	1,953.2	8.9	13.79
1983	521.0	9.8	2,187.7	12.0	12.04
1984	552.1	6.0	2,378.4	8.7	12.71
1985	619.8	12.3	2,576.0	8.3	11.37
1986	724.4	16.9	2,820.3	9.5	9.02
1987	749.8	3.5	2,922.3	3.6	9.38
1988	786.9	4.9	3,083.5	5.5	9.71
1989	794.2	0.9	3,243.0	5.2	9.26
1990	825.8	4.0	3,356.0	3.5	9.32
1991	897.3	8.7	3,457.9	3.0	8.77
1992	1,024.4	14.2	3,515.3	1.7	8.14
1993	1,128.6	10.2	3,583.6	1.9	7.22
1994	1,148.0	1.7	3,617.0	0.9	7.97
1995	1,123.0	−2.2	3,780.7	4.5	7.59

Source: *Economic Report of the President,* 1996, Tables B-74 and B-75.

SECTION 4 (continued)

MONEY SUPPLY, INTEREST RATES, AND FEDERAL FINANCES

	FEDERAL BUDGET TOTALS (BILLIONS OF DOLLARS)			NATIONAL DEBT	
YEAR	FISCAL YEAR OUTLAYS	FISCAL YEAR RECEIPTS	SURPLUS (+) OR DEFICIT (−)	BILLIONS OF DOLLARS	AS A PERCENT OF GDP
1959	92.1	79.2	−12.8	287.5	59.9
1960	92.2	92.5	0.3	290.5	57.6
1961	97.7	94.4	−3.3	292.6	56.6
1962	106.8	99.7	−7.1	302.9	54.6
1963	111.3	106.6	−4.8	310.3	53.1
1964	118.5	112.6	−5.9	316.1	50.5
1965	118.2	116.8	−1.4	322.3	48.0
1966	134.5	130.8	−3.7	328.5	44.7
1967	157.5	148.8	−8.6	340.4	42.9
1968	178.1	153.0	−25.2	368.7	43.5
1969	183.6	186.9	3.2	365.8	39.5
1970	195.6	192.8	−2.8	380.9	38.7
1971	210.2	187.1	−23.0	408.2	38.8
1972	230.7	207.3	−23.4	435.9	38.0
1973	245.7	230.8	−14.9	466.9	36.6
1974	269.4	263.2	−6.1	483.9	34.5
1975	332.3	279.1	−53.2	541.9	35.9
1976	371.8	298.1	−73.7	629.0	37.3
1977	409.2	355.6	−53.7	706.4	36.8
1978	458.7	399.6	−59.2	776.6	36.0
1979	504.0	463.3	−40.7	829.5	34.1
1980	590.9	517.1	−73.8	909.1	34.4
1981	678.2	599.3	−79.0	994.8	33.6
1982	745.8	617.8	−128.0	1,137.3	36.4
1983	808.4	600.6	−207.8	1,371.7	41.4
1984	851.8	666.5	−185.4	1,564.7	42.3
1985	946.4	734.1	−212.3	1,817.5	45.8
1986	990.3	769.1	−221.2	2,120.6	50.3
1987	1,003.9	854.1	−149.8	2,346.1	52.7
1988	1,064.1	909.0	−155.2	2,601.3	54.1
1989	1,143.2	990.7	−152.5	2,868.0	55.4
1990	1,252.7	1,031.3	−221.4	3,206.6	58.5
1991	1,323.8	1,054.3	−269.5	3,598.5	63.4
1992	1,380.9	1,090.5	−290.4	4,002.1	67.6
1993	1,408.7	1,153.5	−255.1	4,351.4	69.5
1994	1,460.9	1,257.7	−203.2	4,643.7	70.0
1995	1,514.4	1,350.6	−163.8	4,921.0	70.3

SECTION 5

SIZE OF GOVERNMENT AS A SHARE OF GDP, 1959–1994

	FEDERAL, STATE, AND LOCAL GOVERNMENT				
YEAR	EXPENDITURES (PERCENT OF GDP)	REVENUES (PERCENT OF GDP)	PURCHASES OF GOODS AND SERVICES (PERCENT OF GDP)	NON-DEFENSE PURCHASES OF GOODS AND SERVICES (PERCENT OF GDP)	TRANSFER PAYMENTS TO PERSONS (PERCENT OF GDP)
1959	22.9	25.4	22.1	8.0	5.4
1960	23.1	26.4	21.5	8.1	5.6
1961	24.0	26.5	22.2	8.4	6.2
1962	24.1	26.6	22.5	8.6	5.9
1963	24.1	27.1	22.3	8.8	5.9
1964	23.7	26.1	21.8	9.0	5.7
1965	23.4	26.0	21.3	9.1	5.7
1966	24.2	26.7	22.0	9.2	5.8
1967	26.1	27.2	23.3	9.6	6.5
1968	26.8	28.7	23.3	9.8	6.9
1969	26.9	30.0	22.8	10.2	7.1
1970	28.3	28.9	22.8	11.0	8.1
1971	28.7	28.4	22.2	11.3	8.8
1972	28.5	29.5	21.7	11.4	9.0
1973	28.0	29.6	20.8	11.3	9.2
1974	29.3	30.2	21.6	11.8	10.1
1975	31.6	28.7	22.2	12.4	11.6
1976	30.6	29.5	21.2	12.1	11.4
1977	30.0	29.8	20.6	11.9	10.9
1978	28.7	29.6	20.0	11.6	10.4
1979	28.4	29.8	19.8	11.4	10.4
1980	30.2	30.0	20.6	11.7	11.4
1981	30.1	30.6	20.3	11.5	11.6
1982	32.5	30.0	21.1	11.7	12.4
1983	32.4	29.3	20.4	11.5	12.4
1984	31.1	29.3	21.0	11.0	11.5
1985	31.4	29.7	20.9	11.2	11.5
1986	31.6	29.7	21.2	11.4	11.6
1987	31.4	30.5	21.2	11.3	11.4
1988	30.7	30.0	20.4	11.1	11.3
1989	30.5	30.2	20.1	11.2	11.3
1990	31.4	30.0	20.5	11.6	11.8
1991	32.1	30.1	20.7	11.8	12.2
1992	33.1	30.0	20.2	11.8	13.6
1993	32.8	30.3	19.7	11.7	13.8
1994	32.0	30.7	19.0	11.5	13.7

Source: *Economic Report of the President,* 1996, calculated from Tables B-1, B-78, B-79, and B-80.

SECTION 6

BASIC ECONOMIC DATA FOR 58 COUNTRIES

	POPULATION 1994 (MILLIONS)	REAL GDP PER CAPITA 1994 (IN 1985 DOLLARS)	AVERAGE ANNUAL GROWTH RATE OF REAL PER CAPITA GDP 1980–1994	ANNUAL GROWTH RATE OF MONEY SUPPLY 1980–1993[1]	AVERAGE ANNUAL INFLATION RATE 1980–1993	GROSS INVESTMENT AS A SHARE OF GDP 1990–1994
HIGH-INCOME COUNTRIES						
United States	260.7	18,850	1.6	7.2	3.8	20.4
Hong Kong	6.0	17,832	5.0	8.5	7.9	28.5
Canada	27.9	17,510	1.3	8.1	3.9	19.0
Switzerland	7.0	15,980	0.8	6.2	3.8	24.8
Australia	18.0	15,169	1.6	11.5	6.1	20.7
Japan	125.7	15,105	2.9	8.2	1.5	31.0
Germany	80.9	15,005	1.8	6.8	2.7	24.8
Denmark	5.2	14,800	1.9	9.8	4.6	15.6
Singapore	2.9	14,415	5.3	13.5	2.5	40.4
Sweden	8.8	13,930	0.8	6.9	6.9	16.7
France	58.0	13,910	1.4	5.1	5.1	19.8
Belgium	10.0	13,735	1.5	2.4	4.0	19.1
Netherlands	15.4	13,505	1.3	4.5	1.7	20.7
United Kingdom	58.0	13,430	1.9	15.9	5.6	16.3
Austria	7.9	13,250	1.6	7.3	3.6	25.4
Italy	58.0	12,920	1.7	10.5	8.8	20.3
Finland	5.1	12,000	1.0	11.4	5.8	18.9
Spain	39.4	9,990	2.1	11.6	8.4	22.5
AFRICA						
Botswana	1.5	3,350	5.3	25.2	12.3	—
Cameroon	12.9	975	−2.3	3.1	4.0	—
Côte d'Ivoire	13.7	1,065	−3.9	2.5	1.5	7.1
Ghana	16.8	975	−0.5	42.0	37.0	15.0
Kenya	27.5	894	−0.0	16.4	9.9	18.6
Mauritius	1.1	6,650	4.8	21.6	8.8	29.8
Nigeria	107.9	960	−1.3	18.0	20.6	10.9
South Africa	41.5	3,025	−1.3	16.6	14.7	16.8
Tanzania	27.5	470	−0.6	33.1[2]	24.9[2]	47.8
Zambia	9.2	525	−2.1	48.2	58.9	14.0
ASIA AND PACIFIC						
Bangladesh	117.8	1,575	2.2	18.0	8.6	—
China	1208.5	1,865	9.3	25.7	7.0	—
India	918.0	1,335	3.0	16.7	8.7	23.3
Indonesia	190.0	2,310	4.1	26.3	8.5	34.9
Korea (South)	44.7	8,565	7.4	21.9	6.3	36.7

BASIC ECONOMIC DATA FOR 58 COUNTRIES

	POPULATION 1994 (MILLIONS)	REAL GDP PER CAPITA 1994 (IN 1985 DOLLARS)	AVERAGE ANNUAL GROWTH RATE OF REAL PER CAPITA GDP 1980–1994	ANNUAL GROWTH RATE OF MONEY SUPPLY 1980–1993[1]	AVERAGE ANNUAL INFLATION RATE 1980–1993	GROSS INVESTMENT AS A SHARE OF GDP 1990–1994
ASIA AND PACIFIC (continued)						
Malaysia	19.5	6,510	4.1	12.6	2.2	34.8
Pakistan	126.3	1,435	2.7	14.2	7.4	19.7
Philippines	67.3	1,720	−0.8	17.4	13.6	23.1
Taiwan	21.3	10,152	6.1	6.1	3.0	24.1
Thailand	60.0	4,450	6.0	19.2	4.3	41.1
SOUTH/CENTRAL AMERICA						
Argentina	33.9	6,025	0.1	356.7	374.3	16.7
Brazil	159.8	4,118	0.1	673.0	652.7	20.6
Chile	14.0	5,250	2.8	29.1	20.1	26.6
Colombia	34.5	3,495	1.5	24.2	24.9	18.0
Dominican Republic	7.8	2,322	0.2	29.3	25.0	22.5
Guatemala	10.2	2,300	−1.2	19.3	16.8	15.9
Mexico	88.4	6,260	−0.1	57.8	57.9	22.4
Peru	23.3	2,390	−1.3	296.6	316.1	17.8
Venezuela	21.2	6,395	−1.2	22.7	23.9	16.3
MIDDLE EAST/MEDITERRANEAN						
Egypt	57.0	1,915	1.6	21.4	13.6	21.2
Greece	10.5	6,783	0.8	21.5	17.3	19.6
Iran	60.1	3,650	−0.2	18.4	17.1	31.6
Israel	5.3	9,970	1.9	78.6	70.4	22.8
Syria	13.7	4,270	0.2	21.8	14.0	20.9
Turkey	60.9	3,665	2.8	60.6	53.5	24.1
EASTERN EUROPE						
Bulgaria	8.9	5,000	0.6	40.0[3]	42.9	—
Hungary	10.2	4,720	0.2	13.3	12.8	21.7
Poland	38.9	4,150	−0.5	64.1	69.3	24.5
Romania	22.8	2,170	−2.3	18.8	22.4	29.1
Russia	148.7	4,200	−2.0	—	35.4	—

[1]Broad measure of the money supply.
[2]Data are for the years 1987–1993.
[3]Data are for the years 1986–1994.

Source: The per capita GDP data are from Robert Summers and Alan Heston, *Penn World Tables* (Cambridge: National Bureau of Economic Research, 1994). They were derived by the purchasing-power parity method and updated to 1994 by the authors. The other data are from World Bank, *World Development Report, 1995*.

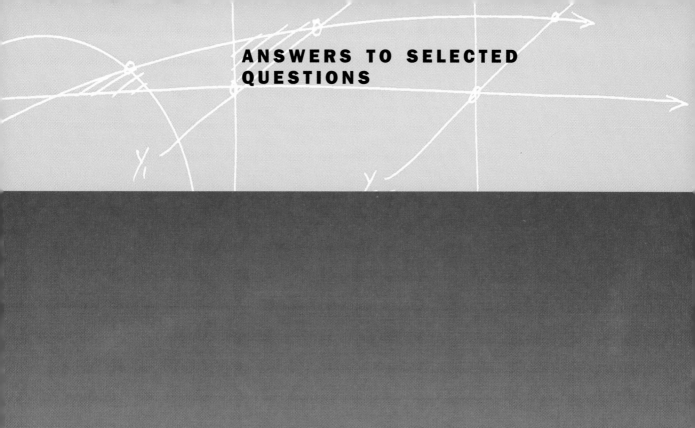

ANSWERS TO SELECTED QUESTIONS

CHAPTER 1

2. Production of scarce goods always involves a cost; there are no free lunches. When the government provides goods without charge to consumers, other citizens (taxpayers) will bear the cost of their provision. Thus, provision by the government affects how the costs will be covered, not whether they are incurred.

4. For most taxpayers, the change will reduce the after-tax cost of raising children. Other things constant, one would predict an increase in the birth rate.

5. False. Intentions do not change the impact of the policy. If the policy runs counter to sound economics, it will lead to a counterproductive outcome even if that was not the intention of the policy. Stupid policies are often advocated by people with good intentions.

7. Raising the price of new cars by requiring safety devices, which customers would not have purchased if given the choice, slows the rate of sales for new cars. Thus the older, less safe cars are driven longer, partially offsetting the safety advantage provided by the newer, safer cars. Also, drivers act a bit differently—they may take more risks—when they believe the safety devices will provide protection should they have an unexpected accident. In fact, economist Gordon Tullock says that the greatest safety device of all might be a dagger built into the center of the steering wheel, pointed directly at the driver's chest!

8. Money has nothing to do with whether an individual is economizing. Any time a person chooses, in an attempt to achieve a goal, he or she is economizing.

9. Positive economics can help one better understand the likely effects of alternative policies. This will help one choose alternatives that are less likely to lead to disappointing results.

CHAPTER 2

2. This is an opportunity cost question. Even though the productivity of painters has changed only slightly, rising productivity in other areas has led to higher wages in other occupations, thereby increasing the opportunity cost of being a housepainter. Since people would not supply house painting services unless they were able to meet their opportunity costs, higher wages are necessary to attract housepainters from competitive (alternative) lines of work.

5. The statement reflects the "exchange is a zero sum game" view. This view is false. No private business can force customers to buy. Neither can a customer force a business to sell. Unless both buyer and seller believe the exchange is in their interest, they will not enter into the exchange. Mutual gain provides the foundation for voluntary exchange.

8. Yes. This question highlights the incentive of individuals to conserve for the future when they have private ownership rights. The market value of the land will increase in anticipation of the future harvest,

as the trees grow and the expected day of harvest moves closer. Thus, with transferable private property, the tree farmer will be able to capture the value added by his planting and holding the trees for a few years, even if the actual harvest does not take place until well after his death.

9. In general, it sanctions all forms of competition except for the use of violence (or the threat of violence), theft, or fraud.

13. If the food from land, now and in the future, is worth more than the housing services from the same land, then developers will not be able to bid the land away from farmers. However, comparative advantage determines the efficient use of a resource; thus, even the best farmland, if situated in the right location, may be far more valuable for buildings. Other, poorer land can always be made more productive by the use of different (and more costly) farming techniques, irrigation, fertilizer, and so on. Physical characteristics alone do not determine the value or the most valuable use of a resource.

15. A large number of people feel that safety is priceless—that no price is too high to pay for something that saves lives. However, there is a problem with this view: It ignores opportunity costs. If we want more safety we will have to give up other things. Sometimes the opportunity cost of the additional safety will exceed its value. Consider travel safety. We could save lives if we cut our current speed limits in half, doubled the width of every road, and allowed only tank-like automobiles on the roads. But we would have to give up other things—things that are valued more highly than the lives saved—if we did. You could reduce your likelihood of accidental death by refusing to travel by automobile, train, or airplane. However, most people do not choose to do this, because they value the travel more than the additional safety. Remember, economics is about trade-offs, not absolutes.

CHAPTER 3

1. Choices a and b would increase the demand for beef; c and d would affect primarily the supply of beef, rather than the demand; e leads to a change in quantity demanded, not a change in demand.

4. a. Reductions in the supply of feed grains and hay led to sharply higher prices; b. the higher feed grain and hay prices increased the cost of maintaining a cattle herd and thereby caused many producers to sell (an increase in current supply), depressing cattle prices in 1988; c. the reduction in the size of cattle herds led to a smaller future supply and higher cattle prices in 1989.

6. Agreement of both buyer and seller is required for an exchange. Price ceilings push prices below equilibrium and thereby reduce the quantity sellers are willing to offer. Price floors push prices above equilibrium and thereby reduce the quantity consumers wish to buy. Both decrease the actual quantity traded in the market.

8. True. "Somebody" must decide who will be the business winners and losers. Neither markets nor the political process leaves the

determination of winners and losers to chance. Under market organization, business winners and losers are determined by the decentralized choices of millions of consumers who use their dollar votes to reward firms that provide preferred goods at a low cost and penalize others who fail to do so. Under political decision making, the winners and losers are determined by political officials who use taxes, subsidies, regulations, and mandates to favor some businesses and penalize others.

10. a. Profitable production increases the value of resources owned by people and leads to mutual gain for resource suppliers, consumers, and entrepreneurs. b. Losses reduce the value of resources, which reduces the well-being of at least some people. c. No.

12. In the absence of trade restrictions, modest price increases in France will attract wheat from other regions, minimizing the effects in the drought region and resulting in slightly higher prices worldwide.

14. Rationing by price encourages future output; waiting in a line does not. Like a higher price, a longer wait in line rations the current supply by increasing the consumer's opportunity cost. However, the consumer's cost of waiting in line is wasted; it generates nothing for suppliers. In contrast, although a higher price also increases the consumer's opportunity cost, this cost transfers resources to suppliers, increases their returns, and thereby encourages them to expand the future availability of the good.

16. a. Demand would increase, rising vertically by $3 per meal—the added per-meal cost previously paid separately. b. Both price and quantity will rise in response to the rise in demand.

CHAPTER 4

2. When payment is not demanded for services, potential customers have a strong incentive to attempt a "free ride." However, when the number of nonpaying customers becomes such that the sales revenues of sellers are diminished (and in some cases eliminated), the sellers' incentive to supply the good is thereby reduced (or eliminated).

5. Disagree. As long as changes in personal costs and benefits influence choices predictably, theories for both market and public-sector action can be developed and tested against real-world events. Theory building and testing are the essential ingredients of a positive science.

6. The antimissile system is a public good for the residents of Washington, D.C. Strictly speaking, none of the other items is a public good since each could be provided to some consumers (paying customers, for example) without being provided to others.

9. In both markets and government, mutual consent is the only conclusive test of whether an action is productive. If all parties affected by an activity agree to it, then it is productive. Projects favored by a majority are not necessarily productive because the cost imposed on the nonconsenting minority may exceed the net gain to the majority.

11. The invisible hand principle is present only when the self-interest of individuals is consistent with the general welfare. Both the special interest effect and the shortsightedness effect indicate that this will not always be the case, even when political choices are made democratically.

12. True. Since individual computer customers both decide the issue (what computer, if any, will be purchased) and bear the consequences of a mistaken choice, they have a strong incentive to acquire information that will help them make a wise choice. In contrast, voters recognize that their choice, even if mistaken, will not decide the congressional election. Thus, they have little incentive to search for information that will help them make a better choice.

CHAPTER 5

2. Local and state governments operate in a more competitive setting than does the federal government. Taxpayers who feel they are paying high taxes and getting little in return can vote with their feet; they can move to another local (or state) governmental unit that offers them more value for their tax dollars. The presence of alternatives—that is, competition among local and state governments—reduces their ability to exploit taxpayer/citizens.

3. User charges differ from general taxation in that they impose the cost of a government activity on users in proportion to their consumption of the good. If you do not use the good, you do not have to pay for it. Taxes earmarked to finance specific activities may approximate user charges, but general taxation does not. The use of general taxes to finance a government activity breaks the link between consumption and payment and thereby forces nonusers to pay for things enjoyed by others. Like market prices, user charges provide valuable information about value relative to cost. If the revenue from a user charge is sufficient to cover opportunity cost, this is strong evidence that consumers value the good more than the alternatives forgone. Conversely, if user charges are insufficient to cover cost, this is evidence that consumers place a higher value on other things that might be produced.

6. True. In addition to the outlay cost of the project, the collection cost of the taxes and the deadweight losses emanating from the taxes implied by the project must also be covered if the project is going to enhance economic welfare.

7. High marginal tax rates make tax-deductible expenditures (for example, business entertainment, elegant offices, or luxury automobiles for business use) cheap to the purchaser (but not to society). A reduction in marginal tax rates will increase the purchaser's cost of deductible expenditures, since the lower rates reduce the tax savings accompanying deductible expenditures. Thus, lower marginal rates will tend to reduce expenditures on deductible items and other forms of tax avoidance.

10. False. Just as businesses do not pay taxes, neither do inanimate objects such as trucks. Only people pay taxes. In this case, the

increased costs accompanying the tax translate into higher freight rates. These costs will be paid by consumers of the products transported (in the form of higher prices), by truck owners (in the form of lower profits), and by trucking employees (in the form of lower earnings).

CHAPTER 6

1. a, c, f, g, and h will exert no impact on GDP; b and d will increase GDP by the amount of the expenditure; and e will increase GDP by $250 (the commission on the transaction).

3. Since the furniture was produced last year, the sale does not affect GDP this year. It reduces inventory investment by $100,000 and increases consumption by $100,000, leaving GDP unchanged.

5. The reliability of GDP comparisons over long periods of time is reduced because the leisure and human costs may change substantially between the two years, and because the types of goods available for consumption during the two years may be vastly different. Likewise, GDP may not be a good index of output differences between countries (for example, the United States and Mexico) for the same reasons. In addition, there may be substantial differences between countries in the production of (a) economic "bads," (b) goods in the household sector, and (c) the size of the underground economy.

7. 250.35

9. a. $1,000; b. $600; c. $200; d. 0; e. $10,000

11. a. False. Inventory investment indicates whether the holdings of unsold goods are rising or falling. A negative inventory investment (economists refer to this as disinvestment) means that inventories were drawn down during the period. b. False. If gross investment is less than the depreciation of capital goods during the period, net investment would be negative. Net investment in the United States was negative for several years during the Great Depression of the 1930s. c. Not necessarily. Rather, it may be the result of an increase in prices, population, or hours worked.

12. Neither the receipts nor the expenditures on payouts would count toward GDP since they are merely transfers—they do not involve production. However, expenditures on operations, administration, and government-provided goods and services from lottery proceeds would add to GDP.

14. a. 0; b. 0; c. $500; d. $300; e. $300; f. 0; g. 0; h. 0

17. Consideration of this question illustrates some of the problems accompanying income comparisons across widely separated time periods when the bundle of goods available differs substantially. Of course, the price level has risen approximately sevenfold since 1929, so that $40,000 of income in 1929 would be comparable to $280,000 in 1989. However, even with $280,000 of income in 1929, you could not have purchased a CD player, color television, personal computer, or an airplane ticket from New York City to Los Angeles. Neither could you have purchased an automobile that would deliver the

service and dependability of even today's economy model. The number of people you could have contacted via telephone would have been limited. Modern household appliances that most people take for granted would have been unavailable. Of course, you could have purchased a lot of other goods, including clothing, land, and wood for heating. Even so, we suspect that many would prefer the choices available today at the lower level of real income.

20. a. $2,260.1 billion; b. $3,384.3 billion; c. 60.4. (You should be able to easily calculate the others.)

CHAPTER 7

2. Job seekers do not know which employers will offer them the more attractive jobs. They find out by searching. Job search is "profitable" and consistent with economic efficiency as long as the marginal gain from search exceeds the marginal cost of searching.

6. One of the most harmful side effects of inflation is the uncertainty it creates with regard to time dimension contracts. As the statement indicates, it tends to undermine the ability of markets to allocate goods and resources to those who value them the most. In effect, it encourages speculation rather than production. The well-known economist who made the statement referred to in the question was John Maynard Keynes. See *The Economic Consequences of Peace* (New York: Harcourt Brace, 1920), pages 235–236.

7. When the actual unemployment rate is equal to the natural rate of unemployment, cyclical unemployment is absent and potential GDP is at its sustainable rate. When the actual unemployment rate is greater (less) than the natural rate of unemployment, cyclical unemployment is positive (negative) and potential GDP is less (greater) than its sustainable rate.

8. a. 60 percent; b. 8.3 percent; c. 55 percent

9. No. No. It means that there were no jobs available at wage rates acceptable to the potential workers who were unemployed. Thus, they continued to search for more attractive opportunities.

10. The inflation will tend to increase the wealth of a and e because it will increase the nominal value of their assets and reduce their real liabilities. It will hurt b, c, and f because their income will rise less rapidly than prices. With regard to d, it depends on whether his indebtedness is at a fixed or variable interest rate. If it is fixed, the inflation will reduce his real indebtedness, but if it is variable (tied to an interest rate that can be expected to increase with the inflation rate), his interest cost will rise with inflation.

13. Each will encourage additional search.

14. The wages people earn are also prices (prices for labor services) and like other prices they usually rise as the general level of prices increases. The statement ignores this factor. It implicitly assumes that money wages are unaffected by inflation—that they would have increased by the same amount (6 percent) even if prices would have been stable. Generally, this will not be the case.

CHAPTER 8

4. If the inflation rate unexpectedly falls from 3 percent to zero, the real wages of union members will rise. If other unions have similar contracts, the unemployment rate will increase because employment costs have risen relative to product prices. Profit margins will be cut and producers will respond by reducing output and laying off workers. In contrast, if the inflation rate rises to 8 percent, profit margins will improve, producers will expand their output, and the unemployment rate will decline.

7. The key things held constant when constructing the demand and supply schedules for a specific good are demand (consumer income, prices of related goods, consumer preferences, expected future price of the good, and number of consumers) and supply (resource prices, technology, and expected future price of the good). Changes in these factors shift the relevant schedule.

   The key things held constant when constructing the aggregate schedules are *AD* (money supply, the government's tax and spending policies, real wealth, real income of one's trading partners, consumer preferences, and the expected future price level); *LRAS* (size of resource base, technology, and institutional structure of the economy); and *SRAS* (factors held constant in the *LR* plus resource prices and the expected price level). Again, changes in these factors will shift the schedules indicated.

10. They are all equal.

11. Negative real interest rates are realized when the money interest rate is less than the inflation rate. This generally occurs when decision makers (particularly lenders) underestimate the future rate of inflation and therefore agree to an inflationary premium that proves to be insufficient to compensate for the effects of inflation. This was the case for many loans in the United States during the sharp acceleration in inflation in the mid-1970s. Negative real interest rates are unlikely to persist because lenders losing real purchasing power will alter their expectations of the inflation rate upward and therefore demand a larger inflationary premium.

12. $10,000; $20,000

13. Inversely; an increase in interest rates is the same thing as a reduction in bond prices.

CHAPTER 9

1. Choice a would decrease *AD*; b, c, and d would increase it; and e would leave it unchanged. For the "why" part of the question, see the Factors That Shift Aggregate Demand section at the beginning of the chapter.

2. a, b, c, and d will reduce *SRAS*; e will increase it.

4. When an economy is operating at less than full employment, weak demand in resource markets will tend to reduce (a) the real rate of interest and (b) resource prices relative to product prices and thereby restore normal profit and the incentive of firms to produce the long-

run potential output level. If resource prices and the real interest rate were inflexible downward, the self-correcting mechanism would not work.

6. At the lower than expected inflation rate, *real* wages (and costs) will increase relative to product prices. This will squeeze profit margins and lead to reductions in output and employment, causing the unemployment rate to rise.

8. Tightness in resource markets will result in rising resource prices relative to product prices, causing the *SRAS* to shift to the left. Profit margins will decline, output rate will fall, and long-run equilibrium will be restored at a higher price level. The above-normal output cannot be maintained because it reflects input prices that people would not have agreed to and output decisions they would not have chosen if they had anticipated the current price level (and rate of inflation). Once they have a chance to correct these mistakes, they do so; and output returns to the economy's long-run potential.

9. Real wages will tend to increase more rapidly when the unemployment rate is low because a tight labor market (strong demand) will place upward pressure on wages.

12. The increase in demand for exports will increase aggregate demand. In the short run, this unanticipated expansion in demand will tend to increase output and employment, while exerting modest upward pressure on the price level. In the long run, the primary impact will be a higher price level, with no change in output and employment.

CHAPTER 10

2. a. Increase current consumption, as the expectation of rising future prices will induce consumers to buy now.
   b. Decrease current consumption, as people will attempt to save more for hard times.
   c. Increase current consumption, as the result of an expansion in disposable income.
   d. May have little effect. However, the tendency will be toward a reduction in consumption, since households have an incentive to save more at the higher interest rate.
   e. Decrease consumption, as falling stock prices will reduce the wealth of consumers.

   f. and g. Increase consumption, as the young and the poor typically have a higher marginal propensity to consume than the elderly and wealthy.

4. It is the concept that a change in one of the components of aggregate demand—investment, for example—will lead to a far greater change in the equilibrium level of income. Since the multiplier equals $1/1 - MPC$, its size is determined by the marginal propensity to consume. The multiplier makes stabilizing the economy more difficult, since relatively small changes in aggregate demand have a much greater impact on equilibrium income.

7. The funds for the additional spending must come from either a decline in saving or an increase in borrowing. The model implicitly assumes one of the following: either (a) the changes in saving and borrowing exert no impact on the real interest rate, or (b) the level of current investment, consumption, and government expenditure is insensitive to changes in the real rate of interest. In essence, the model ignores the interrelation between the goods and services market and the loanable funds market.

9. The statement fails to recognize that association does not imply a direction of causation. The investment demand conditions differ during periods of boom and recession. During an expansionary boom, investment demand is strong. In turn, the strong investment demand pushes interest rates up, not vice versa. Similarly, during a recession, weak investment demand leads to lower interest rates. Thus, it is the fluctuations in investment demand (shifts of the schedule) that explain the pattern of interest rates over the business cycle.

12. You would expect the multiplier to be smaller in Canada because Canadians would be expected to spend a larger share of their additions to income on imports, rather than domestic goods. This will reduce the size of the multiplier.

13. None. The Keynesian model assumes that wages and prices are inflexible downward. It will take an increase in aggregate expenditures to restore full employment.

CHAPTER 11

2. The crowding-out effect is the theory that budget deficits will lead to higher real interest rates, which retard private spending. The crowding-out effect indicates that fiscal policy would not be nearly so potent as the simple Keynesian model implies. The new classical theory indicates that anticipation of higher future taxes (rather than higher interest rates) will crowd out private spending when government expenditures are financed by debt.

4. Automatic stabilizers are built-in features (unemployment compensation, corporate profit tax, progressive income tax) that tend automatically to promote a budget deficit during a recession and a budget surplus (or smaller deficit) during an inflationary boom. Automatic stabilizers have the major advantage of providing needed restraint, or stimuli, without congressional approval—which, in turn, minimizes the problem of proper timing.

8. This statement depicts the views of many economists three decades ago. Today, most economists recognize that it is naive. Given our limited ability to accurately forecast future economic conditions, timing of fiscal policy is more difficult than was previously thought. Political considerations—remember, the government is merely an alternative form of social organization, not a corrective device—reduce the likelihood that fiscal policy will be used as a stabilization tool. Changes in interest rates and private spending may offset fiscal actions and thereby reduce the potency of fiscal policy. All fac-

tors considered, it is clear that the use of fiscal policy to stabilize the economy is both difficult and complex.

10. There is a major defect in this view. If the budget deficits stimulated demand and thereby output and employment, we would have expected the inflation rate to accelerate. This was not the case; in fact, the inflation rate declined. The failure of the inflation rate to accelerate during the expansion of the 1980s strongly suggests that factors other than demand stimulus were at work.

13. This is an accurate statement of what economists refer to as the balanced budget multiplier. It is correct under very restrictive assumptions. However, it ignores the secondary effects in the loanable funds market. If the taxes of consumers rise by $10 billion and consumers reduce their spending by only $7.5 billion, then a $2.5 billion reduction in the supply of loanable funds is implied. This will place upward pressure on the real interest rate, which under normal circumstances will crowd out $2.5 billion dollars of private spending. Thus, when the secondary effects are considered, the validity of the statement is highly questionable.

14. Yes. Only the lower rates would increase the incentive to earn marginal income and thereby stimulate aggregate supply.

CHAPTER 12

1. A liquid asset is one that can easily and quickly be transformed into money without experiencing a loss of its market value. Assets such as high-grade bonds and stocks are highly liquid. In contrast, illiquid assets cannot be easily and quickly converted to cash without some loss of their value. Real estate, a family-owned business, business equipment, and artistic works are examples of illiquid assets.

3. Money is valuable because of its scarcity relative to the availability of goods and services. The use of money facilitates (reduces the cost of) exchange transactions. Money also serves as a store of value and a unit of account. Doubling the supply of money, holding output constant, would simply cause its purchasing power to fall without enhancing the services that it performs. In fact, fluctuations in the money supply would create uncertainty as to its future value and reduce the ability of money to serve as a store of value, accurate unit of account, and medium of exchange for time-dimension contracting.

6. a. No change; currency held by the public increases, but checking deposits decrease by an equal amount. b. Bank reserves decrease by $100. c. Excess reserves decrease by $100, minus $100 multiplied by the required reserve ratio.

8. Answers b, e, and f will reduce the money supply; a and c will increase it; if the Treasury's deposits (or the deposits of persons who receive portions of the Treasury's spending) are considered part of the money supply, then d will leave the money supply unchanged.

10. While the transformation of deposits into currency does not directly affect the money supply, it does reduce the excess reserves of banks. The reduction in excess reserves will cause banks to reduce their

outstanding loans and thereby shrink the money supply. Therefore, an increase in the holding of currency relative to deposits will tend to reduce the supply of money.

12. There are two major reasons. First, the money supply can be altered quietly via open market operations, while a reserve requirement change focuses attention on Fed policy. Second, open market operations are a fine-tuning method, while a reserve requirement change is a blunt instrument. Generally, the Fed prefers quiet, marginal changes to headline-grabbing, blunt changes that are more likely to disrupt markets.

13. a. False; statements of this type often use money when they are really speaking about wealth (or income).
b. False; the checking deposit also counts as money. In addition, the deposit increases the reserves of the receiving bank, and thereby places it in a position to extend additional loans that would increase the money supply.
c. False; only an increase in the availability of goods and services valued by people will improve our standard of living. Without an additional supply of goods and services, more money will simply lead to a higher price level.

17. a. Money supply increases by $100,000; b. $80,000; c. $500,000; d. no; there will be some leakage in the form of additional currency holdings by the public and additional excess reserve holdings by banks.

19. a. Money supply will increase by $2 billion; b. $1.8 billion; c. $20 billion; d. approximately $10.5 billion; e. approximately $8.51 billion; the potential money multiplier was 10, but the actual multiplier was only 4.255; f. the leakages in the form of currency held by the public and additions to bank reserves cause the actual money multiplier to be less than the potential multiplier.

CHAPTER 13

2. Choices a and c would increase your incentive to hold money deposits; b and d would reduce your incentive to hold money.

3. a. The cost of obtaining the house is $100,000, but the cost of holding it is the interest forgone on the $100,000 sales value of the house.
b. The cost of obtaining $1,000 is the amount of goods one must give up in order to acquire the $1,000. For example, if a pound of sugar sells for 50 cents, the cost of obtaining $1,000 in terms of sugar is 2,000 pounds. As in the case of the house, the cost of holding $1,000 is the interest forgone.

7. a. bank reserves will decline; b. real interest rates will rise; c. spending on consumer durables will fall; d. dollar will appreciate because the higher interest rates will attract bond purchases by foreigners; e. exports will decline because the appreciation of the dollar will make U.S. goods more expensive for foreigners; f. the higher real interest rates will tend to reduce real asset prices; and g. real GDP will fall.

10. If the time lag is long and variable (rather than short and highly predictable), it is less likely that policymakers will be able to time changes in monetary policy so that they will exert a countercyclical impact on the economy. The policymakers will be more likely to make mistakes and thereby exert a destabilizing influence.

11. Association does not reveal causation. Decision makers—including borrowers and lenders—will eventually anticipate a high rate of inflation and adjust their choices accordingly. As the expected rate of inflation increases, the demand for loanable funds will increase and the supply will decrease. This will lead to higher nominal interest rates. Thus, economic theory indicates that the causation tends to run the opposite direction from that indicated by the statement.

12. Aggregate demand will decline as individuals and businesses reduce spending in an effort to build up their money balances (demand more money).

13. The change in the money supply (M) plus the change in velocity (V) must equal the change in real output (Y) plus the change in the price level. Historically, the growth rate of real output (Y) in the United States has averaged approximately 3 percent. During the next decade, if real output and velocity both grow at a 3 percent annual rate, then the money supply will have to remain constant (zero growth rate) for price stability to be achieved.

CHAPTER 14

4. Traditional monetary and fiscal policies are designed to maintain a high level of aggregate demand to combat the unemployment problem in the short run. The microapproach, on the other hand, is not such a quick-fix strategy. It emphasizes the relative price effects, the microstructure of the economy, and long-run policy prescriptions. If monetary and fiscal policies cannot permanently reduce the long-run natural rate of unemployment, then the microapproach is a viable substitute for traditional macropolicies.

6. Economists in the mid-1970s thought inflation would reduce unemployment; they failed to recognize that decision makers would eventually come to anticipate the inflation. The modern view of the Phillips curve incorporates expectations into the analysis.

9. Compared to the early views of the Phillips curve, modern theory indicates that inflationary policies will be less attractive. Acceptance of the modern view by policymakers will reduce the likelihood of inflationary policies.

12. Lower unemployment benefits would increase the opportunity cost of continuing job search. Therefore, people would be more likely to accept available jobs rather than continuing to search for something better. Thus, lowering the benefits after a couple of months of job search would reduce both the employment disincentive effects of the benefits and the natural rate of unemployment.

13. With unanticipated inflation, real wages fall because many workers, who did not anticipate the inflation, accepted explicit and implicit

contracts at wage rates they would have found unacceptable had they correctly anticipated the magnitude of the price increase. Job search time will decline because many workers will accept jobs at money wage rates they would have rejected if they had been fully aware of how much inflation had increased money wages. Both of these factors will temporarily reduce the unemployment rate. When the inflation is anticipated, it will be fully reflected in long-term wage agreements. Thus, the inflation will fail to reduce real wage rates. Similarly, job search time will be normal because workers will recognize how much inflation has increased the money wages of potential jobs. Thus, anticipated inflation fails to reduce the unemployment rate.

14. It will reduce the incentive to accept available jobs. Payment for non-work is a substitute for work, particularly employment at a low wage rate. It is not easy to differentiate between unemployed workers and workers out of the labor force. The payments provide persons out of or marginally attached to the labor force with an incentive to indicate that they are available for work in order to receive the benefits. This would increase measured unemployment.

CHAPTER 15

4. Compared with earlier periods, the United States has experienced less economic instability during the last four decades. There is reason to believe that a more stable monetary policy has contributed to the increase in stability. See text Exhibits 15–1 and 15–2.

5. Nonactivists think that a monetary rule would result in less instability from monetary sources. The changing nature of money may reduce the stabilizing effects of a monetary rule.

9. An unexpected shift to more expansionary monetary policy might temporarily reduce real interest rates. However, persistent use of expansionary policy in an attempt to push real interest rates below market levels will result in inflation (and high nominal interest rates). Once decision makers anticipate an inflation rate, even high rates of inflation will fail to reduce real interest rates.

12. In responding to this question, reflect on the following: Will congressional representatives, subject to political pressures, be more or less likely to adopt an anti-inflationary policy than relatively anonymous central banking policymakers (for example, the Board of Governors of the Fed)? The empirical evidence indicates that the politicians will be more likely to adopt inflation-generating policies. The central banks of many countries, particularly those in South America, are under the direct control of the political authorities. The inflation rates in these countries are generally quite high.

CHAPTER 16

1. No. Both private corporations and governments can, and often do, have continual debt outstanding. Borrowers can continue to finance

and refinance debt as long as lenders have confidence in their ability to pay. This will generally be the case as long as the interest liability is small relative to income (or the potential tax base).

4. No. Remember, trade is a positive-sum game. Bonds are sold to foreigners because they are offering a better deal (acceptance of a lower interest rate) than is available elsewhere. Prohibiting the sale of bonds to foreigners would result in higher real interest rates and less investment, both of which would adversely affect Americans.

5. A failure to anticipate fully the future taxes accompanying debt implies an underestimation of the true cost of government. Since politicians will want to exaggerate the benefits and conceal the costs of their actions, the ability of debt to hide the true cost of government increases its attractiveness with vote-seeking politicians.

6. Rather than defaulting, the federal government could, as a last resort, meet its debt obligations by borrowing from the Fed. In essence, this means the government is paying its debts with printing-press money. It would lead to inflation.

8. It increases. Yes, if inflation reduced the real outstanding national debt by a larger amount than the budget deficit. See the next question for an illustration of this point.

10. No. Yes.

14. Lower; voters do not enjoy paying taxes and, therefore, voter dissatisfaction places a restraint on higher taxes, which would also restrain expenditures if the budget had to be balanced. More efficient; the restraint of tax increases would tighten the budget constraint and make the reality of opportunity cost more visible to both voters and politicians.

CHAPTER 17

1. a. Increase demand; b. Decrease demand; c. Decrease incentive to develop nongasoline powered car; d. Leave demand unchanged, quantity demanded increased; e. Increase demand.

3. a. 0.21; 1.2. b. Substitutes; higher fuel oil prices lead to an increase in demand (and consumption) for insulation.

6. Water is usually cheaper than oil because its marginal utility at current consumption levels is less than that of oil. Since water is so abundant relative to oil, the benefit derived from an additional quart of water is less than the benefit from an additional quart of oil, even though the total utility from all units of water is far greater than the total utility from all units of oil. However, the price of a product will reflect marginal utility, not total utility.

7. Both income and time constrain our ability to consume. Since, in a wealthier society, time becomes more binding and income less binding, time-saving actions will be more common in a wealthier society. As we engage in time-saving actions (fast food, automatic appliances, air travel, and so on) in order to shift the time restraint outward, our lives become more hectic.

10. All three statements are true.

11. a. No. Even for things we like, we will experience diminishing returns. Eventually, the cost of additional units of pizza will exceed their benefits. b. Perfection in any activity is generally not worth the cost. For example, reading every page of this text 3, 4, or 5 times may improve your grade, but it may not be worth it. One function of a text is to structure the material (highlighted points, layout of graphs, and so on) so that the reader will be able to learn quickly (at a lower cost).

12. Carole.

13. False. Since the demand for agricultural products is generally inelastic, farm incomes may well increase. But the total utility of farm output reflects not only the sales revenues but also the consumer surplus. For the units produced, the utility is unchanged as the loss of consumer surplus by consumers is exactly offset by higher payments to farmers. However, both the payments to farmers and consumer surplus are lost for those units not produced. Therefore, the decline in production will reduce the total utility of farm output and the nation will be worse off as a result.

16. Deceit and dishonesty will be encouraged by methods of organization that increase the returns to such behavior. The returns to deceitful and dishonest claims will be inversely related to the ease with which they can be countered by rivals. Other things constant, the presence of rivals will tend to reduce deceitful behavior. Is a politician more or less likely to tell the truth when he or she regularly confronts rivals? Is the news media more or less likely to be balanced and trustworthy when it faces rivals in the news business? Is a court witness more or less likely to tell the truth when there are other witnesses and cross-examination can be expected? Is a firm selling automobiles, cough drops, or hamburgers more or less likely to be honest when it faces competitors? Answers to such questions are obvious.

17. The deadweight loss is the loss of the potential gains of buyers and sellers emanating from trades that are squeezed out by the tax. It is an excess burden because even though the exchanges that are squeezed out by the tax impose a cost on buyers and sellers, they do not generate tax revenue (since the trades do not take place).

CHAPTER 18

1. The economic profit of a firm is its total revenues minus the opportunity cost of all resources used in the production process. Accounting profit often excludes the opportunity cost of certain resources—particularly the equity capital of the firm and any labor services provided by an owner-manager. Zero economic profit means that the resources owned by the firm are earning their opportunity cost—that is, the rate of return is as high as the highest valued alternative forgone. Thus, the firm would not gain by pursuing other lines of business.

2. a. Sunk costs are irrelevant; b. There is an opportunity cost of one's house; c. Sunk costs should not affect one's current decision; d. There

is an opportunity cost of public education even if it is provided free to the consumer.

7. (a) and (b) In the short run, marginal cost, not average total cost, is relevant. The firm will increase profit by producing additional units as long as the additional revenue derived from sales exceeds MC. (c) Prior to entry into a business, expected ATC is highly relevant. If an entrepreneur does not expect to cover ATC, the project should not be undertaken.

11. Since owners receive profits, clearly profit maximization is in their interest. Managers, if they are not owners, have no property right to profit and therefore no direct interest in profit maximization. Since a solid record of profitability tends to increase the market value (salary) of corporate managers, they do have an indirect incentive to pursue profits. However, corporate managers may also be interested in power, nice offices, hiring friends, expansion of sales and other activities, which may conflict with profitability. Thus, the potential for conflict between the interests of owners and managers is present.

12. a. The interest payments; b. The interest income forgone. The tax structure encourages debt rather than equity financing since the firm's tax liability is inversely related to its debt/equity ratio.

13. True. If it could produce the output at a lower cost, its profit would be greater.

15. Check list: Did your marginal cost curve cross the ATC and AVC curves at their low points? Does the vertical distance between the ATC and AVC curves get smaller and smaller as output increases? If not, redraw the three curves correctly. See Exhibit 18–6b.

18. $2,500; the $2,000 decline in market value during the year plus $500 of potential interest on funds that could be obtained if the machine were sold new. Costs associated with the decline in the value of the machine last year are sunk costs.

19. Because they believe they will be able to restructure the firm and provide better management so that the firm will have positive net earnings in the future. If the firm is purchased at a low enough price, this will allow the new owners to cover the opportunity cost of their investment and still earn an economic profit. Alternatively, they may expect to sell off the firm's assets, receiving more net revenue than the cost of purchasing the firm.

CHAPTER 19

1. In a highly competitive industry such as agriculture, lower resource prices might improve the rate of profit in the short run, but in the long run, competition will drive prices down until economic profit is eliminated. Thus, lower resource prices will do little to improve the long-run profitability in such industries.

2. New firms will enter the industry and the existing firms will expand output; market supply will expand, causing the market price to fall until economic profit is eliminated.

5. a. Increase; b. Increase; c. Increase. Firms will earn economic profit; d. Rise (compared with its initial level) for an increasing cost industry, but return to initial price for a constant cost industry; e. Increase even more than it did in the short run; f. Economic profit will return to zero.

6. a. Decline; b. Increase; c. Decline; d. Decline.

11. (a) The reduction in supply led to higher prices; (b) since demand is inelastic, the total revenue from sales increased; (c) overall, the profitability of farming increased although some of the producers that were hardest hit by the drought experienced losses because of their sharp reduction in output.

13. b. Six or seven tons; $250 profit. c. Seven or eight tons; $600 profit. d. Five or six tons; $50 loss. Since the firm can cover its variable cost, it should stay in business if it believes that the low ($450) price is temporary.

15. The accountant has ignored the opportunity cost of Emma's labor, which is $50,000 rather than $22,000; from the accounting viewpoint her profit is $80,000 minus $59,000 or $21,000; but for the economist, considering the opportunity cost of her labor, her total cost is $87,000 so she would lose $7,000.

CHAPTER 20

3. The amount of variety is determined by the willingness of consumers to pay for variety relative to the cost of providing it. If consumers value variety highly and the added costs of producing different styles, designs, and sizes is low, there will be a lot of variety. Alternatively, if consumers desire similar products or if variation can be produced only at a high cost, little variety will be present. Apparently, consumers place a substantial value (relative to cost) on variety in napkins, but not in toothpicks.

4. The tax would increase the price of lower quality (and lower priced) automobiles by a larger percentage than higher quality automobiles. Consumers would substitute away from the lower quality autos since their relative price has increased. This substitution would increase the average quality of automobiles sold. Since the funds from the tax are rebated back to citizens through the lottery, one would expect this substitution effect to dominate any possible income effect.

7. No. A firm that maximizes *total* revenue would expand output as long as *marginal* revenue is positive. When marginal costs are positive, the revenue-maximizing price would be lower (and the output greater) than the price that would maximize the firm's profits.

9. Building the new resort is more risky (and less attractive) because if the market analysis is incorrect, and demand is insufficient, it probably will be difficult to find other uses for the newly built resort. If the airline proves unprofitable, however, the capital (airplanes) should be extremely mobile. However, the resort would have one offsetting advantage: If demand were stronger than expected, and

profits larger, it would take competitors longer to enter the market (build a new resort), and they would be more reluctant to make the more permanent investment.

11. In a competitive setting, only the big firms will survive if economies of scale are important. When economies of scale are unimportant, small firms will be able to compete effectively.

15. (a) Total revenue: $0; $8,000; $14,000; $18,000; $20,000; $20,000; Total cost: $0; $5,000; $10,000; $15,000; $20,000; $25,000; Economic profit: $0; $3,000; $4,000; $3,000; $0; −$5,000 (loss)

(b) Marginal revenue: $8,000; $6,000; $4,000; $2,000; $0; Marginal cost: $5,000; $5,000; $5,000; $5,000; $5,000

(c) Profit maximizing price: $7,000

(d) Rod will sell 2 boats at the profit maximizing price of $7,000.

(e) Rod's economic profits will be $4,000 per week.

(f) Yes, boats 1 and 2 are the only boats for which marginal revenue is higher than marginal cost.

(g) Because of the existence of economic profit, more boat dealers will open up in the area. This will result in more competition and lower prices. The entry will continue until boat dealers' economic profits fall to zero.

(h) When demand is elastic, lowering price increases total revenue, thus Rod's demand is elastic between the prices of $9,000 and $5,000. When demand is unitary elastic, lowering price leaves revenues unchanged, thus Rod's demand is unitary elastic between the prices of $5,000 and $4,000. One could also assume that Rod's demand would eventually become inelastic below a price of $4,000 because the elasticity of demand keeps falling as one moves down along a demand curve. When this happens, Rod's total revenues will begin to fall as he continues to lower price. For example, at a price of $3,000 Rod may sell 6 boats per week, resulting in only $18,000 in revenues, which is less than the revenues Rod receives at a price of $4,000.

CHAPTER 21

1. Profits cannot exist in the long run without barriers to entry because without them new entrants seeking the profits would increase supply, drive down price, and eliminate the profits. But as the chapter shows, barriers to entry are no guarantee of profits. Sufficient demand is also a necessary condition.

3. No; No; No.

8. Product variation provides each firm in the oligopoly a change to "cheat" by raising the quality of its products in order to entice customers away from rivals. This raises cost and helps to defeat the purpose, for the oligopolistic group, of controlling price. But if collusion has raised price much above marginal cost, there will be a powerful incentive for each firm to compete in a hidden way to get more customers.

11. Reductions in the cost of transportation generally increase competition because they force firms to compete with distant rivals and per-

mit consumers to choose among a wider range of suppliers. As a result, the U.S. economy today is generally more competitive, in the rivalry sense, than it was 100 years ago.

13. a. $15, profit = $110,000; b. $10.

14. The stock price, when the uncle bought the stock, no doubt reflected the well-known profits of Mammoth. The previous owners of the stock surely would not have sold it at a low price that failed to reflect the future dividends. In the language of the text, the uncle was not an "early bird." It is unlikely that he will profit, in the economic sense, from the purchase.

15. a. 25,000 quarts, $7, each firm produces 25 quarts; b. At $7, each firm wants to produce 45 quarts; c. If all firms cheat, the market becomes competitive. The market-clearing price is $5, 35,000 quarts of honey are produced, and each firm produces 35 quarts.

CHAPTER 22

4. Reduced competition is a potential danger for consumers. But if a merger makes a firm more efficient and better able to undercut the prices of other competitors, it may in effect increase the degree of competition, even as the firm increases its share of the market.

6. Making cars more safe is good, but if the cost has previously kept consumers from demanding the safety measures, it is possible that they are not worth the cost to many consumers. Some very expensive cars, such as Mercedes-Benz, had airbags when there was no requirement, but Volkswagen did not. Should only the more costly cars be sold? If so, then some people, probably the less affluent, will drive older, even less safe cars. This is not a clearcut issue.

8. Profitability may be adversely affected in the short run, but in the long run prices will rise enough for the firms to cover their opportunity cost of production. Consumers bear the cost of such legislation and get the association benefits, large or small.

9. Since this would increase competition from foreign sources, the effect should be to reduce the fears of market power being held by domestic firms. The need for antitrust action should decline.

12. Experts often do know far more about the technical options than do consumers, although consumers can and do read the advice of experts. Suppliers of safer products also make it a point to advertise data and expert opinion indicating their products are indeed safer. Nevertheless, experts usually do understand the technologies better. On the other hand, experts cannot know about how products will be used. A consumer may prefer to pay for a high degree of safety for the family car, which will carry the whole family at high speeds over long distances, while preferring a much cheaper, less reliable car for running errands near home. Such choices are hard to allow if all vehicles are strictly regulated for safety. Decision-maker knowledge (and incentives) is, in some cases, better with consumer choice than with thorough and strict regulation.

15. The statement is essentially true. In the short run, capital may be invested in an industry such that it cannot easily be moved elsewhere. If customer demand is elastic, the industry may bear a large part of the cost burden in the short run. In the long run, however, capital is mobile. Factories don't have to be replaced, for example. If costs in the industry are high, relative to the revenues, then capital will migrate over time to other industries, and supply in the regulated industry will fall until the price buyers will pay is again high enough to provide the market rate of return to capital.

CHAPTER 23

3 a. Five; b. $350; c. Four. The firm will operate in the short run but it will go out of business in the long run unless the market prices rise.

4. Yes. General increases in the productivity of the labor force will cause a general increase in wages. The higher general wage rates will increase the opportunity cost of barbering and cause the supply of barbers to decline. The reduction in the supply of barbers will place upward pressure on the wages of barbers, even if technological change and worker productivity have changed little in barbering.

8. No. The dressmaker needs to employ more capital and less labor because the marginal dollar expenditures on the former are currently increasing output by a larger amount than the latter.

10. Other things constant, a lengthy training requirement to perform in an occupation reduces supply and places upward pressure on the earnings level. However, resource prices, including those for labor services, are determined by both demand and supply. When demand is weak, earnings will be low even though a considerable amount of education may be necessary to perform in the occupation. For example, the earnings of people with degrees in English literature and world history are generally low, even though most people in these fields have a great deal of education.

12. b. 4 c. Employment would decline to 3.

CHAPTER 24

2. U.S. workers are more productive. By investing in human capital, the laborers are somewhat responsible, but the superior tools and physical capital that are available to U.S. workers also contribute to their higher wages.

6. While this statement often made by politicians sounds true, in fact, it is false. Output of goods and services valued by consumers, not jobs, is the key to economic progress and a high standard of living. Real income cannot be high unless real output is high. If job creation was the key to economic progress it would be easy to create millions of jobs. For example, we could prohibit the use of farm machinery. Such a prohibition would create millions of jobs in agriculture. However, it would also reduce output and our standard of living.

8. The opportunity cost of leisure (nonwork) for higher wage workers is greater than for lower wage workers.

9. a. Decreases; b. Increases; c. Decreases; d. Increases.

10. False. Several additional factors including differences in preferences (which would influence time worked, the trade-off between money wage and working conditions, and evaluation of alternative jobs), differences in jobs, and imperfect labor mobility would result in variations in earnings.

12. a., b., e., and f. will generally increase hourly earnings; c. and d. will generally reduce hourly earnings.

13. a. The increase; the cost of employment. Yes. b. Sure, if the higher wages are sufficient to compensate for the absence of the fringe benefits. c. No. Employees pay for them in the form of lower money wages than could be earned on comparable jobs that do not provide the fringe benefits.

15. Hourly wages will be highest in B because the higher wages will be necessary to compensate workers in B for the uncertainty and loss of income during layoffs. Annual earnings will be higher in A in order to compensate workers in A for the additional hours they will work during the year.

16. The employment level of low-skill workers with large families would decline. Some would attempt to conceal the presence of their large family in order to get a job.

18. Not necessarily. Compared with married men, single men tend to be younger, have fewer dependents, are more likely to drop out of the labor force, and less likely to receive earnings-enhancing assistance from another person. All of these factors will reduce their earnings relative to married men.

CHAPTER 25

1. All of the changes would increase interest rates in the United States.

4. No. The average outstanding balance during the year is only about half of $1,000. Therefore, the $200 interest charge translates to almost a 40 percent annual rate of interest.

6. Hints: Which is more risky? Purchasing a bond or a stock? How does risk influence the expected rate of return?

8. 6 percent.

11. a. Mike; b. Yes, people who save a lot are able to get a higher interest rate on their savings as the result of people with a high rate of time preference. c. Yes, people who want to borrow money will be able to do so at a lower rate when there are more people (like Alicia) who want to save a lot.

12. Helped. This question is a lot like prior questions involving Alicia and Mike. Potential gains from trade are present. If obstacles do not restrain trade, the low-income countries will be able to attract savings (from countries with a high saving rate) at a lower interest rate than would exist in the absence of trade. Similarly, people in the high-income countries will be able to earn a higher return than

would otherwise be possible. Both can gain because of the existence of the other.

13. a. Approximately $1.277 million; b. Yes; c. The lottery earnings are less liquid. Since there is not a well-organized market transforming lottery earnings into present income, the transaction costs of finding a "buyer" (at a price equal to the present value of the earnings) for the lottery earnings "rights" may be higher than for the bond, if one wants to sell in the future.

15. No. The present value of the $500 annual additions to earnings during the next ten years is less than the cost of the schooling.

CHAPTER 26

2. If the union is able to raise the wages of the farm workers: (1) The cost of Florida oranges will rise, causing supply to decline and their price to rise in the long run; (b) profits of the Florida orange growers will decline in the short run, but in the long run they will return to the normal rate; (c) mechanization will be encouraged; and (d) the employment of fruit pickers will decline—particularly in the long run.

3. The higher wages in the South would increase the costs of the southern firms and thereby make them less competitive with their northern rivals.

7. If only part of an industry is unionized, the costs of nonunion firms in the industry will be lower than the costs of unionized firms, if the unionized firms have higher wage rates. If the union wages are much higher than nonunion wages, then the unionized firms will be unable to compete successfully.

9. It may be true in the short run but this will not be the case in the long run. Investors do not have to supply capital to an industry. If the expected profit rate of a highly unionized industry is low, then investment funds will flow elsewhere. An unanticipated increase in union wages might reduce profitability in the short run, but it will not be able to do so in the long run. The primary effects of the higher wages will be higher prices. Consumers, rather than investors, will bear the primary cost of high union wages.

10. False. Competition constrains both employers and employees. Employers must compete with other employers for labor services. In order to gain the labor services of an employee, an employer must offer a compensation package superior to what the employee can get elsewhere. If the employer does not offer a superior package, the employee will work for a rival employer or choose self-employment.

Similarly, employees must compete with other employees. Therefore, their ability to demand whatever wage they would like is also restrained. Thus, competition prevents both the payment of low (below market) wages by employers and the imposition of high (above market) wages by employees.

12. Remember, union members compete with other workers, including less skilled workers. An increase in the minimum wage makes

unskilled, low-wage workers more expensive. A higher minimum wage increases the demand for high-skill employees who are good substitutes for the low-skill workers. Union members are over-represented among the high-skill group helped by an increase in the minimum wage. Therefore, while union leaders will generally pitch their support for a higher minimum wage in terms of a desire that all workers be paid a "decent wage," the impact of the legislation on union members suggests that self-interest rather than altruism underlies their support for the legislation.

13. The union and the manufacturer would be most likely to favor the tariff because it would make foreign-produced automobiles more expensive and thereby increase the demand for American-made automobiles and the labor with which they are made. In contrast, the higher gasoline tax makes driving more expensive. In response, the demand for higher-gasoline-consumption automobiles will fall, which will adversely affect both American automobile manufacturers and workers.

15. Not necessarily. Adjustment must be made for differences in (a) the productivity characteristics of the union and nonunion workers and (b) the types of jobs they occupy (for example, work environment, job security, likelihood of layoff, and so on). Adjustment for these factors may either increase or reduce the $1.50 differential.

CHAPTER 27

2. Differences in family size, age of potential workers, nonmoney "income," taxes, and cost-of-living among areas reduce the effectiveness of annual money income as a measure of economic status. In general, high-income families are larger, more likely to be headed by a prime-age worker, have less nonmoney income (including leisure), pay more taxes, and reside in higher cost-of-living areas (particularly large cities). Thus, money income comparison between high-and low-income groups often overstates the economic status of the former relative to the latter.

4. If there were no intergenerational mobility, the diagonal numbers would all be 100 percent. If there were complete equality of opportunity and outcomes, the numbers in each column and row would be 20 percent.

6. No. The increase in marginal tax rates will reduce the incentive of the poor to earn income. Therefore, their income will rise by $1,000 minus the reduction in their personal earnings due to the disincentive effects of the higher marginal tax rates.

7. 67 percent.

10. Here, as in other areas, it is important to remember that government is merely an alternative form of social organization, rather than a corrective device. The structure of income transfers reflects political clout. The elderly, farmers, and business and labor interests are easily identifiable, politically potent interest groups. In contrast, the poor have a low voter participation rate and offer lit-

tle in the way of financial support to politicians. Given these factors, it is not surprising that most income transfers go to the nonpoor.

14. Adjustment of individuals to redistributive programs often leads to unintended side effects. If a higher income from private saving means a lower level of social security benefits, people will save less for retirement. Other things constant, the number of low-income (and therefore high-benefit) elderly will grow. Stated another way, programs that subsidize low-income status (and penalize high-income status) during retirement will expand the number of people in the former category and reduce the number in the latter category with the passage of time.

CHAPTER 28

1. Merely because a resource is unowned and unpriced, it does not follow that its opportunity cost is zero. Use of an unowned, unpriced resource might involve a high opportunity cost. Yet if there is no owner to protect it, or to allocate it to its highest-valued use, then it might indeed be treated as if it had no opportunity cost. This illustrates why private ownership of resources is important for their efficient allocation.

3. The "requirement" of water for the steel industry depends on the value placed on water, as well as on the value placed on steel. Most products can be produced with vastly differing amounts of water (see Exhibit 28–1). Also, steel itself is not indispensable in all its uses, including national defense uses. There are many substitutes, not only for water in the making of steel, but also for steel in the making of tanks, and for tanks in providing national defense. So a given amount of water for steel is not really a requirement.

5. Wells are abandoned by producers when the cost of extracting and delivering additional oil exceeds its value. When the value of crude oil rises, additional oil can be produced since water flooding, steam and chemical measures—all of which are costly—can be paid for by the higher prices gained from the extra oil.

7. Issues for thought: Are resources supplied by nature scarce? If so, what process should be used to ration them among the competing demanders? If a resource is owned by the government rather than privately, how will this affect the incentive to care for, maintain, and conserve it for the future? Do you think that government-owned property like the national forests and parks are better cared for than, for example, Disney World?

9. If an investment, such as leaving the trees to grown another 20 years, yields a higher return than other investments, then the stock price will fall if the trees are cut too soon, or will go higher if a new, more profitable investment path (leaving the trees to grow) is announced. Either way, the stock price immediately rewards good long-term decisions and penalizes bad shortsighted ones.

CHAPTER 29

1. The commons could have been managed politically, without any private ownership. The open access problem is the absence of both private property and of political control of access to the resource.

4. By definition, a public good cannot be marketed, because free riders (nonpayers) can consume it. There is little incentive for the consumer to state his or her true preference, even if asked. So a producer, including government, has a difficult time knowing how much an extra unit of the public good is worth.

6. We expect that private ownership, which concentrates both the costs and the benefits of stewardship on the owner(s), will result in better care than will joint ownership, at least if the joint owners are many. In the latter case, the benefits are spread among the joint owners, while the costs of care fall on the person doing the care—unless, of course, the group arranges to assign and enforce duties, or to jointly pay for care.

7. Permitting all firms to use air and water resources for "free garbage disposal" services reduces the producers' costs of supplying pollution-intensive goods. However, as long as free entry (competition) is present, the lower cost will lead to lower prices, not higher profits. Except for unanticipated changes in pollution control policy, competition will drive the profit rate of all firms, including those in industries that pollute, toward the normal rate of return.

9. Many goods with public-good aspects are provided privately. Free museum admission, free concerts, wildlife preservation, and so on defy the free-rider problem. But the public-good problem is still with us, and we cannot know whether the right amounts are produced when goods have public-good aspects.

10. An inability to exclude nonpaying consumers. Since consumers cannot be prevented (at least not at a low cost) from consuming a public good if they fail to pay, each has an incentive to "free ride," which undermines the private supplier's ability to cover the cost of production.

11. Economics doesn't say what is fair, but corporations—like all firms—want to minimize their costs in order to maximize profits. If they can reduce costs by emitting more pollution into the air and by avoiding costly abatement measures, then they are likely to do so. And those who do will gain a competitive advantage over those who do not, so long as the legal system does not hold polluters responsible for downwind damages. Without effective court procedures or bureaucratic action on behalf of those harmed by the pollution, it would be folly to expect even public-spirited corporate executives to sacrifice profits to gain a public good—air quality—if their competitors were allowed to pollute.

12. Knowing that the firm's national reputation is at stake at every franchise, travelers would probably find the nationally advertised restaurant more appealing. Also, if they had seen the advertising, they would have a better idea of what sort of food is available. Their relative lack of knowledge about the unadvertised place probably

deters them from using it. In contrast, the local people would know more than the travelers about the local restaurant, as the result of personal experience or from talking with friends who had tried it.

CHAPTER 30

1. It is difficult for the voter to know what a candidate will do once elected, and the rationally ignorant voter is usually not willing to spend the time and effort required to understand issues, since his or her vote will not be the decisive one anyway. Special interest voters, on the other hand, will know which candidate has promised them the most on their issue. Also, the candidate who is both competent and prepared to ignore special interests will have a hard time getting these facts to voters without financial support from special interest groups. Each voter has an incentive to be a "free rider" on the "good government" issue. Controlling government on behalf of society as a whole is a public good, requiring much private activity. Like other public goods, it tends to be underproduced.

2. Corporate officers, while they surely care about the next few months and the profits during that time, care also about the value of the firm and its stock price. If the stock price rises sufficiently in the next few months—as it will if investors believe that current investments in future-oriented projects (planting new trees, for example) are sound—then the officers will find their jobs secure even if current profits do not look good. Rights to the profits from those (future) trees are saleable now in the form of the corporation's stock. There is no such mechanism to make the distant fruits of today's investments available to the political entrepreneurs who might otherwise fight for the future-oriented project. Only if the project appeals to today's voters, and they are willing to pay today for tomorrow's benefits, will the program be a political success. In any case, the wealth of the political entrepreneur is not directly enhanced by his or her successful fight for the project.

7. No. The government is merely an alternative form of organization. Government organization does not permit us to escape either scarcity or competition. It merely affects the nature of the competition. Political competition (voting, lobbying, political contributions, taxes, and politically determined budgets) replaces market competition. Neither is there any reason to believe that government organization modifies the importance of personal self-interest.

8. The regulatory and taxation policy toward the liquor industry is usually conducted at the state, rather than at the federal, level. Thus, liquor industry interests will be more likely to use lobbying and campaign contributions to influence the action of state-level politicians.

10. When the welfare of a special interest group conflicts with that of a widely dispersed, unorganized majority, the legislative political process can reasonably be expected to work to the benefit of the special interest.

CHAPTER 31

(Since this chapter focuses on policy, suggested answers are not supplied.)

CHAPTER 32

1. Availability of goods and services, not jobs, is the source of economic prosperity. When a good can be purchased cheaper abroad than it can be produced at home, a nation can expand the quantity of goods and services available for consumption by specializing in the production of those goods for which it is a low-cost producer and trading them for the cheap (relative to domestic costs) foreign goods. Trade restrictions limiting the ability of Americans to purchase low-cost goods from foreigners stifle this process and thereby reduce the living standard of Americans.

3. Answers a and b are not in conflict. Since trade restrictions are typically a special interest issue, political entrepreneurs can often gain by supporting them even when they promote economic inefficiency.

5. True. The primary effect of trade restrictions is an increase in domestic scarcity. This has distributional consequences, but it is clear that as a whole, a nation will be harmed by the increased domestic scarcity accompanying the trade restraints.

6. The quota reduces the supply of sugar to the domestic market and drives up the domestic price of sugar. Domestic producers benefit from the higher prices at the expense of domestic consumers (see Exhibit 32–10). Studies indicate that the quota expanded the gross income of the 11,000 domestic sugar farmers by approximately $130,000 per farm in the mid-1980s, at the expense (in the form of higher prices of sugar and sugar products) of approximately $6 per year to the average domestic consumer. Since the program channels resources away from products for which the United States has a comparative advantage, it reduces the productive capacity of the United States. Both the special interest nature of the issue and rent-seeking theory explain the political attractiveness of the program.

8. a. No. Americans would be poorer if we used more of our resources to produce things for which we are a high opportunity-cost producer and less of our resources to produce things for which we are a low opportunity-cost producer. Employment might either increase or decrease, but the key point is that it is the value of goods produced, not employment, that generates income and provides for the wealth of a nation. The answer to b is the same as a.

9. In thinking about this issue, consider the following points. Suppose the Japanese were willing to give products such as automobiles, electronic goods, and clothing to us free of charge. Would we be worse off if we accepted the gifts? Should we try to keep the free goods out? What is the source of real income—jobs or goods and services? If the gifts make us better off, doesn't it follow that partial gifts would also make us better off?

12. While trade reduces employment in import-competing industries, it expands employment in export industries. On balance, there is no reason to believe that trade either promotes or destroys jobs. The major effect of trade is to permit individuals, states, regions, and nations to generate a larger output by specializing in the things they do well and trading for those things that they would produce only at a high cost. A higher real income is the result.

15. True. If country A imposes a tariff, other countries will sell less to A and therefore acquire less purchasing power in terms of A's currency. Thus, they will have to reduce their purchases of A's export goods.

18. Yes. The price equalization theorem indicates that goods will tend to sell for similar prices in all markets except for differences due to taxes and transport costs. Therefore, except in cases where there is a high tariff (or some other U.S. tax) on a good, it is unlikely that the good will be much cheaper abroad than it is in the United States.

CHAPTER 33

1. The depreciation will make the dollar price of BMWs more expensive, which will reduce the quantity purchased by Americans. If the American demand for BMWs is inelastic (elastic), then the dollar expenditures on BMWs will rise (fall).

4. On February 2, the dollar appreciated against the pound and depreciated against the franc.

5. Answers a and g would cause the dollar to appreciate; b, c, d, e, and h would cause the dollar to depreciate; f would leave the exchange rate unchanged.

9. Each of the changes would reduce the size of the current account deficit.

11. The current account balance will move toward a larger deficit (or smaller surplus) and the dollar will appreciate.

13. The more restrictive monetary policy pushed real interest rates up and reduced the rate of inflation. The higher interest rates induced foreigners to invest more in the United States, which caused the dollar to appreciate. The lower rate of inflation also helped to increase the exchange-rate value of the dollar. In turn, the appreciation of the dollar made foreign goods cheaper for Americans and U.S. exports more expensive to foreigners. Thus, imports increased and exports declined, shifting the current account toward a deficit.

15. False. Flexible exchange rates bring the sum of the current and capital accounts into balance, but they do not necessarily lead to balance for either component.

18. a. No. The exchange rate will bring the sum of the current and capital accounts into balance, but it will not bring about either an overall merchandise trade balance or a trade balance with a specific country.

    b. Compared to the United States, Japan has a high savings rate. High-income countries with high savings rates tend to invest substantially abroad. In order to pay for these investments,

Japan must run a current account surplus. Its trading partners—particularly those with a low saving rate like the United States—will do the opposite. In addition, Japan is a major importer of natural resources and raw materials, two product areas where the United States does not generally have a comparative advantage. Because the United States is generally not a low-cost producer of the primary products imported by the Japanese, the United States tends to export less goods and services to Japan than it imports.

CHAPTER 34

2. There is considerable diversity among the poor nations. The fastest growing economies in the world are all nations that just a few years ago were quite poor. On the other hand, the worst performing economies in the world are also LDCs (see Exhibit 34–4). As the high growth rates of several LDCs illustrate, if they follow sound policies, low-income countries can grow rapidly and reduce the income gap relative to developed economies.

3. A few years ago, many believed that this view was essentially true. However, this is no longer the case. Foreign aid has played an insignificant role in the progress of most of the high-growth LDCs. In some cases, it has adversely affected economies. In the past, aid has disrupted markets and retarded the incentive of producers in less developed countries. Furthermore, attractive investment alternatives will draw investment from abroad even if domestic saving is inadequate. Thus, the efficacy of aid as a tool to promote economic growth is highly questionable.

7. Yes. Trade barriers limit the ability of both businesses and consumers to benefit from economies associated with an expansion in the size of the market. This limitation will be more restrictive for small countries (like Costa Rica) than for larger countries (like Mexico) because the latter will often have sizable domestic markets.

CHAPTER 35

5. Because the prices of goods are also fixed by the planners. Thus, an increase in the supply of money cannot be used to bid up prices. The two major side effects are waiting lines (since prices are fixed below equilibrium) and monetary holdings that go unspent because there is so little to buy.

10. Under capitalism, mass production and market penetration lead to wealth. But you cannot have large-scale production without pricing the product so that it will be affordable to the mass consumer market. Thus, a market system rewards producers who figure out how to make products affordable to lots of consumers rather than just the rich. The careers of Henry Ford and Sir Henry Royce illustrate this point. Ford became a multimillionaire by bringing a low-cost automobile within the budget of mass consumers. In contrast, Royce died

a man of modest wealth. He engineered the Rolls Royce, a car far superior to the Ford, but he designed it for the rich. The market rewarded him accordingly.

12. Points to consider in your answer: What kinds of wealth do the two systems produce? Is there more personal security under socialism? If wealth is acquired from production and exchange that does not involve the use of theft, violence, or fraud, is it fair for the wealth to be taken and given to someone else?

Ability-to-pay principle The equity concept that people with larger incomes (or more consumption or more wealth) should be taxed at a higher rate because their ability to pay is presumably greater. How much higher the rate of taxation should be as income increases is subjective.

Absolute advantage A situation in which a nation, as the result of its previous experience and/or natural endowments, can produce more of a good (with the same amount of resources) than another nation.

Accounting profits The sales revenues minus the expenses of a firm over a designated time period, usually one year. Accounting profits typically make allowances for changes in the firm's inventories and depreciation of its assets. No allowance is made, however, for the opportunity cost of the equity capital of the firm's owners, or other implicit costs.

Activist strategy Deliberate changes in monetary and fiscal policy in order to inject demand stimulus during a recession and apply restraint during an inflationary boom and thereby, it is hoped, minimize economic instability.

Adaptive-expectations hypothesis The hypothesis that economic decision makers base their future expectations on actual outcomes observed during recent periods. For example, according to this view, the rate of inflation actually experienced during the past two or three years would be the major determinant of the rate of inflation expected for next year.

Administrative lag The time period between when the need for a policy change is recognized and when the policy is actually implemented.

Aggregate demand curve A downward-sloping curve indicating an inverse relationship between the price level and the quantity of domestically produced goods and services that households, business firms, governments, and foreigners (net exports) are willing to purchase during a period.

Aggregate supply curve A curve indicating the relationship between the nation's price level and quantity of goods supplied by its producers. In the short run, it is probably an upward-sloping curve, but in the long run most economists believe the aggregate supply curve is vertical (or nearly so).

Allocative inefficiency The use of an uneconomical combination of resources to produce goods and services, or the use of resources to produce goods that are not intensely desired relative to their opportunity cost.

Anticipated change A change that is foreseen by decision makers in time for them to adjust.

Anticipated inflation An increase in the general level of prices that was expected by most decision makers.

Appreciation An increase in the value of a domestic currency relative to foreign currencies. An appreciation increases the purchasing power of the domestic currency for foreign goods.

Asymmetric-information problem A problem arising when either buyers or sellers have important information about the product that is not possessed by the other side in potential transactions.

Automatic stabilizers Built-in features that tend automatically to promote a budget deficit during a recession and a budget surplus during an inflationary boom, even without a change in policy.

Automation A production technique that reduces the amount of labor required to produce a good or service. It is beneficial to adopt the new labor-saving technology only if it reduces the cost of production.

Autonomous expenditures Expenditures that do not vary with the level of income. They are determined by factors (such as business expectations and economic policy) that are outside the basic income-expenditure model.

Average fixed cost Total fixed cost divided by the number of units produced. It always declines as output increases.

Average product The total product (output) divided by the number of units of the variable input required to produce that output level.

Average tax rate (ATR) One's tax liability divided by one's taxable income.

Average total cost Total cost divided by the number of units produced. It is sometimes called *per unit cost*.

Average variable cost The total variable cost divided by the number of units produced.

Balanced budget A situation in which current government revenue from taxes, fees, and other sources is just equal to current government expenditures.

Balance of merchandise trade The difference between the value of merchandise exports and the value of merchandise imports for a nation. The balance of merchandise trade is only one component of a nation's total balance of payments. Also called simply *balance of trade* or *net exports*.

Balance of payments A summary of all economic transactions between a country and all other countries for a specific time period, usually a year. The balance-of-payments account reflects all payments and liabilities to foreigners (debits) and all payments and obligations received from foreigners (credits).

Balance on current account   The import-export balance of goods and services, plus net investment income earned abroad, plus net private and government transfers. If the value of the nation's export-type items exceeds (is less than) the value of the nation's import-type items (plus net unilateral transfers to foreigners), a current-account surplus (deficit) is present.

Balance on goods and services   The exports of goods (merchandise) and services of a nation minus its imports of goods and services.

Bank reserves   Vault cash plus deposits of the bank with Federal Reserve banks.

Barriers to entry   Obstacles that limit the freedom of potential rivals to enter and compete in an industry or market.

Benefit principle   The concept that those who receive government services should pay taxes or user charges for their provision according to the amount of the service or benefit derived from the government activity.

Break-even point   Under a negative income tax plan, the income level at which the reduction in transfers that accompany additional earnings is equal to the base income. Thus, the individual neither pays taxes nor receives supplementary income transfers.

Budget constraint   The constraint that separates the bundles of goods that the consumer can purchase from those that cannot be purchased, given a limited income and the prices of the products.

Budget deficit   A situation in which total government spending exceeds total government revenue during a specific time period, usually one year.

Budget surplus   A situation in which total government spending is less than total government revenue during a time period, usually a year.

Business cycle   Fluctuations in the general level of economic activity as measured by such variables as the rate of unemployment and changes in real GDP.

Capital   Resources that enhance our ability to produce output in the future.

Capital account   Transactions with foreigners that involve either (1) the exchange of ownership rights to real or financial assets or (2) the extension of loans.

Capital formation   The production of buildings, machinery, tools, and other equipment that will enhance the ability of future economic participants to produce. The term can also be applied to efforts to upgrade the knowledge and skill of workers and thereby increase their ability to produce in the future.

Capitalism   An economic system based on private ownership of productive resources and allocation of goods according to the signals provided by market prices.

Cartel   An organization of sellers designed to coordinate supply decisions so that the joint profits of the members will be maximized. A cartel will seek to create a monopoly in the market.

Central bank   A bank that accepts deposits and imposes regulations on private commercial banks. The central bank is responsible for the policies that determine the money supply.

Ceteris paribus   A Latin term meaning "other things constant," used when the effect of one change is being described, recognizing that if other things changed, they also could affect the result. Economists often describe the effects of one change, knowing that in the real world, other things might change and have their effects, too.

Choice   The act of selecting among alternatives.

Civilian labor force   The number of persons 16 years of age and over who are either employed or unemployed. In order to be classified as unemployed one must be looking for a job.

Classical economists   Economists from Adam Smith to the time of Keynes who focused their analyses on economic efficiency and production. With regard to business instability, they thought market prices and wages would decline during a recession quickly enough to bring the economy back to full employment within a short period of time.

Collective bargaining contract   A detailed contract between a group of employees (a labor union) and their employer.

Collective decision making   The method of organization that relies on public-sector decision making (voting, political bargaining, lobbying, and so on). It can be used to resolve the basic economic problems of an economy.

Collusion   Agreement among firms to avoid various competitive practices, particularly price reductions. It may involve either formal agreements or merely tacit recognition that competitive practices will be self-defeating in the long run. Tacit collusion is difficult to detect. In the United States, antitrust laws prohibit collusion and conspiracies to restrain trade.

Commercial banks Financial institutions that offer a wide range of services (for example, checking accounts, savings accounts, and extension of loans) to their customers. Commercial banks are owned by stockholders and seek to operate at a profit.

Common-property resource A resource for which rights are held in common by a group of individuals, none of whom has a transferable ownership interest. Access to the resource may be open (unrestricted), or may be controlled politically.

Comparative advantage The ability to produce a good at a lower opportunity cost than others can produce it. Relative costs determine comparative advantage. A nation will have a comparative advantage in the production of a good when its production costs (other goods forgone) for the good are low relative to the production costs of other nations for the same good.

Compensating wage differentials Wage differences that compensate workers for risk, unpleasant working conditions, and other undesirable nonpecuniary aspects of a job.

Competition as a dynamic process A term that denotes rivalry or competitiveness between or among parties (for example, producers or input suppliers), each of which seeks to deliver a better deal to buyers when quality, price, and product information are all considered. Competition implies a lack of collusion among sellers.

Competitive price-searcher market A market where the firms have a downward-sloping demand curve, and entry into and exit from the market are relatively easy.

Complements Products that are usually consumed jointly (for example, coffee and nondairy creamer), so that a decrease in the price of one will cause a rise in demand for the other.

Concentration ratio The total sales of the four (or sometimes eight) largest firms in an industry as a percentage of the total sales of the industry. The higher the ratio, the greater the market dominance of a small number of firms. The ratio can be seen as a measure of the potential for oligopolistic power.

Conglomerate merger The combining under one ownership of two or more firms that produce unrelated products.

Constant-cost industry An industry for which factor prices and costs of production remain constant as market output is expanded. Thus, the long-run market supply curve is horizontal.

Constant returns to scale Unit costs that are constant as the scale of the firm is altered. Neither economies nor diseconomies of scale are present.

Consumer price index (CPI) An indicator of the general level of prices. It attempts to compare the cost of purchasing the market basket bought by a typical consumer during a specific period with the cost of purchasing the same market basket during an earlier period.

Consumer surplus The difference between the maximum amount a consumer would be willing to pay for a unit of a good, and the payment that is actually made.

Consumption function A fundamental relationship between disposable income and consumption, in which, as disposable income increases, current consumption expenditures rise, but by a smaller amount than the increase in income.

Consumption-opportunity constraint The constraint that separates consumption bundles that are attainable from those that are unattainable. In a money-income economy, this is usually a budget constraint.

Contestable market A market in which the costs of entry and exit are low, so a firm risks little by entering. Efficient production and zero economic profits should prevail in a contestable market. A market can be contestable even if capital requirements are high.

Corporation A business firm owned by shareholders who possess ownership rights to the firm's profits, but whose liability is limited to the amount of their investment in the firm.

Countercyclical policy A policy that tends to move the economy in an opposite direction from the forces of the business cycle. Such a policy would stimulate demand during the contraction phase of the business cycle and restrain demand during the expansion phase.

Credit Funds acquired by borrowing.

Credit unions Financial cooperative organizations of individuals with a common affiliation (such as an employer or labor union). They accept deposits, including checkable deposits, pay interest (or dividends) on them out of earnings, and channel funds primarily into loans to members.

Crowding-out effect A reduction in private spending as a result of higher interest rates generated by budget deficits that are financed by borrowing in the private loanable funds market.

Currency board An entity that (a) issues a currency with a fixed designated value relative to a widely accepted currency (for example, the U.S. dollar), (b) promises to continue to redeem the issued currency at the fixed rate, and

(c) maintains bonds and other liquid assets denominated in the other currency that provides 100 percent backing for all currency issued.

Current account   The record of all transactions with foreign nations that involve the exchange of merchandise goods and services, current income derived from investments, and unilateral gifts.

Cyclical unemployment   Unemployment due to recessionary business conditions and inadequate aggregate demand for labor.

Deadweight loss   A net loss associated with the forgoing of an economic action. The loss does not lead to an offsetting gain for other participants. It thus reflects economic inefficiency.

Decreasing-cost industries   Industries for which costs of production decline as the industry expands. The market supply is therefore inversely related to price. Such industries are atypical.

Demand deposits   Noninterest-earning checking deposits that can either be withdrawn or made payable on demand to a third party. Like currency, these deposits are widely used as a means of payment.

Demand for money   At any given interest rate, the amount of wealth that people desire to hold in the form of money balances—that is, cash and checking-account deposits (or other highly liquid assets in the case of broad measures of the money supply). The quantity demanded is inversely related to the interest rate.

Deposit expansion multiplier   The multiple by which an increase (decrease) in reserves will increase (decrease) the money supply. It is inversely related to the required reserve ratio.

Depository institutions   Businesses that accept checking and saving deposits and use a portion of them to extend loans and make investments. Banks, savings and loan associations, and credit unions are examples.

Depreciation (of a currency)   A reduction in the value of a domestic currency relative to foreign currencies. A depreciation reduces the purchasing power of the domestic currency for foreign goods.

Depreciation (in national income accounting)   The estimated amount of physical capital (for example, machines and buildings) that is worn out or used up producing goods during the period.

Depression   A prolonged and very severe recession.

Derived demand   Demand for an item based on the demand for products the item helps to produce. The demand for resources is a derived demand.

Devaluation   An official act that changes the level of the fixed exchange rate downward in terms of other currencies. In essence, it is a one-step depreciation of a currency under a fixed-exchange-rate system.

Differentiated products   Products distinguished from similar products by such characteristics as quality, design, location, and method of promotion.

Discount rate   The interest rate the Federal Reserve charges banking institutions for borrowing funds.

Discounting   The procedure used to calculate the present value of future income, which is inversely related to both the interest rate and the amount of time that passes before the funds are received.

Discouraged workers   Persons who have given up searching for employment because they believe additional job search would be fruitless. Because they are not currently searching for work, they are not counted among the unemployed.

Discretionary fiscal policy   A change in laws or appropriation levels that alters government revenues and/or expenditures.

Discretionary monetary policy   Changes in monetary policy instituted at the discretion of policymakers. The policy is not predetermined by rules or formulas.

Disposable income   The income available to individuals after personal taxes. It can either be spent on consumption or saved.

Division of labor   A method that breaks down the production of a commodity into a series of specific tasks, each performed by a different worker.

Dumping   The sale of a good by a foreign supplier in another country at a price below that charged by the supplier in its home market.

Economic efficiency   Economizing behavior. When applied to a community, it implies that (1) an activity should be undertaken if the sum of the benefits to the individuals exceeds the sum of their costs and (2) no activity should be undertaken if the costs borne by the individuals exceed the benefits.

Economic good   A good that is scarce. The desire for economic goods exceeds the amount that is freely available from nature.

Economic profit   The difference between the firm's total revenues and total costs.

Economic regulation   Regulation of product price or industrial structure, usually imposed on a specific industry. By and large, the production processes used by the regulated firms are unaffected by this type of regulation.

Economic theory   A set of definitions, postulates, and principles assembled in a manner that makes clear the "cause-and-effect" relationships of economic data.

Economies of scale   Reductions in the firm's per unit costs that are associated with the use of large plants to produce a large volume of output.

Economizing behavior   Choosing with the objective of gaining a specific benefit at the least possible cost. A corollary of economizing behavior implies that, when choosing among items of equal cost, individuals will choose the option that yields the greatest benefit.

Elasticity of supply   The percent change in quantity supplied, divided by the percent change in the price causing that change in quantity supplied.

Employment discrimination   Unequal treatment of persons on the basis of their race, sex, or religion, restricting their employment and earnings opportunities compared to others of similar productivity. Employment discrimination may stem from the prejudices of employers, consumers, and/or fellow employees.

Employment/population ratio   The number of persons 16 years of age and over employed as civilians divided by the total civilian population 16 years of age and over. The ratio is expressed as a percentage.

Entrepreneur   A profit-seeking decision maker who decides which projects to undertake and how they should be undertaken. A successful entrepreneur's actions will increase the value of resources.

Equation of exchange $MV = PY$, where M is the money supply, V is the velocity of money, P is the price level, and Y is the output of goods and services produced.

Equilibrium   A state of balance between conflicting forces, such as supply and demand.

Escalator clause   A contractual agreement that periodically and automatically adjusts money wage rates upward as the price level rises. They are sometimes referred to as cost-of-living adjustments or COLAs.

Eurodollar deposits   Deposits of U.S. dollars by U.S. residents at banks and other financial institutions outside the United States. Although this name originated because of the large amounts of such deposits held at banks in Western Europe, similar deposits in other parts of the world are also called Eurodollars.

Excess burden of taxation   A burden of taxation over and above the burden associated with the transfer of revenues to the government. An excess burden usually reflects losses that occur when beneficial activities are forgone because they are taxed.

Excess reserves   Actual reserves that exceed the legal requirement.

Exchange rate   The domestic price of one unit of foreign currency. For example, if it takes $1.50 to purchase one English pound, the dollar–pound exchange rate is 1.50.

Exchange-rate conversion method   Method that uses the foreign exchange-rate value of a nation's currency to convert that nation's GDP (or GNP) to another monetary unit, such as the U.S. dollar.

Exclusive contract   An agreement between a manufacturer and retailer that prohibits the retailer from carrying the product lines of firms that are rivals of the manufacturer. Such contracts are illegal under the Clayton Act when they "lessen competition."

Expansionary fiscal policy   An increase in government expenditures and/or a reduction in tax rates such that the expected size of the budget deficit expands.

Expansionary monetary policy   A shift in monetary policy designed to stimulate aggregate demand. Bond purchases, creation of additional bank reserves, and an increase in the growth rate of the money supply are generally indicative of a shift to a more expansionary monetary policy.

Expenditure multiplier   The ratio of the change in equilibrium output to the independent change in investment, consumption, or government spending that brings about the change. Numerically, the multiplier is equal to $1 \div (1 - MPC)$ when the price level is constant.

Explicit costs   Payments by a firm to purchase the services of productive resources.

Exports   Goods and services produced domestically but sold to foreigners.

External benefits   Beneficial effects of group or individual action on the welfare of nonpaying secondary parties.

External costs   Harmful effects of an individual's or a group's action on the welfare of a nonconsenting secondary party, not accounted for in market prices.

External debt   The portion of the national debt owed to foreign investors.

Externalities   The side effects, or spillover effects, of an action that influence the well-being of nonconsenting parties. The nonconsenting parties may be either helped (by external benefits) or harmed (by external costs).

Fallacy of composition   Erroneous view that what is true for the individual (or the part) will also be true for the group (or the whole).

Federal Deposit Insurance Corporation (FDIC)   A federally chartered corporation that insures the deposits held by commercial banks and thrift institutions.

Federal funds market   A loanable funds market in which banks seeking additional reserves borrow short-term (generally for seven days or less) funds from banks with excess reserves. The interest rate in this market is called the *federal funds rate.*

Federal Open Market Committee (FOMC)   A 12-member board that establishes Fed policy with regard to the buying and selling of government securities, the primary mechanism used to control the money supply in the United States.

Federal Reserve System   The central bank of the United States; it carries out banking regulatory policies and is responsible for the conduct of monetary policy.

Fiat money   Money that has neither intrinsic value nor the backing of a commodity with intrinsic value; paper currency is an example.

Final market goods and services   Goods and services purchased by their ultimate user.

Fiscal policy   The use of government taxation and expenditure policies for the purpose of achieving macroeconomic goals.

Fixed exchange rates   An exchange rate that is set at a fixed rate by government policy.

Flexible exchange rates   Exchange rates that are determined by the market forces of supply and demand. They are sometimes called *floating exchange rates.*

Foreign exchange market   The market in which the currencies of different countries are bought and sold.

Fractional reserve banking   A system that permits banks to hold reserves of less than 100 percent against their deposits.

Free rider   One who receives the benefit of a good without contributing to its costs. Public goods and commodities that generate external benefits offer people the opportunity to become free riders.

Frictional unemployment   Unemployment due to constant changes in the economy that prevent qualified unemployed workers from being immediately matched up with existing job openings. It results from the scarcity of information and the search activities of both employers and employees for information that will help them make better employment choices.

Fringe benefits   Benefits other than normal money wages that are supplied to employees in exchange for their labor services.

Full employment   The level of employment that results from the efficient use of the labor force after allowance is made for the normal (natural) rate of unemployment due to information cost, dynamic changes, and the structural conditions of the economy. For the United States, full employment is thought to exist when between 94 and 95 percent of the labor force is employed.

GDP deflator   A price index that reveals the cost of purchasing the items included in GDP during the period relative to the cost of purchasing these same items during a base year (currently, 1992). Since the base year is assigned a value of 100, as the GDP deflator takes on values greater than 100, it indicates that prices have risen.

Game theory   Analyzes the strategic choices made by competitors in a conflict situation, such as decisions made by members of an oligopoly.

General Agreement on Tariffs and Trade (GATT)   An organization formed following the Second World War designed to set the rules for the conduct of international trade and reduce barriers to trade among nations.

Going out of business   The sale of a firm's assets and its permanent exit from the market. By going out of business, a firm is able to avoid fixed costs, which would continue during a shutdown.

Goods and services market   A highly aggregated market encompassing the flow of all final-user goods and services. The market counts all items that enter into GDP. Thus, real output in this market is equal to real GDP.

Government failure   Failure of government action to meet the criteria of ideal economic efficiency.

Government purchases   Current expenditures on consumption and investment goods provided by federal, state, and local governments; they exclude transfer payments.

Gross domestic product (GDP)   The total market value of all final goods and services produced domestically during a specific period, usually one year.

Gross national product (GNP)   The total market value of all final goods and services produced by the citizens of a country. It is equal to GDP plus the income the nationals earned abroad minus the income foreigners earned domestically.

Hard budget constraint   A situation in which the enterprise is fully dependent on revenues from sales to cover its costs. The constraint is "hard" because, if losses are present, they will have to be covered by enterprise owners; continuing losses will result in bankruptcy since government subsidies and special grants are unavailable.

Head tax   A lump-sum tax levied on all individuals, regardless of their income, consumption, wealth, or other indicators of economic well-being.

Health and safety regulation   Legislation designed to improve the health, safety, and environmental conditions available to workers and/or consumers. The legislation usually mandates production procedures, minimum standards, and/or product characteristics to be met by producers and employers.

Herfindahl index   A measure of industry concentration, calculated by squaring the percentage share of each firm in the industry, then summing the squares. The index can range from zero to 10,000. It is a more sophisticated measure of concentration than the traditional concentration ratio, and is used by the Justice Department in antitrust policy.

Horizontal merger   The combining of the assets of two or more firms engaged in the production of similar products into a single firm.

Human resources   The abilities, skills, and health of human beings that can contribute to the production of both current and future output. Investment in training and education can increase the supply of human resources.

Impact lag   The time period between when a policy change is implemented and when the change begins to exert its primary effects.

Implicit costs   The opportunity costs associated with a firm's use of resources that it owns. These costs do not involve a direct money payment. Examples include wage income and interest forgone by the owner of a firm who also provides labor services and equity capital to the firm.

Implicit marginal tax rate   The amount of additional (marginal) earnings that must be paid explicitly in taxes or implicitly in the form of a reduction in income supplements. Since the marginal tax rate establishes the fraction of an additional dollar earned that an individual is permitted to keep, it is an important determinant of the incentive to work.

Import quota   A specific quantity (or value) of a good permitted to be imported into a country during a given period.

Imports   Goods and services produced by foreigners but purchased by domestic consumers, investors, and governments.

Income effect   That part of an increase (decrease) in amount consumed that is the result of the consumer's real income (the consumption possibilities available to the consumer) being expanded (contracted) by a reduction (rise) in the price of a good.

Income elasticity   The percent change in the quantity of a product demanded divided by the percent change in consumer income causing the change in quantity demanded. It measures the responsiveness of the demand for a good to a change in income. The sign of the elasticity coefficient is usually positive.

Income mobility   Movement of individuals and families either up or down income-distribution rankings when comparisons are made at two different points in time. When substantial income mobility is present, one's current position will not be a very good indicator as to what one's position will be a few years in the future.

Increasing-cost industries   An industry for which costs of production rise as output is expanded. Thus, even in the long run, higher market prices will be required to induce the firms to expand the total output in such industries. The long-run market supply curve in such industries will slope upward to the right.

Indexed bonds   Bonds that pay a market-determined *real* interest rate plus an inflationary premium equal to the actual rate of inflation that occurs during the period. When the bond is redeemed, the principal is also adjusted for the rate of inflation during the period the bond was outstanding.

Indexing   The automatic increasing of money values as the general level of prices increases. Economic variables that are often indexed include wage rates and tax brackets.

Index of leading indicators   An index of economic variables that historically has tended to turn down prior to the beginning of a recession and turn up prior to the beginning of a business expansion.

Indifference curve   A curve, convex from below, that separates the consumption bundles that are more preferred by an individual from those that are less preferred. The points on the curve represent combinations of goods that are equally preferred by the individual.

Indirect business taxes   Taxes that increase the business firm's costs of production and therefore the prices charged to consumers. Examples would be sales, excise, and property taxes.

Inferior good   A good that has a negative income elasticity, so that, as consumer incomes rise, the demand for that good falls.

Inflation   A continuing rise in the general level of prices of goods and services. The purchasing power of the monetary unit, such as the dollar, declines when inflation is present.

Inflation premium   A component of the money interest rate that reflects compensation to the lender for the expected decrease, due to inflation, in the purchasing power of the principal and interest during the course of the loan. It is determined by the expected rate of future inflation.

Infrastructure   The provision of a legal, monetary, educational, transportation, and communication structure necessary for the efficient operation of an exchange economy.

Innovation   The successful introduction and adoption of a new product or process; the economic application of inventions and marketing techniques.

Intermediate goods   Goods purchased for resale or for use in producing another good or service.

International Monetary Fund (IMF)   An international banking organization, with more than 100 member nations, designed to oversee the operation of the international monetary system. Although it does not control the world supply of money, it does hold currency reserves for member nations and makes currency loans to national central banks.

Invention   The creation of a new product or process, often facilitated by the knowledge of engineering and scientific relationships.

Inventory investment   Changes in the stock of unsold goods and raw materials held during a period.

Investment   The purchase, construction, or development of capital resources, including both physical capital and human capital. Investments increase the supply of capital.

Investment in human capital   Expenditures on training, education, skill development, and health designed to increase the productivity of an individual.

Invisible hand principle   The tendency of market prices to direct individuals pursuing their own interests into productive activities that also promote the economic well-being of the society.

Isocost line   A line representing the various combinations of two factors that can be purchased with a given money budget (cost).

Isoquant   A curve representing the technically efficient combinations of two inputs that can be used to produce a given level of output.

J-curve effect   The tendency of a nation's current-account deficit to widen initially before it shrinks in response to an exchange-rate depreciation. This tendency results because the short-run demand for both imports and exports is often inelastic, even though the long-run demand is almost always elastic.

Labor force participation rate   The number of persons in the civilian labor force 16 years of age or over who are either employed or actively seeking employment as a percentage of the total civilian population 16 years of age and over.

Labor union   A collective organization of employees who bargain as a unit with employers.

Laffer curve   A curve illustrating the relationship between tax rates and tax revenues. The curve reflects the fact that tax revenues are low for both very high and very low tax rates.

Law of comparative advantage   A principle that states that individuals, firms, regions, or nations can gain by specializing in the production of goods that they produce cheaply (that is, at a low opportunity cost) and exchanging those goods for other desired goods for which they are a high-opportunity-cost producer.

Law of demand   A principle that states there is an inverse relationship between the price of a good and the amount of it buyers are willing to purchase.

Law of diminishing marginal utility   The basic economic principle that, as the consumption of a commodity increases, the marginal utility derived from consuming more of the commodity (per unit of time) will eventually decline. Marginal utility may decline even though total utility continues to increase, but at a reduced rate.

Law of diminishing returns   The postulate that, as more and more units of a variable resource are combined with a fixed amount of other resources, employment of additional units of the variable resource will eventually increase output only at a decreasing rate. Once diminishing returns are reached, it will take successively larger amounts of the variable factor to expand output by one unit.

Law of supply   A principle that states there is a direct relationship between the price of a good and the amount of it offered for sale. As the price of a product increases, other things constant, producers will increase the amount of the product supplied to the market.

Less-developed countries (LDCs)   Low-income countries generally characterized by rapid population growth and an agriculture-household sector that dominates the economy. Sometimes these countries are referred to as developing countries.

Liquid asset   An asset that can be easily and quickly converted to purchasing power without loss of value.

Loanable funds market   A general term used to describe the market arrangements that coordinate the borrowing and lending decisions of business firms and households. Commercial banks, savings and loan associations, the stock and bond markets, and insurance companies are important financial institutions in this market.

Logrolling   The exchange between politicians of political support on one issue for political support on another issue.

Long run   A time period of sufficient length to enable decision makers to adjust fully to a market change.

Long run (in production)   A time period long enough to allow the firm to vary all factors of production.

Loss   Deficit of sales revenue relative to the cost of production, once all the resources used have received their opportunity cost. Losses are a penalty imposed on those who use resources in lower, rather than higher, valued uses as judged by buyers in the market.

M1 (money supply)   The sum of (1) currency in circulation (including coins), (2) checkable deposits maintained in depository institutions, and (3) traveler's checks.

M2 (money supply)   Equal to M1 plus (1) savings deposits, (2) time deposits (accounts of less than $100,000) held in depository institutions, and (3) money market mutual fund shares.

M3 (money supply)   Equal to M2, plus (1) time deposits (accounts of more than $100,000) at all depository institutions and (2) large denomination money market mutual funds, (3) overnight loans from customers, and (4) the Eurodollar deposits of U.S. residents.

Macroeconomics   The branch of economics that focuses on how human behavior affects outcomes in highly aggregated markets, such as the markets for labor or consumer products.

Mandated benefits   Fringe benefits that the government forces employers to include in their total compensation package paid to employees.

Marginal   Term used to describe the effects of a change in the current situation. For example, the marginal cost is the cost of producing an additional unit of a product, given the producer's current facility and production rate.

Marginal cost   The change in total cost required to produce an additional unit of output.

Marginal factor cost (MFC)   The cost of employing an additional unit of a resource. When the employer is small relative to the total market, the marginal factor cost is simply the price of the resource. In contrast, under monopsony, marginal factor cost will exceed the price of the resource, since the monopsonist faces an upward-sloping supply curve for the resource because to hire another worker, wages must be raised for all workers.

Marginal product   The increase in the total product resulting from a unit increase in the employment of a variable input—one workday of skilled labor, for example. Mathematically, it is the ratio of the change in total product to the change in the quantity of the variable input.

Marginal propensity to consume (MPC)   Additional current consumption divided by additional current disposable income.

Marginal rate of substitution   The change in the consumption level of one good that is just sufficient to offset a unit change in the consumption of another good without causing a shift to another indifference curve. At any point on an indifference curve, it will be equal to the slope of the curve at that point.

Marginal revenue (MR)   The incremental change in total revenue derived from the sale of one additional unit of a product.

Marginal revenue product (MRP)   The change in the total revenue of a firm that results from the employment of one additional unit of a factor of production. The marginal-revenue product of an input is equal to its marginal product multiplied by the marginal revenue (price) of the good or service produced.

Marginal tax rate (MTR)   Additional tax liability divided by additional income. Thus, if $100 of additional earnings increases one's tax liability by $30, the marginal tax rate is 30 percent.

Marginal utility   The additional utility received by a person from the consumption of an additional unit of a good within a given time period.

Market   An abstract concept that encompasses the trading arrangements of buyers and sellers that underlie the forces of supply and demand.

Market failure   The failure of the market system to attain hypothetically ideal allocative efficiency. This means that potential gain exists that has not been captured. However, the cost of establishing a mechanism that could potentially capture the gain may exceed the benefits. Therefore, it is not always possible to improve the situation.

Market mechanism A method of organization that allows unregulated prices and the decentralized decisions of private property owners to resolve the basic economic problems of consumption, production, and distribution.

Market power The ability of a firm that is not a pure monopolist to earn unusually large profits, indicating that it has some monopoly power. Because the firm has few (or weak) competitors, it has a degree of freedom from the discipline of vigorous competition.

Maximum emission standard The maximum amount of pollution that a polluter is permitted to emit, established by the government or a regulatory authority. Fines are generally imposed on those who are unwilling or unable to comply.

Means-tested income transfers Transfers that are limited to persons or families with an income below a certain cutoff point. Eligibility is thus dependent on low-income status.

Medium of exchange An asset that is used to buy and sell goods or services.

Microeconomics The branch of economics that focuses on how human behavior affects the conduct of affairs within narrowly defined units, such as individual households or business firms.

Middleman A person who buys and sells, or who arranges trades. A middleman reduces transaction costs, usually for a fee or a markup in price.

Minimum wage Legislation requiring that workers be paid at least the stated minimum hourly rate of pay.

Monetarists A group of economists who believe that (1) monetary instability is the major cause of fluctuations in real GDP and (2) rapid growth of the money supply is the major cause of inflation.

Monetary base The sum of currency in circulation plus bank reserves (vault cash and reserves with the Fed). It reflects the stock of U.S. securities held by the Fed.

Monetary policy The deliberate control of the money supply, and, in some cases, credit conditions, for the purposes of achieving macroeconomic goals.

Money interest rate The interest rate measured in monetary units. It overstates the real cost of borrowing during an inflationary period. When inflation is anticipated, an inflationary premium will be incorporated into the nominal value of this rate. The money interest rate is often referred to as the nominal interest rate.

Money market mutual funds Interest-earning accounts offered by brokerage firms that pool depositors' funds and invest them in highly liquid short-term securities. Since these securities can be quickly converted to cash, depositors are permitted to write checks (which reduce their share holdings) against their accounts.

Money rate of interest The rate of interest in monetary terms that borrowers pay for borrowed funds. During periods when borrowers and lenders expect inflation, the money rate of interest exceeds the real rate of intertest.

Monopolistic competition Term often used by economists to describe markets characterized by a large number of sellers that supply differentiated products to a market with low barriers to entry. Essentially, it is an alternative term for competitive price-searcher markets.

Monopoly A market structure characterized by (1) a single seller of a well-defined product for which there are no good substitutes and (2) high barriers to the entry of any other firms into the market for that product.

Monopsony A market in which there is only one buyer. The monopsonist confronts the market supply curve for the resource (or product) bought.

National debt The sum of the indebtedness of the federal government in the form of outstanding interest-earning bonds. It reflects the cumulative impact of budget deficits and surpluses.

National income The total income payments to owners of human (labor) and physical capital during a period. It includes both the domestic and foreign income earned by the nationals (citizens).

Natural monopoly A market situation in which the average costs of production continually decline with increased output. Therefore, average costs of production will be lowest when a single large firm produces the entire output demanded.

Natural rate of unemployment The long-run average unemployment rate due to frictional and structural conditions of labor markets. This rate is affected both by dynamic change and by public policy. It is sustainable into the future. The current natural rate of unemployment in the United States is thought to be between 5 percent and 6 percent.

Negative income tax A system of transferring income to the poor whereby a minimum base level of income is guaranteed to an individual or a family. If nothing is earned, the base income is received in the form of transfers. As additional income is earned, the base income transfer is reduced by some fraction (less than 1) of the additional earnings. An increase in earnings, thus, would always cause disposable income to rise.

Net domestic product (NDP) Gross domestic product minus a depreciation allowance for the wearing out of machines and buildings during the period.

Net exports Exports minus imports.

New classical economists Modern economists who believe there are strong forces pushing a market economy toward full-employment equilibrium and that macroeconomic policy is an ineffective tool with which to reduce economic instability.

Nominal GDP GDP expressed at current prices. It is often called money GDP.

Nominal values Values expressed in current dollars.

Nonactivist strategy The maintenance of the same monetary and fiscal policy—that is, no change in money growth, tax rates, or expenditures—during all phases of the business cycle.

Nonhuman resources The durable, nonhuman inputs that can be used to produce both current and future output. Machines, buildings, land, and raw materials are examples. Investment can increase the supply of nonhuman resources. Economists often use the term *physical capital* when referring to nonhuman resources.

Nonpecuniary job characteristics Working conditions, prestige, variety, location, employee freedom and responsibilities, and other nonwage characteristics of a job that influence how employees evaluate the job.

Normal good A good that has a positive income elasticity, so that, as consumer incomes rise, demand for that good rises also.

Normative economics Judgments about "what ought to be" in economic matters. Normative economic views cannot be proved false, because they are based on value judgments.

Oligopoly A market situation in which a small number of sellers compose the entire industry. It is competition among the few.

Open-access resource A resource to which access is unrestricted. No one has the right to exclude others from using the resource. Overuse and abuse of such a resource is typical.

Open Market Committee A 12-member board that establishes Fed policy with regard to the buying and selling of government securities, the primary mechanism used to control the money supply in the United States.

Open market operations The buying and selling of U.S. government securities (national debt) by the Federal Reserve.

Opportunity cost The highest valued alternative that must be sacrificed as a result of choosing among alternatives.

Opportunity cost of equity capital The implicit rate of return that must be earned by investors to induce them to continue to supply financial capital to the firm.

Other checkable deposits Interest-earning deposits that are also available for checking.

Partnership A business firm owned by two or more individuals who possess ownership rights to the firm's profits and are personally liable for the debts of the firm.

Permanent income hypothesis The hypothesis that consumption depends on some measure of long-run expected (permanent) income rather than on current income.

Personal consumption Household spending on consumer goods and services during the current period. Consumption is a flow concept.

Personal income The total income received by individuals that is available for consumption, saving, and payment of personal taxes.

Phillips curve A curve that illustrates the relationship between the rate of change in prices (or money wages) and the rate of unemployment.

Policy-ineffectiveness theorem The proposition that any systematic policy will be rendered ineffective once decision makers figure out the policy pattern and adjust their decision making in light of its expected effects. The theorem is a corollary of the theory of rational expectations.

Political good Any good (or policy), whether a public good or a private good, supplied through the political process.

Pork-barrel legislation A package of spending projects benefiting local areas at federal expense. The projects typically have costs that exceed benefits, but are intensely desired by the residents of the district getting the benefits without having to pay much of the costs.

Positive economics The scientific study of "what is" among economic relationships.

Positive rate of time preference The desire of consumers for goods now rather than in the future.

Potential deposit expansion multiplier   The maximum potential increase in the money supply as a ratio of the new reserves injected into the banking system. It is equal to the inverse of the required reserve ratio.

Potential output   The level of output that can be achieved and sustained into the future, given the size of the labor force, expected productivity of labor, and natural rate of unemployment consistent with the efficient operation of the labor market. For periods of time, the actual output may differ from the economy's potential.

Poverty threshold income level   The level of money income below which a family is considered to be poor. It differs according to family characteristics (for example, number of family members) and is adjusted when consumer prices change.

Predatory pricing   The practice in which a dominant firm in an industry temporarily reduces prices to damage or eliminate weaker rivals, so that prices can be raised above the level of costs at a later time.

Present value (PV)   The current worth of future income after it is discounted to reflect the fact that revenues in the future are valued less highly than revenues now.

Price ceiling   A legally established maximum price that sellers may charge.

Price discrimination   A practice whereby a seller charges different consumers different prices for the same product or service.

Price elasticity of demand   The percent change in the quantity of a product demanded divided by the percent change in the price causing the change in quantity. Price elasticity of demand indicates the degree of consumer response to variation in price.

Price equalization principle   The tendency for markets, when trade restrictions are absent, to establish a uniform price for each good throughout the world (except for price differences due to transport costs and differential tax treatment of the good).

Price floor   A legally established minimum price that buyers must pay for a good or resource.

Price searchers   Firms that face a downward sloping demand curve for their product. The amount that the firm is able to sell is inversely related to the price that it charges.

Price takers   Sellers who must take the market price in order to sell their product. Because each price taker's output is small relative to the total market, price takers can sell all their output at the market price, but they are unable to sell any of their output at a price higher than the market price.

Principal-agent problem   The incentive problem arising when the purchaser of services (the principal) lacks full information about the circumstances faced by the seller (the agent) and thus cannot know how well the agent performs the purchased services. The agent may to some extent work toward objectives other than those sought by the principal paying for the service.

Private investment   The flow of private sector expenditures on durable assets (fixed investment) plus the addition to inventories (inventory investment) during a period. These expenditures enhance our ability to provide consumer benefits in the future.

Privately held government debt   The portion of the national debt owed to domestic and foreign investors. It does not include bonds held by agencies of the federal government or the Federal Reserve.

Private property rights   Property rights that are exclusively held by an owner, or group of owners, and that can be transferred to others at the owner's discretion.

Production possibilities curve   A curve that outlines all possible combinations of total output that could be produced, assuming (1) the utilization of a fixed amount of productive resources, (2) full and efficient use of those resources, and (3) a specific state of technical knowledge. The slope of the curve indicates the rate at which one product can be traded off to produce more of the other.

Productivity   The average output produced per worker during a specific time period. It is usually measured in terms of output per hour worked.

Profit   An excess of sales revenue relative to the cost of production. The cost component includes the opportunity cost of all resources, including those owned by the firm. Therefore, profit accrues only when the value of the good produced is greater than the sum of the values of the individual resources utilized.

Progressive tax   A tax that requires those with higher taxable incomes to pay a larger percentage of their incomes to the government than those with lower taxable incomes.

Property rights   The right to use, control, and obtain the benefits from a good or service.

Proportional tax   A tax for which individuals pay the same percentage of their income (or other tax base) in taxes, regardless of income level.

Proprietorship   A business firm owned by an individual who possesses the ownership right to the firm's profits and is personally liable for the firm's debts.

Public-choice analysis The study of decision making as it affects the formation and operation of collective organizations, such as governments. The discipline bridges the gap between economics and political science. In general, the principles and methodology of economics are applied to political science topics.

Public goods Jointly consumed goods that are not diminished when one person enjoys their consumption. When consumed by one person, they are also made available to others. National defense, poetry, and scientific theories are all public goods.

Purchasing-power parity method Method of comparing the outputs of different currencies. The amount of each currency required to purchase a typical bundle of goods and services in domestic markets is used to determine the relative purchasing power of different currencies. This information is then used to convert the GDP (or GNP) of each nation to a common monetary unit.

Purely competitive markets Markets characterized by a large number of small firms producing an identical product in an industry (market area) that permits complete freedom of entry and exit. Also called *price-taker markets*.

Quantity theory of money A theory that hypothesizes that a change in the money supply will cause a proportional change in the price level because velocity and real output are unaffected by the quantity of money.

Rate-of-return equalization principle The tendency for capital investment in each market to move toward a uniform, or normal, rate of return. An abnormally high return in a market will attract additional investment, which will drive returns down. Conversely, an abnormally low return will result in investment flight from the market, which will eventually lead to the restoration of normal returns.

Rate of unemployment The percent of persons in the labor force who are unemployed, according to the official definition of "unemployed." Mathematically, it is equal to (Number of persons unemployed ÷ Number in the labor force) × 100

Rational-expectations hypothesis The hypothesis that economic decision makers weigh all available evidence, including information concerning the probable effects of current and future economic policy, when they form their expectations about future economic events (such as the probable future inflation rate).

Rational ignorance effect Voter ignorance resulting from the fact that people perceive their individual votes as unlikely to be decisive. Therefore, they rationally have little incentive to seek the information needed to cast an informed vote.

Rationing An allocation of a limited supply of a good or resource to users who would like to have more of it. Various criteria, including charging a price, can be utilized to allocate the limited supply. When price performs the rationing function, the good or resource is allocated to those willing to give up the most "other things" in order to obtain ownership rights.

Real balance effect The increase in wealth generated by an increase in the purchasing power of a constant money supply as the price level decreases. This wealth effect leads to an inverse relationship between price (level) and quantity demanded in the goods and services market.

Real GDP Gross domestic product adjusted for changes in the price level.

Real interest rate The interest rate adjusted for expected inflation; it indicates the real cost to the borrower (and yield to the lender) in terms of goods and services.

Real rate of interest The money rate of interest minus the expected rate of inflation. The real rate of interest indicates the interest premium, in terms of real goods and services, that one must pay for earlier availability.

Real values Values that have been adjusted for the effects of inflation.

Recession A downturn in economic activity characterized by declining real GDP and rising unemployment. In an effort to be more precise, many economists define a recession as two consecutive quarters in which there is a decline in real GDP.

Recognition lag The time period between when a policy change is needed from a stabilization standpoint and when the need is recognized by policymakers.

Regressive tax A tax that takes a smaller percentage of income as income level increases. Thus, the proportion of income allocated to the tax would be greater for the poor than for the rich.

Rent seeking Actions by individuals and interest groups designed to restructure public policy in a manner that will either directly or indirectly redistribute more income to themselves.

Repeat-purchase item An item purchased often by the same buyer.

Required reserve ratio A percentage of a specified liability category (for example, transaction accounts) that banking institutions are required to hold as reserves against that type of liability.

Required reserves The minimum amount of reserves that a bank is required by law to keep on hand to back up its deposits. Thus, if reserve requirements were 15 percent, banks would be required to keep $150,000 in reserves against each $1 million of deposits.

Residual claimants Individuals who personally receive the excess, if any, of revenues over costs. Residual claimants gain if the firm's costs are reduced or revenues increased.

Resource An input used to produce economic goods. Land, labor, skills, natural resources, and capital are examples. Our history is a record of our struggle to transform available, but limited, resources into things that we would like to have—economic goods.

Resource market (macro) A highly aggregated market encompassing all resources (labor, physical capital, land, and entrepreneurship) that contribute to the production of current output. The labor market forms the largest component of this market.

Resource markets Markets in which business firms demand factors of production (for example, labor, capital, and natural resources) from household suppliers. The resources are then used to produce goods and services. These markets are sometimes called *factor markets* or *input markets*.

Resource mobility A term that refers to the ease with which factors of production are able to move among alternative uses. Resources that can easily be transferred to a different use or location are said to be highly mobile. In contrast, when a resource has few alternative uses, it is immobile. For example, the skills of a trained rodeo rider would be highly immobile, since they cannot be easily transferred to other lines of work.

Restrictive fiscal policy A reduction in government expenditures and/or an increase in tax rates such that the expected size of the budget deficit declines (or the budget surplus increases).

Restrictive monetary policy A shift in monetary policy designed to reduce aggregate demand and place downward pressure on the general level of prices (or the rate of inflation). Bond sales, a decline in bank reserves, and a deceleration in the growth rate of the money supply are generally indicative of a restrictive monetary policy.

Right-to-work laws Laws that prohibit the union shop—the requirement that employees must join a union as a condition of employment. Each state has the option to adopt (or reject) right-to-work legislation.

Samaritan's dilemma General assistance to those with low incomes reduces the opportunity cost of choices that lead to poverty. Thus, there is a conflict between providing income transfers to the poor and discouragement of behavior that increases the incidence of poverty.

Saving Disposable income that is not spent on consumption. Saving is a "flow" concept. Thus, it is generally measured in terms of an annual rate.

Savings and loan associations Financial institutions that accept deposits in exchange for shares that pay dividends. Historically, these funds have been channeled into residential mortgage loans. Under banking legislation adopted in 1980, S&Ls are now permitted to offer a broad range of services similar to those of commercial banks.

Say's Law The view that production creates its own demand. Demand will always be sufficient to purchase the goods produced because the income payments to the resource suppliers will equal the value of the goods produced.

Scarcity Fundamental concept of economics that indicates that a good is less freely available than consumers would like.

Scientific thinking Development of theory from basic postulates and the testing of the implications of that theory as to their consistency with events in the real world. Good theories are consistent with and help explain real-world events. Theories that are inconsistent with the real world are invalid and must be rejected.

Secondary effects Economic consequences of an economic change that are not immediately identifiable but are felt only with the passage of time.

Shirking Working at less than a normal rate of productivity, thus reducing output. Shirking is more likely when workers are not monitored, so that the cost of lower output falls on others than themselves.

Shortage A condition in which the amount of a good offered by sellers is less than the amount demanded by buyers at the existing price. An increase in price would eliminate the shortage.

Short run A time period of insufficient length to permit decision makers to adjust fully to a change in market conditions. For example, in the short run, producers will have time to increase output by using more labor and raw materials, but they will not have time to expand the size of their plants or to install additional heavy equipment.

Short run (in production)   A time period so short that a firm is unable to vary some of its factors of production. The firm's plant size typically cannot be altered in the short run.

Shortsightedness effect   Misallocation of resources that results because public-sector action is biased (1) in favor of proposals yielding clearly defined current benefits in exchange for difficult-to-identify future costs and (2) against proposals with clearly identifiable current costs but yielding less concrete and less obvious future benefits.

Shutdown   A temporary halt in the operation of a business in which the firm anticipates a return to operation in the future and therefore does not sell its assets. The firm's variable cost is eliminated for the duration of the shutdown, but its fixed costs continue.

Social costs   The sum of (1) the private costs incurred by a decision maker and (2) any external costs imposed on nonconsenting secondary parties. If there are no external costs, private and social costs will be equal.

Socialism   A system of economic organization where (1) the ownership and control of the basic means of production rest with the state and (2) the allocation of resources and products is determined by centralized planning rather than by market forces.

Special drawing rights (SDRs)   Supplementary reserves, in the form of accounting entries, established by the International Monetary Fund (also called paper gold). Like gold and foreign currency reserves, they can be used to make payments on international accounts.

Special interest issue   An issue that generates substantial individual benefits to a small minority while imposing a small individual cost on many other voters. In total, the net cost to the majority might either exceed or fall short of the net benefits to the special interest group.

Stagflation   A period during which an economy is experiencing both substantial inflation and either declining or slow growth in output.

Strike   An action of unionized employees in which they (1) discontinue working for the employer and (2) take steps to prevent other potential workers from offering their services to the employer.

Structural unemployment   Unemployment due to the structural characteristics of the economy that make it difficult for job seekers to find employment and employers to hire workers. Although job openings are available, they generally require skills that differ from those of the unemployed workers.

Substitutes   Products that are related such that an increase in the price of one will cause an increase in demand for the other (for example, butter and margarine, Chevrolets and Fords).

Substitution effect   That part of an increase (decrease) in amount consumed that is the result of a good being cheaper (more expensive) in relation to other goods because of a reduction (increase) in price.

Sunk costs   Costs that have already been incurred as a result of past decisions. They are sometimes referred to as historical costs.

Supply shock   An unexpected event that temporarily either increases or decreases aggregate supply.

Supply-side economists   Modern economists who believe that changes in marginal tax rates exert important effects on aggregate supply.

Surplus   A condition in which the amount of a good that sellers are willing to offer is greater than the amount that buyers will purchase at the existing price. A decline in price would eliminate the surplus.

Tariff   A tax levied on goods imported into a country.

Tax base   The level of the activity that is taxed. For example, if an excise tax is levied on each gallon of gasoline, the tax base is the number of gallons of gasoline sold. Because higher tax rates generally make the taxed activity less attractive, the size of the tax base is inversely related to the rate at which the activity is taxed.

Tax incidence   The manner in which the burden of the tax is distributed among economic units (consumers, employees, employers, and so on). The tax burden does not always fall on those who pay the tax.

Tax rate   The per unit or percentage rate at which an economic activity is taxed.

Team production   A process of production wherein employees work together under the supervision of the owner or the owner's representative.

Technological advancement   The introduction of new techniques or methods of production that enable a greater output per unit of input.

Technology   The technological knowledge available at any given time. The level of technology establishes the relationship between inputs and the maximum output they can generate.

Total cost   The costs, both explicit and implicit, of all the resources used by the firm. Total cost includes an imputed normal rate of return for the firm's equity capital.

Total fixed cost   The sum of the costs that do not vary with output. They will be incurred as long as a firm continues in business and the assets have alternative uses.

Total product   The total output of a good that is associated with alternative utilization rates of a variable input.

Total variable cost   The sum of those costs that rise as output increases. Examples of variable costs are wages paid to workers and payments for raw materials

Transaction accounts   Accounts including demand deposits, and interest-earning checkable deposits against which the account holder is permitted to transfer funds for the purpose of making payment to a third party.

Transaction costs   The time, effort, and other resources needed to search out, negotiate, and consummate an exchange.

Transfer payments   Payments to individuals or institutions that are not linked to the current supply of a good or service by the recipient.

Trust   In American history, an arrangement in which the assets of several firms were placed in the custody of trustees who managed the trust for the benefit of the owners. Trusts were used to form cartels in the United States in the late 1800s.

Unanticipated change   A change that decision makers could not reasonably foresee. Thus, choices made prior to the event did not take the event into account.

Unanticipated inflation   Increase in the general level of prices that was not expected by most decision makers.

Underground economy   Unreported barter and cash transactions that take place outside recorded market channels. Some are otherwise legal activities undertaken to evade taxes. Others involve illegal activities, such as trafficking in drugs and prostitution.

Union-shop provision   The requirement that all employees join the recognized union and pay dues to it within a specified length of time (usually 30 days) after their employment with the firm begins.

Unemployed   The term used to describe a person not currently employed who is either (1) actively seeking employment or (2) waiting to begin or return to a job.

User charge   A payment that users (consumers) are required to make if they want to receive certain services provided by the government.

Utility   The benefit or satisfaction expected from a choice or course of action.

Value marginal product (VMP)   The marginal product of a resource multiplied by the selling price of the product it helps to produce. Under pure competition, a firm's marginal revenue product (MRP) will be equal to the value marginal product (VMP).

Velocity of money   The average number of times a dollar is used to purchase final goods and services during a year. It is equal to GDP divided by the stock of money.

Vertical merger   The creation of a single firm from two firms, one of which was a supplier or customer of the other—for example, a merger of a lumber company with a furniture manufacturer.

Voluntary export restraint (VER)   An agreement by foreign firms to limit their own exports.

World Trade Organization   The new name given to GATT in 1994; it is currently responsible for monitoring and enforcing the multilateral trade agreements among the 117 member countries.

	POPULATION AND LABOR FORCE				MONEY SUPPLY (M2)	
YEAR	CIVILIAN NONINSTITUTIONAL POPULATION AGE 16 AND OVER (MILLIONS)	CIVILIAN LABOR FORCE PARTICIPATION RATE (PERCENT)	RATE OF UNEMPLOYMENT (PERCENT)	CIVILIAN EMPLOYMENT/ POPULATION RATIO (PERCENT)	MONEY SUPPLY M2 (BILLIONS)	ANNUAL CHANGE IN M2
1959	115.3	59.3	5.5	56.0	297.8	—
1960	117.2	59.4	5.5	56.1	312.3	4.9
1961	118.8	59.3	6.7	55.4	335.5	7.4
1962	120.1	58.8	5.5	55.5	362.7	8.1
1963	122.4	58.7	5.7	55.4	393.2	8.4
1964	124.5	58.7	5.2	55.7	424.8	8.0
1965	126.5	58.9	4.5	56.2	459.3	8.1
1966	128.1	59.2	3.8	56.9	480.0	4.5
1967	130.0	59.6	3.8	57.3	524.3	9.2
1968	132.0	59.6	3.6	57.5	566.3	8.0
1969	134.3	60.1	3.5	58.0	589.5	4.1
1970	137.1	60.4	4.9	57.4	628.1	6.5
1971	140.2	60.2	5.9	56.6	712.7	13.5
1972	144.1	60.4	5.6	57.0	805.2	13.0
1973	147.1	60.8	4.9	57.8	861.0	6.9
1974	150.1	61.3	5.6	57.8	908.5	5.5
1975	153.2	61.2	8.5	56.1	1,023.2	12.6
1976	156.2	61.6	7.7	56.8	1,163.7	13.7
1977	159.0	62.3	7.1	57.9	1,286.5	10.6
1978	161.9	63.2	6.1	59.3	1,388.6	7.9
1979	164.9	63.7	5.8	59.9	1,496.9	7.8
1980	167.7	63.8	7.1	59.2	1,629.3	8.8
1981	170.1	63.9	7.6	59.0	1,793.3	10.1
1982	172.3	64.0	9.7	57.8	1,953.2	8.9
1983	174.2	64.0	9.6	57.9	2,187.7	12.0
1984	176.4	64.4	7.5	59.5	2,378.4	8.7
1985	178.2	64.8	7.2	60.1	2,576.0	8.3
1986	180.6	65.3	7.0	60.7	2,820.3	9.5
1987	182.8	65.6	6.2	61.5	2,922.3	3.6
1988	184.6	65.9	5.5	62.3	3,083.5	5.5
1989	186.4	66.5	5.3	63.0	3,243.0	5.2
1990	188.0	66.4	5.5	62.7	3,356.0	3.5
1991	189.8	66.0	6.7	61.6	3,457.9	3.0
1992	191.6	66.3	7.4	61.4	3,515.3	1.7
1993	193.6	66.2	6.8	61.6	3,583.6	1.9
1994	196.8	66.6	6.1	62.5	3,617.0	0.9
1995	198.6	66.6	5.6	62.9	3,780.7	4.5

Source: *Economic Report of the President, 1996.*